# WEEKLY UPDATES!

**For only 27 cents a day***

→ Get the *Hollywood Creative Directory* On-Line!

# www.hcdonline.com

AF333362

**Call for a FREE Trial**

*$99.00 a year for *Hollywood Creative Directory*

**ALSO AVAILABLE:**
*Hollywood Agents & Managers Directory*
*Hollywood Distributors Directory*

**BONUS:**
BUY ALL THREE AND GET FREE
*Hollywood New Media Directory*

310·315·4815

800·815·0503
(outside California)

# losangeles independent filmfestival

## congratulations
to all of our
### filmmakers

and **thank you**
to all of our
### sponsors.

## Mark Your Calendars...
## laiff '99: april 15–20

presenting sponsor '98

# sundance
channel™

founding sponsors '98

2nd
cycle of
**The Production Grant Program**

Grant submission period runs from May 25–August 28

Production Grant Program provides:

- **PRODUCTION ASSISTANCE** A package of goods, services and promotional support
- **INDUSTRY RECOGNITION** Grant finalists are selected by
- **PROFESSIONAL SCRIPT COVERAGE** Available to all applicants

Project Partners include: Kodak, CFI, Panavision, Todd A/O and Imperial Bank.
Call 213.960.9460 for an application.

SUMMER 1998 • VOLUME 34 • PUBLISHED TRI-ANNUALLY

# CONTENTS



**HOLLYWOOD CREATIVE DIRECTORY**

3000 W. Olympic Blvd. • Suite 2525
Santa Monica, CA 90404
Phone: 310.315.4815 or 800.815.0503 (outside CA)
Fax: 310.315.4816  Email: hcd@hcdonline.com
Website: www.hcdonline.com

## * next to a listing denotes a new entry

Remarkably simple to use, the Amtel system allows executives and their assistants to silently communicate via a special visual device located next to their phones. After answering the telephone and determining the identity of the caller, the assistant/receptionist inputs the caller's name and information using the Amtel keyboard; this information instantly appears on the LCD display of the executive's Amtel unit. The executive can then instruct the assistant on what steps should be taken, such as "ask him to hold" or take a message," using one of 21 rapid-reply preprogrammed action response keys, all of which can be customized to fit the executive's needs.

Companies, large and small, have found Amtel to be an effective tool for eliminating annoying interruptions and costly phone tag. Amtel systems are used by Merrill Lynch, Walt Disney Studios, Cantor Fitzgerald, MCA and The Law Offices of Beck Dicorso to name just a few.

## HCD STAFF

*Editor / VP , Research*
BARBARA DUGAN

*VP, Marketing & Advertising*
D.V. LAWRENCE

*Dir., Research*
KENYA BARBER

*Dir., Operations*
VALENCIA MCKINLEY

*Research*
JP

*Office Manager*
SHAWN THORNTON

*Operations / Sales*
CHERISH HERNDON

*Advertising Sales*
KATHLEEN WILCOX

*Data Entry*
KATHLEEN FASSBENDER

*Art Director*
DOTTI ALBERTINE

...............

*Advertising & Marketing*
dvlaw@hcdonline.com

*Research*
research@hcdonline.com

*Sales*
hcd@hcdonline.com

*Telephone*
310-315-4815
800-815-0503 (outside CA)

*Fax*
310-315-4816

*Website*
www.hcdonline.com

# A FEW WORDS FROM THE EDITOR

You've got a script that's ready to shoot. Most of the story takes place at a remote ski resort, about two miles from the nearest town. In Colorado. Or maybe Oregon. You need to do a cost, zoning and services analysis. Luckily, Colorado and Oregon, as well as most other states, have established film commissions to help make your life much easier. They're staffed with local experts whose job it is to work one on one with you to help you realize your vision and make location scouting in their state accessible. They keep databases of local talent and production services. They can provide information on anything you may wish to know, from what kind of weather to expect during your shoot, to where to hire a babysitter for your newborn, or where you might find a veggie burger.

In this issue, we pay tribute to those very same film commissions by including a special section. This was done in cooperation with the **ASSOCIATION OF FILM COMMISSIONERS INTERNATIONAL** (AFCI-see resource guide.) We hope this section will encourage you to use these offices and their resources in your future scouting. Also, don't forget about the recently added TV SHOW section (Section E.) It includes the show's running time, network, production company, show runners and other contact information. Keep in mind that some of the shows for the new season are not yet staffed and/or do not yet have official offices.

Lastly, we proudly introduce our new web page, which is up at www.hcdonline.com. It's now easier to use and contains the *Hollywood New Media Directory*, which was also recently published in book form. If you haven't done so, please call us for a free one week trial of the online database.

As always, we value your comments. Send correspondence via fax to 310-315-4794 or email bdugan@hcdonline.

Sincerely,

Barbara E. Dugan
Editor

# All Directors Guild members read DGA Magazine!

## So do Producers, Executives and Industry Professionals...

## Do they know something you don't?

**Subscribe Today!**

1 YEAR/6 ISSUES $24 (CANADA & MEXICO $35; FOREIGN $50)
CALL 800 421-4173, x5306 OR WRITE:
DGA MAGAZINE, 7920 SUNSET BLVD
LOS ANGELES, CA 90046-0907, USA
http://dga.org/dga/dganews/dganews.html

**Advertise Now!**

FOR RATES AND INFORMATION CONTACT:
SCOTT BURNELL AND ASSOCIATES
TEL 213 936-0672 • FAX 213 936-9188

THE MAGAZINE OF THE DIRECTORS GUILD OF AMERICA

# STUDIOS · NETWORKS AND MAJORS AT A GLANCE

**ABC ENTERTAINMENT**
2040 Avenue of the Stars
Los Angeles, CA  90067-4785
**310-557-7777**

**CASTLE ROCK ENTERTAINMENT**
335 N. Maple Drive #135
Beverly Hills, CA  90210-3867
**310-285-2300**

**CBS ENTERTAINMENT**
Los Angeles, CA  90036-2188
**323-975-2345**

**COMEDY CENTRAL**
1775 Broadway
New York, NY  10019
**212-767-8600**

**DREAMWORKS SKG**
100 Universal Plaza Bldg. 10
Universal City, CA  91608-1085
**818-733-7000**

**FOX BROADCASTING CO.**
10201 W. Pico Blvd.
Los Angeles, CA  90035
**310-369-1000**

**HBO (LA)**
2049 Century Park East   #4100
Los Angeles, CA  90067-3215
**310-201-9300**

**HBO (NY)**
1100 Avenue of the Americas
New York, NY  10036
**212-512-1000**

**METRO GOLDWYN MAYER/U.A.**
2500 Broadway St.
Santa Monica, CA  90404-3061
**310-449-3000**

**MIRAMAX FILMS  (LA)**
7966 Beverly Blvd.
Los Angeles, CA 90048
**213-951-4200**

**MIRAMAX FILMS (NY)**
375 Greenwich St.
New York, NY  10013-2338
**212-941-3800**

**MTV NETWORKS (LA)**
2600 Colorado Avenue
Santa Monica, CA 90404
**310-752-8000**

**MTV NETWORKS (NY)**
1515 Broadway
New York, NY  10036
**212-258-8000**

**NBC ENTERTAINMENT**
3000 W. Alameda Avenue
Burbank, CA  91523-0001
**818-840-4444**

**NEW LINE CINEMA (LA)**
116 N. Robertson #200
Los Angeles, CA  90048
**310-854-5811**

**NEW LINE CINEMA (NY)**
888 7th Avenue
New York, NY  10106
**212-649-4900**

**NICKELODEON/NICK AT NITE**
1515 Broadway, 38th Floor
New York, NY  10036
**212-258-7500**

**PARAMOUNT STUDIOS**
5555 Melrose Avenue
Los Angeles, CA  90038-3197
**323-956-5000**

**PBS**
1320 Braddock Place
Alexandria, VA  22314-1698
**703-739-5000**

**SHOWTIME NETWORKS INC.**
10880 Wilshire Blvd., Stes 1500 & 1600
Los Angeles, CA 90024
**310-234-5200**

**SHOWTIME NETWORKS INC (NY)**
1633 Broadway
New York, NY 10019
**212-708-1600**

**SONY PICTURES ENTERTAINMENT**
10202 W. Washington Blvd.
Culver City, CA  90232-3195
**310-244-4000**

**TURNER NETWORK TELEVISION (TNT) (LOS ANGELES)**
1888 Century Park East, 14th Fl.
Los Angeles, CA  90067
**310-551-6300**

**TURNER ENTERTAINMENT GROUP (ATLANTA)**
1050 Techwood Drive, NW
Atlanta, GA  30318-5604
**404-827-1500**

**TWENTIETH CENTURY FOX**
10201 W. Pico Blvd.
Los Angeles, CA  90035
**310-369-1000**

**UNITED PARAMOUNT NETWORK (UPN)**
11800 Wilshire Blvd.
Los Angeles, CA  90025
**310-575-7000**

**UNIVERSAL**
100 Universal City Plaza
Universal City, CA  91608-1085
**818-777-1000**

**VIACOM ENTERTAINMENT GROUP**
5555 Melrose Avenue
Hollywood, CA 90038
**323-956-5000**

**W.B. TELEVISION NETWORK**
4000 Warner Blvd., Bldg. 34-R
Burbank, CA  91522-0001
**818-977-5000**

**THE WALT DISNEY COMPANY**
500 South Buena Vista St.
Burbank, CA  91521-0001
**818-560-1000**

**WARNER BROS. STUDIOS**
4000 Warner Blvd.
Burbank, CA  91522-0001
**818-954-6000**

# These days, many AOL users are finding themselves S.O.L.

**AOL: America Off Line?**

Even though AOL is by far the largest online service, it now costs more and continues to be among the least accessible. The fact is, many subscribers still wait to get on AOL far longer and more often than with other providers.

Access, of course, is everything. And if you're looking to AOL to provide it, you're *?!# out of luck. With EarthLink, you'll find that we're up 99.9% of the time. You also won't be burdened with the annoying busy signals and disconnects AOL is famous for (nor their high prices: we're still $19.95 a month). And because we have more local access numbers than any other Internet Service Provider, you can also get on the Net more easily. Speaking of easily, that's how you can get in touch with us. Our phone number is cleverly listed below. Talk to you soon.

| PC MAGAZINE ISP RATINGS (9/97) | EarthLink | AOL |
| --- | --- | --- |
| Call Rate Success | Good | Poor |
| Average Throughput (download speed) | Excellent | Poor |
| Web Throughput Success | Excellent | Good |
| Overall Performance | Good | Poor |

EarthLink **Still** $19.95 PER MONTH

(888) QUIT-AOL, ext. 3966
784-8265

www.earthlink.net

# RESOURCE GUIDE

## GUILDS/UNIONS/ASSOCIATIONS

**ACADEMY OF MOTION PICTURE ARTS AND SCIENCES (AMPAS)**
8949 Wilshire Blvd.
Beverly Hills, CA 90211-1972
**310-247-3000 / FAX 310-859-9351**
**www.oscars.org**

**ACADEMY OF TELEVISION ARTS & SCIENCES**
5220 Lankershim Blvd.
N. Hollywood, CA 91601
**818-754-2800 / FAX 818-761-2827**
**www.emmys.org**

**ACTORS EQUITY ASSOCIATION**
5757 Wilshire Bl, Ste. 1
Los Angeles, CA 90036
**213-634-1750 / FAX 213-634-1777**

165 West 46th St.
New York, NY 10036
**212-869-8530 / FAX 212-719-9815**

**THE ACTORS FUND OF AMERICA**
4727 Wilshire Blvd., Ste. 310
Los Angeles, CA 90010
**213-933-9244 / FAX 213-933-7615**

1501 Broadway, Ste. 518
New York, NY 10036 5697
**212-221-7300 / FAX 212-764-0238**

**ALLIANCE OF MOTION PICTURE & TELEVISION PRODUCERS**
15503 Ventura Blvd.
Encino, CA 91436
**818-995-3600 / FAX 818-382-1793**

**AMERICAN FEDERATION OF TELEVISION AND RADIO ARTISTS (AFTRA)**
5757 Wilshire Blvd., Ste. 900
Los Angeles, CA 90036
**213-634-8100 / FAX 213-634-8246**

260 Madison Avenue, 7th Floor
New York, NY 10016
**212-532-0800 / FAX 212-545-1238**

**AMERICAN FILM MARKETING ASSOCIATION**
10850 Wilshire Blvd., 9th Floor
Los Angeles, CA 90024
**310-446-1000 / FAX 310-446-1600**
**www.afma.com**

**AMERICAN FILM INSTITUTE (AFI)**
2021 N. Western Ave.
Los Angeles, CA 90027
**213-856-7600 / FAX 213-467-4578**
**www.afionline.org**

**AMERICAN WOMEN IN RADIO & TELEVISION, INC. (AWRT)**
1650 Tysons Blvd., Ste. 200
McLean, VA 22102
**703-506-3290 / FAX 703-506-3266**
**www.awrt.org**

**ASCAP**
7920 Sunset Blvd., 3rd Floor
Los Angeles, CA 90046
**213-883-1000 / FAX 213-883-1049**
**www.ascap.com**

1 Lincoln Plaza
New York, NY 10023
**212-621-6000**

**ASSOCIATION OF FILM COMMISSIONERS INTERNATIONAL (AFCI)**
7060 Hollywood Blvd.
Los Angeles, CA 90028
**213-462-6092 / FAX 213-462-6091**
**www.afciweb.org**

**BMI**
8730 Sunset Blvd., 3rd Floor W.
Los Angeles, CA 90069
**310-659-9109 / FAX 310-657-6947**
**www.bmi.com**

320 W. 57th Street
New York, NY 10019
**212-586-2000 / FAX 212-489-2368**

*(continued on page 10)*

*(continued on page 13)*

The **Story Project** is a program for inner city young adults. It is about exchanging, sharing and communicating their own voices while learning the art of story telling. In an intimate setting in the heart of the city, youths will interact with professionals in the entertainment industry.

Professionals will share their own stories and experiences, then listen to the teenagers tell of experiences growing up in challenging surroundings.

We expect to succeed in inspiring our participants, who have limited avenues, to learn and express themselves by completing writing and story telling assignments. This will also improve their literacy skills and promote healthy self esteem.

**For more information on this mentoring program, please call Debbie Vandermeulen at 310·277·0707.**

# Read It! Do It!

## CREATIVE SCREENWRITING

"THERE ARE NOW A FEW FINE SCREENWRITING JOURNALS. CREATIVE SCREENWRITING IS NOT FINE. IT IS THE BEST!!"

LEW HUNTER (*SCREENWRITING 434*)

"I HAVE NOTHING BUT PRAISE FOR YOUR PUBLICATION. OTHER PUBLICATIONS CAN ONLY ASPIRE TO BE CREATIVE SCREENWRITING. I KNOW, I SUBSCRIBE TO MOST OF THEM."

DANIEL THOMPSON

"CREATIVE SCREENWRITING IS AN INVALUABLE RESOURCE FOR WRITING AND MARKETING YOUR SCREENPLAY, WHICH I HIGHLY RECOMMEND TO ALL MY READERS AND STUDENTS."

MICHAEL HAUGE (*WRITING SCREENPLAYS THAT SELL*)

## CREATIVE SCREENWRITING
### THE SCREENWRITER'S JOURNAL

## Subscribe Today!
## 800-SCRNWRT

## Don't Miss the July/August Issue on Writing Science Fiction
### Interviews with Bruce Joel Rubin, Carrie Fisher, Essay by Harlan Ellison

Available at Barnes and Noble, B. Dalton, Borders, and Hastings Bookstores

# Why Score in L.A.?

## It's Fast.

When you have
a schedule to keep,
it makes sense to score
in the home of the motion
picture industry.

It also makes sense to work with professional
musicians. They can save both time and expense by getting
the music you need fast. Better quality and a better bottom line...
after all, that's what being professional is all about!

817 Vine Street, Suite 209
Hollywood, California 90038
(213) 462-4762 • Fax (213) 462-2406

*Call for the free 300 page L.A. RMA Directory Sourcebook*

817 Vine Street
Hollywood, California 90038
(213) 993-3173 • Fax (213) 461-5260

# RESOURCE GUIDE

*(continued frompage 10)*

## SCREEN ACTORS GUILD (SAG)
5757 Wilshire Blvd.
Los Angeles, CA 90036-3600
**213-954-1600 / FAX 213-954-6603**

1515 Broadway, 44th Floor
New York, NY 10036
**212-944-1030 / FAX 212-944-6774**
**www.sag.com**

## SCREEN ACTORS GUILD CONTRACTS
Industrial / Educational / Interactive
CD Rom . . . . . . . . . . . . . . . . . . . . . . . .213-549-6850
Commercial / Music Videos / Infomercials . .213-549-6858

### PRODUCTION SERVICES
Extras . . . . . . . . . . . . . . . . . . . . . . . . .213-549-6811
Singers Rep . . . . . . . . . . . . . . . . . . . . . .213-549-6864
Television Contracts . . . . . . . . . . . . . . .213-549-6842
Theatrical Contracts . . . . . . . . . . . . . . .213-549-6828

### OTHER DEPARTMENTS
Actors to Locate . . . . . . . . . . . . . . . . . .213-549-6737
Affirmative Action . . . . . . . . . . . . . . . .213-549-6644
Communications . . . . . . . . . . . . . . . . . .213-549-6654
Dues Information . . . . . . . . . . . . . . . . .213-549-6755
SAG Foundation . . . . . . . . . . . . . . . . . .213-549-6773
Legal Affairs . . . . . . . . . . . . . . . . . . . .213-549-6627
Membership Services . . . . . . . . . . . . . .213-549-6778
New Memberships . . . . . . . . . . . . . . . .213-549-6769
Residuals . . . . . . . . . . . . . . . . . . . . . . .213-549-6505
Station 12 . . . . . . . . . . . . . . . . . . . . . .213-549-6794
Signatory Records . . . . . . . . . . . . . . . .213-549-6869
SAG Pension & Health . . . . . . . . . . . . .818-954-9400
Safety Hotline . . . . . . . . . . . . . . . . . . .213-954-1600

## SESAC
421 West 54 St., 4th Floor
New York, NY  10019-4405
**212-586-3450 / FAX 212-489-5699**

55 Music Square East
Nashville, TN 37203
**615-320-0055 / FAX 615-329-9627**

## SOCIETY OF COMPOSERS AND LYRICISTS
400 S. Beverly Drive, Ste. 214
Beverly Hills, CA 90212
**310-281-2812 / FAX 310-990-0601**

## WOMEN IN FILM
6464 Sunset Blvd. #1080
Los Angeles, CA 90028
**213-463-6040 / FAX 213-463-0963**
**www.wif.org**

## WRITER'S GUILD OF AMERICA WEST (WGAW)
7000 W. 3rd St.
Los Angeles, CA 90048
**213-951-4000 / FAX 213-782-4800**
**Agency Listing: 213-782-4502**
**www.wga.org**

## WRITER'S GUILD OF AMERICA EAST (WGAE)
555 West 57th St., Suite 1230
New York, NY 10019
**212-767-7800 / FAX 212-582-1909**
**www.wgaeast.org**

## LIBRARIES

## BEVERLY HILLS PUBLIC LIBRARY
444 N. Rexford Dr.
Beverly Hills, CA 90210
**REFERENCE: 310-288-2244**

## MARGARET HERRICK LIBRARY
## ACADEMY OF MOTION PICURE ARTS & SCIENCES
333 S. La Cienega Blvd.
Beverly Hills, CA 90211
**REFERENCE: 310-247-3020 / FAX 310-657-5193**

## NEW YORK CITY LIBRARY
476 5th Ave.
New York, NY 10018
**TELEPHONE REFERENCE AND GENERAL INFORMATION:**
**212-340-0849**
**www.nypl.org**

## NEW YORK PUBLIC LIBRARY FOR THE PERFORMING ARTS
## — DANCE, DRAMA & FILM DEPT.
40 Lincoln Center Plaza
New York, NY 10023-7498
**212-870-1630**

## MUSEUM OF TELEVISION & RADIO
465 N. Beverly Dr.
Beverly Hills, CA 90210
**310-786-1000 / FAX 310-786-1086**
**www.mtr.org**

## JAMES R. WEBB MEMORIAL LIBRARY
## WRITERS GUILD FOUNDATION
7000 W. Third Street
Los Angeles, CA 90048-4329
**213-782-4544 / FAX 213-782-4695**
**wgafound@mail.directnet.com**

*(continued on page 17)*

# Take a Meeting

## With Hollywood's Hottest Writers

## Best Overall
### Trade Publication

## Most Improved
### Trade Publication

## Best Special Interest
### Trade Publication

**1998 MAGGIE AWARDS/
WESTERN PUBLICATIONS ASSOCIATION**

# Written By

THE JOURNAL OF THE WRITERS GUILD OF AMERICA, WEST

# RESOURCE GUIDE

## TERMS & TYPES

*The information contained in the **Hollywood Creative Directory** is provided to us directly by the companies listed in the book. We do not engage in guess work or editorializing. For example, if a company tells us they produced The XYZ Film and they did not, we cannot be held responsible. If any information does indeed appear incorrectly, it was likely due to human error or misrepresentation of facts by the listee and for that we apologize. Furthermore, telephone numbers and addresses continually change. These are things that we cannot control, unless we were to reprint the book every day. That's why we created hcdonline (www.hcdonline.com) to provide our readers with weekly updates. Call us for a free trial!*

## TERMS

**CREDIT:** A released feature film or broadcast television program which was produced by the company or one of its principals.

**DEAL:** An on-going development deal such as an exclusive, non-exclusive, or first-look right to the company's projects for a period of time.

## TYPES

**ANIMATION:** The company produces animated motion pictures or television programming.

**DOCUMENTARIES:** The company produces film or television programs portraying actual events or the lives of real people.

**FEATURES DIRECT TO VIDEO:** Full-length films which are released on video, but not shown in theaters.

**INTERACTIVE MULTIMEDIA:** The catch-all phrase for new media: CD-ROM, on-line, kiosk, games, etc.

**MOTION PICTURES:** Full-length feature films which have had a theatrical release.

**SYNDICATION**

**TELEVISION:** Commercially broadcast entertainment programming.



17

# THE BENEFITS OF WORKING WITH PROFESSIONALS

**by Linda Taylor Hutchison**

*"The more I see of our film...the more I realize how much we have been kidding ourselves in feeling that we could get really effective stuff on the back lot that should have been shot on location... Frankly, I am now terribly sorry we didn't build Tara on location... "*
— DAVID 0. SELZNICK MEMO, MARCH 9, 1939

As it was then, there will always be scripts and scenes that deserve and demand the authenticity, texture, mood or sheer sweep of nature that a real location offers.

If David O. Selznick were making "Gone With the Wind" today, finding the perfect location for Tara would be a breeze. With one call to **The Association of Film Commissioners International** (AFCI), he could find more than 260 film commissioners around the world eager to be of service, without charge.

The first film commission was formed in the late 1940s in response to the need for film companies to have an on-the-spot government liaison who could coordinate local services such as police, road and highway departments, fire departments, park rangers and other essential production elements.

The pioneers in location filming found that when local governments and location managers worked together, it was a win-win situation. The studio benefited from having a local expert at its disposal; the location benefited from the money the studio spent while on location, plus discovering that exposure in popular films could be priceless billboards for tourism long after the production had wrapped.

Since then, film commissions have been established in 23 countries around the globe, generating billions of dollars for their local economies while contributing to the creative richness and smooth production of thousands of major feature films, documentaries, music videos, television programs, commercials and photo shoots.

The AFCI is an international, non-profit, educational organization of government employees serving as film commissioners. Its members provide, without fee, core services including: location scouting assistance; liaison services with local industry facilities, services and government; and, location research. They are "one-stop shops" to assist with a myriad of elements essential to location and location production decisions.

AFCI members are committed to upholding high standards of professionalism. They are responsive to the needs of a producer, knowledgeable about production practices, and have an excellent understanding of how to get things done in their jurisdiction.

To ensure optimal assistance from a film commission, make contact at the earliest feasible stage of the pre-

(continued from page 19)

# SINCE THEN, FILM COMMISSIONS HAVE BEEN ESTABLISHED IN 23 COUNTRIES AROUND THE GLOBE, GENERATING BILLIONS OF DOLLARS FOR THEIR LOCAL ECONOMIES.

possible. Provide a script, outline or story board if you can, together with information about the production time frame, special effects requirements and any other conditions that are integral to the production process.

Arranging for permits is still an important film commission function. As government-supported organizations, film commissions have well-established working relationships with other governmental agencies and can therefore facilitate the permitting process.

Aside from permitting, a film commission can offer a wealth of information about local resources such as lodging, transportation, rentals, specialized equipment, crew, production facilities and more. Many film commissions produce resource guides covering a wide array of production services and resources in the area and many have websites, as well.

Because AFCI film commission members are prohibited from having any financial interest in any business or service benefiting from production, and cannot be a labor union, private business or proprietary commercial entity, the producer is assured that no conflicts of interest exist.

So, chances are, wherever your production requirements may take you, you can count on an AFCI film commission to assist you and facilitate the shoot in four important ways:

**(1)** THEY CAN SAVE YOU PRODUCTION TIME AND MONEY;

**(2)** THEY ACT AS YOUR LIAISON WITH BOTH GOVERNMENT AND THE PRIVATE SECTOR;

**(3)** THEY KNOW THE TERRITORY; AND

**(4)** THEY WORK WITHOUT FEE.

(continued on page 22)

## FILM IN YOUR BACKYARD

J ust two hours from Los Angeles, Big Bear Lake offers some of the most beautiful scenery in Southern California with our pristine alpine lakes, rugged wilderness, high desert terrain and breathtaking mountain vistas.

For more information on filming in Big Bear Lake, please contact the Big Bear Lake Film Office at 909-878-3040.

BIG BEAR LAKE FILM OFFICE • P.O. BOX 10000 • BIG BEAR LAKE, CA 92315 • 909-878-3040

The makers of *Ace Ventura: When Nature Calls* discovered that the Dark Continent is just down the road from us. And what's really wild is that this resort ranch supplied a lot of the exotic game animals for the filming. So if you're hunting for an affordable location that's right out of Africa, shoot San Antonio. With your camera, of course.



1-800-447-3372 (Ask for Kathy Rhoads), P.O. Box 2277
San Antonio, TX 78298-2277 (210) 207-6700 • www.SanAntonioCVB.com

# THE PIONEERS IN LOCATION FILMING FOUND THAT WHEN LOCAL GOVERNMENTS AND LOCATION MANAGERS WORKED TOGETHER, IT WAS A WIN-WIN SITUATION.

production process. Then, keep the lines of communication open, creating a partnership of trust that allows the film commission to provide service and support from the start to the close of production.

The more the film commission knows, the more it will be able to provide production options and resources for consideration, so supply as much information as

*(continued on page 20)*

## MONUMENTAL SITES IN ONE GREAT LOCATION



Obviously, there are more than 20 monumental reasons to shoot here in the nation's Capital. But, there are other advantages, too. Beyond the Capital dome and Washington Monument is a multicultural city full of historic sites, diverse neighborhoods and charming vistas, just waiting to be captured on film. You need only look around our 67 square mile "back lot." It's all here. ✪ The Office of Motion Picture & Television Development (OMPTD) will assist you in discovering all the hidden treasures in Washington, DC. We invite you to explore our unique city and we are sure you will agree that "Washington, DC is Picture Perfect" for your monumental project.

**District of Columbia, Office of Motion Picture & Television Development**
**410 Eighth Street, N.W., Washington, DC 20004**
Phone: 202-727-6608 • Fax: 202-727-3787 • E-mail: tvfilm@erols.com • Web site: www.erols.com/tvfilm

© AAA Reproduced by permission.

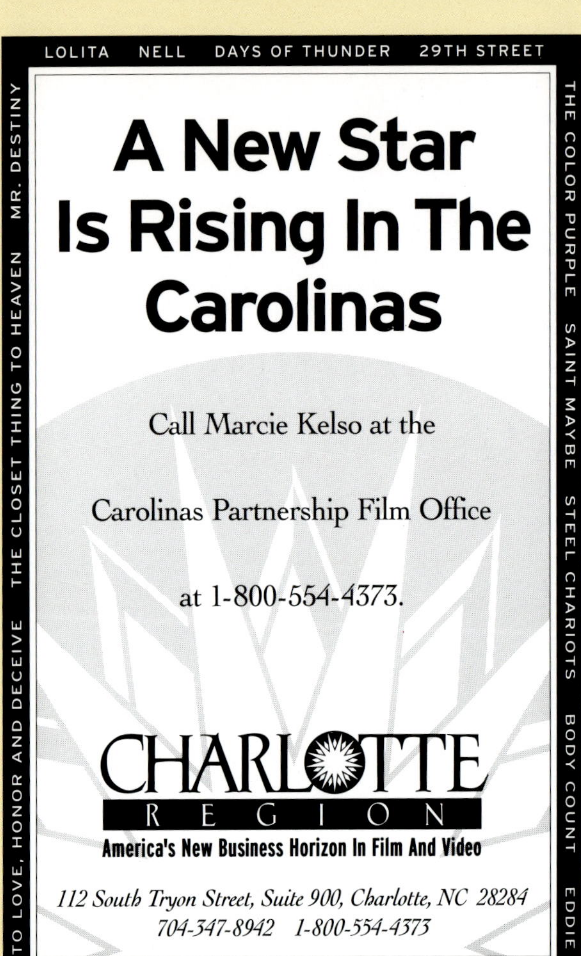


(continued from page 20)

A tip to feature film producers: Film commissioners will appreciate an acknowledgment in the end credits; it's the only compensation they accept from filmmakers for their hard work.

In addition to offering a directory of its members, the AFCI also produces the only annual trade show for worldwide location production services; "Locations '99" is scheduled for February 19-21, 1999, at the Los Angeles Convention Center. Admission is free to entertainment industry professionals.

**For more information, contact:**
**ASSOCIATION OF FILM COMMISSIONERS INTERNATIONAL (AFCI)**
**7060 Hollywood Blvd., Los Angeles, CA 90028**
TELEPHONE    **(213) 462-6092**
FAX    **(213) 462-6091**
AFCI WEBSITE    **www.afciweb.org**

*Linda Taylor Hutchison is President of the Association of Film Commissioners International (AFCI) and Director of the New Mexico Film Commission.*

## Need to film in the Oval Office and can't get security clearance?

**Virginia has an Oval Office set** and

**Architecture in Richmond doubles for**

**a facade of the 1860's Lincoln White House**

**Washington, D.C.**

**No problem.**

Consider Virginia first when your projects **call** for the nation's capital.

**VIRGINIA THE FILM OFFICE**

Oval Office information:
804.957.4200
Virginia production information:
800.854.6233

Lance Henriksen as Abraham Lincoln in the TNT original, THE DAY LINCOLN WAS SHOT.  photo: Andrew Eccles

# HOLLYWOOD CREATIVE DIRECTORY

## FILM COMMISSION ADVERTISERS

**BIG BEAR LAKE FILM OFFICE**
399707 Big Bear Blvd.
P.O. Box 10000
Big Bear Lake, CA  92315
Phone:  909-878-3040
Fax:  909-866-6766
Pager:  909-514-2161
Email:  **bblfilm@citybigbearlake.com**
Web:  **www.citybigbearlake.com/film.html**
Staff:  Ranee Ruble, Manager
Credits:  *Parent Trap, The Opposite of Sex
Dr. Dolittle.*

**CHARLOTTE REGION FILM OFFICE**
112 S. Tryon Street, Suite 900
Charlotte, NC  28284
Email:  **mkelso@charlotteregion.com**
Web:  **www.charlotteregion.com**
Staff:  Marcie Kelso, Director
Beth Petty, Location Coordinator
Credits:  *Black Dog, He Got Game, Saint Maybe*

**CHICAGO FILM OFFICE**
One North LaSalle Street, Suite 2165
Chicago, IL  60602
Phone:  312-744-6415
Fax:  312-744-1378
Email:  **FilmOffice@ci.chi.il.us**
Web:  **www.ci.chi.il.us.**
Staff:  Richard Moskal, Director

**COLORADO MOTION PICTURE
AND TELEVISION COMMISSION**
1625 Broadway, Suite 1700
Denver, CO  80202-4729
Phone:  303-620-4500
800-SCOUT US
Fax:  303-620-4545
Email:  **coloradofilm@state.co.us**
**www.coloradofilm.org**
Staff:  Michael Klein, Director
Stephanie Two Eagles, Location Specialist
Mary Crawford, Location Specialist
Patti Bonnet, Location Specialist
Lora Mihelic,  Program Assistant
Andrea Winter, Administration Assistant

# Unmatched Resources, and a Fast Clip to Boot.

One of the great things about shooting in the Dallas-Ft.Worth area is the outstanding quality of the local backup support. With resources such as the Irving Texas Film Commission and the Studios at Las Colinas, you'll have everything you need on location right at your fingertips. Which means we can get you in and out. Fast. And since we've got everything here that you've got there, you won't have to worry about getting everything from there, here. So pack light. Just don't forget the boots. **1.800.2.IRVING**

## IRVING TEXAS FILM COMMISSION
Irving Convention and Visitors Bureau

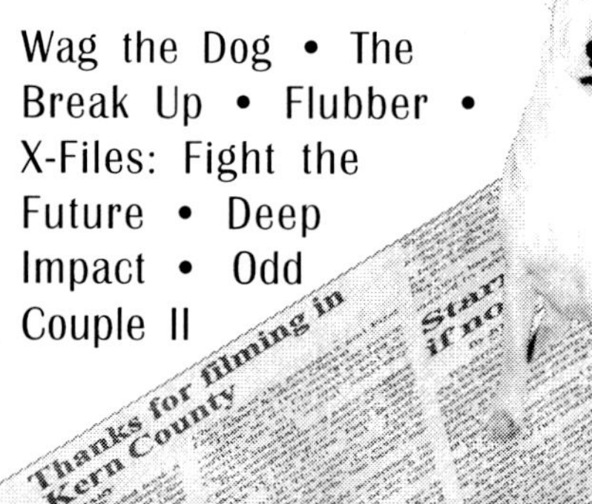


(continued from page 24)

## COLORADO SPRINGS FILM COMMISSION
104 South Cascade Avenue, Suite 104
Colorado Springs, CO  80903
Phone:   719-635-7506 x131
         800-368-4748 x131
Fax:     719-635-4968
Email:   **eforeman@coloradosprings-travel.com**
Web:     **www.film@coloradosprings-travel.com**
Staff:   Edwina A. Forman, Film Commissioner, Mgr.
         Steve Ladden, Film Commissioner
Credits: *StrangeLand, Adventures with a Duchess*

## GEORGIA FILM & VIDEOTAPE OFFICE
285 Peachtree Center Avenue, Suite 1000
Atlanta, GA  30303
Phone:   404-656-3591
Fax:     404-651-9063
Email:   **gafilm@georgia.org**
Web:     **www.Georgia.org**
Staff:   Greg Torre, Director
         Lee Thomas, Project Manager
         A.B. Cooper, Public Relations &
           Information Specialist
         Carri Gibbs Luse, Field Representative
         John Findley, Field Representative
Credits: *Black Dog, Scream 2*
         *Midnight in the Garden of Good and Evil*

## GREATER PHILADELPHIA FILM OFFICE
1600 Arch Street, 12th Floor
Philadelphia, PA  19103
Phone:   215-686-2668
Fax:     215-686-3659
Email:   **mail@film.org**
Web:     **www.film.org**
Staff:   Sharon Pinkenson, Executive Director
         Peter Leokum, Deputy Director
         Dena Robbins, Director of Resources
         Joan Bressler, Projects Coordinator
         Joan Gerstie, Secretary
         Heather Seok, Assistant to the Executive
           Director
         Cheri Zucca, Staff Assistant

## IRVING TEXAS FILM COMMISSION
6309 N. O'Connor Road, Suite 222
Irving, TX  75039
Phone:   972-869-0303
         800-2-IRVING
Fax:     972-869-4609
Email:   **itfc@airmail.net**
Web:     **www.irvingtexas.com**
Staff:   Ellen Sandoloski Mayers, Director
         Nancy Cunningham, Assistant Director
Credits: *Walker, Texas Ranger, Wishbone, Barney*

(continued on page 28)

# SCOUT LOUISIANA

**State of Louisiana Office of Film and Video    P.O. Box 44320    Baton Rouge, LA 70804-4320**

(continued from page 26)

**KANSAS FILM COMMISSION**
700 SW Harrison Street, Suite 1300
Topeka, KS  66603
Phone:   785-296-4927
Fax:       785-296-6988
Email:    **vhenley@KDOCH.STATE.KS.US**
Web:      **www.kansascommerce.com**
Staff:    Vicky Henley, Manager
            Mary McCaffrey, Assistant Manager
            Keith Russell, Secretary
Credits:  *Ride with the Devil, Monday After the
            Miracle, Mars Attacks!*

**KERN COUNTY BOARD OF TRADE**
2101 Oak Street
Bakersfield, CA  93268
Phone:   805-861-2367
 800-500-KERN
Fax:       805-861-2017
Email:    **tourism@lightspeed.net**
Staff:    Ann Gutcher, Film Commissioner
            Aimee Bajaras, Marketing Associate
            Dave Hook, Marketing Associate
Credits:  *Wag the Dog, X-Files: The Movie
            Deep Impact*

**OMAHA/DOUGLAS COUNTY FILM COMMISSION**
6800 Mercy Road, Suite 202
Omaha, NE 68106-2627
Phone:   402-444-7736
            402-444-7737
Fax:       402-444-4511
Email:    **shootomaha@juno.com**
Web:      **www.visitomaha.com**
Staff:    Julie Ginsberg, Film Commissioner
            Kathy Sheppard, Film Commissioner
Credits:  *Too Wong Foo, Citizen Ruth, O Pioneers*

**OREGON FILM & VIDEO OFFICE**
One World Trade Center
121 SW Salmon Street, Suite 1205
Portland, OR  97204
Phone:   503-229-5832
Fax:       503-229-6869
Email:    **Shoot@OregonFilm.org**
Web:      **www.OregonFilm.org**
Staff:    David Woolson, Executive Director
            Veronica Rinard, Assistant Director
            Kaja Zaloudek, Project Manager
            Patty Frazier, Office Manager
            Bona Huston, Special Projects
Credits:  *Zero Effect, Mr. Holland's Opus
            The River Wild*

(continued on page 30)

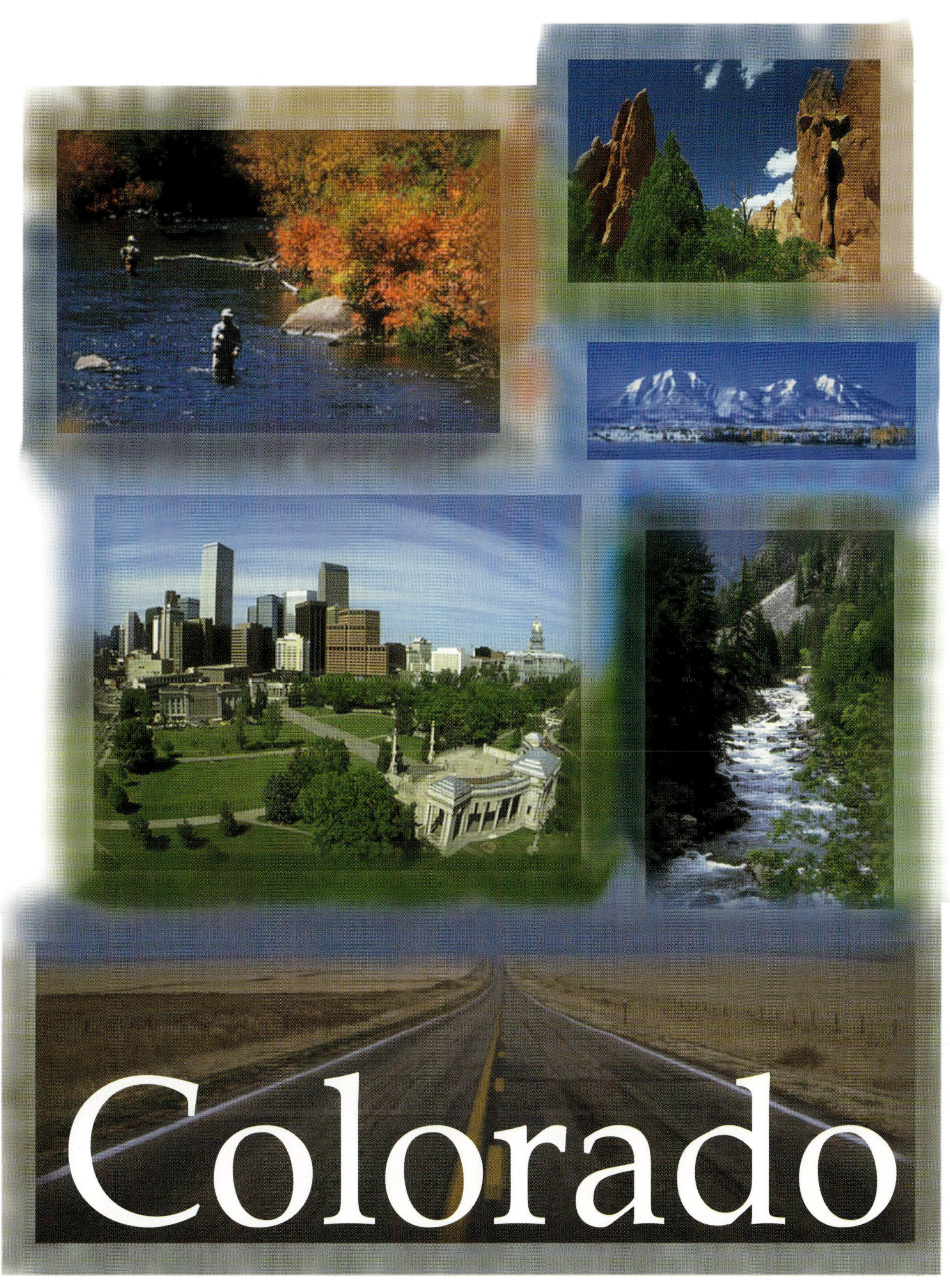


Colorado Motion Picture and Television Commission
1-800-SCOUT US   www.coloradofilm.org

(continued from page 28)

## NEVADA FILM OFFICE
555 E. Washington Ave., Suite 5400
Las Vegas, NV 89101
5151 S. Carson Street
Carson City, NV 89701
Phone: 800-336-1600
        702-486-2711
Fax:    702-786-2712
        702-687-4450
Email:  **ccnmp@bizopp.state.nv.us**
Web:    **nevada-mpd.state.nv.us**
Staff:  Charles Geocan, Director
        Robin Holabird, Deputy Director
Credits: *Lethal Weapon 4, Jane Austen's Mafia!*

## SAN ANTONIO FILM COMMISSION
P.O. Box 2277
San Antonio, TX 78298
203 S. St. Mary's, 2nd Floor
San Antonio, TX 78205
Phone: 210-207-6700
Fax:   210-207-6843
Email: **filmsa@sanantoniocvb.com**
Web:   **www.sanantoniocvb.com**
Staff: Kathy Rhoads, Director
       Sonia Guardiola, Account Executive
Credits: *Selena, Eddie*
         *Ace Ventura: When Nature Calls*

## SANTA BARBARA CONFERENCE AND VISITORS BUREAU & FILM COMMISSION
12 East Carrillo Street
Santa Barbara, CA 93101
Phone: 805-966-9222
Fax:   805-966-1728
Email: **sbfilmcomm@aol.com**
Web:   **sbfilmcomm.com**
Staff: Elizabeth Melley Genolio, Film Commissioner
Credits: *The Odd Couple II, GI Jane, Face/Off*

## VIRGINIA FILM OFFICE
901 E. Byrd Street
Richmond, VA 23210-4048
Phone: 804-371-8204
       800-854-6233
Fax:   804-317-8177
Email: **Vafilm@vedp.state.va .us**
Web:   **Film.Virginia.Org**
Staff: Rita D. McClenny, Director
       Rebecca Albert, Marketing Manager
       Mary Nelson, Communications Manager
       Andrew Edmonds, Location Manager
       Tammie Blockburger, Staff Assistant
Credits: *Deep Impact, GI Jane, The Jackal*

# IT'S IN THE KAN

# Shoot Omaha!

"Skip, babe. Hey, it's me, Cliff. I've found the perfect location for that last scene."

Skip closed his eyes at the sound of the voice coming from the speakerphone and placed the flat of his hand over his high forehead. Cliff, his cost-unconscious and cocky location manager, was blessed with the innate ability to ruin an otherwise good day.

"Refresh my memory," Skip sighed and leaned forward against his desk. "I've got a half-dozen films in the can."

In an overly enthusiastic voice, Cliff said, "The train station scene. You know, where the German spy gets gunned down by the secret agent - single father of three."

*I've got to start producing better films*, Skip thought to himself. "Yeah, I remember." Skip nodded his head weakly. "I also remember that part of the film being too expensive to shoot. Something about the high price the train station people wanted to charge to rent the joint."

"Yeah, well, thanks to Julie and Kathy, two film commissioners *everyone* in this crazy industry should meet, I've got the train station, *and* I got it at less than half the price."

Skip was beginning to like Cliff, his overindulgent location manager. But something he said wasn't quite right. "Wait a minute. Who's Julie? And who's Kathy? They're not with our Film Commission. And how can they promise us the train station so cheaply?"

Cliff chuckled out loud. *I should be the one producing movies*, he thought to himself. "No, no, no," he groaned. "Julie and Kathy are in Omaha, with the Film Commission. And it's the Omaha Union Station. Do you believe that price?"

Skip quickly picked up the phone. He was on to something, and he wanted to keep it a secret. "Cliff," he whispered determinedly in the phone. "You tell anyone about Omaha and the low cost of shooting movies there, I'll personally see to it that your next location scout will be for a cable access series. Now go secure that last location… in Omaha."

The dawn of digital effects.

# Special effects are

If you can dream it, we can deliver it. Our effects facilities are
absolutely leading edge. And more importantly, they're fueled

# a Georgia specialty.

by the limitless imaginations of the people who work here. Call
the Georgia Film and Videotape Office at (404) 651-8570.
With our attitude, everything is possible.



**EVERYTHING YOU'RE SHOOTING FOR.**

# COMPANIES NEW TO THIS ISSUE 

*This new feature to the HCD should be a time-saver. No more weekends on the couch highlighting new companies. We have compiled a list of those companies for you. Some of these companies are recently established. Other companies have been around for a while, and are just now being listed or have come back after a hiatus from the book. They still appear within the "Companies and Staff" section with asterisks next to their listings.*

Amphion/Nitestar Productions
Auerbach Company Baltimore Pictures, Inc.
Bauer Company, The
Beach House
Bigel/Mailer Films
Bleecker Street Films
Blue Bay Productions
Blue Horizon
Borchers, Donald P.
Bristol Cities
BThree Films
Buckeye Entertainment Group
Burlage/Edell Productions, Inc.
Capo Productions
Carreras Productions
Carter Company, The Thomas
Cartoon Network
CinePoint Productions, Inc.
Cinewest Productions
Cobblestone Films
Cohen & Ryan Films, Inc.
Cohen Productions Inc., Herman
Cohen Productions, Martin B.
Common Ground Entertainment
Comsky Group Productions
cTonic Fliks
Edelson Productions
Enchantment Films, Inc.
Everyman Pictures
Fields Co., The
FilmSaavy
First Cold Press Productions
First Entertainment LLC
First Folio Films
Flying Freehold Productions
Fortis Films
Fresh Produce Company
Freyer Productions, Ellen
Front Street Productions
Gallo Entertainment, Inc.
Germain Productions, Stephanie
Glatzer Productions

Gleneagle Productions
Goldbar Entertainment
Goldwyn Films Inc.
Greenblatt Janollari Studio, The
Greif Company
Gross Management, Ken
Hellman Productions, Jerome
Hunt-Tavel Productions
Iwerks Entertainment
Jericho Entertainment
Jersey Shore
Jinks/Cohen Company, The
Kedzie Productions
Lake Como Pictures
Latitude Films
Legend Entertainment
Levinson/Fontana Company, LLC, The
Lexington Road Productions
Lions Gate Films Production
LookAlike Productions
Lower East Side Films
Madguy Films
Magic Hour Pictures
MakeMagic Productions
Mandalay Television
March Hare Entertainment
Mary Ann-LaGlo Productions
Master Thespian Productions
Material
Mendillo/Form Productions
Mindless Entertainment
Miranda Entertainment
Mischel Co., The
More/Medavoy Management
Motor City Films
Mount Royal Entertainment
MPH Entertainment, Inc.
Mutant Enemy, Inc.
Nava Films
Newmarket Capital Group
Ocelot Films, Inc.
One Story Pictures
Out of the Blue . . . Entertainment

Overbrook Entertainment
Palomar Pictures
Panamort Television
Paramount International Television
Picture Factory, The
Proud Mary Entertainment
Raskin Productions, Bonnie
Rat Entertainment
Raylin Entertainment
Razors Edge Productions, Inc.
Red Mullet, Inc.
Rehme Productions
Ridini Entertainment Corporation
RKO Pictures, Inc.
Saphier Productions
Schiff Productions, Paul
Sellers Productions, Dylan
Simian Films
Sladek Entertainment
Snapdragon Films Inc.
Spanky Pictures, Inc.
Startz Productions, Inc., Jane
State Street Pictures
Studios USA
Studios USA Pictures
Studios USA Talk Television
Studios USA Television
TBS Superstation
Team Todd
Telvan Productions
Terra Bella Entertainment
Traveler's Rest Films
Trinity Pictures, Inc.
Tse Productions, Simon
Two Stepp Productions
UBU Productions
Utopia Films
Voight Entertainment, Jon
Westwind Productions, Inc.
Whidbey Island Films, Inc.
Write Place Write Time
York Company, The

# HAVE YOU BEEN ASKED TO COPY THIS BOOK?

## COPYRIGHT INFRINGEMENT IS A FEDERAL CRIME.

We offer rewards on information of illegal photocopying or distribution of any of our books. Please call our office.

*Your identity will be protected.*

**310-315-4815**

# SECTION A.

# Companies and Staff

NOTE: Paramount was in the process of changing area codes at press time. All companies on the Paramount lot will eventually change from 213 to 323. If a 213 area code does not work, try 323.

# COMPANIES AND STAFF

## 1492 PICTURES
PHONE . . . . . . . . . . . . . . . . . . . . . . . . . . . . . . 310-369-2368
10201 W. Pico Blvd., Bldg. 86, 2nd Fl.
Los Angeles, CA 90035

| | |
|---|---|
| TYPE | Motion Pictures + Television |
| CREDITS | Nine Months - Jingle All The Way |

Chris Columbus . . . . . . . . . . . . . . . . Writer/Director/Producer/Partner
Mark Radcliffe . . . . . . . . . . . . . . . . . . . . . . . . . Producer/Partner
Michael Barnathan . . . . . . . . . . . . . . . . . . President/Producer/Partner
Paula DuPre-Pesmen . . . . . . . . . . . . . . . . . . . . Associate Producer
Jennifer Blum . . . . . . . . . . . . . . . . . . . . . . . . VP, Creative Affairs
James Mulay . . . . . . . . . . . . . . . . . . . . . . . . VP, Creative Affairs
Karen Swallow . . . . . . . . . . . . . . . . . . . . . . . . . . Chief of Staff
Elizabeth Devereux . . . . . . . . . . . . . . . . . . . Asst. to Mr. Columbus
Jeanne Austin . . . . . . . . . . . . . . . . . . . . . . Asst. to Mr. Radcliffe
Lesley Howard . . . . . . . . . . . . . . . . . . . . . . . Asst. to Mr. Mulay
Pamela McIntyre . . . . . . . . . . . . . . . . . . . . Asst. to Mr. Barnathan
Michelle Miller . . . . . . . . . . . . . . . . . . . . . . . Asst. to Ms. Blum

## 3 ARTS ENTERTAINMENT
PHONE . . . . . . . . . . . . . . . . 310-888-3200/212-262-6565
FAX . . . . . . . . . . . . . . . . . . 310-888-3210/212-246-1522
9460 Wilshire Blvd., 7th Fl.
Beverly Hills, CA 90212

| | |
|---|---|
| TYPE | Motion Pictures + Television |
| CREDITS | Chris Rock Show - King of the Hill |

Dave Becky . . . . . . . . . . . . . . . . . . . . . . . . . . . . . New York
Jeff Golenberg . . . . . . . . . . . . . . . . . . . . . . . . . . . No Title
Howard Klein . . . . . . . . . . . . . . . . . . . . . . . . . . . . No Title
Raelle Koota . . . . . . . . . . . . . . . . . . . . . . . . . . . New York
Molly Madden . . . . . . . . . . . . . . . . . . . . . . . . . . . No Title
David Miner . . . . . . . . . . . . . . . . . . . . . . . . . . . New York
Daniel Rappaport . . . . . . . . . . . . . . . . . . . . . . . . . No Title
Michael Rotenberg . . . . . . . . . . . . . . . . . . . . . . . . . No Title
Mark Schulman . . . . . . . . . . . . . . . . . . . . . . . . . . . No Title
Rich Silverman . . . . . . . . . . . . . . . . . . . . . . . . . . . No Title
Scott Solomon . . . . . . . . . . . . . . . . . . . . . . . . Co-Head, Film
Lainie Sorkin . . . . . . . . . . . . . . . . . . . . . . . . . . . No Title
Erwin Stoff . . . . . . . . . . . . . . . . . . . . . . . . . . . . No Title
Wendy Wanderman . . . . . . . . . . . . . . . . . . . . . . Co-Head, Film

## 360 ENTERTAINMENT
PHONE . . . . . . . . . . . . . . . . . . . . . . . . . . 213-461-6360
FAX . . . . . . . . . . . . . . . . . . . . . . . . . . . . 213-461-6330
WEBSITE . . . . . . . . . . . . . . . . http://www.360entertainment.com
536 N. Larchmont Blvd.
Los Angeles, CA 90004

| | |
|---|---|
| TYPE | Motion Pictures + Feature Direct to Video + Television |
| CREDITS | Last Gasp- Within The Rock- Ravager |

Stanley Isaacs . . . . . . . . . . . . . . . . . . . . . Producer/Writer/Partner
Scott McGinnis . . . . . . . . . . . . . . . . . . . . Director/Producer/Partner
Robert Patrick . . . . . . . . . . . . . . . . . . . . . . Actor/Producer/Partner

## 40 ACRES & A MULE FILMWORKS INC.
PHONE . . . . . . . . . . . . . . . . 718-624-3703/310-276-2116
FAX . . . . . . . . . . . . . . . . . . . . . . . . . . . . /310-276-2164
124 Dekalb Ave.
Brooklyn, NY 11217

| | |
|---|---|
| TYPE | Motion Pictures |
| DEAL | Columbia Pictures |
| CREDITS | Clockers - Malcolm X - Crooklyn - Girl 6 - Get on the Bus - 4 Little Girls - He Got Game - Do the Right Thing |
| COMMENTS | Also: 8899 Beverly Blvd., Ste. 401, LA, CA 90048 |

Spike Lee . . . . . . . . . . . . . . . . . . . . . . . . . . . . . Chairman
Sam Kitt . . . . . . . . . . . . . . . . . . . . . . . . . . . President (LA)
Karen Firestone . . . . . . . . . . . . . . . . . . . . . VP, Development (LA)
Andre Hereford . . . . . . . . . . . . . . . . . . . . . Dir., Development (NY)
Heather Parish . . . . . . . . . . . . . . . . . . . . . . . Business Manager
Ross Martin . . . . . . . . . . . . . . . . . . . . . . . . . Story Editor (NY)

## 44 BLUE PRODUCTIONS, INC.
PHONE . . . . . . . . . . . . . . . . . . . . . . . . . . 818-760-4442
FAX . . . . . . . . . . . . . . . . . . . . . . . . . . . . 818-760-1509
EMAIL . . . . . . . . . . . . . . . . . . . . . . . . presidiopx@aol.com
4040 Vineland Ave., Ste. 105
Studio City, CA 91604

| | |
|---|---|
| TYPE | Documentaries + Motion Pictures + Television + Syndication |
| DEAL | Discovery Networks/A & E Television Networks |
| CREDITS | And Now This - Elite Choppers: Birds of Prey - ESPN Presents: All Americans |
| COMMENTS | Also deals with ESPN & The Travel Channel. |

Rasha Drachkovitch . . . . . . . . . . . . . . . President/Exec. Producer
Lasta Drachkovitch . . . . . . . . . . . . . . . . . . . . . . . Sr. Producer
Dick Noonan . . . . . . . . . . . . . . . . . . . . . . . . . . . Producer
David R. Hale . . . . . . . . . . . . . . . . . . . . . . Associate Producer

## 54TH STREET PRODUCTIONS
PHONE . . . . . . . . . . . . . . . . . . . . . . . . . . 310-445-5484
10880 Wilshire Blvd., Ste. 2080
Los Angeles, CA 90024

| | |
|---|---|
| TYPE | Motion Pictures |

Lindsay Conner . . . . . . . . . . . . . . . . . . . . . . . . . . Principal

## A & E TELEVISION NETWORKS
PHONE . . . . . . . . . . . . . . . . . . . . . . . . . . 212-210-1400
WEBSITE . . . . . . . . . . . . . . . . . . . . . . . http://www.AandE.com
235 E. 45th St.
New York, NY 10017

| | |
|---|---|
| TYPE | Television + Feature Direct to Video + Documentaries |
| CREDITS | A&E's Biography- American Justice - Investigative Reports - Mystery Movies |
| COMMENTS | Launched the History Channel 1/95. www.Biography.com, www.HistoryChannel.com, and www.HistoryTravel.com. |

Nickolas Davatzes . . . . . . . . . . . . . . . . . . . . . . . President/CEO
Seymour Lesser . . . . . . . . . . . . . . . . . . . . Chief Financial Officer
Daniel E. Davids . . . . . . . . . Exec. VP/General Manager, The History Channel
Brooke Bailey Johnson . . . . . . . . . Exec. VP/General Manager, A&E Network
Michael Cascio . . . . . . . . . . . . . . . . . . . . . . Sr. VP, Programming
Abbe Raven . . . . . . . . . . . . . Sr. VP, Programming, The History Channel
Delia Fine . . . . . . . . . . . . . . . . . . VP, Drama & Film Programming
Bill Harris . . . . . . . . . . . . . . . . . . . . . . VP, Production Services

## A BAND APART
PHONE . . . . . . . . . . . . . . . . . . . . . . . . . . 213-951-4600
FAX . . . . . . . . . . . . . . . . . . . . . . . . . . . . 213-951-4601
7966 Beverly Blvd.
Los Angeles, CA 90048

| | |
|---|---|
| TYPE | Motion Pictures |
| DEAL | Miramax Films |
| CREDITS | Pulp Fiction - Reservoir Dogs - From Dusk Till Dawn - Good Will Hunting - Jackie Brown |

Quentin Tarantino . . . . . . . . . . . . . . . . . . . . . . Writer/Director
Lawrence Bender . . . . . . . . . . . . . . . . . . . . . . . . . Producer
Julie Kirkham . . . . . . . . . . . . . . . . . . . . . . Sr. VP, Production
Courtney McDonnell . . . . . . . . . . . . . . . . . . . . . VP, Production
Nicole Pennington . . . . . . . . . . . . . . . . . Development Executive
Victoria Lucai . . . . . . . . . . . . . . . . . . . . Asst. to Mr. Tarantino
Jeff Swafford . . . . . . . . . . . . . . . . . . . . . . Asst. to Mr. Bender

## ABATEMARCO PRODUCTIONS, FRANK
PHONE . . . . . . . . . . . . . . . . . . . . . . . . . . 213-954-4560
FAX . . . . . . . . . . . . . . . . . . . . . . . . . . . . 213-954-4550
EMAIL . . . . . . . . . . . . . . . . . . . . . fabatemarco@hillfields.com
4500 Wilshire Blvd. 3rd Floor
Los Angeles, CA 90010

| | |
|---|---|
| TYPE | Motion Pictures + Television |
| CREDITS | I Can Make You Love Me: The Stalking of Laura Black - A Tangled Web |
| COMMENTS | Email Also: maxleader@aol.com |

Frank Abatemarco . . . . . . . . . . . . . . . . . . . . . . Producer/Writer
Erik Adams . . . . . . . . . . . . . . . . . . . . . . . Mgr., Development

## ABC DAYTIME
PHONE . . . . . . . . . . . . . . . . 212-456-7777/310-557-7777
77 West 66 St.
New York, NY 10023

| | |
|---|---|
| TYPE | Television |
| COMMENTS | Also: 4151 Prospect Ave., Los Angeles, CA 90067 |

Patricia Fili-Krushel . . . . . . . . . . . . . . . . . . . . . . . President
Dona Cooper . . . . . . . . . . . . . . . . . Sr. VP, Daytime Programing
Valerie Schaer . . . . . . . . . . . . Sr. VP, Production & Reality Programming
Harriet Abraham . . . . . . . . . . . . . . . . . VP, Programming Operations
Barbara Bloom . . . . . . . . . . . . . . . . . . . . . . . VP, Programming
Holly Jacobs . . . . . . . . . . . . . VP, Reality Programming, Daytime
Dominick Nuzzi . . . . . . . . . . . . . . . . . . . . . . . VP, Production
Jill Farren Phelps . . . . . . . . . . . . . Exec. Producer, One Life to Live
Bill Geddie . . . . . . . . . . . . . . . . . Exec. Producers, The View
Barbara Walters . . . . . . . . . . . . . . . . . Exec. Producer, The View
Francesca James . . . . . . . . . . . . . . Exec. Producer, All My Children
Wendy Riche . . . . . . . . . . Exec. Producer, General Hospital & Port Charles

# COMPANIES AND STAFF

**ABC ENTERTAINMENT**
PHONE . . . . . . . . . . . . . . . . . . . . . . . . . . . . . . . . . . 310-557-7777
WEBSITE . . . . . . . . . . . . . . . . . . . . . . . . . . . . . http://abc.com
2040 Ave. of the Stars
Los Angeles, CA 90067-4785

TYPE          Television
Stuart Bloomberg . . . . . . . . . . . . . . . . . . . . . . . . . . . . . . Chairman
Jamie Tarses . . . . . . . . . . . . . . . . . . . . . . . . . . . . . . . . President
David Westin . . . . . . . . . . . . . . . . . . . . . . . . . . . . Pres., ABC News
Preston Padden . . . . . . . . . . . . . . . . . . . . . . . Pres., ABC TV Network
Michael Davies . . . . . . . . . . . . . . Exec. VP, Alternative Series & Specials
Susan Lyne . . . . . . . . . . . . . . . . . . . . . . Exec. VP, Movies & Miniseries
Brian McAndrews . . . . . . . . . . . . . . . . . . . . . . . Exec. VP, Production
Mark Pedowitz . . . . . . . . . Sr. VP, Business Affairs & Contracts, West Coast
John Wolters . . . . . . . . . . . . . Sr. VP, Finance/Controller, East Coast
Jeff Bader . . . . . . . . . . . . . . . . VP, Program Planning & Scheduling
Maura Dunbar . . . . . . . . . . . . . . . . . VP, Miniseries & Special Projects
Carolyn Ginsburg . . . . . . . . . . . . . . . . . VP, Comedy Series Programming
Christine Hikawa . . . . . . . VP, Broadcast Standards & Practices, East Coast
Susan Leeper . . . . . . . . . . . . . . . . . . . . . . VP, Comedy Programming
Stephen Tao . . . . . . . . . . . . . . . . . . . . . . . . VP, Drama Programming
Brett White . . . . . . . . . . . . . . Broadcast Standards & Practices, West Coast
Michael Becker . . . . . . . . . . . . . . . . . . . . Exec. Dir., Comedy Programming
Suzanne Bukinik . . . . . . . . . . . . . . . . . . Exec. Dir., Comedy Programming
Stephanie Leifer . . . . . . . . . . . . . . . . . . Exec. Dir., Comedy Programming
Jackie Lyons . . . . . . . . . . . . . . . . . . . . . . . . Exec. Dir., Drama
Philippe Perebinossoff . . . . . . . . . . . Exec. Dir., Motion Pictures for TV
Kim Rozenfeld . . . . . . . . . . Exec. Dir., Comedy Series Programming
Quinn Taylor . . . . . . . . . . . . . . . . Exec. Dir., Motion Pictures for TV
Nancy Cotton . . . . . . . . . . . . . . . . . . . . Dir., Drama Programming
Wendell Foster . . . . . . . . . Dir., Program Planning & Scheduling
Sonja Piper . . . . . . . . . . . . . . . . . . . . . . . . . . . . . . . . . Director
Susan Rovner . . . . . . . . . . . . . . . . . . . . . . . . Dir., Movies for TV
Tom Sherman . . . . . . . . . . . . . . . . . . . . . . . Dir., Drama Programming
Adam Wolman . . . . . . . . . . . . . . . . . . . . . . . . Dir., Comedy Series
Alex Kreisler . . . . . . . . . . . . . . . . . . . . . . . . . Mgr., Comedy Series
Scott Rhodes . . . . . . . . . . . . . . . . . . . . . . . . . . Music Supervisor
Greg Yantek . . . . . . . . . . . . . . . . . . . . . . . . . . . Music Supervisor

**ABC PICTURES**
PHONE . . . . . . . . . . . . . . . . . . . . . . . . . . . . . . . . . 310-557-6806
FAX . . . . . . . . . . . . . . . . . . . . . . . . . . . . . . . . . . . . 310-557-6021
2020 Ave. of the Stars, 5th Floor
Los Angeles, CA 90067

TYPE          Television
COMMENTS   Movies and Mini-Series
Didier Pietri . . . . . . . . . . . . . . . . . . . . . . . . . . . Sr. Vice President
Dennis Brown . . . . . . . . . . . . . . . . . . . . . . . . . . . . VP, Production
John McGuire . . . . . . . . . . . . . . . . . . . . . . . . . VP, Business Affairs
Darren Frankel . . . . . . . . . . . . . . . . . . . . Exec. Dir., Post Production
Brian Colgan . . . . . . . . . . . . . . . . . . . . . . . . . Mgr., Business Affairs
Kristen Arthur . . . . . . . . . . . . . . . . . . . . . . . . . Development Executive
Michael Sluchan . . . . . . . . . . . . . . . . . . . . . . . Development Executive

**ABILENE PICTURES**
PHONE . . . . . . . . . . . . . . . . . . . . . . . . . . . . . . . . . 310-888-3550
FAX . . . . . . . . . . . . . . . . . . . . . . . . . . . . . . . . . . . . 310-888-3540
Castle Rock Entertainment
335 N. Maple Dr., Ste. 135
Beverly Hills, CA 90210

TYPE          Motion Pictures + Television
DEAL          New Line Cinema/Castle Rock Entertainment
CREDITS       Primal Fear - Fallen
Gregory Hoblit . . . . . . . . . . . . . . . . . . . . . . . . . . . . . . . Director
Beverly Graf . . . . . . . . . . . . . . . . . . . . . . . . . . . . VP, Development
Patricia Graf . . . . . . . . . . . . . . . . . . . . . . . . . Associate Producer

**ABOUT FACE PRODS.**
PHONE . . . . . . . . . . . . . . . . . . . . . . . . . . . . . . . . . 310-278-6886
FAX . . . . . . . . . . . . . . . . . . . . . . . . . . . . . . . . . . . . 310-457-4315
626 Santa Monica Blvd., Ste. 303
Santa Monica, CA 90401-1066

TYPE          Motion Pictures + Television + Documentaries
CREDITS       Perfect Moment - One or the Other - What Can Be Shown
Nicholas Hondrogen . . . . . . . . . . . . . . . . . . . . . Producer/Director
George Bennett . . . . . . . . . . . . . . . . . . . . . . . . . . . Business Affairs
Edwin Oro . . . . . . . . . . . . . . . . . . . . . . . . . . . . . . No title (LA)

**ACAPPELLA PICTURES**
PHONE . . . . . . . . . . . . . . . . . . . . . . . . . . . . . . . . . 213-782-8200
FAX . . . . . . . . . . . . . . . . . . . . . . . . . . . . . . . . . . . . 213-782-8210
8271 Melrose Ave., Ste. 101
Los Angeles, CA 90046

TYPE          Motion Pictures
CREDITS       Second Son - The Brave - The House of Mirth
Charles Evans Jr. . . . . . . . . . . . . . . . . . . . . . . . Director/Producer
Carroll Kemp . . . . . . . . . . . . . . . . . . . . . . . . . . . . . . . Producer
Ron Cogan . . . . . . . . . . . . . . . Development/Production Executive
Leigh Rodwick . . . . . . . . . . . . . . . . . . . . . . . . . . . . . . Assistant

**ACT III PRODUCTIONS**
PHONE . . . . . . . . . . . . . . . . . . . . . 213-956-8587/310-553-3636
FAX . . . . . . . . . . . . . . . . . . . . . . . . 213-862-1185/310-551-4070
Jerry Lewis Annex
5555 Melrose Ave.
Los Angeles, CA 90038

TYPE          Motion Pictures + Television
DEAL          Paramount Television Group/PolyGram Filmed Ent.
CREDITS       Fried Green Tomatoes - Powers That Be - 704 Hauser
COMMENTS      Motion Pict. Division: 1999 Ave. of the Stars, Ste. 500 LA
              90067
Norman Lear . . . . . . . . . . . . . . . . . . Chairman/CEO, Act III Comm.
John Baskin . . . . . . . . . . . . . . . . . . . . . . . . . . . . . . . President
George Waud . . . . . . . . . . . . . . . . . . . . . . . . . . VP, Motion Pictures
Rachel Davidson . . . . . . . . . . . . . . VP, Television & Motion Pictures
Craig Cochrane . . . . . . . . . . . . . . . . . . . . . . Dir., TV Development
Jill Ettinger . . . . . . . . . . . . . . . . . . . . . . . . . . Creative Executive
Lisa Abramowitz . . . . . . . . . . . . . . . . . Exec. Asst. to Mr. Lear
Ana Maria Geraldino . . . . . . . . . . . . . . . Exec. Asst. to Mr. Baskin
Lee Spragens . . . . . . . . . . . . . . . . . Exec. Asst. to Ms. Davidson
Andrew Zinnes . . . . . . . . . . . . . . . . . . Exec. Asst. to Mr. Waud
Troy Hutchinson . . . . . . . . . . . . . . . . . . . Asst. to Lear Office

**ACTION AMERICA ENTERTAINMENT**
PHONE . . . . . . . . . . . . . . . . . . . . . . . . . . . . . . 818-881-1515
FAX . . . . . . . . . . . . . . . . . . . . . . . . . . . . . . . . . 818-881-7977
EMAIL . . . . . . . . . . . . . . . . . . . . . actionrk@westworld.com
5061 Avenida Hacienda
Tarzana, CA 91356-4222

TYPE          Motion Pictures + Television
Robert Kesler . . . . . . . . . . . . . . . . . . . . . . . . . . . . . . . Producer
Robin Lombardo . . . . . . . . . . . . . . . . . . . . . . . . . . . . . Producer
Robyn Hall . . . . . . . . . . . . . . . . . . . . . . . . . . . . . . . . . Assistant

**ACTIVE ENTERTAINMENT**
PHONE . . . . . . . . . . . . . . . . . . . . . . . . . . . . . . 805-963-4230
FAX . . . . . . . . . . . . . . . . . . . . . . . . . . . . . . . . . 805-963-7590
EMAIL . . . . . . . . . . . . . . . . . . . . . . . . . kbadish@aol.com
3 W. Carrillo St., Ste. 205
Santa Barbara, CA 93101

TYPE          Motion Pictures + Interactive Multimedia + Feature Direct
              to Video
CREDITS       Laurel & Hardy - For Love or Mummy - Ernest in the
              Army - Ernest Goes to Africa
Ken Badish . . . . . . . . . . . . . . . . . . . . . . . . . . . . . . . President

**ADAM PRODUCTIONS**
PHONE . . . . . . . . . . . . . . . . . . . . . . . . . . . . . . 310-442-3580
FAX . . . . . . . . . . . . . . . . . . . . . . . . . . . . . . . . . 310-207-2680
11777 San Vicente Blvd., Ste. 880
Los Angeles, CA 90049

TYPE          Television
CREDITS       Hearts Afire - Anything But Love - Only Way Out -
              Dreamer of Oz
John Ritter . . . . . . . . . . . . . . . . . . . . . . . . . . . . . . Actor/Producer
Tim Stephen . . . . . . . . . . . . . . . . . . . . . . . . . . . . . . . President
Robert Myman . . . . . . . . . . . . . . . . . . . . . . . . . . . . . . Producer

**ADDIS FILMS, MICHAEL**
PHONE . . . . . . . . . . . . . . . . . . . . . . . . . . . . . . 213-931-8076
FAX . . . . . . . . . . . . . . . . . . . . . . . . . . . . . . . . . 213-965-7690
EMAIL . . . . . . . . . . . . . . . . . . . . . . mikeaddis@loop.com
WEBSITE . . . . . . . . . . . . . http://www.geocities.com/hollywood/2920
620 S. La Jolla Ave.
Los Angeles, CA 90048-4819

TYPE          Motion Pictures + Television + Syndication + Animation +
              Interactive Multimedia
CREDITS       Die Wholesale - True Comedy - Cozy Cabin - Ritual Abuse
              The Dale Akiki Story - Poor White Trash
COMMENTS      Also: Sitcoms, Commercials and Music Videos
Michael Addis . . . . . . . . . . . . . . . . . . . . . . . . . . . . . . . President
Phil Shuster . . . . . . . . . . . . . . . . . . . . . . . . . . . . Dir., Development

# COMPANIES AND STAFF

**ADELSON ENTERTAINMENT**
PHONE . . . . . . . . . . . . . . . . . . . . . . . . . . . . . . 310-586-2160
FAX . . . . . . . . . . . . . . . . . . . . . . . . . . . . . . . . 310-586-2161
2121 Cloverfield Blvd., Ste. 202
Santa Monica, CA 90404

TYPE       Motion Pictures + Television + Interactive Multimedia
CREDITS    Hiroshima - Critical Choices - Love In Another Town - Thanks of a Grateful Nation

Andrew Adelson . . . . . . . . . . . . . . . . . . . . Partner/Exec. Producer (x2165)
Tracey Alexander . . . . . . . . . . . . . . . . . . . Partner/Exec. Producer (x2166)
Laurie Arent . . . . . . . . . . . . . . . . . . . . . . . . Dir., Development (x2167)
Jennifer Sadeghi . . . . . . Exec. Asst. to Andy Adelson/Office Manager (x2169)

**ADELSON PRODUCTIONS, ORLY**
PHONE . . . . . . . . . . . . . . . . . . . . . . . . . . . . . . 310-399-5552
FAX . . . . . . . . . . . . . . . . . . . . . . . . . . . . . . . . 310-399-6668
EMAIL . . . . . . . . . . . . . . . . . . . . . . . . . . . . oap@pacbell.net
3330 Ocean Park Blvd., Ste. 115A
Santa Monica, CA 90405

TYPE       Motion Pictures + Television
CREDITS    Murder Between Friends- Desperate Rescue - The Perfect Mother - A Chance of Snow

Orly Adelson . . . . . . . . . . . . . . . . . . . . . . . . . . . . . . President
Scott Goldman . . . . . . . . . . . . . . . . . . . . . . . . Dir., Development

**AEI-ATCHITY EDIT./ENT. INTL. INC.**
PHONE . . . . . . . . . . . . . . . . . . . . . . . . . . . . . . 213-932-0407
FAX . . . . . . . . . . . . . . . . . . . . . . . . . . . . . . . . 213-932-0321
EMAIL . . . . . . . . . . . . . . . . . . . . . . . . . . aeikja@lainet.com
WEBSITE . . . . . . . . . . . . . . . . . . . . . . . . http://aeionline.com
9601 Wilshire Blvd., Box 1202
Beverly Hills, CA 90210

TYPE       Motion Pictures + Television + Feature Direct to Video
CREDITS    Shadow of Obsession - Shades of Love - Meg - Amityville: The Evil Escapes - The Last Valentine
COMMENTS   Literary management and MP Production

Ken Atchity . . . . . . . . . . . . . . . . . . . . . . Writer/Producer/Partner
Chi-Li Wong . . . . . . . . . . . . . Exec. VP, Development and Production/Partner
Vincent Atchity . . . . . . . . . . . . . . . . . . . Exec. VP, Writers Lifeline
Andrea McKeown . . Exec. VP, Editorial, Novels (Kansas City) (913-897-4124)
David Angsten . . . . . . . . . . . . . . . . . . . . . . . . . VP, Development
Graham Moes . . . . . . . . . . . . . . . . . . . Development Administrator

**AFFRIME PRODUCTIONS, MINDY**
PHONE . . . . . . . . . . . . . . . . . . . . . . . . . . . . . . 213-661-4481
FAX . . . . . . . . . . . . . . . . . . . . . . . . . . . . . . . . 213-644-0680
EMAIL . . . . . . . . . . . . . . . . . . . . . . . . . minaffrime@aol.com
1429 Avon Park Terrace
Los Angeles, CA 90026

TYPE       Motion Pictures
CREDITS    Female Perversions - In The Zone - Wrestling With Alligators

Mindy Affrime . . . . . . . . . . . . . . . . . . . . . . President/Producer

**AGAMEMNON FILMS INC.**
PHONE . . . . . . . . . . . . . . . . . . . . . . . . . . . . . . 213-960-4066
650 N. Bronson Ave., Ste. B-225
Los Angeles, CA 90004

TYPE       Motion Pictures + Television
CREDITS    Treasure Island - C. Heston Presents The Bible

Fraser C. Heston . . . . . . . . . . . . . . . . . . . . . . . . . President
John Stronach . . . . . . . . . . . . . . . . . . . . . . . . Vice President
Alex Butler . . . . . . . . . . . . . . . . . . . . . . . . . . . . Producer
Timothy Colvin . . . . . . . . . . . . . . . . . . . . . . . . Development

**ALAN SMITHEE FILMS**
PHONE . . . . . . . . . . . . . . . . . . . . . . . . . . . . . . 213-850-8926
EMAIL . . . . . . . . . . . . . . . . . . . . . . . . . SmitheeFlm@aol.com
WEBSITE . . . . . . . . . . . . . . . . . . . . . http://www.smithee.com/films
7510 Sunset Blvd., Ste. 525
Hollywood, CA 90046

TYPE       Motion Pictures + Television
CREDITS    Dudley's Kitchen - The Base - Treasure Hunt

Fred Smythe . . . . . . . . . . . . . . . . . . . . . . . . . . . . Director
Michael Runstrom . . . . . . . . . . . . . . . . . . . . . Associate Director

**ALBERT PRODS. INC., SYDELL**
PHONE . . . . . . . . . . . . . . . . . . . . . . . . . . . . . . 213-850-1044
FAX . . . . . . . . . . . . . . . . . . . . . . . . . . . . . . . . 213-850-7551
6716 Hillpark Dr., Ste. 305
Los Angeles, CA 90068

TYPE       Motion Pictures + Television + Syndication + Documentaries + Animation
CREDITS    Preppy Murder (ABC)- Last Rites (Universal) - One of Her Own (ABC)

Sydell Albert . . . . . . . . . . . . . . . . . . . . . . . . . . . . Producer
Rafaell Nola . . . . . . . . . . . . . . . . . . . . . . . . . VP, Development

**ALBRECHT & ASSOCS. INC.**
PHONE . . . . . . . . . . . . . . . . . . . . . . . . . . . . . . 818-222-4836
FAX . . . . . . . . . . . . . . . . . . . . . . . . . . . . . . . . 818-222-5835
3442 Dorothy Road
Topanga, CA 90290-4105

TYPE       Motion Pictures + Television
CREDITS    Mickey Mouse's 60th Bday/NBC - Scandals/ABC - CBS Comedy Bloopers

J.A. Albrecht . . . . . . . . . . . . . . . . President/Producer/Director/Writer

**ALBRECHT/READ MANAGEMENT**
PHONE . . . . . . . . . . . . . . . . . . . . . . . . . . . . . . 213-461-3200
FAX . . . . . . . . . . . . . . . . . . . . . . . . . . . . . . . . 213-461-3468
737 Seward St. #1
Hollywood, CA 90028

TYPE       Television
DEAL       HBO Original Programming
CREDITS    HBO Comedy Judy Gold/Bob Smith - Drop Dead Gorgeous - Juror #5 (HBO)

Annie Albrecht . . . . . . . . . . . . . . . . . . . . . Producer/Manager
Bob Read . . . . . . . . . . . . . . . . . . . . . . . . . Producer/Manager
April Fletcher . . . . . . . . . . . . . . . . . . . . . . . . . . . Development

**ALEXANDER/ENRIGHT & ASSOCS.**
PHONE . . . . . . . . . . . . . . . . . . . . . . . . . . . . . . 310-458-3003
FAX . . . . . . . . . . . . . . . . . . . . . . . . . . . . . . . . 310-393-7238
201 Wilshire Blvd., 3rd Fl.
Santa Monica, CA 90401

TYPE       Motion Pictures + Television
CREDITS    Our Son The Matchmaker - Family Pictures - Caroline - Ice

Les Alexander . . . . . . . . . . . . . . . . . . . . . . Executive Producer
Don Enright . . . . . . . . . . . . . . . . . . . . . . . Executive Producer
Karin Aurino . . . . . . . . . . . . . . . . . . . . . . . . . . . Producer
Tami Gunloy . . . . . . . . . . . . . . . . . . . . . Dir., Administration
Frederique Fechner . . . . . . . . . . . . . . . . . . Production Associate
Sarah Koepple . . . . . . . . . . . . . . . . . . . Development Associate

**ALIVE FILMS**
PHONE . . . . . . . . . . . . . . . . . . . . . . . . . . . . . . 808-891-0022
FAX . . . . . . . . . . . . . . . . . . . . . . . . . . . . . . . . 808-879-2734
EMAIL . . . . . . . . . . . . . . . . . . . . . . . . . alivewow@maui.net
3264 S. Kihei
Kihei, HI 96753

TYPE       Motion Pictures

Shep Gordon . . . . . . . . . . . . . . . . . . . . . . . . . . . Chairman

**ALL AMERICAN COMMUNICATIONS, INC.**
PHONE . . . . . . . . . . . . . . . . . . . . . . . . . . . . . . 310-656-1100
FAX . . . . . . . . . . . . . . . . . . . . . . . . . . . . . . . . 310-656-7400
EMAIL . . . . . . . . . . . . . . . . . . . . . . . . . allamcom@aol.com
808 Wilshire Blvd., 4th Floor
Santa Monica, CA 90401

TYPE       Television + Syndication
CREDITS    Baywatch - Baywatch Nights - Sinbad

Myron Roth . . . . . . . . . . . . . . . . . . . . . . . . . President/COO
Syd Vinnedge . . . . . . . . . . . . . . . . . . . Sr. Exec. Vice President

**ALL AMERICAN TELEVISION, INC.**
PHONE . . . . . . . . . . . . . . . . . . . . . . . . . . . . . . 212-541-2800
FAX . . . . . . . . . . . . . . . . . . . . . . . . . . . . . . . . 212-541-2810
1325 Avenue of the Americas
New York, NY 10019

TYPE       Television

Larry Lamattina . . . . . . . . . . . . . . . . . . . . . . . . President/CEO
John Storrier . . . . . . . . . . . . . . . . . . . . Chief Operating Officer
Rand Stoll . . . . . . . . . . . . . . . . . . Exec. VP, Programming, East Coast

# COMPANIES AND STAFF

**ALL GIRL PRODS.**
PHONE . . . . . . . . . . . . . . . . . . . . . . . . . . . . . . . . . . . . 818-777-7776
FAX . . . . . . . . . . . . . . . . . . . . . . . . . . . . . . . . . . . . . . 818-866-5871
100 Universal Plaza, Prod. Bldg. 507 #4D
Universal City, CA 91608

TYPE          Motion Pictures
DEAL          Universal Pictures
CREDITS     Beaches- Gypsy - Man of The House - Diva Las Vegas
Bette Midler . . . . . . . . . . . . . . . . . . . . . . . . . . . . Actress/Producer
Bonnie Bruckheimer . . . . . . . . . . . . . . . . . . . . . . . . . . . Producer
Yvette Taylor . . . . . . . . . . . . . . . . VP, Production (818-777-9623)
Dabney Lee . . . . . . . . . . . . . . . VP, Creative Affairs (818-777-5851)
Martin Navis . . . . . . . . . . . . . . . . . Dir., Development (818-777-5856)
Merle Elias . . . . . . . . . . . . . . . . . . . . . . . . . Asst. to B. Bruckheimer
Robert Nguyen . . . . . . . . . . . . . . . . . . . . . . . . . Production Assistant
Rob Thomas . . . . . . . . . . . . . Development Assistant (818-777-9610)

**ALLEGRO FILMS**
PHONE . . . . . . . . . . . . . . . . . . . . 310-888-3499/514-529-0320
FAX . . . . . . . . . . . . . . . . . . . . . . . 310-859-7173/514-529-0328
9107 Wilshire Blvd., Ste. 625
Beverly Hills, CA 90210

TYPE          Motion Pictures + Television + Syndication + Animation +
                   Documentaries
CREDITS     Screamers- Little Men- The Assignment - Deadbolt
COMMENTS   ALSO: 2187 Lariviere St., Montreal, Quebec H2K 1P5
Jacques Methe . . . . . . . . . . . . . . . . . . . . . . . . . President, Montreal
Stephane Reichel . . . . . . . . . . . . . . . . . . . . . . Exec. VP, Montreal
Allan Joli-Coeur . . . . . . . . . . . . . . . VP, Business & Legal (Montreal)
Elissa McBride . . . . . . . . . . . . . . . . . VP, Creative Affairs (LA)

**ALLIANCE PICTURES**
PHONE . . . . . . . . . . . . . . . . . . . . 310-275-5501/416-967-1174
FAX . . . . . . . . . . . . . . . . . . . . . . . 310-275-5502/416-960-0971
EMAIL . . . . . . . . . . . . . . . . . . . . . . . alliance1@worldnet.att.net
WEBSITE . . . . . . . . . . . . . . . . . . . . . . . . http://www.alliance.ca/
301 N. Canon Dr., Ste. 321
Beverly Hills, CA 90210

TYPE          Motion Pictures
CREDITS     eXistenZ - The Sweet Hereafter - Crash - Johnny
                   Mnemonic - Exotica - When Night Is Falling
COMMENTS   121 Bloor St., East, Ste. 1400, Toronto, Ontario
                   CANADA M4W 3M5
Robert Lantos . . . . . . . . . . . . . . . . Chairman/CEO, Alliance Comm. Corp.
David R. Ginsburg . . . . . . . . . . . . . . . Pres., Filmed Entertainment
Andras Hamori . . . . . . . . . . . . . . . . . . . . . . . . . . . . . . . . . . . President
Mark A. Horowitz . . . . . . . . . . . . . . . . . Pres., Alliance Picts. Intl.
Levy Antal . . . . . . . . . . . . . . . . . . . . . . . . . . . Project Executive (LA)
Charlotte Mickie . . . . . . . . . Sr. VP, Alliance Independent Films (Toronto)
Andrea Wood . . . . . . . . . . . . . Sr. VP, Business & Legal Affairs (Toronto)
Ted East . . . . . . . . . . . . . VP, Production & Acquisitions (Toronto)
Julia Rosenberg . . . . . . . . . Dir., Development & Production (Toronto)
Michael Coutanche . . . . . . . . . . Mgr., Development & Acquisitions (Toronto)

**ALLIANCE TELEVISION PRODUCTIONS**
PHONE . . . . . . . . . . . . . . . . . . . . 310-275-5501/416-967-1174
FAX . . . . . . . . . . . . . . . . . . . . . . . 310-275-5502/416-960-0971
EMAIL . . . . . . . . . . . . . . . . . . . . . . . alliance1@worldnet.att.net
WEBSITE . . . . . . . . . . . . . . . . . . . . . . . . http://www.alliance.ca/
301 N. Canon Dr., Ste. 321
Beverly Hills, CA 90210

TYPE          Motion Pictures + Television
CREDITS     Due South - ReBoot - Blackjack - Once A Thief - Total
                   Recall - Sins of the City - BelaVille - Shadow Warriors II
COMMENTS   Also: 121 Bloor St., East., Ste. 1400, Toronto, Ontario
                   CANADA M4W 3M5
Michael Weisbarth . . . . . . . . . . . . . . . . . Pres., Alliance Television
Laurie Pozmantier . . . . . . . . . . . . . . . . . . . . Exec. Vice President
Ian McDougall . . . . . . . . . . . . . . . . Sr. VP, Production (Toronto)
John Morayniss . . . . . . . . . . . . . Sr. VP, Business & Legal Affairs
Christine Shipton . . . . . . . . . . . . Sr. VP, Creative Affairs (Toronto)
Ted Gold . . . . . . . . . . . . . . . . . . . . . . . . . . . VP, Creative Affairs
Noreen Halpern . . . . . . . . . . . . . . . . . . . . . VP, Creative Affairs

**ALLIANCE/LEMONDE ENTERTAINMENT**
PHONE . . . . . . . . . . . . . . . . . . . . 310-275-5501/416-967-1174
FAX . . . . . . . . . . . . . . . . . . . . . . . 310-275-5502/416-960-0971
EMAIL . . . . . . . . . . . . . . . . . . . . . marc_forby@notes.alliance.ca
WEBSITE . . . . . . . . . . . . . . . . . . . . . . . . http://www.alliance.ca/
301 N. Canon Dr., Ste 321
Beverly Hills, CA 90210

TYPE          Motion Pictures + Television
CREDITS     The Fall - It Came from the Sky - Hidden Agenda - Laser
                   Hawk
John Fremes . . . . . . . . . . . . . . . . . . . . . . . . . . . . . . . . . . President
Marc Forby . . . . . . . . . . . . . . . . . . . . . . . . . . Dir., Creative Affairs

**ALLIED STARS**
PHONE . . . . . . . . . . . . . . . . . . . . . . . . . . . . . . . . . . . . 310-244-5188
FAX . . . . . . . . . . . . . . . . . . . . . . . . . . . . . . . . . . . . . . 310-244-6499
Sony Pictures
10202 W. Washington Blvd., Lean, #219
Culver City, CA 90232-3195

TYPE          Motion Pictures + Television
DEAL          Columbia Pictures
CREDITS     Hook - FX - FX2 - Chariots of Fire - The Scarlet Letter
Melissa Henning . . . . . . . . . . . . . . . . . . . . . . . Sr. VP, Production
Kelley Jones . . . . . . . . . . . . . . . . . . . . . . . . . . . . VP, Development

**ALLYN FILMS**
PHONE . . . . . . . . . . . . . . . . . . . . . . . . . . . . . . . . . . . . 213-937-8162
FAX . . . . . . . . . . . . . . . . . . . . . . . . . . . . . . . . . . . . . . 213-937-8164
5850 Canoga Ave.
Woodland Hills, CA 91367

TYPE          Motion Pictures + Television
CREDITS     Rich and Famous - Cousins - Spring Awakening (CBS)
Sandra Smith Allyn . . . . . . . . . . . . . . . . . . . . . . . Writer/Producer
William Allyn . . . . . . . . . . . . . . . . . . . . . . . . . . . Producer/Owner

**ALPHAVILLE**
PHONE . . . . . . . . . . . . . . . . . . . . . . . . . . . . . . . . . . . . 213-956-4803
FAX . . . . . . . . . . . . . . . . . . . . . . . . . . . . . . . . . . . . . . 213-862-1616
EMAIL . . . . . . . . . . . . . . . . . . . . . . . . . . . firstname@aville.com
5555 Melrose Ave., Jerry Lewis Bldg.
Hollywood, CA 90038-3197

TYPE          Motion Pictures
DEAL          Paramount Pictures- Motion Picture Group
CREDITS     Hard Target - Tombstone - Dazed and Confused - Michael
                   - The Jackal
Sean Daniel . . . . . . . . . . . . . . . . . . . Producer/Partner (213-956-4805)
Jim Jacks . . . . . . . . . . . . . . . . . . . . . Producer/Partner (213-956-4830)
Caldecot Chubb . . . . . . . . . . . . . . . . Pres., Production (213-956-4846)
Amanda Moose . . . . . . . . . . . . . . . Sr. VP, Production (213-956-4864)
Roy Lee . . . . . . . . . . . . . . . . . . Dir., Development (213-956-4868)
Brian Gerber . . . . . . . . . . . . . . . . . . Creative Executive (213-956-4876)
Samantha Hochman . . . . . . . . . . . Asst. to Caldecot Chubb (213-956-4846)
Angelina Fontana Miller . . . . . . . . . . Asst. to Sean Daniel (213-956-4805)
Jennifer Moyer . . . . . . . . . . . . . . . . . Asst. to Jim Jacks (213-956-4830)
Michael Reisman . . . . . . . . . . . . . . Asst. to Amanda Moose (213-956-4864)

**ALPINE PICTURES**
PHONE . . . . . . . . . . . . . . . . . . . . . . . . . . . . . . . . . . . . 818-909-5207
FAX . . . . . . . . . . . . . . . . . . . . . . . . . . . . . . . . . . . . . . 818-782-4565
EMAIL . . . . . . . . . . . . . . . . . . . . . . . . . . . alpine@primenet.com
WEBSITE . . . . . . . . . . . . . . . . . . . . . . . . http://www.alpinepix.com
6919 Valjean Ave.
Van Nuys, CA 91406

TYPE          Motion Pictures + Television + Feature Direct to Video
CREDITS     Witchboard - Season of Fear - Lord Protector
Roland Carroll . . . . . . . . . . . . . . . . . . . . . . . . . . . CEO/Co-Partner
Paul L. Miller . . . . . . . . . . . . . . . . . . . . . Chief Operations Officer
Ryan J. Carroll . . . . . . . . . . . . . . . Exec. Producer/Co-Partner
George Peirson . . . . . . . . . . . . . Exec. VP, Production/Co-Producer
Jed Nolan . . . . . . . . . . . . . . . . . . . . . . . . . . . . Sr. VP, Production
Don Barnes . . . . . . . . . . . . . . . . . Dir., Development/Acquisitions
Philip K. Hammond . . . . . . . . . . . . . . . . . Chief Financial Officer
Patricia Monville . . . . . . . . . . . . . . . . . . . Unit Production Manager

**AM PRODUCTIONS & MANAGEMENT**
PHONE . . . . . . . . . . . . . . . . . . . . . . . . . . . . . . . . . . . . 310-275-9081
FAX . . . . . . . . . . . . . . . . . . . . . . . . . . . . . . . . . . . . . . 310-275-9082
EMAIL . . . . . . . . . . . . . . . . . . . . . . . . . . . AMPROD1@aol.com
8899 Beverly Blvd., Ste. 713
Los Angeles, CA 90048

TYPE          Motion Pictures + Television
CREDITS     Seduced by Madness - Following Her Heart - Nobody's
                   Children
Ann-Margret . . . . . . . . . . . . . . . . . . . . . . . . . Exec. Producer/Actor
Alan Margulies . . . . . . . . . . . . . . . . . . . . . . . . . Executive Producer
Burt Reynolds . . . . . . . . . . . . . . . . . Exec. Producer/Director/Actor
Roger Smith . . . . . . . . . . . . . . . . . . . . . . . . . . . Producer/Writer
Karri Bowman . . . . . . . . . . . . . . . . . . . . . . . Administrative Director

## AMEN RA FILMS
PHONE . . . . . . . . . . . . . . . . . . . . . . . . . . . . . . . 310-246-6510
FAX . . . . . . . . . . . . . . . . . . . . . . . . . . . . . . . . . 310-550-1932
9460 Wilshire Blvd., Ste. 400
Beverly Hills, CA 90212

| | |
|---|---|
| TYPE | Motion Pictures |
| CREDITS | Blade - John Henrik Clarke: A Great and Mighty Walk - The Big Hit - Down in the Delta |

Wesley Snipes . . . . . . . . . . . . . . . . . . . . . . . . . Actor/Producer
Kimiko Jackson . . . . . . . . . . . . . . . . . . . . . . . . Sr. VP/Producer
Victor McGauley . . . . . . . . . . . . . . . . . . . . . . . . . . . Producer
Glennis Bastien . . . . . . . . . . . . . . . Exec. Asst. to Mr. McGauley
Sandra Farrior . . . . . . . . . . . . . . Personal Asst. to Mr. Snipes (NY)
Justine Hah . . . . . . . . . . . . . . . . . . . Exec. Asst. to Ms. Jackson
Tatiana Saunders . . . . . . . . . . . . . . . . . . . . . . Exec. Assistant
Carrie Seeley . . . . . . . . . . . . . . . . Personal Asst. to Mr. Snipes
Trudy Snipes . . . . . . . . . . . . . . . . . . . . . . . . . Office Manager

## AMERICA NATIONAL NETWORK, INC.
PHONE . . . . . . . . . . . . . . . . . . . . . . . . . . . . . 310-820-7767
FAX . . . . . . . . . . . . . . . . . . . . . . . . . . . . . . . . 310-442-9850
EMAIL . . . . . . . . . . . . . . . . . . . . . . ANNPatriot@Earthlink.net
12304 Santa Monica Blvd., Ste. 100
Los Angeles, CA 90025

| | |
|---|---|
| TYPE | Motion Pictures + Television + Documentaries |
| CREDITS | Stars of Tommorow - Trapper County War - The Nutcracker |
| COMMENTS | Constructive, pro-American, positive value, pro-family programming only. |

Michael W. Leighton . . . . . . . . . . . . . . . . . . . President/COO
Stephen Kutner . . . . . . . . . . . . . . . . . . . Chief Executive Officer
Sheldon I. Altfeld . . . . . . . . . . . . . . . . VP, Network Operations
Gary A. Lowe . . . . . . . . . . . . . . . . . . . . . . VP, Production
Rita Saiz . . . . . . . . . . . . . . . . . . . . . . . . VP, Development
Rich Weathers . . . . . . . . . . . . . . . . VP, Network Development
Bud Roberson . . . . . . . . . . . . . . . Exec. in Charge of Production
William G. Schneider . . . . . . . . . . . . . . . . . Dir., Finance
Michael Shane Leighton . . . . . . . . . . . . Dir., Affiliate Relations
Deborah J. Taylor . . . . . . . . . . . . . . . . . . . . Dir., Operations

## AMERICAN FILMWORKS
PHONE . . . . . . . . . . . . . . . . . . . . . . . . . . . . . 310-288-0569
FAX . . . . . . . . . . . . . . . . . . . . . . . . . . . . . . . . 310-288-0578
EMAIL . . . . . . . . . . . . . . . . . . . . . . . . . . AmFilm@aol.com
222 N. Canon Dr., Ste. 201
Beverly Hills, CA 90210

| | |
|---|---|
| TYPE | Motion Pictures + Television |
| CREDITS | Jack the Bear - China Syndrome - On Golden Pond - 9 to 5 - Coming Home - Glory & Honor |

Bruce Gilbert . . . . . . . . . . . . . . . . . . . . . . . President/Producer

## AMERICAN MOVIE CLASSICS/ROMANCE CLASSIC
PHONE . . . . . . . . . . . . . . . . . . . . . . . . . . . . . 516-396-3000
FAX . . . . . . . . . . . . . . . . . . . . . . . . . . . . . . . . 516-364-2246
150 Crossways Park West
Woodbury, NY 11797

| | |
|---|---|
| TYPE | Television + Documentaries |
| CREDITS | AMC In Concert - Blacklist:Hollywood on Trial - The Hollywood Soundtrack Story - Remember WENN |

Katie McEnroe . . . . . . . . . . . . . . . . . . President, AMC Networks
Marc Jurus . . . . . . . Sr. VP, Original Programming, Pkg. & Prod. (AMC)
Nancy McKenna . . . . . . . . . . . . . Exec. In Charge of Production
Paula Connelly-Skorka . . . . . . . . . . . . . VP, Series & Development

## AMERICAN NEW WAVE FILMS
PHONE . . . . . . . . . . . . . . . . . . . . . . . . . . . . . 213-850-1700
FAX . . . . . . . . . . . . . . . . . . . . . . . . . . . . . . . . 213-850-1788
7775 Sunset Blvd., Ste. 150
Hollywood, CA 90046

| | |
|---|---|
| TYPE | Motion Pictures + Television + Feature Direct to Video |
| CREDITS | Taxi Dancers - Midnight - King of the City (A.K.A. Club Life) - Frightmare |

Norman Thaddeus Vane . . . . . . . . . . Writer/Director/Producer
Henry Von Seyfried . . . . . . . . . . . . . . . . . Executive Producer
Rheinhardt Schreiner . . . . . . . . . . . . . . . . . . Line Producer
Gus Ramos . . . . . . . . . . . . . . . . . . . . Production Coordinator

## AMERICAN WORLD PICTURES
PHONE . . . . . . . . . . . . . . . . . . . . . . . . . . . . . 818-710-7717
FAX . . . . . . . . . . . . . . . . . . . . . . . . . . . . . . . . 818-710-7718
21800 Oxnard St., Ste. 480
Woodland Hills, CA 91367

| | |
|---|---|
| TYPE | Motion Pictures + Feature Direct to Video |
| CREDITS | The Ex- Public Enemy #1- Night of the Running Man - Misbegotten - The Base |
| COMMENTS | Also:  Acquisitions |

Mark L. Lester . . . . . . . . . . . . . . . . . . . . . . . . President
Dana Dubovsky . . . . . . . . . . . . . . . . . . . . . VP, Production
Brian R. Etting . . . . . . . . . . . . . . . . . . . Head, Development

## AMERICAN ZOETROPE
PHONE . . . . . . . . . . . . . . . 415-788-7500/310-385-4218
FAX . . . . . . . . . . . . . . . . . . . 415-989-7910/310-385-4204
WEBSITE . . . . . . . . . . . . . . . . . . http://www.zoetrope.com
916 Kearny St.
San Francisco, CA 94133

| | |
|---|---|
| TYPE | Motion Pictures + Television |
| CREDITS | Bram Stoker's Dracula - The Rainmaker - The Odyssey |
| COMMENTS | TV Office:  9333 Wilshire Blvd., Beverly Hills, CA 90210 |

Fred Fuchs . . . . . . . . . . . . . . . . . . . . . . . . . President
Tom Luddy . . . . . . . . . . . . . . . . . . . . . . . . . . Producer
Jay Shoemaker . . . . . . . . . . . . . . . . . . Chief Executive Officer
Kevin Cooper . . . . . . . . . . . . . . . . . . Exec. VP, Television
Julie Costanzo . . . . . . . . . . . . . . . . . VP, Production & Film
Tara McCann . . . . . . . . . . . . . . . . . . . Dir., Development
Genevieve Haag . . . . . . . . . . . . . . . . . . Asst. to Mr. Fuchs
Shannon Lail . . . . . . . . . . . . . . . . Asst. to Francis Coppola

## *AMPHION/NITESTAR PRODUCTIONS
PHONE . . . . . . . . . . . . . . . . . . . . . . . . . . . . . 805-260-1135
FAX . . . . . . . . . . . . . . . . . . . . . . . . . . . . . . . . 805-260-1195
EMAIL . . . . . . . . . . . . . . . . . . . . . . AmphionPro@aol.com
25399 The Old Road, 15-201
Stevenson Ranch, CA 91381

| | |
|---|---|
| TYPE | Motion Pictures + Television |
| CREDITS | Solstice (Lifetime) |
| COMMENTS | Also: Music Videos. Jvasilatos@nitestar.com |

Jerry Vasilatos . . . . . . . . . . . . . . . . . . . Producer/Director
Sara Coover Caldwell . . . . . . . . . . . . . . . . . Producer/Writer

## AMUSE PRODUCTIONS
PHONE . . . . . . . . . . . . . . . . . . . . . . . . . . . . . 310-209-6155
FAX . . . . . . . . . . . . . . . . . . . . . . . . . . . . . . . . 310-209-6160
10900 Wilshire Blvd., Ste. 950
Los Angeles, CA 90024

| | |
|---|---|
| TYPE | Motion Pictures + Television |
| DEAL | Miramax Films |
| CREDITS | Hook - It Could Happen To You - Universal Soldier |

Gary Adelson . . . . . . . . . . . . . . . . . . . . . . . . Producer
Valerie Letton . . . . . . . . . . . . . . Exec. Asst. to Gary Adelson

## ANDERSON PRODS., CRAIG
PHONE . . . . . . . . . . . . . . . . . . . . . . . . . . . . . 310-841-2555
FAX . . . . . . . . . . . . . . . . . . . . . . . . . . . . . . . . 310-841-5934
EMAIL . . . . . . . . . . . . . . . . . . . . . . . . CAPPix@aol.com
10202 W. Washington Blvd.
Meralta Plaza, Ste. 308
Culver City, CA 90232

| | |
|---|---|
| TYPE | Motion Pictures + Television |
| DEAL | Columbia TriStar Television |
| CREDITS | True Women - The Piano Lesson - O'Pioneers! - Dead By Sunset - The Staircase |
| COMMENTS | Messenger Delivery: 9696 Culver Blvd., Ste. 308 |

Craig Anderson . . . . . . . . . . . . . . . . . . . Executive Producer
Wendy Kram . . . . . . . . . . . . . . . . . . . Sr. Vice President
Helene Lynn-Nash . . . . . . . . . . . . . . . . . VP, Development
Marty E. Schwartz . . . . . . . . . . . . . . . . . . . . Production
Robert C. Edgar . . . . . . . . . . . . . . . . . . . Creative Executive

## ANDRE PRODS., INC., BLUE
PHONE . . . . . . . . . . . . . . . . . . . . . . . . . . . . . 213-874-3750
FAX . . . . . . . . . . . . . . . . . . . . . . . . . . . . . . . . 213-878-0548
14140 Ventura Blvd., Ste. 110
Sherman Oaks, CA 91423

| | |
|---|---|
| TYPE | Motion Pictures + Television |
| CREDITS | Pancho Barnes - Unnatural Causes - While Justice Sleeps - Adrift |

Blue Andre . . . . . . . . . . . . . . . . . . President/Exec. Producer
Bruce Hickey . . . . . . . . . . . . . . . . . . . Mgr., Development

## ANGEL ARK PRODUCTIONS
```
PHONE ................................................ 818-777-2529
FAX ................................................... 818-866-3493
```
100 Universal City Plaza, Bldg. 507, 4A
Universal City, CA 91608

| | |
|---|---|
| TYPE | Motion Pictures + Television |
| DEAL | Universal Television & Networks Group |
| CREDITS | Dunston Checks In- Bye Bye Birdie- For Better or Worse |

```
Jason Alexander ........................... Producer/Director/Actor
Jenny Birchfield-Eick ............................. Vice President
Christophe Abiragi ...................................... Assistant
Cydrice Myers .......................................... Assistant
```

## ANGEL/BROWN PRODS.
```
PHONE ................................................ 213-960-8014
```
5358 Melrose Ave., West Office, 3rd Fl.
Hollywood, CA 90038

| | |
|---|---|
| TYPE | Motion Pictures + Television |
| DEAL | Henson Company, Jim |
| CREDITS | Goosebumps - Body Bags - X-Files - Animorphs |
| COMMENTS | Also: Cable |

```
Dan Angel ......................................... Writer/Producer
Billy Brown ....................................... Writer/Producer
```

## APATOW PRODUCTIONS
```
PHONE ................................................ 310-656-9122
FAX ................................................... 310-656-9132
```
1351 3rd St., Ste. 300
Santa Monica, CA 90401

| | |
|---|---|
| TYPE | Motion Pictures |
| DEAL | New Line Cinema |
| CREDITS | The Cable Guy |

```
Judd Apatow ....................................... Writer/Producer
Mia Apatow ...................................... Dir., Development
Chris Cowles .................................... Creative Executive
Temil Marmon ................................. Asst. to Mr. Apatow
John Hayes .................................. 2nd Asst. to Mr. Apatow
```

## APOSTLE PICTURES
```
PHONE ................................................ 212-541-4323
FAX ................................................... 212-541-4330
EMAIL ........................................ apostlepix@aol.com
```
The Ed Sullivan Theater
1697 Broadway, Ste. 300
New York, NY 10019

| | |
|---|---|
| TYPE | Motion Pictures + Television |
| DEAL | DreamWorks SKG |

```
Denis Leary ............................... Actor/Director/Producer
Jim Serpico ................... Pres., Motion Pictures & Television
Tom Sellitti ...................................... Creative Executive
Joe Lipa ................................... Administrative Assistant
```

## APPLE & HONEY PRODUCTIONS, LTD.
```
PHONE ................................................ 310-556-5639
FAX ................................................... 310-556-1295
```
1530 Edris Dr.
Los Angeles, CA 90035

| | |
|---|---|
| TYPE | Motion Pictures + Television |
| CREDITS | The Quarrel - My Life As A Dog |

```
David Brandes ..................................... Producer/Writer
Dan Williams ................................... Dir., Development
```

## APPLEDOWN FILMS, INC.
```
PHONE ................................................ 310-552-1833
FAX ................................................... 310-552-1331
```
9687 W. Olympic Blvd.
Beverly Hills, CA 90212

| | |
|---|---|
| TYPE | Motion Pictures |
| CREDITS | Remo Williams - Sunchaser |

```
Larry Spiegel ..................................... Producer/Writer
Judy Goldstein ......................................... Producer
```

## ARAMA ENTERTAINMENT
```
PHONE ................................................ 818-788-6400
FAX ................................................... 818-990-9344
EMAIL ....................................... Aramaent@aol.com
```
15821 Ventura Blvd., Ste. 635
Encino, CA 91436

| | |
|---|---|
| TYPE | Motion Pictures |
| CREDITS | Triumph of the Spirit - Eminent Domain - Warrior - Black Eagle - The Last Word |

```
Shimon Arama .............................. Chairman/Producer
Elaine Ford Arama ............................... Co-Chairman
Dama Chasle ........................... VP, Business & Legal
Suzanne Jealous ................... VP, Finance & Accounting
Vidette Shine ................... VP, Development & Operations
```

## ARBUS PRODS., INC., LOREEN
```
PHONE ................................................ 213-930-1244
FAX ................................................... 213-930-0186
```
8075 W. 3rd St., Ste. 410
Los Angeles, CA 90048

| | |
|---|---|
| TYPE | Television + Documentaries + Syndication |
| CREDITS | Case Closed(USA) - In the Name of Love(Lifetime) - Crimes of Passion |
| COMMENTS | Nonfiction series, movies & specials. |

```
Loreen Arbus ..................... Exec. Producer/President
Rick Gough ................................ VP, Development
Carey Campbell ....................... Executive Assistant
```

## ARKOFF INTL. PICTURES
```
PHONE ................................................ 818-558-2199
FAX ................................................... 818-848-7634
```
Walt Disney Studios
500 S. Buena Vista, Ste. 660
Burbank, CA 91521-7471

| | |
|---|---|
| TYPE | Motion Pictures + Television |
| CREDITS | Amityville Horror - Mad Max - Dressed to Kill |

```
Samuel Z. Arkoff ................................. President
Shann Dornhecker ..................... Dir., Development
```

## ARNOLD PRODUCTIONS, INC., JUDY
```
PHONE ................................................ 818-981-3541
FAX ................................................... 818-990-2379
```
13251 Ventura Blvd., Ste. 1
Studio City, CA 91604

| | |
|---|---|
| TYPE | Motion Pictures + Television |
| CREDITS | Good Bad But Beautiful - Walking to Waldheim |
| COMMENTS | ALSO: Theater - The Disputation - The Eleventh |

```
Judy Arnold ......................................... Producer
Leesa Freed ............................... Associate Producer
Bari Hochwald ......................... Dir., Development
Susan Sullivan ........................... Executive Assistant
```

## ARROW ENTERTAINMENT
```
PHONE ................................................ 212-258-2200
FAX ................................................... 212-245-1252
EMAIL ................................... arrow@arrowfilms.com
WEBSITE .......................... http://www.arrowfilms.com
```
135 W. 50th St., Ste. 1925
New York, NY 10020

| | |
|---|---|
| TYPE | Motion Pictures |
| CREDITS | Jack & His Friends - Rule #3 - Abducted 2 |

```
Dennis Friedland ................................. President
Wayne Keeley ........................... Exec. Vice President
Andy Pressman ..................... VP, Technical Operations
```

# COMPANIES AND STAFF

## ARTISAN ENTERTAINMENT
PHONE . . . . . . . . . . . . . . . . . . 310-449-9200/212-577-2400
FAX . . . . . . . . . . . . . . . . . . . . . 310-255-3920/310-255-3970
EMAIL . . . . . . . . . . . . . . . . . . name@live-entertainment.com
2700 Colorado Ave., 2nd Floor
Santa Monica, CA 90404

TYPE     Motion Pictures + Television  
CREDITS     Reservoir Dogs - T2 - Dirty Dancing - The Substitute - The Arrival - Trees Lounge  
COMMENTS     Also: 157 Chambers Street, New York, NY 10007 p: 212-577-2400, f: 212-577-2890

Bill Block . . . . . . . . . . . . . . . . . . . . . . . . . . . . . . President  
Amir Malin . . . . . . . . . . . . . . . . . . . . . . . . . . . . . President  
Mark A. Curcio . . . . . . . . . . . . . . . . . . . Chief Executive Officer  
Ken Schapiro . . . . . . . . . . . . . . . . . . . . . . Exec. Vice President  
Tony Amatullo . . . . . . . . . . . . . . . . . . . . . Sr. VP, Production  
Karen E. Levin . . . . . . . . . . . . . . . . VP, Legal & Business Affairs  
Meltem Demirer . . . . . . . . . . . . . . . . . Dir., Production/Finance  
Leilani Forby . . . . . . . . . . . . . . . . . . Dir., Production/Acquisitions  
Beck Sloca . . . . . . . . . . . . . . . . . . . . . Mgr., Business Affairs  
Cybelle Greenman . . . . . . . . . . . . Mgr., Development/Production  
Dana Reid . . . . . . . . . . . . . . . . . Mgr., Development/Production  
Sean Cardinalli . . . . . . . . . . . . . . . . . . . . . . . Story Editor

## ASCATO ENTERTAINMENT
PHONE . . . . . . . . . . . . . . . . . . . . . . . . . 213-658-5091
FAX . . . . . . . . . . . . . . . . . . . . . . . . . . . . 213-658-5092
EMAIL . . . . . . . . . . . . . . . . counterisco@earthlink.com
8222 Melrose Ave., Ste. 302
Los Angeles, CA 90046

TYPE     Motion Pictures + Television  
CREDITS     Laurel Ave. - Lily In Winter - White Mile - Grand Ave. - Scattering Dad - Profiler - From The Earth To The Moon

Anthony Santa Croce . . . . . . . . . . . . . . . . . . . . . . Producer  
Tony To . . . . . . . . . . . . . . . . . . . . . . . . . . . . . . Producer  
Kimberly Dickens . . . . . . . . . . . . . . . . . . Dir., Development

## ASIS PRODUCTIONS
PHONE . . . . . . . . . . . . . . . . . . . . . . . . . 310-824-0133
FAX . . . . . . . . . . . . . . . . . . . . . . . . . . . 310-824-2131
1033 Gayley Ave., Ste. 111
Los Angeles, CA 90024

TYPE     Motion Pictures + Television  
CREDITS     American Heart - Hidden In America

Jeff Bridges . . . . . . . . . . . . . . . . . . . . . . . . . President  
Neil Koenigsberg . . . . . . . . . . . . . . . . . . . . . . Executive

## ASPECT RATIO FILMS
PHONE . . . . . . . . . . . . . . . . . . . . . . . . . 310-458-4330
FAX . . . . . . . . . . . . . . . . . . . . . . . . . . . 310-319-6563
1148 4th St., #203
Santa Monica, CA 90403

TYPE     Motion Pictures + Television + Documentaries  
CREDITS     Bachelor Party - Ace Ventura - I Love You To Death - The Runner  
COMMENTS     No unsolicited submissions, please.

Bob Israel . . . . . . . . . . . . . . . . . . . . . . . . . . . . Producer  
Neal Israel . . . . . . . . . . . . . . . . . . . . . . . . . . . Producer  
Ron Moler . . . . . . . . . . . . . . . . . . . . . . . . . . . Producer  
Juliette Capretta . . . . . . . . . . . . . . . . . . Sr. VP, Production  
John Vresilovic . . . . . . . . . . . . . . . . . . . . . Story Analyst

## ASSEYEV PRODS. INC., TAMARA
PHONE . . . . . . . . . . . . . . . . . . . . . . . . . 213-656-4731
FAX . . . . . . . . . . . . . . . . . . . . . . . . . . . 213-656-2211
1355 N. Laurel Ave., Ste. 11
Los Angeles, CA 90046

TYPE     Motion Pictures + Television  
CREDITS     I Wanna Hold Your Hand - Norma Rae - Life of Beryl Markham - Big Wednesday

Tamara Asseyev . . . . . . . . . . . . . . . . . . . . . . . . Producer  
Constance Mead . . . . . . . . . . . . . . . . . . Asst. to Producer

## ASSOCIATED PRODUCERS GROUP, INC.
PHONE . . . . . . . . . . . . . . . . . . . . . . . . . 310-888-8023
FAX . . . . . . . . . . . . . . . . . . . . . . . . . . . 310-888-8070
EMAIL . . . . . . . . . . . . . . . . . . . . . . . . . apg@aol.com
9028 Sunset Blvd., Penthouse #1
W. Hollywood, CA 90069

TYPE     Documentaries + Motion Pictures + Television  
CREDITS     Swimming With Sharks - Back In Business - Stalin - Police Academy 1-6

J. David Riva . . . . . . . . . . . . . . . . . . . President/Producer  
William J. Bateman . . . . . . . . . . . . . . . . . . . . . . Producer  
Brian Garcia . . . . . . . . . . . . . . . . . . . . . . . . . . Producer  
Kai Hand . . . . . . . . . . . . . . . . . . . . . . . . . . . . Producer  
Stephen Isreal . . . . . . . . . . . . . . . . . . . . . . . . Producer  
Donald West . . . . . . . . . . . . . . . . . . . . . . . . . Producer  
Ryan Glasgow . . . . . . . . . . . . . . . . . . Asst. to Mr. Riva  
Jack Winch . . . . . . . . . . . . . . . . . . . . . . . . . . Assistant

## ASYLUM FILMS
PHONE . . . . . . . . . . . . . . . . . . . . . . . . . 212-570-4491
25 E. End Ave.
New York, NY 10028

TYPE     Motion Pictures + Television + Syndication  
CREDITS     Strangers Kiss - Consenting Adults - Citizen X  
COMMENTS     No submissions of unsolicited scripts or treatments.

Matthew Chapman . . . . . . . . . . . . . . Writer/Director/Producer

## ATELIER PICTURES
PHONE . . . . . . . . . . . . . . . . 310-888-7727/805-466-4660
FAX . . . . . . . . . . . . . . . . . . 310-888-7726/805-466-4729
EMAIL . . . . . . . . . . . . . . . . . . . . webm@atelierpix.com
WEBSITE . . . . . . . . . . . . . . . . http://www.atelierpix.com
280 S. Beverly Dr., #500
Beverly Hills, CA 90212

TYPE     Motion Pictures + Interactive Multimedia + Television + Documentaries + Feature Direct to Video  
CREDITS     Please Don't Walk Around in The Nude - Starfish - Everyman  
COMMENTS     Also: 10420 San Marcos Rd., Atascadero, CA 93422

Paul T. Gray . . . . . . . . . . . . . . . . Director/Exec. Producer  
Robert Dimitrijevich . . . . . . . . . . . Exec. VP, Business Affairs  
Gretchen G. Gray . . . . . . . . . . . . . Exec. VP, Creative Affairs  
Tom FitzGibbon . . . . . . . . . . . . . . . . . . . Dir., Development

## ATKINSON WAY FILMS
PHONE . . . . . . . . . . . . . . . . . . . . . . . . . 213-666-4300
FAX . . . . . . . . . . . . . . . . . . . . . . . . . . . 213-666-2026
2406 N. Catalina Street
Los Angeles, CA 90027

TYPE     Motion Pictures + Television  
CREDITS     Journey of August King - iHelp! - Star Maps

Sam Waterston . . . . . . . . . . . . . . . . . . . . . . . . Producer  
Beth Colt . . . . . . . . . . . . . . . . . . . . . . . . . . . Producer

## ATLANTIS FILMS
PHONE . . . . . . . . . . . . . . . . . . . . . . . . . 310-576-7719
FAX . . . . . . . . . . . . . . . . . . . . . . . . . . . 310-576-0799
WEBSITE . . . . . . . . . . . . . . . . http://www.Atlantis.ca
227 Broadway, Ste. 300
Santa Monica, CA 90401

TYPE     Television

Peter Sussman . . . . . . . . . . . . . . . . . . . . . . . . President  
Janine Coughlin . . . . . . . . . . . . . . . . VP/Series Development  
Ed Gernon . . . . . . . . . . . . . . . . VP/TV Movies and Mini-series  
Vickie Montoya . . . . . . . . . . . . . Exec. Asst. to Peter Sussman

## ATLAS ENTERTAINMENT
PHONE . . . . . . . . . . . . . . . . . . . . . . . . . 310-724-7350
FAX . . . . . . . . . . . . . . . . . . . . . . . . . . . 310-724-7345
9169 Sunset Blvd.
Los Angeles, CA 90069

TYPE     Motion Pictures + Television  
DEAL     Warner Bros. Pictures  
CREDITS     12 Monkeys - Cool Runnings - Sister Act II - City of Angeles - Fallen

Charles Roven . . . . . . . . . . . . Producer/Partner (310-724-7310)  
Douglas Segal . . . . . . . . . . . . Exec. VP, Production (310-724-7330)  
Kelley Smith-Wait . . . . . . . . . Sr. VP, Physical Production (310-724-7325)  
Richard Suckle . . . . . . . . . . . . . . . VP, Production (310-724-7327)  
Alan Glazer . . . . . . . . . . . . Dir., Physical Production (310-724-7335)  
Kim Franklin . . . . . . . . . . . Exec. Asst. to Mr. Roven (310-724-7310)  
Tom Brennan . . . . . . . . . . . . . Asst. to Mr. Segal (310-724-7330)  
Gloria Fan . . . . . . . . . . . . . . . Asst. to Mr. Suckle (310-724-7327)

# COMPANIES AND STAFF

**ATMAN ENTERTAINMENT**
PHONE . . . . . . . . . . . . . . . . . . . . . . . . . . . . . . . . . 310-979-4868
FAX . . . . . . . . . . . . . . . . . . . . . . . . . . . . . . . . . . . . 310-571-1259
12210 Nebraska Ave., Ste. 15
Los Angeles, CA 90025
| | |
| --- | --- |
| TYPE | Motion Pictures |
| CREDITS | Fight Club - Great White Hype - Sky is Falling - Lambs of God |

Ross Grayson Bell . . . . . . . . . . . . . . . . . . . . . . . . . . . . . . Producer
Martin della Valle . . . . . . . . . . . . . . . . . . . . . . . . Creative Executive

**ATMOSPHERE ENTERTAINMENT INC.**
PHONE . . . . . . . . . . . . . . . . . . . . . . . . . . . . . . . . . 310-434-0066
FAX . . . . . . . . . . . . . . . . . . . . . . . . . . . . . . . . . . . . 310-434-0036
EMAIL . . . . . . . . . . . . . . . . . . . . . . . . . . . main@filmwave.com
1558 10th Street
Santa Monica, CA 90401
| | |
| --- | --- |
| TYPE | Motion Pictures + Television + Feature Direct to Video + Interactive Multimedia |
| CREDITS | Lured Innocence - Dish Dogs - La Cucaracha - Romantic Moritz |
| COMMENTS | Formerly Filmwave Pictures. |

Adam Fast . . . . . . . . . . . . . . . . . . . . . . . . . . . VP, International
Christopher J. Fries . . . . . . . . . . . . . . . . . . . . . . . . . Producer
Amanda Goodwin . . . . . . . . . . . . . . . . . . . . . . . . . Development
Jerry Kohn . . . . . . . . . . . . . . . . . . . . . . . . . . . . Business Affairs

***AUERBACH COMPANY**
PHONE . . . . . . . . . . . . . . . . . . . . . . . . . . . . . . . . . 310-478-1700
FAX . . . . . . . . . . . . . . . . . . . . . . . . . . . . . . . . . . . . 310-478-2202
Hearst Entertainment
1640 S. Sepulveda Blvd., 4th Fl.
Los Angeles, CA 90025
| | |
| --- | --- |
| TYPE | Motion Pictures + Television |
| DEAL | Hearst Entertainment |
| CREDITS | Mortal Sins - Marilyn & Bobby - Nightbreaker - Babies Having Babies - No Means No - A Chance of Snow |

Jeffrey Auerbach . . . . . . . . . . . . . . . . . . . . . Executive Producer
Audrey George . . . . . . . . . . . . . . . . . . . . . . . . Creative Executive

**AURORA PRODUCTIONS**
PHONE . . . . . . . . . . . . . . . . . . . . . . . . . . . . . . . . . 310-854-6900
FAX . . . . . . . . . . . . . . . . . . . . . . . . . . . . . . . . . . . . 310-854-0583
8642 Melrose Ave., Ste. 200
Los Angeles, CA 90069
| | |
| --- | --- |
| TYPE | Motion Pictures + Television |
| CREDITS | The Rock - Eddie & the Cruisers - Heart Like a Wheel |

William Stuart . . . . . . . . . . . . . . . . . . . . . . . . . . . . . . President
Al Septien . . . . . . . . . . . . . . . . . . . . . . . . . . . . Writer/Producer
Turi Meyer . . . . . . . . . . . . . . . . . . . . . . . . . . . . Writer/Director
Nancy Best . . . . . . . . . . . . . . . . . . . . . . . . . . Dir., Development

**AVANTI ENTERPRISES**
PHONE . . . . . . . . . . . . . . . . . . . . . . . . . . . . . . . . . 213-466-2266
6922 Hollywood Blvd.
Los Angeles, CA 90028-6133
| | |
| --- | --- |
| TYPE | Motion Pictures + Television |
| DEAL | Fries Productions, Inc., Chuck |
| CREDITS | Troop Beverly Hills - Born Famous |

Ava Fries . . . . . . . . . . . . . . . . . . . . . . . . . . . . . . . . President

**AVENUE PICTURES**
PHONE . . . . . . . . . . . . . . . . . . . . . . . . . . . . . . . . . 310-996-6800
FAX . . . . . . . . . . . . . . . . . . . . . . . . . . . . . . . . . . . . 310-473-4376
EMAIL . . . . . . . . . . . . . . . . . . . . . . . . . . . . . avepix@aol.com
WEBSITE . . . . . . . . . . . . . . http://www.avenue-entertainment.com
11111 Santa Monica Blvd., Ste. 2110
Los Angeles, CA 90025-3355
| | |
| --- | --- |
| TYPE | Motion Pictures + Television |
| DEAL | Pearson Television Productions |
| CREDITS | Short Cuts - The Player - Restoration - Drugstore Cowboy - Finding Graceland |

Cary Brokaw . . . . . . . . . . . . . . . . . . . . . . . . . . . Chairman/CEO
J.J. Jamieson . . . . . . . . . . . . . . . . . . . . . . . . . Pres., Television
Sheri Halfon . . . . . . . . . . . . . . . . . . . . . . . . . . . . Sr. VP/CFO
Michael Feldman . . . . . . . . . . . . . . . . . . . . Exec. Vice President
Nick Veronis . . . . . . . . . . . . . . . . . . . . . . . . Sr. Vice President
Judy Geletko . . . . . . . . . . . . . . . . . . . . . . . . . . . . . Controller
Michael Zoumas . . . . . . . . . . . . . . . . . . . . . . . . VP, Production
Sal Capone . . . . . . . . . . . . . . . . . . . . . . . Dir., Feature Development
Rachel Frazin . . . . . . . . . . . . . . . . . . . . . Dir., Feature Development
Lynn Novatt . . . . . . . . . . . . . . . . . . . . . . . Dir., Development TV

**AVIATOR FILMS LLC**
PHONE . . . . . . . . . . . . . . . . . . . . . . . . . . . . . . . . . 818-558-5880
FAX . . . . . . . . . . . . . . . . . . . . . . . . . . . . . . . . . . . . 818-556-2899
EMAIL . . . . . . . . . . . . . . . . . . . . . . . . . . aviatorpix@aol.com
4150 Riverside Dr., #201
Toluca Lake, CA 91505
| | |
| --- | --- |
| TYPE | Television + Motion Pictures |
| DEAL | Warner Bros. Pictures/Warner Bros. Television Productions |
| CREDITS | Us Begins With You |

Anthony Edwards . . . . . . . . . . . . . . . . . . . . . . . . . . . . Partner
Dante di Loreto . . . . . . . . . . . . . . . . . . . . . . . . . . . . . Partner
Jane Ridley . . . . . . . . . . . . . . . . . . . . . . . . . . . . . Story Editor
Frank Pavich . . . . . . . . . . . . . . . . . . . . . . . . . . . . . Associate

**AVNET-KERNER CO.**
PHONE . . . . . . . . . . . . . . . . . . . . . . . . . . . . . . . . . 310-838-2500
FAX . . . . . . . . . . . . . . . . . . . . . . . . . . . . . . . . . . . . 310-204-4208
3815 Hughes Ave.
Culver City, CA 90232-2715
| | |
| --- | --- |
| TYPE | Motion Pictures + Television |
| DEAL | Walt Disney Pictures/Touchstone Pictures |
| CREDITS | When a Man Loves a Woman- The War- George of The Jungle - Up Close and Personal - Red Corner |

Jon Avnet . . . . . . . . . . . . . . . . . . . . . . . . . . Producer/Director
Jordan Kerner . . . . . . . . . . . . . . . . . . . . . . . . . . . . Producer
Lisa Lindstrom . . . . . . . . . . . . . . Sr. VP, Development & Production
Susan Reiner . . . . . . . . . . . . . . . . . Sr. VP, Series Development
Elizabeth Stephen . . . . . . . . . . . . Sr. VP, Development & Production
Carol Chacamaty . . . . . . . . . . . . . VP, Finance & Administration
Marsha Oglesby . . . . . . . . . . . . . . VP, Development & Production
Shari Kimoto . . . . . . . . . . . . . . . . . . . . . . . Creative Executive
Jason Abril . . . . . . . . . . . . . . . . . . . Story Editor - MOW's/TV
Dorothy Davis . . . . . . . . . . . . . . Creative Asst. to Susan Reiner
Swanna MacNair . . . . . . . . . . . . Creative Asst. to Lisa Lindstrom
Lisa McCampbell . . . . . . . . . . Creative Asst. to Elizabeth Stephen
Jonna Smith . . . . . . . . . . . . . . . . . Creative Asst. to Jon Avnet
Carla Gambles . . . . . . . . . . . . . . . . . Asst. to Jordan Kerner
Sonia Norville . . . . . . . . . . . . . . . . . . Asst. to Jordan Kerner

**AXELROD/WIDDOES PRODUCTIONS**
PHONE . . . . . . . . . . . . . . . . . . . . . . . . . . . . . . . . . 818-777-8544
FAX . . . . . . . . . . . . . . . . . . . . . . . . . . . . . . . . . . . . 818-866-0355
100 Universal City Plaza, Bldg 507-1C
Universal City, CA 91608
| | |
| --- | --- |
| TYPE | Motion Pictures + Television |
| CREDITS | Dave's World - Can't Hurry Love - A Day With... - Late Bloomer (CBS) |

Jonathan Axelrod . . . . . . . . . . . . . . . . . . . . Executive Producer
James Widdoes . . . . . . . . . . . . . . . . . . Director/Exec. Producer
Nicole Gold . . . . . . . . . . . . . . . . . . . . . . . . . . . . . Assistant
Carrie Mitchell . . . . . . . . . . . . . . . . . . . . . . . . . . . . Assistant

**AXELSON-WEINTRAUB PRODUCTIONS**
PHONE . . . . . . . . . . . . . . . . . . . . . . . . . . . . . . . . . 310-788-9381
FAX . . . . . . . . . . . . . . . . . . . . . . . . . . . . . . . . . . . . 310-788-0476
EMAIL . . . . . . . . . . . . . . . . . . . . . aw-prods@earthlink.net
1900 Ave. of the Stars, Ste. 1440
Los Angeles, CA 90067
| | |
| --- | --- |
| TYPE | Television + Motion Pictures + Documentaries |
| CREDITS | Affectionate Look Fatherhood - Really Naked Truth - New Adventures Robin Hood |

John Axelson . . . . . . . . . . . . . . . . . Exec. Producer/Director
Barbara Weintraub . . . . . . . . . . . . . . . . . . Executive Producer
Eric Streit . . . . . . . . . . . . . . . . . . . . . . . . . Creative Associate

**B.S. COMPANY, INC., THE**
PHONE . . . . . . . . . . . . . . . . . . . . . . . . . . . . . . . . . 310-457-8098
EMAIL . . . . . . . . . . . . . . . . . . . . . . . . bobshayne@worldnet.att.net
WEBSITE . . . . . . . . . . . . http://www.hollywoodnetwork.com/bobshayne
29229 Heathercliff Rd. #1
Malibu, CA 90265
| | |
| --- | --- |
| TYPE | Motion Pictures + Television + Documentaries |
| CREDITS | Frog Prince - Return of Sherlock Holmes - Staying Afloat |

Bob Shayne . . . . . . . . . . . . . . . . . . . . . . . . Producer/Writer
Bonnie De Souza . . . . . . . . . . . . . . . . . . . . VP, Development
Dylan Shayne . . . . . . . . . . . . . . . . . . . . . . . . VP, Production

# COMPANIES AND STAFF

## BADHAM CO., THE

| | |
|---|---|
| PHONE | 818-990-9495 |
| FAX | 818-981-9163 |
| EMAIL | BadhamC.@ix.netcom.com |

3344 Clerendon Road
Beverly Hills, CA 90210

| | |
|---|---|
| TYPE | Motion Pictures |
| DEAL | Paramount Pictures- Motion Picture Group |
| CREDITS | Drop Zone - Nick of Time - Stakeout 1&2 - War Games |
| COMMENTS | Representation: Lee Rosenberg, William Morris Agency |

John Badham . . . . . . . . . . . . . . . . . . . . . . . . Director/Producer
Cammie Crier . . . . . . . . . . . . . . . . . . . Co-Producer/Development

## BAER ANIMATION CO. INC.

| | |
|---|---|
| PHONE | 818-760-8666 |
| FAX | 818-760-8698 |
| EMAIL | baer@baeranimation.com |
| WEBSITE | http://www.baeranimation.com |

3765 Cahuenga Blvd. West
Studio City, CA 91604-3504

| | |
|---|---|
| TYPE | Motion Pictures + Television + Animation + Interactive Multimedia + Feature Direct to Video |
| CREDITS | Roger Rabbit - The Prince & the Pauper - Annabelle's Wish |
| COMMENTS | Animation integrated w/live action specialists. |

Jane Baer . . . . . . . . . . . . . . . . . . . . President/Exec. Producer
Hope Parker . . . . . . . . . . . . . . . . . . . . VP/Dir., Operations
Steve Walby . . . . . . . . . . . . . . . . . . . . Production Manager
Don Hibbard . . . . . . . . . . . . . . . . . . . . . . . Project Manager

## BAER ENTERTAINMENT GROUP

| | |
|---|---|
| PHONE | 310-777-3680/212-605-9107 |
| FAX | 310-777-3685/212-644-3906 |

9229 Sunselt Blvd., Ste. 412
West Hollywood, CA 90069

| | |
|---|---|
| TYPE | Motion Pictures |
| DEAL | October Films |
| COMMENTS | Also: c/o Universal Studios, 445 Park Avenue, 8th Fl., NY, NY 10022. Division of Steinhardt Baer Picts. Co. |

Thomas Baer . . . . . . . . . . . . . . . . . . . . . . . . . . . Producer
Michael Steinhardt . . . . . . . . . . . . . . . . . . . . . . . . . Partner
Mario E. Acosta . . . . . . . . . . . . . . . . . . . . . . . . Story Editor

## BAERWALD PRODS., SUSAN

| | |
|---|---|
| PHONE | 310-476-6221 |
| FAX | 310-476-1436 |

132 S. Anita Ave.
Los Angeles, CA 90049

| | |
|---|---|
| TYPE | Television |
| CREDITS | Blind Faith - Lucky/Chances - Cruel Doubt - Inflammable - A Time to Heal |

Susan Baerwald . . . . . . . . . . . . . . . . . . . . Executive Producer

## BAKULA PRODUCTIONS, INC.

| | |
|---|---|
| PHONE | 213-960-4005 |

5555 Melrose Ave.
Hollywood, CA 90038

| | |
|---|---|
| TYPE | Motion Pictures + Television |
| DEAL | Paramount Network Television |
| CREDITS | Mr. & Mrs. Smith - The Bachelor's Baby - Prowler |
| COMMENTS | Also: Theatre |

Scott Bakula . . . . . . . . . . . . . . . . . . . . . . . . CEO/Producer
Tom Spiroff . . . . . . . . . . . . . . . . . . . . . President/Producer
Ron Cortes . . . . . . . . . . . . . . . . . . . . . . Creative Executive
Amy Gardner . . . . . . . . . . Exec. Asst. to Mr. Bakula & Mr. Spiroff

## BALDWIN/COHEN PRODUCTIONS

| | |
|---|---|
| PHONE | 310-248-6360 |
| FAX | 310-248-6370 |

9200 Sunset Blvd., Ste. 418
Los Angeles, CA 90069

| | |
|---|---|
| TYPE | Motion Pictures + Television |
| CREDITS | Mystery Alaska - The Patriot - Sudden Death - From the Hip - Gideon's Web - Resurrection |

Howard Baldwin . . . . . . . . . . . . . . . . . . . . . . . . . President
Richard Cohen . . . . . . . . . . . . . . . . . . . . . . . . . . . Partner
Karen Baldwin . . . . . . . . . . . . . . . . . . . . Exec. Vice President
Jack Gilardi Jr. . . . . . . . . . . . . . . . . . . . . . . VP, Production
William Papriella . . . . . . . . . . . . . . . . . . . . VP, Development
Nick Ruta . . . . . . . . . . . . . . . . . . . VP, Finance & Legal Affairs
Paul Pompian . . . . . . . . . . . . . . Production Supervisor/Producer
Carmen Garcia . . . . . . . . . . . . . . . . . Exec. Asst. to President
Jonathan McFadden . . . . . . . . . . . . Exec. Asst. to Vice President
Cecille Zagala . . . . . . . . . . . . . . . . . . Bookkeeper/Legal Affairs
Simon Fischler . . . . . . . . . . . . . . . . . . . . Production Assistant

## BALLPARK PRODUCTIONS

| | |
|---|---|
| PHONE | 310-827-1328 |
| FAX | 310-577-9626 |
| EMAIL | 105614.270@Compuserve.com |

PO Box 508
Venice, CA 90294

| | |
|---|---|
| TYPE | Motion Pictures + Television |
| DEAL | Interscope Communications Inc. |
| CREDITS | Crimson Tide - Colors - The Peacemaker |

Michael Schiffer . . . . . . . . . . . . . . . . . . . Producer/Writer
Sally Allen . . . . . . . . . . . . . . . . . . . . . . . VP, Development
Caleb Dewart . . . . . . . . . . . . . . . . . . . . . Creative Assistant

## BALLYHOO, INC.

| | |
|---|---|
| PHONE | 310-244-8193 |
| FAX | 310-244-7898 |

10202 W. Washington Blvd., Capra 100
Culver City, CA 90232

| | |
|---|---|
| TYPE | Motion Pictures + Television |
| CREDITS | Seven Years in Tibet - The Opposite of Sex |

Michael Besman . . . . . . . . . . . . . . . . . . . President/Producer
Jess Siegler . . . . . . . . . . . . . . . Vice President (310-244-6593)
Heather Arnold . . . . . . . . . . . . Creative Executive (310-244-5261)
Will Farnan . . . . . . . . . . . . Asst. to Jess Siegler (310-244-4074)
Andrew Federici . . . . . . . . . Asst. to Michael Besman (310-244-8247)

## *BALTIMORE PICTURES, INC.

| | |
|---|---|
| TYPE | Motion Pictures + Television |
| COMMENTS | Also: See Baltimore/Spring Creek Pictures, LLC or the Levinson/Fontana Company, LLC. |

## BALTIMORE/SPRING CREEK PICTURES, LLC

| | |
|---|---|
| PHONE | 818-954-1210/818-954-2666 |
| FAX | 818-954-2737/818-954-2693 |
| EMAIL | www.levinson.com |

4000 Warner Blvd.
Burbank, CA 91522-0768

| | |
|---|---|
| TYPE | Motion Pictures |
| DEAL | Warner Bros. Pictures |
| CREDITS | Analyze This (in production) |
| COMMENTS | Formerly Baltimore Pictures, Inc. and Spring Creek Productions, Inc. |

Barry Levinson . . . . . . . . . . . . . . . Director/Writer/Producer
Paula Weinstein . . . . . . . . . . . . . . . . . . . . . . . . . Producer
Amy Solan . . . . . . . . . . . . . . . . . . . . CFO/Business Affairs
Len Amato . . . . . . . . . . . . . . . . . . . . . Exec. Vice President
Robin Forman . . . . . . . . . . . . . . . . . . . . Exec. Vice President
Dana Goldberg . . . . . . . . . . . . . . . . . . . . . . Vice President
Vanessa Coifman . . . . . . . . . . . . . . . . . . . . Dir., Development

## BANDEIRA ENTERTAINMENT

| | |
|---|---|
| PHONE | 213-866-3535 |
| FAX | 213-866-3599 |

8447 Wilshire Blvd., Ste. 212
Beverly Hills, CA 90211

| | |
|---|---|
| TYPE | Motion Pictures |
| DEAL | DreamWorks SKG |
| CREDITS | johns - The House of Yes - Little City - Judas Kiss - Life During Wartime - Starf*cker - Coming Soon |

Beau Flynn . . . . . . . . . . . . . . . . . . . . . . . . . . . Producer
Stefan Simchowitz . . . . . . . . . . . . . . . . . . . . . . . Producer
Jane Park . . . . . . . . . . . . . . . . . . . . . . . . VP, Development
Laura Mueller . . . . . . . . . . . . . . . . . . . Asst. to Jane Park
Jeff Wallace . . . . . . . . . . . . . . . . . . . . . Asst. to Jon King
Marc Weitzman . . . . . . . . . . . . . . . . . . . Asst. to Beau Flynn

## BANNER ASSOCS., BOB

| | |
|---|---|
| PHONE | 213-936-5188 |
| FAX | 213-936-5189 |

535 S. Curson Avenue, #9L
Los Angeles, CA 90036

| | |
|---|---|
| TYPE | Television |
| CREDITS | Showtime at the Apollo - Angel Flt. Down - Happy Birthday George Gershwin |

Bob Banner . . . . . . . . . . . . . . . . . . . . . . . . . . . President
Chuck Banner . . . . . . . . . . . . . . . . . . . . . . Vice President
Chris Rowe . . . . . . . . . . . . . . . . . . . Development Associate
Rae Whitney . . . . . . . . . . . . . . . . . . . . . . . . . . Associate

# COMPANIES AND STAFF

**BANNER ENTERTAINMENT**
PHONE . . . . . . . . . . . . . . . . . . . . . . . . . . . . . . 213-848-7500
FAX . . . . . . . . . . . . . . . . . . . . . . . . . . . . . . . . 213-848-7501
8000 Sunset Blvd., 3rd Fl.
Los Angeles, CA 90046

TYPE        Motion Pictures
CREDITS     Telling Lies In America - Under Heaven - Go - Delivered
Mickey Liddell . . . . . . . . . . . . . . . . . . . . . . . . . . . . President
Robert Campbell . . . . . . . . . . . . . . . . . . . . . Creative Executive
Stacy C. Wilson . . . . . . . . . . . . . . . . . Dir., Financial Operations
Matt Hannon . . . . . . . . . . . . . . . . . . . . . . . . . Post Production

**BARNETTE PRODUCTIONS, ALAN**
PHONE . . . . . . . . . . . . . . . . . . . . . . . . . . . . . . 310-369-1000
Fox Studios
10201 W. Pico Blvd.
Los Angeles, CA 90035

TYPE        Motion Pictures + Television + Feature Direct to Video
DEAL        Twentieth Century Fox
CREDITS     Somebody Has To Shoot The Picture - Off Limits - Sliders
Alan Barnette . . . . . . . . . . . . . . . . . . . . . . . Executive Producer
Chris Severson . . . . . . . . . . . . . . . . . . . . . . Executive Assistant

**BARNSTORM FILMS**
PHONE . . . . . . . . . . . . . . . . . . . . . . . . . . . . . . 310-396-5937
FAX . . . . . . . . . . . . . . . . . . . . . . . . . . . . . . . . 310-450-4988
73 Market St.
Venice, CA 90291

TYPE        Motion Pictures
CREDITS     Untamed Heart - Five Corners - My Bodyguard - Taxi
            Driver - The Sting
Tony Bill . . . . . . . . . . . . . . . . . . . . . . . . . Producer/Director
Helen Bartlett . . . . . . . . . . . . . . . . . . . . . . . . . . . Producer

**BARRON/PENNETTE PRODS.**
PHONE . . . . . . . . . . . . . . . . . . . . . . . . . . . . . . 818-655-5960
FAX . . . . . . . . . . . . . . . . . . . . . . . . . . . . . . . . 818-655-4120
CBS Studio Center
4024 Radford Ave., Norvet Bldg., 4th Fl.
Studio City, CA 91604

TYPE        Television
DEAL        NBC Studios
CREDITS     Caroline In The City - Union Square
Fred Barron . . . . . . . . . . . . . . . . . . . . . . . Executive Producer
Marco Pennette . . . . . . . . . . . . . . . . . . . . . Executive Producer

**BARTLETT PRODS., JUANITA**
PHONE . . . . . . . . . . . . . . . . . . . . . . . . . . . . . . 818-753-5785
FAX . . . . . . . . . . . . . . . . . . . . . . . . . . . . . . . . 818-753-0232
15445 Ventura Blvd., Ste. 1005
Sherman Oaks, CA 91413

TYPE        Motion Pictures + Television
CREDITS     In the Heat of the Night - Spenser for Hire - Rockford
            Files(MOW)
Juanita Bartlett . . . . . . . . . . . . . . . . . . Exec. Producer/Writer
Kathy L. Ezso . . . . . . . . . . . . . . . . . . . . . . Executive Assistant

**BARWOOD FILMS**
PHONE . . . . . . . . . . . . . . . . . . . . . . . . . . . . . . 212-765-7191
FAX . . . . . . . . . . . . . . . . . . . . . . . . . . . . . . . . 212-765-6988
330 W. 58th St.
New York, NY 10019

TYPE        Motion Pictures + Television
DEAL        Columbia Pictures
CREDITS     Serving in Silence- Nuts - Prince of Tides - The Mirror Has
            Two Faces - Yentl - The Rescuers
Barbra Streisand . . . . . . . . . . . . . Owner/Actress/Producer/Director
Cis Corman . . . . . . . . . . . . . . . . . . . . . . . . . . . . President
Jennifer Raucher . . . . . . . . . . . . . . . . . . . . . Dir., Development
Erin Hennicke . . . . . . . . . . . . . . . . . . . . . . . . . Story Editor

**BATES ENTERTAINMENT**
PHONE . . . . . . . . . . . . . . . . . . . . . . . . . . . . . . 213-962-9204
137 N. Larchmont Blvd., Ste. 805
Los Angeles, CA 90004

TYPE        Motion Pictures + Television + Interactive Multimedia
CREDITS     Fall Time - Last Time I Committed Suicide - Whacked
Edward J. Bates . . . . . . . . . . . . . . . . . . . . Producer/President
Rochelle Bates . . . . . . . . . . . . . . . . . . . . Dir., Development/VP

**BATFILM PRODS., INC.**
PHONE . . . . . . . . . . . . . . . . . . . . . . . . . . . . . . 212-302-2688
FAX . . . . . . . . . . . . . . . . . . . . . . . . . . . . . . . . 212-302-2696
EMAIL . . . . . . . . . . . . . . . . . . . . . . . . . . batfilm@aol.com
123 W. 44th St., Ste. 10-K
New York, NY 10036

TYPE        Motion Pictures + Television + Interactive Multimedia +
            Animation
CREDITS     Batman - Batman Forever - Batman Returns - Carmen
            Sandiego - Batman & Robin
Benjamin Melniker . . . . . . . . . . . . . . . . . . . . . . . . Producer
Michael Uslan . . . . . . . . . . . . . . . . . . . . . . . . . . Producer
F.J. DeSanto . . . . . . . . . . . . . . . . . . . . . . . . . Development

**BATJAC PRODUCTIONS, INC.**
PHONE . . . . . . . . . . . . . . . . . . . . . . . . . . . . . . 310-278-9870
FAX . . . . . . . . . . . . . . . . . . . . . . . . . . . . . . . . 213-272-7381
9595 Wilshire Blvd., #610
Beverly Hills, CA 90212-2506

TYPE        Motion Pictures
CREDITS     Hondo - McLintock - The Green Berets - The Alamo - Big
            Jake
Michael A. Wayne . . . . . . . . . . . . . . . . . . . . . . . . President

***BAUER COMPANY, THE**
PHONE . . . . . . . . . . . . . . . . . . . . . . . . . . . . . . 310-247-3880
FAX . . . . . . . . . . . . . . . . . . . . . . . . . . . . . . . . 310-247-3881
9465 Wilshire Blvd., Ste. 620
Beverly Hills, CA 90212

TYPE        Motion Pictures + Television
Martin R. Bauer . . . . . . . . . . . . . . . . . . . . . . . . . Producer
Robert Marsala . . . . . . . . . . . . . . . . Development Executive
Cheryl Anthony . . . . . . . . . . . . . . . . . Asst. to Martin Bauer

**BAUM PRODUCTIONS, CAROL**
PHONE . . . . . . . . . . . . . . . . . . . . . . . . . . . . . . 310-550-4575
FAX . . . . . . . . . . . . . . . . . . . . . . . . . . . . . . . . 310-550-2088
8899 Beverly Blvd., Ste. 721
Los Angeles, CA 90048

TYPE        Motion Pictures
CREDITS     Father of the Bride - Dead Ringers- Kicking & Screaming -
            Fly Away Home
COMMENTS    No Unsolicited Submissions
Carol Baum . . . . . . . . . . . . . . . . . . . . . . . . . . . Producer
George Gatins . . . . . . . . . . . . . . . . . . . . . . Creative Executive

**BAUMGARTEN/PROPHET ENTERTAINMENT**
PHONE . . . . . . . . . . . . . . . . . . . . . . . . . . . . . . 310-996-1885
FAX . . . . . . . . . . . . . . . . . . . . . . . . . . . . . . . . 310-996-1892
1640 S. Sepulveda #218
Los Angeles, CA 90025

TYPE        Motion Pictures + Television
CREDITS     Jade - Hook - It Could Happen To You - Blank Check -
            Univeral Soldier - Esmeralda
Craig Baumgarten . . . . . . . . . . . . . . . . . . . . Producer/Partner
Melissa Prophet . . . . . . . . . . . . . . . . . . . . . Producer/Partner
David Fleming . . . . . . . . . . . . . . . . . . . . . . . . . . Producer
Randy Shafton . . . . . . . . . . . . . . . . . . . . . . . Office Manager
Claudine Vacca . . . . . . . . . . . . . . . . . . . Asst. to Mr. Fleming
Karen Woodward . . . . . . . . . . . . . . . Asst. to Craig Baumgarten
Susan Yoo . . . . . . . . . . . . . . . . . . . . . . Asst. to Ms. Prophet

**BAY FILMS**
PHONE . . . . . . . . . . . . . . . . . . . . . . . . . . . . . . 310-829-7799
FAX . . . . . . . . . . . . . . . . . . . . . . . . . . . . . . . . 310-829-7099
2110 Broadway
Santa Monica, CA 90404

TYPE        Motion Pictures + Television
DEAL        Walt Disney Company, The
CREDITS     Armageddon - The Rock - Bad Boys
Michael Bay . . . . . . . . . . . . . . . . . . . . . . . Director/Producer
Jennifer Klein . . . . . . . . . . . . . . . . . . . . . . . Vice President
Kevin K. Cooper . . . . . . . . . . . . . . . . . . . . Dir., Development
Brad Sisk . . . . . . . . . . . . . . . . . . . . . . Asst. to Michael Bay
Kristin Lowe . . . . . . . . . . . . . . . . . . . Asst. to Jennifer Klein

# COMPANIES AND STAFF

***BEACH HOUSE**
PHONE . . . . . . . . . . . . . . . . . . . . . . . . . . . . . . . . 310-260-8870
FAX . . . . . . . . . . . . . . . . . . . . . . . . . . . . . . . . . . 310-260-8867
225 Santa Monica Blvd., Ste. #404
Santa Monica, CA 90401

TYPE       Documentaries + Motion Pictures + Television + Syndication
CREDITS    Welcome to Hollywood - Casualties - Undercover Comics
Tony Markes . . . . . . . . . . . . . . . . . . . . . . . . . . . Producer/Director

**BEACON PICTURES**
PHONE . . . . . . . . . . . . . . . . . . . . . . . . . . . . . . . . 213-850-2651
FAX . . . . . . . . . . . . . . . . . . . . . . . . . . . . . . . . . . 213-850-2613
Warner-Hollywood Studios
1041 N. Formosa Ave.
Hollywood, CA 90046-6798

TYPE       Motion Pictures + Television
CREDITS    Commitments - A Midnight Clear - Air Force One - A Thousand Acres

Armyan Bernstein . . . . . . . . . . . . . . . . . . . . . . . . . Chairman
Marc Abraham . . . . . . . . . . . . . . . . . . . . . . . . . . . President
Thomas Bliss . . . . . . . . . . . . . . . . . . . . . COO/Exec. Vice President
Jon Shestack . . . . . . . . . . . . . . . . . . . . . . Exec. VP, Production
Cindy McWethy . . . . . . . . . . . . . . . . . . . . . . . . . VP, Finance
Caitlin Scanlon . . . . . . . . . . . . . . . . . . . . . . Head, Development
Debbie Von Arx . . . . . . . . . . . . . . . . . VP, Business & Legal Affairs
Peter Almond . . . . . . . . . . . . . . . . . . . . . . . . . . . Producer
Suzann Ellis . . . . . . . . . . . . . . . . . . . . . . . . Creative Executive
Scott Lew . . . . . . . . . . . . . . . . . . . . . . . . . Dir., Development
Linda Mack . . . . . . . . . . . . . . . . . . . . . . . . Dir., Legal Affairs
Rob Mitchell . . . . . . . . . . . . . . . . . . . . . . . . . Dir., Finance
Max Wong . . . . . . . . . . . . . . . . . . . . . . . . . Dir., Development
Susan Jizba-Peterson . . . . . . . . . . . . . . . . . . . Financial Analyst
Cynthia Moon . . . . . . . . . . . . . . . . Mgr., Business & Legal Affairs
Merry Rose . . . . . . . . . . . . . . . . . . . . . Mgr., Human Resources
Katherine Bishop . . . . . . . . . . . . . . . . . . . . Asst. to Mr. Bliss
Sara Endsley . . . . . . . . . . . . . . . . . . . 1st Asst. to Mr. Bernstein
A.B. Fischer . . . . . . . . . . . . . . . . . . . 2nd Asst. to Mr. Bernstein
Misty Green . . . . . . . . . . . . . . . . . . . . . . Asst. to Mr. Abraham

**BEAN AND COD PRODS.**
PHONE . . . . . . . . . . . . . . . . . . . . . . . . . . . . . . . . 213-871-1966
FAX . . . . . . . . . . . . . . . . . . . . . . . . . . . . . . . . . . 213-871-1430
EMAIL . . . . . . . . . . . . . . . . . . . . . . . . comedymgmt@aol.com
6515 Sunset Blvd., Ste. 205
Los Angeles, CA 90028

TYPE       Motion Pictures + Television + Syndication
COMMENTS  Comedy Shows.

Barry Newman . . . . . . . . . . . . . . . . . . . Exec. Producer/Actor
Harvey Elkin . . . . . . . . . . . . . . . . . . . . . . Executive Producer
David Rich . . . . . . . . . . . . . . . . . . . . . . . Dir., Development

**BEDFORD FALLS CO., THE**
PHONE . . . . . . . . . . . . . . . . . . . . . . . . . . . . . . . . 310-394-5022
FAX . . . . . . . . . . . . . . . . . . . . . . . . . . . . . . . . . . 310-394-5825
409 Santa Monica Blvd., PH
Santa Monica, CA 90401

TYPE       Motion Pictures + Television
DEAL       ABC Entertainment/Twentieth Century Fox-Fox 2000 (LA)
CREDITS    My So-Called Life - thirtysomething - Legends of the Fall - Against All Enemies - Dangerous Beauty

Marshall Herskovitz . . . . . . . Exec. Producer/Writer/Director (310-394-5355)
Edward Zwick . . . . . . . . . . Exec. Producer/Writer/Director (310-394-2697)
Richard Solomon . . . . . . . . . . . . . . . . . . . . President (310-394-5643)
Lisa Moiselle . . . . . . . . . . . . . . . . Sr. VP, Production (310-394-4502)
Robin Budd . . . . . . . . . . . . . . . . . Creative Exec. to Mr. Zwick
Michelle Herman . . . . . . . . . . . . . Creative Exec. to Mr. Solomon
Joshua Gummersall . . . . . . . . . . . Creative Exec. to Mr. Herskovitz
AJ Marcantonio . . . . . . . . . . . . . Creative Exec. to Ms. Moiselle
Nicholas Theodoropoulos . . . . . . . . . . . . . . . . . . Road Warrior

**BELISARIUS PRODS.**
PHONE . . . . . . . . . . . . . . . . . . . . . . . . . . . . . . . . 213-956-8660
FAX . . . . . . . . . . . . . . . . . . . . . . . . . . . . . . . . . . 213-862-0250
Paramount
5555 Melrose Ave., Clara Bow Bldg. #204
Los Angeles, CA 90038-3197

TYPE       Television + Motion Pictures
DEAL       Paramount Pictures- Motion Picture Group
CREDITS    Quantum Leap- Magnum, P.I.- Last Rites- JAG
COMMENTS  A division of Viacom.

Donald P. Bellisario . . . . . . . . . . . Writer/Exec. Producer/Director
Stephen Zito . . . . . . . . . . . . . . . . Co-Exec. Producer/Writer
David Bellisario . . . . . . . . . . . . . . . . . . . . . . . . . Producer
Avery Drewe . . . . . . . . . . . . . . . . . . . . . . . . . . . Producer
Mark Horowitz . . . . . . . . . . . . . . . . . . . . . . . . . . Producer
Julie Watson . . . . . . . . . . . . . . . . . . . . . . . . . . . Producer
R. Scott Gemmill . . . . . . . . . . . . . . . . . . . . Producer/Writer
Tina Albanese . . . . . . . . . . . . . . . . . . . . . Associate Producer
Shari Ramsey . . . . . . . . . . . . . . . . . . . . . . Script Coordinator
Beth Tracy . . . . . . . . . . . . . . Exec. Asst. to Donald Bellisario
Mickey Silberman . . . . . . . . . . 2nd Asst. to Donald Bellisario
Nina Bunche Pierce . . . . . . . . . . Asst. to Chas. Floyd Johnson

**BELL AND ASSOCIATES, DAVE**
PHONE . . . . . . . . . . . . . . . . . . . . . . . . . . . . . . . . 213-851-7801
FAX . . . . . . . . . . . . . . . . . . . . . . . . . . . . . . . . . . 213-851-9349
EMAIL . . . . . . . . . . . . . . . . . . . . . . . . . . . DBATV@aol.com
3211 Cahuenga Blvd. West
Los Angeles, CA 90068

TYPE       Motion Pictures + Television + Syndication + Documentaries
CREDITS    LAPD - Worlds Most Dangerous Animals - Deep Red - Long Walk Home - Night Visitors

David L. Bell . . . . . . . . . . . . . . . . . . . . . . . . . . . President
Cynthia B. Shapiro . . . . . . . . . . . . . . . . . . . . . Vice President
Shari Cookson . . . . . . . . . . . . . . . VP, Documentary Production
Garrett Cohen . . . . . . . . . . . . . . . . . . . . . . . . . . Producer
Ben Moses . . . . . . . . . . . . . . . . . Executive Producer/Writer
Christine Good . . . . . . . . . . . . . . . . . . . . . Dir., Development

**BELL-PHILLIP TV PRODS., INC.**
PHONE . . . . . . . . . . . . . . . . . . . . . . . . . . . . . . . . 213-852-4138
FAX . . . . . . . . . . . . . . . . . . . . . . . . . . . . . . . . . . 213-655-8760
7800 Beverly Blvd., Ste. 3371
Los Angeles, CA 90036-2188

TYPE       Television
CREDITS    The Bold and the Beautiful

William J. Bell . . . . . . . . . . . . . . . . . . . . . . . . . . . Creator
Lee Phillip Bell . . . . . . . . . . . . . . . . . . . . . . . . Co-Creator
Bradley Bell . . . . . . . . . . . . . . . Executive Producer/Head Writer
Ron Weaver . . . . . . . . . . . . . . . . . Sr. Coordinating Producer
Deveney Kelly . . . . . . . . . . . . . . . . . . . . . . . . . . Producer
John Zak . . . . . . . . . . . . . . . . . . . . . . Supervising Producer
Rhonda Friedman . . . . . . . . . . . . . . . . Coordinating Producer

**BELLADONNA PRODUCTIONS**
PHONE . . . . . . . . . . . . . . . . . . . . . . . . . . . . . . . . 310-452-0399
2704 11th Street
Santa Monica, CA 90405

TYPE       Motion Pictures
CREDITS    Never Leave Nevada
Diane Campbell . . . . . . . . . . . . . . . . . . . . . Producer/Writer

**BENEDETTI PRODUCTIONS, INC., ROBERT**
PHONE . . . . . . . . . . . . . . . . . . . . . . . . . . . . . . . . 310-664-0912
FAX . . . . . . . . . . . . . . . . . . . . . . . . . . . . . . . . . . 310-664-0932
EMAIL . . . . . . . . . . . . . . . . . . . . . . . . . Benedetti1@aol.com
2533 6th St.
Santa Monica, CA 90405-3707

TYPE       Motion Pictures + Television
CREDITS    Miss Evers' Boys - On Promised Land - Canterville Ghost
COMMENTS  Formerly Anasazi Productions
Robert Benedetti . . . . . . . . . . . . . . . . . . . . . . . . . President

# COMPANIES AND STAFF

**BENJAMIN PRODS. INC.**
PHONE . . . . . . . . . . . . . . . . . . . . . . . . . . . . . . . . . . 818-752-8500
FAX . . . . . . . . . . . . . . . . . . . . . . . . . . . . . . . . . . . . 818-752-4928
12725 Ventura Blvd., Ste. B
Studio City, CA 91604-2437
TYPE          Motion Pictures + Television
CREDITS       La Bamba - Everybody's All American - Mortal Thoughts -
              The Abduction
Stuart Benjamin . . . . . . . . . . . . . . . . . . . . . . . . . . . . . . . . . Producer
Alise Benjamin . . . . . . . . . . . . . . . . . . . . . . . . . . . . . . . . . . Producer
Matthew M. Burns . . . . . . . . . . . . . . . . . . . . . . . . . . . VP, Production
Berit Campion . . . . . . . . . . . . . . . . . . . . . . . . . . . . . . . . . Assistant

**BENNETT PRODUCTIONS, HARVE**
PHONE . . . . . . . . . . . . . . . . . . . . . . . . . . . . . . . . . . 818-733-6977
FAX . . . . . . . . . . . . . . . . . . . . . . . . . . . . . . . . . . . . 818-733-6950
DreamWorks Television Animation
1000 Flower St.
Glendale, CA 91201-3007
TYPE          Television + Motion Pictures + Animation
CREDITS       Star Trek II-V - Rich Man, Poor Man - Time Trax -
              Invasion America
Harve Bennett . . . . . . . . . . . . . . . . . . Executive Producer/Writer
Marianne Tyler . . . . . . . . . . . . . . . . Development/Research (310-306-7198)
Richard Thompson . . . . . . . . . . . . . . . Business Affairs (310-859-6839)
Craig Kyle . . . . . . . . . . . . . . . . . . . . . . . . . . . Asst. to Mr. Bennett

**BENT OUTTA SHAPE PRODUCTIONS**
PHONE . . . . . . . . . . . . . . . . . . . . . . . . . . . . . . . . . . 818-954-1978
FAX . . . . . . . . . . . . . . . . . . . . . . . . . . . . . . . . . . . . 818-954-7400
Warner Bros. Television
4000 Warner Blvd., Bldg. 136
Burbank, CA 91522
TYPE          Television
DEAL          Warner Bros. Television Productions
CREDITS       Jamie Foxx Show
Bentley Kyle Evans . . . . . . . . . . . . . . . . . . . . . . . . . . . President

**BERK SCHWARTZ BONANN PRODUCTIONS**
PHONE . . . . . . . . . . . . . . . . . . . . . . . . . . . . . . . . . . 310-302-9135
FAX . . . . . . . . . . . . . . . . . . . . . . . . . . . . . . . . . . . . 310-302-9189
5433 Beethoven St.
Los Angeles, CA 90066
TYPE          Motion Pictures + Television + Interactive Multimedia +
              Syndication
CREDITS       Baywatch - Thunder In Paradise - Baywatch Nights -
              Assault on Devil's Island - Steel Chariots
Michael Berk . . . . . . . . . . . . . . . . . . . . . . . . . . Executive Producer
Gregory J. Bonann . . . . . . . . . . . . . . . . . . . . . . Executive Producer
Douglas Schwartz . . . . . . . . . . . . . . . . . . . . . . . Executive Producer
Kevin Beggs . . . . . . . . . . . . . . . . . . . . . . . . . . . . VP, Development
Jon Valenti . . . . . . . . . . . . . . . . . . . . . . . . Development Associate

**BERMAN PRODUCTIONS, RICK**
PHONE . . . . . . . . . . . . . . . . . . . . . . . . . . . . . . . . . . 213-956-5037
FAX . . . . . . . . . . . . . . . . . . . . . . . . . . . . . . . . . . . . 213-862-1076
5555 Melrose Ave., Ste. 232
Los Angeles, CA 90038
TYPE          Motion Pictures + Television + Syndication
DEAL          Paramount Television Group/Paramount Pictures- Motion
              Picture Group
CREDITS       Star Trek: Deep Space Nine-Star Trek: First Contact - Star
              Trek: Voyager
Rick Berman . . . . . . . . . . . . . . . . . . . . . . . . . . Executive Producer
Dave Rossi . . . . . . . . . . . . . . . . . . . . . Supervor, Star Trek Projects
Maril Davis . . . . . . . . . . . . . . . . . . . . . . . . . . Asst. to Rick Berman
Jose Munoz . . . . . . . . . . . . . . . . . . . . . . . . . . . Asst. to Producers

**BERNBAUM, PAUL**
PHONE . . . . . . . . . . . . . . . . . . . . . . . . . . . . . . . . . . 310-234-5085
FAX . . . . . . . . . . . . . . . . . . . . . . . . . . . . . . . . . . . . 310-234-5059
Viacom Productions
10880 Wilshire Blvd., Ste. 1101
Los Angeles, CA 90024
TYPE          Television
DEAL          Viacom Productions
CREDITS       Rent a Kid - Deadly Games - Connections - Royce - Family
              Plan
Paul Bernbaum . . . . . . . . . . . . . . . . . . . . . . . . . Executive Producer
Michelle Wilkerson . . . . . . . . . . . . . . . . . . . . Asst. to Paul Bernbaum

**BERNER FILMS, FRED**
PHONE . . . . . . . . . . . . . . . . . . . . . . . . . . . . . . . . . . 212-592-0673
FAX . . . . . . . . . . . . . . . . . . . . . . . . . . . . . . . . . . . . 212-592-0696
401 Fifth Ave., Fifth Floor
New York, NY 10016
TYPE          Motion Pictures + Television
CREDITS       The Great White Hype- Ballad of Little Jo - Vanya on
              42nd Street - The Farmhouse
Fred Berner . . . . . . . . . . . . . . . . . . . . . . . . . . . . . . . . . President
Elaine Frontain Bryant . . . . . . . . . . . . . . . . . Dir., Creative Affairs
Ann C. Young . . . . . . . . . . . . . . . . . . . . . . . . Creative Associate

**BERNSEN PRODS. INC., HARRY**
PHONE . . . . . . . . . . . . . . . . . . . . . . 213-463-7659/310-203-8810
FAX . . . . . . . . . . . . . . . . . . . . . . . . . . . . . . . . . . . . 213-878-6769
2001 S. Barrington Ave., Ste. 210
Los Angeles, CA 90025
TYPE          Motion Pictures + Television
CREDITS       El Diluvio Que Viene - The Awakening Land - There is
              Nothing Like 2 Dames
COMMENTS      Also: Theatre
Harry Bernsen . . . . . . . . . . . . . . . . . . . . . . . President/Producer
Collin Bernsen . . . . . . . . . . . . . . . . . . . . . . . . . . VP, Production
Roger N. Golden . . . . . . . . . . . . . . . . . . VP, Legal & Financial
Caren Wilson . . . . . . . . . . . . . . . . . . . . . . . . . . VP, Development

**BERNSTEIN PRODUCTIONS, JAY**
PHONE . . . . . . . . . . . . . . . . . . . . . . . . . . . . . . . . . . 310-858-1485
FAX . . . . . . . . . . . . . . . . . . . . . . . . . . . . . . . . . . . . 310-858-1607
P.O. Box 1148
Beverly Hills, CA 90213
TYPE          Motion Pictures + Television + Syndication + Feature
              Direct to Video
CREDITS       Mike Hammer - Sunburn - Diamond Trap - Double
              Jeopardy
COMMENTS      Also: Personal Manager.
Jay Bernstein . . . . . . . . . . . . . . . Pres./Prod./Director/Writer

**BESAME MUCHO PICTURES**
PHONE . . . . . . . . . . . . . . . . . . . . . . . . . . . . . . . . . . 818-954-4555
FAX . . . . . . . . . . . . . . . . . . . . . . . . . . . . . . . . . . . . 818-954-4033
4000 Warner Blvd., Prods. 2, Ste. 1105
Burbank, CA 91522
TYPE          Motion Pictures
DEAL          Warner Bros. Pictures
CREDITS       Little Princess- Solo Con Tu Pareja - Fallen Angels: Murder
              Obliquely - Great Expectations
Alfonso Cuaron . . . . . . . . . . . . . . . . . . . . . . Director/President
Bryan A. Kenny . . . . . . . . . . . . . . . . . . . . . . . . . . Vice President
Victoria Dew . . . . . . . . . . . . . . . . . . . . . . Asst. To Alfonso Cuaron

**BETTINA PRODS. LTD.**
PHONE . . . . . . . . . . . . . . . . . . . . . . . . . . . . . . . . . . 213-937-2101
FAX . . . . . . . . . . . . . . . . . . . . . . . . . . . . . . . . . . . . 213-937-2103
624 S. June St.
Los Angeles, CA 90005
TYPE          Motion Pictures + Television
CREDITS       Stone Cold - Rope of Sand - Kentucky Woman
Walter Doniger . . . . . . . . . . . . . . . . . . . . . . . . . . . . . . President

**BICKLEY PRODS.**
PHONE . . . . . . . . . . . . . . . . . . . . . . . . . . . . . . . . . . 818-954-2782
FAX . . . . . . . . . . . . . . . . . . . . . . . . . . . . . . . . . . . . 818-954-4326
4000 Warner Blvd., Bldg. 36, #152
Burbank, CA 91522
TYPE          Television
DEAL          Warner Bros. Television Productions
CREDITS       Hangin with Mr. Cooper - Family Matters - Step by Step -
              Kirk
William Bickley . . . . . . . . . . . . . . . . . . . . . . . . . Executive Producer

**BIG BANG FILMS**
PHONE . . . . . . . . . . . . . . . . . . . . . . . . . . . . . . . . . . 818-505-6100
FAX . . . . . . . . . . . . . . . . . . . . . . . . . . . . . . . . . . . . 818-505-6106
EMAIL . . . . . . . . . . . . . . . . . . . . . . . . . . . Gayne1024@aol.com
3965 Carpenter Ave.
Studio City, CA 91604
TYPE          Motion Pictures
CREDITS       City of Industry
COMMENTS      Also: Large Format.
Matthew Gayne . . . . . . . . . . . . . . . . . . . . . . . . . . . . . President

# COMPANIES AND STAFF

**BIG DADDY PRODUCTIONS**
PHONE . . . . . . . . . . . . . . . . . . . . . . . . . . . . . . . . . 818-238-2038
FAX . . . . . . . . . . . . . . . . . . . . . . . . . . . . . . . . . . . . 818-238-2088
3601 West Olive Avenue, First Floor
Burbank, CA 91505
TYPE        Television
CREDITS     My Indian Summer - TV's Funniest Families I & II
Kerri Friedland . . . . . . . . . . . . . . . . . . . . . . . . . . . Executive Producer
Scott Friedland . . . . . . . . . . . . . . . . . . . . . . . . . . . Executive Producer
Julie Ward . . . . . . . . . . . . . . . . . . . . . . . . . . . . . . . . . . . Development

**BIG SHOES PRODUCTIONS**
PHONE . . . . . . . . . . . . . . . . . . . . . . . . . . . . . . . . . 310-573-1701
FAX . . . . . . . . . . . . . . . . . . . . . . . . . . . . . . . . . . . . 310-573-9683
249 Mabery Rd.
Santa Monica, CA 90402
TYPE        Motion Pictures + Television + Documentaries
CREDITS     Andre - The Blue Yonder - Dangerous Intentions
Annette Handley . . . . . . . . . . . . . . . . . . . . . . . . . . . . . . . Producer

**BIG SKY ENTERTAINMENT**
PHONE . . . . . . . . . . . . . . . . . . . . . . . . . . . . . . . . . 310-609-7369
27422 Laurel Glen Circle
Valencia, CA 91354
TYPE        Motion Pictures + Television + Documentaries +
                 Animation + Feature Direct to Video
Todd A. Miller . . . . . . . . . . . . . . . . . . . . . . . . Chief Executive Officer
Matt Kleinman . . . . . . . . . . . . . . . . . . . . . . . . . . . . . . . . . President
Marilyn Jones . . . . . . . . . . . . . . . . . . . . . . . . . . . . . . . Development
Traci E. Miller . . . . . . . . . . . . . . . . . . . . . . . . . . . Associate Producer

**BIG TICKET TELEVISION**
PHONE . . . . . . . . . . . . . . . . . . . . . . . . . . . . . . . . . 213-860-7400
FAX . . . . . . . . . . . . . . . . . . . . . . . . . . . . . . . . . . . . 213-468-4176
Sunset Gower Studios
1438 N. Gower St., Box 45, Bldg. 35
Hollywood, CA 90028-8362
TYPE        Television + Syndication
CREDITS     Moesha - Judge Judy - Judge Joe Brown
COMMENTS   Subsidiary of Spelling Entertainment
Larry Lyttle . . . . . . . . . . . . . . . . . . . . . . . . . . . . . . . . . . President
Bill Sanders . . . . . . . . . . . . . . . . . . . . . . . . . . . Exec. Vice President
Deborah Curtan . . . . . . . . . . . . . . . . . . . . Sr. VP, Current Programs
Bruce Kerner . . . . . . . . . . . . . . . . . . . . . . . . . . . Sr. VP, Production
Roger Kirman . . . . . . . . . . . . . . . . . . . . . . Sr. VP, Business Affairs
Laura Schrock . . . . . . . . . . . . . . . . . . . . Sr. VP, Series Development
Dawn Steinberg . . . . . . . . . . . . . . . . . . . . Sr. VP, Talent & Casting
Mark S. Johnson . . . . . . . . . . . . . . . . . . . . . . . . . . VP, Production
Fred Paccone . . . . . . . . . . . . . . . . . . . . . . . . . . . . . . VP/Controller
Paul Shapiro . . . . . . . . . . . . . . . . . . . . . . . . . . . Dir., Development
Amy Slaughter . . . . . . . . . . . . . . . . . . . . . . . Dir., Creative Affairs
John Westphal . . . . . . . . . . . . . . . . . . . . . . . Mgr., Creative Affairs
Warren Coulter . . . . . . . . . . . . . . . . . . . . . . . . . . . . . Development
Cindy Bernstein . . . . . . . . . . . . . . . . . Coordinator, Office of President

**BIG TOWN PRODUCTIONS**
PHONE . . . . . . . . . . . . . . . . . . . . . . . . . . . . . . . . . 310-888-3506
FAX . . . . . . . . . . . . . . . . . . . . . . . . . . . . . . . . . . . . 310-888-3595
Castle Rock Entertainment
335 N. Maple Dr., Ste. 135
Beverly Hills, CA 90210
TYPE        Motion Pictures
DEAL        Castle Rock Entertainment
Bill Pullman . . . . . . . . . . . . . . . . . . . . . . . . . . . . Actor/Producer
Ruth Fainberg . . . . . . . . . . . . . . . . . . . . . . . . . . . VP, Development
Jennifer Deaton . . . . . . . . . . . . . . . . . . . . . . . . . Dir., Development
Karen Goldstein . . . . . . . . . . . . . . . . . . . . . . . Asst. to Bill Pullman

***BIGEL/MAILER FILMS**
PHONE . . . . . . . . . . . . . . . . . . . . . . . . . . . . . . . . . 212-343-7916
FAX . . . . . . . . . . . . . . . . . . . . . . . . . . . . . . . . . . . . 212-343-9572
EMAIL . . . . . . . . . . . . . . . . . . . . . . . . . . dbigel@bigelmailer.com
WEBSITE . . . . . . . . . . . . . . . . . . . . . . . http://www.bigelmailer.com
443 Greenwich St., Ste. 3A
New York, NY 10013
TYPE        Motion Pictures
CREDITS     Two Girls and a Guy - Casanova Falling - The Money Shot
Daniel Bigel . . . . . . . . . . . . . . . . . . . . . . . Chief Executive Officer
Michael Mailer . . . . . . . . . . . . . . . . . . . . . . . . . . . . . . . President

**BILL OAKLEY & JOSH WEINSTEIN**
PHONE . . . . . . . . . . . . . . . . . . . . . . . . . . . . . . . . . 310-888-3529
Castle Rock Entertainment
335 N. Maple Dr., Ste. #135
Beverly Hills, CA 90210
TYPE        Television
DEAL        Castle Rock Entertainment
CREDITS     The Simpsons
Bill Oakley . . . . . . . . . . . . . . . . . . . . . . . . . . . . . . . . . Producer
Josh Weinstein . . . . . . . . . . . . . . . . . . . . . . . . . . . . . . . Producer

**BLACK & WHITE PRODUCTIONS**
PHONE . . . . . . . . . . . . . . . . . . . . . . . . . . . . . . . . . 310-641-8086
6308 W. 89th St., Ste. 211
Los Angeles, CA 90045
TYPE        Motion Pictures + Television
Jasmine Guy . . . . . . . . . . . . . . . . . . . . . . . . . . Executive Producer
Tambre Hemstreet . . . . . . . . . . . . . . . . . . . . . . . . . . . . . Producer

**BLACK ENTERTAINMENT TV**
PHONE . . . . . . . . . . . . . . . . 202-608-2000/818-566-9948
FAX . . . . . . . . . . . . . . . . . . . . . . . . . . . . . . . . . . . . 818-566-1655
One BET Plaza, 1900 W. Place NE
Washington, DC 20018-1211
TYPE        Television
COMMENTS   ALSO: 2801 W. Olive Ave., Burbank, CA 91505
Robert Johnson . . . . . . . . . . . . . . . . . . . . . . . . . . . Chairman/CEO
Debra Lee . . . . . . . . . . . . . . . . . . . . . . . . . . . . . President/COO
Shelia Frazier . . . . . . . . . . . . . . . . . . . . . . . . . . . . Producer (LA)
Curtis Gadson . . . . . . . . VP, Net. Ops. & Programming/Exec. Producer (LA)
Cindy Mahmoud . . . . . . . . . . . . . . . . . . . . . . . . . VP, Syndication
Deborah Tang . . . . . . . . . . . . . . . . . VP, Entertainment and News
Lynne Harris Taylor . . . . . . . . . . . . . . . . Director/Sr. Producer (LA)
Andre Barnwell . . . . . . . Dir., Net Ops & Programming/Exec. Producer (LA)

**BLACK SHEEP ENTERTAINMENT**
PHONE . . . . . . . . . . . . . . . . . . . . . . . . . . . . . . . . . 213-830-2622
FAX . . . . . . . . . . . . . . . . . . . . . . . . . . . . . . . . . . . . 213-850-2650
EMAIL . . . . . . . . . . . . . . . . . . . . . . . . blacksheep@artnet.net
Warner Hollywood Studios, Writers Bldg.
1041 N. Formosa, Ste. 31B
West Hollywood, CA 90046
TYPE        Motion Pictures
CREDITS     The Big Gig - The Cottonwood - It Had To Be You
Steven Feder . . . . . . . . . . . . . . . . Partner/Writer/Director/Producer
Neil Kaplan . . . . . . . . . . . . . . . . . . . . . . . . . . . Partner/Producer
Jeff Mazzola . . . . . . . . . . . . . . . . . . . . . . . . . . . . . . . . Producer
Tracey Morton . . . . . . . . . . . . . . . . . . . Development Executive

**BLACK, LAWRENCE & SILVERHARDT ENT.**
PHONE . . . . . . . . . . . . . . . . . . . . . . . . . . . . . . . . . 310-229-9555
FAX . . . . . . . . . . . . . . . . . . . . . . . . . . . . . . . . . . . . 310-229-9558
EMAIL . . . . . . . . . . . . . . . . . . . . . . . . . . . . blasela@aol.com
10350 Santa Monica Blvd., #295
Los Angeles, CA 90025
TYPE        Motion Pictures + Television
CREDITS     Marker - Born To Run - Heaven or Vegas
Christopher Black . . . . . . . . . . . . . . . . . . . . . . . . . . . . . Partner
Barbara Lawrence . . . . . . . . . . . . . . . . . . . . . . . . . . . . . Partner
Jerald J. Silverhardt . . . . . . . . . . . . . . . . . . . . . . . . . . . Partner
Michael Corbin . . . . . . . . . . . . . . . . . . . . . . . . . . . . . Associate
Jenna Anderson . . . . . . . . . . . . . . . . . . . . . . . . . . . . . Assistant
Andrew Dainoff . . . . . . . . . . . . . . . . . . . . . . . . . . . . . Assistant

**BLACK/MARLENS COMPANY, THE**
PHONE . . . . . . . . . . . . . . . . . . . . . . . . . . . . . . . . . 310-772-8264
P.O. Box 1166
Malibu, CA 90265
TYPE        Motion Pictures + Television
CREDITS     The Wonder Years - Laurie Hill - Ellen
Carol Black . . . . . . . . . . . . . . . . . . . . . . Writer/Producer/Director
Neal Marlens . . . . . . . . . . . . . . . . . . . . . Writer/Producer/Director

**BLAKE PRODS., TIMOTHY**
PHONE . . . . . . . . . . . . . . . . . . . . . . . . . . . . . . . . . 310-657-4136
1643 Sunset Plaza Drive
Los Angeles, CA 90069
TYPE        Motion Pictures + Television
Timothy Blake . . . . . . . . . . . . . . . . . . . . . . . . . . . . . . President
Patrick Strong . . . . . . . . . . . . . . . . . . . . . . . . . . . Vice President
Hillary Morgan . . . . . . . . . . . . . . . . . . . . . . . . . . . Development

## BLANKI & BODI PRODS., INC.
```
PHONE ............................ 818-753-7644/213-969-0366
FAX ........................................ 213-969-8644
EMAIL ................................. BandB03@aol.com
```
3599 Cahuenga Blvd. W., Ste. 440
Los Angeles, CA 90068

| | |
|---|---|
| TYPE | Television + Syndication |
| CREDITS | Where Are They Now '97 - Ladies Home Journal: Most Fascinating Women of '97 - American Originals (TNN) |

```
Susan Winston .......................... Executive Producer
Dan Funk .............................. Executive Producer
Vivian Sampson ......................... Executive Assistant
```

## *BLEECKER STREET FILMS
```
PHONE ........................................ 213-993-7386
FAX .......................................... 213-993-7387
EMAIL ......................... bleeckerstr@earthlink.net
```
1438 N. Gower St., Ste. 267
Los Angeles, CA 90028

| | |
|---|---|
| TYPE | Motion Pictures + Television |
| DEAL | Turner Network Television |
| CREDITS | A Bright Shining Lie - Two for Texas - Lakota Woman - Broken Trust |
| COMMENTS | Also: Features for Cable |

```
Lois Bonfiglio ............................... President
Nellie Kurtzman ................... Development Associate
```

## *BLUE BAY PRODUCTIONS
```
PHONE ........................................ 310-440-9904
FAX .......................................... 310-440-9924
EMAIL ................................. berisky@aol.com
```
Rodney Liber
1119 Colorado Ave., Ste. 100
Santa Monica, CA 90401

| | |
|---|---|
| TYPE | Motion Pictures |
| CREDITS | Wild Things - Dunston Checks In |
| COMMENTS | Independent Financing/Development. |

```
Rodney Liber ................................. Producer
Jennifer Hughes ....................... Creative Executive
Dana Murray .......................... Office Assistant
```

## *BLUE HORIZON
```
PHONE ........................................ 310-656-6177
FAX .......................................... 310-656-6196
```
919 Santa Monica Blvd., 2nd Floor
Santa Monica, CA 90401

| | |
|---|---|
| TYPE | Motion Pictures |
| DEAL | Twentieth Century Fox |
| CREDITS | Titanic |

```
Jon Landau .................................. Producer
Brooks Ferguson ..................... Exec. VP, Production
Loren Shertzer ........... Asst. to Jon Landau (310-666-6156)
Mark Botvinick ........ Development Assistant (310-656-6180)
```

## BLUE RELIEF, INC.
```
PHONE ........................................ 818-560-2255
FAX .......................................... 818-567-4092
EMAIL ................................. bluerelief@aol.com
```
500 S. Buena Vista St., Animation 1C6
Burbank, CA 91521-1620

| | |
|---|---|
| TYPE | Motion Pictures + Television |
| DEAL | Propaganda Films/Alliance Entertainment |
| CREDITS | Northern Lights |
| COMMENTS | No Unsolicited Submissions. |

```
Diane Keaton .................... Director/Producer/Actor
Bill Robinson ............................... Producer
Amanda McHugh ...................... Dir., Development
Laura Citrano ..................... Asst. to Diane Keaton
Emily Lenzner ..................... Asst. to Bill Robinson
```

## BLUE RIDER PICTURES
```
PHONE ........................................ 310-314-8246
FAX .......................................... 310-581-4352
EMAIL ......................... 74774,2454@compuserve.com
WEBSITE ..................... http://www.blueriderpictures.com
```
2800 28th St., Ste. 105
Santa Monica, CA 90405

| | |
|---|---|
| TYPE | Motion Pictures + Television + Feature Direct to Video + Animation + Documentaries |
| DEAL | Hallmark Entertainment |
| CREDITS | Call of The Wild - Shergar - Evolver - Silverwolf - Children of the Corn 5 |

```
Jeff Geoffray .......................... Producer/Partner
Walter Josten .......................... Producer/Partner
Murray Schultz ......................... Pres., International
Sirod ................................. Creative Director
Craig Nicholls ......................... Dir., Development
Gerald Gottesman ...................... Dir., Business Affairs
```

## BLUE TULIP PRODUCTIONS
```
PHONE ........................................ 310-752-7900
FAX .......................................... 310-752-7920
```
1658 10th St.
Santa Monica, CA 90404

| | |
|---|---|
| TYPE | Motion Pictures + Television + Animation |
| DEAL | Twentieth Century Fox |
| CREDITS | Speed - Twister - SLC-Punk - Matilda |

```
Jan De Bont ................................. President
Michael Peyser ............................... Partner
Randy Auerbach ...................... VP, Creative Affairs
Robert Green .......................... Dir., Development
Peter Ward ............................ Dir., Production
Christopher Collet .................... Asst. Mr. De Bont
Glen Salloum ......................... Associate Producer
Brad Simonsen ...................... Development/Production
```

## BLUE TURTLE, INC.
```
PHONE ........................................ 213-654-7797
FAX .......................................... 213-654-7722
EMAIL ................................. labti@aol.com
```
2304 Sunset Plaza Drive
West Hollywood, CA 90069

| | |
|---|---|
| TYPE | Motion Pictures + Television |
| CREDITS | Pontiac Moon - Diggstown |
| COMMENTS | No Unsolicited Submissions Please. |

```
Youssef Vahabzadeh ..................... Owner/Producer
Tamiko D. Theros ....... VP, Development & Production/Co-Producer
Michael Pisano ...................... Development Assistant
```

## BLUE WOLF PRODS. INC.
```
PHONE ........................................ 310-451-8890
FAX .......................................... 310-451-4886
```
725 Arizona Ave., Ste. 202
Santa Monica, CA 90401

| | |
|---|---|
| TYPE | Motion Pictures |
| DEAL | Walt Disney Motion Pictures Group |
| CREDITS | Mrs. Doubtfire - Jakob the Liar |

```
Robin Williams ............................... No Title
Marsha Williams .............................. No Title
Barry Sabath ................................. No Title
Cyndi Margolis ............................... No Title
Jennifer Garces Cerchiai ...................... No Title
Liz Condren .................................. No Title
```

## BLUELINE PRODUCTIONS
```
PHONE ........................................ 310-887-1812
FAX .......................................... 310-887-1815
```
8899 Beverly Blvd., Ste. 811
Los Angeles, CA 90048

| | |
|---|---|
| TYPE | Motion Pictures + Television |
| CREDITS | Frankie The Fly - Bat 21 - El Diablo - Nightbreaker - The Personals |

```
Peter Markle ......................... Director/Producer
Graham Jones ......................... Dir., Development
```

                    ©1998 Hollywood Creative Directory Vol. 34

## BLUM PRODUCTIONS, HOWARD
PHONE . . . . . . . . . . . . . . . . . . . . . . . . . . . . . . . . . . . 310-285-2300
FAX . . . . . . . . . . . . . . . . . . . . . . . . . . . . . . . . . . . . . . 310-888-3516
335 N. Maple Dr., Ste. 135
Beverly Hills, CA 90210
TYPE     Motion Pictures + Television
DEAL     Mandalay Pictures/Columbia TriStar Television/Castle Rock Entertainment
CREDITS     A Family of Spies: The Walker Spy Ring

Howard Blum . . . . . . . . . . . . . . . . . . . . . . . . . . . . . Producer/Writer
Geoffrey Mattson . . . . . . . . . . . . . . . Vice President (310-285-2392)
Tara Sullivan . . . . . . . . . . . . . . . . . . . . . . . . . . . . . . . . No Title

## BLUMBERG PRODUCTIONS
PHONE . . . . . . . . . . . . . . . . . . . . . . . . . . . . . . . . . . . 310-472-6410
FAX . . . . . . . . . . . . . . . . . . . . . . . . . . . . . . . . . . . . . . 310-472-5705
833 Moraga Dr., #12
Los Angeles, CA 90049
TYPE     Motion Pictures
CREDITS     Sensation - The West Side Waltz - Plato's Run

Mitch Blumberg . . . . . . . . . . . . . . . . . . . . . . . . . . . . . . . Producer

## BLURCO
PHONE . . . . . . . . . . . . . . . . . . . . . . . . . . . . . . . . . . . 213-938-2719
FAX . . . . . . . . . . . . . . . . . . . . . . . . . . . . . . . . . . . . . . 213-938-2719
1208 S. Stanley Ave.
Los Angeles, CA 90019
TYPE     Motion Pictures
CREDITS     Nowhere - The Doom Generation - Color of a Brisk & Leaping Day - Desert Blue

Andrea Sperling . . . . . . . . . . . . . . . . . . . . . . . . . . . . . . . Producer
Narween Otto . . . . . . . . . . . . . . . . . . . . . . . . Asst. to Ms. Sperling

## BOARDWALK ENT./ALAN WAGNER PRODS., INC.
PHONE . . . . . . . . . . . . . . . . . . . . . . . . . . . . . . . . . . . 212-679-3800
FAX . . . . . . . . . . . . . . . . . . . . . . . . . . . . . . . . . . . . . . 212-679-3816
EMAIL . . . . . . . . . . . . . . . . . . . . . . . . boardwalk@infohouse.com
210 E. 39th St.
New York, NY 10016
TYPE     Motion Pictures + Television
CREDITS     Wounded Heart - Hearts Adrift - Reasons of the Heart - Four Spenser movies
COMMENTS     No unsolicited submissions.

Alan Wagner . . . . . . . . . . . . . . . . . . . . . . . . . . . . . . . . Chairman
Susan Wagner . . . . . . . . . . . . . . . . . . . . . . . . . . . . . . . President
Ann-Cathrin Schmidt . . . . . . . . . . . . . VP, In Charge of Production
Elizabeth Wagner . . . . . . . . . . . . . . . . . . . . . VP, Creative Affairs
Marti Wagner . . . . . . . . . . . . . . . . . . . . . . . Dir., Story Department

## BOBKER FILMS, DANIEL
PHONE . . . . . . . . . . . . . . . . . . . . . . . . . . . . . . . . . . . 213-933-5555
FAX . . . . . . . . . . . . . . . . . . . . . . . . . . . . . . . . . . . . . . 213-933-3908
369 N. Spaulding Ave., Ste. 1
Los Angeles, CA 90036
TYPE     Motion Pictures
CREDITS     Blood & Chocolate

Daniel Bobker . . . . . . . . . . . . . . . . . . . . . . . . . . . . . . . . Producer

## BOCHCO PRODS., STEVEN
PHONE . . . . . . . . . . . . . . . . . . . . . . . . . . . . . . . . . . . 310-369-2400
FAX . . . . . . . . . . . . . . . . . . . . . . . . . . . . . . . . . . . . . . 310-369-3236
10201 W. Pico Blvd., Bldg. 1
Los Angeles, CA 90035
TYPE     Television
DEAL     CBS Entertainment/ABC Entertainment
CREDITS     NYPD Blue - Total Security - Brooklyn South

Steven Bochco . . . . . . . . . . . . . . . . . . . . . . . . . . . Chairman/CEO
Dayna Flanagan . . . . . . . . . . . . . . . . . President, TV Production
Franklin B. Rohner . . . . . . . . . . . . . . . . . . . . . . . President/CFO
Sheldon Mittleman . . . . . . . . . . . . . . . . . Sr. VP, Business Affairs
James A. Roach . . . . . . . . . . . . . . . . . . . . . . . . . . . . VP, Finance
Maureen Milligan . . . . . . . . . . . . . . . . . . . . . . VP, Administration
William Phillips . . . . . . . . . . . . . . . . . . . . . . . . . . VP, Production
Moira Dekker . . . . . . . . . . . . . . . . . . . . . . . . . . Dir., Development
Bernadette McNamara . . . . . . . . . . . . Associate Dir., Development

## BODEGA BAY PRODS., INC.
PHONE . . . . . . . . . . . . . . . . . . . . . . . . . . . . . . . . . . . 310-273-3157
FAX . . . . . . . . . . . . . . . . . . . . . . . . . . . . . . . . . . . . . . 310-271-5581
EMAIL . . . . . . . . . . . . . . . . . . . . . . . . . . . . bodegabay@msn.com
9301 Wilshire Blvd., Ste. 310
Beverly Hills, CA 90210-5424
TYPE     Motion Pictures + Television
CREDITS     Bill & Ted's Excellent Adventure - Munsters - Celebrity Island Videos - The Last Best Sunday
COMMENTS     Large Format Films.

Michael Murphey . . . . . . . . . . . . . . . . . . . . . . . . . . . . Producer
Chip Garofalo . . . . . . . . . . . . . . . . . . Producer, Large Format
Julie Fay . . . . . . . . . . . . . . . . . . . . . Production & Development
Joel Peterson . . . . . . . . . . . . . . . . . . Production & Development

## BOKU FILMS
PHONE . . . . . . . . . . . . . . . . . . . . . . . . . . . . . . . . . . . 213-993-2033
FAX . . . . . . . . . . . . . . . . . . . . . . . . . . . . . . . . . . . . . . 213-465-6709
EMAIL . . . . . . . . . . . . . . . . . . . . . . . . . . . . . . apoul1@aol.com
3185 Deronda Drive
Los Angeles, CA 90068
TYPE     Motion Pictures + Television
DEAL     Propaganda Films
CREDITS     Thursday - More Tales of the City - Woman on Top

Alan Poul . . . . . . . . . . . . . . . . . . . . . . . . . . . . . . . . . . Producer
David Gilby . . . . . . . . . . . . . . . . . . . . . . . . . . . . . . . . Assistant

## BONA FIDE PRODUCTIONS
PHONE . . . . . . . . . . . . . . . . . . . . . . . . . . . . . . . . . . . 310-273-6782
FAX . . . . . . . . . . . . . . . . . . . . . . . . . . . . . . . . . . . . . . 310-273-7821
8899 Beverly Blvd., Ste. 804
Los Angeles, CA 90048
TYPE     Motion Pictures
CREDITS     King of the Hill - Jack the Bear - Crumb - Election - The Wood - Cold Mountain

Albert Berger . . . . . . . . . . . . . . . . . . . . . . . . . . . . . . . . Producer
Ron Yerxa . . . . . . . . . . . . . . . . . . . . . . . . . . . . . . . . . . Producer

## BONNEVILLE WORLDWIDE ENTERTAINMENT
PHONE . . . . . . . . . . . . . . . . . . . . 818-379-9400/801-575-3680
FAX . . . . . . . . . . . . . . . . . . . . . . 818-379-8511/818-379-8501
EMAIL . . . . . . . . . . . . . . . . . . . . . . . . . . . . nduff@bwela.com
WEBSITE . . . . . . . . . . . . . . . . . . . . . . . . http://www.bwwe.com
16255 Ventura Blvd., Ste. 1100
Encino, CA 91436
TYPE     Motion Pictures + Television + Interactive Multimedia + Feature Direct to Video
CREDITS     The Christmas Box - Summer Of The Monkeys - Coming Unglued - The Staircase
COMMENTS     Also: 55 N. 300 West, Broadcast House #325, Salt Lake City, Utah 84110 Fax: 801-575-3699

Allan W. Henderson . . . . . . . . . . . . . . . . . . . . . President (SLC)
Chris Harding . . . . . . . . . . . . . . . Exec. VP/General Manager (SLC)
Michael C. Green . . . . . . . . . . . . . . . Exec. VP, Film & TV (LA)
Robin Montgomery . . . . . . . . . . . . . . . Exec. VP, Home Video (LA)
Andrew Richter . . . . . . . . . . Sr. VP, TV Acquisitions & Development (LA)
Ilyssa Goodman . . . . . . VP, Motion Picture Acquisitions & Co-Prod. (LA)
Eric Poticha . . . . . . . . . . . . VP, TV Acquistions & Development (LA)
Scott Iverson . . . . . . . . Dir., Acquisitions & Development, Home Video (LA)

## BOOKER PRODUCTIONS, BOB
PHONE . . . . . . . . . . . . . . . . . . . . . . . . . . . . . . . . . . . 310-914-1441
FAX . . . . . . . . . . . . . . . . . . . . . . . . . . . . . . . . . . . . . . 310-914-1441
11811 W. Olympic Blvd.
Los Angeles, CA 90064
TYPE     Television
CREDITS     Out of This World - Anything For A Laugh - Foul-ups Bleeps & Blunders

Bob Booker . . . . . . . . . . . . . . . . . . . . . . . . . . . . . . . . . No Title

## *BORCHERS, DONALD P.
PHONE . . . . . . . . . . . . . . . . . . . . . . . . . . . . . . . . . . . 213-467-3838
PO Box 93039
Hollywood, CA 90093
TYPE     Motion Pictures
CREDITS     Two Moon Junction - Crimes of Passion - Motorama

Donald P. Borchers . . . . . . . . . . . . . . . . . . . . . . . . . . . Producer

**BOTTOM LINE STUDIO, INC.**
PHONE . . . . . . . . . . . . . . . . . . . . . . . . . . . 818-954-3215
FAX . . . . . . . . . . . . . . . . . . . . . . . . . . . . . 818-945-7399
EMAIL . . . . . . . . . . . . . . . . . . . . . bottln@ix.netcom.com
Warner Bros.
4000 Warner Blvd., Bldg. 4
Burbank, CA 91522
TYPE      Motion Pictures + Feature Direct to Video + Television + Syndication
CREDITS   Kill Squad - Savage Instinct - Ground Rules - Roughcut - Parole Violators

Sean Donahue . . . . . . . . . . . . . . . . Writer/Producer/Director
Patrick Donahue . . . . . . . . . . . . . . Writer/Dir., Development
Kathy Shaw . . . . . . . . . . . . . . . . . . . . . . . . . . . Producer

**BOYLE-TAYLOR PRODS.**
PHONE . . . . . . . . . . . . . . . . . . . . . . . . . . . 213-954-4260
FAX . . . . . . . . . . . . . . . . . . . . . . . . . . . . . 213-954-4270
6320 Commodore Sloat Drive
Los Angeles, CA 90048
TYPE      Motion Pictures + Television
CREDITS   Mrs. Munck - Bottle Rocket - Phenomenon - Instinct
Barbara Boyle . . . . . . . . . . . . . . . . . . . . . . . . . . Producer
Michael Taylor . . . . . . . . . . . . . . . . . . . . . . . . . Producer
Tiger Bela . . . . . . . . . . . . . . . . . . . . . . . . . . . Assistant
Adam Dugas . . . . . . . . . . . . . . . . . . . . . . . . . . Assistant

**BOYMAN PRODUCTIONS, INC.**
PHONE . . . . . . . . . . . . . 310-205-6250/416-733-3000
FAX . . . . . . . . . . . . . . . 310-205-6264/416-733-1900
EMAIL . . . . . . . . . . . . . . . . . . . . . . . . marc ami@aol.com
Quadra
130 So. El Camino
Beverly Hills, CA 90212
TYPE      Motion Pictures + Television
CREDITS   The Incubus - The Fly - Dead Ringers - 1492
COMMENTS  Also: 4711 Yonge St., Ste. 1101 Toronto, ON Canada M2N6K8

Marc Boyman . . . . . . . . . . . . . . . . . . . . . . . . . Producer
Karen McClellan . . . . . . . . . . . . . . . . . . . Creative Executive

**BOZ PRODUCTIONS**
PHONE . . . . . . . . . . . . . . . . . . . . . . . . . . . 310-235-5401
FAX . . . . . . . . . . . . . . . . . . . . . . . . . . . . . 310-235-5766
EMAIL . . . . . . . . . . . . . . . . . . . . . . . . . boz51@aol.com
10960 Wilshire Blvd., Ste. 734
Los Angeles, CA 90024
TYPE      Motion Pictures + Television
DEAL      Saban Entertainment
CREDITS   Wrong Exit - Bodywaves - Thick as a Brick
Bo Zenga . . . . . . . . . . . . . . . . . Writer/Director/Producer
Jeff Monarch . . . . . . . . . . . . . . . . . . . . . . . Story Editor
Julie Visvydas . . . . . . . . . . . . . . . . . . . Asst. to Mr. Zenga

**BRADFORD ENTERPRISES & GEMMY PRODS.**
PHONE . . . . . . . . . . . . . . . . . . . . . . . . . . . 212-308-7390
FAX . . . . . . . . . . . . . . . . . . . . . . . . . . . . . 212-935-1636
450 Park Ave., Ste. 1903
New York, NY 10022
TYPE      Television
CREDITS   Hold The Dream - Voice of the Heart - Remember - Everything to Gain - Love In Another Town
Robert Bradford . . . . . . . . . . . . . . . . . President/Producer
Barbara Taylor Bradford . . . . . . . . . . . . . . Director/Novelist
Susan Schuhart-Zito . . . . . . . . . Exec. Assistant/Corp. Secretary
Rosemarie Cerutti . . . . . . . . . . Exec. Assistant/Office Manager

**BRAGA PRODUCTIONS**
PHONE . . . . . . . . . . . . . . . . . . . . . . . . . . . 213-956-5799
FAX . . . . . . . . . . . . . . . . . . . . . . . . . . . . . 213-862-8503
Paramount Pictures
5555 Melrose Ave., Hart. Bldg. #205
Hollywood, CA 90038
TYPE      Motion Pictures + Television
DEAL      Paramount Network Television/Paramount Pictures-Motion Picture Group
CREDITS   Star Trek: Voyager - Star Trek: The Next Generation - Star Trek Generations - Star Trek First Contact
COMMENTS  Also:  One hour dramas.
Brannon Braga . . . . . . . . . . . . . . . . . . . . . . . President
Michael O'Halloran . . . . . . . . . . . . . . Asst. to Brannon Braga

**BRAINSTORM MEDIA**
PHONE . . . . . . . . . . . . . . . . . . . . . . . . . . . 310-285-0812
FAX . . . . . . . . . . . . . . . . . . . . . . . . . . . . . 310-285-0772
EMAIL . . . . . . . . . . . . . . . . . . . . . brainmedia@aol.com
9000 W. Sunset Blvd., Ste. 506
Los Angeles, CA 90069
TYPE      Motion Pictures + Television
CREDITS   Kid Cop - Little Men - The Truth About Lying
Meyer Shwarzstein . . . . . . . . . . . . . . . . . . . . . . President
Jennifer Glianna . . . . . . . . . . . . . . . . Mgr., Creative Affairs

**BRANDMAN PRODS.**
PHONE . . . . . . . . . . . . . . . . . . . . . . . . . . . 213-463-3224
FAX . . . . . . . . . . . . . . . . . . . . . . . . . . . . . 213-463-0852
2062 N. Vine St., Ste. 5
Los Angeles, CA 90068
TYPE      Motion Pictures + Television
CREDITS   The Heidi Chronicles - Last Stand At Saber River - Alone
Michael Brandman . . . . . . . . . . . . . . . . . . . . . . President
Joanna Miles . . . . . . . . . . . . . . . . . . . . . . Vice President
JoAnn Rink . . . . . . . . . . . Dir., Story Dev./Asst. to Producer

**BRAUBACH PRODUCTIONS**
PHONE . . . . . . . . . . . . . . . . . . . . . . . . . . . 310-230-1804
EMAIL . . . . . . . . . . . . . . . . . . . . . braubach@att.net
3050 Airport Ave. #C
Santa Monica, CA 90405
TYPE      Motion Pictures + Television
CREDITS   A Great Bunch of Girls - Four Days In September - Last Stand At Saber River
Mary Ann Braubach . . . . . . . . . . . . . . . . . . . . . Producer
Nickole Kerner . . . . . . . . . . . . . . . . . . Dir., Development

**BRAUN ENTERTAINMENT GROUP, INC.**
PHONE . . . . . . . . . . . . . . . . . . . . . . . . . . . 310-888-7727
FAX . . . . . . . . . . . . . . . . . . . . . . . . . . . . . 310-888-7726
EMAIL . . . . . . . . . . . . . . . . . . . . . BraunEnt@aol.com
280 S. Beverly Dr., Ste. 500
Beverly Hills, CA 90212
TYPE      Motion Pictures + Television
CREDITS   Tour of Duty - Abducted: A Father's Love - Menendez: Killing in Beverly Hills
Zev Braun . . . . . . . . . . . . . . . . . President/Exec. Producer
Philip M. Krupp . . . . . . . . . . . . . . . VP, Production/Producer
Sonia Apodaca-Harms . . . . . . . . . . . Sr. Executive Assistant

**BRAUN PRODUCTIONS, DAVID**
PHONE . . . . . . . . . . . . . . . . . . . . . . . . . . . 310-453-0089
2530 Wilshire Blvd., 3rd Fl.
Santa Monica, CA 90403-4616
TYPE      Motion Pictures + Television + Interactive Multimedia + Animation
CREDITS   Seduction in Travis County - Labyrinth: A Life of Kafka - Myth Quest
David Braun . . . . . . . . . . . . . . . . . . . . . . . . . President
Doug Guarino . . . . . . . . . . . . . . . . . Vice President/CFO
Lissa Sanders . . . . . . . . . . . . . . . . . . VP, Creative Affairs
Peter Zinner . . . . . . . . . . . . . . . . . . . . . VP, Production
Denise Weeks . . . . . . . . . . . . . . . . . . . . Producer/Writer

**BRAYTON/CARLUCCI PRODUCTIONS**
PHONE . . . . . . . . . . . . . . . . . . . . . . . . . . . 310-478-1700
FAX . . . . . . . . . . . . . . . . . . . . . . . . . . . . . 310-478-2202
Hearst Entertainment
1640 S. Sepulveda Blvd.
Los Angeles, CA 90025
TYPE      Television
DEAL      Hearst Entertainment
CREDITS   Donato & Daughter - Not Our Son - Unforgivable - When Husbands Cheat
Anne Carlucci . . . . . . . . . . . . . . . . . . . Executive Producer
Marian Brayton . . . . . . . . . . . . . . . . . . Executive Producer
Larry Grimaldi . . . . . . . . . . . . . . . . . . Mgr., Development

## BREEN PRODS., PAULETTE
| | |
|---|---|
| PHONE | 818-342-0228 |
| FAX | 818-342-0228 |

6920 Texhoma Avenue, Ste. 100
Van Nuys, CA 91406

| | |
|---|---|
| TYPE | Television + Motion Pictures |
| CREDITS | 83 Hrs. - Separated By Murder - Abducted: Father's Love - Stranger Within |
| COMMENTS | Also: Cable. |

Paulette Breen . . . . . . . . . . . . . . . . . . . . . . . . . . . President/Producer
Diane Biederbeck . . . . . . . . . . . . . . . . . . . . . . . VP, Creative Affairs
Kathy Page . . . . . . . . . . . . . . . . . . . Creative Asst./Office Administrator

## BREGMAN ENTERTAINMENT CO., THE
| | |
|---|---|
| PHONE | 213-833-6207 |
| FAX | 213-876-1957 |
| EMAIL | BudBoy@pacbell.net |
| WEBSITE | http://http://home.pacbell.net/budboy/budboy.htwl |

269 S. Beverly Dr., Ste. 380
Beverly Hills, CA 90212

| | |
|---|---|
| TYPE | Motion Pictures + Television |
| DEAL | Genx Entertainment |
| CREDITS | 9 Ball - The Know-It-All - Prez  - Small Town Games |
| COMMENTS | Also: Music Videos |

Buddy Bregman . . . . . . . . . . . . . . . . . . . Producer/Director/Writer
Marie de Puthod . . . . . . . . . . . . . . . . . . . . . . . . . . . Writer/Director

## BREGMAN PRODUCTIONS
| | |
|---|---|
| PHONE | 818-954-9988 |
| FAX | 818-954-9989 |

859 N. Hollywood Way, Ste. 462
Burbank, CA 91505

| | |
|---|---|
| TYPE | Motion Pictures |
| CREDITS | Nothing To Lose- Carlito's Way- Sea Of Love- Scarface |

Martin Bregman . . . . . . . . . . . . . . . . . . . . . . . . . . . . . . . . Producer
Michael Bregman . . . . . . . . . . . . . . . . . . . . . . . . . . . . . . . . Producer

## BRIGGLE PRODS., STOCKTON
| | |
|---|---|
| PHONE | 310-557-2565 |
| FAX | 310-557-2565 |

9434 Gregory Way
Beverly Hills, CA 90212

| | |
|---|---|
| TYPE | Motion Pictures + Television + Syndication |
| CREDITS | Her Hidden Truth  Willing to Kill  Bridge to Silence |

Stockton Briggle . . . . . . . . . . . . . . . . . . . . . . . . . Executive Producer

## BRIGHT STREET PICTURES
| | |
|---|---|
| PHONE | 716-884-6771 |
| FAX | 716-884-6772 |

150 Lexington Avenue
Buffalo, NY 14222

| | |
|---|---|
| TYPE | Motion Pictures + Television + Documentaries + Syndication |
| CREDITS | Doing Time on Maple Drive - Any Mother's Son - A Father for Brittany |

Joseph A. DiPasquale . . . . . . . . . . . . . . . . . . . . . Executive Producer
Don Elick . . . . . . . . . . . . . . . . . . . . . . . . . . . . . . . . VP, Production

## BRIGHT-KAUFFMAN-CRANE PRODS.
| | |
|---|---|
| PHONE | 818-977-7777 |
| FAX | 818-977-7999 |

4000 Warner Blvd., Bldg. 160, Ste. 750
Burbank, CA 91522

| | |
|---|---|
| TYPE | Television |
| DEAL | Warner Bros. Television Productions |
| CREDITS | Friends - Dream On - Veronica's Closet - All My Life |

Kevin S. Bright . . . . . . . . . . . . . . . . . . . . . . . . . Executive Producer
David Crane . . . . . . . . . . . . . . . . . . . . . . . . . . . Executive Producer
Marta Kauffman . . . . . . . . . . . . . . . . . . . . . . . . Executive Producer
Debby Kaplan . . . . . . . . . . . . . . . . . . . . . . . . . . . Dir., Development

## BRILLSTEIN-GREY ENT.
| | |
|---|---|
| PHONE | 310-275-6135 |
| FAX | 310-275-6180 |

9150 Wilshire Blvd., Ste. 350
Beverly Hills, CA 90212

| | |
|---|---|
| TYPE | Motion Pictures + Television + Interactive Multimedia |
| DEAL | ABC Entertainment/Universal Pictures |
| CREDITS | NewsRadio - Just Shoot Me - Steve Harvey Show |

Bernie Brillstein . . . . . . . . . . . . . . . . . . . . . . . . . . . . . . Consultant
Brad Grey . . . . . . . . . . . . . . . . . . . . . . . . . . . . . . . . Chairman/CEO
Steve Blume . . . . . . . . . . . . . . . . . . . . . . . Chief Financial Officer
Sandy Wernick . . . . . . . . . . . . . . . . . . . . . Sr. Exec. Vice President
Matthew Baer . . . . . . . . . . . . . . . . . . . Co-Head, Motion Picture Division
Michael Siegel . . . . . . . . . . . . . . . . . Co-Head, Motion Picture/Literary
Marc Gurvitz . . . . . . . . . . . . . . . . . . . . . . . . . Exec. VP, Television
Kevin Reilly . . . . . . . . . . . . . . . . . . . . . . . . Exec. Vice President
Susie Fitzgerald . . . . . . . . . . . . . . . . . . . . . . . Sr. VP, Television
Michael Rosenfeld . . . . . . . . . . . . . . . . . . . . . . Sr. Vice President
Peter Traugott . . . . . . . . . . . . . . . . . . . . . . . . . Sr. VP, Television
Tony Carey . . . . . . . . . . . . . . . . . . . . . VP, Production, Television
Laura Hopper . . . . . . . . . . . . . . . . . . . . . . . VP, Motion Pictures
Denise Stewart . . . . . . . . . . . . . . . . . . . . . . VP, Motion Pictures
George McFetridge . . . . . . . . . . . . . . . . . . . . . . Business Affairs
Jeff Zella . . . . . . . . . . . . . . . . . . . . . . . . . . . . Business Affairs
Jennifer Faltings . . . . . . . . . . . . . . . . . . . . . . . Dir., Television
Marianne Cracchiolo . . . . . . . . . . . . . . . . . . . . . Mgr., Television
Becky Jackson . . . . . . . . . . . . . . . . . . . . . . . . . Mgr., Television
Sean White . . . . . . . . . . . . . . . . . . . . . . . . . . . Mgr., Television

## *BRISTOL CITIES
| | |
|---|---|
| PHONE | 323-956-3513 |
| FAX | 323-862-1172 |
| EMAIL | BrstlCty@aol.com |

Paramount Pictures
5555 Melrose Ave., Swanson Bldg. Rm. 105
Los Angeles, CA 90038

| | |
|---|---|
| TYPE | Motion Pictures + Television |
| DEAL | Paramount Television Group |
| COMMENTS | Developing movies for television; series & feature films. |

Jane Leeves . . . . . . . . . . . . . . . . . . . . . . . . . . . Actress/Producer
Peri Gilpin . . . . . . . . . . . . . . . . . . . . . . . . . . . Actress/Producer
Doug Collins . . . . . . . . . . . . . . . . . . . . . . . . VP, Creative Affairs

## BRITISH LION
| | |
|---|---|
| PHONE | 818-789-9112 |
| FAX | 818-789-2901 |

5302 Ethel Ave.
Sherman Oaks, CA 91401

| | |
|---|---|
| TYPE | Motion Pictures + Television |
| CREDITS | Man For All Seasons - Don't Look Now - Wicker Man - Lady Jane |
| COMMENTS | Founded 1927 - ALSO: Pinewood Studios, Iver.Bucks England, SLO ONH |

Peter R. E. Snell . . . . . . . . . . . . . . . . . . . . . . . . . . Chairman/CEO
Toni Pinnolis . . . . . . . . . . . . . . . . . . . Vice President (West Coast)

## BRITT ALLCROFT CO., THE
| | |
|---|---|
| PHONE | 212-463-9623 |
| FAX | 212-463-9626 |
| EMAIL | brittall@aol.com |
| WEBSITE | http://www.thomasthetankengine.com |

1133 Broadway, Ste. 1520
New York, NY 10010

| | |
|---|---|
| TYPE | Motion Pictures + Television + Animation + Interactive Multimedia |
| CREDITS | Magic Adventures of Mumfie - Shining Time Station - Thomas the Tank Engine & Friends |

Britt Allcroft . . . . . . . . . . . . . . . . . . . . . . . . . . . Deputy Chairman
Charles Falzon . . . . . . . . . . . . . . . . . . . Group President, Entertainment
Jeanne Perry . . . . . . . . . . . . . . . . . . . . . . . . . . . General Manager
William Harris . . . . . . . . . . . . . . . . . . . . . . . . . . Managing Director

# COMPANIES AND STAFF

**BROADWAY PICTURES (LA)**
PHONE . . . . . . . . . . . . . . . . . . . . . . . . . . . . . . . . 213-956-5729
FAX . . . . . . . . . . . . . . . . . . . . . . . . . . . . . . . . . . 213-862-8605
Paramount Studios
5555 Melrose Ave., Dressing Rm #109
Los Angeles, CA 90038-3197
TYPE            Motion Pictures
DEAL            Paramount Pictures- Motion Picture Group
CREDITS         Wayne's World II - Kids in the Hall - Coneheads - Night at
                the Roxbury
COMMENTS        Subsidary of Broadway Video.
Lorne Michaels . . . . . . . . . . . . . . . . . . . . . . . . . . . . . . Chairman
Bob Weiss . . . . . . . . . . . . . . . . . . . . . . . . . . . . . . . . President
Carr D'Angelo . . . . . . . . . . . . . . . . . . . . . . . . . . VP, Production
Kyu Kahn . . . . . . . . . . . . . . . . . . . . . . . . . . . Asst. to Bob Weiss

**BROADWAY VIDEO (NY)**
PHONE . . . . . . . . . . . . . . . . . . . . . . . . . . . . . . 212-265-7621
WEBSITE . . . . . . . . . . . . . . . . . . . http://www.broadwayvideo.com/
1619 Broadway, 9th Fl., Brill Bldg.
New York, NY 10019
TYPE            Television + Interactive Multimedia + Motion Pictures
DEAL            NBC Studios/Paramount Pictures- Motion Picture Group
CREDITS         Saturday Night Live - Kids in the Hall - Night Music - Late
                Night with Conan O'Brien
Barry Grieff . . . . . . . . . . . . . . . . . . . . . . . . . . . . .Co-President
Bob Kreek . . . . . . . . . . . . . . . . . . . . . . . . . . . . . .Co-President
James Biederman . . . . . . . . . . . . . . . . . . . . . VP, Creative Affairs
David Lang . . . . . . . . . . . . . . . . . . . . . . . . . . . VP, Creative Group
Mark Offitzer . . . . . . . . . . . . . . . . VP, Special Event Programming
Erin Fraser . . . . . . . . . . . . . . . . . . . . . . . . . Dir., Creative Affairs

**BROIDO @ ALEXANDER/ENRIGHT & ASSOC.**
PHONE . . . . . . . . . . . . . . . . . . . . . . . . . . . . . . 310-458-3003
FAX . . . . . . . . . . . . . . . . . . . . . . . . . . . . . . . . 310-393-7238
201 Wilshire Blvd., 3rd Fl.
Santa Monica, CA 90401
TYPE            Television
Joe Broido . . . . . . . . . . . . . . . . . . . . . . . . . . . Executive Producer

**BROOKSFILMS, LTD.**
PHONE . . . . . . . . . . . . . . . . . . . . . . . . . . . . . . 310-202-3292
FAX . . . . . . . . . . . . . . . . . . . . . . . . . . . . . . . . 310-202-3225
Culver Studios
9336 W. Washington Blvd.
Culver City, CA 90232
TYPE            Motion Pictures
CREDITS         My Favorite Year - Elephant Man - The Fly I & II - Frances
Mel Brooks . . . . . . . . . . . . . . . . . . . . . . . . . . . . . . . President
Leah Zappy . . . . . . . . . . . . . . . . . . . . . VP, Production Services
Patricia Lewis . . . . . . . . . . . . . . . . . . . . . . . Asst. to Mr. Brooks

**BROOKWELL MCNAMARA ENTERTAINMENT**
PHONE . . . . . . . . . . . . . . . . . . . . . . . . . . . . . . 310-914-3315
FAX . . . . . . . . . . . . . . . . . . . . . . . . . . . . . . . . 310-914-9755
EMAIL . . . . . . . . . . . . . . . . . . . . . . . . . . . bmemail@aol.com
2050 Granville Avenue
Los Angeles, CA 90025
TYPE            Motion Pictures + Television + Feature Direct to Video
CREDITS         The Adventures of Capricorn - Casper: A Spirited
                Beginning - Treehouse Hostage
David Brookwell . . . . . . . . . . . . . . . . . . . . . . . Executive Producer
Sean McNamara . . . . . . . . . . . . . . . . . . . . . . . Executive Producer
Leonard Koss . . . . . . . . . . . . . . . . . . . . . . . Production Executive
Karen Sachs . . . . . . . . . . . . . . . . . . . . . . . Production Associate

**BROWN GROUP, THE**
PHONE . . . . . . . . . . . . . . . . . . . . . . . . . . . . . . 310-581-4354
FAX . . . . . . . . . . . . . . . . . . . . . . . . . . . . . . . . 310-452-0699
EMAIL . . . . . . . . . . . . . . . . . . . . . . . . . . . jbdead@aol.com
2800 28th St., Ste. 105
Santa Monica, CA 90405
TYPE            Motion Pictures + Television + Syndication + Interactive
                Multimedia
DEAL            Ruddy Morgan Organization, Inc., The
CREDITS         The Tie That Binds
Jon Brown . . . . . . . . . . . . . . . . . . . . . . . . . . . . . . . President
Jeff Goldenberg . . . . . . . . . . . . . . . . . . . . . . Development Associate

**BROWNHOUSE PRODUCTIONS**
PHONE . . . . . . . . . . . . . . . . . . . . . . . . . . . . . . 213-650-2670
FAX . . . . . . . . . . . . . . . . . . . . . . . . . . . . . . . . 213-656-7928
8439 Sunset Blvd. Ste. 106
W. Hollywood, CA 90069
TYPE            Motion Pictures + Television
DEAL            Touchstone Pictures
CREDITS         Rodgers & Hammerstein's Cinderella
Whitney Houston . . . . . . . . . . . . . . . . . . . . . . . . . . . . President
Debra Martin Chase . . . . . . . . . . . . . . . . . . . Exec. Vice President
Steve Lapuk . . . . . . . . . . . . . . . . . . . . . . . . . . Dir., Development
Leah Hunter . . . . . . . . . . . . . . . . . . . . . . . . Executive Assistant

**BRUCKHEIMER FILMS, JERRY**
PHONE . . . . . . . . . . . . . . . . . . . . . . . . . . . . . . 310-664-6260
1631 10th St.
Santa Monica, CA 90404
TYPE            Motion Pictures + Television + Syndication
DEAL            Walt Disney Pictures/Touchstone Pictures
CREDITS         Top Gun - The Rock - Con Air - Crimson Tide -
                Armageddon - Enemy of the State
Jerry Bruckheimer . . . . . . . . . . . . . . . . . . . . Producer (310-664-6262)
Jonathan Littman . . . . . . . . . . . . Exec. VP, Television (310-664-6295)
Chad Oman . . . . . . . . . . . . . . . . Exec. Vice President (310-664-6264)
Jennifer Worthington . . . . . . . . . . Vice President (310-664-6265)
Charlie Banks . . . . . . . . . . . . . . . Creative Executive (310-664-6266)
Todd Marrero . . . . . . . . . . . . . . . Creative Executive (310-664-6238)
Tripp Vinson . . . . . . . . . . . . . . . Creative Executive (310-664-6241)

**BRYAN FILMS, JAMES**
PHONE . . . . . . . . . . . . . . . . . . . . . . . . . . . . . . 818-361-0374
FAX . . . . . . . . . . . . . . . . . . . . . . . . . . . . . . . . 818-361-0374
P.O. Box 790
San Fernando, CA 91341
TYPE            Motion Pictures
CREDITS         Don't Go In The Woods
James Bryan . . . . . . . . . . . . . . . . . . . . . . . . . Producer/Director
Suzette Gomez . . . . . . . . . . . . . . . . . . . . . . . . . . . . Producer

***BTHREE FILMS**
PHONE . . . . . . . . . . . . . . . . . . . . . . . . . . . . . . 310-358-8114
FAX . . . . . . . . . . . . . . . . . . . . . . . . . . . . . . . . 310-414-0444
EMAIL . . . . . . . . . . . . . . . . . . . . . . . . . . . DBb3Film@aol.com
P.O. Box 2125
Manhattan Beach, CA 90267
TYPE            Motion Pictures
CREDITS         Perfect Prey - When the Bough Breaks
Denise Ballew . . . . . . . . . . . . . . . . . . . . . . . . . . . . Producer

**BUBBLE FACTORY, THE**
PHONE . . . . . . . . . . . . . . . . . . . . . . . . . . . . . . 310-358-3000
FAX . . . . . . . . . . . . . . . . . . . . . . . . . . . . . . . . 310-358-3299
8840 Wilshire Blvd., 3rd Floor
Beverly Hills, CA 90211
TYPE            Motion Pictures + Feature Direct to Video
CREDITS         Flipper - McHale's Navy - Stinkers - That Old Feeling - The
                Pest - A Simple Wish - For Richer or Poorer
Sid Sheinberg . . . . . . . . . . . . . . . . . . . . . . . . . . . . . . Partner
Bill Sheinberg . . . . . . . . . . . . . . . . . . . . . . . . . . . . . . Partner
Jon Sheinberg . . . . . . . . . . . . . . . . . . . . . . . . . . . . . . Partner
Bret Magpiong . . . . . . . . . . . . . . . . . . . Chief Financial Officer
Gerald S. Barton . . . . . . . . . . . . . . . . . . Exec. VP, Business Affairs
Gerard Bocaccio . . . . . . . . . . . . . . . . . . Sr. VP, Creative Affairs
Tom Prince . . . . . . . . . . . . . . . . . . . . . . . . Sr. VP, Production
Gwen Osborne . . . . . . . . . . . . . . . . . . . . . . Dir., Development
Kevin D. Forester . . . . . . . . . . . . . . Mgr., Finance & Operations
Marsha L. Alexander . . . . . . . . . . . . Exec. Asst. to S. Sheinberg
Wendy Brennan . . . . . . . . . . . . . . . Exec. Asst. to B. Sheinberg
Mindy Cross . . . . . . . . . . . . . . . . . . . Exec. Asst. to G. Barton
Lisa Giambarberee . . . . . . . . . . . . . Exec. Asst. to J. Sheinberg
Kimberly Gross . . . . . . . . . . . . . . . Exec. Asst. to B. Magpiong
Jordan Lichtman . . . . . . . . . . . . . . . Exec. Asst. to T. Prince
Marcellus Marsh . . . . . . . . . . . . . . Exec. Asst. to G. Boccacio

***BUCKEYE ENTERTAINMENT GROUP**
PHONE . . . . . . . . . . . . . . . . . . . . . . . 212-777-1987/212-777-2802
FAX . . . . . . . . . . . . . . . . . . . . . . . . . . . . . . . . 212-777-2585
38 East First Street
New York, NY 10003
TYPE            Animation + Documentaries + Motion Pictures +
                Television + Interactive Multimedia
CREDITS         Spanking the Monkey - Hairspray - Up at the Villa - Joe
                Glory
Stanley F. Buchthal . . . . . . . . . . . . . . . . . . . . . . . . . . . President
Jeffrey H. Campagna . . . . . . . . . . . . . . . . . . . . . Dir., Development

## BUENA VISTA PRODUCTIONS
PHONE . . . . . . . . . . . . . . . . . . . . . . . . . . . . . . . . 818-560-1000
FAX . . . . . . . . . . . . . . . . . . . . . . . . . . . . . . . . . . 818-842-9046
WEBSITE. . . . . . . . . . . . . . . . . . . . . . . http://www.disney.com
Walt Disney Studios
500 S. Buena Vista St., Team Disney Bldg
Burbank, CA 91521-0001
TYPE            Television
Walter Liss . . . . . . . . . . . . . . . . . . . . . Chairman, Buena Vista Television
Mort Marcus . . . . . . . . . . . . . . . . . . . . . . Pres., Buena Vista Television
Stephanie Drachkovitch . . . . . . . . . . . . . . . . . . . . . Sr. VP, Development
Mary Kellogg-Joslyn . . . . . . . . . Sr. VP, Current Programming & Production
Brooke Karzan . . . . . . . . . . . . . . . . . . . . . . . . . . . VP, Development
Hayma (Screech) Washington . . . . . . . . . . . . . . . . . . . VP, Production

## BUNGALOW 78 PRODS.
PHONE . . . . . . . . . . . . . . . . . . . . . . . . . . . . . . . . 213-956-4440
FAX . . . . . . . . . . . . . . . . . . . . . . . . . . . . . . . . . . 213-862-2090
5555 Melrose Ave., Lasky 200
Los Angeles, CA 90038
TYPE            Motion Pictures + Television
DEAL            Paramount Television Group
CREDITS         Coach - Romy & Michelle - Patch Adams
Barry Kemp . . . . . . . . . . . . . . . . . . . . . . . Exec. Producer/Writer
Devorah Moos-Hankin . . . . . . . . . . . . . . . . . Sr. VP, Feature Production
Bess Walkes . . . . . . . . . . . . . . . . Dir., Development, Feature Production
Jill Bowles . . . . . . . . . . . . . . . . . . . . . . . . . . . Asst. to B. Kemp

## BUNIM-MURRAY PRODUCTIONS, INC.
PHONE . . . . . . . . . . . . . . . . . . . . . . . . . . . . . . . . 818-756-5150
FAX . . . . . . . . . . . . . . . . . . . . . . . . . . . . . . . . . . 818-756-5140
EMAIL . . . . . . . . . . . . . . . . . . . . . bmpmail@bunim-murray.com
WEBSITE. . . . . . . . . . . . . . . . . . . . http://www.bunim-murray.com
6007 Sepulveda Blvd.
Van Nuys, CA 91411
TYPE            Television + Syndication + Documentaries
CREDITS         The Real World - Road Rules - Class Reunion
Mary-Ellis Bunim . . . . . . . . . . . . . . . . . . . . . . . Executive Producer
Jonathan Murray . . . . . . . . . . . . . . . . . . . . . . . Executive Producer
Tom Colamarla . . . . . . . . . . . . . . Executive in Charge of Production
Scott Freeman . . . . . . . . . . . . . . . . . . . . . . . . Dir., Development

## *BURLAGE/EDELL PRODUCTIONS, INC.
PHONE . . . . . . . . . . . . . . . . . . . . . . . . . . . . . . . . 310-481-2104
FAX . . . . . . . . . . . . . . . . . . . . . . . . . . . . . . . . . . 310-481-2111
11601 Wilshire Blvd., Ste. 2030
Los Angeles, CA 90025
TYPE            Motion Pictures + Documentaries + Television
Roger Burlage . . . . . . . . . . . . . . . . . . . . . . . . . Producing Partner
Elaine Hastings Edell . . . . . . . . . . . . . . . . . . . . . . Producing Partner
Dan March . . . . . . . . . . . . . . . . . . . . . . . . . . . Executive Assistant

## BURRUD PRODUCTIONS
PHONE . . . . . . . . . . . . . . . . . . . . . . . . . . . . . . . . 714-846-7174
FAX . . . . . . . . . . . . . . . . . . . . . . . . . . . . . . . . . . 714-846-4814
EMAIL . . . . . . . . . . . . . . . . . . . . . . . . burrudprod@aol.com
16902 Bolsa Chica St., Ste. 203
Huntington Beach, CA 92649
TYPE            Motion Pictures + Television + Documentaries +
                Interactive Multimedia
DEAL            Digital Technologies Media
CREDITS         Americas Wonders - Beyond Bizarre - Creatures of the
                Wild
John Burrud . . . . . . . . . . . . . . . . . . . . . . . . . . . President/CEO
Stanley H. Green . . . . . . . . . . . . . . . . . Exec. VP, Business Affairs
Drew Horton . . . . . . . . . . . . . . . . . . . . . . . . . . VP, Production
Linda Karabin-Hecomovich . . . . . . . . . . . . . . . . VP, Administration
Kurt Porter . . . . . . . . . . . . . . . . . . . . . . . . . . . . . . . . Editor
Shannon Mead . . . . . . . . . . . . . . . . Asst. to VP/Production Assistant
Paul Ahn . . . . . . . . . . . . . . . . . . . . . . . . . . . Production Assistant

## BURTON PRODS., AL
PHONE . . . . . . . . . . . . . . . . . . . . . . . . . . . . . . . . 213-954-7865
FAX . . . . . . . . . . . . . . . . . . . . . . . . . . . . . . . . . . 213-934-8718
5900 Wilshire Blvd., 26th Fl.
Los Angeles, CA 90036
TYPE            Television + Syndication
DEAL            Buena Vista Productions/Walt Disney TV/Touchstone TV
CREDITS         The New Lassie - Charles in Charge - Win Ben Stein's
                Money
Al Burton . . . . . . . . . . . . . . . . . . . . . . . . . . . . Executive Producer
Solmaz Ghassemi . . . . . . . . . . . . . . . . . . . . . . . Dir., Development

## BURTON PRODS., TIM
PHONE . . . . . . . . . . . . . . . . . . . . . . . . . . . . . . . . 213-850-3100
FAX . . . . . . . . . . . . . . . . . . . . . . . . . . . . . . . . . . 213-850-3110
1041 N. Formosa Ave, Writers Bldg. 10
West Hollywood, CA 90046
TYPE            Motion Pictures
CREDITS         Ed Wood - Beetlejuice - Batman - Edward Scissorhands -
                Batman Returns - Mars Attacks!
Tim Burton . . . . . . . . . . . . . . . . . . . . . . . . . . Director/Producer
Eva Quiroz . . . . . . . . . . . . . . . . . . . . Executive/Asst. to Mr. Burton

## BUTCHERS RUN FILMS
PHONE . . . . . . . . . . . . . . . . . . . . . . . . . . . . . . . . 818-777-7333
FAX . . . . . . . . . . . . . . . . . . . . . . . . . . . . . . . . . . 818-866-3414
100 Universal City Plaza
Building 507, Ste. 2D
Universal City, CA 91608
TYPE            Motion Pictures + Television
DEAL            October Films/Universal Pictures
CREDITS         A Family Thing - The Man Who Captured Eichmann - The
                Apostle
Robert Duvall . . . . . . . . . . . . . . . . . . Actor/Producer/Director
Rob Carliner . . . . . . . . . . . . . . . . . . . . . . . . . . . . . Producer
Adam Prince . . . . . . . . . . . . . . . . . . . . . . . . . . . Story Editor

## BYCK, DANN
PHONE . . . . . . . . . . . . . . . . . . . . . . . . . . . . . . . . 310-587-3477
FAX . . . . . . . . . . . . . . . . . . . . . . . . . . . . . . . . . . 310-587-3577
EMAIL . . . . . . . . . . . . . . . . . . . . . dannbyck@ix.netcom.com
1033 12th St., Ste. 301
Santa Monica, CA 90403
TYPE            Motion Pictures + Television + Documentaries
CREDITS         The Laundromat - Night, Mother
Dann Byck . . . . . . . . . . . . . . . . . . . . . . . . . . . . . . . Producer

## BYLINE FILMS
PHONE . . . . . . . . . . . . . . . . . . . . . . . . . . . . . . . . 310-451-5260
1221 Marguerita
Santa Monica, CA 90402
TYPE            Motion Pictures
CREDITS         Target Earth (ABC)
COMMENTS        Also: Rastar Prods., 310-244-4412, fax: 310-244-2331
Michael Cieply . . . . . . . . . . . . . . . . . . . . . . . . . . . . Producer
George Mays . . . . . . . . . . . . . . . . . . . . . . . . Dir., Development

## BYRUM POWER & LIGHT
PHONE . . . . . . . . . . . . . . . . . . . . . . . . . . . . . . . . 213-662-5006
FAX . . . . . . . . . . . . . . . . . . . . . . . . . . . . . . . . . . 213-662-4865
2594 Adelbert Avenue
Los Angeles, CA 90039
TYPE            Television + Motion Pictures
CREDITS         Inserts - Razors Edge - Middle Ages - Winnetka Road
COMMENTS        No solicitations by mail!
John Byrum . . . . . . . . . . . . . . . . . . . . . . . Exec. Producer/Writer
Alison Young . . . . . . . . . . . . . . . . . . . . . . . . . . . . . . Assistant

## C.M. TWO PRODUCTIONS
PHONE . . . . . . . . . . . . . . . . . . . . . . . . . . . . . . . . 310-575-1291
FAX . . . . . . . . . . . . . . . . . . . . . . . . . . . . . . . . . . 310-478-2202
Hearst Entertainment
1640 S. Sepulveda Blvd., 4th Floor
Los Angeles, CA 90025
TYPE            Television
DEAL            Hearst Entertainment
CREDITS         Care and Handling of Roses - Lying Eyes
Chuck McLain . . . . . . . . . . . . . . . . . . . . . . . Executive Producer
Charles Morales . . . . . . . . . . . . . . . . . . . . . . Supervising Producer

## C/W PRODUCTIONS
PHONE . . . . . . . . . . . . . . . . . . . . . . . . . . . . . . . . 213-956-8150
FAX . . . . . . . . . . . . . . . . . . . . . . . . . . . . . . . . . . 213-862-1250
5555 Melrose Ave.
Hollywood, CA 90038
TYPE            Motion Pictures
DEAL            Paramount Pictures- Motion Picture Group
CREDITS         Mission Impossible - Pre/Without Limits
Paula Wagner . . . . . . . . . . . . . . . . . . . . . . . . . Partner/Producer
Jonathan Sanger . . . . . . . . . . . . . . . . . . . . . . . . . . . Producer
Nicholas Bogner . . . . . . . . . . . . . . . . . . . . . . Head, Development
Darren Miller . . . . . . . . . . . . . . . . . Prod. & Development Exeutive
Amy Stevens . . . . . . . . . . . . . . . . . . . Prod. & Development Executive
Sebastian Twardosz . . . . . . . . . . . . . . . . . . . . . . Creative Executive
Ryan Warren . . . . . . . . . . . . . . . . . . . . . . . . . Producer's Assistant
Nick Roe . . . . . . . . . . . . . . . . . . . . . . . . Development Assistant

## CAFE PRODUCTIONS
PHONE . . . . . . . . . . . . . . . . . . . . . . . . . . . . . . 213-653-8433
6535 Wilshire Blvd., #256
Los Angeles, CA 90048

TYPE — Motion Pictures + Television
CREDITS — Fun- Strange Love In Little Italy - Red Meat - Kid - Ancient Prophecies - Dr. Giggles - Sonny Boy

Jeff Kirshbaum . . . . . . . . . . . . . . . . . . . . . . . Producer/President
Rod Hamilton . . . . . . . . . . . . . . . . . . . . Producer/Development
Graeme Whifler . . . . . . . . . . . . . . . . . . . . . . . Writer/Director

## CAIRO/SIMPSON PRODUCTIONS, INC.
PHONE . . . . . . . . . . . . . . . . . . . . . . . . . . . 310-557-6939
FAX . . . . . . . . . . . . . . . . . . . . . . . . . . . . . . 310-557-6021
EMAIL . . . . . . . . . . . . . . . . . . . . . MASReelman@aol.com
2020 Avenue of the Stars, 5th Floor
Los Angeles, CA 90067

TYPE — Motion Pictures + Television + Interactive Multimedia
DEAL — ABC Pictures
CREDITS — The Boy King - Her Deadly Rival - Twisted Desire - Perfect Body - What We Did That Night

Judy Cairo . . . . . . . . . . . . . . . . . . . . . . . Executive Producer
Michael A. Simpson . . . . . . . . . . . . . . . . . . . Writer/Director
Day Vinson . . . . . . . . . . . . . . . . . . . Development Executive

## CALM DOWN PRODUCTIONS, INC.
PHONE . . . . . . . . . . . . . . . . . . . . . . . . . . . 818-954-7614
FAX . . . . . . . . . . . . . . . . . . . . . . . . . . . . . . 818-954-7846
Warner Bros. Television
4000 Warner Blvd., Prod. 6, Ste. F
Burbank, CA 91522

TYPE — Motion Pictures + Television
DEAL — Warner Bros. Pictures
CREDITS — Stop With The Kicking - Grant & Lee - The Underworld

Lucy Webb . . . . . . . . . . . . . . . . . . . . . . . . . . . . President
Kevin Pollak . . . . . . . . . . . . . . . . . . . Chief Executive Officer
Susan Garon . . . . . . . . . . . . . . . . . . . . . Executive Assistant

## CAMERA MARC
PHONE . . . . . . . . . . . . . . . . . . . . . . . . . . . 818-753-9901
FAX . . . . . . . . . . . . . . . . . . . . . . . . . . . . . . 818-753-9921
4605 Lankershim Blvd., Ste. 201
North Hollywood, CA 91602

TYPE — Motion Pictures
CREDITS — Stargate - Boiling Point - Murder in the First

Marc Frydman . . . . . . . . . . . . . . . . . . . . . . . CEO/Producer
Marc Rocco . . . . . . . . . . . . . . . . . . . . . Director/Producer
Dominique Forma . . . . . . . . . . . . . . . . . . . VP, Production
James Spies . . . . . . . . . . . . . . . . . . . . . Asst. to Mr. Rocco
Kent Walters . . . . . . . . . . . Asst. to M. Frydman and D. Forma

## CANAL+ (U.S.)
PHONE . . . . . . . . . . . . . . . . . . . . . . . . . . . 310-247-0994
FAX . . . . . . . . . . . . . . . . . . . . . . . . . . . . . . 310-247-0998
301 N. Canon Dr., Ste. 228
Beverly Hills, CA 90210-4723

TYPE — Motion Pictures + Television + Animation
CREDITS — Cliffhanger - Stargate - Murder in the First - Boiling Point

Pierre Lescure . . . . . . . . . . . . . . . . . Chairman/President/CEO
Robert Chamberlain . . . . . . . . . . . . . . Chief Financial Officer
Richard Garzilli . . . . . . . . . . . . . . Exec. VP/General Counsel
Arnaud Duteil . . . . . . . . . . . . . . . . . . . . VP, Business Affairs
Barbara DiNallo . . . . . . . . . . . . . . Dir., Contract Administration

## CANNELL MOTION PICTURES
PHONE . . . . . . . . . . . . . . . . . . . . . . . . . . . 213-856-7330
FAX . . . . . . . . . . . . . . . . . . . . . . . . . . . . . . 213-856-7390
7083 Hollywood Blvd., 6th Floor
Hollywood, CA 90028

TYPE — Motion Pictures

Stephen J. Cannell . . . . . . . . . . . . . . . Chairman (213-465-5800)
Wayne S. Williams . . . . . . . . . . . . . . . . . . . . Vice President
Shannon Spencer . . . . . . . . . . . . . Creative Executive (213-856-7301)

## CANNERY, INC., THE
PHONE . . . . . . . . . . . . . . . . . . . . . . . . . . . 310-396-6943
FAX . . . . . . . . . . . . . . . . . . . . . . . . . . . . . . 310-396-6153
EMAIL . . . . . . . . . . . . . . . . . . . . . . . . . aw@sprynet.com
169 Pier Ave.
Santa Monica, CA 90405

TYPE — Motion Pictures + Documentaries + Animation
CREDITS — Football Stories - Last Call - Dry Manhattan
COMMENTS — Also: Music Videos

David T. Page . . . . . . . . . . . . . . . . . . . President/Producer
Robert R. Ahdoot . . . . . . . . . . . . . . . . . . . . . . . Producer
Tina Wolfson . . . . . . . . . . . . . . . . . . . . . . . . . . Producer
Langdon F. Page . . . . . . . . . . . . . . . . . . . Director/Editor
Luz Maria Vela . . . . . . . . . . . . . . . . . . . Producer/Director

## CANNON & ASSOCIATES, REUBEN
PHONE . . . . . . . . . . . . . . . . . . . . . . . . . . . 213-939-3190
FAX . . . . . . . . . . . . . . . . . . . . . . . . . . . . . . 213-939-7793
EMAIL . . . . . . . . . . . . . . . . . . . . . . . ReubCan@aol.com
5225 Wilshire Blvd., Ste. 526
Los Angeles, CA 90036

TYPE — Motion Pictures + Television
CREDITS — The Women of Brewster Place - Down in the Delta - Good News (UPN) - Get on the Bus

Reuben Cannon . . . . . . . . . . . . . . . . . . . . . . . . . Producer
Eddie Dunlop . . . . . . . . . . . . . Dir., Creative Affairs & Talent

## CANTERBURY FILMS
PHONE . . . . . . . . . . . . . . . . . . . . . . . . . . . 310-550-0100
9903 Santa Monica Blvd.
Beverly Hills, CA 90212

TYPE — Motion Pictures + Television
DEAL — New Regency Television/Ruddy Morgan Organization, Inc., The
CREDITS — Rainbows - The Chameleon

Robert J. DeBrino . . . . . . . . . . . . . . . . . . . . . . . Producer
George Rende . . . . . . . . . . . . . . . . . . . . VP, Development

## CANTON COMPANY, THE
PHONE . . . . . . . . . . . . . . . . . . . . . . . . . . . 818-954-2130
FAX . . . . . . . . . . . . . . . . . . . . . . . . . . . . . . 818-954-2967
Warner Bros.
4000 Warner Blvd., Bldg. 81, Ste. 200
Burbank, CA 91522

TYPE — Motion Pictures + Television
DEAL — Warner Bros. Pictures

Mark Canton . . . . . . . . . . . . . . . . . . . . . . . . . . No Title
Barbara Kalish . . . . . . . . . . . . . . . . . . . . . . . . . No Title
John Goldstone . . . . . . . . . . . . . . . . . . . . . . . . No Title
Anna DeRoy . . . . . . . . . . . . . . . . . . . . . . . . . . . No Title
Jonathan Berg . . . . . . . . . . . . . . . . . . . . . . . . . No Title
Matthew Bakal . . . . . . . . . . . . . . . Asst. to John Goldstone
Chris Farber . . . . . . . . . . . . . . . . . Asst. to Barbara Kalish
Nathan Kahane . . . . . . . . . . . . . . . . Asst. to Mark Canton
Shelbee Mintzer . . . . . . . . . . . . . . . . Asst. to Anna DeRoy

## CANTON PRODUCTIONS, MAJ
PHONE . . . . . . . . . . . . . . . . . . . . . . . . . . . 310-823-1917
655 Oxford Ave.
Venice, CA 90291-4724

TYPE — Motion Pictures + Television
CREDITS — Wife, Mother, Murderer - A Mother's Revenge
COMMENTS — Author: Complete Guide to TV Movies/Miniseries 1984-97

Maj Canton . . . . . . . . . . . . . . . . . . . . . . . . . . . Producer

## CAPELLA FILMS INC.
PHONE . . . . . . . . . . . . . . . . . . . . . . . . . . . 310-247-4700
FAX . . . . . . . . . . . . . . . . . . . . . . . . . . . . . . 310-247-4701
9242 Beverly Blvd., Ste. 280
Beverly Hills, CA 90210-3710

TYPE — Motion Pictures
CREDITS — Austin Powers: Intl. Man of Mystery - Two Bits - Shattered

Rolf Deyhle . . . . . . . . . . . . . . . . . . . . . . . . . . Chairman
David Korda . . . . . . . . . . . . . . Pres., Production/Development
Bridget Hedison . . . . . . . . . . . . . . . . . . . VP, Development

# COMPANIES AND STAFF

**CAPITAL ARTS ENTERTAINMENT**
PHONE . . . . . . . . . . . . . . . . . . . . . . . . . . . . . 310-581-3020
FAX . . . . . . . . . . . . . . . . . . . . . . . . . . . . . . . . 310-581-3023
EMAIL . . . . . . . . . . . . . . . . . . . . . . . . capartsent@aol.com
2950 31st St., Ste. 390
Santa Monica, CA 90405
TYPE         Motion Pictures + Feature Direct to Video + Television
CREDITS     Route 9 - Casper Meets Wendy - Richie Rich - Addams'
                 Family Reunion
Mike Elliott . . . . . . . . . . . . . . . . . . . . . . . . . . . . . . . President
Rob Kerchner . . . . . . . . . . . . . . . . . . . . . . . . . . . . . President
Joe Genier . . . . . . . . . . . . . . . . . . . . . . . . . Head, Production
Abraham Gordon . . . . . . . . . . . . . . . . . . . Creative Executive
Scott Sandin . . . . . . . . . . . . . . . . . . . . . . Creative Executive
Aaron Richmond . . . . . . . . . . . . . . . . . . Production Executive
Naomi Yoelin . . . . . . . . . . . . . . . . . . . . . . . Casting Director

***CAPO PRODUCTIONS**
PHONE . . . . . . . . . . . . . . . . . . . . . . . . . . . . . 310-477-4234
EMAIL . . . . . . . . . . . . . . . . . . . . . . . . . . capoprod@aol.com
1726 Kelton Avenue
Los Angeles, CA 90024
TYPE         Motion Pictures
CREDITS     Isn't It Romantic - Hot Spot
Deborah Capogrosso . . . . . . . . . . . . . . . . . . . . . . . President

**CAPPA PRODUCTIONS**
PHONE . . . . . . . . . . . . . . . . . . . . . . . . . . . . . 212-906-8800
445 Park Ave.
New York, NY 10022
TYPE         Motion Pictures
DEAL         Walt Disney Company, The
CREDITS     Casino - Age of Innocence - Goodfellas - Raging Bull -
                 Kundun
COMMENTS   No unsolicited material.
Martin Scorsese . . . . . . . . . . . . . . . . . . . . . . . . . . Director
Barbara De Fina . . . . . . . . . . . . . . . . . . . . . . . . . . Producer
Shira Levin . . . . . . . . . . . . . . . . . . . . . . . Dir., Development
Gretchen Campbell . . . . . . . . . . . . . . . Asst. to Mr. Scorsese

**CARASCOPE PRODUCTIONS INC.**
PHONE . . . . . . . . . . . . . . . . . . . . . . . . . . . . . 718-442-8626
FAX . . . . . . . . . . . . . . . . . . . . . . . . . . . . . . . . 718-448-6111
EMAIL . . . . . . . . . . . . . . . . . . . . . caraproductions@aol.com
131 Waldron Ave.
Staten Island, NY 10301
TYPE         Motion Pictures + Television + Interactive Multimedia
CREDITS     Sunset Park
Cara Buonincontri . . . . . . . . . . . . . . President/Producer/Writer
Michele Garofano . . . . . . . . . . . . . . . . . . . Dir., Development

**CARAVAN PICTURES**
PHONE . . . . . . . . . . . . . . . . . . . . . . . . . . . . . 310-264-4400
FAX . . . . . . . . . . . . . . . . . . . . . . . . . . . . . . . . 310-264-4404
3000 W. Olympic Blvd., Bldg. 5
Santa Monica, CA 90404
TYPE         Motion Pictures
DEAL         Walt Disney Company, The
CREDITS     Grosse Pointe Blank - The Three Musketeers - While You
                 Were Sleeping - Metro - GI Jane
Roger Birnbaum . . . . . . . . . . . . . . . . . . . Chairman/Producer
Jonathan Glickman . . . . . . . . . . . . . . . . . . Pres., Production
Claudia Sachs . . . . . . . . . . . . . . . . . . . . . . . VP, Production
Derek Evans . . . . . . . . . . . . . . . . . . . . . . . Dir., Development
Marlena Wilkens . . . . . . Exec. Asst. to Mr. Birnbaum/Production Coordinator
Kelly Balfe . . . . . . . . . . . . . . . . . . . . . . . Asst. to Ms. Wilkens
Katie DiMento . . . . . . . . . . . . . . . . . . . Asst. to Mr. Glickman
Alex Sanger . . . . . . . . . . . . . . . . . . . . . . . Asst. to Ms. Sachs
John McKee . . . . . . . . . . . . . . . . . . . . . . . . . Office Assistant

**CARLINER PRODS., MARK**
PHONE . . . . . . . . . . . . . . . . . . . . . . . . . . . . . 818-763-4783
EMAIL . . . . . . . . . . . . . . . . . . . . . . . . . . mcarliner@aol.com
11700 Laurelwood Dr.
Studio City, CA 91604
TYPE         Motion Pictures + Television
CREDITS     Heaven Help Us- George Wallace(TNT)- Crossroads -
                 Stalin- The Shining (ABC Miniseries)
Mark Carliner . . . . . . . . . . . . . . . . . . . . . . . . . . . Producer
BJ Heath . . . . . . . . . . . . . . . . . . . . . . . . . . . . . . . Assistant

**CARLSON, MATTHEW**
PHONE . . . . . . . . . . . . . . . . . . . . . . . . . . . . . 818-760-5054
FAX . . . . . . . . . . . . . . . . . . . . . . . . . . . . . . . . 818-760-6224
Carsey-Werner
4024 Radford Ave., Bldg. 4, Room 201
Studio City, CA 91604
TYPE         Television + Motion Pictures
DEAL         Carsey-Werner Co., The
CREDITS     The Boys Are Back - The Wonder Years - Townies - Men
                 Behaving Badly
Matthew Carlson . . . . . . . . . . . . . . . . . . Executive Producer
Lynette Paradise . . . . . . . . . . . . . . . . . . Executive Assistant

**CARLSON-LEHMAN PRODS.**
PHONE . . . . . . . . . . . . . . . . . . . . . . . . . . . . . 310-280-6000
10000 W. Washington Blvd.
Culver City, CA 90232-2792
TYPE         Motion Pictures + Television
CREDITS     Never So Long Came Dawn - Sarah's Story - Mother
                 Nature
Judith Carlson . . . . . . . . . . . . . . . . . . . . . . Writer/Producer
Naomi Lehman . . . . . . . . . . . . . . . . . . . . . . Writer/Producer
Petra Feinberg . . . . . . . . . . . . . . . . . . . . . . . . Development

**CARLYLE PRODS. & MGMT.**
PHONE . . . . . . . . . . . . . . . . . . . . . . . . . . . . . 213-848-4960
FAX . . . . . . . . . . . . . . . . . . . . . . . . . . . . . . . . 213-650-8249
EMAIL . . . . . . . . . . . . . . . . . . . . . . . carlyle@earthlink.net
P.O. Box 691856
Los Angeles, CA 90069
TYPE         Motion Pictures + Television
CREDITS     Seven- The Accidental Tourist
Phyllis Carlyle . . . . . . . . . . . . . . . . . President/Owner/Producer
Bill Lagan . . . . . . . . . . . . . . . . Associate Producer/VP, Development
Devin Klein . . . . . . . . . . . . . . . . . . . . Asst. to Ms. Carlyle

**CARR ENTERPRISES, ALLAN**
PHONE . . . . . . . . . . . . . . . . . . . . . . . . . . . . . 310-278-2490
FAX . . . . . . . . . . . . . . . . . . . . . . . . . . . . . . . . 310-274-2278
P.O. Box 15568
Beverly Hills, CA 90209-1568
TYPE         Motion Pictures
DEAL         Paramount Pictures- Motion Picture Group
CREDITS     Can't Stop the Music - Grease - Grease 2 - La Cage aux
                 Folles - Cloak & Dagger
COMMENTS   Also: Theater. Do not sent scripts and/or resumes without
                 calling first.
Allan Carr . . . . . . . . . . . . . . . . . . . . . . . Chairman/Producer
Rob Bonet . . . . . . . . . . . . . . . . . . . . Producer/Dir., Development
Joan Hoven . . . . . . . . . . . . . . . . . . . . . . . . Business Affairs

***CARRERAS PRODUCTIONS**
PHONE . . . . . . . . . . . . . . . . . . . . . . . . . . . . . 310-247-1801
FAX . . . . . . . . . . . . . . . . . . . . . . . . . . . . . . . . 310-247-1977
321 N. Palm Drive, Ste. #1
Beverly Hills, CA 90210
TYPE         Motion Pictures
CREDITS     Black Circle Boys (Sundance 97) - Destiny Turns on the
                 Radio - Savoy
Raquel Carreras . . . . . . . . . . . . . . . . . . . . . . . Producer/CEO
Julia Teachey . . . . . . . . . . . . . . . . . . . Development Executive

**CARRIE PRODUCTIONS**
PHONE . . . . . . . . . . . . . . . . . . . . . . . . . . . . . 818-567-3292
FAX . . . . . . . . . . . . . . . . . . . . . . . . . . . . . . . . 818-567-3296
4444 Riverside Dr., Ste. 110
Burbank, CA 91505
TYPE         Motion Pictures + Television
CREDITS     Buffalo Soldiers - Deadly Voyage- America's Dream
COMMENTS   Affiliated with Robey Theatre Company.
Danny Glover . . . . . . . . . . . . . . . . . . . . . Executive Producer
Carolyn McDonald . . . . . . . . . . . . . . . . . Executive Producer

# COMPANIES AND STAFF

## CARSEY-WERNER CO., THE
```
PHONE .............................................. 818-655-5598
FAX ................................................. 818-655-6259
```
4024 Radford Ave., Bldg. 3
Studio City, CA 91604

TYPE         Television + Motion Pictures
CREDITS      Cosby - 3rd Rock From the Sun - Feelin' Alright

Marcy Carsey .................................. Owner/Exec. Producer
Tom Werner .................................... Owner/Exec. Producer
Stuart Glickman ................................ Vice Chairman/CEO
Bob Dubelko ................................ Exec. VP, Finance/CFO
Caryn Mandabach ....................... President/Exec. Producer
Courtney Conte ............................... Exec. VP, Production
Bret Sarnoff ........................................ Sr. VP, Finance
David Tochterman ......................... Sr. VP, Creative Affairs
Dirk W. van de Bunt ........ Exec. VP, Business & Legal Affairs
Polly Platt ................. Producer, Carsey-Werner Moving Picts.

## *CARTER COMPANY, THE THOMAS
```
PHONE ............................................. 310-449-4094
FAX ................................................ 310-449-4069
```
3000 W. Olympic Blvd.
Santa Monica, CA 90404

TYPE         Motion Pictures + Television
CREDITS      Don King: Only in America - Five Desperate Hours - The
                  Uninvited
COMMENTS  TV Movie Deal with Pearson Entertainment.

Thomas Carter .......................................... President
Richard Rothstein ................................... VP, Development
Jana Fain ......................................... Mgr., Development

## *CARTOON NETWORK
```
PHONE ............................................. 404-885-2263
FAX ................................................ 404-885-4312
```
1050 Techwood Dr., NW
Atlanta, GA 30318

TYPE         Television
COMMENTS  AOL Keywords: Cartoon Network.

Betty Cohen ................... President, Cartoon Network Worldwide
Rob Sorcher .................................... Exec. Vice President
Mike Lazzo ................... Sr. VP, Programming & Production
Michael Ouweleen ......................... Sr. VP/Creative Director
Keith Crofford .................................... VP, Production
Mark Norman ............................. VP, Business Operations
Linda Simensky ......................... VP, Original Animation

## CARUSO-MENDELSOHN PRODS.
```
PHONE ............................................. 212-941-4036
FAX ................................................ 212-941-3997
```
Tribeca Film Center
375 Greenwich St.
New York, NY 10013

TYPE         Motion Pictures + Television
CREDITS      Through an Open Window - Little Red Riding Hood - Judy
                  Berlin

Rocco Caruso ........................................... Producer
Eric Mendelsohn ................................... Writer/Director

## CASTLE ROCK ENTERTAINMENT
```
PHONE ............................................. 310-285-2300
FAX ................................................ 310-285-2345
WEBSITE ........................... http://www.castle-rock.com
```
335 N. Maple Dr., Ste. 135
Beverly Hills, CA 90210-3867

TYPE         Motion Pictures + Television
CREDITS      A Few Good Men - City Slickers - In The Line of Fire -
                  Misery - Seinfeld
COMMENTS  Also: Cable

Alan Horn ......................................... Chairman/CEO
Rob Reiner ..................................... Producer/Director
Glenn Padnick ..................... Pres., Castle Rock Television
Andrew Scheinman ............................. Producer/Director
Martin Shafer ....................... Pres., Castle Rock Pictures
Greg Paul ................................. Chief Operating Officer
Liz Glotzer ............... Pres., Production, Castle Rock Pictures
Jeffrey Stott ..................... Exec. VP, Production Management
Jess Wittenberg ............................... Exec. Vice President
David Goodman ................ Sr. VP, Business & Legal Affairs
Robin Green ..................... Sr. VP, Castle Rock Television
Steven Rabiner ................................... Sr. VP, Production
Jessica Roddy ................ Sr. VP, Business & Legal Affairs
Carlos Perez .................................... VP, Administration
James Campbell ................... Dir., Financial Administration
Kerry Leary ..................... Dir., Castle Rock Television
Sharon Lignier ................ Dir., Business Affairs Administration
Brady Thomas ...................................... Story Editor

## CATAPULT FILMS
```
PHONE ............................................. 310-395-1470
FAX ................................................ 310-395-3740
```
832 Third St., Ste. 303
Santa Monica, CA 90403-1155

TYPE         Motion Pictures + Television
Lawrence Levy ............................................. Producer
Lisa Stromer .............................................. Producer

## CATES/DOTY PRODUCTIONS
```
PHONE ............................................. 310-208-2134
```
10920 Wilshire Blvd., Ste. 830
Los Angeles, CA 90024

TYPE         Motion Pictures + Television
CREDITS      Innocent Victims - Confessions:Two Faces of Evil -
                  Absolute Strangers - Call Me Anna

Gilbert Cates ................................... Producer/Director
Dennis Doty ............................................ Producer
Peggy Griffin ................................. Associate Producer

## CATFISH PRODUCTIONS
```
PHONE ............................................. 310-456-5365
FAX ................................................ 310-456-8325
```
24955 Pacific Coast Highway,  Ste. C304
Malibu, CA 90265

TYPE         Motion Pictures + Television
DEAL         CBS Entertainment
CREDITS      The Absolute Truth - A Passion For Justice - The Stars Fell
                  on Henrietta

James Keach ......................... Actor/Producer/Director
Jane Seymour ............................... Actress/Producer
Tatum Cook-Reiner ................ VP, Creative Development
Kiana Kang .............................................. Assistant

## CBS CORPORATION
```
PHONE .............................................. 212-975-4321
```
51 W. 52 St.
New York, NY 10019

Michael H. Jordan ................................. Chairman/CEO
Mel Karmazin ..................................... President/COO
Leslie Moonves ........... Pres./CEO, CBS Television & Pres., CBS Cable
Fred Reynolds .................................... Exec. VP/CFO
Louis Briskman ............... Exec., Vice President/General Counsel
Susan J. Holliday ................ Sr. VP/Deputy General Counsel
Martin P. Messinger ............... Sr. VP/Deputy General Counsel
Derk Zimmerman ........ Sr. VP, New Ventures & Business Development
Robert Freedline ....................................... Controller

## CBS ENTERPRISES
```
PHONE ............................................. 310-446-6000
FAX ................................................ 310-446-6066
```
10877 Wilshire Blvd.
Los Angeles, CA 90024

Ed Wilson .................... President, CBS Enterprises/Eyemark
Bob Cook..................... Exec. VP, CBS Enterprises/Eyemark
Marvin Shirley ............... Exec. VP, CBS Enterprises/Eyemark
Rainer Siek ............... Exec. VP/Pres., CBS Broadcast Intl.

# COMPANIES AND STAFF

## CBS ENTERTAINMENT
PHONE . . . . . . . . . . . . . . . . . . . . . . . . . . . . . . . . . 323-575-2345
WEBSITE . . . . . . . . . . . . . . . . . . . . . . . . . . . http://www.cbs.com
7800 Beverly Blvd.
Los Angeles, CA 90036-2188

TYPE            Television
COMMENTS   ALSO: 51 W. 52nd St., 6th Fl., NY, NY 10019
Leslie Moonves . . . . . . . . . . . . . . . . . . . . . Pres./CEO, CBS Television
Nancy Tellem . . . . . . Exec. VP, Business Affairs/Exec. VP, CBS Productions
Marc J. Graboff . . . . . . . . . . . . . . . . . . . . . Sr. VP, Business Affairs
Lucy Johnson . . . . . . . Sr. VP, Daytime/Children's Programs & Spec. Projects
Gary Silver . . . . . . . . . . . . . . . . . . . . . . . . . . . VP, Business Affairs
Anita Addison . . . . . . . . . . . . . . . . VP, Dramatic Series Development
Terry Botwick . . . . . . . . . . . . . . . . . . VP, Current Programs & Specials
Martin Garcia . . . . . . VP, Business Affairs/Program & Rights Negotiations
Peter Golden . . . . . . . . . . . . . . . . . . . . . . . . VP, Talent & Casting
Wendi Goldstein . . . . . . VP, Special Comedy Programs/Dir., Comedy Devel.
Joan Harrison . . . . . . . . . . . . . . . . . . . . . . . . . . . VP, Mini-Series
Sunta Izzicupo . . . . . . . . . . . . . . . . . . . . . . VP, Movies for Television
Kelly Kahl . . . . . . . . . . . . . . . . . . VP, Program Planning & Scheduling
Rob Kaplan . . . . . . . . . . VP, Nontraditional Prog./Dir., Drama Series Dev.
Sidney H. Lyons . . . . . . . VP, Bus. Affairs, Long Form Contracts & Acquisitions
Brian O'Neal . . . . . . . . . . . . . . . . . . . . . . VP, Children's Programs
Madeline Peerce . . . . . . VP, Creative Services/Artist Relations
Mitchell R. Semel . . . . . . . . . . . . . . . . VP, Programming  (East Coast)
Gene Stein . . . . . . . . . . . . . . . . . . . VP, Comedy Series Development
Anne R. Nelson . . . . . . . . . . . . . . . . . . . . Sr. VP, Business Affairs
Cindy Badell-Slaughter . . . . . . . . . . . . . . . Dir., Music Operations
Bela Bajaria . . . . . . . . . . . . . . . . . . . . . . Dir., Movies for Television
Ruthe Benton . . . . . . . . . . . . . . . . . . . . . . Dir., Movies for Television
Cyndy Brown . . . . . . . . . . . . . . . . . . . . . . . . . . Dir., Planning
Julianna Carnessale . . . . . . . . . . . . . . . . . . . Dir., Business Affairs
Lucy Cavallo . . . . . . . . . . . . . . . . . . . . . . . . . . . . Dir., Casting
Carolyn Ceslik . . . . . . . . . . . . Dir., Childrens Programs (East Coast)
Chris Davidson . . . . . . . . . . . . . . . . . . . . . Dir., Current Programs
Vincent P. Favale . . . . . . . . . . . . Dir., Late Night Programs (East Coast)
Wendy Fishman . . . . . . . . . . . . . . . . Dir., Daytime Programs, (NY)
Deborah Gale . . . . . . . . . . . . . . . . . . . . . . . . . . . Dir., Casting
Dorian Hannaway . . . . . . . . . Dir., Late Night Programming, (West Coast)
Greg Harris . . . . . . . . . . . . . . . . . . . . . . . . Dir., Current Programs
Monique Hart . . . . . . . . . . . . . . . . Dir., Specials/Feature Films
Amy Herzig . . . . . . . . . . . . . . . . . . . . . . . . Dir., Casting (East Coast)
Sherry Hilber . . . . . . . . . . . . . . . . . . . . . . . Dir., Current Programs
Michael A. Katcher . . . . . . . . . . . . . . . . . . . . . . . Dir., Casting
Dick Kirschner . . . . . . . . . . . . . . . . . . . . . . Dir., Current Programs
Jim McKairnes . . . . . . . . . . . . . Dir., Program Planning & Scheduling
Laverne McKinnon . . . . . . . . . Dir., Childrens Programs (West Coast)
Myra Model . . . . . . . . . . . . . . . . . . . . . . . . . . Dir., Mini-Series
Fern Orenstein . . . . . . . . . . . . . . . . . . . . . . . . . . . Dir., Casting
Alison Rinzel . . . . . . . . . . . . . . . Dir., Daytime Casting (East Coast)
Matt Ross . . . . . . . . . . . . . . . . . . . . . . . . . Dir., Business Affairs
Chris Ryan . . . . . . . . . . . . . . . . . . . . . . . . . Dir., Business Affairs
Patricia Saphier . . . . . . . . . . . . . . . . . . . Dir., Movies for Television
Sam Semon . . . . . . . . . . . . . . . . . . . . . . . . . Dir., Business Affairs
Roger Senders . . . . . . . . . . . . . . . . . . . . . . . Dir., Business Affairs
Margot Wain . . . . . . . . . . . . . . Dir., Daytime Programs (West Coast)
Barbara Hunter Welsh . . . . . . . Dir., Daytime Programming (West Coast)
Michael Wright . . . . . . . . . . . . . . . . . . . . Dir., Movies for Television
Joan Yee . . . . . . . . . . . . . . . . . . . . . . . . . . Dir., Movies for Television
Laurie Zaks . . . . . . . . . . . . . . . . . . . . . . . . . . Dir., Current Programs

## CBS PRODUCTIONS
PHONE . . . . . . . . . . . . . . . . . . . . . . . . . . . . . . . . . 323-575-2345
WEBSITE . . . . . . . . . . . . . . . . . . . . . . . . . . . http://www.cbs.com
7800 Beverly Blvd.
Los Angeles, CA 90036-2188

TYPE            Television
Nancy Tellem . . . . . . . . . . . . . . . . . . . . . Executive Vice President
Robert Gros . . . . . . . . . . . . . . . . . . . . . . . . . Sr. Vice President
Maria Rastatter . . . . . . . . . . . . . . . . . . . . . . Sr. VP, Comedy
Nina Tassler . . . . . . . . . . . . . . . . . . . . . . . . . Sr. VP, Drama
Glenn Adilman . . . . . . . . . . . . . . . . . . . . . . . . Vice President
Leola Gorius . . . . . . . . . VP, Talent & Guild/Negotiations/Business Affairs
Ann McGrail . . . . . . . . . . . . . . . . . . . . . . Dir., Primetime Series

## CECCHI GORI PICTURES
PHONE . . . . . . . . . . . . . . . . . . . . . . . . . . . . . . . . . 310-442-4777
FAX . . . . . . . . . . . . . . . . . . . . . . . . . . . . . . . . . . . . 310-442-9507
WEBSITE . . . . . . . . . . . . . . . . . . . . . http://www.cecchigori.com
11990 San Vicente Blvd., Ste. 200
Los Angeles, CA 90049

TYPE            Motion Pictures + Television
CREDITS         Il Postino - The Star Maker - Mediterraneo
Gianni Nunnari . . . . . . . . . . . . . . . . . . . . . . . . . . . . President
Anna Gross . . . . . . . . . . . . . . . . . . . . . . . . . . . . Vice President

## CENTROPOLIS STREAMLINE
PHONE . . . . . . . . . . . . . . . . . . . . . . . . . . . . . . . . . 310-828-3422
FAX . . . . . . . . . . . . . . . . . . . . . . . . . . . . . . . . . . . . 310-828-1512
WEBSITE . . . . . . . . . . . . . . . . . . . . . . . . http://centropolis.com
2700 Colorado Ave., 3rd Floor
Santa Monica, CA 90404

TYPE            Motion Pictures
CREDITS         13th Floor
COMMENTS   Science Fiction.
Ute Emmerich . . . . . . . . . . . . . . . . . . . . . . . . . . . Co-President
Marco Weber . . . . . . . . . . . . . . . . . . . . . . . . . . . Co-President
Vanessa Jordan . . . . . . . . . . . . . . . . . . . . . Executive Assistant
Rachel Rose . . . . . . . . . . . . . . . . . . . . . . . Executive Assistant

## CHAKO FILM INTERNATIONAL
PHONE . . . . . . . . . . . . . . . . . . . . . . . . . . . . . . . . . 310-275-1543
FAX . . . . . . . . . . . . . . . . . . . . . . . . . . . . . . . . . . . . 310-271-3786
EMAIL . . . . . . . . . . . . . . . . . . . . . . . . . . . chakofilm@aol.com
369 S. Doheny Drive, #1202
Beverly Hills, CA 90211

TYPE            Motion Pictures
DEAL            Twentieth Century Fox
CREDITS         Forever and Beyond - Piranha - Raging Angels - Dentsu
                Inc.
Chako Van Leeuwen . . . . . . . . . . . . . . . . . . . . . . . . Producer
Stens Christensen . . . . . . . . . . . . . . . . . . . Associate Producer
David Markov . . . . . . . . . . . . . . . . . . . . . . . . Dir., Production
Mark Devendorf . . . . . . . . . . . . . . . . . . . . . . . Creative Affairs

## CHANCELLOR ENTERTAINMENT
PHONE . . . . . . . . . . . . . . . . . . . . . . . . . . . . . . . . . 310-474-4521
FAX . . . . . . . . . . . . . . . . . . . . . . . . . . . . . . . . . . . . 310-470-9273
10600 Holman Ave., Ste. 1
Los Angeles, CA 90024

TYPE            Motion Pictures + Television
CREDITS         Idol Maker - The Razor's Edge - Letter to Three Wives -
                Smilin' Jack
Robert P. Marcucci . . . . . . . . . . . . . . . . . . . . . . . . President
Joan Muraskin . . . . . . . . . . . . . . . . . Sr. VP, Talent & Development

## CHANNEL PRODUCTIONS
PHONE . . . . . . . . . . . . . . . . . . . . . . . . . . . . . . . . . 310-454-8498
FAX . . . . . . . . . . . . . . . . . . . . . . . . . . . . . . . . . . . . 310-454-2598
EMAIL . . . . . . . . . . . . . . . . . . . . . . . . . . . sloane01@aol.com
1223 Wilshire Blvd., #857
Santa Monica, CA 90403

TYPE            Motion Pictures
CREDITS         St. Elmo's Fire - Sixteen Candles - The Breakfast Club -
                Guarding Tess
Ned Tanen . . . . . . . . . . . . . . . . . . . . . . . . . . . . . . Producer

## CHANNING FILMS LLC
PHONE . . . . . . . . . . . . . . . . . . . . . . . . . . . . . . . . . 310-836-9000
FAX . . . . . . . . . . . . . . . . . . . . . . . . . . . . . . . . . . . . 310-836-9292
EMAIL . . . . . . . . . . . . . . . . . . . . . . . . . . . kelley@musicosm.com
8693 Wilshire Blvd., Ste. 300
Beverly Hills, CA 90211

TYPE            Motion Pictures
CREDITS         Secrets & Lies - Retroactive - Musicosm Rex
Simon Channing-Williams . . . . . . . . . . . . . . . . . . . . . Partner
Kelley Feldsott Reynolds . . . . . . . . . . . . . . . . . . . . . . Partner

## CHANTICLEER FILMS
PHONE . . . . . . . . . . . . . . . . . . . . . . . . . . . . . . . . . 213-462-4705
FAX . . . . . . . . . . . . . . . . . . . . . . . . . . . . . . . . . . . . 213-462-1603
EMAIL . . . . . . . . . . . . . . . . . . . . . . . . . . . antihil@aol.com
1680 N. Vine St., Ste. 1212
Hollywood, CA 90028

TYPE            Motion Pictures
DEAL            Alliance Television Productions
CREDITS         Directed By... - Gold Coast - Advanced Guard
Jana Sue Memel . . . . . . . . . . . . . . . . . . . . . President/Producer
Larry Hymes . . . . . . . . . . . . . . VP, Development & Production/Producer
Hillary Anne Ripps . . . . . . . . . . . . . . VP, Prod. Admin./Producer
Michelle Rowe . . . . . . . . . . . . . . . . . . . . Development Assistant

## CHARLES-BURROWS-CHARLES

PHONE . . . . . . . . . . . . . . . . . . . . . . . . . . 213-956-5961
Paramount TV
5555 Melrose Ave., Ball 203
Los Angeles, CA 90038-3197

TYPE — Television
DEAL — Paramount Television Group
CREDITS — Cheers

James Burrows . . . . . . . . . . . . . . . . . . . Exec. Producer/Director
Glen Charles . . . . . . . . . . . . . . . . . . . . . . . Executive Producer
Les Charles . . . . . . . . . . . . . . . . . . . . . . . . Executive Producer

## CHARTOFF PRODUCTIONS

PHONE . . . . . . . . . . . . . . . . . . . . . . . . . . 310-319-1960
1250 Sixth St., Ste. 101
Santa Monica, CA 90401

TYPE — Motion Pictures
CREDITS — Rocky Movies - The Right Stuff - Raging Bull - Straight Talk
COMMENTS — Also: Cable films.

Robert Chartoff . . . . . . . . . . . . . . . . . . . . . . . . CEO/President
Lynn Hendee . . . . . . . . . . . . . . . . . . . . . Exec. Vice President
Lori Imbler Vernon . . . . . . . . . . . . . . . . . . Production Associate

## CHASE PRODS., STANLEY

PHONE . . . . . . . . . . . . . . . . . . . . . . . . . . 310-475-4236
FAX . . . . . . . . . . . . . . . . . . . . . . . . . . . . . 310-474-5720
1937 S. Beverly Glen Blvd., Ste. 20
Los Angeles, CA 90025

TYPE — Motion Pictures + Television
CREDITS — Mack the Knife - The Guardian - Grace Kelly - American Xmas Carol

Stanley Chase . . . . . . . . . . . . . . . . . . . . . . . . . . President
Dorothy Rice . . . . . . . . . . . . . . . . . . . . . . . . Vice President

## CHERRY ALLEY PRODUCTIONS

PHONE . . . . . . . . . . . . . . . . . . . . . . . . . . 310-458-8886
225 Arizona Ave., Ste. 350
Santa Monica, CA 90401

TYPE — Motion Pictures + Television + Interactive Multimedia
CREDITS — Hope - The Out of Towners
COMMENTS — No unsolicited submissions accepted.

Goldie Hawn . . . . . . . . . . . . . . . . . . Chief Executive Officer
Teri Schwartz . . . . . . . . . . . . . . . . . . . . . . . . . President
Philip E. Thomas . . . . . . . . . . . . . . . . . . . . VP, Production
Deloris Horn . . . . . . . . . Executive Production Coordinator to Ms. Hawn
Priscilla Valldejuli . . . . . . . . . . . . . . . Asst. to Ms. Schwartz

## CHESLER/PERLMUTTER PRODUCTION

PHONE . . . . . . . . . . . . . . . . . . . . . . . . . . 310-887-5600
FAX . . . . . . . . . . . . . . . . . . . . . . . . . . . . . 310-887-5259
EMAIL . . . . . . . . . . . . . . . . . . . . . . . . chesperl@aol.com
301 N. Canon Dr., Ste. 203
Beverly Hills, CA, CA 90210

TYPE — Motion Pictures + Television
CREDITS — Hitchhiker - Hidden Room - Strangers - Ms. Bear - Bone Daddy - Sins of the City - Betaville
COMMENTS — Also: UPN Movies. Also: 129 Yorkville Ave., #200 Toronto, Ontario M5R 1C4 Canada.

Lewis Chesler . . . . . . . . . . . . . . . . . Chairman/Exec. Producer
David Perlmutter . . . . . . . . . . . . . . . . . . . . . . . . Chairman
Steve Ujlaki . . . . . . . . . . . . . . . . . President, Motion Pictures
Hank McCann . . . . . . . . . . . . . . . . Sr. VP, Talent & Production
Kevin Commins . . . . . . . . . . . . . . . . . . . . . VP, Development
Jiles Fitzgerald . . . . . . . . . . . . . . . . . . . . . . VP, Sci-Fi Dept.
Meredith Freeman . . . . . . . . . . . . . . . . . VP, Story Department
Gail Glaze . . . . . . . . . . . . . . . . . . . . . . . . . VP, Story Dept.
Robert Vaughn . . . . . . . . . . . . . . . . . . . VP, Motion Pictures
Dan Collins . . . . . . . . . . . . . . . . . . . . . . . Dir., Production
Andrew Goodman . . . . . . . . . . . . . . . . . . . . Dir., Production
Roberta Harron . . . . . . . . . . . . . . . . . . . . Dir., Administration
Carrie Iglehart . . . . . . . . . . . . . . . . . Dir., Family Entertainment
Gaille LeDrew . . . . . . . . . . . . . . . Dir., Contract Administration
Donalda Palmer . . . . . . . . . . . . . . . . . . . . . . . . Accounting

## CHESTERFIELD FILM CO., THE

PHONE . . . . . . . . . . . . . . . . . . . . . . . . . . 310-260-6112
FAX . . . . . . . . . . . . . . . . . . . . . . . . . . . . . 310-260-6116
EMAIL . . . . . . . . . . . . . . . . . . . Email_route50@aol.com
WEBSITE . . . . . . . . . . . . . . . http://www.chesterfield_co.com
1351 4th St., Ste. 201
Santa Monica, CA 90401

TYPE — Motion Pictures + Television
DEAL — Kennedy/Marshall Company
CREDITS — Requiem - Black Circle Boys - Digging to China
COMMENTS — Writer's Film Project. Screenwriting Fellowship.

Kenneth S. Orkin . . . . . . . . . . . . . . . . . . . . . . . . President
Sondra Baker . . . . . . . . . . . . . . . . . . . . . . . . . . Producer
Douglas Rosen . . . . . . . . . . . . . . . . . . . Dir., Development

## CHESTNUT HILL PRODS.

PHONE . . . . . . . . . . . . . . . . . . . . . . . . . . 310-260-1400
FAX . . . . . . . . . . . . . . . . . . . . . . . . . . . . . 310-260-1406
1460 4th St., Ste. 210
Santa Monica, CA 90401

TYPE — Motion Pictures + Television + Interactive Multimedia
CREDITS — I Love You to Death- V.I. Warshawski- Foxfire - State of Emergency

Jeffrey Lurie . . . . . . . . . . . . . . . . . . . . . . . . . President
John P. Marsh . . . . . . . . . . . . . . . . . . . Sr. VP, Production
Andrea Mia . . . . . . . . . . . . . . . . . . . . . . Dir., Development

## CHEYENNE 7 PRODS.

PHONE . . . . . . . . . . . . . . . . . . . . . . . . . . 818-954-7310
Warner Bros. Television
4000 Warner Blvd., Bldg. 137, Room 1068
Burbank, CA 91522

TYPE — Motion Pictures + Television
DEAL — MTV Networks/Warner Bros. Television Productions
CREDITS — Sliders - Star Trek - Intruders - Fire In The Sky - Kung Pow (MTV)

Tracy Torme . . . . . . . . . . . . . . . . President/Producer/Writer
Clint Milby . . . . . . . . . . . . . . . . . . . . . . . . . Story Editor

## CHIARAMONTE FILMS, INC.

PHONE . . . . . . . . . . . . . . . . . . . . . . . . . . 310-578-7363
FAX . . . . . . . . . . . . . . . . . . . . . . . . . . . . . 310-578-1704
EMAIL . . . . . . . . . . . . . . . . . . . . . . . . monte711@aol.com
681 Washington Blvd.
Marina del Rey, CA 90292

TYPE — Motion Pictures + Feature Direct to Video
CREDITS — Twogether

Andrew Chiaramonte . . . . . . . . . . . . . . Writer/Producer/Director

## CHICAGOFILMS

PHONE . . . . . . . . . . . . . . . . . . . . . . . . . . 212-307-0050
FAX . . . . . . . . . . . . . . . . . . . . . . . . . . . . . 212-307-9066
EMAIL . . . . . . . . . . . . . . . . . . . . . . . . chifilms@aol.com
250 West 57th Street, Ste. 2217
New York, NY 10107

TYPE — Motion Pictures + Television
CREDITS — The Last Good Time - Parents

Bob Balaban . . . . . . . . . . . . . . . . . . . Actor/Director/Producer
Riaz Patel . . . . . . . . . . . . . . . . . . . . . . . Dir., Development

## CHILDREN'S TELEVISION WORKSHOP

PHONE . . . . . . . . . . . . . . . . . . . . . . . . . . 212-595-3456
FAX . . . . . . . . . . . . . . . . . . . . . . . . . . . . . 212-875-6104
WEBSITE . . . . . . . . . . . . . . . . . . . . http://www.ctw.org
One Lincoln Plaza, 4th Fl.
New York, NY 10023

TYPE — Television + Feature Direct to Video
CREDITS — Sesame Street - Big Bag - CRO - Ghostwriter - New Ghostwriter Mysteries - Dragontales

David Britt . . . . . . . . . . . . . . . . . . . . . . . . . . President
Gary Knell . . . . . . . . . . . . . . . . . . . . Exec. VP/Operations
Ann Sardini . . . . . . . . . . . . . . . . . . . . . . . Exec. VP/CFO
Daniel Victor . . . . . . . . Exec. VP, Legal & Business Affairs & Gen. Counsel
Nina Elias . . . . . . . . . . . . Exec. Producer, Big Bag, Dragontales
Marjorie Kalins . . . . . . . . . Exec. Producer, Elmo in Grouchland
Michael Loman . . . . . . . . . . . Exec. Producer, Sesame Street
Jeffrey Nelson . . . . . . . . . . . . . . . . . . . . . Exec. Producer
Taska Carrigan . . . . . . . . . . . . . . VP, Legal & Business Affairs
David Chan . . . . . . . . . . . . . . . . VP, Legal & Business Affairs
Joseph T. Diaz . . . . . . . . . . . . . . VP, Legal & Business Affairs
Jodi Nussbaum . . . . . . . . . . . . . . . . . . . . . VP, Production
Jeneane Fountaine Murray . . . . . . . . . . . . . . . . Sr. Counsel

# COMPANIES AND STAFF

**CHOTZEN/JENNER PRODUCTIONS**
PHONE . . . . . . . . . . . . . . . . . . . . . . . . . . . . . 213-465-9877
FAX . . . . . . . . . . . . . . . . . . . . . . . . . . . . . . . . 213-460-6451
Jaffe-Braunstein Films
7920 Sunset Blvd., Ste. 444
Los Angeles, CA 90046
TYPE       Motion Pictures + Television + Feature Direct to Video
DEAL       Jaffe/Braunstein Films Ltd.
CREDITS       Lies He Told - Prison of Secrets - Matter of Justice - My Father's Shadow

Yvonne Chotzen . . . . . . . . . . . . . . . . . . . . . . . Producer/Partner
William Jenner . . . . . . . . . . . . . . . . . . . . . . . . Producer/Partner
Dominique Azusa . . . . . . . . . . . . . . . . . . . . . . Development

**CHRIS/ROSE PRODS.**
PHONE . . . . . . . . . . . . . . . . . . . . . . . . . . . . . 310-840-8384
FAX . . . . . . . . . . . . . . . . . . . . . . . . . . . . . . . . 310-840-8392
9050 W. Washington Blvd., Ste. 3201
Culver City, CA 90232
TYPE       Motion Pictures + Television
DEAL       Columbia TriStar Television
CREDITS       Treasure of Dos Santos - Long Island Incident - Home Invasion - Down in the Delta

Robert W. Christiansen . . . . . . . . . . . . . . . . Producer/Exec. Producer
Rick Rosenberg . . . . . . . . . . . . . . . . . . . . . . Producer/Exec. Producer
Corina A. Sandru . . . . . . . . . . . . . . . . . . . . . Asst. to Producers

**CHRISTMAS TREE ENTERTAINMENT, INC.**
PHONE . . . . . . . . . . . . . . . . . . . . . . . . . . . . . 310-840-8370
FAX . . . . . . . . . . . . . . . . . . . . . . . . . . . . . . . . 310-840-8385
CSOB
9050 W. Washignton Blvd., Ste. 1108
Culver City, CA 90232
TYPE       Television + Motion Pictures
DEAL       Columbia TriStar Television
CREDITS       Matt Waters

Thomas D. Tannenbaum . . . . . . . . . . . . . . . Pres./Exec. Producer
Paul Lancer . . . . . . . . . . . . . . . . . . . . . . . . . VP, Development

**CINE. GRANDE. ENTERTAINMENT**
PHONE . . . . . . . . . . . . . . . . . . . . . . . . . . . . . 310-358-2240
FAX . . . . . . . . . . . . . . . . . . . . . . . . . . . . . . . . 310-659-0071
EMAIL . . . . . . . . . . . . . . . . . 76027,1212@compuserve.com
554 Norwich Dr.
Los Angeles, CA 90048
TYPE       Motion Pictures
CREDITS       Sub Down - Talos the Mummy

Silvio Muraglia . . . . . . . . . . . . . . . . . . . . . . . Chairman/CEO
Marian Salas . . . . . . . . . . . . . . . . . . . . . . . . . Financial Affairs

**CINE PARIS**
PHONE . . . . . . . . . . . . . . . . . . . . . . . . . . . . . 213-874-3534
FAX . . . . . . . . . . . . . . . . . . . . . . . . . . . . . . . . 818-789-0954
EMAIL . . . . . . . . . . . . . . . . . cinebank@confessionstv.com
5152 Sepulveda #125
Sherman Oaks, CA 91403-9999
TYPE       Motion Pictures + Television
CREDITS       Terminal Velocity - Bleeder & Bates - Dead Right - Confessions - Diary

Stephen Mitchell . . . . . . . . . . . . . . . . . . . . . Writer/Producer/Director
Kathi Carey . . . . . . . . . . . . . . . . . . . . . . . . . . Writer/Producer/Director
David Manship . . . . . . . . . . . . . . . . . . . . . . . Writer/Producer/Director

**CINECITY PICTURES**
PHONE . . . . . . . . . . . . . . . . . . . . . . . . . . . . . 310-559-7410
FAX . . . . . . . . . . . . . . . . . . . . . . . . . . . . . . . . 310-559-7452
EMAIL . . . . . . . . . . . . . . . . . . . . cinecity@cinecity.com
1925 Century Park East, 5th Floor
Los Angeles, CA 90067
TYPE       Motion Pictures
CREDITS       Bopha!

Lawrence Taubman . . . . . . . . . . . . . . . . . . . Producer
Stacy Katz . . . . . . . . . . . . . . . . . . . . . . . . . . . Dir., Development

**CINEMA SEVEN PRODS.**
PHONE . . . . . . . . . . . . . . . . . . . . . . . . . . . . . 212-315-1060
FAX . . . . . . . . . . . . . . . . . . . . . . . . . . . . . . . . 212-315-1085
EMAIL . . . . . . . . . . . . . . . . . . . . . . . cin7prod@aol.com
Carnegie Hall
154 W. 57th St., Ste. 112/1214
New York, NY 10019
TYPE       Motion Pictures
CREDITS       Where Eagles Dare - Angel Heart - The Long Goodbye - Love Is All There Is

Elliott Kastner . . . . . . . . . . . . . . . . . . . . . . . . President
George Pappas . . . . . . . . . . . . . . . . . . . . . . . Sr. Vice President
Chantal Ribeiro . . . . . . . . . . . . . . . . . . . . . . . Vice President
Lea Blackman . . . . . . . . . . . . . . . . . . . . . . . . Executive Accountant
Pasquale Botta . . . . . . . . . . . . . . . . . . . . . . . Executive Assistant

***CINEPOINT PRODUCTIONS, INC.**
PHONE . . . . . . . . . . . . . . . . . . . . . . . . . . . . . 310-937-1535
FAX . . . . . . . . . . . . . . . . . . . . . . . . . . . . . . . . 310-798-9443
EMAIL . . . . . . . . . . . . . . . . . cinepoint@worldnet.att.net
111 N. Sepulveda Blvd., Ste. 250
Manhattan Beach, CA 90266
TYPE       Motion Pictures

Michael Russell . . . . . . . . . . . . . . . . . . . . . . Co-President
Stephen LoCascio . . . . . . . . . . . . . . . . . . . . Co-President

**CINEQUANON PICTURES INTL. INC.**
PHONE . . . . . . . . . . . . . . . . . . . . . . . . . . . . . 213-658-6043
FAX . . . . . . . . . . . . . . . . . . . . . . . . . . . . . . . . 213-658-6087
EMAIL . . . . . . . . . . . . . . . . . . . . info@cinequanon.com
WEBSITE . . . . . . . . . . . . . . . . . http://www.cinequanon.com
8057 Beverly Blvd., 2nd Floor
Los Angeles, CA 90048
TYPE       Motion Pictures
CREDITS       The Treat - Lost Valley - I Woke Up Early The Day I Died - Wild Blue - Woundings - Dark Side of the Sun - Facade

Daniel Sales . . . . . . . . . . . . . . . . . . . . . . . . . President
Jennifer Peckham . . . . . . . . . . . . . . . . . . . . . Exec. Vice President
Marc Barson . . . . . . . . . . . . . . . . . . Sr. VP, Business & Legal Affairs
Kathleen Haase . . . . . . . . . . . . . . . . VP, Production & Acquisitions
Erik Jensen . . . . . . . . . . . . . . . . . . . . . . . VP, Sales & Acquisitions
Vester Mapp . . . . . . . . . . . . . . . . . . . . . . . . . VP, Finance
Drew Phillips . . . . . . . . . . . . . . . . . . . . . . . . . VP, Production
Greg Kim . . . . . . . . . . . . . . . . . . . . . Dir., Development & Acquisitions
Lisa Simone . . . . . . . . . . . . . . . . . . Mgr., Contract Administration
Alex Klyusner . . . . . . . . . . . . . . . . . . . . . . . . Story Editor

**CINERGI PICTURES ENTERTAINMENT INC.**
PHONE . . . . . . . . . . . . . . . . . . . . . . . . . . . . . 310-315-6000
FAX . . . . . . . . . . . . . . . . . . . . . . . . . . . . . . . . 310-828-0443
2308 Broadway
Santa Monica, CA 90404-2916
TYPE       Motion Pictures
CREDITS       Die Hard With A Vengeance - Nixon - Evita

Andrew Vajna . . . . . . . . . . . . . . . . . . . . . . . . Chairman/CEO
Samuel Falconello . . . . . . . . . . . . . . . . . . . . Sr. VP, Finance
Brett Fain . . . . . . . . . . . . . . . . . . . . . . . VP., Creative Affairs
Gabriel Benson . . . . . . . . . . . . . . . . . . . . . . . Story Editor
Susan Koscinski . . . . . . . . . . . . . . . . . . . . . . Controller

**CINESTAGE PRODUCTIONS**
PHONE . . . . . . . . . . . . . . . . . . . . . . . . . . . . . 213-465-1000
5935 Canyon Heights Lane
Los Angeles, CA 90068-2425
TYPE       Motion Pictures
CREDITS       Seduced By Evil - Snitch - Undercurrents
COMMENTS       Also: Theatre

Richard Polak . . . . . . . . . . . . . . . . . . . . . . . . Partner
Anthony DeSantis . . . . . . . . . . . . . . . . . . . . . Development

**CINETEL FILMS**
PHONE . . . . . . . . . . . . . . . . . . . . . . . . . . . . . 213-654-4000
FAX . . . . . . . . . . . . . . . . . . . . . . . . . . . . . . . . 213-650-6400
8255 Sunset Blvd.
Los Angeles, CA 90046-2432
TYPE       Motion Pictures
CREDITS       Carried Away - Where the Day Takes You - Past Midnight

Paul Hertzberg . . . . . . . . . . . . . . . . . . . . . . . President/CEO
Nick Gorenc . . . . . . . . . . . . . . . . . . . . . . . . . Chief Financial Officer
Lisa Hansen . . . . . . . . . . . . . . . . . . . . . . . . . Exec. Vice President
J.P. Pettinato . . . . . . . . . . . . . . . . . . . . . . . . VP, Post Production
Rick Alvarez . . . . . . . . . . . . . . . . . . . . . . . . . Dir., Development

# COMPANIES AND STAFF

**CINEVILLE INC.**
PHONE . . . . . . . . . . . . . . . . . . . . . . . . . . . . . . . . 310-394-4699
FAX . . . . . . . . . . . . . . . . . . . . . . . . . . . . . . . . . . 310-394-3052
EMAIL . . . . . . . . . . . . . . . . . . . . . . . . . . cineville@aol.com
225 Santa Monica Blvd.
Santa Monica, CA 90401
TYPE            Motion Pictures
CREDITS         Velocity of Gary - The Whole Wide World - Swimming
                with Sharks - Cafe Society- Gas Food Lodging

Carl-Jan Colpaert . . . . . . . . . . . . . . . . . . . . . . . . . Administration
Christopher Henkel . . . . . . . . . . . . . . . . . . . . . . . . Administration
Susan Shapiro . . . . . . . . . . . . . . . . . . . . . . . Pres., Production
Kathryn Arnold . . . . . . . . . . . . . . . . . . . . . . . . . . . . . . Producer
Gina Carollo . . . . . . . . . . . . . . . . . . . . . . Dir., Business Affairs
Harvey Greenberg . . . . . . . . . . . . . . . . . . . Dir., Post Production

***CINEWEST PRODUCTIONS**
PHONE . . . . . . . . . . . . . . . . . . . . . . . . . . . . . . . . 619-435-5520
FAX . . . . . . . . . . . . . . . . . . . . . . . . . . . . . . . . . . 619-435-0691
EMAIL . . . . . . . . . . . . . . . . . . . . . . . . . . cinewest@aol.com
WEBSITE . . . . . . . . . . . . . . . . . . . . . . http://www.lovealways.com
700 Adella Lane
Coronado, CA 92118
TYPE            Documentaries + Motion Pictures + Television
CREDITS         Love Always - Break of Dawn - Ballad of an Unsung Hero

Jude Pauline Eberhard . . . . . . . . . . . . . . Director/Writer/Producer
Isaac Artenstein . . . . . . . . . . . . . . . . . . . Writer/Producer/Director

**CINNAMON PRODS. INC.**
PHONE . . . . . . . . . . . . . . . . . . . . . . . . . . . . . . . . 203-221-0613
FAX . . . . . . . . . . . . . . . . . . . . . . . . . . . . . . . . . . 203-227-0840
EMAIL . . . . . . . . . . . . . . . . . . . . . . . . . cinnaprods@aol.com
19 Wild Rose Rd.
Westport, CT 06880
TYPE            Motion Pictures + Television + Documentaries
CREDITS         To Protect Mother Earth - Brainstorm - Jeremy

Joel L. Freedman . . . . . . . . . . . . . . . . . . . . CEO/Producer/Director
Alan Eisenberg . . . . . . . . . . . . . . . . . . . . . . . . . Producer/Director
Ken Golden . . . . . . . . . . . . . . . . . . . . . . . . . . . . . . . . Producer
Linda Cummins . . . . . . . . . . . . . . . . . Dir., Creative Development
John C. May . . . . . . . . . . . . . . . . . . . . . . . . Creative Executive

**CITADEL ENTERTAINMENT., LLC**
PHONE . . . . . . . . . . . . . . . . . . . . . . . . . . . . . . . . 310-887-0112
FAX . . . . . . . . . . . . . . . . . . . . . . . . . . . . . . . . . . 310-887-0187
301 North Canon Dr., Ste. 321
Beverly Hills, CA 90210
TYPE            Motion Pictures + Television
CREDITS         Citizen X - Roswell - Pandora's Clock - Rasputin - Hidden
                In America

Judy Ranan . . . . . . . . . . . . . . . . . . . . . . . . Exec. Vice President
Anne Morea . . . . . . . . . . . . . . . . . . . . . . . . VP, Business Affairs
Patti Singer . . . . . . . . . . . . . . . . . . . . . . . . . . . . VP, Production
Vicky Choy . . . . . . . . . . . . . . . . . . . . . . . . . Dir., Development

**CITY ENTERTAINMENT**
PHONE . . . . . . . . . . . . . . . . . . . . . . . . . . . . . . . . 310-273-3101
FAX . . . . . . . . . . . . . . . . . . . . . . . . . . . . . . . . . . 310-273-3676
266 1/2  S. Rexford Dr.
Beverly Hills, CA 90212
TYPE            Motion Pictures + Television + Documentaries
CREDITS         Dead Men Can't Dance - Howard Street - The Dorothy
                Dandridge Story (HBO Pictures) - Exodus 1947

Joshua D. Maurer . . . . . . . . . . . . . . . . . . . . . . . . . President
Alixandre Witlin . . . . . . . . . . . . . . . . . . . . . . . . Vice President

**CITY LIGHT FILMS**
PHONE . . . . . . . . . . . . . . . . . . . . . . . . . . . . . . . . 310-314-3500
FAX . . . . . . . . . . . . . . . . . . . . . . . . . . . . . . . . . . 310-314-3525
2110 Main St., Ste. 200
Santa Monica, CA 90405
TYPE            Motion Pictures
CREDITS         Scent of a Woman - Midnight Run

Martin Brest . . . . . . . . . . . . . . . . . . . . . . . . . Director/Producer
David J. Wally . . . . . . . . . . . . . . . . . . . . . . . . . . VP/Co-Producer
Beth Deitchman . . . . . . . . . . . . . . . . . . . . . . . . . Story Editor
Stephen Whelan . . . . . . . . . . . . . . . . . . . . Production Associate
Remy Chong . . . . . . . . . . . . . . . . . . . . . . . . . Executive Assistant
Jeff Berger . . . . . . . . . . . . . . . . . . . . . . . . Asst. to Martin Brest

**CLARK PRODS., INC., DICK**
PHONE . . . . . . . . . . . . . . . . . . . . . . . . . . . . . . . . 818-841-3003
FAX . . . . . . . . . . . . . . . . . . . . . . . . . . . . . . . . . . 818-954-8609
3003 W. Olive Ave.
Burbank, CA 91505-7811
TYPE            Television + Syndication
DEAL            CBS Entertainment/ABC Entertainment/NBC Studios
CREDITS         American Music Awards - Golden Globes - Academy of
                Country Music Awards

Dick Clark . . . . . . . . . . . . . . . . . . . . . . . . . . . . Chairman/CEO
Francis La Maina . . . . . . . . . . . . . . . . . . . . . . . President/COO
Bill Simon . . . . . . . . . . . . . . . . . . . . . . . . . . CFO/VP, Finance
Neil Stearns . . . . . . . . . . . . . . . . . . . . . . . Sr. VP, Film Group
Tom Frank . . . . . . . . . . . . . . . . Sr. VP, Television Programming
Al Schwartz . . . . . . . . . . . . . . . . . . . . . . . Sr. VP, Production
Andrew Suser . . . . . . . . . . . . . . . . . . . . Sr. VP, Business Affairs
Gene Weed . . . . . . . . . . . . . . . . . . . . . . . Sr. VP, Television
Barry Adelman . . . . . . . . . . . . . . . . . . . . . VP, TV Development
Don Wollman . . . . . . . . . . . . . . . . . . . . . . . . . . VP, Production
Michael Compton . . . . . . . . . . . . . . . . . . Dir., Business Affairs
Heidi Atherton . . . . . . . . . . . . . . Mgr., Programming & Development

**CLC PRODUCTIONS, INC.**
PHONE . . . . . . . . . . . . . . . . . . . . . . . . . . . . . . . . 310-454-0664
FAX . . . . . . . . . . . . . . . . . . . . . . . . . . . . . . . . . . 310-459-2889
WEBSITE . . . . . . . . . . . . . . . . . . . . . http://www.cathylee.com
1223 Wilshire Blvd., Ste. 404
Santa Monica, CA 90403
TYPE            Motion Pictures + Television
CREDITS         One Child - Cathy Lee Crosby Beautiful Body Workout -
                When The Cradle Falls - Lost Treasure of Dos Santos
COMMENTS        Also: Literary/Publishing. "Let the Magic Begin", the book.

Cathy Lee Crosby . . . . . . . . . . . . . . . . . . . . . . . President
Brooke Channon . . . . . . . . . . . . . . . . . . . . . VP, Development
Robbyn Benjamin . . . . . . . . . . . . . . . . . . . Dir., Development
Curt Abramson . . . . . . . . . . . . . . . . . . . . . . . . . . . . . CPA

**CLEAN BREAK PRODUCTIONS**
PHONE . . . . . . . . . . . . . . . . . . . . . . . . . . . . . . . . 818-777-5977
FAX . . . . . . . . . . . . . . . . . . . . . . . . . . . . . . . . . . 818-866-1018
MCA/Universal
100 Universal City Plaza, Bldg 507, 1B
Universal City, CA 91608
TYPE            Motion Pictures + Television
DEAL            Universal Pictures
CREDITS         The Tom Show

Tom Arnold . . . . . . . . . . . . . . . . . . . . . . . . President/Producer
Erin Simon . . . . . . . . . . . . . . . . . . . . . . . . . Head, Development
Courtney Thompson . . . . . . . . . . . . . . . . . . . Head, Production

**CLIFFORD PRODS., PATRICIA**
PHONE . . . . . . . . . . . . . . . . . . . . . . . . . . . . . . . . 310-234-5074
FAX . . . . . . . . . . . . . . . . . . . . . . . . . . . . . . . . . . 310-234-5094
Viacom Productions
10880 Wilshire Blvd., Ste. 1101
Los Angeles, CA 90024
TYPE            Motion Pictures + Television
DEAL            Viacom Productions
CREDITS         To Dance with the White Dog-A Husband, A Wife & A
                Lover - Jack Reed: A Killer Amongst Us

Patricia Clifford . . . . . . . . . . . . . . . . . . . . . . . . . . Producer
Peter Karabats . . . . . . . . . . . . . . . . . . . . . . . Dir., Development

**COBALT FILMS INTERNATIONAL**
PHONE . . . . . . . . . . . . . . . . . . . . . . . . . . . . . . . . 310-550-6150
FAX . . . . . . . . . . . . . . . . . . . . . . . . . . . . . . . . . . 310-274-5354
468 N. Camden Dr., Ste., 200
Beverly Hills, CA 90210
TYPE            Motion Pictures + Television
CREDITS         Nick & Jane

Damon F. Barone . . . . . . . . . . . . . . . . . . . . . . . . . Producer
Jason Douglas . . . . . . . . . . . . . . . . . . . . . . Business Development
Kevin Fry . . . . . . . . . . . . . . . . . . . . . . Motion Picture Development

# COMPANIES AND STAFF

**COBALT MOON**
PHONE . . . . . . . . . . . . . . . . . . . . . . . . . . . . . . . . . . 310-656-8020
FAX . . . . . . . . . . . . . . . . . . . . . . . . . . . . . . . . . . . . . 310-656-8030
EMAIL . . . . . . . . . . . . . . . . . . . . . . . . admin@cobaltmoon.com
WEBSITE . . . . . . . . . . . . . . . . . . . . http://www.cobaltmoon.com
1640 5th St.
Santa Monica, CA 90401
TYPE          Television + Interactive Multimedia
Will Hobbs . . . . . . . . . . . . . . . . . . . . . . . . . . . . . . . . . . . No Title
Matti Leshem . . . . . . . . . . . . . . . . . . . . . . . . . . . . . . . . . No Title
Joe Orr . . . . . . . . . . . . . . . . . . . . . . . . . . . . . . . . . . . . . . No Title
Tim Bennett . . . . . . . . . . . . . . . . . . . . . . . . . . . . VP, Development
Cathy Hoyle . . . . . . . . . . . . . . . . . . . . . . . . . . . Head, Production

***COBBLESTONE FILMS**
PHONE . . . . . . . . . . . . . . . . . . . . . . . . . . . . . . . . . . 310-552-1727
FAX . . . . . . . . . . . . . . . . . . . . . . . . . . . . . . . . . . . . . 310-552-1727
1484 Reeves Street, Ste. #203
Los Angeles, CA 90035
TYPE          Motion Pictures + Television + Feature Direct to Video +
              Syndication + Animation
Ben Adler . . . . . . . . . . . . . . . . . . . . . . . . . . . . . . . . . . . Producer
Jacqui Adler . . . . . . . . . . . . . . . . . . . . . . . . . . . . . . . . . Producer

**CODIKOW FILMS**
PHONE . . . . . . . . . . . . . . . . . . . . . . . . . . . . . . . . . . 310-246-9388
FAX . . . . . . . . . . . . . . . . . . . . . . . . . . . . . . . . . . . . . 310-246-9877
EMAIL . . . . . . . . . . . . . . . . . . . . . . . . . codikowflm@aol.com
WEBSITE . . . . . . . . . . . . . . . http://http://www.codikowfilms.com
8899 Beverly Blvd., Ste. 719
Los Angeles, CA 90048
TYPE          Motion Pictures + Television
CREDITS       Under The Hula Moon - To Kill For - Lonely Place - Fatal
              Instinct
Stacy Codikow . . . . . . . . . . . . . . . . . . . . . . . Producer/Writer
Lara Moon . . . . . . . . . . . . . . . . . . . . . . . . . . . Dir., Development
Kevin Vermilion . . . . . . . . . . . . . . . . . . . Asst. to Stacy Codikow
Keith Warner . . . . . . . . . . . . . . . . . . . . . . . Executive Assistant

**COFFEY/BALLANTINE**
PHONE . . . . . . . . . . . . . . . . . . . . . . . . . . . . . . . . . . 310-442-6315
FAX . . . . . . . . . . . . . . . . . . . . . . . . . . . . . . . . . . . . . 310-826-1058
WEBSITE . . . . . . . . . . . . . . . . . . http://www.coffeyballantine.com
12400 Wilshire Blvd., Ste. 1200
Santa Monica, CA 90025
TYPE          Motion Pictures + Television + Animation + Interactive
              Multimedia
DEAL          King World Productions
CREDITS       The Ren & Stimpy Show - Rugrats - Doug - Rocko's
              Modern Life - The Little Rascals Show
Jim Ballantine . . . . . . . . . . . . . . . . . . . . CEO/Exec. Producer
Vanessa Coffey . . . . . . . . . . . . . . . . . . President/Exec. Producer

***COHEN & RYAN FILMS, INC.**
PHONE . . . . . . . . . . . . . . . . . . . . . . . . . . . . . . . . . . 310-657-4034
FAX . . . . . . . . . . . . . . . . . . . . . . . . . . . . . . . . . . . . . 310-657-4121
EMAIL . . . . . . . . . . . . . . . . . . . . . . . . . . . jryanIIII@aol.com
8601 Wilshire Blvd., Ste. 604
Beverly Hills, CA 90211-3018
TYPE          Motion Pictures + Television
CREDITS       Never Met Picasso - Lie Down with Dogs
H. Jason Cohen Esq. . . . . . . . . . . . . . . . . . Co-President/Producer
Jennifer Ryan-Shearman . . . . . . . . . . . . . . . Co-President/Producer

***COHEN PRODUCTIONS INC., HERMAN**
PHONE . . . . . . . . . . . . . . . . . . . . . . . . . . . . . . . . . . 213-466-3388
FAX . . . . . . . . . . . . . . . . . . . . . . . . . . . . . . . . . . . . . 213-653-4875
650 N. Bronson Ave., #116
Hollywood, CA 90004
TYPE          Animation + Motion Pictures + Television
CREDITS       Beserk - Trog - Craze
Herman Cohen . . . . . . . . . . . . . . . . . . . . . . . . . . . . President
Didier Chatelain . . . . . . . . . . . . . . . . . . . . Exec. Vice President

***COHEN PRODUCTIONS, MARTIN B.**
PHONE . . . . . . . . . . . . . . . . . . . . . . . . . . . . . . . . . . 310-552-2958
FAX . . . . . . . . . . . . . . . . . . . . . . . . . . . . . . . . . . . . . 310-552-2958
9962 Durant Drive
Beverly Hills, CA 90212
TYPE          Motion Pictures
Martin B. Cohen . . . . . . . . . . . . . . . . . . . . . . Producer/Director
Shannon Brennan . . . . . . . . . . . . . . . . . . . . . Creative Executive
Amie Vines . . . . . . . . . . . . . . . . . . . . . Development Executive

**COLLETON COMPANY, THE**
PHONE . . . . . . . . . . . . . . . . . . . . . . . . . . . . . . . . . . 818-560-7190
500 S. Buena Vista St., Anim. 2F-4
Burbank, CA 91521
TYPE          Motion Pictures
DEAL          Touchstone Pictures
CREDITS       Renaissance Man
Sara Colleton . . . . . . . . . . . . . . . . . . . . . . . . . . . President
Jonah Brown . . . . . . . . . . . . . . . . . . . . . . . . VP, Development
Yolanda Person . . . . . . . . . . . . . . . . . . . Asst. to Sara Colleton

**COLMANO PRODUCTIONS, MARINO**
PHONE . . . . . . . . . . . . . . . . . . . . . . . . . . . . . . . . . . 818-764-8580
FAX . . . . . . . . . . . . . . . . . . . . . . . . . . . . . . . . . . . . . 818-764-5752
EMAIL . . . . . . . . . . . . . . . . . . . . . . . . . . macbravo@loop.com
WEBSITE . . . . . . . . . . . . . . . http://www.zpub.com/bus/bravo/
7120 Alcove Ave.
N. Hollywood, CA 91605
TYPE          Documentaries + Feature Direct to Video + Motion
              Pictures + Television
CREDITS       Reservoirs of Strength (PBS) - End of the Rainbow - The
              Danger Zone (Home Video)
COMMENTS      Also:  Promotionals
Marino Colmano . . . . . . . . . . . . . . President/Producer/Director/Writer
Michael Britton . . . . . . . . . . . . . . Charge of Production/Producer/Writer

**COLOMBY/KEATON**
PHONE . . . . . . . . . . . . . . . . . . . . . . . . . . . . . . . . . . 310-399-8881
FAX . . . . . . . . . . . . . . . . . . . . . . . . . . . . . . . . . . . . . 310-392-1323
2110 Main St., Ste. 302
Santa Monica, CA 90405
TYPE          Motion Pictures
Harry Colomby . . . . . . . . . . . . . . . . . . . . . . . . . . . Producer
Michael Keaton . . . . . . . . . . . . . . . . . . . . . . . . . . . Producer
Jennifer Keohane . . . . . . . . . . . . . . . . . . . . Dir., Development
Susan Johnson . . . . . . . . . . . . . . . . . . . . . Executive Assistant

**COLOSSAL PICTURES**
PHONE . . . . . . . . . . . . . . . . . . . . . . . . . . . . . . . . . . 415-643-1799
FAX . . . . . . . . . . . . . . . . . . . . . . . . . . . . . . . . . . . . . 415-643-1699
WEBSITE . . . . . . . . . . . . . . . . . . . . http://www.colossal.com
2800 Third St.
San Francisco, CA 94107
TYPE          Motion Pictures + Interactive Multimedia + Animation +
              Television
CREDITS       MTV's Liquid TV
COMMENTS      Also: Special Effects.
Drew Takahashi . . . . . . . . . . . . . . Chairman/Chief Creative Officer
Jan Bauman . . . . . . . . . . . . . . . . . . . . . Chief Financial Officer
Jana Canellos . . . . . . . . . . . . . . . . . . . . . . . Executive Producer

# COMPANIES AND STAFF

## COLUMBIA PICTURES
PHONE . . . . . . . . . . . . . . . . . . . . . . . . . . . . . . . 310-244-4000
FAX . . . . . . . . . . . . . . . . . . . . . . . . . . . . . . . . . 310 244 2626
WEBSITE . . . . . . . . . . . . . . . . . . . . . http://www.spe.sony.com/
10202 W. Washington Blvd.
Culver City, CA 90232-3195

TYPE       Motion Pictures
COMMENTS    See also Columbia TriStar Motion Pict. Group, & Sony Picts.

Lucy Fisher . . . . . . . . . . Vice Chairman, Columbia TriStar Motion Picts. Group
Gareth Wigan . . . . . . . . Co-Vice Chair, Columbia TriStar Motion Picts. Group
Kenneth Lemberger . . . . . . . President, Columbia TriStar Motion Picts. Group
Amy Pascal . . . . . . . . . . . . . . . . . . . . . . . . . . . . . President
Christopher Lee . . . . . . . . . . . . . . . . . . . . . . Pres., Production
Liz Aschenbrenner . . . . . . . . . . . . . . . . Exec. VP, Legal Affairs
Amy Baer . . . . . . . . . . . . . . . . . . . . . . . Exec. VP, Production
Robert Geary . . . . . . . . . . . . . . . . . . Exec. VP, Business Affairs
Bryan Lee . . . . . . . . . . . Exec. VP, Business Affairs & Operations
Lauren Lloyd . . . . . . . . . . . . . . . . . . . . . Exec. VP, Production
Doug Belgrad . . . . . . . . . . . . . . . . . . . . . . Sr. VP, Production
Michael Costigan . . . . . . . . . . . . . . . . . . . . Sr. VP, Production
Jon Gibson . . . . . . . . . . . . . . . . . . . Sr. VP, Business Affairs
Gary Hirsch . . . . . . . . . . . . . . . . . . . Sr. VP, Business Affairs
Alan Krieger . . . . . . . . . . . . . . . . . . . Sr. VP, Business Affairs
John S. Levy . . . . . . . . . . . . . . . . . . . Sr. VP, Business Affairs
Matthew Tolmach . . . . . . . . . . . . . . . . . . . . Sr. VP, Production
Roger Toll . . . . . . . . . . . . . . . . . . . . . Sr. VP, Legal Affairs
Luis Allen . . . . . . . . . . . . . . . . . . . . . . . VP, Legal Affairs
Deborah Bruenell . . . . . . . . . . . . . . . . . . . . VP, Legal Affairs
Lori Goldklang-Furie . . . . . . . . . . . . . . . . . . . . VP, Production
Mark B. Horowitz . . . . . . . . VP, Business Affairs Administration
Carrie Richman . . . . . . . . . . . . . . . . . . . . . . . VP, Production
Michelle Schultz . . . . . . . . . . . . . . . . . . . . VP, Legal Affairs
Thomas Stack . . . . . . . . . . VP, Business Affairs & Contract Administration
Ricky Strauss . . . . . . . . . . . . . . . . . . . . . . . VP, Prodution
Mark Wyman . . . . . . . . . . . . . . . . . . . VP, Business Affairs
Ben Cosgrove . . . . . . . . . . . . . . . . . . . . . Dir., Development
Susan Avallon . . . . . . . . . . . . . . . . . . . . . Creative Executive
Andrea Giannetti . . . . . . . . . . . . . . . . . . . Creative Executive
Walter Hamada . . . . . . . . . . . . . . . . . . . . Creative Executive
Rachel O'Connor . . . . . . . . . . . . . . . . . . . Creative Executive
Grace Benn . . . . . . . . . . . . . . . . . . . . . . . . . Story Editor

## COLUMBIA TRISTAR MOTION PICTURE GROUP
PHONE . . . . . . . . . . . . . . . . . . . . . . . . . . . . . . . 310-244-4000
FAX . . . . . . . . . . . . . . . . . . . . . . . . . . . . . . . . . 310-244-2626
10202 W. Washington Blvd.
Culver City, CA 90232
COMMENTS    Also: Columbia Picts. & Sony Picts.

Lucy Fisher . . . . . . . . . . . . . . . . . . . . . . . . . . . Vice Chairman
Gareth Wigan . . . . . . . . . . . . . . . . . . . . . . . Co-Vice Chairman
Kenneth Lemberger . . . . . . . . . . . . . . . . . . . . . . . President
Gary Martin . . . . . . . . . . . . . . . . . Pres., Production Administration
Jimmy Honore . . . . . . . . . . . . . . . . . Exec. VP, Post Production
Paul Smith . . . . . . . . . . . . . . . . . . . . . . Exec. Vice President
Bill Ewing . . . . . . . . . . . . . . . . . Sr. VP, Production Administration
Ray Zimmerman . . . . . . . . . . . . . . Sr. VP, Production Administration
Pete Corral . . . . . . . . . . . . . . . . . . VP, Production Administration
Diana Hawkins . . . . . . . . . . . . . . . . . . . VP, Creative Affairs
Kathy McDermott . . . . . . . . . . . . . . . . . VP, Production Administration
Russ Paris . . . . . . . . . . . . . . . . . . . . . . . VP, Post Production
Karen Moy . . . . . . . . . . . . . . . . . . . Exec. Dir., Creative Affairs
Suzanne Potts . . . . . . . . . . . . . . . . . . . . Creative Executive

## COLUMBIA TRISTAR TELEVISION
PHONE . . . . . . . . . . . . . . . . . . . . . . . . . . . . . . . 310-202-1234
FAX . . . . . . . . . . . . . . . . . . . . . . . . . . . . . . . . . 310-244-2626
WEBSITE . . . . . . . . . . . . . . . . . . . . . http://www.spe.sony.com/
9336 W. Washington Blvd.
Culver City, CA 90232

TYPE       Television
Jon Feltheimer . . . . . . . . . . . President, Columbia TriStar Television Group
Andrew J. Kaplan . . . . . . . . . . Exec. VP, Columbia TriStar Television Group
Eric Tannenbaum . . . . . . . . . . . . . . . . . . . . . . . . . President
Helene Michaels . . . . . . . . . . . . . . . . . . . . . Exec. Vice President
Edward Lammi . . . . . . . . . . . . . . . . . . . . Exec. VP, Production
Sander Schwartz . . . . . . . . . Exec. VP, Children's Programming
Sandra Stern . . . . . . . . . . . . . . . Exec. VP, Business Affairs
Helen Verno . . . . . . . . . . . . . . Exec. VP, Movies & Miniseries
Jeanie Bradley . . . . . . . . . . . . . . . . . . . . Sr. VP, Programming
Richard Glosser . . . . . . . . . . . . . . Sr. VP, Interactive Programming
Kim Haswell . . . . . . . . . . . . . . . . Sr. VP, Comedy Development
Ruth-Ann Huvane . . . . . . . . . . . . . . . . . . . . Sr. VP, Talent
Beverly Nix . . . . . . . . . . . . . . . . . . . Sr. VP, Business Affairs
Sarah Timberman . . . . . . . . . . . . . . . Sr. VP, Drama Development
Peggy Becker . . . . . . . . . . . . . . . . . VP, Animation Production
Carolyn Bernstein . . . . . . . . . . . . . . . . VP, Drama Development
Christina Friedgen . . . . . . . . . . . . . . . . . . . VP, Post Production
Amy S. Gittelsohn . . . . . . . . . . . . . . . . . . VP, Business Affairs
Bob Higgins . . . . . . . . . . VP, Creative Affairs, Children's Programming
David Holman . . . . . . . . . . . . . . . . VP, Production Operations
Robert Hunka . . . . . . . . . . . . . . . . . . . . . . VP, TV Music
Michael Kohn . . . . . . . . . . . . . . . . . . . . VP, Business Affairs
Joanne Mazzu . . . . . . . . . . . . . . . . . . . . VP, Business Affairs
John A. Morrissey . . . . . . . . . . . . . . . . . . VP, Film Production
Winifred White Neisser . . . . . . . . . . . . VP, Movies & Miniseries
John Spector . . . . . . . . . . . . . . . . . . . . . . . VP, Production
Phil Squyres . . . . . . . . . . . . . . . . . . . VP, Technical Operations
Jamie Erlicht . . . . . . . . . . . . . . . . . Dir., Current Programming
Jocelyn Freid . . . . . . . . . . . . . . . . Dir., Comedy Development
Danielle S. Stokdyk . . . . . . . . . . . . . . Dir., Current Programming
Susan Wycoff . . . . . . . . . . . . . . . . . Dir., Current Programming
Laura Levinsky . . . . . . . . . . . . . . . . . . . . Mgr., TV Music

## COMEDY CENTRAL
PHONE . . . . . . . . . . . . . . . . . . . . 212-767-8600/310-201-9515
FAX . . . . . . . . . . . . . . . . . . . . . . 212-767-8592/310-201-9387
WEBSITE . . . . . . . . . . . . . . . . . . . . . http://comedycentral.com
1775 Broadway
New York, NY 10019

TYPE       Television
CREDITS     Dr. Katz- The Daily Show - South Park - Viva Variety
COMMENTS    Also: 2049 Century Park East, Ste. 2295, LA 90067

Doug Herzog . . . . . . . . . . . . . . . . . . . . . . . . . President/CEO
John Cucci . . . . . . . . . . . . . . . . . . . . . CFO/Sr. Vice President
Eileen Katz . . . . . . . . . . . . . . . . . . . . . Sr. VP, Programming
Joan Aceste . . . . . . . . . . . . . . . . . VP, Legal & Business Affairs
Kent Alterman . . . . . . . . . . . . . . . . . . . . . VP, Development
Michele Ganeless . . . . . . . . . . . . . . . . . . . . VP, Programming
Lauren Gray . . . . . . . . . . . . . . . . . . . . . . . VP, Production
Beth Hisler . . . . . . . . . . . . . . . . . . . . VP, Human Resources
Larry Lieberman . . . . . . VP, Strategic Planning/New Business Development
Deborah Liebling . . . . . . . . VP, West Coast Development & Production (LA)
Shari Patrick . . . . . . . . . VP/General Counsel, Legal & Business Affairs
Chris Pergola . . . . . . . . . . . . . . . . . . . . VP/Asst. Controller
Jim Walley . . . . . . . . . . . . . . . . . . VP, Information Technology
Dave Serwatka . . . . . . . . . . West Coast Production & Development
Patty Newburger . . . . . . . . . . . . . . . . . Dir., Corporate Affairs
Frank Quinn . . . . . . . . . . . . . . . . . Dir., New Business Development

## COMMON CREED ENTERTAINMENT CORP.
PHONE . . . . . . . . . . . . . . . . . . . . . . . . . . . . . . . 310-281-7084
FAX . . . . . . . . . . . . . . . . . . . . . . . . . . . . . . . . . 949-955-3556
EMAIL . . . . . . . . . . . . . . . . . . . . . . . comcreed@aol.com
269 S. Beverly Dr., No. 202
Beverly Hills, CA 90212

TYPE       Motion Pictures + Television
CREDITS     Star Trek 4-6 - High Incident - Mighty Joe Young - Left Behind

Ralph Winter . . . . . . . . . . . . . . . . . . . . . . . . . . . . Producer
Jeff Weber . . . . . . . . . . . . . . . . . . . . Producer (949-955-3555)
Holly Schiffer . . . . . . . . . . . . . . . . . . . . . . . . . . Assistant

# COMPANIES AND STAFF

***COMMON GROUND ENTERTAINMENT**
PHONE . . . . . . . . . . . . . . . . . . . . . . . . . . . . . . . . . . . . . 310-274-5186
FAX . . . . . . . . . . . . . . . . . . . . . . . . . . . . . . . . . . . . . . . . 310-274-3850
9107 Wilshire Blvd., #500
Beverly Hills, CA 90210
TYPE  Motion Pictures + Television
DEAL  Twentieth Century Fox-Fox 2000 (LA)/Fox Animation Studios
CREDITS Bram Stoker's Dracula - Hook - Contact - Mary Shelley's Frankenstien - Muppet Treasure Island
James V. Hart . . . . . . . . . . . . . . . . . . . . . . . . . . . . Writer/Producer
Valerie Kerns . . . . . . . . . . . . . . . . . . . . . . . . . . President/Producer
Manuel Oteyza . . . . . . . . . . . . . . . . . . . . . . . . . . . . Story Editor

**COMMUNICATIONS CORP. OF AMERICA**
PHONE . . . . . . . . . . . . . . . . . . . . . . . . . . . . . . . . . . 773-348-0001
2501 N. Sheffield
Chicago, IL 60614-2216
TYPE  Motion Pictures + Television + Documentaries + Interactive Multimedia
CREDITS Last Full Measure of Devotion - State of the City (Chicago)
COMMENTS Political Debates for TV & major special events. Documentary Film Crews for German TV-Chicago/NY/Miami.
Fred Strauss . . . . . . . . . . . . . . . . . . . . . . . . . . . Executive Producer

***COMSKY GROUP PRODUCTIONS**
PHONE . . . . . . . . . . . . . . . . . . . . . . . . . . . . . . . . . . 310-278-5575
FAX . . . . . . . . . . . . . . . . . . . . . . . . . . . . . . . . . . . . . . . 310-278-3797
1027 Cove Way
Beverly Hills, CA 90210
TYPE  Motion Pictures + Television + Syndication
CREDITS Pandora's Clock - Medusa's Child
COMMENTS Also:  Theater.
Cynthia Comsky . . . . . . . . . . . . . . . . . . . . . . . . . Executive Producer
David Comsky . . . . . . . . . . . . . . . . . . . . . . . . . . . Executive Producer

**CONCORDE/NEW HORIZONS CORP.**
PHONE . . . . . . . . . . . . . . . . . . . . . . . . . . . . . . . . . . 310-820-6733
FAX . . . . . . . . . . . . . . . . . . . . . . . . . . . . . . . . . . . . . . . 310-207-6816
11600 San Vicente Blvd.
Los Angeles, CA 90049
TYPE  Motion Pictures
CREDITS Star Quest - Carnosaur - Bloodfist 1-8 - Brothers In Arms - Black Scorpion
Roger Corman . . . . . . . . . . . . . . . . . . . . . . . . . . . . . President/CEO
Ryan Kirk . . . . . . . . . . . . . . . . . . . . . . . . Worldwide Music Operations
Julie Corman . . . . . . . . . . . . . . . . . . . . . . . . . . Exec. VP/Producer
Cheryl Parnell . . . . . . . . . . . . . . . . . . . . . . . . Exec. Vice President
Frances Doel . . . . . . . . . . . . . . . . . . . . . . . . . . . VP, Development
Jan Glaser . . . . . . . . . . . . . . . . . . . . . . . . . . . . VP, Casting, CSA
Goly Jamshidi . . . . . . . . . . . . . . . . . . . . . . . . . . . . . VP, Finance
Edward Reilly Jr. . . . . . . . . . . . . . . . . . . VP, Business & Legal Affairs
Marta Mobley . . . . . . . . . . . . . . . . . . . . . . . . . . . . Head, Studio

**CONCOURSE PRODS.**
PHONE . . . . . . . . . . . . . . . . . . . . . . . . . . . . . . . . . . 310-306-0502
EMAIL . . . . . . . . . . . . . . . . . . . . . . . . . . . concourse@earthlink.net
171 Pier Ave. #354
Santa Monica, CA 90405
TYPE  Motion Pictures + Television + Syndication
CREDITS For the Boys - Intersection - On Golden Pond - Crime of the Century
Mark Rydell . . . . . . . . . . . . . . . . . . . . . . . . . . Producer/Director
Dustin Castleberry . . . . . . . . . . . . . . . . . . . . . . . . . Development

**CONNECTION III ENTERTAINMENT CORP.**
PHONE . . . . . . . . . . . . . . . . . . . . . . . . . . . . . . . . . . 213-653-3400
8489 W. Third St.
Los Angeles, CA 90048
TYPE  Motion Pictures + Television
CREDITS Phat Beach - What About Your Friends? - The Garage Club
Cleveland O'Neal . . . . . . . . . . . . . . . . . . . . . . . . . . . . Producer
Donna Shirazi . . . . . . . . . . . . . . . Assoc. Producer/Dir., Development
Mahsa Shirazi . . . . . . . . . . . . . . . . . . . . . . . . Production Supervisor

**CONSTANTIN FILM DEVELOPMENT INC.**
PHONE . . . . . . . . . . . . . . . . . . . . . . . . . . . . . . . . . . 310-247-0300
FAX . . . . . . . . . . . . . . . . . . . . . . . . . . . . . . . . . . . . . . . 310-247-0305
9200 Sunset Blvd., Ste. 730
Los Angeles, CA 90069
TYPE  Motion Pictures
CREDITS Smilla's Sense of Snow - House of Spirits - Last Exit to Brooklyn - Name of the Rose
Bernd Eichinger . . . . . . . . . . . . . . . . . . . . . . . . . . . . . . No Title
Russel Fischer . . . . . . . . . . . . . . . . . . . . . . . . . . . . . . . No Title
Lisa Kregness . . . . . . . . . . . . . . . . . . . . . . . . . . . . . . . No Title
Robert Kulzer . . . . . . . . . . . . . . . . . . . . . . . . . . . . . . . No Title
Marsha Metz . . . . . . . . . . . . . . . . . . . . . . . . . . . . . . . . No Title
Cynthia Pruett . . . . . . . . . . . . . . . . . . . . . . . . . . . . . . . No Title

**COOK FILMS**
PHONE . . . . . . . . . . . . . . . . . . . . . . . . . . . . . . . . . . 213-463-6020
FAX . . . . . . . . . . . . . . . . . . . . . . . . . . . . . . . . . . . . . . . 213-463-5009
EMAIL . . . . . . . . . . . . . . . . . . . . . . . . . . . . cookfilms@aol.com
2830 Belden Drive
Los Angeles, CA 90068
TYPE  Motion Pictures + Television + Documentaries
CREDITS The Boys Next Door - Geronimo - The January Man
Chris Cook . . . . . . . . . . . . . . . . . . . . . . . . . . . . . . . . Producer

**COPP AND GOODMAN**
PHONE . . . . . . . . . . . . . . . . . . . . . . . . . . . . . . . . . . 310-288-4545
CAA
9830 Wilshire Blvd.
Beverly Hills, CA 90212
TYPE  Motion Pictures + Television
CREDITS Captain Zoom - Flying Blind - Dream-On - Wings - Team Knight Rider - Spy Girls
Rick Copp . . . . . . . . . . . . . . . . . . . . . . . . . . . . Writer/Producer
David A. Goodman . . . . . . . . . . . . . . . . . . . . . . . . Writer/Producer

**COPPER SKY PRODUCTIONS**
PHONE . . . . . . . . . . . . . . . . . . . . . . . . . . . . . . . . . . 310-827-9766
FAX . . . . . . . . . . . . . . . . . . . . . . . . . . . . . . . . . . . . . . . 310-306-6039
110 Topsail Mall
Marina del Rey, CA 90292
TYPE  Motion Pictures + Television
DEAL  Warner Bros. Pictures
CREDITS With Honors
Abe Milrad . . . . . . . . . . . . . . . . . . . . . . . . . . . . . . . . Producer
B.J. Markel . . . . . . . . . . . . . . . . . . . . . . . . . VP, Creative Affairs
Sid Plavin . . . . . . . . . . . . . . . . . . . . . . . . . . . . . . VP, Finance
Adrienne Armstrong . . . . . . . . . . . . . . . . . . . . Dir., Development

**CORT/MADDEN COMPANY, THE**
PHONE . . . . . . . . . . . . . . . . . . . . . . . . . . . . . . . . . . 213-956-5884
FAX . . . . . . . . . . . . . . . . . . . . . . . . . . . . . . . . . . . . . . . 213-862-1110
5555 Melrose Ave., Chevalier Bldg. 203
Hollywood, CA 90038
TYPE  Motion Pictures + Television
DEAL  Paramount Pictures- Motion Picture Group
CREDITS Odd Couple II - Out of Towners
Robert Cort . . . . . . . . . . . . . . . . . . . . . . . . . . . . . . . . Producer
David Madden . . . . . . . . . . . . . . . . . . . . . . . . . . . . . . . Producer
Keri Selig . . . . . . . . . . . . . . . . . . . . . . . . . . . . . Vice President
Scarlett Lacey . . . . . . . . . . . . . . . . . . . . . . . . Creative Executive
Chris Shellen . . . . . . . . . . . . . . . . . . . . . . . . . Creative Executive
Edgar Cayago . . . . . . . . . . . . . . . . . . . . . . . . . . . . . . . Creative
Eric Hetzel . . . . . . . . . . . . . . . . . . . . . . . . . . . . . . . . Creative
Patty MacDonald . . . . . . . . . . . . . . . . . . . . . . . . . . . . Creative
Catherine Purves . . . . . . . . . . . . . . . . . . . . . . . . . . . . Creative

**CORYMORE PRODS.**
PHONE . . . . . . . . . . . . . . . . . . . . . . . . . . . . . . . . . . 818-777-1181
FAX . . . . . . . . . . . . . . . . . . . . . . . . . . . . . . . . . . . . . . . 818-866-1573
Universal Studios
100 Universal City Plaza, Bldg 426
Universal City, CA 91608
TYPE  Television
DEAL  Universal Television & Networks Group
CREDITS Murder She Wrote - Mrs. 'Arris Goes To Paris - Positive Moves - Mrs. Santa Claus - South by Southwest - Mrs. Pollifax
Angela Lansbury . . . . . . . . . . . . . . . . . . . . . . . Actress/Producer
David Shaw . . . . . . . . . . . . . . . . . . . . . . . . . . . . . . . President
Anthony Shaw . . . . . . . . . . . . . . . . . . . . . . . . . . . . . . Director

## COSGROVE-MEURER PRODS.
PHONE . . . . . . . . . . . . . . . . . . . . . . . . . . . . . . . . . 818-843-5600
FAX . . . . . . . . . . . . . . . . . . . . . . . . . . . . . . . . . . . 818-843-8585
WEBSITE . . . . . . . . . . . . . . . . . . . . . . http://www.unsolved.com
4303 W. Verdugo Ave.
Burbank, CA 91505

TYPE            Motion Pictures + Television
CREDITS         Voice From The Grave - A Friend's Betrayal - Unsolved
                Mysteries - The Inheritance

Terry Meurer . . . . . . . . . . . . . . . . . . . . . . . . . . . . . . . President
John Cosgrove . . . . . . . . . . . . . . . . . . . . Chief Executive Officer
Rebecca Whittington . . . . . . . . . . . . . . . . . . . . . VP, Development
Jolene Dodson . . . . . . . . . . . . . . . . . . . . . . . . . Dir., Development
Heather Hecker . . . . . . . . . . . . . . . . . . . . . Development Associate
Christine Lenig . . . . . . . . . . . . . . Asst. to T. Meurer & J. Cosgrove

## COSSETTE PRODUCTIONS
PHONE . . . . . . . . . . . . . . . . . . . . . . . . . . . . . . . . . 310-278-3366
FAX . . . . . . . . . . . . . . . . . . . . . . . . . . . . . . . . . . . 310-278-6587
8899 Beverly Blvd., Ste. 100
Los Angeles, CA 90048

TYPE            Motion Pictures + Television + Documentaries
CREDITS         Grammy Awards - The Scarlet Pimpernel
COMMENTS        Also: Theatre

Pierre Cossette . . . . . . . . . . . . . . . . . . . . . . . . . . . . Chairman
John Cossette . . . . . . . . . . . . . . . . . . . . . . . . . . . . . President
Mary Cossette . . . . . . . . . . . . . . . . . . . . . VP, Creative Affairs
Andrea Dossa . . . . . . . . . . . . . . . . . . . . Production Coordinator
Maureen Meany . . . . . . . . . . . . . . . . . . . . . Executive Assistant

## COWLIP PRODUCTIONS
PHONE . . . . . . . . . . . . . . . . . . . . . . . . . . . . . . . . . 818-954-3403
FAX . . . . . . . . . . . . . . . . . . . . . . . . . . . . . . . . . . . 818-954-4912
300 Television Pl, Bldg. 136 #105
Burbank, CA 91505

TYPE            Television
DEAL            Warner Bros. Television Productions
CREDITS         Sisters - An Early Frost (Emmy) - The Love She Sought
                (MOW)

Ron Cowen . . . . . . . . . . . . . . . . . . . . . . . . . . Executive Producer
Daniel Lipman . . . . . . . . . . . . . . . . . . . . . . . . Executive Producer
Adam Newman . . . . . . . . . . . . . . Dir., Development (818-954-2766)

## COYOTE PASS PRODUCTIONS
PHONE . . . . . . . . . . . . . . . . . . . . . . . . . . . . . . . . . 626-794-4463
FAX . . . . . . . . . . . . . . . . . . . . . . . . . . . . . . . . . . . 626-798-9930
EMAIL . . . . . . . . . . . . . . . . . . . . . . . coyotep@earthlink.net
WEBSITE . . . . . . . . . . . . . . http://home.earthlink.net/~coyotep/
P.O. Box 6318
Altadena, CA 91003-6318

TYPE            Motion Pictures + Television
CREDITS         Out of Order - Beneath The News - Juan For All - Who
                The Hell Is Chip Glass?
COMMENTS        Specializing in Latino Char. & Themes

Beth Dolan . . . . . . . . . . . . . . . . . . . . . . . . . . Executive Producer
Luis Remesar . . . . . . . . . . . . . . . . . . . . . . . . . Executive Producer

## CPC ENTERTAINMENT
PHONE . . . . . . . . . . . . . . . . . 310-652-8194/212-554-6447
FAX . . . . . . . . . . . . . . . . . . . . . . . . . . . . . . . . . . . 310-652-4998
EMAIL . . . . . . . . . . . . . . . . . . . . . chane@compuserve.com
840 N. Larrabee St., Ste. 2322
Los Angeles, CA 90069-4528

TYPE            Motion Pictures + Television + Animation
CREDITS         In the Eyes of a Stranger - The Gourmet Kid - Capital
                Offense
COMMENTS        ALSO: 353 W. 57th St. #2411, New York NY
                10019-3100

Peggy Howard Chane . . . . . . . . . . . . . . . . . . . Producer/Director
Meri Howard . . . . . . . . . . . . . . . . . . . Exec. VP, Creative Affairs
Sylvie De La Riviere . . . . . . . . . . . . . . . VP, Development (Paris)
Kirsten Zauber . . . . . . . . . . . . . . . . . . . . . . . Mgr., Development

## CRAVEN FILMS, WES
PHONE . . . . . . . . . . . . . . . . . . . . . . . . . . . . . . . . . 818-752-0197
FAX . . . . . . . . . . . . . . . . . . . . . . . . . . . . . . . . . . . 818-752-1789
11846 Ventura Blvd., Ste. 208
Studio City, CA 91604

TYPE            Interactive Multimedia + Television + Motion Pictures
DEAL            Miramax Films/Dimension Films
CREDITS         Scream- Scream 2

Wes Craven . . . . . . . . . . . . . . . . . . . . . . . . . . . . . . . Director
Marianne Maddalena . . . . . . . . . . . . . . . . . President/Producer
Alix Taylor . . . . . . . . . . . . . . . . . . . . . . . . . . . VP, Development
David Baden . . . . . . . . . . . . . . . . . . . . . Asst. to Mr. Craven
Jana Conley . . . . . . . . . . . . . . . . . . . . Asst. to Ms. Maddalena

## CREATIVE GROUP PRODS., INC.
PHONE . . . . . . . . . . . . . . . . . . . . . . . . . . . . . . . . . 818-508-8212
FAX . . . . . . . . . . . . . . . . . . . . . . . . . . . . . . . . . . . 818-506-4184
EMAIL . . . . . . . . . . . . . . . . . . . . . . . . . . . pmkla@aol.com
WEBSITE . . . . . . . . . . . . . . . . . . . . http://www.filmlinks.com
6126 Rhodes Ave.
North Hollywood, CA 91606

TYPE            Motion Pictures + Television
CREDITS         Miles From Home - Key Exchange - The Gingerbread Man
                - Looking for an Echo - Tinseltown
COMMENTS        Feature film finance, production & line producing services.

Paul Kurta . . . . . . . . . . . . . . . . . . . . . . . . . Producer/President
Jacqueline Burnham-Kurta . . . . . . . . . . . . . . . . . Vice President
Tim Christenson . . . . . . . . . . . . . . . . . . . . . Production Executive

## CREATIVE ROAD CORP.
PHONE . . . . . . . . . . . . . . . . . . . . . . . . . . . . . . . . . 213-658-7224
FAX . . . . . . . . . . . . . . . . . . . . . . . . . . . . . . . . . . . 213-658-7228
8222 Melrose Ave., Ste. 301
Los Angeles, CA 90046

TYPE            Motion Pictures + Television + Interactive Multimedia
CREDITS         Metalbeast - Tales from the Darkside - Double Revenge -
                Hot Flashes

T.J. Castronovo . . . . . . . . . . . . . . . . . . . . . . . . . . . President
Michael Carazza . . . . . . . . . . . . . . . . . . Chief Financial Officer
Ray Rappa . . . . . . . . . . . . . . . . . . . . . . . VP, Business Affairs

## CREW PRODS., DICK
PHONE . . . . . . . . . . . . . . . . . . . . . . . . . . . . . . . . . 213-851-1466
FAX . . . . . . . . . . . . . . . . . . . . . . . . . . . . . . . . . . . 213-851-7459
EMAIL . . . . . . . . . . . . . . . . . . . . . . . . . . . . sfe@scifi.com
WEBSITE . . . . . . . . . . . . . . http://www.scifi.com/entertainment
3575 Cahuenga Blvd. West, Ste. 630
Los Angeles, CA 90068

TYPE            Television
CREDITS         Masters of Fantasy - Sci-Fi Entertainment (SciFi Channel)
COMMENTS        Currently produces Sci-Fi Channel Shows.

Dick Crew . . . . . . . . . . . . . . . . . . . . . . . . . . Executive Producer
Lee Olson . . . . . . . . . . . . . . . . . . . . . . . . . . . . . . Sr. Producer
David DiSarro . . . . . . . . . . . . . . . . . . . . . . Associate Producer
Curtis Paine . . . . . . . . . . . . . . . . . . . . . . . . . . . . . Producer
John Platt . . . . . . . . . . . . . . . . . . . . . . . . . . . . . . . Producer
Maureen O'Keefe . . . . . . . . . . . . . . . . . . Production Coordinator
Steve Sabellico . . . . . . . . . . . . . . . . . . . Production Coordinator

## CROSBY/LEVY CO., THE
PHONE . . . . . . . . . . . . . . . . . . . . . . . . . . . . . . . . . 310-360-0110
FAX . . . . . . . . . . . . . . . . . . . . . . . . . . . . . . . . . . . 310-360-9990
8500 Melrose Ave., Ste. 215
Los Angeles, CA 90069

TYPE            Motion Pictures + Television + Interactive Multimedia
CREDITS         Eye For An Eye - Prelude To A Kiss - Gardens of Stone -
                Gotcha - Article 99
COMMENTS        Also: Management company.

John Crosby . . . . . . . . . . . . . . . . . . . . . . . . Producer/Manager
Michael I. Levy . . . . . . . . . . . . . . . . . . . . . . Producer/Manager
Zack Estrin . . . . . . . . . . . . . . . . . . . . . . . . . . VP, Development
Stephen F. Macias . . . . . . . . . . . . . . . . . . . Creative Assistant

## CROWN INTERNATIONAL PICTURES
PHONE . . . . . . . . . . . . . . . . . . . . . . . . . . . . . . . . . 310-657-6700
FAX . . . . . . . . . . . . . . . . . . . . . . . . . . . . . . . . . . . 310-657-4489
8701 Wilshire Blvd.
Beverly Hills, CA 90211

TYPE            Motion Pictures
CREDITS         My Mom's a Werewolf - My Tutor - My Chauffeur - Lena's
                Holiday

Mark Tenser . . . . . . . . . . . . . . . . . . . . . . . . . . . President/CEO
Marilyn J. Tenser . . . . . . . . . . . . . . . . . . . . . . . . . . Producer
Scott E. Schwimer . . . . . . . . . . . . . . . . . . . Sr. Vice President

# COMPANIES AND STAFF

**CRYSTAL BEACH ENTERTAINMENT**
PHONE . . . . . . . . . . . . . . . . . . . . . . . . . . . . . 310-840-8358
FAX . . . . . . . . . . . . . . . . . . . . . . . . . . . . . . . 310-840-8427
9050 W. Washington Blvd., CB2103
Culver City, CA 90232

| | |
|---|---|
| TYPE | Motion Pictures + Television |
| DEAL | Columbia TriStar Television |
| CREDITS | Medicine Ball - Gabriel's Fire - Under Suspicion - Abandoned and Deceived |

Robert Lieberman . . . . . . . . . . . . . . . . . . . . . . . . President
Marilu Henner . . . . . . . . . . . . . . . . . . . . . . . . . President
Elizabeth Carney . . . . . . . . . . . . . VP, Production/Development
John Priemer . . . . . . . . . . . . . . . . . . . . . Executive Assistant

**CRYSTAL PYRAMID PRODUCTIONS**
PHONE . . . . . . . . . . . . . . . . . . . . . . . . . . . . . 310-822-8434
FAX . . . . . . . . . . . . . . . . . . . . . . . . . . . . . . . 310-822-9491
EMAIL . . . . . . . . . . . . . . . . . . . . . . . . . klc1313@aol.com
8 Avenue 23 #201
Venice, CA 90291

| | |
|---|---|
| TYPE | Documentaries + Television + Syndication |
| COMMENTS | International Consulting for Broadcast & Cable. Also: Internet Content Provider. |

Karen Lee Copeland . . . . . . . . . . . . . . . President/Exec. Producer

***CTONIC FLIKS**
PHONE . . . . . . . . . . . . . . . . . . . 213-957-7824/213-957-7825
FAX . . . . . . . . . . . . . . . . . . . . . . . . . . . . . . . 213-957-8735
EMAIL . . . . . . . . . . . . . . . . . . . . . . . . ctonic@yahoo.com
5540 Hollywood Blvd., 2nd Floor
Los Angeles, CA 90028

| | |
|---|---|
| TYPE | Motion Pictures + Television |

Catalaine Knell . . . . . . . . . . . . . . . . . . . . . . . . . Producer

**CUDDIHY, CHRISTOPHER A.**
PHONE . . . . . . . . . . . . . . . . . . . . . . . . . . . . . 310-396-2455
FAX . . . . . . . . . . . . . . . . . . . . . . . . . . . . . . . 310-396-4993
2811 2nd Street
Santa Monica, CA 90405

| | |
|---|---|
| TYPE | Motion Pictures + Television |
| CREDITS | Blessing |

Christopher Cuddihy . . . . . . . . . . . . . . . . . . . . . . Producer

**CULVER FILMS, CARMEN**
PHONE . . . . . . . . . . . . . . . . . . . . . . . . . . . . . 310-458-2770
FAX . . . . . . . . . . . . . . . . . . . . . . . . . . . . . . . 310-458-2770
1148 4th St., Ste. 103
Santa Monica, CA 90403

| | |
|---|---|
| TYPE | Motion Pictures + Television |
| CREDITS | The Thorn Birds - The Ring - Seduced by Madness |

Carmen Culver . . . . . . . . . . . . . . . . President/Producer/Writer
Cordelia Culver . . . . . . . . . . . . . . . . . . . . Dir., Development

**CUNNINGHAM PRODS. INC.**
PHONE . . . . . . . . . . . . . . . . . . . . . . . . . . . . . 818-995-1585
EMAIL . . . . . . . . . . . . . . . . . . . . . . . . sscfilms@aol.com
4420 Hayvenhurst Ave.
Encino, CA 91436

| | |
|---|---|
| TYPE | Motion Pictures + Television |
| DEAL | New Line Cinema |
| CREDITS | My Boyfriend's Back - Deep Star Six - House - Friday the 13th |

Sean S. Cunningham . . . . . . . . . . . . . . . . . Producer/Director
Noel Cunningham . . . . . . . . . . . . . . . . . . . . VP, Production
Mark Haslett . . . . . . . . . . . . . . . . . . . . . . VP, Development
Todd Farmer . . . . . . . . . . . . . . . . . . . . . Creative Executive

**CURTIS PRODS., DAN**
PHONE . . . . . . . . . . . . . . . . . . . . . . . . . . . . . 310-575-8999
FAX . . . . . . . . . . . . . . . . . . . . . . . . . . . . . . . 310-575-9299
11766 Wilshire Blvd., Ste. 1410
Los Angeles, CA 90025

| | |
|---|---|
| TYPE | Motion Pictures + Television |
| CREDITS | Winds of War - War and Remembrance - Dark Shadows - The Love Letter |

Dan Curtis . . . . . . . . . . . . . . . . . . . . . . Producer/Director
David Kennedy . . . . . . . . . . . . . . . . . . Exec. Vice President
Katherine Stuart . . . . . . . . . . . . . . . . . . . . VP, Development
Deborah Lewin . . . . . . . . . . . . . . . . . . . . . Office Manager
Martha Sanchez . . . . . . . . . . . . . . . . . . . . . . . . Assistant

**DAKOTA NORTH ENT./DAKOTA FILMS**
PHONE . . . . . . . . . . . . . . . . . . . . . . . . . . . . . 213-871-8424
FAX . . . . . . . . . . . . . . . . . . . . . . . . . . . . . . . 213-871-8429
EMAIL . . . . . . . . . . . . . . . . . . . . dakota@dakotafilms.com
WEBSITE . . . . . . . . . . . . . . . . . http://www.dakotafilms.com
Hollywood Center Studios
1040 N. Las Palmas, Bldg. 27, Ste. 125
Los Angeles, CA 90038

| | |
|---|---|
| TYPE | Motion Pictures + Television |
| CREDITS | Mr. Show with Bob and David - Oscar's Opening Film Sequence - MTV's Movie Awards Film |
| COMMENTS | Accepts no unsolicited material. |

Troy Miller . . . . . . . . . . . . . . . . . . . . . . Producer/Director
John Saade . . . . . . . . . . . . . . . . . . . . . . Producer/Director
Thomas Sherren . . . . . . . . . . . . . Producer/Production Executive
Steve Welch . . . . . . . . . . . . . . . . . . . . . . Post Production
Dora Rosas . . . . . . . . . . . . . . . . . . . . . . . Post Production
Wendy Wilkins . . . . . . . . . . . . . . . . . . . . . . Development
Tracey Krasno . . . . . . . . . . . . . . . . . . . . . . Unit Manager
Sean Suhl . . . . . . . . . . . . . . . . . . . . . . Dir., New Media

**DALY-HARRIS PRODUCTIONS**
PHONE . . . . . . . . . . . . . . . . . . . . . . . . . . . . . 213-956-8930
FAX . . . . . . . . . . . . . . . . . . . . . . . . . . . . . . . 213-862-1067
Paramount Pictures
5555 Melrose, Marx Bros. #208
Los Angeles, CA 90038

| | |
|---|---|
| TYPE | Motion Pictures + Television |
| DEAL | Paramount Television Group |
| CREDITS | Denise Calls Up - Lewis & Clark & George - Bad Manners - Digging to China |

Tim Daly . . . . . . . . . . . . . . . . . . . . . . . . Actor/Producer
Amy Van Nostrand . . . . . . . . . . . . . . . . . . . Actor/Producer
J. Todd Harris . . . . . . . . . . . . . . . . . . . . Producer/Partner
Stephen Burleigh . . . . . . . . . . . . . . . . . . VP, Creative Affairs
Tom Traub . . . . . . . . . . . . . . . . . . . . . . Dir., Development
Craig Davis Roth . . . . . . . . . . . . . . . . . . . Creative Executive

**DANCING ASPARAGUS PRODS.**
PHONE . . . . . . . . . . . . . . . . . . . . . . . . . . . . . 310-652-6054
FAX . . . . . . . . . . . . . . . . . . . . . . . . . . . . . . . 310-652-6055
WEBSITE . . . . . . . . . . . . . . . . . http://www.ASPARAGUS.com
264 S. La Cienega Blvd., Ste. 238
Beverly Hills, CA 90211

| | |
|---|---|
| TYPE | Motion Pictures + Feature Direct to Video |
| CREDITS | Vipor - True Blood - Land of Doom |

Grant Thomas . . . . . . . . . . . . . . . . . . . . . . . . . Producer
Brian Pogue . . . . . . . . . . . . . . . . . . . . . . . . . . Producer
Robert Weinberg . . . . . . . . . . . . . . . . VP, Business & Legal
Jodi Tucker . . . . . . . . . . . . . . . . . . . . . . VP, Development
Barbara Schiffman . . . . . . . . . . . . . . . . . . . . Story Editor
Rachel Lefleur . . . . . . . . . . . . . . . . . . . Asst. to Mr. Thomas

**DANGER FILMWORKS**
PHONE . . . . . . . . . . . . . . . . . . . . . . . . . . . . . 212-982-1399
FAX . . . . . . . . . . . . . . . . . . . . . . . . . . . . . . . 212-982-1399
54 East. 3rd St., Ste. 1
New York, NY 10003

| | |
|---|---|
| TYPE | Motion Pictures |
| CREDITS | I Like It Like That - I Think I Do - Cooking Tandoori Chicken - Fool's Gold - Just One Time |

Lane Janger . . . . . . . . . . . . . . . . . . . . . . . . . . Producer
Joshua Arnell . . . . . . . . . . . . . . . . . . . . . Asst. to Producer

**DANIEL PRODUCTIONS, JAY**
PHONE . . . . . . . . . . . . . . . . . . . . . . . . . . . . . 818-760-5959
FAX . . . . . . . . . . . . . . . . . . . . . . . . . . . . . . . 818-508-2335
4024 Radford Ave., Admin. Bldg., 280
Studio City, CA 91604

| | |
|---|---|
| TYPE | Television |
| DEAL | Brillstein-Grey Ent. |
| CREDITS | The Naked Truth - Cybill - Roseanne - Moonlighting |

Jay Daniel . . . . . . . . . . . . . . . . . . . . . . Executive Producer
Melissa Gelineau . . . . . . . . . . . . . . . . Producer/Development
Dina Sidebottom . . . . . . . . . . . . . . . . . . Executive Assistant

# COMPANIES AND STAFF

**DANIELSON - ROSENTHAL PRODUCTIONS**
PHONE . . . . . . . . . . . . . . . . . . . . . . . . . . . . . 310-205-5566
FAX . . . . . . . . . . . . . . . . . . . . . . . . . . . . . . . 310-205-5577
EMAIL . . . . . . . . . . . . . . . . . . . . . LDRosentha@aol.com
1500 San Ysidro Dr.
Beverly Hills, CA 90210
TYPE          Motion Pictures + Television
CREDITS       The West Side Waltz - Nickel & Dime - Marilyn Life After
              Death - 1,000 Men and a Baby
Lynn Danielson . . . . . . . . . . . . . . . . . . . . . . . . . . Producer
Jamie Mayes . . . . . . . . . . . . . . . . . . . . . Development Associate

**DANIKA PRODUCTIONS, INC.**
PHONE . . . . . . . . . . . . . . . . . . . . . . . . . . . . . 818-995-8095
FAX . . . . . . . . . . . . . . . . . . . . . . . . . . . . . . . 818-995-3589
EMAIL . . . . . . . . . . . . . . . . . . . . . . . . . cinewa2@aol.com
14636 Sutton St.
Sherman Oaks, CA 91403
TYPE          Motion Pictures
CREDITS       The Vanishing - I Love You To Death - V.I. Warshawski -
              Dance with Me
Lauren C. Weissman . . . . . . . . . . . . . . . . President/Producer
Lee Smith . . . . . . . . . . . . . . . . . . . . . . . . . . VP, Production

**DANJAQ INC.**
PHONE . . . . . . . . . . . . . . . . . . . . . . . . . . . . . 310-449-3185
FAX . . . . . . . . . . . . . . . . . . . . . . . . . . . . . . . 310-449-3189
MGM Plaza
2401 Colorado Ave., Ste. 330
Santa Monica, CA 90404
TYPE          Motion Pictures
DEAL          MGM/UA
CREDITS       The James Bond Films - Chitty Chitty Bang Bang
Dana Broccoli . . . . . . . . . . . . . . . . . . . . . . . . Co-Chairman
Michael Wilson . . . . . . . . . . . . . . . . . . . . . . . President/CEO
David Pope . . . . . . . . . . . . . . . . . . . Chief Operating Officer
Barbara Broccoli . . . . . . . . . . . . . . VP, Production/Development
Michael Tavares . . . . . . . . . . . . . . . . . . . . Asst. to Producers

**DARK HORSE ENT.**
PHONE . . . . . . . . . . . . . . . . . . . . . . . . . . . . . 818-777-5830
FAX . . . . . . . . . . . . . . . . . . . . . . . . . . . . . . . 818-866-5939
WEBSITE . . . . . . . . . . . . . . . . . . . . . . http://www.dhorse.com
100 Universal City Plaza, Bldg. 507-3F
Universal City, CA 91608
TYPE          Motion Pictures + Television + Animation + Interactive
              Multimedia
DEAL          Universal Studios/Columbia TriStar Television
CREDITS       The Mask - TimeCop - Virus
Mike Richardson . . . . . . . . . . . . . . . . . . . President/Producer
Scott Faye . . . . . . . . . . . . . . . . . . . . . . . . . VP, Production
Steven Gilder . . . . . . . . . . . . . . . . . . . . VP, Creative Affairs
Kevin Hageman . . . . . . . . . . . . . . . . . . Development Associate

**DARK MATTER PRODUCTIONS**
PHONE . . . . . . . . . . . . . . . . . . . . . . . . . . . . . 310-364-3391
FAX . . . . . . . . . . . . . . . . . . . . . . . . . . . . . . . 310-271-8646
EMAIL . . . . . . . . . . . . . . . . . . . . . . . . . drkmattr@aol.com
Davis Entertainment Classics
2121 Avenue of the Stars
Los Angeles, CA 90067
TYPE          Motion Pictures + Television
CREDITS       Denise Calls Up - Lewis & Clark & George
COMMENTS      for dev. proposals, contact via email or fax preferred.
Dan Gunther . . . . . . . . . . . . . . . . . . . . . . . . Actor/Producer

**DAVID LADD FILMS**
PHONE . . . . . . . . . . . . . . . . . . . . . . . . . . . . . 310-449-3410
FAX . . . . . . . . . . . . . . . . . . . . . . . . . . . . . . . 310-586-8272
MGM
2450 Broadway Street
Santa Monica, CA 90404
TYPE          Motion Pictures
DEAL          MGM/UA
CREDITS       Serpent And The Rainbow - Mod Squad
David Ladd . . . . . . . . . . . . . . . . . . . . . . . . . . . . President
Shannon Gaulding . . . . . . . . . . . . . . . . . . . . Vice President
Danielle Laff . . . . . . . . . . . . . . . . . . . . . . Dir., Development
Homa Alamdari . . . . . . . . . . . . . . . . . . . Asst. to David Ladd

**DAVIS CLASSICS**
PHONE . . . . . . . . . . . . . . . . . . . . . . . . . . . . . 310-551-2266
FAX . . . . . . . . . . . . . . . . . . . . . . . . . . . . . . . 310-556-3760
Davis Entertainment
2121 Ave. of the Stars, Ste. 2900
Los Angeles, CA 90067
TYPE          Motion Pictures
DEAL          Davis Entertainment Co.
CREDITS       Denise Calls Up - Cadillac Ranch - Lewis & Clark &
              George - Digging To China - Bad Manners
COMMENTS      Also: Cable.
Todd Harris . . . . . . . . . . . . . . . . . . . . . . . . . . . Producer
Frederick E. Salmo . . . . . . . . . . . . . . . . . . Dir., Development
Kevin Ruskin . . . . . . . . . . . . . . . . . . . . . Creative Executive
Sam Dehghani . . . . . . . . . . . . . . . . . . Development Associate

**DAVIS ENTERTAINMENT CO.**
PHONE . . . . . . . . . . . . . . . . . . . . . . . . . . . . . 310-556-3550
FAX . . . . . . . . . . . . . . . . 310-556-3688/310-556-3760
EMAIL . . . . . . . . . . . . . . . . . . . . . . . . . davisent@aol.com
2121 Ave. of the Stars, Ste. 2900
Los Angeles, CA 90067
TYPE          Motion Pictures
CREDITS       Predator I & II - The Firm - Grumpy Old Men - Waterworld
              - The Chamber - Out To Sea - Dr. Doolittle
John A. Davis . . . . . . . . . . Chairman, Davis Ent. Co. & Davis Ent. TV
Bruce Sallan . . . . . . . . . . . . . . Pres., Davis Ent. TV (310-551-2206)
Teddy Zee . . . . . . . . . . . . . . . . . . . . President (310-282-6917)
Wyck Godfrey . . . . . . . . . . . . . Exec. VP, Production (310-282-6906)
Anya Kochoff . . . . . . . . . . . . . . Sr. Vice President (310-282-6913)
Craig Berenson . . . . . . . . . . . . . . VP, Production (310-282-6969)
Brooke Brooks . . . . . . . . . . . . . . . . . . . VP, Administration
Stacy Kolker . . . . . . . . . . . . . . VP, Creative Affairs (310-551-2291)
William Sherak . . . . . . . . . . . . Creative Executive (310-282-6920)
Brad Hisey . . . . . . . . . . . . . . . . . . . . . Asst. to John Davis
Michael Savas . . . . . . . . . . . . . . . . . . . Asst. to Bruce Sallan
Nancy Jo Buck . . . . . . . . . Development Assistant (310-282-6922)
Jennifer Danska . . . . . . . . . Development Assistant (310-282-6909)
Lil Phillips . . . . . . . . . . . . . . Development Assistant (310-282-6910)

**DAYBREAK PRODS.**
PHONE . . . . . . . . . . . . . . . . . . . . . . . . . . . . . 818-777-0278
FAX . . . . . . . . . . . . . . . . 818-866-0285/818-866-0381
Universal Studios
100 Universal City Plaza, Bung. 124
Universal City, CA 91608
TYPE          Motion Pictures
DEAL          Universal Pictures
CREDITS       Waterworld - Die Hard 1 & 2 - Field of Dreams - Rocket
              Boys
Charles Gordon . . . . . . . . . . . . . . . . Producer (818-777-9557)
Marc Sternberg . . . . . . . . . . . . . . . . . President (818-777-0277)
Peter Cramer . . . . . . . . . . . . . . Sr. Vice President (818-777-0282)

**DAYDREAM PRODUCTIONS INC.**
PHONE . . . . . . . . . . . . . . . . . . . . . . . . . . . . . 310-285-9677
FAX . . . . . . . . . . . . . . . . . . . . . . . . . . . . . . . 310-201-0257
WEBSITE . . . . . . . . . . . . . . . . http://daydream@earthlink.net
8969 Sunset Blvd.
Los Angeles, CA 90069
TYPE          Television
CREDITS       Best Men - Two Sheets to the Wind - Leaves of Grass
COMMENTS      Also: Children's Television & MOW's.
Sheryl Steinman . . . . . . . . . . . . . . . . . . . President/Producer
Alan Steinman . . . . . . . . . . . . . . . . . . . . . . . VP, Production
Kathleen Barnett . . . . . . . . . . . . . . . . . . . Dir., Development

**DE LAURENTIIS COMPANY, DINO**
PHONE . . . . . . . . . . . . . . . . . . . . . . . . . . . . . 310-289-6100
FAX . . . . . . . . . . . . . . . . . . . . . . . . . . . . . . . 310-855-0562
EMAIL . . . . . . . . . . . . . . . . . . . . . . . . . ddlco@worldsite.net
8670 Wilshire Blvd., Ste. 300
Beverly Hills, CA 90211
TYPE          Motion Pictures + Television
CREDITS       Breakdown - Bound - U-571
Dino De Laurentiis . . . . . . . . . . . . . . . . . . . . . . Consultant
Martha De Laurentiis . . . . . . . . . . . . . . . . President/Producer
Roberta Shintani . . . . . . . . . . . . . . . . Chief Financial Officer
Stuart Boros . . . . . . . . . . . . . . . . . . . . . . . Business Affairs
Shirley Delovich . . . . . . . . . . . . . . . . . . . . . . Story Editor
Christy Humphrey . . . . . . . . . . . . . . . . . . . Story Consultant
Hector Freeman . . . . . . . . . . . . . . . . . . . . . . Asst. to DDL

**DE PASSE ENTERTAINMENT**
PHONE . . . . . . . . . . . . . . . . . . . . . . . . . . . . . . . . . . . . . . . 213-965-2580
FAX . . . . . . . . . . . . . . . . . . . . . . . . . . . . . . . . . . . . . . . . . . 213-965-2598
5750 Wilshire Blvd., Ste. 640
Los Angeles, CA 90036

TYPE             Motion Pictures + Television + Syndication
CREDITS          Lonesome Dove - Sister, Sister - Smart Guy - Buffalo Girls
Suzanne de Passe . . . . . . . . . . . . . . . . . . . . . . . . . . . . . . Chairman/CEO
Suzanne Coston . . . . . . . . . . . . . . . . . . . . . . . . . . . . . . . . . President
Toni Patillo . . . . . . . . . . . . . . . . . . . . . . . . . . . . . . . Exec. Vice President
Vinette Bond . . . . . . . . . . . . . . . VP, Business Affairs & Administration
Eric Buchanan . . . . . . . . . . . . . . . . . . . . . . . . . . . . . . VP, Development
Keith Wixson . . . . . . . . . . . . . . . . . . . . . . . . . . . . . . . . Story Advisor

**DEE GEE ENTERTAINMENT**
PHONE . . . . . . . . . . . . . . . . . . . . . . . . 310-652-0999/312-750-8459
FAX . . . . . . . . . . . . . . . . . . . . . . . . . . 310-652-0718/310-920-2477
368 N. La Cienega Blvd.
Los Angeles, CA 90048-1925

TYPE             Motion Pictures
CREDITS          Simple Justice- Ricochet River - Vultures - The Wedding
                 Planner
COMMENTS  ALSO: 200 W. Madison St. #3604, Chicago IL 60606
Deborah Del Prete . . . . . . . . . . . . . . . . . . . . . . . . . . . . . . . Producer
Gigi Pritzker . . . . . . . . . . . . . . . . . . . . . . . . . . . . . . . . . . . Producer
Andrew Francis . . . . . . . . . . . . . . . . . . . . . . . . . . . Creative Executive
Amy Hurdelbrink . . . . . . . . . . . . . . . . . . . . . Assistant to Producers

**DEF PICTURES**
PHONE . . . . . . . . . . . . . . . . . . . . . . . . . . . . . . . . . . . . . . . 310-205-5430
FAX . . . . . . . . . . . . . . . . . . . . . . . . . . . . . . . . . . . . . . . . . . 310-205-5433
9171 Wilshire Blvd., Ste. 400
Beverly Hills, CA 90210

TYPE             Motion Pictures
COMMENTS  Production Deal with PolyGram Filmed Ent.
Russell Simmons . . . . . . . . . . . . . . . . . . . . . . . . . . . . . . Co-Chairman
Stan Lathan . . . . . . . . . . . . . . . . . . . . . . . . . . . . . . . . . Co-Chairman
Preston Holmes . . . . . . . . . . . . . . . . . . . . . . . . . . . . . . . . President
Darrien Michele Gipson . . . . . . . . . . . . . . . . . . . . Dir., Development
Terrence Meyers . . . . . . . . . . . . . . . . . . . . . . . . . . Creative Executive
Robert Johnson . . . . . . . . . . . . . . . . . . . . . . . . Asst. to Co-Chairman
Allison Joseph . . . . . . . . . . . . . . . . . . . . . . . . . Asst. to Co-Chairman
Tyrone D. Dixon . . . . . . . . . . . . . . . . . . . . . . . . . Asst. to President
Camille Irons . . . . . . . . . . . . . . . . . . . . . . . Asst. to Dir., Development

**DEJA VIEW PRODUCTIONS, INC.**
PHONE . . . . . . . . . . . . . . . . . . . . . . . . . . . . . . . . . . . . 818-704-9185
FAX . . . . . . . . . . . . . . . . . . . . . . . . . . . . . . . . . . . . . . 818-704-6001
EMAIL . . . . . . . . . . . . . . . . . . . . . . . . . . . dejavprods@aol.com
7603 Atron Ave.
West Hills, CA 91304

TYPE             Motion Pictures + Television
CREDITS          Virus - Outbreak - Pacific Heights
COMMENTS  Also: Made For Cable.
Robyn Evans-Jones . . . . . . . . . . . . . . . . . . . . . . Producer/Partner
Dennis E. Jones . . . . . . . . . . . . . . . Line Producer/UPM/Partner

**DELAWARE PICTURES**
PHONE . . . . . . . . . . . . . . . . . . . . . . . . . . . . . . . . . . . . 213-465-9984
FAX . . . . . . . . . . . . . . . . . . . . . . . . . . . . . . . . . . . . . . 213-465-9372
EMAIL . . . . . . . . . . . . . . . . . . . . . . . . . delaware_pix@yahoo.com
WEBSITE . . . . . . . . . . . http://www.members.xoom.com/DELAWARE
1147 N. Vine St., 2nd Fl.
Hollywood, CA 90038

TYPE             Motion Pictures + Television
CREDITS          Hatfields & McCoys - The Alamo - No Drums, No Bugles -
                 Human Error - 300 Miles for Stephanie
COMMENTS  Formerly Millican/Delaware Productions.
Clyde Ware . . . . . . . . . . . . . . . . . . . . . . . . . . . . . . Writer/Director
Judy Landfield . . . . . . . . . . . . . . . . . . . . . . . . . . . . . . . . Producer
Chip Mills . . . . . . . . . . . . . . . . . . . . . . . . . . . . . . . . . . . Producer
Steve Beden . . . . . . . . . . . . . . . . . . . . . . . . . . . Executive Producer
Stephane Mermet . . . . . . . . . . . . . . . . . . . . . . . . . . . . . Creative
Pepe Serna . . . . . . . . . . . . . . . . . . . . . . . . . . . . . . . . . . Creative
Angela Durrell . . . . . . . . . . . . . . . . . . . . . . . . . . . . . . . Associate

**DEMBERG PRODUCTIONS, LISA**
PHONE . . . . . . . . . . . . . . . . . . . . . . . . . . . . . . . . . . . . 310-557-6908
FAX . . . . . . . . . . . . . . . . . . . . . . . . . . . . . . . . . . . . . . 310-557-6021
ABC Pictures
2020 Ave. of The Stars, 5th Floor
Los Angeles, CA 90067

TYPE             Motion Pictures + Television
DEAL             ABC Pictures
CREDITS          Murder Live! - Thrill - Promised A Miracle - Indiscretion Of
                 An American Wife - Different
COMMENTS  MOWs, Miniseries, Cable
Lisa Demberg . . . . . . . . . . . . . . . . . . . . . . . . . . . Executive Producer
Shanna Rosen . . . . . . . . . . . . . . . Dir., Development (310-557-6889)
Jason Pinchuk . . . . . . . . . . . . . . . . . . . . . . Development Assistant

**DEMO PRODUCTIONS, INC.**
PHONE . . . . . . . . . . . . . . . . . . . . . . . . . . . . . . . . . . . . 818-341-1484
FAX . . . . . . . . . . . . . . . . . . . . . . . . . . . . . . . . . . . . . . 818-341-1526
21704 Devonshire St., #300
Chatsworth, CA 91311

TYPE             Motion Pictures + Television
CREDITS          Wishmaster - From Dusk Till Dawn - The Demolitionist
Robert Kurtzman . . . . . . . . . . . . . . . . . . . . . Producer/Writer/Director
Anne Kurtzman . . . . . . . . . . . . . . . . . . . . . . . . . . . . . . President

**DEPEW PRODUCTIONS**
PHONE . . . . . . . . . . . . . . . . . . . . . . . . . . . . . . . . . . . . 213-654-5300
EMAIL . . . . . . . . . . . . . . . . . . . . . . . . . . . . . . gdepew@aol.com
1444 N. Laurel Ave.
Los Angeles, CA 90046

TYPE             Motion Pictures
CREDITS          Children of the Corn III & IV - The Hard Truth - The
                 Willies
Gary DePew . . . . . . . . . . . . . . . . . . . . . . . . . . . . . . . . . Producer

**DESERT HEART PRODS.**
PHONE . . . . . . . . . . . . . . . . . . . . . . . . . . . . . . . . . . . . 310-399-0013
FAX . . . . . . . . . . . . . . . . . . . . . . . . . . . . . . . . . . . . . . 310-396-4047
EMAIL . . . . . . . . . . . . . . . . . . . . . . deserthearts@earthlink.com
685 Venice Blvd.
Venice, CA 90291

TYPE             Motion Pictures + Television
CREDITS          Desert Hearts- Women of Brewster Place- Prison Stories
Donna Deitch . . . . . . . . . . . . . . . . . . . . . . . . . . . Director/Producer
Frank Smith . . . . . . . . . . . . . . . . . . . . . . . . . . . Executive Assistant

**DI BONA PRODS., VIN**
PHONE . . . . . . . . . . . . . . . . . . . . . . . . . . . . . . . . . . . . 310-442-5600
FAX . . . . . . . . . . . . . . . . . . . . . . . . . . . . . . . . . . . . . . 310-442-5605
12233 W. Olympic Blvd., Ste. 170
Los Angeles, CA 90064

TYPE             Television
CREDITS          I Survived a Disaster - Sherman Oaks - America's Funniest
                 Home Videos
Vin Di Bona . . . . . . . . . . . . . . . . . . . . . . . . . . . . . . . . . Chairman
Richard C. Brustein . . . . . . . . . . . . . . . . . . . . . . . . . . . . President
Siow Vigman . . . . . . . . . . . . . . . . Exec. In Charge of Production/CFO
Lloyd Weintraub . . . . . . . . . . . . . . . . . Exec. VP, Creative Affairs
Honi Almond . . . . . . . . . . . . . . . . Sr. VP, Business/Legal Affairs
Dan Lux . . . . . . . . . . . . . . . . . . . . . . . . . . . . . . VP, Development
Cara DiBona . . . . . . . . . . . . . . . . . . . . Mgr., Children's Programs
Katharine Linke . . . . . . . . . . . . . . . . . . Mgr., Children's Programs
John Goldhammer . . . . . . . . . . . . . . . . . . . . . Creative Consultant

**DI NOVI PICTURES**
PHONE . . . . . . . . . . . . . . . . . . . . . . . . . . . . . . . . . . . . 310-581-1355
FAX . . . . . . . . . . . . . . . . . . . . . . . . . . . . . . . . . . . . . . 310-399-0499
3110 Main St. #220
Santa Monica, CA 90405

TYPE             Motion Pictures
DEAL             Warner Bros. Pictures
CREDITS          Batman Returns - Edward Scissorhands - Ed Wood - Little
                 Women
Denise Di Novi . . . . . . . . . . . . . . . . . . . . . . . . . . . . . . . Producer
Pete Czernin . . . . . . . . . . . . . . . . . . . . . . . . . . . . . . . . . President
Marc Wolf . . . . . . . . . . . . . . . . . . . . . . . . . . . . VP, Development
Brad Wiss . . . . . . . . . . . . . . . . . . . . . . . . . . . . . . . . Story Editor

# COMPANIES AND STAFF

**DIAMOND HEART PRODUCTIONS**
PHONE . . . . . . . . . . . . . . . . . . . . . . . 310-369-3753
FAX . . . . . . . . . . . . . . . . . . . . . . . . . . 310-369-8861
Twentieth Century Fox
10201 W. Pico Blvd., Bldg. 667
Los Angeles, CA 90035
TYPE        Motion Pictures
DEAL        Twentieth Century Fox-Fox 2000 (LA)
Leslie Morgan . . . . . . . . . . . . . . . . . . . . . . . . . . . Producer
Matt Luber . . . . . . . . . . . . . . . . . . . . . . . VP, Development
Lorne Volat . . . . . . . . . . . . . . . . . . . . . . . . . Story Editor

**DIAMONDBACK ENTERTAINMENT**
PHONE . . . . . . . . . . . . . . . . . . . . . . . 310-659-2117
EMAIL . . . . . . . . . . . . . . . . . . . diamond@starone.com
8221 Sunset Blvd.
Los Angeles, CA 90046
TYPE        Motion Pictures
CREDITS     The Tuskegee Airmen - Rude Awakening - Off And
            Running
Bill Carraro . . . . . . . . . . . . . . . . . . . . . . . . . . . Producer
David Keith . . . . . . . . . . . . . . . . . . . . . . Actor/Director
Jenna Chandler-Ward . . . . . . . . . . . . . . . . . Development

**DIANA KEREW PRODUCTIONS**
PHONE . . . . . . . . . . . . . . . . . . . . . . . 310-575-1272
FAX . . . . . . . . . . . . . . . . . . . . . . . . . . 310-478-6067
Hearst Ent.
1640 S. Sepulveda Blvd., 4th Fl.
Los Angeles, CA 90025
TYPE        Television
DEAL        Hearst Entertainment
CREDITS     Fifteen and Pregnant - Paris Trout - Ed McBain's 87th
            Precinct - My Breast
COMMENTS    Movies for Television.
Diana Kerew . . . . . . . . . . . . . . . . . . . . . . . . . Producer
Linda Carolei . . . . . . . . . . . . . . . . . . . Dir., Development
Ellen Graham . . . . . . . . . . . . . . . . . . . Asst. to Producer

**DIC ENTERTAINMENT**
PHONE . . . . . . . . . . . . . . . . . . . . . . . 818-955-5400
FAX . . . . . . . . . . . . . . . . . . . . . . . . . . 818-955-5696
EMAIL . . . . . . . . . . . . . . . . . . . . . VincenP@abc.com
303 N. Glenoaks Blvd.
Burbank, CA 91502
TYPE        Television + Animation + Feature Direct to Video +
            Motion Pictures
DEAL        Walt Disney Pictures/Touchstone Pictures
CREDITS     Carmen Sandiego - Inspector Gadget - Madeline -
            Mummies Alive! - Tex Avery - Meet the Deedles
COMMENTS    Also: Live Action.
Andy Heyward . . . . . . . . . . . . . . . . . . . . . . President/CEO
Jeff Wernick . . . . . . . . . . . . . . . COO/Exec. VP, Operations
Dene Stratton . . . . . . . . . . . . General Manager/Sr. Vice President
Roger Omae . . . . . . . . . . . . . . . . . . . . . . . . . . Controller
Robby London . . . . . . . . . . . . . . Exec. VP, Creative Affairs
Michael Maliani . . . . . . . . . . . . . . . Exec. VP, Development
Stacey Gallishaw . . . . . . . . . . . . . . . . . . . VP, Production
Michael Helfand . . . . . . . . . . . VP, Legal & Business Affairs
Aaron Meyerson . . . . . . . . . . . . . . . . . . VP, Motion Picture
Karyn Ulman . . . . . . . . . . . . . . . . . . . . . . . . . VP, Music
Riley Ellis . . . . . . . . . . . . . . . . . . . . . . . . . . . Producer

**DIMENSION FILMS**
PHONE . . . . . . . . . . . . . . . 212-941-3800/213-951-4200
FAX . . . . . . . . . . . . . . . . . . 212-941-3949/213-951-4218
WEBSITE . . . . . . . . . . . . . . . http://www.dimensionfilms.com
Miramax Films
375 Greenwich St.
New York, NY 10013-2338
TYPE        Motion Pictures
CREDITS     Nightwatch - Scream - Scream 2 - Phantoms - Mimic - The
            Crow - Senseless
COMMENTS    Also: 7966 Beverly Blvd. Los Angeles, CA  90048
Bob Weinstein . . . . . . . . . . . . . . . . . . . Co-Chairman (NY)
Cary Granat . . . . . . . . . . . . . . . . . . . . . . . President (NY)
Kevin Hyman . . . . . . . . . . . . Sr. VP, Physical Production (NY)
Richard Potter . . . . . . . . . . Sr. VP, Production & Development (NY)
Andrew Rona . . . . . . . . . . . . Sr. VP, Production & Development (NY)
Cary Meadow . . . . . . . . . . . . . . . . . VP, Business Affairs
Dan Gross . . . . . . . . . . . . . . . . . . . . . . . . VP, Production
Clark Henderson . . . . . . . . . . . . . . . VP, Post Production
Jennifer Sherwood . . . . . . . . . . . . Production Executive (NY)
Beth Calabro . . . . . . . . . . . Dir., Production & Development (NY)
David Jordan . . . . . . . . . . . . . Dir., Production & Development
Peter Schwerin . . . . . . . . . . . . . . Production Executive (NY)

**DINAMO ENTERTAINMENT**
PHONE . . . . . . . . . . . . . . . . . . . . . . . 310-473-1311
FAX . . . . . . . . . . . . . . . . . . . . . . . . . . 310-473-8233
EMAIL . . . . . . . . . . . . . . . . . . . dinamo@earthlink.net
1954 Cotner Avenue
Los Angeles, CA 90025
TYPE        Motion Pictures + Television
CREDITS     Suicide Kings - The Substitute - Bad Influence - Apartment
            Zero
Morrie Eisenman . . . . . . . . . . . . . . . . . . . . . . President
Charles Chiara . . . . . . . . . . . . . . . . . . . . . VP, Production
Taedra Kogan . . . . . . . . . . . . . . . . Dir., Creative Affairs

**DISCOVERY NETWORKS**
PHONE . . . . . . . . . . . . . . . . . . . . . . . 301-986-1999
WEBSITE . . . . . . . . . . . . . . . . . http://www.discovery.com
7700 Wisconsin Ave.
Bethesda, MD 20814
TYPE        Television
CREDITS     Titanic: Anatomy of a Disaster - The Ultimate Guide
John Hendricks . . . . . . . . . . . . . . . . Founder/Chairman/CEO
Judith McHale . . . . . . . . . . . . . . . . . . . President/COO
Greg Moyer . . . . . . . . . President/Chief Editorial/Creative Officer
Johnathan Rodgers . . . . . . . . President, Discovery Networks (US)
Michela English . . . . . . . . President, Discovery Enterprises Worldwide
Donald Wear . . . . . . . . . President, Discovery Networks (International)
Greg Durig . . . . . . . . . . . . . . . . . . . . . . . Exec. VP/CFO
Clark Bunting . . . . . . . . Sr. VP/General Manager, Animal Planet
Tim Cowling . . . . . . . . Sr. VP/Sr. Exec. Producer, Discovery Networks (US)
Jay Feldman . . . . . . . . Sr. VP/General Manager, Travel Channel
John Ford . . . . . . . . Sr. VP/General Manger, The Learning Channel
Chuck Gingold . . . . . Sr. VP/GM, Daytime Programming, Dis. Networks
Mike Quattrone . . . . . . Sr. VP/General Manager, Dis. Channel

**DISNEY CHANNEL**
PHONE . . . . . . . . . . . . . . . . . . . . . . . 818-569-7500
FAX . . . . . . . . . . . . . . . . . . . . . . . . . . 818-558-1241
WEBSITE . . . . . . . . . . . . . . . http://www.disneychannel.com
3800 W. Alameda Avenue
Burbank, CA 91505-4398
TYPE        Television
Anne Sweeney . . . . . . . . . . . . . . . . . . . . . . . . President
Frederick Kuperberg . . . . . . . . . . Sr. VP, Business & Legal Affairs
Patrick T. Lopker . . . . . . . . . . Sr. VP, Finance & Administration
Gary K. Marsh . . . . . . . . . . . . Sr. VP, Original Programming
Rich Ross . . . . . . . . . . . . . Sr. VP, Programming & Production
Jill Casagrande . . . . . . . . . VP, Scheduling & Program Planning
Peggy J. Christianson . . . . . . . . . . . . . . VP, Creative Affairs
Michael Healy . . . . . . . . . . . . . . . . . . VP, Original Movies
Susette Hsiung . . . . . . . . . . . . . . . . . . . . VP, Production
Chuck Kent . . . . . . . . . . . . . . . . . . . VP, Business Affairs
Sandra Wax . . . . . . . . . . . . . . . VP, Research & Planning

**DISNEY TELEFILMS**
PHONE . . . . . . . . . . . . . . . . . . . . . . . 818-560-1000
FAX . . . . . . . . . . . . . . . . . . . . . . . . . . 818-566-8736
WEBSITE . . . . . . . . . . . . . . . . . http://www.disney.com
500 S. Buena Vista St.
Burbank, CA 91521-0001
TYPE        Television
CREDITS     The Wonderful World of Disney
Charles Hirschhorn . . . . . . . . . . . . . . . . . . . . President
Peter Green . . . . . . . . . . . . . . . . . . . . . . VP, Production
Leah Keith . . . . . . . . . . . . . . . . . . . . . . . VP, Production
Gail Levin . . . . . . . . . . . . . . . . . . . . . . . . . VP, Casting
Joe Del Hierro . . . . . . . . . . . . . . . . . . . . . . . . Director
Nancy D. Silverman . . . . . . . . . . . . . . . . . . . . . Director

**DISTANT HORIZON**
PHONE . . . . . . . . . . . . . . . . . . . . . . . 213-848-4140
FAX . . . . . . . . . . . . . . . . . . . . . . . . . . 213-848-4144
EMAIL . . . . . . . . . . . . . . . . . . . distanth@ix.netcom.com
8282 Sunset Blvd., Ste. A
Los Angeles, CA 90046
TYPE        Motion Pictures + Television + Syndication
CREDITS     Sarafina!- Chain of Desire- Cry, The Beloved Country -
            Scorpion Spring- Captives - Face - Theory of Flight
Anant Singh . . . . . . . . . . . . . . . . . . . . . . . . . President
Brian Cox . . . . . . . . . . . . . . . . . . . . . . . . . . . Producer
James Pendorf . . . . . . . . . . . . . . . . Production Coordinator

## DOCKRY PRODUCTIONS
PHONE . . . . . . . . . . . . . . . . . . . . . . . . . . . . . . 310-274-0761
FAX . . . . . . . . . . . . . . . . . . . . . . . . . . . . . . . 310-274-0762
2528 Hutton Dr.
Beverly Hills, CA 90210

| | |
|---|---|
| TYPE | Motion Pictures + Television + Syndication + Feature Direct to Video + Documentaries + Animation |
| CREDITS | Murder One - China Love - Bakshish |
| COMMENTS | Parent Co. is International Productions, a consortium of 27 companies from 27 countries |

Nancy Dockry . . . . . . . . . . . . . . . . . . . . . . . . . . . . President
Walter Edwards . . . . . . . . . . . . . . . . . . . . . . . VP, Production
Edward Hope . . . . . . . . . . . . . . . . . . . . . . . VP, Acquisitions
Sue Cazen . . . . . . . . . . . . . . . . . . . . . . . . . VP, Development
Peter Brownet . . . . . . . . . . . . . . . . . . . . Dir., Video Projects
Tad Clancy . . . . . . . . . . . . . . . . . . . . . . . . Dir., Comedy TV
Jack Dillman . . . . . . . . . . . . . . . . . . . . . . . . Dir., Features
John Firste . . . . . . . . . . . . . . . . . . . . . . . . . Dir., Drama TV
Linda Pele . . . . . . . . . . . . . . . . . . . . . . . . . Dir., Animation
James Mark . . . . . . . . . . . . . . . . . . . . . . . . . Legal Affairs
Jeremy Chu . . . . . . . . . . . . . . . . . . . . . Financial Consultant
Adolph Kaczynski . . . . . . . . . . . . . . . . . . . . . . . . Treasurer

## DOGSMILE PICTURES
PHONE . . . . . . . . . . . . . . . . . . . . . . . . . . . . . . 310-551-2258
FAX . . . . . . . . . . . . . . . . . . . . . . . . . . . . . . . 310-556-3760
Davis Entertainment
2121 Ave. of the Stars, Ste. 2900
Los Angeles, CA 90067

| | |
|---|---|
| TYPE | Motion Pictures + Television |
| DEAL | Davis Entertainment Co. |
| CREDITS | Eden - Lovelife - Love Stinks - Meeting Daddy - The Settlement |

Todd Hoffman . . . . . . . . . . . . . . . . . . . . . . . . . . Producer
Dane Gillibrand . . . . . . . . . . . . . . . . . . . . . . . Development
Bruce Bullock . . . . . . . . . . . . . . . . . Development Assistant

## DOGSTAR FILMS
PHONE . . . . . . . . . . . . . . . . . . . . . . . . . . . . . . 310-552-1518
FAX . . . . . . . . . . . . . . . . . . . . . . . . . . . . . . . 310-552-2310
EMAIL . . . . . . . . . . . . . . . . . . . . . . . . . dogstar@fox.com
10390 Santa Monica Blvd., #350
Los Angeles, CA 90025

| | |
|---|---|
| TYPE | Motion Pictures + Television |
| DEAL | Twentieth Century Fox-Fox 2000 (LA) |
| CREDITS | 200 Cigarettes - Best Laid Plans |

Mike Newell . . . . . . . . . . . . . . . . . . . . . . . Director/Partner
Alan Greenspan . . . . . . . . . . . . . . . . . . . . . Producer/Partner
Betsy Beers . . . . . . . . . . . . . . . . . . . . . . . Pres., Production
Julie Vallely . . . . . . . . . . . . . . . . . . . . . . . Dir., Development
Chip Brantley . . . . . . . . . . . . . . Story Editor/Asst. to Betsy Beers
Devorah Herbert . . . . . . . . . . . . . . . . Asst. to Alan Greenspan

## DON BAER PRODS. INC.
PHONE . . . . . . . . . . . . . . . . . . . . . . . . . . . . . . 303-786-9223
FAX . . . . . . . . . . . . . . . . . . . . . . . . . . . . . . . 303-786-9223
22 Pine Brook Rd.
Boulder, CO 80304

| | |
|---|---|
| TYPE | Motion Pictures + Television |
| CREDITS | The Boy Who Drank Too Much - Fighting Back - Tomorrow's Child |

Don Baer . . . . . . . . . . . . . . . . . . . . . . . . . . . . Producer

## DONLEY PRODUCTIONS, MAUREEN
PHONE . . . . . . . . . . . . . . . . . . . . . . . . . . . . . . 310-369-5418
FAX . . . . . . . . . . . . . . . . . . . . . . . . . . . . . . . 310-369-7423
Twentieth Century Fox
10201 W. Pico Blvd., Bldg. 15, Rm. O
Los Angeles, CA 90035

| | |
|---|---|
| TYPE | Motion Pictures |
| DEAL | Fox 2000 |
| CREDITS | Anastasia |
| COMMENTS | Specializes in live action motion pictures. |

Maureen Donley . . . . . . . . . . . . . . . . . . . . . . . . Producer
Lauren Sands . . . . . . . . . . . . . . . . . . . . . . . Dir., Development
Mark Misch . . . . . . . . . . . . . . . . . . . . . . . . . . Assistant

## DONNER/SHULER-DONNER PRODS.
PHONE . . . . . . . . . . . . . . . . . . . . . . . . . . . . . . 818-954-ext
FAX . . . . . . . . . . . . . . . . . . . . . . . . . . . . . . . 818-954-4908
Warner Bros. Pictures
4000 Warner Blvd., Bldgs. 102 & 103 #4
Burbank, CA 91522-0001

| | |
|---|---|
| TYPE | Motion Pictures + Television + Animation |
| DEAL | Warner Bros. Pictures |
| CREDITS | Dave - Lady Hawke - Free Willy - Maverick - Lethal Weapon 1-3 - Consipiracy Theory - Volcano |

Richard Donner . . . . . . . . . . . . . . . . . . No Title (x3961)
Lauren Shuler-Donner . . . . . . . . . . . . . . . No Title (x3611)
Julie Durk . . . . . . . . . . . . . . . . . . . . . . No Title (x3611)
Mills Goodloe . . . . . . . . . . . . . . . . . . . . No Title (x3961)
Cynthia Neber . . . . . . . . . . . . . . . . . . . . No Title (x3961)
Kathy Liska . . . . . . . . . . . . . . . . . . . . . No Title (x3611)
Michael Aguilar . . . . . . . . . . . . . . . . . . . No Title (x3284)
David Cervantes . . . . . . . . . . . . . . . . . . . No Title (x3961)
Kevin Feige . . . . . . . . . . . . . . . . . . . . . No Title (x3611)
Marti Garcia . . . . . . . . . . . . . . . . . . . . . No Title (x3961)
Laura Holstein . . . . . . . . . . . . . . . . . . . . No Title (x3611)
Geoff Johns . . . . . . . . . . . . . . . . . . . . . No Title (x3961)
Deon Wilkes . . . . . . . . . . . . . . . . . . . . . No Title (x3284)
Kevin Donahue . . . . . . . . . . . . . . . . . . . . No Title (x3961)

## DORE PRODUCTIONS, BONNY
PHONE . . . . . . . . . . . . . . . . . . . . . . . . . . 310-274-7136
FAX . . . . . . . . . . . . . . . . . . . . . . . . . . . 310-274-7390
EMAIL . . . . . . . . . . . . . . . . . . . . bdore81647@aol.com
9454 Wilshire Blvd., Penthouse
Beverly Hills, CA 90212

| | |
|---|---|
| TYPE | Motion Pictures + Television + Syndication + Interactive Multimedia |
| CREDITS | Captive - Sins - Glory, Glory! - The Jill Ireland Story - Rainbow Warrior |

Bonny Dore . . . . . . . . . . . . . . . . . President/Exec. Producer

## DOUBLE A FILMS
PHONE . . . . . . . . . . . . . . . . . . . . . . . . . . 212-741-8500
FAX . . . . . . . . . . . . . . . . . . . . . . . . . . . 212-741-0424
EMAIL . . . . . . . . . . . . . . . . . . . . . . aafilms@aol.com
180 Varick St., 10th Fl.
New York, NY 10014

| | |
|---|---|
| TYPE | Motion Pictures |
| CREDITS | Sunday - At Sundance - Nadja |

Andrew Fierberg . . . . . . . . . . . . . . . . . . . . . President
Amy Hobby . . . . . . . . . . . . . . . . . . . . . . . . President
Lori Cheatle . . . . . . . . . . . . . . . . . . . Creative Executive
Rene Veilleux . . . . . . . . . . . . . . . . . . . VP, Development

## DOUBLE EAGLE ENT.
PHONE . . . . . . . . . . . . . . . . . . . . . . . . . . 310-246-1690
FAX . . . . . . . . . . . . . . . . . . . . . . . . . . . 310-246-1693
EMAIL . . . . . . . . . . . . . . . . . Rowlandperk@earthlink.net
433 N. Camden Dr., #888
Beverly Hills, CA 90210

| | |
|---|---|
| TYPE | Motion Pictures + Television + Syndication + Feature Direct to Video + Animation + Interactive Multimedia |
| CREDITS | Hiroshima (Showtime) - Code Name: Wolverine (Fox) - Psychic Chronicles (UPN) |

Rowland Perkins . . . . . . . . . . . . . . . . . . Chairman/President
Stephen Saltzman . . . . . . . . . Exec. VP, Operations/Business Affairs

## DOUBLE WHAMMY PRODUCTIONS
PHONE . . . . . . . . . . . . . . . . . . . . . . . . . . 310-859-8853
FAX . . . . . . . . . . . . . . . . . . . . . . . . . . . 310-859-2490
345 N. Maple Dr., Ste. 280
Beverly Hills, CA 90210

| | |
|---|---|
| TYPE | Motion Pictures + Television |

Pamela Beck . . . . . . . . . . . . . . . . . . . . . Writer/Producer
Barbara Guggenheim . . . . . . . . . . . . . . . . . . . . . Producer
Jorge Jazan . . . . . . . . . . . . . . . . . . . . . Dir., Development
Pari Joundourian . . . . . . . . . . . . . . . . . Asst. to Ms. Beck
Erin Stickle . . . . . . . . . . . . . . . . . Asst. to Ms. Guggenheim

## DOUMANIAN PRODS., JEAN
PHONE . . . . . . . . . . . . . . . . . . . . . . . . . . . . . . . . . . . . 212-486-2626
FAX . . . . . . . . . . . . . . . . . . . . . . . . . . . . . . . . . . . . . . . 212-688-6236
595 Madison Ave., Ste. 2200
New York, NY 10022

| | |
|---|---|
| TYPE | Motion Pictures + Television + Documentaries |
| CREDITS | Everyone Says I Love You - SNL - Deconstructing Harry - The Spanish Prisoner |
| COMMENTS | Also: Theatre. Credits include Off-Broadway play, "Dinah Was". |

Jean Doumanian . . . . . . . . . . . . . . . . . . . . . . . . . . . . . . President
John Logigian . . . . . . . . . . . . . . . . . . . . . . Exec. Vice President
Letty Aronson . . . . . . . . . . . . . . . . . . . . . . . . . . Vice President
Adam Schlesinger . . . . . . . . . . . . . . . . . . . . Dir., Development
Etan Frankel . . . . . . . . . . . . . . . . . . . . . . . . . . . . . Story Editor

## DOUTHIT PRODUCTIONS LTD.
PHONE . . . . . . . . . . . . . . . . . . . . . . . . . . . . . . . . 310-917-1194
FAX . . . . . . . . . . . . . . . . . . . . . . . . . . . . . . . . . . . 310-451-5033
801 Ocean Ave., Ste. 302
Santa Monica, CA 90403

| | |
|---|---|
| TYPE | Television + Motion Pictures |
| DEAL | Big Ticket Television |
| CREDITS | Larry King Live - Crossfire - Jenny Jones - Judge Judy - Judge Joe - The Treat - Honey |

Randy Douthit . . . . . . . . . . . . . . . . . . . President/Exec. Producer
Patrice Jones . . . . . . . . . . . . . . . . . . . . . . . . . . . . VP/Producer

## DRAGON PICTURES
PHONE . . . . . . . . . . . . . . . . . 213-935-6967/011-44-171-734-6303
FAX . . . . . . . . . . . . . . . . . . . . 213-935-6910/011-44-171-734-6202
181 N. Mansfield Ave.
Los Angeles, CA 90036

| | |
|---|---|
| TYPE | Motion Pictures |
| CREDITS | Debt Collector - Splendor - Welcome to Sarajevo - Gridlock'd |
| COMMENTS | ALSO: 23 Golden Square, London, WIR 3PA. Deal with Channel Four Films. |

Damian Jones . . . . . . . . . . . . . . . . . . . . . . . . . . . . . . . Producer
Graham Broadbent . . . . . . . . . . . . . . . . . . . . . . . . . . . Producer
Elaine Chin . . . . . . . . . . . . . . . . . . . . . . . . . . . . . . Development
Katie Goodson . . . . . . . . . . . . . . . . . . . . . . . . . . Development

## DRAIZIN CO., THE
PHONE . . . . . . . . . . . . . . . . . . . . . . . . . . . . . . . . 818-972-4756
FAX . . . . . . . . . . . . . . . . . . . . . . . . . . . . . . . . . . . 818-972-4765
500 S. Buena Vista St.
Burbank, CA 91521-7280

| | |
|---|---|
| TYPE | Television + Motion Pictures + Animation |
| DEAL | Walt Disney Pictures/Touchstone Pictures/Walt Disney TV/Touchstone TV |
| CREDITS | Fools Rush In - Spy Hard - Safety Patrol - Stretch Armstrong |
| COMMENTS | Delivery Address: 2600 W. Olive Ave., Ste. 1047 Burbank, CA 91505 |

Doug Draizin . . . . . . . . . . . . . . . . . . . . . . . . . . . . . . President
Scott Bernstein . . . . . . . . . . . . . . . . . . . . . . Dir., Development

## DREAM CITY FILMS
PHONE . . . . . . . . . . . . . . . . . . . . . . . . . . . . . . . . 213-223-4169
FAX . . . . . . . . . . . . . . . . . . . . . . . . . . . . . . . . . . . 213-226-9929
216 Mt. Washington Drive
Los Angeles, CA 90065

| | |
|---|---|
| TYPE | Television + Motion Pictures + Interactive Multimedia |
| CREDITS | Bachelor's Baby- Dancing in the Dark- Bonds of Love |

Heidi Wall . . . . . . . . . . . . . . . . . . . . . . . . . . Executive Producer
Harry Chandler . . . . . . . . . . . . . . . . . . . . . . . . . . . . . President

## DREAMWORKS SKG
PHONE . . . . . . . . . . . . . . . . . . . . . . . . . . . . . . . . 818-733-7000
100 Universal Plaza, Bldg. 10
Universal City, CA 91608-1085

| | |
|---|---|
| TYPE | Motion Pictures + Television + Animation + Interactive Multimedia |

David Geffen . . . . . . . . . . . . . . . . . . . . . . . . . . . Administration
Jeffrey Katzenberg . . . . . . . . . . . . . . . . . . . . . Administration
Steven Spielberg . . . . . . . . . . . . . . . . . . . . . . . Administration
Helene Hahn . . . . . . . . . . . . . . . . . . . . . . . . . . . Administration
Ron Nelson . . . . . . . . . . . . . . . . . . . . . . . . . . . . Administration
Bob Brassel . . . . . . . . . . . . . . . . . . . . . . Theatrical Production
Margaret French Issac . . . . . . . . . . . . . . Theatrical Production
Adam Goodman . . . . . . . . . . . . . . . . . . . Theatrical Production
Michael Grillo . . . . . . . . . . . . . . . . . . . . . Theatrical Production
Marc Haimes . . . . . . . . . . . . . . . . . . . . . . Theatrical Production
Jason Hoffs . . . . . . . . . . . . . . . . . . . . . . . Theatrical Production
Asa Hung . . . . . . . . . . . . . . . . . . . . . . . . . Theatrical Production
Suzanne Jurva . . . . . . . . . . . . . . . . . . . . Theatrical Production
Karen Kushell . . . . . . . . . . . . . . . . . . . . . Theatrical Production
Paul Lister . . . . . . . . . . . . . . . . . . . . . . . . Theatrical Production
Laurie MacDonald . . . . . . . . . . . . . . . . . Theatrical Production
Andrea McCall . . . . . . . . . . . . . . . . . . . . Theatrical Production
Steven R. Molen . . . . . . . . . . . . . . . . . . . Theatrical Production
Walter Parkes . . . . . . . . . . . . . . . . . . . . . Theatrical Production
Grey Rembert . . . . . . . . . . . . . . . . . . . . . Theatrical Production
Glenn Williamson . . . . . . . . . . . . . . . . . Theatrical Production
Bruce Cranston . . . . . . . . Head, Develop., Television Animation
Gary Krisel . . . . . . . . . . . . . . . . . Head, Television Animation
David L. Simon . . . . . . . . . . . . . . . Head, Television Animation
Penney Finkelman Cox . . . . . . . . . . . . . . . . . . . . . Animation
Sandy Rabins . . . . . . . . . . . . . . . . . . . . . . . . . . . . . Animation
Bonne Radford . . . . . . . . . . . . . . . . . . . . . . . . . . . Animation
Dan McDermott . . . . . . . . . . . . . . . . . . . . . Head, Television
Justin Falvey . . . . . . . . . . . . . . . . . . . . . . . . . . . . Television
Darryl Frank . . . . . . . . . . . . . . . . . . . . . . . . . . . . . Television
Charles Segars . . . . . . . . . . . . . . . . . . . . . . . . . . . Television
Michael Ostin . . . . . . . . . . . . . . . . . . . . . . . . . . . . . . . Music
Mo Ostin . . . . . . . . . . . . . . . . . . . . . . . . . . . . . . . . . . . Music
Lenny Waronker . . . . . . . . . . . . . . . . . . . . . . . . . . . . . Music
Tony Hull . . . . . . . . . . . . . . . . . . . . . . . . . . . . . . . . Financial
Laura Fox . . . . . . . . . . . . . . . Theatrical Business Affairs
Art Frazier . . . . . . . . . . . . . . . . . . . . . . . . . Business Affairs
Alan Myerson . . . . . . . . . . . . . . . . Animation Business Affairs
Lisa Pongracic . . . . . . . . . . . . . . . Television Business Affairs
Clara Ukai . . . . . . . . . . . . . . . . . . . . . . . . . . . . Legal Affairs

## DREYFUSS/JAMES PRODS.
PHONE . . . . . . . . . . . . . . . . . . . . . . . . . . . . . . . . 213-850-3140
FAX . . . . . . . . . . . . . . . . . . . . . . . . . . . . . . . . . . . 213-850-3141
EMAIL . . . . . . . . . . . . . . . . . . . greg@djprods.claris.com
Warner-Hollywood Studios
1041 Formosa Ave., Pickford Bldg. Rm.110
West Hollywood, CA 90046

| | |
|---|---|
| TYPE | Motion Pictures |
| CREDITS | Quiz Show- Mad Dog Time - Mr. Holland's Opus |

Richard Dreyfuss . . . . . . . . . . . . . . . . . . Owner/Exec. Producer
Judith James . . . . . . . . . . . . . . . . . . . . . . Owner/Exec. Producer
Audrey Bamber . . . . . . . . . . . . . . . . . . . . Asst. to Mr. Dreyfuss
Greg Szimonisz . . . . . . . . . . . . . . . . . . . . Asst. to Judith James

## DRISKILL ENTERTAINMENT
PHONE . . . . . . . . . . . . . . . . . . . . . . . . . . . . . . . . 818-222-5800
FAX . . . . . . . . . . . . . . . . . . . . . . . . . . . . . . . . . . . 818-222-5821
EMAIL . . . . . . . . . . . . . . . . . . . . . . . . . . . driskent@aol.com
2899 Agoura Rd., Ste. 533
Calabasas, CA 91361

| | |
|---|---|
| TYPE | Motion Pictures + Television |
| CREDITS | 100 Hours - Tailhook - Hits - Words Up |

Martha D. Humphreys . . . . . . . . . . . . . . . . . President/Producer
Una Hart . . . . . . . . . . . . . . . . . . . . . . . . . . . VP, Creative Affairs
Marcus Wernig . . . . . . . . . . . . . . . . . . . . . . . . . . . . . . Director
Katharine Haggerty . . . . . . . . . . . . . . . . . . . . . . . Story Editor

## DRYER PRODS., FRED
PHONE . . . . . . . . . . . . . . . . . . . . . . . . . . . . . . . . 818-505-6620
FAX . . . . . . . . . . . . . . . . . . . . . . . . . . . . . . . . . . . 818-505-6630
EMAIL . . . . . . . . . . . . . . . . . . . . . . . . . . . . . . wcfdp@idt.net
4117 Radford Ave.
Studio City, CA 91604

| | |
|---|---|
| TYPE | Motion Pictures + Television + Syndication |
| CREDITS | Lands End - Day of Reckoning - Return of Hunter |

Fred Dryer . . . . . . . . . . . . . . . . . . . . . . . . Actor/Exec. Producer
Victor Schiro . . . . . . . . . . . . . . . . . . . . . . . Executive Producer
Wally Caddow . . . . . . . . . . . . . . . . . . Creative Assistant/Admin.
Derek Chase . . . . . . . . . . . . . . . . . . . Creative Assistant/Admin.

# COMPANIES AND STAFF

**DUCKS IN A ROW ENTERTAINMENT CORPORATION**
PHONE . . . . . . . . . . . . . . . . . . . . . . . . . . . . . . . . . . . 310-557-2444
FAX . . . . . . . . . . . . . . . . . . . . . . . . . . . . . . . . . . . . . . 310-557-0017
EMAIL . . . . . . . . . . . . . . . . . . . . . . . . . . . . . ducksinrow@aol.com
Wilshire Court Productions
1840 Century Park East., Ste. 400
Los Angeles, CA 90067-2105
TYPE            Motion Pictures + Television + Syndication
DEAL            Wilshire Court Productions
Anat Baron . . . . . . . . . . . . . . . . . . . . . . . . . . . . Executive Producer

**DUNAS PRODS., RONALD S.**
PHONE . . . . . . . . . . . . . . . . . . . . . . . . . . . . . . . . . . . 310-273-4712
FAX . . . . . . . . . . . . . . . . . . . . . . . . . . . . . . . . . . . . . . 310-275-1647
9060 Santa Monica Blvd., Ste. 370
West Hollywood, CA 90069
TYPE            Motion Pictures
CREDITS         Dr. Phibes - Scorned & Swindled - Bells - Boys of '68
Ronald Dunas . . . . . . . . . . . . . . . . . . . . President/Writer/Producer
Kolleen White . . . . . . . . . . . . . . . . Creative Asst./Office Administrator

**E! ENTERTAINMENT TELEVISION**
PHONE . . . . . . . . . . . . . . . . . . . . . . . . . . . . . . . . . . . 213-954-2400
FAX . . . . . . . . . . . . . . . . . . . . . . . . . . . . . . . . . . . . . . 213-954-2660
WEBSITE . . . . . . . . . . . . . . . . . . . . . . . . http://www.eonline.com
5670 Wilshire Blvd.
Los Angeles, CA 90036
TYPE            Television
CREDITS         E! News Daily - Talk Soup - Gossip Show - Howard Stern -
                E! True Hollywood Story
COMMENTS        24-hour entertainment network
Lee Masters . . . . . . . . . . . . . . . . . . . . . . . . . . . . . President/CEO
William Keenan . . . . . . . . . . . . . . . . . . . . . . . . . . . Sr. VP/CFO
Chris Fager . . . . . . . . . . . . . . . . . . . Sr. VP, International Development
Mark Feldman . . . . . . . . . . . . . . . . . Sr. VP, Business & Legal Affairs
Fran Shea . . . . . . . . . . . . . . . . . . . . . . . . . Sr. VP, Programming
Jon Helmrich . . . . . . . . . . . . . . . . . . VP, International Development
John Rieber . . . . . . . . . . . . . . . . . . . . . . . VP, Special Projects
Doug Sylvester . . . . . . . . . VP, Planning and New Business Development
Marta Tracy . . . . . . . . . . . . . . . . VP, Programming & Development
Gail McClellan . . . . . . . . . . . . . . . . . . Dir., Corporate Planning
Barbara Pepe . . . . . . . . . . . . . . . . . . . . . . Dir., Intl. Production
Antonio Ruiz . . . . . . . . . . . . . . . . . . . . . . . . Dir., Live Events
Gary Snegaroff . . . . . . . . . . . . . . . . . . . . . . Dir., Special Projects

**EAGLE NATION FILMS**
PHONE . . . . . . . . . . . . . . . . . . . . . . . . . . . . . . . . . . . 213-956-5989
EMAIL . . . . . . . . . . . . . . . . . . . . . . . . . . . . . enation@aol.com
5555 Melrose Ave., Gower Mill, Ste. 117
Los Angeles, CA 90038
TYPE            Television + Motion Pictures
DEAL            Paramount Pictures- Motion Picture Group/Paramount
                Television Group
CREDITS         Reading Rainbow
LeVar Burton . . . . . . . . . . . . . . . . . . . . . . . . . . . . . . President
Julia Roberson . . . . . . . . . . . . . . . . . . . . . . . . . . VP/Producer
Olivia Barham . . . . . . . . . . . . . . . . . . Associate Development Exec.

**EARTHBOURNE FILMS, INC.**
PHONE . . . . . . . . . . . . . . . . . . . . . . . . . . . . . . . . . . . 310-582-9180
FAX . . . . . . . . . . . . . . . . . . . . . . . . . . . . . . . . . . . . . . 310-582-9183
EMAIL . . . . . . . . . . . . . . . . . . . . . . . . . . . . . . kaktis@idt.net
1150 Yale St., Ste. 2
Santa Monica, CA 90403
TYPE            Motion Pictures + Television + Documentaries
CREDITS         Touch
Fida Attieh . . . . . . . . . . . . . . . . . . . . . . . . . . . . . . . Producer
Amanda Burton . . . . . . . . . . . . . . . . . . . . . . . . . . . . Associate

**EARTHWORKS FILMS, INC.**
PHONE . . . . . . . . . . . . . . . . . . . . . . . . . . . . . . . . . . . 818-990-2261
FAX . . . . . . . . . . . . . . . . . . . . . . . . . . . . . . . . . . . . . . 818-990-2265
EMAIL . . . . . . . . . . . . . . . . . . . . . . . . . earthwrx@primenet.com
13527 Contour Drive
Sherman Oaks, CA 91423
TYPE            Motion Pictures + Documentaries + Television
CREDITS         Broken Rainbow
COMMENTS        Academy Award Best Documentary Feature
Maria Florio . . . . . . . . . . . . . . . . . . . . . . . . . . . . . . . Producer
Victoria Mudd . . . . . . . . . . . . . . . . . . . . . . . . . . . . . . Producer

**EAST WEST FILM PARTNERS**
PHONE . . . . . . . . . . . . . . . . . . . . . . . . . . . . . . . . . . . 310-858-3091
FAX . . . . . . . . . . . . . . . . . . . . . . . . . . . . . . . . . . . . . . 310-858-0703
EMAIL . . . . . . . . . . . . . . . . . . . . . . . . . EASTWESTFP@aol.com
270 N. Canon Dr., Ste. 1329
Beverly Hills, CA 90210
TYPE            Motion Pictures
CREDITS         Good Luck - Joe's Rotten World - Grim Prairie Tales
Richard Hahn . . . . . . . . . . . . . . . . . . . . . . . President/Producer
Shirley Honickman Hahn . . . . . . . . . . . . . . . . . . . . . . Producer
Andrew Kamrowski . . . . . . . . . . . . . . . . . . . . . . . . . . Producer

**EDELMAN PRODUCTIONS, ABRA**
PHONE . . . . . . . . . . . . . . . . . . . . . . . . . . . . . . . . . . . 310-724-8969
FAX . . . . . . . . . . . . . . . . . . . . . . . . . . . . . . . . . . . . . . 310-724-8970
9157 Sunset Blvd., Ste. 200
Los Angeles, CA 90069
TYPE            Motion Pictures
CREDITS         Bulletproof Heart - Underworld - Changing Habits - Some
                Girls
Abra Edelman . . . . . . . . . . . . . . . . . . . . . . . . . . . . . . Producer

***EDELSON PRODUCTIONS**
PHONE . . . . . . . . . . . . . . . . . . . . . . . . . . . . . . . . . . . 818-733-0616
EMAIL . . . . . . . . . . . . . . . . . . . . . . . . . . . . . edelsonp@aol.com
100 Universal City Plaza, 473, 205
Universal City, CA 91608
TYPE            Television
DEAL            Universal Studios
CREDITS         Prey - Promised Land - Darrow
COMMENTS        Agent:  Jack Dytman 310-274-8844
William Schmidt . . . . . . . . . . . . . . . . . . . . . . . . . . . . Producer
Nayiri Ishakian . . . . . . . . . . . . . . . . . . . . . . . Dir., Development

**EDMONDS ENTERTAINMENT**
PHONE . . . . . . . . . . . . . . . . . . . . . . . . . . . . . . . . . . . 213-860-1550
FAX . . . . . . . . . . . . . . . . . . . . . . . . . . . . . . . . . . . . . . 213-860-1554
1635 N. Cahuenga Blvd.
Los Angeles, CA 90028
TYPE            Motion Pictures + Television
DEAL            Twentieth Century Fox-Fox 2000 (LA)
CREDITS         Soul Food - Hav Plenty
Kenneth "Babyface" Edmonds . . . . . . . . . . . . . . . . President/CEO
Tracey E. Edmonds . . . . . . . . . . . . . . . . . . . . . . President/CEO
Bridget D. Davis . . . . . . . . . . . . . . . . . . . . . . . . . . VP, Film
Andrew J. Horne . . . . . . . . . . . . . . . . . . . . . . VP, Television
Patrik-Ian Polk . . . . . . . . . . . . . . . . . . . . . Creative Executive
Stacy D. Bodden . . . . . . . . . . . . . . . . . . . . Asst./Manager, TV
LaShan R. Brown . . . . . . . . . . . . . . . . . . . . . Asst./Story Editor

**EDWARDS CO., BLAKE**
PHONE . . . . . . . . . . . . . . . . . . . . . . . . . . . . . . . . . . . 310-207-5455
FAX . . . . . . . . . . . . . . . . . . . . . . . . . . . . . . . . . . . . . . 310-207-9305
10520 Wilshire Blvd., Ste. 1002
Los Angeles, CA 90024
TYPE            Motion Pictures
CREDITS         Switch - Victor/Victoria - Son of the Pink Panther
Blake Edwards . . . . . . . . . . . . . . . . . . . . . . . . . . . . Chairman

**EDWARDS YELLEN ENTERTAINMENT**
PHONE . . . . . . . . . . . . . . . . . . . . 213-466-3013/818-990-6299
FAX . . . . . . . . . . . . . . . . . . . . . . . . . . . . . . . . . . . . . . 213-467-1258
6399 Wilshire Blvd., Ste. 406
Los Angeles, CA 90048
TYPE            Motion Pictures + Television
DEAL            ABC Entertainment
CREDITS         The Companion (USA)-One Special Victory (NBC) - I
                Know What You Did (ABC)-In A Workmanlike Manner
                (CBS)
COMMENTS        Also:  Literary Management & Theatre.
Rona Edwards . . . . . . . . . . . . . . . . . . . . . . . . . . . . . . Producer
Nicholas Yellen . . . . . . . . . . . . . . . . . . . . . . . . . . . . . Producer

**EFFE FILMS, INC.**
PHONE . . . . . . . . . . . . . . . . . . . . . . . . . . . . . . . . . . . 310-277-7351
FAX . . . . . . . . . . . . . . . . . . . . . . . . . . . . . . . . . . . . . . 310-556-0253
501 S. Beverly Dr., 3rd Fl.
Beverly Hills, CA 90212
TYPE            Motion Pictures + Television
CREDITS         Flashback - Monkey Trouble
Franco Amurri . . . . . . . . . . . . . . . . . . . . . . . . . . . Writer/Director

# COMPANIES AND STAFF

**EGG PICTURES**
PHONE . . . . . . . . . . . . . . . . . . . . . . . . . . . . . . . . . . . 213-845-0300
FAX . . . . . . . . . . . . . . . . . . . . . . . . . . . . . . . . . . . . . 213-845-0301
7920 Sunset Blvd., Ste. 200
Los Angeles, CA 90046
| | |
|---|---|
| TYPE | Motion Pictures |
| DEAL | PolyGram Filmed Ent. |
| CREDITS | Nell - Home For the Holidays |

Jodie Foster . . . . . . . . . . . . . . . . . . . . . . . . . . . Actress/Director/Producer
Stuart Kleinman . . . . . . . . . . . . . . . . . . . . . . . . . . . . . . . . . President
Meg LeFauve . . . . . . . . . . . . . . . . . . . . . . . . . . . . . . . . Vice President
Lisa Buono . . . . . . . . . . . . . . . . . . . . . . . . . . . . . . Creative Executive
Erin O'Donnell . . . . . . . . . . . . . . . . . . . . . . . . . . Executive Assistant
Kate Wilson . . . . . . . . . . . . . . . . . . . . . . . . . . . . Executive Assistant
Lida Nassif . . . . . . . . . . . . . . . . . . . . . . . . . . . Development Assistant

**EL DORADO PICTURES**
PHONE . . . . . . . . . . . . . . . . . . . . . . . . . . . . . . . . . 310-244-8464
FAX . . . . . . . . . . . . . . . . . . . . . . . . . . . . . . . . . . . 310-244-2155
10202 W. Washington Blvd., Lean #220
Culver City, CA 90232
| | |
|---|---|
| TYPE | Motion Pictures |
| DEAL | Columbia TriStar Television/Castle Rock Entertainment |
| CREDITS | The Confession |

Alec Baldwin . . . . . . . . . . . . . . . . . . . . . . . . . . . . . . . . . . Producer
Corrinne Mann . . . . . . . . . . . . . . . . . . . . . . . . . . . . . . . . . Producer
India Osborne . . . . . . . . . . . . . . . . . . . . . . . . . . . . Dir., Development
Greg Pace . . . . . . . . . . . . . . . . . . . . . . . . . . . . . . . Dir., Production
T. Vincent . . . . . . . . . . . . . . . . . . . . . . . . . . . . Asst. to Alec Baldwin

**ELEPHANT WALK ENTERTAINMENT**
PHONE . . . . . . . . . . . . . . . . . . . . . . . . . . . . . . . . . 310-887-3977
EMAIL . . . . . . . . . . . . . . . . . . . . . elephantwalk@earthlink.net
9200 Sunset Blvd., #430
Los Angeles, CA 90069
| | |
|---|---|
| TYPE | Motion Pictures + Television |
| DEAL | Twentieth Century Fox/Columbia TriStar Television |
| CREDITS | Jason's Lyric - New Jack City - Malcolm & Eddie - A Thin Line Between Love & Hate |
| COMMENTS | Also: Music & Talent Management. |

Doug McHenry . . . . . . . . . . . . . . . . . . . . . . . . . . . Producer/Director
Rob Lee . . . . . . . . . . . . . . . . . . . . . . . . . . . . . . . . . . . . Producer
Suzanne Broderick . . . . . . . . . . . . . . . . . . . . . . Exec. VP, Production
Lana Campbell . . . . . . . . . . . . . . . . . . . Exec. Asst. to Mr. McHenry
Melissa Friedman . . . . . . . . . . . . . . . . . . . . . . Exec. Asst. to Mr. Lee

**ELEVENTH DAY ENTERTAINMENT**
PHONE . . . . . . . . . . . . . . . . . . . . . . . . . . . . . . . . . 818-784-6403
FAX . . . . . . . . . . . . . . . . . . . . . . . . . . . . . . . . . . . 818-784-6421
EMAIL . . . . . . . . . . . . . . . . . . . . . . eleventhday@earthlink.net
17003 Ventura Blvd., Ste. 200
Encino, CA 91316
| | |
|---|---|
| TYPE | Documentaries + Television |
| CREDITS | Sex and The Silver Screen - MGM When The Lion Roars - CBS-1st 50 Years |
| COMMENTS | Also: Commercials |

Frank Martin . . . . . . . . . . . . . . . . . . . . . . . . . . . . Producer/Director
Rudy Poe . . . . . . . . . . . . . . . . . . . . . . . . . . . . . . . Producer/Director
Jack Masters . . . . . . . . . . . . . . . . . VP, Development/Business Affairs

**ELKINS ENTERTAINMENT**
PHONE . . . . . . . . . . . . . . . . . . . . . . . . . . . . . . . . . 310-285-0700
FAX . . . . . . . . . . . . . . . . . . . . . . . . 310-273-4999/310-273-1251
EMAIL . . . . . . . . . . . . . . . . . . . . . . . . . . . . elkinsent@msn.com
8306 Wilshire Blvd., Ste. 438
Beverly Hills, CA 90211-2382
| | |
|---|---|
| TYPE | Motion Pictures + Television |
| CREDITS | Dolls House - Richard Pryor Live - A New Leaf - Inside |
| COMMENTS | Also: Theatre. A management & production corp. |

Hillard Elkins . . . . . . . . . . . . . . . . . . . . . . . . . . . President/Producer
Sandi Love . . . . . . . . . . . . . . . . . . . . . . . . . . . . . . . . . Vice President
Greg Hausmann . . . . . . . . . . . . . . . Exec. Asst. to Mr. Elkins/Office Mgr.
Ivan Rivas . . . . . . . . . . . . . . . . . . . . . . . . . . . . . . . . . . . . Assistant

**ELLIS MILLER FILMS, ROBERT**
PHONE . . . . . . . . . . . . . . . . . . . . . . . . . . . . . . . . . 213-655-5156
FAX . . . . . . . . . . . . . . . . . . . . . . . . . . . . . . . . . . . 213-655-3001
8170 Beverly Blvd., Ste. 100
Los Angeles, CA 90048
| | |
|---|---|
| TYPE | Motion Pictures |
| CREDITS | Reuben, Reuben - Any Wednesday - Hawks - The Heart is a Lonely Hunter |

Robert Ellis Miller . . . . . . . . . . . . . . . . . . . . . . . . Producer/Director
Brian Black . . . . . . . . . . . . . . . . . . . . . . . . . . . . . . . . . Development

**ELLISON, BOB**
PHONE . . . . . . . . . . . . . . . . . . . . . . . . . . . . . . . . . 213-956-4859
FAX . . . . . . . . . . . . . . . . . . . . . . . . . . . . . . . . . . . 213-862-1691
Paramount TV
5555 Melrose Ave., Clara Bow Bldg. 200
Los Angeles, CA 90038-3197
| | |
|---|---|
| TYPE | Television |
| DEAL | Paramount Television Group |
| CREDITS | Caroline in the City - Wings - Dear John - Cheers |

Bob Ellison . . . . . . . . . . . . . . . . . . . . . . . . . . . . . . Writer/Producer

**EMBY EYE**
PHONE . . . . . . . . . . . . . . . . . . . . . . . . . . . . . . . . . 310-315-4826
FAX . . . . . . . . . . . . . . . . . . . . . . . . . . . . . . . . . . . 310-315-4879
3000 W. Olympic Blvd., Ste. 1431
Santa Monica, CA 90404
| | |
|---|---|
| TYPE | Motion Pictures + Television + Feature Direct to Video |
| CREDITS | Three of Hearts- When The Party's Over- Edie & Pen - Alphabet City |

Matthew Irmas . . . . . . . . . . . . . . . . . . . . . . . . . . . . . . . President

**EMK PRODUCTIONS**
PHONE . . . . . . . . . . . . . . . . . . . . . . . . . . . . . . . . . 213-954-4066
FAX . . . . . . . . . . . . . . . . . . . . . . . . . . . . . . . . . . . 213-954-1483
EMAIL . . . . . . . . . . . . . . . . . EMKPRODUCTIONS@prodigy.net
955 S. Carrillo Dr., Ste. 200
Los Angeles, CA 90048
| | |
|---|---|
| TYPE | Motion Pictures + Television + Documentaries |
| CREDITS | Other People's Money - The Kathy & Mo Show - A Lesson Before Dying |

Ellen M. Krass . . . . . . . . . . . . . . . . . . . . . . . . . . Executive Producer
Daniel Bernstein . . . . . . . . . . . . . . . . . . . . . . . . . . Dir., Development

**EMPIRE PICTURES INC.**
PHONE . . . . . . . . . . . . . . . . . . . . . . . . . . . . . . . . . 213-463-1618
FAX . . . . . . . . . . . . . . . . . . . . . . . . . . . . . . . . . . . 213-957-9762
Propaganda Films
940 N. Mansfield Ave.
Los Angeles, CA 90038
| | |
|---|---|
| TYPE | Motion Pictures + Television + Interactive Multimedia |
| DEAL | PolyGram Filmed Ent. |
| CREDITS | Keys to Tulsa |

Michael Birnbaum . . . . . . . . . . . . . . . . . . . . . . President/Producer
Nikki Corda . . . . . . . . . . . . . . . . . . . . . . . . . . . . Creative Executive

**ENCHANTER ENTERTAINMENT**
PHONE . . . . . . . . . . . . . . . . . . . . . . . . . . . . . . . . . 212-586-2020
FAX . . . . . . . . . . . . . . . . . . . . . . . . . . . . . . . . . . . 212-586-1020
EMAIL . . . . . . . . . . . . . . . . . . . . . . . . . . . enchant101@aol.com
101 W. 55th St., Ste. 12H
New York, NY 10019
| | |
|---|---|
| TYPE | Motion Pictures + Television |
| CREDITS | The Gingerbread Man |

Glen Tobias . . . . . . . . . . . . . . . . . . . . . . . . . . . . Executive Producer
Jeremy Tannenbaum . . . . . . . . . . . . . . . . . . . . . . Executive Producer
Brenda Simon . . . . . . . . . . . . . . . . . . . . . . . . . . . . Creative Affairs

***ENCHANTMENT FILMS, INC.**
PHONE . . . . . . . . . . . . . . . . . . . . . . . . . . . . . . . . . 213-467-8352
FAX . . . . . . . . . . . . . . . . . . . . . . . . . . . . . . . . . . . 213-467-8319
EMAIL . . . . . . . . . . . . . . . . . . . . . . . . . . . efilms13@aol.com
6525 Sunset Blvd., Ste. 303
Hollywood, CA 90028
| | |
|---|---|
| TYPE | Motion Pictures |
| CREDITS | South Central - Dead Men Can't Dance |
| COMMENTS | Produced Columbia Pictures, Chanticlear Films Discovery Program |

Steve Anderson . . . . . . . . . . . . . . . . . . . . . Writer/Director/Producer

**ENLIGHTENED WITNESS, INC./LEVINE MGMT.**
PHONE . . . . . . . . . . . . . . . . . . . . . . . . . . . . . . . . . 310-275-0875
FAX . . . . . . . . . . . . . . . . . . . . . . . . . . . . . . . . . . . 310-275-1540
EMAIL . . . . . . . . . . . . . . . . . . . . . . . . . . levinemgmt@aol.com
9028 Sunset Blvd., PH 1
Los Angeles, CA 90069
| | |
|---|---|
| TYPE | Motion Pictures + Television |
| CREDITS | Shame: The Secret - Nothing Personal |
| COMMENTS | Please no unsolicited submissions or phone calls. Also: MOW's/Series Television. |

Amanda Donohoe . . . . . . . . . . . . . . . . Writer/Producer/Director/Actor
Michael P. Levine . . . . . . . . . . . . . . . . . . . . . . . Manager/Producer
Arnold Fram . . . . . . . . . . . . . . . . . . . . . . . . Chief Financial Officer

## ENTERAKTION, INC.
PHONE . . . . . . . . . . . . . . . . . . . . . . . . . . . . . . . . 310-459-1262
FAX . . . . . . . . . . . . . . . . . . . . . . . . . . . . . . . . . . 310-459-4497
EMAIL . . . . . . . . . . . . . . . . . . . . . . . . . . . EnterAk@aol.com
15200 Sunset Blvd., Ste. 208
Pacific Palisades, CA 90272
TYPE          Motion Pictures + Television + Animation + Interactive Multimedia
CREDITS     Denial - We Dare You - Mismatch - House to House - The Arrival
Tom Walsh . . . . . . . . . . . . . . . CEO/Producer/Director/Co-Chairman
Ronald Hilton . . . . . . . . . . . . . . . . . . . . . . . . . . . Co-Chairman
Lloyd Gross . . . . . . . . . . . . . . . . . . . . . . . . . Producer/Director
Martina Ritt . . . . . . . . . . . . . . . . . . . . . . . . . . . . . . Producer
Adriana Walsh . . . . . . . . VP, Intl. Co-Productions & Creative Affairs
Don Waters . . . . . . . . . . . . . . . . . . . . . . . . . . Dir., Digital
James Ripley . . . . . . . . . . . . . . . . . . . . . . . . . Artist Digital
Elizabeth Flower . . . . . . . . . . . . . . . . . Exec. Asst. to Mr. Walsh

## ENTERTAINMENT ALLIANCE, INC., THE
PHONE . . . . . . . . . . . . . . . . . . . . . . . . . . . . . . . . 310-821-2627
FAX . . . . . . . . . . . . . . . . . . . . . . . . . . . . . . . . . . 310-821-2627
EMAIL . . . . . . . . . . . . . . . . . . . . . . . . . . heatherdo@aol.com
2554 Lincoln Blvd. #644
Marina del Rey, CA 90291
TYPE          Motion Pictures + Television
COMMENTS   Please call first before faxing.
Alan R. Green . . . . . . . . . . . . . . . . . . . . . . President/Producer
Heather Barton . . . . . . . . . . . . . . . Dir., Development/Production
Katina Weaver . . . . . . . . . . . Development/Production Associate

## ENTERTAINMENT GROUP, THE
PHONE . . . . . . . . . . . . . . . . . . . . . . . . . . . . . . . . 212-925-9300
FAX . . . . . . . . . . . . . . . . . . . . . . . . . . . . . . . . . . 212-925-9603
270 Lafayette St., Ste. 610
New York, NY 10012
TYPE          Motion Pictures + Television
CREDITS     The Pentagon Wars - Flashback - Remember WENN - The Paramour
Howard Meltzer . . . . . . . . . . . . . . . . . . . . . . . . . . President
Emily Murphy . . . . . . . . . . . . . . . . . . . . . . Dir., Development
Andrea Weir . . . . . . . . . . . . . . . . . . . . Asst. Dir., Development

## ENTPRO, INC.
PHONE . . . . . . . . . . . . . . . . . . . . . . . . . . . . . . . . 310-440-4829
1015 Gayley Ave., Ste. 1149
Los Angeles, CA 90024-3424
TYPE          Motion Pictures + Television
CREDITS     Rescue Me - False Witness - A Friendship in Vienna - The Sisters
COMMENTS   Also: Theatre.
Richard Alfieri . . . . . . . . . . . . . . . . . . . . . . . Writer/Producer
Arthur Allan Seidelman . . . . . . . . . . . . . . . . . Director/Producer
Joseph Eastwood . . . . . . . . . . . . . . . . . . . . . . . Development

## ENZO FILMS
PHONE . . . . . . . . . . . . . . . . . . . . . . . . . . . . . . . . 213-957-6622
FAX . . . . . . . . . . . . . . . . . . . . . . . . . . . . . . . . . . 213-957-7590
Raleigh Studios
650 N. Bronson Ave., Ste. 215
Los Angeles, CA 90004
TYPE          Motion Pictures + Television + Documentaries
CREDITS     Stormy Summer - Sweet Revenge - A Business Affair
Charlotte Brandstrom . . . . . . . . . . . . . . . . . . . . Writer/Director

## EO PRODUCTIONS INTERNATIONAL, INC.
PHONE . . . . . . . . . . . . . . . . . . . . . . . . . . . . . . . . 310-264-5566
FAX . . . . . . . . . . . . . . . . . . . . . . . . . . . . . . . . . . 310-453-9469
EMAIL . . . . . . . . . . . . . . . . . . . . . . . . . . . . . eopi@aol.com
3025 W. Olympic Blvd.
Santa Monica, CA 90404
TYPE          Motion Pictures + Television + Documentaries + Feature Direct to Video
CREDITS     Williams Syndrome - ...and then there is hope - Goldilocks
Albert Mons . . . . . . . . . . . . . . . . . . . . . . Chief Executive Officer
Nickolas Barris . . . . . . . . . . . . . . . . . . . . . Pres., Development
Geert Heetebrij . . . . . . . . . . . . . . . . . . . . . . . . Story Editor
Christy Gauger . . . . . . . . . . . . . . . . . Development Coordinator

## EPIPHANY PRODUCTIONS, INC.
PHONE . . . . . . . . . . . . . . . . . . . . . . . . . . . . . . . . 310-815-1266
FAX . . . . . . . . . . . . . . . . . . . . . . . . . . . . . . . . . . 310-815-1269
EMAIL . . . . . . . . . . . . . . . . . . . . . . . Roadog@concentric.net
10625 Esther Ave.
Los Angeles, CA 90064
TYPE          Motion Pictures + Television
CREDITS     Picture Windows- Rosemary- Road Dogs - Rebs - Behind The Lines - The African
Scott JT Frank . . . . . . . . . . . . . . . . . . . . . . Producer/Director
Dan Halperin . . . . . . . . . . . . . . . . . . . . . . . Producer/Director

## EPSTEIN PRODUCTIONS, STEFANIE
PHONE . . . . . . . . . . . . . . . . . . . . . . . . . . . . . . . . 310-444-8310
FAX . . . . . . . . . . . . . . . . . . . . . . . . . . . . . . . . . . 310-996-6123
1440 S. Sepulveda Blvd., Ste. 314
Los Angeles, CA 90025
TYPE          Motion Pictures + Television
CREDITS     Abduction of Innocence - Postal Police - What Men Want Most
Stefanie Epstein . . . . . . . . . . . . . . . . . . . . . . . . . . Producer
Joanna Lovinger . . . . . . . . . . . . . . . . . . . . . . . . Development

## EQUINOX ENTERTAINMENT LTD.
PHONE . . . . . . . . . . . . . . . . . . . . . . . . . . . . . . . . 818-788-2500
FAX . . . . . . . . . . . . . . . . . . . . . . . . . . . . . . . . . . 818-528-1488
15030 Ventura Blvd., #815
Sherman Oaks, CA 91403
TYPE          Motion Pictures + Television
Mark Michopoulos . . . . . . . . . . . . . . . . Exec. Producer/Producer
Bob Manning . . . . . . . . . . . . . . . . . . . . . . . . . . Co-Producer
Ben Carpenter . . . . . . . . . . . . . . . . . . . . . . . Dir., Operations
Alex Ellis . . . . . . . . . . . . . . . . . . . . . . . . . . Dir., Development
Mandy Goldberg . . . . . . . . . . . . . . Dir., Research & Acquisitions
Tim Mathos . . . . . . . . . . . . . . . . . . . . . . . Dir., Creative Affairs
Amy Segal . . . . . . . . . . . . . . . . . . . . . . . . . . Dir., Production
Samantha Wagner . . . . . . . . . . . . . . . . . Dir., Business Affairs
Lauren Worth . . . . . . . . . . . . . Dir., Finance/Marketing/Distribution
Nick Andraos . . . . . . . . . . . . . . . . . . . . . . . . . Story Editor
Ryan Sahlberg . . . . . . . . . . . . . Assoc. Prod./Dir., Talent & Casting
Lisa Logan . . . . . . . . . . . . . . . . . Exec. Asst. to Mr. Michopoulos
Jennifer Mancini . . . . . . . . . . . . . Exec. Asst. to Mr. Michopoulos
Evan Cartwright . . . . . . . . . . . . . . . . . . . . Asst./Story Editor
Sara Palmer . . . . . . . . . . . . . . . . . . . . . Asst./Talent & Casting
C.J. Pillsbury . . . . . . . . . . . . . . . . . . . . . . Asst./Development
Max Shepherd . . . . . . . . . . . . . . . Asst./Research & Acquisitions

## EQUUS ENTERTAINMENT
PHONE . . . . . . . . . . . . . . . . . . . . . . . . . . . . . . . . 310-551-2262
FAX . . . . . . . . . . . . . . . . . . . . . . . . . . . . . . . . . . 310-556-3760
2121 Ave. of the Stars, 29th Floor
Los Angeles, CA 90067
TYPE          Motion Pictures
DEAL          Twentieth Century Fox/Davis Entertainment Co.
CREDITS     What If Guy - Icemen - Flawless - Fifth Access - Confidence Men
Adam J. Gibgot . . . . . . . . . . . . . . . . . . . . . . . Writer/Producer
Brian Hochman . . . . . . . . . . . . . . Development (310-551-2271)

## ERRATIC ENTERTAINMENT, INC.
PHONE . . . . . . . . . . . . . . . . . . . . . . . . . . . . . . . . 310-657-0922
FAX . . . . . . . . . . . . . . . . . . . . . . . . . . . . . . . . . . 310-657-1360
1131 Alta Loma Rd., #331
Los Angeles, CA 90069
TYPE          Motion Pictures + Television
CREDITS     The Call Of The Wild
Graham Ludlow . . . . . . . . . . . . . . . . . . . . . . Producer/Partner
Sam Okun . . . . . . . . . . . . . . . . . . . . . . . . . . Producer/Partner
Tom Damien . . . . . . . . . . . . . . . . . . . . . . . . Dir., Development
Jon Hamilton . . . . . . . . . . . . . . . . . . . . . . . Creative Executive

# COMPANIES AND STAFF

**ESPARZA-KATZ PRODS.**
PHONE . . . . . . . . . . . . . . . . . . . . . . . . . . . . . . . 310-281-3770
FAX . . . . . . . . . . . . . . . . . . . . . . . . . . . . . . . . . . 310-281-3777
8899 Beverly Blvd., Ste. 506
Los Angeles, CA 90048

TYPE    Motion Pictures + Television
CREDITS   Avenging Angel- Selena - Gettysburg - Milagro Beanfield War- Disappearance of Garcia Lorca - Butter - Rough Riders
COMMENTS   Developing Asian-American Features.

Moctesuma Esparza . . . . . . . . . . . . . . . . . . . . . . . . . . . Producer
Robert Katz . . . . . . . . . . . . . . . . . . . . . . . . . . . . . . . . . . Producer
Micheal Campus . . . . . . . . . . . . . . . . . . . . . . . . . . . . . Producer
Julian Fowles . . . . . . . . . . . . . . . . . . . . . . . . . . . . . . . Producer
Jacki Kong . . . . . . . . . . . . . . . . . . . . . . . . . . . . . . . . . Producer
Steve Kalb . . . . . . . . . . . . . . . . . . . . . . . VP, Business Affairs
Ligiah Villalobos . . . . . . . . . . . . . . . . . . . . VP, Creative Affairs
Xavier Salinas . . . . . . . . . . . . Production Executive/Development
Greg Gomez . . . . . . . . . . . . . . . . . . . . . . . . . . . . Development
Anamarie Esparza . . . . . . . . . . . . . . . Production Coordinator
Yesenia Collazo . . . . . . . . . . . . . . . . . . . . . . . . . . . . Assistant

**ESTEVEZ PRODUCTIONS**
PHONE . . . . . . . . . . . . . . . . . . . . . . . . . . . . . . . 310-264-4199
FAX . . . . . . . . . . . . . . . . . . . . . . . . . . . . . . . . . . 310-264-4196
3000 W. Olympic Blvd., Bldg. 5,Ste. 2215
Santa Monica, CA 90404

TYPE    Motion Pictures
DEAL    Walt Disney Company, The/Touchstone Pictures
CREDITS   The War at Home

Emilio Estevez . . . . . . . . . . . . . . . . . . . . . . Producer/Director
Mickey McDermott . . . . . . . . . . . . . Exec. Asst. to Mr. Estevez

**ETERNITY PICTURES, INC**
PHONE . . . . . . . . . . . . . . . . . . . . . . . . . . . . . . . 310-571-4443
FAX . . . . . . . . . . . . . . . . . . . . . . . . . . . . . . . . . . 310-571-9222
EMAIL . . . . . . . . . . . . . . . . . . . . . . . . . EternityP@aol.com
11440 San Vicente Blvd., Ste. 102
Los Angeles, CA 90049

TYPE    Motion Pictures
CREDITS   Afterglow - Laws Of Deception - Roadblock

Willi E. Baer . . . . . . . . . . . . . . . . . . . . . . . . . . . . . . Producer
Carmen M. Miller . . . . . . . . . . . . . . . . . . . . . . . . . . Producer
Zana Ross . . . . . . . . . . . . . . . . . . . . . . Asst. to CMM & WEB

**EVANS CO., THE ROBERT**
PHONE . . . . . . . . . . . . . . . . . . . . . . . . . . . . . . . 213-956-8800
FAX . . . . . . . . . . . . . . . . . . . . . . . . . . . . . . . . . . 213-862-0070
Paramount Studios
5555 Melrose Ave., Lubitsch #117
Los Angeles, CA 90038-3197

TYPE    Motion Pictures + Television
DEAL    Paramount Pictures- Motion Picture Group
CREDITS   The Saint - Chinatown - The Godfather - Sliver - The Phantom

Robert Evans . . . . . . . . . . . . . . . . . . . . . . . . . . . . . Chairman
Christine Forsyth-Peters . . . . . . . . . . . . . . . . . . . . President
Robin Guthrie . . . . . . . . . . . . . . . . . . . . Exec. Vice President
Shannon McNulty . . . . . . . . . . . . . . . . . . . . . . . Development

**EVANS PRODUCTIONS, INC., CHARLES**
PHONE . . . . . . . . . . . . . . . . . . . . . . . . . . . . . . . 212-755-2782
FAX . . . . . . . . . . . . . . . . . . . . . . . . . . . . . . . . . . 212-371-0768
745 Fifth Ave.
New York, NY 10151

TYPE    Motion Pictures
CREDITS   Tootsie - Monkey Shines - Showgirls - Bloodlines

Charles Evans . . . . . . . . . . . . . . . . . . . . . . . . . . . President
Alice Shure . . . . . . . . . . . . . . . . . . . . . . . . . . Vice President
Linda Munson . . . . . . . . . . . . . . . . . . . . . . . . . . . Secretary

***EVERYMAN PICTURES**
PHONE . . . . . . . . . . . . . . . . . . . . . . . . . . . . . . . 310-244-8932
FAX . . . . . . . . . . . . . . . . . . . . . . . . . . . . . . . . . . 310-244-0458
10202 W. Washington Blvd.
Culver City, CA 90232

TYPE    Motion Pictures
DEAL    Walt Disney Pictures/Touchstone Pictures
CREDITS   Mystery, Alaska

Jay Roach . . . . . . . . . . . . . . . . . . . . . . . . . . . . . . President
Shauna Robertson . . . . . . . . . . . . . . . . . . . . . Vice President

**EVOLVE ENTERTAINMENT**
PHONE . . . . . . . . . . . . . . . . . . . . . . . . . . . . . . . 310-273-6676
FAX . . . . . . . . . . . . . . . . . . . . . . . . . . . . . . . . . . 310-273-0478
EMAIL . . . . . . . . . . . . . . . . . . . . . . . . . . evolveent@aol.com
9100 Wilshire Blvd., Ste. 540 East Tower
Beverly Hills, CA 90212

TYPE    Motion Pictures + Television + Documentaries
CREDITS   Family of Spies - David's Mother - Rivals Series - Choices of the Heart: The Margaret Sanger Story

Gerald W. Abrams . . . . . . . . . . . . . . . . . . . . . . Co-Chairman
Jennifer Alward . . . . . . . . . . . . . . . . . . . . . . . . Co-Chairman
Philip Kruener . . . . . . . . . . . . . . . . . . . . . . Dir., Development
Michael Goldstein . . . . . . . . . . . . . . . . . . Creative Executive

**EXCELSIOR PICTURES CORP.**
PHONE . . . . . . . . . . . . . . . . . . . . . . . . . . . . . . . 310-289-8220
FAX . . . . . . . . . . . . . . . . . . . . . . . . . . . . . . . . . . 310-358-8768
EMAIL . . . . . . . . . . . . . . . . . . . . . . . . . . ExcelPict@aol.com
8544 Melrose Ave.
West Hollywood, CA 90069

TYPE    Motion Pictures + Television
CREDITS   It Rained All Night the Day I Left - Girls - Reckless - Riding Fast - Lucky Star

Christopher Harbonville . . . . . . . . . . . . . . . President/Producer
Simon Edery . . . . . . . . . . . . . . . . . . . . . . . . . . . . Producer
Olivier Prat . . . . . . . . . . . . . . . . . . VP, Business Affairs CDN
Jonathan Paul . . . . . . . . . . . . . . . . . . . . . . Dir., Development
David Raphael . . . . . . . . . . . . . . . . . . . . . . . Business Affairs

**EXILE ENTERTAINMENT**
PHONE . . . . . . . . . . . . . . . . . . . . . . . . . . . . . . . 310-244-3239
FAX . . . . . . . . . . . . . . . . . . . . . . . . . . . . . . . . . . 310-244-8886
Sony Pictures - David Lean Bldg.
10202 W. Washington Blvd., #230
Culver City, CA 90232

TYPE    Motion Pictures

Gary Ungar . . . . . . . . . . . . . . . . . . . . . . . . . . . . . . Producer

**EXPECT MIRACLES, INC.**
PHONE . . . . . . . . . . . . . . . . . . . . . . . . . . . . 213-882-8452
1710 N. Fuller Ave., Ste. 105
Los Angeles, CA 90046

TYPE    Motion Pictures + Television
CREDITS   The Private Files of J. Edgar Hoover - Bone - God Told Me To

Desmond Towey . . . . . . . . . . . . . . . . . . . . . . . . President
Janelle Webb . . . . . . . . . . . . . . . . . . . . . . . Vice President
Jill Gatsby . . . . . . . . . . . . . . . . . . . . . . . . Head, Development

**EYEMARK ENTERTAINMENT**
PHONE . . . . . . . . . . . . . . . . . . . . . . . . . . . . . . . 310-446-6000
FAX . . . . . . . . . . . . . . . . . . . . . . . . . . . . . . . . . . 310-446-6066
10877 Wilshire Blvd., 9th Floor
Los Angeles, CA 90024-4341

TYPE    Television + Syndication
CREDITS   Pensacola: Wings of Gold - Jackie Collins' Hollywood

Ed Wilson . . . . . . . . . . . . . . . . . . . . . . . . . . . . President
Robert Cook . . . . . . . . . . . . . . . . . . . . Exec. Vice President
Marvin Shirley . . . . . . . . . . . . . . . . . . . . Exec. Vice President
Barry Wallach . . . . . . . . . . . . . . . . . Exec. VP, Syndication
Robb Dalton . . . . . . . . . Sr. VP, Business and Program Development
Jim Dauphinee . . . . . . . . Sr. VP, Programming & Development (NY)
Elaine Bauer . . . . . . . . . . . . . . VP, Programming & Development

**F.R. PRODUCTIONS**
PHONE . . . . . . . . . . . . . . . . . . . . . . . . . . . . . . . 310-470-9212
FAX . . . . . . . . . . . . . . . . . . . . . . . . . . . . . . . . . . 310-470-4905
2980 Beverly Glen Circle
Los Angeles, CA 90077

TYPE    Motion Pictures
CREDITS   Godfather 2&3 - Black Stallion - Barfly - The Secret Garden - Town and Country

Fred Roos . . . . . . . . . . . . . . . . . . . . . . . . Producer/President
Anne Edgar . . . . . . . . . . . . . . . . . . . . . . . . Dir., Development

# COMPANIES AND STAFF

**FACE PRODUCTIONS**
PHONE . . . . . . . . . . . . . . . . . . . . . . . . . . . 310-285-2300
FAX . . . . . . . . . . . . . . . . . . . . . . . . . . . . . 310-285-2386
Castle Rock Entertainment
335 N. Maple Dr., Ste. 135
Beverly Hills, CA 90210
TYPE            Motion Pictures
DEAL            Castle Rock Entertainment
CREDITS         City Slickers I & II - Mr. Saturday Night - Forget Paris - My Giant

Billy Crystal . . . . . . . . . . . . . . . . . . . . . Actor/Producer
Annette Mathews . . . . . . . . . . . . . . . . . . . . . Story Editor
Carol Sidlow . . . . . . . . . . . . . . . . . Asst. to Billy Crystal

**FAIRDINKUM PRODS.**
PHONE . . . . . . . . . . . . . . . . . . . . . . . . . . . 310-586-8471
FAX . . . . . . . . . . . . . . . . . . . . . . . . . . . . . 310-586-8469
EMAIL . . . . . . . . . . . . . . . . . . . . . sbettencourt@mgm.com
MGM
2500 Broadway St., Bldg. E-5108
Santa Monica, CA 90404
TYPE            Motion Pictures + Television
DEAL            Walt Disney TV/Touchstone TV
CREDITS         MacGyver - Sightings - Dead Man's Gun

Henry Winkler . . . . . . . . . . Actor/Exec. Producer/Director
Sheryl Bettencourt . . . . . . . . . . Exec. Asst. to Mr. Winkler

**FANARO-NATHAN PRODS.**
PHONE . . . . . . . . . . . . . . . . . . . . . . . . . . . 213-956-8870
FAX . . . . . . . . . . . . . . . . . . . . . . . . . . . . . 213-862-0270
Paramount TV
5555 Melrose Ave.
Los Angeles, CA 90038-3197
TYPE            Motion Pictures + Television
DEAL            Paramount Television Group
CREDITS         Golden Girls - Fanelli Boys - Pacific Station - Kingpin
Barry Fanaro . . . . . . . . . . . . . . Exec. Producer/Writer
Mort Nathan . . . . . . . . . . . . . . . Exec. Producer/Writer
Sarah Krasney . . . . . . . . . . . . . . . . . . . . . . . . Assistant

**FARRELL/MINOFF PRODS.**
PHONE . . . . . . . . . . . . . . . . . . . . . . . . . . . 818-789-5766
FAX . . . . . . . . . . . . . . . . . . . . . . . . . . . . . 818-789-7459
14011 Ventura Blvd., Ste. 401
Sherman Oaks, CA 91423
TYPE            Motion Pictures + Television + Documentaries + Feature Direct to Video
CREDITS         Dominick & Eugene - Sins of the Mind - Patch Adams
Mike Farrell . . . . . . . . . . . . . . Actor/Producer/Director
Marvin Minoff . . . . . . . . . . . . . . . . . . . . . . . . Producer

**FAT CHANCE FILMS**
PHONE . . . . . . . . . . . . . . . . . . . . . . . . . 213-882-4130
EMAIL . . . . . . . . . . . . . . . . . . fatchancefilm@juno.com
P.O. Box 34928
Los Angeles, CA 90034
TYPE            Motion Pictures + Television
CREDITS         One Last Time- Circle of Pain- Why Colors - Some of My Best Friends
Bobby Mardis . . . . . . . . . . . . . . . . . Producer/Director

**FATIMA PRODUCTION**
PHONE . . . . . . . . . . . . . . . . . . . . . . . . . . . 212-633-0440
FAX . . . . . . . . . . . . . . . . . . . . . . . . . . . . . 212-633-7008
P.O. Box 1207
New York, NY 10011
TYPE            Television
CREDITS         St. Elsewhere - Tattinger's - Homicide: Life on the Street - OZ
Tom Fontana . . . . . . . . . . . . . . . . . Executive Producer
James Finnerty . . . . . . . . . . . . . . Co-Executive Producer
Sunil Nayar . . . . . . . . . . . . . . . . . . . . Asst. Mr. Fontana

**FEIGELSON PRODS., INC., J.D.**
PHONE . . . . . . . . . . . . . . . . . . . . . . . . . . . 310-273-7769
9171 Wilshire Blvd., Ste. 541
Beverly Hills, CA 90210-5564
TYPE            Motion Pictures + Television + Feature Direct to Video
CREDITS         Dark Night of the Scarecrow - Chiller - Gone to Texas - The Lake
J.D. Feigelson . . . . . . . . . . . . . . Owner/Exec. Producer
Dick deBlois . . . . . . . . . . . . . . . . . . . . Business Manager
Thea Kerman . . . . . . . . . . . . Legal Affairs (310-657-7007)
Wayne Mejia . . . . . . . . . . . . . . . . . . . . Business Manager

**FELDMAN CO., EDWARD S.**
PHONE . . . . . . . . . . . . . . . . . . . . . . . . . . . 818-972-3304
FAX . . . . . . . . . . . . . . . . . . . . . . . . . . . . . 818-972-3309
EMAIL . . . . . . . . . . . . . . . . . . . . . esfeldman@aol.com
Walt Disney Co.
500 S. Buena Vista St.
Burbank, CA 91521-7254
TYPE            Motion Pictures
CREDITS         The Doctor - Witness - Green Card - Forever Young - 101 Dalmations - The Truman Show
Ed Feldman . . . . . . . . . . . . . . . . President/Producer
Winship Cook . . . . . . . . . . . . . . . . Creative Associate

**FENADY ASSOCIATES, INC.**
PHONE . . . . . . . . . . . . . . . . . . . . . . . . . . . 213-466-6375
FAX . . . . . . . . . . . . . . . . . . . . . . . . . . . . . 213-466-6376
249 N. Larchmont, Ste. 6
Los Angeles, CA 90004
TYPE            Motion Pictures + Television
CREDITS         Chisum - The Sea Wolf - Yes Virginia, There Is a Santa Claus
Andrew Fenady . . . . . . . . . . . . . . . . . . . . . President
John Duke Fenady . . . . . . . . . . . . . VP, Creative Affairs
Tri Fritz . . . . . . . . . . . . . . . . . . . . . . . Dir., Development

**FEURY ENTERTAINMENT, JOSEPH**
PHONE . . . . . . . . . . . . . . . . . . . . . . . . . . . 212-221-9090
FAX . . . . . . . . . . . . . . . . . . . . . . . . . . . . . 212-221-0606
230 W. 41st St., Ste. 1400
New York, NY 10036
TYPE            Motion Pictures + Television + Documentaries
CREDITS         Seasons of the Heart - Staying Together - Say It! Fight It! Cure It!
Joseph Feury . . . . . . . . . . . . . . . . . . . . . . . . Producer
Lee Grant . . . . . . . . . . . . . . . . . . . . . Actress/Director

**FGM ENTERTAINMENT**
PHONE . . . . . . . . . . . . . . . . . . . . . . . . . . . 310-358-1370
FAX . . . . . . . . . . . . . . . . . . . . . . . . . . . . . 310-358-1380
EMAIL . . . . . . . . . . . . . . . . . . HometownCa@aol.com
8670 Wilshire Blvd., Ste. 301
Beverly Hills, CA 90211
TYPE            Motion Pictures
DEAL            MGM/UA
CREDITS         Species - Internal Affairs - Ronin
Frank Mancuso Jr. . . . . . . . . . . . . Producer/President
Marjorie Lewis . . . . . . . . . . . . . . Exec. VP, Devlopment
Jenni Villegas . . . . . . . . . . . . Exec. Asst. to Mr. Mancuso
Wendi Hyde . . . . . . . . . . . . . . . . Development Assistant

**FIELDS & HELLMAN CO., THE**
PHONE . . . . . . . . . . . . . . . . . . . . . . . . . . . 310-276-6555
FAX . . . . . . . . . . . . . . . . . . . . . . . . . . . . . 310-385-7441
345 N. Maple Dr., Ste. 205
Beverly Hills, CA 90210
TYPE            Motion Pictures
CREDITS         Glory - Crimes of the Heart - Midnight Cowboy - Mosquito Coast
Freddie Fields . . . . . . . . . . . . . . . . . . . . . . . . Producer
Jerome Hellman . . . . . . . . . . . . . . . . . . . . . . . . Producer

***FIELDS CO., THE**
PHONE . . . . . . . . . . . . . . . . . . . . . . . . . . . 310-276-6555
FAX . . . . . . . . . . . . . . . . . . . . . . . . . . . . . 310-276-1640
1005 Benedict Canyon Dr.
Beverly Hills, CA 90210
TYPE            Motion Pictures
CREDITS         Glory - Crimes of the Heart - Victory
COMMENTS        Also: Series Talk Shows
Freddie Fields . . . . . . . . . . . . . . . . . . . . . . . . Producer
Fred Iberri . . . . . . . . . . . . . . . . . . . Production Executive

**FIELDS PRODUCTIONS, ADAM**
PHONE . . . . . . . . . . . . . . . . . . . . . . . . . . . 310-369-1959
FAX . . . . . . . . . . . . . . . . . . . . . . . . . . . . . 310-369-8610
20th Century Fox
10201 W. Pico Blvd., Bldg 6, Rm. 105
Los Angeles, CA 90035
TYPE            Motion Pictures
CREDITS         Great Balls of Fire - Money Train - Vision Quest
Adam Fields . . . . . . . . . . . . . . . . . . . . . . . . No Title
Ilana Gutman . . . . . . . . . . . . . . . . . . . Dir., Development

# COMPANIES AND STAFF

**FILM AND GENERAL PRODS.**
PHONE . . . . . . . . . . . . . . . . . . . . . . . . . . . . . . . . 310-274-4773
FAX . . . . . . . . . . . . . . . . . . . . . . . . . . . . . . . . . . 213-874-9854
P.O. Box 46097
Los Angeles, CA 90046
TYPE          Motion Pictures
CREDITS       Gregory's Girl - Other People's Money - A Business Affair - Comfort & Joy - True Blue
Clive Parsons . . . . . . . . . . . . . . . . . . . . . . . . . . . . . . . . . Partner
Davina Belling . . . . . . . . . . . . . . . . . . . . . . . . . . . . . . . . Partner

**FILM GARDEN ENTERTAINMENT**
PHONE . . . . . . . . . . . . . . . . . . . . . . . . . . . . 818-783-3456
FAX . . . . . . . . . . . . . . . . . . . . . . . . . . . . . . 818-753-2545
EMAIL . . . . . . . . . . . . . . . . . . . . filmgarden@pacificnet.net
4215 Coldwater Canyon Blvd.
Studio City, CA 91604
TYPE          Television + Documentaries
CREDITS       The Secret World Of - Real Romance
Nancy Jacobs Miller . . . . . . . . . . . . . . . . . . President/Exec. Producer
Michelle Van Kempen . . . . . . . . . . . . . . . . . . . . Exec. Vice President
Ronnie Weinstock . . . . . . . . . . . . . . . . . . . . . Supervising Producer
Lauren Lexton . . . . . . . . . . . . . . . . . . . . . . . . . . . . Story Editor
Tom Rogan . . . . . . . . . . . . . . . . . . . . . . . . . . . . . Line Producer
Virginia Casey . . . . . . . . . . . . . . . . . . . . . . . . . . Development

**FILM KITCHEN**
PHONE . . . . . . . . . . . . . . . . . . . . . . . . . . . . . 213-936-6677
FAX . . . . . . . . . . . . . . . . . . . . . . . . . . . . . . . 213-936-7101
EMAIL . . . . . . . . . . . . . . . . . 74631,2335@compuserve.com
7223 Beverly Blvd., Ste. 203
Los Angeles, CA 90036-2536
TYPE          Motion Pictures + Documentaries
CREDITS       Chain of Desire - Shelf Life - Bar Girls - Shooting Porn - My Sweet Killer - Circus Lives - Angel's Ladies
COMMENTS      Proponents of American auteur cinema.
Doug Lindeman . . . . . . . . . . . . . . . . . . . . . . . . . . . . Producer
Kirk Harris . . . . . . . . . . . . . . . . . . . . . . . . . . . . . . Producer
Jack Rubio . . . . . . . . . . . . . . . . . . . . . . . . . . . . . . Producer

**FILM ROMAN, INC.**
PHONE . . . . . . . . . . . . . . . . . . . . . . . . . . . . . 818-761-2544
FAX . . . . . . . . . . . . . . . . . . . . . . . . . . . . . . . 818-985-2973
12020 Chandler Blvd., Ste. 200
North Hollywood, CA 91607
TYPE          Motion Pictures + Television + Animation + Syndication + Feature Direct to Video + Interactive Multimedia
CREDITS       C-Bear & Jamal - Garfield - Bobby's World - Simpsons - King of the Hill
Phil Roman . . . . . . . . . . . . . . . . . . . . . . . . . . Chairman/Founder
David B. Pritchard . . . . . . . . . . . . . . . . . . . . . . . . President/CEO
Greg Arsenault . . . . . . . . . . . . . . . Sr. VP, Finance & Administration
Jon Vein . . . . . . . . . . . . . . . . . . . . . . . . . . . . Sr. Vice President
Lolee Aries . . . . . . . . . . . . . . . . . . . . . . . . . . . VP, Production
Andi Copley . . . . . . . . . . . . . . . . . . . . . . . . . . . VP, Development
Danica Katz . . . . . . . . . . . . . . . . . . . . . . . . . . . VP, Development
Guy Vasilovich . . . . . . . . . . . Exec. Dir., Development & Creative Affairs

**FILMATIC ADVENTURES INC.**
PHONE . . . . . . . . . . . . . . . . . . . . . . . . . . 213-655-8200
7510 Sunset Blvd., Ste. 543
Los Angeles, CA 90046
TYPE          Motion Pictures + Television + Animation
CREDITS       1996 Fox Kid's Network Bumpers - Space Jam - Furry Creatures (UPN Pilot)
COMMENTS      Specialization in animation /live action inc. Agent Submissions only.
Michael Lander . . . . . . . . . . . . . . . . . . . . President/Exec. Producer

**FILMCOLONY, LTD.**
PHONE . . . . . . . . . . . . . . . . . . . . . . . . . . . . . 213-951-4650
FAX . . . . . . . . . . . . . . . . . . . . . . . . . . . . . . . 213-951-4660
7966 Beverly Blvd.
Los Angeles, CA 90048
TYPE          Motion Pictures
DEAL          Miramax Films
CREDITS       54 - Jackie Brown - The Crossing Guard - Pulp Fiction - Reservoir Dogs
Richard N. Gladstein . . . . . . . . . . . . . . . . . . Producer/President
Mitchell Solomon . . . . . . . . . . . . . . . . . . . . . Sr. VP, Production
Adam Robinson . . . . . . . . . . . . . . . . . . . . . . Dir., Development
Lila Yacoub . . . . . . . . . . . . . . . . . . . . . . . Production Executive
Sophie McMenamin . . . . . . . . . . . . . . . . . . Asst. to Mr. Gladstein

**FILMLIGHT**
PHONE . . . . . . . . . . . . . . . . . . . . . . . . . . . . . 310-887-2970
FAX . . . . . . . . . . . . . . . . . . . . . . . . . . . . . . . 310-887-2995
9100 Wilshire Blvd., Ste. 615E
Beverly Hills, CA 90212
TYPE          Motion Pictures + Television + Animation + Interactive Multimedia
CREDITS       Lawnmower Man - Hideaway - Virtuosity - T-Rex (IMAX)
Brett Leonard . . . . . . . . . . . . . . . . . . . . . . . . Director/Partner
Steve Freedman . . . . . . . . . . . . . . . . . . . . . . . Producer/Partner
Gimel Everett . . . . . . . . . . . . . . . . . . . . . . . . Producer/Writer
Dawn Gray . . . . . . . . . . . . . . . . . . . . . . . . . . . Development

**FILMOPOLIS PICTURES**
PHONE . . . . . . . . . . . . . . . . . . . . . . . . . . . . . 310-914-1776
FAX . . . . . . . . . . . . . . . . . . . . . . . . . . . . . . . 310-914-1777
EMAIL . . . . . . . . . . . . . . . . . . . . . . . . . . polyfilm@aol.com
WEBSITE . . . . . . . . . . . . . . . . . http://www.filmopolis.com
11300 W. Olympic Blvd., Ste. 625
Los Angeles, CA 90064
TYPE          Motion Pictures + Television + Syndication + Feature Direct to Video + Documentaries
CREDITS       My Favorite Season - The Stranger - Son of Gascogne
COMMENTS      Also: Theatrical distribution of American independent and Foreign films.
Zachary Lovas . . . . . . . . . . . . . . . . . . . . . . . . . . . President
Ray Kavandi . . . . . . . . . . . . . . . . . . . . . . . VP, US Operations
Jason Lovas . . . . . . . . . . . . . . . . . . . . . Exec. VP, Production

**FILMROOS**
PHONE . . . . . . . . . . . . . . . . . . . . . . . . . . . . . 310-205-5490
FAX . . . . . . . . . . . . . . . . . . . . . . . . . . . . . . . 310-205-0217
EMAIL . . . . . . . . . . . . . . . . . . . . . . . . . . info@filmroos.com
8899 Beverly Blvd., 6th Floor
Los Angeles, CA 90048
TYPE          Motion Pictures + Television + Documentaries
CREDITS       Biography - In Search of History - Top Secret - Crimes In Time
COMMENTS      Cable Ace Nominee for Best Documentary Series.
Bram Roos . . . . . . . . . . . . . . . . . . . . . . . . . Executive Producer
Morgan Bateman . . . . . . . . . . . . . . . . . . . . . . . . Executive Office
Ellen Curtis . . . . . . . . . . . . . . . . . . . . . . . . . . . . . . Controller
Yun Lingner . . . . . . . . . . . . . . . . . . Dir., Development/Operations

**FILMS BY JOVE**
PHONE . . . . . . . . . . . . . . . . . . . . . . . . . . . . . 818-506-0550
FAX . . . . . . . . . . . . . . . . . . . . . . . . . . . . . . . 818-752-0387
EMAIL . . . . . . . . . . . . . . . . . . . . . . . . . . . . vidov@aol.com
11325 Sunshine Terrace
Studio City, CA 91604
TYPE          Television + Animation
CREDITS       Stories From My Childhood- Masters of Russian Animation - The Animated Classic Showcase
Joan Borsten . . . . . . . . . . . . . . . . . . . . . . . . . . . . . Principal
Oleg Vidov . . . . . . . . . . . . . . . . . . . . . . . . . . . . . . Principal
Sonia Konbrandt . . . . . . . . . . . . . . . Dir., CIS/Russina Operations

***FILMSAAVY**
PHONE . . . . . . . . . . . . . . . . . . . . . . . . . . . . . 818-895-8515
FAX . . . . . . . . . . . . . . . . . . . . . . . . . . . . . . . 818-895-8415
EMAIL . . . . . . . . . . . . . . . . . . . . . . . . . FilmSaavy@aol.com
16931 Dearborn Street
Northridge, CA 91343
TYPE          Motion Pictures + Television
CREDITS       Rhapsody in Bloom - At First Sight - Two Guys Talkin' About Girls - Closer and Closer
Craig M. Saavedra . . . . . . . . . . . . . . . . . . . . Director/Producer

**FILMSMITH**
PHONE . . . . . . . . . . . . . . . . . . . . . . . . . . . . . 310-260-8866
FAX . . . . . . . . . . . . . . . . . . . . . . . . . . . . . . . 310-260-8867
EMAIL . . . . . . . . . . . . . . . . . . . . . . . filmsmith@bravado.com
225 Santa Monica Blvd., 4th Floor
Santa Monica, CA 90401
TYPE          Motion Pictures + Documentaries + Television
CREDITS       Welcome to Hollywood! - Glam - French Exit - California Convertible
COMMENTS      Also: Large Format
Zachary Matz . . . . . . . . . . . . . . . . . . . . . . . . Producer/Owner
Lisa Larrivee . . . . . . . . . . . . . . . . . . . . . Dir., Creative Affairs
Melissa Brabetz . . . . . . . . . . . . . . . . . . Administrative Coordinator

## FILMWERKS
PHONE . . . . . . . . . . . . . . . . . . . . . . . . . . . . . . . . 310-452-8429
FAX . . . . . . . . . . . . . . . . . . . . . . . . . . . . . . . . . . 310-452-8431
2800 28th St., #155
Santa Monica, CA 90405
TYPE      Motion Pictures + Feature Direct to Video + Television
CREDITS   Mean Guns - Blast - Omega Doom - Adrenalin - Nemsis
        Series - Crazy Six - Postmortem

Tom Karnowski . . . . . . . . . . . . . . . . . . . . . . . . . . . . . . . Production
Gary Schmoeller . . . . . . . . . . . . . . . . . . . . . . . . . . . . . . Production
Teri Blythe . . . . . . . . . . . . . . . . . . . . . . . . . . . . . . . Development

## FINE LINE FEATURES
PHONE . . . . . . . . . . . . . . . . . . . . 212-649-4800/310-854-5811
FAX . . . . . . . . . . . . . . . . . . . . . . 212-956-1942/310-659-1453
WEBSITE . . . . . . . . . . . . . . . . . . . . . . . . . . http://www.flf.com
888 7th Ave.
New York, NY 10106
TYPE      Motion Pictures + Documentaries
CREDITS   Shine - Love!Valour!Compassion! - Crash - Roseanna's
        Grave - Deconstructing Harry - The Sweet Hereafter
COMMENTS  Also:  116 N. Robertson Blvd., Ste. 200 Los Angeles, CA
        90048

Mark Ordesky . . . . . . . . . . . . . . . . . . . . . . . . . . . . . . President
Rachael Horovitz . . . . . . . . . . Sr. VP, Production & Acquisitions (NY)
Paul Federbush . . . . . . . . . . . VP, Acquisitions & Co-Prods. (LA)
Emma Clarke . . . . . . . . . . . . . Sr. Creative Executive (London)
John Barnes . . . . . . . . . . . . . . . . . . . . . . . Dir., Development
Matt Alvarez . . . . . . . . . . . . . Mgr., Acquisitions & Co-Prods. (LA)
Arianna Bocco . . . . . . . . . . . . Mgr., Acquisitions & Co-Prods. (LA)
Kate McCreery . . . . . . . . . . . . . . . . Creative Executive (London)
Joe Revitte . . . . . . . . . . . . . . . . . . . . . Creative Executive (NY)
Ann Chervisnky . . . . . . . . . . . . . . . . . . . . . Story Editor (LA)
Renee Witt . . . . . . . . . . . . . . . . . . . . . . . . Story Editor (NY)

## FINERMAN PRODS., WENDY
PHONE . . . . . . . . . . . . . . . . . . . . . . . . . . . . . . . . 310-244-4650
FAX . . . . . . . . . . . . . . . . . . . . . . . . . . . . . . . . . . 310-244-1495
Sony Studios
10202 W. Washington Blvd., TriStar #224
Culver City, CA 90232-3195
TYPE      Motion Pictures
CREDITS   I Like It Like That - Forrest Gump - The Fan - Fairy
        Tale...A True Story

Wendy Finerman . . . . . . . . . . . . . . . . . . . . . . . . . . . . . Producer
Greg Mooradian . . . . . . . . . . . . . . . . . . . . . Pres., Production
Lindsay Williams . . . . . . . . . . . . . . . . . . . . . . . VP, Production
Erin Lacey . . . . . . . . . . . . . . . . . . . . . . . . . . . . . . Story Editor
Timothy Record . . . . . . . . . . . . . . . Office Manager/ Story Asst.
Chandra Joy Hagopian . . . . . . . . . . . . . Asst. to Wendy Finerman
Lisa Zupan . . . . . . . . . . . . . . . . . . . . . Asst. to Wendy Finerman

## FINNEGAN-PINCHUK COMPANY
PHONE . . . . . . . . . . . . . . . . . . . . . . . . . . . . . . . . 818-508-5614
FAX . . . . . . . . . . . . . . . . . . . . . . . . . . . . . . . . . . 818-985-3853
4225 Coldwater Canyon
Studio City, CA 91604
TYPE      Motion Pictures + Television
CREDITS   Reality Bites- Fabulous Baker Boys - A Father For Charlie
Patricia Finnegan . . . . . . . . . . . . . . . . . . . . . . Executive Producer
William Finnegan . . . . . . . . . . . . . . . . . . . . . . Executive Producer
Sheldon Pinchuk . . . . . . . . . . . . . . . . . . . . . . Executive Producer
Dauri Chase . . . . . . . . . . . . . . . . . . . . . . . . . VP, Development
Lori-Etta Taub . . . . . . . . . . . . . . . . . . . . . . . . . . . . . Producer
Kim Cybulski . . . . . . . . . . . . . . . . . . . . . . Asst. to the Producers

## FIREBRAND PRODUCTIONS
PHONE . . . . . . . . . . . . . . . . . . . . . . . . . . . . . . . . 213-845-0550
FAX . . . . . . . . . . . . . . . . . . . . . . . . . . . . . . . . . . 213-845-0555
6767 Forest Lawn Dr., Ste. 115
Los Angeles, CA 90068
TYPE      Motion Pictures + Television
CREDITS   The Good Old Boys - Four Eyes & Six Guns - The New
        Adventures of Spin & Marty: Suspect Behavior
Salli Newman . . . . . . . . . . . . . . . . . . . . . . . . . . . . . . Producer
Kathy Menzies . . . . . . . . . . . . . . . . . . . . . . Dir., Development
Amanda Micallef . . . . . . . . . . . . . . . . . . . Asst. to Ms. Newman

## FIRESTORM PICTURES, LTD.
PHONE . . . . . . . . . . . . . . . . . . . . . . . . . . . . . . . . 310-358-2244
FAX . . . . . . . . . . . . . . . . . . . . . . . . . . . . . . . . . . 310-358-2249
554 Norwich Dr.
West Hollywood, CA 90048
TYPE      Motion Pictures
Richard G. Abramson . . . . . . . . . . . . . . . . . . . . . . . . Producer
Martin Landau . . . . . . . . . . . . . . . . . . . . . . . . . . . . . Producer
Billy Mancini . . . . . . . . . . . . . . . . . . . . . . . . . . . . . . Producer
Silvio Muraglia . . . . . . . . . . . . . . . . . . . . . . . . . . . . Producer
Bradley R. Bernstein . . . . . . . . . Pres., Development & Production
Alisandra M. Rand . . . . . . . . . . . . VP, Development & Production
Ara Apcar . . . . . . . . . . . . . . . . . . . . . . . . . Executive Assistant

## *FIRST COLD PRESS PRODUCTIONS
PHONE . . . . . . . . . . . . . . . . . . . . . . . . . . . . . . . . 212-444-3215
FAX . . . . . . . . . . . . . . . . . . . . . . . . . . . . . . . . . . 212-888-2175
Rysher Entertainment
885 Second Ave., 30th Floor
New York, NY 10017
TYPE      Motion Pictures
DEAL      October Films
CREDITS   The Impostors - Big Night
COMMENTS  Address will change in next several months.
Stanley Tucci . . . . . . . . . . . . . . . . . . . . . . . . Producer/Director
Beth Alexander . . . . . . . . . . . . . . . . . . . . . . . . . . . . . Producer
Jennifer Craig . . . . . . . . . . . . . . . Dir., Development/Assistant

## *FIRST ENTERTAINMENT LLC
PHONE . . . . . . . . . . . . . . . . . . . . . . . . . . . . . . . . 310-449-1130
FAX . . . . . . . . . . . . . . . . . . . . . . . . . . . . . . . . . . 310-449-9213
952 18th St., Ste. 4
Santa Monica, CA 90403
TYPE      Motion Pictures + Television
CREDITS   The First to Go - Married To It - Bingo
COMMENTS  Also:  Personal Management.
John Jacobs . . . . . . . . . . . . . . . . . . . . . . . . . . . . . . . Partner
Preston Keogh . . . . . . . . . . . . . . . . . . . . . . . . . . . . . Partner
John Clay Evans . . . . . . . . . . . . . . . . . . . . . . . . . . Executive

## *FIRST FOLIO FILMS
PHONE . . . . . . . . . . . . . . . . . . . . . . . . . . . . . . . . 818-840-7741
FAX . . . . . . . . . . . . . . . . . . . . . . . . . . . . . . . . . . 818-840-7519
NBC Studios
330 Bob Hope Dr., Catalina Bldg. C-117
Burbank, CA 91523
TYPE      Television + Motion Pictures
DEAL      NBC Studios/NBC Television Network
CREDITS   Working
COMMENTS  Also:  Thisby Entertainment
Andrew Tsao . . . . . . . . . . . . . . . . . . . . . . . . . . . Director/CEO
Theresa McCarthy . . . . . . . . . . . . . . . . . . . . . . VP, Production

## FIRST KISS PRODUCTIONS
PHONE . . . . . . . . . . . . . . . . . . . . . . . . . . . . . . . . 310-244-5171
FAX . . . . . . . . . . . . . . . . . . . . . . . . . . . . . . . . . . 310-244-2131
Columbia Pictures
10202 W. Washington Blvd., Capra #106
Culver City, CA 90232
TYPE      Motion Pictures
DEAL      Columbia Pictures
Alicia Silverstone . . . . . . . . . . . . . . . . . . . . . . Actress/Producer
Carolyn Kessler . . . . . . . . . . . . . . . . . . . . . . . . Mgr./Producer
Matt Miranda . . . . . . . . . . . . . . . . . . . . . . . . Creative Executive

## FIRST LIGHT
PHONE . . . . . . . . . . . . . . . . . . . . . . . . . . . . . . . . 310-777-3178
FAX . . . . . . . . . . . . . . . . . . . . . . . . . . . . . . . . . . 310-777-4698
Working Title Films
9333 Wilshire Blvd.
Beverly Hills, CA 90210
TYPE      Motion Pictures
CREDITS   Set-Up - The Loveless - Near Dark - Blue Steel - Point
        Break - Strange Days
Kathryn Bigelow . . . . . . . . . . . . . . . . . . . . . . . . . . . . Director
Wei Koh . . . . . . . . . . . . . . . . . . . . . . . . . . . . . VP, Development
Jason Wesche . . . . . . . . . . . . . . . . . . . . . . Asst. to Ms. Bigelow

## FIRST LOOK PICTS./OVERSEAS FILMGROUP
PHONE . . . . . . . . . . . . . . . . . . . . . . . . . . . . . . . . . . . 310-855-1199
FAX . . . . . . . . . . . . . . . . . . . . . . . . . . . . . . . . . . . . . 310-855-0719
EMAIL . . . . . . . . . . . . . . . . . . . . . . . . . . . . . . . . . info@ofg.com
WEBSITE . . . . . . . . . . . . . . . . . . . . . . . . . . . . http://www.ofg.com
8800 Sunset Blvd., 3rd Floor
Los Angeles, CA 90069

TYPE       Motion Pictures + Syndication + Feature Direct to Video + Documentaries
CREDITS    Illuminata - Alegria - Waking Ned
COMMENTS   Additional Website: http://www.flp.com
Robert Little . . . . . . . . . . . . . . . . . . . . . . . . . . . Co-Chairman/Co-CEO
Ellen Little . . . . . . . . . . . . . . . . . . . . . . . . . . . . . Co-Chair/Co-CEO
William Lischak . . . . . . . . . . . . . . . . . . . . . . . . . . . . . . . . CFO/COO
Deborah Chiaramonte . . . . . . . . . . . . . . VP, Legal & Business Affairs
Maud Nadler . . . . . . . . . . . . . . . . . . . . . . . . . . VP, Creative Affairs
Jeanne Moy Joe . . . . . . . . . . . . . . . . . . . . . . . . Dir., Creative Affairs
Doug McClure . . . . . . . . . . . . . . . . . . . . . Dir., Legal & Busines Affairs
Linda Moglovkin . . . . . . . . . . . . . . . . . . . . . . . . . . . . . . . Controller
Dana Lambert . . . . . . . . . . . . . . . . . . . . Coordinator, Creative Affairs
Carla Schwam . . . . . . . . . . . . . . . . . . . . Coordinator, Creative Affairs

## FIRST STREET FILMS, INC.
PHONE . . . . . . . . . . . . . . . . . . . . . . . . . . . . . . . . . . . 310-244-7891
FAX . . . . . . . . . . . . . . . . . . . . . . . . . . . . . . . . . . . . . 310-244-2373
Sony Studios
10202 W. Washington Bl.
Culver City, CA 90232

TYPE       Motion Pictures + Television
DEAL       Columbia Pictures
CREDITS    Get On The Bus - Desperado - Excess Baggage - La Bamba
Bill Borden . . . . . . . . . . . . . . . . . . . . . . . . . . . . . . . . . . . . Producer
Barry Rosenbush . . . . . . . . . . . . . . . . . . . . . . . . . . . . . . . . Producer
Jenny Manriquez . . . . . . . . . . . . . . . . . . VP, Production & Development
Karen Borja . . . . . . . . . . . . . . . . . . . . . . . . . . . . Asst. to Producers
John Keel . . . . . . . . . . . . . . . . . . . . . . . . . . . . . Asst. to Producers

## FISCHER CO., PRESTON STEPHEN
PHONE . . . . . . . . . . . . . . . . . . . . . . . . . . . . . . . . . . . 310-578-9587
FAX . . . . . . . . . . . . . . . . . . . . . . . . . . . . . . . . . . . . . 310-823-3548
EMAIL . . . . . . . . . . . . . . . . . . . . . . . . . . . . . . . psfco@aol.com
13078 Mindanao Way, PH 313
Marina Del Rey, CA 90292

TYPE       Motion Pictures + Television
CREDITS    Intensity - Outrage - The Two Mrs. Grenvilles - White Fang II
Preston Fischer . . . . . . . . . . . . . . . . . . . . . . . . . . . . . . . . . Producer

## FITZGERALD PRODS. & MGT.
PHONE . . . . . . . . . . . . . . . . . . . . . . . . . . . . . . . . . . . 505-466-1186
FAX . . . . . . . . . . . . . . . . . . . . . . . . . . . . . . . . . . . . . 505-466-1186
84 Monte Alto Rd.
Santa Fe, NM 87505

TYPE       Motion Pictures + Television
CREDITS    Extremely Weird
COMMENTS   No faxed queries please.
Lisa FitzGerald . . . . . . . . . . . . . . . . . . . . . . . . . . . . . . . . . Producer

## FLASHPOINT ENTERTAINMENT
PHONE . . . . . . . . . . . . . . . . . . . . . . . . . . . . . . . . . . . 310-472-3332
1247 N. Bundy Dr.
Los Angeles, CA 90049-1514

TYPE       Motion Pictures + Television
CREDITS    Helium 3
Andrew R. Tennenbaum . . . . . . . . . . . . . . . . . . . . . . . . . . . . . . . Producer

## FLAT PENNY FILMS
PHONE . . . . . . . . . . . . . . . . . . . . . . . . . . . . . . . . . . . 213-933-0991
FAX . . . . . . . . . . . . . . . . . . . . . . . . . . . . . . . . . . . . . 213-933-3515
114 N. Mansfield, 2nd Fl.
Los Angeles, CA 90036

TYPE       Motion Pictures + Television
DEAL       Twentieth Century Fox-Fox 2000 (LA)/Universal Pictures
CREDITS    State of the Union- The Cherry Orchard - Spyglass - Lovers Leap - Micho
Amy Lanier . . . . . . . . . . . . . . . . . . . . . . . . . . . . . President/Owner

## FLEECE FILMS
PHONE . . . . . . . . . . . . . . . . . . . . . . . . . . . . . . . . . . . 213-462-6400
FAX . . . . . . . . . . . . . . . . . . . . . . . . . . . . . . . . . . . . . 213-463-7874
Propaganda Films
940 N. Mansfield Ave.
Los Angeles, CA 90038

TYPE       Motion Pictures
CREDITS    Your Friends and Neighbors
Jason Patric . . . . . . . . . . . . . . . . . . . . . . . . . . . . Actor/Producer
Alix Madigan . . . . . . . . . . . . . . . . . . . . . . . . . . . . . . . . Executive

## FLOWER FILMS, INC.
PHONE . . . . . . . . . . . . . . . . . . . . . . . . . . . . . . . . . . . 310-285-0200
FAX . . . . . . . . . . . . . . . . . . . . . . . . . . . . . . . . . . . . . 310-285-0827
9220 Sunset Blvd., #309
Los Angeles, CA 90069

TYPE       Motion Pictures
DEAL       Twentieth Century Fox-Fox 2000 (LA)
Drew Barrymore . . . . . . . . . . . . . . . . . . . . . . . . . . . . . . . . Partner
Nancy Juvonen . . . . . . . . . . . . . . . . . . . . . . . . . . . . . . . . . Partner
Stephanie Savage . . . . . . . . . . . . . . . . . . . . . . . Dir., Development
Gwenn Stroman . . . . . . . . . . . . . . . . . . . . . . . . . . Office Manager
Christie Milliken . . . . . . . . . . . . . . . . . . . . Development Assistant
Nina Lenders . . . . . . . . . . . . . . . . . . . . . . . . . . . . . . . . Assistant
Catherine Engel . . . . . . . . . . . . . . . . . . . . . . . . . . . . . . Assistant

## FLOYD JOHNSON PRODUCTIONS, CHARLES
PHONE . . . . . . . . . . . . . . . . . . . . . . . . . . . . . . . . . . . 213-956-3606
FAX . . . . . . . . . . . . . . . . . . . . . . . . . . . . . . . . . . . . . 213-862-1175
Paramount
5555 Melrose Ave., Clara Bow Bldg. 203
Los Angeles, CA 90038-3197

TYPE       Television
DEAL       Paramount Television Group
CREDITS    The Rockford Files - Quantum Leap - Magnum P.I. - JAG
Chas. Floyd Johnson . . . . . . . . . . . . . . . . . . . . . Executive Producer
Anne Burford . . . . . . . . . . . . . . . . . . . . . . . . . . . Vice President
Nina Bunche Pierce . . . . . . . . . . . . . . . . . . . Asst. to Mr. Johnson

## *FLYING FREEHOLD PRODUCTIONS
PHONE . . . . . . . . . . . . . . . . . . . . . . . . . . . . . . . . . . . 213-956-8838
FAX . . . . . . . . . . . . . . . . . . . . . . . . . . . . . . . . . . . . . 213-862-1031
Paramount Pictures
5555 Melrose Ave., Clara Bow #120
Los Angeles, CA 90038-3197

TYPE       Motion Pictures
DEAL       Paramount Pictures- Motion Picture Group
Patrick Stewart . . . . . . . . . . . . . . . . . . . . . Chief Executive Officer
Wendy Neuss . . . . . . . . . . . . . . . . . . . . . . . . . . . . . President
James Johnston . . . . . . . . . . . . . . . . . . . . . . . . Creative Executive
Jackie Edwards . . . . . . . . . . . . . . . . . . Exec. Asst. to Patrick Stewart

## FOGWOOD FILMS
PHONE . . . . . . . . . . . . . . . . . . . . . . . . . . . . . . . . . . . 818-560-2880
FAX . . . . . . . . . . . . . . . . . . . . . . . . . . . . . . . . . . . . . 818-841-4954
500 S. Buena Vista St., Animation 3B-9
Burbank, CA 91521-1814

TYPE       Motion Pictures + Television + Documentaries
DEAL       Walt Disney Company, The
CREDITS    The Christmas Tree - The Lost Children of Berlin
Sally Field . . . . . . . . . . . . . . . . . . . . . . . . . . . . . . . . . . . . Producer
Wendy Japhet . . . . . . . . . . . . . . . . . . . . . . . . . . . . . . . . . . Producer
Barbara J. Bloom . . . . . . . . . . . . . . . . . . . . . . . . . . VP, Television
Selena McAfee . . . . . . . . . . . . . . . . . . . . . . Development Associate
Michelle Stone . . . . . . . . . . . . . . . . . . . . . . Development Associate

## FORCE TEN PRODUCTIONS
PHONE . . . . . . . . . . . . . . . . . . . . . . . . . . . . . . . . . . . 310-394-8105
FAX . . . . . . . . . . . . . . . . . . . . . . . . . . . . . . . . . . . . . 310-394-8205
12957 San Vicente
Los Angeles, CA 90049

TYPE       Motion Pictures + Television
John Roach . . . . . . . . . . . . . . . . . . . . . . . . . . . . . . . . . . . . Producer
Elizabeth Karl . . . . . . . . . . . . . . . . . . . . . . . . . . . . . . . . . . Producer
Carol Drechsler . . . . . . . . . . . . . . . . . . . . . . . . . . . . . . . Executive

## FORRESTER FILMS
PHONE . . . . . . . . . . . . . . . . . . . . . . . . . . . . . . . . . . . 310-836-1710
FAX . . . . . . . . . . . . . . . . . . . . . . . . . . . . . . . . . . . . . 310-836-3126
2803 Forrester Dr.
Los Angeles, CA 90064-4663

TYPE       Motion Pictures + Television
CREDITS    Reflections In the Dark - Henry Hamilton, Graduate Ghost
Barbara Klein . . . . . . . . . . . . . . . . . . . . . . . . . . . . . . . . . . Producer
Rebecca Justice . . . . . . . . . . . . . . . . . . . . . . . . . . Dir., Development

# COMPANIES AND STAFF

***FORTIS FILMS**
PHONE . . . . . . . . . . . . . . . . . . . . . . . . . . . . 310-659-4533
FAX . . . . . . . . . . . . . . . . . . . . . . . . . . . . . 310-659-4373
8581 Santa Monica Blvd., Ste. 1
W. Hollywood, CA 90069

| | |
|---|---|
| TYPE | Motion Pictures |
| DEAL | Warner Bros. Pictures |
| CREDITS | Hope Floats - Making Sandwiches - Our Father |

Sandra Bullock . . . . . . . . . . . . . . . . . . . . . . . . . . . . Owner
John Bullock . . . . . . . . . . . . . . . . . . . . . . . . President/CEO
Gesine Bullock . . . . . . . . . . . . . . . . . . Exec. Vice President
Maggie Biggar . . . . . . . . . . . . . . . . . . . Production Executive
Lillian Dean . . . . . . . . . . . . . . . . . . . . . . . Dir., Development

**FORTUNE MEDIA GROUP, INC.**
PHONE . . . . . . . . . . . . . . . . . . . . . . . . . . 818-777-3063
FAX . . . . . . . . . . . . . . . . . . . . . . . . . . . . . 818-866-1572
Universal - Bldg. 507
100 Universal City Plaza, Ste. 3H
Universal City, CA 91608

| | |
|---|---|
| TYPE | Motion Pictures |
| DEAL | Universal Pictures |
| CREDITS | Dona Barbara |

Peter Rawley . . . . . . . . . . . . . . . . . . . . . . . President/CEO
Anthony Beaudoin . . . . . . . . . . . . . . Dir., Business & Legal Affairs
Jose-Maria Iturralde . . . . . . . . . . . . . . . . . Dir., Development
Rowena Li . . . . . . . . . . . . . . . . . . . . . . . . Dir., Development
Kari Neumeyer . . . . . . . . . . . . . . . . . . . . . Dir., Development
Beth Bodo . . . . . . . . . . . . . . . . . . . . . . . Executive Assistant

**FORWARD PASS, INC.**
PHONE . . . . . . . . . . . . . . . . . . . . . . . . . . 310-571-3443
12233 W. Olympic Blvd., Ste. 224
Los Angeles, CA 90064

| | |
|---|---|
| TYPE | Motion Pictures |
| DEAL | Walt Disney Company, The |
| CREDITS | Last of the Mohicans - Manhunter - Thief - Drug Wars - Heat - Jericho Mile |

Michael Mann . . . . . . . . . . . . . . . . Writer/Producer/Director
Nancy Peardon . . . . . . . . . . . . . . . Exec. Asst. to Mr. Mann

**FOSTER PRODUCTIONS, DAVID**
PHONE . . . . . . . . . . . . . . . . . . . . . . . . . . 310-244-4635
FAX . . . . . . . . . . . . . . . . . . . . . . . . . . . . . 310-244-2255
Sony Studios
10202 W. Washington Bl. Myrna Loy #4
Culver City, CA 90232

| | |
|---|---|
| TYPE | Motion Pictures + Television |
| CREDITS | The Mask of Zorro - The River Wild - The Getaway 1 & 2 - Running Scared - Short Circuit 1 & 2 |

David Foster . . . . . . . . . . . . . . . . . . . . . . . . . . Producer
Ben Sussman . . . . . . . . . . . . . . . . . . . . . Creative Executive

**FOUNDRY FILM PARTNERS**
PHONE . . . . . . . . . . . . . . 212-977-9597/310-289-4907
FAX . . . . . . . . . . . . . . . . 212-977-9525/310-289-1914
EMAIL . . . . . . . . . . . . . . . . . foundrycom@foundrycom.com
WEBSITE . . . . . . . . . . . . . . . . http://www.foundrycom.com
130 W. 57th St., #8B
New York, NY 10019

| | |
|---|---|
| TYPE | Motion Pictures |
| CREDITS | Bullets Over Broadway- Big- Preacher's Wife - Mom's Up On The Roof |
| COMMENTS | Also: 8800 Sunset Blvd., 3rd Floor LA, CA 90069 |

Robert Greenhut . . . . . . . . . . . . . . . . . . Partner/Producer
Jon Ein . . . . . . . . . . . . . . . . . . . . . . . . . Managing Partner
Jo Levi . . . . . . . . . . . . . . . Dir., Development & Acquisitions
Stefanie Berk . . . . . . . . . . . . . . . . . . . Production Associate

**FOUNTAINBRIDGE FILMS**
PHONE . . . . . . . . . . . . . . . . . . . . . . . . . . 213-782-1177
FAX . . . . . . . . . . . . . . . . . . . . . . . . . . . . . 213-852-9327
8428 Melrose Place, Unit C
Los Angeles, CA 90069

| | |
|---|---|
| TYPE | Motion Pictures + Television |
| DEAL | Columbia Pictures |
| CREDITS | Just Cause |

Sean Connery . . . . . . . . . . . . . . . . . . . . . Actor/Producer
Rhonda Tollefson . . . . . . . . . . . . . . . . . President/Producer
Richard Brassel . . . . . . . . . . . . . . . . Dir., Creative Affairs
Lynnette Ramirez . . . . . . . . . . . . . . . Development Assistant
Laura Netscher . . . . . . . . . . . . . . . . . . Executive Assistant
Joyce Tollefson . . . . . . . . . . . . Office Manager/Receptionist

**FOURTH AVENUE FILMS**
PHONE . . . . . . . . . . . . . . . . . . . . . . . . . . 310-392-0224
209 4th Avenue #3
Venice, CA 90291

| | |
|---|---|
| TYPE | Motion Pictures + Television |

Tamara Kaiser . . . . . . . . . . . . . . . . . . . . Producer/Partner
Victoria Sterling . . . . . . . . . . . . . . . . . . Producer/Partner

**FOX ANIMATION STUDIOS**
PHONE . . . . . . . . . . . . . . . . . . . . . . . . . . 310-369-1000
FAX . . . . . . . . . . . . . . . . . . . . . . . . . . . . . 310-369-3907
WEBSITE . . . . . . . . . . . . . . . . . . . . http://www.fox.com/
10201 W. Pico Blvd., Bldg. 58
Los Angeles, CA 90035

| | |
|---|---|
| TYPE | Motion Pictures + Animation + Feature Direct to Video |

Chris Meledandri . . . . . . . . . . . . . . President (310-369-3068)
Kevin Bannerman . . . . . . . . . Sr. VP, Production (310-369-1431)
Barbara Zipperman . . . . . . . Sr. VP, Business Affairs (310-369-5762)
Melissa Cobb . . . . . . . . . . . . . VP, Production (310-369-3258)

**FOX BROADCASTING CO.**
PHONE . . . . . . . . . . . . . . . . . . . . . . . . . . 310-369-1000
FAX . . . . . . . . . . . . . . . . . . . . . . . . . . . . . 310-369-1283
WEBSITE . . . . . . . . . . . . . . . . . . . http://www.foxworld.com
10201 W. Pico Blvd.
Los Angeles, CA 90035

| | |
|---|---|
| TYPE | Television |

Rupert Murdoch . . . . . . . . . . . . . . . Chairman/CEO, News Corp.
Chase Carey . . . . . . . . Chairman/CEO, Fox Television/Co-COO, News Corp.
Peter Chernin . . . President/COO, News Corp./Chairman/CEO, The Fox Grp.
David Hill . . . . . . . . . . . . . . Chairman/CEO, Fox Broadcasting Co.
Peter Roth . . . . . . . . . . . . President, Fox Entertainment Group
Larry Jacobson . . . . . . . . . . . . . . President, Fox TV Networks
Rob Dwek . . . . . . . . . . . . . Exec. VP, Comedy & Drama Series
Ira Kurgan . . . . . . . . . . . . Exec. VP, Network Business Operations
Jon Nesvig . . . . . . . . . . . . . . . . . . . . Exec. VP, Fox TV
Eric Yeldell . . . . . . . . . . . . . . . . . . Exec. VP, Legal Affairs
Cheryl Bayer . . . . . . . . . . . . . . . . Sr. VP, Comedy Development
Danielle Claman . . . . . . . . . . . Sr. VP, Drama Series Programming
Mike Darnell . . . . . . . . . . . Sr. VP, Specials & Alternative Prog.
Karen Fox . . . . . . . . . . . . . . . . . . Sr. VP, Business Affairs
Gary Hoffman . . . . . . . . . . . . . . . Sr. VP, Movies & Miniseries
Susanne Horenstein . . . . . . . . . . . . . . . . Sr. VP, Scheduling
Del Mayberry . . . . . . . . . . . . . . . . . . . . . Sr. VP, Finance
Minna Taylor . . . . . . . . . . . . . . . . . . Sr. VP, Legal Affairs
Richard Vokulich . . . . . . . . . . . . . . . Sr. VP, Business Affairs
Jeff Eckerle . . . . . . . . . . . . . VP, Current Drama Programming
Sandy Gong . . . . . . . . . . . . . . . . . . . . . . . VP, Finance
Leslie Kolins-Small . . . . . VP, Alternative & Late Night Programming
MJ LaVaccare . . . . . . . . . . . . . . . . . . . . . . VP, Scheduling
Lance B. Taylor . . . . . . . . . . . . VP, Current Comedy Programming
Peter T. Johnson . . . . . . . . . . . . . . . . Development Executive
Megan Callaway . . . . . . . . . . . . . . . Dir., Movies & Miniseries
Michael Clements . . . . . . . . . . . . . . . Dir., Comedy Development
Kathy Edrich . . . . . . . . . . . . . . . . . . . Dir., Business Affairs
Craig H. Erwich . . . . . . . . . . . . . . . Dir., Current Programming
Haya Handel . . . . . . . . . . . . . . . . . . Dir., Business Affairs
Deborah Service . . . . . . . . . . . . . . . Dir., Movies and Miniseries
Tom Sheets . . . . . . . . . . . . . . . . . . . . Dir., FOX Specials
Jason Stewart . . . . . . . . . . . . . . . . Dir., Current Programming
Barbara Wall . . . . . . . . . . . . . . . . Dir., Current Programming
Jeff Brustrom . . . . . . . . . . . . . . . . Mgr., Comedy Development
Gavin Glynn . . . . . . . . . . . . . . . . . . . . Mgr., FOX Specials
Connie Jones . . . . . . . . . . . . . . . . . . Mgr., Business Affairs
Paul Lewis . . . . . . . . . . . . . . . . . Mgr., Current Programming
Anne Schwarz . . . . . . . . . . . . . . . . . . . Mgr., Scheduling
Donna Weiser . . . . . . . . . . . . . . . . . Mgr., Movies & Miniseries

# COMPANIES AND STAFF

**FOX FAMILY CHANNEL**
PHONE . . . . . . . . . . . . . . . . . . . . . . . . . . . . . . . . 310-235-5100
FAX . . . . . . . . . . . . . . . . . . . . . . . . . . . . . . . . . . . . 310-235-5102
EMAIL . . . . . . . . . . . . . . . . . . viewer_mail@familychannel.com
WEBSITE . . . . . . . . . . . . . . . . . . http://www.familychannel.com
10960 Wilshire Blvd.
Los Angeles, CA 90025
TYPE       Television
CREDITS       Mary Higgins Clark's Moonlight Becomes You - The
           Ditchdigger's Daughter

Haim Saban . . . . . . . . . . . . . . . . . . . . . . . . . . . Chairman/CEO
Mel Woods . . . . . . . . . . . . . . . . . . . . . . . . . . . President/COO
Gus Lucas . . . . . . . . . . . . . . . . . Consultant, Fox Family Channel
Lance H. Robbins . . . . . . . Pres., TV, Movies & Series, Saban Entertainment
Joel Andryc . . . . . . . . . . . . . . . . Sr. VP, Children's Programming
Eytan Keller . . . . . . . . . . . Sr. VP, Reality Programming & Specials
Julia Gilbert . . . . . . . . . . VP, Production, Reality Programming & Specials
Julie Resh . . . . . . . . . . VP, Development, Reality Programming & Specials
Dan Smith . . . . . . . . . . VP, Development, Reality Programming & Specials
Tom Halleen . . . . . . . . . . . . . . . . . . . . . . . . . Dir., Programming
Kim Millimaki . . . . . . . . . . . . . . . . . . . . . . . . Dir., Programming

**FOX KIDS NETWORK**
PHONE . . . . . . . . . . . . . . . . . . . . . . . . . . . . . . . . 310-235-9600
FAX . . . . . . . . . . . . . . . . . . . . . . . . . . . . . . . . . . . . 310-235-5102
10960 Wilshire Blvd.
Los Angeles, CA 90024
TYPE       Television
CREDITS       Power Rangers - Goosebumps - Life with Louie
Haim Saban . . . . . . . . . . . . . . . . . . . . . . . . . . . Chairman/CEO
Mel Woods . . . . . . . . . . . . . . . . . . . . . . . . . . . President/COO
Maureen Smith . . . . . . . . . . GM/Exec. VP, Fox Family Worldwide
Donna Cunningham . . . . . . . . . . . . . . Sr. VP, Business Affairs
Mark Ittner . . . . . . . . . . . . . . . . . . . . . . . . Sr. VP, Finance
Eytan Keller . . . . . . . . . . . . Sr. VP, Reality-Based Programming
Steve Leblang . . . . . . . . . . . . . . . . . . . . . Sr. VP, Research
Carol Monroe . . . . . . . . . . . . . . . . . . . . . . Sr. VP, Programming
Marni Bernstein . . . . . . . . . . . . . . . . . VP, On-Air Promotions
Gary Brand . . . . . . . . . . . . . VP, On-Air Promotions & Family Programming
Karen DiNoto . . . . . . . . . . . . . VP, Programming & Development
Greg Economos . . . . . . . . . . . . . . . VP, Business & Legal Affairs
Rhonda Gail . . . . . . . . . . . . . . . . . VP, Business & Legal Affairs
Jacqui Grunfeld . . . . . . . . . . . . . . . VP, Business & Legal Affairs
Stacy Lifton . . . . . . . . . . . . . . . . . . . . . VP, Business Affairs
Donna Mitroff . . . . . . . . VP, Educational Policies & Program Practices
Bill Nault . . . . . . . . . . . . . . . . . . . . . . . . VP, Finance Planning
Angie Small . . . . . . . . . . . . . . . . . . . . . . . VP, Legal Affairs
Hubert Smith . . . . . . . . . . . . . . . . . . . . . VP, Business Affairs

**FOX PRODUCTIONS, TED**
PHONE . . . . . . . . . . . . . . . . . . . . . . . . . . . . . . . . 310-659-5016
FAX . . . . . . . . . . . . . . . . . . . . . . . . . . . . . . . . . . . . 310-659-5023
EMAIL . . . . . . . . . . . . . . . . . . . . . . . . . . . tfoxprod@aol.com
8900 Thrasher Ave.
Los Angeles, CA 90069
TYPE       Motion Pictures + Television + Syndication + Feature
           Direct to Video
DEAL       Unapix Entertainemnt
CREDITS       Soulmates - Love Is Like That - Deadfall - Little Cobras -
           Monkey Business - Dark Nova - Quick & Easy
COMMENTS       Also: Music Videos.
Ted Fox . . . . . . . . . . . . . . . . . . . . . . . . . . President/Producer
Sharon Craig . . . . . . . . . . . . . . . . . . . . . . Dir., Development
Jeff Carlis . . . . . . . . . . . . . . . . . . . . . . . . . . . . Aquisitions
Jhoanna Trias . . . . . . . . . . . . . . . . . . . . . . . . . Story Editor

**FOX TELEVISION STUDIOS**
PHONE . . . . . . . . . . . . . . . . . . . . . . . . . . . . . . . . 310-369-1000
FAX . . . . . . . . . . . . . . . . . . . . . . . . . . . . . . . . . . . . 310-369-7378
10201 W. Pico Blvd., Bldg. 41
Beverly Hills, CA 90213-0900
TYPE       Television
David Grant . . . . . . . . . . . . . . . . . . . . . . . . . . . . . President
Lisa Berger . . . . . . . . . . . . . . . . . Exec. VP, Creative Affairs
Mindy Herman . . . . . . . . . . . . . Exec. VP, Program Enterprises
Eric Jacobson . . . . . . . . . . . . . . . . VP, Business & Legal Affairs
Sheila Johnson . . . . . . . . . . . . . . . VP, Business & Legal Affairs
Diane Klein . . . . . . . . . . . . . . . . VP, Finance & Administration
Jim Sharp . . . . . . . . . . . . . . . . . . . . . . . . . . VP, Production
Daniela Welteke . . . . . . . . . . . . . . VP, Program Enterprises
Martin Carlson . . . . . . . . . . . . . . Dir., Business & Legal Affairs
Cindy Hochman . . . . . . . . . Dir., Business Affairs Administration
Lou Wallach . . . . . . . . . . . . . . . . . . . Dir., Creative Affairs
Marci Pool . . . . . . . . . . Sr. VP, Development, Movies & Minis
Bob Lemchen . . . . . . . . . . . . VP, Development, Movies & Minis
Kimberly Myers . . . . . . . . . . . VP, Development, Movies & Minis
Debra Harkin . . . . . . . . . . . . . . . Story Editor, Movies & Minis

**FOXBORO COMPANY, INC., THE**
PHONE . . . . . . . . . . . . . . . . . . . . . . . . . . . . . . . . 212-755-6690
FAX . . . . . . . . . . . . . . . . . . . . . . . . . . . . . . . . . . . . 212-888-6470
133 E. 58th St., #301
New York, NY 10022
TYPE       Motion Pictures + Television + Feature Direct to Video
CREDITS       In The Presence of Mine Enemies (Showtime) - A Town
           Has Turned to Dust (Sci-Fi) - Pictures of Baby Jane Doe
COMMENTS       Also: Television Movies.
Nelle Nugent . . . . . . . . . . . . . . . President/Executive Producer
Kenneth Teaton . . . . . . . . . . . . VP, Operations/Co-Producer
Alan Taglianetti . . . . . . . . . . . . . . . . . . . Operations Manager

**FOXSTAR PRODUCTIONS**
PHONE . . . . . . . . . . . . . . . . . . . . . . . . . . . . . . . . 310-369-1709
FAX . . . . . . . . . . . . . . . . . . . . . . . . . . . . . . . . . . . . 310-369-4507
EMAIL . . . . . . . . . . . . . . . . . . . . . . . . scotthar@foxinc.com
WEBSITE . . . . . . . . . . . . . . . . . . . . . http://www.foxstar.com
10201 W. Pico Blvd., Bldg. 41, Ste. 501
Los Angeles, CA 90035
TYPE       Television + Syndication + Documentaries
CREDITS       A & E Biography - 20th Cent. Fox: The First 50 Years -
           Rodgers & Hammerstein: The Sound of Movies
COMMENTS       Made for TV Movies/Specials/Emmy nominated specials.
Kevin J. Burns . . . . . . . . . . . . . . . . . . . Sr. Vice President
Scott Hartford . . . . . . . . . . . . . . . . . . . . Dir., Development

**FRANCHISE PICTURES INC.**
PHONE . . . . . . . . . . . . . . . . . . . . . . . . . . . . . . . . 213-822-0730
FAX . . . . . . . . . . . . . . . . . . . . . . . . . . . . . . . . . . . . 213-822-2169
8228 Sunset Blvd.
Los Angeles, CA 90046
TYPE       Motion Pictures
CREDITS       Double Impact - The White Raven - A Murder of Crows
COMMENTS       Also: Phoenician Entertainment, 13801 Ventura Blvd.,
           Sherman Oaks, CA 91423 818-905-8480
Ashok Amritraj . . . . . . . . . . . . . . . . . . . . . . . Co-Chairman
Andrew Stevens . . . . . . . . . . . . . . . . . . . . . . . . . President

**FRANKOVICH PRODS., INC., PETER**
PHONE . . . . . . . . . . . . . . . . . . . . . . . . . . . . . . . . 310-447-3670
FAX . . . . . . . . . . . . . . . . . . . . . . . . . . . . . . . . . . . . 310-447-3672
12140 W. Olympic Blvd., Ste. 23
Los Angeles, CA 90064
TYPE       Motion Pictures + Television
DEAL       Finnegan-Pinchuk Company
CREDITS       Ride The Wind - The Unspoken Truth - Her Costly Affair -
           The Lake (NBC-MOW)
Peter Frankovich . . . . . . . . . . . . . . . . . . President/Producer
David Mandel . . . . . . . . . . . . . . . . . . Asst. to the President

**FRASER PRODS., WOODY**
PHONE . . . . . . . . . . . . . . . . . . . . . . . . . . . . . . . . 818-505-6050
FAX . . . . . . . . . . . . . . . . . . . . . . . . . . . . . . . . . . . . 818-505-6052
WEBSITE . . . . . . . . . . . . . . . . . http://www.homeandfamily.com
Home and Family
100 Universal City Plaza
Universal City, CA 91608
TYPE       Television + Syndication
DEAL       Fox Family Channel
CREDITS       Home & Family - The Home Show (ABC) - That's
           Incredible - The Richard Simmons Show
Woody Fraser . . . . . . . . . . . . . . . . . . . . Executive Producer
Bob George . . . . . . . . . . . . . . . Exec. in Charge of Production
Lee Cadorette . . . . . . . . . . . . . . . . . . Production Manager
Cathy Masamitsu . . . . . . . . . . . . . . . . Asst. to Mr. Fraser

**FREE RANGE PICTURES**
PHONE . . . . . . . . . . . . . . . . . . . . . . . . . . . . . . . . 360-379-9382
FAX . . . . . . . . . . . . . . . . . . . . . . . . . . . . . . . . . . . . 360-379-9384
218 Polk St.
Port Townsend, WA 98368
TYPE       Motion Pictures
CREDITS       The Breakfast Club - Fried Green Tomatoes - Birdy
Andy Meyer . . . . . . . . . . . . . . . . . . . . . . . . . . . . Producer
Gil Friesen . . . . . . . . . . . . . . . . . . . . . . . . . . . . Producer

# COMPANIES AND STAFF

**FREEDMAN PRODS., JACK**
PHONE . . . . . . . . . . . . . . . . . . . . . . . . . . . . . . 818-789-9306
FAX . . . . . . . . . . . . . . . . . . . . . . . . . . . . . . . . . 818-789-2632
14225 Ventura Blvd., Ste. 200
Sherman Oaks, CA 91423
TYPE          Motion Pictures + Television
CREDITS       Toy Soldiers - Body Parts - Mother's Boys
Jack Freedman . . . . . . . . . . . . . . . . . . . . Chairman of the Board
Patricia Herskovic . . . . . . . . . . . . . . . . . . . . . . . . . President
Barry Greenfield . . . . . . . . . . . . . . . . . . . . . . . . . . Producer
Bret McCartney . . . . . . . . . . . . . . . . . . . . VP, Creative Affairs

***FRESH PRODUCE COMPANY**
PHONE . . . . . . . . . . . . . . . . . . . . . . . . . . . . . . 213-931-3700
FAX . . . . . . . . . . . . . . . . . . . . . . . . . . . . . . . . . 213-931-8908
EMAIL . . . . . . . . . . . . . . . . . . . . . . . . . . . MPFPC@aol.com
5820 Wilshire Blvd., Ste. 400
Los Angeles, CA 90036
TYPE          Motion Pictures
CREDITS       Still Breathing
Marshall Persinger . . . . . . . . . . . . . . . . . . . . . . . . . Producer
Joyce Schweickert . . . . . . . . . . . . . . . . . . . Executive Producer
Julie Lynn . . . . . . . . . . . . . . . . . . . . . . . . . . . . VP, Production
Kira Lewis . . . . . . . . . . . . . . . . . . . . . . . . Production Associate

***FREYER PRODUCTIONS, ELLEN**
PHONE . . . . . . . . . . . . . . . . . . . . . . . . . . . . . . 213-936-1826
FAX . . . . . . . . . . . . . . . . . . . . . . . . . . . . . . . . . 213-936-1827
EMAIL . . . . . . . . . . . . . . . . . . . . . . elnsmp@mainnet.com
1154 Alvira St.
Los Angeles, CA 90035
TYPE          Animation + Feature Direct to Video + Motion Pictures +
              Television
CREDITS       Anatole (CBS) - Summer of the Monkey's (WD Video) -
              Whipping Boy (Disney Channel)
COMMENTS      Children's and Family Entertainment
Ellen Freyer . . . . . . . . . . . . . . . . . . . . Producer/Executive Producer

**FRIED FILMS**
PHONE . . . . . . . . . . . . . . . . . . . . . . . . . . . . . . 310-244-8727
FAX . . . . . . . . . . . . . . . . . . . . . . . . . . . . . . . . . 310-244-2166
Sony Pictures Entertainment
10202 W. Washington Blvd., Capra 113A
Culver City, CA 90232-3195
TYPE          Motion Pictures + Television
DEAL          Columbia Pictures/HBO
CREDITS       Rudy - So I Married An Axe Murderer - Only You
Robert Fried . . . . . . . . . . . . . . . . . . . . . . . . . . . . Producer
Richard Zinman . . . . . . . . . . . . . . . . . . . . . . . . . . Producer
Geri Robert . . . . . . . . . . . . . . . . . . . . . . . . . Vice President
Alex Close . . . . . . . . . . . . . . . . . . . . . . . . . Creative Associate

**FRIED PRODUCTIONS, DANIEL**
PHONE . . . . . . . . . . . . . . . . . . . . . . . . . . . . . . 310-827-6342
FAX . . . . . . . . . . . . . . . . . . . . . . . . . . . . . . . . . 310-827-6595
EMAIL . . . . . . . . . . . . . . . . . . . . . . . . . . kidfried@aol.com
5455 Centinela Ave., 3rd Floor
Los Angeles, CA 90066
TYPE          Motion Pictures
CREDITS       American Knight - What We Do is Secret - Big Packages
Daniel Fried . . . . . . . . . . . . . . . . . . . . . . . . . . . . Producer

**FRIENDLY PRODUCTIONS**
PHONE . . . . . . . . . . . . . . . . . . . . . . . . . . . . . . 310-369-3973
FAX . . . . . . . . . . . . . . . . . . . . . . . . . . . . . . . . . 310-369-7436
10201 W. Pico Blvd., Bldg. 41
Los Angeles, CA 90035
TYPE          Motion Pictures
DEAL          Twentieth Century Fox-Fox 2000 (LA)
CREDITS       Dr. Dolittle - Out To Sea - Courage Under Fire
David T. Friendly . . . . . . . . . . . . . . . . . . . . . . . . . No Title
David W. Higgins . . . . . . . . . . . . . . No Title (310-369-4132)
Michael McGahey . . . . . . . . . . . . . . . . . . . . . . . . No Title
Elisabeth Caren . . . . . . . . . . . . . . . No Title (310-369-4132)

**FRIES FILM GROUP, INC.**
PHONE . . . . . . . . . . . . . . . . . . . . . . . . . . . . . . 818-888-3052
FAX . . . . . . . . . . . . . . . . . . . . . . . . . . . . . . . . . 818-888-3042
22817 Ventura Blvd., #909
Woodland Hills, CA 91364
TYPE          Motion Pictures + Feature Direct to Video + Television
CREDITS       Call of the Wild - Progeny - Owd Bob - Under Current -
              Nico The Unicorn
Charles M. Fries . . . . . . . . . . . . . . . . . . . . . . . . . President
Michael Kananack . . . . . . . . . . . . . . . VP, Sales & Acquisitions
Patti Perlstein . . . . . . . . . . . . . . . . . . . . . Dir., Business Affairs

**FRIES PRODUCTIONS, INC., CHUCK**
PHONE . . . . . . . . . . . . . . . . . . . . . . . . . . . . . . 213-466-2266
FAX . . . . . . . . . . . . . . . . . . . . . . . . . . . . . . . . . 213-465-7835
6922 Hollywood Blvd.
Los Angeles, CA 90028-6133
TYPE          Motion Pictures + Television
CREDITS       Screamers- Deadly Web- Queen of Mean Leona Helmsley
COMMENTS      Fries Film Co., Inc./Fries Sales Co., Inc. Fries Worldwide
              Consulting
Charles W. Fries . . . . . . . . . . . . . . . Chairman/President/CEO
Benjamin Meltzer . . . . . . . . . . . . . . . . . . Executive Assistant

***FRONT STREET PRODUCTIONS**
PHONE . . . . . . . . . . . . . . . . . . . . . . . . . . . . . . 310-450-0440
FAX . . . . . . . . . . . . . . . . . . . . . . . . . . . . . . . . . 310-450-0488
2656 29th St., Ste. 208
Santa Monica, CA 90405
TYPE          Motion Pictures + Television
CREDITS       Divided By Hate - Eden - The Break Up
Jonas Goodman . . . . . . . . . . . . . . . . . . . . . . . . . . Producer
Harvey Kahn . . . . . . . . . . . . . . . . . . . . . . . . . . . . Producer
Tom Fortuna . . . . . . . . . . . . . . . . . . . . . . VP, Development

**FROST PRODS., MARK**
PHONE . . . . . . . . . . . . . . . . . . . . . . . . . . . . . . 213-939-1983
P.O. Box 1723
Studio City, CA 91604
TYPE          Motion Pictures + Television
CREDITS       Twin Peaks - American Chronicles - Storyville
Mark Frost . . . . . . . . . . . . . . . . . . . Chairman/Exec. Producer
Ken Scherer . . . . . . . . . . . . . . . . . . . . . . . . . . . President

**FTM PRODUCTIONS**
PHONE . . . . . . . . . . . . . . . . . . . . . . . . . . . . . . 310-550-0400
FAX . . . . . . . . . . . . . . . . . . . . . . . . . . . . . . . . . 310-550-0412
EMAIL . . . . . . . . . . . . . . . . . . . . . . . . . FTMprod@aol.com
9200 Sunset Blvd., Ste. 1209
Los Angeles, CA 90069
TYPE          Motion Pictures + Television
CREDITS       Flinch - Passport To Murder - The Girl Next Door
Tony Masucci . . . . . . . . . . . . . . . . . . . . . . . . . . . President

**FULL CIRCLE ENT. AKA SUZANNE BAUMAN PROD**
PHONE . . . . . . . . . . . . . . . . . . . . . . . . . . . . . . 310-557-1932
FAX . . . . . . . . . . . . . . . . . . . . . . . . . . . . . . . . . 310-557-1521
1551 S. Robertson Blvd., Ste. 204
Los Angeles, CA 90035
TYPE          Motion Pictures + Television + Documentaries
CREDITS       Animal Adventures - La Belle Epoque - River of Dreams -
              Edge of the Bonfire - Jackie Behind the Myth
COMMENTS      Also: Theater.
Suzanne Bauman . . . . . . . . . . . . . . . . . . . Producer/Director
Elliott Easton . . . . . . . . . . . . . . . . . . . . . . . . . . . Producer
Beth Laity Lerch . . . . . . . . . . . . . . . . . . . . . . . . . Producer
Brian Oppenheimer . . . . . . . . . . . . . . . . . . Dir., Development

**FULL MOON & HIGH TIDE PRODS. INC.**
PHONE . . . . . . . . . . . . . . . . . . . . . . . . . . . . . . 213-852-2626
269 South Beverly Dr., Ste. 383
Beverly Hills, CA 90212
TYPE          Motion Pictures + Television
DEAL          King World Productions
Roseanne . . . . . . . . . . . . . . . . . . . . . . . . . . . Owner/Writer
Allan Stephan . . . . . . . . . . . . . . . . . . . . . Head, Development

# COMPANIES AND STAFF

**FURST FILMS**
PHONE . . . . . . . . . . . . . . . . . . . . . . . . . . . . . . . . . . . . . . . 310-278-6468
FAX . . . . . . . . . . . . . . . . . . . . . . . . . . . . . . . . . . . . . . . . . . . 310-278-7401
EMAIL . . . . . . . . . . . . . . . . . . . . . . . . . . . . . . . . furstbyrd@aol.com
8954 West Pico Blvd., 2nd Floor
Los Angeles, CA 90035
TYPE           Motion Pictures + Television
CREDITS        No Limit - Shepherd
Sean Furst . . . . . . . . . . . . . . . . . . . . . . . . . . . . . . . . . . . . . . . Producer
Josh Samson . . . . . . . . . . . . . . . . . . . . . . . . . . . . . . . . . Development
Bryan Furst . . . . . . . . . . . . . . . . . . . . . . . . . . . . . . . . . . Development

**FX NETWORKS, LLC**
PHONE . . . . . . . . . . . . . . . . . . . . . . 310-444-8123/212-802-4000
FAX . . . . . . . . . . . . . . . . . . . . . . . . . 310-444-8160/212-802-4348
WEBSITE . . . . . . . . . . . . . . . . . . . . . http://www.fxnetworks.com
1440 S. Sepulveda Blvd.
Los Angeles, CA 90025
TYPE           Television
COMMENTS       Also: 212 Fifth Ave., NY, NY 10010
Mark Sonnenberg . . . . . . . . . . . . . . . . . . . . . . . . Exec. Vice President
Bob Boden . . . . . . . . . . . . . . . . . . . . . . VP, Development/Production
Chris Fahland . . . . . . . . . . . . . . . . . . . . . Dir., Development/Production
Christy Dees . . . . . . . . . . . . . . . . . . . . . Mgr., Development/Production
Michael Koegel . . . . . . . . . . Exec. in Charge of Development/Production (NY)

**GALAN ENTERTAINMENT**
PHONE . . . . . . . . . . . . . . . . . . . . . . . . . . . . . . . . . . 310-452-8400
FAX . . . . . . . . . . . . . . . . . . . . . . . . . . . . . . . . . . . . . 310-452-5154
915 Electric Ave., Bldg. C
Venice, CA 90291
TYPE           Motion Pictures + Television + Documentaries +
               Interactive Multimedia
CREDITS        Loco Slam - Bravo Awards - Fox Kids
Nely Galan . . . . . . . . . . . . . . . . . . . . . . . . . . . . . . . . President/CEO
Yogini Purohit . . . . . . . . . . . . . . . . . . . . . . . . Chief Financial Officer
Kathleen Bedoya . . . . . . . . . . . . . . . . . . . . . . . . . Creative Director
Roland Ballester . . . . . . . . . . . . . . . . . . . . . . . . . VP, Business Affairs
Derek Bond . . . . . . . . . . . . . . . . . . . . . . . . . . . . . . . VP, Production
Barbara Farmer . . . . . . . . . . . . . . . . . . . . . . . . . . Dir., Development
Diana Mogollon . . . . . . . . . . . . . . . . . . . . . . . . . . Dir., Development
Denise Garcia . . . . . . . . . . . . . . . . . . . . . . . . . . . Mgr., Development

**GALANTY & COMPANY**
PHONE . . . . . . . . . . . . . . . . . . . . . . . . . . . . . . . 310-451-2525
EMAIL . . . . . . . . . . . . . . . . . . . . . . . . . Galanty @ix.netcom.com
1640 5th St., Ste. 202
Santa Monica, CA 90401
TYPE           Television
CREDITS        Fonda's Favorite Fat Burners - Stefanie Powers' Broadway
               Workout
COMMENTS       Permanent exhibits at the L.A. Museum of Tolerance.
Mark Galanty . . . . . . . . . . . . . . . . . . . . . . . . . . . . Executive Producer
Sidney Galanty . . . . . . . . . . . . . . . . . . . . Exec. Producer/Director
Sanja Brizic Ilic . . . . . . . . . . . . . . . . . . . . . . . . Associate Producer

**GALLANT ENTERTAINMENT, INC.**
PHONE . . . . . . . . . . . . . . . . . . . . . . . . . . . . . . . . . . 818-905-9848
FAX . . . . . . . . . . . . . . . . . . . . . . . . . . . . . . . . . . . . . 818-906-9965
EMAIL . . . . . . . . . . . . . . . . . . . . . . . . GALLANTENT@aol.com
16161 Ventura Blvd., #347
Encino, CA 91436-2504
TYPE           Motion Pictures + Television
CREDITS        Stompin' At The Savoy - Bionic Ever After
Michael O. Gallant . . . . . . . . . . . . . . . . . . . . . . . . . . . President
Kathleen Gallant . . . . . . . . . . . . . . . . . . . . . VP, Business Affairs
David Cohen . . . . . . . . . . . . . . . . . . . . . . . . . . . Dir., Development

***GALLO ENTERTAINMENT, INC.**
PHONE . . . . . . . . . . . . . . . . . . . . . . . . . . . . . . . 310-277-8107
FAX . . . . . . . . . . . . . . . . . . . . . . . . . . . . . . . . . . 310-277-1828
1421 Ambassador St., #101
Los Angeles, CA 90035
TYPE           Television + Motion Pictures
CREDITS        Hustling - Mafia Princess - The Lookalike - Princess Daisy
Lillian Gallo . . . . . . . . . . . . . . . . . . . . . . . . . . . . Producer/Partner
Lew Gallo . . . . . . . . . . . . . . . . . . . . . . . . . . . . . Producer/Partner
Andi Carreiro . . . . . . . . . . . . . . . . . . . . . . . . . . . . . . . Associate

**GASLIGHT PICTURES**
PHONE . . . . . . . . . . . . . . . . . . . . . . . . . . . . . . . . . . 818-379-8518
FAX . . . . . . . . . . . . . . . . . . . . . . . . . . . . . . . . . . . . . 818-379-9679
EMAIL . . . . . . . . . . . . . . . . . . . . . . . . . gaslitepic@aol.com
16255 Ventura Blvd., Ste. 204
Encino, CA 91436
TYPE           Motion Pictures + Television
DEAL           Bonneville Worldwide Entertainment
CREDITS        The Perfect Getaway (ABC) - Nightmare In Big Sky
               Country (Lifetime)
Shanna Tyndall . . . . . . . . . . . . . . . . . . . . . . . . . Producer/Partner
Greg Gugliotta . . . . . . . . . . . . . . . . . . . . . . . . . . Producer/Partner
Dru Homer . . . . . . . . . . . . . . . . . . . . . . Development Associate

**GAUMONT**
PHONE . . . . . . . . . . . . . . . . . . . . . . . . . . . . . . . . . . 310-281-5804
FAX . . . . . . . . . . . . . . . . . . . . . . . . . . . . . . . . . . . . . 310-281-5808
9151 Sunset Blvd.
West Hollywood, CA 90069
TYPE           Television + Motion Pictures + Animation
CREDITS        The Fifth Element- The Professional- Highlander -
               Skydancers
Marla Ginsburg . . . . . . . . . Exec. Producer, Intl. TV Co-Prod. (Paris & LA)
Yvonne Styles . . . . . . . . . . . . . . . . . . . . . . . . Dir., Development

**GEKKO FILM CORP**
PHONE . . . . . . . . . . . . . . . . . . . . . . . . . . . . . . . . . . 604-654-1690
FAX . . . . . . . . . . . . . . . . . . . . . . . . . . . . . . . . . . . . . 604-654-2900
MGM Worldwide Television, Inc.
2500 Broadway St.
Santa Monica, CA 90404
TYPE           Motion Pictures + Television
CREDITS        MacGyver - Legend - Stargate-SG1
COMMENTS       Also: 2400 Boundary Rd., Burnaby, BC V5M 3Z3
Richard Dean Anderson . . . . . . . . . . . . . . . . . . Chief Executive Officer
Michael Greenburg . . . . . . . . . . . . . . . . . . . . . . . . . . . . President
Jenny McDonell . . . . . . . . . . . . . . . . . . Exec. Dir., Development

**GELFAND PRODUCTIONS, JANNA E.**
PHONE . . . . . . . . . . . . . . . . . . . . . . . . . . . . . . . . . . 310-826-2345
FAX . . . . . . . . . . . . . . . . . . . . . . . . . . . . . . . . . . . . . 310-826-6268
EMAIL . . . . . . . . . . . . . . . . . . . . . . . . jegprods@earthlink.net
960 S. Westgate #108
Los Angeles, CA 90049
TYPE           Motion Pictures + Television
CREDITS        Kissing Miranda
Janna E. Gelfand . . . . . . . . . . . . . . . . . . . . . . . . . . . . . . Producer
Kathy Rodriguez . . . . . . . . . . . . . . . . . . . . Development Assistant
Tom Black . . . . . . . . . . . . . . . . . . . . . . . . . . . . . . . . . . . . Reader
Tammy Rae . . . . . . . . . . . . . . . . . . . . . . . . . . . . . . . . . . . Reader

**GENDECE FILM CO.**
PHONE . . . . . . . . . . . . . . . . . . . . . . . . . . . . . . . . . . 213-960-4734
FAX . . . . . . . . . . . . . . . . . . . . . . . . . . . . . . . . . . . . . 213-960-4735
Raleigh Studios
5300 Melrose Ave., Bung. 110
Hollywood, CA 90038
TYPE           Motion Pictures + Television
CREDITS        Runaway Train - American Ninja - Cyborg
COMMENTS       Also: Soundtracks.
Brian Gendece . . . . . . . . . . . . . . . . . . . . . Producer/Partner/Writer
Richard Gordon . . . . . . . . . . . . . . . . . . . . . . . . . . . . . Producer

**GEORGE LITTO PICTURES**
PHONE . . . . . . . . . . . . . . . . . . . . . . . . . . . . . . . . . . 310-358-3160
FAX . . . . . . . . . . . . . . . . . . . . . . . . . . . . . . . . . . . . . 310-358-3111
8840 Wilshire Blvd., Ste. 101
Beverly Hills, CA 90211
TYPE           Motion Pictures
CREDITS        Kansas - Blow Out - Dressed to Kill - Over the Edge
George Litto . . . . . . . . . . . . . . . . . . . . . . . . . . . . . . . . . . . Owner
Jim Bullard . . . . . . . . . . . . . . . . . . . . . . CFO/Exec. Vice-President
Pamela Godfrey . . . . . . . . . . . . . . . . . . . . . . VP, Creative Affairs
Andria Litto . . . . . . . . . . . . . . . . . . . . . . . . . . . Creative Executive
Hilary Ryan . . . . . . . . . . . . . . . . . . . . . . . . . . . Creative Executive

**GEORGE STREET PICTURES**
PHONE . . . . . . . . . . . . . . . . . . . . . . . . . . . . . . 818-954-4361
FAX . . . . . . . . . . . . . . . . . . . . . . . . . . . . . . . . 818-954-3682
4000 Warner Blvd., Bldg. 81, Rm. 203
Burbank, CA 91522
TYPE        Motion Pictures
DEAL        Warner Bros. Pictures
Chris O'Donnell . . . . . . . . . . . . . . . . . . . . . . . . . President
Bing Howenstein . . . . . . . . . . . . . . . . . . . . . Vice President
Julie Lane . . . . . . . . . . . . . . . . . . . . . . . . . Dir., Development

**GEORGIAN BAY PRODS.**
PHONE . . . . . . . . . . . . . . . . . . . . . . . . . . . . . . 818-843-7704
FAX . . . . . . . . . . . . . . . . . . . . . . . . . . . . . . . . 818-843-0528
EMAIL . . . . . . . . . . . . . . . . . . . . . . . . . georgnbay@aol.com
3815 W. Olive Ave., Ste. 202
Burbank, CA 91505-4648
TYPE        Motion Pictures + Television
CREDITS     Maid in America - Word of Honor - Jimmy B & Andre
Alex Karras . . . . . . . . . . . . . . . . . . . . . . . . Producer/Actor
Susan Clark . . . . . . . . . . . . . . . . . . . . . . Producer/Actress
Catherine Lincoln . . . . . . . . . . . . . . . . . Producer/Development

***GERMAIN PRODUCTIONS, STEPHANIE**
PHONE . . . . . . . . . . . . . . . . . . . . . . . . . . . . . . 818-766-2610
FAX . . . . . . . . . . . . . . . . . . . . . . . . . . . . . . . . 818-766-7423
von Zerneck-Sertner Films
12001 Ventura Place, Ste. 400
Studio City, CA 91604
TYPE        Motion Pictures + Television
DEAL        Von Zerneck-Sertner Films
CREDITS     Holiday In Your Heart - Mother Knows Best - No One
            Would Tell
Stephanie Germain . . . . . . . . . . . . . . . . . . . . . . . Producer
Miriam Diaz-Santana . . . . . . . . . . . . . . . . Asst. to Ms. Germain

**GERREN PRODUCTIONS**
PHONE . . . . . . . . . . . . . . . . . . . . . . . . . . . . . . 213-292-1600
FAX . . . . . . . . . . . . . . . . . . . . . . . . . . . . . . . . 213-293-8214
EMAIL . . . . . . . . . . . . . . . . . . . . . . . . . RGerren207@aol.com
3640 W. 63rd St., Ste. 1A
Los Angeles, CA 90043-3706
TYPE        Motion Pictures + Television + Documentaries +
            Animation + Interactive Multimedia
CREDITS     Diversity Awards - The Nation - Gospel Soul Search - Get
            to Go - Jazz at Drew - Reggae Sunsplash - Black Business
            Expo
Rudy Gerren . . . . . . . . . . . . . . . . . . . . . . . . . CEO/President
Conrad Bullard . . . . . . . . . . . . . . . . . . . . . . VP, Production
Jamal Gerren . . . . . . . . . . . . . . . . . . . . . . VP, Development
Michele Gerren . . . . . . . . . . . . . . . . . . . . . Special Projects
Lara McGee . . . . . . . . . . . . . . . . . . . . . . . . . . . Accounting

**GIBBONS ENTERPRISES, LEEZA**
PHONE . . . . . . . . . . . . . . . . . . . . . . . . . . . . . . 213-956-4972
FAX . . . . . . . . . . . . . . . . . . . . . . . . . . . . . . . . 213-862-0110
5555 Melrose Ave., Mae West 115
Hollywood, CA 90038
TYPE        Television
DEAL        Paramount Television Group
CREDITS     Leeza - ET on Radio - Top 25 Count - Intimate Portrait of
            JFK Jr. - Straight From The Heart
Leeza Gibbons . . . . . . . . . . . . . . . . . . . CEO/Exec. Producer
Kaye Zusmann . . . . . . . . . . . . . . . . . . . . . Sr. Vice President
Joe Lupariello . . . . . . . . . . . . . . . . . . . . . . . Vice President

**GIDDINGS IMAGES INC., AL**
PHONE . . . . . . . . . . . . . . . . . . . . . . . . . . . . . . 406-333-4300
FAX . . . . . . . . . . . . . . . . . . . . . . . . . . . . . . . . 406-333-4308
EMAIL . . . . . . . . . . . . . . . . . . . . . . . . . algiddings@aol.com
75 Bridger Hollow Road
Pray, MT 59065
TYPE        Television + Documentaries + Motion Pictures +
            Interactive Multimedia
CREDITS     Blue Whale: Lgst. Animal On Earth - Galapagos: Beyond
            Darwin - Titanic
Al Giddings . . . . . . . . . . . . . . . . . . President/Director/Producer
Lindy Moore . . . . . . . . . . . . . . . . . . . . . Asst. to Al Giddings

**GILBERT ASSOCIATES, RON**
PHONE . . . . . . . . . . . . . . . . . . . . . . . . . . . . . . 213-954-4540
FAX . . . . . . . . . . . . . . . . . . . . . . . . . . . . . . . . 213-954-4550
4500 Wilshire Blvd., 2nd Floor
Los Angeles, CA 90010
TYPE        Motion Pictures + Television
CREDITS     Blind Ambition - Long Hot Summer - Night Stalker -
            Matter of Justice
Ron Gilbert . . . . . . . . . . . . . . . . . . . . . . . . . . . President
Corrinne Olivo . . . . . . . . . . . . Vice President (213-954-4576)

**GILLEN & PRICE**
PHONE . . . . . . . . . . . . . . . . 310-394-3131/213-655-8047
FAX . . . . . . . . . . . . . . . . . . . . . . . . . . . . . . . . 310-394-3133
301 Arizona Ave., Ste. 303
Santa Monica, CA 90401
TYPE        Motion Pictures + Television
CREDITS     Fried Green Tomatoes
Jody Price . . . . . . . . . . . . . . . . . . . . . . . . . . . . Producer

**GIMBEL PRODUCTIONS, INC., ROGER**
PHONE . . . . . . . . . . . . . . . . . . . . . . . . . . . . . . 310-459-3838
FAX . . . . . . . . . . . . . . . . . . . . . . . . . . . . . . . . 310-459-6940
EMAIL . . . . . . . . . . . . . . . . . . . . gimpixl@ix.netcom.com
1675 Old Oak Road
Los Angeles, CA 90049
TYPE        Motion Pictures + Television
DEAL        Turner Network Television
CREDITS     Montana - Chernobyl: The Final Warning - Murder
            Between Friends - The Perfect Mother
Roger Gimbel . . . . . . . . . . . . . . President/Exec. Producer
Mark Trabulus . . . . . . . . . . . . . . . . . . . . . . . . . Producer
Lorraine DeVille . . . . . . . . . . . . . . Exec. Asst. to Mr. Gimbel

**GINTY FILMS**
PHONE . . . . . . . . . . . . . . . . . . . . . . . . . . . . . . 310-277-1408
FAX . . . . . . . . . . . . . . . . . . . . . . . . . . . . . . . . 310-274-1065
EMAIL . . . . . . . . . . . . . . . . . . . . . . . . . rwginty@aol.com
16133 Ventura Blvd., #800
Encino, CA 91436
TYPE        Motion Pictures + Television
CREDITS     China Beach - Dream On - Early Edition - Fame L.A. -
            Nash Bridges- Xena- Honey I Shrunk The Kids
Robert Ginty . . . . . . . . . . . . . . . Producer/Director/CEO
Christine Porter . . . . . . . . . . . . . . . . . . Executive Assistant
Kathryn Seno . . . . . . . . . . . . . . . . . . . . Executive Assistant

**GITLIN PRODUCTIONS**
PHONE . . . . . . . . . . . . . . . . . . . . . . . . . . . . . . 310-550-0212
FAX . . . . . . . . . . . . . . . . . . . . . . . . . . . . . . . . 310-550-7092
415 N. Camden Drive
Beverly Hills, CA 90210
TYPE        Motion Pictures
CREDITS     White Squall - Browning Version - Monkey Trouble -
            Thelma & Louise - 1492
Mimi Polk Gitlin . . . . . . . . . . . . . . . . . . . . . . . . . Producer
Stephanie Williams . . . . . . . . . . . . . . . . . Dir., Development
Caspar Uniacke . . . . . . . . . . . . . . . . . Development Assistant

**GITTES, INC.**
PHONE . . . . . . . . . . . . . . . . . . . . . . . . . . . . . . 310-244-4333
FAX . . . . . . . . . . . . . . . . . . . . . . . . . . . . . . . . 310-244-1711
Columbia Pictures
10202 W. Washington Blvd., Poitier #1200
Culver City, CA 90232-3195
TYPE        Motion Pictures
DEAL        Columbia Pictures
CREDITS     Little Nikita - Breaking In - Goin' South
Harry Gittes . . . . . . . . . . . . . . . . . . . . . . . . . . . Producer
Edward C. Wang . . . . . . . . . Dir., Development (310-244-4334)

**GIV'EN FILMS**
PHONE . . . . . . . . . . . . . . . . . . . . . . . . . . . . . . 212-965-0128
FAX . . . . . . . . . . . . . . . . . . . . . . . . . . . . . . . . 212-965-0485
51 Wooster Street
New York, NY 10013
TYPE        Motion Pictures
CREDITS     Hurricane Streets- Myth America - Restaurant
Galt Niederhoffer . . . . . . . . . . . . . . . . President/Producer
Paul Mezey . . . . . . . . . . . . . . . . . . . . . . . . VP/Producer
Susannah Ludwig . . . . . . . . . . Assoc., Production/Operations
Alexander Orlovsky . . . . . . . . . . . . . . . . Project Coordinator

# COMPANIES AND STAFF

## *GLATZER PRODUCTIONS
PHONE . . . . . . . . . . . . . . . . . . . . . . . . . . . . . . 310-248-2786
FAX . . . . . . . . . . . . . . . . . . . . . . . . . . . . . . . . 310-278-7401
8954 W. Pico Blvd., 2nd Floor
Los Angeles, CA 90035

TYPE        Motion Pictures
CREDITS      The Grave - Deceiver - Shepherd

Peter Glatzer . . . . . . . . . . . . . . . . . . . . . . . . . . . Producer
Joshua Samson . . . . . . . . . . . . . . . . . . . . Production Associate

## *GLENEAGLE PRODUCTIONS
PHONE . . . . . . . . . . . . . . . . . . . . . . . . . . . . . . 310-478-1700
FAX . . . . . . . . . . . . . . . . . . . . . . . . . . . . . . . . 310-478-6067
EMAIL . . . . . . . . . . . . . . . . . . gleneagle_productions@msn.com
1640 Sepulveda, 4th Fl.
Los Angeles, CA 90025

TYPE        Motion Pictures + Television + Syndication
DEAL        Hearst Entertainment

Chad S. Hoffman . . . . . . . . . . . . . . . . . . . . . Executive Producer
Robert Schwartz . . . . . . . . . . . . . . . . . . . . . Executive Producer
Elizabeth Yost . . . . . . . . . . . . . . . . . . . . . . . Dir., Development

## GLOBAL ENTERTAINMENT NETWORK, INC.
PHONE . . . . . . . . . . . . . . . . . . . . . . . . . . . 516-262-1757
FAX . . . . . . . . . . . . . . . . . . . . . . . . . . . . . 516-262-1760
EMAIL . . . . . . . . . . . . . . . . . . . . . . . . . geneast@erols.com
34 Harbor Heights Dr.
Centerport, NY 11721

TYPE        Motion Pictures + Television
CREDITS      Just Your Luck - Pink As The Day She Was Born

Stan Bernstein . . . . . . . . . . . . . . . . . . . . . . . . . President
Mary Hughes . . . . . . . . . . . . . . . . . . . . . . Asst. to President

## GLORY MONTY PRODS.
PHONE . . . . . . . . . . . . . . . . . . . . . . . . . . . . . . 310-274-4924
FAX . . . . . . . . . . . . . . . . . . . . . . . . . . . . . . . . 213-383-0932
3550 Wilshire Blvd., Ste. 840
Los Angeles, CA 90010-2409

TYPE        Television
DEAL        Grosso-Jacobson Productions, Inc.
CREDITS      The Hamptons- The Imposter- Remember Me - While My
              Pretty One Sleeps

Gloria Monty . . . . . . . . . . . . . . . . . . . . . . . . . President

## GMR PRODUCTIONS, INC.
PHONE . . . . . . . . . . . . . . . . . . . . . . . . . . . . . . 310-823-3650
FAX . . . . . . . . . . . . . . . . . . . . . . . . . . . . . . . . 310-823-3651
EMAIL . . . . . . . . . . . . . . . . . . . . . . . . . . . gmres@aol.com
214 South Venice Blvd.
Venice, CA 90291

TYPE        Motion Pictures
CREDITS      Clockwatchers - Female Perversions

Gina Resnick . . . . . . . . . . . . . . . . . . . . . . . . . . Producer

## GOAT CAY PRODUCTIONS, INC.
PHONE . . . . . . . . . . . . . . . . . . . . . . . . . . . . . . 212-247-6493
FAX . . . . . . . . . . . . . . . . . . . . . . . . . . . . . . . . 212-247-6599
EMAIL . . . . . . . . . . . . . . . . . . . . . . . . . goatcay@bway.net
200 W. 57th St., Ste. 1306
New York, NY 10019

TYPE        Motion Pictures + Television
DEAL        Twentieth Century Fox
COMMENTS   No Unsolicited Material.

Sigourney Weaver . . . . . . . . . . . . . . . . . . President/Producer/Actor
Mary Robbins . . . . . . . . . . . . . . . . . . . . Development Executive
Laura Valdivia . . . . . . . . . . . . . . . . . . . . . . . . . . Assistant

## GOATSINGERS, THE
PHONE . . . . . . . . . . . . . . . . . . . . . . . . . . . 212-966-3045
FAX . . . . . . . . . . . . . . . . . . . . . . . . . . . . . 212-966-4362
179 Franklin ST., 6th Fl.
New York, NY 10013

TYPE        Motion Pictures + Television
DEAL        October Films

Harvey Keitel . . . . . . . . . . . . . . . . . . . . . . . . . . President
Peggy Gormley . . . . . . . . . . . . . . . . . . . . . . . . . . Partner
Kerri Courtney . . . . . . . . . . . . . . . . . . . . . Executive Assistant

## GOEPP CIRCLE PRODUCTIONS
PHONE . . . . . . . . . . . . . . . . . . . . . . . . . . . 213-956-4620
FAX . . . . . . . . . . . . . . . . . . . . . . . . . . . . . 213-862-1119
Paramount Pictures
5555 Melrose Ave., Cooper #116
Los Angeles, CA 90038

TYPE        Motion Pictures + Television
DEAL        Paramount Pictures- Motion Picture Group
CREDITS      Star Trek: First Contact

Jonathan Frakes . . . . . . . . . . . . . . . . . . . . . Director/Producer
Lisa J. Olin . . . . . . . . . . . . . . . . . . . . . . . Pres., Production
Ellen Hornstein . . . . . . . . . . . . . . . . . . . . . . . Story Editor
Molly Mandell . . . . . . . . . . . . . . . . . . . . . . . . Story Editor

## GOLCHAN PRODS., FREDERIC
PHONE . . . . . . . . . . . . . . . . . . . . . . . . . . . 310-854-1133
FAX . . . . . . . . . . . . . . . . . . . . . . . . . . . . . 310-854-9028
EMAIL . . . . . . . . . . . . . . . . . . . . . . . . . . fgfilm@aol.com
8787 Shoreham Dr., Ste. 1001
West Hollywood, CA 90069

TYPE        Motion Pictures + Television
CREDITS      Intersection - Quick Change - In The Deep Woods - The
              Associate

Frederic Golchan . . . . . . . . . . . . . . . . . . . . . . . President
Nanette Julian . . . . . . . . . . . . . . . . . . . . . Executive Assistant

## GOLD'N HEN PRODUCTIONS
PHONE . . . . . . . . . . . . . . . . . . . . . . . . . . . 310-820-1308
FAX . . . . . . . . . . . . . . . . . . . . . 310-820-1398/212-689-4261
12301 Wilshire Blvd., Ste. 402
Los Angeles, CA 90025

TYPE        Motion Pictures + Television
CREDITS      Replacing Dad - God Bless The Moon - Spy Girl - Fiesta at
              Twilight
COMMENTS   Also: 370 Lexington Ave. #808, NY, NY 10017. Also:
              Movies of the week.

Joel Goldstein . . . . . . . . . . . . . . . . . . . . . Chairman (NY)
Judy Henry . . . . . . . . . . . . . . . . . . . . . . . President (NY)
Dale Eldridge Kaye . . . . . . . . . . . . . . . . . . Vice President (LA)
Giles Felton . . . . . . . . . . . . . . . . . . . . . . Development (NY)
Jamie Goldstein . . . . . . . . . . . . . . . . . . . . Development (LA)

## *GOLDBAR ENTERTAINMENT
PHONE . . . . . . . . . . . . . . . . . . . . . . . . . . . 310-478-8080
FAX . . . . . . . . . . . . . . . . . . . . . . . . . . . . . 310-478-6432
EMAIL . . . . . . . . . . . . . . . . . . . . . . . GoldbarEnt@aol.com
11620 Wilshire Blvd., Ste. 400
Los Angeles, CA 90025

TYPE        Feature Direct to Video + Motion Pictures + Television
CREDITS      Diary of a Serial Killer - The Girl Gets Moe - Other Voices

Harel Goldstein . . . . . . . . . . . . . . . . . . . . . . Co-Chairman
Bill Barnett . . . . . . . . . . . . . . . . . . . . . . . . Co-Chairman

## GOLDCREST FILMS INTERNATIONAL, INC.
PHONE . . . . . . . . . . . . . . . 213-650-4551/011441714378696
FAX . . . . . . . . . . . . . . . . . 213-650-3581/011441714374448
EMAIL . . . . . . . . . . . . . . . . . mailbox@goldcrest-films.com
1240 Olive
Los Angeles, CA 90069

TYPE        Motion Pictures
CREDITS      Rock-A-Doodle - Black Rainbow - Clockwatchers - No Way
              Home
COMMENTS   ALSO: 65/66 Dean St., London W1V 6PL

John Quested . . . . . . . . . . . . . . . . . . . . . Chairman (London)
Stephen R. Johnston . . . . . . . . . . . . . . . . . . . President (LA)
Dawn Arroyo . . . . . . . . . . . . . . . . Production & Acquisitions (LA)
Patty Tapanes . . . . . . . . . . . . . . . . . . . Business Affairs (LA)

## GOLDEN & ASSOCIATES INC., PETER
PHONE . . . . . . . . . . . . . . . . . . . . . . . . . . . 818-907-9566
FAX . . . . . . . . . . . . . . . . . . . . . . . . . . . . . 818-907-9567
EMAIL . . . . . . . . . . . . . . . . . . . . . . . Broadlawn@aol.com
16350 Ventura Blvd., Ste. 181
Encino, CA 91436

TYPE        Motion Pictures + Television
CREDITS      The Operation/CBS - Just Words/HBO Spec.
COMMENTS   Also: Management

Peter Golden . . . . . . . . . . . . . . . . . . . . . . . . . . Producer

# COMPANIES AND STAFF

**GOLDEN HARVEST FILMS**
PHONE . . . . . . . . . . . . . . . . . . . . . . . . . . . . . . . . 310-203-0722
FAX . . . . . . . . . . . . . . . . . . . . . . . . . . . . . . . . . . . 310-556-3214
9884 Santa Monica Blvd.
Beverly Hills, CA 90212

| | |
|---|---|
| TYPE | Motion Pictures |
| CREDITS | Teenage Mutant Ninja Turtles I, II & III |

Thomas K. Gray . . . . . . . . . . . . . . . . . . . . . . . Sr. VP, Production
Roberta Chin . . . . . . . . . . . . . . . . . . . . . . . . . . . . Vice President
John W. Stuart . . . . . . . . . . . . . . . . . . . . . . . . . . . VP, Finance

**GOLDEN QUILL**
PHONE . . . . . . . . . . . . . . . 310-274-5016/212-387-9656
FAX . . . . . . . . . . . . . . . . . . 310-274-5028/212-387-9632
8899 Beverly Blvd., Ste. 702
Los Angeles, CA 90048

| | |
|---|---|
| TYPE | Motion Pictures |
| CREDITS | In-Laws - Love Story - The Babe - Outrageous Fortune |
| COMMENTS | ALSO: 65 Bleecker St., 12th Fl., New York, NY 10012 |

Arthur Hiller . . . . . . . . . . . . . . . . . . . . . . . . . . Director/Producer
Hassan Ildari . . . . . . . . . . . . . Exec. VP, Acquisitions/Development
Brenda White . . . . . . . . . . . . . . . . . . . . . . . . . Executive Assistant

**GOLDENRING PRODUCTIONS**
PHONE . . . . . . . . . . . . . . . . . . . . . . . . . . . . . . . . 818-560-7605
FAX . . . . . . . . . . . . . . . . . . . . . . . . . . . . . . . . . . . 818-841-3819
Walt Disney Studios
500 S. Buena Vista St.
Burbank, CA 91521-1812

| | |
|---|---|
| TYPE | Motion Pictures + Television |
| DEAL | Walt Disney Company, The |
| CREDITS | On The Second Day Of Christmas |

Jane Goldenring . . . . . . . . . . . . . . . . . . . . . . . . . . . . . President
Vivien Mejia . . . . . . . . . . . . . . . . . . . . . . . . . Dir., Development
Victoria Farwell . . . . . . . . . . . . . . . . . . . . . . . . . Exec. Assistant

**GOLDHEART PICTURES CORP.**
PHONE . . . . . . . . . . . . . . . . . . . . . . . . . . . . . . . . 212-924-7270
FAX . . . . . . . . . . . . . . . . . . . . . . . . . . . . . . . . . . . 212-924-7198
EMAIL . . . . . . . . . . . . . . . . . . . . . . . . goldhart@interport.net
186 5th Ave., 5th Floor
New York, NY 10010

| | |
|---|---|
| TYPE | Motion Pictures |
| CREDITS | The Substance Of Fire - Angela - Harvest - Walking to the Waterline - Better Living |

Ron Kastner . . . . . . . . . . . . . . . . . . . . . . . Co-President/Producer
Lemore Syvan . . . . . . . . . . . . . . . . . . . . . . Co-President/Producer

**GOLDSMITH COMPANY, THE**
PHONE . . . . . . . . . . . . . . . . . . . . . . . . . . . . . . . . 213-466-2266
FAX . . . . . . . . . . . . . . . . . . . . . . . . . . . . . . . . . . . 213-465-7835
EMAIL . . . . . . . . . . . . . . . . . . . . . . . . . . . goldco8@aol.com
6922 Hollywood Blvd., 12th Fl.
Hollywood, CA 90028

| | |
|---|---|
| TYPE | Television + Motion Pictures |
| CREDITS | Cocaine: One Man's Seduction - She's the Sheriff - Families in Crisis |
| COMMENTS | Also: Family Films. |

David Goldsmith . . . . . . . . . . . . . . . . . . . . . . . . . . . . President
Nancy Gregory . . . . . . . . . . . . . . . . . . . . . . . . . Creative Affairs

**GOLDSMITH ENTERTAINMENT COMPANY**
PHONE . . . . . . . . . . . . . . . . . . . . . . . . . . . . . . . . 310-440-3711
FAX . . . . . . . . . . . . . . . . . . . . . . . . . . . . . . . . . . . 310-440-3715
141 South Barrington, Ste. E
Los Angeles, CA 90049

| | |
|---|---|
| TYPE | Motion Pictures + Television |
| CREDITS | In the Mood - One Against the Wind - Dalva |

Russell Goldsmith . . . . . . . . . . . . . . . . . . . . . . . . . . . President
Karen Mack . . . . . . . . . . . . . . . . . . . . . . . Producer/Vice President

**GOLDSTEIN CO., THE**
PHONE . . . . . . . . . . . . . . . . . . . . . . . . . . . . . . . . 310-659-9511
FAX . . . . . . . . . . . . . . . . . . . . . . . . . . . . . . . . . . . 310-659-8779
1644 Courtney Avenue
Los Angeles, CA 90046

| | |
|---|---|
| TYPE | Motion Pictures |
| CREDITS | Under Siege - Pretty Woman - The Hunted - Under Siege II |

Gary W. Goldstein . . . . . . . . . . . . . . . . . . . . . . . . . . . Producer
David Bales . . . . . . . . . . . . . . . . . . . . . . . . . . . . . . . . Producer
Ryan Pilon . . . . . . . . . . . . . . . . . . . . . . . . Production Associate

**GOLDSTREET PICTURES INC.**
PHONE . . . . . . . . . . . . . . . . . . . . . . . . . . . . . . . . 310-452-0262
FAX . . . . . . . . . . . . . . . . . . . . . . . . . . . . . . . . . . . 310-452-7349
1930 Ocean Ave., Ste. 307
Santa Monica, CA 90405

| | |
|---|---|
| TYPE | Motion Pictures + Television |
| CREDITS | Vampire's Kiss - Motorama - Wigstock: The Movie - HBO's Real Sex |

Barry Shils . . . . . . . . . . . . . . . . . . . . . . . . . . Producer/Director
Joanne Lara . . . . . . . . . . . . . . . . . . . . . . . . . . . . Vice President

**GOLDWYN COMPANY, THE SAMUEL**
PHONE . . . . . . . . . . . . . . . . . . . . . . . . . . . . . . . . 310-552-2255
FAX . . . . . . . . . . . . . . . . . . . . . . . . . . . . . . . . . . . 310-284-8493
10203 Santa Monica Blvd.
Los Angeles, CA 90067

| | |
|---|---|
| TYPE | Motion Pictures |
| CREDITS | Big Night - Madness of King George - Welcome Woop Woop - Bent |

Samuel Goldwyn Jr. . . . . . . . . . . . . . . . . Chairman of the Board/CEO
Meyer Gottlieb . . . . . . . . . . . . . . . . . . . . . . . . . . President/COO
John Manulis . . . . . . . . . . . . . . . Head, Worldwide Prod. & Acquisitions
Monica Chuo . . . . . . . . . . . . . . . . Dir., Development & Acquisitions
Gregg Goldman . . . . . . . . . . . . . . . Dir., Development & Acquisitions
Elicia Delazerda . . . . . . . . . . . . . . . . Asst. to Samuel Goldwyn, Jr.
Laura Coleman . . . . . . . . . . . . . . . . . . . Asst. to Meyer Gottlieb
Suzanne Brodsky . . . . . . . . . . . . . . . . . . . Asst. to John Manulis
Tom Quinn . . . . . . . . . . . . . . . . . . . . . . . . . . . . . . . . Assistant

***GOLDWYN FILMS INC.**
PHONE . . . . . . . . . . . . . 310-449-3000/44-171-333-8877
FAX . . . . . . . . . . . . . . . 310-586-8358/44-171-333-8878
2500 Broadway
Santa Monica, CA 90404-3061

| | |
|---|---|
| TYPE | Motion Pictures |
| CREDITS | The Hanging Garden - Live Flesh - Velvet Goldmine |
| COMMENTS | Also: 10 Stephen Mews, London, W1P 1PP, United Kingdom |

Larry Gleason . . . . . . . . . . . . . . . . . . . . . . . . . . . . . . Director
Gerry Rich . . . . . . . . . . . . . . . . . . . . . . . . . . . . . . . . Director
Wendy Palmer . . . . . . . . . . . . . . . . . . . . . . . . . . CEO (London)
Fiona Mitchell . . . . . . . . . . . . . . Sr. Exec. Vice President (London)
Francois Thos . . . . . . . . . . . . . . . Chief Financial Officer (London)
Sara Rose . . . . . . . . . . . . . . . . . . . . VP, Acquistions & Production
Tom Strudwick . . . . . . . . . . VP, Acquisitions & Production (London)
Andrew Weiner . . . . . . . . . . . . . . . . . . . . Acquistions Coordinator

**GOOD MACHINE**
PHONE . . . . . . . . . . . . . . . . . . . . . . . . . . . . . . . . 212-343-9230
FAX . . . . . . . . . . . . . . . . . . . . . . . . . . . . . . . . . . . 212-343-9645
EMAIL . . . . . . . . . . . . . . . . . . . . . . . . GoodMachin@aol.com
WEBSITE . . . . . . . . . . . . . . . . . . . http://www.goodmachine.com
417 Canal, 4th Floor
New York, NY 10013

| | |
|---|---|
| TYPE | Motion Pictures |
| DEAL | Twentieth Century Fox-Searchlight Picts. |
| CREDITS | The Ice Storm - No Looking Back - Walking and Talking - The Wedding Banquet - The Brothers McMullen |
| COMMENTS | Email = name@goodmachine.com |

Ted Hope . . . . . . . . . . . . . . . . . . . . . . . . . . . . . . Co-Chairman
James Schamus . . . . . . . . . . . . . . . . . . . . . . . . . . Co-Chairman
Anthony Bregman . . . . . . . . . . . . . . . . . . . . . . . VP, Production
Anne Carey . . . . . . . . . . . . . . . . . . . . . . . . . . . VP, Development
Mary Jane Skalski . . . . . . . . . . . . . . . . . . . . . VP, Creative Affairs
Noreen Ward . . . . . . . . . . . . . . . . . . . . . . . . . . . . . . Controller
Glen Basner . . . . . . . . . . . . . . . . . . . . . . . Dir., Business Affairs
Cielo Cerezo . . . . . . . . . . . . . . . . . . . . Development Coordinator

**GOODMAN-ROSEN PRODS.**
PHONE . . . . . . . . . . . . . . . . . . . . . . . . . . . . . . . . 310-309-5332
FAX . . . . . . . . . . . . . . . . . . . . . . . . . . . . . . . . . . . 310-309-5246
2401 Colorado Ave., Ste. 200
Santa Monica, CA 90404

| | |
|---|---|
| TYPE | Motion Pictures + Television |
| CREDITS | Cisco Kid - Police Academy - Christmas Everyday - Highlander - Wagons East |

Gary Goodman . . . . . . . . . . . . . . . . . . . . . . . . . . . . . . . Partner
Barry Rosen . . . . . . . . . . . . . . . . . . . . . . . . . . . . . . . . . Partner
Barbara Wellner . . . . . . . . . . . . . . . . . . Pres., Longform Television
Ford Lytle Gilmore . . . . . . . . . . . . . . . . Dir., Feature Development

## GORDON PRODS., DAN

| | |
|---|---|
| PHONE | 805-496-2566 |

2060-D Ave. Los Arboles, #256
Thousand Oaks, CA 91362-1361

| TYPE | Motion Pictures + Television |
|---|---|
| CREDITS | The Assignment - Murder in the First - Wyatt Earp - Passenger 57 - Gotcha |

Dan Gordon . . . . . . . . . . . . . . . . . . . . . . . . . . . Writer/Producer
Lenore R. Lewis . . . . . . . . . . . . . . . . . . . . . . . . . . . Development

## GOTHAM ENTERTAINMENT

PHONE . . . . . . . . . . . . . . . . . . . . . . . . . . 213-512-5094

3212 Nichols Canyon
Los Angeles, CA 90046

| TYPE | Motion Pictures + Television + Documentaries |
|---|---|
| CREDITS | Woo - Martin Lawrence Concert Film - True Class - Ritual |

Beth Gotham Hubbard . . . . . . . . . . . . . . . . . . . . . . Producer
Michael Hubbard . . . . . . . . . . . . . . . . . . . . . . . . . Producer
Dan Curnow . . . . . . . . . . . . . . . . . . . . . . . Dir., Development

## GRACIE FILMS

PHONE . . . . . . . . . . . . . . . . . . . . . . . . . . 310-244-4222
FAX . . . . . . . . . . . . . . . . . . . . . . . . . . . . 310-244-1530

Sony Film Corp.
10202 W. Washington Blvd.
Culver City, CA 90232

| TYPE | Motion Pictures + Television + Animation |
|---|---|
| DEAL | Sony Pictures Entertainment |
| CREDITS | Big - Jerry Maguire - Broadcast News - As Good As It Gets - BottleRocket - The Simpsons |
| COMMENTS | ALSO: 10201 W. Pico Blvd, LA, CA 90035 |

James L. Brooks . . . . . . . . . . . . . . . Producer/Writer/Director
Richard Sakai . . . . . . . . . . . . . . . . . President, Gracie Films
Julie Ansell . . . . . . . . . . . . . . . . . . Pres., Motion Pictures
Denise Sirkot . . . . . . . . . . . . . . . . . Exec. Vice President
Kelly R. Kulchak . . . . . . . . . . . . . . . . . . . VP, Production

## GRADE A ENTERTAINMENT

PHONE . . . . . . . . . . . . . . . . . . . . . . . . . . 310-471-0228
FAX . . . . . . . . . . . . . . . . . . . . . . . . . . . . 310-440-0409
EMAIL . . . . . . . . . . . . . . . . . . . . gradeaprod@aol.com

11718 Barrington Ct., Ste. 411
Los Angeles, CA 90049

| TYPE | Motion Pictures + Television |
|---|---|
| CREDITS | Captain Ron - It Takes Two - A Chance of Snow |

Andy Cohen . . . . . . . . . . . . . . . . . . . . Producer/Manager
Courtney Winn . . . . . . . . . . . . . . . . . . . . . . . . . Assistant

## GRAMMNET PRODUCTIONS

PHONE . . . . . . . . . . . . . . . . . . . . . . . . . . 213-956-5547
FAX . . . . . . . . . . . . . . . . . . . . . . . . . . . . 213-862-1774

Paramount Pictures
5555 Melrose Ave., Lucy Bung. 206
Los Angeles, CA 90038-3197

| TYPE | Television + Motion Pictures |
|---|---|
| DEAL | Paramount Television Group |
| CREDITS | Fired Up - The Innocent - Kelsey Grammer Salutes Jack Benny |

Kelsey Grammer . . . . . . . . . . . . . . . . Actor/Producer/CEO
Rudy Hornish . . . . . . . . . . . . . . . . . . Exec. Vice President
Cheryl Dolins . . . . . . . . . . . . . . . . . . . . . VP, Development
Xochitl L. Olivas . . . . . . . . . . . . . . . . . Production Manager

## GRANADA ENTERTAINMENT USA

PHONE . . . . . . . . . . . . . . . . . . . . . . . . . . 310-689-4777
FAX . . . . . . . . . . . . . . . . . . . . . . . . . . . . 310-689-4789

11812 San Vicente Blvd., Ste. 503
Los Angeles, CA 90049

| TYPE | Television |
|---|---|
| CREDITS | Cracker |
| COMMENTS | The London Television Centre, Upper Ground, London SE1 9LT |

Scott Siegler . . . . . . . . . . . . . . . . . . . . . . President (US)
Antony Root . . . . . . . . . . . . . . . . Head, Intl. Drama (UK)
Jon Cowan . . . . . . . . . . . . . . . . . . Exec. Producer/Writer
Robert Rovner . . . . . . . . . . . . . . . . Exec. Producer/Writer
Craig McNeil . . . . . . . . . . . . . . . . . . . Sr. VP, Production
Gary Robinson . . . . . . . . . Sr. VP, Business & Legal Affairs
Dan Pasternack . . . . . . . . . . . . . . . VP, Creative Affairs(US)

## GRANADA FILM

PHONE . . . . . . . . . . . . . . . . . . . . . . . . . . 213-692-9940
FAX . . . . . . . . . . . . . . . . . . . . . . . . . . . . 213-692-9944
EMAIL . . . . . . . . . . . . . . Granada_Film_USA@Compuserve.com

5225 Wilshire Blvd., Ste. 603
Los Angeles, CA 90036

| TYPE | Motion Pictures |
|---|---|
| CREDITS | My Left Foot - The Field - August |
| COMMENTS | The London Television Centre, Upper Ground, London SE1 9LT |

Lissa Lebel . . . . . . . . . . . . . . . . . . . . . Coordinator (US)
Janette Day . . . . . . . . . . . . . . . . . . . . . . Producer (UK)
Pippa Cross . . . . . . . . . . . . . . . . . . . . . Head, Film (UK)
Tessa Gibbs . . . . . . . . . . . . . . . . . Head, Development (UK)
Rebecca Hodgson . . . . . . . . . . . . . . . . . Development (UK)

## GRAND DESIGNS ENTERTAINMENT

PHONE . . . . . . . . . . . . . . . . . . . . . . . . . . 310-656-7575
FAX . . . . . . . . . . . . . . . . . . . . . . . . . . . . 310-656-7574

530 Wilshire Blvd., Ste. 304
Santa Monica, CA 90401

| TYPE | Motion Pictures + Television + Animation |
|---|---|
| DEAL | Miramax Films/Dimension Films |
| CREDITS | For The Cause - Allied Forces |

Kia Jam . . . . . . . . . . . . . . . . . . . . . . . . Producer/CEO
David March Douglas . . . . . . . . . . . . . . . . . . . . . Director
Christopher Holt . . . . . . . . . . . . . . . . . . Dir., Photography
Tim Douglas . . . . . . . . . . . . . . . . Visual Effects Supervisor
Robert Henny . . . . . . . . . . . . . . . . . . . . . . . Development

## GRAND PRODUCTIONS, INC.

PHONE . . . . . . . . . . . . . . . . . . . . . . . . . . 310-887-5645
FAX . . . . . . . . . . . . . . . . . . . . . . . . . . . . 310-887-5626
EMAIL . . . . . . . . . . . . . . . . . . . . . . gar0908@aol.com

301 N. Canon Dr., Ste. 321
Beverly Hills, CA 90210

| TYPE | Motion Pictures + Television |
|---|---|
| DEAL | Citadel Entertainment., LLC |
| CREDITS | The Round Table - Adventure, Inc. - Leaving LA - Beauty |

Gary Randall . . . . . . . . . . . . . . . . . . . President/Owner
Wili Baronet . . . . . . . . . . . . . . . . . . . Executive Producer
Mark Israel . . . . . . . . . . . . . . . . . . . . Executive Producer
Michael Akers . . . . . . . . . . . . . . . . . . Mgr., Development

## GRANT PRODUCTIONS, BUD

PHONE . . . . . . . . . . . . . . . . . . . . . . . . . . 213-650-3953
FAX . . . . . . . . . . . . . . . . . . . . . . . . . . . . 213-650-3859

1495 Stone Canyon Rd.
Los Angeles, CA 90077

| TYPE | Television + Motion Pictures |
|---|---|
| CREDITS | Cutters - Sydney - I Love Lucy 1st Show |

Bud Grant . . . . . . . . . . . . . . . . . . . . . . . . . . President

## GRANT, GIL

PHONE . . . . . . . . . . . . . . . . . . . . . . . . . . 310-309-5544

Rysher Entertainment
2401 Colorado, Ste. 200
Santa Monica, CA 90404

| TYPE | Television |
|---|---|
| DEAL | Rysher Entertainment |
| CREDITS | Oldest Rookie - Covington Cross - McKenna - Hull High - The Cape |

Gil Grant . . . . . . . . . . . . . . . . . . . . . . Writer/Producer
Charles Heit . . . . . . . . . . . . . . . . . . . . . Creative Affairs

## GRAY FOX FILMS

PHONE . . . . . . . . . . . . . . . . . . . . . . . . . . 310-888-0090
FAX . . . . . . . . . . . . . . . . . . . . . . . . . . . . 310-858-5858

205 S. Beverly Dr., Ste. 212
Beverly Hills, CA 90212

| TYPE | Motion Pictures + Television |
|---|---|

Stephan Gray . . . . . . . . . . . . . . . . . Chief Executive Officer
Priscilla Pesci . . . . . . . . . . . . . . . . . . . . . . . President
Kelly Ann Ward . . . . . . . . . . . . . . . . . . . VP, Development

# COMPANIES AND STAFF

**GRB ENTERTAINMENT**
PHONE . . . . . . . . . . . . . . . . . . . . . . . . . . . . . 818-753-3400
FAX . . . . . . . . . . . . . . . . . . . . . . . . . . . . . . . 818-753-3401
EMAIL . . . . . . . . . . . . . . . . . . . . . . . . . . info@grbtv.com
WEBSITE . . . . . . . . . . . . . . . . . . . . . http://www.grbtv.com
12001 Ventura Place, Ste. 600
Studio City, CA 91604

TYPE  Television + Documentaries + Syndication
CREDITS Movie Magic - World of Wonder - Hollywood's Greatest
   Stunts - SeaTek - Without Warning - Storm Warning!
COMMENTS Also:  Home Video.
Gary R. Benz . . . . . . . . . . . . . . . . . . . . . . . . . . . . . President
Michael Branton . . . . . . . . . . . . . . . . . Sr. VP, Creative Affairs
Debby Reid Levin . . . . . . . . . . . . . . . . . . . . . . VP, Production

**GREEN COMMUNICATIONS**
PHONE . . . . . . . . . . . . . . . . . . . . . . . . . . . . . 818-557-0050
FAX . . . . . . . . . . . . . . . . . . . . . . . . . . . . . . . 818-557-0056
EMAIL . . . . . . . . . . . . . . . . . . . . . . . . info@greenfilms.com
WEBSITE . . . . . . . . . . . . . . . . . . . . http://www.greenfilms.com
3407 W. Olive Ave.
Burbank, CA 91505

TYPE  Motion Pictures + Television + Animation
CREDITS Ground Control - Living In Peril - Space Marines - The
   Time of Her Time
COMMENTS Also: Mini-Series.
Talaat Captan . . . . . . . . . . . . . . . . . . . . . . . . . . . President
Marion Captan . . . . . . . . . . . . . . . . . . . Exec. Vice President
Vince Ravine . . . . . . . . . . . . . . . . . . . . . . Sr. Vice President
Daryl DequetteVille . . . . . . . . . . . VP, Production & Acquisitions
Ron Schmidt . . . . . . . . . . . . . . . . . . . . . VP, Post Production

**GREEN GRASS BLUE SKY COMPANY, INC.**
PHONE . . . . . . . . . . . . . . . 818-763-4182/011-396-331-4045
EMAIL . . . . . . . . . . . . . . . . . . frankcatalano@msn.com
10700 Ventura Blvd., Ste. D
Studio City, CA 91604

TYPE  Motion Pictures
DEAL  Warner Bros. Pictures
CREDITS Almost Classix- Bed Time Stories- Icarus Mission -
   Adventures of Dynamo Duck- Autumn Sweet
COMMENTS Also: 156 Viale Cortina D'Ampezzo, Rome, Italy
Frank Catalano . . . . . . . . . . . . . . . . . . . . . . . . . President
Anthony Catalano . . . . . . . . . . . Business Affairs/Intl. Co-Productions (LA)
Gregory Snegoff . . . . . . . . . . . . . . . . . Writer/Producer (Rome)
Sandra Carlson . . . . . . . . . . . . . . . . . . Creative Development
Ronald J. Wong . . . . . . . . . . . . . . . . . . Creative Development

**GREEN MANAGEMENT & PRODUCTIONS, JOAN**
PHONE . . . . . . . . . . . . . . . . . . . . . . . . . . . . . 213-878-0484
FAX . . . . . . . . . . . . . . . . . . . . . . . . . . . . . . . 213-878-0492
1836 Courtney Terrace
Los Angeles, CA 90046

TYPE  Motion Pictures + Television
CREDITS Mother, May I Sleep With Danger - Dare To Love
Joan Green . . . . . . . . . . . . . . . . . . . . . . . . . . . President
Jill Crowley . . . . . . . . . . . . . . . . . . . . . . . . . . . Assistant

**GREEN MOON PRODUCTIONS**
PHONE . . . . . . . . . . . . . . . . . . . . . . . . . . . . . 310-450-6111
FAX . . . . . . . . . . . . . . . . . . . . . . . . . . . . . . . 310-450-1333
EMAIL . . . . . . . . . . . . . . . . . . . . . . name@greenmoon.com
3110 Main St., Ste. 205
Santa Monica, CA 90405

TYPE  Motion Pictures + Television + Documentaries +
   Animation
DEAL  Warner Bros. Pictures
Antonio Banderas . . . . . . . . . . . . . . . . . . . Producer/Actor
Melanie Griffith . . . . . . . . . . . . . . . . . . . . Producer/Actor
Diane Sillan . . . . . . . . . . . . . . . . . . . . . . . . . . President
Nadine Taloni . . . . . . . . . . . . . . . . . . . . Dir., Development
Sam Gaglani . . . . . . . . . . . . . . . . . . . . . Creative Executive
Leda Cianfarini . . . . . . . . . . . . . . . . . Development Assistant

**GREEN/EPSTEIN PRODS.**
PHONE . . . . . . . . . . . . . . . . . . . . . . . . . . . . . 818-753-9080
FAX . . . . . . . . . . . . . . . . . . . . . . . . . . . . . . . 818-753-9481
EMAIL . . . . . . . . . . . . . . . . . . . . . . grenepstn@aol.com
12103 Maxwellton Rd.
Studio City, CA 91604

TYPE  Motion Pictures + Television
CREDITS Stephen King's It - And the Sea Will Tell - Doublecrossed
Jim Green . . . . . . . . . . . . . . . . . . . . . . . . Executive Producer
Allen Epstein . . . . . . . . . . . . . . . . . . . . . . Executive Producer
Mark Bacino . . . . . . . . . . . . . . . . . . . . . . . . . . . Producer
Val McLeroy . . . . . . . . . . . . . . . . . VP, Development/Producer
Vivienne Kaplin . . . . . . . . . . . . . . . . . Production Coorinator
Jack S. Kimball . . . . . . . . . . . . . . . . . . Executive Assistant

***GREENBLATT JANOLLARI STUDIO, THE**
PHONE . . . . . . . . . . . . . . . . . . . . . . . . . . . . . 310-369-2026
FAX . . . . . . . . . . . . . . . . . . . . . . . . . . . . . . . 310-369-0368
2121 Avenue of the Stars, #1200
Los Angeles, CA 90067

TYPE  Motion Pictures + Television
DEAL  Fox Television Studios
Robert Greenblatt . . . . . . . . . . . . . . . . . . . . . . . President
David Janollari . . . . . . . . . . . . . . . President (310-369-0367)
Theresa Edy . . . . . . . . . . . Exec. VP/Creative Affairs (310-369-4694)
Holly Powell . . . . . . . . . . . . Head, Talent & Casting (310-369-7743)
Jim Sharp . . . . . . . . . . . . . . . . . . . . . . . Head, Production

**GREENE PRODS., VANESSA**
PHONE . . . . . . . . . . . . . . . . . . . . . . . . . . . . . 213-852-4425
7800 Beverly Blvd.
Los Angeles, CA 90036

TYPE  Television
DEAL  CBS Entertainment
CREDITS Under The Influence - Nothing Lasts Forever - Stolen
   Women
Vanessa Greene . . . . . . . . . . . . . . . . . . . . . . . . Producer

**GREENHOUSE FILM GROUP LTD., THE**
PHONE . . . . . . . . . . . . . . . 310-652-1777/212-288-9200
FAX . . . . . . . . . . . . . . . . . . . . . . . . . . . . . . . 310-385-7106
662A N. Robertson Blvd.
Los Angeles, CA 90069

TYPE  Motion Pictures + Television + Documentaries
CREDITS Choices - Monster Mash, The Movie - Frankenstein Sings -
   The Loft
COMMENTS ALSO: 32 East 64th St. New York, NY  10021
Michael Kates . . . . . . . . . . . . . . . . . . . . . . . . . . Producer
Nathaniel Kramer . . . . . . . . . . . . . . . . . . . . . . . . Producer
Holden Kaufman . . . . . . . . . . . . . . . . . . Dir., Development

**GREENWALD PRODS., ROBERT**
PHONE . . . . . . . . . . . . . . . . . . . . . . . . . . . . . 310-204-0404
FAX . . . . . . . . . . . . . . . . . . . . . . . . . . . . . . . 310-204-0174
WEBSITE . . . . . . . . . . . . . . . . . . . . http://rgprod@aol.com
10510 Culver Blvd.
Culver City, CA 90232-3400

TYPE  Motion Pictures + Television
CREDITS Woman of Independent Means - Breaking Up - The Day
   Lincoln Was Shot
Robert Greenwald . . . . . . . . . . . . . . . . . . . . . . . President
Philip Kleinbart . . . . . . . . . . . . . . . . . Exec. Vice President
Kimberly Rubin . . . . . . . . . . . . . . . . . . Executive Producer
Elizabeth Selzer . . . . . . . . . . . . . . . VP, Feature Development
Bradley Gordon . . . . . . . . . . . . . . . . . Production Executive
Elizabeth Missan Yost . . . . . . . . . . . . . Mgr., TV Development

**GREENWICH ENTERTAINMENT**
PHONE . . . . . . . . . . . . . . . . . . . . . . . . . . . . . 310-285-5342
FAX . . . . . . . . . . . . . . . . . . . . . . . . . . . . . . . 310-285-5358
468 N. Camden Dr.
Beverly Hills, CA 90210

TYPE  Motion Pictures + Television
CREDITS Graveyard Shift - Family Prayers - Dark Horse
Rosalyn Bazar . . . . . . . . . . . . . . . . . . . . . . . . . . Partner
Bonnie Sugar . . . . . . . . . . . . . . . . . . . . . . . . . . Partner

# COMPANIES AND STAFF

**GREENWOOD AVENUE ENTERTAINMENT**
PHONE . . . . . . . . . . . . . . . . . . . . . . . . . . . . . . . . . . 310-454-9984
FAX . . . . . . . . . . . . . . . . . . . . . . . . . . . . . . . . . . . . . 310-454-9984
2004 Palisades Drive
Pacific Palisades, CA 90272
TYPE            Television + Syndication
CREDITS         Baywatch - Baywatch Nights - Thunder In Paradise
David W. Hagar . . . . . . . . . . . . . . . . . . . . . . . Exec. Producer/Director
Cathy Dwyer . . . . . . . . . . . . . . . . . . . . . . . . . . . Executive Producer

**GREGORY PRODUCTIONS, INC.**
PHONE . . . . . . . . . . . . . . . . . . . . . . . . . . . . . . . . . . 601-781-3885
FAX . . . . . . . . . . . . . . . . . . . . . . . . . . . . . . . . . . . . . 601-781-3340
864 Goodman Road, East
Southaven, MS 38671
TYPE            Motion Pictures
CREDITS         The Spitfire Grill
Roger Courts . . . . . . . . . . . . . . . . . . . . . . . . Chief Executive Officer
Mark Ratay. . . . . . . . . . . . . . . . . . . . . . . . Creative Affairs Executive

***GREIF COMPANY**
PHONE . . . . . . . . . . . . . . . . . . . . . . . . . . . . . . . . . . 310-385-1200
FAX . . . . . . . . . . . . . . . . . . . . . . . . . . . . . . . . . . . . . 310-385-1207
EMAIL . . . . . . . . . . . . . . . . . . . . . greifcompany@earthlink.net
9233 W. Pico Blvd., Ste. 218
Los Angeles, CA 90035
TYPE            Motion Pictures + Television + Documentaries
CREDITS         Walker: Texas Ranger - Keys to Tulsa - Intimate Portraits
Leslie Greif . . . . . . . . . . . . . . . . . . . President/Producer/Director/Writer
Kenny Golde . . . . . . . . . . . . . . . . . . . . . . . . . . . . . . VP/Producer
Tom Owen . . . . . . . . . . . . . . . . . . . . . . . . . . Creative Associate

**GREYSTONE COMMUNICATIONS GROUP, INC.**
PHONE . . . . . . . . . . . . . . . . . . . . . . . . . . . . . . . . . . 818-762-2900
FAX . . . . . . . . . . . . . . . . . . . . . . . . . . . . . . . . . . . . . 818-762-1626
EMAIL . . . . . . . . . . . . . . . . . . . . . . . . info@greystoneonline.com
WEBSITE. . . . . . . . . . . . . . . . . . . http://http://www.greystoneonline.com
4705 Laurel Canyon Blvd., 5th Fl.
Valley Village, CA 91607
TYPE            Television + Documentaries
CREDITS         Civil War Journal - Prophecies - A&E Biography - TNN
                Life and Times of... - Ancient Mysteries
COMMENTS  Also: Greystone Films, Fax 818-762-8418, Ste. 201
Craig Haffner . . . . . . . . . . . . . . . . . . President/Exec. Producer/Writer
Donna E. Lusitana . . . . . . . . . . . . Exec. VP, Production/Producer/Director
Shinaan Krakowsky . . . . . . . . . . . . . . . . . . . . . . . . General Counsel
Rick Brookwell . . . . . . . . . VP, Corporate Counsel/New Business Development

**GREYSTONE FILMS**
PHONE . . . . . . . . . . . . . . . . . . . . . . . . . . . . . . . . . . 818-762-2900
FAX . . . . . . . . . . . . . . . . . . . . . . . . . . . . . . . . . . . . . 818-762-8418
EMAIL . . . . . . . . . . . . . . . . . . . . . cadiz@greystoneonline.com
WEBSITE. . . . . . . . . . . . . . . . . . . http://http://www.greystoneonline.com
4705 Laurel Canyon Blvd., Ste. 201
Valley Village, CA 91607
TYPE            Motion Pictures + Television + Feature Direct to Video +
                Documentaries
CREDITS         Lunker Lake - Left Luggage
Craig Haffner . . . . . . . . . . . . . . . . . . . . . . . . . . . . . . . President
Brad Wilson . . . . . . . . . . . . . . . . . . . . . . . . VP, Film Production
Sandra Cadiz . . . . . . . . . . . . . . Exec. Asst. to Mr. Haffner & Mr. Wilson
Caryn Silver . . . . . . . . . . . . . . . . . . . . . . . . . . . Creative Affairs

**GRINNING DOG PICTURES**
PHONE . . . . . . . . . . . . . . . . . . . . . . . . . . . . . . . . . . 610-259-5650
FAX . . . . . . . . . . . . . . . . . . . . . . . . . . . . . . . . . . . . . 610-259-5653
EMAIL . . . . . . . . . . . . . . . . . . . . . . . . grinnindog@aol.com
525 Mildred Ave., Studio C
Primos, PA 19018
TYPE            Television + Documentaries
CREDITS         Science Frontiers - Jessica Savitch Bio - Wolfman's Myth
                & Science
Connie Bottinelli . . . . . . . . . . . . . . . . . . . . . . Executive Producer
Warren Weidner . . . . . . . . . . . . . . . . . . . . . . . . . Executive Producer

***GROSS MANAGEMENT, KEN**
PHONE . . . . . . . . . . . . . . . . . . . . . . . . . . . . . . . . . . 310-552-8480
FAX . . . . . . . . . . . . . . . . . . . . . . . . . . . . . . . . . . . . . 310-229-9282
10345 W. Olympic Blvd., Penthouse
Los Angeles, CA 90064
TYPE            Motion Pictures + Television
CREDITS         Dead by Midnight
COMMENTS  Also: A Management Company.
Kenneth H. Gross . . . . . . . . . . . . . . . . President/Producer/Manager
Stephanie Gaines . . . . . . . . . . . . . . . . . . . . . Development Associate

**GROSS POINTS ENTERTAINMENT**
PHONE . . . . . . . . . . . . . . . . . . . . . . . . . . . . . . . . . . 310-289-4766
FAX . . . . . . . . . . . . . . . . . . . . . . . . . . . . . . . . . . . . . 310-312-0870
1511 Sawtelle Blvd., Ste. 343
Los Angeles, CA 90025
TYPE            Motion Pictures + Television
CREDITS         Matthew Modine's 12 Angry Men - Profiles of
                Extraordinary Friendships
Renee Dupont . . . . . . . . . . . . . . . . . . . . . . . . . . . . . . Producer
Michelle Dupont . . . . . . . . . . . . . . . . . . . . . . . . Writer/Director
Sarah Bingham . . . . . . . . . . . . . . . . . . . . . . . . . . . . . . Writer
Iris Dawn Alonzo . . . . . . . . . . . . . . . . . . . . Assoc. to Ms. Dupont

**GROSS-WESTON PRODS.**
PHONE . . . . . . . . . . . . . . . . . . . . . . . . . . . 213-466-2266 x18
FAX . . . . . . . . . . . . . . . . . . . . . . . . . . . . . . . . . . . . . 213-465-7835
6922 Hollywood Blvd., Ste. 922
Hollywood, CA 90028
TYPE            Motion Pictures + Television
CREDITS         Country Gold - A Place for Annie - Billionaire Boys Club
Marcy Gross . . . . . . . . . . . . . . . . . . . . . . . . . . Executive Producer
Ann Weston . . . . . . . . . . . . . . . . . . . . . . . . . . . Executive Producer
Lisa Donovan . . . . . . . . . . . . . . . . . . . . . . Dir., Development

**GROSSBARD PRODUCTIONS, BETH**
PHONE . . . . . . . . . . . . . . . . . . . . . . . . . . . . . . . . . . 818-758-2500
FAX . . . . . . . . . . . . . . . . . . . . . . . . . . . . . . . . . . . . . 818-705-7366
5168 Otis Ave.
Tarzana, CA 91356
TYPE            Motion Pictures + Television
CREDITS         No One Could Protect Her
Beth Grossbard . . . . . . . . . . . . . . . . . . . . . . . . . . . . . Producer
Michelle Habash . . . . . . . . . . . . . . . . . . . Development Assistant

**GROSSBART, BARNETT PRODUCTIONS**
PHONE . . . . . . . . . . . . . . . . . . . . . . . . . . . . . . . . . . 310-275-5800
FAX . . . . . . . . . . . . . . . . . . . . . . . . . . . . . . . . . . . . . 310-275-5818
9255 Sunset Blvd., Ste. 1010
Los Angeles, CA 90069
TYPE            Television + Motion Pictures + Syndication
CREDITS         A Father for Brittany - The Alison Gertz Story -
                Unforgivable - Any Mother's Son
Joan Barnett . . . . . . . . . . . . . . . . . . . . Co-President/Exec. Producer
Jack Grossbart . . . . . . . . . . . . . . . . . . . . Co-President/Exec. Producer
Linda L. Kent . . . . . . . . . . . . . . . . . . . . Sr. VP, Development
Daniel Blatt . . . . . . . . . . . . . . . . . . . . . . . . Executive Assistant
Cheryl Cedrone . . . . . . . . . . . . . . . . . . . . . . Executive Assistant
Jason Friedlander . . . . . . . . . . . . . . . . . . . . . Production Assistant

**GROSSO-JACOBSON PRODUCTIONS, INC.**
PHONE . . . . . . . . . . . . . . . . . . . . . . . . . . . . . . . . . . 212-644-6909
FAX . . . . . . . . . . . . . . . . . . . . . . . . . . . . . . . . . . . . . 212-355-3178
767 Third Ave., 27th Fl.
New York, NY 10017
TYPE            Motion Pictures + Television
CREDITS         While My Pretty One Sleeps - Let Me Call You Sweetheart
                - Moonlight Becomes You
Sonny Grosso . . . . . . . . . . . . . . . . . . . . . . . . Executive Producer
Lawrence S. Jacobson . . . . . . . . . . . . . . . . . . . . . Executive Producer
Keith Johnson . . . . . . . . . . . . . . . . . . . . . . VP, Development
Christina Avis Krauss . . . . . . . . . . . . . . . . . Development Coordinator

# COMPANIES AND STAFF

**GRUB STREET PRODS.**
PHONE . . . . . . . . . . . . . . . . . . . . . . . . . . . . . 213-956-4657
Paramount TV
5555 Melrose Ave., Wilder #101
Los Angeles, CA 90038-3197

| | |
|---|---|
| TYPE | Television + Syndication |
| DEAL | Paramount Television Group |
| CREDITS | Wings - Frasier - Pursuit of Happiness - Encore! Encore! |
| COMMENTS | Also: Development. |

David Angell . . . . . . . . . . . . . . . . . . . . . . . Creator/Exec. Producer
Peter Casey . . . . . . . . . . . . . . . . . . . . . . . Creator/Exec. Producer
David Lee . . . . . . . . . . . . . . . . . . . . . . . . Creator/Exec. Producer
Christopher Lloyd . . . . . . . . . . . . . . . . . Exec. Producer (Frasier)
Maggie Randell . . . . . . . . . . . . . . . . . . . . . . . Producer (Frasier)
Mary Fukuto . . . . . . . . . . . . . . . . . . . Producer (Encore! Encore!)

**GUERRERO & COMPANY, DAN**
PHONE . . . . . . . . . . . . . . . . . . . . . . . . . . 213-960-5370
FAX . . . . . . . . . . . . . . . . . . . . . . . . . . . . 213-960-5385
Hollywood Center Studios
5842 Sunset Blvd., Bldg. 11
Hollywood, CA 90028

| | |
|---|---|
| TYPE | Television + Motion Pictures |
| CREDITS | Loco Slam (HBO) - NBC Vida Awards - Concert of the Americas (PBS) |
| COMMENTS | Also: Los Angeles International Latino Film Festival |

Dan Guerrero . . . . . . . . . . . . . . . . . . . . . . . . . . . . . . . Producer

**GULLANE PICTURES**
PHONE . . . . . . . . . . . . . . . . . 310-451-5111/212-463-9623
FAX . . . . . . . . . . . . . . . . . . . 310-451-5321/212-463-9626
1351 Third Street Promenade, Ste 200
Santa Monica, CA 90401

| | |
|---|---|
| TYPE | Motion Pictures + Television + Syndication + Animation |
| CREDITS | Shining Time Station - Adventures of Mumfie - Shadow Zone: Teacher Ate My Homework - Universal Soldier II & III |
| COMMENTS | Also: 1133 Broadway, Ste. 1520, NY, NY 10011 |

Britt Allcroft . . . . . . . . . . . . . . . . . . . . . . . . . . . Co-Chairperson
Charles Falzon . . . . . . . . . . . . . . . . . . . . . . . . . . Co-Chairperson
Jeanne Perry . . . . . . . . . . . . . . . . . . VP, Business Affairs (NY)
Deborah Strichartz . . . . . . . . . . VP, Original Programming (LA)
Jesse Stovin . . . . . . . . . . . . . . . . . . . . . . . . Dir., Development (LA)
Shelley Harkin . . . . . . . . . . . . . . . . . . Production Coordinator (NY)
Lisa M. Consales . . . . . . . . . . . . . . . . . . . Executive Assistant (LA)

**GUNNING CO., THE**
PHONE . . . . . . . . . . . . . . . . . . . . . . . . . . . 310-271-7825
9005 Cynthia St., Ste. 219
West Hollywood, CA 90069

| | |
|---|---|
| TYPE | Television |
| CREDITS | My Boyfriend's Back - Crossing The Mob - Tricks |
| COMMENTS | Please do not send any unsolicited material. |

Barbara Gunning . . . . . . . . . . . . . . . . . . . . . President/Producer

**H. BEALE COMPANY**
PHONE . . . . . . . . . . . . . . . . . . . . . . . . . . . 310-235-1198
FAX . . . . . . . . . . . . . . . . . . . . . . . . . . . . 310-235-1073
11755 Wilshire Blvd., Ste. 2200
Los Angeles, CA 90025

| | |
|---|---|
| TYPE | Motion Pictures + Television + Interactive Multimedia + Syndication |
| COMMENTS | Relocating at Press Time. |

Lilly Tartikoff . . . . . . . . . . . . . . . . . . . . . . . . . . . . . . President
Kim Fleary . . . . . . . . . . . . . . . . . . . . Head, Television Development

**H.R.D. PRODS.**
PHONE . . . . . . . . . . . . . . . . . . . . . . . . . . . 213-850-3595
FAX . . . . . . . . . . . . . . . . . . . . . . . . . . . . 213-850-3596
Warner Hollywood Studios
1041 N. Formosa Ave.
West Hollywood, CA 90046

| | |
|---|---|
| TYPE | Motion Pictures |
| CREDITS | Pretty in Pink - Article 99 - Grumpier Old Men - Odd Couple II |

Howard Deutch . . . . . . . . . . . . . . . . . . . . . . . . . . . . . . Director
Carrie Shackelford . . . . . . . . . . . . . . . . . . . . . . . . . . . Assistant

**H2 PRODUCTIONS**
PHONE . . . . . . . . . . . . . . . . . . . . . . . . . . . 310-839-7927
FAX . . . . . . . . . . . . . . . . . . . . . . . . . . . . 310-394-6510
212 San Vicente Blvd., Ste. H
Santa Monica, CA 90402

| | |
|---|---|
| TYPE | Motion Pictures + Television |
| CREDITS | Peacock Blues - The Subsititute - Tell About The South - The Substitute 2 |

Steven Bakalar . . . . . . . . . . . . . . . . . . . . . . . . . Producer/Writer
Devorah Cutler-Rubenstein . . . . . . . . . . . Producer/Writer/Director
Ariel Reiss . . . . . . . . . . . . . . . . . . . . . . . . . . . Dir., Development
T.C. Gunter . . . . . . . . . . . . . . . . . . . . . . . . . . . . Story Associate
Kamafi Adio-Byrd . . . . . . . . . . . . . . . . . . . . . Research Associate

**HAFT ENTERTAINMENT**
PHONE . . . . . . . . . . . . . . 212-586-3881/818-777-5925
FAX . . . . . . . . . . . . . . . 212-459-9798/818-866-3414
130 W. 57th St., Ste. 5-E
New York, NY 10019

| | |
|---|---|
| TYPE | Motion Pictures + Television + Documentaries |
| DEAL | Universal Pictures |
| CREDITS | Hocus Pocus - Dead Poets Society - The Last Dance - Emma |
| COMMENTS | Also: 100 Universal City Plaza, Bldg. 507, Ste. 2D Universal City, CA 91608 |

Steven Haft . . . . . . . . . . . . . . . . . . . . . . . . . . . . . . . . Producer
Judi Farkas . . . . . . . . . . . . . . . . . Exec. VP/Head of Production
Amanda Schreiber . . . . . . . . . . . . Dir., Development (East Coast)
Jason Hallock . . . . . . . . . . . . . . . . . . Story Editor (West Coast)

**HAINES COMPANY, RANDA**
PHONE . . . . . . . . . . . . . . . . . . . . . . . . . . . 310-889-1843
FAX . . . . . . . . . . . . . . . . . . . . . . . . . . . . 310-889-1873
11693 San Vicente Blvd., Ste. 389
Los Angeles, CA 90049

| | |
|---|---|
| TYPE | Motion Pictures |
| CREDITS | Children of a Lesser God- The Doctor - Wrestling Ernest Hemingway - A Family Thing - Dance with Me |

Randa Haines . . . . . . . . . . . . . . . . . . . . . . . Director/Producer
Margaret Gracla . . . . . . . . . . . . . . . . . . . . . . . VP, Production
Michelle Romaine . . . . . . . . . . . . . . . . . . . . Creative Associate

**HALE PRODUCTIONS, CORKY**
PHONE . . . . . . . . . . . . . . . . . . . . . . . . . . . 310-274-6587
FAX . . . . . . . . . . . . . . . . . . . . . . . . . . . . 310-274-4878
9100 Oriole Way
Los Angeles, CA 90069

| | |
|---|---|
| TYPE | Television + Documentaries + Motion Pictures |
| CREDITS | Lullaby of Broadway - Twist of Fate - Give 'Em Hell, Harry |
| COMMENTS | Also: Stage. |

Corky Hale . . . . . . . . . . . . . . . . . . . . . . . . . . . . . . . President
Barbara Marcus . . . . . . . . . . . . . . . . . . . . . . Executive Assistant

**HALLET STREET PRODS.**
PHONE . . . . . . . . . . . . . . . . . . . . . . . . . . . 213-874-3000
FAX . . . . . . . . . . . . . . . . . . . . . . . . . . . . 310-275-7223
EMAIL . . . . . . . . . . . . . . . . . . . . . . . andrews@loop.com
519 N. Arden Dr.
Beverly Hills, CA 90210-3507

| | |
|---|---|
| TYPE | Motion Pictures + Television + Syndication + Feature Direct to Video + Documentaries |
| CREDITS | The Ginger Tree - A Woman Called Golda - Do You Remember Love? |

Marilyn Hall . . . . . . . . . . . . . . . . . . . . . . . . . . . . . . . President
Carol Andrews . . . . . . . . . . . . . . . . . . . . . . Executive Assistant

**HALLMARK ENTERTAINMENT (LA)**
PHONE . . . . . . . . . . . . . . . . . . . . . . . . . . . 213-634-8972
FAX . . . . . . . . . . . . . . . . . . . . . . . . . . . . 213-549-0197
EMAIL . . . . . . . . . . . . . . . . . . . . . . . tvmovies@aol.com
6100 Wilshire Blvd., Ste. 1400
Los Angeles, CA 90048

| | |
|---|---|
| TYPE | Television |
| CREDITS | The Odyssey - In Cold Blood - Gulliver's Travels - Moby Dick |

Pamela Murphy . . . . . . . . . . . . . . . . . . . . . . . VP, Development
S. Nicole Brown . . . . . . . . . . . . . . . . . . . . . . . . . . . . Assistant

# COMPANIES AND STAFF

## HALLMARK ENTERTAINMENT (NY)

PHONE . . . . . . . . . . . . . . . . . . . . . . . . . . . . . . . . . . . 212-977-9001
FAX . . . . . . . . . . . . . . . . . . . . . . . . . . . . . . . . . . . . . 212-977-7407
1325 Ave. of the Americas, 21st Floor
New York, NY 10019

TYPE — Television + Feature Direct to Video + Animation
CREDITS — Scarlett - Gypsy - Lonesome Dove - Gulliver's Travels - The Odyssey - Moby Dick - Merlin - Mrs. Santa Claus - In Cold Blood
COMMENTS — ALSO: 6100 Wilshire Blvd., Ste. 1400, LA, CA 90048

Robert Halmi Sr. . . . . . . . . . . . . . . . . . . . . . . . . . . . . . Chairman
Robert Halmi Jr. . . . . . . . . . . . . . . . . . . . . . . . . . . President/CEO
Peter von Gal . . . . . . . . . . . . . . . . . . . . . . . . . . . Exec. VP/COO
Dan Martin . . . . . . . . . . . . . . . . . . . . . . . . . Exec. VP, Production
Timothy Clyne . . . . . . . . . . . . . . . . . . . . . . . . . Sr. VP, Finance
Tony Guido . . . . . . . . . . . . . . . . . Sr. VP, Legal & Business Affairs
Janet Jacobson . . . . . . . . . . . . Sr. VP, Co-Production Programming
Lynn Holst . . . . . . . . . . . . . . . . . . . . . . . . . . . VP, Development
Mike Isaacson . . . . . . . . . . . . . . . . . . . . . . . . . . . VP, Finance
Margret Louis . . . . . . . . . . . . . . . . . . VP, Legal & Business Affairs
Mary-Liz McDonald . . . . . . . . . . . . . . . . . . . . . . VP, Development
Alan Lewis . . . . . . . . . . . . . . . . . . Sr. Dir., Legal & Business Affairs
Dawne Mann . . . . . . . . . . . Dir., Legal & Business Affairs Admin.
Whitney Vliet . . . . . . . . . . . . . . . . . . . Dir., Business Development

## HALLMARK HALL OF FAME PRODUCTIONS, INC.

PHONE . . . . . . . . . . . . . . . . . . . . . . . . . . . . . . . . . . . 818-505-9191
FAX . . . . . . . . . . . . . . . . . . . . . . . . . . . . . . . . . . . . . 818-505-9842
11969 Ventura Blvd., Ste. 102
Studio City, CA 91604

TYPE — Television
CREDITS — What the Deaf Man Heard - Ellen Foster - Old Man

Brad R. Moore . . . . . . . . . . . . . . . . . . . . . . . . . . . . . President
Jan Parkinson . . . . . . . . . . . . . . . . . . . . . . . . . . Vice President
Richard E. Welsh . . . . . . . . . . . . . . . . . . . . . Executive Producer
Brent Shields . . . . . . . . . . . . . . . . . . . . . . . . . . . . . Producer
Paul Muterspaugh . . . . . . . . . . . Asst. to Richard E. Welsh & Brent Shields
Myra Morris . . . . . . . . . . . . . . . . . . . . . . . . . . Dir., Development

## HAMILTON ENTERTAINMENT, INC., DEAN

PHONE . . . . . . . . . . . . . . . . . . . . . . . . . . . . . . . . . . . 310-459-4816
FAX . . . . . . . . . . . . . . . . . . . . . . . . . . . . . . . . . . . . . 310-459-1186
EMAIL . . . . . . . . . . . . . . . . . . . . . . . . . . HEGI@earthlink.net
WEBSITE . . . . . . . . . . . . . . . . . . . . . . http://supermodelsInc.com
7351 Sunset Blvd., Ste. 102
Pacific Palisades, CA 90272

TYPE — Motion Pictures + Documentaries + Interactive Multimedia + Television
CREDITS — The Road Home - Supermodels in the Rainforest - Savage Land - The Dream Team

Dean Hamilton . . . . . . . . . . . . . . . . . Producer/Director/President
Jim Townsend . . . . . . . . . . . . . . . Sr. VP, Production & Development
Ronnie Hadar . . . . . . . . . . . . . . . . . . . . . . . . . . . . . Producer
Donald Borza II . . . . . . . . . . . . . . . VP, Production & Development
Vikki Boyer . . . . . . . . . . . . . . . . . . . . . . Development Associate

## HAMPTON FILMS, INC.

PHONE . . . . . . . . . . . . . . . . . . . . . . . . . . . . . . . . . . . 617-536-8177
FAX . . . . . . . . . . . . . . . . . . . . . . . . . . . . . . . . . . . . . 617-536-1732
486 Shawmut Ave.
Boston, MA 02118

TYPE — Motion Pictures + Television + Documentaries
CREDITS — Eyes On The Prize I & II - The Great Depression - War On Poverty

Henry Hampton . . . . . . . . . . . . . . . . . . . . . . . . . . . . Chairman
W. Michael Greene . . . . . . . . . . . . . . . . . . . . . . . . . . President

## HAMPTONS FILM COMPANY, THE

PHONE . . . . . . . . . . . . . . . . . . . . . . . . . . . . . . . . . . . 213-663-2565
FAX . . . . . . . . . . . . . . . . . . . . . . . . . . . . . . . . . . . . . 213-669-0510
4455 Los Feliz Blvd.
Los Angeles, CA 90027

TYPE — Motion Pictures + Television
CREDITS — Up Above The World So High - Mariette In Ecstasy
Alba Francesca . . . . . . . . . . . . . . . . . . . . . Producer/Writer/Director

## HANDPRINT ENTERTAINMENT

PHONE . . . . . . . . . . . . . . . . . . . . . . . . . . . . . . . . . . . 213-655-2400
FAX . . . . . . . . . . . . . . . . . . . . . . . . . . . . . . . . . . . . . 213-655-8555
8436 W. 3rd St., Ste. 650
Los Angeles, CA 90048-4186

TYPE — Motion Pictures + Television + Documentaries
DEAL — Miramax Films
CREDITS — Fresh Prince of Bel Air - Above The Rim - Booty Call

Benny Medina . . . . . . . . . . . . . . . . . . . . . . . . . . . . . Partner
Jeff Pollack . . . . . . . . . . . . . . . . . . . . . . . . . . . . . . . Partner
David Guillod . . . . . . . . . . . . . . . . . . . . . . . . . . . . . . Partner

## HANSEN, EDWARD D.

PHONE . . . . . . . . . . . . . . . . . . . . . . . . . . . . . . . . . . . 626-447-3168
FAX . . . . . . . . . . . . . . . . . . . . . . . . . . . . . . . . . . . . . 626-447-3168
437 Harvard Dr.
Arcadia, CA 91007-2639

TYPE — Motion Pictures + Television + Documentaries + Feature Direct to Video
CREDITS — Bikini Carwash - Disney's Rocky & Bullwinkle - Young Elvis

Ed Hansen . . . . . . . . . . . . . . . . . . . President/Writer/Director
Buck Flower . . . . . . . . . . . . . . . . . . . . . . Sr. VP, Development
Rose Mary Morelli . . . . . . . . . . . . . . . . . . VP, Intl./Production
Steve Essig . . . . . . . . . . . . . . . . . . . . . . Production Executive
Carl Irwin . . . . . . . . . . . . . . . . . . . . . . . . Managing Producer

## HARBOR LIGHTS PRODUCTIONS

PHONE . . . . . . . . . . . . . . . . . . . . . . . . . . . . . . . . . . . 818-222-2875
FAX . . . . . . . . . . . . . . . . . . . . . . . . . . . . . . . . . . . . . 818-222-2947
EMAIL . . . . . . . . . . . . . . . . . . . . . . movierock@aol.com
4400 Coldwater Canyon, #215
Studio City, CA 91423

TYPE — Motion Pictures + Television + Syndication
CREDITS — White Squall - Titanic (CBS Mini-series) - Nervous Ticks - Race For Glory

Rocky Lang . . . . . . . . . . . . . . . . . . . . Writer/Producer/Director

## HARDING, DAVE

PHONE . . . . . . . . . . . . . . . . . . . . . . . . . . . . . . . . . . . 818-905-0046
4011 Hopevale Dr.
Sherman Oaks, CA 91403

TYPE — Television + Motion Pictures + Syndication
CREDITS — Most Dangerous - Cyberlife - Murderous Intent - Doomsday - Yes, Virginia - Rescue of Flight 232 - Busted on Job - Red-Handed - Secrets Revealed

Dave Harding . . . . . . . . . . . . . . . . . . . . . . . . . . . . . Producer

## HARGROVE PRODS., DEAN

PHONE . . . . . . . . . . . . . . . . . . . . . . . . . . . . . . . . . . . 310-838-6841
FAX . . . . . . . . . . . . . . . . . . . . . . . . . . . . . . . . . . . . . 310-838-4167
10202 W. Washington Blvd.
Culver City, CA 90232

TYPE — Television
DEAL — Columbia TriStar Television
CREDITS — Matlock - Perry Mason Movies - Diagnosis Murder

Dean Hargrove . . . . . . . . . . . . . . . . . . . . . . Executive Producer
Doris Stockstill . . . . . . . . . . . . . . . . . Exec. Asst. to Mr. Hargrove

## HARMONY GOLD

PHONE . . . . . . . . . . . . . . . . . . . . . . . . . . . . . . . . . . . 213-851-4900
FAX . . . . . . . . . . . . . . . . . . . . . . . . . . . . . . . . . . . . . 213-851-5599
7655 Sunset Blvd.
Los Angeles, CA 90046

TYPE — Television
CREDITS — Shaka Zulu - Around the World in 80 Days - Lost World - Heidi
COMMENTS — Also: Live Action & Episodic Animation. Screening Room, 250 seat theater.

Frank Agrama . . . . . . . . . . . . . . . . . . . . . . . . Chairman/CEO
Joanne Hoffman . . . . . . . . . . . . . . . . VP, Business & Legal Affairs

## HARMONY PICTURES

PHONE . . . . . . . . . . . . . . . . . . . . . . . . . . . . . . . . . . . 213-960-1400
FAX . . . . . . . . . . . . . . . . . . . . . . . . . . . . . . . . . . . . . 213-960-1415
WEBSITE . . . . . . . . . . . . . . . . . . http://www.HarmonyPictures.com
6806 Lexington Ave.
Hollywood, CA 90038

TYPE — Motion Pictures + Television
CREDITS — Flatliners - Made in America - Radio Flyer

Jan Wieringa . . . . . . . . . . . . . . . . . . . . . . . . . . . . . President
Tony Frere . . . . . . . . . . . . . . . . . . . . Executive Producer (NY)
Kay Millet . . . . . . . . . . . . . . . . . . . . . . . . Executive Producer

# COMPANIES AND STAFF

**HARPO FILMS INC.**
PHONE . . . . . . . . . . . . . . . . . . . . . . . . . . . 310-278-5559
345 N. Maple Dr., Ste. 315
Beverly Hills, CA 90210

TYPE          Motion Pictures + Television
DEAL          ABC Entertainment/Walt Disney Company, The
CREDITS       There Are No Children Here - The Wedding - Before
              Women Had Wings - Beloved
COMMENTS  ALSO: 110 N. Carpenter, Chicago, IL 60607
Oprah Winfrey . . . . . . . . . . . . . . . . . . . . . . . . . Chairman/CEO
Jeffrey Jacobs . . . . . . . . . . . . . . . . . . . . . . . . . . . President
Kate Forte . . . . . . . . . . . . Exec. VP, Development & Production (LA)
Susan Heyer . . . . . . . . . . . . . . . Dir., Development, Television (LA)
Valerie Scoon . . . . . . . . . . . . . . . . Dir., Development, Features (LA)
Tim Tortora . . . . . . . . . . . . . . . . . . . . . Dir., Production (LA)
Mark Maynard . . . . . . . . . . . . . . . . . . Development Assistant (LA)
Stephanie Harris . . . . . . . . . . . . Exec. Assistant/Office Mgr. (LA)

**HARRIS & COMPANY**
PHONE . . . . . . . . . . . . . . . . . . . . . . . . . . . 818-777-3717
FAX . . . . . . . . . . . . . . . . . . . . . . . . . . . . . 818-866-0290
EMAIL . . . . . . . . . . . . . . . . . . . . . . . . . . jim@korris.com
100 Universal City Plaza, Bldg. 507-3C
Universal City, CA 91608

TYPE          Motion Pictures + Television
DEAL          Universal Television & Networks Group
CREDITS       Indian in the Cupboard - Twilight Man - Atlantis - Dad's
              Week Off- Not In This Town
COMMENTS  Email for Robert Harris rharris@mca.com
Robert Harris . . . . . . . . . . . . . . . . . . . . . . . . . . President
Jim Korris . . . . . . . . . . . . . . . . . . . . . . . Exec. Vice President
Heather Wordham . . . . . . . . . . . . . . . . . . . . . . Story Editor
Shirley Morningstar . . . . . . . . . . . . . . . . . . Asst. to R. Harris

**HART ENTERTAINMENT**
PHONE . . . . . . . . . . . . . . . . . . . . . . . . . . . 818-504-4864
FAX . . . . . . . . . . . . . . . . . . . . . . . . . . . . . 818-615-1849
15030 Ventura Blvd., Ste. 905
Sherman Oaks, CA 91403

TYPE          Motion Pictures + Television
CREDITS       Final Decision
Geno Hart . . . . . . . . . . . . . . . . . . . . . . Chief Executive Officer
Steve Larson . . . . . . . . . . . . . . . . . . . . . Dir., Development

**HART SHARP ENTERTAINMENT, INC.**
PHONE . . . . . . . . . . . . . . . . . . . . . . . . . . . 212-475-7555
FAX . . . . . . . . . . . . . . . . . . . . . . . . . . . . . 212-475-1717
EMAIL . . . . . . . . . . . . . . . . . . . . . jsharp@hartsharp.com
380 Lafayette St., Ste. 304
New York, NY 10003

TYPE          Motion Pictures
CREDITS       Safe - Drunks - Office Killer - Dark Harbor
COMMENTS  Theatre/Film/Management.
John Hart . . . . . . . . . . . . . . . . . . . . . . . . . . . . . Principal
Jeff Sharp . . . . . . . . . . . . . . . . . . . . . . . . . . . . . Principal
Jeffrey Roda . . . . . . . . . . . . . . . . . . . . . . . . . . . . Principal
Gretchen Hayduk Wroblewski . . . . . . . . . . . . Development Director
Peter Burns . . . . . . . . . . . . . . . . . . . . . Development Assistant

**HARVEY ENTERTAINMENT COMPANY**
PHONE . . . . . . . . . . . . . . . . . . . . . . . . . . . 310-789-1990
FAX . . . . . . . . . . . . . . . . . . . . . . . . . . . . . 310-789-1991
WEBSITE . . . . . . . . . . . . . . . . . . . . http://www.harvey.com
1999 Ave. of the Stars, Ste. 2050
Los Angeles, CA 90067-6055

TYPE          Television + Animation + Motion Pictures + Feature Direct
              to Video
CREDITS       Casper - Richie Rich - Casper Meets Wendy - Baby Huey
              Show
Anthony J. Scotti . . . . . . . . . . . . . . . . . . Interim CEO/President
Michael S. Hope . . . . . . . . . . . . Interim Chief Financial Officer
Kerry Broom . . . . . . . . . . . . . . . . . . . . . VP, Creative Affairs
Sean Gorman . . . . . . . . . . . . . . . . . . . . Dir., Creative Affairs

**HASSITT FILMS, NICHOLAS**
PHONE . . . . . . . . . . . . . . . . . . . . . . . . . . . 213-654-8183
1345 N. Hayworth Ave., Ste. 210
W. Hollywood, CA 90046

TYPE          Motion Pictures
CREDITS       In The Army Now - Kangaroo Court - Toy Soldiers
Nicholas Hassitt . . . . . . . . . . . . . . . . . . . . . . . . . Producer
Simon Ledworth . . . . . . . . . . . . . . . . . . . . . . . . . Associate

**HAUGLAND PRODUCTIONS, DAVID**
PHONE . . . . . . . . . . . . . . . . . . . . . . . . . . . 310-550-1556
FAX . . . . . . . . . . . . . . . . . . . . . . . . . . . . . 310-550-1584
EMAIL . . . . . . . . . . . . . . . . . . . . . . . . intrepidla@aol.com
8961 Sunset Blvd., Ste. 2D
West Hollywood, CA 90069

TYPE          Motion Pictures + Television + Documentaries
CREDITS       The Portrait - Changing Our Minds - World & Time
              Enough
David Haugland . . . . . . . . . . . . . . . . . . . . Producer/Director

**HAVING HAD PRODS., INC.**
PHONE . . . . . . . . . . . . . . . . . . . . . . . . . . . 760-340-2736
FAX . . . . . . . . . . . . . . . . . . . . . . . . . . . . . 760-340-9206
75209 Kiowa Dr.
Indian Wells, CA 92210

TYPE          Motion Pictures
CREDITS       Never Forget - Neil Simon's Broadway Bound - Ghost Dad
Terry Nelson . . . . . . . . . . . . . . . . . . . . . . . . . . . Producer

**HAVOC INC.**
PHONE . . . . . . . . . . . . . . . . . . . . . . . . . . . 212-924-1629
FAX . . . . . . . . . . . . . . . . . . . . . . . . . . . . . 212-924-3105
16 W 19th St., 12th Floor
New York, NY 10011

TYPE          Motion Pictures + Documentaries
DEAL          PolyGram Filmed Ent./Working Title Films
CREDITS       Bob Roberts - Dead Man Walking - The Typewriter the
              Rifle and the Movie Camera
Tim Robbins . . . . . . . . . . . . . . . . Producer/Director/Writer/Actor
Allison Hebble . . . . . . . . . . . . . . . . . . . . . Asst. to Mr. Robbins
Chris Talbott . . . . . . . . . . . . . . . . . . . . . . . . Office Manager
Nadia Benamara . . . . . . . . . . . . . . . . . . . . . Office Assistant

**HBO**
PHONE . . . . . . . . . . . . . . . . . . . . . . . . . . . 212-512-1000
FAX . . . . . . . . . . . . . . . . . . . . . . . . . . . . . 212-512-5517
WEBSITE . . . . . . . . . . . . . . . . . . . . . http://www.hbo.com
1100 Ave. of the Americas
New York, NY 10036

TYPE          Television
Jeff Bewkes . . . . . . . . . . . . . . . . . . . . . . . . President/CEO

**HBO ANIMATION**
PHONE . . . . . . . . . . . . . . . . . . . . . . . . . . . 310-229-1100
FAX . . . . . . . . . . . . . . . . . . . . . . . . . . . . . 310-229-1125
WEBSITE . . . . . . . . . . . . . . . . . . . . . http://www.hbo.com
2049 Century Park East, 41st Floor
Los Angeles, CA 90067

TYPE          Animation + Television
CREDITS       Spawn - Spicy City
Carmi Zlotnik . . . . . . . . . . . . . . . . . . . . . Sr. Vice President

**HBO INDEPENDENT PRODUCTIONS**
PHONE . . . . . . . . . . . . . . . . . . 310-201-9200/212-512-1000
WEBSITE . . . . . . . . . . . . . . . . . . . . . http://www.hbo.com
2049 Century Park East, Ste. 4200
Los Angeles, CA 90067

TYPE          Television
CREDITS       Everybody Loves Raymond
Chris Albrecht . . . . . . . . . . . Pres., Original Prg. & Independent Prod. (LA)
Lowell Mate . . . . . . . . . . . . . . . . . . . Exec VP, Creative Affairs
Russell Schwartz . . . . . . . . . . . . . . . Sr. Exec. VP, Business & Planning
Carmi Zlotnik . . . . . . . . . . . . . . . . . . . Sr. VP, Production (LA)
Carolyn Strauss . . . . . . . . . VP, Comedy Series, Specials & Late Night (LA)

# COMPANIES AND STAFF

**HBO NYC PRODUCTIONS**
PHONE . . . . . . . . . . . . . . . . . . . . . . . . . . . . 212-512-1000
FAX . . . . . . . . . . . . . . . . . . . . . . . . . . . . . . 212-512-5009
WEBSITE . . . . . . . . . . . . . . . . . . . . . http://www.hbo.com
1100 Ave. of the Americas
New York, NY 10036

TYPE          Motion Pictures + Television

John Matoian . . . . . . . . . . . . . . . . . . . President (310-201-9405)
Colin Callender . . . . . . . . . . . . . . . Exec. Vice President (212-512-5779)
Frank Doelger . . . . . . . . . . . VP, Production & Development (212-512-1770)
Kerith Putnam . . . . . . . . . . . VP, Production & Development (212-512-1901)
Tracey Kemble . . . . . . . . . . . . . . . VP, Development (212-512-1564)
Carrie Frazier . . . . . . . . . . . . . VP, Talent & Casting (310-201-9537)
Alan Grabelsky . . . . . . . . . . . . . . . . VP, Production (212-512-1431)
Bruce Grivetti . . . . . . . . . VP, East Coast Bus. Affairs Admin. (212-512-1664)
Karen Levinson . . . . . . . . . . VP, East Coast Bus. Affairs (212-512-1245)
Sharon Werner . . . . . . . . . . VP, East Coast Bus. Affairs (212-512-1474)
Jessika Borsiczky . . . . . . . . . . . . . . Dir., Development (212-512-1107)
Judith Brown . . . . . . . . . . . . . . . . Dir., Post-Production (212-512-1410)
Jane Evans . . . . . . . . . . . . . . . . . . . Dir., Production (212-512-1419)
Nellie Nugiel . . . . . . . . . . . . . . . . . . Dir., Production (212-512-1840)
Susan Israelson . . . . . . . . . . . . . . . . Dir., Literary Dept. (212-512-5893)
Amy Berman . . . . . . . . . . . . . Mgr., Talent & Casting (310-201-9543)
Ani Gasti . . . . . . . . . . . . . . . . . . . Project Coordinator (212-512-1706)
Nicolas Karlson . . . . . . . . . . . . . . . . Project Coordinator (212-512-8704)
Kristel Crews . . . . . . . . . . . . Operations Administrator (212-512-5614)

**HBO ORIGINAL PROGRAMMING**
PHONE . . . . . . . . . . . . . . . . . . . 310-201-9300/212-512-1000
FAX . . . . . . . . . . . . . . . . . . . . . . . . . . . /212-512-5517
WEBSITE . . . . . . . . . . . . . . . . . . . . . http://www.hbo.com
2049 Century Park East, Ste. 4200
Los Angeles, CA 90067

TYPE          Motion Pictures + Television
CREDITS       Larry Sanders Show - Dennis Miller Live - Arliss
COMMENTS      Also: 1100 Ave. of the Americas, New York, NY 10036

Chris Albrecht . . . . . . . . . . . . Pres., Original Prg. & Independent Prod. (LA)
Sheila Nevins . . . . . . . . . Sr. VP, Family Programming & Documentaries (NY)
Nancy Geller . . . . . . . . . . VP, Original Prog./Sr.VP, Downtown Prod. (NY)
Nancy Abraham . . . . . . . . . . . . . VP, Documentary Programming (NY)
Kary Antholis . . . . . . . . . . . VP, Dramatic Mini-Series & Events (NY)
Sarah Condon . . . . . . . . . VP, Comedy Series, Specials & Late Night (LA)
Susan Ennis . . . . . . . . . VP, Longterm Planning & Original Programming
John Fisher . . . . . . . . . . . . . . . . . VP, Downtown Prods. (NY)
Michael Lombardo . . . . . . . . . . . . . . . . VP, Business Affairs
Anthony Radziwill . . . . . . . . . . VP, Documentary Programming (NY)
Carole Rosen . . . . . . . . . . . . . . VP, Family Programming (NY)
Carolyn Strauss . . . . . . . . VP, Series, Specials & Late Night (LA)
Anne Thomopoulos . . . . . . . VP, Dramatic Mini-Series & Events (LA)
Carmi Zlotnik . . . . . . . . . . . . . VP, Creative Ops. & Prod. (LA)
Jackie Glover . . . . . . . . . . . Dir., Documentary Programming (NY)
Nina Rosenstein . . . . . . . . Dir., Development, HBO Downtown Prods. (NY)
Laurie Sykes . . . . . . . . . . . . . . . . . . . Dir., Music Events
Miranda Heller . . . . . . . . . . . . . . . . . Mgr., Drama Series (LA)
Katie McLaughlin . . . . . . . . . . . . Mgr., Family Programming (NY)
John Murchison . . . . . . . . Mgr., Dramatic Mini-Series & Events (LA)
Daria Overby . . . . . . . . . . . Mgr., Comedy Series, Specials & Late Night (LA)
Melanie Roy . . . . . Mgr., Development & Talent, HBO Downtown Prods. (NY)
Elizabeth White . . . . . . . . . . . . . . . . . Dir., Business Affairs
Donny Yankelevits . . . . . . . . . . . . . . . . Dir., Business Affairs

**HBO PICTURES**
PHONE . . . . . . . . . . . . . . . . . . . . . . . . . . . 310-201-9200
WEBSITE . . . . . . . . . . . . . . . . . . . . . http://www.hbo.com
2049 Century Park East, Ste. 3600
Los Angeles, CA 90067-3215

TYPE          Motion Pictures

John Matoian . . . . . . . . . . . . . . . . . . President (310-201-9405)
Ellen Collett . . . . . . . . . . VP, Production & Development (310-201-9277)
Michael Halpern . . . . . . . VP, Production & Development (310-201-9536)
Gaye Hirsch . . . . . . . . . . VP, Production & Development (310-201-9284)
Glenn Whitehead . . . . . . . VP, Business Affairs & Production (310-201-9291)
Suzanne Young . . . . . . . . . . . . . . VP, Business Affairs (310-201-9353)
Molly Wilson . . . . . . . . . . VP/Chief Counsel (West Coast Prog.) (310-201-9375)
Jeff Guthrie . . . . . . . . . . VP/Sr. Counsel (West Coast Prog.) (310-201-9315)
Jay Roewe . . . . . . . . . . . . . . . . . . VP, Production (310-201-9401)
Rich Battaglia . . . . . . . . . . . VP, Finance/Asst. Controller (310-201-9202)
Carrie Frazier . . . . . . . . . . . . . VP, Talent & Casting (310-201-9537)
Matt Prager . . . . . . . . . . . . . . . . Dir., Development (310-201-9307)
Paige Smith . . . . . . . . . . . . . . . . . Dir., Development (310-201-9522)
Sherry Fadely . . . . . . . . . . . . . . . . . Dir., Production (310-201-9403)
Janet Graham . . . . . . . . . . . . . . . . . Dir., Production (310-201-9404)
Cynthia Kanner . . . . . . . . . . . . . . . . Dir., Production (310-201-9456)
Susan Israelson . . . . . . . . . Dir., Literary Development (212-512-5893)
Ellen Rudolph . . . . . . . . . . . . . . . . Dir., Operations (310-201-9549)
Amy Berman . . . . . . . . . . . . . Mgr., Talent & Casting (310-201-9543)
Lisa Neeley . . . . . . . . . . . . . . . . Creative Executive (310-201-9318)
Bettina Moss . . . . . . . . . . . . . . . . . . Story Editor (310-201-9302)
Donna Pearlmutter . . . . . . . . . . . . Production Supervisor (310-201-9464)

**HEARST ENT. LICENSING & FAMILY PROG.**
PHONE . . . . . . . . . . . . . . . . . . . . . . . . . . . 310-478-1700
FAX . . . . . . . . . . . . . . . . . . . . . . . . . . . . . 310-478-7579
WEBSITE . . . . . . . . . . . . . . . . . . http://www.hearstcorp.com
1640 S. Sepulveda Blvd., 4th Floor
Los Angeles, CA 90025

TYPE          Animation
COMMENTS      Live Action/Animated Features, Live Action/Animated
              Television, Entertainment Licensing.

Rick Karo . . . . . . . . . . . . . . . . . . . . Exec. Vice President
Leslie M. Levine . . . . . . . . . . . . . . . VP, Entertainment Licensing
Timothy P. Walker . . . . . . . . . . . . . . . Administrative Assistant

**HEARST ENTERTAINMENT**
PHONE . . . . . . . . . . . . . . . . . . . . . . . . . . . 310-478-1700
FAX . . . . . . . . . . . . . . . . . . . . . . . . . . . . . 310-478-2202
1640 S. Sepulveda Blvd., 4th Fl.
Los Angeles, CA 90025-7510

TYPE          Television

Glenda Grant . . . . . . . . . . . . . . . . . . . . . . . President
Mel Bishop . . . . . . . . . . . . . . . . . . . Exec. VP, Production
Marvin S. Katz . . . . . . . . . . . Exec. VP, Business Affairs & Admin.
Jerry Shevick . . . . . . . . . . . . . . . Sr. VP/Reality Programming
Mary Ann Spero . . . . . . . . . . . . . Sr. VP, Movies & Mini-Series
Ronald Ulloa . . . . . . . . . . . . . . . . . Sr. VP, Business Affairs
Paul Goldman . . . . . . . . . . . VP, Production & Post Production
BJ Markus . . . . . . . . . . . . . . . . . VP, Production Finance
Joe Lawlor . . . . . . . . . . . . . . . . . . Dir., Movies & Miniseries

**HELIOS PRODS.**
PHONE . . . . . . . . . . . . . . . . . . . . . . . . . . . 213-934-5454
FAX . . . . . . . . . . . . . . . . . . . . . . . . . . . . . 213-939-3711
5514 Wilshire Blvd., 11th Floor
Los Angeles, CA 90036

TYPE          Television
CREDITS       What Happened To Bobby Earl? - Crash Landing - Born
              Into Exile

Joseph Maurer . . . . . . . . . . . . . . . . . . . . Writer/Producer
Bradley Wigor . . . . . . . . . . . . . . . . . . . Director/Producer

**HELLER PRODS., PAUL**
PHONE . . . . . . . . . . . . . . . . . . . . . . . . . . . 310-275-4477
FAX . . . . . . . . . . . . . . . . . . . . . . . . . . . . . 310-275-1406
1666 N. Beverly Dr.
Beverly Hills, CA 90210

TYPE          Motion Pictures + Interactive Multimedia
CREDITS       Withnail & I - David & Lisa - Skirball Cultural Center - My
              Left Foot

Paul Heller . . . . . . . . . . . . . . . . . . . . . . . . Producer
Kathy Zebrowski-Heller . . . . . . . . . . . . . . . . . . President
Michael Peters . . . . . . . . . . . . . . . . . . . . . Development

## HELLER PRODS., ROSILYN
PHONE ................................ 213-876-2820
2237 Nichols Canyon Rd.
Los Angeles, CA 90046

TYPE      Motion Pictures + Television
CREDITS   Ice Castles - Who's That Girl - American Heart - Beans of Egypt, Maine
COMMENTS  Also: Cable.

Rosilyn Heller ........................... President/Producer

## HELLINGER FILMS
PHONE ................................ 310-446-6338
10573 West Pico Blvd., Ste. 865
Los Angeles, CA 90064

TYPE      Motion Pictures + Television + Documentaries
CREDITS   The Violent Heart/RKO

Laura A.S. Phillips ........................... Producer
Charlotte McKenna ........................... Assistant

## *HELLMAN PRODUCTIONS, JEROME
PHONE ................................ 310-205-6317
FAX ................................ 310-205-6318
9300 Hazen Drive
Beverly Hills, CA 90210

TYPE      Motion Pictures
CREDITS   Midnight Cowboy - Mosquito Coast - Coming Home

Jerome Hellman ........................... Producer
Hilary Six ........................... Exec. Asst./Development

## HENSON COMPANY, JIM
PHONE ................ 213-960-4096/212-794-2400
FAX ................ 213-960-4935/212-570-1147
WEBSITE ........................ http://www.henson.com
Raleigh Studios
5358 Melrose Ave., Ste. 300 W
Hollywood, CA 90038

TYPE      Motion Pictures + Television + Animation + Feature Direct to Video + Interactive Multimedia
CREDITS   Muppet Treasure Island - Bear in the Big Blue House - World of Dr. Seuss
COMMENTS  Also: 117 E. 69th St., NY, NY 10021 Also: 30 Oval Rd., Camden, London NW1 7DE

Brian Henson ........................... President/CEO
Charles H. Rivkin ........................... President/COO
Margaret Loesch ........... President, Jim Henson TV Group
Martin G. Baker ........... Exec. VP, Physical Production, Worldwide
Peter Schube ...... Exec. VP, Business & Legal Affairs/General Counsel
Peter Coogan ........................... Production Executive
Linda Govreau ........... Sr. VP, Finance & Administration
Marcy Ross ........................... Sr. VP, Creative Affairs
Peter van Roden ..... Sr. VP, New York Production & Themed Entertainment
Angus Fletcher ........... VP, International Dev. & Co-Production
Cheryl Henson ........................... VP, CTW Relations
Rita Peruggi ........................... VP, Production, Worldwide
Halle Stanford Grossman ........................... VP, Creative Affairs
John Stephenson ...... Creative Supervisor/VP, Creature Shop, Worldwide
Craig Allen ........... General Mgr., Henson On-Line/Henson.com
Matt Britton ........... General Manager, L.A. Creature Shop
David Barrington Holt ........... Creative Supervisor, LA Creature Shop
Jim Lewis ........................... Writer

## HENSON PICTURES, JIM
PHONE ................................ 213-960-4096
FAX ................................ 213-960-4780
WEBSITE ........................ http://www.henson.com
5358 Melrose Ave., Ste. 300W
Hollywood, CA 90038

TYPE      Motion Pictures
DEAL      Sony Pictures Entertainment
CREDITS   Buddy

Stephanie Allain ........................... Pres., Production
Kristine Belson ........................... Production
Jill L. Smith Esq. ........... VP, Business & Legal Affairs
Louis M. Phillips ........................... Production/Administration
Rob Valois ........................... Story Editor
Paul Davidson ........................... Production Coordinator
Maura Dooley ........................... London Consultant
Jenny Klion ........................... New York Consultant
Marti Bircoll ........................... Reader
Jere Douglass ........................... Asst. to Ms. Smith
Tom Supa ........................... Asst. To Ms. Allain

## HERMAN PRODUCTIONS, VICKY
PHONE ................................ 213-656-4207
8001 Highland Trail
Los Angeles, CA 90046

TYPE      Motion Pictures + Television
CREDITS   A Dangerous Affair - Trial By Fire - Holiday Affair

Vicky Herman ........................... Producer
David Markland ........................... Dir., Development

## HERO ENTERTAINMENT, INC.
PHONE ................................ 213-654-7849
FAX ................................ 213-654-7849
1601 No. Kings Rd.
Los Angeles, CA 90069

TYPE      Motion Pictures + Television
CREDITS   Roger Ramjet - Blank Check

Blake Snyder ........................... President/CEO

## HICKOX PRODUCTIONS, INC., BRYAN
PHONE ................................ 904-354-3027
FAX ................................ 904-354-5753
EMAIL ........................ sbryanh@aol.com
Jacksonville Production Center
851 N. Market St.
Jacksonville, FL 32202-2798

TYPE      Motion Pictures + Television
CREDITS   CCPD - ABC Family Theater - Sudden Terror: The Hijacking of Miami School Bus Cx-17 - and Ride

S. Bryan Hickox ........................... Producer/Co-Owner
Joanne Kraemer ........................... Chief Financial Officer
Dan H. Hinds ........................... Dir., Development
Peter Bengston ........................... SAG Casting
Michael Stark ........................... SAG Casting
Terry Vanderwier ........................... Non-SAG Casting
Nancy Fankhauser ........................... Asst. to Mr. Hickox

## HIGH HORSE FILMS
PHONE ................................ 213-461-4948
FAX ................................ 213-461-7884
533 N. McCadden Place
Los Angeles, CA 90004

TYPE      Motion Pictures + Television
CREDITS   Hard Promises - Keep the Change

Cynthia Chvatal ........................... Producer
William Petersen ........................... Actor/Producer
Ann Russell ........................... Assistant

## HIGH ROAD PRODUCTIONS
PHONE ................................ 213-276-0349
5750 Wilshire Blvd., Ste. 580
Los Angeles, CA 90036

TYPE      Motion Pictures + Television
CREDITS   Pontiac Moon - Diggstown - Jacknife - Table For Five
COMMENTS  Direct submissions and inquiries to Sharon Roesler.

Robert Schaffel ........................... Producer/Writer
Sharon Roesler ........................... Producer
E.J. Campfield ........................... Writer

## HILL PRODUCTIONS, DEBRA
PHONE ................................ 310-319-0052
FAX ................................ 310-260-8502
1250 6th St., Ste. 205
Santa Monica, CA 90401

TYPE      Motion Pictures + Television
CREDITS   Escape From LA - Halloween - The Fisher King

Debra Hill ........................... Writer/Producer/Director
Barri Evins ........................... President
Patrick List ........................... Dir., Development
Jeff Howard ........................... Development Assistant

## HILL/FIELDS ENT.
PHONE ................................ 213-954-4500
FAX ................................ 213-954-4550
4500 Wilshire Blvd.
Los Angeles, CA 90010

TYPE      Motion Pictures + Television
CREDITS   A Matter of Justice - Long Hot Summer - Gone In The Night - Detention

Leonard Hill ........................... Executive Producer
Joel Fields ........................... Executive Producer
Alys Shanti ........................... Dir., Development
Debbie Siegel ........................... Controller
Linda Ferrero ........................... Production Coordinator
Tim Winteringham ........................... Auditor

# COMPANIES AND STAFF

**HIMBER ENTERTAINMENT**
PHONE . . . . . . . . . . . . . . . . . . . . . . . . . . . . . . . . . . . . . . 310-276-2500
FAX . . . . . . . . . . . . . . . . . . . . . . . . . . . . . . . . . . . . . . . . . 310-276-2538
EMAIL . . . . . . . . . . . . . . . . . . . . . . . . . . . . HimBerEnt@aol.com
211 S. Beverly Dr., Ste. 208
Beverly Hills, CA 90212

TYPE          Motion Pictures + Television
Steve Himber . . . . . . . . . . . . . . . . . . . . . . . . . . . . . . . . . . . . . .Producer
Rick Faigin . . . . . . . . . . . . . . . . . . . . . . . . . . . . . . . . . . . . . . .Producer
Sheree Cohen . . . . . . . . . . . . . . . . . . . . . . . . . . . . . . . . . . . .Producer

**HINTERLAND ENTERTAINMENT**
PHONE . . . . . . . . . . . . . . . . . . . . . . . . . . . . . . . . . . . . . . 818-786-9923
FAX . . . . . . . . . . . . . . . . . . . . . . . . . . . . . . . . . . . . . . . . . 818-786-9028
EMAIL . . . . . . . . . . . . . . . . . . . . . . . . . . . . HINTERENT@aol.com
13601 Ventura Blvd., Ste. 294
Sherman Oaks, CA 91423

TYPE          Motion Pictures + Television
CREDITS     American Samurai - Destination Vegas - Mr. Atlas
Karen Lee Arbeeny . . . . . . . . . . . . . . . . . . . . . . . . . . Director/Producer
Elaine Chekich . . . . . . . . . . . . . . . . . . . . . . . . . . . . . . Producer/Writer

**HIRSCH COMPANY, INC., S.**
PHONE . . . . . . . . . . . . . . . . . . . . . . . . . . . . . . . . . . . . . . 310-854-4436
FAX . . . . . . . . . . . . . . . . . . . . . . . . . . . . . . . . . . . . . . . . . 310-854-4437
EMAIL . . . . . . . . . . . . . . . . . . . . . . . tomwoosley@shirschco.com
8490 Sunset Blvd., Ste. 500
West Hollywood, CA 90069

TYPE          Motion Pictures
Steven Hirsch . . . . . . . . . . . . . . . . . . . . . . . . . . . . . . . .President/CEO
Tom Woosley . . . . . . . . . . . . . . . . . . VP, Development & Acquisitions

**HISTORY CHANNEL, THE**
PHONE . . . . . . . . . . . . . . . . . . . . . . . . . . . . . . . . . . . . . . 212-210-1400
FAX . . . . . . . . . . . . . . . . . . . . . . . . . . . . . . . . . . . . . . . . . 212-210-9016
WEBSITE . . . . . . . . . . . . . . . . . . . . . . http://HistoryChannel.com
235 E. 45th St.
New York, NY 10017

TYPE          Television + Documentaries
CREDITS     History Alive - In Search of History - Movies in Time -
                  Trains Unlimited - Modern Marvels
COMMENTS  24 hr. historical docum./movies/miniseries cable channel.
Daniel E. Davids . . . . . . . . . . . . . . . . . . . . Exec. VP/General Manager
Seymour Lesser . . . . . . . . . . . . . . . . . . Exec. VP/General Manager, Intl.
Abbe Raven . . . . . . . . Sr. VP, Programming, History Ch. & History Ch. Intl.
Charles Maday . . . . . . . . . . . . . . . . . . . . . . . . VP, Historical Programming
Joe LaPolla . . . . . . . . . . . . . . . . . . Dir., Program Acquisitions & Scheduling

**HIT & RUN PRODUCTIONS, INC.**
PHONE . . . . . . . . . . . . . . . . . . . . . . . . . . . . . . . . . . . . . . 212-974-8400
FAX . . . . . . . . . . . . . . . . . . . . . . . . . . . . . . . . . . . . . . . . . 212-974-8443
EMAIL . . . . . . . . . . . . . . . . . . . . . . . . . . . . HitRunProd@aol.com
150 W. 56th St., Ste. 5606
New York, NY 10019

TYPE          Motion Pictures
CREDITS     Eye of the Beholder
COMMENTS  Also: London, Los Angeles
Tony Smith . . . . . . . . . . . . . . . . . . . . . . . . . . . . . . . . . . . . . Chairman
Hilary Shor . . . . . . . . . . . . . . . . . . . . . . . . . . . . . . Pres., Production
Grant Lee . . . . . . . . . . . . . . . . . . . . . . . . . . . . . . Associate (London)
Barbara Ghammaski . . . . . . . . . . . . . . . . . . . . . . Asst. to Hilary Shor
Cynthia L. Gitter . . . . . . . . . . . . . . . . . . . . . . . . . . . . . . Story Editor

**HKM FILMS**
PHONE . . . . . . . . . . . . . . . . . . . . . . . . . . . . . . . . . . . . . . 213-465-9191
FAX . . . . . . . . . . . . . . . . . . . . . . . . . . . . . . . . . . . . . . . . . 213-464-3574
EMAIL . . . . . . . . . . . . . . . . . . . . . . . . . . . . . . . . . films@hkm.com
1641 N. Ivar Avenue
Hollywood, CA 90028

TYPE          Motion Pictures
CREDITS     F.T.W. - Mobsters - The Silent War
Graham Henman . . . . . . . . . . . . . . . . . . . . . . . . . . Producer/Director
Michael Karbelnikoff . . . . . . . . . . . . . . . . . . . . . . . . Producer/Director
Alexis Magagni-Seely . . . . . . . . . . . . . . . Producer/Sr. VP, Creative Affairs

**HOBEL PRODUCTIONS**
PHONE . . . . . . . . . . . . . . . . . . . . . . . . . . . . . . . . . . . . . . 212-246-5522
FAX . . . . . . . . . . . . . . . . . . . . . . . . . . . . . . . . . . . . . . . . . 212-246-5525
EMAIL . . . . . . . . . . . . . . . . . . . . . . . . . . . . thecinemag@aol.com
WEBSITE . . . . . . . . . . . . . . . http://www.cinemaguild.com/cinemaguild
1697 Broadway, Ste. 506
New York, NY 10019-5904

TYPE          Motion Pictures + Television + Documentaries +
                  Syndication + Interactive Multimedia
CREDITS     Tender Mercies - Kennedys Don't Cry - Surfacing
Mary-Ann Hobel . . . . . . . . . . . . . . . . . . . . . . . . . . . . . . . . Producer
Philip Hobel . . . . . . . . . . . . . . . . . . . . . . . . . . . . . . . . . . . . Producer

**HOLCOMB-SPEED PRODUCTIONS**
PHONE . . . . . . . . . . . . . . . . . . . . . . . . . . . . . . . . . . . . . . 818-954-2006
FAX . . . . . . . . . . . . . . . . . . . . . . . . . . . . . . . . . . . . . . . . . 818-954-2711
Warner Bros.
4000 Warner Blvd., Producers 6, Ste. E
Burbank, CA 91522

TYPE          Motion Pictures + Television
CREDITS     ER (pilot) - China Beach (pilot) - Wise Guy (pilot)
Rod Holcomb . . . . . . . . . . . . . . . . . . . . . . . . . . . . Producer/Director
Lizz Speed . . . . . . . . . . . . . . . . . . . . . . . . . . . . . . . . . . . . Producer
Melissa Anderson . . . . . . . . . . . . . . . . . . . . . . . . . . . . . . . Assistant

**HOLLANE CORP.**
PHONE . . . . . . . . . . . . . . . . . . . . . . . . . . . . . . . . . . . . . . 213-876-8873
FAX . . . . . . . . . . . . . . . . . . . . . . . . . . . . . . . . . . . . . . . . . 213-876-8892
P.O. Box 17137
Beverly Hills, CA 90209-3137

TYPE          Motion Pictures + Television
CREDITS     Diana, Her True Story - Lion in Winter - Nighthawks
Martin Poll . . . . . . . . . . . . . . . . . . . . . . . . . . . . President/Producer
Shirley Mellner . . . . . . . . . . . . . . . . . . . . . . . Exec. VP, Creative
Aliana Scurlock . . . . . . . . . . . . . . . . . . . . . . . . Executive Assistant

**HOLLYWOOD LITERARY RETREAT/ZOOM ENT.**
PHONE . . . . . . . . . . . . . . . . . . . . . . . . . . . . . . . . . . . . . . 310-358-3211
FAX . . . . . . . . . . . . . . . . . . . . . . . . . . . . . . . . . . . . . . . . . 310-358-3299
c/o The Bubble Factory
8840 Wilshire Blvd., 2nd Fl.
Beverly Hills, CA 90211

TYPE          Motion Pictures + Television + Documentaries
CREDITS     I Love You To Death - Hollywood Goes Back To Story -
                  Bordello - Youngblood - Maui Heat
COMMENTS  310-268-6618 for the retreat in association with Writers'
                  Boot Camp.
Lynn Isenberg . . . . . . . . . . . . . . . . . . . . . . President/Writer/Producer

**HOLLYWOOD NETWORK, INC.**
PHONE . . . . . . . . . . . . . . . . . . . . . . . . . . . . . . . . . . . . . . 310-288-1882
FAX . . . . . . . . . . . . . . . . . . . . . . . . . . . . . . . . . . . . . . . . . 310-475-0193
EMAIL . . . . . . . . . . . . . . . . . . . . hollyinfo@hollywoodnetwork.com
WEBSITE . . . . . . . . . . . . . . . . . . . . http://hollywoodnetwork.com
433 N. Camden Dr., Ste. 600
Beverly Hills, CA 90210

TYPE          Motion Pictures + Interactive Multimedia + Feature Direct
                  to Video
CREDITS     Power Brokers - Justice...On Trial
COMMENTS  A division of CCS Entertainment.
Carlos de Abreu . . . . . . . . . . . . . . . . . . . . . . . . President/Producer
Janice de Abreu . . . . . . . . . . . . . . . . . . . . . . . . . . . . . . . Producer
Michael Almeida . . . . . . . . . . . . . . . . . . . . . . . . . . VP, International
John Jacobson . . . . . . . . . . . . . . . . . . . . . . . . . . . . VP, New Media

**HOLMES RUN ENTERTAINMENT**
PHONE . . . . . . . . . . . . . . . . . . . . . . . . . . . . . . . . . . . . . . 310-471-7585
219 South Thurston Ave.
Los Angeles, CA 90049-3123

TYPE          Motion Pictures + Television + Animation + Interactive
                  Multimedia
Herbert S.H. Holmes . . . . . . . . . . . . . . . . . . . . . . . . . . . . President

**HORSEPOWER ENTERTAINMENT**
PHONE . . . . . . . . . . . . . . . . . . . . . . . . . . . . . . . . . . . . . . 818-980-9455
FAX . . . . . . . . . . . . . . . . . . . . . . . . . . . . . . . . . . . . . . . . . 818-752-3941
4063 Radford Ave., Ste. 206
Studio City, CA 91604

TYPE          Motion Pictures + Television
CREDITS     Debt - The Core - Best Laid Plans
Sean Bailey . . . . . . . . . . . . . . . . . . . . . . . . . . . . . . . . . . . . . Partner
Cooper Layne . . . . . . . . . . . . . . . . . . . . . . . . . . . . . . . . . . . . Partner

## HORSESHOE BAY PRODUCTIONS
```
PHONE .............................................. 310-587-0787
FAX ................................................ 310-899-4259
```
710 Wilshire Blvd., Ste. 600
Santa Monica, CA 90401

| | |
|---|---|
| TYPE | Motion Pictures |
| DEAL | Walt Disney Company, The |
| CREDITS | Sleepless In Seattle - Tin Cup - Grumpy Old Men - Small Miracle |

```
Gary S. Foster ........................................ Producer
Mark Steven Johnson ................... Writer/Director/Producer
Josie Rosen ........................................... President
Julie Beckett ................................... Vice President
Amberwren Briskey-Cohen .................... Creative Associate
Erik Baiers ....................................... Story Editor
Christopher Adams .................... Exec. Asst. to Ms. Rosen
Brian Rankel ....................... Exec. Asst. to Mr. Johnson
```

## HOWARD PRODS. INC., AL
```
PHONE .............................................. 213-960-2431
FAX ................................................ 213-960-2533
```
Hollywood Center Studios
1040 N. Las Palmas, #236
Los Angeles, CA 90038

| | |
|---|---|
| TYPE | Television |
| CREDITS | Supermarket Sweep - Sale of the Century |

```
Al Howard ............................. President/Exec. Producer
Joel Stein ........................................... Producer
Chris Darley .......................................... Director
Jim Rossi ........................... Exec. in Charge of Production
```

## HSI ENTERTAINMENT
```
PHONE .............................................. 310-452-9999
FAX ................................................ 310-396-2128
EMAIL ............................... films@hsiproductions.com
```
1611 Electric Ave.
Venice, CA 90291

| | |
|---|---|
| TYPE | Motion Pictures |
| DEAL | Warner Bros. |

```
Stavros Merjos ....................................... President
Adam Rosenfelt .......................... Exec. Vice President
Chad Snopek ...................... Sr. VP, Production/Manager
Mike Kobayashi ............................ Creative Executive
```

## HSX FILMS, INC.
```
PHONE .............................................. 310-458-5256
FAX ................................................ 310-458-3792
WEBSITE ............................... http://www.hsx.com
```
225 Arizona Avenue, Ste. 250
Santa Monica, CA 90401

| | |
|---|---|
| TYPE | Motion Pictures |
| CREDITS | Six String Samurai - Desert Blue - Mixed Signals - Possums - Dancer - TX pop. 81 - The Suburbans |
| COMMENTS | Soon to be Ignite Entertainment. |

```
Michael Burns ........................................ Chairman
Leanna Creel ............................... Pres., Production
Marc Butan ............................. VP, Business Affairs
Cassandra Leonard .................................. Controller
Leon Marucci ........................... Asst. to Leanna Creel
```

## *HUNT-TAVEL PRODUCTIONS
```
PHONE .............................................. 310-244-3144
FAX ................................................ 310-244-0164
```
10202 W. Washington, Capra 105
Culver City, CA 90232

| | |
|---|---|
| TYPE | Motion Pictures + Television |
| DEAL | Columbia Pictures |

```
Helen Hunt ............................................. Partner
Connie Tavel .......................................... Partner
Dana Jackson .................................... Vice President
Stacey Berns ............................... Asst. to Ms. Hunt
Jason D. Scott .......................... Asst. to Ms. Jackson
```

## HUNT/JAFFE PRODS.
```
PHONE .............................................. 818-841-6750
FAX ................................................ 818-841-0883
```
2625 W. Olive
Burbank, CA 91505

| | |
|---|---|
| TYPE | Television |
| CREDITS | You Don't Say - Top 40 Videos - Urban Nights |
| COMMENTS | Top 40 Fax 818-841-0883. Urban Nights Fax 818-841-0883. Also: Post Production. |

```
Gary Hunt ..................................... Writer/Producer
Barry Jaffe .................................. Writer/Producer
```

## HYAMS PRODS., INC., PETER
```
PHONE .............................................. 310-393-1553
FAX ................................................ 310-393-1554
```
1453 Third St. Promenade, Ste. 315
Santa Monica, CA 90401-2397

| | |
|---|---|
| TYPE | Motion Pictures |
| CREDITS | Sudden Death - The Relic - Timecop - Narrow Margin |

```
Peter Hyams .................................. Director/Writer
Jonathan Wilson ............................. Dir., Development
```

## HYPERFILMS
```
PHONE .............................................. 818-777-5617
FAX ................................................ 818-866-3633
```
Universal Studios
100 Universal City Plaza, Bldg. 507-3G
Universal City, CA 91608

| | |
|---|---|
| TYPE | Motion Pictures |
| DEAL | Universal Pictures |

```
Lynwood Spinks ....................................... Producer
Steven Roffer .................................. Co-President
Melinda Farrell ............................... Co-President
Kim Surowicz .............. Executive Assistant (818-777-5624)
```

## HYPERION ENTERTAINMENT
```
PHONE .............................................. 818-244-4704
FAX ................................................ 818-244-4713
WEBSITE .................... http://www.hyperion-studio.com
```
111 N. Maryland Ave., Ste. 200
Glendale, CA 91206

| | |
|---|---|
| TYPE | Motion Pictures + Television + Animation + Interactive Multimedia + Feature Direct to Video |
| CREDITS | Dancing About Architecture - Tom's Midnight Garden - Brave Little Toaster - Life with Louie |

```
Thomas Wilhite ....................................... President
Willard Carroll .................. Co-Owner/Writer/Director
Kurt Albrecht .................................. VP, Production
John W. Lanza Jr. .................... VP, Multimedia Production
Corey Powell .......................... VP, Creative Affairs
Russell Marleau ...................................... Producer
```

## ICON PRODUCTIONS INC.
```
PHONE .............................................. 818-954-2960
FAX ................................................ 818-954-4212
```
Warner Bros. Picts.
4000 Warner Blvd.
Burbank, CA 91522-0001

| | |
|---|---|
| TYPE | Motion Pictures |
| DEAL | Paramount Pictures- Motion Picture Group/Warner Bros. Pictures |
| CREDITS | Hamlet - Man Without a Face - Immortal Beloved - Braveheart - 187 - Payback |

```
Bruce Davey .......................................... President
Steve McEveety ...................................... Producer
Vicki Christianson ............. VP, Finance & Business Affairs
Dana Ginsburg ............... VP, Legal & Business Affairs
Jim Lemley ............... VP, Production/Associate Producer
Karen J. Glasser ............................... VP, Development
Eveleen Bandy ............................... Dir., Development
Bonnie Watkins ............................. Asst. to B. Davey
Doug Weaver ............................... Executive Assistant
```

## IDEAL ENTERTAINMENT, INC.
```
PHONE .............................................. 213-939-3399
FAX ................................................ 213-939-3009
EMAIL ................................... shapiro@flash.net
```
100 Universal City Plaza
Bldg. 506, Ste. E
Universal City, CA 91608

| | |
|---|---|
| TYPE | Motion Pictures + Television + Animation |
| CREDITS | Richie Rich |

```
Jon Shapiro ............................... President/Producer
Peter Shapiro ......................... Vice President/Producer
```

## IDEAL MOVIE SHOPPE, LLC, THE
```
PHONE .............................................. 818-223-8089
FAX ................................................ 818-776-9293
EMAIL ................................... mw@earthlink.net
```
23901 Calabasas Rd., #1051
Calabasas, CA 91302

| | |
|---|---|
| TYPE | Television + Animation + Syndication |
| CREDITS | The Angry Beavers - GI Joe: Extreme |

```
Lee Gunther ............................... Executive Producer
Michael Wahl .............................. Executive Producer
```

# COMPANIES AND STAFF

## IF/X PRODUCTIONS
PHONE . . . . . . . . . . . . . . . . . . . . . . . . . . . . . . 818-501-1822
FAX . . . . . . . . . . . . . . . . . . . . . . . . . . . . . . . . 818-501-4526
5103 Gloria Ave.
Encino, CA 91436

| | |
|---|---|
| TYPE | Motion Pictures + Television + Interactive Multimedia |
| CREDITS | Peter and the Wolf - Rhythm & Jam - Bugs Bunny on Broadway - Magical World of Chuck Jones |
| COMMENTS | Also: Concerts. |

George Daugherty . . . . . . . . . . . . . . . . . . . . . . . President/Director
David Wong . . . . . . . . . . . . . . . . . . . . . Producer/Sr. Vice President
Bruce Triplett . . . . . . . . . . . . . . . . . . . . . . . . . VP, Development
Isabelle Zakin . . . . . . . . . . . . . . . . . . . . . . . . . . Vice President

## IFM FILM ASSOCIATES, INC.
PHONE . . . . . . . . . . . . . . . . . . . . . . . . . . . . . . 213-874-4249
FAX . . . . . . . . . . . . . . . . . . . . . . . . . . . . . . . . 213-874-2654
EMAIL . . . . . . . . . . . . . . . . . . . . . . . . . . . ifmfilm@aol.com
1541 N. Gardner St.
Los Angeles, CA 90046-2807

| | |
|---|---|
| TYPE | Motion Pictures + Television |
| CREDITS | Sally Marhsall's Not an Alien - The Whole of the Moon |

Antony I. Ginnane . . . . . . . . . . . . . . . . . . . . . . . . . . President
Ann Lyons . . . . . . . . . . . . . . . . . . . . . . . . . . Exec. Vice President

## ILLUSION ENTERTAINMENT GROUP
PHONE . . . . . . . . . . . . . . . . . . . . . . . . . . . . . . 310-458-7747
FAX . . . . . . . . . . . . . . . . . . . . . . . . . . . . . . . . 310-458-1597
201 Santa Monica Blvd., Ste. 625
Santa Monica, CA 90401

| | |
|---|---|
| TYPE | Motion Pictures + Television + Documentaries |
| CREDITS | Nixon - Assassinated: The Last Days of Kennedy & King - The Corruptor - U-Turn |

Oliver Stone . . . . . . . . . . . . . . . . . . . . . Writer/Director/Producer
Dan Halsted . . . . . . . . . . . . . . . . . . . . . . . . . . . . President
Jonathan Krauss . . . . . . . . . . . . . . . . . . . . . . . . . Vice President
Brennan Rees . . . . . . . . . . . . . . . . . . . . . Development Executive
Mikko Alanne . . . . . . . . . . . . . . . . . . . . . . . . . . . Story Editor
Katherine Ku . . . . . . . . . . . . . . . . . . Exec. Asst. to Dan Halsted
Rob Wilson . . . . . . . . . . . . . . . . . . . . Exec. Asst. to Oliver Stone
Becky Kuhns . . . . . . . . . . . . . . . . . . . . . Asst. to Oliver Stone
Rick Lubaroff . . . . . . . . . . . . . . . . . . . . . Asst. to Dan Halsted

## IMAGE ORGANIZATION, INC.
PHONE . . . . . . . . . . . . . . . . . . . . . . . . . . . . . . 310-278-8751
FAX . . . . . . . . . . . . . . . . . . . . . . . . . . . . . . . . 310-278-3967
9000 Sunset Blvd., Ste. 915
Los Angeles, CA 90069

| | |
|---|---|
| TYPE | Motion Pictures + Television |
| CREDITS | Wishmaster - Table for One - Captured |

Larry Goebel . . . . . . . . . . . . . . . . . . . . . . . . . . . . President
Clark Peterson . . . . . . . . . . . . . . . . . . . Sr. VP, Creative Affairs
Noel Zanitsch . . . . . . . . . . . . . . . . . . . . . . . Sr. VP, Production
Carol Diesel Allison . . . . . . . . . . . . . . . . Chief Financial Officer
Ken Sanders . . . . . . . . . . . . . . . . . . . . . . . . VP, Creative Affairs
Cheri Turner . . . . . . . . . . . . . . VP, Acquisitions & Co-Productions

## IMAGEMOVERS
PHONE . . . . . . . . . . . . . . . . . . . . . . . . . . . . . . 818-733-8313
FAX . . . . . . . . . . . . . . . . . . . . . . . . . . . . . . . . 818-733-8333
Universal Pictures
100 Universal City Plaza, Bung. 127
Universal City, CA 91608

| | |
|---|---|
| TYPE | Motion Pictures |
| DEAL | DreamWorks SKG |
| CREDITS | Forrest Gump - Back To The Future 1-3 - Who Framed Roger Rabbit - Death Becomes Her - Contact |

Robert Zemeckis . . . . . . . . . . . . . . . . . . Writer/Director/Producer
Jack Rapke . . . . . . . . . . . . . . . . . . . . . . . . . . . . . Producer
Steve Starkey . . . . . . . . . . . . . . . . . . . . . . . . . . . Producer
Jennifer Perini . . . . . . . . . . . . . . . . . . . . . . . . Dir., Development

## IMAGERIES ENTERTAINMENT
PHONE . . . . . . . . . . . . . . . . . . . . . . . . . . . . . . 310-244-6119
FAX . . . . . . . . . . . . . . . . . . . . . . . . . . . . . . . . 310-278-5085
10202 W. Washington Blvd.
Culver City, CA 90232

| | |
|---|---|
| TYPE | Motion Pictures + Television |
| DEAL | Columbia Pictures |
| CREDITS | The New Adventures of Pippi Longstocking - Men of Respect - Friday The 13th, Part VII |

Gary Mehlman . . . . . . . . . . . . . . . . . . . . . . . Producer/Partner
John Buechler . . . . . . . . . . . . . . . . . . . Writer/Director/Partner

## IMAGINARY FORCES
PHONE . . . . . . . . . . . . . . . . . . . . . . . . . . . . . . 213-957-6868
FAX . . . . . . . . . . . . . . . . . . . . . . . . . . . . . . . . 213-957-9577
EMAIL . . . . . . . . . . . . . . . . . . . . michel@imaginaryforces.com
WEBSITE . . . . . . . . . . . . . . . . . . http://www.imaginaryforces.com
6526 Sunset Blvd.
Hollywood, CA 90028

| | |
|---|---|
| TYPE | Motion Pictures + Television |
| CREDITS | Juice - Boys - Blade |
| COMMENTS | Also: Conceptual design and marketing - title design and corporate branding. |

Peter Frankfurt . . . . . . . . . . . . . . . . . . . . . . . Executive Producer
Chip Houghton . . . . . . . . . . . . . . . . . . . . . . . Executive Producer
Kyle Cooper . . . . . . . . . . . . . . . . . . . . . . . . . Creative Director
Saffron Kenny . . . . . . . . . . . . . . . . . . . . . . . . Head, Production

## IMAGINATION FACTORY INC.
PHONE . . . . . . . . . . . . . . . . . . . . . . . . . . . . . . 818-993-4448
FAX . . . . . . . . . . . . . . . . . . . . . . . . . . . . . . . . 818-993-5553
EMAIL . . . . . . . . . . . . . . . . . . . . . . . . . . . imagfac@aol.com
9340 Eton St.
Chatsworth, CA 91311-5879

| | |
|---|---|
| TYPE | Motion Pictures + Television + Animation + Feature Direct to Video + Interactive Multimedia |
| CREDITS | Bad Baby - Brute Force - TerraTopia - Jerry's Insane Fish |
| COMMENTS | Licensing. |

Stanford Blum . . . . . . . . . . . . . . . . . . . . . . . . . President/CEO
Peter Devoy . . . . . . . . . . . . . . . . . . . . . . . . . . Vice President

## IMAGINATION PRODUCTIONS INC.
PHONE . . . . . . . . . . . . . . . . . . . . . . . . . . . . . . 310-315-4760
3000 W. Olympic Blvd., Ste. 1400
Santa Monica, CA 90404

| | |
|---|---|
| TYPE | Motion Pictures + Television |
| DEAL | Showtime Networks Inc. |
| CREDITS | Natl. Lampoon's Favorite Deadly Sins- The Ratings Game - The Godfather's Analyst- Mastergate |

David Jablin . . . . . . . . . . . . . . . . . . . . Exec. Producer/Director
Cybele May . . . . . . . . . . . . . . . . . . . . . . . . Associate Producer

## IMAGINAZIUM
PHONE . . . . . . . . . . . . . . . . . . . . . . . . . . . . . . 818-995-0471
EMAIL . . . . . . . . . . . . . . . . . . . . . . . . . . imaginazm@aol.com
15718 Milbank St.
Encino, CA 91436

| | |
|---|---|
| TYPE | Television + Interactive Multimedia |
| CREDITS | What To Do When There's Nothing To Do - Imagics: Games That Stretch Your Imagination |
| COMMENTS | Educational entertainment for children - books & audio Also: imaginazium@choicemail.com |

Leah Kalish . . . . . . . . . . . . . . . . . . . . . . . . . Executive Producer
Diane Spahn . . . . . . . . . . . . . . . . . . . . . . . . Dir., Development

## IMAGINE ENTERTAINMENT
PHONE . . . . . . . . . . . . . . . . . . . . . . . . . . . . . . 310-277-1665
FAX . . . . . . . . . . . . . . . . . . . . . . . . . . . . . . . . 310-785-0107
1925 Century Park East, Ste. 2300
Los Angeles, CA 90067-2734

| | |
|---|---|
| TYPE | Motion Pictures |
| CREDITS | The Nutty Professor - Liar, Liar - From the Earth to the Moon |

Brian Grazer . . . . . . . . . . . . . . . . . . . . . . . . . . Co-Chairman
Ron Howard . . . . . . . . . . . . . . . . . . . . . . . . . . Co-Chairman
Karen Kehela . . . . . . . . . . . . . . . . . . Co-Chairman, Imagine Films
Michael Bostick . . . . . . . . . . . . . . . . . President, Imagine Films
Michael Rosenberg . . . . . . . . . . . . President, Imagine Entertainment
Robin Barris . . . . . . . . . . . . . . . . Sr. VP, Administration & Operations
Jan Geniesse . . . . . . . . . . . . . . . . . . . . . . . . VP, Motion Pictures
Julie Glucksman . . . . . . . . . . . . . . . . . . . . . . VP, Motion Pictures
Maureen Peyrot . . . . . . . . . . . . . . . . . . . . . . VP, Motion Pictures
Jim Whitaker . . . . . . . . . . . . . . . . . . . . . . . . VP, Motion Pictures
Sarah Bowen . . . . . . . . . . . . . . . . . . . Mgr., Creative Research
Suzy Gilstrap . . . . . . . . . . . . . . . . . . . . . . . . . Story Editor
David Bernardi . . . . . . . . . . . . . . . . . . . . . . . Creative Executive

# COMPANIES AND STAFF

**IMAGINE TELEVISION**
PHONE . . . . . . . . . . . . . . . . . . . . . . . . . . . . . . . . 310-277-1665
FAX . . . . . . . . . . . . . . . . . . . . . . . . . . . . . . . . . . . 310-785-0107
1925 Century Park East, 23rd Fl.
Los Angeles, CA 90067

| | |
|---|---|
| TYPE | Television |
| CREDITS | Felicity - The PJ's - Sports Night |

Brian Grazer . . . . . . . . . . . . . . . . . . . . . . . . . . . . . Co-Chairman
Ron Howard . . . . . . . . . . . . . . . . . . . . . . . . . . . . . . Co-Chairman
Tony Krantz . . . . . . . . . . . . . . . . . . . . . . . . . . Co-Chairman/CEO
Skip Chasey . . . . . . . . . . . . . . . . . . Sr. VP, Business Affairs
Nena Rodrigue . . . . . . . . . . . . . . . . . . . . . . Sr. Vice President
Sally DeSipio . . . . . . . . . . . . . . . . . . . . . . . . . . Vice President
Gayle Pillsbury . . . . . . . . . . . . . . . . . . . . . VP, Talent & Casting

**IMAX CORPORATION**
PHONE . . . . . . . . . . . . . . . . . . . . . . . . . . . . . . . . 310-571-1800
FAX . . . . . . . . . . . . . . . . . . . . . . . . . . . . . . . . . . . 310-571-1810
WEBSITE . . . . . . . . . . . . . . . . . . . . . . . . . http://www.imax.com
11454 San Vicente Blvd. 1st Floor
Los Angeles, CA 90049

| | |
|---|---|
| TYPE | Documentaries + Motion Pictures |
| CREDITS | The Dream Is Alive - Into The Deep - Rolling Stones at the Max |
| COMMENTS | Large Format Films. |

Andrew Gellis . . . . . . . . . . . . . . . . . . Sr. VP, Film/Distribution
Barry Kemper . . . . . . . . . . . . . . . . . VP, Attractions Development
Patrick Murray . . . . . . . . . . . . . . . . . . . VP, Film Operations
Wendi Mirabella . . . . . . . . . . . . . . . . Dir., Film Development

**IMMORTAL FILMS**
PHONE . . . . . . . . . . . . . . . . . . . . . . . . . . . . . . . . 310-582-8300
FAX . . . . . . . . . . . . . . . . . . . . . . . . . . . . . . . . . . . 310-582-8301
1650 21st Street
Santa Monica, CA 90404

| | |
|---|---|
| TYPE | Motion Pictures + Television + Interactive Multimedia |
| DEAL | Motion Pict. Corp. of America |
| CREDITS | The Last Party - MOB Story - Shiny New Enemies |
| COMMENTS | Also: Soundtracks |

Eric Cahan . . . . . . . . . . . . . . . . . . . . . . . . . . . . . . . . Partner
Happy Walters . . . . . . . . . . . . . . . . . . . . . . . . . . . . . Partner
Manish Raval . . . . . . . . . . . . . . . . . . . . . . Head, Soundtracks
Tom Wolfe . . . . . . . . . . . . . . . . . . . . . . . . Head, Soundtracks

**IMPERIAL ENTERTAINMENT**
PHONE . . . . . . . . . . . . . . . . . . . . . . . . . . . . . . . . 818-762-0005
FAX . . . . . . . . . . . . . . . . . . . . . . . . . . . . . . . . . . . 818-762-0006
11846 Ventura Blvd., 3rd Floor
Studio City, CA 91604

| | |
|---|---|
| TYPE | Motion Pictures + Television + Feature Direct to Video + Interactive Multimedia |
| CREDITS | Angel Town - Nemesis - Double Dragon - To The Ends of Time - Sabotage - Lionheart - Late Last Night - Boogie Boy |

Sunil R. Shah . . . . . . . . . . . . . . . . . . . . . . . . . . . . . President
Clem Gatmaitan . . . . . . . . . . . . . . . . . Chief Financial Officer
Sundip R. Shah . . . . . . . . . . . . . . . . . . . Exec. Vice President
Ash R. Shah . . . . . . . . . . . . . . . . . . . . . . Exec. VP, Production
Dolly M. Vergara . . . . . . . . . . . . . . . . . Dir., Business Affiars

**IN BLACK WORLD**
PHONE . . . . . . . . . . . . . . . . . . . . . . . . . . . . . . . . 213-878-5547
P.O. Box 93425
Los Angeles, CA 90093

| | |
|---|---|
| TYPE | Motion Pictures + Television |
| CREDITS | One Last Time- Circle of Pain- Some...Best Friends |
| COMMENTS | Also: Legitimate Theatre |

T'Keyah Crystal Keymah . . . . . . . . . . . . . . Producer/Actress
Lynora Miller . . . . . . . . . . . . . . . . . . . . . . . . . . . . Consultant

**INDICAN PRODUCTIONS**
PHONE . . . . . . . . . . . . . . . . . . . . . . . . . . . . . . . . 212-274-1880
FAX . . . . . . . . . . . . . . . . . . . . . . . . . . . . . . . . . . . 212-274-1869
588 Broadway, Ste. 1103
New York, NY 10012

| | |
|---|---|
| TYPE | Motion Pictures |
| DEAL | Twentieth Century Fox-Searchlight Picts. |
| CREDITS | Calling The Ghosts |
| COMMENTS | Formerly Ormond Productions |

Julia Ormond . . . . . . . . . . . . . . . . . . . . . President/Producer
Milton Justice . . . . . . . . . . . . . . . . . . . . . . . . . . . Producer
Lamia Guellati . . . . . . . . . . . . . . . . . Story Editor/Administrator
Jennifer Storey . . . . . . . . . . . . . . . . . . . . Executive Assistant

**INDIEGAL PRODUCTIONS, LLC**
PHONE . . . . . . . . . . . . . . . . . . . . 310-889-9024/914-657-7273
FAX . . . . . . . . . . . . . . . . . . . . . . . 310-889-9034/914-657-9625
EMAIL . . . . . . . . . . . . . . . . . . . . . . . . . pgtt40a@prodigy.com
11733 Montana Ave., Ste. 107
Los Angeles, CA 90049

| | |
|---|---|
| TYPE | Motion Pictures + Television + Interactive Multimedia |
| CREDITS | To Protect and Serve - The Iron Triangle - He's My Girl |
| COMMENTS | Also: 492 Ohayo Mountain Rd. Woodstock, NY 12498 |

Angela P. Schapiro . . . . . . . . . . . . . . . . . . . . . . . . Partner
Laura Keats . . . . . . . . . . . . . . . . . . . . . . . . . . . . . . . Partner
Gail Harris . . . . . . . . . . . . . . . . . . . . . . . . . . . . . . . . Partner
Deborah Zimmerly . . . . . . . . . . . . . . . . . . VP, Development

**INDUSTRY ENTERTAINMENT**
PHONE . . . . . . . . . . . . . . . . . . . . . . . . . . . . . . . . 213-954-9000
FAX . . . . . . . . . . . . . . . . . . . . . . . . . . . . . . . . . . . 213-954-9009
955 S. Carrillo Dr., 3rd Floor
Los Angeles, CA 90048

| | |
|---|---|
| TYPE | Motion Pictures + Television |
| DEAL | Sony Television/New Line Cinema |
| CREDITS | sex, lies & videotape - Drugstore Cowboy - The Player - Eve's Bayou |
| COMMENTS | Company formerly known as Addis-Wechsler & Associates. |

Keith Addis . . . . . . . . . . . . . . . . . . . . . . . . . . . . Co-Chairman
Nick Wechsler . . . . . . . . . . . . . . . . . . . . . . . . . Co-Chairman
Julie Yorn . . . . . . . . . . . . . . . . . . . . . . . . . . . . Co-President
Rick Yorn . . . . . . . . . . . . . . . . . . . . . . . . . . . . Co-President
Julia Chasman . . . . . . . . . . . . . . . . . . . Exec. VP, Production
David Carmel . . . . . . . . . . . . . . . . . . . . Production Executive
Marc Evans . . . . . . . . . . . . . . . . . . . . . . Production Executive
Amy Mason . . . . . . . . . . . . . Dir., Operations/Human Resources
Ryan Jaffe . . . . . . . . . . . . . . . . . . . . . . . . . . . . Story Editor

**INFRONT PRODUCTIONS**
PHONE . . . . . . . . . . . . . . . . . . . . . . . . . . . . . . . . 310-369-5890
FAX . . . . . . . . . . . . . . . . . . . . . . . . . . . . . . . . . . . 310-369-8356
10201 West Pico Blvd., Bldg. 3
Los Angeles, CA 90035

| | |
|---|---|
| TYPE | Television + Motion Pictures |
| DEAL | Twentieth Century Fox |
| CREDITS | Mad About You - Good Advice - Roseanne - The 3 Stooges - Two Guys, A Girl and a Pizza Place |

Danny Jacobson . . . . . . . . . . . . . . . . . . . . Writer/Producer
Marjorie Weitzman . . . . . . . . . . . . . . . . . . . . . . . Producer
Jennifer Hertrich . . . . . . . . . . . . . . . . . . . VP, Development

**INITIAL ENTERTAINMENT GROUP**
PHONE . . . . . . . . . . . . . . . . . . . . . . . . . . . . . . . . 213-658-5603
FAX . . . . . . . . . . . . . . . . . . . . . . . . . . . . . . . . . . . 213-658-5605
6380 Wilshire Blvd., Ste. 1600
Los Angeles, CA 90048

| | |
|---|---|
| TYPE | Motion Pictures + Television + Feature Direct to Video + Interactive Multimedia |
| CREDITS | Savior - Little City - Montana - The Florentine - Very Bad Things |

Cindy Cowan . . . . . . . . . . . . . . . Pres., Production & Acquisitions
Colin Cotter . . . . . . . . . . . . . . . . . . . Chief Financial Officer
Shelly Glasser . . . . . . . . . . . . . . Sr. VP, Production & Acquisitions
Carole McGorrian . . . . . . . . . . . . . . . . . . . . . . Dir., Production
Frank Salvino . . . . . . . . . . . . . . . . . . . . . . . . Dir., Production
Gary Wax . . . . . . . . . . . . . . . . . . Mgr., Production & Acquisitions
Margo Campillo . . . . . . . . . . . . . Asst., Production & Distribution

**INK TANK, THE**
PHONE . . . . . . . . . . . . . . . . . . . . . . . . . . . . . . . . 212-869-1630
FAX . . . . . . . . . . . . . . . . . . . . . . . . . . . . . . . . . . . 212-764-4169
EMAIL . . . . . . . . . . . . . . . . . . . . . . . . inktank@interport.net
2 West 47th Street
New York, NY 10036

| | |
|---|---|
| TYPE | Motion Pictures + Television + Animation |
| CREDITS | L'Histoire du Soldat (PBS) - Big Bag - Ka-Blam! |
| COMMENTS | Also: itank@aol.com |

R.O. Blechman . . . . . . . . . . . . . . . . . . . . . . Creative Director
Brian O'Connell . . . . . . . . . . . . . . . . . . . . Executive Producer

# COMPANIES AND STAFF

**INTERLAND ENTERTAINMENT**
PHONE . . . . . . . . . . . . . . . . . . . . . . . . . . . . 310-899-9416
FAX . . . . . . . . . . . . . . . . . . . . . . . . . . . . . 310-899-9516
EMAIL . . . . . . . . . . . . . . . . . . . . . jt5300c@earthlink.net
1017 Euclid Street, Ste. 2
Santa Monica, CA 90403

TYPE          Motion Pictures + Television

James Terry Hayes . . . . . . . . . . . . . . . . . . . . . . Executive Producer
Katherine Vallin . . . . . . . . . . . . . . . . Co-Exec. Prod./Dir., Intl. Develop.

**INTERNATIONAL FILMMAKERS MANAGEMENT, INC**
PHONE . . . . . . . . . . . . . . . . . . . . . . . . . . . . 310-451-7486
FAX . . . . . . . . . . . . . . . . . . . . . . . . . . . . . 310-451-7463
520 Broadway, Ste. 600
Santa Monica, CA 90401

TYPE          Motion Pictures + Television + Documentaries
CREDITS       Whispers In The Dark - Big Showdown In Little Tokyo -
              Pentathalon

Martin Caan . . . . . . . . . . . . . . . . . . . . . . . . . . . . . Producer
Todd Sharp . . . . . . . . . . . . . . . . . . . . . . . . . . . . Associate

**INTERSCOPE COMMUNICATIONS INC.**
PHONE . . . . . . . . . . . . . . . . . . . . . . . . . . . . 310-208-8525
FAX . . . . . . . . . . . . . . . . . . . . . . . . . . . . . 310-208-1764
EMAIL . . . . . . . . . . . . . . . . . . . . . . intercomm1@aol.com
10900 Wilshire Blvd., Ste. 1400
Los Angeles, CA 90024

TYPE          Motion Pictures
DEAL          PolyGram Filmed Ent.
CREDITS       Jumanji - Mr. Holland's Opus - What Dreams May Come
Ted W. Field . . . . . . . . . . . . . . . . . . . . . . . . . . . Chairman/CEO
Michael Helfant . . . . . . . . . . . Exec. VP/Head, Operations & Acquisitions
Scott Kroopf . . . . . . . . . . . . . . . . Exec. VP/ Head, Production
Richard Lewis . . . . . . . . . . . . . . . . . . . . . . . . . . . . VP/CFO
Jonathan Bader . . . . . . . . . . . . . . . Sr. VP, Business & Legal Affairs
Andrew Gumpert . . . . . . . . . . . . . . . . VP, Business & Legal Affairs
Margaret Mitchell . . . . . . . . . . . . . . . . . VP, Production Finance
Michelle Wright . . . . . . . . . . . . . . . . . VP, Physical Production
Tom Engelman . . . . . . . . . . . . . . . . . . . Production Executive
Erica Huggins . . . . . . . . . . . . . . . . . . . Production Executive
Gary S. Goodman . . . . . . . . . . . . . . . . . . Creative Director
Kaye Popofsky . . . . . . . . . . . . . . . . . . . Creative Director
Kym Wulfe . . . . . . . . . . . . . . . . . Dir., Business & Legal Affairs

**INTL. HOME ENTERTAINMENT**
PHONE . . . . . . . . . . . . . . . . . . . . . . . . . . . . 213-460-4545
FAX . . . . . . . . . . . . . . . . . . . . . . . . . . . . . 213-663-2820
1440 Veteran Ave., Ste. 650
Los Angeles, CA 90024

TYPE          Motion Pictures + Television
CREDITS       Stars of Sports! - Soap Stars Confidental - Soap Opera
              Hall of Fame
Robert Levinson . . . . . . . . . . . . . . . . . . . . . . . . . . President
Sandra S. Levinson . . . . . . . . . . . . . . . . . . . . VP, Production
Jed Leland Jr. . . . . . . . . . . . . . . . . . . . . . Asst. to President

**INTREPIDUS**
PHONE . . . . . . . . . . . . . . . . . . . . . . . . . . . . 310-315-4805
FAX . . . . . . . . . . . . . . . . . . . . . . . . . . . . . 310-315-4806
EMAIL . . . . . . . . . . . . . . . . . . . . . . info@intrepidus.com
WEBSITE . . . . . . . . . . . . . . . . . http://www.intrepidus.com
3000 W. Olympic Blvd., Bldg. 4
Santa Monica, CA 90404-5041

TYPE          Motion Pictures + Television + Documentaries +
              Interactive Multimedia
George Woods Baker . . . . . . . . . . . . . . . . . . CEO/Executive Producer
Charles Salmon . . . . . . . . . . . . . . . . . . . . . Producer (UK)
Kristine K. Pike . . . . . . . . . . . . . . . . . . . Creative Associate
Christina L. Sims . . . . . . . . . . . . . . . . . . . . . Coordinator

**ISAAC PRODUCTIONS, SANDY**
PHONE . . . . . . . . . . . . . . . . . . . . . . . . . . . . 310-369-3528
FAX . . . . . . . . . . . . . . . . . . . . . . . . . . . . . 310-369-5688
Twentieth Century Fox
10201 W. Pico Blvd., Bldg. 6, Room 201
Los Angeles, CA 90035

TYPE          Motion Pictures + Television
DEAL          Twentieth Century Fox-Fox 2000 (LA)
CREDITS       To Die For - Hero
Sandy Isaac . . . . . . . . . . . . . . . . . . . . . . . . . . . . Producer
David J. Zelman . . . . . . . . . . . . . Dir., Development (310-369-5613)

**ISLAND-IN-THE-SKY PICTURES**
PHONE . . . . . . . . . . . . . . . . . . . . . . . . . . . . 310-276-5000
FAX . . . . . . . . . . . . . . . . . . . . . . . . . . . . . 310-659-8895
8831 Sunset Blvd., Ste. 203
Los Angeles, CA 90069

TYPE          Motion Pictures
COMMENTS      Production End of World Markets Network, Inc. (Literary
              Rights Managements).
Jerome Lapara . . . . . . . . . . . . . . . . . . . . . . . . . . . President
Martin Ondrus . . . . . . . . . . . . . . . . . . . . . . Vice President
Richard Clar . . . . . . . . . . . . . . . . . . . . . . Business Affairs

**ITASCA PICTURES, INC.**
PHONE . . . . . . . . . . . . . . . . . . . . . . . . . . . . 310-273-6505
FAX . . . . . . . . . . . . . . . . . . . . . . . . . . . . . 310-273-1475
345 N. Maple Dr., Ste. 278
Beverly Hills, CA 90210

TYPE          Motion Pictures + Television
CREDITS       At Sachem Farm - Powder - Blind Fury
Daniel L. Grodnik . . . . . . . . . . . . . . . . . . . . Producer/CEO
Robert Snukal . . . . . . . . . . . . . . . . . . . . Producer/Chairman
Kandice Stroh . . . . . . . . . . . . . . . . . . . . Dir., Development

**ITB CINEGROUP/TELEVISION**
PHONE . . . . . . . . . . . . . . . . . . . . . . . . . . . . 213-254-9414
FAX . . . . . . . . . . . . . . . . . . . . . . . . . . . . . 213-951-1283
EMAIL . . . . . . . . . . . . . . . . . . . . . . . quixotic@att.net
816 Idaho Ave.
Santa Monica, CA 90403

TYPE          Motion Pictures + Television
CREDITS       Criminal Act - Deception - Cyber Challenge - The Comedy
              Hour
Frank Antonelli . . . . . . . . . . . . . . . . . . . . . . Writer/Producer
Mark Byers . . . . . . . . . . . . . . . . . . Director/Producer/Writer
Jeffrey Berman . . . . . . . . . . . . . . . . . . . . . Writer/Producer
Michael Ciccolini . . . . . . . . . . . . . . . . . . . . . . . . Writer
Heather Ashley . . . . . . . . . . . . . . . . . . . . . . Development

***IWERKS ENTERTAINMENT**
PHONE . . . . . . . . . . . . . . . . . . . . . . . . . . . . 818-841-7766
FAX . . . . . . . . . . . . . . . . . . . . . . . . . . . . . 818-840-7462
4540 Valerio
Burbank, CA 91505

TYPE          Animation + Documentaries + Motion Pictures
CREDITS       Dino Island - Super Speedway - Superstition
COMMENTS      360 degrees, 15-70, 8-70 Large Format.
Don Iwerks . . . . . . . . . . . . . . . . . . . . . . . . . . Founder/CTO
Jon Corfino . . . . . . . . . . . . . . . . . . . . . . . . VP, Attractions
Mix Ryan . . . . . . . . . . . . . . . . . . . . . . VP, Film Production
Douglas Yellin . . . . . . . . . . . . . . . . . . . Production Supervisor
Scott Shepley . . . . . . . . . . . . . . . . . . Film Technical Director
Greg Meador . . . . . . . . . . . . . . . . . . Post-Production Coordinator
Paul Piepeir . . . . . . . . . . . . . . . . . Editor, Motion Programmer
Trish Mauris . . . . . . . . . . . . . . . . . . . Production Coordinator
Blane Betts . . . . . . . . . . . . . . . . . . . . . Motion Programmer
Leslie Wilcox . . . . . . . . . . . . . . . . . . Administrative Assistant

**IXL**
PHONE . . . . . . . . . . . . . . . . . . . . . . . . . . . . 310-235-3900
FAX . . . . . . . . . . . . . . . . . . . . . . . . . . . . . 310-235-3999
EMAIL . . . . . . . . . . . . . . . . . . . . . . . . . info@ixl.com
WEBSITE . . . . . . . . . . . . . . . . . . . . http://www.ixl.com
10960 Wilshire Blvd., Ste. 1550
Los Angeles, CA 90024

TYPE          Television + Interactive Multimedia
CREDITS       Planet Hollywood - Billboard Music Awards - Extreme
              Magic
COMMENTS      Also: Web Development, Web Maintenance, Web Hosting
              Video Chat Software, Cyberchat Production.
Kevin Wall . . . . . . . . . . . . . . . . . . . . . . Chief Executive Officer
Lisa Janzen . . . . . . . . . . . . . . . . . . . . . . General Manager

**JACOBS PRODS., MICHAEL**
PHONE . . . . . . . . . . . . . . . . . . . . . . . . . . . . 818-560-6290
FAX . . . . . . . . . . . . . . . . . . . . . . . . . . . . . 818-567-0415
500 S. Buena Vista St., Anim. 2A
Burbank, CA 91521-1701

TYPE          Motion Pictures + Television
DEAL          Walt Disney Company, The
CREDITS       Quiz Show - Boy Meets World - Dinosaurs - The
              Torkelsons - Zoe Bean
Michael Jacobs . . . . . . . . . . . . . . . . . . . . . . Executive Producer
Jeff McCracken . . . . . . . . . . . . . . . . . . . . . . . . . President
Ann Johnson . . . . . . . . . . . . . . . . . . . . . . VP, Development

# COMPANIES AND STAFF

## JACOBS/MUTRUX PRODS.

| | |
|---|---|
| PHONE | 310-369-3181 |
| FAX | 310-369-8538 |

Twentieth Century Fox
10201 W. Pico Blvd., Bldg 667
Los Angeles, CA 90035

| | |
|---|---|
| TYPE | Motion Pictures |
| DEAL | Twentieth Century Fox-Fox 2000 (LA) |
| CREDITS | Getting Even with Dad - Donnie Brasco - Quiz Show - A Cool, Dry Place |

Katie Jacobs . . . . . . . . . . . . . . . . . . . . . . . . . . . Producer
Gail Mutrux . . . . . . . . . . . . . . . . . . . . . . . . . . . Producer
Ned Gusick . . . . . . . . . . . . . . . . . . . . . . . . VP, Production
Valerie Dean . . . . . . . . . . . . . . . . . . . . Creative Executive
Marianne Gray . . . . . . . . . . . . . . . . . . . Production Executive
Julie Carideo . . . . . . . . . . . . . . . . . . . Asst. to Katie Jacobs

## JACOBSON COMPANY, THE

| | |
|---|---|
| PHONE | 818-560-1600 |
| FAX | 818-567-4010 |

Walt Disney Studios
500 S. Buena Vista, Animation 2C-7
Burbank, CA 91521-1733

| | |
|---|---|
| TYPE | Motion Pictures |
| DEAL | Walt Disney Company, The |
| CREDITS | Mighty Joe Young |

Tom Jacobson . . . . . . . . . . . . . . . . . . . . . . . . . . . Producer
Jim Wedaa . . . . . . . . . . . . . Exec. Vice President (818-560-6653)
Eric Newman . . . . . . . . . . . VP, Creative Affairs (818-560-1625)
Tom Hoffman . . . . . . . . . . . Dir., Creative Affairs (818-560-1669)
Scott Benton . . . . . . . . . . . . . . . . . . . . . . Executive Assistant
Rebecca Garrett . . . . . . . . . . . . . . . . . . . . Executive Assistant
Rachel Kaiser . . . . . . . . . . . . . . . . . . . . . Executive Assistant

## JAFFE/BRAUNSTEIN FILMS LTD.

| | |
|---|---|
| PHONE | 213-464-4100 |
| FAX | 213-878-0871 |

7920 Sunset Blvd., Ste. 444
Los Angeles, CA 90046

| | |
|---|---|
| TYPE | Television |
| CREDITS | No Further Questions (USA) - Mind Prey (ABC) - My Father's Shadow (CBS) |

Michael Jaffe . . . . . . . . . . . . . . . . . . . . . . . . . . . Partner
Howard Braunstein . . . . . . . . . . . . . . . . . . . . . . . Partner
Barbara Carswell . . . . . . . . . . . . . . . . . . . Business Manager
Amy Berkenbile . . . . . . . . . . . . . . Asst. to Howard Braunstein
Lynn Delaney . . . . . . . . . . . . . . . . . . . . . Asst. to Mr. Jaffe

## JAFFILMS

| | |
|---|---|
| PHONE | 310-244-4700/212-262-4700 |
| FAX | 310-244-8448/212-262-4729 |

10202 W. Washington Blvd., Lean 119
Culver City, CA 90232

| | |
|---|---|
| TYPE | Motion Pictures |
| DEAL | Sony Pictures Entertainment |
| CREDITS | Madeline - Taps - Kramer Vs. Kramer - Fatal Attraction |
| COMMENTS | Also: 152 W. 57th St., 52nd Floor NY, 10019 |

Stanley R. Jaffe . . . . . . . . . . . . . . . . . . . . . . . . . . Producer
Bob Jaffe . . . . . . . . . . . . . . . . . . . . . . . . . . . . . Producer
Allyn Stewart . . . . . . . . . . . . . . . . . . . . . . . . . . . Producer
Wendy Silbert . . . . . . . . . . . . . . . . Production Executive (NY)
Kimberley Guidone . . . . . . . . . . . . . . . . . . . Story Editor (NY)
Maggie Constantinidis . . . . . . . . . . . Asst. to Stanley Jaffe (NY)
Lucinda Gould . . . . . . . . . . . . . . . . . Asst. to Allyn Stewart
Michelle Mikolajczak . . . . . . . . . . . . . . . . . Asst. to Bob Jaffe

## JAKE FILMS

| | |
|---|---|
| PHONE | 818-760-6601 |
| FAX | 818-760-6616 |
| EMAIL | JAKE306@aol.com |

5130 Bellair Avenue
North Hollywood, CA 91607

| | |
|---|---|
| TYPE | Motion Pictures |

Robert Fields . . . . . . . . . . . . . . . . . . . . . . . . . . . Producer
B.J. Robbins . . . . . . . . . . . . . . . . . . . . . . . . . . . Producer
Jeff Singer . . . . . . . . . . . . . . . . . . . . . . . . Head, Development

## JASON COMPANY, MELINDA

| | |
|---|---|
| PHONE | 310-472-8309 |
| FAX | 310-471-5106 |
| EMAIL | elfbrain@aol.com |

216 S. Carmelina Ave.
Los Angeles, CA 90049

| | |
|---|---|
| TYPE | Motion Pictures + Television |
| CREDITS | The First Power - Eve of Destruction - Body of Evidence - Killer |

Melinda Jason . . . . . . . . . . . . . . . . . . . President/Producer
Minh Dang . . . . . . . . . . . . . . . . . . . . . . . . . . . Assistant

## JAYGEE PRODUCTIONS INC.

| | |
|---|---|
| PHONE | 213-658-7224 |
| FAX | 213-658-7228 |

8222 Melrose Ave. #301
Los Angeles, CA 90046

| | |
|---|---|
| TYPE | Television |
| CREDITS | Green Acres (MOW) - Perfect Score - Tales From the Darkside |
| COMMENTS | Network, Syndication and Cable. |

Jerry Golod . . . . . . . . . . . . . . . . . . . . . . . . . . . President
Carol Stanley . . . . . . . . . . . . . . . . . Exec. VP, Production

## JAZZ PICTURES, INC.

| | |
|---|---|
| PHONE | 310-888-2412 |
| FAX | 310-888-2454 |

202 N. Beverly Dr.
Beverly Hills, CA 90210-5303

| | |
|---|---|
| TYPE | Motion Pictures |
| CREDITS | Bad Company - Little Boy Blue - Claudine's Return |

Amedeo A. Ursini . . . . . . . . . . . . . . . . . President/Producer

## JCS ENTERTAINMENT INC.

| | |
|---|---|
| PHONE | 310-575-1262/404-815-8889 |
| FAX | 310-478-2202/404-815-8890 |
| EMAIL | jcsent@earthlink.com (LA) |

Hearst Entertainment
1640 S. Sepulveda Blvd., 4th Floor
Los Angeles, CA 90025-7510

| | |
|---|---|
| TYPE | Television + Motion Pictures + Syndication |
| DEAL | Hearst Entertainment |
| CREDITS | Stay the Night - Something Borrowed/Blue - America's Greatest Pets: Amazing But True - Robert Ripley: BION |
| COMMENTS | Also: 576 Armour Circle, Atlanta, GA 30324 |

J C Shardo . . . . . . . . . . . . . . . . . . Exec. Producer/President
Victoria Grove . . . . . . . . . . . . . . . . . Mgr., Development (LA)
Lisa Ferrell . . . . . . . . . . . . . . . . Creative Assistant (Atlanta)

## JD PRODUCTIONS

| | |
|---|---|
| PHONE | 310-244-7590 |
| FAX | 310-244-2060 |
| EMAIL | Jdprod@aol.com |

Columbia Pictures
10202 W. Washington Blvd., Poitier 3206
Culver City, CA 90232

| | |
|---|---|
| TYPE | Motion Pictures + Television |
| DEAL | Columbia Pictures |
| CREDITS | Natural Born Killers - Apt Pupil - Permanent Midnight |

Jane Hamsher . . . . . . . . . . . . . . . . . . . . . . . . . . Producer
Don Murphy . . . . . . . . . . . . . . . . . . . . . . . . . . . Producer
Richard Benattar . . . . . . . . . . . . . . . . . . . Creative Executive

## *JERICHO ENTERTAINMENT

| | |
|---|---|
| PHONE | 310-282-6924 |
| FAX | 310-556-3760 |
| EMAIL | TheJoshs@aol.com |

Davis Entertainment
2121 Ave. of the Stars, Ste. 2900
Los Angeles, CA 90067

| | |
|---|---|
| TYPE | Motion Pictures + Television + Feature Direct to Video |
| DEAL | Davis Entertainment Co. |
| COMMENTS | Also: Literary and Talent Management |

Joshua Silver . . . . . . . . . . . . . . . . . . . . . . . . . . . Partner
Josh Kesselman . . . . . . . . . . . . . . . . . . . . . . . . . . Partner
Christopher M. Mills . . . . . . . . . . . . . . . . . Dir., Development

# COMPANIES AND STAFF

**JERSEY FILMS**
PHONE . . . . . . . . . . . . . . . . . . . . . . . . . . . . . . . 310-203-1000
FAX . . . . . . . . . . . . . . . . . . . . . . . . . . . . . . . . . 310-203-1010
10351 Santa Monica Blvd., Ste. 200
Los Angeles, CA 90025

| | |
|---|---|
| TYPE | Motion Pictures |
| DEAL | Universal Pictures |
| CREDITS | Reality Bites - Pulp Fiction - Get Shorty - Hoffa - 8 Seconds - Feeling Minnesota - Sunset Park - Matilda - Gattaca |

Danny DeVito . . . . . . . . . . . . . . . . . . . . . . . . . . . . Co-Chairman
Michael Shamberg . . . . . . . . . . . . . . . . . . . . . . . . Co-Chairman
Stacey Sher . . . . . . . . . . . . . . . . . . . . . . . . . . . . . Co-Chairman
Gail Lyon . . . . . . . . . . . . . . . . . . . . . . . . Exec. VP, Production
Pamela Abdy . . . . . . . . . . . . . . . . . . . . . . . . . . VP, Production
Grace Evans . . . . . . . . . . . . . . . . . . . VP, Operations/Controller
Josh Levinson . . . . . . . . . . . . . . . . . . . . VP, Physical Production
Carla Santos Shamberg . . . . . . . . . . . . . . . VP, Special Projects
Jennifer Kuczaj . . . . . . . . . . . . . . . . . . . . . . . . . . Story Editor
Lisa Cisneroz . . . . . . . . . . . . . . . . . . . Exec. Asst. to Mr. DeVito
Jud Hudgins . . . . . . . . . . . . . . . . . . . Exec. Asst. to Mr. Shamberg
Julian Andraus . . . . . . . . . . . . . . . . . . . . . Asst. to Mr. DeVito
Katie Felton . . . . . . . . . . . . . . . . . . . . . . . Asst. to Ms. Lyon
Rich Jones . . . . . . . . . . . . . . . . . . . . . . . . Asst. to Mr. DeVito
Lisa Kearns . . . . . . . . . . . . . . . . . . . . . . Asst. to Mrs. Evans
Tracey Mayer . . . . . . . . . . . . . . . . . . . . Asst. to Mr. Shamberg
Amy Palmer . . . . . . . . . . . . . . . . . . . . . . . . Asst. to Ms. Sher
Beverly Griffith . . . . . . . . . . . . . . . . . . . . . . Office Manager
Laurie Record . . . . . . . . . . . . . . . . . . . . . . . Office Assistant

***JERSEY SHORE**
PHONE . . . . . . . . . . . . . . . . . . . . . . . . . . . . . . . 212-333-3377
FAX . . . . . . . . . . . . . . . . . . . . . . . . . . . . . . . . . 212-333-3346
130 West 57th Street, Ste. 11B
New York, NY 10019

Jonathan Weisgal . . . . . . . . . . . . . . . . . . . . . . . . President
Kevin Kennedy . . . . . . . . . . . . . . . . . . . . . Creative Executive
Drew Filus . . . . . . . . . . . . . . . . . . . . . . Asst. to Mr. Weisgal
Regina Gilgan . . . . . . . . . . . . . . . . . . . . . . . . Receptionist

***JINKS/COHEN COMPANY, THE**
PHONE . . . . . . . . . . . . . . . . . . . . . . . . . . . . . . . 213-650-6447
FAX . . . . . . . . . . . . . . . . . . . . . . . . . . . . . . . . . 213-650-4567
EMAIL . . . . . . . . . . . . . . . . . . . . . . . . . . bruciec@aol.com
8292 Hollywood Blvd.
Los Angeles, CA 90069

| | |
|---|---|
| TYPE | Motion Pictures |
| CREDITS | Mouse Hunt - Nothing to Lose - The Flintstones |

Dan Jinks . . . . . . . . . . . . . . . . . . . . . . . . . . . . . Producer
Bruce Cohen . . . . . . . . . . . . . . . . . . . . . . . . . . . . Producer

**JLT PRODUCTIONS**
PHONE . . . . . . . . . . . . . . . . . . . . . . . . . . . . . . . 213-852-1215
FAX . . . . . . . . . . . . . . . . . . . . . . . . . . . . . . . . . 213-852-1217
8489 W. 3rd St., Ste. 1046
Los Angeles, CA 90048

| | |
|---|---|
| TYPE | Motion Pictures |
| CREDITS | Free Willy I, II , III - Lethal Weapon I, II, III - Star Kid - Scrooged |

Jennie Lew Tugend . . . . . . . . . . . . . . . . . . . . . . . Producer
Jennifer Gero . . . . . . . . . . . . . . . . . . Asst. to Ms. Lew Tugend

**JOHNSON ENTERTAINMENT, MAGIC**
PHONE . . . . . . . . . . . . . . . . . . . . . . . . . . . . . . . 310-369-1000
FAX . . . . . . . . . . . . . . . . . . . . . . . . . . . . . . . . . 310-369-7394
2121 Ave. of the Stars, Ste. 860
Los Angeles, CA 90067

| | |
|---|---|
| TYPE | Motion Pictures + Television |
| DEAL | Twentieth Century Fox |

Magic Johnson . . . . . . . . . . . . . . . . . Producer (310-369-0770)
Lon Rosen . . . . . . . . . . . . . . . . . . . . Producer (310-369-1481)
Tamara Gregory . . . . . . . . . . . . Sr. VP, MP Production (310-369-1579)
Charles Murray . . . . . . . . . . . . Creative Executive, MP (310-369-1523)
Michael Leslie DeJan . . . . . . . . . . . . . . . Development Mgr., TV
Kyona Beatty . . . . . . . . . . . . . . . . Asst. to Magic Johnson (310-369-0770)

**JOHNSON PRODS., DON**
PHONE . . . . . . . . . . . . . . . . . . . . . . . . . . . . . . . 818-238-2200
WEBSITE . . . . . . . . . . . . . . . . . . . . . . http://www.thenetshow.com
3400 Riverside Dr. #100
Burbank, CA 91505

| | |
|---|---|
| TYPE | Motion Pictures + Television |
| DEAL | Rysher Entertainment |
| CREDITS | In the Co. of Darkness - The Horatio Alger Awards - The Marshall - Nash Bridges |

Don Johnson . . . . . . . . . . . . . . . . . CEO/Executive Producer
Marc Granirer . . . . . . . . . . . . . . . . . COO/Exec., Production
David Buelow . . . . . . . . . . . . . . . . . Exec. VP, Creative Affairs

**JOHNSON PRODUCTIONS, MARK**
PHONE . . . . . . . . . . . . . . . . . . . . . . . . . . . . . . . 818-733-9872
FAX . . . . . . . . . . . . . . . . . . . . . . 818-733-9870/818-733-9606
DreamWorks
100 Universal City Plaza, Bldg. 10
Universal City, CA 91608

| | |
|---|---|
| TYPE | Motion Pictures |
| DEAL | DreamWorks SKG |
| CREDITS | Donnie Brasco - A Little Princess - A Perfect World - Bugsy - Rain Man |

Mark Johnson . . . . . . . . . . . . . . . . . . . . . . . . . . . Producer
Elizabeth Cantillon . . . . . . . . . . . . . . . . . . . . . . . President
Tiffany Daniel . . . . . . . . . . . . . . . . . . . . . . . . VP, Production
Hogan Sheffer . . . . . . . . . . . . Creative Executive (Fax: 818-733-9606)
Aditya Sood . . . . . . . . . . . . . . . . Story Editor (Fax: 818-733-9606)
Cheryl Donaldson . . . . . . . . . . . . . . Executive Asst. to Mr. Johnson
Leah Tarpy . . . . . . . . . . . . . . . . . . Asst. to Elizabeth Cantillon

**JONES ENTERTAINMENT GROUP**
PHONE . . . . . . . . . . . . . . . . . . . . . . . . . . . . . . . 303-784-8250
FAX . . . . . . . . . . . . . . . . . . . . . . . . . . . . . . . . . 303-790-9021
9697 East Mineral Ave.
Englewood, CO 80112

| | |
|---|---|
| TYPE | Motion Pictures + Television + Documentaries + Interactive Multimedia |
| DEAL | A & E Television Networks |
| CREDITS | Household Saints - The Secret of Roan Inish - Charlton Hestons's Bible |

Glenn R. Jones . . . . . . . . . . . . . . . . . . . . . . . . . President
David K. Zonker . . . . . . . . . . . . . . . . . Group Managing Dir.
Joyce McDaniel . . . . . . . . . . . . . . . . . Operations Specialist

**JOYFUL NOISE UNLIMITED, A**
PHONE . . . . . . . . . . . . . . . . . . . . . . . . . . . . . . . 310-859-4327
William Morris Agency
151 El Camino Dr.
Beverly Hills, CA 90212

| | |
|---|---|
| TYPE | Motion Pictures + Television |
| CREDITS | LBJ: The Early Years - Almost Golden: The Jessica Savitch Story - The Image |

Peter H. Werner . . . . . . . . . . . . . . . . . . . . . . . . . President

**JPH PRODUCTIONS**
PHONE . . . . . . . . . . . . . . . . . . . . . . . . . . . . . . . 213-874-7254
3469 Wonder View Place
Los Angeles, CA 90068

| | |
|---|---|
| TYPE | Motion Pictures + Television |
| CREDITS | Truth or Consequences, N.M. - Legalese |

J. Paul Higgins . . . . . . . . . . . . . . . . . . . . . . . . . . Producer

**JUMBO PICTURES, INC.**
PHONE . . . . . . . . . . . . . . . . . . . . . . . . . . . . . . . 212-337-0077
FAX . . . . . . . . . . . . . . . . . . . . . . . . . . . . . . . . . 212-337-0437
WEBSITE . . . . http://www.disney.com/DisneyT/One_Saturday_M/doug/index.html
161 Ave. of the Americas, 15th Fl.
New York, NY 10013

| | |
|---|---|
| TYPE | Television + Animation |
| CREDITS | Disney's Doug, The Movie - PB&J Otter - 101 Dalmations, the Series - Allegra's Window |
| COMMENTS | Subsidiary of Disney Also:  Animation & Live Action. |

Jim Jinkins . . . . . . . . . . . . . . . . . . . . . . . . Creator/President
David Campbell . . . . . . . . . . . . . . . . . . . Exec. VP/Producer
Bill Gross . . . . . . . . . . . . . . . . . . . Sr. VP/General Manager
Ellie Copeland . . . . . . . . . . . . . . . . . . . . . . . . VP, Finance
Beldeen Fortunato . . . . . . . . . . . . . . . . . . VP, Administration
Martha Ripp . . . . . . . . . . . . . . . . . . . . . . . . VP, Live Action
Jack Spillum . . . . . . . . . . . . . . . . . . . . . . . . VP, Animation
Melanie Grisanti . . . . . . . . . . . . . . . . . . . Producer, Animation

**JUNCTION ENTERTAINMENT**
PHONE . . . . . . . . . . . . . . . . . . . . . . . . . . . 818-560-2800
FAX . . . . . . . . . . . . . . . . . . . . . . . . . . . . . 818-560-2828
500 S. Buena Vista St., Animation 1-B
Burbank, CA 91521-1616
TYPE          Motion Pictures
DEAL          Walt Disney Company, The
Jon Turteltaub . . . . . . . . . . . . . . . . . No Title (818-560-2070)
Christina Steinberg . . . . . . . . . . . . . . No Title (818-560-6020)
Mary Mooney . . . . . . . . . . . . . . . . . . No Title (818-560-3670)
Nikki Reed . . . . . . . . . . . . . . . . . . . . . . . . . . . . No Title
Chris Skinner . . . . . . . . . . . . . . . . . . . . . . . . . . . No Title

**JURIST PRODUCTIONS**
PHONE . . . . . . . . . . . . . . . . . . . . . . . . . . . 212-627-4660
FAX . . . . . . . . . . . . . . . . . . . . . . . . . . . . . 212-242-9056
215 W. 20th St.
New York, NY 10011
TYPE          Motion Pictures + Television + Documentaries
CREDITS       Without Warning: Terror In The Towers
Madelon Rosenfeld . . . . . . . . . . . . . . . . . Producer/President
Ira Block . . . . . . . . . . . . . . . . . . . . . . . . . . Vice President

**JUST BETZER FILMS INC.**
PHONE . . . . . . . . . . . . . . . . . . . . . . . . . . . 760-772-5544
FAX . . . . . . . . . . . . . . . . . . . . . . . . . . . . . 760-772-5773
76954 Tomahawk Run
Indian Wells, CA 92210
TYPE          Motion Pictures + Television + Syndication
CREDITS       Babette's Feast - The Girl in a Swing - A Day in October
Just Betzer . . . . . . . . . . . . . . . . . . . . . . . President/CEO

**KAHN POWER PICTURES(FORMERLY ODESSA PIC)**
PHONE . . . . . . . . . . . . . . . . . . . . . . . . . . . 310-967-6566
FAX . . . . . . . . . . . . . . . . . . . . . . . . . . . . . 310-289-8313
EMAIL . . . . . . . . . . . . . . . . . . . . . . . . . iampower@gte.net
New Line Television
116 N. Robertson, Ste. 710
Los Angeles, CA 90048
TYPE          Television + Motion Pictures
DEAL          New Line Television
CREDITS       Stalin - Fatherland - Roswell - White Mile - Gia - Buffalo
              Soldiers
Ilene Kahn Power . . . . . . . . . . . . . . . . . President/Producer
Derek Power . . . . . . . . . . . . . . . . . . . . . . . . . . . Partner
Heather Sullivan . . . . . . . . . . . . . . . . . . Creative Executive

**KAHN PRODUCTIONS, RONALD J.**
PHONE . . . . . . . . . . . . . . . . . . . . . . . . . . . 516-466-8394
FAX . . . . . . . . . . . . . . . . . . . . . . . . . . . . . 516-466-8349
87 Old Mill Road
Great Neck, NY 11023
TYPE          Motion Pictures + Television
CREDITS       The Prodigious Hickey - American Playhouse - A Child's
              Cry For Help (NBC)
Ronald J. Kahn . . . . . . . . . . . . . . . . . . . . . . . . Producer
Jan Jaffe Kahn . . . . . . . . . . . . . . . . . . . . . . . . . . Writer

**KAPLAN, MARTY**
PHONE . . . . . . . . . . . . . . . . . . . . . . . . . . . 213-740-9945
FAX . . . . . . . . . . . . . . . . . . . . . . . . . . . . . 213-740-3772
EMAIL . . . . . . . . . . . . . . . . . . . . . . . mkaplan@aol.com
3502 Watt Way
Los Angeles, CA 90089-0281
TYPE          Motion Pictures
CREDITS       Noises Off - The Distinguished Gentelman
Marty Kaplan . . . . . . . . . . . . . . . . . . . . . . . . . President

**KARDANA FILMS, INC.**
PHONE . . . . . . . . . . . . . . . . . . . . . . . . . . . 212-255-9680
FAX . . . . . . . . . . . . . . . . . . . . . . . . . . . . . 212-255-9648
285 Hudson St., 2nd Floor
New York, NY 10013
TYPE          Motion Pictures
CREDITS       Office Killer - Drunks - Kiss Me Guido - Safe - Arresting
              Gena - The Blood Oranges
Tom Carouso . . . . . . . . . . . . . . . . . . . . . . . . . Producer
Barry Schindel . . . . . . . . . . . . . . . . . . . . Producer/Writer
Noah Baylin . . . . . . . . . . . . . . . . . . . Dir., Creative Affairs
Mark Almadrones . . . . . . . . . . . . . . . . . . Creative Executive

**KAREEM PRODUCTIONS**
PHONE . . . . . . . . . . . . . . . . . . . . . . . . . . . 310-201-7960
EMAIL . . . . . . . . . . . . . . . . . . . . . . . GRAFFIOS@aol.com
2049 Century Park East, #1200
Los Angeles, CA 90067
TYPE          Motion Pictures + Television
COMMENTS   Theatrical Agent: Mike Eisenstadt 213-939-1188
Kareem Abdul-Jabbar . . . . . . . . . . . . . . . . . . . . . President

**KARZ ENTERTAINMENT**
PHONE . . . . . . . . . . . . . . . . . . . . . . . . . . . 818-560-4260
FAX . . . . . . . . . . . . . . . . . . . . . . . . . . . . . 818-567-1634
500 S. Buena Vista, 1E12 Animation Bldg
Burbank, CA 91521
TYPE          Motion Pictures + Television
DEAL          Walt Disney TV/Touchstone TV
CREDITS       My Date with the President's Daughter
Mike Karz . . . . . . . . . . . . . . . . . . . . . . . . . . . Producer
Russell Hollander . . . . . . . . . . . Creative Executive (818-560-5555)

**KASSIRER MEYER ENTERTAINMENT**
PHONE . . . . . . . . . . . . . . . . . . . . . . . . . . . 310-273-7773
FAX . . . . . . . . . . . . . . . . . . . . . . . . . . . . . 310-859-7500
301 N. Canon #300
Beverly Hills, CA 90210
TYPE          Motion Pictures + Television
CREDITS       Snapdragon- North Shore Fish
COMMENTS   Also:  Series, Cable & Network.
Allan M. Kassirer . . . . . . . . . . . . . . . . . . Producer/Manager
Ellen Meyer . . . . . . . . . . . . . . . . . . . . . Producer/Manager
Matt Presser . . . . . . . . . . . . . . . . . . . . . . . . Development

**KATIE FACE PRODS.**
PHONE . . . . . . . . . . . . . . . . . . . . . . . . . . . 310-244-6788
FAX . . . . . . . . . . . . . . . . . . . . . . . . . . . . . 310-244-1828
Sony Pictures Studios
10202 W. Washington Blvd., D. Lean #103
Culver City, CA 90232
TYPE          Television
DEAL          Sony Pictures Entertainment
CREDITS       Hudson Street - Before They Were Stars - Bermuda
              Triangle - Crowned and Dangerous
Tony Danza . . . . . . . . . . . . . . . . . . . . . . . . . . Principal
Melissa Goldsmith . . . . . . . . . . . . . . . . . . . . . . President
Tamara Holmes . . . . . . . . . . . . . . . . . . . . VP, Television
Troy Westergaard . . . . . . . . . . . . . . . . . Dir., Development

**KATZ ENTERTAINMENT GROUP, BARRY**
PHONE . . . . . . . . . . . . . . . . . 212-977-1000/213-977-1000
1776 Broadway Ste. 2001
New York, NY 10019
TYPE          Television + Motion Pictures
DEAL          Walt Disney TV/Touchstone TV
COMMENTS   Also: 2600 W. Olive, Ste. 1056, Burbank CA
              91505-7284
Barry Katz . . . . . . . . . . . . . . . . . . . . . . . . . . President
Matt Frost . . . . . . . . . . . . . . . . . . . . . . . . . . Associate
Vincent Nastri . . . . . . . . . . . . . . . . . . . . . . . . Associate
Debbie Segal . . . . . . . . . . . . . . . . . . . . . . . . . Associate
Maureen Taran . . . . . . . . . . . . . . . . . . . . . . . . Associate

**KATZ PRODS., MARTY**
PHONE . . . . . . . . . . . . . . . . . . . . . . . . . . . 310-260-8501
FAX . . . . . . . . . . . . . . . . . . . . . . . . . . . . . 310-260-8502
1250 6th St., Ste. 205
Santa Monica, CA 90401
TYPE          Motion Pictures
CREDITS       Man Of The House - Lost In America - Mr. Wrong
Marty Katz . . . . . . . . . . . . . . . . . . . . . . . . . . Producer
Frederick Levy . . . . . . . . . . . . . . . . . . . . VP, Development
Campbell Katz . . . . . . . . . . . . . . . . . Development Associate
James Krisel . . . . . . . . . . . . . . . . . . . . . . . . Story Editor

**KATZ PRODUCTIONS, PERRY**
PHONE . . . . . . . . . . . . . . . . . . . . . . . . . . . 818-981-0232
FAX . . . . . . . . . . . . . . . . . . . . . . . . . . . . . 818-981-6451
100 Universal City Plaza, Bldg. 507, #3H
Universal City, CA 91608
TYPE          Motion Pictures
DEAL          Universal Pictures
CREDITS       Flipper - McHale's Navy
Perry Katz . . . . . . . . . . . . . . . . . . . . . . . . . . President

# COMPANIES AND STAFF

**KATZ/RUSH ENTERTAINMENT**
PHONE . . . . . . . . . . . . . . . . . . . . . . . . . . . . . . . . . . . . 310-273-4211
FAX . . . . . . . . . . . . . . . . . . . . . . . . . . . . . . . . . . . . . . . 310-246-5444
345 N. Maple Dr., Ste. 297
Beverly Hills, CA 90210

TYPE            Motion Pictures + Television + Syndication + Interactive
                Multimedia
CREDITS         Miss America Behind the Crown - Montel Williams - Susan
                Powter Show
Herman Rush . . . . . . . . . . . . . . . . . . . . . . . . . . . . Partner (310-246-5431)
Raymond Katz . . . . . . . . . . . . . . . . . . . . . . . . . . . . . . . . . . . . Partner
Beverly Callison . . . . . . . . . . . . . . . . . . . . . . . . . . . Associate Manager

**KAUFMAN CO., THE**
PHONE . . . . . . . . . . . . . . . . . . . . . . . . . . . . . . . . . . . . 310-887-0150
FAX . . . . . . . . . . . . . . . . . . . . . . . . . . . . . . . . . . . . . . . 310-887-0155
301 N. Canon Dr., Ste. 321
Beverly Hills, CA 90210

TYPE            Motion Pictures + Television
DEAL            Citadel Entertainment., LLC
CREDITS         Thirst - A Promise to Carolyn - Emma's Wish
Paul A. Kaufman . . . . . . . . . . . . . . . . . . . . . . . . . . . . . . . . Producer
Gregg Tilson . . . . . . . . . . . . . . . . . . . . . Dir., Development (310-887-0151)
Scott Michael Morgan . . . . . . . . . . . . . . . . . . . . . . . . . . . . . Assistant

**KAYLOR COMPANY, THE (AKA EDGE ENTER.)**
PHONE . . . . . . . . . . . . . . . . . . . . . . . . . . . . . . . . . . . . 818-762-6600
EMAIL . . . . . . . . . . . . . . . . . . . . . . . . . . . . . . . longbowkk@aol.com
4181 Sunswept, Ste. 100
Studio City, CA 91604

TYPE            Television + Motion Pictures
DEAL            Longbow Productions
CREDITS         The Cutting Edge - Safe Sex - If I Can't Have You -
                Mermaids in Manhattan - The Devil and Danny Webster
COMMENTS        Relocating at Press Time.
Kristi Kaylor . . . . . . . . . . . . . . . . . . . . . . . . . . . . President/Producer

***KEDZIE PRODUCTIONS**
PHONE . . . . . . . . . . . . . . . . . . . . . . . . . . . . . . . . . . . . 818-954-5454
FAX . . . . . . . . . . . . . . . . . . . . . . . . . . . . . . . . . . . . . . . 818-954-3352
Warner Bros. Television - Bldg. 137
300 Television Plaza, Rm. 1057
Burbank, CA 91505

TYPE            Television
DEAL            Warner Bros. Television Productions
CREDITS         Courthouse - Lois and Clark - Dawson's Creek (Pilot) -
                Anyday Now
Deborah Joy LeVine . . . . . . . . . . . . . . . . . . . Exec. Producer/Writer
Kevin Raymond . . . . . . . . . . . . . . . . . . . . . . . . . . . . . . . . . Assistant

**KEESHEN PRODUCTIONS, JIM**
PHONE . . . . . . . . . . . . . . . . . . . . . . . . . . . . . . . . . . . . 310-478-7230
FAX . . . . . . . . . . . . . . . . . . . . . . . . . . . . . . . . . . . . . . . 310-478-5142
EMAIL . . . . . . . . . . . . . . . . . . . . . . . . . . . . . . . animatics@aol.com
WEBSITE . . . . . . . . . . . . . . . . . . . . . . http://www.jfkproductions.com
1950 Sawtelle Blvd., Ste. 220
Los Angeles, CA 90025

TYPE            Motion Pictures + Television + Animation
CREDITS         Nickelodeon (IDS) - Monkey Love (Short) - Locomotion
                (IDS)
COMMENTS        Also: Commercials, Animatics & Motion-Controlled
                camera.
James F. Keeshen . . . . . . . . . . . . . . . . . . . . . President/Producer
Barbara Ziering . . . . . . . . . . . . . . . . . . VP, Development/Creative Affairs

**KEEYUMAH FILMS**
PHONE . . . . . . . . . . . . . . . . . . . . . . . . . . . . . . . . . . . . 301-217-0113
217 Lynn Manor Dr.
Rockville, MD 91403

TYPE            Motion Pictures + Television + Syndication
CREDITS         Guy - On The Run - Dead In a Heartbeat
Claudia Crown Ades . . . . . . . . . . . . . . . . . . . . . . . . . . . . Producer
Richard Ades . . . . . . . . . . . . . . . . . . . . . . . . . . . . . . . . . . . Producer

**KEITH BARISH PRODS.**
PHONE . . . . . . . . . . . . . . . . . . . . . . . . . . . . . . . . . . . . 310-777-0096
FAX . . . . . . . . . . . . . . . . . . . . . . . . . . . . . . . . . . . . . . . 310-777-0081
9454 Wilshire Blvd., Ste. 901
Beverly Hills, CA 90212

TYPE            Motion Pictures + Television
CREDITS         Running Man - 9-1/2 Weeks - Ironweed - Sophie's Choice
                - Fugitive
Keith Barish . . . . . . . . . . . . . . . . . . . . . . . . . . . . . . . . . Chairman
G. Evan Todd . . . . . . . . . . . . . . . . . . . . . . . . . . . . . Vice President

**KELLER ENTERTAINMENT GROUP**
PHONE . . . . . . . . . . . . . . . . . . . . . . . . . . . . . . . . . . . . 818-981-4950
FAX . . . . . . . . . . . . . . . . . . . . . . . . . . . . . . . . . . . . . . . 818-501-6224
14225 Ventura Blvd.
Sherman Oaks, CA 91423

TYPE            Motion Pictures + Television + Syndication
CREDITS         Conan (Series) - Tarzan (Series) - Acapulco Heat (Series)
Max Keller . . . . . . . . . . . . . . . . . . . . . . . . . . . . . . . . . . Chairman
Micheline Keller . . . . . . . . . . . . . . . . . . . . . . . . . . . . . . President
Steve Hayes . . . . . . . . . . . . . . . . . . . . . . . . . . . . VP, Development
Carol Rossi . . . . . . . . . . . . . . . . . . . . . . . . . . . . VP, Administration
Cord Douglas . . . . . . . . . . . . . . . . . . . . . . . . . . . Dir., Development
Jeannine Imperiale . . . . . . . . . . . . . . . . . . . . . . . . . . . Comptroller
Jim Toll . . . . . . . . . . . . . . . . . . . . . . . . . . . . Chief Financial Officer
Allen Klein . . . . . . . . . . . . . . . . . . . Business Affairs Administration

**KELLEY PRODUCTIONS, DAVID E.**
PHONE . . . . . . . . . . . . . . . . . . . . . . . . . . . . . . . . . . . . 310-369-3717
WEBSITE . . . . . . . . . . . . . . . . . . . . . . . . . . . . . . http://abc.com
Fox
10201 W. Pico Blvd.
Los Angeles, CA 90035

TYPE            Television + Motion Pictures
CREDITS         Picket Fences - L.A. Law - Chicago Hope - The Practice -
                Lake Placid - Ally McBeal - Mystery - Alaska
David E. Kelley . . . . . . . . . . . . . . . . . . . . CEO/Writer/Exec. Producer
Jeffrey Kramer . . . . . . . . . . . . . . . . . . . . . President/Co-Exec. Producer
Pamela Wisne . . . . . . . . . . . . . . . . . . . . . Exec. VP/Co-Producer
Bob Breech . . . . . . . . . . . . . . . . . . . VP/Supervising Producer/Producer
Roseann M. Keris . . . . . . . . . . . . . . . . . . . . . . . . Mgr., Productions
Neely Swanson . . . . . . . . . . . . . . . . . . . . . . Mgr., Business Affairs

**KENNEDY/MARSHALL COMPANY**
PHONE . . . . . . . . . . . . . . . . . . . . . . . . . . . . . . . . . . . . 310-656-8400
FAX . . . . . . . . . . . . . . . . . . . . . . . . . . . . . . . . . . . . . . . 310-656-8430
1351 4th St., 4th Floor
Santa Monica, CA 90401

TYPE            Motion Pictures
DEAL            Walt Disney Company, The
CREDITS         Milk Money - Congo - The Indian In The Cupboard
Kathleen Kennedy . . . . . . . . . . . . . . . . . . . . . . . . . . . . Producer
Frank Marshall . . . . . . . . . . . . . . . . . . . . . . . . . Producer/Director
Clyde Derrick . . . . . . . . . . . . . . . . . . . . . . . . . Creative Executive
Jay Derrah . . . . . . . . . . . . . . . . . . . . . . . . . . . . . . . Development
Darin Moiselle . . . . . . . . . . . . . . . . . . . . . . . . . . . . . Story Editor
Alyse Rubin . . . . . . . . . . . . . . . . . . . . . . . . . . . . . . . Development

**KENWOOD PRODS., INC.**
PHONE . . . . . . . . . . . . . . . . . . . . . . . . . . . . . . . . . . . . 707-833-2829
FAX . . . . . . . . . . . . . . . . . . . . . . . . . . . . . . . . . . . . . . . 707-833-2829
P.O. Box 217
Kenwood, CA 95452

TYPE            Motion Pictures + Television
CREDITS         Fatal Vision - The Case of the Hill Side Strangler
Mike Rosenfeld . . . . . . . . . . . . . . . . . . . . . . . . . Executive Producer
Carole Coates . . . . . . . . . . . . . . . . . . . . . . . . . . . . Writer/Producer

**KETTLEDRUM FILMS, INC**
PHONE . . . . . . . . . . . . . . . . . . . . . . . . . . . . . . . . . . . . 818-506-7525
FAX . . . . . . . . . . . . . . . . . . . . . . . . . . . . . . . . . . . . . . . 818-506-2405
4961 Agnes Ave.
Valley Village, CA 91607

TYPE            Motion Pictures
CREDITS         Monty Python And Now For Something Completely
                Different - Point Blank - Negatives - Deep End - The
                Marsailles Contract - Double Trouble
Judd Bernard . . . . . . . . . . . . . . . . . . . . . . . . . . . . . . . President
Patricia Casey . . . . . . . . . . . . . . . . . . . . . . . . . Exec. VP, Creative
Alicia Richards . . . . . . . . . . . . . . . . . . . . . . . . . . . VP, UK Europe

## KILLER FILMS, INC.
PHONE . . . . . . . . . . . . . . . . . . . . . . . . . . . . . . . . . . . 212-473-3950
FAX . . . . . . . . . . . . . . . . . . . . . . . . . . . . . . . . . . . . . 212-473-6152
EMAIL . . . . . . . . . . . . . . . . . . . . . . . . . . . . killerfilm@aol.com
380 Lafayette St., #302
New York, NY 10003

TYPE          Motion Pictures + Television + Documentaries
DEAL          Goldwyn Films Inc.
CREDITS       Safe - I Shot Andy Warhol - Kids - Velvet Goldmine -
              Happiness
COMMENTS      Also:  Music Videos.
Pamela Koffler . . . . . . . . . . . . . . . . . . . . . . . . . . . . . . . . . Producer
Christine Vachon . . . . . . . . . . . . . . . . . . . . . . . . . . . . . . . Producer
Eva Kolodner . . . . . . . . . . . . . . . . . . . . . . . . . . . Dir., Development
Katie Roumel . . . . . . . . . . . . . . . . . . . . . . . . . . . Head, Production
Bradford Simpson . . . . . . . . . . . . . . . . . . . . . Production Executive
Laird Adamson . . . . . . . . . . . . . . . . . . . . . . . . Asst. to C. Vachon
Ramsey Fong . . . . . . . . . . . . . . . . . . . . . . . . . . . . . . . . Assistant

## KIMINA ENTERTAINMENT
PHONE . . . . . . . . . . . . . . . . . . . . . . . . . . . . . . . 310-550-0824
EMAIL . . . . . . . . . . . . . . . . . . . . . . . . . . . kiminaent@aol.com
8807 W. Pico Blvd., Ste. 208
Los Angeles, CA 90035

TYPE          Motion Pictures + Television
DEAL          Castle Rock Entertainment/Universal Pictures
CREDITS       American Reel - Coach - First Dog - Dudes - Never Talk to
              Strangers
Darrell Griffin . . . . . . . . . . . . . . . . . . . . . . . . . . . . Co-Chairman
Jordan Rush . . . . . . . . . . . . . . . . . . . . . . . . . . . . . Co-Chairman
Suzanne Fenton . . . . . . . . . . . . . . . . . . . . . . . . . Vice President
Clifford Numark . . . . . . . . . . . . . . . . . . . . . . . VP, Development
Margo Ileen . . . . . . . . . . . . . . . . . . . . . . . . . . . . . Story Editor

## KING WORLD PRODUCTIONS
PHONE . . . . . . . . . . . . . . . 310-826-1108/212-315-4000
FAX . . . . . . . . . . . . . . . . . . . . . . . . . . . . . . . . 310-207-2179
12400 Wilshire Blvd., Ste. 1200
Los Angeles, CA 90025-1019

TYPE          Television + Syndication
CREDITS       American Journal -  Inside Edition
COMMENTS      Also: 1700 Broadway, 32nd & 33rd Fl., NY, NY 10019
Roger King . . . . . . . . . . . . . . . . . . . . . . . . . . . . . . . . Chairman
Michael King . . . . . . . . . . . . . . . . . . . . . . . . Vice Chairman/CEO
Jules Haimovitz . . . . . . . . . . . . . . . . . . . . . . . . . President/COO
Fred Cohen . . . . . . . . . . . . . . . . . . . . . . . Pres., King World Intl.
Andy Friendly . . . . . . . . . . . . . . . . Exec. VP, Programming & Production
Steven LoCascio . . . . . . . . Sr. VP, Chief Financial Officer(201-376-1313)
Merrill H. Karpf . . . . . . . . . . . . . . . . . . . Sr. VP, Network Programming
Steven Nalevansky . . . . . . . . . . . . Sr. VP, Programming & Production
Sean E. Perry . . . . . . . . . . . . . . . . . . . . . . . . . Sr. VP, Development
Jon Birkhahn . . . . . . . . . . . . . . VP, General Counsel/Business Affairs (NY)
Donna Lee Ebbs . . . . . . . . . . . . . . . . . . VP, Network Programming
Ralph Goldberg . . . . . . . . VP, Legal Affairs, Reality-Based Programming (NY)
Pamela Miller . . . . . . . . . . . . VP, Business & Legal Affairs, West Coast
Tim Sullivan . . . . . . . . . . . . . . . VP, Business Affairs, K.W. Direct (LA)
Sylvester Russo . . . . . . . . . . . . . . . . . . . . . Controller(201-376-1313)

## KINGMAN FILMS INTERNATIONAL
PHONE . . . . . . . . . . . . . . . . . . . . . . . . . . . . . . . 818-548-3456
FAX . . . . . . . . . . . . . . . . . . . . . . . . . . . . . . . . . 818-548-3899
EMAIL . . . . . . . . . . . . . . . . . . . . . . . . info@kingmanfilms.com
WEBSITE . . . . . . . . . . . . . . . . . . http://www.kingmanfilms.com
801 North Brand Blvd., Ste. 630
Glendale, CA 91203

TYPE          Motion Pictures
CREDITS       FrontLine
Arthur Chang . . . . . . . . . . . . . . . . . . . . . . . . . . . Founder/CEO
Eric Miller . . . . . . . . . . . . . . . . . . . . . . . . . . . VP, Acquisitions
Peter Rosten . . . . . . . . . . . . . . . . . . . . . . . . . . . VP, Production
Mandy Safavi . . . . . . . . . . . . . . . . . . . . . . . . Dir., Development

## KINGS ROAD ENTERTAINMENT INC.
PHONE . . . . . . . . . . . . . . . . . . . . . . . . . . . . . . . 310-552-0057
FAX . . . . . . . . . . . . . . . . . . . . . . . . . . . . . . . . . 310-277-4468
EMAIL . . . . . . . . . . . . . . . . . . . . . . . . . . kingsrdent@aol.com
1901 Ave. of the Stars, Ste. 1545
Los Angeles, CA 90067

TYPE          Motion Pictures
CREDITS       Enemy Mine - Kickboxer - Big Easy - All of Me - Jacknife
COMMENTS      Publicly traded @ KREN.
Kenneth Aguado . . . . . . . . . . . . . . . . . . Chief Executive Officer
Christopher Trunkey . . . . . . . . . . . . . . . Chief Financial Officer

## KINGSGATE FILMS, INC.
PHONE . . . . . . . . . . . . . . . . . . . . . . . . . . . . . . . 310-244-7004
FAX . . . . . . . . . . . . . . . . . . . . . . . . . . . . . . . . . 310-244-6918
10202 W. Washington Blvd.
Frankovich Bldg., Ste. 108
Culver City, CA 90232-3195

TYPE          Motion Pictures
DEAL          Phoenix Pictures
Nick Nolte . . . . . . . . . . . . . . . . . . . . . . . . . . Actor/Producer
Greg Shapiro . . . . . . . . . . . . . . . . . . . . . . . . . . . . . Producer
Joel Lubin . . . . . . . . . . . . . . . . . . . . . . . . . . . . . . . Producer
Marisa Forrest . . . . . . . . . . . . . . . . . . . . . Executive Assistant

## KINGSIZE ENTERTAINMENT
PHONE . . . . . . . . . . . . . . . . . . . . . . . . . . . . . . . 213-467-7199
FAX . . . . . . . . . . . . . . . . . . . . . . . . . . . . . . . . . 213-467-7201
EMAIL . . . . . . . . . . . . . . . . . . . . . . . . kingsize@primenet.com
WEBSITE . . . . . . . . . . . . . . . . . . http://www.Kingsize-Ent.com
639 N. Larchmont Blvd., Ste. 201
Los Angeles, CA 90004

TYPE          Motion Pictures
CREDITS       Plump Fiction - Single Action - Bravo
Mark Roberts . . . . . . . . . . . . . . . . . . . . . . . . . . . . . Producer
Lorena David . . . . . . . . . . . . . . . . . . . . . . . Director/Producer
Carlos Gallardo . . . . . . . . . . . . . . . . . . . . . . Actor/Director

## KIRSCHNER PRODS., DAVID
PHONE . . . . . . . . . . . . . . . . . . . . . . . . . . . . . . . 818-553-5511
FAX . . . . . . . . . . . . . . . . . . . . . . . . . . . . . . . . . 818-553-4920
EMAIL . . . . . . . . . . . . . . . . . . . . . . . . . . dkprods@aol.com
611 N. Brand Blvd., 5th Floor
Glendale, CA 91203

TYPE          Motion Pictures
DEAL          Warner Bros. Feature Animation
CREDITS       An American Tail - Child's Play - The Flintstones - Cats
              Don't Dance
David Kirschner . . . . . . . . . . . . . . . . . . . . . . . . . . . . Producer
Paul Gertz . . . . . . . . . . . . . . . . . . . . . . . . . President/Producer
Corey Sienega . . . . . . . . . . . VP, Development (818-553-5648)
Susan Roberts . . . . . . . . . . . . . . . Production Office Supervisor

## KLASKY CSUPO INC.
PHONE . . . . . . . . . . . . . . . . . . . . . . . . . . . . . . . 213-463-0145
FAX . . . . . . . . . . . . . . . . . . . . . . . . . . . . . . . . . 213-463-0804
1258 N. Highland Ave.
Hollywood, CA 90038-1243

TYPE          Animation + Television
CREDITS       Real Monsters - Rugrats - Duckman - Santo Bugito - The
              Simpsons
COMMENTS      Also:  Commercials.
Gabor Csupo . . . . . . . . . . . . . . . . . . . . . . . . . . Co-Chairman
Arlene Klasky . . . . . . . . . . . . . . . . . . . . . . . . . . Co-Chairman
Terry Thoren . . . . . . . . . . . . . . . . . . . . . . . . . President/CEO
Eryk Casemiro . . . . . . . . . . . . . . . . . . . . VP, Creative Affairs
Cella Duffy . . . . . . . . . . . . . . . . . . . . . . . . . . . VP, Production
Laslo Nosek . . . . . . . . . . . . . . . . VP/Dir., Creative Services
Christine Ferriter . . . . . . . . . . . . . . . . . . . . . . . . . . Producer
Vicki Ariyasu . . . . . . . . . . . . . . . . . . . . . . . Dir., Development

## KLEISER PRODS., RANDAL
PHONE . . . . . . . . . . . . . . . . . . . . . . . . . . . . . . . 213-850-5511
FAX . . . . . . . . . . . . . . . . . . . . . . . . . . . . . . . . . 213-850-1074
EMAIL . . . . . . . . . . . . . . . . . . . . . . . . rkprods@earthlink.net
3050 Runyon Canyon Rd.
Los Angeles, CA 90046

TYPE          Motion Pictures
CREDITS       Grease - Getting It Right - White Fang - It's My Party
Randal Kleiser . . . . . . . . . . . . . . . . . . . . . . Director/Producer
Gregory Hinton . . . . . . . . . . . . . . . . . . . . . Executive Producer

## KLINE PRODUCTIONS, ADAM
PHONE . . . . . . . . . . . . . . . . . . . . . . . . . . . . . . . 310-312-4814
FAX . . . . . . . . . . . . . . . . . . . . . . . . . . . . . . . . . 310-312-4816
EMAIL . . . . . . . . . . . . . . . . . . . . . . . . . . . . arkpix@aol.com
11925 Wilshire Blvd., 3rd Floor
Los Angeles, CA 90025

TYPE          Motion Pictures + Television
CREDITS       Shadow of Doubt
Adam Kline . . . . . . . . . . . . . . . . . . . . . . . . . . . . . . . Producer

# COMPANIES AND STAFF

**KNICKERBOCKER FILMS**
PHONE . . . . . . . . . . . . . . . . . . . . . . . . . . . 310-369-3946
FAX . . . . . . . . . . . . . . . . . . . . . . . . . . . . . 310-369-8515
20th Century Fox
10201 W. Pico, Bldg. 86, Rm. 101
Los Angeles, CA 90035
TYPE          Motion Pictures
DEAL          Twentieth Century Fox-Fox 2000 (LA)
CREDITS       Melvin and Howard - Fast Times At Ridgemont High - The
              Untouchables - Heat - The Edge - Great Expectations
Art Linson . . . . . . . . . . . . . . . . . . . . . . . . . . . . . . . . Producer
Patti Roberts Nelson . . . . . . . . . . . . . . . . . . VP, Administration
John Linson . . . . . . . . . . . . . . . . . . . . . . . . . . . . . . . Producer
Kareem Elseify . . . . . . . . . . . . . . . . . . . . . . . . . . Development
Jordanna Fraiberg . . . . . . . . . . . . . . . . . . . . . . . . Development

**KNIGHT COMPANY, THE**
PHONE . . . . . . . . . . . . . . . . . . . . . . . . . . . 310-395-7100
FAX . . . . . . . . . . . . . . . . . . . . . . . . . . . . . 310-395-7099
EMAIL . . . . . . . . . . . . . . . . . . . . . . . cknight447@aol.com
1337 Ocean Ave., South Penthouse
Santa Monica, CA 90401
TYPE          Motion Pictures + Television + Animation + Interactive
              Multimedia
CREDITS       The Dream Team - Winners Take All
Christopher W. Knight . . . . . . . . . . . . . . . . . . . . . . . President
Wendy A. Goldman . . . . . . . . . . . . . . . . . . Dir., Development
Ken Kravec . . . . . . . . . . . . . . . . . . . . . . . . . Office Manager

**KOCH CO., THE**
PHONE . . . . . . . . . . . . . . . . . . . . . . . . . . . 213-956-8219
FAX . . . . . . . . . . . . . . . . . . . . . . . . . . . . . 213-862-0048
EMAIL . . . . . . . . . . . . . . . . . . . . . . . . TheKochCo@aol.com
Paramount Comm.
5555 Melrose Ave., Lubitsch 106
Los Angeles, CA 90038-3197
TYPE          Motion Pictures
CREDITS       Losing Isaiah - Wayne's World I & II - Primal Fear - The
              Beautician and the Beast
Howard W. "Hawk" Koch Jr. . . . . . . . . . . . . . . . . . . Producer
Carol Ann Blinken . . . . . . . . . . . . . . . . . . VP, Creative Affairs
Janice Jordan . . . . . . . . . . . . . . . . . . . . . . . . . . Story Editor
Heather Jennings . . . . . . . . . . . . . . . . . . . . Asst. to Mr. Koch

**KOLAR PRODUCTIONS, INC.**
PHONE . . . . . . . . . . . . . . . . . . . . . . . . . . . 818-505-6100
FAX . . . . . . . . . . . . . . . . . . . . . . . . . . . . . 818-505-6106
3965 Carpenter Ave.
Studio City, CA 91604
TYPE          Motion Pictures + Television
CREDITS       Delta of Venus - Surf Ninjas - Bat 21 - Street Smart - City
              of Industry
COMMENTS      Also providing production services in Czech Republic.
Evzen Kolar . . . . . . . . . . . . . . . . . . . . . . . . President/Producer
Deborah Shaw-Kolar . . . . . . . . . . . . . . VP, Creative Affairs/Producer
Scott Rogers . . . . . . . . . . . . . . . . . . . . . . . . . Asst. to Mr. Kolar

**KONIGSBERG CO., THE**
PHONE . . . . . . . . . . . . . . . . . . . . . . . . . . . 213-845-1000
FAX . . . . . . . . . . . . . . . . . . . . . . . . . . . . . 213-845-1020
7919 Sunset Blvd., 2nd Floor
Los Angeles, CA 90046
TYPE          Motion Pictures + Television
CREDITS       The Last Don - Titanic - Bella Mafia
Frank Konigsberg . . . . . . . . . . . . . . . . . . . . Executive Producer
Michael Elias . . . . . . . . . . . . . . . . . . . . . . Associate Producer
Drew Smith . . . . . . . . . . . . . . . . . . . . Development Executive

**KONRAD PICTURES**
PHONE . . . . . . . . . . . . . . . . . . . . . . . . . . . 818-560-2700
FAX . . . . . . . . . . . . . . . . . . . . . . . . . . . . . 818-848-0369
Disney
500 S. Buena Vista St., An. 2F-8
Burbank, CA 91521-1767
TYPE          Motion Pictures
DEAL          Miramax Films
CREDITS       Killing Mrs. Tingle - Scream 2 - Scream - Copland - Citizen
              Ruth - Beautiful Girls - Kids
Cathy Konrad . . . . . . . . . . . . . . . . . . Producer (818-560-4703)
Megan Wolpert . . . . . . . . . . . . . . . Dir., Development (818-560-7872)
David J. Levine . . . . . . . . . . . . . . . Dir., Development (818-560-4080)
Jonathan Friedman . . . . . . . . . . . . . . . Story Editor (818-560-2706)
Brad Minnich . . . . . . . . . . . Exec. Asst. to Cathy Konrad (818-560-3343)
Danny Pellegrini . . . . . . . . . Exec. Asst. to Cathy Konrad (818-560-3344)
Chris Lapin . . . . . . . . . . . . Development Assistant (818-560-7325)

**KOPELSON ENTERTAINMENT**
PHONE . . . . . . . . . . . . . . . . 310-369-7500/212-556-8565
FAX . . . . . . . . . . . . . . . . . . 310-369-7501/212-730-2635
2121 Ave. of the Stars, Ste. 1400
Los Angeles, CA 90067
TYPE          Motion Pictures + Television
CREDITS       Seven - Fugitive - Falling Down - A Perfect Murder -
              Platoon - U.S. Marshals - Devil's Advocate - Outbreak
COMMENTS      Also: 1211 Ave. of the Americas, 16th Fl., NY NY 10036
Arnold Kopelson . . . . . . . . . . . . . . . . . . Producer/CEO (310-369-7555)
Anne Kopelson . . . . . . . . . . . . . . . . . . Producer/COO (310-369-7575)
Stephen J. Brown . . . . . . . . . . . . . . Pres., Production (310-369-7522)
Nana Greenwald . . . . . . . . . . . . . Pres., Creative Affairs (310-369-7511)
Damian Stevenson . . . . . . . . . . . . . Sr. VP, Production (310-369-7507)
Heather Byer . . . . . . . . . . . . . . . VP, Literary Acquisitions (NY)
Matthew Gross . . . . . . . . . . . . . . . . VP, Production (310-369-7520)
Maria Norman . . . . . . . . . . . . . . . VP, Administration (310-369-7566)
Ruth Pomerance . . . . . . . . . . . . . . VP, Literary Acquisitions (NY)
Aaron Lubin . . . . . . . . . . . . . . . . Creative Executive (310-369-7505)
Brad Follmer . . . . . . . . . . . . . . . . . Story Editor (310-369-7508)
Natalya Murakhver . . . . . . . . . . . . . . Dir., Development (NY)
Lara Wood . . . . . . . . . . . . . . Story Dept. Coordinator (310-369-7510)
Claudia O'Hehir . . . . . . . . Exec. Asst. to Mrs. Kopelson (310-369-7575)

**KOROVA ENTERTAINMENT**
PHONE . . . . . . . . . . . . . . . . . . . . . . . . . . . 213-654-5519
FAX . . . . . . . . . . . . . . . . . . . . . . . . . . . . . 213-654-5519
1010 North Orange Grove, #3
Los Angeles, CA 90046
TYPE          Motion Pictures
Jane Gurtiza . . . . . . . . . . . . . . . . . . . . . . . . . . . . . . No Title
Steven Johnson . . . . . . . . . . . . . . . . . . . . . . . . . . . . No Title

**KORSHAK COMPANY, THE**
PHONE . . . . . . . . . . . . . . . . . . . . . . . . . . . 818-882-2051
FAX . . . . . . . . . . . . . . . . . . . . . . . . . . . . . 818-882-4284
EMAIL . . . . . . . . . . . . . . . . . . . . . . . . . korshak@ibm.net
808 Hillcrest Road
Beverly Hills, CA 90210
TYPE          Motion Pictures
CREDITS       Gable & Lombard - Sheila Levine - Hit
Harry Korshak . . . . . . . . . . . . . . . . . . . . . . . . . . . . . Producer

**KOSBERG PRODS., ROBERT**
PHONE . . . . . . . . . . . . . . . . . . . . . . . . . . . 310-285-1345
FAX . . . . . . . . . . . . . . . . . . . . . . . . . . . . . 310-858-7956
The Griffin Group
9860 Wilshire Blvd.
Beverly Hills, CA 90210
TYPE          Motion Pictures + Television
DEAL          Griffin Group, The
CREDITS       Commando - Man's Best Friend - Twelve Monkeys
Robert Kosberg . . . . . . . . . . . . . . . . . . . . . . . . . . . Producer
Kira Mason . . . . . . . . . . . . . . . . . . . . . . . . Creative Executive

**KOUF-BIGELOW PRODS.**
PHONE . . . . . . . . . . . . . . . . . . . . . . . . . . . 818-508-1010
FAX . . . . . . . . . . . . . . . . . . . . . . . . . . . . . 818-508-1079
EMAIL . . . . . . . . . . . . . . . . . . . . . . . . . doublek@aol.com
10061 Riverside Dr., #1024
Toluca Lake, CA 91602
TYPE          Motion Pictures + Television
CREDITS       Stakeout I&II - Kalifornia - Disorganized Crime - Gang
              Related - ConAir
Jim Kouf . . . . . . . . . . . . . . . . . . . . Writer/Director/Producer
Lynn Bigelow-Kouf . . . . . . . . . . . . . . . . . . . . . . . . . Producer

**KRAININ PRODUCTIONS INC.**
PHONE . . . . . . . . . . . . . . . . . . . . . . . . . . . 914-359-0445
FAX . . . . . . . . . . . . . . . . . . . . . . . . . . . . . 914-359-0446
EMAIL . . . . . . . . . . . . . . . . . . . . . . krainin@rockland.net
8 Century Rd.
Palisades, NY 10964
TYPE          Motion Pictures + Television + Documentaries
CREDITS       To America - Disaster at Silo 7 - Quiz Show - George
              Wallace
Julian Krainin . . . . . . . . . . . . . . . . . . Producer/Director/President
Michael Lawrence . . . . . . . . . . . . . . . . . . . Producer/Director
Martye Wayne . . . . . . . . . . . . . . VP, Development & Production
Todd Philips . . . . . . . . . . . . . . Assoc. in Charge of Development

# COMPANIES AND STAFF

**KRANE GROUP, THE JONATHAN**
PHONE . . . . . . . . . . . . . . . . . . . . . . . 310-278-0142
FAX . . . . . . . . . . . . . . . . . . . . . . . . . 310-278-0925
9255 Sunset Blvd., Ste. 1111
Los Angeles, CA 90069
TYPE       Motion Pictures
DEAL       Twentieth Century Fox-Fox 2000 (LA)
CREDITS       Look Who's Talking- Chocolate War - Michael - Blind Date - Face-Off
Jonathan D. Krane . . . . . . . . . . . . . . Producer/CEO/Chairman
Lori Weintraub . . . . . . . . . . . . . . . . Exec. Vice President
Kimberlyn M. Lucken . . . . . . . . . . . . . . . . . . Development
Edward Oleschak . . . . . . . . . . . . . . . . . . . . . Production
Brad Blondheim . . . . . . . . . . . . . . . Asst. to Ms. Weintraub
Maria Vallen . . . . . . . . . . . . . . . . . . . Asst. to Mr. Krane

**KRANTZ PRODS., STEVE**
PHONE . . . . . . . . . . . . . . . . . . . . . . . 213-549-6940
FAX . . . . . . . . . . . . . . . . . . . . . . . . . 213-937-3161
166 Groverton Place
Los Angeles, CA 90077
TYPE       Television
CREDITS       Jack Reed - Dazzle - Deadly Matrimony - Children of the Dark
Steve Krantz . . . . . . . . . . . . . . . . Exec. Producer/President

**KROFFT PICTURES CORP., SID & MARTY**
PHONE . . . . . . . . . . . . . . . . . . . . . . . 213-467-3125
FAX . . . . . . . . . . . . . . . . . . . . . . . . . 213-932-6332
419 N. Larchmont Blvd., Ste. 11
Los Angeles, CA 90004
TYPE       Motion Pictures + Television
CREDITS       H.R. Pufnstuf - Land of the Lost - D.C. Follies
COMMENTS       Children's Home Video.
Marty Krofft . . . . . . . . . . . . . . . . . . . . . . . . President
Sid Krofft . . . . . . . . . . . . . . . . . . . . Exec. Vice President
Randy Pope . . . . . . . . . . . . . Sr. VP, Production & Development

**KROST/CHAPIN**
PHONE . . . . . . . . . . . . . . . . . . . . . . . 310-278-0648
FAX . . . . . . . . . . . . . . . . . . . . . . . . . 310-278-0937
9465 Wilshire Blvd., Ste. 430
Beverly Hills, CA 90212
TYPE       Motion Pictures + Television
CREDITS       What's Love Got To Do With It - Dave's World - Love! Valour! Compassion!
COMMENTS       Also: Music.
Doug Chapin . . . . . . . . . . . . . . . . . . . . . . . . . Partner
Barry Krost . . . . . . . . . . . . . . . . . . . . . . . . . Partner
Ira Koslow . . . . . . . . . . . . . . . . . . Pres., Music Division
Leslie Lipton . . . . . . . . . . . . . . . . . . . Sr. VP, Television
Jose Delgado . . . . . . . . . . . . . . . . . . . . Music Manager
Ken Iwamasa . . . . . . . . . . . . . . . . . . . . . . . Associate
Karyn Wulbrun . . . . . . . . . . . . . . . . . . . . . . Associate
Brandi Whitmore . . . . . . . . . . . . . . . . Asst. to Ira Koslow
George Collins . . . . . . . . . . . . . . . . . . . . . Office Asst.

**KSPRODUCTIONS**
PHONE . . . . . . . . . . . . . . . . . . . . . . . 310-914-4830
FAX . . . . . . . . . . . . . . . . . . . . . . . . . 310-914-4131
EMAIL . . . . . . . . . . . . . . . . . . mitoutnom@earthlink.net
11844 West Pico Blvd., Second Floor
Los Angeles, CA 90064
TYPE       Motion Pictures + Television + Feature Direct to Video
Kathryn Sommer Parry . . . . . . . . . . . . . . . . . . . Producer
Mark Mishkin . . . . . . . . . . . . . . . . . . . . . . Story Editor

**KUSHNER-LOCKE CO.**
PHONE . . . . . . . . . . . . . . . . . . . . . . . 310-481-2000
FAX . . . . . . . . . . . . . . . . . . . . . . . . . 310-481-2101
EMAIL . . . . . . . . . . . . . . . . . . . . kl@kuschner-locke.com
WEBSITE . . . . . . . . . . . . . . . http://www.kushner-locke.com
11601 Wilshire Blvd., 21st Fl.
Los Angeles, CA 90025
TYPE       Motion Pictures + Television + Syndication + Interactive Multimedia + Animation + Feature Direct to Video
CREDITS       Andre- Princess In Love- Jack Reed 3, 4, 5 - Cracker - Pinocchio - Gun
Donald Kushner . . . . . . . . . . . . . . . . . . . . Co-Chairman
Peter Locke . . . . . . . . . . . . . . . . . . . . . . Co-Chairman
Bruce St. J. Lilliston . . . . . . . . . . . . . . . . President/COO
Robert Swan . . . . . . . . . . . . . . . . Chief Financial Officer
Frank Hildebrand . . . . . . . . . . . . . . Exec. VP, Production
Phil Mittleman . . . . . . . . . . . . . . . Exec. VP, Feature Films
Andrew Steinberg . . . . . . . . . . . . . . Exec. VP, Television
Richard Marks . . . . . . . . . . . Sr. VP, Business Affairs/Features
Annette Benson . . . . . . . . . . . . . . . . . . . . VP, Casting
Steve Rosen . . . . . . . . . . . . . . . . VP, Production Finance
Jerry Rubin . . . . . . . . . . . . . . . . . . VP, Business Affairs
Dana Scanlan . . . . . . . . . . . . . . . . . . . . . VP, Features
Sherry Mills . . . . . . . . . . . . . . . . . Dir., Human Resources
Rosemary Tarquinio . . . . . . . . . . . . . . Dir., TV Development
Bob Wenokur . . . . . . . . . . . . . . . . . Dir., Post Production

**KUZUI ENTERPRISES, INC.**
PHONE . . . . . . . . . . . . . . . . . . . . . . . 213-650-1045
FAX . . . . . . . . . . . . . . . . . . . . . . . . . 213-650-1772
EMAIL . . . . . . . . . . . . . . . . . . . uskuzui@earthlink.net
8480 Sunset Blvd., Ste. B
Los Angeles, CA 90069
TYPE       Motion Pictures + Television
CREDITS       Buffy the Vampire Slayer - Tokyo Pop - Telling Lies In America - Orgazmo
Kaz Kuzui . . . . . . . . . . . . . . . . . . . . . . . . President
Fran Rubel Kuzui . . . . . . . . . . . . . . . Exec. Vice President
Laurie Fisher . . . . . . . . . . . VP, Acquisitions & Co-Production
Dawn Haber . . . . . . . . . . . . . . . . . . . Mgr., Operations

**L.A. ANIMATION**
PHONE . . . . . . . . . . . . . . . . . . . . . . . 818-224-4888
FAX . . . . . . . . . . . . . . . . . . . . . . . . . 818-224-4148
EMAIL . . . . . . . . . . . . . mightykong@mail.earthlink.net
23501 Park Sorrento, Ste. 207
Calabasas, CA 91302
TYPE       Animation + Motion Pictures + Television + Feature Direct to Video
CREDITS       Timberwood Tales - The Mighty Kong - Space Warriors - Kong, The TV Series
Lyn Henderson . . . . . . . . . . . . . . . . . . . . . . President
Denis de Vallance . . . . . . . . . . . . . VP, Production/Director
Craig Martin . . . . . . . . . . . . . . . . Production Executive
Art Scott . . . . . . . . . . . . . . . . . . . . Animation Director
Jim Simon . . . . . . . . . . . . . . . . . . . . Animation Director

**LA LUNA FILMS**
PHONE . . . . . . . . . . . . . . . . . . . . . . . 310-285-9696
FAX . . . . . . . . . . . . . . . . . . . . . . . . . 310-285-9691
335 N. Maple Dr., Ste. 235
Beverly Hills, CA 90210
TYPE       Motion Pictures + Television + Animation + Interactive Multimedia
DEAL       Pacifica Entertainment
CREDITS       Mermaids- Butcher's Wife- Drop Zone- Dream Lover - Fires Within- Shadow Ops (UPN) - 6 Days/7 Nights
Wallis Nicita . . . . . . . . . . . . . . . . . . . . . . . Producer

**LA-MONT COMMUNICATIONS INC.**
PHONE . . . . . . . . . . . . . . . . . . . . . . . 310-577-6725
FAX . . . . . . . . . . . . . . . . . . . . . . . . . 310-577-6727
13323 Washington Blvd., Ste. 205
Los Angeles, CA 90066
TYPE       Motion Pictures + Television
DEAL       Telescene Film Group/AAN
CREDITS       Hiroshima - Sirens- Witchboard III- The Hunger - Thunderpoint - Alaye' 96, 97, & 98
Willie Gault . . . . . . . . . . . . . . . . . . . . . . . President
Bruce Jones . . . . . . . . . . . . . . . . . . . Vice President
Pamela Exum . . . . . . . . . . . . . . . . . Creative Director

## LADD COMPANY, THE
PHONE . . . . . . . . . . . . . . . . . . . . . . . . . . . . . . . 213-956-8203
FAX . . . . . . . . . . . . . . . . . . . . . . . . . . . . . . . . . . 213-862-1115
Paramount
5555 Melrose Ave., Chevalier 117
Los Angeles, CA 90038-3112

TYPE — Motion Pictures
DEAL — Paramount Pictures- Motion Picture Group
CREDITS — The Brady Bunch - Braveheart - The Phantom - A Very Brady Sequel

Alan Ladd Jr. . . . . . . . . . . . . . . . . . . . . . . President (213-956-8055)
Toby Jaffe . . . . . . . . . . . . . . . . . . . . . . . . Producer (213-956-8095)
Kelliann Ladd . . . . . . . . . . . . . . . . . . . . . Producer (213-956-8036)
Damon Lindelof . . . . . . . . . . . . . . . . . Creative Executive (213-956-8060)
Natalia Chydzik . . . . . . . . . . . . . Asst. to Alan Ladd, Jr. (213-956-3854)
Anne Mitchell . . . . . . . . . . . . . . Asst. to Alan Ladd, Jr. (213-956-8055)
Rhoades Rader . . . . . . . . . . . . . . . . Asst. to Toby Jaffe (213-956-3885)
Paul Keith . . . . . . . . . . . . . . . . . . Asst. to Kelliann Ladd (213-956-3082)

## LADD PRODUCTIONS, INC., DIANE
PHONE . . . . . . . . . . . . . . . . . . . . . . . . . . . . . . . 310-271-0626
FAX . . . . . . . . . . . . . . . . . . . . . . . . . . . . . . . . . . 310-271-5152
EMAIL . . . . . . . . . . . . . . . . . . . . . . . . . . . dlprods@aol.com
P.O. Box 17111
Beverly Hills, CA 90209-3111

TYPE — Motion Pictures + Television + Syndication
CREDITS — Little Girl Lost - Mrs. Munck - Woman Inside

Diane Ladd . . . . . . . . . . . . . . . . . . . . . . . Actress/Director/Producer
Robert C. Hunter . . . . . . . . . . . . . . . . . . . Chief Executive Officer
Scott Alsop . . . . . . . . . . . . . . . . . . . . . . . . . Affiliate Producer
Elizabeth Paulson . . . . . . . . . . . . Personal Assistant/Head, Development
Craig Parker . . . . . . . . . . . . . . . . . . . . . . . . . . . . . Assistant

## *LAKE COMO PICTURES
PHONE . . . . . . . . . . . . . . . . . . . . . . . . . . . . . . . 310-289-5462
FAX . . . . . . . . . . . . . . . . . . . . . . . . . . . . . . . . . . 310-274-7957
EMAIL . . . . . . . . . . . . . . . . . . . . . . . . . . LakeComoCo@aol.com
270 North Canon Drive, Ste. 1568
Beverly Hills, CA 90210

TYPE — Documentaries + Motion Pictures + Television
COMMENTS — A Division of The Lake Como Company, Inc.

John Saler . . . . . . . . . . . . . . . . . . . . . . . President/Exec. Producer
Ellen Steloff . . . . . . . . . . . . . . . . . . . . . . . . Executive Producer
Jay Hernandez . . . . . . . . . . . . . . . . . . . . . . . Dir., Development

## LAKESHORE ENTERTAINMENT CORP.
PHONE . . . . . . . . . . . . . . . . . . . . . . . . . . . . . . . 213-956-4222
FAX . . . . . . . . . . . . . . . . . . . . . . . . . . . . . . . . . . 213-862-1190
Paramount Pictures
5555 Melrose - Gloria Swanson Bldg.
Hollywood, CA 90038

TYPE — Motion Pictures
DEAL — Paramount Pictures- Motion Picture Group
CREDITS — Arlington Road - 200 Cigarettes - Next Best Thing - Passion of Mind

Thomas Rosenberg . . . . . . . . . . . . . . . . . . . Co-Chairman/CEO
Ted Tannebaum . . . . . . . . . . . . . . . . . . . . . . Co-Chariman
Sigurjon Sighvatsson . . . . . . . . . . . . . . . . . . . . . President
Peter Rogers . . . . . . . . . . . . . . . . . . President, Lakeshore International
Eric Reid . . . . . . . . . . . . . . . . Exec. VP, Business & Legal Affairs
Richard Wright . . . . . . . . . . . . . . . . Sr. VP/Head of Production
Robert Benun . . . . . . . . . . . . . . . . . VP, Business & Legal Affairs
Julie Golden . . . . . . . . . . . . . . . . . . . . VP, Development (MP)
Andre Lamal . . . . . . . . . . . . . . . . . . VP, Physical Production (MP)
Renee Mancuso . . . . . . . . . . . . . . . . . . . . . . . . VP, Finance
Christine Buckley . . . . . . . . . . . . . . Dir., Business & Legal Affairs
David Stein . . . . . . . . . . . . . . . . . . . . . . . . Dir., Development
Elizabeth Schimmel . . . . . . . . . . . . . . . . Production Coordinator (MP)
Bic Tran . . . . . . . . . . . . . . . . . . . . . . . Development/Acquistions
James Anderson . . . . . . . . . . Exec. Asst. to Mr. Rosenberg/Human Resources
Matt Rudolph . . . . . . . . . . . . . . . . . . . . . . Asst. to Ms. Golden
Jeff Sommerville . . . . . . . . . . . . . . . . . . . . . Asst. to Mr. Wright
Alex Sulaimani . . . . . . . . . . . . . . . . . . . . Asst. to Mr. Sighvatsson
Yumi Yoshinaga . . . . . . . . . . . . . . . . . . Asst. to Legal/Mr. Reid

## LANCASTER GATE ENT.
PHONE . . . . . . . . . . . . . . . . . . . . . . . . . . . . . . . 818-995-6000
FAX . . . . . . . . . . . . . . . . . . . . . . . . . . . . . . . . . . 818-905-8164
4702 Hayvenhurst Ave.
Encino, CA 91436

TYPE — Motion Pictures + Television
CREDITS — December - Grumpy Old Men - Angel Flight Down - Grumpier Old Men

Richard C. Berman . . . . . . . . . . . . . . . . . . . . . . . . . Producer
Brian K. Schlichter . . . . . . . . . . . . . . . . . . . . Dir., Development

## LANCASTER PRODUCTIONS, DAVID
PHONE . . . . . . . . . . . . . . . . . . . . . . . . . . . . . . . 213-874-1415
FAX . . . . . . . . . . . . . . . . . . . . . . . . . . . . . . . . . . 213-874-7749
EMAIL . . . . . . . . . . . . . . . . . . . . . . . . . . laninco@earthlink.net
3356 Bennett Dr.
Los Angeles, CA 90068-1704

TYPE — Motion Pictures + Television
CREDITS — 'night Mother - Woman Undone - Persons Unknown - Sadness of Sex - Caracara - Scam
COMMENTS — No unsolicited manuscripts will be accepted. Write first.

David Lancaster . . . . . . . . . . . . . . . . . . . . . . . . . . . Producer
John Shoenfelt . . . . . . . . . . . . . . . . . . . . . . . . . . . Associate

## LANCIT MEDIA ENT. MOTION PICTURES
PHONE . . . . . . . . . . . . . . . . . . . . . . . . . . . . . . . 310-315-1499
FAX . . . . . . . . . . . . . . . . . . . . . . . . . . . . . . . . . . 310-315-1487
1524 Cloverfield Blvd., Ste. E
Santa Monica, CA 90404

TYPE — Motion Pictures
CREDITS — The Giver - Taxi Dog - Fenwick's Suit
COMMENTS — Also: Good Medicine Films, Inc.

David Michaels . . . . . . . . . . . . . . . Producer/Sr. VP, Motion Pictures

## LANCIT MEDIA ENTERTAINMENT, LTD.
PHONE . . . . . . . . . . . . . . . . . . . . 212-977-9100/310-275-0724
FAX . . . . . . . . . . . . . . . . . . . . . . 212-977-9164/310-275-0724
601 W. 50th St., 6th Fl.
New York, NY 10019

TYPE — Television
CREDITS — The Puzzle Place - Reading Rainbow - Backyard Safari

Susan L. Solomon . . . . . . . . . . . . . . . . . . . . . . Chairman/CEO
Laurence A. Lancit . . . . . . . . . . . . . . . . . . . . . . Co-President
Cecily Truett . . . . . . . . . . . . . . . . . . . . . . . . . Co-President
Jane M. Abernethy . . . . . . . . . . . Sr. VP, Legal & Business Affairs
Orly Berger-Wiseman . . . . . . . . . . . . . . . . Sr. VP, Production
David Michaels . . . . . . . . . . . . . . . . Sr. VP, Motion Pictures (LA)
Noel Resnick . . . . . . . . . . . . . . . . . . Sr. VP, Development (LA)

## LANDMARK ENTERTAINMENT GROUP
PHONE . . . . . . . . . . . . . . . . . . . . . . . . . . . . . . . 818-753-6700
FAX . . . . . . . . . . . . . . . . . . . . . . . . . . . . . . . . . . 818-753-6767
EMAIL . . . . . . . . . . . . . . . . . . . landmark@landmarkusa.com
WEBSITE . . . . . . . . . . . . . . http://www.landmark.hollywood.ca.us
5200 Lankershim Blvd., Ste. 700
North Hollywood, CA 91601

TYPE — Motion Pictures + Television
CREDITS — Ghostbusters Show - Star Trek The Experience - Samsung Pavillion (Expo 93)
COMMENTS — Also: Theme Parks/Licensing /Theatre.

Tony Christopher . . . . . . . . . . . . . . . . . . . . . . CEO/President
Gary Goddard . . . . . . . . . . . . . . . . . . . . . . . . . . . Chairman

## LANDSBURG CO., THE
PHONE . . . . . . . . . . . . . . . . . . . . . . . . . . . . . . . 310-478-7878
FAX . . . . . . . . . . . . . . . . . . . . . . 310-477-7166/310-473-6776
EMAIL . . . . . . . . . . . . . . . . . . . . . . . . . . . . tlcpix@aol.com
11811 W. Olympic Blvd.
Los Angeles, CA 90064-1113

TYPE — Television + Documentaries
DEAL — CBS Corporation/NBC Entertainment/ABC Entertainment
CREDITS — If Someone Had Known - The Secret of... - The Lottery - Country Justice

Alan Landsburg . . . . . . . . . . . . . . . . . . . . . . . . Chairman/CEO
Howard Lipstone . . . . . . . . . . . . . . . . . . . . . . President/COO
Linda Otto . . . . . . . . . . . . . . . . . . . . . . . . Producer/Director
Leslie Lipton . . . . . . . . . . . . . . . . . . . . . . . VP, Development
Gloria L. Morris . . . . . . . . . . . . . . . . . . . . Mgr., Development
Diane Skwarek . . . . . . . . . . . . . . . . . . . Asst. to Mr. Lipstone

# COMPANIES AND STAFF

**LANGLEY PRODS.**
PHONE . . . . . . . . . . . . . . . . . . . . . . . . . . . . 310-449-5300
FAX . . . . . . . . . . . . . . . . . . . . . . . . . . . . . . 310-449-5330
EMAIL . . . . . . . . . . . . . . . elena@langleyproductions.com
WEBSITE. . . . . . . . . . . . . . . . . . . http://www.cops.com
2225 Colorado Ave.
Santa Monica, CA 90404

TYPE            Motion Pictures + Television + Documentaries +
                Syndication + Interactive Multimedia
DEAL            Twentieth Century Fox/New Line Cinema
CREDITS         Cops - Code 3 - Wild Side - Cop Files - Dog Watch
COMMENTS        Also: Video Distribution.

John Langley . . . . . . . . . . . . . . President/Exec. Prod./Dir./Writer
Murray Jordan . . . . . . . . . . . . . . . . . . . . . Producer (COPS)
Elie Cohn . . . . . . . . . . . . . . . . . . . . . Producer, Features
Karen Hori . . . . . . . . . . . . . . . . . . VP, Development, TV
Joanna Lancaster . . . . . . . . . . . . VP, Development, Movies
Maria Remiro-Jordan . . . . . . . . . . Associate Producer, Cops

**LANTANA PRODUCTIONS**
PHONE . . . . . . . . . . . . . . . . . . . . . . . . . . 310-315-4777
FAX . . . . . . . . . . . . . . . . . . . . . . . . . . . . 310-315-4778
3000 W. Olympic Blvd., Ste. 1300
Santa Monica, CA 90404-5041

TYPE            Motion Pictures + Television
CREDITS         Swing Shift - Stanley & Iris - Circle of Friends

Arlene Sellers . . . . . . . . . . . . . . . . . . . . . . . . Producer
Alex Winitsky . . . . . . . . . . . . . . . . . . . . . . . . . Producer

**LARCO PRODUCTIONS, INC.**
PHONE . . . . . . . . . . . . . . . . . . . . . . . . . . 310-550-7942
EMAIL . . . . . . . . . . . . . . . . . gatsby10@netcom.com
2111 Coldwater Canyon
Beverly Hills, CA 90210

TYPE            Motion Pictures + Television
CREDITS         It's Alive - The Stuff - Q - J. Edgar Hoover - Best Seller

Larry Cohen . . . . . . . . . . . . . . President/Writer/Producer/Director

**LARGO ENTERTAINMENT**
PHONE . . . . . . . . . . . . . . . . . . . . . . . . . . 310 203 0055
FAX . . . . . . . . . . . . . . . . . . . . . . . . . . . . 310-203-0254
2029 Century Park East, Ste. 2500
Los Angeles, CA 90067

TYPE            Motion Pictures
CREDITS         Time Cop - White Squall - Mulholland Falls - G.I. Jane

Barr Potter . . . . . . . . . . . . . . . . . . . . . . . . . Chairman/CEO
Peter Elson . . . . . . . . . . . . . . . . . . . . . . . . . . President
Bruce Vann . . . . . . . . . . . . . . Sr. VP, Legal & Business Affairs
Robert Corzo . . . . . . . . . . . . . . . . . . . . . . . . VP, Finance
Frank K. Isaac . . . . . . . . . . . . . . . . . VP, Prod./Dist. Services
Chris Taylor . . . . . . . . . . . . . . VP, Acquisitions & Business Affairs

**LASHER, MCMANUS & ROBINSON**
PHONE . . . . . . . . . . . . . . . . . . . . . . . . . . 310-446-1466
FAX . . . . . . . . . . . . . . . . . . . . . . . . . . . . 310-446-1566
2372 Veteran Ave., Ste. 102
Los Angeles, CA 90064

TYPE            Motion Pictures
CREDITS         The Last Time I Committed Suicide

Estelle Lasher . . . . . . . . . . . . . . . . . . . . . . . No Title
Marsha McManus . . . . . . . . . . . . . . . . . . . . . . No Title
Elizabeth Robinson . . . . . . . . . . . . . . . . . . . . No Title
Ilan Breil . . . . . . . . . . . . . . . . . . . . . . . . . . . No Title
Elizabeth Feldman . . . . . . . . . . . . . . . . . . . . . No Title
Rebekah Slotnick . . . . . . . . . . . . . . . . . . . . . . No Title

**LASKAY DRIVE**
PHONE . . . . . . . . . . . . . . . . . . . . . . . . . . 310-828-2805
1107 19th St., C
Santa Monica, CA 90403

TYPE            Motion Pictures
CREDITS         Razor's Edge

Jason Laskay . . . . . . . . . . . . . . . . . . Writer/Director/Producer
Bambi Lynn Scott . . . . . . . . . . . . . . . . . . Dir., Development

**LAST STAND PICTURES, INC.**
PHONE . . . . . . . . . . . . . . . . . . . . . . . . . . 310-724-5700
FAX . . . . . . . . . . . . . . . . . . . . . . . . . . . . 310-385-0363
124 S. Lasky Dr., First Floor
Beverly Hills, CA 90212

TYPE            Motion Pictures + Television + Interactive Multimedia
CREDITS         Dances With Wolves - 500 Nations - X: The Unheard
                Music

Michael Blake . . . . . . . . . . . . . . . . . Writer/Director/Producer
William Morgan . . . . . . . . . . . . . . . . . Writer/Director/Producer

***LATITUDE FILMS**
PHONE . . . . . . . . . . . . . . . . . . . . . . . . . . 310-442-1128
11740 Montana Ave., Ste. 401
Los Angeles, CA 90049

TYPE            Motion Pictures + Television

Curtis Burch . . . . . . . . . . . . . . . . . . . . . . Producer/Writer

**LAUREN PRODUCTIONS, ANDREW**
PHONE . . . . . . . . . . . . . . . . . . . . . . . . . . 212-639-1975
FAX . . . . . . . . . . . . . . . . . . . . . . . . . . . . 212-639-9476
EMAIL . . . . . . . . . . . . . . . . . alprod@earthlink.net
114 E. 70th St., #3
New York, NY 10021

TYPE            Motion Pictures

Andrew Lauren . . . . . . . . . . . . . . . . . . President/Producer
Ian Jeffers . . . . . . . . . . . . . . . . . . . . . . . . . Producer
Jordan Hoffman . . . . . . . . . . . . . . . . . . Dir., Development
Alan Choi . . . . . . . . . . . . . . . . . . . . Development Assistant

**LAVIN ENTERTAINMENT GROUP**
PHONE . . . . . . . . . . . . . . . . . . . . . . . . . . 910-772-9916
FAX . . . . . . . . . . . . . . . . . . . . . . . . . . . . 910-772-9918
EMAIL . . . . . . . . . . . . . . . . . lavinet@aol.com
P.O. Box 2847
Wilmington, NC 28402

TYPE            Motion Pictures + Television + Syndication
CREDITS         Room for Two - The Rose Garden
COMMENTS        Agent: Joel Dean, Agency for the Performing Arts
                310-888-4235.

Linda Lavin . . . . . . . . . . . . . . . Actress/Director/Producer
Elle Puritz . . . . . . . . . . . . . . . . . . . . . Executive Director

**LEACH ENT. ENTERPRISES, INC.**
PHONE . . . . . . . . . . . . . . . . . . . . . . . . . . 212-759-8787
FAX . . . . . . . . . . . . . . . . . . . . . . . . . . . . 212-838-4364
1 Dag Hammarskjold Plz/885 2nd Av. 25 Fl
New York, NY 10017

TYPE            Television + Syndication
CREDITS         Lifestyles - Gourmet Getaways - TVFN - Heroes America -
                Miracles & Wonders

Robin Leach . . . . . . . . . . . . . . . . . . . . Executive Producer
Rob Hess . . . . . . . . . . . . . . . . . . . . . . . . . Producer
Nick LaPenna . . . . . . . . . . . . . . . . . . . . . . . Producer

**LEE PRODUCTIONS, MICHELE**
PHONE . . . . . . . . . . . . . . . . . . . . . . . . . . 213-852-4094
FAX . . . . . . . . . . . . . . . . . . . . . . . . . . . . 213-852-4261
CBS Television City
7800 Beverly Blvd.
Los Angeles, CA 90036

TYPE            Motion Pictures + Television
DEAL            CBS Entertainment
CREDITS         When No One Would Listen - The Dottie West Story -
                Color Me Perfect
COMMENTS        Also: Theatre.

Michele Lee . . . . . . . . . . . . . . . . . President/Exec. Producer
Richard Ostlund . . . . . . . . . . . . . . Dir., Development/Producer
Ken Dusick Esq . . . . . . . . . . . . . . . . . . . Business Affairs

**LEFRAK PRODS.**
PHONE . . . . . . . . . . . . . . . . . . . . . . . . . . 212-541-9444
FAX . . . . . . . . . . . . . . . . . . . . . . . . . . . . 212-974-8205
40 W. 57th St., Ste. 409
New York, NY 10019

TYPE            Motion Pictures + Television
DEAL            Alliance Television Productions
CREDITS         Mi Vida Loca - Miss Rose White - The Infiltrator - Shot
                Through the Heart

Francine LeFrak . . . . . . . . . . . . . . . . . . . . . President
Katerina Georgiou . . . . . . . . . . . . . . . . Development Executive
Kris Mihelik . . . . . . . . . . . . . . . . . . . . Creative Executive
Rick Friedberg . . . . . . . . . . . . . . Dir., Business & Legal Affairs

**LEGACY ENTERTAINMENT INC.**
PHONE . . . . . . . . . . . . . . . . . . . . . . . . . . 310-285-2300
FAX . . . . . . . . . . . . . . . . . . . . . . . . . . . . 310-285-2345
335 N. Maple Dr., Ste. 135
Beverly Hills, CA 90210

TYPE            Motion Pictures + Television
DEAL            Castle Rock Entertainment

Andrew Susskind . . . . . . . . . . . . . . . . . . . . . President
Gayle Prezioso . . . . . . . . . . . . . . . . . . . Dir., Development

# COMPANIES AND STAFF

***LEGEND ENTERTAINMENT**
PHONE . . . . . . . . . . . . . . . . . . . . . . . . . . . . . . . . . . . . . . . . 310-888-2244
FAX . . . . . . . . . . . . . . . . . . . . . . . . . . . . . . . . . . . . . . . . . . . 310-859-7173
9107 Wilshire Blvd., Ste. 625
Beverly Hills, CA 90210
TYPE　　　　Motion Pictures + Television
Tom Berry . . . . . . . . . . . . . . . . . . . . . . . . . . . . . . . . . . . . . . . . President
Barbara Javitz . . . . . . . . . . . . . . . . . . . . . . . . . . . . Sr. Vice President
Elissa McBride . . . . . . . . . . . . . . . . . . . . . . . . . . VP, Creative Affairs
Richard Lowry . . . . . . . . . . . . . . . . . . . . . . . . . . . . Executive Producer

**LEIDER CO., THE JERRY**
PHONE . . . . . . . . . . . . . . . . . . . . . . . . . . . . . . . . . . . . . . . . 310-820-3161
FAX . . . . . . . . . . . . . . . . . . . . . . . . . . . . . . . . . . . . . . . . . . . 310-820-4323
11661 San Vicente Blvd., Ste. 702
Los Angeles, CA 90049
TYPE　　　　Motion Pictures + Television
CREDITS　　My Favorite Martian - Trucks - Payne
Jerry Leider . . . . . . . . . . . . . . . . . . . . . . . . . . . . . . . . . . . . . . President
Greg Griffin . . . . . . . . . . . . . . . . . . . . . . . . Development (310-820-4722)

**LEMON SKY PRODUCTIONS, INC.**
PHONE . . . . . . . . . . . . . . . . . . . . . . . . . . . . . . . . . . . . . . . . 212-957-9642
FAX . . . . . . . . . . . . . . . . . . . . . . . . . . . . . . . . . . . . . . . . . . . 212-957-8022
357 W. 55th St.
New York, NY 10019
TYPE　　　　Motion Pictures + Television
CREDITS　　Lemon Sky - Living In Oblivion - The Real Blonde
Marcus Viscidi . . . . . . . . . . . . . . . . . . . . . . . . . . . . . . . . . . . . President
Samantha Bell . . . . . . . . . . . . . . . . . . . . . . . . . . . . . VP, Development
John Parker . . . . . . . . . . . . . . . . . . . . . . . . . . . . . . . . . . VP, Finance

**LEO FILMS**
PHONE . . . . . . . . . . . . . . . . . . . . . . . . . . . . . . . . . . . . . . . . 213-666-7140
FAX . . . . . . . . . . . . . . . . . . . . . . . . . . . . . . . . . . . . . . . . . . . 213-666-7414
EMAIL . . . . . . . . . . . . . . . . . . . . . . . . . . . . . . . . . . . . . lustgar@idt.net
WEBSITE . . . . . . . . . . . . . . . . . . . . http://http://www.movies-online.com
6249 Landgdon Ave.
Van Nuys, CA 91411
TYPE　　　　Feature Direct to Video + Motion Pictures
CREDITS　　American Taboo - Power Slide - Smart Alex with Steve
　　　　　　Oedekerk
Steve Lustgarten . . . . . . . . . . . . . . . . . . . . . . . . . . . . . . . . . President

**LEO PRODUCTIONS, MALCOLM**
PHONE . . . . . . . . . . . . . . . . . . . . . . . . . . . . . . . . . . . . . . . . 213-464-4448
FAX . . . . . . . . . . . . . . . . . . . . . . . . . . . . . . . . . . . . . . . . . . . 213-856-8755
6536 Sunset Blvd.
Hollywood, CA 90028
TYPE　　　　Motion Pictures + Television + Documentaries +
　　　　　　Syndication
DEAL　　　　Paramount Pictures- Motion Picture Group
CREDITS　　This Is Elvis - Laverne & Shirley Reunion - Rolling Stone
　　　　　　Anniv. - Best of Hollywood Palace
COMMENTS　Produced highest rated TV reunion, Happy Days.
Malcolm Leo . . . . . . . . . . . . . . . . . . Exec. Producer/Director/President
Bonnie Peterson . . . . . . . . . . . . . . . . . . . . . . . . . . Supervising Producer
David Fairfield . . . . . . . . . . . . . . . . . . . . . . . . . Development Supervisor
R. Merrick . . . . . . . . . . . . . . . . . . . . . . . . . . . . . . Librarian/Research

**LEUCADIA FILM CORP.**
PHONE . . . . . . . . . . . . . . . . . . . . . . . . . . . . . . . . . . . . . . . . 801-521-1094
FAX . . . . . . . . . . . . . . . . . . . . . . . . . . . . . . . . . . . . . . . . . . . 801-524-1760
535 East S. Temple
Salt Lake City, UT 84102
TYPE　　　　Motion Pictures
CREDITS　　Address Unknown - Wish Upon A Star - Just In Time
H.E. Scruggs . . . . . . . . . . . . . . . . . . . . . . . . . . . . . . . Chairman/CEO
Jeff Crane . . . . . . . . . . . . . . . . . . . . . . . . . . . Chief Financial Officer
Monty Magleby . . . . . . . . . . . . . . . . . . . . . . . . . . . . . Vice President

**LEVINSON PRODS., RON**
PHONE . . . . . . . . . . . . . . . . . . . . . . . . . . . . . . . . . . . . . . . . 310-559-2470
7201 Raintree Circle
Culver City, CA 90230
TYPE　　　　Motion Pictures + Television
CREDITS　　In the Arms of a Killer
Ron Levinson . . . . . . . . . . . . . . . . . . . . . . . . . . . . . . . . . . . . Producer

**LEVINSON, MARK**
PHONE . . . . . . . . . . . . . . . . . . . . . . . . . . . . . . . . . . . . . . . . 310-573-1968
FAX . . . . . . . . . . . . . . . . . . . . . . . . . . . . . . . . . . . . . . . . . . . 310-573-1077
P.O. Box 1536
Pacific Palisades, CA 90272
TYPE　　　　Motion Pictures
CREDITS　　Home Alone - Mystic Pizza - Killer
Mark Levinson . . . . . . . . . . . . . . . . . . . . . . . . . . . . . . . . . . Producer
Charmian Jago . . . . . . . . . . . . . . . . . . . . . . . . . . . . VP, Development

***LEVINSON/FONTANA COMPANY, LLC, THE**
PHONE . . . . . . . . . . . . . . . . . . . . . . . . . . . . . . . . . . . . . . . . 212-206-3585
FAX . . . . . . . . . . . . . . . . . . . . . . . . . . . . . . . . . . . . . . . . . . . 212-206-3581
WEBSITE . . . . . . . . . . . . . . . . . . . . . . . . . . http://www.levinson.com
P.O. Box 1207
New York, NY 10011
TYPE　　　　Documentaries + Television + Syndication
DEAL　　　　Rysher Entertainment
CREDITS　　TV: Homicide: Life on the Street (NBC) - Oz (HBO)
Barry Levinson . . . . . . . . . . . . . . . . . . . Exec. Producer/Director/Writer
Tom Fontana . . . . . . . . . . . . . . . . . . . . . . . . Exec. Producer/Writer
Amy Solan . . . . . . . . . . . . . . . . . . . . . . . . . . . CFO/Business Affairs
Sunil Nayar . . . . . . . . . . . . . . . . . . . . . . . Asst. to Exec. Producer
Shannon Logan-Torres . . . . . . . . . . . . . . . . . . . . . . Staff Assistant

**LEVY-GARDNER-LAVEN PRODS.**
PHONE . . . . . . . . . . . . . . . . . . . . . . . . . . . . . . . . . . . . . . . . 310-278-9820
FAX . . . . . . . . . . . . . . . . . . . . . . . . . . . . . . . . . . . . . . . . . . . 310-278-2632
9595 Wilshire Blvd., Ste. 610
Beverly Hills, CA 90212
TYPE　　　　Motion Pictures + Television
CREDITS　　Gator - White Lightning - Geronimo - Brannigan
Jules Levy . . . . . . . . . . . . . . . . . . . . . . . . . . . . . . . . . . . . . . President
Arthur Gardner . . . . . . . . . . . . . . . . . . . . . VP/Secretary/Treasurer
Arnold Laven . . . . . . . . . . . . . . . . . . . . . . . . . . . . . . Vice President

**LEVY/WEISS PRODUCTIONS**
PHONE . . . . . . . . . . . . . . . . . . . . . . . . . . . . . . . . . . . . . . . . 310-260-1404
FAX . . . . . . . . . . . . . . . . . . . . . . . . . . . . . . . . . . . . . . . . . . . 310-260-1406
1460 4th St., Ste. 210
Santa Monica, CA 90401-3414
TYPE　　　　Motion Pictures
Barbara Levy . . . . . . . . . . . . . . . . . . . . . . . . . . . . . . . . . . . . Producer
Christina Weiss Lurie . . . . . . . . . . . . . . . . . . . . . . . . . . . . . Producer

**LEWIS PRODS., SIMON**
PHONE . . . . . . . . . . . . . . . . . . . . . . . . . . . . . . . . . . . . . . . . 818-906-7677
FAX . . . . . . . . . . . . . . . . . . . . . . . . . . . . . . . . . . . . . . . . . . . 818-906-2836
16002 Meadowcrest Rd.
Sherman Oaks, CA 91403-4716
TYPE　　　　Motion Pictures
CREDITS　　Look Who's Talking - The Chocolate War - Age Old
　　　　　　Friends
Simon R. Lewis . . . . . . . . . . . . . . . . . . . . . . . . . . . . . . . . . President

***LEXINGTON ROAD PRODUCTIONS**
PHONE . . . . . . . . . . . . . . . . . . . . . . . . . . . . . . . . . . . . . . . . 310-248-4854
FAX . . . . . . . . . . . . . . . . . . . . . . . . . . . . . . . . . . . . . . . . . . . 310-248-4990
9014 Melrose Ave.
Los Angeles, CA 90069
TYPE　　　　Motion Pictures + Television
CREDITS　　Men With Guns
COMMENTS　Family Entertainment.
Lou Gonda . . . . . . . . . . . . . . . . . . . . . . . . . . . . . . . . . . . . . . . Partner
Kelly Gonda . . . . . . . . . . . . . . . . . . . . . . . . . . . . . . . . . . . . . . Partner
Karen Dare . . . . . . . . . . . . . . . . . . . . . . . . . . . . . . . . Vice President

**LICHT/MUELLER FILM CORP.**
PHONE . . . . . . . . . . . . . . . . . . . . . . . . . . . . . . . . . . . . . . . . 310-205-5500
FAX . . . . . . . . . . . . . . . . . . . . . . . . . . . . . . . . . . . . . . . . . . . 310-205-5590
132A S. Lasky Dr., Ste. 200
Beverly Hills, CA 90212
TYPE　　　　Motion Pictures + Television
CREDITS　　The Cable Guy - Idle Hands - Waterworld
Andrew Licht . . . . . . . . . . . . . . . . . . . . . . . . . . . . . . . . . . . . Producer
Jeffrey Mueller . . . . . . . . . . . . . . . . . . . . . . . . . . . . . . . . . . Producer
Elizabeth Hackett . . . . . . . . . . . . . . . . . . . . . . . . . . Dir., Development
Winston Stromberg . . . . . . . . . . . . . . . . . . . . . . . . Creative Assistant

# COMPANIES AND STAFF

## LIFETIME TELEVISION (LA)
PHONE . . . . . . . . . . . . . . . . . . . . . . . . 310-556-7500
2049 Century Park East, Ste. 840
Los Angeles, CA 90067

TYPE          Television
CREDITS       Almost Golden: The Jessica Savitch Story - Sophie & The
              Moonhanger - Any Mother's Son

Laurette Hayden . . . . . . . . . . . . . . . . . . VP, Original Movies
Kelly Goode . . . . . . . . . . . . . . . . . . Head, Creative Affairs
Rick Jacobs . . . . . . . . . . . . . . . . . . . . . Head, Talent
Nancy McCabe . . . . . . . . . . . . . . . . . . Dir., Original Movies
Robin Palmer . . . . . . . . . . . . . . . . . . Dir., Original Movies
Marian Effinger . . . . . . . . . . . Dir., Creative Affairs (West Coast)
Dana Laughlin . . . . . . . . . . . . . . . . . . Mgr., Original Movies
Allison Teicher . . . . . . . . . . . . . . . . . . . . . Mgr., Series

## LIFETIME TELEVISION (NY)
PHONE . . . . . . . . . . . 212-424-7000/718-706-3501
WEBSITE . . . . . . . . . . . . . . . . http://www.lifetimetv.com
Worldwide Plaza
309 West 49th St.
New York, NY 10019

TYPE          Television
CREDITS       Debt - New Attitudes - Next Door with Katie Brown
COMMENTS      Studio: 34-12 36th St., Astoria, NY 11106

Douglas McCormick . . . . . . . . . . . . . . . . . . President/CEO
James Wesley . . . . . . . . . . . . . . . . . . Sr. VP, Financial/CFO
Jane Tollinger . . . . . . . . . . . . . . . . . . Executive Vice President
Patrick Guy . . . . . . . . . . . . . . . Sr. VP, Business & Legal Affairs
Dawn Tarnofsky . . . . . . . . . . . . Sr. VP, Programming & Production
Amy Introcaso-Davis . . . . . . . . . . . . . VP, Series, East Coast
Jean Rigg . . . . . . . . . . . . . . . VP, Business & Legal Affairs
Jeffrey Smith . . . . . . . . . . . . . . VP, Business & Legal Affairs
Steve Warner . . . . . VP, Program Planning, Scheduling & Acquisitions
Julie Falk . . . . . . . . . . . . . . . . . . Dir., Original Programming
Paul Noble . . . . . . . . . . . . . . . . . . . Dir., Feature Films
Todd Schwartz . . . . . . . . . . . . . . . . Dir., Original Programming
Beth Sosin . . . . . . . . . . . . . . . . Dir., Original Programming
Rosemary Sykes . . . . . . . . . . . . . . Dir., Original Programming
Dorian Winship . . . . . . . . . . . . . . . . . . Dir., Production
Allison Teicher . . . . . . . Mgr., Specials, Documentaries, Daytime
Barbara Rothkin . . . . . . . . . . . Exec. Asst. to Mr. McCormick

## LIGHTHOUSE ENTERTAINMENT
PHONE . . . . . . . . . . . . . . . . . . . . . . . . 310-246-0499
FAX . . . . . . . . . . . . . . . . . . . . . . . . . . 310-246-0899
409 N. Camden Dr., Ste. 202
Beverly Hills, CA 90210

TYPE          Motion Pictures + Television
CREDITS       The Rookie - Gridlock'd - Fun

Steven Siebert . . . . . . . . . . . . . . . . . . . . . . . Producer

## LIGHTHOUSE PRODUCTIONS
PHONE . . . . . . . . . . . . . . . . . . . . . . . . 310-859-4923
FAX . . . . . . . . . . . . . . . . . . . . . . . . . . 310-859-7511
EMAIL . . . . . . . . . . . . . . . . . . . . . . lighthouse@jfr.com
120 El Camino Dr., Ste. 212
Beverly Hills, CA 90212

TYPE          Motion Pictures + Television + Feature Direct to Video +
              Interactive Multimedia
CREDITS       The Sting - Close Encounters - Taxi Driver - The Flamingo
              Kid - Mimic

Michael Phillips . . . . . . . . . . . . . . . . . . . . . Producer
Juliana Maio . . . . . . . . . . . . . . . . . . . . . . . Producer
John Frank Rosenblum . . . . . . . . . . . . . . . . . . . Producer
Mary Jo Flynn . . . . . . . . . . . . . . . . . . . . . Development

## LIGHTSTORM ENTERTAINMENT
PHONE . . . . . . . . . . . . . . . . . . . . . . . . 310-656-6100
FAX . . . . . . . . . . . . . . . . . . . . . . . . . . 310-656-6102
919 Santa Monica Blvd.
Santa Monica, CA 90401

TYPE          Motion Pictures
CREDITS       Aliens - Terminator - Abyss - T2 - True Lies - Strange Days
              - Titanic

James Cameron . . . . . . . . . . . . . . . . . . . Chairman/CEO
Rae Sanchini . . . . . . . . . . . . . . . . . . . . . . President
Carol Henry . . . . . . . . . . . . . . . . . . Chief Financial Officer
Stacy Maes . . . . . . . . . . . . . . . . . . . . VP, Development
Jay Sanders . . . . . . . . . . . . . . . . . . . Dir., Development
Tom Cohen . . . . . . . . . . . . . . . . . . . Asst./Story Editor
Nancy Hobson . . . . . . . . . . . . . . . . . Asst. to Mr. Cameron
Kim Troy . . . . . . . . . . . . . . . . . . . Asst. to Ms. Sanchini

## LIGHTVIEW ENTERTAINMENT
PHONE . . . . . . . . . . . . . . . . . . . . . . . . 310-820-6194
FAX . . . . . . . . . . . . . . . . . . . . . . . . . . 310-820-3670
EMAIL . . . . . . . . . . . . . . . . . . . . Lightview1@aol.com
11853 Nebraska Ave.
Los Angeles, CA 90025

TYPE          Motion Pictures + Television
CREDITS       Galatea's Wish - Hope's Creek - Disturbing The Peace

Thomas Patrick Smith . . . . . . . . . . Director/President/Partner
Greg Smith . . . . . . . . . . . . . . . . . . . . Vice President
Ned Doyle . . . . . . . . . . . . . . . . . . . Producer/Partner

## LILAC PRODUCTIONS
PHONE . . . . . . . . . . . . . . . . . . . . . . . . 818-762-8641
FAX . . . . . . . . . . . . . . . . . . . . . . . . . . 818-762-0330
9911 W. Pico Blvd.
Los Angeles, CA 90035

TYPE          Television + Motion Pictures + Syndication +
              Documentaries

Nancy Malone . . . . . . . . . . . . . . . . . . . . . . President

## LINDEN PRODS.
PHONE . . . . . . . . . . . . . . . . . . . . . . . . 310-474-2234
FAX . . . . . . . . . . . . . . . . . . . . . . . . . . 310-474-8773
10850 Wilshire Blvd., Ste. 250
Los Angeles, CA 90024

TYPE          Motion Pictures + Television + Documentaries

Pippa Scott . . . . . . . . . . . . . . . . . . . . . . President
Glory Friend . . . . . . . . . . . . . . . . . . . . . Development

## *LIONS GATE FILMS PRODUCTION
PHONE . . . . . . . . . . . . . . . . . . . . . . . . 212-966-4670
FAX . . . . . . . . . . . . . . . . . . . . . . . . . . 212-966-2544
EMAIL . . . . . . . . . . . . . . . . . krosin@lionsgatefilms.com
WEBSITE . . . . . . . . . . . . . . . http://www.lionsgatefilms.com
561 Broadway, Ste. 12B
New York, NY 10012

TYPE          Motion Pictures
CREDITS       Jerry & Tom - Buffalo 66 - I'm Losing You
COMMENTS      Produce 8-10 Independent Features per year.

Michael Paseornek . . . . . . . . . . . . . . . . . . . President
Lauren McLaughlin . . . . . . . . . . . . . . . . . Vice President
Carrie Walkup . . . . . . . . . . . . . . . Dir., Creative Affairs
Katherine Rosin . . . . . . . . . . . . . . . . . . . Coordinator

## LIPPER PRODUCTIONS, KEN
PHONE . . . . . . . . . . . . . 310-385-6000/212-883-6333
FAX . . . . . . . . . . . . . . 310-248-2449/212-682-7762
9465 Wilshire Blvd., Ste. 880
Beverly Hills, CA 90210

TYPE          Motion Pictures
CREDITS       City Hall - The Winter Guest
COMMENTS      Also: 101 Park Ave., 6th Floor, New York, NY 10178

Ken Lipper . . . . . . . . . . . . . . . . . . . . . . President
John Miranda . . . . . . . . . . . . . . . . . . . . VP, Production
Brenda Arechiga . . . . . . . . . . . . . . . . . VP, Development

## LIPTON PRODS., JAMES
PHONE . . . . . . . . . . . . . . . . . . . . . . . . 212-535-9500
FAX . . . . . . . . . . . . . . . . . . . . . . . . . . 212-772-1126
159 E. 80th St.
New York, NY 10021

TYPE          Television
CREDITS       Copacabana - Mirrors - Bob Hope Specials - Inside the
              Actors' Studio

James Lipton . . . . . . . . . . . . . . . . . . . . Writer/Producer

## LIROFF PRODUCTIONS, MARCI
PHONE . . . . . . . . . . . . . . . . . . . . . . . . 213-876-3900
FAX . . . . . . . . . . . . . . . . . . . . . . . . . . 213-876-3900
P.O. Box 48498
Los Angeles, CA 90048

TYPE          Motion Pictures
CREDITS       The Spitfire Grill

Marci Liroff . . . . . . . . . . . . . . . . . . President/Producer

## LISTEN TO YOUR MOTHER PRODS., INC.
PHONE . . . . . . . . . . . . . . . . . . . . . . . . . . . . . 714-376-7094
EMAIL . . . . . . . . . . . . . . . . . . . . . . . . . . kipzone@aol.com
1224 Cerritos Drive
Laguna Beach, CA 92651
TYPE        Motion Pictures + Television + Interactive Multimedia
CREDITS     Miss Evers' Boys
Kip Konwiser . . . . . . . . . . . . . . . . . . . . . . . . . . . . . President
Anabel Konwiser . . . . . . . . . . . . . . . . . . . . . . . . . CFO/Mom
Kern Konwiser . . . . . . . . . . . . . . . . . . . . . . . . . Vice President

## LITTLE BEAR FILMS, INC.
PHONE . . . . . . . . . . . . . . . . . . . . . . . . . 212-226-0814
FAX . . . . . . . . . . . . . . . . . . . . . . . . . . . 212-334-5180
135 Watts Street
New York, NY 10013
TYPE        Motion Pictures + Documentaries
CREDITS     Broken Noses - Let's Get Lost - Back Yard Movie - Gentle
            Giants
Nan Bush . . . . . . . . . . . . . . . . . . . . . . . . . . . . . Principal
Bruce Weber . . . . . . . . . . . . . . . . . . . . . . . . . . . Principal
Elizabeth Kline . . . . . . . . . . . . Development & Production Coordinator
Andrew Rose . . . . . . . . . . . . . . . . . . . . . . . Film Department

## LITVINOFF PRODUCTIONS, SI
PHONE . . . . . . . . . . . . . . . . . . . . . . . . . 213-848-6907
2825 Woodstock Rd.
Los Angeles, CA 90046
TYPE        Motion Pictures
CREDITS     Clockwork Orange - Walkabout - The Man Who Fell to
            Earth - The Queen
Si Litvinoff . . . . . . . . . . . . . . . . . . . . . . . . . . . . . Producer
Paul Madden . . . . . . . . . . . . . . . . . . . . . . . . Creative Affairs

## LIVE ACTION PICTURES
PHONE . . . . . . . . . . . . . . . . . . . . . . . . . 310-276-8196
P.O. Box 5155
Beverly Hills, CA 90210
TYPE        Motion Pictures
CREDITS     Sanctuary - The Resurrection of Broncho Billy (AA) - Agro
            & York: Moon Monkeys
June Breidt . . . . . . . . . . . . . . . . . . . . . . . . Writer/Producer
John Longenecker . . . . . . . . . . . . . . . . . . . . Writer/Producer

## LOBELL-BERGMAN PRODS.
PHONE . . . . . . . . . . . . . . . . . . . . . . . . . 818-777-9944
FAX . . . . . . . . . . . . . . . . . . . . . 818-866-3460/818-866-3456
100 Universal City Plaza, Bung. 301
Universal City, CA 91608
TYPE        Motion Pictures
DEAL        Universal Pictures
CREDITS     Striptease - It Could Happen To You - The Freshman -
            Honeymoon In Vegas
Andrew Bergman . . . . . . . . . . . . . . . . . Producer/Writer/Director
Mike Lobell . . . . . . . . . . . . . . . . . . . . . . . . . . . . Producer
Catherine Schulman . . . . . . . . . . . . . . . Sr. VP, Production (818-777-9906)
Steve Barnett . . . . . . . . . . . . . . . . . . Vice President (818-777-8667)
Laura Lichstein . . . . . . . . . . . . . . . . Dir., Development (818-777-9902)
Alex Barder . . . . . . . . . . . Asst. to Mike Lobell & Andrew Bergman
Grant Calof . . . . . . . . . . . . . . . Asst. to Ms. Schulman (818-777-9906)
John Sacchi . . . . . . . . . . . . . . . . . . . . Asst. to Laura Lichstein
Josh Schaer . . . . . . . . . . . . . . . . . . . . Asst. to Steve Barnett

## LOCK 'N LOAD (UBIQUITOUS) PICS.
PHONE . . . . . . . . . . . . . . . . . . . . . . . . . 818-769-4565
FAX . . . . . . . . . . . . . . . . . . . . . . . . . . . 818-769-1917
12041 Hoffman St.
Studio City, CA 91604
TYPE        Motion Pictures
CREDITS     Kill Thy Neighbor - Beam Me Up, Scotty - Distortions -
            Fate Loves The Fearless
Daniel Kuhn . . . . . . . . . . . . . . . . . . . . . . . . Producer/Writer
Susan Coppola . . . . . . . . . . . . . . . . . . Producer/Writer/Director

## LOGANWORKS LTD.
PHONE . . . . . . . . . . . . . . . . . . . . . . . . . 818-760-7151
FAX . . . . . . . . . . . . . . . . . . . . . . . . . . . 818-760-1114
WEBSITE . . . . . . . . . . . . . . . . . http://www.LOGANWORKS.com
3880 Reklaw Dr.
Studio City, CA 91604
TYPE        Motion Pictures + Television
CREDITS     Repossessed - Meatballs IV - Up Your Alley
Bob Logan . . . . . . . . . . . . . . . . . . . . Writer/Director/Producer
Stephen Goepel . . . . . . . . . . . . . . . . . . . . . . VP, Production
Daniel Linck . . . . . . . . . . . . . . . . VP, Production & Development

## LOGO ENTERTAINMENT
PHONE . . . . . . . . . . . . . . . . . . . . . . . . . 310-276-6700
FAX . . . . . . . . . . . . . . . . . . . . . . . . . . . 310-284-3290
EMAIL . . . . . . . . . . . . . . . . . . . . . logoent@earthlink.net
1888 Century Park East, Ste. 1900
Los Angeles, CA 90067
TYPE        Motion Pictures + Television + Documentaries +
            Syndication + Feature Direct to Video
DEAL        Proctor & Gamble Prods. Inc.
CREDITS     To Dance With Olivia - A Father for Charlie - The
            Inspectors
Louis Gossett Jr. . . . . . . . . . . . . . . . . . Actor/Executive Producer
Dennis Considine . . . . . . . . . . . . . . . . . . . . Executive Producer
Laurie Ferneau . . . . . . . . . . . . . . . . . . . . Executive Assistant
Otis Harper . . . . . . . . . . . . . . . . . . Asst. to Louis Gossett, Jr.

## LONDINE PRODUCTIONS
PHONE . . . . . . . . . . . . . . . . . . . . . . . . . 310-281-7540
EMAIL . . . . . . . . . . . . . . . . . . . . . . . cassiusII@aol.com
1626 N. Wilcox Ave., Ste. 480
Hollywood, CA 90028-6273
TYPE        Motion Pictures + Television + Feature Direct to Video
CREDITS     D.C. Cab - 24/7 Radio
COMMENTS    Also: Music Videos.
Cassius Vernon Weathersby . . . . . . . . . . . . President/Producer
Nadine Weathersby . . . . . . . . . . . . . . . . . . . . . VP/Producer

## LONDON COMPANY, BARRY
PHONE . . . . . . . . . . . . . . . . . . . . . . . . . 213-956-5066
FAX . . . . . . . . . . . . . . . . . . . . . . . . . . . 213-862-2305
Paramount Pictures
5555 Melrose Ave., Bob Hope #200
Hollywood, CA 90038
TYPE        Motion Pictures + Television
DEAL        Paramount Pictures- Motion Picture Group
Barry London . . . . . . . . . . . . . . . . . . . . . . . . . . Producer
Mark Jacobson . . . . . . . . . . . . . . . . . . . . . . Vice President
Kimberly Hughes . . . . . . . . . . . Development Coordinator/Exec. Asst.

## LONG ROAD PRODUCTIONS
PHONE . . . . . . . . . . . . . . . . . . . . . . . . . 310-271-9292
FAX . . . . . . . . . . . . . . . . . . . . . . . . . . . 310-271-9497
130 S. El Camino
Beverly Hills, CA 90212
TYPE        Motion Pictures
CREDITS     Maximum Risk - The Quest - Sudden Death - Timecop -
            Universal Soldier - Double Team
Jean-Claude Van Damme . . . . . . . . . . . . . . . . . . . President
Richard G. Murphy . . . . . . . . . . . . . . . . . . VP, Development

## LONGBOW PRODUCTIONS
PHONE . . . . . . . . . . . . . . . . . . . . . . . . . 818-762-6600
EMAIL . . . . . . . . . . . . . . . . . . . . . . longbowprd@aol.com
4181 Sunswept Drive, Ste. 100
Studio City, CA 91604-2335
TYPE        Motion Pictures + Television
CREDITS     A Private Matter - A League of Their Own - Forever Love -
            The Summer of Ben Tyler
Richard Kughn . . . . . . . . . . . . . . . . . . . . . . . . . Chairman
Sharon Cicero . . . . . . . . . . . . . . . . . . . . . . . . . . Partner
Ronnie D. Clemmer . . . . . . . . . . . . . . . . . . . . . . . Partner
Bill Pace . . . . . . . . . . . . . . . . . . . . . . . . . . . . . Partner
Marla White . . . . . . . . . . . . . . . . . . . . . Dir., Development
Gregory Maxey . . . . . . . . . . . . . . . . . . . . . . . Production
Jonathan Foster . . . . . . . . . . . . . . . . . . . Asst. to Ms. Cicero
Victoria Villandry . . . . . . . . . . . . . . . . . Administrative Assistant

## LONGFELLOW PICTURES
PHONE . . . . . . . . . . . . . . . . . . . . . . . . . 212-431-5550
FAX . . . . . . . . . . . . . . . . . . . . . . . . . . . 212-431-5822
EMAIL . . . . . . . . . . . . . . . . . . . . . . LongPics@aol.com
145 Hudson St., 12th Floor
New York, NY 10013
TYPE        Motion Pictures
DEAL        Sidney Kimmel Entertainment
CREDITS     Princess Caraboo - Prince of Tides - The Rachel Papers -
            Curtain Call - Town and Country
Andrew Karsch . . . . . . . . . . . . . . . . . . . . Producer/President
Tara Connaughton . . . . . . . . . . . . . . . Dir., Creative Development

# COMPANIES AND STAFF

**LONGRIDGE ENTERPRISES**
PHONE . . . . . . . . . . . . . . . . . . . . . . . . . . . 818-783-6251
FAX . . . . . . . . . . . . . . . . . . . . . . . . . . . . . 818-783-6518
15250 Ventura Blvd., Ste. 800
Sherman Oaks, CA 91403

TYPE        Television
CREDITS     You Must Remember (PBS) - Fairy Tales For Every Child
            (HBO)

Robert Guillaume . . . . . . . . . . . . President/Actor/Executive Producer
Donna Brown Guillaume . . . . . . . . . . . . . . . . . . . . VP/Producer
Jack La Zard Jr. . . . . . . . . . . . . . . . . . . . . . . . . . . . . Producer

***LOOKALIKE PRODUCTIONS**
PHONE . . . . . . . . . . . . . . . . . . . . . . . . . . . 310-444-8650
FAX . . . . . . . . . . . . . . . . . . . . . . . . . . . . . 310-444-8272
EMAIL . . . . . . . . . . . annepo@foxinc.com/LisaJ@foxinc.com
Fox Television Studios
10210 West Pico Blvd., Bldg. 41
Los Angeles, CA 90035

TYPE        Documentaries + Television
DEAL        Fox Television Studios

Nancy Stern . . . . . . . . . . . . . Exec. Producer/Sr. VP, Fox TV Studios
Anne M. Powell . . . . . . . . . . . . . . . . Producer/Mgr., Development
Lisa Jackson . . . . . . . . . . . . . . . . . . . . . . . Producer/Development

**LOOKING GLASS PRODUCTIONS**
PHONE . . . . . . . . . . . . . . . . . . . . . . . . . . . 310-281-7598
FAX . . . . . . . . . . . . . . . . . . . . . . . . . . . . . 213-661-8139
2118 Wilshire Blvd., Ste. 760
Santa Monica, CA 90403-5784

TYPE        Motion Pictures + Television + Animation
CREDITS     Sand Trap - The Thing at Pete and Julie's - The Rundown
COMMENTS    Also: Theatre.

Jerry Rapp . . . . . . . . . . . . . . . . . . . . Writer/Director/Producer
Jacqueline Harris . . . . . . . . . . . . . . . . . . . . . . . . . Producer
Linda Miller . . . . . . . . . . . . . . . . . . . . . . . . . . . . . Producer
Karen Hayden-Jaffe . . . . . . . . . . . . . . . . . . . Dir., Development

**LORD/WEAVER PRODS.**
PHONE . . . . . . . . . . . . . . . . . . . . . . . . . . . 310-244-6160
FAX . . . . . . . . . . . . . . . . . . . . . . . . . . . . . 310-244-6169
EMAIL . . . . . . . . . . . . . . . . . . . . . . . . . . lwprod@aol.com
WEBSITE . . . . . . . . . . . . . . . . . . . http://www.lordweaver.com
Columbia Pictures
10202 W. Washington Blvd., Lean # 430
Culver City, CA 90232

TYPE        Motion Pictures + Television

Tony Lord . . . . . . . . . . . . . . . . . . . . . . . . . Producer/Partner
Matthew Weaver . . . . . . . . . . . . . . . . . . . . . . Producer/Partner
Joshua Rafofsky . . . . . . . . . . . . . . . . . . . . . Creative Executive
Ara Soghomonian . . . . . . . . . . . . . . . . . . Asst. to the Producers

**LORING PRODUCTIONS, LYNN**
PHONE . . . . . . . . . . . . . . . . . . . . . . . . . . . 310-274-1575
FAX . . . . . . . . . . . . . . . . . . . . . . . . . . . . . 310-276-5562
EMAIL . . . . . . . . . . . . . . . . . . . . . . . . . lynn3939@aol.com
506 N. Camden Drive
Beverly Hills, CA 90210

TYPE        Motion Pictures + Television + Syndication + Interactive
            Multimedia
CREDITS     Mr. Mom - Best Little Girl In The World

Lynn Loring . . . . . . . . . . . . . . . . . . . . President/Exec. Producer
Brett Tracy . . . . . . . . . . . . . . . . . . . . . . . . . Creative Assistant

**LOTUS PICTURES**
PHONE . . . . . . . . . . . . . . . . . . . . . . . . . . . 310-577-8027
FAX . . . . . . . . . . . . . . . . . . . . . . . . . . . . . 310-577-0194
EMAIL . . . . . . . . . . . . . . . . . . . . . . . . . LotusPics@aol.com
415 Washington Blvd., #1004
Marina del Rey, CA 90292

TYPE        Motion Pictures + Television
CREDITS     Legacy

Michele Berk . . . . . . . . . . . . . . . . . . . . . . . . . . . . Producer
Jennifer Stein . . . . . . . . . . . . . . . . . . . . . . . Dir., Development

**LOVELL, DYSON**
PHONE . . . . . . . . . . . . . . . . . . . . . . . . . . . 310-854-3833
FAX . . . . . . . . . . . . . . . . . . . . . . . . . . . . . 310-854-0211
EMAIL . . . . . . . . . . . . . . . . . dyson@lovlev.demon.co.uk
HGL
760 N. La Cienega Blvd.
Los Angeles, CA 90069

TYPE        Motion Pictures + Television
CREDITS     Jane Eyre - The Champ - Cotton Club - Lonesome Dove -
            Hamlet - The Odyssey - Merlin - Mary Stuart - Alice in
            Wonderland - Farragut's Crime

Dyson Lovell . . . . . . . . . . . . . . . . . . . . . . . . . . . . . Producer

***LOWER EAST SIDE FILMS**
PHONE . . . . . . . . . . . . . . . . . . . . . . . . . . . 212-966-0111
FAX . . . . . . . . . . . . . . . . . . . . . . . . . . . . . 212-966-0555
EMAIL . . . . . . . . . . . . . . . . . . . . . . . . . . lesfilms@aol.com
443 Broadway, 5th Floor
New York, NY 10013

TYPE        Animation + Motion Pictures + Television

John Leguizamo . . . . . . . . . . . . . . . . . . . . . . . . . . . Partner
David Bar Katz . . . . . . . . . . . . . . . . . . . . . . . . . . . . Partner
Kathy De Marco . . . . . . . . . . . . . . . . . . . . . . Head, Production
Barbara Hammond . . . . . . . . . . . . . . . . . . . . . . Story Editor
Juan Caceres . . . . . . . . . . . . . . . . . . . . . . . . . . . . Assistant

**LOWRY PRODUCTIONS, HUNT**
PHONE . . . . . . . . . . . . . . . . . . . . . . . . . . . 818-560-6790
FAX . . . . . . . . . . . . . . . . . . . . . . . . . . . . . 818-560-6798
EMAIL . . . . . . . . . . . . . . . . . . . . . . . lowryprods@aol.com
Walt Disney Studios
500 S. Buena Vista St.
Burbank, CA 91521

TYPE        Motion Pictures
DEAL        Walt Disney Company, The
CREDITS     A Time To Kill - First Knight - The Last of the Mohicans

Hunt Lowry . . . . . . . . . . . . . . . . . . . . . . . . . . . . . Producer
Casey La Scala . . . . . . . . . . . . . Sr. VP, Production (818-560-2917)
Stacy Cohen . . . . . . . . . . . . . . . . Dir., Development (818-560-6184)
Victor H. Constantino . . . . . . . . . . . . . . . Asst. to Mr. Lowry
Alexandra Sorota . . . . . . . . . . . . . . . . . . . Asst. To Mr. La Scala

**LUCCHESI PRODS., GARY**
PHONE . . . . . . . . . . . . . . . . . . . . . . . . . . . 310-888-3400
FAX . . . . . . . . . . . . . . . . . . . . . . . . . . . . . 310-888-3401
345 N. Maple Dr., Ste. 120
Beverly Hills, CA 90210

TYPE        Motion Pictures
CREDITS     Jennifer 8 - Virtuosity - 3 Wishes - Primal Fear - Gotti
COMMENTS    And Cable - Also: The Really Useful Film Company Inc.

Gary Lucchesi . . . . . . . . . . . . . . . . . . . . . . . . . . . Producer
Robert McMinn . . . . . . . . . . . . . . . . . . . . . Sr. VP, Production
Arnold Rudnick . . . . . . . . . . . . . . . . . . . . . Dir., Development
Leigh Oblinger . . . . . . . . . . . . . . . . . . . Asst. to Gary Lucchesi

**LUGER PRODUCTIONS, INC., LOIS**
PHONE . . . . . . . . . . . . . . . . . . . . . . . . . . . 213-937-8996
FAX . . . . . . . . . . . . . . . . . . . . . . . . . . . . . 213-938-3801
800 S. Curson Ave.
Los Angeles, CA 90036

TYPE        Motion Pictures + Television + Feature Direct to Video
CREDITS     Terror In The Shadows - The Danger of Love - Divided By
            Hate

Lois Luger . . . . . . . . . . . . . . . . . . . . . . . President/Producer
Wendy Arthur . . . . . . . . . . . . . . . . . . . . . Creative Executive

**LUMIERE FILMS INC.**
PHONE . . . . . . . . . . . . . . . . . . . . . . . . . . . 213-653-7878
FAX . . . . . . . . . . . . . . . . . . . . . . . . . . . . . 213-653-8877
EMAIL . . . . . . . . . . . . . . . . . . . rpitts@lumierefilms.com
8442 Melrose Place
Los Angeles, CA 90069

TYPE        Motion Pictures
CREDITS     Leaving Las Vegas - Fresh - Touch

Randolph Pitts . . . . . . . . . . . . . . . . . . Chief Executive Officer
Lila Cazes . . . . . . . . . . . . . . . . . . . Head, Worldwide Production
Beth Voiku . . . . . . . . . . . . . . . . . . . . . . . . . . Office Manager
Melissa Morgan . . . . . . . . . . . . . . . . . . . . Executive Assistant

# COMPANIES AND STAFF

**LUNARIA FILMS**
PHONE . . . . . . . . . . . . . . . . . . . . . . . . . . . 310-581-9212
FAX . . . . . . . . . . . . . . . . . . . . . . . . . . . . . 310-581-9512
2922 2nd St., #E
Santa Monica, CA 90405-5433
TYPE        Motion Pictures + Television + Animation
CREDITS     Kicking & Screaming - Black Circle Boys - The Only Thrill
            - Vig
Erin E. Martin . . . . . . . . . . . . . . . . . . . . . . . . . . . . Producer

**LUPOVITZ PRODS.**
PHONE . . . . . . . . . . . . . . . . . . . . . . . . . . . 310-276-4923
FAX . . . . . . . . . . . . . . . . . . . . . . . . . . . . . 310-276-4923
1501 S. Holt Ave.
Los Angeles, CA 90035
TYPE        Motion Pictures + Television
CREDITS     Search and Destroy - The Velocity of Gary - Mrs. Cage
Dan Lupovitz . . . . . . . . . . . . . . . . . . . . . . . . . . . Producer
Rudy Benjamin . . . . . . . . . . . . . . . . . . . . . . . . . Associate
Randy Albelda . . . . . . . . . . . . . . . . . . . . Head, Development

**LUSSIER, PAUL**
PHONE . . . . . . . . . . . . . . . . . . . . . . . . . . . 818-954-4483
FAX . . . . . . . . . . . . . . . . . . . . . . . . . . . . . 818-954-4407
4000 Warner Blvd., Bldg. 138, Rm. 1202A
Burbank, CA 91522
TYPE        Television
DEAL        Warner Bros. Television Productions
CREDITS     Doing Time on Maple Drive - Blue Rodeo - Based on an
            Untrue Story
Paul Lussier . . . . . . . . . . . . . . . . . . . President/Exec. Producer
Marguerite Topping . . . . . . . . . . . . . . . . . . . Development

**LUX PICTURES**
PHONE . . . . . . . . . . . . . . . . . . . . . . . . . . . 310-314-3898
FAX . . . . . . . . . . . . . . . . . . . . . . . . . . . . . 310-314-3892
EMAIL . . . . . . . . . . . . . . . . . . . . . . . . . luxpix@aol.com
1318 Pacific Ave.
Venice, CA 90291-3608
TYPE        Motion Pictures + Documentaries
COMMENTS    Also: Completion financing.
Martin Kistler . . . . . . . . . . . . . . . . . . . . . . . . . . . Producer
James Magowan . . . . . . . . . . . . . . . . . . . . . . . . . Producer
Manuel Ruiz . . . . . . . . . . . . . . . . . . . . . . . . . . . Controller

**LYLES PRODS., A.C.**
PHONE . . . . . . . . . . . . . . . . . . . . . . . . . . . 213-956-5819
FAX . . . . . . . . . . . . . . . . . . . . . . . . . . . . . 213-862-0256
Paramount Pictures
5555 Melrose Ave.
Los Angeles, CA 90038-3197
TYPE        Motion Pictures + Television + Documentaries
DEAL        Paramount Pictures- Motion Picture Group
CREDITS     Conversations with the President - The Last Day - Dear
            Mr. President
A.C. Lyles . . . . . . . . . . . . . . . . . . . . . . . Executive Producer
Mary-Ann Dunlap . . . . . . . . . . . . . . . . . . . Asst. to Mr. Lyles

**LYNCH ENTERTAINMENT**
PHONE . . . . . . . . . . . . . . . . . . . . . . . . . . . 310-473-5217
FAX . . . . . . . . . . . . . . . . . . . . . . . . . . . . . 310-473-9847
2001 S. Barrington Ave., Ste. 200
Los Angeles, CA 90025
TYPE        Television + Motion Pictures
CREDITS     Night Tracks - Kids Inc - Xuxa - Secret World of Alex Mack
            - NFAA Award - Journey of Allen Strange
Tom Lynch . . . . . . . . . . . . . . . . . . . . . CEO/Exec. Producer
John Lynch . . . . . . . . . . . . . . . . . . President/Exec. Producer
Brian Altounian . . . . . . . . . . . . . . . . . . . . . . VP, Finance
Gary Stephenson . . . . . . . . . . . . . . . . . . . . VP, Production
Brandy Lynn . . . . . . . . . . . . . . . . . . . Production Supervisor
Naomi Rothberg . . . . . . . . . . . . . . . . . . Dir., Development
Seena Greenwald . . . . . . . . . . . . . Exec. Asst. to Mr. Lynch
Jonas Agin . . . . . . . . . . . . . . . . . . . . . . . . . . . . . Assistant
Anthony Cipriano . . . . . . . . . . . . . . . . . . . . . . . . Assistant

**LYNN PRODUCTIONS, TAMI**
PHONE . . . . . . . . . . . . . . . . . . . . . . . . . . . 818-888-8264
FAX . . . . . . . . . . . . . . . . . . . . . . . . . . . . . 818-888-8267
EMAIL . . . . . . . . . . . . . . . . . . . . . tamilynn@webtv.com
20411 Chapter Drive
Woodland Hills, CA 91364
TYPE        Motion Pictures + Documentaries
DEAL        Columbia Pictures/Warner Bros. Pictures
CREDITS     Vibrations - Healing Hands - Given A Chance - Claudine's
            Return - All My Life
COMMENTS    In association with Kim Tam & Healing Hands
            Productions.
Tami Lynn . . . . . . . . . . . . . . . . . . . . . President/Producer
Kim Marriner . . . . . . . . . . . . . . . . . . . . . . . . . . . Producer
Marc Alexander . . . . . . . . . . . . . . . . . . . . . . . . . Producer
Robert D'Amato . . . . . . . . . . . . . . . . . . Asst. to Ms. Lynn

**MACDONALD PRODS**
PHONE . . . . . . . . . . . . . . . . . . . . . . . . . . . 310-229-9590
FAX . . . . . . . . . . . . . . . . . . . . . . . . . . . . . 310-229-9826
10100 Santa Monica Blvd., Ste. 910
Los Angeles, CA 90067
TYPE        Motion Pictures + Television
CREDITS     Sliver - Jade - The Saint - Rough Riders - One Man's Hero
William J. Macdonald . . . . . . . . . . . . . . . . . . . . . Producer
Kristine Harlan . . . . . . . . . . . . . . . . . . . . . . . . . . Producer
Lola Butler . . . . . . . . . . . . . . . . . . . . . . . . . . . . Assistant
Erik Mountain . . . . . . . . . . . . . . . . . . . . . . . . . . Assistant

**MACHT ENT. GROUP, INC.**
PHONE . . . . . . . . . . . . . . . . . . . . . . . . . . . 310-449-4096
FAX . . . . . . . . . . . . . . . . . . . . . . . . . . . . . 310-449-4097
3000 W. Olympic Blvd., Bldg. 4
Stes. 1370-4
Santa Monica, CA 90404
TYPE        Motion Pictures + Television
CREDITS     Best of Comedy Live
Jon Macht . . . . . . . . . . . . . . . . . . . . . . . Writer/Producer
Sheila Conlin . . . . . . . . . . . . . . . . . . . . . . . . . . Producer
Mark Rains . . . . . . . . . . . . . . . . . . . . . . . . . . . Producer
Alan Carter . . . . . . . . . . . . . . . . . . . . . . . . . . . . Director
Tom Harmon . . . . . . . . . . . . . . . . . . . . . . . . . Animation
Theone Masoner . . . . . . . . . . . . . . . . . . . . . . . . . Writer
JJ Bertelzen . . . . . . . . . . . . . . . . . . . . . . . . . . . Assistant
Ian Wright . . . . . . . . . . . . . . . . . . . . . . . . . . . . Assistant

**MAD CHANCE**
PHONE . . . . . . . . . . . . . . . . . . . . . . . . . . . 818-954-3803
FAX . . . . . . . . . . . . . . . . . . . . . . . . . . . . . 818-954-3447
EMAIL . . . . . . . . . . . . . . . . . . madchance@sprintmail.com
Warner Bros.
4000 Warner Blvd., Bldg. 81, Ste. 209
Burbank, CA 91522
TYPE        Motion Pictures
DEAL        Warner Bros. Pictures
CREDITS     Astronaut's Wife - Bound - Assassins - The Things I Hate
            About You
Andrew Lazar . . . . . . . . . . . . . . . . . . . . . . . . . . . Producer
Jody Hedien . . . . . . . . . . . . . . . . . . . . . . . . . Co-Producer
Doug Davison . . . . . . . . . . . . . . . . . . . Dir., Development
Far Shariat . . . . . . . . . . . . . . . . . . . Dir., Creative Affairs
Alexander Ankeles . . . . . . . . . . . . . . . Asst. to Jody Hedien
Gym Hinderer . . . . . . . . . . . . . . . . . Asst. to Andrew Lazar
Sean Wicks . . . . . . . . . . . . . . . . . . . . . Creative Assistant

***MADGUY FILMS**
PHONE . . . . . . . . . . . . . . . . . . . . . . . . . . . 310-777-6515
FAX . . . . . . . . . . . . . . . . . . . . . . . . . . . . . 310-777-6528
9348 Civic Center Dr.
Beverly Hills, CA 90210
TYPE        Motion Pictures
DEAL        Warner Bros. Pictures
Madonna . . . . . . . . . . . . . . . . . . . . . . . . . . . . . No Title
Guy Oseary . . . . . . . . . . . . . . . . . . . . . . . . . . . No Title
Caresse Norman . . . . . . . . . . . . . . . . . . . . . . . No Title
Gary Ventimiglia . . . . . . . . . . . . . . . . . . . . . . . No Title
Daniel Rosenfeld . . . . . . . . . . . . . . . Development Assistant

# COMPANIES AND STAFF

## MADSEN PRODUCTIONS, BILL
```
PHONE ............................................ 310-475-8811
```
1015 Gayley Ave., Ste. 230
Los Angeles, CA 90025

| | |
|---|---|
| TYPE | Motion Pictures |
| CREDITS | Citizen Hero - Lady Lake |

Bill Madsen ............................................ Producer
Ann Forester ............................... Executive Assistant

## MAGAR FILMS, INC., GUY
```
PHONE ............................................ 213-461-9009
FAX .............................................. 213-876-9809
```
7185 Woodrow Wilson Drive
Los Angeles, CA 90068

| | |
|---|---|
| TYPE | Motion Pictures + Television |
| CREDITS | Showdown - Stepfather III - Retribution |

Guy Magar ....................... Director/Writer/Producer

## *MAGIC HOUR PICTURES
```
PHONE ............................................ 310-286-7208
FAX .............................................. 310-286-0518
```
1801 Ave. of the Stars, #1200
Los Angeles, CA 90067

| | |
|---|---|
| TYPE | Motion Pictures + Television + Feature Direct to Video + Syndication |
| CREDITS | Indiscreet - The Beneficiary - The Hit List |
| COMMENTS | International Distribution: 310-286-0530. |

Marc Greenberg ....................................... President
Rich Goldberg ................................... Vice President
Marc Bienstock .......................... Producer/Director
Pierre Kurland ....................................... Controller

## MAGNUM MOTION PICTURES, INC.
```
PHONE ............................................ 213-656-3922
FAX .............................................. 213-656-4738
EMAIL ............................... wlustig@primenet.com
```
1287-G N. Crescent Heights Blvd.
W. Hollywood, CA 90046-5022

| | |
|---|---|
| TYPE | Motion Pictures + Television + Feature Direct to Video |
| DEAL | Hammer Film Productions Limited/Anchor Bay Entertainment |
| CREDITS | Vigilante- Maniac Cop 1 & 2- Relentless- Uncle Sam - Maniac - Hit List - Naked City |
| COMMENTS | Also: Home Video Distribution. |

William Lustig ............................. Producer/Director

## MAIA PRODUCTIONS
```
PHONE ............................................ 310-289-1705
FAX .............................................. 310-289-7885
EMAIL ............................... sasha@pacbell.net
```
1158 26th St., Ste. 422
Santa Monica, CA 90403

| | |
|---|---|
| TYPE | Motion Pictures + Television + Interactive Multimedia |
| CREDITS | The Doors - Street Fighter - High School High - Cadillacs & Dinosaurs (CBS) |

Sasha Harari ......................................... President
Ari Shofet ............................... Dir., Development

## MAIN LINE PICTURES
```
PHONE ............................................ 213-851-5555
FAX .............................................. 213-851-2191
```
7920 Sunset Blvd., Ste. 250
Los Angeles, CA 90046

| | |
|---|---|
| TYPE | Motion Pictures |
| CREDITS | Boxing Helena - Body Count |

James Schaeffer ..................................... Chairman
Carl Mazzocone ..................................... President
Susan Lenser .......................... Production Executive
Liz Hecht-Ward ..................................... Controller

## *MAKEMAGIC PRODUCTIONS
```
PHONE ............................................ 213-653-3108
FAX .............................................. 213-653-3144
```
8489 W. 3rd St., #1002
Los Angles, CA 90048

| | |
|---|---|
| TYPE | Motion Pictures + Television |
| CREDITS | Lady Killer - Snoopy the Musical |
| COMMENTS | Co-Production deal with Acropolis Entertainment, Inc. |

Denise David .............................. President/Producer
Michael L. Grace ............................ Writer/Producer

## MALPASO PRODS.
```
PHONE ............................................ 818-954-3367
FAX .............................................. 818-954-4803
```
Warner Bros. Inc.
4000 Warner Blvd., Bldg. 81
Burbank, CA 91522-0811

| | |
|---|---|
| TYPE | Motion Pictures + Television + Documentaries + Interactive Multimedia |
| DEAL | Warner Bros. Pictures |
| CREDITS | The Bridges of Madison County - Unforgiven - Bird - Midnight In The Garden Of Good And Evil |

Clint Eastwood ................... Producer/Actor/Director
Tom Rooker ............................ Associate Producer
Melissa Rooker .......................... Dir., Development
Joel Cox ................................................ Editor
Andrew White ...................... Production Coordinator

## MANDALAY PICTURES
```
PHONE ............................................ 310-244-2400
FAX .............................................. 310-244-2151
```
10202 W. Washington Blvd., Astaire 3rd
Culver City, CA 90232

| | |
|---|---|
| TYPE | Motion Pictures |

Peter Guber .......................................... Chairman
Paul Schaeffer ................................. Vice Chairman
Adam Platnick ....................................... President
Darrell Walker ................. Exec. VP, Business Affairs
John Zabel ..................................... Exec. VP/CFO
Karen Teicher ........... Exec. VP, Motion Picture Production
David Zelon ................. Sr. VP, Production Administration
Chantal Feghali ......................... VP, Post Production
Ori Marmur ..................... VP, Motion Picture Production
Tracy Andreen ........................... Dir., Development
Michelle DiRaffaele ......... Dir., Business Affairs Administration

## *MANDALAY TELEVISION
```
PHONE ............................................ 310-244-2400
FAX .............................................. 310-244-2220
```
10202 W. Washington Blvd.
Culver City, CA 90232

| | |
|---|---|
| TYPE | Television + Documentaries |
| COMMENTS | MOW's, Mini-series, Series. |

Peter Guber .......................................... Chairman
Tom Patricia ................................. Pres., TV Pictures
Scott Sanders ................................. Pres., Series TV
Joe Voci ........................... Exec. Producer, Series TV
Steven Lewis ................. Sr. VP, Nonfiction Television
Ellen Burditt ................. Sr. VP, Television Pictures
Chris Selak .............. Assoc. Dir., Development, Series TV
Margie Moreno .......................... Mgr., TV Pictures

## MANDEVILLE FILMS
```
PHONE ............................................ 818-560-1000
FAX .............................................. 818-842-4066
```
Walt Disney Studios
500 S. Buena Vista St.
Burbank, CA 91521-1829

| | |
|---|---|
| TYPE | Motion Pictures |
| DEAL | Walt Disney Company, The |
| CREDITS | Mr. Wrong - The Sixth Man - George of the Jungle - The Negotiator |

David Hoberman ....................................... President
Albert Beveridge ................................. Vice President
Cristi Limm ............................... Dir., Development
Cookie Carosella ................. Asst. to David Hoberman
Trilby Sheeser ................... Asst. to David Hoberman
David Jung ........................... Asst. to Cristi Limm

## MANDY FILMS, INC.
```
PHONE ............................................ 310-246-0500
FAX .............................................. 310-246-0350
```
9201 Wilshire #206
Beverly Hills, CA 90210

| | |
|---|---|
| TYPE | Motion Pictures + Television |
| DEAL | Paramount Pictures- Motion Picture Group |
| CREDITS | Sleeping With the Enemy - War Games - Distinguished Gentleman - Double Jeopardy |

Leonard Goldberg ................. President/Exec. Producer
Heather Neely ................................. Vice President
Amy Mitchell ...................... Exec. Asst. to President
Martina Papinchak .......... Exec. Asst. to Vice President

## MANHATTAN PICTURES LTD.
PHONE . . . . . . . . . . . . . . . . . . . . . . . . . . . . . . . . 818-706-1729
FAX . . . . . . . . . . . . . . . . . . . . . . . . . . . . . . . . . 818-706-6034
18653 Ventura Blvd., Ste. 312
Tarzana, CA 91356

TYPE          Motion Pictures + Television
Rob Silver . . . . . . . . . . . . . . . . . . . . . . . . . . . . . . Executive Producer
Stephen A. Tate . . . . . . . . . . . . . . . . . . . . . . . . . . . . . . Producer
Thomas H. Marshall . . . . . . . . . . . . . . . . . . . . . . . . . . . . . . Producer
Raymond Stella . . . . . . . . . . . . . . . . . . . . . . . . . Production Executive
Marvin Vogel . . . . . . . . . . . . . . . . . . . . . . . . . . . . Dir., Development
Shoshanna Tate . . . . . . . . . . . . . . . . . . . . . . . . . Executive Assistant
Greg Cruise . . . . . . . . . . . . . . . . . . . . . . . . . . . . Executive Assistant

## MANHATTAN PROJECT LTD., THE
PHONE . . . . . . . . . . . . . . . . . . . . . . . . . . . . . . . . 212-258-2541
FAX . . . . . . . . . . . . . . . . . . . . . . . . . . . . . . . . . 212-258-2546
1775 Broadway, Ste. 410
New York, NY 10019-1903

TYPE          Motion Pictures + Television + Syndication + Feature
                 Direct to Video
CREDITS     Jaws - The Verdict - The Player - A Few Good Men - Deep
                 Impact
COMMENTS   Also: Theater.
David Brown . . . . . . . . . . . . . . . . . . . . . . . . President/Producer (NY)
Kit Golden . . . . . . . . . . . . . . . . . . Sr. VP, Production (NY) (212-258-2543)
Doris Wood . . . . . . . . . . . . . . . . . Exec. Asst. to David Brown (NY)

## MANHEIM COMPANY, THE
PHONE . . . . . . . . . . . . . . . . . . . . . . . . . . . . . . . . 310-456-7272
FAX . . . . . . . . . . . . . . . . . . . . . . . . . . . . . . . . . 310-456-3790
15237 Sunset Blvd.
Pacific Palisades, CA 90272

TYPE          Motion Pictures + Television
CREDITS     Leap of Faith - Roe vs. Wade - Zooman - Trial By Fire -
                 Jitters
Michael Manheim . . . . . . . . . . . . . . . . . . . . . . . . . . . . . President
Ronda Berkeley . . . . . . . . . . . . . . . . . . . . . . . . . . . VP, Development
Aaron Pelman . . . . . . . . . . . . . . . . . . . . . . . . . Development Associate

## MANIFEST FILM COMPANY
PHONE . . . . . . . . . . . . . . . . . . . . . . . . . . . . . . . . 310-244-4900
FAX . . . . . . . . . . . . . . . . . . . . . . . . . . . . . . . . . 310-244-1461
10202 W. Washington Bl., Crawford Bldg.
Culver City, CA 90232

TYPE          Motion Pictures + Television
DEAL          Columbia Pictures
CREDITS     People vs. Larry Flynt - Joy Luck Club - Zero Effect
Lisa Henson . . . . . . . . . . . . . . . . . . . . Producer/Partner (310-244-4928)
Janet Yang . . . . . . . . . . . . . . . . . . . . Producer/Partner (310-244-4959)
Naomi Despres . . . . . . . . . . . . . . . . . . . . . Vice President (310-244-4962)
Mark Levine . . . . . . . . . . . . . . . . . . . . Dir., Development (310-244-4965)
Kathy Hicks . . . . . . . . . . . . . . . . Office Mgr./Exec. Asst. to Lisa Henson
Danny Brown . . . . . . . . . . . . . . . . . . . . . . . . . . Asst. to Janet Yang
Jill Wakeman . . . . . . . . . . . . . . . . . . . . . . . . . . Asst. to Ms. Despres

## MANOS PRODS., INC., JAMES
PHONE . . . . . . . . . . . . . . . . . . . . . . . . . . . . . . . . 213-857-1630
FAX . . . . . . . . . . . . . . . . . . . . . . . . . . . . . . . . . 213-857-1465
5410 Wilshire Blvd., Ste. 602
Los Angeles, CA 90036

TYPE          Motion Pictures + Television
CREDITS     The Positively True Alleged Cheerleader Murdering Mom -
                 Apollo 11 - The Ditchdiggers Daughters
James Manos Jr. . . . . . . . . . . . . . . . . . . . . . . . . . . Writer/Producer
Cynthia Mann . . . . . . . . . . . . . . . . . . . . . . Asst. to James Manos, Jr.

## MAPLE PALM PRODUCTIONS
PHONE . . . . . . . . . . . . . . . . . . . . . . . . . . . . . . . . 310-458-8163
FAX . . . . . . . . . . . . . . . . . . . . . . . . . . . . . . . . . 310-451-9754
EMAIL . . . . . . . . . . . . . . . . . . . . . . . . . mpalm@ix.netcom.com
429 Santa Monica Blvd., Ste. 500
Santa Monica, CA 90401

TYPE          Motion Pictures + Television + Interactive Multimedia +
                 Syndication
CREDITS     Inside America's Lifestyles - Family Challenge - Ambushed
Dave Thomas . . . . . . . . . . . . . . . . . . . . . . . . . . . . . . . Chairman
Bill Bromiley . . . . . . . . . . . . . . . . . . . . . . . . . . . . . . . President
Jonathan Josell . . . . . . . . . . . . . . . . . . . . . . . . . . . . VP, Production
Mark Barbolak . . . . . . . . . . . . . . . . . . . . . . . . . . . Vice President
Lisa Gooding . . . . . . . . . . . . . . . . . . . . . . . . . . . Dir., Development
Kristen Kahl . . . . . . . . . . . . . . . . . . . . . . . . . Mgr., Special Projects

## MARADAY PRODS.
PHONE . . . . . . . . . . . . . . . . . . . . . . . . . . . . . . . . 310-277-1266
FAX . . . . . . . . . . . . . . . . . . . . . . . . . . . . . . . . . 310-277-4331
10110 Empyrean Way, Ste. 304
Los Angeles, CA 90067

TYPE          Motion Pictures
COMMENTS   NO UNSOLICITED MATERIAL.
Mariette Hartley . . . . . . . . . . . . . . . . . . . Executive Producer/Actress
Arlene L. Dayton . . . . . . . . . . . . . . . . . . . . . . . . Executive Producer
Judy L. Milrad . . . . . . . . . . . . . . . . . . . . . . . . . . Dir., Development

## *MARCH HARE ENTERTAINMENT
PHONE . . . . . . . . . . . . . . . . . . . . . . . . . . . . . . . . 213-464-4100
FAX . . . . . . . . . . . . . . . . . . . . . . . . . . . . . . . . . 213-878-0871
Jaffe/Braunstein Films
7920 Sunset Blvd., 4th Floor
Los Angeles, CA 90046

TYPE          Television + Syndication
DEAL          Jaffe/Braunstein Films Ltd.
CREDITS     Ken Folletts' The Third Twin
Sally Jessy Raphael . . . . . . . . . . . . . . . . CEO/Executive Producer
Ellyn Williams . . . . . . . . . . . . . . . . . President/Co-Exec. Producer

## MARINO FILM GROUP, INC.
PHONE . . . . . . . . . . . . . . . . . . . . . . . . . . . . . . . . 818-848-4564
FAX . . . . . . . . . . . . . . . . . . . . . . . . . . . . . . . . . 818-843-6174
EMAIL . . . . . . . . . . . . . . . . . . . . . . . . . marinofilm@aol.com
4127 Warner Blvd.
Burbank, CA 91505

TYPE          Motion Pictures + Television
CREDITS     Forgotten Heroes
Jack Marino . . . . . . . . . . . . . . . . . . . . Pres./CEO/Producer/Director/Writer

## MARK PRODS., LAURENCE
PHONE . . . . . . . . . . . . . . . . . . . . . . . . . . . . . . . . 818-560-6280
Walt Disney Co./Touchstone
500 S. Buena Vista St./Anim 1F-4
Burbank, CA 91521-1664

TYPE          Motion Pictures
DEAL          Sony Pictures Entertainment
CREDITS     Working Girl - Jerry Maguire - Romy & Michele - Deep
                 Rising - As Good As It Gets - The Object of My Affection
Laurence Mark . . . . . . . . . . . . . . . . . . . . . . President/Producer
John Baldecchi . . . . . . . . . . . . . . . . . Pres., Creative Affairs (818-560-6285)
Jonathan King . . . . . . . . . . . . . . . . . . . . . . . . . . . . . . . Producer
Deborah Cincotta . . . . . . . . . . . . . . Dir., Development, TV (818-560-2417)
John McNamara . . . . . . . . . . . . . Dir., Feature Development (818-560-4774)
Fernanda Niven . . . . . . . . . . . . . . . . . . . . . Story Editor (818-560-2758)
Petra Alexandria . . . . . . . . . . . . . . . . . . . Exec. Asst. to Laurence Mark
Eric Mansur . . . . . . . . . . . . . . . . . . . . . . . Asst. to Laurence Mark
Chad Ahrendt . . . . . . . . . . . . . . . . . . . . . . . Asst. to Laurence Mark
David Zerr . . . . . . . . . . . . . . . . . . . . . . . . . Asst. to John Baldecchi

## MARKS PRODUCTIONS, JOAN
PHONE . . . . . . . . . . . . . . . . . . . . . . . . . . . . . . . . 310-434-9179
930 Euclid, #103
Santa Monica, CA 90404

TYPE          Television
CREDITS     In The Company of Darkness - A Bunny's Tale - Violation
                 of Sarah McDavid
Joan Marks . . . . . . . . . . . . . . . . . . . . . . . . President/Exec. Producer

## MARMONT PRODS. INC.
PHONE . . . . . . . . . . . . . . . . . . . . . . . . . . . . . . . . 310-659-0768
FAX . . . . . . . . . . . . . . . . . . . . . . . . . . . . . . . . . 310-659-0826
1022 Palm Ave., Ste. 3
Los Angeles, CA 90069

TYPE          Motion Pictures + Television
CREDITS     Mountains of the Moon - Blood & Wine - Poodle Springs -
                 The Postman Always Rings Twice
COMMENTS   Agency: Ken Kamins ICM 310-550-4327
Bob Rafelson . . . . . . . . . . . . . . . . . . . . . . . . . . . Director/Producer
Jolene Wolff . . . . . . . . . . . . . . . . . . . . . . . . . . . . . Vice President

# COMPANIES AND STAFF

**MARS PRODS. CORP.**
PHONE . . . . . . . . . . . . . . . . . . . . . . . . . . . . 818-980-8011
FAX . . . . . . . . . . . . . . . . . . . . . . . . . . . . . . 818-980-1900
10215 Riverside Dr.
Toluca Lake, CA 91602-2501
TYPE            Motion Pictures + Television + Documentaries + Feature
                Direct to Video
CREDITS         James Dean: Race With Destiny - Rise and Fall of The
                Soviet Union - Zane Grey
Mr. Mardi Rustam . . . . . . . . . . . . . . . . . . . President/Producer
Mark Delo . . . . . . . . . . . . . . . . . . . . . . Production Executive
Sarah Rustam . . . . . . . . . . . . . . . . . . . . . Executive Producer

**MARSH ENTERTAINMENT**
PHONE . . . . . . . . . . . . . . . . . . . . . . . . . . . . 310-476-3198
FAX . . . . . . . . . . . . . . . . . . . . . . . . . . . . . . 310-476-6198
216 S. Carmelina Ave.
Los Angeles, CA 90049
TYPE            Motion Pictures + Television
CREDITS         Crazy from the Heart (TNT)
Sherry Marsh . . . . . . . . . . . . . . . . . . . . . . . .Owner/Manager
Debra Bowland . . . . . . . . . . . . . . . . . . . Asst. to Ms. Marsh

**MARSTAR PRODS.**
PHONE . . . . . . . . . . . . . . . . . . . . . . . . . . . . 310-820-7210
FAX . . . . . . . . . . . . . . . . . . . . . . . . . . . . . . 310-820-1850
EMAIL . . . . . . . . . . . . . . . . . . . . . . . . . marstar@idt.net
12100 Wilshire Blvd., Ste. 670
Los Angeles, CA 90025
TYPE            Motion Pictures
CREDITS         Mask - Sophie's Choice - On Golden Pond - Escape from
                Sobibor
Martin Starger . . . . . . . . . . . . . . . . . . . . . . . . President
Howard Alston . . . . . . . . . . . . . . . . . . . Sr. VP, Production
Darren Reagan . . . . . . . . . . . . . . . . . . . . . . Development
Diana K. Maitland . . . . . . . . Executive/Admin. Asst. to the President

**MARVEL STUDIOS**
PHONE . . . . . . . . . . . . . . . . . . . . . . . . . . . . 310-441-5404
FAX . . . . . . . . . . . . . . . . . . . . . . . . . . . . . . 310-441-2667
WEBSITE . . . . . . . . . . . . . . . http://www.marvelonline.com
10880 Wilshire Blvd., Ste. 1400
Los Angeles, CA 90024
TYPE            Motion Pictures + Television + Animation
CREDITS         Spider-Man - X-Men - Fantastic Four - Iron Man - Silver
                Surfer - Hulk - Blade
Stan Lee . . . . . . . . . . . . . . . . . . . . . . . . . . . Chairman
Gary Gittelsohn . . . . . . . . . . . . . . . . . . . . . . . President
Matthew Edelman . . . . . . . . . . . . . . VP, Production & Development
Scott Thomas . . . . . . . . . . . . . . . . . . . . Creative Director
Nicholas Glover . . . . . . . . . . . . . . . . . . . Creative Executive
Donna Boswell . . . . . . . . . . . . . . . . . Exec. Asst. to Mr. Lee
Carlynn Chapman . . . . . . . . . . . . Exec. Asst. to Mr. Gittelsohn
Michael Kelly . . . . . . . . . . . . . . . . . Exec. Asst. to Mr. Lee

**MARVIN PRODUCTIONS, NIKI**
PHONE . . . . . . . . . . . . . . . . . . . . . . . . . . . . 310-274-6320
FAX . . . . . . . . . . . . . . . . . . . . . . . . . . . . . . 310-274-3890
8919 Harratt Street, Ste. 304
Los Angeles, CA 90069
TYPE            Motion Pictures + Television
CREDITS         The Shawshank Redemption - Buried Alive I & II -
                Nightmare on Elm Street 3
Niki Marvin . . . . . . . . . . . . . . . . . . . . . . . . President

**MARX PRODS., INC., TIMOTHY**
PHONE . . . . . . . . . . . . . . . . . . . . . . . . . . . . 818-789-4344
17177 Adlon Rd.
Encino, CA 91436
TYPE            Motion Pictures + Television
CREDITS         Citizen X - Passed Away - Smooth Talk - Arli$$
Timothy Marx . . . . . . . . . . . . . . . . . . . . . . . .Producer

***MARY ANN-LAGLO PRODUCTIONS**
PHONE . . . . . . . . . . . . . . . . . . . . . . . . . . . . 310-274-5222
FAX . . . . . . . . . . . . . . . . . . . . . . . . . . . . . . 818-508-1616
EMAIL . . . . . . . . . . . . . . . . . . . . . . . cedricyuki@att.net
P.O. Box 3038
Beverly Hills, CA 90212
TYPE            Motion Pictures + Television
CREDITS         Mandela and deKlerk - To Sir With Love 2 - Free of Eden
Cedric Scott . . . . . . . . . . . . . . . . . . . . . . CEO/Producer
Emmanuel Knowles . . . . . . . . . . . . . . . Dir., Creative Affairs
Joy Thale . . . . . . . . . . . . . . . . . . . . . . Executive Assistant

**MASE/KAPLAN PRODUCTIONS, INC.**
PHONE . . . . . . . . . . . . . . . . . . . . . . . . . . . . 213-304-5267
FAX . . . . . . . . . . . . . . . . . . . . . . . . . . . . . . 818-385-0817
EMAIL . . . . . . . . . . . . . . . . . . . . . . . . filmator@aol.com
5314 Wortser Ave.
Sherman Oaks, CA 91401
TYPE            Motion Pictures + Television
CREDITS         Red Shoe Diaries - Strangers - Lawnmower Man 2 - She's
                So Lovely - The Patriot - Buffalo 66 - Belly - Beyond Belief
Avram Butch Kaplan . . . . . . . . . . . . . . . . . . . . . Producer
Suzanna Lezama . . . . . . . . . . . . . . . . . . . Dir., Development

***MASTER THESPIAN PRODUCTIONS**
PHONE . . . . . . . . . . . . . . . . . . . . . . . . . . . . 818-560-7711
FAX . . . . . . . . . . . . . . . . . . . . . . . . . . . . . . 818-563-6298
Walt Disney
500 S. Buena Vista St.
Burbank, CA 91521-1719
TYPE            Motion Pictures
DEAL            Walt Disney Company, The
Jon Lovitz . . . . . . . . . . . . . . . . . . . . . . . . . . President
Wayne Rice . . . . . . . . . . . . . . . . . . . . . . . . . President
Michelle Cox . . . . . . . . . . . . . . . . . . . . Dir., Development

***MATERIAL**
PHONE . . . . . . . . . . . . . . . . . . . . . . . . . . . . 818-954-1551
FAX . . . . . . . . . . . . . . . . . . . . . . . . . . . . . . 818-954-5299
EMAIL . . . . . . . . . . . . . . . . . . . . . . . . material@gte.net
4000 Warner Blvd., 139/27
Burbank, CA 91522
TYPE            Motion Pictures
DEAL            Warner Bros.
Jorge Saralegui . . . . . . . . . . . . . . . . . . . . . . .Producer
Channing Dungey . . . . . . . . . . . . . . . . Sr. VP, Production
Zanthe Taylor . . . . . . . . . . . . . . . Asst. to Jorge Saralegui
Kat Scudder . . . . . . . . . . . . . . . . . . . . . . . Story Editor

**MATINEE ENTERTAINMENT**
PHONE . . . . . . . . . . . . . . . . . . . . . . . . . . . . 310-246-9044
FAX . . . . . . . . . . . . . . . . . . . . . . . . . . . . . . 310-246-9066
EMAIL . . . . . . . . . . . . . . . . . . . . . general@matinee.com
WEBSITE . . . . . . . . . . . . . . . . . . http://www.matinee.com
345 N. Maple Dr., Ste. 285
Beverly Hills, CA 90210
TYPE            Television + Animation + Interactive Multimedia
CREDITS         Kampung Boy
COMMENTS        Also: Animation Direct to Video.
Michael I. Yanover . . . . . . . . . . . . . . . . . . . . . President
Frank Saperstein . . . . . . . . . . . . . . . . . . Producer/Director

**MATOVICH PRODUCTIONS**
PHONE . . . . . . . . . . . . . . . . . . . . . . . . . . . . 805-250-0644
FAX . . . . . . . . . . . . . . . . . . . . . . . . . . . . . . 805-250-0167
26438 Oak Highland Dr.
Santa Clarita, CA 91321
TYPE            Motion Pictures + Television
CREDITS         Lightning In A Bottle - I Don't Buy Kisses Anymore -
                Social Suicide
Mitchel Matovich . . . . . . . . . . . . . . . . . . President/Producer

**MATTHAU COMPANY, INC., THE**
PHONE . . . . . . . . . . . . . . . . . . . . . . . . . . . . 310-557-2727
1999 Ave. of the Stars, Ste. 2100
Los Angeles, CA 90067
TYPE            Motion Pictures + Television
CREDITS         The Grass Harp - Grumpier Old Men - Mrs. Lambert
                Remembers Love - Doin' Time on Planet Earth
Walter Matthau . . . . . . . . . . . . . . . . . . . . . . . Chairman
Charles Matthau . . . . . . . . . . . . . . . . . . . . . . . President
Lana Morgan . . . . . . . . . . . . . . . . . . Dir., Creative Affairs
Judy Raleigh . . . . . . . . . . . . . . . . . . Dir., Business Affairs
Rich Connor . . . . . . . . . . . . . . . . . . . . . . . Story Editor

**MAYNARD PRODS., RICHARD**
PHONE . . . . . . . . . . . . . . . . . . . . . . . . . . . . 310-441-0893
FAX . . . . . . . . . . . . . . . . . . . . . . . . . . . . . . 310-441-1233
1568 Manning Ave. #4
Los Angeles, CA 90024
TYPE            Motion Pictures + Television
CREDITS         Normal Life - Stompin' at the Savoy - Mission of the Shark
Richard Maynard . . . . . . . . . . . . . . . . . . . . . . .Producer
George Stoddard . . . . . . . . . . . Story Editor (NY) (212-570-6290)
Eileen Nelson . . . . . . . . . . . . Dir., Creative Affairs & Production

# COMPANIES AND STAFF

**MAYO/GREGG ENTERTAINMENT**
PHONE . . . . . . . . . . . . . . . . . . . . . . . . . . . . 310-475-3333
EMAIL . . . . . . . . . . . . . . . . . . . . . mayoent@earthlink.net
1818 Thayer Ave., Ste. 303
Los Angeles, CA 90025-4962
TYPE            Motion Pictures + Television
CREDITS         The Parsley Garden - Aftermath - The Fear Inside
COMMENTS        Also: Management
Faye Nuell Mayo . . . . . . . . . . . . . . . . . . . . . . . . . . . . . Producer
Judie Gregg . . . . . . . . . . . . . . . . . . . . . . . . . . . . . . . . Producer

**MAYSVILLE PICTURES**
PHONE . . . . . . . . . . . . . . . . . . . . . . . . . . . . 818-954-4840
FAX . . . . . . . . . . . . . . . . . . . . . . . . . . . . . . 818-954-4860
Warner Bros.
4000  Warner Blvd., Bldg. 81 Rm. 117
Burbank, CA 91522
TYPE            Motion Pictures + Television
DEAL            Warner Bros. Pictures
CREDITS         Down Periscope- Clueless- Die Hard With A Vengeance
George Clooney . . . . . . . . . . . . . . . . . . . . . . . Actor/Producer
Robert Lawrence . . . . . . . . . . . . . . . . . . . . . . . . CEO/Producer
Anne Helmstadter . . . . . . . . . . . . . . . . . . . . . VP, Development
Amy Cohen . . . . . . . . . . . . . . . . . . . . Asst. to George Clooney
Kevin Field . . . . . . . . . . . . . . . . . . . . Asst. to George Clooney
Tim Grierson . . . . . . . . . . . . . . . . . . Asst. to Anne Helmstadter
Megan Weiss . . . . . . . . . . . . . . . . . . . Asst. to Robert Lawrence

**MCKISSICK/GREGORY PRODS.**
PHONE . . . . . . . . . . . . . . . . . . . . . . . . . . . . 918-747-9848
FAX . . . . . . . . . . . . . . . . . . . . . . . . . . . . . . 918-747-9801
EMAIL . . . . . . . . . . . . . . . . . . . . . . . . mgprod@ionet.net
2617 E. 58th St.
Tulsa, OK 74105
TYPE            Motion Pictures + Television
Pam McKissick . . . . . . . . . . . . . . . . . . Exec. Producer/Writer
Cheryl Gregory . . . . . . . . . . . . . . . . . . . Exec. Producer/Writer

**MDP WORLDWIDE**
PHONE . . . . . . . . . . . . . . . . . . . . . . . . . . . . 310-226-8300
FAX . . . . . . . . . . . . . . . . . . . . . . . . . . . . . . 310-226-8350
1925 Century Park East, Ste. 1700
Los Angeles, CA 90067
TYPE            Motion Pictures + Television + Syndication
CREDITS         Deceiver - Knockoff - Orgazmo - Jungle Book
Mark Damon . . . . . . . . . . . . . . . . . . . . . . . . . Chairman/CEO
Richard Kiratsoulis . . . . . . . . . . . . . . . . . . . . President/COO
Stephen Monas . . . . . . . . . . . . . . . . . . . Exec. Vice President
Nathan Scott . . . . . . . . . . . . . . . . . . . . . VP, Finance/Treasurer

**MEDIA FINANCIAL CORPORATION**
PHONE . . . . . . . . . . . . . . . . . . . . . . . . . . . . 617-338-1570
FAX . . . . . . . . . . . . . . . . . . . . . . . . . . . . . . 617-338-1565
EMAIL . . . . . . . . . . . . . . . . . . . . . hd@mediainancial.com
162 Columbus Ave., 3rd Floor
Boston, MA 02116
TYPE            Motion Pictures
CREDITS         Lakeboat - Next Stop Wonderland - Squeeze - Sudden
                Death
COMMENTS        Finance & Production.
William Minot . . . . . . . . . . . . . . . . . . . . . . . . . Chairman/CEO
Ari Newman . . . . . . . . . . . . . . . . . . . . . . . . . . . . President
Kathryn Albert . . . . . . . . . . . . . . . . . . . . VP, Creative Affairs

**MEDIA FOUR**
PHONE . . . . . . . . . . . . . . . . . . . . . . . . . . . . 310-556-5445
FAX . . . . . . . . . . . . . . . . . . . . . . . . . . . . . . 310-556-5440
2029 Century Pk. East., Ste. 3250
Los Angeles, CA 90067
TYPE            Motion Pictures + Television
CREDITS         Before They Were Stars - George - Whereabouts of Jenny
Pam Prince . . . . . . . . . . . . . . . . . . . . . . . . . . Founding Partner
Steve Sauer . . . . . . . . . . . . . . . . . . . . . . . . . Founding Partner
Ricki-Jean Bass . . . . . . . . . . . . . . . . . . . . . Executive Assistant
Teka Ludovico . . . . . . . . . . . . . . . . . . . . . . Executive Assistant

**MEERSON-KRIKES**
PHONE . . . . . . . . . . . . . . . . . . . . . . . . . . . . 310-858-0552
FAX . . . . . . . . . . . . . . . . . . . . . . . . . . . . . . 310-858-0554
427 N. Canon Dr., Ste. 216
Beverly Hills, CA 90210
TYPE            Motion Pictures
CREDITS         Star Trek IV - Back to the Beach - Double Impact
Peter Krikes . . . . . . . . . . . . . . . . . . . . . . . . . Writer/Producer
Steve Meerson . . . . . . . . . . . . . . . . . . . . . . . . Writer/Producer

**MEGA FILMS, INC.**
PHONE . . . . . . . . . . . . . . . . . . . . . . . . . . . . 818-985-6342
FAX . . . . . . . . . . . . . . . . . . . . . . . . . . . . . . 818-985-6333
P.O. Box 6732
Beverly Hills, CA 90212-6732
TYPE            Motion Pictures + Television
James A. Chory . . . . . . . . . . . . . . . . . . . President/Producer
Russ Albert . . . . . . . . . . . . . . . . . . . . . . . . . . . . Producer
Evan R. Bell . . . . . . . . . . . . . . . . . . . . . . . . . . . . Producer
Bill Sheridan . . . . . . . . . . . . . . . . . . . . . . . . . . . Producer
Elizabeth Chory . . . . . . . . . . . . . . . . . . . . . . . Development

**MELENDEZ PRODUCTIONS, BILL**
PHONE . . . . . . . . . . . . . . . . . . . . . . . . . . . . 213-463-4101
FAX . . . . . . . . . . . . . . . . . . . . . . . . . . . . . . 213-469-0195
EMAIL . . . . . . . . . . . . . . . . . . . . . bmpi@primenet.com
439 N. Larchmont Blvd.
Los Angeles, CA 90004
TYPE            Television + Animation
CREDITS         Peanuts Characters Worldwide
Bill Melendez . . . . . . . . . . . . . . . . . . . . . . . . . . President
Leo Moran . . . . . . . . . . . . . . . . . . . . . . . Creative Director
Carol Neal . . . . . . . . . . . . . . . . . . . . . . Financial Supervisor
Sandy Arnold . . . . . . . . . . . . . . . . . . . . . . . . . Production
Joanna Coletta . . . . . . . . . . . . . . . . . . . . . . . . Production

**MELROSE PRODS.**
PHONE . . . . . . . . . . . . . . . . . . . . . . . . . . . . 805-295-3333
FAX . . . . . . . . . . . . . . . . . . . . . . . . . . . . . . 805-295-3334
27420 Avenue Scott, Stage #A
Santa Clarita, CA 91355
TYPE            Television
CREDITS         Melrose Place
Frank South . . . . . . . . . . . . . . . . . . . . . . Executive Producer
Carol Mendelsohn . . . . . . . . . . . . . . . . Co-Executive Producer
Chuck Pratt . . . . . . . . . . . . . . . . . . . . Co-Executive Producer
Chip Hayes . . . . . . . . . . . . . . . . . . . . . . . . . . . Producer
Hynndie Wali . . . . . . . . . . . . . . . . . . . . . Associate Producer
James Kahn . . . . . . . . . . . . . . . . . . . . . Supervising Producer

**MELTZER PRODUCTIONS, MICHAEL**
PHONE . . . . . . . . . . . . . . . . . . . . . . . . . . . . 310-289-0702
FAX . . . . . . . . . . . . . . . . . . . . . . . . . . . . . . 310-289-0436
EMAIL . . . . . . . . . . . . . . . . . . . . . . melmax@aol.com
8530 Holloway Dr., Ste. 327
Los Angeles, CA 90069
TYPE            Motion Pictures + Television + Feature Direct to Video +
                Interactive Multimedia
CREDITS         The Hidden - Up The Creek - Dead Heat - Carnival Of
                Souls
Michael L. Meltzer . . . . . . . . . . . . . . . . . . . . . . . . Producer

**MENDEL PRODUCTIONS, BARRY**
PHONE . . . . . . . . . . . . . . . . . . . . . . . . . . . . 818-560-6747
FAX . . . . . . . . . . . . . . . . . . . . . . . . . . . . . . 818-566-9821
500 S. Buena Vista St.
Burbank, CA 91521-1655
TYPE            Motion Pictures
DEAL            Walt Disney Pictures/Touchstone Pictures
CREDITS         Sixth Sense - Rushmore - Flora Plum
Barry Mendel . . . . . . . . . . . . . . . . . . . . . . . . . . No Title
Michael Schulman . . . . . . . . . . . . . . . No Title (818-560-6779)
Jennifer Simpson . . . . . . . . . . . . . . . . No Title (818-560-6649)
Jason Miller . . . . . . . . . . . . . . . . . . . . . . . . . . . . No Title
Heather Magee . . . . . . . . . . . . . . . . . . . . . . . . . . No Title

***MENDILLO/FORM PRODUCTIONS**
PHONE . . . . . . . . . . . . . . . . . . . . . . . . . . . . 213-960-8066
FAX . . . . . . . . . . . . . . . . . . . . . . . . . . . . . . 213-960-8068
EMAIL . . . . . . . . . . . . . . . . . . . . . Fafilms@aol.com
Raleigh Studios
650 N. Bronson
Hollywood, CA 90004
TYPE            Motion Pictures + Television
CREDITS         Trading Favors - Kissing a Fool
Stephen Tag Mendillo . . . . . . . . . . . . . . . . Partner/Writer/Producer
Andrew Form . . . . . . . . . . . . . . . . . . . . . . Partner/Producer
Neil (Elmo) Elman . . . . . . . . . . . . . . . . . . . Creative Executive
Warren Kohler . . . . . . . . . . . . . . . . . . . . . . Business Affairs

## MERCHANT-IVORY
PHONE . . . . . . . . . . . . . . . . . . . . . . . . . . . . . . . 212-582-8049
FAX . . . . . . . . . . . . . . . . . . . . . . . . . . . . . . . . . 212-459-9201
250 W. 57th St., Ste. 1913A
New York, NY 10107

TYPE — Motion Pictures
CREDITS — Howards End - Room With A View - Surviving Picasso - Remains of the Day - The Proprietor

Ismail Merchant . . . . . . . . . . . . . . . . . . . . Co-President/Producer
James Ivory . . . . . . . . . . . . . . . . . . . . . . . Co-President/Director
Richard Hawley . . . . . . . . . . . . . . . . . Exec. VP/Exec. Producer
Dara McQuillan . . . . . . . . . . Production Supervisor/Asst. to President
Marla L. Shelton . . . . . . . . . Production Supervisor/Asst. to President

## MERCURY-JET PICTURES
PHONE . . . . . . . . . . . . . . . . . . . . . . . . . . . . . . . 818-971-7181
12100 Valley Spring Ln, #302
Studio City, CA 91604

TYPE — Motion Pictures
CREDITS — Up at the Corner - Tulipmania - Cuffdunk & Roundtree

Stuart Lerner . . . . . . . . . . . . . . . . . . . . . . . . . . . . . President
Louis Zivot . . . . . . . . . . . . . . . . . . . . . . . . . . . Vice President
Lynette Morrow . . . . . . . . . . . . . . . . . . . Administrative Assistant

## MERIDIAN ENTERTAINMENT, LLC
PHONE . . . . . . . . . . . . . . . . . . . . . . . . . . . . . . . 310-552-2200
FAX . . . . . . . . . . . . . . . . . . . . . . . . . . . . . . . . . 310-552-0196
WEBSITE . . . . . . . . . . . . . . . . . http://www.MERIDIAN-ENT.com
10323 Santa Monica Blvd., Bungalow 101
Los Angeles, CA 90025

TYPE — Animation + Syndication + Motion Pictures + Television
CREDITS — Homage - Mind Games - Some Girls - Postal Worker - Sweetwater

John King . . . . . . . . . . . . . . . . . . . . . . . . . . . . . . . Producer
Tim Wesley . . . . . . . . . . . . . . . . . . . . . . . . . . . . . . Producer
Josh Woodward . . . . . . . . . . . . . . . . . . . . . . . . . . . Producer

## MERIDIAN FILMS
PHONE . . . . . . . . . . . . . . . . . . . . . . . . . . . . . . . 310-394-1617
FAX . . . . . . . . . . . . . . . . . . . . . . . . . . . . . . . . . 310-821-2191
EMAIL . . . . . . . . . . . . . . . . . . . . . . . . . merfilms@aol.com
233 Wilshire Blvd., #400
Santa Monica, CA 90401

TYPE — Motion Pictures + Television
CREDITS — Twice Dead - Mom

Bernard Demers . . . . . . . . . . . . . . . . . . . . . . . . . . . President
Robert McDonnell . . . . . . . . . . . . . . . . . . . . . . Writer/Producer
Lori Rosene . . . . . . . . . . . . . . . . . . . . . . . . . Head, Acquisitions
Jose Novo . . . . . . . . . . . . . . . . . . . . . . . . . . Dir., Development
Jennifer Evans . . . . . . . . . . . . . . . . . . . . . . . . . . . . Assistant

## MERKO MOTION PICTURES
PHONE . . . . . . . . . . . . . . . . . . . . . . . . . . . . . . . 213-653-4749
FAX . . . . . . . . . . . . . . . . . . . . . . . . . . . . . . . . . 213-653-9762
EMAIL . . . . . . . . . . . . . . . . . . . . . . . . . merkomp@aol.com
1059 South Alfred Street
Los Angeles, CA 90035

TYPE — Motion Pictures
CREDITS — Homecoming - Kiss of Death - Single White Female - Barfly

Jack Baran . . . . . . . . . . . . . . . . . . . . . . . . . . . . . . President
Linda Leeds . . . . . . . . . . . . . . . . . . . . . . VP, Creative Affairs
Michael Pariser . . . . . . . . . . . . . . . . . . . . . . . . VP, Production

## MERLIN ENTERTAINMENT
PHONE . . . . . . . . . . . . . . . . . . . . . . . . . . . . . . . 310-246-0240
FAX . . . . . . . . . . . . . . . . . . . . . . . . . . . . . . . . . 310-246-1655
9145 Sunset Blvd., 2nd Floor
Los Angeles, CA 90069

TYPE — Motion Pictures + Television
CREDITS — Super Mario Bros. - Rolling Thunder

Brad Weston . . . . . . . . . . . . . . . . . . . . . . . . . . . . . Producer
Peter Speakman . . . . . . . . . . . . . . . . . . . . . . Dir., Development

## MERV GRIFFIN PRODUCTIONS
PHONE . . . . . . . . . . . . . . . . . . . . . . . . . . . . . . . 310-664-3000
FAX . . . . . . . . . . . . . . . . . . . . . . . . . . . . . . . . . 310-664-3001
9860 Wilshire Boulevard
Beverly Hills, CA 90210

TYPE — Motion Pictures + Television
CREDITS — The Christmas List - Click! - Merv Griffin's New Years Special - Who Makes You Laugh - Jackie Mason at the London Palladium
COMMENTS — Numbers to change shortly after press time.

Ernest Chambers . . . . . . . . . . . . . . . . . . . . . Sr. VP, Production
Roger Lefkon . . . . . . . . . . . VP, Programming & Business Affairs
Peter Marino . . . . . . . . . . . . . Exec. Producer/VP, Creative Affairs
Diana Redmon . . . . . . . . . . . . . . . . . . . . Contract Administrator
Karen Naimy . . . . . . . . . . . . . . . . . . . . Asst. to Mr. Chambers

## MESMERIZE STUDIOS
PHONE . . . . . . . . . . . . . . . . . . . . . . . . . . . . . . . 310-656-1250
FAX . . . . . . . . . . . . . . . . . . . . . . . . . . . . . . . . . 310-656-1220
EMAIL . . . . . . . . . . . . . . . . . . . . . jkramer@mesmerize.com
WEBSITE . . . . . . . . . . . . . . . . . . . . http://www.mesmerize.com
701 Santa Monica, Ste. 300
Santa Monica, CA 90401

TYPE — Television + Syndication + Documentaries
CREDITS — Screen Actors Guild Awards - Sinbad Live - Moonwalker - The A-List - Ricky Jay - Eddie Griffin - Voodoo Child
COMMENTS — Also: Comedy Specials & Award Shows.

Jerry Kramer . . . . . . . . . . . . . . . . . . . . . . . . . . . . . President
Lara Karchmer . . . . . . . . . . . . . . . . . . . . . Asst. to Mr. Kramer

## MESSINA CAPTOR FILMS
PHONE . . . . . . . . . . . . . . . . . . . . . . . . . . . . . . . 310-587-2644
FAX . . . . . . . . . . . . . . . . . . . . . . . . . . . . . . . . . 310-587-2646
225 Santa Monica Blvd., 7th Fl.
Santa Monica, CA 90401

TYPE — Motion Pictures + Television
CREDITS — Dead on Sight - Home Sweet Homeless (MOW-CBS)

Roxanne Messina Captor . . . . . . . . . . . . . . . . . Producer/Director
Tracy Gossett . . . . . . . . . . . . . . . . . . . . . . . Creative Executive

## MESTRES PRODUCTIONS, RICARDO
PHONE . . . . . . . . . . . . . . . . . . . . . . . . . . . . . . . 818-560-Ext.
FAX . . . . . . . . . . . . . . . . . . . . . . . . . . . . . . . . . 818-953-4238
500 S. Buena Vista St., Anim. Bldg 2E8
Burbank, CA 91521

TYPE — Motion Pictures
DEAL — Walt Disney Company, The
CREDITS — 101 Dalmations - Jack - Flubber - Home Alone III

Ricardo Mestres . . . . . . . . . . . . . . . . . . Producer (Ext. 6040)
Danny Davids . . . . . . . . . . . . . . . . . . . . Creative (Ext. 4367)
Andrew Gunn . . . . . . . . . . . . . . . . . . . . Creative (Ext. 6156)
Ann Marie Sanderlin . . . . . . . . . . . . . . . Creative (Ext. 4160)
Nicole Casagrande . . . . . . . . . . . . . . . . . . Creative Associate
Heijin Chung . . . . . . . . . . . . . . Creative Associate (Ext. 5494)
Stephanie Jakubiak . . . . . . . . . . . . . . . . . Creative Associate
Channing Work . . . . . . . . . . . Creative Associate (Ext. 4311)

## METAFILMICS INC.
PHONE . . . . . . . . . . . . . . . . . . . . . . . . . . . . . . . 818-734-9320
FAX . . . . . . . . . . . . . . . . . . . . . . . . . . . . . . . . . 213-656-2932
4250 Wilshire Blvd.
Los Angeles, CA 90010

TYPE — Motion Pictures + Television
CREDITS — What Dreams May Come

Barnet Bain . . . . . . . . . . . . . . . . . . . . . . . . . . . . . Producer
Stephen Simon . . . . . . . . . . . . . . . . . . . . . . . . . . . Producer
Alicia Gargaro . . . . . . . . . . . . . . . . . . . . . . Dir., Development

## METRO-GOLDWYN-MAYER PICTURES
PHONE . . . . . . . . . . . . . . . . . . . . . . . . . . . . . 310-449-3000
WEBSITE. . . . . . . . . . . . . . . http://www.mgm.com/motionpictures
2500 Broadway St.
Santa Monica, CA 90404-3061
CREDITS       Dirty Work - Disturbing Behavoir - At First Sight - Be the
              Man - Super Dave

Frank Mancuso . . . . . . . . . . . . . . . . . . . . . . . . . . Chairman/CEO
Michael Nathanson . . . . . . . . . . . . . . . . . . . . . . . . . . President
Robert Relyea . . . . . . . . . . . . . . . . . . . . . . . . Pres., Production
Michael G. Corrigan . . . . . . . . . . . . . . . . . . . Sr. Exec. VP/CFO
Darcie Denkert . . . . . . . . . . . . . . . . . Sr. Exec. VP, Business Affairs
David Johnson . . . . . . . . . . . . . . . . . Sr. Exec. VP/General Counsel
William Jones . . . . . . . . . . . Sr. Executive Vice President/Secretary
Charles Cohen . . . . . . . . . . Exec. VP, Finance & Corporate Development
Gregory A. Foster . . . . . . . . . . . . . . . . . . . . . Exec. VP, Production
Daniel Rosett . . . . . . . . Exec. VP, Studio Finance & Operations
Dan Taylor . . . . . . . . . . . . . . . . Exec. VP, Corporate Finance
Donald Brada . . . . . . . . . . . . . Sr. VP/Deputy, General Counsel
Jeffrey Coleman . . . . . . . . . . . . . . . . . . . . . Sr. VP, Production
Mark Fleisher . . . . . . . . . . . . . Sr. VP/Deputy, General Counsel
Rebecca Ford . . . . . . . . . . . . . Sr. VP/Deputy, General Counsel
Garret G. Gerlich . . . . . . . . . . . . . . . . Sr. VP, Post Production
Elizabeth Carroll . . . . . . . . . . . . . . . . . . . . . . . . VP, Production
Damon Lee . . . . . . . . . . . . . . . . . . . . . . . . . . . VP, Production
Yalda Tehranian . . . . . . . . . . . . . . . . . . . . . . . VP, Production

## METRO-GOLDWYN-MAYER/WORLDWIDE TV
PHONE . . . . . . . . . . . . . . . . . . . . . . . . . . 310-449-3000
WEBSITE. . . . . . . . . . . . . . . . . . . . . . . http://www.mgm.com
2500 Broadway St.
Santa Monica, CA 90404-3061
TYPE          Television
CREDITS       L.A.P.D. - The Magnificent Seven - Outer Limits -
              Poltergeist: The Legacy - Star Gate SG-1

John Symes . . . . . . . . . . . . . . . . . . . . . . . . . . . . President
Hank Cohen . . . . . . . . . . . . . . . . . . Exec. VP, Creative Affairs
Tom Malanga . . . . . . . . . . . . . . . . . Exec. VP, Finance & Strategic Planning
Mel Swope . . . . . . . . . . . . . . . . . . . . . Exec. VP, Production
Jay Fukuto . . . . . . . . . . . . . . . . . . . . Sr. VP, MGM Animation
Craig Roessler . . . . . . . . . . . . . . . . . Sr. VP, Creative Affairs
Albert Spevak . . . . . . . . . . . . . . . . . Sr. VP, Business Affairs
Shelley Brown . . . . . . . . . . . . VP, Finance & Administration
Robert Curran . . . . . . . . . . . . . . . . . . . . . . . . VP, Production
Michael Hartounian . . . . . . . . . . . . . . . . VP, Business Affairs
Hudson Hickman . . . . . . . . . . . . . . . . . . VP, Post Production
Peter Kiwitt . . . . . . . . . . . . . . . . . . . . . . . Dir., Production
Tony Optican . . . . . . . . . . . . . . . . . . . . Dir., Creative Affairs
Scott Spungin . . . . . . . . . . . . . . . . . . . Dir., Business Affairs
Stephanie Wise . . . . . . . . . . . . . . . . . . Dir., Post Production
Tina Wlasic . . . . . . . . . . . . . . . . . . . . . Dir., Business Affairs
Jayson Raitt . . . . . . . . . . . . . . . Mgr., Creative Affairs, MGM Animation

## MEYER PRODS., PATRICIA K.
PHONE . . . . . . . . . . . . . . . . . . . . . . . . . . 310-392-0422
FAX . . . . . . . . . . . . . . . . . . . . . . . . . . . 310-581-0859
EMAIL . . . . . . . . . . . . . . . . . . . . . . . . . pkmeyer@aol.com
2617 5th St.
Santa Monica, CA 90405
TYPE          Motion Pictures + Television
CREDITS       The Women of Brewster Place - This Is My Life - Home
              Song - Take Me Home Again
Patricia K. Meyer . . . . . . . . . . . . . . . . . . . . Writer/Producer

## MEYER/JAFFE PRODS.
PHONE . . . . . . . . . . . . . . . . . . . . . . . . . . 213-956-5841
FAX . . . . . . . . . . . . . . . . . . . . . . . . . . . 213-862-4827
Paramount Pictures
5555 Melrose Ave., Marx Bros. #107
Los Angeles, CA 90038-3197
TYPE          Motion Pictures
DEAL          Paramount Pictures- Motion Picture Group
CREDITS       Star Trek 2,4,6 - Time After Time - Sommersby - 7%
              Solution
Nicholas Meyer . . . . . . . . . . . . . . . . Writer/Director/Producer
Rebecca Floeter . . . . . . . . . . . . . . . . . . . Dir., Development

## MEYERS/SHYER CO., THE
PHONE . . . . . . . . . . . . . . . . . . . . . . . . . . 818-560-4810
FAX . . . . . . . . . . . . . . . . . . . . . . . . . . . 818-563-4290
Walt Disney Pictures
500 S. Buena Vista St., Anim. Bldg. 1G
Burbank, CA 91521-1675
TYPE          Motion Pictures
DEAL          Walt Disney Pictures/Touchstone Pictures
CREDITS       Father of the Bride I & II - Baby Boom - Private Benjamin -
              The Parent Trap

Charles Shyer . . . . . . . . . . . . . . . . . Writer/Producer/Director
Nancy Meyers . . . . . . . . . . . . . . . . . Writer/Producer/Director
Bruce Block . . . . . . . . . . . . . . . . . . . . . . . . . . . Producer
Stacey Attanasio . . . . . . . . . . . . . . . . . . Exec. Vice President
Lani Pollock . . . . . . . . . . . . . . . . . . . . . . Creative Executive
Suzanne Farwell . . . . . . . . . . . . Creative Asst. to Nancy Meyers
Jessica Hochman . . . . . . . . . . . . Creative Asst. to Charles Shyer

## MICHAEL/FINNEY PRODS., INC.
PHONE . . . . . . . . . . . . . . . . . . . . . . . . . . 310-201-0700
FAX . . . . . . . . . . . . . . . . . . . . . . . . . . . 310-201-9854
EMAIL . . . . . . . . . . . . . . . . . . . . . michael/finney@usa.net
264 S. La Cienega Blvd., Ste. 131
Beverly Hills, CA 90211
TYPE          Motion Pictures + Television + Syndication
CREDITS       Maximum Risk - Fall - If Lucy Fell - Peroxide Passion -
              There's No Fish Food in Heaven
Richard Finney . . . . . . . . . . . . . . . . Co-Chairman/Producer
Terence Michael . . . . . . . . . . . . . . . . Co-Chairman/Producer
Sean Elliott . . . . . . . . . . . . . . . . . . . . . Dir., Development

## MIDDLE FORK PRODUCTIONS
PHONE . . . . . . . . . . . . . . . . . . . . . . . . . . 310-271-4200
FAX . . . . . . . . . . . . . . . . . . . . . . . . . . . 310-271-8200
10877 Wilshire Blvd., Ste. 1810
Los Angeles, CA 90024
TYPE          Motion Pictures
CREDITS       Anaconda
Verna Harrah . . . . . . . . . . . . . . . . . . . . . . . . . Chairman
Susan Ruskin . . . . . . . . . . . . . . . . . . . . . . Pres., Production
Andy Fickman . . . . . . . . . . . . . . . . . . . . Sr. VP, Production
Betsy Sullenger . . . . . . . . . . . . . . . . . . . Creative Executive

## MIDNIGHT SUN PICTURES
PHONE . . . . . . . . . . . . . . . . . . . . . . . . . . 213-850-2670
FAX . . . . . . . . . . . . . . . . . . . . . . . . . . . 213-850-2661
EMAIL . . . . . . . . . . . . . . . . . . info@midnightsunpix.com
Warner Hollywood Studios
1041 N. Formosa
West Hollywood, CA 90046
TYPE          Motion Pictures + Television + Animation + Interactive
              Multimedia
CREDITS       Speechless - Cliffhanger - Long Kiss Goodnight - Die Hard
              2 - Blast from the Past
Renny Harlin . . . . . . . . . . . . . . . . . . . . . Director/Producer
Amanda Stern . . . . . . . . . . . . . . . . . . . . . . . . . President
Rebecca Spikings . . . . . . . . . . . . . . . . Production Executive
Jennifer Gilbert . . . . . . . . . . . . . . . . . . . . Creative Assistant
Michael Lindenbaum . . . . . . . . . . . . . 1st Asst. to Renny Harlin
Lisa Stott . . . . . . . . . . . . . . . . . . . . 2nd Asst. to Renny Harlin

## MILESTONE PICTURES INC.
PHONE . . . . . . . . . . . . . . . . . . . . . . . . . . 310-478-6273
FAX . . . . . . . . . . . . . . . . . . . . . . . . . . . 310-478-6273
EMAIL . . . . . . . . . . . . . . . . . . . . . . . . filmphd@aol.com
12021 Wilshire Blvd., Ste. 416
Los Angeles, CA 90025
TYPE          Motion Pictures + Television + Interactive Multimedia
CREDITS       Mindwalk - Mattel's Barbie CD Rom - Spawn
Adrianna A.J. Cohen . . . . . . . . . . . . . . . . . . . . . Producer
Andrea Miloro . . . . . . . . . . . . . . . . . . . . . . . . . Producer

## MILLENNIUM MEDIAWORKS, INC.
PHONE . . . . . . . . . . . . . . . . . . . . . . . . . . 310-288-5838
FAX . . . . . . . . . . . . . . . . . . . . . . . . . . . 310-285-9692
335 North Maple Drive, Ste. 235
Beverly Hills, CA 90210
TYPE          Motion Pictures
Chris Sierernich . . . . . . . . . . . . . . . . . . . . . . . President
Chris Dubrow . . . . . . . . . . . . . . . . . . . . . VP, Development
Matt Milich . . . . . . . . . . . . . . . . . . . . Executive Assistant

## MILLER ENTERTAINMENT GROUP, INC.
```
PHONE . . . . . . . . . . . . . . . . . . . . . . . . . . . . 212-980-4180
FAX . . . . . . . . . . . . . . . . . . . . . . . . . . . . . . 212-980-6439
EMAIL . . . . . . . . . . . . . . . . . MillerEntertainment@msn.com
306 East 50th Street
New York, NY 10022
TYPE        Motion Pictures + Television
CREDITS     River Red - Easter
David Miller . . . . . . . . . . . . . . . . . . . . . . . . . . . . President
```

## MILLER/BOYETT/WARREN PRODUCTIONS
```
PHONE . . . . . . . . . . . . . . . . . . . . . . . . . . . . 818-954-7700
FAX . . . . . . . . . . . . . . . . . . . . . . . . . . . . . . 818-954-7712
Warner Bros.
4000 Warner Blvd., Bldg. #1
Burbank, CA 91522
TYPE        Motion Pictures + Television
DEAL        Warner Bros. Pictures
CREDITS     Step By Step - Family Matters - Full House - Laverne &
            Shirley - Happy Days - Mork & Mindy
Thomas L. Miller . . . . . . . . . . . . . . . . . . Executive Producer
Robert L. Boyett . . . . . . . . . . . . . . . . . . Executive Producer
Michael Warren . . . . . . . . . . . . . . . . . . . Executive Producer
Diane Murphy . . . . . . . . . . . . . . . . . . Dir., Miller/Boyett
Debbie Baker . . . . . . . . . . . . . . . . . . . Executive Assistant
Ophir Adar . . . . . . . . . . . . . . . . . . . . . . . . . . Assistant
Jeremy Casper . . . . . . . . . . . . . . . . . . . . . . . . Assistant
John Fulton . . . . . . . . . . . . . . . . . . . . . . . . . Assistant
Brandon Starling . . . . . . . . . . . . . . . . . . . . . . Assistant
```

## MILLS PRODS., DONNA
```
PHONE . . . . . . . . . . . . . . . . . . . . . . . . . . . . 310-275-1446
FAX . . . . . . . . . . . . . . . . . . . . . . . . . . . . . . 310-205-0985
12711 Ventura Blvd., Ste. 330
Studio City, CA 91604
TYPE        Television
CREDITS     World's Oldest Bridesmaid - Element of Truth - My Name
            Is Kate
Donna Mills . . . . . . . . . . . . . . . . . . . . President/Producer
```

## *MINDLESS ENTERTAINMENT
```
PHONE . . . . . . . . . . . . . . . . . . . . . . . . . . . . 310-444-8549
FAX . . . . . . . . . . . . . . . . . . . . . . . . . . . . . . 310-231-0476
1440 S. Sepulveda, Ste. 333
Los Angeles, CA 90025
TYPE        Motion Pictures + Television + Syndication
DEAL        Fox Television Studios
CREDITS     The Howard Stern Show - Singled Out - The Judger - Big
            Deal - Just Your Luck
Gary Auerbach . . . . . . . . . . . . . . . . . . . . . . Co-President
Mark Cronin . . . . . . . . . . . . . . . . . . . . . . . Co-President
Heather Mason . . . . . . . . . . . . . . . Development Associate
```

## MINISTRY OF FILM INC., THE
```
PHONE . . . . . . . . . . . . . . . . . . . . . . . . . . . . 310-271-5400
FAX . . . . . . . . . . . . . . . . . . . . . . . . . . . . . . 310-271-3479
P.O. Box 5767
Beverly Hills, CA 90209
TYPE        Motion Pictures + Television + Interactive Multimedia
CREDITS     Timecop - The Getaway - Pacific Blue - Digging To China
COMMENTS    Also: Soundtracks.
Alan Mruvka . . . . . . . . . . . . . . . . . . . . . . . Co-Chairman
Marilyn Vance . . . . . . . . . . . . . . . . . . . . . . Co-Chairman
Edward Hazan . . . . . . . . . . . . . . . Chief Financial Officer
Cathy Goodman-Robbins . . . . . . . . . . . . . . VP, Operations
Ladd Vance . . . . . . . . . . . . . . . . . . . . . . . VP, Production
Josh Levitan . . . . . . . . . . . . . . . . . . . . . . . Story Editor
```

## MIRACLE PICTURES
```
PHONE . . . . . . . . . . . . . . . . . . . . . . . . . . . . 310-392-3011
FAX . . . . . . . . . . . . . . . . . . . . . . . . . . . . . . 310-392-2021
1625 Olympic Blvd., Ste. 200
Santa Monica, CA 90404
TYPE        Motion Pictures
CREDITS     The Ghost and the Darkness - J.F.K. - Born on the 4th of
            July
A. Kitman Ho . . . . . . . . . . . . . . . . . . . . . . . . President
Laurie Hansen . . . . . . . . . . . VP, Development/Production
Michael R Hoffman . . . . . . . . . . . . . . . . Asst. to Mr. Ho
```

## MIRACLE PRODUCTIONS, INC.
```
PHONE . . . . . . . . . . . . . . . . . . 213-845-0756/805-494-6833
EMAIL . . . . . . . . . . . . . robert_loves_stefanie@worldnet.att
1428 N. Curson, #7
Los Angeles, CA 90046
TYPE        Motion Pictures
CREDITS     The Life & Times of Charlie Putz
Robert Rothbard . . . . . . . . . . . . . . . . . . . Writer/Director
Greg Lipari . . . . . . . . . . . . . . . . . . . . . Dir., Development
```

## MIRAGE ENTERPRISES
```
PHONE . . . . . . . . . . . . . . . . . . . . . . . . . . . . 310-244-2044
FAX . . . . . . . . . . . . . . . . . . . . . . . . . . . . . . 310-244-0044
Sony Pictures Entertainment
10202 W. Washington Blvd., Lean Bldg.
Culver City, CA 90232-3195
TYPE        Motion Pictures
DEAL        Sony Pictures Entertainment
CREDITS     Sabrina - Sense & Sensibility - The Firm - Fallen Angels
Sydney Pollack . . . . . . . . . . . . . . . . . . Producer/Director
William Horberg . . . . . . . . . . . . . . . . . . . . . . . Producer
David Rubin . . . . . . . . . . . . . . . . . . . . . . . . . Producer
Geoff Stier . . . . . . . . . . . . . . . . . . . VP, Creative Affairs
Jenny McLaren . . . . . . . . . . . . . . . . . . . Office Manager
Donna Ostroff . . . . . . . . . . . . . . . . . Asst. to Mr. Pollack
```

## MIRAMAX FILMS
```
PHONE . . . . . . . . . . . . . . . . . . 212-941-3800/213-951-4200
FAX . . . . . . . . . . . . . . . . . . . . 212-941-3949/213-951-4211
WEBSITE . . . . . . . . . . . . . . . . . . http://www.miramax.com
Tribeca Film Center
375 Greenwich St.
New York, NY 10013-2338
TYPE        Motion Pictures
CREDITS     Good Will Hunting - Jackie Brown - Copland - Emma -
            The English Patient
COMMENTS    ALSO: 7966 Beverly Blvd. Los Angeles CA 90048
Harvey Weinstein . . . . . . . . . . . . . . . . Co-Chairman (NY)
Bob Weinstein . . . . . . . . . . . . . . . . . . Co-Chairman (NY)
Rick Sands . . . . . . . . . . . . . . . . President, International (NY)
Robert Osher . . . . . . . . . . . . . . . . Co-Pres., Production
Meryl Poster . . . . . . . . . . . . . . Co-Pres., Production (NY)
Mark Gill . . . . . . . . . . . . . . . . . . . President, Miramax LA
Francesca Hickson . . . . . . . . . . . . Chief Financial Officer (NY)
Jack Lechner . . . . . . . . . . . . . . . . Exec. VP, Development (NY)
Agnes Mentres . . . . . . . . . . . Exec. VP, Acquisitions/Co-Prod. (NY)
Jason Blum . . . . . . . . . . . . . . . . . . Sr. VP, Acquisitions (NY)
Vicki Cherkas . . . . . . . . . . . Sr. VP, Business & Legal Affairs (NY)
Julie Goldstein . . . . . . . . . . Sr. VP, Production & Development
Jonathan Gordon . . . . . . . . . . . . . . . Sr. VP, Production (NY)
Andrew Herwitz . . . . . . . . Sr. VP, Acquisitions & Business Affairs (NY)
Steven Hutensky . . . . . . . . Sr. VP, Business & Legal Affairs (NY)
Amy Israel . . . . . . . . . . . . . . . . . . . Sr. VP, Acquisitions (NY)
Brian Burkin . . . . . . . . . . . . . . . VP, Business & Legal Affairs (NY)
Bobby Cohen . . . . . . . . . . . . . . . . . . . . VP, Production (NY)
Michael Cole . . . . . . . . . . . . . VP, Acq. & Strategic Planning
Jeremy Kramer . . . . . . . . . . . . . . . . . . . . . . VP, Production
Cary Meadow . . . . . . . . . . . . . . . . . . VP, Business Affairs
Jill Messick . . . . . . . . . . . . . . . . . . . . . . VP, Development
Teresa Moneo . . . . . . . . . . . . . . . . . . VP, Acquisitions (UK)
Louis Anderman . . . . . . . . . . . . . . . . . . Dir., Development
Jennifer Berman . . . . . . . . . . . . . . . . Dir., Development (NY)
Robbie Brenner . . . . . . . . . . . . . . . . . . Dir., Development
Matt Brodlie . . . . . . . . . . . . . . . . . . . . Dir., Acquisitions
Robert Kessel . . . . . . . . . . . . . . . . . Dir., Acquisitions (NY)
Laura Madden . . . . . . . . . . . . . . . . . Dir., Acquisitions (UK)
Michell Raimo . . . . . . . . . . . . . . . . . Dir., Development (NY)
Beth Rosenblatt . . . . . . . Dir., MP Music Affairs (212-941-2446)
Amy Slotnick . . . . . . . . . . . . . . Dir., Production/Casting (NY)
Alyson Wellins . . . . . . . . . Music Coordinator (212-941-2446)
```

## *MIRANDA ENTERTAINMENT
```
PHONE . . . . . . . . . . . . . . . . . . . . . . . . . . . . 213-851-9126
FAX . . . . . . . . . . . . . . . . . . . . . . . . . . . . . . 213-851-5350
EMAIL . . . . . . . . . . . . . . . . . . . . lorenz@westworld.com
1818 Outpost Drive
Los Angeles, CA 90068
TYPE        Motion Pictures
CREDITS     Prince Valiant - Stalker
Carsten Lorenz . . . . . . . . . . . . . . . . . . . . . . . . No Title
```

# COMPANIES AND STAFF

**MIRISCH CORPORATION**
PHONE . . . . . . . . . . . . . . . . . . . . . . . . . . . . . . . 818-777-1271
FAX . . . . . . . . . . . . . . . . . . . . . . . . . . . . . . . . . 818-866-1422
Universal Studios
100 Universal City Plaza, Bldg. 507 #2C
Universal City, CA 91608-1085
TYPE          Motion Pictures + Television + Animation
CREDITS       West Side Story - The Apartment - Pink Panther Movies
Marvin Mirisch . . . . . . . . . . . . . . . . . . . . . . . . . . . . . . Producer
Walter Mirisch . . . . . . . . . . . . . . . . . . . . . . . . . . . . . . Producer

**MIRKIN VISION**
PHONE . . . . . . . . . . . . . . . . . 310-369-1963/818-954-4181
FAX . . . . . . . . . . . . . . . . . . . . 310-369-3963/818-954-4912
The Simpsons/20th Century Fox
10201 W. Pico Blvd., Bung. 42, Rm. 8
Los Angeles, CA 90035
TYPE          Television + Motion Pictures
DEAL          Warner Bros. Television Productions
CREDITS       The Simpsons - Get A Life - Romy & Michele's High
              School Reunion
COMMENTS      Also: 4000 Warner Blvd., Bldg. 136, Rm. 109 Burbank
              CA 91522
David Mirkin . . . . . . . . . . . . . . . . . . . Exec. Producer/Writer/Director
Jane Yamashita . . . . . . . . . . . . . . . . . . . . . . . . . . . . . . Assistant

***MISCHEL CO., THE**
PHONE . . . . . . . . . . . . . . . . . . . . . . . . . . . . . . . 310-526-0321
FAX . . . . . . . . . . . . . . . . . . . . . . . . . . . . . . . . . 310-526-0322
1610 Broadway
Santa Monica, CA 90404
TYPE          Motion Pictures + Television + Animation +
              Documentaries
DEAL          Film Roman, Inc.
CREDITS       Suicide Kings - Littlest Angel - Strangely, Pennsylvania
COMMENTS      Also: Commercials.
Rick Mischel . . . . . . . . . . . . . . . . . . . . . . . . . . . . . President
Braxton Pope . . . . . . . . . . . . . . . . . . . Dir., Acquisitions/Production
Jared Glazer . . . . . . . . . . . . . . . . . . . . . . . . . . . . . . Assistant

**MISCHER PRODUCTIONS, DON**
PHONE . . . . . . . . . . . . . . . . . . . . . . . . . . . . . . . 310-276-2093
FAX . . . . . . . . . . . . . . . . . . . . . . . . . . . . . . . . . 310-276-0098
8899 Beverly Blvd., Ste. 902
Los Angeles, CA 90048
TYPE          Television
CREDITS       '96 Olympics Open/Close Ceremony - Emmys - Kennedy
              Center Honors
Don Mischer . . . . . . . . . . . . . . . . . . . . . . . . . . . . . President

**MISS UNIVERSE L.P., LLLP**
PHONE . . . . . . . . . . . . . . . . . . . . . . . . . . . . . . . 310-553-2555
FAX . . . . . . . . . . . . . . . . . . . . . . . . . . . . . . . . . 310-553-0234
1801 Century Park East., Ste. 2100
Los Angeles, CA 90067-2323
TYPE          Television
CREDITS       Miss Universe - Miss USA - Miss Teen USA Pageants
Molly Miles . . . . . . . . . . . . . . . . . . . . . . . Chief Executive Officer
Maureen J. Reidy . . . . . . . . . . . . . . . . . . . . . . . . . . . President
Dee Baker . . . . . . . . . . . . . . . . . . . . . . . . . . . . VP, Production
Maureen Murray Quinn . . . . . . . . . . . . . . . . . . . . VP, Marketing
Gail Rosenblum . . . . . . . . . . . . . . . . . VP, Legal & Business Affairs
Carl Allison . . . . . . . . . . . . . . . . . . . . . . . . . . . . . Controller

**MISSEL PRODS., RENEE**
PHONE . . . . . . . . . . . . . . . . . . . . . . . . . . . . . . . 805-565-0888
FAX . . . . . . . . . . . . . . . . . . . . . . . . . . . . . . . . . 805-565-3091
EMAIL . . . . . . . . . . . . . . . . . . . . . . . . . . . filmtao@aol.com
1860 Eucalyptus Hill Rd., Ste. A
Santa Barbara, CA 93108
TYPE          Motion Pictures
CREDITS       Resurrection - Defenseless - The Main Event - Nell - Guy
Renee Missel . . . . . . . . . . . . . . . . . . . . . . . . . . . . . . Producer
Nadja Zubrick . . . . . . . . . . . . . . . . . . . . . . . . . . . Story Editor

**MK PRODUCTIONS**
PHONE . . . . . . . . . . . . . . . . . . . . . . . . . . . . . . . 310-315-6035
FAX . . . . . . . . . . . . . . . . . . . . . . . . . . . . . . . . . 310-315-6015
2308 Broadway
Santa Monica, CA 90404
TYPE          Motion Pictures
Mario Kassar . . . . . . . . . . . . . . . . . . . . . . . . . . . . . President
Joel B. Michaels . . . . . . . . . . . . . . . . . . . . . . Pres., Production
Tim Roche . . . . . . . . . . . . . . . . . . . . . . . . Asst. to Mr. Kassar
Peggy Vargas . . . . . . . . . . . . . . . . . . . . . Asst. to Mr. Michaels

**MKD PRODS.**
PHONE . . . . . . . . . . . . . . . . . . . . . . . . . . . . . . . 805-965-5454
FAX . . . . . . . . . . . . . . . . . . . . . . . . . . . . . . . . . 805-965-4954
EMAIL . . . . . . . . . . . . . . . . . . . . . . . . . . . muffettk@aol.com
1257 Ferrelo Rd.
Santa Barbara, CA 93103
TYPE          Motion Pictures + Television + Documentaries
CREDITS       Phenomenology - March Fire - Choosing Victory - It's
              Your Call
Muffett Kaufman . . . . . . . . . . . . . . . . . . . . . . Producer/Director
Barbara Pearlman . . . . . . . . . . . . . . . . . . . . . . . Vice President

**MOFFITT ASSOCIATES, WILLIAM**
PHONE . . . . . . . . . . . . . . . . . . . . . . . . . . . . . . . 626-791-2559
FAX . . . . . . . . . . . . . . . . . . . . . . . . . . . . . . . . . 626-791-3092
EMAIL . . . . . . . . . . . . . . . . . . . . . . . . . . . info@lonehorse.com
WEBSITE . . . . . . . . . . . . . . . . . . . . . http://www.lonehorse.com
747 N. Lake Ave.
Pasadena, CA 91104
TYPE          Television + Documentaries + Animation + Interactive
              Multimedia
CREDITS       Seeds For The Harvest - Three Faces of Love
COMMENTS      Also: Industrials & Commercials
Lynne Moffitt . . . . . . . . . . . . . . . . . . . . . . . Executive Producer
William Moffitt . . . . . . . . . . . . . . . . . . . . . . . . . . . . Director

**MOFFITT-LEE PRODS.**
PHONE . . . . . . . . . . . . . . . . . . . . . . . . . . . . . . . 213-463-6646
FAX . . . . . . . . . . . . . . . . . . . . . . . . . . . . . . . . . 213-467-2946
1438 N. Gower St., Ste. 250
Hollywood, CA 90028-8306
TYPE          Television
CREDITS       Comic Relief - Not Necessarily the News - U.S. Comedy
              Arts Festival
John Moffitt . . . . . . . . . . . . . . . . . . . . . . . . Executive Producer
Pat Tourk Lee . . . . . . . . . . . . . . . . . . . . . . . Executive Producer
Nancy Kurshner . . . . . . . . . . . . . . . . . . . . . Supervising Producer
Jeff Thorsen . . . . . . . . . . . . . . . . . . . . . . . . Associate Producer

**MOJO FILMS**
PHONE . . . . . . . . . . . . . . . . . . . . . . . . . . . . . . . 310-248-6070
FAX . . . . . . . . . . . . . . . . . . . . . . . . . . . . . . . . . 310-385-0475
9021 Melrose Ave., Suite 302
Los Angeles, CA 90069
TYPE          Motion Pictures
DEAL          New Line Cinema
Gary Fleder . . . . . . . . . . . . . . . . . . . . . . . . . Producer/Director
Amber Stevens . . . . . . . . . . . . . . . . . . . . . . . Dir., Development
Benji White . . . . . . . . . . . . . . . . . . . . . Executive Asst./Story Editor

**MOLL/BEALLOR PRODUCTIONS**
PHONE . . . . . . . . . . . . . . . . . . . . . . . . . . . . . . . 818-777-9000
FAX . . . . . . . . . . . . . . . . . . . . . . . . . . . . . . . . . 818-866-2161
Dream Works SKG
100 Universal City Plaza, Bldg. 477
Universal City, CA 91608
TYPE          Motion Pictures + Documentaries + Television
DEAL          DreamWorks SKG
CREDITS       Survivors of the Holocaust - The Lost Children of Berlin
June Beallor . . . . . . . . . . . . . . . . . . . . . . . . . . . . . . Producer
James Moll . . . . . . . . . . . . . . . . . . . . . . . . . . Producer/Director
Susan M. Baker . . . . . . . . . . . . . . . . . . . . . . . Dir., Development
Aaron Zarrow . . . . . . . . . . . . . . . . . . . . . . . Associate Producer
Christopher Pavlick . . . . . . . . . . . . . . . . . . . . Asst. to James Moll
Serina Tremayne . . . . . . . . . . . . . . . . . . . . . Asst. to June Beallor

**MONARCH PICTURES**
PHONE . . . . . . . . . . . . . . . . . . . . . . . . . . . . . . . . 310-369-1668
10201 W. Pico Blvd., Bldg. 50
Los Angeles, CA 90035

TYPE  Motion Pictures
DEAL  Twentieth Century Fox-Fox 2000 (LA)
CREDITS Devil in a Blue Dress - One False Move - One True Thing - Laurel Avenue

Carl Franklin . . . . . . . . . . . . . . . . . . . . . . . . . . . . . . . . Director
Jesse Beaton . . . . . . . . . . . . . . . . . . . . . . . . . . . . . . . . Producer
Karen Kaufman . . . . . . . . . . . . . . . . . . . . . . . . VP, Development
Abdul Williams . . . . . . . . . . . . . . . . . . . . Development Assistant
Jeni-Lynn DeBow . . . . . . . . . . . . . . . . . . . . . Executive Assistant

**MONT BLANC PRODS.**
PHONE . . . . . . . . . . . . . . . . . . . . . . . . . . . . . . . . 310-394-2327
FAX . . . . . . . . . . . . . . . . . . . . . . . . . . . . . . . . . . . 310-394-1764
EMAIL . . . . . . . . . . . . . . . . . . . . . . . . . . boothprods@aol.com
425 San Vicente Blvd., Ste. C
Santa Monica, CA 90402

TYPE  Motion Pictures + Television
CREDITS Terminal Velocity - Extreme - Team Xtreme

Ron Booth . . . . . . . . . . . . . . . . . . . . . . . . . . . . . . . . Producer
Andrew Wainrib . . . . . . . . . . . . . . . . . . . . . . . . . . . Producer
Didier LaFond . . . . . . . . . . . . . . . . . . . . . . . . . . . . . Director

**MONTAGE ENTERTAINMENT**
PHONE . . . . . . . . . . . . . . . . . . . . . . . . . . . . . . . . 310-966-0222
FAX . . . . . . . . . . . . . . . . . . . . . . . . . . . . . . . . . . . 310-966-0223
2118 Wilshire Blvd., #297
Santa Monica, CA 90403-5784

TYPE  Motion Pictures + Television
CREDITS Acting On Impulse - Marshal Law - Mi Vida Loca - Gas, Food, Lodging

David Peters . . . . . . . . . . . . . . . . . . . . . . . . . . . . . . Producer
Bill Ewart . . . . . . . . . . . . . . . . . . . . . . . . . . . . . . . . Producer
Jim Mercurio . . . . . . . . . . . . . . . . . . . . . . . Dir., Development

**MONTAN PRODUCTIONS, CHRIS**
PHONE . . . . . . . . . . . . . . . . . . . . . . . . . . . . . . . . 818-560-7485
FAX . . . . . . . . . . . . . . . . . . . . . . . . . . . . . . . . . . . 818-560-2500
Walt Disney Studios
500 S. Buena Vista St., Animation 2E-16
Burbank, CA 91521-1759

TYPE  Motion Pictures + Television + Animation
DEAL  Walt Disney Company, The
CREDITS Rodgers and Hammerstein's Cinderella (Disney)

Chris Montan . . . . . . . . . . . . . . . . . Producer (818-560-7495)
Melissa Bachrach . . . . . . . . . . . . . . . . . Sr. VP, Production
Michael Koopman . . . . . . . . . . . . Creative Executive (818-560-6686)
Jill Iverson . . . . . . . . . . . . . . . Production Associate (818-560-7495)

**MONTIVAGUS PRODS.**
PHONE . . . . . . . . . . . . . . . . . . . . . . . . . . . . . . . . 818-782-1212
FAX . . . . . . . . . . . . . . . . . . . . . . . . . . . . . . . . . . . 818-782-1931
13930 Burbank Blvd., Ste. 100
Sherman Oaks, CA 91401-5046

TYPE  Motion Pictures
CREDITS The Second Room - Along for the Ride - In Therapy
Timothy T. Miller . . . . . . . . . . . . . . . . . . . President/Producer
Bryan W. Simon . . . . . . . . . . . . . . . . . . . . Producer/Director
Marjorie Engesser . . . . . . . . . . . . . . . . . . . Producer/Writer
Douglas Coler . . . . . . . . . . . . . . . . . . . . . . . Creative Affairs

**MOONSTONE ENTERTAINMENT**
PHONE . . . . . . . . . . . . . . . . . . . . . . . . . . . . . . . . 310-247-6060
FAX . . . . . . . . . . . . . . . . . . . . . . . . . . . . . . . . . . . 310-247-6061
335 N. Maple Dr., Ste. 222
Beverly Hills, CA 90210

TYPE  Motion Pictures + Television
CREDITS Afterglow - The Only Thrill - Digging to China
Ernst Etchie Stroh . . . . . . . . . . . . . . . . . . . . . . . . President
Yael Stroh . . . . . . . . . . . . . . . . . . . . . . Exec. Vice President

***MORE/MEDAVOY MANAGEMENT**
PHONE . . . . . . . . . . . . . . . . . . . . . . . . . . . . . . . . 213-969-0700
FAX . . . . . . . . . . . . . . . . . . . . . . . . . . . . . . . . . . . 213-969-9340
7920 Sunset Blvd., Ste. 401
Los Angeles, CA 90046

TYPE  Motion Pictures + Television
DEAL  Twentieth Century Fox
CREDITS Dharma & Greg - Just Shoot Me - Getting Personal - The Single Guy

Erwin More . . . . . . . . . . . . . . . . . . . . . . . . . . . . . . . . Partner
Brian Medavoy . . . . . . . . . . . . . . . . . . . . . . . . . . . . . Partner
Gina Rugolo-Judd . . . . . . . . . . . . . . . . . . . . . . . . VP, Talent
Cheryl Stanley . . . . . . . . . . . . . . . . . . . . . VP, Creative Affairs

**MORESS-NANAS-HART ENTERTAINMENT**
PHONE . . . . . . . . . . . . . . . 310-820-9897/615-329-9945
FAX . . . . . . . . . . . . . . . . . 310-820-7375/615-321-3457
12424 Wilshire Blvd., Ste. 840
Los Angeles, CA 90025

TYPE  Motion Pictures + Television
CREDITS 2 Days in the Valley - Mother - Defending Your Life
COMMENTS ALSO: Music Management. ALSO: 1102 18th Ave. South, Nashville TN 37212

Scott Hart . . . . . . . . . . . . . . . . . . Producer/Personal Manager
Stan Moress . . . . . . . . . . . . . . . . . Producer/Personal Manager
Herb Nanas . . . . . . . . . . . . . . . . . Producer/Personal Manager
Ana Guttierez . . . . . . . . . . . . . . . . . . . . . . Asst. to Mr. Hart
Katherine Hyder . . . . . . . . . . . . . . . . . . . Asst. to Mr. Moress
Fran Messer . . . . . . . . . . . . . . . . . . . . . . Asst. to Mr. Nanas

**MORGAN CREEK PRODS.**
PHONE . . . . . . . . . . . . . . . . . . . . . . . . . . . . . . . . 818-954-4800
FAX . . . . . . . . . . . . . . . . . . . . . . . . . . . . . . . . . . . 818-954-4811
4000 Warner Blvd., Bldg. 76
Burbank, CA 91522

TYPE  Motion Pictures
CREDITS Robin Hood - Ace Ventura I & II - Major League I & II - Diabolique - Wild America

James G. Robinson . . . . . . . . . . . . . . . . . . . . Chairman/CEO
Howard Kaplan . . . . . . . . . . . . . . . . . . Chief Financial Officer
Jonathan A. Zimbert . . . . . . . . . . . . . . . . . Pres., Production
Richard Klubeck . . . . . . . . . . Sr. VP, Business Affairs/General Counsel
Hilary Galanoy . . . . . . . . . . . . . . . . . . . . . . . VP, Development
Drew Larner . . . . . . . . . . . . . . . . . . . . VP, Morgan Creek Intl.
Joe Martino . . . . . . . . . . . . . . . . . . . . . . . . VP, Development

**MORRA, BREZNER, STEINBERG & TENENBAUM**
PHONE . . . . . . . . . . . . . . . . . . . . . . . . . . . . . . . . 310-385-1820
FAX . . . . . . . . . . . . . . . . . . . . . . . . . . . . . . . . . . . 310-385-1834
345 N. Maple Dr., Ste. 200
Beverly Hills, CA 90210

TYPE  Motion Pictures + Television
DEAL  Walt Disney Pictures/Touchstone Pictures
CREDITS Throw Momma from the Train - Good Morning Vietnam - Krippendorf's Tribe

Larry Brezner . . . . . . . . . . . . . . . . . . . . . . . . . . . . . . Partner
Mike Marcus . . . . . . . . . . . . . . . . . . . . . . . . . . . . . . . Partner
Buddy Morra . . . . . . . . . . . . . . . . . . . . . . . . . . . . . . . Partner
David Steinberg . . . . . . . . . . . . . . . . . . . . . . . . . . . . Partner
Stephen Tenenbaum . . . . . . . . . . . . . . . . . . . . . . . . . Partner
Jonathan Brandstein . . . . . . . . . . . . . . . . . . . . . . . . No Title
Ross Canter . . . . . . . . . . . . . . . . . . . . . . . . . . . . . . . No Title
Scott Fedro . . . . . . . . . . . . . . . . . . . . . . . . . . . . . . . No Title
Julie James . . . . . . . . . . . . . . . . . . . . . . . . . . . . . . . No Title
Aghi Koh . . . . . . . . . . . . . . . . . . . . . . . . . . . . . . . . . No Title

**MORROW-HEUS PRODUCTIONS**
PHONE . . . . . . . . . . . . . . . . . . . . . . . . . . . . . . . . 310-815-9973
FAX . . . . . . . . . . . . . . . . . . . . . . . . . . . . . . . . . . . 310-815-9975
EMAIL . . . . . . . . . . . . . . . . . . . . . . . . . . morrowheus@aol.com
8800 Venice Blvd., Ste. 209
Los Angeles, CA 90034

TYPE  Motion Pictures + Television + Documentaries
CREDITS Race The Sun - The Disappearance of Vonnie - Christmas on Division Street

Barry Morrow . . . . . . . . . . . . . . . . . . . . . . . . Writer/Producer
Richard Heus . . . . . . . . . . . . . . . . . . . . . . . . . . . . . . Producer
Julia Rask . . . . . . . . . . . . . . . . . . . . . . . . . . . . . . . . No Title
Paul Shrater . . . . . . . . . . . . . . . . . . . . . . . . Dir., Development

# COMPANIES AND STAFF

**MORTON PRODS., JEFF**
PHONE . . . . . . . . . . . . . . . . . . . . . . . . . . . . . . . . . . . 818-986-4539
FAX . . . . . . . . . . . . . . . . . . . . . . . . . . . . . . . . . . . . . . 818-981-4152
5027 Noeline Ave.
Encino, CA 91436
TYPE          Motion Pictures + Television
CREDITS       Caracara - Second Skin - Double Jeopardy
Jeff Morton . . . . . . . . . . . . . . . . . . . . . . . . . . . . . . . . . . . Producer

**MOSTOW/LIEBERMAN**
PHONE . . . . . . . . . . . . . . . . . . . . . . . . . . . . . . . . . . . 818-777-4444
FAX . . . . . . . . . . . . . . . . . . . . . . . . . . . . . . . . . . . . . . 818-866-1328
Universal Pictures
100 Universal City Plaza, Bung. 414
Universal City, CA 91608
TYPE          Motion Pictures
CREDITS       Breakdown - The Jackal - The Game - Flight of Black
              Angel - U-571 - New Jersey Turnpikes
Hal Lieberman . . . . . . . . . . . . . . . . . . . . . . . . . . . . . . . . Partner
Jonathan Mostow . . . . . . . . . . . . . . . . . . . . . . . . . . . . . Partner
Abby Wolf . . . . . . . . . . . . . . . . . . . . . . . . . . . . . . . . . . President
Jed Blaugrund . . . . . . . . . . . . . . . . . . . . . . . . . . . . . . . No Title
Paul Neesan . . . . . . . . . . . . . . . . . . . . . . . . . . . . . . . . No Title
Debbie Levy . . . . . . . . . . . . . . . . . . . . . . Asst. to Hal Lieberman
Annie Rhodes . . . . . . . . . . . . . . . . . . . Asst. to Jonathan Mostow
Paul Brehme . . . . . . . . . . . . . . . . . . . . Asst. to Jonathan Mostow
Marnie Breeker . . . . . . . . . . . . . . . . . . Dev. Asst. to Abby Wolf
Jeff Lew . . . . . . . . . . . . . . . . . . . . . . . . . Asst. to Jed Blaugrund
Graham Reed . . . . . . . . . . . . . . . . . . . . . . Asst. to Paul Neesan
Dresden Shumaker . . . . . . . . . . . . . . . . . . . . . . . . . . . Assistant
Alec Pederson . . . . . . . . . . . . . . . . . . . . . . . . . Office Assistant

**MOTION PICT. CORP. OF AMERICA**
PHONE . . . . . . . . . . . . . . . . . . . . . . . . . . . . . . . . . . . 310-319-9500
FAX . . . . . . . . . . . . . . . . . . . . . . . . . . . . . . . . . . . . . . 310-319-9501
1401 Ocean Ave., Ste. 301
Santa Monica, CA 90401
TYPE          Motion Pictures
CREDITS       Kingpin - Beverly Hills Ninja - Dumb And Dumber
Brad Krevoy . . . . . . . . . . . . . . . . . . . . . . . . . . . . . Co-President
Steve Stabler . . . . . . . . . . . . . . . . . . . . . . . . . . . . Co-President
Jeff Ivers . . . . . . . . . . . . . . . . . . . . . . . . . . Exec. Vice President
Brent Baum . . . . . . . . . . . . . . . . . . . . . . . . . Exec. Vice President
Brad Jenkel . . . . . . . . . . . . . . . . . . . . . . . . Exec. VP/Producer
John Bertolli . . . . . . . . . . . . . . . . . . . . Sr. VP, Production/Producer
Bradley Thomas . . . . . . . . . . . . . . . . . . Sr. VP, Production/Producer
David Bixler . . . . . . . . . . . . . . . . VP, Acquisitions & Production/Producer
Tim Foster . . . . . . . . . . . . . . . . . . . . . . . VP, Production/Producer
Scott Niemeyer . . . . . . . . . . . . . . . . . . . . VP, Finance/Production
Danielle Parsons . . . . . . . . . . . . . . . . VP, Creative Affairs/Producer
Jade Ramsey . . . . . . . . . . . . . . . . . VP, Production/Business Affairs
Michael Nadeau . . . . . . . . . . . . . . . . . . . . . . . . . . . . . . Producer
Lawrence Grey . . . . . . . . . . . . . . . . . . . . . Dir., Creative Affairs
Mark Morgan . . . . . . . . . . . . . . . . . . . . . . . . . Dir., Development
Doug Morton . . . . . . . . . . . . . . . . . . . . . . . . . Dir., Development
Warren Davis . . . . . . . . . . . . . . . . . . . . . . . . Creative Executive
Brian Grushcow . . . . . . . . . . . . . . . . . . . . . . . . . . . Story Editor

***MOTOR CITY FILMS**
PHONE . . . . . . . . . . . . . . . . . . . . . . . . . . . . . . . . . . . 310-369-0360
FAX . . . . . . . . . . . . . . . . . . . . . . . . . . . . . . . . . . . . . . 310-369-0359
Twentieth Century Fox
10201 W. Pico Blvd., Bldg. 12, Rm. 133
Los Angeles, CA 90035
TYPE          Motion Pictures
DEAL          Fox 2000
CREDITS       Gridlock'd
Vondie Curtis Hall . . . . . . . . . . . . . . . . . . . Producer/Director
Steven Siebert . . . . . . . . . . . . . . . . . . . . . . . . . . . . . . Producer
Helena Echegoyen . . . . . . . . . . . . . . . . . . . . . . . . . . . Producer
Alexandria Nabatoff . . . . . . . . . . . . . . . . . . . Creative Executive
Raye Dowell . . . . . . . . . . . . . . . . . . . . . . . . Asst. to Mr. Hall

**MOUNT OLYMPUS ENTERTAINMENT**
PHONE . . . . . . . . . . . . . . . . . . . . . . . . . . . . . . . . . . . 310-202-6798
FAX . . . . . . . . . . . . . . . . . . . . . . . . . . . . . . . . . . . . . . 310-559-1644
3221 Overland Ave., Ste. 1233
Los Angeles, CA 90034
TYPE          Motion Pictures + Television
Daniel Harris . . . . . . . . . . . . . . . . . . . . . . . . . . . . . . . Partner
Costantino Magnatta . . . . . . . . . . . . . . . . . . . . . . . . . Partner

***MOUNT ROYAL ENTERTAINMENT**
PHONE . . . . . . . . . . . . . . . . . . . . . . . . . . . . . . . . . . . 310-656-9382
FAX . . . . . . . . . . . . . . . . . . . . . . . . . . . . . . . . . . . . . . 310-656-9385
1542 15th Street
Santa Monica, CA 90404
TYPE          Motion Pictures
CREDITS       Dead Man's Curve - Limbo
Michael Amato . . . . . . . . . . . . . . . . . . . . . . . . . . . . No Title
Jeremy Lew . . . . . . . . . . . . . . . . . . . . . . . . . . . . . . No Title
William Mercer . . . . . . . . . . . . . . . . . . . . . . . . . . . No Title
Ted Schipper . . . . . . . . . . . . . . . . . . . . . . . . . . . . . No Title

**MOUNT/KRAMER COMPANY, THE**
PHONE . . . . . . . . . . . . . . . . . . . . . . . . . . . . . . . . . . . 310-226-8374
FAX . . . . . . . . . . . . . . . . . . . . . . . . . . . . . . . . . . . . . . 310-226-8343
1925 Century Park E., #1700
Los Angeles, CA 90067
TYPE          Motion Pictures
DEAL          MDP/Behaviour Worldwide
CREDITS       Night Falls on Manhattan - Death & The Maiden - Bull
              Durham
Josh Kramer . . . . . . . . . . . . . . . . . . . . . . . . . . . . . . . Partner
Thom Mount . . . . . . . . . . . . . . . . . . . . . . . . . . . . . . . Partner
Rodman Gregg . . . . . . . . . . . . . . . . . . . . Pres., M/K Television
Patrick Olmstead . . . . . . . . . . . . . . . . . . . . Creative Executive
Raquel Carreras . . . . . . . . . . . . . . . . . . . . . . . . . . . . Producer
Dominick Rappa . . . . . . . . . . . . . . . . . . . . Asst. to Josh Kramer
Kenneth Ross . . . . . . . . . . . . . . . . . . . . . Asst. to Thom Mount

**MOUNTAIN DRIVE**
PHONE . . . . . . . . . . . . . . . . . . . . . . . . . . . . . . . . . . . 310-395-6200
FAX . . . . . . . . . . . . . . . . . . . . . . . . . . . . . . . . . . . . . . 310-458-6664
625 Arizona Ave.
Santa Monica, CA 90401
TYPE          Television + Interactive Multimedia + Motion Pictures
CREDITS       Deepak Chopra Specials - Virtual Set Productions - Dr.
              Andrew Weil Specials
Sandra Hay . . . . . . . . . . . . . . . . . . . . . . . . . Executive Producer
John G. Otto . . . . . . . . . . . . . . . . . . . . . . . . . Dir., Development

**MOVICORP HOLDINGS, INC.**
PHONE . . . . . . . . . . . . . . . . . . . . . . . . . . . . . . . . . . . 310-553-4300
FAX . . . . . . . . . . . . . . . . . . . . . . . . . . . . . . . . . . . . . . 310-553-1159
WEBSITE . . . . . . . . . . . . . . . . . . . . . . . . http://www.movicorp.com
9887 Santa Monica Blvd. #200
Beverly Hills, CA 90212-1604
TYPE          Motion Pictures + Television + Feature Direct to Video
DEAL          Universal Television & Networks Group
CREDITS       Infamous Dorothy Parker - Rebel - Hemingway - In Love,
              In War, In The Movies
COMMENTS      Owns Cable Network Oasis TV.
Robert Schnitzer . . . . . . . . . . . . . . . . . . . . . . . . Chairman/CEO
Toni Serritello . . . . . . . . . . . . . . . . . . . . . . . VP, Creative Affairs
Larry Haber . . . . . . . . . . . . . . . . . . . . . . . . . Financial Consultant

**MOVIE DEVELOPMENT CORP.**
PHONE . . . . . . . . . . . . . . . . . . . . . 818-753-8399/914-723-5100
FAX . . . . . . . . . . . . . . . . . . . . . . . . 818-753-2088/914-723-6207
EMAIL . . . . . . . . . . . . . . . . . . . . . . . . . . . . . . mibuntz@aol.com
3626 Laurel Canyon Blvd.
Studio City, CA 91604
TYPE          Motion Pictures + Television
CREDITS       The Exterminator - Love Kills
COMMENTS      ALSO: 1075 Central Park Ave. #410, Scarsdale NY
              10583
Mark Buntzman . . . . . . . . . . . . . . . . . . . . . Producer/President

**MOVIE GROUP, THE**
PHONE . . . . . . . . . . . . . . . . . . . . . . . . . . . . . . . . . . . 310-556-2830
FAX . . . . . . . . . . . . . . . . . . . . . . . . . . . . . . . . . . . . . . 310-277-1490
1900 Ave. of the Stars, Ste. 1425
Los Angeles, CA 90067
TYPE          Motion Pictures
CREDITS       Cadence - Best of the Best I, II & III - By the Sword -
              Kickboxer
COMMENTS      Finances and distributes independently produced films. Int.
              Distribution- Features, All Media. Intl.
Peter E. Strauss . . . . . . . . . . . . . . . . . . . . . . . . President/CEO
Ann Oliver . . . . . . . . . . . . . . . . . . . . . . Chief Financial Officer
Randy Klinenberg . . . . . . . . . . . . . . . . . . . . . . VP, Operations

# COMPANIES AND STAFF

## MOVING PICTURES
PHONE . . . . . . . . . . . . . . . . . . . . . . . . . . . . . . . . . 310-576-0577
FAX . . . . . . . . . . . . . . . . . . . . . . . . . . . . . . . . . . 310-576-0527
1453 Third St., Ste. 420
Santa Monica, CA 90401

TYPE           Motion Pictures + Television
DEAL           Universal Pictures
CREDITS     Now & Then - If These Walls Could Talk - GI Jane - Austin Powers

Demi Moore . . . . . . . . . . . . . . . . . . . . . . . . . . . . . . . . . . . . . Partner
Daneen Conroy . . . . . . . . . . . . . . . . . . . . . . . . . . . . . . . . . . Partner
David Marko . . . . . . . . . . . . . . . . . . . . . . . . . . . Dir., Development
Cathryn Stanley . . . . . . . . . . . . . . . . . . . . . . . . . . . . Coordinator
Mark Hunter Reinking . . . . . . . . . . . . . . . . . . . . Asst. to Demi Moore
Karen Thumm . . . . . . . . . . . . . . . . . . . . . . . . Development Assistant
Harry Saltz . . . . . . . . . . . . . . . . . . . . . . . . The Guy Who Gets Stuff

## MOZARK PRODUCTIONS
PHONE . . . . . . . . . . . . . . . . . . . . . . . . . . . . . . . . . 818-655-5779
4024 Radford Ave., Bldg. 5 #104
Studio City, CA 91604

TYPE           Television + Motion Pictures
DEAL           DreamWorks SKG/CBS Entertainment
CREDITS     Hearts Afire - Women of the House - Evening Shade - Designing Women

Linda Bloodworth-Thomason . . . . . . . . . . . . . . . Executive Producer/Writer
Harry Thomason . . . . . . . . . . . . . . . . . . . . . Executive Producer/Director

## *MPH ENTERTAINMENT, INC.
PHONE . . . . . . . . . . . . . . . . . . . . . . . . . . . . . . . . . 818-761-4211
FAX . . . . . . . . . . . . . . . . . . . . . . . . . . . . . . . . . . 818-761-4929
EMAIL . . . . . . . . . . . . . . . . . . . . . . . . MPHENT@earthlink.net
4400 Coldwater Canyon Ave., Ste. 300
Studio City, CA 91604

TYPE           Motion Pictures + Television + Documentaries
Jim Milio . . . . . . . . . . . . . . . . . . . . . . . . . . . . . . . . . President
Mark Hufnail . . . . . . . . . . . . . . . Vice President/Chief Financial Officer
Melissa Jo Peltier . . . . . . . . . . . . . . . . . . . . . . . . . Vice President

## MR. MUDD
PHONE . . . . . . . . . . . . . . . . . . . . . . . . . . . . . . . . . 213-932-5656
FAX . . . . . . . . . . . . . . . . . . . . . . . . . . . . . . . . . . 213-932-5666
5225 Wilshire Blvd., Ste. 604
Los Angeles, CA 90036

TYPE           Motion Pictures
DEAL           Granada Entertainment USA
CREDITS     Of Mice and Men - Queens Logic - The Witness - Man In the Iron Mask

John Malkovich . . . . . . . . . . . . . . . . . . . . . . . . . Producer/Director
Lianne Halfon . . . . . . . . . . . . . . . . . . . . . . . . . . . . . . Producer
Russ Smith . . . . . . . . . . . . . . . . . . . . . . . . . . . . . . . . Producer
Shannon Clark . . . . . . . . . . . . . . . . . . . . . . . . . Creative Associate
David Hopper . . . . . . . . . . . . . . . . . . . . . . . . . . Creative Associate

## MTV FILMS
PHONE . . . . . . . . . . . . . . . . . . . . . . . . . . . . . . . . . 323-956-8023
FAX . . . . . . . . . . . . . . . . . . . . . . . . . . . . . . . . . . 323-862-1386
WEBSITE . . . . . . . . . . . . . . . . . . . . . . . . . http://www.mtv.com
Paramount Studios
5555 Melrose Ave., Studio H, # 200
Los Angeles, CA 90038

TYPE           Motion Pictures
DEAL           Paramount Pictures- Motion Picture Group
CREDITS     Election - Dead Man on Campus - 200 Cigarettes - Varsity Blues - The Wood
COMMENTS  Production fax line: 323-862-2020.

Van Toffler . . . . . . . . . . . . . . . . GM, MTV Networks/Pres., MTV Prods.
David M. Gale . . Head, MTV Films/Sr. Vice President, MTV (213-956-4390)
Elysa Koplovitz . . . . . . . . . . . . . . . Dir., Development (213-956-3275)
Momita Sengupta . . . . . . . . . . . . . . . MTV Films Production Manager
Tajamika Paxton . . . . . . . . . . . . . . . . . . . . . . . Creative Executive
Amie Steir . . . . . . . . . . . . . . . . . . . Story Editor (212-846-4886)

## MTV NETWORKS
PHONE . . . . . . . . . . . . . . . . . . . 212-258-8000/310-752-8000
FAX . . . . . . . . . . . . . . . . . . . . . . 212-258-8303/310-752-8001
WEBSITE . . . . . . . . . . . . . . . . . . . . . . . . . http://www.mtv.com
1515 Broadway Ave.
New York, NY 10036

TYPE           Television
CREDITS     Beavis & Butthead - Choose Or Lose '96 - House of Style - Singled Out
COMMENTS  Also: 2600 Colorado Ave., Santa Monica CA 90404

Thomas E. Freston . . . . . . . . . . . . . . . . Chairman/CEO, MTV Networks
Mark Rosenthal . . . . . . . . . . . . . . . . . . . . . . . . . President/COO
Judith McGrath . . . . . . . . . . . . . . . . . . . . . . . . President, MTV
William Roedy . . . . . . . . . . . . . . . . . . . . . . President, Intl.
Abby Terkuhle . . . . . . . . Pres., MTV Anim./Creative Dir., MTV & MTV Prod
Van Toffler . . . . . . . . . . . . . . . . General Manager, MTV Networks
Betsy Frank . . . . . . . . . . . . . . . . Exec. VP, Research & Development
Brian Graden . . . . . . . . . . . . . . . Exec. VP, Television Programming
Greg Ricca . . . . . . . . . . . . . . . . . . . . . . . Exec. VP, MTVN
James M. Shaw . . . . . . . . . . . . . . . . . . Executive Vice President
Matt Farber . . . . . . . . . . . . . . Sr. VP, New Business & Programming
Patty Galuzzi . . . . . . . . . . . . . . . . . . Sr. VP, Music Programming
Robin Berlin . . . . . . . . . . . . VP, Celebrity Talent & Specials (LA)
Catherine Houser . . . . . . . . . . . . VP, Human Resources (West Coast)
Lewis Largent . . . . . . . . . . . . . . . . VP, Music & Artist Development
Lauren Levine . . . . . . . . . . VP/Exec. Producer MTV Video Programming
Harriet Shultz . . . . . . . . . . . . . . . . VP, West Coast Operations (LA)
Kurt Steffek . . . . . . . . . . . . VP, Music Programming (212-258-8836)

## MULBERRY SQUARE PRODUCTIONS, INC.
PHONE . . . . . . . . . . . . . . . . . . . . . . . . . . . . . . . . . 919-933-2575
FAX . . . . . . . . . . . . . . . . . . . . . . . . . . . . . . . . . . 919-933-1721
310 1/2 W. Franklin St.
Chapel Hill, NC 27516

TYPE           Motion Pictures + Television
CREDITS     Benji - For The Love of Benji - Oh Heavenly Dog - The Hunted

Joseph Camp . . . . . . . . . . . . . . . . . . . . . . . . . . . . . . President
Angela W. McNeill . . . . . . . . . . . . . . . . . . . . . . . General Manager

## MUNDY LANE ENTERTAINMENT
PHONE . . . . . . . . . . . . . . . . . . . . . . . . . . . . . . . . . 310-369-5940
FAX . . . . . . . . . . . . . . . . . . . . . . . . . . . . . . . . . . 310-369-8330
10201 W. Pico Blvd., Bldg. 31, Room 300
Los Angeles, CA 90035

TYPE           Motion Pictures
DEAL           Twentieth Century Fox
CREDITS     The Preacher's Wife - Devil in A Blue Dress - Hank Aaron Documentary

Denzel Washington . . . . . . . . . . . . . . . . . . . . . . . . . . . No Title
Cecil C. Cox . . . . . . . . . . . . . . . . . . . . . . . . . . . . . . No Title
Deidra L. Colvin . . . . . . . . . . . . . . . . . . . . . . Executive Assistant

## MURPHY PRODS., EDDIE
PHONE . . . . . . . . . . . . . . . . . . . . . . . . . . . . . . . . . 212-399-9900
FAX . . . . . . . . . . . . . . . . . . . . . . . . . . . . . . . . . . 212-399-0555
152 W. 57th St., 47th Fl.
New York, NY 10019

TYPE           Motion Pictures
DEAL           Caravan Pictures
CREDITS     Metro - Beverly Hills Cop II & III - Vampire In Brooklyn - Nutty Professor - Dr. Dolittle

Eddie Murphy . . . . . . . . . . . . . . . . . . . . . . . . . . CEO/President
Ray Murphy Jr. . . . . . . . . . . . . . . . . . . . . . . . . . VP, Production
Charles Murphy . . . . . . . . . . . . . . . . . Creative Consultant/Writer
Clint Smith . . . . . . . . . . . . . . . . . . . . . . . . . Creative Consultant
Vernon Lynch Jr. . . . . . . . . . . . . . . . . . . . . . . Creative Consultant
Charisse Hewitt . . . . . . . . . . . . . . . . . Exec. Asst. to Mr. Murphy

## MUSE PRODUCTIONS, INC.
PHONE . . . . . . . . . . . . . . . . . . . . . . . . . . . . . . . . . 310-306-2001
FAX . . . . . . . . . . . . . . . . . . . . . . . . . . . . . . . . . . 310-574-2614
EMAIL . . . . . . . . . . . . . . . . . . . . . . . . . musefilm@aol.com
15 Brooks Ave., Unit B
Venice, CA 90291

TYPE           Motion Pictures + Interactive Multimedia
CREDITS     Trees Lounge - Two Girls and A Guy - Buffalo 66 - Revenant - Freeway

Chris Hanley . . . . . . . . . . . . . . . . . . . . . . . . President/Producer
Jordan Gertner . . . . . . . . . . . . . . . . . . . . . . . . . . VP/Producer
Timothy Peternel . . . . . . . . . . . . . . . . . . VP, Development/Producer
Roberta Hanley . . . . . . . . . . . . . . . . . . . Actress/Writer/Producer

***MUTANT ENEMY, INC.**
PHONE . . . . . . . . . . . . . . . . . . . . . . . . . . . . . . . . . . . 310-579-5180
FAX . . . . . . . . . . . . . . . . . . . . . . . . . . . . . . . . . . . . . 310-579-5380
P.O. Box 900
Beverly Hills, CA 90213-0900

| | |
|---|---|
| TYPE | Animation + Motion Pictures + Television |
| DEAL | Twentieth Century Fox Film Corp. |
| CREDITS | Buffy the Vampire Slayer (TV Series) - Buffy the Vampire Slayer (Feature) - Toy Story - Alien Resurrection |

Joss Whedon . . . . . . . . . . . . . . . . . . . . . . . . . . Chief Executive Officer
Jeff Bynum . . . . . . . . . . . . . . . . . . . . Sr. Vice President (310-579-5181)
George Snyder . . . . . . . . . . . . . . . . . Dir., Development (310-579-5182)
Diego Gutierrez . . . . . . . . . . . . . . . . . . . . . . . . . Asst. to Joss Whedon
Laura Kotcharian . . . . . . . . . . . . . . . . . Asst. to Jeff Bynum (310-579-5183)
Adam Wilson . . . . . . . . . . . . . . . Asst. to George Snyder (310-579-5184)

**MUTUAL FILM CO.**
PHONE . . . . . . . . . . . . . . . . . . . . . . . . . . . . . . . . . . . 213-871-5690
FAX . . . . . . . . . . . . . . . . . . . . . . . . . . . . . . . . . . . . . 213-871-5689
EMAIL . . . . . . . . . . . . . . . . . . . . . . . . . . . . info@mutualfilm.com
Raleigh Studios
650 N. Bronson Ave., Clinton Bldg.
Hollywood, CA 90004

| | |
|---|---|
| TYPE | Motion Pictures + Television |
| DEAL | Paramount Pictures- Motion Picture Group |
| CREDITS | Saving Private Ryan - Paulie - 12 Monkeys - Broken Arrow - Speed |
| COMMENTS | Also: Foreign Distribution |

Mark Gordon . . . . . . . . . . . . . . . . . . . . . . . . . . . . . . . . . . . Principal
Gary Levinsohn . . . . . . . . . . . . . . . . . . . . . . . . . . . . . . . . . Principal
Allison Segan . . . . . . . . . . . . . . . . . . . . . . . . . . . . Pres., Production
Ed Maguire . . . . . . . . . . . . . . . . . . . . . . . . . . . . VP, Administration
Eric Suddelson . . . . . . . . . . . . . . . . . . VP, Business & Legal Affairs
Michael Dahan . . . . . . . . . . . . . . . . . . . . . . . Development Executive
Tania Landau . . . . . . . . . . . . . . . . . . . . . . . . . Development Executive
Suzanne Patmore . . . . . . . . . . . . . . . . . . . . . . Development Executive
Kristin Dardano . . . . . . . . . . . . . . . . . . . . . . . . . . . . . Story Editor
Steve Asbell . . . . . . . . . . . . . . . . . . . . . . . . . . . Asst. to S. Patmore
Kaz Brecher . . . . . . . . . . . . . . . . . . . . . . . . . . Asst. to G. Levinsohn
Antonio Daniel . . . . . . . . . . . . . . . . . Asst. to M. Dahan & T. Landau
Adam Fratto . . . . . . . . . . . . . . . . . . . . . . . . . . . . . Asst. to A. Segan
Cindy Holland . . . . . . . . . . . . . . . . . . . . . . . . . Asst. to G. Levinsohn
Karen Jacobs . . . . . . . . . . . . . . . . . . . . . . . . . . . Asst. to M. Gordon
Josh Baizer . . . . . . . . . . . . . . . . . . . . . . . . . . . . . . . . Receptionist

**MWG PRODS.**
PHONE . . . . . . . . . . . . . . . . . . . . . . . . . . . . . . . . . . . 213-469-8290
FAX . . . . . . . . . . . . . . . . . . . . . . . . . . . . . . . . . . . . . 213-469-8304
EMAIL . . . . . . . . . . . . . . . . mwgproductions@mindspring.com
WEBSITE . . . . . . . . . . . . . . . . . . . . . . http://www.AlaskaDQ.com
2317 Vasanta Way
Los Angeles, CA 90068

| | |
|---|---|
| TYPE | Motion Pictures + Television + Interactive Multimedia |
| CREDITS | Nine - Alaska |
| COMMENTS | Also: goldenson@mindspring.com/wynne9@aol.com |

Max Goldenson . . . . . . . . . . . . . . . . . . . . . . . . President/Producer
Melissa Wylie . . . . . . . . . . . . . . . . . . . . . . . . . . . Dir., Development

**MYERSON ENTERTAINMENT**
PHONE . . . . . . . . . . . . . . . . . . . . . . . . . . . . . . . . . . . 310-550-7383
FAX . . . . . . . . . . . . . . . . . . . . . . . . . . . . . . . . . . . . . 310-550-7391
275 S. Beverly Dr., Ste. 210
Beverly Hills, CA 90212

| | |
|---|---|
| TYPE | Motion Pictures + Television |
| DEAL | Columbia TriStar Television |
| CREDITS | The Mahabharata |

Edward Myerson . . . . . . . . . . . . . . . . . . . . . . . . . . . . . . . Producer
Rachel Tabori Myerson . . . . . . . . . . . . . . . . . . . . . . . . . . . Producer
Steve Oxman . . . . . . . . . . . . . . . . . . . . . . . . . . . . VP, Development

**MYRON PRODUCTIONS, BEN**
PHONE . . . . . . . . . . . . . . . . . . . . . . . . . . . . . . . . . . . 310-360-1144
FAX . . . . . . . . . . . . . . . . . . . . . . . . . . . . . . . . . . . . . 310-360-1145
1024 W. Palm Ave.
W. Hollywood, CA 90069

| | |
|---|---|
| TYPE | Motion Pictures + Television |
| DEAL | Universal Pictures |
| CREDITS | One False Move - Leave It To Beaver - An Alan Smithee Film - Mr. Magoo |

Ben Myron . . . . . . . . . . . . . . . . . . . . . . . . . . . . . . . . . . Producer
Sean McDermott . . . . . . . . . . . . . . . . . . . . . . . . . . . . Development
Marilyn Belknap . . . . . . . . . . . . . . . . . . . . . . . . Executive Assistant

**NASH ENTERTAINMENT**
PHONE . . . . . . . . . . . . . . . . . . . . . . . . . . . . . . . . . . . 213-993-7384
FAX . . . . . . . . . . . . . . . . . . . . . . . . . . . . . . . . . . . . . 213-993-7385
Sunset Gower Studios
1438 N. Gower St., Bldg. 35, Ste. 13
Hollywood, CA 90028

| | |
|---|---|
| TYPE | Television |

Bruce Nash . . . . . . . . . . . . . . . . . . . . . . . . . . . . Executive Producer
Robyn Nash . . . . . . . . . . . . . . . . . . . . . . . . . . . . . . . . . . Producer
Dan Goldberg . . . . . . . . . . . . . . . . . Exec. In Charge of Production

**NASSER ENTERTAINMENT GROUP**
PHONE . . . . . . . . . . . . . . . . . . . . . . . . . . . . . . . . . 818-505-8030
FAX . . . . . . . . . . . . . . . . . . . . . . . . . . . . . . . . . . . 818-505-1102
EMAIL . . . . . . . . . . . . . . . . . . . . . . . . . . . nassent@pacbell.net
11350 Ventura Blvd., Ste. 101
Studio City, CA 91604

| | |
|---|---|
| TYPE | Motion Pictures + Television |
| DEAL | Warner Bros. Pictures |
| CREDITS | Out of Nowhere - A Stranger to Love - Blaze of Glory - Disappearing Act |
| COMMENTS | Also: Distribution, Made for TV Movies & Series. |

Jack Nasser . . . . . . . . . . . . . . . . . . . . . . . . . . . . . . . . . President
Steve Pine . . . . . . . . . . . . . . . . . . . . . . . . Chief Financial Officer
Brian Bloom . . . . . . . . . . . . . . . . . . . . . . . . . . . . . . VP, Features
Joe Nasser . . . . . . . . . . . . . . . . . . . . . . . . . . . . . Vice President
Jason Ward . . . . . . . . . . . . . . . . . . . . . . . . . Mgr., Development
Kathleen Durso . . . . . . . . . . . . . . . . . . . . . . . . . Office Manager
Rita Saigh . . . . . . . . . . . . . . . . . . . . . . . . . . . . . . . . Accounting
Christina Debeenie . . . . . . . . . . . . . . . . . . . . . . . . . . . Assistant
Jacki Schur . . . . . . . . . . . . . . . . . . . . . . . . . . . . . . . . Assistant

**NATIONAL GEOGRAPHIC FEATURE FILMS**
PHONE . . . . . . . . . . . . . . . . . . . . . . . . . . . . . . . . . 818-506-2420
FAX . . . . . . . . . . . . . . . . . . . . . . . . . . . . . . . . . . . 818-506-2416
4370 Tujunga Ave., Ste. 330
Studio City, CA 91604

| | |
|---|---|
| TYPE | Motion Pictures + Television |
| CREDITS | Forbidden Territory: Stanley's Search for Livingstone |

Hank Palmieri . . . . . . . . . . . . . . . . . . . . . . . Head, Feature Films
Richard Marks . . . . . . . . . . . . . . . . . . . . . . . . . . . . Story Editor
Christine Whitaker . . . . . . . . . . . . . . . . . Development Executive
John Dombrow . . . . . . . . . . . . . . . . . . . . . . . . . . . . . . Assistant

**NATIONAL GEOGRAPHIC TELEVISION**
PHONE . . . . . . . . . . . . . . . . . . . . . . . . . . . . . . . . . 818-506-8300
FAX . . . . . . . . . . . . . . . . . . . . . . . . . . . . . . . . . . . 818-506-8200
EMAIL . . . . . . . . . . . . . . . . . . . . . . . . . . . . shutchis@ngs.org
WEBSITE . . . . . . . . . . . . . . . . http://www.nationalgeographic.com
4370 Tujunga Ave., Ste. 300
Studio City, CA 91604

| | |
|---|---|
| TYPE | Television + Documentaries + Motion Pictures + Interactive Multimedia |
| CREDITS | Explorer - Specials |
| COMMENTS | ALSO: 1145 17th St., NW Washington DC 20036 |

Tim Kelly . . . . . . . . . . . . . . . . . . . . . . . . . Pres., Television (DC)
Ken Ferguson . . . . . . . . . . . . . CFO/Chief Administrative Officer (DC)
Nicolas Noxon . . . . . . . . . . . . . . . . Exec. Producer, Specials (LA)
Teresa Koenig . . . . . . . . . . . . . . . . . . Sr. Producer, Specials (LA)
Barry Nye . . . . . . . . . . . . . . . . Supervising Producer, Specials (LA)
Michael Rosenfeld . . . . . . . . . . . . . Exec. Producer, Explorer (DC)
Andrew Carl Wilk . . . . . . . . . . . . . Sr. VP, Programming/Production (DC)
Susan Borke . . . . . . . . . . . . General Counsel/VP, Bus. & Legal Affairs (DC)
Janelle Balnicke . . . . . . . . . . . . . . Dir., Specials Development (LA)
Megan Bevan . . . . . . . . . . . . . . . . . . . Dir., Programming (DC)
Maryanne Culpepper . . . . . . . . . . . . . Dir., Development, Explorer (DC)

**NATIONAL LAMPOON**
PHONE . . . . . . . . . . . . . . . . . . . . . . . . . . . . . . . . . 310-474-5252
FAX . . . . . . . . . . . . . . . . . . . . . . . . . . . . . . . . . . . 310-474-1219
10850 Wilshire Blvd., Ste. 1000
Los Angeles, CA 90024

| | |
|---|---|
| TYPE | Motion Pictures + Television + Animation + Feature Direct to Video + Interactive Multimedia + Syndication |
| CREDITS | Loaded Weapon I - Vacation - Animal House - NL's Senior Trip |
| COMMENTS | National Lampoon Magazine - Books. |

James P. Jimirro . . . . . . . . . . . . . . . . . . . . . . . . . . . President/CEO

# COMPANIES AND STAFF

## *NAVA FILMS
PHONE . . . . . . . . . . . . . . . . . . . . . . . . . . . . . . . . . 213-850-3155
FAX . . . . . . . . . . . . . . . . . . . . . . . . . . . . . . . . . . . 213-850-3152
Warner Hollywood
1041 N. Formosa, Writers Bldg., Rm. 8
Los Angeles, CA 90046

TYPE       Motion Pictures
DEAL       Warner Bros.
CREDITS       El Norte - Mi Familia - Selena - Why Do Fools Fall in Love
Gregory Nava . . . . . . . . . . . . . . . . . . . . . . . . . . . Director/Producer
Susana R. Zepeda . . . . . . . . . . . . . . . . . . . . . . . . VP, Development
Francisco Hernandez . . . . . . . . . . . . . . . . . . . . Asst. to Mr. Nava

## NBC ENTERTAINMENT
PHONE . . . . . . . . . . . . . . . . . . . . . . . . . . . . . . . . 818-840-4444
3000 W. Alameda Ave.
Burbank, CA 91523-0001

TYPE       Television
Don Ohlmeyer . . . . . . . . . . . . . . . . . . . . . President, NBC West Coast
Warren Littlefield . . . . . . . . . . . . . . . . . . . . President, NBC Entertainment
Harold Brook . . . . . . . . . . Exec. VP, Bus. Affairs, NBC Entertainment & Studios
Preston Beckman . . . . . . . . . . . . . Exec VP, Program Planning & Scheduling
Lindy De Koven . . . Exec.VP,Mini-Ser.&TV Mov./Longform Prog. NBC Stud.
Karey Burke . . . . . . . . . . . . . . . . . . . . . . . Sr. VP, Primetime Series
Susan D. Lee . . . . . . . . . . . . . . . . . . . . . . . Sr. VP, Daytime Programs
Richard Ludwin . . . . . . . Sr. VP, Specials, Prime Time & Late Night Programs
David Nevins . . . . . . . . . . . . . . . . . . . . . . . Sr. VP, Primetime Series
Bridget Potter . . . . . . . . . . Sr. VP, Entertainment Programs, East Coast
Michael Tenzer . . . . . . . . . . . . . . . Sr. VP, Business Affairs & Administration
Joanna Brockway . . . . . . . . . . . . . . . . . . VP, TV Movies & Miniseries
Bari Carrelli . . . . . . . . . . . . . . . . . . . . . . VP, TV Movies & Miniseries
Ted Frank . . . . . . . . . . . . . . . . . . . . . . . . . . VP, Primetime Series
Geoffrey Harris . . . . . . . . . . . . VP, Story & Writer Development
Kate Juergens . . . . . . . . . . . . . . . . . . . . . . VP, Primetime Series
Gary Kessler . . . . . . . . . . . . . . . VP, Miniseries & Motion Picts. for TV
Annamarie Kostura . . . . . . . . . . . . . . . . . VP, Daytime Programs
John Landgraf . . . . . . . . . . . . . . . . . . . . . . VP, Primetime Series
Robert Levy . . . . . . . . . . . . . . . . . . . . . . . VP, Primetime Series
Shelley McCrory . . . . . . . . . . . . . . . . . . . . VP, Primetime Series
Charisse McGhee-Lazarou . . . . . . . . . . . . . . VP, Primetime Series
Stephen McPherson . . . . . . . . . . . . . . . . . . VP, Primetime Series
Robin Schwartz . . . . . . . . . VP, Sat. Morning & Family Programs
Flody Suarez . . . . . . . . . . . . . . . . . . . . . . . VP, Primetime Series
Chris Conti . . . . . . . . . . . . . . . . . . . . . . . Dir., Primetime Series
Michael Morrison . . . . . . . . . Dir., NBC Entertainment Programs (East Coast)
Rick Olshansky . . . . . . . . . . . . . . . . . . . . . . Dir., Business Affairs
Richard Rothstein . . . . . . . . . . . . . . . . . Dir., TV Movies & Mini-Series
Kathy Talbert-Weller . . . . . . . . . . Dir., Daytime Programs (East Coast)
Bruce A. Evans . . . . . . . . . . . . . . . . . . . . . . Mgr., Primetime Series

## NBC STUDIOS
PHONE . . . . . . . . . . . . . . . . . . . . . . . . . . . . . . . . 818-840-7500
FAX . . . . . . . . . . . . . . . . . . . . . . . . . . . . . . . . . . 818-840-6510
WEBSITE . . . . . . . . . . . . . . . . . . . . . . . . . http://www.nbc.com
3000 W. Alameda Ave. #124
Burbank, CA 91523

TYPE       Television
Harold Brook . . . . . . . . . . . . . . . . . . . . . . Exec. VP, Business Affairs
Lindy De Koven . . . . . . . . . . . . . . . Exec. VP, Longform Programming
David Bartis . . . . . . . . . . . . . . . . . . . . . . Sr. VP, Primetime Series
Stephen J. Sass . . . . . . . . . . . . . . . . . . . . Sr. VP, Business Affairs
JoAnn Alfano . . . . . . . . . . . . . . . . . . . . . VP, Prime Time Series
Angela Bromstad . . . . . . . . . . . . . . . . . VP, Movies & Miniseries
Michael Forman . . . . . . . . . . . . . . . . . . . . VP, Prime Time Series
Christopher Saranec . . . . . . . . . Composer/Music Supervisor (818-840-3532)
Joshua Berman . . . . . . . . . . . . . . . . . . . . . Dir., Primetime Series
Charles Freericks . . . . . . . . . . . . . . . . . . . Dir., Movies & Mini-Series
Larry Hancock . . . . . . . . . . . . . . . . . . . . . Dir., Primetime Series
Martha Hanrahan . . . . . . . . . . . . Dir., Music Services (818-840-3532)
Kim Hershman . . . . . . . . . . . . . . . . . . . . . Dir., Primetime Series
Debbie Teicher . . . . . . . . . . . . . . . . . . . . Dir., Movies & Mini-Series
Loretta Desmond . . . . . . . . . . . . . . . . . . Mgr., Music Licensing (NY)
Gwen Potiker . . . . . . . . . . . . . . . . . . . . . Mgr., Movies & Mini-Series

## NEDERLANDER TELEVISION & FILM
PHONE . . . . . . . . . . . . . . . . . . . . . . . . . . . . . . . . 212-664-0033
FAX . . . . . . . . . . . . . . . . . . . . . . . . . . . . . . . . . . 212-765-8159
1650 Broadway, Ste. 408
New York, NY 10019

TYPE       Motion Pictures + Television
CREDITS       Next Door - When Will I Be Loved - General Motors
           Playwright Theatre
COMMENTS       Theatre, one act plays for television.
Gladys Nederlander . . . . . . . . . . . . . . . . . . . . . Executive Producer
Manjari Prakash . . . . . . . . . . . . . . . . . . . . . . . . . . . Development

## NEILA INC.
PHONE . . . . . . . . . . . . . . . . . . . . . . . . . . . . . . . . 310-559-7826
FAX . . . . . . . . . . . . . . . . . . . . . . . . . . . . . . . . . . 310-559-3969
EMAIL . . . . . . . . . . . . . . . . . . . . . sross@almaak.usc.edu
P.O. Box 3605
Beverly Hills, CA 90212

TYPE       Motion Pictures + Interactive Multimedia
CREDITS       A Thing of Beauty - Hilarious - Saturday Matinee
COMMENTS       ALSO: Legitimate Theatre.
Stanley Ralph Ross . . . . . . . . . . . . . . . . . . Exec. Vice President
Lisa M. Ross . . . . . . . . . . . . . . . . . . . . VP, Literary Acquisition
Nancy M. Ross . . . . . . . . . . . . . . . . . . VP, Education & Training

## NELVANA ENTERTAINMENT
PHONE . . . . . . . . . . . . . . . . 213-549-4222/416-588-5571
FAX . . . . . . . . . . . . . . . . . . . . . . . . . . . . . . . . . . 213-549-4232
EMAIL . . . . . . . . . . . . . . . . . . . . . . . . nelvana@aol.com
4500 Wilshire Blvd., 1st Floor
Los Angeles, CA 90010

TYPE       Motion Pictures + Television + Animation
CREDITS       Sam & Max - Nancy Drew - Hardy Boys - Little Bear -
           Magic School Bus - Babar
COMMENTS       Also: 32 Atlantic Ave., Toronto, Ontario M6K1X8
Michael Hirsh . . . . . . . . . . . . . . . . . . Co-Chief Executive Officer
Patrick Loubert . . . . . . . . . . . . . . . . . Co-Chief Executive Officer
Toper Taylor . . . . . . . . . . . . . . . . . . . . . . . . . . . . President
Sarah Maizes . . . . . . . . . . . . . . . . . . . . . . . . . VP, Development
Barry Levy . . . . . . . . . . . . . . . . . . . . . . . . . Dir., Development
Kristin Hawley . . . . . . . . . . . . . Development/Asst. to Toper Taylor

## NEO MOTION PICTURES, INC.
PHONE . . . . . . . . . . . . . . . . . . . . . . . . . . . . . . . . 213-653-6007
FAX . . . . . . . . . . . . . . . . . . . . . . . . . . . . . . . . . . 213-653-0409
EMAIL . . . . . . . . . . . . . . . . . . . . . . . . . new2u@aol.com
8315 Beverly Blvd.
Los Angeles, CA 90048-2607

TYPE       Motion Pictures + Television + Interactive Multimedia
CREDITS       Infinity - The Prophecy - Phantoms
Joel Soisson . . . . . . . . . . . . . . . . . . . . . . . . . . . President
Don Phillips . . . . . . . . . . . . . . . . . . . . . . . . . . . Producer
W.K. Border . . . . . . . . . . . . . . . . . . . . . . . . VP, Development
Mike Leahy . . . . . . . . . . . . . . . . . . . . . . . . . VP, Production
Lori Leahy . . . . . . . . . . . . . . . . . . . . . . . . . . . . Finance
Jason Mundy . . . . . . . . . . . . . . . . . . . . . . . . . . Production
Jen Conroy . . . . . . . . . . . . . . . . . . . . . . . . . Administration
Jamison Goci . . . . . . . . . . . . . . . . . . . . . . . Digital Effects
Jennifer Lane . . . . . . . . . . . . . . . . . . . . . . . Post Production

## NEPOTISM PRODUCTIONS
PHONE . . . . . . . . . . . . . . . . . . . . . . . . . . . . . . . . 818-508-3449
FAX . . . . . . . . . . . . . . . . . . . . . . . . . . . . . . . . . . 818-508-3476
EMAIL . . . . . . . . . . . . . . . . . . . FAMI13E@prodigy.com
12711 Ventura Blvd., Ste. 320
Studio City, CA 91604

TYPE       Television
Bernard Oseransky . . . . . . . . . . . . . . . . . . . . . . . . Producer
Gregg Houston . . . . . . . . . . . . . . . . . . . . . . . VP, Development

## NETTER DIGITAL ENTERTAINMENT
PHONE . . . . . . . . . . . . . . . . . . . . . . . . . . . . . . . . 818-753-1990
FAX . . . . . . . . . . . . . . . . . . . . . . . . . . . . . . . . . . 818-753-7655
EMAIL . . . . . . . . . . . . . . . . . . . . . . . . . ndei@aol.com
5125 Lankershim Blvd.
North Hollywood, CA 91601

TYPE       Motion Pictures + Television + Documentaries
CREDITS       Siringo - The Wild West - Babylon 5 - Hypernauts
COMMENTS       Also: Visual Effects Animation
Douglas Netter . . . . . . . . . . . . . . . . . . Chief Executive Officer
John Copeland . . . . . . . . . . . . . . . . . . . . Exec. Vice President
Jamie Smith . . . . . . . . . . . . . . . . . . . . . . . . VP, Development
Jason Netter . . . . . . . . . . . . . . . . . . Dir., Business Development
Tracie Drenning . . . . . . . . . . . . . . . . . . . . . Asst. to the CEO

## NETWORK GRAPHICS LTD.
PHONE . . . . . . . . . . . . . . . . . . . . . . . . . . . . . . . . 310-810-1120
FAX . . . . . . . . . . . . . . . . . . . . . . . . . . . . . . . . . . 310-471-5843
EMAIL . . . . . . . . . . . . . . . . . . . netgraph@earthlink.net
WEBSITE . . . . . . . . . . . . . . . . . http://www.firstdegreeburn.com
948 Stone Canyon Rd.
Los Angeles, CA 90077

TYPE       Motion Pictures + Television
CREDITS       Blackjack - First Degree Burn - Missing Persons
Peter Lance . . . . . . . . . . . . . . . . . . . . . . . . . Writer/Producer
Hay Tanning . . . . . . . . . . . . . . . . . . . . . . . . . . Co-Producer

# COMPANIES AND STAFF

**NEU-MAN-FILMS, INC.**
PHONE . . . . . . . . . . . . . . . . . . . . . . . . . . . . . . . 818-346-9004
FAX . . . . . . . . . . . . . . . . . . . . . . . . . . . . . . . . . . 818-346-1023
EMAIL . . . . . . . . . . . . . . . . . . . neumanfilms@compuserve.com
21321 W. Lighthill Drive
Topanga, CA 90290-4442

TYPE          Motion Pictures + Television
CREDITS       Under Siege 2:Dark Territory - Never Talk To Strangers -
              Sunstroke - Islanders - Across Apple Lake

Jeffrey R. Neuman . . . . . . . . . . . . . . . . . . . . . . President/Producer
Susan Clary . . . . . . . . . . . . . . . . . Exec. VP, Business Affairs

**NEUFELD PRODUCTIONS, MACE**
PHONE . . . . . . . . . . . . . . . . . . . . . . . . . . . . . . . 213-956-4816
FAX . . . . . . . . . . . . . . . . . . . . . . . . . . . . . . . . . . 213-862-2571
Paramount Pics.
5555 Melrose Ave., Dressing #112
Hollywood, CA 90038-3197

TYPE          Motion Pictures + Television
DEAL          Paramount Pictures- Motion Picture Group
CREDITS       The Saint - Clear and Present Danger - Patriot Games -
              Hunt for Red October

Mace Neufeld . . . . . . . . . . . . . . . . . . . . . . . . . . . . . . . Principal
Dan Rissner . . . . . . . . . . . . . . . . . . . . . . . . Exec. Vice President
Elisabeth Kern . . . . . . . . . . . . . . . . . . . . . . Associate Producer
Innes Weir . . . . . . . . . . . . . . . . . . . . . . . . . . . . VP, Production
Kel Symons . . . . . . . . . . . . . . . . . . . . . . . . . . . . Story Editor
Kathy Day . . . . . . . . . . . . . Exec. Asst. to Mr. Neufeld/Office Mgr.
Marsha Nadler . . . . . . . . . . . . . . . Exec. Asst. to Mr. Rissner
Braden Kuhlman . . . . . . . . . . . . . . . . . . . . . . . . . . . Assistant

**NEVER A DULL MOMENT PRODS.**
PHONE . . . . . . . . . . . . . . . . . . . . . . . . . . . . . . . 310-455-1651
FAX . . . . . . . . . . . . . . . . . . . . . . . . . . . . . . . . . . 310-455-1893
EMAIL . . . . . . . . . . . . . . . . . . . . . . . . . . . . . ndull@aol.com
1406 N. Topanga Canyon Blvd.
Topanga, CA 90290

TYPE          Motion Pictures + Television + Documentaries + Feature
              Direct to Video
CREDITS       Midnight's Child - Deadly Love - Synapse - It's Not Me, It's
              My OCD

David N. Gottlieb . . . . . . . . . . . . . . . . . . . Producer/Director
Lisa Hallas Gottlieb . . . . . . . . . . . . . . . . . . . . . . . . . Producer

**NEVERLAND FILMS, INC.**
PHONE . . . . . . . . . . . . . . . . . . . . . . . . . . . . . . . 310-772-0008
10323 Santa Monica Blvd., Ste. 106
Los Angeles, CA 90025

TYPE          Motion Pictures
CREDITS       Desperate Measures - A Brothers Kiss - Palmetto

Al Corley . . . . . . . . . . . . . . . . . . . . . . . . . . . . . . . Producer
Eugene Musso . . . . . . . . . . . . . . . . . . . . . . . . . . . . Producer
Bart Rosenblatt . . . . . . . . . . . . . . . . . . . . . . . . . . . Producer
James R. Millican . . . . . . . . . . . . . . . . . . . . . . . . No Title

**NEW AMSTERDAM ENTERTAINMENT, INC.**
PHONE . . . . . . . . . . . . . . . . . . . . . . . . . . . . . . . 212-922-1930
FAX . . . . . . . . . . . . . . . . . . . . . . . . . . . . . . . . . . 212-922-0674
EMAIL . . . . . . . . . . . . . newamsterdamnyc@worldnet.att.net
WEBSITE . . . . . . . . . . http://http://home.att.net/~newamsterdamnyc/
675 Third Ave., Ste. 2521
New York, NY 10017

TYPE          Motion Pictures + Television
CREDITS       Pet Sematary - The Stand - Vernon Johns Story

Richard P. Rubinstein . . . . . . . . . . . . . . . . . . . Chairman/CEO
Mitchell Galin . . . . . . . . . . . . . . . . . . . . . . . . . President/COO
Michael Messina . . . . . . . . . . Asst. to Richard P. Rubinstein
Maya Slobin . . . . . . . . . . . . . . . . . . . Asst. to Mitchell Galin

**NEW CRIME PRODUCTIONS**
PHONE . . . . . . . . . . . . . . . . . . . . . . . . . . . . . . . 310-396-2199
FAX . . . . . . . . . . . . . . . . . . . . . . . . . . . . . . . . . . 310-396-4249
EMAIL . . . . . . . . . . . . . . . . . . . . . . . . . . . newcrime@aol.com
555 Rose Ave.
Venice, CA 90291

TYPE          Motion Pictures
DEAL          Castle Rock Entertainment
CREDITS       Grosse Pointe Blank

John Cusack . . . . . . . . . . . . . . . . . . . . . . . . . Writer/Producer
Steve Pink . . . . . . . . . . . . . . . . . . . . . . . . . . . Writer/Producer
Doug Dearth . . . . . . . . . . . . . . . . . . . Production Executive
D.V. DeVincentis . . . . . . . . . . . . . . . . . . . . . Writer/Producer
Grace Loh . . . . . . . . . . . . . . . . . . . . . . . . . . . Dir., Operations
Brian Powell . . . . . . . . . . . . . . . . . . . . . . . Dir., Development

**NEW ENGLAND PRODS., INC.**
PHONE . . . . . . . . . . . . . . . . . . . . . . . . . . . . . . . 310-839-8583
FAX . . . . . . . . . . . . . . . . . . . . . . . . . . . . . . . . . . 310-839-1644
3024 Motor Avenue
Los Angeles, CA 90064-4716

TYPE          Motion Pictures + Television
CREDITS       Medusa's Child - Friends At Last - Out of Darkness - Metro

George W. Perkins . . . . . . . . . . . . . . . . . . . . . . . . . . Producer

**NEW LINE CINEMA**
PHONE . . . . . . . . . . . . . . . . 310-854-5811/212-649-4900
FAX . . . . . . . . . . . . . . . . . . 310-854-1824/212-649-4966
WEBSITE . . . . . . . . . . . . . . . . . . http://www.newline.com
116 N. Robertson Blvd., Ste. 200
Los Angeles, CA 90048

TYPE          Motion Pictures
CREDITS       Wag the Dog - The Wedding Singer - Pleasantville - Blade
COMMENTS   ALSO: 888 Seventh Avenue, New York, NY 10106

Robert Shaye . . . . . . . . . . . . . Chairman/CEO, New Line Cinema (NY & LA)
Michael Lynne . . . . . . . . . . . . . Pres./COO, New Line Cinema (NY)
Sara Risher . . . . . . . . . . . . . . . Chairman, New Line Prods.
Michael De Luca . . . . . . . . . . . . President/COO, New Line Prods.
Stephen Einhorn . . . . . . . . . . . President, New Line Home Video
Robert Friedman . . . . . . . . . . President, New Line Television (NY)
Rolf Mittweg . . . . . . . . . . . . . President, New Line International
Toby Emmerich . . . . . . . . . . . President, New Line Music (NY)
Stephen Abramson . . . . . . . . . . Chief Financial Officer (NY)
Carla Fry . . . . . . . . . . . . . . . Exec. VP, Production Admin.
Camela Galano . . . . . . . . . Exec. VP, European Supervisor New Line Intl.
Lynn Harris . . . . . . . . . . . . . . . Exec. VP, Production
Diane J. Keating . . . . . . . . . . . Exec. VP, New Line TV Intl. (NY)
Claire Rudnick Polstein . . . . . . . . . . . Exec. VP, Production
Richard Saperstein . . . . . . . . . . . Exec. VP, New Line Prods.
Ben Zinkin . . . . . . . . . . . . . . Exec. VP, Business Affairs
Laura Armstrong . . . . . . . Sr. VP, Production & Development, New Line TV
Judd Funk . . . . . . . . . . . . . . . Sr. VP, Business Affairs
Erik Holmberg . . . . . . . . . . . . . . Sr. VP, Production
Cindy Hornickel . . . . . . . . . . . . Sr. VP, TV Production
Suzanne Rosencrans . . . . . . . . . Sr. VP, Business Affairs
Jay Stern . . . . . . . . . . . . . . . . Sr. VP, Production
Sonya Thompsen . . . . . . . . . . . Sr. VP, Business Affairs
Mark Tusk . . . . . . . . Sr. VP, Production & Development (East Coast)
Paul Broucek . . . . . . . . . . . . . . . . . . . VP, Music (LA)
Leon Dudevoir . . . . . . . . . . . . . VP, Physical Production
Evan Edelist . . . . . . . . . . . . . . . VP, Post Production
Paul Federbush . . . . . . . . . . . . . . . VP, Acquisition
Sara Frith . . . . . . . . . . . . . . . . VP, Business Affairs
Amy Henkels . . . . . . . . . . VP, Production & Development (NY)
Mark S. Kaufman . . . . . . . . . . VP, Music/Business Affairs (NY)
Brent Kaviar . . . . . . . . . . . . . . VP, Post Production Services
Richard Keeley . . . . . . . . . . . . . . VP, Post Production
Sara King . . . . . . . . . . . . . . . . VP, Post Production
Donna Langley . . . . . . . . . . . . . . . VP, Production
Ginny Martino . . . . . . . . . . VP, Business Affairs Admin. (NY)
Andrew Matthews . . . . . . . . . VP, Finance & Intl. Affairs
Valerie McCaffrey . . . . . . . . . . . VP, Features Casting
Jon McHugh . . . . . . . . . . . . . . VP, Soundtracks (LA)
Patrick Moran . . . . . . . . . . . . VP, New Line Television
Dana Sano . . . . . . . . . . . . . . . . VP, Music (LA)
Lori Silfen . . . . . . . . . . . . . . . VP, Business Affairs
Brian Witten . . . . . . . . . . . . . . . . VP, Production
Cindy Guidry . . . . . . . . . . . . . . . Creative Executive
Carolyn Manetti . . . . . . . . . . . . . Creative Executive
Renee Witt . . . . . . . . . . . . . . . Creative Executive (NY)
Janis Chaskin . . . . . . . . . . Exec. Dir., Creative Affairs
Richard Brener . . . . . . . . . . . . . . . Dir., Development
Emily Glatter . . . . . . . . . . . . . . . . Dir., Production
Scott Kanyuck . . . . . . . . . . . . Dir., Business Affairs Admin.
Michael D. Lewis . . . . . . . . . . Dir., Business & Legal Affairs
David Sporn . . . . . . . . . . . . . Dir., Business Affairs Admin.
Dan Treinish . . . . . . . . . . . . . Dir., Business Affairs Admin.
Julia Kay . . . . . . . . . . . . . . . Mgr., Business Development
Stephanie Striegel . . . . . . . . . . . . . . . . . . . . Story Editor

# COMPANIES AND STAFF

**NEW REGENCY PRODS.**
PHONE . . . . . . . . . . . . . . . . . . . . . . . . . 818-954-3044
FAX . . . . . . . . . . . . . . . . . . . . . . . . . . . 818-954-3295
WEBSITE . . . . . . . . . . . . . . . . http://www.newregency.com
4000 Warner Blvd., Bldg. 66
Burbank, CA 91522-0001

TYPE · Motion Pictures + Television
DEAL · Twentieth Century Fox
CREDITS · L.A. Confidential - Devil's Advocate - Under Seige II - Free Willy II - A Time To Kill - Tin Cup - Heat - Cobb
COMMENTS · Regency Vision.

Arnon Milchan . . . . . . . . . . . . . . . . . . . . . . . . . Producer
Gail Berman . . . . . . . . . . . . . . President, Regency Television
Bridget Johnson . . . . . . . . . . . . . . . President, Production
David Matalon . . . . . . . . . . . . . . . . . . . President/CEO
Patrick Crowley . . . . . . . . . . . . . . Exec. VP, Production
Louis Santor . . . . . . . . . . . . . . . . . . Exec. VP/CFO
William S. Weiner . . . . . . . . Exec. VP, Bus. & Legal Affairs/General Counsel
Bonnie Daniels . . . . . . . . . . . . . VP, Production Accounting
Kara Francis . . . . . . . . . . . . . . . . . VP, Creative Affairs
Jon Katzman . . . . . . . . VP, Longform Programming, Regency Television
Dan Levine . . . . . . . . . . . . . . . . . . . . VP, Production
Elissa Loparco . . . . . . . . . . . . . . . . VP, Post Production
Alexandra Milchan . . . . . . . . . . . . . . VP, Regency Vision
Maggie Murphy . . . . . . VP, Drama Development, Regency Television
Jacqueline Dollard . . . . . . . . . . . . . . . . . Story Editor
Carole Nix . . . . . . . . . . . . . . . . Production Supervisor

**NEW SCREEN CONCEPTS, INC.**
PHONE . . . . . . . . . . . . . . 203-961-0670/310-557-7486
FAX . . . . . . . . . . . . . . . . 203-961-0831/310-557-7487
EMAIL . . . . . . . . . . . . . . . . . . . newscren@aol.com
WEBSITE . . . . . . . . . . . . http://www.bodyhuman2000.com
84 West Park Place
Stamford, CT 06901

TYPE · Television + Documentaries
DEAL · ABC Entertainment
CREDITS · The Senior Prom - Body Human 2000 Series - I Am Your Child - Siegfried & Roy - Weddings of a Lifetime - Yearbook
COMMENTS · Also: 2020 Avenue of the Stars, Ste. #500, LA CA 90067

Charles Bangert . . . . . . . . . . . . . . . . . . . . . Chairman
Louis Gorfain . . . . . . . . . . . . . . . . . . . . . . President
Hank O'Karma . . . . . . . . . . . . . . . . . . . . . Producer
Janis Biewend . . . . . . . . . . . . . . . . Associate Producer
Curt Northrup . . . . . . . . . . . . . . . . Dir., Development
Mitchell Horn . . . . . . . . . . . . . . . Production Supervisor
Ken Krausgill . . . . . . . . . . . . . Finance/Business Affairs

**NEWLAND-RAYNOR PRODS., INC.**
PHONE . . . . . . . . . . . . . . . . . . . . . 310-470-6785
10450 Wilshire Blvd.
Los Angeles, CA 90024

TYPE · Motion Pictures + Television
CREDITS · The Execution(NBC) - Arch of Triumph(CBS) - Too Good to Be True(NBC)

Milton T. Raynor . . . . . . . . . . . . President/Exec. Producer
John Newland . . . . . . . . . . . . . . . . . . . . . Producer

**NEWMAN PRODS., LAUNA**
PHONE . . . . . . . . . . . . . . 310-442-5667/310-234-1010
FAX . . . . . . . . . . . . . . . . . . . . . . 310-234-0101
10520 Wilshire Blvd., Penthouse 2
Los Angeles, CA 90024

TYPE · Television + Documentaries + Interactive Multimedia + Motion Pictures
DEAL · ABC Entertainment
CREDITS · I Survived A Disaster I, II, III & IV
COMMENTS · Co-Venture with Vin Di Bona Productions

Launa Newman-Minson . . . . . . . . . . . . . . Executive Producer
Erik Fleming . . . . . . . . . . . . . . . . . . VP, Development

**NEWMAN PRODUCTIONS, CARROLL**
PHONE . . . . . . . . . . . . . . . . . . . . . 310-235-5165
FAX . . . . . . . . . . . . . . . . . . . . . . 310-235-5767
Saban Entertainment
10960 Wilshire Blvd.
Los Angeles, CA 90024

TYPE · Motion Pictures + Television
CREDITS · House Arrest - Wildflower - A Different Kind of Christmas

Carroll Newman . . . . . . . . . . . . . . . . Executive Producer
Melissa Barrett . . . . . . . . . . . . . . . . . . . . Producer
Jenifer Newman . . . . . . . . . . . . . . . . Mgr., Development

**NEWMAN/TOOLEY FILMS**
PHONE . . . . . . . . . . . . . . . . . . . . . 310-777-8733
FAX . . . . . . . . . . . . . . . . . . . . . . 310-777-8730
WEBSITE . . . . . . . . . . http://newmantooley@earthlink.net
101 S. Robertson Blvd.
Los Angeles, CA 90048

TYPE · Feature Direct to Video + Motion Pictures
CREDITS · Viciouse Circle - Fait Accompli - Sound Man

Vincent Newman . . . . . . . . . . . . . . . . Managing Member
Tucker Tooley . . . . . . . . . . . . . . . . . Managing Member
Joyce Marie Brusasco . . . . . . . . Dir., Development/Production
Jake Woods . . . . . . . . . . . . . . . . . Executive Assistant

***NEWMARKET CAPITAL GROUP**
PHONE . . . . . . . . . . . . . . . . . . . . . 310-858-7472
FAX . . . . . . . . . . . . . . . . . . . . . . 310-858-7473
202 North Canon Dr.
Beverly Hills, CA 90210

TYPE · Motion Pictures

Brent Amelingmeier . . . . . . . . . . . . . . . . . . . No Title
Chris Ball . . . . . . . . . . . . . . . . . . . . . . . No Title
Linda Hawkins . . . . . . . . . . . . . . . . . . . . . No Title
Rene Hom . . . . . . . . . . . . . . . . . . . . . . . No Title
Cindy Kirven . . . . . . . . . . . . . . . . . . . . . No Title
Debra Pollack . . . . . . . . . . . . . . . . . . . . . No Title
Aaron Ryder . . . . . . . . . . . . . . . . . . . . . . No Title
William Tyrer . . . . . . . . . . . . . . . . . . . . . No Title

**NEWSTAR MEDIA**
PHONE . . . . . . . . . . . . . . . . . . . . . 310-786-1600
FAX . . . . . . . . . . . . . . . . . . . . . . 310-246-6544
WEBSITE . . . . . . . . . . . http://www.doveaudio.com/dove/
8955 Beverly Blvd.
Los Angeles, CA 90048

TYPE · Motion Pictures + Television + Documentaries + Feature Direct to Video + Interactive Multimedia
DEAL · NewStar Television
COMMENTS · Also: Audio Book, Book Publishing and Film Distribution.

Ron Lightstone . . . . . . . . . . . . . . . . . . . President/CEO
Noil Topham . . . . . . . . . . . . . . . . Chief Financial Officer
Ron Ziskin . . . . . . . . . . . . . . . . . . Pres., Television
John Brady . . . . . . . . . . . . . Finance Executive, Television
Doug Field . . . . . . . . . . . . . . . . . VP, Business Affairs
Geoff Hannell . . . . . . . . . . . . . . . . . . VP, Publisher
Robert Murray . . . . . . . . . . . . . . . VP, General Counsel
Stefan Rudnicki . . . . . . . . Exec. Producer/Audio Production (310-786-1636)
Shauna Zurbrugg . . Producer/Sr. Abridger, Audio Production (310-786-1609)
Gabrielle DeCuir . . . . Producer/Abridger, Audio Production (310-786-1621)
Rick Penn-Kraus . . . . . . . Creative Director, Art Department (310-786-1629)

**NEWSTAR TELEVISION**
PHONE . . . . . . . . . . . . . . . . . . . . . 310-786-1600
FAX . . . . . . . . . . . . . . . . . . . . . . 310-247-2929
8955 Beverly Blvd.
Los Angeles, CA 90048

TYPE · Television + Syndication
CREDITS · Make Me Laugh - Unnatural History - FutureSport - Amazing America - Unwed Father - By Dawn's Early Light

Ron Ziskin . . . . . . . . . . . . . . . . . . . President/COO
Dave Collins . . . . . . . . . . . . VP, TV Development (310-786-1659)
Jack Wartlieb . . . . . . . . . . . . . VP, Production & Operations
Eric Cowger . . . . . . . . . . . . . . Dir., Development, MOW
Michael Tetrick . . . . . . . . Post-Production Facilities Manager (310-786-1685)
Jim Wargowski . . . . . . . . . . . . . . . Engineer, Editing Facilities
Shawn Dwyer . . . . . . . . . . . . . Asst. Editor, Editing Facilities
Wendy O'Dea . . . . . Exec. Coord., TV Development & Music (310-786-1657)

**NEXUS ENTERTAINMENT, INC.**
PHONE . . . . . . . . . . . . . . . . . . . . . 213-460-7413
FAX . . . . . . . . . . . . . . . . . . . . . . 213-654-0441
8033 Sunset Blvd., Ste. 1800
Los Angeles, CA 90046

TYPE · Motion Pictures + Television
CREDITS · Bobby Garwood, The Last P.O.W.? - Stuck With Each Other - Kids Like These

Georg Stanford Brown . . . . . . . . . . . . . . Producer/Director
Tracey Washington . . . . . . . . . . . . . . . . . . . No Title

<h1 style="text-align:center">COMPANIES AND STAFF</h1>

**NICHOL MOON FILMS**
PHONE . . . . . . . . . . . . . . . . . . . . . . . . . . . . . 213-845-0320
FAX . . . . . . . . . . . . . . . . . . . . . . . . . . . . . . . . 213-876-6410
EMAIL . . . . . . . . . . . . . . . . . . . . . . . . . . . nme@emoon.com
WEBSITE . . . . . . . . . . . . . . . . . . . http://www.nicholmoon.com
2604 Devista Place
Los Angeles, CA 90046

| | |
|---|---|
| TYPE | Motion Pictures + Feature Direct to Video + Interactive Multimedia |
| CREDITS | Farewell to Flanders Field |

Michael Philip . . . . . . . . . . . . . . . . . . . . . . . . . Chief Executive Officer
Marc Dorfman . . . . . . . . . . . . . . . . . . . . . . . . . Chief Operating Officer
Matthew Grimaldi . . . . . . . . . . . . . . . . . . . . . . . . . . . . . President
Chris Ver Wiel . . . . . . . . . . . . . . . . . . . . . . . . . . . . . . . . . Partner

**NICKELODEON MOVIES**
PHONE . . . . . . . . . . . . . . 212-258-4985/213-956-8663
FAX . . . . . . . . . . . . . . . . 212-846-1769/213-862-1663
1515 Broadway, 37th Floor
New York, NY 10036

| | |
|---|---|
| TYPE | Motion Pictures |
| DEAL | Paramount Pictures- Motion Picture Group |
| CREDITS | Harriet The Spy - Good Burger - Rugrats: The Movie |
| COMMENTS | Also: Paramount Picts. 5555 Melrose Ave., Wilder Bldg., #107, Hollywood, CA  90038 |

Albie Hecht . . . . . . . . . . . . . . . . . . . . . . . President, Nickelodeon Movies
Julia Pistor . . . . . . . . . . . . . . . . . . . . . Vice President (212-258-6576)
Kathrin Seitz . . . . . . . . . . . . . . . . . . . . . . . . Vice President (LA)
Joe D'Ambrosia . . . . . . . . . . . . . . . . . . . . Dir., Development (LA)
Rebecca Poole . . . . . . . . . . . . . . . . Creative Executive, Animation (LA)
Damon Ross . . . . . . . . . . . . . . . . . . Creative Executive (212-258-6569)

**NICKELODEON/NICK AT NITE**
PHONE . . . . . . . . . . . . . . . . . . . . . . . . . . . . . 212-258-7500
FAX . . . . . . . . . . . . . . . . . . . . . . . . . . . . . . . . 212-258-7705
WEBSITE . . . . . . . . . . . . . . . . . . http://nickatnitestvland.com
1515 Broadway, 38th Fl.
New York, NY 10036

| | |
|---|---|
| TYPE | Television |
| COMMENTS | Nick online on America Online keyword: NOL Nick at Nite TV land on America Online Keyword: NAN. |

Herb Scannell . . . . . . . . . . . . . . . . . . . . . . . . . . . . . . . . . President
Albie Hecht . . . . . . . . . . . . . . . . . . . . . Pres., Film & TV Entertainment
Jeff Dunn . . . . . . . . . . . . . . . . . . . . . . . . . Chief Operating Officer
Ann Sarnoff . . . . . . . . Exec. VP, Consumer Products & Business Development
Cyma Zarghami . . . . . . . . . . . . . . General Manager/Exec. VP, Programming
Brown Johnson . . . . . . Exec. Prod./SVP, Production & Development, Nick Jr

**NIDES PRODUCTIONS, TINA**
PHONE . . . . . . . . . . . . . . . . . . . . . . . . . . . . . 818-788-3935
FAX . . . . . . . . . . . . . . . . . . . . . . . . . . . . . . . . 818-501-5215
4120 Dixie Cyn. Ave.
Sherman Oaks, CA 91423

| | |
|---|---|
| TYPE | Motion Pictures |

Tina Nides . . . . . . . . . . . . . . . . . . . . . . . . . . . . . . . . . Producer

**NIGHT FLIGHT INC.**
PHONE . . . . . . . . . . . . . . . . . . . . . . . . . . . . . 805-667-3900
FAX . . . . . . . . . . . . . . . . . . . . . . . . . . . . . . . . 805-653-7170
5301 Ventura Ave.
Ventura, CA 93001

| | |
|---|---|
| TYPE | Television |
| CREDITS | Night Flight (series) - Nash & Zullo's Offbeat Sports |

Mark Phillips . . . . . . . . . . . . . . . . . . . . . . . . . . . . . . . . . President
Steve Grass . . . . . . . . . . . . . . . . . . . . . . . . Producer, Night Flight

**NINE BY NINE**
PHONE . . . . . . . . . . . . . . . . . . . . . . . . . . . . . 213-464-8930
FAX . . . . . . . . . . . . . . . . . . . . . . . . . . . . . . . . 213-464-1940
EMAIL . . . . . . . . . . . . . . . . . . . . . . . . . . . filmeight@aol.com
WEBSITE . . . . . . . . . . . . http://www.santafe.edu/~kurt/blueskies.html
1770 N. Highland, Ste. 770
Los Angeles, CA 90028

| | |
|---|---|
| TYPE | Motion Pictures |
| CREDITS | Blue Skies Are A Lie - George B. - Hollywood (and Vine) |

Keith Brunsmann . . . . . . . . . . . . . . . . . . . . . . . . . . . . . . . . Partner
Wade W. Danielson . . . . . . . . . . . . . . . . . . . . . . Partner/Producer
Gregory Ruzzin . . . . . . . . . . . . . . . . . . . . Partner/Writer/Director
Susan Karasic . . . . . . . . . . . . . . . . . . . . . . . . Dir., Development

**NO PRISONERS**
PHONE . . . . . . . . . . . . . . . . . . . . . . . . . . . . . 310-396-5937
FAX . . . . . . . . . . . . . . . . . . . . . . . . . . . . . . . . 310-450-4988
EMAIL . . . . . . . . . . . . . . . . . . . . . . . . nopris@earthlink.net
73 Market Street
Venice, CA 90291

| | |
|---|---|
| TYPE | Motion Pictures + Television + Interactive Multimedia |
| CREDITS | Time Cop - Barb Wire - Virus - Wing Commander |
| COMMENTS | also: c/o Cryo Interactive Entertainment, 24 rue Marc Seguin, 75018 Paris |

Todd Moyer . . . . . . . . . . . . . . . . . . . . . . . . . . Producer/Partner
Jean-Martial Lefranc . . . . . . . . . . . . . . . . . . . . Producer/Partner
Chris Kibbey . . . . . . . . . . . . . . . . . . . . . . . . . . . . . . . Associate
Michael Abbott . . . . . . . . . . . . . . . . . . . . Development Assistant

**NOBLE PRODUCTIONS INC.**
PHONE . . . . . . . . . . . . . . . . . . . . . . . . . . . . . 310-552-2934
FAX . . . . . . . . . . . . . . . . . . . . . . . . . . . . . . . . 310-552-3508
1615 S. Crest Dr.
Los Angeles, CA 90035-3315

| | |
|---|---|
| TYPE | Motion Pictures |
| CREDITS | Last Nazi At Large - Mission Killfast - Dervishes - Massacre At Noon |

Ika Panajotovic . . . . . . . . . . . . . . . . . . . . . . . . . . . . . . . . . President

**NOLAN/LAMONTE-ITG**
PHONE . . . . . . . . . . . . . . . . . . . . . . . . . . . . . 310-656-9100
FAX . . . . . . . . . . . . . . . . . . . . . . . . . . . . . . . . 310-656-9104
EMAIL . . . . . . . . . . . . . . . . . . . . . . . . . . . . intvg@aol.com
1322 Second St.
Santa Monica, CA 90401

| | |
|---|---|
| TYPE | Television |
| CREDITS | Cat on A Hot Tin Roof |

Lou LaMonte . . . . . . . . . . . . . . . . . . President/Executive Producer
Laurie Nolan . . . . . . . . . . . . . . . . . . . VP, Production/Development

**NOMAD PRODUCTIONS**
PHONE . . . . . . . . . . . . . . . . . . . . . . . . . . . . . 310-282-0660
FAX . . . . . . . . . . . . . . . . . . . . . . . . . . . . . . . . 310-282-0990
10351 Santa Monica Blvd., #402
Los Angeles, CA 90025

| | |
|---|---|
| TYPE | Motion Pictures |
| DEAL | Gaumont |
| CREDITS | Vatel |

Roland Joffe . . . . . . . . . . . . . . . . . . . . . . . . . . . . . . . . . . . Partner
Alain Goldman . . . . . . . . . . . . . . . . . . . . . . . . . . . . . . . . . . Partner
Van Spurgeon . . . . . . . . . . . . . . . . . . . . . . . VP, Creative Affairs
Cynthia Matzger . . . . . . . . . . . . . . . . . . . . . . . . . Asst. to R. Joffe
Brian King . . . . . . . . . . . . . . . . . . . . . . . Development Associate
Kevin Wyatt . . . . . . . . . . . . . . . . . . . . . . . Asst. to Van Spurgeon

**NORAH FILMS**
PHONE . . . . . . . . . . . . . . . . . . . . . . . . . . . . . 213-960-3458
EMAIL . . . . . . . . . . . . . . . . . . . . . . . . . . Norahfi@aol.com
662 N. Van Ness Ave., Ste. 301/302
Los Angeles, CA 90004

| | |
|---|---|
| TYPE | Motion Pictures |

Roee Sharon . . . . . . . . . . . . . . . . . . . . . . . . . . . . . . . . . Producer
Robert Lazar . . . . . . . . . . . . . . . . . . . . . . . . . . . VP, Development

**NORANN ENTERTAINMENT**
PHONE . . . . . . . . . . . . . . . . . . . . . . . . . . . . . 818-752-8474
FAX . . . . . . . . . . . . . . . . . . . . . . . . . . . . . . . . 818-752-3279
4370 Tujunga Ave., Suite 120
Studio City, CA 91604

| | |
|---|---|
| TYPE | Motion Pictures + Television |
| CREDITS | The Joyriders |

Norm Miller . . . . . . . . . . . . . . . . . . Chairman/CEO/Executive Producer
Anne Miller . . . . . . . . . . . . . . . . . . . . . . . . . . . Executive Producer
Cindy Bond . . . . . . . . . . . . . . . . . . . . . . . . President/Producer
Ted Voltmer . . . . . . . . . . . . . . . . . . . . . . . . . VP, Business Affairs

**NORTH HALL PRODUCTIONS**
PHONE . . . . . . . . . . . . . . . . . . . . . . . . . . . . . 310-558-5040
FAX . . . . . . . . . . . . . . . . . . . . . . . . . . . . . . . . 310-558-5091
3000 S. Robertson Blvd., Ste. 240
Los Angeles, CA 90034

| | |
|---|---|
| TYPE | Television + Motion Pictures + Syndication |
| CREDITS | Pacific Blue - Brothers - American Detective - Time Trax |

Bill Nuss . . . . . . . . . . . . . . . . . . . . . . . . . . . . . Executive Producer

# COMPANIES AND STAFF

**NORTHERN LIGHTS ENT.**
PHONE . . . . . . . . . . . . . . . . . . . . . . . . . . . . . . . . 818-777-8080
FAX . . . . . . . . . . . . . . . . . . . . . . . . . . . . . . . . . . 818-866-0689
100 Universal City Plaza, Bldg. 489
Universal City, CA 91608
TYPE           Motion Pictures + Animation
CREDITS        Beethoven - Ghostbusters - Dave - Space Jam - 6 Days/7
               Nights - Private Parts
COMMENTS       Formerly Ivan Reitman Prods.
Ivan Reitman . . . . . . . . . . . . . . . . . . . . . Exec. Producer/Director
Dan M. Goldberg . . . . . . . . . . . . . . . . . . . . . . . . . . . . . Producer
Joe Medjuck . . . . . . . . . . . . . . . . . . . . . . . . . . . . . . . . Producer
Sheldon Kahn . . . . . . . . . . . . . . . . . . . . . . . . . . Producer/Editor
Michael Chinich . . . . . . . . . Dir., Development/Casting Exec./Producer
Terry Norton . . . . . . . . . . Associate Producer/Asst. to Mr. Reitman
Laurie Sheldon . . . . . . . . . . . . . . . . . . . . . . . Asst. to Mr. Chinich
Susan Seferian . . . . . . . . . . . . . . . . . . . . . . Asst. to Mr. Medjuck
Darci Gardner . . . . . . . . . . . . . . . . . . . . . . . Asst. to Terry Norton

**NORTHSTAR ENTERTAINMENT**
PHONE . . . . . . . . . . . . . . . . . . . . . . . . . . . . . . . 818-980-8881
4315 Coldwater Canyon, Ste. 9
Studio City, CA 91604
TYPE           Motion Pictures + Television + Feature Direct to Video
CREDITS        The Random Factor - Turn of the Blade - American
               Comedy Awards
COMMENTS       No Unsolicited Calls.
Bryan Michael Stoller . . . . . . . . . . . . . . . . . . Northstar Entertainment

**NU IMAGE**
PHONE . . . . . . . . . . . . . . . . . . . . . . . . . . . . . . . 310-246-0240
FAX . . . . . . . . . . . . . . . . . . . . . . . . . . . . . . . . . 310-246-1655
9145 Sunset Blvd., 2nd Floor
Los Angeles, CA 90069
TYPE           Motion Pictures
CREDITS        Shadrach - Lesser Prophets - Some Girl - Oct. 22nd
Avi Lerner . . . . . . . . . . . . . . . . . . . . . . . . . . . . . . . . Chairman
Danny Dimbort . . . . . . . . . . . . . . . . . . . . . . . . . . . . President
Trevor Short . . . . . . . . . . . . . . . . . . . . . . . . . . . . Consultant
Boaz Davidson . . . . . . . . . . . . . . . . . . . . . . . . Head, Production

**O'HARA-HOROWITZ PRODUCTIONS**
PHONE . . . . . . . . . . . . . . . . . . . . . . . . . . . . . . . 818-986-7150
FAX . . . . . . . . . . . . . . . . . . . . . . . . . . . . . . . . . 818-986-8226
EMAIL . . . . . . . . . . . . . . . . . . . . . . . . . . . ohpsouth@aol.com
16633 Ventura Blvd., Ste. 1330
Encino, CA 91436-1840
TYPE           Television
DEAL           NBC Entertainment/ABC Entertainment
CREDITS        Moment of Truth - Franchise - Switched at Birth - A
               Child's Wish
COMMENTS       ALSO: 900 Welch Rd., Ste. 210, Palo Alto, CA 94304
Michael O'Hara . . . . . . . . . . . . . . . . . President/Executive Producer
Lawrence Horowitz . . . . . . . . . . . . . . . . . . CEO/Executive Producer
Jim Fitzgerald . . . . . . . . . . . . . . . . . . . . . Chief Financial Officer
Kristine Bamattre . . . . . . . . . . . . . . . . . Post Production Supervisor
Robert Shaw . . . . . . . . . . . . . . . . . . . . . . Los Angeles Coordinator
Shawnee Meeks . . . . . . . . . . . . . . . . . . . . . . Asst. to Dr. Horowitz

**OAK ISLAND FILMS, INC.**
PHONE . . . . . . . . . . . . . . . . . . . . . . . . . . . . . . . 310-246-1466
FAX . . . . . . . . . . . . . . . . . . . . . . . . . . . . . . . . . 310-246-9936
8581 Santa Monica Blvd.
Los Angeles, CA 90069
TYPE           Motion Pictures
CREDITS        The Winner - Ice House - American Intellectuals
Kenneth Schwenker . . . . . . . . . . . . . . . . . . . . . . . . . President
Ronell Venter . . . . . . . . . . . . . . . . . . . . . . . . Creative Executive

**OBST PRODS., LYNDA**
PHONE . . . . . . . . . . . . . . . . . . . . . . . . . . . . . . . 310-369-2993
FAX . . . . . . . . . . . . . . . . . . . . . . . . . . . . . . . . . 310-369-2983
Twentieth Century Fox
10201 W. Pico Blvd., Bldg. 43
Los Angeles, CA 90035
TYPE           Motion Pictures + Television
DEAL           Fox Broadcasting Co.
CREDITS        Sleepless in Seattle - The Fisher King - One Fine Day -
               Contact - Hope Floats
Lynda Obst . . . . . . . . . . . . . . . . . . . . . . . . . . . . . . . Producer
Lisa Fielding . . . . . . . . . . . . . . . . . . . . . . . . . . . . Development
Rio Hernandez . . . . . . . . . . . . . . . . . . . . . Development Assistant
Amy Rardin . . . . . . . . . . . . . . . . . . . . . . . Development Assistant
Mark Russ . . . . . . . . . . . . . . . . . . . . . . . . Development Assistant

**OCEAN PICTURES**
PHONE . . . . . . . . . . . . . . . . . . . . . . . . . . . . . . . 310-369-0093
FAX . . . . . . . . . . . . . . . . . . . . . . . . . . . . . . . . . 310-369-7742
10201 W. Pico Blvd., Bldg. 12, Room 123
Los Angeles, CA 90035
TYPE           Motion Pictures
CREDITS        Caddyshack - Groundhog Day - Multiplicity
Harold Ramis . . . . . . . . . . . . . . . . . . . . Director/Writer/Producer
Trevor Albert . . . . . . . . . . . . . . . . . . . . . . . . . . . . . Producer
Whitney White . . . . . . . . . . . . . . . . . . . . . . . . VP, Development
Suzanne Herrington . . . . . . . . . . . . . . . . . . . . . Dir., Development
Emily Hodges . . . . . . . . . . . . . . . . . . . . . . Development Assistant
Brian M. Schwartz . . . . . . . . . . . . . . . . . . . . Development Assistant
Andrew Stephan . . . . . . . . . . . . . . . . . . . . . Development Assistant

***OCELOT FILMS, INC.**
PHONE . . . . . . . . . . . . . . . . . . . . . . . . . . . . . . . 213-934-5353
FAX . . . . . . . . . . . . . . . . . . . . . . . . . . . . . . . . . 213-934-5354
EMAIL . . . . . . . . . . . . . . . . . . . . . . . . . . . ocelotfilm@aol.com
179 So. Detroit Street
Los Angeles, CA 90036
TYPE           Motion Pictures
CREDITS        The Pompatus of Love - Sunday - Cement
D.J. Paul . . . . . . . . . . . . . . . . . . . . . . . . . . . . . . . President

**OCKRENT PRODUCTIONS, LTD.**
PHONE . . . . . . . . . . . . . . . . . . . . . . . . . . . . . . . 212-636-5820
FAX . . . . . . . . . . . . . . . . . . . . . . . . . . . . . . . . . 212-636-5820
EMAIL . . . . . . . . . . . . . . . . . . mike_ockrent@warnerbros.com
1325 Ave. of the Americas, 29th Fl.
New York, NY 10019
TYPE           Animation + Motion Pictures
DEAL           Warner Bros. Pictures
CREDITS        Dancin' Thru the Dark - Money for Nothing - Quest for
               Camelot
Mike Ockrent . . . . . . . . . . . . . . . . Producer/Director (212-636-5039)
Priscilla Elliott . . . . . . . . . . . . . . . Dir., Development (212-636-5681)
Jill Green . . . . . . . . . . . . . . . . . . . . . . . . . . U.K. Representative

**OCTOBER FILMS**
PHONE . . . . . . . . . . . . . . . . . . . 212-539-4000/310-248-6222
FAX . . . . . . . . . . . . . . . . . . . . . 212-539-4099/310-248-6226
WEBSITE . . . . . . . . . . . . . . . . . . . . http://www.octoberfilms.com
65 Bleecker St.
New York, NY 10012
TYPE           Motion Pictures
CREDITS        Secrets & Lies - Lost Highway - The Apostle - Breaking
               the Waves
COMMENTS       Also: 9229 Sunset Blvd. #615, W. Hollywood, CA 90069
Scott Greenstein . . . . . . . . . . . . . . . . . . . . . . . . . Co-President
Bingham Ray . . . . . . . . . . . . . . . . . . . . . . . . . . . Co-President
John Schmidt . . . . . . . . . . . . . . . . . . . . . . . . . . . Co-President
Dan Lieblein . . . . . . . . . . . . . . . . . . . . . Chief Financial Officer
Avy Eschenasy . . . . . . . . . . . . . . . . . Sr. VP, Business/Legal Affairs
Randy Ostrow . . . . . . . . . . . . . . . . . . Sr. VP, Physical Production
Susan Glatzer . . . . . . . . . . . . . . . . . . . . . . VP, Acquisitions (LA)
Patrick Gunn . . . . . . . . . . . . . . . . . . . . . . . . . VP, Acquisitions
Matt Wall . . . . . . . . . . . . . . . . . . . . . . . . VP, Acquisitions (LA)
Peter Kalmbach . . . . . . . . . . . . . . . . . . . . . . . Dir., Acquisitions
Amanda Klein . . . . . . . . . . . . . . . . . . Dir., Acquisitions/Production

**OFFROAD ENTERTAINMENT**
PHONE . . . . . . . . . . . . . . . . . . . . . . . . . . . . . . . 213-956-4425
FAX . . . . . . . . . . . . . . . . . . . . . . . . . . . . . . . . . 213-862-1120
Paramount Pictures
5555 Melrose Ave., Drier #209
Hollywood, CA 90038
TYPE           Motion Pictures + Television
DEAL           Paramount Pictures- Motion Picture Group
CREDITS        Three Ninjas Kickback - Jury Duty
Steven L. Bernstein . . . . . . . . . . . . . . . . . . . . . . . . . Producer
Pat Bernard . . . . . . . . . . . . . . . . . . . . . . . . . Dir., Development
Lucky Baxter . . . . . . . . . . . . . . . . . . . . . . . . Story Department

**OLD BEANTOWN FILMS**
PHONE . . . . . . . . . . . . . . . . . . . . . . . . . . . . . . . 310-576-7719
FAX . . . . . . . . . . . . . . . . . . . . . . . . . . . . . . . . . 310-576-0799
Atlantis Films
227 Broadway, Ste. 300
Santa Monica, CA 90401
TYPE           Television
DEAL           Atlantis Films
Brenda Friend . . . . . . . . . . . . . . . . . . . . . . . . . . . . Producer

# COMPANIES AND STAFF

**OLIVER PRODUCTIONS, LIN**
PHONE . . . . . . . . . . . . . . . . . . . . . . . . . . . . . . . . 310-859-2727
FAX . . . . . . . . . . . . . . . . . . . . . . . . . . . . . . . . . . 310-859-4877
EMAIL . . . . . . . . . . . . . . . zuccny@aol.com or lin02@juno.com
345 N. Maple Dr., Ste. 296
Beverly Hills, CA 90210

TYPE        Motion Pictures + Television + Feature Direct to Video
CREDITS     Harry & the Hendersons - Corduroy - Trumpet of the
            Swan - Aliens
COMMENTS    Family feature films and longform television/Children's
            Television/Children's Publishing.
Lin Oliver . . . . . . . . . . . . . . . . . . . . . . . . . . . . Producer/Executive
Allan Baker . . . . . . . . . . . . . . . . . . . . . . . . . VP, Creative Affairs
Christopher Risucci . . . . . . . . . . . . Production Coordinator/Exec. Assistant

**OLMOS PRODUCTIONS INC.**
PHONE . . . . . . . . . . . . . . . . . . . . . . . . . . . . . . . 310-557-7010
FAX . . . . . . . . . . . . . . . . . . . . . . . . . . . . . . . . . 310-557-6276
EMAIL . . . . . . . . . . . . . . . . . . . . . . . . . . . . . . olmos@abc.com
2020 Ave. of the Stars, Ste. 500
Century City, CA 90067

TYPE        Motion Pictures + Documentaries + Television
DEAL        ABC Entertainment
CREDITS     Roosters - American Me - Lives in Hazard - It Ain't Love
Edward James Olmos . . . . . . . . . . . . . . . . . . . . . . . . . . Chairman
Bill Miller . . . . . . . . . . . . . . . . . . . . . . . . . . . . . . . . President
Fernando Cubillas . . . . . . . . . . . . . . . . . . . . Production Manager
Nick Athas . . . . . . . . . . . . . . . . . . . . . . . . . . . . . . . Producer
Danny Haro . . . . . . . . . . . . . . . . . . . . . . . . . . . . . . Producer

**OMEGA ENTERTAINMENT**
PHONE . . . . . . . . . . . . . . . . . . . . . . . . . . . . . . . 310-855-0516
FAX . . . . . . . . . . . . . . . . . . . . . . . . . . . . . . . . . 310-652-2044
EMAIL . . . . . . . . . . . . . . . . . . . . . . . . . . . . . . InhausP@aol.com
8760 Shoreham Dr.
Los Angeles, CA 90069

TYPE        Motion Pictures + Feature Direct to Video
CREDITS     Hired to Kill - In the Cold of the Night - The Naked Truth
COMMENTS    Production & Distribution.
Nico Mastorakis . . . . . . . . . . . . . President/CEO/Writer/Producer/Director
Carole Mishkind . . . . . . . . . . . . . . . . . . . . . . . . VP, International
Christy Pokarney . . . . . . . . . . . . . . . . . . . . . . Vice President
Bill Cunningham . . . . . . . . . . . . . . . . . . . . . . Executive Assistant

**OMNIBUS**
PHONE . . . . . . . . . . . . . . . . . . . . . . . . . . . . . . . 310-369-7226
FAX . . . . . . . . . . . . . . . . . . . . . . . . . . . . . . . . . 310-369-7225
Twentieth Century Fox
P.O. Box 900
Beverly Hills, CA 90213

TYPE        Motion Pictures + Television
DEAL        Twentieth Century Fox
CREDITS     Cousin Bette - Sportsnight
COMMENTS    2121 Ave. of the Stars, Ste. 860, LA, CA 90067
Rob Scheidlinger . . . . . . . . . . . . . . . . . . . . . Producer/President
Jason Weiss . . . . . . . . . . . . . . . . . . . . . . . . . . . VP, Development

**OMS - ONE MIND SOUND PRODUCTIONS**
PHONE . . . . . . . . . . . . . . . . . . . . . . . . . . . . . . . 310-474-6160
FAX . . . . . . . . . . . . . . . . . . . . . . . . . . . . . . . . . 310-474-3086
EMAIL . . . . . . . . . . . . . . . . . . . . . . . . . . kzatoms@earthlink.net
Rubenstein and Associates
5850 Canoga Ave., St. 400
Woodland Hills, CA 91367

TYPE        Motion Pictures + Television + Interactive Multimedia
CREDITS     Parallel Lives - Chantilly Lace - Suicide Prevention Line
Kathy Zotnowski . . . . . . . . . . . . . . . . . . . . . . . . . . . . Producer

**ON STILTS PRODUCTIONS**
PHONE . . . . . . . . . . . . . . . . . . . . 818-759-8164/310-391-6053
EMAIL . . . . . . . . . . . . . . . . . . . . . . . . . . . . . PStelzer@aol.com
22647 Ventura Blvd., #447
Woodland Hills, CA 91364

TYPE        Motion Pictures
CREDITS     On Promised Land - Miss Evers' Boys - An Affectionate
            Look At Fatherhood
Peter Stelzer . . . . . . . . . . . . . . . . . . . . . . . . . . . . . Producer

**ONCE UPON A TIME FILMS, LTD.**
PHONE . . . . . . . . . . . . . . . . . . . . . . . . . . . . . . . 310-582-1220
FAX . . . . . . . . . . . . . . . . . . . . . . . . . . . . . . . . . 310-582-0098
EMAIL . . . . . . . . . . . . . . . . . . . . . . . . . . oncupnatim@aol.com
2314 Michigan Ave.
Santa Monica, CA 90404

TYPE        Motion Pictures + Television
CREDITS     Murder At My Door - A Dream Is A Wish - The Opposite
            Sex  - Too Close to Home
Stanley M. Brooks . . . . . . . . . . . . . . . . . . . . . . . Exec. Producer
Scott Anderson . . . . . . . . . . . . . . . . VP, Development & Production
Andrew Cohen . . . . . . . . . . . . . . . VP, Production & Business Affairs
Hallie Einhorn . . . . . . . . . . . . . . . . . . . . . . . Mgr., Development
Victor Santana . . . . . . . . . . . . . Mgr., Production & Business Affairs
Ted Hiatt . . . . . . . . . . . . . . . . . . . . . . . . . Assistant to Mr. Brooks

**ONE EIGHT FIVE FILM PRODUCTIONS, INC.**
PHONE . . . . . . . . . . . . . . . . . . . . . . . . . . . . . . . 818-769-6437
FAX . . . . . . . . . . . . . . . . . . . . . . . . . . . . . . . . . 818-769-0746
EMAIL . . . . . . . . . . . . . . . . . . . . . . . . . . . lurehead@aol.com
12409 Ventura Ct., #A
Studio City, CA 91604

TYPE        Television
CREDITS     Montana Crossroads - Long Road Home - Teenage
            Confidential
Regge Bulman . . . . . . . . . . . . . . . . . . . . . . . . . . . . President
Melanie Mihal . . . . . . . . . . . . . . . . . . . . . . . . . . . . Producer
Clay Eide . . . . . . . . . . . . . . . . . . . . . . . . . . Writer/Director

***ONE STORY PICTURES**
PHONE . . . . . . . . . . . . . . . . . . . . . . . . . . . . . . . 310-822-2895
FAX . . . . . . . . . . . . . . . . . . . . . . . . . . . . . . . . . 310-822-2895
1670 Electric Ave.
Venice, CA 90291

TYPE        Motion Pictures
CREDITS     Arachnophobia - Double Team - Blue Thunder (ABC)
Don Jakoby . . . . . . . . . . . . . . . . . . . . . . . . . . Writer/Producer
David Rodgers . . . . . . . . . . . . . . . . . . . . . . . . . . . . Producer
Christine Rodgers . . . . . . . . . . . . . . . . . . . . . . . . Development

**ONE VOICE ENTERTAINMENT, INC.**
PHONE . . . . . . . . . . . . . . . . . . . . . . . . . . . . . . . 818-398-1643
FAX . . . . . . . . . . . . . . . . . . . . . . . . . . . . . . . . . 818-398-0026
1838 N. Madison Ave.
Pasadena, CA 91104

TYPE        Motion Pictures + Television
CREDITS     Elegies - Storm Warning - Aeiou Sometimes y
Robert Ozn . . . . . . . . . . . . . . . . . . . . . . . . . . . Writer/Producer

**ONELIGHT PICTURES**
PHONE . . . . . . . . . . . . . . . . . . . . . . . . . . . . . . . 213-938-9919
641 N. Poinsettia Pl.
Los Angeles, CA 90036

TYPE        Motion Pictures
CREDITS     Changing Habits - Quest of the Delta Knights - Deadly
            Rivals - Deadlock
James Dodson . . . . . . . . . . . . . . . . . . . . . . . Producer/Director
John Elk . . . . . . . . . . . . . . . . . . . . . . . . . Production Executive
Michael Hamm . . . . . . . . . . . . . . . . . . . . . . Production Manager

**OPEN DOOR ENTERTAINMENT**
PHONE . . . . . . . . . . . . . . . . . 310-777-8851/48-601-36-6767
FAX . . . . . . . . . . . . . . . . . . . . . 310-777-8861/48-22-621-4810
EMAIL . . . . . . . . . . . . . . . . . . opendoorkai@compuserve.com
162 North Doheny Drive
Beverly Hills, CA 90211

TYPE        Motion Pictures + Television
COMMENTS    Also: Aleja Szucha 16/33, 00-582 Warsaw Poland. 1861
            S. Bundy Dr., Ste. 308, 310-315-5371/Fx:5205
Dale Pollock . . . . . . . . . . . . . . . . . . . . . . Co-President/Producer
Kai P. Schoenhals . . . . . . . . . . . . . . . . . . . . Co-President/Producer
Igor Ostrowski . . . . . . . . . . . . . . . . . . . . . Legal Counsel (Poland)
Joanna Strzelecka . . . . . . . . . . . . . . . . . . . . Associate in Poland

# COMPANIES AND STAFF

## OPEN ROAD PRODS., LTD.
PHONE . . . . . . . . . . . . . . . . . . . . . . . . . . . 818-980-1100
FAX . . . . . . . . . . . . . . . . . . . . . . . . . . . . . 818-980-9862
EMAIL . . . . . . . . . . . . . . . . . . OPEN_ROAD@msn.com
6101 Morella Ave.
North Hollywood, CA 91606

TYPE       Motion Pictures + Television + Documentaries + Feature Direct to Video  
CREDITS      Pastime (aka One Cup of Coffee) - The Man Who Stayed Behind - Shadow of a Bull

Robin B. Armstrong . . . . . . . . . . . . . . . . Director/Producer  
Paul Tamasy . . . . . . . . . . . . . . . . . . . Development Executive  
Joshua Crooch . . . . . . . . . . . . . . . . . Development Assistant

## ORBIT ENTERTAINMENT GROUP
PHONE . . . . . . . . . . . . . . . . . . . . . . . . . . . 323-525-2626
FAX . . . . . . . . . . . . . . . . . . . . . . . . . . . . . 323-525-2627
EMAIL . . . . . . . . . . . . . . . . . . orbit-1@orbit-grp.com
714 N. La Brea Ave.
Hollywood, CA 90038

TYPE       Motion Pictures + Television  
CREDITS      The Seventh Coin - Platinum Blonde  
COMMENTS   Subsidiaries:  Orbit Pictures & Orbit Productions

Dror Soref . . . . . . . . . . . . . . . Partner/President/Director  
Lee Nelson . . . . . . . . . . . . . Partner/Co-CEO/Exec. Producer  
Kevin Moreton . . . . . . . . . . . . . . . . VP, Orbit Pictures

## ORENDA FILMS
PHONE . . . . . . . . . . . . . . . . . . . . . . . . . . . 212-228-8716
FAX . . . . . . . . . . . . . . . . . . . . . . . . . . . . . 212-228-5931
WEBSITE . . . . . . . . . . . . . http://www.tiac.net/users/openfilm/
3 Washington Square Vill., #10-P
New York, NY 10012

TYPE       Motion Pictures  
CREDITS      No Way Home - Search for One-Eyed Jimmy

Robert Nickson . . . . . . . . . . . . . . . . . . . . . . Producer  
Lisa Bruce . . . . . . . . . . . . . . . . . . . . . . . . . Producer  
Sara Bernstein . . . . . . . . . . . . . . . . . . . . . Acquisitions

## ORIGINAL FILM
PHONE . . . . . . . . . . . . . . . . . . . . . . . . . . . 310-445-9000
FAX . . . . . . . . . . . . . . . . . . . . . . . . . . . . . 310-445-9191
2045 S. Barrington Ave.
Los Angeles, CA 90025

TYPE       Motion Pictures  
DEAL       Columbia TriStar Motion Picture Group  
CREDITS      Volcano - Juice - I Know What You Did Last Summer I & II - Cruel Inventions - Rat Pack - Urban Legend

Neal Moritz . . . . . . . . . . . . . . . . . . . . . . . . Producer  
Stokely Chaffin . . . . . . . . . . . . . . . . Sr. VP, Production  
Brad Luff . . . . . . . . . . . . . . . . . . . . Sr. VP, Production  
Heather Zeegen . . . . . . . . . . . . . . . . . Dir., Development  
Sean O'Keefe . . . . . . . . . . . . . . . . . Creative Executive  
Moe Jelline . . . . . . . . . . . . . . . . . . . . . Story Editor  
Carrie Cook . . . . . . . . . . . . . . . . . Development Assistant  
Mike Harlow . . . . . . . . . . . . . . . . . Development Assistant

## ORIGINAL VOICES, INC.
PHONE . . . . . . . . . . . . . . . . . . . . . . . . . . . 310-264-4259
FAX . . . . . . . . . . . . . . . . . . . . . . . . . . . . . 310-264-4258
3000 W. Olympic Blvd., Ste. 1463
Santa Monica, CA 90404

TYPE       Motion Pictures  
CREDITS      The Brady Bunch Movie - Rasputin - Big Night - The Opposite of Sex - Bruno

David Kirkpatrick . . . . . . . . . . . . . . . . President/Producer  
Douglas Kirkpatrick . . . . . . . . . . . . Chief Financial Officer  
Andrew Carey . . . . . . . . . . . . . . . . . . . . VP, Production  
Lontih Khatami . . . . . . . . . . . . . . . . . . VP, Development

## *OUT OF THE BLUE . . . ENTERTAINMENT
PHONE . . . . . . . . . . . . . . . . . . . . . . . . . . . 310-244-7800
FAX . . . . . . . . . . . . . . . . . . . . . . . . . . . . . 310-244-1539
Sony Pictures Entertainment
10202 W. Washington Blvd.
Culver City, CA 90232-3195

TYPE       Motion Pictures + Television  
DEAL       Columbia Pictures  
CREDITS      Guy Gets Kid - I Dream of Jeannie  
COMMENTS   NO UNSOLICITED MATERIAL.

Sid Ganis . . . . . . . . . . . . . . . . . . . . . . . . . No Title  
Alex Siskin . . . . . . . . . . . . . . . . . . . . . . . . No Title  
Michelle Archer . . . . . . . . . . . . . . . . . . . . . No Title  
Tom McNulty . . . . . . . . . . . . . . . . . . . . . . . No Title  
Jennifer Todhunter . . . . . . . . . . . . . . . . . . . No Title  
Peter Calabrese . . . . . . . . . . . . . . . . . . . . Television  
Karen Robinson Hunte . . . . . . . . . . . . . . . . . Television

## OUTERBANKS ENTERTAINMENT
PHONE . . . . . . . . . . . . . 310-979-8747/310-202-3399
FAX . . . . . . . . . . . . . . . . . . . . . . . . . . . . . 310-202-3511
12233 W. Olympic Blvd., Ste. 210
Los Angeles, CA 90064

TYPE       Motion Pictures + Television  
DEAL       Miramax Films  
CREDITS      Scream 1 & 2 - Dawson's Creek - Killing Mrs. Tingle  
COMMENTS   Moving at press time - new address unknown.

Kevin Williamson . . . . . . . . . . . . . Writer/Director/Producer  
Julie Plec . . . . . . . . . . . . . . . VP, Production/Development  
David Blanchard . . . . . . . . . . . . Asst. to Kevin Williamson  
Albert Bianchini . . . . . . . . . . . . Asst. to Kevin Williamson  
Ty Williams . . . . . . . . . . . . . . . . . Asst. to Julie Plec

## OUTLAW PRODUCTIONS
PHONE . . . . . . . . . . . . . . . . . . . . . . . . . . . 310-777-2000
FAX . . . . . . . . . . . . . . . . . . . . . . . . . . . . . 310-777-2010
827 N. Hilldale Ave.
Los Angeles, CA 90069

TYPE       Motion Pictures  
DEAL       Warner Bros. Pictures  
CREDITS      Santa Clause - sex, lies, and videotape - Don Juan DeMarco - Addicted To Love - Three to Tango

Robert Newmyer . . . . . . . . . . . . . . . Producer (310-777-2001)  
Jeffrey Silver . . . . . . . . . . . . . . . . . . . . . . Producer  
Scott Strauss . . . . . . . . . . . . . . Pres., Production (310-777-2011)  
Susan Novick . . . . . . . . . . . . . . . . . Associate Producer  
Orin Woinsky . . . . . . . . . . . . . . VP, Production (310-777-2019)  
Alex Litvak . . . . . . . . . . . . . . . VP, Production (310-777-2017)  
Jeanne Allgood . . . . . . . . . . . . . Story Editor (310-777-2018)  
Tom Forrest . . . . . . . . . . . . . . . . . . . . . . . Production  
Nikol Plass . . . . . . . . . . . . . . Exec. Asst. to Mr. Newmyer  
Brad Ley . . . . . . . . . . . . . . . . . . Asst. to Mr. Strauss  
Jennifer Barnard . . . . . . . . . . . . . Administrative Assistant

## *OVERBROOK ENTERTAINMENT
PHONE . . . . . . . . . . . . . . . . . . . . . . . . . . . 818-777-2224
FAX . . . . . . . . . . . . . . . . . . . . . . . . . . . . . 818-866-5440
100 Universal City Plaza, 507A, PH2
Universal City, CA 91608

TYPE       Motion Pictures + Feature Direct to Video + Animation + Documentaries  
DEAL       Universal Pictures  
COMMENTS   Also: Music. Music Deal w/ Interscope Records.

Will Smith . . . . . . . . . . . . . . . . . . . . . . . . . Partner  
James Lassiter . . . . . . . . . . . . . . . . . . . . . . Partner  
Bradford W. Smith . . . . . . . . . . Exec. VP, Feature Development  
Lori Zuker . . . . . . . . . . . . . . . . . . . Dir., Development  
Glendon Palmer . . . . . . . . . . . . . . . . Creative Executive

## OVITZ PRODUCTIONS, MARK H.
PHONE . . . . . . . . . . . . . . . . . . . . . . . . . . . 818-526-2882
FAX . . . . . . . . . . . . . . . . . . . . . . . . . . . . . 310-454-1894
101 S. 1st St., 2nd Fl., Ste. C
Burbank, CA 91502

TYPE       Motion Pictures + Television + Feature Direct to Video  
COMMENTS   Moving at Press Time.

Mark H. Ovitz . . . . . . . . . . . . . . . . . . . . . . Producer

<h1 style="text-align:center">COMPANIES AND STAFF</h1>

**OZMA PRODUCTIONS**
PHONE . . . . . . . . . . . . . . . . . . . . . . . . . . . . . . . 310-656-1100
FAX . . . . . . . . . . . . . . . . . . . . . . . . . . . . . . . . . 310-656-7422
808 Wilshire Blvd., 3rd Floor
Santa Monica, CA  90401, CA 90401

TYPE  Motion Pictures + Television
DEAL  Pearson All American
CREDITS Rambling Rose - Out To Sea - Valley Girl - Lost In Yonkers - Three Wishes

Martha Coolidge . . . . . . . . . . . . . . . . . . . . . . . . Director/Producer
Sarahbeth Grossman . . . . . . . . . . . . . . . VP, Production/Development
April Fitzsimmons . . . . . . . . . . . . . . . . . . . . . . . . . . . . Assistant

**P.A.T. PRODUCTIONS**
PHONE . . . . . . . . . . . . . . . . . . . . . . . . . . . . . . . 310-244-8881
FAX . . . . . . . . . . . . . . . . . . . . . . . . . . . . . . . . . 310-244-1210
Columbia TriStar Television
10202 W. Washington Blvd.
Culver City, CA 90232

TYPE  Television + Motion Pictures + Syndication
DEAL  Columbia TriStar Television
CREDITS Angus & The Ducks (Short)

Pat Sajak . . . . . . . . . . . . . . . . . . . . . . . . . . . . . . . President
David S. Williger . . . . . . . . . . . . . . . . . . . . Exec. Vice President
Gary Templeton . . . . . . . . . . . . . . . . . Dir., Children's Programming
Renee Macisco . . . . . . . . . . . . . . . . . . . . . . . . Executive Assistant

**P.E.A. FILMS, INC.**
PHONE . . . . . . . . . . . . . . . . . . . . . . . . . . . . . . . 310-573-0063
FAX . . . . . . . . . . . . . . . . . . . . . . . . . . . . . . . . . 310-230-4467
18 W. 55th Street
New York, NY 10019

TYPE  Motion Pictures
CREDITS The Good, The Bad & The Ugly - Last Tango in Paris - 1900

Maurizio Grimaldi . . . . . . . . . . . . . . . . . . . . President/Producer

**P.O.V. CO.**
PHONE . . . . . . . . . . . . . . . . . . . . . . . . . . . . . . . 818-707-2644
FAX . . . . . . . . . . . . . . . . . . . . . . . . . . . . . . . . . 818-707-3557
3033 Three Springs Dr.
Westlake Village, CA 91361

TYPE  Motion Pictures + Television
CREDITS Kennedys of Massachusettes - True Women - Glory & Honor - The Love Letter

Lynn Raynor . . . . . . . . . . . . . . . . . . . . . . . . . . . . . Producer

**PACHYDERM ENTERTAINMENT**
PHONE . . . . . . . . . . . . . 212-840-8400/213-883-0993
FAX . . . . . . . . . . . . . . . . . . . . . . . . . . . . . . . . . 212-840-1124
1560 Broadway, Ste. 400
New York, NY 10036

TYPE  Motion Pictures + Television
CREDITS Zooman - The Trial of Bernard Goetz

James B. Freydberg . . . . . . . . . . . . . . . . . . . . . . . . Partner
Kenneth Feld . . . . . . . . . . . . . . . . . . . . . . . . . . . . . Partner
Caralyn Fuld . . . . . . . . . . . . . . . . . . . . . . . . VP, Development
Doug MacArthur . . . . . . . . . . . . . . . . . . . . Producing Associate

**PACIFIC DATA IMAGES**
PHONE . . . . . . . . . . . . . . . . . . . . . . . . . . . . . . . 650-846-8100
FAX . . . . . . . . . . . . . . . . . . . . . . . . . . . . . . . . . 650-846-8101
EMAIL . . . . . . . . . . . . . . . . . . . . . . . . . . . . . . info@pdi.com
WEBSITE . . . . . . . . . . . . . . . . . . . . . . http://www.pdi.com
3101 Park Boulevard
Palo Alto, CA 94306

TYPE  Motion Pictures + Animation
DEAL  DreamWorks SKG
CREDITS The Simpsons Homer 3-D - Batman & Robin - The Peacemaker - ANTZ
COMMENTS Also digital effects.

Carl Rosendahl . . . . . . . . . . . . . . . . . . . . . . . . . . . President
Cindy Cosenzo . . . . . . . . . . . . . . . . Exec. Producer, Commercials
Les Hunter . . . . . . . . . . . . . . . . . . . . . . . . . . . . Sr. Producer
Brad Lewis . . . . . . . . . . . . . . . . . . . . . . . . VP/Exec. Producer
Richard Chuang . . . . . . . . . . . VP/Senior Visual Effects Supervisor
Patty Wooton . . . . . . . . . . . . . . . . . . . . VP/Head, Production
Larry Bafia . . . . . . . . . . . . . . . . . . . . . . . . . . Dir., Animation
Cliff Boule . . . . . . . . . . . . . . . . . . . . . . . . . Designer/Director

**PACIFIC MOTION PICTURES**
PHONE . . . . . . . . . . . . . . . . . . . . . . . . . . . . . . . 310-659-5898
FAX . . . . . . . . . . . . . . . . . . . . . . . . . . . . . . . . . 310-659-6755
450 N. Robertson Blvd.
W. Hollywood, CA 90048

TYPE  Motion Pictures + Television
CREDITS Magic In The Water - In Cold Blood - Masterminds
COMMENTS ALSO: 45 Dunlevy Ave., Vancouver, BC V6A3A3

Tony Allard . . . . . . . . . . . . . . . . . . . . . Chairman/CEO (Vancouver)
Matthew O'Connor . . . . . . . . . . . . . . . . . . President (Vancouver)
Tom Rowe . . . . . . . . . . . . . . . . Sr. VP, Creative Affairs (Vancouver)
George Horie . . . . . . . . . . . . . . . . . . VP, Production (Vancouver)
Lisa Richardson . . . . . . . . . . . . . . . . . . . . VP, Business Affairs
Lizzy Shaw . . . . . . . . . . . . . . . . . . . . . . . . VP, Television (LA)
Tara Twigg . . . . . . . . . . . . . . . . . . VP, Development (Vancouver)
Amanda James . . . . . . . . . . . . . . . . . . Development Assistant

**PACIFIC WESTERN PRODS.**
PHONE . . . . . . . . . . . . . . . . . . . . . . . . . . . . . . . 213-956-8601
FAX . . . . . . . . . . . . . . . . . . . . . . . . . . . . . . . . . 213-862-1101
EMAIL . . . . . . . . . . . . . . . . . . . . . . james_rossow@paramount.com
Paramount
5555 Melrose Ave., Lubitsch Annex 119
Los Angeles, CA 90038-3197

TYPE  Motion Pictures + Television
DEAL  Paramount Pictures- Motion Picture Group
CREDITS Aliens - Terminator 1 & 2 - Dante's Peak - The Waterdance - The Ghost & the Darkness - Armageddon

Gale Anne Hurd . . . . . . . . . . . . . . . . . . . . . . . . . Producer
Julie Thomson . . . . . . . . . . . Sr. VP, Finance & Business Affairs
Maggie Malina . . . . . . . . . . . . . . . . . . . . . . . . VP, Production
Kristy Scanlan . . . . . . . . . . . . . . . . . . . . . . Dir., Development
Jim Rossow . . . . . . . . . . . . . . . . . . . . . . . . . . . Story Editor
Mick Kelly . . . . . . . . . . . . . . . . . . . . . . . . Asst. to Ms. Hurd
Maureen Egan . . . . . . . . . . . . . . . . . . . . Asst. to Ms. Malina
Joke Fincioen . . . . . . . . . . . . . . . . . . . . Asst. to Ms. Thomson

**PACIFICA ENTERTAINMENT**
PHONE . . . . . . . . . . . . . . . . . . . . . . . . . . . . . . . 310-285-9696
FAX . . . . . . . . . . . . . . . . . . . . . . . . . . . . . . . . . 310-285-9691
EMAIL . . . . . . . . . . . . . . . . . . . . . . . . . pacent@pacbell.net
335 N. Maple Dr., Ste. 235
Beverly Hills, CA 90210

TYPE  Motion Pictures
CREDITS Clay Pigeons - Where the Money Is

Moritz Borman . . . . . . . . . . . . . . . . . . . . . . . . . Co-President
Chris Sievernich . . . . . . . . . . . . . . . . . . . . . . . . Co-President
Chris Dubrow . . . . . . . . . . . . . . . . . . . . . . VP, Development
Fran McGivern . . . . . . . . . . . . . . . . Exec. Asst. to Mr. Dubrow
Matt Milich . . . . . . . . . . . . . . . . . Exec. Asst. to Mr. Sievernich
Laura K. Miller . . . . . . . . . . . . . . . . . Exec. Asst. to Mr. Borman

**PAIGE ASSOC., INC., GEORGE**
PHONE . . . . . . . . . . . . . . . . . . . . . . . . . . . . . . . 310-315-4835
FAX . . . . . . . . . . . . . . . . . . . . . . . . . . . . . . . . . 310-315-4836
EMAIL . . . . . . . . . . . . . . . . . . . . . . . GPACORP@aol.com
3000 W. Olympic Blvd., Ste. 1407
Santa Monica, CA 90404-5041

TYPE  Motion Pictures + Television + Interactive Multimedia
CREDITS Abbott & Costello Meet Jerry Seinfeld - Martin & Lewis - 3 Stooges Greatest Hits

George Paige . . . . . . . . . . . . . . . . . . . . . . . . . . . President
James Tumminia . . . . . . . . . . . . . . . . . . . . . . . . . Producer

**PAKULA PRODS., INC.**
PHONE . . . . . . . . . . . . . . . . . . . . . . . . . . . . . . . 212-664-0640
FAX . . . . . . . . . . . . . . . . . . . . . . . . . . . . . . . . . 212-397-1344
330 W. 58th St., Ste. 508
New York, NY 10019

TYPE  Motion Pictures
CREDITS Presumed Innocent - Sophie's Choice - The Pelican Brief
COMMENTS Story Dept. Phone: 212-399-9822

Alan J. Pakula . . . . . . . . . . . . . . . . . . Producer/Director/Writer
Holly Frederick . . . . . . . . . . . . . . . . . . . . . . Dir., Development
Catherine Solt . . . . . . . . . . . . . . . . . Exec. Asst. to Mr. Pakula
Peter Phillips . . . . . . . . . . . . . . . . . . . . . Asst. to Mr. Pakula

## PALISADES PICTURES
PHONE . . . . . . . . . . . . . . . . . . . . . . . . . . . . . . 310-576-6655
FAX . . . . . . . . . . . . . . . . . . . . . . . . . . . . . . . 310-576-6836
225 Santa Monica Blvd., Ste. 610
Santa Monica, CA 90401

TYPE       Motion Pictures
CREDITS      Loved - Zebrahead - Fern Gully...The Last Rain Forest
Jeff Dowd . . . . . . . . . . . . . . . . . . . . . . . . . . . . . . . . . Partner
Gary Palermo . . . . . . . . . . . . . . . . . . . . . . . . . . . . . . . Partner
Mark Severini . . . . . . . . . . . . . . . . . . . . . . . . . . . . . . . Partner
Peter Torres . . . . . . . . . . . . . . . . . . . . . . . . . . . . . . Executive

## *PALOMAR PICTURES
PHONE . . . . . . . . . . . . . . . . . . . . . . . . . . . . . . 213-525-2900
FAX . . . . . . . . . . . . . . . . . . . . . . . . . . . . . . . 213-525-2912
5657 Wilshire Blvd., 5th Floor
Los Angeles, CA 90036

TYPE       Motion Pictures + Documentaries + Television + Interactive Multimedia
CREDITS      Always Outnumbered - I Just Wasn't Made for These Times
Anne-Marie Mackay . . . . . . . . . . . . . . . . . Producer/Co-President & CEO
Jonathon Ker . . . . . . . . . . . . . . . . . . . . Producer/Co-President & CEO
Tony Shiff . . . . . . . . . . . . . . . . . . . . . . . . . . . . Producer/COO
Skot Bright . . . . . . . . . . . . . . . . . . . . . . . . . . Head, Production
Helen McCusker . . . . . . . . . . . . . . . . . . . . . . . . Head, Development

## PAMPLIN-FISHER COMPANY
PHONE . . . . . . . . . . . . . . . . . . . . . . . . . . . . . . 407-224-6671
FAX . . . . . . . . . . . . . . . . . . . . . . . . . . . . . . . 407-224-6672
EMAIL . . . . . . . . . . . . . . . . . . . . . . . . . . . pfcfilm@aol.com
Universal Studios Florida
1000 U.S. Plaza, Bldg. 22, Ste. 215
Orlando, FL 32819-7610

TYPE       Motion Pictures + Television
CREDITS      Michael Winslow Live - Hoover - Magic 4 Morons
Rick Pamplin . . . . . . . . . . . . . . . . . . . . Producer/Writer/Director
Robert W. Fisher . . . . . . . . . . . . . . . . . . . . . . . Producer/Writer
Joseph T. Lyons . . . . . . . . . . . . . . . . . . . . . . . . . . Co-Producer
William L. Whitacre . . . . . . . . . . . . . . . . . . . . Executive Producer
Ellen Fisher . . . . . . . . . . . . . . . . . . . . . . . . . . . . Co-Producer
Matt Green . . . . . . . . . . . . . . . . . . . . . . . . . . . . . Co-Producer

## *PANAMORT TELEVISION
PHONE . . . . . . . . . . . . . . . . . . 310-557-6920/212-541-6337
FAX . . . . . . . . . . . . . . . . . . . . 310-557-7153/212-541-6233
2020 Ave. of the Stars, Fifth Fl.
Los Angeles, CA 90067

TYPE       Television
DEAL       ABC Entertainment
COMMENTS    Also: 888 Seventh Ave., Ste. 3405, New York, NY 10106
Robert Morton . . . . . . . . . . . . . . . . . President/Exec. Producer
Jeremy Gold . . . . . . . . . . . . . . . . . . . . VP, Talent & Development
Jennifer Cunningham . . . . . . . . . Dir., Talent & Development (East Coast
Jaime Panoff . . . . . . . . . . . . . . . . . . . . . . Asst. to J. Gold (NY)
Alexandra Soffer . . . . . . . . . . . . . . . . . . Asst. to R. Morton (LA)

## PAPAZIAN-HIRSCH ENTERTAINMENT
PHONE . . . . . . . . . . . . . . . . . . . . . . . . . . . . . . 818-887-2400
FAX . . . . . . . . . . . . . . . . . . . . . . . . . . . . . . . 818-887-2450
6625 Variel Ave.
Canoga Park, CA 91303

TYPE       Television + Motion Pictures
DEAL       Rysher Entertainment
CREDITS      Hart to Hart - L.A. Firefighters - The Pest - The Burning Zone - Nash Bridges
Robert Papazian . . . . . . . . . . . . . . . . . . . . Executive Producer
James G. Hirsch . . . . . . . . . . . . . . . . . Exec. Producer/Writer

## PARACHUTE ENTERTAINMENT, LLC.
PHONE . . . . . . . . . . . . . . . . . . . . . . . . . . . . . . 212-691-1697
FAX . . . . . . . . . . . . . . . . . . . . . . . . . . . . . . . 212-929-6061
156 Fifth Ave., Ste. 325
New York, NY 10010

TYPE       Motion Pictures + Television
DEAL       Hollywood Pictures/Viacom
CREDITS      Ghost of Fear Street - Goosebumps
Joan Waricha . . . . . . . . . . . . . . . . . . . . . . . . Chairman/CEO
Jane Stine . . . . . . . . . . . . . . . . . . . . . . . . . . . . . President

## PARADOX PROD., INC.
PHONE . . . . . . . . . . . . . . . . . . . . . . . . . . . . . . 818-623-2855
FAX . . . . . . . . . . . . . . . . . . . . . . . . . . . . . . . 818-623-2856
11846 Ventura Blvd., Ste. 202
Studio City, CA 91604

TYPE       Motion Pictures + Television
DEAL       Walt Disney Company, The
CREDITS      The Santa Clause - Home Improvement - Roseanne - L.A. Law - Jungle 2 Jungle
John Pasquin . . . . . . . . . . . . . . . . . . . . . Director/President
Kimberly Brent . . . . . . . . . . . . . . . . . . . . . . VP, Production
Monica Gelardo . . . . . . . . . . . . . . . . . . . . . . Story Editor

## PARALLEL PICTURES
PHONE . . . . . . . . . . . . . . . . . . . . . . . . . . . . . . 310-284-8500
FAX . . . . . . . . . . . . . . . . . . . . . . . . . . . . . . . 310-284-8778
417 S. Beverly Dr., Ste. 203
Beverly Hills, CA 90212

TYPE       Motion Pictures
CREDITS      Quest for Fire - Prelude to a Kiss - My Favorite Year
Michael Gruskoff . . . . . . . . . . . . . . . . . . . President/Partner
Gary A. Rosenberg . . . . . . . . . . . . . . . . . . President/Partner
Tom Kemper . . . . . . . . . . . . . . . . . . . . . . . . Story Editor

## PARAMI PRODUCTIONS
PHONE . . . . . . . . . . . . . . . . . . . . . . . . . . . . . . 818-508-3475
FAX . . . . . . . . . . . . . . . . . . . . . . . . . . . . . . . 818-508-3476
EMAIL . . . . . . . . . . . . . . . . . . . . . . parami@media23.com
12711 Ventura Blvd., Ste. 335
Studio City, CA 91604

TYPE       Motion Pictures + Television
CREDITS      L.A. Law - Dad, The Angel & Me - Pretender
Rick Wallace . . . . . . . . . . . . . . . . . . . . . Producer/Director
Dennis Blomquist . . . . . . . . . . . . . . . . . . . Dir., Development

## PARAMOUNT DOMESTIC TV
PHONE . . . . . . . . . . . . . . . . . . . . . . . . . . . . . . 323-956-5000
WEBSITE . . . . . . . . . . . . . . . . . . . http://www.paramount.com
5555 Melrose Ave.
Los Angeles, CA 90038-3197

TYPE       Television
Joel Berman . . . . . . . . . . . . . . . . . . . Co-President, Domestic TV
Frank Kelly . . . . . . . . . . . . . . . . . . . Co-President, Domestic TV
Bobbee Gabelmann . . . . . . . . . . . Exec. VP, Current Programming
Larry Forsdick . . . . . . . . . . . . . . . . . . . Sr. VP, Programming
Mike Mellon . . . . . . . . . . . . . . . . . . . . . . Sr. VP, Research
Phillip Murphy . . . . . . . . . . . . . . . . Sr. VP, Group Operations
Bruce Pottash . . . . . . . . . . . . . . Sr. VP, Business & Legal Affairs
Dawn Abel . . . . . . . . . . . . . . . . . . . . . . . VP, Programming
Clancy Collins . . . . . . . . . . . . . . . . . . . . . VP, Development
Lynn Fero . . . . . . . . . . . . . . . . . . . VP, Business Affairs Admin.
Peter Kane . . . . . . . . . . . . . . . . . . . . . . VP, Business Affairs
Karen Kanemoto . . . . . . . . . . . . . . . . . . . . . . . VP, Finance
Robert Mendez . . . . . . . . . . . . . . . . . . . . VP, Business Affairs
Cynthia Teele . . . . . . . . . . . . . . . . . . . . . . . . . . VP, Legal

## *PARAMOUNT INTERNATIONAL TELEVISION
PHONE . . . . . . . . . . . . . . . . . . . . . . . . . . . . . . 323-956-5000
FAX . . . . . . . . . . . . . . . . . . . . . . . . . . . . . . . 323-862-3938
EMAIL . . . . . . . . . . . . . . . . . . . . . . . . . . . paramount.com
Paramount Pictures
5555 Melrose Avenue
Hollywood, CA 90038-3197

TYPE       Television
Gary Marenzi . . . . . . . . . . . . . . . . . . . . . . . . . . President
James M. Dowaliby . . . . . . . . . . . . . . . . . . . . . VP, Production
Lyle Stewart . . . . . . . . . . . . . . . . . . . . . . Development Asst.

# COMPANIES AND STAFF

## PARAMOUNT NETWORK TELEVISION

PHONE . . . . . . . . . . . . . . . . . . . . . . . . . . . 323-956-5000
WEBSITE . . . . . . . . . . . . . . . . . . . . http://www.paramount.com
5555 Melrose Ave.
Los Angeles, CA 90038-3197

TYPE            Television

Garry Hart . . . . . . . . . . . . . . . . . . President, Network Television
Jake Jacobson . . . . . . . . . . . . . . . . . Exec. VP, Business Affairs
Tom Mazza . . . . . . . . Exec. VP, Current Programming & Strategic Planning
Dan Fauci . . . . . . . . . . . . . . . . . . . Sr. VP, Comedy Development
Kathy Lingg . . . . . . . . . . . . . . . . . . . Sr. VP, Drama Development
Milinda McNeely . . . . . . . . . . . . . . . Sr. VP, Legal, Network TV
Helen Mossler . . . . . . . . . . . . . . . . Sr. VP, Talent & Casting
Tom Russo . . . . . . . . . . . . . . . . . Sr. VP, Long Form Programming
Reid Shane . . . . . . . . . . . . . . . . . . . . . . Sr. VP, Production
Steve Stark . . . . . . . . . . . . . . . . . . Sr. VP, Current Programs
David Grossman . . . . . . . . . . . . . . . . . . . . . VP, TV Music
Hal Harrison . . . . . . . . . . . . . . . . . . . . VP, Post Production
Eileen Ige-Wong . . . . . . . . . . . . . . . . . VP, Production Finance
Brett King . . . . . . . . . . . . . . . . . . . . . VP, Current Programs
J.R. McGinnis . . . . . . . . . . . . . . . . . . . . VP, Business Affairs
Rose Catherine Pinkney . . . . . . . . . . . VP, Comedy Development
Cheryl Birch Rothschild . . . . . . . . . . . . . VP, Business Affairs
Scott Vila . . . . . . . . . . . . . . . . . . . . VP, Drama Development
Jody Zucker . . . . . . . . . . . . . . . . . . . . . . . . VP, Legal

## PARAMOUNT PICTURES- MOTION PICTURE GROUP

PHONE . . . . . . . . . . . . . . . . . . . . . . . . . . . 323-956-5000
WEBSITE . . . . . . . . . . . . . . . . . . . . http://www.paramount.com
5555 Melrose Ave.
Los Angeles, CA 90038-3197

Sherry Lansing . . . . . . . . . . . . . Chairman, Motion Picture Group
Robert G. Friedman . . . . . . . . . . . Vice Chairman, Motion Picture Group
John Goldwyn . . . . . . . . . . . . . President, Paramount Motion Pictures
Joanna Johnson . . . . . . . . . . . . . . Exec. VP, Intl. Motion Pictures
John Ferraro . . . . . . . . . . . Sr. VP, Worldwide Acquisitions & Co-Prod.

## PARAMOUNT PICTURES- PRODUCTION DIVISION

PHONE . . . . . . . . . . . . . . . . . . . . . . . . . . . 323-956-5000
WEBSITE . . . . . . . . . . . . . . . . . . . . http://www.paramount.com
5555 Melrose Ave.
Los Angeles, CA 90038-3197

TYPE            Motion Pictures

Michelle Manning . . . . . . . . . . . . . . . . . . . Pres., Production
Fred T. Gallo . . . . . . . . . . . . . Exec. VP, Feature Production Mgmt.
Donald Granger . . . . . . . . . . . . . . . . . . Exec. VP, Production
Paul Haggar . . . . . . . . . . . . . . . . . Exec. VP, Post Production
E. Barry Haldeman . . . . . . . Exec. VP In Charge of Business Affairs
Karen Rosenfelt . . . . . . . . . . . . . . . . . . Exec. VP, Production
Richard Fowkes . . . . . . . . . Sr. VP In Charge of Business Affairs
Deborah Aquila . . . . . . . . . . . . . . . Sr. VP, Features Casting
Mark Bakshi . . . . . . . . . . . . Sr. VP, Feature Production Mgmt.
Rochel Blachman . . . . . . . . . . . . . . . Sr. VP, Business Affairs
Harlan Goodman . . . . . . . . . . . . . . . . . . . Sr. VP, Music
Alan B. Heppel . . . . . . . . . . . . . . . . . . . . Sr. VP, Legal
Kevin Koloff . . . . . . . . . . . . Sr. VP, Business Affairs, Music
Thomas Levine . . . . . . . . . . . . . . . . . . . Sr. VP, Production
Karen Magid . . . . . . . . . . . . . . . . . . . . . . Sr. VP, Legal
Linda Wohl . . . . . . . . . . . . . . . . . . . Sr. VP, Music Legal
Fran M. Black . . . . . . . . . . . . . . . . . . . . . . VP, Legal
Patricia Burke . . . . . . . . . . . . . . . . VP, Literary Affairs (NY)
Lynn Flaisher . . . . . . . . . . . . . . . . . . . . . . VP, Legal
Dede Gardner . . . . . . . . . . . . . . . . . . . . . VP, Production
Michael Hill . . . . . . . . . . . . . . . . . . VP, Production Finance
Brad Kessell . . . . . . . . . . . . . . . . . . . VP, Creative Affairs
Claudia Martin . . . . . . . . . . VP, Credit & Title Administration
Scott Martin . . . . . . . . . . . . . . . . VP, Intellectual Properties
Nan Morales . . . . . . . . . . . . . . VP, Feature Prod. Management
Fera Mostow . . . . . . . . . . . . . . . . . . . . VP, Music Legal
Linda Springer . . . . . . . . . . . . . . . . . VP, Music Production
Eldridge Walker . . . . . . . . . . . . . . . . . VP, Music Clearance
John Wiseman . . . . . . . . . . . . . . . . . . VP, Post Production

## *PARAMOUNT SPECIALTY DIVISION

PHONE . . . . . . . . . . . . . . . . . . . . . . . . . . . 323-956-5000
FAX . . . . . . . . . . . . . . . . . . . . . . . . . . . . 323-862-1204
WEBSITE . . . . . . . . . . . . . . . . . . . . http://www.paramount.com
5555 Melrose Ave.
Los Angeles, CA 90038-3197

David Dinerstein . . . . . . . . . . . . . . . . . . . . . . Co-President
Ruth Vitale . . . . . . . . . . . . . . . . . . . . . . . . . Co-President

## PARAMOUNT TELEVISION GROUP

PHONE . . . . . . . . . . . . . . . . . . . . . . . . . . . 323-956-5000
WEBSITE . . . . . . . . . . . . . . . . . . . . http://www.paramount.com
5555 Melrose Ave.
Los Angeles, CA 90038-3197

TYPE            Television

Kerry McCluggage . . . . . . . . . . . . . Chairman, Paramount Television Group
Steven Goldman . . . . . . . . . . . . . . . Exec. VP/Chief Admin. Officer
Richard Lindheim . . . . . . . . . . . . . . . Exec. VP, Television Group
Robert Sheehan . . . . . . . . . . . . . . . Exec. VP, Business Affairs/Finance

## PARAVIEW INC.

PHONE . . . . . . . . . . . . . . . . . . . . . . . . . . . 212-489-5343
FAX . . . . . . . . . . . . . . . . . . . . . . . . . . . . 212-489-5371
EMAIL . . . . . . . . . . . . . . . . . . . . . . . paraview@inch.com
1674 Broadway, Ste. 4A & 4B
New York, NY 10019

TYPE        Motion Pictures + Television + Documentaries
DEAL        Icon Productions Inc.
CREDITS     The Power of Dreams - Cowgirls: Glamour, Grit and Glory
            - Intuition

Sandra Martin . . . . . . . . . . . . . . . . Exec. Producer/President
Lars Bjornlund . . . . . . . . . . . . . . . . . . . . . . . . Producer
Lisa Hagan . . . . . . . . . . . . . . . . . . . . . . . VP, Production
Karla Murthy . . . . . . . . . . . . . . . . . . . Dir., Graphic Art

## PARKWAY PRODUCTIONS

PHONE . . . . . . . . . . . . . . . . . . . . . . . . . . . 818-777-7107
FAX . . . . . . . . . . . . . . . . . . . . . . . . . . . . 818-866-4616
EMAIL . . . . . . . . . . . . . . . . . . . . . . parkway@earthlink.net
100 Universal Plaza, Bungalow 105
Universal City, CA 91608

TYPE        Motion Pictures + Television
DEAL        Universal Pictures
CREDITS     Big - A League of Their Own - Renaissance Man - The
            Preacher's Wife - Awakenings

Penny Marshall . . . . . . . . . . . . . . . . . . . . . . . Director
Amy Lemisch . . . . . . . . . . . . . . . . . . . . . . . . Producer
Sean Corrigan . . . . . . . . . . . . . . . . Chief Operating Officer
Andrea Asimow . . . . . . . . . . . . . . . . . . . . VP, Production
Adele Fitzgerald . . . . . . . . . . . . . . . . . Asst. to Mr. Corrigan
Kristin Larson . . . . . . . . . . . . . . . . . . Asst. to Ms. Marshall
Scott Nemes . . . . . . . . . . . . . . . . . Development Assistant
Curt Pratt . . . . . . . . . . . . . . . . . . . . . . . . . . Assistant

## PARKWOOD PICTURES

PHONE . . . . . . . . . . . . . . . . . . . . . . . . . . . 310-551-2216
FAX . . . . . . . . . . . . . . . . . . . . . . . . . . . . 310-286-9359
2121 Ave. of the Stars, Ste. 2800
Los Angeles, CA 90067

TYPE            Motion Pictures

Gregg Davis . . . . . . . . . . . . . . . . . . . . . . . . President
Walt Becker . . . . . . . . . . . . . . Writer/Director (310-551-2292)
Cary Tusan . . . . . . . . . . . . . Dir., Development (310-551-2217)

## PATCHETT KAUFMAN ENTERTAINMENT

PHONE . . . . . . . . . . . . . . . . . . . . . . . . . . . 310-838-7000
FAX . . . . . . . . . . . . . . . . . . . . . . . . . . . . 310-838-8430
8621 Hayden Place
Culver City, CA 90232

TYPE        Television
CREDITS     In the Line of Duty Franchise - Dean Koontz's Mr. Murder
            - The Patron Saint of Liars

Tom Patchett . . . . . . . . . . . . . . . . . . . . . . . . Chairman
Kenneth Kaufman . . . . . . . . . . . . . . . . . . . President/COO
Ann Kindberg . . . . . . . . . . . . Sr. VP, Production & Business Affairs
Ed Solorzano . . . . . . . . . . . . . . . . . . Sr. VP, Development
Debra Smith-Cannold . . . . . . . . . . . . . VP, Production Services

## PATRIOT PICTURES

PHONE . . . . . . . . . . . . . . . . . . . . . . . . . . . 310-551-7340
FAX . . . . . . . . . . . . . . . . . . . . . . . . . . . . 310-556-3145
2029 Century Park East, Ste. 3900
Los Angeles, CA 90067

TYPE        Motion Pictures
CREDITS     One Tough Cop

Michael Mendelsohn . . . . . . . . . . . . . . . . . Chairman/CEO
Marika Lumi Morgan . . . . . . . . . . . . . . . Executive Assistant

## PAULIST PRODS.
PHONE . . . . . . . . . . . . . . . . . . . . . . . . . . . . . . . . . . . . . 310-454-0688
FAX . . . . . . . . . . . . . . . . . . . . . . . . . . . . . . . . . . . . . . . 310-459-6549
EMAIL . . . . . . . . . . . . . . . . . . . . . . . . . . . . . . paulistpic@aol.com
WEBSITE . . . . . . . . . . . . . . . http://www.members.aol.com/paulistpic
17575 Pacific Coast Highway, P.O. 1057
Pacific Palisades, CA 90272-1057
TYPE        Motion Pictures + Television
CREDITS     Entertaining Angels: The Dorothy Day Story - 4th
            Wiseman - Romero - We Are the Children - Insight
Father Ellwood E. Kieser C.S.P. . . . . . . . . . . . . . . Pres./Executive Producer
Enid N. Sevilla . . . . . . . . . . . . . . . General Manager/Financial Officer
Barbara R. Nicolosi . . . . . . . . . . . . . . . . . . . . . . . Dir., Development

## PAULSON PRODS., DANIEL L.
PHONE . . . . . . . . . . . . . . . . . . . . . . . . . . . . . . . 310-234-5270
FAX . . . . . . . . . . . . . . . . . . . . . . . . . . . . . . . . . 310-234-5059
10880 Wilshire Blvd., Ste. 1101
Los Angeles, CA 90024
TYPE        Motion Pictures + Television
DEAL        Showtime Networks Inc.
CREDITS     Mr. and Mrs. Loving - Passenger 57 - Comes A Horseman
            - Sunset Park
Daniel L. Paulson . . . . . . . . . . . . . . . . . . . . . . . . . . . . President
Bob Chmiel . . . . . . . . . . . . . . . . VP, Creative Affairs (310-234-5267)
Steve A. Kennedy . . . . . . . . . . . . . . Dir., Adminstration (310-234-5360)
Wendy Saatjian . . . . . . . . . . . . . . Development Associate (310-234-5313)
Eileen McDermott . . . . . . . . . . . . . . . . . . . . . Development Assistant

## PB MANAGEMENT
PHONE . . . . . . . . . . . . . . . . . . . . . . . . . . . . . . . 213-653-7284
FAX . . . . . . . . . . . . . . . . . . . . . . . . . . . . . . . . . 213-653-5285
EMAIL . . . . . . . . . . . . . . . . . . . . . . . . . . . capnett@pacbell.net
6523 W. 6th Street
Los Angeles, CA 90048
TYPE        Motion Pictures + Television
DEAL        HBO Original Programming
Paul Bennett . . . . . . . . . . . . . . . . . . . . . . . . . . . . . . President
Barbara Caplan . . . . . . . . . . . . . . . . . . . . . . . . . VP, Development

## PBS
PHONE . . . . . . . . . . . . . . . . . . . . . . . . . . . . . . . 703-739-5000
FAX . . . . . . . . . . . . . . . . . . . . . . . . . . . . . . . . . 703-739-0775
WEBSITE . . . . . . . . . . . . . . . . . . . . . . . . . . http://www.pbs.org
1320 Braddock Place
Alexandria, VA 22314-1698
TYPE        Television
Ervin S. Duggan . . . . . . . . . . . . . . . . . . . . . . . . . President/CEO
Robert G. Ottenhoff . . . . . . . . . . . . . . . . . . . . . . . Exec. VP/COO
John C. Hollar . . . . . . . . . . . . . . . . . Exec. VP, PBS Learning Ventures
Kathy Quattrone . . . . . . . . . . Exec. VP, Programming/Chief Prog. Executive
Jonathan C. Abbott . . . . . . . . . . Sr. VP, Development & Corporate Relations
M. Peter Downey . . . . . . . . . . . . . . . . Sr. VP, Program Business Affairs
Elizabeth Wolfe . . . . . . . . . . . . . . . . . . . . . . . . . . Sr. VP/CFO
Michael Diefenbach . . . . . . . . . . . . . . . . . . . VP, Sponsor Development
Nanette Dudar . . . . . . . . . . . . . . . . . . . . . VP, Finance & Treasurer
Alan Foster . . . . . . . . . . . . . . VP, Fundraising & Syndicated Programming
Jim Guerra . . . . . . . . . . . . . . . . . . . . . VP, Program Business Affairs
Pat Hunter . . . . . . . VP, Programming Administration & Communication
Cindy Johanson . . . . . . . . . . . . . . . . . . . . . . . . . . VP, PBS Online
Donald Thoms . . . . . . . . . . . . . . . . . . . . VP, Program Management
John Wilson . . . . . . . . . . . . VP, Program Scheduling & Editorial Mgmt.
Steven Gray . . . . . . . . . . . . . . Sr. Dir., Scheduling, Planning & Standards
Alice Cahn . . . . . . . . . . . . . . . . . . . Dir., Children's Programming
Jack Dougherty . . . . . . . . . . . . . . . . Dir., Program Business Affairs
Sandy Heberer . . . . . . . . . . . . . Dir., News & Information Programming
Jennifer McCormick . . . . . . . . . . . . . . . . Dir., Sponsor Development
Mary Jane McKinven . . . . . Dir., Science, Natural History & Exploration Prog.
James Scalem . . . . . . . . . . . . . . Project Exec., Fundraising Programming
Glenn DuBose . . . . . . . Dir., Drama, Performance & Arts Programming
Dick Hanratty . . . . . . . . . . . . . . . . Dir., PBS Plus & PBS Select
Lauren Kalos . . . . . . . . . . . . . . . . . . Dir., Program Operations

## PDQ DIRECTIONS, INC.
PHONE . . . . . . . . . . . . . . . . . . . . . . . . . . . . . . . 310-552-1470
FAX . . . . . . . . . . . . . . . . . . . . . . . . . . . . . . . . . 310-552-1469
2160 Century Park East, Ste. 1409
Los Angeles, CA 90067
TYPE        Motion Pictures + Television + Documentaries + Feature
            Direct to Video
CREDITS     Malibu Bikini Shop - Kandyland - Listen to the Music
Leo Leichter . . . . . . . . . . . . . . . . . . . . . . . . . . Owner/Producer
Barbra Hudson . . . . . . . . . . . . . . . . . . . . . . Creative Development
Jon Leichter . . . . . . . . . . . . . . . . . . . . . . . . . . Business Affairs

## PEACOCK FILMS/1ST MIRACLE PICTURES
PHONE . . . . . . . . . . . . . . . . . . . . . . . . . . . . . . . 213-874-6000
FAX . . . . . . . . . . . . . . . . . . . . . . . . . . . . . . . . . 213-874-4252
3439 West Cahuenga Blvd.
Hollywood, CA 90068
TYPE        Motion Pictures + Feature Direct to Video + Television +
            Syndication
CREDITS     Freedom Deep - Desperation Highway - Tangled - Never
            Look Back
COMMENTS    Production & Distribution.
Moshe Bibiyan . . . . . . . . . . . . . . . . . . . . Chief Executive Officer
Simon Bibiyan . . . . . . . . . . . . . . . . . . . . . . . . . . . President
Jefferson Donald . . . . . . . . . . . . . . Sr. VP, Production & Acquisitions
Lloyd Korn . . . . . . . . . . . . . . . . . . . . VP, Business & Legal Affairs

## PEAK PRODUCTIONS
PHONE . . . . . . . . . . . . . . . . . . . . . . . . . . . . . . . 310-315-5371
FAX . . . . . . . . . . . . . . . . . . . . . . . . . . . . . . . . . 310-315-5205
1861 S. Bundy Dr., Ste. #308
West Los Angeles, CA 90025
TYPE        Motion Pictures + Television
CREDITS     Set It Off - Blaze - Midnight Clear - The Mighty Quinn
COMMENTS    Affiliated with Open Door Entertainment.
Dale Pollock . . . . . . . . . . . . . . . . . . . . . . . . . . . . President
Ada Gorn . . . . . . . . . . . . . . . . . . . . . . . . . . . Creative Executive
Patricia Finneran . . . . . . . . . . . . . . . . . . . . . . . Creative Executive

## PEARSON ALL AMERICAN
PHONE . . . . . . . . . . . . . . . . . . . . . . . . . . . . . . . 310-656-1100
FAX . . . . . . . . . . . . . . . . . . . . . . . . . . . . . . . . . 310-656-7400
EMAIL . . . . . . . . . . . . . . . . . . . . . . . . . . . allamcom@aol.com
808 Wilshire Blvd., 3rd Floor
Santa Monica, CA 90401-1810
TYPE        Television
CREDITS     Baywatch - Family Feud - Sinbad - Ghost Stories
David Gerber . . . . . . . . . . . . . . . . . . . . . . . . . . . . President
Lou Festa . . . . . . . . . . . . . . . . . . . . . . . . . . . . . . . . CFO
Bill Lincoln . . . . . . . . . . . . . . . . . . . . . Exec. VP, Productions
Catherine MacKay . . . . . . . . . . . . . Exec. VP, Operations (NY)
Jamie Waldron . . . . . . . . . . . . . . . . . . . Exec. Vice President
Anne Bartnett . . . . . . . . . . . . . . . . . . . . . VP, Business Affairs
John Janisch . . . . . . . . . . . . . . . . . . . . VP, Production Finance
Lorin B. Salob . . . . . . . . . . . . . . . . . . . . . . . . VP, Production
Geoff Silverman . . . . . . . VP, Drama & Syndication & Development
Helen Stringer . . . . . . . . . . . . . . . . . . . Dir., Creative Affairs
Kathi Weissberger . . . . . . . . . Exec. Asst. to the Pres./Administrative Mgr.

## PEARSON TELEVISION PRODUCTIONS
PHONE . . . . . . . . . . . . . . . . . . . . . . . . . . . . . . . 310-656-1100
FAX . . . . . . . . . . . . . . . . . . . . . . . . . . . . . . . . . 310-656-7400
808 Wilshire Blvd., 3rd Fl.
Santa Monica, CA 90401
TYPE        Television
CREDITS     Man O'Man - Sale of the Century - Small Talk
COMMENTS    Formerly ACI/Reg Grundy Productions.
Juliet Blake . . . . . . . . . . . . . . . . . . . . . . . . VP, Programming
Ruth Caruso . . . . . . . . . . . . . . . . . . . . . . . Dir., Programming
Jill Schwartz . . . . . . . . . . . . . . . Dir., Programming & Development
Nigel Caaro . . . . . . . . . . . . . . . . . Exec. Asst./Development

## PERENNIAL PICTURES FILM CORP.
PHONE . . . . . . . . . . . . . . . . . . . . . . . . . . . . . . . 317-253-1519
FAX . . . . . . . . . . . . . . . . . . . . . . . . . . . . . . . . . 317-257-2166
EMAIL . . . . . . . . . . . . . . . . . . . . . . . . . . . . . perpix@aol.com
2102 E. 52nd Street
Indianapolis, IN 46205-1408
TYPE        Television + Animation + Feature Direct to Video
CREDITS     O. Ratz - Ugly Duckling's Christmas Wish - The First
            Easter Egg
Jerry Reynolds . . . . . . . . . . . . . . . . . . . . . . . . . . . President
Russ Harris . . . . . . . . . . . . . . . . . . . . . . . . . . Sr. Vice President

## PERISCOPE PICTURES
PHONE . . . . . . . . . . . . . . . . . . . . . . . . . . . . . . . 310-858-8659
FAX . . . . . . . . . . . . . . . . . . . . . . . . . . . . . . . . . 310-858-0194
EMAIL . . . . . . . . . . . . . . . . . . . . . . . . . periscope@earthlink.net
152 N. Lapeer Dr.
Los Angeles, CA 90048
TYPE        Motion Pictures
CREDITS     Dickwad - Under The Hula Moon - Gunshy
Jim B. Hodge . . . . . . . . . . . . . . . . . . . . . . . . . CEO/Chairman
Jeff Celentano . . . . . . . . . . . . . . . . . . President/Writer/Director
Whitney Hunter . . . . . . . . . . . . . . . . VP, Development & Production
Kim Meade . . . . . . . . . . . . . . . . . . . . . . . . . Executive Assistant

# COMPANIES AND STAFF

**PERLMAN PRODUCTIONS**
PHONE . . . . . . . . . . . . . . . . . . . . . . . . . . . . . . . . . . . 310-301-1613
FAX . . . . . . . . . . . . . . . . . . . . . . . . . . . . . . . . . . . . . . 310-823-1654
1990 S. Bundy Dr., Ste. 200
Los Angeles, CA 90025-5240
TYPE        Motion Pictures + Television
CREDITS     Vital Signs - Lucky Stiff - Big Girls Don't Cry...They Get
            Even
Laurie Perlman . . . . . . . . . . . . . . . . . . . . . . . . . . . . . . . . . . Producer
Marvin V. Acuna . . . . . . . . . . . . . . . . . . . . . . . . . Dir., Development

**PERMUT PRESENTATIONS**
PHONE . . . . . . . . . . . . . . . . . . . . . . . . . . . . . . . . . . . 310-248-2792
FAX . . . . . . . . . . . . . . . . . . . . . . . . . . . . . . . . . . . . . . 310-248-2797
9150 Wilshire Blvd., Ste. 247
Beverly Hills, CA 90212
TYPE        Motion Pictures + Television
CREDITS     Face-Off - Eddie - Dragnet - Blind Date
David Permut . . . . . . . . . . . . . . . . . . . . . . . . Producer/President
Steven A. Longi . . . . . . . . . . . . . . . . . . . . . . . . . . VP, Development
Michael Alfieri . . . . . . . . . . . . . . . . . . . . . . Development Associate
Scot Ginsberg . . . . . . . . . . . . . . . . . . . . . . . . Executive Assistant

**PERSISTENT PICTURES, INC.**
PHONE . . . . . . . . . . . . . . . . . . . . . . . . . . . . . . . . . . . 213-960-1444
FAX . . . . . . . . . . . . . . . . . . . . . . . . . . . . . . . . . . . . . . 213-960-1434
EMAIL . . . . . . . . . . . . . . . . . . . . . . . . mail@persistentpictures.com
WEBSITE . . . . . . . . . . . . . . . . . . . . http://www.persistentpictures.com
6464 Sunset Blvd., Ste. 990
Hollywood, CA 90028
TYPE        Motion Pictures + Television + Interactive Multimedia
CREDITS     Life During Wartime - Dust and Stardust - Standoff
Dan Stone . . . . . . . . . . . . . . . . . . . . . . No Title (213-960-1446)
Henry M. Shea Jr. . . . . . . . . . . . . . . . . . . . . . . . . . . . . No Title
Devorah Barkan . . . . . . . . . . . . . . . . . . . . . . . . . . . . . No Title
Matthew Rhodes . . . . . . . . . . . . . . . . . . . . . . . . . . . . . No Title
Richard Williams . . . . . . . . . . . . . . . . . . . . . . . . . . . . Assistant

**PERSKY PRODS., LESTER**
PHONE . . . . . . . . . . . . . . . . . . . . . . . . . . . . . . . . . . . 310-278-1995
FAX . . . . . . . . . . . . . . . . . . . . . . . . . . . . . . . . . . . . . . 310-278-1910
EMAIL . . . . . . . . . . . . . . . . . . . . . . . . . . . . . . . . . jnnla@aol.com
9910 Tower Lane
Beverly Hills, CA 90210
TYPE        Motion Pictures + Television
CREDITS     Liz - A Woman Named Jackie - Poor Little Rich Girl - Hair
Lester Persky . . . . . . . . . . . . . . . . . . President/Exec. Producer
Tomlinson Dean . . . . . . . . . . . . . . . . . . . . . . . . . VP/Producer
Camille Pollock . . . . . . . . . . . . . . . . . . . . . . . . . . . Controller
Jonas A. Neilson . . . . . . . . . . . . . . . . . . . . . Dir., Development

**PET FLY PRODS.**
PHONE . . . . . . . . . . . . . . . . . . . . . . . . . . . . . . . . . . . 818-843-3594
FAX . . . . . . . . . . . . . . . . . . . . . . . . . . . . . . . . . . . . . . 818-526-0906
EMAIL . . . . . . . . . . . . . . . . . . . . . . . . . . . . . . . . . pettfly@aol.com
3100 W. Burbank Blvd., #201
Burbank, CA 91505
TYPE        Motion Pictures + Television
DEAL        Paramount Television Group
CREDITS     The Rocketeer - The Wrong Guys - Viper - The Flash -
            The Sentinel
Danny Bilson . . . . . . . . . . . . . . . . . . Writer/Exec. Producer/Director
Paul De Meo . . . . . . . . . . . . . . . . . . . . . . . Writer/Exec. Producer
Joe Lauer . . . . . . . . . . . . . . . . . . . . . . . . . . . . . . . . . President
Michael Lacoe . . . . . . . . . . . . . . . . . . . VP, Production/Producer
Lisa Beard . . . . . . . . . . . . . . . . . . . . . . . Production Associate

**PETERS ENTERTAINMENT**
PHONE . . . . . . . . . . . . . . . . . . . . . . . . . . . . . . . . . . . 818-954-2441
FAX . . . . . . . . . . . . . . . . . . . . . . . . . . . . . . . . . . . . . . 818-954-4976
4000 Warner Blvd., Bldg. 15
Burbank, CA 91522
TYPE        Motion Pictures
DEAL        Columbia Pictures/Warner Bros. Pictures
CREDITS     Batman - Rainman - Money Train - Rosewood - My Fellow
            Americans
Jon Peters . . . . . . . . . . . . . . . . . . . . Chairman (818-954-4960)
Brian D. Manis . . . . . . . . . . . . . . . . . . . . . . . Creative Executive
Stacy Zand . . . . . . . . . . . . . . . . . . . . . . . . . Creative Executive
Loretta Walsh-Gruber . . . . . . . . . . . . . . . . . Asst. to Jon Peters

**PETRIE JR. & CO., DANIEL**
PHONE . . . . . . . . . . . . . . . . . . . . . . . . . . . . . . . . . . . 818-623-1600
FAX . . . . . . . . . . . . . . . . . . . . . . . . . . . . . . . . . . . . . . 818-623-1606
4400 Coldwater Canyon Ave., Ste. 202
Studio City, CA 91604
TYPE        Motion Pictures + Television
DEAL        Paramount Television Group
CREDITS     In the Army Now - Toy Soldiers - B.H. Cop - Turner &
            Hooch - Dead Silence
Dan Petrie Jr. . . . . . . . . . . . . . . . . . . . . Director/Writer/Producer
Jon Lucas . . . . . . . . . . . . . . . . . . . . . . . . . . . . . . . . Associate

**PETRIE PRODS., INC., DOROTHEA G.**
PHONE . . . . . . . . . . . . . . . . . . . . . . . . . . . . . . . . . . . 310-394-2608
FAX . . . . . . . . . . . . . . . . . . . . . . . . . . . . . . . . . . . . . . 310-395-8530
13201 Haney Place
Los Angeles, CA 90049
TYPE        Motion Pictures + Television
CREDITS     Caroline - Getting Out - Face on the Milk Carton - Captive
            Heart
Dorothea G. Petrie . . . . . . . . . . . . . . . . . . . . . . . Producer/Writer

**PFILMCO, INC.**
PHONE . . . . . . . . . . . . . . . . . . . . . . . . . . . . . . . . . . . 310-571-9191
FAX . . . . . . . . . . . . . . . . . . . . . . . . . . . . . . . . . . . . . . 310-571-9222
11440 San Vicente Blvd., Ste. 102
Los Angeles, CA 90049
TYPE        Motion Pictures + Television
CREDITS     The Winner - Men of War - The Entity - Thick as Thieves -
            The Big Brass Ring
Andrew Pfeffer . . . . . . . . . . . . . . . . . . . . . . . . . . . . . Producer

**PHASE I PRODUCTIONS**
PHONE . . . . . . . . . . . . . . . . . . . . . . . . . . . . . . . . . . . 310-393-6217
FAX . . . . . . . . . . . . . . . . . . . . . . . . . . . . . . . . . . . . . . 310-260-1498
EMAIL . . . . . . . . . . . . . . . . . . . . . . . . . . . . . . Phase1P@aol.com
429 Santa Monica Blvd., Ste. 610
Santa Monica, CA 90401
TYPE        Motion Pictures
DEAL        Paramount Pictures- Motion Picture Group
CREDITS     Kiss The Girls - Dunston Checks In - Fire In The Sky -
            Wrestling Ernest Hemingway
COMMENTS    Affiliated with Wizan Film Properties.
Joe Wizan . . . . . . . . . . . . . . . . . . . . . . . . . . . . . . . . . . Partner
Don Schneider . . . . . . . . . . . . . . . . . . . . . . . . . . . . . . . Partner
Steve Wizan . . . . . . . . . . . . . . . . . . . . . . . . . . . . . . . President
Lonnie Ramati . . . . . . . . . . . . . . . . . . . . . . VP, Business Affairs
Kristine J. Schwarz . . . . . . . . . . . . . . . . . . . . VP, Creative Affairs
Edward M. Needham . . . . . . . . . . . . . . . . Dir., Creative Affairs
Leroy Logan . . . . . . . . . . . . . . . . . . . . . . . . . . . . Development
Dru A. Ransom . . . . . . . . . . . . . . . . . . . . . . Creative Executive
Chase Adams . . . . . . . . . . . . . . . . . . . . . . . . . . . . . . Assistant
Beppe Brezzo . . . . . . . . . . . . . . . . . . . . . . . . . . . . . . No Title

**PHIL ALDEN ROBINSON**
PHONE . . . . . . . . . . . . . . . . . . . . . . . . . . . . . . . . . . . 818-777-5055
FAX . . . . . . . . . . . . . . . . . . . . . . . . . . . . . . . . . . . . . . 818-866-1575
Universal Pictures
100 Universal City Plaza, Bung. 70
Universal City, CA 91608-1085
TYPE        Motion Pictures
CREDITS     Sneakers - Field of Dreams - All of Me
Phil Alden Robinson . . . . . . . . . . . . . . . . . Writer/Director/Producer
Margaret Solow . . . . . . . . . . . . . . . . . . . . . Dir., Creative Affairs
Lale Arpaci . . . . . . . . . . . . . . . . . . . . . . Asst. to Mr. Robinson

**PHILIPICO PICTURES CO.**
PHONE . . . . . . . . . . . . . . . . . . . . . . . . . . . . . . . . . . . 213-874-1555
EMAIL . . . . . . . . . . . . . . . . . . . . . . . . . . . . . . . philipico@aol.com
3575 Cahuenga Blvd. West, 2nd Floor
Los Angeles, CA 90068
TYPE        Motion Pictures + Television + Feature Direct to Video +
            Animation + Syndication
CREDITS     The Hired Heart - The Haunting of Lisa- Shoot To Kill
COMMENTS    Affiliate:  Century Park Pictures Corp.
Phil Rogers . . . . . . . . . . . . . . . . . . . . . . . . . . Principal/Producer
Stephanie Rogers . . . . . . . . . . . . . . . . . . . . . . . . . . . Principal

## PHOENICIAN FILMS
PHONE . . . . . . . . . . . . . . . . . . . . . . . . . . . . . . . . . . . . 213-848-3444
FAX . . . . . . . . . . . . . . . . . . . . . . . . . . . . . . . . . . . . . . 213-848-9612
8228 Sunset Blvd., Ste. 311
Los Angeles, CA 90046

TYPE      Motion Pictures
CREDITS      Free Money - A Murder of Crows - 20 Dates

Elie Samaha . . . . . . . . . . . . . . . . . . . . . . . . . . . . . . . . . . Chairman
Tia Carrere . . . . . . . . . . . . . . . . . . . . . . . . . . . . . . . . . . President
Tracee Stanley . . . . . . . . . . . . . . . . . . . . . . . . . Pres., Development
Mark McGarry . . . . . . . . . . . . . . . . . . . . . . . Sr. VP, Production
Dawn Miller . . . . . . . . . . . . . . . . . . . . . . . . . . . VP, Development
Geno Havens . . . . . . . . . . . . . . . . . . . . . . . . . Creative Executive
Paul D. Brown . . . . . . . . . . . . . . . . . . . . . . . Executive Assistant
Malee Nerenhausen . . . . . . . . . . . . . . . . . . . . Executive Assistant

## PHOENIX PICTURES
PHONE . . . . . . . . . . . . . . . . 310-244-6100/212-245-7309
FAX . . . . . . . . . . . . . . . . . . . 310-839-8915/212-245-7847
10125 W. Washington Blvd., Frankovich
Culver City, CA 90232

TYPE      Motion Pictures + Television
CREDITS      The People vs Larry Flynt - U-Turn - Apt Pupil - Thin Red Line - Urban Legend
COMMENTS    Also: 712 Fifth Ave., 40th Fl, NY NY 10019

Mike Medavoy . . . . . . . . . . . . . . . . . . . . . . . . . . . . . Chairman/CEO
Arnold Messer . . . . . . . . . . . . . . . . . . . . . . President (310-244-6101)
Rick Hess . . . . . . . . . . . . . . . . . . Sr. Exec. Vice President (310-244-6888)
Lawrence Bernstein . . . . . . . . . . Exec. VP, Business & Legal Affairs
Lindsey Bayman . . . . . . . . . Sr. VP, Business & Legal Affairs (310-244-6120)
Christy Prunier . . . . . . . . . . . . . . . Sr. VP, Production (310-244-6102)
Diane Sokolow . . . . . . . . . . . . . . . . . Sr. VP, East Coast Production
Edward Teets . . . . . . . . . . . . Sr. VP, Physical Production (310-244-6413)
Judith Garinger . . . . . . . . . . . . . . . . . . . . VP/Controller (310-244-6382)
Marc Lorber . . . . . . . . . . . . . . . . . . . . . VP, Television (310-244-6138)
Nicholas Morton . . . . . . . . . . . . . . . VP, Development (310-244-6104)
Nick Osborne . . . . . . . . . . . . . . . . . VP, Development (310-244-6194)
Eric Paquette . . . . . . . . . . . . . . . . Dir., Development (310-244-6131)
Tom Kane . . . . . . . . . . . . . . . . . . . . . . . . . . . . . . . . . . Story Editor
Chad Miller . . . . . . . . . . Exec. Asst. to Mike Medavoy (310-244-6540)
Ian Smith . . . . . . . . . . . . . . . . . . . . . . . . . . . . . . . . . . Jr. Publicist

## PICO CREEK PRODS.
PHONE . . . . . . . . . . . . . . . . . . . . . . . . . . . . . . . . . . . . 310-394-7522
FAX . . . . . . . . . . . . . . . . . . . . . . . . . . . . . . . . . . . . . . 310-394-5825
409 Santa Monica Blvd., 2nd Fl.
Santa Monica, CA 90401

TYPE      Motion Pictures + Television
DEAL      Warner Bros. Television Productions
CREDITS      The Cure- thirtysomething - Extreme Close Up - Birdland- Murder Live

Peter Horton . . . . . . . . . . . . . . . . . . . . . . . . . . Director/Actor
Kristin Friedrich . . . . . . . . . . . . . . . . . . . . . . . Creative Executive

## *PICTURE FACTORY, THE
PHONE . . . . . . . . . . . . . . . . . . . . . . . . . . . . . . . . . . . . 213-874-4247
FAX . . . . . . . . . . . . . . . . . . . . . . . . . . . . . . . . . . . . . . 213-874-7542
P.O. Box 931567
Los Angeles, CA 90093

TYPE      Motion Pictures + Television

David Lynch . . . . . . . . . . . . . . . Writer/Director/Partner/Exec. Producer
Mary Sweeney . . . . . . . . . . . . . . . . . . . . . . . . . Producer/Partner
Neal Edelstein . . . . . . . . . . . . . . . . . . . . . . . . Producer/Partner

## PICTUREMAKER PRODS.
PHONE . . . . . . . . . . . . . . . . . . . . . . . . . . . . . . . . . . . . 203-629-6253
FAX . . . . . . . . . . . . . . . . . . . . . . . . . . . . . . . . . . . . . . 203-622-7133
5855 Topanga Cyn. Blvd. #410
Woodland Hills, CA 91367

TYPE      Motion Pictures + Television
CREDITS      Clean & Sober - Moonlighting - Wilder Napalm - Love Affair - Picture Perfect

Glenn Gordon Caron . . . . . . . . . . . . . . . Writer/Director/Producer
Diane Salzberg . . . . . . . . . . . . . . . . . . . . . . . Asst. to Mr. Caron

## PIERCE CO., THE FREDERICK S.
PHONE . . . . . . . . . . . . . . . . . . . . . . . . . . . . . . . . . . . . 213-964-7800
FAX . . . . . . . . . . . . . . . . . 213-964-7818/914-948-0427
5670 Wilshire Blvd., Ste. 1350
Los Angeles, CA 90036

TYPE      Motion Pictures + Television
CREDITS      Witness to Execution - Substitute Wife - Cheerleader - Moneytrain - The Absolute Truth - 20,000 Leagues

Frederick S. Pierce . . . . . . . . . . . . . . . . . . . . . . . Chairman/CEO
Keith Pierce . . . . . . . . . . . . . . . . . . . . . . . . . . Executive Producer
Richard Pierce . . . . . . . . . . . . . . . . . . . . . . . . Executive Producer

## PILOT BOY PRODUCTIONS
PHONE . . . . . . . . . . . . . . . . . . . . . . . . . . . . . . . . . . . . 818-560-2853
FAX . . . . . . . . . . . . . . . . . . . . . . . . . . . . . . . . . . . . . . 818-563-9887
500 S. Buena Vista St., Anim. 1C, Rm.1-2
Burbank, CA 91521-1626

TYPE      Motion Pictures + Television
DEAL      Touchstone Pictures

David Chappelle . . . . . . . . . . . . . . . . . . . . . . . . . . . President
Vikki Jackson . . . . . . . . . . . . . . . . . . . . . . . Dir., Development

## PIRROMOUNT PICTURES
PHONE . . . . . . . . . . . . . . . . . . . . . . . . . . . . . . . . . . . . 818-994-3262
WEBSITE . . . . . . . . . . . . . . . . . . http://www.loop.com/~pirro
P.O. Box 7520
Van Nuys, CA 91405

TYPE      Motion Pictures + Feature Direct to Video + Documentaries
CREDITS      Color Blinded - Nudist Colony of the Dead - Polish Vampire in Burbank
COMMENTS    Also: Commercials.

Mark Pirro . . . . . . . . . . . . . . . . . . . . . . Writer/Producer/Director
Louis Gerstel . . . . . . . . . . . . . . . . . . . . . . . . Head, Development
Ron Curtiss . . . . . . . . . . . . . . . . . . . . . . . . . Associate Producer
Jim Rainey . . . . . . . . . . . . . . . . . . . . . . . . . Associate Producer
Lee Neville . . . . . . . . . . . . . . . . . . . . . . . . Production Associate

## PIXAR ANIMATION STUDIOS
PHONE . . . . . . . . . . . . . . . . . . . . . . . . . . . . . . . . . . . . 510-236-4000
FAX . . . . . . . . . . . . . . . . . . . . . . . . . . . . . . . . . . . . . . 510-236-0388
WEBSITE . . . . . . . . . . . . . . . . . . . . . . . http://www.pixar.com
1001 West Cutting Blvd.
Richmond, CA 94804

TYPE      Motion Pictures
DEAL      Walt Disney Motion Pictures Group
COMMENTS    Produced Toy Story, the first fully computer animated feature film.

Steven P. Jobs . . . . . . . . . . . . . . . . . . . . . . . . . . Chairman/CEO
Dr. Edwin E. Catmull . . . . . . . . . . . . . . . . . . . . Exec. VP/CTO
Lawrence B. Levy . . . . . . . . . . . . . . . . . . . . . . Exec. VP/CFO
John Lasseter . . . . . . . . . . . . . . . . . . VP, Creative Development
Sarah McArthur . . . . . . . . . . . . . . . . . . . . . . . VP, Production

## PLANET GIRL PICTURES
PHONE . . . . . . . . . . . . . . . . . . . . . . . . . . . . . . . . . . . . 310-559-6424
FAX . . . . . . . . . . . . . . . . . . . . . . . . . . . . . . . . . . . . . . 310-559-6366
EMAIL . . . . . . . . . . . . . . . . . . . . . . . planetgirl@loop.com
Box 6311
Beverly Hills, CA 90212

TYPE      Motion Pictures + Television + Documentaries + Interactive Multimedia
CREDITS      Island Girl - One Man's Heaven
COMMENTS    Film Financing, Entertainment, Ventures Financing.

Sherry Joniff . . . . . . . . . . . . . . . . . . . . . . . . . Producer/Partner
Steph Horzepa . . . . . . . . . . . . . . . . . . . . . . . . Writer/Partner
Janice Kahn . . . . . . . . . . . . . . . . . . . . Production/Creative Asst.

## PLASTER CITY PRODUCTIONS
PHONE . . . . . . . . . . . . . . . . . . . . . . . . . . . . . . . . . . . . 213-951-0985
FAX . . . . . . . . . . . . . . . . . . . . . . . . . . . . . . . . . . . . . . 213-951-0986
EMAIL . . . . . . . . . . . . . . . . . . . . . . c.coppola@plastercity.com
WEBSITE . . . . . . . . . . http://http://home.earthlink.net/~plastercity
100 N. La Cienega Blvd., Ste. 110
Los Angeles, CA 90048

TYPE      Motion Pictures + Television
CREDITS      Deadfall - Ballad of a Gunfighter - Palmer's Pickup - Black Stallion Rebels

Christopher Coppola . . . . . . . . . . . . . . . . . . . . . . . . . President
Adrienne Coppola . . . . . . . . . . . . . . . . . . . . . . . Vice President
Alain Silver . . . . . . . . . . . . . . . . . . . . . . . . . . . . . . Producer
Nick Johnson . . . . . . . . . . . . . . . . . Prouction Executive/Writer
Mark Dziak . . . . . . . . . . . . . . . . . . . . . . . . Production Executive

## PLATFORM ENTERTAINMENT
PHONE . . . . . . . . . . . . . . . . . . . . . . . . . . . . . . . . . . . . 310-996-3108
FAX . . . . . . . . . . . . . . . . . . . . . . . . . . . . . . . . . . . . . . . 310-996-9520
11811 W. Olympic Blvd.
Los Angeles, CA 90067

TYPE  Motion Pictures + Television
CREDITS  Dante's View

Daniel Levin . . . . . . . . . . . . . . . . . . . . . . . . . . . . . . . . Producer
Steven Brooksbank . . . . . . . . . . . . . . . . . . . . . . . Casting Director
Fazia Michele . . . . . . . . . . . . . . . . . . . . . . . Production Supervisor
Mark Butler . . . . . . . . . . . . . . . . . . . . . . . . . . . . . . Story Editor

## PLATINUM STUDIOS, LLC
PHONE . . . . . . . . . . . . . . . . . . . . . . . . . . . . . . . . . . . . 310-276-3900
FAX . . . . . . . . . . . . . . . . . . . . . . . . . . . . . . . . . . . . . . . 310-276-2799
EMAIL . . . . . . . . . . . . . . . . . . . . . . . . . . info@platinumstudios.com
9744 Wilshire Blvd., Ste. 400
Beverly Hills, CA 90212

TYPE  Animation + Motion Pictures + Television + Interactive
Multimedia
DEAL  Sony Television
CREDITS  Men In Black (feature) - Night Man - Men In Black
(animated series) - Cowboys & Aliens
COMMENTS  Live Action.

Scott Mitchell Rosenberg . . . . . . . . . . . . . . . . . . . . . . . Chairman
Ervin Rustemagic . . . . . . . . . . . . . . . . . . . . . . . . . . . . President
Gregory Noveck . . . . . . . . . . . . . . . . . . . . . . . . . . VP, Production
Paul Benjamin . . . . . . . . . . . . . . . . . . . . . . Dir., Creative Affairs
Jake Friedman . . . . . . . . . . . . . . . . . . . . . . . . . . Dir., Development
Bill Kunkel . . . . . . . . . . . . . . . . . . . . . Dir., Interactive Development
Caryn Antonini . . . . . . . . . . . . . . . . . . . . . Development Assistant

## PLAYBOY ENTERTAINMENT GROUP INC.
PHONE . . . . . . . . . . . . . . . . . . . . . . . . . . . . . . . 310-246-4000
FAX . . . . . . . . . . . . . . . . . . . . . . . . . . . . . . . . 310-246-4050
WEBSITE . . . . . . . . . . . . . . . . . . . . . . . . http://www.playboy.com
9242 Beverly Blvd.
Beverly Hills, CA 90210

TYPE  Feature Direct to Video
COMMENTS  Parent Company - Alta Loma.

Anthony J. Lynn . . . . . . . . . . . . . . . . . . . . . . . . . . . President
Richard P. Rosetti . . . . . . . . . . . . . . . Pres., Worldwide Production
James English . . . . . . . . . . . . . . . . Pres., Playboy Network Worldwide
Richard Bencivengo . . . . . . . . Exec. VP, Programming & Prod., Alta Loma Ent.
Myron DuBow . . . . . . . . . . . . . . Sr. VP, Business & Legal Affairs
Jeffrey Lai . . . . . . . . . . . . . . . . . Sr. VP, Business & Legal Affairs
Stuart Kricun . . . . . . . . . . . . . . . . . VP, Business & Legal Affairs
Catherine Zulfer . . . . . . . . . . . . . . . . . . . . . . . VP/Controller
Sahara Riley . . . . . . . . . . . . . . . . Dir., Feature Film Development
Steve Hajdu . . . . . . . . . . . . . . . . . . . . . . . . . . . Story Editor

## PLAYTIME PRODUCTIONS
PHONE . . . . . . . . . . . . . . . . . . . . . 310-203-1360/213-960-9446
FAX . . . . . . . . . . . . . . . . . . . . . . . . 310-652-6055/213-653-4605
EMAIL . . . . . . . . . . . . . . . . . . . . playtimeproductions@usa.net
264 S. La Cienega Blvd., Ste. 326
Beverly Hills, CA 90211

TYPE  Motion Pictures + Television + Animation
COMMENTS  ALSO: Raleigh Studios, 5400 Melrose Ave., LA, CA
90038

Brett A. Liebman . . . . . . . . . . . . . . . . . . . . . . . Producer/Writer
Danny Goldwyn . . . . . . . . . . . . . . . . . . . . . Production Executive
Annie Simon . . . . . . . . . . . . . . . . . . . . . Development Executive
Addie Brooks . . . . . . . . . . . . . . . . . Development Exec./Animation
Tom Hilman . . . . . . . . . . . . . . . . . . . . . . . . Executive Assistant
Jill Tannenbaum . . . . . . . . . . . . . . . . . . . . . . Executive Assistant

## PLOTPOINT INC.
PHONE . . . . . . . . . . . . . . . . . . . . . . . . . . . . . . . 818-509-9464
12600 Kling St.
Studio City, CA 91604

TYPE  Motion Pictures
CREDITS  Whispers in the Dark - A Case for Murder - Road to Ruin
Rick Gitelson . . . . . . . . . . . . . . . . . . . . . . . . . . . . . . Producer

## PLURABELLE FILMS
PHONE . . . . . . . . . . . . . . . . . . . . . . . . . . . . . . . 310-244-6782
FAX . . . . . . . . . . . . . . . . . . . . . . . . . . . . . . . . 310-842-7364
10125 W. Washington Blvd., #205
Culver City, CA 90232

TYPE  Motion Pictures + Documentaries + Television
DEAL  Phoenix Pictures
CREDITS  Into the West - Last of the High Kings - In the Name of the
Father

Gabriel Byrne . . . . . . . . . . . . . . . . . . . . . . . . Actor/Producer
Amy Singer . . . . . . . . . . . . . . . . . . . . . . . . Sr. Vice President
Christina Giffen . . . . . . . . . . . . . . . . . . . . . . . Vice President

## POCO PRODUCTIONS
PHONE . . . . . . . . . . . . . . . . . . . . . . . . . . . . . . . 310-385-4219
FAX . . . . . . . . . . . . . . . . . . . . . . . . . . . . . . . . 310-385-4205
9333 Wilshire Blvd., 3rd Floor
Beverly Hills, CA 90210

TYPE  Motion Pictures + Television
CREDITS  Dragon: The Bruce Lee Story - Daylight - Dragonheart -
The Rat Pack

Rob Cohen . . . . . . . . . . . . . . . . . . . . Director/Producer/Writer
David Reeder . . . . . . . . . . . . . . . . . . . . . . . . . VP, Development
Creighton Bellinger . . . . . . . . . . . . . . . . . . Asst. to Rob Cohen
Aaron Huffman . . . . . . . . . . . . . . . . . 2nd Asst. to Rob Cohen

## POGUEFILM
PHONE . . . . . . . . . . . . . . . . . . . . . . . . . . . . . . . 213-658-5041
FAX . . . . . . . . . . . . . . . . . . . . . . . . . . . . . . . . 213-651-3536
824 N. Kilkea Drive
Los Angeles, CA 90046

TYPE  Motion Pictures

John Pogue . . . . . . . . . . . . . . . . . . . . . . . . Writer/Producer
Marilyn Roberts . . . . . . . . . . . . . . . . . . . . . Dir., Development

## POLA CO PRODUCTIONS
PHONE . . . . . . . . . . . . . . . . . . . . . . . . . . . . . . . 213-655-5156
FAX . . . . . . . . . . . . . . . . . . . . . . . . . . . . . . . . 213-655-3001
8170 Beverly Blvd., Ste. 100
Los Angeles, CA 90048

TYPE  Television
CREDITS  Backstage at the Zoo - Sleep from A to Zzzz - Winners
Pola Miller . . . . . . . . . . . . . . . . . . . . . . . President/Producer
Cyndi Sayre . . . . . . . . . . . . . . . . . . . . Development Assistant

## POLAKOFF PRODS., CAROL
PHONE . . . . . . . . . . . . . . . . . . . . . . . . . . . . . . . 213-368-8009
100 N. La Cienega, Ste. 110
Los Angeles, CA 90048

TYPE  Motion Pictures + Television
CREDITS  Sexual Advances - Sis & Jerry Levin Story
Carol Polakoff . . . . . . . . . . . . . . . . . . . . . . . . . . . . . . Producer

## POLONE COMPANY, THE
PHONE . . . . . . . . . . . . . . . . . . . . . . . . . . . . . . . 310-309-5707
FAX . . . . . . . . . . . . . . . . . . . . . . . . . . . . . . . . 310-309-5206
5750 Wilshire Blvd.
Los Angeles, CA 90036

TYPE  Motion Pictures + Television
DEAL  Mandalay Entertainment
CREDITS  Riot - The Perfect Body - What We Did That Night
Judith A. Polone . . . . . . . . . . . . . . . . . . . . . Executive Producer
Lindsey Hughes . . . . . . . . . . . . . . . . . . . . . . Dir., Development
Jaynie Smeerin . . . . . . . . . . . . . . . . . Exec. Asst. to Judy Polone

## POLSON COMPANY, THE
PHONE . . . . . . . . . . . . . . . . . . . . . . . . . . . . . . . 626-405-0080
FAX . . . . . . . . . . . . . . . . . . . . . . . . . . . . . . . . 626-795-9039
391 South Madison Avenue
Pasadena, CA 91101

TYPE  Motion Pictures + Television
CREDITS  Timepiece - The Christmas Box - Message From Holly
Beth Polson . . . . . . . . . . . . . . . . . . . . . . . . Executive Producer
Leah Goodman . . . . . . . . . . . . . . . . . . . . . . Executive Assistant

# COMPANIES AND STAFF

## POLYGRAM FILMED ENT.
PHONE . . . . . . . . . . . . . . . . . . 310-777-7700/011-44-171-747-4000
FAX . . . . . . . . . . . . . . . . . . 310-777-7709/011-44-171-747-4499
WEBSITE . . . . . . . . . . . . . . . . . . http://www.reellife.com\pfe
9333 Wilshire Blvd
Beverly Hills, CA 90210
TYPE      Motion Pictures + Television + Syndication
CREDITS      Fargo - The Game - Bean
COMMENTS      Also: 8 St. James's Sq., London United Kingdom SW1Y4JU

Michael Kuhn . . . . . . . . . . . . . . . . . . Chief Executive Officer
Stuart Ells . . . . . . . . . . . . . . . . . . CFO, Worldwide
Stewart Till . . . . . . . . . . . . . . . . . . President, International (UK)
Rick Finkelstein . . . . . . . . . . . . . . . . . . Exec. Vice President
Zanne Devine . . . . . . . . . . . . . . . . . . Sr. Vice President
Jacquie Perryman . . . . . . . . . . . . Sr. VP, Soundtracks (213-856-6631)
Dawn Soler . . . . . . . . . . . . . . . . . . Sr. VP, Music
Shauna Hellewell . . . . . . . . . . VP, Creative Affairs & Acquisitions
Caroline Southey . . . . . . . . . . . . . . . VP, Literary Rights (NY)

## POLYGRAM TELEVISION
PHONE . . . . . . . . . . . . . . . . . . 310-385-4200
FAX . . . . . . . . . . . . . . . . . . 310-385-4201
9333 Wilshire Blvd.
Beverly Hills, CA 90210
TYPE      Television
CREDITS      Big Easy - Motown Live

Bob Sanitsky . . . . . . . . . . . . . . . . . . President
Deana Elwell . . . . . . . . . . . . . . Exec. Vice President & COO
John Huncke . . . . . . . . . . . . . . . . Sr. VP & General Counsel
G. Michael Novelly . . . . . . . . . . . Sr. VP & Chief Financial Officer
Karen Danaher-Dorr . . . . . . . . . . Sr. VP, Movies & Mini-Series
Stephen Gelber . . . . . . . . . . . . Sr. VP, Series Development
Mark Lieber . . . . . . . . . . . . . Sr. VP, Children's Programming
Betsy Braun . . . . . . . . . . . . . . . . . . VP, Research
Michele Moshay . . . . . . . . . . . . . Exec. Asst. to President

## POMPIAN PRODUCTIONS, PAUL
PHONE . . . . . . . . . . . . . . . . . . 310-476-0404
FAX . . . . . . . . . . . . . . . . . . 310-476-9212
EMAIL . . . . . . . . . . . . . . . . . . spycatchp@aol.com
11804 Bel Terrace Street
Los Angeles, CA 90049
TYPE      Motion Pictures + Television
CREDITS      Weekend War - Prepple Murder - Captive City - The Shooter - Time Served

Paul Pompian . . . . . . . . . . . . . . . . . . Producer
John Burrows . . . . . . . . . . . . . . . . . . VP, Production
Polly Middleton . . . . . . . . . . . . . . . . . . VP, Development
Ed Dogans . . . . . . . . . . . . . . . . . . Executive Assistant

## POPULAR ARTS ENT., INC.
PHONE . . . . . . . . . . . . . . . . . . 818-562-6366
FAX . . . . . . . . . . . . . . . . . . 818-562-6373
EMAIL . . . . . . . . . . . . . . . . . . popartstv@aol.com
2006 W. Olive Ave.
Burbank, CA 91506
TYPE      Motion Pictures + Television + Syndication + Interactive Multimedia + Feature Direct to Video + Animation
CREDITS      Popular Arts Ent. News Service - Going Wild With Jeff Corwin - Dr. Katz

Tim Braine . . . . . . . . . . . . . . . . . . Producer/Partner
Kevin Meagher . . . . . . . . . . . . . . . . . . Producer/Partner
Thomas Guttry . . . . . . . . . . . . . . . Business Affairs Manager

## POPULUXE PICTURES
PHONE . . . . . . . . . . . . . . . . . . 213-272-5537
FAX . . . . . . . . . . . . . . . . . . 310-275-1853
EMAIL . . . . . . . . . . . . . . . . . . broad@earthlink.net
9601 Wilshire Blvd., Ste. 1150
Beverly Hills, CA 90210
TYPE      Motion Pictures + Feature Direct to Video
DEAL      Vega 7 Entertainment/Storm Entertainment
CREDITS      Sexbomb - Area 51

Jeff Broadstreet . . . . . . . . . . . . . . . . . . Director/Producer
R.C. Rosenbalm . . . . . . . . . . . . . . . . . . Writer/Development

## PORCHLIGHT ENTERTAINMENT
PHONE . . . . . . . . . . . . . . . . . . 310-477-8400
FAX . . . . . . . . . . . . . . . . . . 310-477-5555
EMAIL . . . . . . . . . . . . . . . . . . porchlt@aol.com
11777 Mississippi Ave.
Los Angeles, CA 90025
TYPE      Motion Pictures + Television + Animation + Feature Direct to Video + Interactive Multimedia
CREDITS      Adventures From The Book of Virtues - Night of the Twisters - Inside The Cold War - Jay Jay the Jet Plane

Bruce D. Johnson . . . . . . . . . . . . . . . . . . President/CEO
William T. Baumann . . . . . . . . . . . . . . . . . . Exec. VP/CFO
Tom Gleason . . . . . . . . . . . . . . . . . . VP, Post Production
Michael D. Jacobs . . . . . . . . . . . . . . . . . . Vice President
Fred Schaefer . . . . . . . . . . . . . . . . . . VP, Animation
Lauren Stogel . . . . . . . . . . . . . . . . . . VP, Business Affairs
Andy Tompkins . . . . . . . . . . . . . . . . . . Associate Producer
Aurora Winter . . . . . . . . . . . . . VP, Development & Production
Karen Butler . . . . . . . . . . . . . Exec. Prod/Dir., Interactive

## PORT STREET FILMS
PHONE . . . . . . . . . . . . . . . . . . 213-850-2555
1041 N. Formosa
W. Hollywood, CA 90046
TYPE      Motion Pictures + Television
CREDITS      One Special Victory - The John Larroquette Show

John Larroquette . . . . . . . . . . . . . . . . . . Actor/Producer
LeeAnn Lambright . . . . . . . . . . . . . . Development/Production

## POST OFFICE, THE
PHONE . . . . . . . . . . . . . . . . . . 818-508-2422
FAX . . . . . . . . . . . . . . . . . . 818-508-2442
EMAIL . . . . . . . . . . . . . . . . . . tpollc@aol.com
5729 Cahuenga Blvd.
N. Hollywood, CA 91601
TYPE      Animation + Documentaries + Motion Pictures + Television + Feature Direct to Video
COMMENTS      Audio, Video and Music Post Production.

Glenn Aulepp . . . . . . . . . . . . . . . . . . Producer
Glen Matisoff . . . . . . . . . . . . . . . . . . Producer

## POWER COMPANY, THE DEREK
PHONE . . . . . . . . . . . . . . . . . . 310-472-4647
FAX . . . . . . . . . . . . . . . . . . 310-472-1705
EMAIL . . . . . . . . . . . . . . . . . . iampower@gte.net
11450 Albata St., Ste. 150
Los Angeles, CA 90049
TYPE      Motion Pictures + Television
CREDITS      The Hot Spot- The Funhouse- The Last Wave
COMMENTS      Intl. Co-productions. Also: Film Music Mgmt. Affiliate of Kahn Power Pictures.

Derek Power . . . . . . . . . . . . . . . . . . President/Partner
Ilene Kahn Power . . . . . . . . . . . . . . . . . . Partner
Sarah Christie Bellwood . . . . . . . . . . . . . . . . . . VP, Development
Marilyn Hooper . . . . . . . . . . . . . . . Chief Financial Officer

## PRATT ENT., INC., CHARLES
PHONE . . . . . . . . . . . . . . . . . . 213-634-1122
FAX . . . . . . . . . . . . . . . . . . 213-634-1131
5700 Wilshire Blvd., Ste. 478
Los Angeles, CA 90036
TYPE      Television
CREDITS      Melrose Place - Life Goes On - Gabriel's Fire - Models Inc. - Sunset Beach

Charles Pratt Jr. . . . . . . . . . . . . . . . . . . Writer/Producer
Jonathan Cycmanick . . . . . . . . . . . . . . . . . . Asst. to Mr. Pratt

## PRELUDE PICTURES
PHONE . . . . . . . . . . . . . . . . . . 561-835-4063
1000 Southern Blvd., Ste. 201
West Palm Beach, FL 33405
TYPE      Motion Pictures + Television
CREDITS      Judicial Consent - Lost In Space - Black Dog

Mark W. Koch . . . . . . . . . . . . . . . . . . Chairman/CEO

# COMPANIES AND STAFF

**PREMIER ATTRACTIONS**
PHONE . . . . . . . . . . . . . . . . . . . . . . . . . . . . 310-281-7308
EMAIL . . . . . . . . . . . . . . . . . . . . premier@relaypoint.net
8306 Wilshire Blvd., Ste. 1030
Beverly Hills, CA 90211

TYPE       Motion Pictures + Feature Direct to Video +
           Documentaries + Interactive Multimedia
CREDITS    Play to Win - Bounty Hunter - Hot Tips - The Main Room
COMMENTS   Deal with Atlantic Syndication Network.
Michael Edwards . . . . . . . . . . . . . . . . . . . . . . Producer/Director/President

**PRESSMAN FILM CORP., EDWARD R.**
PHONE . . . . . . . . . . . . . . . . . 310-271-8383/212-489-3333
FAX . . . . . . . . . . . . . . . . . . . 310-271-9497/212-489-2103
EMAIL . . . . . . . . . . . . . . . . . . . . . pressman@earthlink.com
WEBSITE . . . . . . . . . . . . . . . . . . . http://www.Pressman.com
130 El Camino Dr.
Beverly Hills, CA 90212

TYPE       Motion Pictures
CREDITS    City Hall - The Crow - Reversal of Fortune - Conan - Wall
           Street - Two Girls & A Guy
COMMENTS   ALSO: 130 West 57th St., Ste. 3B N.Y., N.Y. 10019
Edward R. Pressman . . . . . . . . . . . . . . . . . . . . . . . . . . . . President
Christian Halsey Solomon . . . . . . . . . . . . . . Co-Chief Operating Officer
Gregory Woertz . . . . . . . . Co-Chief Operating Officer/Chief Financial Officer
Tom Torii . . . . . . . . . . . . . . . . . . . . . . . . . . . . . . . . . . Controller
Lisa Shapiro . . . . . . . . . . . . . . . . . . . . VP, Business & Legal Affairs
Alessandro Camon . . . . . . . . . . . . . . . . . . . . Sr. VP, Production
Erin O'Rourke . . . . . . . . . . . . . . . . . Dir., Development, East Coast
Zach Schiff-Abrams . . . . . . . . . . . . . . . . . . . . . Creative Affairs
Emily Zalenski . . . . . . . . . . . . . . . . . . . . . . . . Dir., Marketing
Jeff Conner . . . . . . . . . . . . . . . . . . . . . . . . . . VP, Publishing

**PRINCIPAL PRODS., VICTORIA**
PHONE . . . . . . . . . . . . . . . . . . . . . . . . . . . . 310-278-3097
FAX . . . . . . . . . . . . . . . . . . . . . . . . . . . . . . 310-278-1870
120 S. Spalding Dr., Ste. 205
Beverly Hills, CA 90212

TYPE       Television
CREDITS    Don't Touch My Daughter - Inner Sanctum - Sparks -
           Midnight's Child
Victoria Principal . . . . . . . . . . . . . . . . . . . . . . Actress/Producer
Nancy J. Tom . . . . . . . . . . . . . . . . . . . . . . . . . . . . . Assistant

**PRODUCER & MANAGEMENT ENT. GROUP**
PHONE . . . . . . . . . . . . . . . . . . . . . . . . . . . . 213-466-5319
FAX . . . . . . . . . . . . . . . . . . . . . . . . . . . . . . 213-466-1892
6255 Sunset Blvd., Ste. 2000
Los Angeles, CA 90028

TYPE       Motion Pictures
Jerry Goldstein . . . . . . . . . . . . . . . . . . . . . . . . . . . President
Mike Flint . . . . . . . . . . . . . . . . . . . . . . . VP, Creative Affairs
Richard Robbins . . . . . . . . . . . . . . . . . . . . VP, Business Affairs
Curtis Farmer . . . . . . . . . . . . . . . . . . . . . Dir., Creative Affairs
Keith Pusavat . . . . . . . . . . . . . . . . . . . . . . . Dir., Development

**PRODUCERS ENT. GROUP, LTD., THE**
PHONE . . . . . . . . . . . . . . . . . . . . . . . . . . . . 213-634-8634
FAX . . . . . . . . . . . . . . . . . . . . . . . . . . . . . . 213-634-8635
WEBSITE . . . . . . . . . . . . . . . . . . . . . . . . http://tpeg.com
5757 Wilshire Blvd., Penthouse 1
Los Angeles, CA 90036

TYPE       Motion Pictures + Television + Syndication
CREDITS    Sorrow Floats (Showtime) - Passion of Ayn Rand
           (Showtime) - Legion of Fire: Killer Ants (FBC)
Irwin Meyer . . . . . . . . . . . . . . . . . . . . . Chief Executive Officer
Sonny Grosso . . . . . . . . . . . . . . . . . . . . Chief Operating Officer
Lawrence S. Jacobson . . . . . . . . . . . . . . . . . . . . . . . . President
Arthur H. Bernstein . . . . . . . . . . . . . . . . . . . Exec. Vice President
Dick Berg . . . . . . . . . . . . . . . . . . . . . . . . Executive Producer
Peter Crane . . . . . . . . . . . . . . . . . . . . . . . Executive Producer
Allan Marcil . . . . . . . . . . . . . . . . . . . . . . . Executive Producer
Linda Wexelblatt . . . . . . . . . . . . . . . . . . . . Executive Producer
Rhonda Bloom . . . . . . . . . . . . . . . . . . . . . . . VP, Development
Tracy Quinn . . . . . . . . . . . . . . . . . . . . . . . Mgr., Development
Kirt Eftekhar . . . . . . . . . . . . . . . . . . . . . . . Dir., Development

**PRODUCERS GROUP STUDIOS**
PHONE . . . . . . . . . . . . . . . . . . . . . . . . . . . . 719-632-2463
FAX . . . . . . . . . . . . . . . . . . . . . . . . . . . . . . 719-634-6987
EMAIL . . . . . . . . . . . . . . . . . . . . . RUSTYKERN@aol.com
2430-A West Colorado Ave.
Colorado Springs, CO 80904

TYPE       Motion Pictures + Television
CREDITS    Spittin Image - Planet Gone Mad - Pools of Anger
Russell S. Kern . . . . . . . . . . . . . . . . . . . . . . Producer/Director
Steven R. Flanigan . . . . . . . . . . . . . . Producer/Dir. of Photography

**PRODUCTION PARTNERS, INC.**
PHONE . . . . . . . . . . . . . . . . . . . . . . . . . . . . 818-556-5065
4421 Riverside Dr., Ste. 206
Burbank, CA 91505

TYPE       Television + Motion Pictures
CREDITS    Chris Rock - Adam Sandler - Janeane Garofalo - Steve
           Oedekerk.com - David Spade
Sandy Chanley . . . . . . . . . . . . . . . . . . . . . . Producer/Writer
Tom Bull . . . . . . . . . . . . . . . . . . . . . . . . . . . . . . Producer
Keith Truesdell . . . . . . . . . . . . . . . . . . . . . . . . . . . Director

**PRODUCTION SERVICES**
PHONE . . . . . . . . . . . . . . . . . . . . . . . . . . . . 310-394-0047
FAX . . . . . . . . . . . . . . . . . . . . . . . . . . . . . . 310-394-0047
522 Wilshire Blvd., Ste. H
Santa Monica, CA 90401

TYPE       Motion Pictures + Television
CREDITS    My Tutor - Don't Answer The Phone - Unseen Hollywood
Michael Castle . . . . . . . . . . . . . . . . . . . . . . . . . . . President
Allen H. Jones . . . . . . . . . . . . . . . . . . . . . . VP, Creative Affairs
Sylvia Merschel . . . . . . . . . . . . . . . . . . . . . . Dir., Development

**PROFT, PAT**
PHONE . . . . . . . . . . . . . . . . . . . . . . . . . . . . 310-449-4008
FAX . . . . . . . . . . . . . . . . . . . . . . . . . . . . . . 310-449-4011
3000 W. Olympic Blvd., Ste. 1271
Santa Monica, CA 90404

TYPE       Motion Pictures
CREDITS    Hot Shots- Hot Shots Part Deux - Naked Gun 1, 2 1/2 &
           33 1/3 - Wrongfully Accused
COMMENTS   Agent: c/o Bill Block, ICM. No Unsolicited Material!
Pat Proft . . . . . . . . . . . . . . . . . . . . . . Writer/Producer/Director
Patty Sachs . . . . . . . . . . . . . . . . . . . . . . . Asst. to Mr. Proft

**PROMARK ENTERTAINMENT GROUP**
PHONE . . . . . . . . . . . . . . . . . . . . . . . . . . . . 213-878-0404
FAX . . . . . . . . . . . . . . . . . . . . . . . . . . . . . . 213-878-0486
EMAIL . . . . . . . . . . . . . . . . . . . . . promark@ix.netcom.com
3599 Cahuenga Blvd. W., 3rd Fl.
Los Angeles, CA 90068

TYPE       Motion Pictures + Television + Feature Direct to Video
CREDITS    The Invader - The Shadowmen - Johnny 2.0 - The Vivero
           Letter - Breed Apart
COMMENTS   Also: TV films & TV series.
Jonathan Kramer . . . . . . . . . . . . . . . . . . . . . . . . . . President
Steve Beswick . . . . . . . . . . . . . . . . . . . . . . . . . VP, Production
Gil-Adrienne Wishnick . . . . . . . . . . . . . . . . . VP, Creative Affairs
Rick Shane . . . . . . . . . . . . . . . . . . . . . . Chief Financial Officer
Amy Krell . . . . . . . . . . . . . . . . . . . . . . . . Production Executive

# COMPANIES AND STAFF

**PROPAGANDA FILMS**
PHONE . . . . . . . . . . . . . . . . . . . . . . . . . . . . . . . . . . . . . 213-462-6400
FAX . . . . . . . . . . . . . . . . . . . . . . . . . . . . . . . . . . . . . . . . 213-463-7874
940 N. Mansfield Ave.
Los Angeles, CA 90038-3197

| | |
|---|---|
| TYPE | Motion Pictures + Television |
| CREDITS | The Game - The Portrait of a Lady - Sleepers - A Thousand Acres - Your Friends and Neighbors |
| COMMENTS | A Division of PolyGram. Also: Music Videos and Commericals. |

Steve Golin . . . . . . . . . . . . . . . . . . . . . . . . . . . . . . . . . . . Chairman
James Tauber . . . . . . . . . . . . . . . . . . . . . . . . . . . . . . President/COO
Clive Ellis . . . . . . . . . . . . . . . . . . . . . . . . . . . . . Chief Financial Officer
Stephen Dickstein . . . . . . . . . . . . . . . . . . Pres., Commercial Division
Paul H. Green . . . . . . . . . . . . . . . . . . . . . . . . . . Exec. Vice President
Laurie Malaga . . . . . . . . . . . . . . Exec. Producer, Music Video Division
Elizabeth Lane . . . . . . . . . . . . . . . . . . . . . . . Sr. VP, Motion Picts.
David Boyle . . . . . . . . . . . . . . . . . . . VP, Legal & Business Affairs
Guymon Casady . . . . . . . . . . . . . . . . . . . . . VP, Creative Affairs
Jenna Cooper . . . . . . . . . . . . . . . . . . . . . . . VP, Creative Affairs
Tim Clawson . . . . . . . . . . . . . . . . . . . . . . . . . Head, Production
Beth Holden . . . . . . . . . . . . . . . . . . . Head, Management Division
Laurie Ross . . . . . . . . . . . . . . . . . . . . . . . . . . . Dir., Development
Melissa Sagerian . . . . . . . . . . . . . . . Dir., Contract Administration
Glenn Gregory . . . . . . . . . . . . . . . . . . . . . . . . . . . . Story Editor

***PROUD MARY ENTERTAINMENT**
PHONE . . . . . . . . . . . . . . . . . . . . . . . . . . . . . . . . . . . 213-658-0458
FAX . . . . . . . . . . . . . . . . . . . . . . . . . . . . . . . . . . . . . 213-658-7247
EMAIL . . . . . . . . . . . . . . . . . . . . . . . . . proudmaryent@earthlink.net
Saban Entertainment
8306 Wilshire Blvd., Ste. 460
Beverly Hills, CA 90211

| | |
|---|---|
| TYPE | Motion Pictures + Television + Animation |
| DEAL | Saban Entertainment |

Mary L. Aloe . . . . . . . . . . . . . . . . . . . . . . . . . . Executive Producer
Jay Jacobs . . . . . . . . . . . . . . . . . . . . . . . . . . . Dir., Development
John Downey III . . . . . . . . . . . . . . . . . . . . . . . . . . . . Producer
Richard A. Teeter . . . . . . . . . . . . . . . . . . . . . . . Executive Assistant

**PRUFROCK PICTURES**
PHONE . . . . . . . . . . . . . . . . . . . . . . . . . . . . . . . . . . . 310-285-2360
FAX . . . . . . . . . . . . . . . . . . . . . . . . . . . . . . . . . . . . . 310-888-3595
335 N. Maple Dr., Ste. 135
Beverly Hills, CA 90210

| | |
|---|---|
| TYPE | Motion Pictures + Television |
| DEAL | Castle Rock Entertainment/PolyGram Television |
| CREDITS | French Kiss - Northern Lights |

Meg Ryan . . . . . . . . . . . . . . . . . . . . . . . . . . . . Actress/Producer
Nina R. Sadowsky . . . . . . . . . . . . . . . . . . . . . . . . . . President
Michael Gorak . . . . . . . . . . . . . . . . . . . . . . . . . VP, Development
Ali Woodward . . . . . . . . . . . . . . . . . . . . . . . . . Dir., Development
Cathy Hutchinson . . . . . . . . . . . . . . . . . . Development Assistant
Leslie Adler . . . . . . . . . . . . . . . . . . . . . . . . . Asst. to Meg Ryan

**PUNCH PRODUCTIONS**
PHONE . . . . . . . . . . . . . . . . 212-595-8800/310-442-4888
EMAIL . . . . . . . . . . . . . . . . . . . . . . . . maureenf@punch21.com
1926 Broadway #305
New York, NY 10023

| | |
|---|---|
| TYPE | Motion Pictures |
| CREDITS | Outbreak - Death of a Salesman - American Buffalo - Tootsie - Mad City - The Blouse Man - Wag the Dog |
| COMMENTS | Also: Punch 21 at 11661 San Vicente Blvd., Los Angeles, CA 90049 |

Dustin Hoffman . . . . . . . . . . . . . . . . . . . . . . . . . . . . . Owner
Jay Cohen . . . . . . . . . . . . . . . . . . . . . . . . . . . . . Partner (LA)
Lee Gottsegen . . . . . . . . . . . . . . . . . . . . . . . . . . . . President
Joanne Moore . . . . . . . . . . . . . . . . . . . Pres., Production (LA)
Laura Gherardi . . . . . . . . . . . . . . . . . . . . . . . . VP, Production
Christopher Santos . . . . . . . . . . . . . . . . . . . . . . VP, Development
Jay Schinderman . . . . . . . . . . . . . . . . . Development Associate (LA)
Murray Schisgal . . . . . . . . . . . . . . . . . . . . . . . . . . . Producer

**QUINCE PRODS., INC.**
PHONE . . . . . . . . . . . . . . . . . . . . . . . . . . . . . . . . . . . 213-436-0677
FAX . . . . . . . . . . . . . . . . . . . . . . . . . . . . . . . . . . . . . 213-436-0246
12400 Ventura Blvd., Suite 371
Studio City, CA 91604

| | |
|---|---|
| TYPE | Motion Pictures + Television |
| CREDITS | Payback |

Edward Asner . . . . . . . . . . . . . . . . . . President/Exec. Producer
Patricia Egan . . . . . . . . . . . . . . . . . . . . . . . Executive Assistant

**QUINCY JONES*DAVID SALZMAN ENTERTAINMENT**
PHONE . . . . . . . . . . . . . . . . . . . . . . . . . . . . . . . 213-874-2009
FAX . . . . . . . . . . . . . . . . . . . . . . . . . . . . . . . . . 213-874-3364
3800 Barham Blvd., Ste. 503
Los Angeles, CA 90068

| | |
|---|---|
| TYPE | Motion Pictures |
| CREDITS | Fresh Prince of Bel Air - Jenny Jones - In The House - Mad TV - Academy Awards |

Quincy Jones . . . . . . . . . . . . . . . . . . . . Co-Chief Executive Officer
David Salzman . . . . . . . . . . . . . . . . . . . Co-Chief Executive Officer
Jerry Gottlieb . . . . . . . . . . . . . . . . . . . . Chief Operating Officer
Rita Katsotis . . . . . . . . . . . . . . . . . . . . . . . . . . VP, Production
Jay Imamoto . . . . . . . . . . . . . . . . . . Exec. Dir., Financial Services

**QUINN PRODUCTIONS**
PHONE . . . . . . . . . . . . . . . . . . . . . . . . . . . . . . . 818-787-5952
FAX . . . . . . . . . . . . . . . . . . . . . . . . . . . . . . . . . 818-787-5952
P.O. Box 8415
Van Nuys, CA 91409

| | |
|---|---|
| TYPE | Motion Pictures + Television |
| CREDITS | Broken Rose - Cheerleader Camp - Fallen Angel - Goldy 1, 2 & 3 |

John Quinn . . . . . . . . . . . . . . . . . . . . . . . . . . . . . . President
Kimberlee Duplechien . . . . . . . . . . . . . . . . . . . Dir., Development

**R. EDWARDS PRODS./R. EDWARDS FILMS**
PHONE . . . . . . . . . . . . . . . . . . . . . . . . . . . . . . . 213-462-2212
6922 Hollywood Blvd., Ste. 415
Hollywood, CA 90028

| | |
|---|---|
| TYPE | Television + Motion Pictures + Animation |
| CREDITS | People's Court - This Is Your Life - Bzzz - Truth or Consequences - Annabelle's Wish |
| COMMENTS | Edwards/Billett - TV only, R. Edwards - TV, MP & Animation. |

Ralph Edwards . . . . . . . . . . . Executive Producer/Pres. Ralph Edwards Prods.
Stu Billett . . . . . . . . . . . . . . Executive Producer/Pres. Stu Billett Prods.
Barbara Dunn-Leonard . . . . . . . . . . . . . . . . . . . Executive Producer
James B. Pollock . . . . . . . . . . . . . . . . . . . General Counsel/COO
Gary Edwards . . . . . . . . . . . . . . . . . . . . . VP/Executive Producer

**R.A.M.M. ENTERTAINMENT, INC**
PHONE . . . . . . . . . . . . . . . . . . . . . . . . . . . . . . . 818-713-8144
FAX . . . . . . . . . . . . . . . . . . . . . . . . . . . . . . . . . 818-888-7083
EMAIL . . . . . . . . . . . . . . . . . . . . . . . . rammfilms@aol.com
6301 DeSoto Avenue, Ste. D
Woodland Hills, CA 91367

| | |
|---|---|
| TYPE | Animation + Documentaries + Feature Direct to Video + Motion Pictures + Television + Syndication |
| CREDITS | Blood Thirsty - The Man in the Iron Mask - Pariah |
| COMMENTS | Production & Distribution company with on-site post-production facility. Financing. |

Glen Hartford . . . . . . . . . . . . . . . . . . . . . . . . . . . . . President
Rowan Sutherland . . . . . . . . . . . . . . . . . . . VP, TV Development
Alicia Hollinger . . . . . . . . . . . . . Dir., Co-Productions/Acquisitions
Jennifer Nakamori . . . . . . . . . . . . . . . . . . . Assistant to President

**RADIANT PRODUCTIONS**
PHONE . . . . . . . . . . . . . . . . . . . . . . . . . . . . . . . 310-656-1400
FAX . . . . . . . . . . . . . . . . . . . . . . . . . . . . . . . . . 310-656-1408
914 Montana Ave., 2nd Floor
Santa Monica, CA 90403

| | |
|---|---|
| TYPE | Motion Pictures + Television |
| DEAL | Sony Pictures Entertainment |
| CREDITS | Air Force One - Outbreak - In The Line of Fire - Das Boot |

Wolfgang Petersen . . . . . . . . . . . . . . . . . . . . Director/Producer
Gail Katz . . . . . . . . . . . . . . . . . . . . . . . . . . President/Producer
Samuel Dickerman . . . . . . . . . . . . . . . . . . . . . . Vice President
Susan Stein . . . . . . . . . . . . . . . . . . . . . . . . Creative Executive
Anthony Dickson . . . . . . . . . . . . . . . . . . . Asst. to Mr. Dickerman
Jacqueline King . . . . . . . . . . . . . . . . . . . . Asst. to Mr. Petersen
Dave Markus . . . . . . . . . . . . . . . . . . . . . . . . Asst. to Ms. Katz

**RADIO...WITH PICTURES**
PHONE . . . . . . . . . . . . . . . . . . . . . . . . . . . . . . . 213-462-7261
FAX . . . . . . . . . . . . . . . . . . . . . . . . . . . . . . . . . 213-462-3432
1956 N. Cahuenga Blvd.
Hollywood, CA 90068

| | |
|---|---|
| TYPE | Motion Pictures + Television + Syndication |
| CREDITS | Why Planes Go Down - Inside A Crash - The Players (CNN) |

Peter Isacksen . . . . . . . . . . . . . . . . . . . . . . . . . . . . . Partner
Bert Berdis . . . . . . . . . . . . . . . . . . . . . . . . . . . . . . . Partner
Deborah Kennedy . . . . . . . . . . . . . . . . . . . . . . . . . . Producer
Martha Sloan . . . . . . . . . . . . . . . . . . . . . . . Associate Producer
Dean Howser . . . . . . . . . . . . . . . . . . . . . . . Production Assistant

**RADLERFILM**
PHONE . . . . . . . . . . . . . . . . . . . . . . . . . . . 805-374-1913
EMAIL . . . . . . . . . . . . . . . . . . . . . . . . . bobrad@aol.com
1393 La Granada Dr.
Thousand Oaks, CA 91362

TYPE         Motion Pictures + Television
CREDITS      Best of the Best 1 & 2 - Soldier of Fortune (TV Series) -
             TNT (HBO World Premiere Movie)
COMMENTS     Not accepting scripts at this time.
Kitty Radler . . . . . . . . . . . . . . . . . . . . . . . . . . . . . Producer
Robert Radler . . . . . . . . . . . . . . . . . . . . . . . Producer/Director

**RADMIN COMPANY, THE**
PHONE . . . . . . . . . . . . . . . . . . . . . . . . . . . 310-274-9515
FAX . . . . . . . . . . . . . . . . . . . . . . . . . . . . . 310-274-0739
EMAIL . . . . . . . . . . . . . . . . . . . . . . . . . radminco@aol.com
9201 Wilshire Blvd., Ste. 305
Beverly Hills, CA 90210

TYPE         Motion Pictures + Television
CREDITS      The Fantasticks - Mastermind - Next Best Thing - Witch
             Hunt - One Neck
Linne Radmin . . . . . . . . . . . . . . . . . . . . . . . . . . . . . Producer
Stacy Abrams . . . . . . . . . . . . . . . . . . . . . . . . . . . . . Producer
Jeanne O'Brien . . . . . . . . . . . . . . . . . . . . . . . . . . . . Producer
Greg Clark . . . . . . . . . . . . . . . . . . . . . . Development Assistant
Ryan McCoy . . . . . . . . . . . . . . . . . . . . . . Development Assistant

**RAFFAELLA PRODUCTIONS, INC.**
PHONE . . . . . . . . . . . . . . . . . . . . . . . . . . . 818-777-2655
FAX . . . . . . . . . . . . . . . . . . . . . . . . . . . . . 818-866-1571
Universal City Studios
100 Universal City Plaza, Bung. 73
Universal City, CA 91608-1085

TYPE         Motion Pictures + Television
CREDITS      Daylight - Dragonheart - Kull - Dragon: Bruce Lee Story
Raffaella De Laurentiis . . . . . . . . . . . . . . . . President/Producer
Hester Hargett . . . . . . . . . . . . . . . . . . . . Exec. VP/Co-Producer
Ed Wacek . . . . . . . . . . . . . . . . . . . . . . . . . Sr. VP, Production
Steve O'Corr . . . . . . . . . . . . . . . . . . . . . . . . VP, Operations
Erik Jessen . . . . . . . . . . . . . . . . . . . . . . . . . . Story Editor

**RAINBOW FILM CO./RAINBOW RELEASING**
PHONE . . . . . . . . . . . . . . . . . . . . . . . . . . . 310-271-0202
FAX . . . . . . . . . . . . . . . . . . . . . . . . . . . . . 310-271-2753
EMAIL . . . . . . . . . . . . . . . . . . . . rainbow@webstorm.com
WEBSITE . . . . . . . . . . . . . . . . . . . . . http://www.jaglom.com
9165 Sunset Blvd., Ste. 300
Los Angeles, CA 90069

TYPE         Motion Pictures
CREDITS      Last Summer In The Hamptons - Babyfever - Eating - Deja
             Vu - New Year's Day
COMMENTS     Also Distribution. Deal with Revere Ent., London.
Henry Jaglom . . . . . . . . . . . . . . . . . . . . . . . . . . . President
Judith Wolinsky . . . . . . . . . . . . . . . . . . Producer/Development

**RAINCITY**
PHONE . . . . . . . . . . . . . . . . . . . . . . . . . . . 310-578-2114
FAX . . . . . . . . . . . . . . . . . . . . . . . . . . . . . 310-578-2248
2554 Lincoln Blvd., Ste. 545
Marina del Rey, CA 90291

TYPE         Motion Pictures
CREDITS      Afterglow - The Moderns - Choose Me - Mrs. Parker and
             the Vicious Circle
Alan Rudolph . . . . . . . . . . . . . . . . . . . . . . . . . . . Director
David Blocker . . . . . . . . . . . . . . . . . . . . . . . . . . . Producer

**RAINDANCE PICTURES**
PHONE . . . . . . . . . . . . . . . . . . . . . . . . . . . 201-444-9700
FAX . . . . . . . . . . . . . . . . . . . . . . . . . . . . . 201-444-6486
45 N. Broad St., Ste. 402
Ridgewood, NJ 07450

TYPE         Motion Pictures
CREDITS      A Chill In The Air
Fred Strype . . . . . . . . . . . . . . . . . . . . . . . Producer/Partner

**RAJSKI PRODUCTIONS, PEGGY**
PHONE . . . . . . . . . . . . . . . . . . . . . . . . . . . 310-829-0173
FAX . . . . . . . . . . . . . . . . . . . . . . . . . . . . . 310-829-0193
924 Yale St.
Santa Monica, CA 90403

TYPE         Motion Pictures
CREDITS      Home For the Holidays - Used People - Little Man Tate
Peggy Rajski . . . . . . . . . . . . . . . . . . . . . . . Producer/Director

**RAMBALDI ENTERPRISES, DAVID**
PHONE . . . . . . . . . . . . . . . . . . . . . . . . . . . 909-584-2453
FAX . . . . . . . . . . . . . . . . . . . . . . . . . . . . . 909-584-2453
P.O. Box 3248
Big Bear Lake, CA 92314

TYPE         Motion Pictures + Television
CREDITS      Eyes of The Beholder - Rainy Day - Slave Master
David Rambaldi . . . . . . . . . . . . . . . . . . . . . . . . . President
Neil Rambaldi . . . . . . . . . . . . Sr. VP, Creative Affairs/Creative Consultant

**RANDAN PRODS., INC.**
PHONE . . . . . . . . . . . . . . . . . . . . . . . . . . . 310-838-8883
EMAIL . . . . . . . . . . . . . . . . . . . . . . . . . randfilms@aol.com
10424 Cheviot Dr.
Los Angeles, CA 90064-4408

TYPE         Motion Pictures + Television
CREDITS      Suspect - Race For Glory - Impromptu - Donor - All Lies
             End In Murder
COMMENTS     Distribution Deal with Hamdon Entertainment.
Daniel A. Sherkow . . . . . . . . . . . . . . . . . . . . . . . President
Randi Sunshine . . . . . . . . . . . . . . . . . . . . . . VP, Development

**RANDWELL PRODUCTIONS**
PHONE . . . . . . . . . . . . . . . . . . . . . . . . . . . 310-399-2980
FAX . . . . . . . . . . . . . . . . . . . . . . . . . . . . . 310-399-5501
1608 Pacific Ave., Ste. 205
Venice, CA 90291

TYPE         Motion Pictures + Television
CREDITS      Two Mother Fight for Zachery - Amelia Earhart: - The
             Final Flight - Almost Perfect Bank Robbery
COMMENTS     Distribution deal through Hamdon Entertainment.
Randy Robinson . . . . . . . . . . . . . . . President/Executive Producer
Tom Kageff . . . . . . . . . . . . . . . . . . . . . . . . VP, Development

**RANKIN/BASS PRODUCTIONS**
PHONE . . . . . . . . . . . . . . . . . . . . . . . . . . . 212-582-4017
24 W. 55th St.
New York, NY 10019

TYPE         Motion Pictures + Animation + Television
DEAL         Morgan Creek Prods.
CREDITS      The Hobbit - The Last Unicorn - Thundercats - The King
             & I
COMMENTS     Animated motion pictures.
Arthur Rankin . . . . . . . . . . . . . . . . . . . . . . . . President/CEO
Peter Bakalian . . . . . . . . . . . . . . Sr. VP, Production & Development
Norman Topper . . . . . . . . . . . . . . . . . . Vice President/Treasurer

**RANSOHOFF PRODUCTIONS, INC., MARTIN**
PHONE . . . . . . . . . . . . . . . . . . . . . . . . . . . 310-551-2680
FAX . . . . . . . . . . . . . . . . . . . . . . . . . . . . . 310-551-2094
400 South Beverly Drive, Ste. 308
Beverly Hills, CA 90212

TYPE         Motion Pictures
CREDITS      Guilty As Sin - Jagged Edge - Switching Channels - Class
Martin Ransohoff . . . . . . . . . . . . . . . . . . . . . . . . . Producer
Bob Robinson . . . . . . . . . . . . . . . . . . . . . . . Vice President
Carol Gronner . . . . . . . . . . . . . . . . . Creative Asst./Operations

***RASKIN PRODUCTIONS, BONNIE**
PHONE . . . . . . . . . . . . . . . . . . . . . . . . . . . 818-840-7571
FAX . . . . . . . . . . . . . . . . . . . . . . . . . . . . . 818-840-7519
330 Bob Hope Drive, Ste. 117
Burbank, CA 91523

TYPE         Television
DEAL         NBC Studios
CREDITS      Killing Mr. Griffin
Bonnie Raskin . . . . . . . . . . . . . . . . . . . . . Executive Producer
Amy Schultz . . . . . . . . . . . . . . . . . . . . Development Assistant

**RASKOFF PRODUCTIONS, KEN**
PHONE . . . . . . . . . . . . . . . . . . . . . . . . . . . 310-557-7700
FAX . . . . . . . . . . . . . . . . . . . . . . . . . . . . . 310-557-6021
ABC Pictures
2020 Avenue of the Stars, 5th Floor
Los Angeles, CA 90067

TYPE         Television
DEAL         ABC Pictures
Ken Raskoff . . . . . . . . . . . . . . . . . . . . . . Executive Producer
Curtis Chin . . . . . . . . . . . . . . . . . . . . . . . . . Development

# COMPANIES AND STAFF

**RASTAR PRODUCTIONS**
PHONE . . . . . . . . . . . . . . . . . . . . . . . . . . . . . . 310-244-7871
FAX . . . . . . . . . . . . . . . . . . . . . . . . . . . . . . . 310-244-2331
Sony Pictures Studios
10202 W. Washington Blvd., Hepburn West
Culver City, CA 90232-3195
TYPE        Motion Pictures
DEAL        Columbia Pictures
CREDITS     To Gillian on Her 37th Birthday - Steel Magnolias - Harriet
            The Spy

Ray Stark . . . . . . . . . . . . . . . . . . . . . . . . . . . . . Chairman
Marykay Powell . . . . . . . . . . . . . . . . . . . . . . . . . . President
Janet Garrison . . . . . . . . . . . . . . . . . . . . . . . VP, Administration
Andrew Lee . . . . . . . . . . . . . . . . . . . . . . . . . Dir., Development
Michael Cieply . . . . . . . . . . . . . . . . . . . . . . . . . . Consultant
Don Safran . . . . . . . . . . . . . . . . . . . . . . . . . . . . Consultant
Michael Sudmeier . . . . . . . . . . . . . . . . . . . . . . . . . Consultant
Theresa De La Paz . . . . . . . . . . . . . . . . . . . . Asst. to Mr. Stark
Arden Doss . . . . . . . . . . . . . . . . . . . . . . . . Asst. to Ms. Powell

***RAT ENTERTAINMENT**
PHONE . . . . . . . . . . . . . . . . . . . . . . . . . . . . . . 310-248-6040
FAX . . . . . . . . . . . . . . . . . . . . . . . . . . . . . . . 310-858-8921
9060 Santa Monica Blvd., Ste. 350
Los Angeles, CA 90069
TYPE        Motion Pictures
DEAL        New Line Cinema
CREDITS     Money Talks - Rush Hour

Brett Ratner . . . . . . . . . . . . . . . . . . . . . . . Director/Producer
Alyss Dixson . . . . . . . . . . . . . . . . . . . . . . . Dir., Development
John Cheng . . . . . . . . . . . . . . . . . . . . . Development Associate
Anita Chang . . . . . . . . . . . . . . . . . . . . Exec. Asst. to Mr. Ratner

***RAYLIN ENTERTAINMENT**
PHONE . . . . . . . . . . . . . . . . . . . . . . . . . . . . . . 818-777-6434
FAX . . . . . . . . . . . . . . . . . . . . . . . . . . . . . . . 818-866-2526
100 Universal City Plaza
Bldg. 473, Ste. 301
Universal City, CA 91608
TYPE        Animation + Motion Pictures + Television + Syndication
DEAL        Universal Pictures
CREDITS     Ricki Lake - Missing Persons

Kevin Makowski . . . . . . . . . . . . . . . . . . . . . . . . . . Producer
Leslie Thomas . . . . . . . . . . . . . . . . . . . . . . . . . . . Assistant

***RAZORS EDGE PRODUCTIONS, INC.**
PHONE . . . . . . . . . . . . . . . . . . . . . . . . . . . . . . 213-634-8920
FAX . . . . . . . . . . . . . . . . . . . . . . . . . . . . . . . 213-634-8921
EMAIL . . . . . . . . . . . . . . . . . . . . . . . . ageorge@r-edge.com
5225 Wilshire Blvd., Ste. 611
Los Angeles, CA 90036
TYPE        Motion Pictures + Television
CREDITS     Demolition Man - Richie Rich

Jacqueline George . . . . . . . . . . . . . . . . . . . . . . . . President
Trevor Waterson . . . . . . . . . . . . . . . . . . . . . . . VP, Production
Amber George . . . . . . . . . . . . . . . . . . . . . . . . . Story Editor

**REALLY BIG SHOE PRODS.**
PHONE . . . . . . . . . . . . . . . . . . . . . . . . . . . . . . 818-985-8008
FAX . . . . . . . . . . . . . . . . . . . . . . . . . . . . . . . 818-985-7117
4852 Morella Ave.
Valley Village, CA 91607
TYPE        Motion Pictures + Television + Documentaries
CREDITS     Word

Mindy Molinary . . . . . . . . . . . . . . . . . . . . . . President/Producer

**REARGUARD PRODUCTIONS, INC.**
PHONE . . . . . . . . . . . . . . . . . . . . . . . . . . . . . . 213-937-1570
FAX . . . . . . . . . . . . . . . . . . . . . . . . . . . . . . . 213-937-0564
6030 Wilshire Blvd., Ste. 300
Los Angeles, CA 90036-3617
TYPE        Motion Pictures + Television + Syndication
CREDITS     Tales From the Crypt - Survive the Savage Sea - Land
            That Time Forgot - Rock, Rock, Rock!

Max J. Rosenberg . . . . . . . . . . . . . . . . . . . . President/Producer
Julie G. Moldo Jones . . . . . . . . . . . . . . . . . Exec. Vice President

**RECORDED PICTURE COMPANY**
PHONE . . . . . . . . . . . . . . . . . 213-460-4747/0171-6362251
FAX . . . . . . . . . . . . . . . . . . . 213-936-4913/0171-6362261
7001 Melrose Ave.
Los Angeles, CA 90038
TYPE        Motion Pictures
CREDITS     The Last Emperor - Stealing Beauty - Crash - Blood &
            Wine - Little Buddha - The Brave
COMMENTS    ALSO: 24 Hanway St., London W1P 9DD

Jeremy Thomas . . . . . . . . . . . . . . . . . . . . Producer/Chairman
Hercules Bellville . . . . . . . . . . . . . . . . . . . Head, Development
Chris Auty . . . . . . . . . . . . . . . . . . . . . . . Managing Director
Alexandra Stone . . . . . . . . . . . . . . . . . . . . Sr. Vice President
Stephan Mallmann . . . . . . . . . . . . . . . . . . . . Head, Finance
Peter Watson . . . . . . . . . . . . . . . . . . . Head, Business Affairs
Jocelyn Jones . . . . . . . . . . . . . Exec. Asst. to Jeremy Thomas
Leoni Cotgrove . . . . . . . . . . . . . . . . . . . Asst. to Chris Auty
Stuart Cooke . . . . . . . . . . . . . . . . . . . . Company Accountant
Simon Gosling . . . . . . . . . . . . . . . . . . . Production Assistant

**RED DIAMOND COMPANY, THE**
PHONE . . . . . . . . . . . . . . . . . . . . . . . . . . . . . . 310-285-9533
FAX . . . . . . . . . . . . . . . . . . . . . . . . . . . . . . . 310-285-0955
9507 Santa Monica Blvd. Ste. 217
Beverly Hills, CA 90210
TYPE        Motion Pictures + Television

Rene Sheridan . . . . . . . . . . . . . . . . . . . . . . . . . . . Producer

**RED HEN PRODUCTIONS**
PHONE . . . . . . . . . . . . . . . . . . . . . . . . . . . . . . 818-560-1716
FAX . . . . . . . . . . . . . . . . . . . . . . . . . . . . . . . 818-563-9887
EMAIL . . . . . . . . . . . . . . . . . . . . . . redhen@earthlink.com
500 S. Buena Vista St., Anim.Bldg.#1F-15
Burbank, CA 91521
TYPE        Motion Pictures + Feature Direct to Video + Interactive
            Multimedia
DEAL        Walt Disney Pictures/Touchstone Pictures
CREDITS     Honey I Shrunk/Blew Up the Kid - Re-Animator - Fortress
            - Space Truckers - Ice Cream Suit

Stuart Gordon . . . . . . . . . . . . . . . . . . Director/Writer/Producer
Scott Watson . . . . . . . . . . . . . . . . . . . . . . . . . . Development

**RED HOUR FILMS**
PHONE . . . . . . . . . . . . . . . . . . . . . . . . . . . . . . 310-289-2565
FAX . . . . . . . . . . . . . . . . . . . . . . . . . . . . . . . 310-289-5988
193 N. Roberston Blvd.
Beverly Hills, CA 90211
TYPE        Motion Pictures + Television
DEAL        Twentieth Century Fox-Fox 2000 (LA)
CREDITS     The Ben Stiller Show - Reality Bites - The Cable Guy -
            There's Something About Mary - The Suburbans

Ben Stiller . . . . . . . . . . . . . . . . . . . . . . . Filmmaker/Actor
George Linardos . . . . . . . . . . . . . . . . . . . . . . . . . Producer
Dara Cohen . . . . . . . . . . . . . . . . . . . . . . . Creative Executive
Erin Alexander . . . . . . . . . . . . . . . . . . . . . Asst. to Ben Stiller
Maggie Carroll . . . . . . . . . Asst. to George Linardos/Story Editor

***RED MULLET, INC.**
PHONE . . . . . . . . . . . . . . . . . . . . . . . . . . . . . . 310-244-3364
FAX . . . . . . . . . . . . . . . . . . . . . . . . . . . . . . . 310-244-0390
Sony Pictures Entertainment
10202 W. Washington Blvd., Lean #315
Culver City, CA 90232
TYPE        Motion Pictures
DEAL        Sony Pictures Entertainment
CREDITS     Leaving Las Vegas - One Night Stand - Death & Loss of
            Sexual Innocence - Internal Affairs

Mike Figgis . . . . . . . . . . . . . . . . . . . . . . . Director/Producer
Annie Stewart . . . . . . . . . . . . . . . . . . . . . . . . . . Producer
Doug Van Doren . . . . . . . . . . . . . . . . . . . . . . . Development

**RED STROKES ENTERTAINMENT**
PHONE . . . . . . . . . . . . . . . . . . . . . . . . . . . . . . 310-786-7887
9465 Wilshire Blvd., Ste. 511
Beverly Hills, CA 90212
TYPE        Motion Pictures

Garth Brooks . . . . . . . . . . . . . . . . . . . . . . . Talent/Producer
Lisa Sanderson . . . . . . . . . . . . . Development Executive/Producer

# COMPANIES AND STAFF

**RED WAGON PRODS.**
PHONE . . . . . . . . . . . . . . . . . . . . . . . . . . . . . . . . . . 310-244-4466
FAX . . . . . . . . . . . . . . . . . . . . . . . . . . . . . . . . . . . . . 310-244-1480
Sony Studios
10202 W. Washington Blvd., Capra, #112
Culver City, CA 90232-3195

TYPE       Motion Pictures + Television + Animation
DEAL       Sony Pictures Entertainment
CREDITS       Wolf - Working Girl - The Craft

Doug Wick . . . . . . . . . . . . . . . . . . . . . . . . . . Producer/President
Donald Laventhall . . . . . . . . . . . . . . . . . Exec. VP, Production
Melissa Reid . . . . . . . . . . . . . . . . . . . . . . . . Dir., Development
Karen White . . . . . . . . . . . . . . . . . . . . . . . . . . . . . Story Editor
Ilyse McKimmie . . . . . . . . . . . . . . . . . . . Asst. To D. Laventhall
Nancy Safran . . . . . . . . . . . . . . . . . . . . . . . . . Asst. to D. Wick

**REDEEMABLE FEATURES**
PHONE . . . . . . . . . . . . . . . . . . . . . . . . . . . . . . . . 212-685-8585
FAX . . . . . . . . . . . . . . . . . . . . . . . . . . . . . . . . . . . 212-685-1455
EMAIL . . . . . . . . . . . . . . . . . . . . information@redeemable.com
WEBSITE . . . . . . . . . . . . . . . . . . . . . . . http://www.redeemable.com
381 Park Ave. South, PH
New York, NY 10016

TYPE       Motion Pictures
CREDITS       Kiss Me Guido - Smoke - The Hairy Bird - Lulu on the Bridge

Ira Deutchman . . . . . . . . . . . . . . . . . . . . . . . . . . . . . . . Partner
Greg Johnson . . . . . . . . . . . . . . . . . . . . . . . . . . . . . . . . Partner
Peter Newman . . . . . . . . . . . . . . . . . . . . . . . . . . . . . . . Partner
Melissa Chesman . . . . . . . . . . . . . . . . . . . . . Dir., Development
Brad Grossman . . . . . . . . . . . . . . . . . . . . Asst. to the Producers

**REDLER ENTERTAINMENT, DAN**
PHONE . . . . . . . . . . . . . . . . . . . . . . . . . . . . . . . . 818-776-0938
FAX . . . . . . . . . . . . . . . . . . . . . . . . . . . . . . . . . . . 818-705-6870
18730 Hatteras St., Unit 8
Tarzana, CA 91356

TYPE       Motion Pictures + Television + Feature Direct to Video
CREDITS       Profile for Murder - In His Father's Shoes

Dan Redler . . . . . . . . . . . . . . . . . . . . . . . . . . . . . . . . Producer

**REEL LIFE WOMEN**
PHONE . . . . . . . . . . . . . . . . . . . . . . . . . . . . . . . . 310-271-4722
FAX . . . . . . . . . . . . . . . . . . . . . . . . . . . . . . . . . . . 310-274-0503
EMAIL . . . . . . . . . . . . . . . . . ReelLifeWomen@compuserve.com
10158 Hollow Glen Circle
Bel Air, CA 90077-2112

TYPE       Motion Pictures + Television
CREDITS       NAVY SEALS - The Healing Force
COMMENTS       Women oriented pictures/MOW's & Mini-series.

Brenda Feigen . . . . . . . . . . . . . . . . . . . Co-President/Producer
Joanne Parrent . . . . . . . . . . . . . . Co-President/Writer/Producer

**REES ASSOCS., MARIAN**
PHONE . . . . . . . . . . . . . . . . . . . . . . . . . . . . . . . . 818-508-5599
FAX . . . . . . . . . . . . . . . . . . . . . . . . . . . . . . . . . . . 818-508-8012
EMAIL . . . . . . . . . . . . . . . . . . . . . . . . . vantage@primenet.com
3708 Vantage Ave.
Studio City, CA 91604

TYPE       Television
CREDITS       When The Vows Break - Keeping The Promise - Ruby Bridges

Marian Rees . . . . . . . . . . . . . . . . . . Exec. Producer/President
Anne Hopkins . . . . . . . . . . . . . . . . . Producer/VP, Development
Dyan Conway . . . . . . . . . . . . . . . . . . . . . . . . . Business Affairs
Jenny Cowen . . . . . . . . . . . . . . . . . . . . . . . . . . . . . . Assistant
Tom Domingues . . . . . . . . . . . . . . . . . . . . . . . . . . . . Assistant

**REGAN COMPANY, THE**
PHONE . . . . . . . . . . . . . . . . . . . . . . . . . . . . . . . . 212-207-7400
FAX . . . . . . . . . . . . . . . . . . . . . . . . . . . . . . . . . . . 212-207-6951
EMAIL . . . . . . . . . . . . . . . . . . . . . . . . www.harpercollins.com
10 E. 53rd St.
New York, NY 10022

TYPE       Motion Pictures + Television
CREDITS       Ruby Ridge: An American Tragedy (CBS) - Microserfs (Universal) - A Man & His Mother (CBS)
COMMENTS       Also: Publishing.

Judith Regan . . . . . . . . . . . . . . . . . . . . . . . President/Publisher

**REGENT ENTERTAINMENT, INC.**
PHONE . . . . . . . . . . . . . . . . . . . . . . . . . . . . . . . . 310-446-4577
FAX . . . . . . . . . . . . . . . . . . . . . . . . . . . . . . . . . . . 310-446-4599
EMAIL . . . . . . . . . . . . . . . . . . . . . . regentpx@ix.netcom.com
1762 Westwood Blvd., #400
Los Angeles, CA 90024

TYPE       Motion Pictures + Television + Feature Direct to Video
CREDITS       The Twilight of the Golds - Gods & Monsters - Doomsday Rock

Paul Colichman . . . . . . . . . . . . . . . . . . . . . . . . . . . . . . Partner
Mark R. Harris . . . . . . . . . . . . . . . . . . . . . . . . . . . . . . . Partner
Jeff Schenck . . . . . . . . . . . . . . . . . . . . . . . . . . VP, Development

***REHME PRODUCTIONS**
PHONE . . . . . . . . . . . . . . . . . . . . . . . . . . . . . . . . 310-477-5811
FAX . . . . . . . . . . . . . . . . . . . . . . . . . . . . . . . . . . . 310-477-3881
11030 Santa Monica Blvd., Ste. 109
Los Angeles, CA 90025

TYPE       Motion Pictures + Television
DEAL       Phoenix Pictures
CREDITS       Patriot Games - Clear & Present Danger

Robert Rehme . . . . . . . . . . . . . . . . . . . . . . . . . . . . . Principal
Nick Grillo . . . . . . . . . . . . . Exec. Vice President (310-477-1991)
Susan Woods . . . . . . . . . . . . . . VP, Development (310-477-1991)
Robin Meier . . . . . . . . . . . . . . . . . . . . Development Associate
Jamie Dinsmore . . . . . . . . . . . . . . . . . . . Asst. to Robert Rehme

**REID PRODUCTIONS, INC., TIM**
PHONE . . . . . . . . . . . . . . . . . . . . . . . . . . . . . . . . 310-231-3400
FAX . . . . . . . . . . . . . . . . . . . . . . . . . . . . . . . . . . . 310-231-3404
1640 S. Sepulveda Blvd., Ste. 311
Los Angeles, CA 90025-7510

TYPE       Television + Motion Pictures
CREDITS       About Sarah

Tim Reid . . . . . . . . . . . . . . . . . . . . . . . . . . . . . . . . President
Michele Sacharow . . . . . . . . . . . . . . . . . Exec. VP, Television
Tori L. Reid . . . . . . . . . . . . . . . . . . . Administrative Assistant

**REINERT PICTURES, RICK**
PHONE . . . . . . . . . . . . . . . . . . . . . . . . . . . . . . . . 818-889-8977
FAX . . . . . . . . . . . . . . . . . . . . . . . . . . . . . . . . . . . 818-889-9097
32107 Lindero Canyon Rd., Ste. 224
Westlake Village, CA 91361

TYPE       Motion Pictures + Television + Animation
CREDITS       Captain O.G. Readmore Series - Winnie The Pooh - Precious Moments - Best Birthday

Rick Reinert . . . . . . . . . . . . . . . . . . . . . . . . . . . . . . . Producer
Carole Reinert . . . . . . . . . . . . . . . . . . . . . VP, Business Affairs
Dave Bennett . . . . . . . . . . . . . . . . . . . . . . . . . . Dir., Animation

**REMOTE CONTROL PRODUCTIONS**
PHONE . . . . . . . . . . . . . . . . . . . . . . . . . . . . . . . . 310-656-9356
FAX . . . . . . . . . . . . . . . . . . . . . . . . . . . . . . . . . . . 310-260-3172
EMAIL . . . . . . . . . . . . . . . . . . . . . . . . . . . . flix@rcprods.com
1547 14th St.
Santa Monica, CA 90404

TYPE       Animation + Motion Pictures + Television
DEAL       DreamWorks SKG

Karla Murray . . . . . . . . . . . . . . . . . . . . . . . . . . . . . . Producer

**RENAISSANCE PICTURES**
PHONE . . . . . . . . . . . . . . . . . . . . . . . . . . . . . . . . 818-777-0088
FAX . . . . . . . . . . . . . . . . . . . . . . . . . . . . . . . . . . . 818-866-0223
100 Universal City Plaza, Bldg. 78
Universal City, CA 91608

TYPE       Motion Pictures + Television + Feature Direct to Video + Syndication
DEAL       Studios USA Television
CREDITS       Evil Dead - Darkman - Hard Target - American Gothic - Hercules - Xena - Young Hercules

Sam Raimi . . . . . . . . . . . . . . . . . . . . . . . . . . Director/Producer
Robert Tapert . . . . . . . . . . . . . . . . . . . . . . . . . . . . . . Producer
David Eick . . . . . . . . . . . . . . . . . . . . . . . . . . . . . . . President
Liz Friedman . . . . . . . . . . . . . . . . . . . . . . . . . . VP, Television
Cynthia Hsiung . . . . . . . . . . . . . . . . . . . . Production Executive
Susan Binder . . . . . . . . . . . . . . . . . . . . . . . . Business Manager
Teresa Rowlee . . . . . . . . . . . . . . . . . . . . . . Creative Associate
Kevin Blank . . . . . . . . . . . . . . . . . . . . . . . Mgr., Special Effects
Mike McDonald . . . . . . . . . . . . . . . . . . . . . . Mgr., Development
Melissa Blake . . . . . . . . . . . . . . . . . . . . . Asst. to Rob Tapert
Jeff Cruce . . . . . . . . . . . . . . . . . . . . . . . . Asst. to David Eick
Grant Curtis . . . . . . . . . . . . . . . . . . . . . . Asst. to Sam Raimi
Erika Gingold . . . . . . . . . . . . . . . . . . Asst. to Cynthia Hsiung
David Pollison . . . . . . . . . . . . . . . . . . . . . . . . . . . . . . Assistant

# COMPANIES AND STAFF

**RENFIELD PRODS.**
PHONE . . . . . . . . . . . . . . . . . . . . . . . . 818-733-0707
FAX . . . . . . . . . . . . . . . . . . . . . . . . . . 818-866-2621
100 Universal City Plaza, Bungalow 113
Universal City, CA 91608

TYPE        Motion Pictures + Television
DEAL        Walt Disney TV/Touchstone TV
CREDITS     Gremlins 1 & 2- Innerspace - Deceived - Matinee - 2nd
                 Civil War

Joe Dante . . . . . . . . . . . . . . . . . . . . . . . . . . . . Director
Michael Finnell . . . . . . . . . . . . . . . . . . Producer/President
John Morgan . . . . . . . . . . . . . . . . . . . . . VP, Development
Betty Moos . . . . . . . . . . . . . . . . . . Asst. to Dante & Finnell

**REVELATIONS ENTERTAINMENT**
PHONE . . . . . . . . . . . . . . . . . . . . . . . . 310-394-3131
FAX . . . . . . . . . . . . . . . . . . . . . . . . . . 310-394-3133
EMAIL . . . . . . . . . . . . . . . mccreary@revelationsent.com
WEBSITE . . . . . . . . . . . . . . http://www.revelationsent.com
301 Arizona Ave., Ste. 303
Santa Monica, CA 90401

TYPE        Motion Pictures + Interactive Multimedia
CREDITS     Bopha!

Morgan Freeman . . . . . . . . . . . . . . . Actor/Director/Producer
Lori McCreary . . . . . . . . . . . . . . . President/CEO/Producer
Anne Marie Gillen . . . . . . . . . . . . . Chief Operating Officer
Jules A. Levy . . . . . . . . . . . . . . . . . . . . VP, Development
Zina Ponder . . . . . . . . . . . . . . . . . Dir., Creative Affairs
S. Russell Werkman . . . . . . . . . . . . . . . . . . . . Associate

**REVOLUTION ENTERTAINMENT**
PHONE . . . . . . . . . . . . . . . . . . . . . . . . 310-288-0303
FAX . . . . . . . . . . . . . . . . . . . . . . . . . . 310-288-0404
EMAIL . . . . . . . . . . . . . . . . . . . revfilms@aol.com
275 S. Beverly Dr., Ste. 200
Beverly Hills, CA 90212

TYPE        Motion Pictures + Television
CREDITS     Sleep With Me - Freeway - The Locusts - Ten Things I
                 Hate About You - Brown's Requiem

Marc Ezralow . . . . . . . . . . . . . . . . . . . Partner/Producer
Seth Jaret . . . . . . . . . . . . . . . . . . . . . Partner/Producer
Erik Kritzer . . . . . . . . . . . . . . . . . . . . Partner/Producer
Sarah Amundson . . . . . . . . . . . . . . . Executive Assistant
Jennifer Barg . . . . . . . . . . . . . . . . Asst. to Erik Kritzer

**RIALTO FILMS**
PHONE . . . . . . . . . . . . . . . . . . . . . . . . 818-501-3121
FAX . . . . . . . . . . . . . . . . . . . . . . . . . . 818-501-3818
EMAIL . . . . . . . . . . . . . . . . . . bnchmrk144@aol.com
13333 Ventura Blvd., Ste. 206
Sherman Oaks, CA 91423

TYPE        Motion Pictures + Television
CREDITS     Family Blessings (CBS) - Alibi (ABC)

Arthur Axelman . . . . . . . . . . . . . . . . . . . CEO/Producer
Matt Axelman . . . . . . . . . . . . . . . . . . . . . Development

**RICE & BEANS PRODS.**
PHONE . . . . . . . . . . . . . . . . . . . . . . . . 626-792-9171
FAX . . . . . . . . . . . . . . . . . . . . . . . . . . 626-792-9171
EMAIL . . . . . . . . . . . . . . . . . . . vin88@pacbell.net
30 N. Raymond., Ste. 605
Pasadena, CA 91103

TYPE        Motion Pictures + Television + Feature Direct to Video
DEAL        Columbia TriStar Television/Fox Broadcasting Co.
CREDITS     In The House - Night Court - Growing Pains - Roc -
                 Married With Children - Empty Nest - Between Brothers -
                 The Steve Harvey Show

Vince Cheung . . . . . . . . . . . . . . . . . . . Writer/Producer
Ben Montanio . . . . . . . . . . . . . . . . . . . Writer/Producer

**RICH PRODUCTIONS, LEE**
PHONE . . . . . . . . . . . . . . . . . . . . . . . . 213-956-2570
FAX . . . . . . . . . . . . . . . . . . . . . . . . . . 213-862-3502
Paramount Pictures
5555 Melrose Ave., Dressing Rm. Bl. #318
Hollywood, CA 90038

TYPE        Motion Pictures + Television
CREDITS     Just Cause - Desperate Measures - Gloria
COMMENTS   Also: Mini-series & MOW's.

Lee Rich . . . . . . . . . . . . . . . . . . . . . . . . . . . Chairman
Veronica Brice . . . . . . . . . . . . . . . Exec. Asst. to Lee Rich

**RICHE/LUDWIG PRODUCTIONS**
PHONE . . . . . . . . . . . . . . . . . . . . . . . . 213-850-2777
Warner Hollywood Studios
1041 N. Formosa Ave., Formosa Bldg. #5
West Hollywood, CA 90046

TYPE        Motion Pictures
DEAL        Warner Bros. Pictures
CREDITS     Empire Records - Mouse Hunt - The Mod Squad

Tony Ludwig . . . . . . . . . . . . . . . . . . . . . . . . . Producer
Alan Riche . . . . . . . . . . . . . . . . . . . . . . . . . . Producer
Geoff Shaevitz . . . . . . . . . . . . . . . . . Dir., Development

**RICHULCO, INC.**
PHONE . . . . . . . . . . . . . . . . . . . . . . . . 310-477-1464
FAX . . . . . . . . . . . . . . . . . . . . . . . . . . 310-966-1975
11041 Santa Monica Blvd., Ste. 511
Los Angeles, CA 90025

TYPE        Motion Pictures + Television
CREDITS     Within The Lines - Mulligan Men - Jekyll Island

Richard Hull . . . . . . . . . . . . . . . . . . . President/Producer

***RIDINI ENTERTAINMENT CORPORATION**
PHONE . . . . . . . . . . . . . . . . . . . . . . . . 213-874-1582
FAX . . . . . . . . . . . . . . . . . . . . . . . . . . 213-874-1381
EMAIL . . . . . . . . . . . . . . . ridinifilm@earthlink.net
6728 Hillpark Drive, Ste. 305
Los Angeles, CA 90068

TYPE        Motion Pictures + Television
CREDITS     Falling Fire - Convict 762 - Future Fear - Shepherd
COMMENTS   Ridini Ent. is also a Public Relations Firm handling a variety
                   of entertainment clients.

Maryann Ridini . . . . . . . . . . . . . . . . . . . . . . . Producer

**RIDIO PRODS., INC., ANTHONY**
PHONE . . . . . . . . . . . . . . . . . . . . . . . . 310-316-8652
500 Avenue G
Redondo Beach, CA 90277

TYPE        Motion Pictures + Television
CREDITS     Free Jack - Hellbound

Anthony Ridio . . . . . . . . . . . . . . . . . . . . CEO/Producer
Ian Rabin . . . . . . . . . . . . . . . . . . . VP/Dir., Development
Stephanie Nichols . . . . . . . . . . . . . . . . . . . Development
Kelly Ridio . . . . . . . . . . . . . . . . . . . . . . . Development
Rosemary Torigian . . . . . . . . . . . . . . . . . . Story Editor

**RIVE GAUCHE INTERNATIONAL TV**
PHONE . . . . . . . . . . . . . . . . . . . . . . . . 818-784-9912
FAX . . . . . . . . . . . . . . . . . . . . . . . . . . 818-784-9916
15442 Ventura Blvd., Ste. 101
Sherman Oaks, CA 91403

TYPE        Documentaries + Television + Syndication
DEAL        Nash Entertainment
CREDITS     Komodo's Dragons - Animal Tales - Sulfur Slaves
COMMENTS   Also: Network Specials / Deal with Pie Town Prods.

Ronald Glazer . . . . . . . . . . . . . . . . . . . . . . . President
Christiane Nicolini . . . . . . . . . . . . . . . . . Vice President
Sharon Beverly . . . . . . . . . . . . . . . . . . Dir., Development

**RIVER MILL PRODUCTIONS**
PHONE . . . . . . . . . . . . . . . 612-399-1343/800-935-5705
FAX . . . . . . . . . . . . . . . . . . . . . . . . . . 612-866-3001
EMAIL . . . . . . . . . . . . . . . . . . Oimages@pclink.com
WEBSITE . . . . . . . . . . . . . . . . . . http://www.funkytown.com
404 Washington Ave. N., Ste. 200
Minneapolis, MN 55401

TYPE        Motion Pictures + Television + Documentaries
CREDITS     Youngblood - I Love You To Death - FunkyTown - The
                 Personals
COMMENTS   Also: turkscott@hotmail.com

Patrick C. Wells . . . . . . . . . . . . . . . . . . . . . . Producer
Chris Ohlsen . . . . . . . . . . . . . . . . . . Producer/Director
Craig Rice . . . . . . . . . . . . . . . . . . . . Producer/Director
Scott A. Turk . . . . . . . . . . . . . . . . . . . Head, Development

## RIVER ONE FILMS
PHONE . . . . . . . . . . . . . . . . . . . . . . . . . . . . . . 212-956-2455
FAX . . . . . . . . . . . . . . . . . . . . . . . . . . . . . . . . 212-956-1519
EMAIL . . . . . . . . . . . . . . . . . . . . . . . . . BillyGith@aol.com
1619 Broadway, Ste. 574
New York, NY 10019

TYPE        Motion Pictures
CREDITS    Watch It - Black Caeser - Colin Fitz - How To Marry A Black Man

Thomas J. Mangan IV . . . . . . . . . . . . . . . . . President/Producer
William E. Githens . . . . . . . . . . . . . . VP/Production Executive
John C. McGinley . . . . . . . . . . . . . . . . . . . . . . . Producer
Emily Blavatnik . . . . . . . . . . . . . . . . . . . . . . . . Creative
Tania Campbell . . . . . . . . . . . . . . . . Post Production Executive
Seth I. Shire . . . . . . . . . . . . . . . . . Post Production Executive

## *RKO PICTURES, INC.
PHONE . . . . . . . . . . . . . 310-277-0707/212-644-0600
FAX . . . . . . . . . . . . . . . . . . . . . . . . . . . . 310-226-2490
1875 Century Park East, Ste. 2140
Los Angeles, CA 90067

TYPE        Motion Pictures + Television
CREDITS    Mighty Joe Young - Beyond a Reasonable Doubt - The Locked Room
COMMENTS  Also: 551 Madison Ave., 14th Fl., New York, NY 10022.

Ted Hartley . . . . . . . . . . . . . . . . . . . . . . . . . . Chairman/CEO
Dina Merrill . . . . . . . . . . . . . . . . . . . . . . . . Vice Chairman
Arthur Horan . . . . . . . . . . . . . Exec. VP, Business/Legal Affairs
Julia Halperin . . . . . . . . . . . . . . . . . VP, Feature Development
Laurel Lees-Gonzalez . . . . . . . . . . . . VP, Finance & Administration
Inge Van Herle . . . . . . . . . . . . . . VP/Asst. General Counsel
Inness Wei . . . . . . . . . . . . . . . . . . . . VP, TV Development
Doris Schwartz . . . . . . . . . . . . . . . . . Production Executive
Lauren Iungerich . . . . . . . . . . . . . . . . . Creative Executive
Jennifer Kirschenbaum . . . . . . . . . . . . . . . Creative Assistant

## ROADKILL FILMS
PHONE . . . . . . . . . . . . . . . . . . . . . . . . . . . . . 213-962-0295
FAX . . . . . . . . . . . . . . . . . . . . . . . . . . . . . . . 310-475-0034
EMAIL . . . . . . . . . . . . . . . . . . . . . . . . . sofagirl@aol.com
6305 Yucca St., 7th Fl.
Hollywood, CA 90028

TYPE        Motion Pictures
DEAL        Sneak Preview Entertainment, Inc.
CREDITS    Blue - Tollbooth - Fast Sofa - An Occassional Hell

Salome Breziner . . . . . . . . . . . . . . . . . . . . Director/Writer

## ROARING FORK PRODUCTIONS
PHONE . . . . . . . . . . . . . . . . . . . . . . . . . . . . . 310-887-5643
FAX . . . . . . . . . . . . . . . . . . . . . . . . . . . . . . . 310-887-5626
Citadel Entertainment. L.L.C.
301 N. Canon, Ste. 321
Beverly Hills, CA 90210

TYPE        Motion Pictures + Television
DEAL        Citadel Entertainment., LLC
CREDITS    Chance of a Lifetime - Love, Lies and Murder - Fatal Vows - Armed and Innocent
COMMENTS  Also: MOW's.

Tim Hill . . . . . . . . . . . . . . . . . . . . . . . . Executive Producer
Danielle Hill . . . . . . . . . . . . . . . . . . . . Executive Producer
Jonathan Eskenas . . . . . . . . . . . . . . . Assistant to Producers

## ROARING MOUSE ENTERTAINMENT, INC.
PHONE . . . . . . . . . . . . . . . . . . . . . . . . . . . . . 805-373-8131
FAX . . . . . . . . . . . . . . . . . . . . . . . . . . . . . . . 805-373-8133
EMAIL . . . . . . . . . . . . . . . . . . . . . . . dlm@roaringmouse.com
WEBSITE . . . . . . . . . . . . . . . . http://http://www.roaringmouse.com
1800 Bridgegate St., #103
Westlake Village, CA 91361

TYPE        Animation + Documentaries + Feature Direct to Video + Motion Pictures + Television + Interactive Multimedia
CREDITS    Breakfast of Aliens - Zoo-opolis

David L. Miller . . . . . . . . . . . . . . . . Producer/Writer/Director
Bill Patterson . . . . . . . . . . . . . . . . . Producer/Director/Editor

## ROBBINS ENTERTAINMENT
PHONE . . . . . . . . . . . . . . . . . . . . . . . . . . . . . 617-964-2555
FAX . . . . . . . . . . . . . . . . . . . . . . . . . . . . . . . 617-964-9640
EMAIL . . . . . . . . . . . . . . . . . . . mitchrobb@mindspring.com
2150 Washington St.
Newton, MA 02162

TYPE        Motion Pictures
CREDITS    Squeeze - The Darien Gap - Next Stop Wonderland

Mitchell B. Robbins . . . . . . . . . . . . . . . . . . . . . President
Laura Bernieri . . . . . . . . . . . . . . . . . . . VP, Creative Affairs

## ROBINSON ENTERTAINMENT, DOLORES
PHONE . . . . . . . . . . . . . . . . . . . . . . . . . . . . . 310-441-7300
FAX . . . . . . . . . . . . . . . . . . . . . . . . . . . . . . . 310-441-7310
10683 Santa Monica Blvd.
Los Angeles, CA 90025

TYPE        Motion Pictures + Television
DEAL        Warner Bros. Television Productions
CREDITS    Matt Waters (CBS)- Southern Fried Ice (ABC pilot) - Between Brothers

Dolores Robinson . . . . . . . . . . . . . . . . . President/Producer
Michael Valeo . . . . . . . . . . . . . . . . . . . . VP, Development

## ROBINSON PRODUCTIONS, AMY
PHONE . . . . . . . . . . . . . . . . . . . . . . . . . . . . . 212-262-5500
FAX . . . . . . . . . . . . . . . . . . . . . . . . . . . . . . . 212-262-4940
250 W. 57th St., Ste. 2217
New York, NY 10107

TYPE        Motion Pictures
CREDITS    With Honors - Once Around - Running on Empty

Amy Robinson . . . . . . . . . . . . . . . . . . . . . . . . Producer
Andrew Dansby . . . . . . . . . . . . . . . Development Associate

## ROBSON ENTERTAINMENT
PHONE . . . . . . . . . . . . . . . . . . . . . . . . . . . . . 310-246-4688
FAX . . . . . . . . . . . . . . . . . . . . . . . . . . . . . . . 310-247-8882
345 N. Maple Dr., Ste. 208
Beverly Hills, CA 90210-3867

TYPE        Motion Pictures
CREDITS    Gordy

Sybil A. Robson . . . . . . . . . . . . . . . . . . . . . . . Producer
Aurelio Christian . . . . . . . . . . . . . . Exec. Asst. to Ms. Robson

## ROCKET PICTURES
PHONE . . . . . . . . . . . . . . . . . . . . . . . . . . . . . 310-247-7600
FAX . . . . . . . . . . . . . . . . . . . . . . . . . . . . . . . 310-550-1126
EMAIL . . . . . . . . . . . . . . . . . . . . . RocketPix_@msn.com
9601 Wilshire Blvd., Ste. 1109
Beverly Hills, CA 90210

TYPE        Motion Pictures + Feature Direct to Video + Interactive Multimedia
CREDITS    The Lovemaster - Cannesman - Rodney Dangerfield's Guide to Golf Style & Etiquette - It Came from the Sky

Danny Kopels . . . . . . . . . . . . . . . . . . . . . . . . President

## ROCKING HORSE PRODS.
PHONE . . . . . . . . . . . . . . . . . . . . . . . . . . . . . 310-315-4868
FAX . . . . . . . . . . . . . . . . . . . . . . . . . . . . . . . 818-905-9919
EMAIL . . . . . . . . . . . . . . . . . . . penny.perry@mci2000.com
P.O. Box 57677
Sherman Oaks, CA 91413

TYPE        Motion Pictures + Television
CREDITS    Stranger In The Kingdom

Eugene Davis . . . . . . . . . . . . . . . . . . President/Producer
Penny Perry Davis . . . . . . . . . . . . . . . . . . Vice President

## RODAN PRODS., INC.
PHONE . . . . . . . . . . . . . . . . . . . . . . . . . . . . . 310-207-4427
FAX . . . . . . . . . . . . . . . . . . . . . . . . . . . . . . . 310-207-4427
855 S. Bundy Dr.
Los Angeles, CA 90049

TYPE        Motion Pictures + Television
CREDITS    Elvis Presley's Comeback Special - Diana Ross in Central Park - Virtual Ed Sullivan

Steve Binder . . . . . . . . . . . . . . . . . . Producer/Director/Writer

## ROGERS ENTERTAINMENT
PHONE . . . . . . . . . . . . . . . . . . . . . . . . . . . . . . 310-820-0073
EMAIL . . . . . . . . . . . . . . . . . . . . . . . at1with@earthlink.net
11680 Montana
Los Angeles, CA 90049

TYPE      Motion Pictures + Television + Interactive Multimedia
DEAL      Greenblatt-Junollari/The Sullivan Co./Atlantis Films
CREDITS      Tommy Davidson Special - Sarah Stanley Show - Alonzo Borden Show

Diane Berger-Rogers . . . . . . . . . . . . . . . . . . . . . . Vice President
Heather Schliewen . . . . . . . . . . . . . . . . . . . . . Dir., Development

## ROGOW PRODUCTIONS, STAN
PHONE . . . . . . . . . . . . . . . . . . . . . . . . . . . . . . 818-560-5807
FAX . . . . . . . . . . . . . . . . . . . . . . . . . . . . . . . . 818-848-0167
Walt Disney Co.
500 S. Buena Vista, Animation Bl. 1E-6
Burbank, CA 91521-1651

TYPE      Television + Motion Pictures
DEAL      Walt Disney Company, The
CREDITS      Nowhere to Hide - Shannon's Deal - Middle Ages - Nowhere Man - The Defenders

Stan Rogow . . . . . . . . . . . . . . . . . . . . . . . . . Executive Producer
Todd Kravitz . . . . . . . . . . . . . . . . . . . . . . . . Asst. to Mr. Rogow

## ROSA ENTERTAINMENT
PHONE . . . . . . . . . . . . . . . . . . . . . . . . . . . . . . 310-659-7592
EMAIL . . . . . . . . . . . . . . . . . . . . . . . ssfilm@earthlink.net
7274 Sunset Blvd., Suite 4
Los Angeles, CA 90046

TYPE      Motion Pictures + Television + Documentaries + Interactive Multimedia
CREDITS      The Legend of Billy the Kid - The Tunnel - Survivors of the Holocaust

Sidney Sherman . . . . . . . . . . . . . . . . . . . . . . . . . . . . Producer
Kathy S. Pomerantz . . . . . . . . . . . . . . . . . . . . . . . . . . Producer

## ROSCOE ENTERPRISES, INC.
PHONE . . . . . . . . . . . . . . . . . . . . . . . . . . . . . . 310-449-4066
FAX . . . . . . . . . . . . . . . . . . . . . . . . . . . . . . . . 310-264-4158
3000 W. Olympic Blvd., Ste. 2276
Santa Monica, CA 90404

TYPE      Motion Pictures
CREDITS      Usual Suspects - Hard Eight - Serpent's Kiss
COMMENTS      Also: Blue Parrot, Inc. and Gardens Square Production, Inc.

Hans Brockmann . . . . . . . . . . . . . . . . . . . . . . . . . . . Principal
Francois Duplat . . . . . . . . . . . . . . . . . . . . . . . . . . . Principal
Alexandra Schultze . . . . . . . . . . . . . . . . . . . . Managing Director

## ROSE PRODS. INC., ALEX
PHONE . . . . . . . . . . . . . . . . . . . . . . . . . . . . . . 213-654-8662
FAX . . . . . . . . . . . . . . . . . . . . . . . . . . . . . . . . 213-654-0196
8291 Presson Pl.
Los Angeles, CA 90069

TYPE      Motion Pictures + Television + Documentaries
CREDITS      Frankie & Johnny - Nothing In Common - Norma Rae - Overboard
COMMENTS      Currently in Post Production for "The Other Sister" at Touchstone Pictures.

Alex Rose . . . . . . . . . . . . . . . . . . . . . . . . . . . . . . . Producer
Ilan Arboleda . . . . . . . . . . . . . . . . . . . . . . . . . . . Story Editor

## ROSE PRODUCTIONS, LEE
PHONE . . . . . . . . . . . . . . . . . . . . . . . . . . . . . . 310-659-2050
FAX . . . . . . . . . . . . . . . . . . . . . . . . . . . . . . . . 310-659-6755
450 N. Robertson Blvd.
W. Hollywood, CA 90048

TYPE      Motion Pictures + Television
DEAL      Universal Television
CREDITS      A Mother's Prayer - Nothing Personal - An Unexpected Family

Lee Rose . . . . . . . . . . . . . . . . . . . . . . . Exec. Producer/Writer
Aisha Prigann . . . . . . . . . . . . . . . . . . . . . . . . . . . . Assistant

## ROSEMONT PRODS. INTERNATIONAL LTD.
PHONE . . . . . . . . . . . . . . . . . . . . . . . . . . . . . . 818-528-2300
FAX . . . . . . . . . . . . . . . . . . . . . . . . . . . . . . . . 818-528-2301
16255 Ventura Blvd., Ste. 900
Encino, CA 91436

TYPE      Motion Pictures + Television
CREDITS      The Secret Garden - What Love Sees - Riders of the Purple Sage

Norman Rosemont . . . . . . . . . . . . . . . . . . . . . . Executive Producer
David A. Rosemont . . . . . . . . . . . . . . . . . . . . . Executive Producer
Susan Zachary . . . . . . . . . . . . . . . . Producer/Exec. VP, Production
Robert Coppini . . . . . . . . . . . . . . . . . . . . . . . . . . . Operations
Kristen Gaines . . . . . . . . . . Exec. Asst. to Norman and David A. Rosemont
Sheri Brummond . . . . . . . . . . . . . . . . . . . Development Assistant

## ROSEN/BENDER PRODS.
PHONE . . . . . . . . . . . . . . . . . . . . . . . . . . . . . . 213-650-1385
FAX . . . . . . . . . . . . . . . . . . . . . . . . . . . . . . . . 213-650-1385
EMAIL . . . . . . . . . . . . . . . . . . . . mergatroyed@earthlink.net
1541 N. Laurel Ave., Ste. 205
Los Angeles, CA 90046

TYPE      Motion Pictures + Feature Direct to Video
CREDITS      Midnight Kiss

Manette Beth Rosen . . . . . . . . . . . . . . . . . . . . . . . . . . Producer
Joel Bender . . . . . . . . . . . . . . . . . . . . . . . . . . . . . . . Director

## ROSENBERG, HELENA HACKER
PHONE . . . . . . . . . . . . . . . . . . . . . . . . . . . . . . 310-276-7788
FAX . . . . . . . . . . . . . . . . . . . . . . . . . . . . . . . . 310-276-4314
HHR Productions
9000 Cynthia St., Ste. 406
Los Angeles, CA 90069

TYPE      Motion Pictures + Television
CREDITS      Aftermath - The Fear Inside - The Conviction of Kitty Dodds - Nightmare Street

Helena Hacker Rosenberg . . . . . . . . . . . . . . . . . . Executive Producer

## ROSENBLOOM PRODS., RICHARD
PHONE . . . . . . . . . . . . . . . . . . . . . . . . . . . . . . 805-650-3500
FAX . . . . . . . . . . . . . . . . . . . . . . . . . . . . . . . . 805-650-0937
2925 Surfrider Ave.
Ventura, CA 93001

TYPE      Television
CREDITS      Sinatra, the Mini-Series - Scarlett (miniseries)

Richard Rosenbloom . . . . . . . . . . . . . . . . . . . . . . . . . . Producer

## ROSENMAN PRODUCTIONS, HOWARD
PHONE . . . . . . . . . . . . . . . . . . . . . . . . . . . . . . 310-659-2100
EMAIL . . . . . . . . . . . . . . . . . . . . . . . . . BIG2R@aol.com
635A Westbourne Drive
Los Angeles, CA 90069

TYPE      Motion Pictures + Documentaries + Television
CREDITS      Father of the Bride - Buffy the Vampire Slayer - The Celluloid Closet - Common Threads

Howard Rosenman . . . . . . . . . . . . . . . . . . . . . . . . . . . President

## ROSS PRODUCTION, GARY
PHONE . . . . . . . . . . . . . . . . . . . . . . . . . . . . . . 818-623-8200
FAX . . . . . . . . . . . . . . . . . . . . . . . . . . . . . . . . 818-623-8700
10045 Riverside Dr., 2nd Fl.
Toluca Lake, CA 91602

TYPE      Motion Pictures
CREDITS      Trial & Error - Pleasantville

Gary Ross . . . . . . . . . . . . . . . . . . . . . . . . . . . . . . . No Title
Robin Bissell . . . . . . . . . . . . . . . . . . . . . . . . . . . . . Assistant
Amy Lamare . . . . . . . . . . . . . . . . . . . . . . . . . . . . . . Assistant

## ROSS PRODUCTIONS, HAL
PHONE . . . . . . . . . . . . . . . . . . . . . . . . . . . . . . 310-471-8321
FAX . . . . . . . . . . . . . . . . . . . . . . . . . . . . . . . . 310-471-0495
991 Oakmont Drive
Los Angeles, CA 90049

TYPE      Motion Pictures + Television
COMMENTS      Former WMA Sr. VP. All deals now in development.

Hal Ross . . . . . . . . . . . . . . . . . . . . . . . . . . . . . . . President

# COMPANIES AND STAFF

**ROSS, HERBERT**
PHONE . . . . . . . . . . . . . . . . . . . . . . . . . . . . . 310-278-4201
FAX . . . . . . . . . . . . . . . . . . . . . . . . . . . . . . . 310-278-5330
F. Altman & Co.
9255 Sunset Blvd., Ste. 901
Los Angeles, CA 90069

TYPE            Motion Pictures
CREDITS         The Turning Point - Steel Magnolias - Boys On The Side
Herbert Ross . . . . . . . . . . . . . . . . . . . . . . . . . Director/Producer

**ROSSU ENTERTAINMENT**
PHONE . . . . . . . . . . . . . . . . . . . . . . . . . . . . . 310-578-5015
8833 Sunset Blvd., Ste. 304
Los Angeles, CA 90069

TYPE            Motion Pictures + Television
CREDITS         Big Trouble in Little China - Critical Masses
COMMENTS        Formerly Fortis Entertainment
Alex Rossu . . . . . . . . . . . . . . . . . . . . . . . Writer/Director/Producer
David Weinstein . . . . . . . . . . . . . . . . . . . . . . . . Writer/Producer
Jane Austen . . . . . . . . . . . . . . . . . . . . . . . . . . VP, Development
Andrew Bullas . . . . . . . . . . . . . . . . . . . . . . . VP, Business Affairs
Tony Saintex . . . . . . . . . . . . . . . . . . . . . . . . . Dir., Development

**ROTH/ARNOLD PRODS.**
PHONE . . . . . . . . . . . . . . . . . . . . . . . . . . . . . 310-315-4830
FAX . . . . . . . . . . . . . . . . . . . . . . . . . . . . . . . 310-315-4832
3000 W. Olympic Blvd., Bldg. 4, #2208
Santa Monica, CA 90404

TYPE            Motion Pictures
DEAL            DreamWorks SKG
CREDITS         Grosse Pointe Blank - Unstrung Heroes - Benny & Joon
Susan Arnold . . . . . . . . . . . . . . . . . . . . . . . . . . . . . Producer
Donna Roth . . . . . . . . . . . . . . . . . . . . . . . . . . . . . . Producer
Jennifer Leshnick . . . . . . . . . . . . . . . . . . . . . . . . VP, Development
Jodi Targon . . . . . . . . . . . . . . . . . . . . . . . . . . . . . Assistant
Megan Weaver . . . . . . . . . . . . . . . . . . . . . . . . . . . . Assistant
Nora Zuckerman . . . . . . . . . . . . . . . . . . . Asst. to Jennifer Leshnick

**ROTHSTEIN PRODS., FREYDA**
PHONE . . . . . . . . . . . . . . . . . . . . . . . . . . . . . 310-575-1264
FAX . . . . . . . . . . . . . . . . . . . . . . . . . . . . . . . 310-478-6067
Hearst Entertainment
1640 S. Sepulveda Blvd., 4th Fl.
Los Angeles, CA 90025-7510

TYPE            Motion Pictures + Television
DEAL            Hearst Entertainment
CREDITS         The Reef - Two Voices - And Then There Was One
Freyda Rothstein . . . . . . . . . . . . . . . . . . . . . . . Executive Producer
Deborah Wolsh . . . . . . . . . . . . . . . . . . . . . . . VP, Creative Affairs
Renee A. Siemann . . . . . . . . . . . . . . . . . . . . . . Executive Assistant

**ROTMAN PRODUCTIONS, DAVID**
PHONE . . . . . . . . . . . . . . . . . . . . . . . . . . . . . 310-369-4476
FAX . . . . . . . . . . . . . . . . . . . . . . . . . . . . . . . 310-969-1399
10201 W. Pico, Bldg. 89, Rm. 131
Los Angeles, CA 90035

TYPE            Motion Pictures + Television
CREDITS         Dragonheart - Cliffhanger - Stranger Things
David Rotman . . . . . . . . . . . . . . . . . . . . . . . . . . . . . Producer
Alan Plotner . . . . . . . . . . . . . . . . . . . . . . . . . . . Vice President
Jane Rose . . . . . . . . . . . . . . . . . . . . . . . . . . Asst. to David Rotman

**ROUGH DIAMOND PRODUCTIONS**
PHONE . . . . . . . . . . . . . . . . . . . . . . . . . . . . . 213-848-2900
FAX . . . . . . . . . . . . . . . . . . . . . . . . . . . . . . . 213-848-8142
EMAIL . . . . . . . . . . . . . . . . . . . . . . . . roughdi@aol.com
1424 N. Kings Rd.
Los Angeles, CA 90069

TYPE            Motion Pictures + Feature Direct to Video
CREDITS         Temptation - The Set Up - Past Perfect - A Matter of Trust
                - A Breed Apart - Detour
Julia Verdin . . . . . . . . . . . . . . . . . . . . . . . . President/Producer
Brent Morris . . . . . . . . . . . . . . . . . . . . . . . . . Partner/Producer
Tim Bond . . . . . . . . . . . . . . . . . . . . . . . . . . . Director/Producer
Jonathan Heap . . . . . . . . . . . . . . . . . . . . . . . . Director/Producer
James Hickox . . . . . . . . . . . . . . . . . . . . . . . . . Director/Producer
Danny Huston . . . . . . . . . . . . . . . . . . . . . . . . . Director/Producer
Paul Papadeas . . . . . . . . . . . . . . . . . . . . . . . . Dir., Development

**ROUNDELAY PRODS.**
PHONE . . . . . . . . . . . . . . . . . . . . . . . . . . . . . 310-288-4545
Creative Artists Agency/Glenn Bickel
9830 Wilshire Blvd.
Beverly Hills, CA 90210

TYPE            Television
CREDITS         Bodies of Evidence - Homefront - Knots Landing - Dallas -
                Moloney
David Jacobs . . . . . . . . . . . . . . . . . Exec. Producer/Director/Writer

**ROXABOXEN**
PHONE . . . . . . . . . . . . . . . . . . . . . . . . . . . . . 310-559-9192
FAX . . . . . . . . . . . . . . . . . . . . . . . . . . . . . . . 310-559-3518
EMAIL . . . . . . . . . . . . . . . . . . . . . . . . . . www.roxaboxen.com
4319 Keystone Ave.
Culver City, CA 90232

TYPE            Motion Pictures + Television
DEAL            Batson Enterprises/Oceans 2 Ent.
Diane Batson-Smith . . . . . . . . . . . . . . . . . . . . . . . . . Producer
Debra J. Kleid . . . . . . . . . . . . . . . . . . . . . . . Creative Associate
Ron Wechsler . . . . . . . . . . . . . . . . . . . . . . . . . . . . . Producer

**RSO FILMS**
PHONE . . . . . . . . . . . . . . . . . . . . . . . . . . . . . 212-975-0700
122 E. 42nd St., #810
New York, NY 10168

TYPE            Motion Pictures
CREDITS         Evita - Saturday Night Fever - Grease
Robert Stigwood . . . . . . . . . . . . . . . . . . . . . . . . . . Chairman

**RUBIN * BURKE PRODUCTIONS**
PHONE . . . . . . . . . . . . . . . . . . . . . . . . . . . . . 310-275-8488
FAX . . . . . . . . . . . . . . . . . . . . . . . . . . . . . . . 310-275-9264
361 N. Canon Drive, Ste. 6
Beverly Hills, CA 90210-4704

TYPE            Motion Pictures + Television
Shawn Burke . . . . . . . . . . . . . . . . . . . . . . . . . Producer/Partner
Marjorie Rubin . . . . . . . . . . . . . . . . . . . . . . . . Producer/Partner
Dagney Cardinale . . . . . . . . . . . . . . . . . . . . . . . . . . Assistant

**RUBY-SPEARS PRODS.**
PHONE . . . . . . . . . . . . . . . . . . . . . . . . . . . . . 818-840-1234
FAX . . . . . . . . . . . . . . . . . . . . . . . . . . . . . . . 818-840-1258
EMAIL . . . . . . . . . . . . . . . . . . . rubyspears@earthlink.net
710 S. Victory Blvd., Ste. 201
Burbank, CA 91502-2425

TYPE            Motion Pictures + Television + Animation + Syndication
CREDITS         Skysurfer Strike Force - Jirimpimbira - Rumpelstiltskin -
                Megaman
Joseph Ruby . . . . . . . . . . . . . . . . . . . President/Exec. Producer
Kenneth Spears . . . . . . . . . . . . . . . . . . . . . . VP/Exec. Producer
Loretta High . . . . . . . . . . . . . . . . . . . . . . . . Production Manager
Cesar De Castro . . . . . . . . . . . . . . . . . . . . . . . . Art Director

**RUDDY MORGAN ORGANIZATION, INC., THE**
PHONE . . . . . . . . . . . . . . . . . . . . . . . . . . . . . 310-271-7698
FAX . . . . . . . . . . . . . . . . . . . . . . . . . . . . . . . 310-278-9978
9300 Wilshire Blvd., Ste. 508
Beverly Hills, CA 90212

TYPE            Motion Pictures + Television
CREDITS         The Scout - Heaven's Prisoners - Mr. Magoo - Walker:
                Texas Ranger - Married To A Stranger
Andre Morgan . . . . . . . . . . . . . . . . . . . . . . . . . . . . . Producer
Al Ruddy . . . . . . . . . . . . . . . . . . . . . . . . . . . . . . . Producer
Traci Dalke . . . . . . . . . . . . . . . . . . . . . . . . . . Creative Director
Lucas Oliver-Frost . . . . . . . . . . . . . . . . . . . . . . Creative Director
Philip Marr . . . . . . . . . . . . . . . . . . . . . . . . . . . Story Editor
Pam Paul . . . . . . . . . . . . . . . . . . . . . . . . . . . Office Manager

## RUDIN PRODS., SCOTT
PHONE . . . . . . . . . . . . . . . . . . . . . . . 213-956-4600/212-704-4600
FAX . . . . . . . . . . . . . . . . . . . . . . . . . 213-862-0262/212-869-8557
Paramount Pictures
5555 Melrose Ave., DeMille Bldg. #200
Los Angeles, CA 90038

TYPE     Motion Pictures
DEAL     Paramount Pictures- Motion Picture Group
CREDITS     Ransom - First Wives Club - Clueless - The Firm - Mother - In and Out - The Truman Show
COMMENTS     ALSO: 120 W. 45th St., 10th Fl., New York, NY 10036

Scott Rudin . . . . . . . . . . . . . . . . . . . . . . . . . Producer
Adam Schroeder . . . . . . . . . . . . . . . . President (213-956-4644)
Eric Steel . . . . . . . . . . . . . . . . . . . VP, Development (NY)
Ian McGloin . . . . . . . . . . . . . . . . . . . Dir., Development (NY)
Molly Rain . . . . . . . . . . . . . . . Dir., Development (LA) (213-956-4295)
Gregory Lessans . . . . . . . . . . . Exec. Asst. to Scott Rudin (LA)
Lucia Murillo . . . . . . . . . . . Exec. Asst. to Adam Schroeder (LA)
Mark Roybal . . . . . . . . . . . . . . Exec. Asst. to Scott Rudin
Edward Goemans . . . . . . . . . . . . . . Asst. to Scott Rudin (NY)
Tina Hay . . . . . . . . . . . . . . . . . . . . . . . Development (LA)

## RUMBLESEAT PRODS.
PHONE . . . . . . . . . . . . . . . . . . . . . . . . . . 310-785-0170
FAX . . . . . . . . . . . . . . . . . . . . . . . . . . . 310-785-0174
501 S. Beverly Dr., 3rd Fl.
Beverly Hills, CA 90212

TYPE     Motion Pictures
CREDITS     Deadly Games - The Good Mother - Never Forget - 3 Men and A Baby

Leonard Nimoy . . . . . . . . . . . . . . . . . . . . . . . President
Simone D. Rodman . . . . . . . . . . . . . . . . . Production Associate

## RUPERT PRODUCTIONS, INC.
PHONE . . . . . . . . . . . . . . . . . . . . . . . . . . 310-390-9360
FAX . . . . . . . . . . . . . . . . . . . . . . . . . . . 310-390-9620
3760 Grandview Blvd.
Los Angeles, CA 90066

TYPE     Motion Pictures + Television + Syndication
CREDITS     Electra - Glide-in-Blue - Last Dragon - Wolfen - Jaws 3-D - Snakes and Ladders - Backstreet Dreams - Night Visitor - Nowhere Land

Rupert Hitzig . . . . . . . . . . . . . . . . . . . . . . . President

## RUSSELL PRODUCTIONS, NEIL
PHONE . . . . . . . . . . . . . . . . . . . . . . . . . . 310-827-2121
FAX . . . . . . . . . . . . . . . . . . . . . . . . . . . 310-827-6965
EMAIL . . . . . . . . . . . . . . . . . . . . . . . . nrprod@aol.com
5455 Centinela Ave., Ste. 300
Los Angeles, CA 90066

TYPE     Television + Motion Pictures
CREDITS     Soldier of Fortune - Donato & Daughter - Not Our Son

Neil Russell . . . . . . . . . . . . . . . . . . . . . . . President

## RUST PRODUCTIONS, PATRICIA
PHONE . . . . . . . . . . . . . . . . . . . . . . . . . . 818-386-1383
FAX . . . . . . . . . . . . . . . . . . . . . . . . . . . 818-784-1325
EMAIL . . . . . . . . . . . . . . . . . . . . . . . dauphine2@aol.com
12021 Wilshire Blvd., Ste. 924
Los Angeles, CA 90025

TYPE     Motion Pictures + Television + Animation + Feature Direct to Video
CREDITS     Four Your Love - Legs - I Really Can Cook
COMMENTS     Produces own projects. Does not accept unsolicited material. Children's TV.

Patricia Rust . . . . . . . . . . . . . . . . President/Creative Director
Aryn Kennedy . . . . . . . . . . . . . . . . . Development Associate

## RYSHER ENTERTAINMENT
PHONE . . . . . . . . . . . . . . . . . . . . . . . . . . 310-309-5200
FAX . . . . . . . . . . . . . . . . . . . . . . . . . . . 310-309-5266
EMAIL . . . . . . . . . . . . . . . . . . . . . . . rysher@aol.com
WEBSITE . . . . . . . . . . . . . . . . . . . http://www.rysher.com
2401 Colorado Ave., Ste. 200
Santa Monica, CA 90404

TYPE     Television + Syndication + Feature Direct to Video
CREDITS     Primal Fear - Evening Star - Nash Bridges - Big Night - The Saint - Private Parts - Judge Mills Lane - S.O.S.
COMMENTS     A division of Cox Enterprises Inc.

Tim Helfet . . . . . . . . . . . . . . . . . . . . . . CEO/President
Rob Kenneally . . . . . . . . . . . . . . . . . Pres., Creative Affairs
Franklin Johnson . . . . . . . . . . . . . . . CFO/Sr. VP, Finance
Jeff Matloff . . . . . . . . . . . . . . . Sr. VP, Business/Legal Affairs
Barbara M. Rubin . . . . . . . . . . . Sr. VP, TV Business/Legal Affairs
Marcia Carter . . . . . . . . . . . . . . . . VP, Corporate Controller
Mel Effros . . . . . . . . . . . . . . . . . . . . Sr. VP, Production
Gwen Gale . . . . . . . . . . . . . . . . . . VP, International Finance
George Majewski . . . . . . . . . VP, International Business/Legal Affairs
Andrew Plotkin . . . . . . . . . . . . . . . . . . VP, Creative Affairs
Julie Shapiro . . . . . . . . . . . . . VP, TV Business/Legal Affairs
Jeff Thomas . . . . . . . . . . . . . . . . . . . . . . VP, Finance

## S.E.R. FILMWORKS
PHONE . . . . . . . . . . . . . . . . . . . . . . . 757-625-7647
EMAIL . . . . . . . . . . . . . . . . . . . . . . filmwrks@erols.com
500 Botetourt St., Ste 401
Norfolk, VA 23510-1101

TYPE     Motion Pictures + Television
CREDITS     Never Say Goodbye - Mother's Day - If I Die Before I Wake - About Sarah
COMMENTS     Represented by The Irv Schecter Co. (Fax by modem, please call ahead)

Susan Rohrer . . . . . . . . . . . . . . . Producer/Writer/Director

## SABAN ENTERTAINMENT
PHONE . . . . . . . . . . . . . . . . . . . 310-235-5100/212-779-7760
FAX . . . . . . . . . . . . . . . . . . . . 310-235-5102/212-779-7751
10960 Wilshire Blvd.
Los Angeles, CA 90024

TYPE     Motion Pictures + Television + Animation
CREDITS     Power Rangers - Addams Family Reunion - The All New Captain Kangaroo
COMMENTS     ALSO: 432 Park Ave. South, #1301, NY, NY 10016. Partners with Fox Family Channel, Fox Kids.

Haim Saban . . . . . . . . . . . . . . . . . . . . . . Chairman/CEO
Mel Woods . . . . . . . . . . . . . . . . . . . . . . President/COO
Stan Golden . . . . . . . . . . . . . President (Saban Intl. Services)
Shuki Levy . . . . . . . . . . . . . . . . . . . Pres., Production
Lance H. Robbins . . . . . . . . . . . . . Pres., TV, Movies & Series
Joel Andryc . . . . . . . . . . . . . . . . . . . Sr. VP, Development
Mark Ittner . . . . . . . . . . . . . . . . . . . . . Sr. VP, Finance
Bill Josey . . . . . . . . . . . . . . . . . Sr. VP/General Counsel
Eric Rollman . . . . . . . . . . . . Sr. VP, Production/Postproduction
Julie Ashton . . . . . . . . . . . . . . . . . . . . . . VP, Casting
Dana Booton . . . . . . . . . . . . . . . . . . . . . VP, Animation
Abbie A. Charette . . . . . . . . . . . . . . . VP, Live Action Series
Beth Cleary . . . . . . . . . . . . VP, Human Resources & Administration
Susan Cooper . . . . . . . . . . . . . . . . . . . VP, Acquisitions
Rodd Feingold . . . . . . . . . . . . . . . . . VP, Physical Production
Amy Goldberg . . . . . . . . . . . . . . . . . . . VP, Motion Pictures
Cheryl McDermott . . . . . . . . . . . . VP, Business Affairs (Saban Intl.)
Judith Merians . . . . . . . . . . . . VP, Business & Legal (Saban Intl.)
Robert L. Palmer . . . . . . . . . . . . . . . VP, Production Operations
Kim Christianson . . . . . . . . . . . . . . . . . . Dir., Development
Ann Knapp . . . . . . . . . . . . . . . . . . Dir., Program Development
Kim Millimaki . . . . . . . . . . . . . . . Dir., Development MP & TV
Barry Scaton . . . . . . . . . . . . . . . . . . Dir., Business Affairs
Cori Stern . . . . . . . . . . . . Dir., Development & Programming
Laura Wegner . . . . . . . . . . . . . . . . . . . Dir., Development
Johanna Candido . . . . . . . . . . . . . . . . Mgr., Business Affairs
Michael Cutler . . . . . . . . . . . . . . . . . Mgr., Business Affairs
Tanya Valentine . . . . . . . . . . . Coordinator, Motion Pictures & TV
Sadaf Cohen . . . . . . . . . . . . . . Exec. Asst. to Lance Robbins

## SACHNOFF-LIPMAN ENTERTAINMENT
PHONE . . . . . . . . . . . . . . . . . . . . . . . . . . 310-286-6728
FAX . . . . . . . . . . . . . . . . . . . . . . . . . . . 310-556-1658
1551 S. Robertson Blvd.
Los Angeles, CA 90035

TYPE     Documentaries + Television
CREDITS     Strange Science - Finnegan's Crossing
COMMENTS     Also, MOW's & Children's Programming

Marc Sachnoff . . . . . . . . . . . . . . . . . . . Executive Producer
Joel Lipman . . . . . . . . . . . . . . . . . . . . Executive Producer
Emilie Hall . . . . . . . . . . . . . . . . . . . . Executive Assistant

# COMPANIES AND STAFF

## SACHS PRODUCTIONS, GABE

PHONE . . . . . . . . . . . . . . . . . . . . . . . . . . . . . . . . 818-380-3481
FAX . . . . . . . . . . . . . . . . . . . . . . . . . . . . . . . . . . 818-761-5600
EMAIL . . . . . . . . . . . . . . . . . . . . . . . . . cooper8789@aol.com
11271 Ventura Blvd., Ste. 345
Studio City, CA 91604

TYPE        Television + Motion Pictures
CREDITS     Street Match- Pranks - Damian Cromwell's Postcards from
America

Gabe Sachs . . . . . . . . . . . . . . . . . . . Exec. Producer/Writer/Director
Liat Goodson . . . . . . . . . . . . . . . . . . . . . . . . . . . . . . . . Assistant

## SACKS PRODUCTIONS INC., ALAN

PHONE . . . . . . . . . . . . . . . . . . . . . . . . . . . . . . . . 213-654-4430
FAX . . . . . . . . . . . . . . . . . . . . . . . . . . . . . . . . . . 213-654-3893
EMAIL . . . . . . . . . . . . . . . . . . . . . . . . . . . . sax2409@aol.com
8205 Santa Monica Blvd, Ste. 1227
Los Angeles, CA 90046

TYPE
CREDITS     Welcome Back Kotter - Cowboy Poetry Gathering - Riders
In The Sky - Me And My Hormones

Alan Sacks . . . . . . . . . . . . . . . . . . . . . . . . . . . . . . . . Producer
Teena Portier . . . . . . . . . . . . . . . . . . . . . . . Asst. to Producer

## SAGA PICTURES CORPORATION

PHONE . . . . . . . . . . . . . . . . . . . . . . . . . . . . . . . . 310-278-5200
FAX . . . . . . . . . . . . . . . . . . . . . . . . . . . . . . . . . . 310-278-5511
8899 Beverly Blvd., Ste. 813
Los Angeles, CA 90048

TYPE        Motion Pictures
CREDITS     Johnny Mnemonic - Total Eclipse - Another 9 1/2 Weeks

Yanko Damboulev . . . . . . . . . . . . . . . . . . . . . . . . Chairman/CEO
Staffan Ahrenberg . . . . . . . . . . . . . . . . . . . . . . . . . Consultant

## SALTIRE ENTERTAINMENT

PHONE . . . . . . . . . . . . . . . . . . . . . . . . . . . . . . . . 213-469-3893
FAX . . . . . . . . . . . . . . . . . . . . . . . . . . . . . . . . . . 213-469-3839
EMAIL . . . . . . . . . . . . . . . . . . . . . . . . . . . . . saltire@aol.com
2256 Holly Drive
Hollywood, CA 90068

TYPE        Motion Pictures
CREDITS     Stone of Destiny - Blue Thunder - One of The Hollywood
Ten

Stuart Pollok . . . . . . . . . . . . . . . . . . . . . . . . Owner/Producer

## SAMOSET INC./SACRET INC.

PHONE . . . . . . . . . . . . . . . . . . . . . . . . . . . . . . . . 310-458-1618
FAX . . . . . . . . . . . . . . . . . . . . . . . . . . . . . . . . . . 310-458-4037
127 Broadway, Ste. 220
Santa Monica, CA 90401

TYPE        Motion Pictures + Television
CREDITS     Orleans - Texarkana - VR5 - Romero - Testament - China
Beach - Thanks of A Grateful Nation

John Sacret Young . . . . . . . . . . . . . . . . . Writer/Director/Producer
Staci Hayes . . . . . . . . . . . . . . . . . . . Exec. Asst. to Mr. Young

## SAMUELS ENT. INC., RON

PHONE . . . . . . . . . . . . . . . . . . . . . . . . . . . . . . . . 310-273-8964
120 El Camino Dr., Penthouse
Beverly Hills, CA 90212

TYPE        Motion Pictures + Television
CREDITS     Ravenhawk - Iron Eagle 1-3 - Scruples - A Different Affair
Ron Samuels . . . . . . . . . . . . . . . . . . . . . . . . . . . . . . . Producer

## SAMUELSON PRODUCTIONS

PHONE . . . . . . . . . . . . . . . . . . . . . . . . . . . . . . . . 310-208-1000
FAX . . . . . . . . . . . . . . . . . . . . . . . . . . . . . . . . . . 310-208-2809
EMAIL . . . . . . . . . . . . . . . . . . . . . . . . . . . petersam@who.net
WEBSITE . . . . . . . . . . . . . . . . . . . . . http://www.oscarwilde.com
10401 Wyton Dr.
Los Angeles, CA 90024-2527

TYPE        Motion Pictures + Television
DEAL        Showtime Networks Inc.
CREDITS     Wilde - Revenge of the Nerds - Tom & Viv - Turk 182 -
Dog's Best Friend - The Commissioner - Arlington Road
COMMENTS   23 W Smithfield, London EC1A9HY; phone:
171-236-5532 Fx236-5504

Peter Samuelson . . . . . . . . . . . . . . . . . . . . . . . . Partner (U.S.)
Marc Samuelson . . . . . . . . . . . . . . . . . . . . . . . . . Partner (U.K.)
Rachel Cuperman . . . . . . . . . . . . . . . . . Executive Assistant (U.K.)
Daniela Ryan . . . . . . . . . . . . . . . . . . . Executive Assistant (U.S.)
Saryl Hirsch . . . . . . . . . . . . . . . . . . . . . . . . . . Controller (U.S.)
Ian Thompson . . . . . . . . . . . . . . . . . . . . . . . . . . Assistant (U.K.)

## SANDOLLAR PRODS.

PHONE . . . . . . . . . . . . . . . . . . . . . . . . . . . . . . . . 818-560-5820
FAX . . . . . . . . . . . . . . . . . . . . . . . . . . . . . . . . . . 818-566-7666
EMAIL . . . . . . . . . . . . . . . . . . . . . . . sandollar1@earthlink.net
Walt Disney Studios
500 S. Buena Vista St. Animation I-D-9
Burbank, CA 91521

TYPE        Motion Pictures + Television
DEAL        Walt Disney Pictures/Touchstone Pictures
CREDITS     Father of the Bride - Sabrina - I.Q. - Social Studies - Fly
Away Home - Buffy the Vampire Slayer - All American
Girl

Dolly Parton . . . . . . . . . . . . . . . . . . . . . . . . . . . . . . . . Owner
Sandy Gallin . . . . . . . . . . . . . . . . . . . . . . . . . . . . . . . . Owner
Scott Immergut . . . . . . . . . . . . . . . . . . . . . . . . . . . President
Tracy Katsky . . . . . . . . . . . . . . . . . VP, Television (818-560-4254)
Lisa Reid . . . . . . . . . . . . . . . . . . . Creative Executive (818-560-4289)
David Koga . . . . . . . . . . . . . Devel. Asst. to Scott Immergut (818-560-7147)
Allison Slater . . . . . . . . . . . . . Dev., Asst. to Tracy Katsky (818-560-4254)

## SANFORD/PILLSBURY PRODS.

PHONE . . . . . . . . . . . . . . . . . . . . . . . . . . . . . . . . 310-393-5225
FAX . . . . . . . . . . . . . . . . . . . . . . . . . . . . . . . . . . 310-393-8665
EMAIL . . . . . . . . . . . . . . . . . . . . . . . sanpills@earthlink.net
1459 Sixth St.
Santa Monica, CA 90401

TYPE        Motion Pictures + Television
DEAL        DreamWorks SKG
CREDITS     And the Band Played On - How To Make An American
Quilt - Desperately Seeking Susan
COMMENTS   Also: Cable

Sarah Pillsbury . . . . . . . . . . . . . . . . . . . . . . . . . . . . Producer
Midge Sanford . . . . . . . . . . . . . . . . . . . . . . . . . . . . Producer
Holly Thro . . . . . . . . . . . . . . . . . . . . . . . . Creative Executive

## SANTA MONICA PICTURES

PHONE . . . . . . . . . . . . . . . . . . . . . . . . . . . . . . . . 310-264-5566
FAX . . . . . . . . . . . . . . . . . . . . . . . . . . . . . . . . . . 310-264-5572
3025 Olympic Blvd.
Santa Monica, CA 90404

TYPE        Motion Pictures
CREDITS     Goldilocks And The Three Bears
COMMENTS   Produces original films.  Distributes own films as well as
acquires other completed films.

David Rose . . . . . . . . . . . . . . . . . . . . . . Chief Executive Officer
Todd Hess . . . . . . . . . . . . . . . . . . . . . . . . . . . . . President
Marina Muhlfriedel . . . . . . . . . . . . . . . . . . . . . . VP, Development
Peter Manoogian . . . . . . . . . . . . . . . . . Director/Producer/Writer
Tim Montgomery . . . . . . . . . . . . . . . . . . . . . . Producer/Writer

## SANTIAGO FILMS

PHONE . . . . . . . . . . . . . . . . . . . . . . . . . . . . . . . . 310-449-4049
FAX . . . . . . . . . . . . . . . . . . . . . . . . . . . . . . . . . . 310-449-4016
Lantana Center
3000 W. Olympic Blvd.
Santa Monica, CA 90404

TYPE        Motion Pictures
CREDITS     Kissing Miranda - Sweethearts

Aleks Horvat . . . . . . . . . . . . . . . . . . . . . . . . . . Writer/Director

## *SAPHIER PRODUCTIONS

PHONE . . . . . . . . . . . . . . . . . . . . . . . . . . . . . . . . 818-501-6646
FAX . . . . . . . . . . . . . . . . . . . . . . . . . . . . . . . . . . 818-995-6554
EMAIL . . . . . . . . . . . . . . . . . . . . . . . . . . . Psaphier@aol.com
4245 Valley Meadow Road
Encino, CA 91436

TYPE        Motion Pictures + Television
CREDITS     Black Dog - Scarface

Peter Saphier . . . . . . . . . . . . . . . . . . . . . . . . . . . . . Principal

## SARABANDE PRODS.

PHONE . . . . . . . . . . . . . . . . . . . . . . . . . . . . . . . . 310-395-4842
FAX . . . . . . . . . . . . . . . . . . . . . . . . . . . . . . . . . . 310-395-7079
530 Wilshire Blvd., Ste. 308
Santa Monica, CA 90401

TYPE        Motion Pictures + Television
CREDITS     Nothing Sacred - Thicker Than Blood - Nightjohn - Birdy -
Bring on the Night - Mad Love

David Manson . . . . . . . . . . . . . . . . . . . . . . . . . . . President
Arla Sorkin Manson . . . . . . . . . . . . . . . . . . Exec. Vice President
Sarah Dohrmann . . . . . . . . . . . . . . . . . . Development Associate
Melissa Sherman . . . . . . . . . . . . . . . . . . Development Associate

# COMPANIES AND STAFF

**SARATOGA ENTERTAINMENT**
PHONE . . . . . . . . . . . . . . . . . . . . . . . . . . . . . . . . 310-664-9633
FAX . . . . . . . . . . . . . . . . . . . . . . . . . . . . . . . . . . . 310-664-0144
EMAIL . . . . . . . . . . . . . . . . . . . . . . . . . saratogapr@aol.com
508 Pier Avenue
Santa Monica, CA 90405
TYPE Motion Pictures + Television
CREDITS GO
Paul Rosenberg . . . . . . . . . . . . . . . . . . . . . . . . . . . . . . . Producer
David Hosbein . . . . . . . . . . . . . . . . . . . . . . . . . VP, Production
Lee Sosin . . . . . . . . . . . . . . . . . . . . . . . . . . . Dir., Development

**SARKISSIAN PRODUCTIONS, ARTHUR**
PHONE . . . . . . . . . . . . . . . . . . . . . . . . . . . . . . . . 310-385-1486
FAX . . . . . . . . . . . . . . . . . . . . . . . . . . . . . . . . . . . 310-385-1489
9465 Wilshire Blvd., Ste. 980
Beverly Hills, CA 90212
TYPE Motion Pictures + Television
CREDITS Wanted Dead or Alive - While You Were Sleeping - Last Man Standing - Rush Hour
Arthur Sarkissian . . . . . . . . . . . . . . . . . . . . . . . . . . . . . . Producer
Rick Joseph . . . . . . . . . . . . . . . Executive Assistant/Development

**SATURN FILMS**
PHONE . . . . . . . . . . . . . . . . . . . . . . . . . . . . . . . . 310-887-0900
FAX . . . . . . . . . . . . . . . . . . . . . . . . . . . . . . . . . . . 310-248-2965
9000 Sunset Blvd., #911
West Hollywood, CA 90069
TYPE Motion Pictures
DEAL Walt Disney Pictures/Touchstone Pictures
Nicolas Cage . . . . . . . . . . . . . . . . . . . . . . . President/Producer
Jeff Levine . . . . . . . . . . . . . . . . . . . . . . . . . . . . . . . . . . Producer
Norm Golightly . . . . . . . . . . . . . . . . . . . . . . VP, Creative Affairs
Jack Oliver . . . . . . . . . . . . . . . . . . . . . . . . . Corporate Operations
Stephen Bures . . . . . . . . . . . . . . . . . . . . . . . Asst. to Mr. Cage
Morgan Gregory . . . . . . . . . . . . . . . . . Asst. to Norm Golightly

**SAUCE ENTERTAINMENT**
PHONE . . . . . . . . . . . . . . . . . . . . . . . . . . . . . . . . 212-343-3000
FAX . . . . . . . . . . . . . . . . . . . . . . . . . . . . . . . . . . . 212-343-8503
EMAIL . . . . . . . . . . . . . . . . . . . . . . . . . . . . sauceent@aol.com
WEBSITE . . . . . . . . . . . . . . . . . . . . http://www.saucenyc.com
100 Varick St., 3rd Floor
New York, NY 10013
TYPE Motion Pictures + Documentaries + Animation + Interactive Multimedia
CREDITS I Like It Like That - Village Idiots - The Naked Man
COMMENTS Also: Music Videos & Commercials.  Graphics Department & Post Production.
Marcus Englefield . . . . . . . . . . . . . . . . . Chief Executive Officer
Aida Ashenafi . . . . . . . . . . . . . . . . . . . . . . . . . . . . . . President
Kenji Mitsuka . . . . . . . . . . . . . . . . . . . . . . . . . . . . . . . Producer

**SAVAGE STUDIOS LTD.**
PHONE . . . . . . . . . . . . . . . . . . . . . . . . . . . . . . . . 818-560-2316
FAX . . . . . . . . . . . . . . . . . . . . . . . . . . . . . . . . . . . 818-567-1873
500 S. Buena Vista, Anim. 1C8
Burbank, CA 91521
TYPE Animation + Motion Pictures + Television
DEAL Walt Disney Television
Savage Steve Holland . . . . . . . . . . . . . . . Producer/Writer/Director
Melanie Shea . . . . . . . . . . . . . . . . . . . . . . . . . Dir., Development

**SAVOIR FAIRE PRODUCTIONS**
PHONE . . . . . . . . . . . . . . . . . . . . . . . . . . . . . . . . 310-459-6191
FAX . . . . . . . . . . . . . . . . . . . . . . . . . . . . . . . . . . . 310-459-6491
EMAIL . . . . . . . . . . . . . . . . . . . . . . . . . . savfair@earthlink.net
1025 Chautaugua Blvd.
Pacific Palisades, CA 90272
TYPE Documentaries + Motion Pictures + Television
COMMENTS Also: Team Studio A.S.
Rebekah Jorgensen . . . . . . . . . . . . . . . . . . . . . . . . . . President
Allen Karlin . . . . . . . . . . . . . . . . . . . . . . . . . . . . Vice President
Kenneth Ussenko . . . . . . . . . . . . . . . . . . . . . . . . Head Writer

**SAY UNKEL ENTERTAINMENT**
PHONE . . . . . . . . . . . . . . . . . . . . . . . . . . . . . . . . 818-506-6015
FAX . . . . . . . . . . . . . . . . . . . . . . . . . . . . . . . . . . . 818-752-0709
10413 Bloomfield Street
Toluca Lake, CA 91602
TYPE Motion Pictures + Television
DEAL Paramount Pictures- Motion Picture Group
Robert Unkel . . . . . . . . . . . . . . . . . . . . . . . . . . . . . . President
John Mekrut . . . . . . . . . . . . . . . . . . . . . . . . . VP, Development

**SCARLET FIRE FILMS**
PHONE . . . . . . . . . . . . . . . . . . . . . . . . . . . . . . . . 818-972-9900
FAX . . . . . . . . . . . . . . . . . . . . . . . . . . . . . . . . . . . 818-972-9992
EMAIL . . . . . . . . . . . . . . . . . . . . . . . . . . . . . fireflix@aol.com
4231 W. McFarlane Ave.
Burbank, CA 91505
TYPE Motion Pictures + Feature Direct to Video
CREDITS Breathe - Resolution
Robert Steinberg . . . . . . . . . . . . . . . Executive Producer/President
Josh Nadel . . . . . . . . . . . . . . . . . . . . . . . . . . . VP, Production
Straw Weisman . . . . . . . . . . . . . . . . . . . . . . . VP, Development
Laura Cayouette . . . . . . . . . . . . . . . . . . . . . Writer/Development
Trisha Zigler . . . . . . . . . . . . . . . . . . . . . . Executive Assistant

**SCHACHTER ENTERTAINMENT, INC.**
PHONE . . . . . . . . . . . . . . . . . . . . . . . . . . . . . . . . 310-277-6108
FAX . . . . . . . . . . . . . . . . . . . . . . . . . . . . . . . . . . . 310-277-6602
EMAIL . . . . . . . . . . . . . . . . . . . . . . . . . schachtert@aol.com
10264 Rochester Ave.
Los Angeles, CA 90024-5331
TYPE Motion Pictures + Television
CREDITS Homeboys In Outer Space - Bela Donna
COMMENTS Also: Comedy.
Ted Schachter . . . . . . . . . . . . . . . . . . . . . . . . . . . . . . Principal
Michael Tribuch . . . . . . . . . . . . . . . . . . . . . . . . . Development

**SCHEIMER PRODS., LOU**
PHONE . . . . . . . . . . . . . . . . . . . . . . . . . . . . . . . . 818-884-2810
FAX . . . . . . . . . . . . . . . . . . . . . . . . . . . . . . . . . . . 818-884-1824
20300 Ventura Blvd., Ste. 145
Woodland Hills, CA 91364
TYPE Motion Pictures + Television + Animation + Feature Direct to Video
CREDITS He-Man & She-Ra - Fat Albert
COMMENTS Family Entertainment & Children's Programs.
Lou Scheimer . . . . . . . . . . . . . . . . . . . . . . . . . . . . . . President
Erika Scheimer . . . . . . . . . . . . . . . . . . . . . . VP, Creative Affairs

**SCHERICK ASSOCS., EDGAR J.**
PHONE . . . . . . . . . . . . . . . . . . . . . . . . . . . . . . . . 310-996-2376
FAX . . . . . . . . . . . . . . . . . . . . . . . . . . . . . . . . . . . 310-996-2392
1950 Sawtelle Blvd., Ste. 282
Los Angeles, CA 90025
TYPE Motion Pictures + Television
CREDITS Rambling Rose - Ruby Ridge - The Wall
Edgar J. Scherick . . . . . . . . . . . . . . . . . Exec. Producer/President
Liza Leeds . . . . . . . . . . . . . . . . . . . . . . . . . . . VP, Development
Sandi Carrillo . . . . . . . . . . . . . . . . . . . . . . . Asst. to Mr. Scherick
Neill MacLeod-Hunter . . . . . . . . . . . . . . . . . Asst. To Mr. Scherick

***SCHIFF PRODUCTIONS, PAUL**
PHONE . . . . . . . . . . . . . . . . . . . . . . . . . . . . . . . . 818-560-4423
FAX . . . . . . . . . . . . . . . . . . . . . . . . . . . . . . . . . . . 818-842-5749
500 S. Buena Vista St.
Burbank, CA 91521-1770
TYPE Motion Pictures
DEAL Walt Disney Company, The
CREDITS My Cousin Vinny - Young Guns I & II
Paul Schiff . . . . . . . . . . . . . . . . . . . . . . . President/Producer
Matt Berenson . . . . . . . . . . . . . . Sr. VP, Production (818-560-3392)
Samantha Sprecher . . . . . . . . . . . . Creative Executive (818-560-3346)

**SCHINDLER PRODS., DEBORAH**
PHONE . . . . . . . . . . . . . . . . . . . . . . . . . . . . . . . . 212-265-7760
FAX . . . . . . . . . . . . . . . . . . . . . . . . . . . . . . . . . . . 212-581-3617
110 W. 57th St., Ste. 401
New York, NY 10019
TYPE Motion Pictures
DEAL Twentieth Century Fox
CREDITS Waiting to Exhale - Prelude to A Kiss - How Stella Got Her Groove Back
Deborah Schindler . . . . . . . . . . . . . . . . . . . . . . . . . . . Producer
Tad Floridis . . . . . . . . . . . . . . . . . . . . . . . . Dir., Literary Affairs
Patricia Jones . . . . . . . . . . . . . . . . . . . . . . . . . . . Story Editor
Tom Heller . . . . . . . . . . . . . . . . . . . . Asst. to Deborah Schindler

## SCHLATTER PRODS., GEORGE
```
PHONE ........................................... 213-655-1400
FAX ............................................. 213-852-1640
```
8321 Beverly Blvd.
Los Angeles, CA 90048

| | |
|---|---|
| TYPE | Television |
| DEAL | Fox Entertainment Company |
| CREDITS | American Comedy Awards - Sinatra: 80 Years My Way - Laugh In - Real People |

```
George Schlatter ............................... Executive Producer
Maria S. Schlatter ................................. Co-Producer
Donn Hoyer ....................................... Co-Producer
Gary Necessary ...................... Exec. In Charge of Production
Nathan Golden ........................................ Accounting
Suzzanne Stangel ........................... Production Manager
```

## SCHOLASTIC ENTERTAINMENT
```
PHONE ........................................... 212-343-7500
FAX ....................... 212-343-7888/212-343-7566
EMAIL ......................... sdonaldson@scholastic.com
WEBSITE .......................... http://www.scholastic.com
```
555 Broadway
New York, NY 10012-3999

| | |
|---|---|
| TYPE | Motion Pictures + Television + Syndication + Animation + Interactive Multimedia |
| CREDITS | The Magic School Bus - Indian in the Cupboard - Goosebumps |
| COMMENTS | Also: Live Action Animation. |

```
Deborah Forte ........................... Division Head/Exec. VP
Linda Kahn ................. Sr. VP, Programming & Distribution
Ginger McGuire ................... VP, Finance & Business Affairs
Andrea Sporer ................................ VP, Legal Affairs
Martha Atwater ...................... Exec. Dir., Development
Maria Gillen .............................. Dir., Development
```

## SCHUMACHER PRODS., JOEL
```
PHONE ........................................... 818-954-2508
FAX ............................................. 818-954-2509
```
Warner Bros.
4000 Warner Blvd., Bldg. 81, Rm. 207
Burbank, CA 91522-1332

| | |
|---|---|
| TYPE | Motion Pictures |
| DEAL | Warner Bros. Pictures |
| CREDITS | Batman & Robin - A Time To Kill - Batman Forever |

```
Joel Schumacher ....................................... Owner
Claire Baker ................... Exec. Asst. to Joel Schumacher
Eli Richbourg .................... Asst. to Joel Schumacher
```

## SCHWARTZ PRODUCTIONS, BERNARD
```
PHONE ........................................... 310-277-3700
```
1900 Ave. of the Stars, Ste. 1800
Los Angeles, CA 90067

| | |
|---|---|
| TYPE | Motion Pictures + Television |
| CREDITS | Sweet Dreams - Coal Miner's Daughter - St. Elmo's Fire |

```
Bernard Schwartz ..................................... Producer
Sandra Jones ......................................... Assistant
```

## SCHWARTZ PRODUCTIONS, STEVEN
```
PHONE ........................................... 860-868-0627
FAX ............................................. 860-868-0504
EMAIL ..................................... ssflix@aol.com
```
53 Curtiss Rd.
New Preston, CT 06777

| | |
|---|---|
| TYPE | Motion Pictures + Television + Documentaries |
| CREDITS | Critical Care - A Raisin in the Sun - Likely Stories |

```
Steven Schwartz .............................. Writer/Producer
Nicki Miller ............................... Dir., Development
```

## SCHWARTZBERG & COMPANY
```
PHONE ........................................... 818-508-1833
FAX ............................................. 818-508-1253
```
12700 Ventura Blvd., 4th Floor
Studio City, CA 91604

| | |
|---|---|
| TYPE | Documentaries + Motion Pictures + Television + Interactive Multimedia + Animation |
| CREDITS | Oceans of Air - Discovery Channel |
| COMMENTS | Also: Black Light Films. Also: Commericals. |

```
Louis Schwartzberg ............... Director/Cinematographer
Henry Winkler ......................................... Director
```

## SCOTT FREE PRODUCTIONS
```
PHONE ........................................... 310-888-4100
FAX ............................................. 310-888-4111
```
9348 Civic Center Dr., Mezzanine Floor
Beverly Hills, CA 90210

| | |
|---|---|
| TYPE | Motion Pictures + Television |
| DEAL | Polygram Filmed Entertainment |
| CREDITS | White Squall - Crimson Tide - Thelma & Louise - Enemy of the State - GI Jane |

```
Ridley Scott ......................................... Co-Chairman
Tony Scott ........................................... Co-Chairman
Chris Zarpas ........................................... President
Robert Norton ....................... COO/Exec. Vice President
Lou Spoto ......................... Exec. VP, Business Affairs
Christopher Dorr ........................... Sr. VP, Production
Diane Minter Lewis ......................... Sr. VP, Production
Shaun Williams ....................... Controller/Dir., Finance
Steven Kent Foster ........................ Dir., Development
Jerry Heiss ...................... Exec. Asst. to Tony Scott
Edwin Kashiba ................. Story Editor/Asst. to D. Minter
Anne Lai ...................... Exec. Asst. to Ridley Scott
Mark Nelson ........... Dir., Business Affairs Admin./Asst. to Lou Spoto
Peg Shearer ..................... Exec. Asst. to Chris Zarpas
Pete Toumasis ..................... Exec. Asst. to Tony Scott
Ashley Fondrevay ........................... Asst. to C. Dorr
Molly Ann Howard ............ Office Manager/Asst. to R. Norton
Denise Huth ......................................... Accountant
```

## SCRIPPS HOWARD PRODS.
```
PHONE ........................................... 310-264-3000
FAX ............................................. 310-264-3111
```
The Water Garden
2425 Olympic Blvd., Ste. 5005
Santa Monica, CA 90404

| | |
|---|---|
| TYPE | Motion Pictures + Television + Documentaries + Syndication |
| CREDITS | Tycoon - Buried Secrets - The Prosecutors - Suddenly - Night Sins - When Secrets Kill |

```
David Percelay ................................... President/CEO
Michele Brustin ............... Sr. Exec. Producer, Entertainment
Craig Leake .............. Sr. Exec. Producer, Non-Fiction
Richard Brams ................ Exec. in Charge of Production
Nina Weinstein .................... Sr. Producer, Non-Fiction
Allan Chalfin ............ VP, Production, Finance & Adminstration
Dana Walker ................ VP, Business & Legal Affairs
Jane Jacobs ......................... Mgr., Business Affairs
Trish McGee ..................................... Office Manager
Maggie DeFina ...................... Creative Affairs Associate
Paul Raney ........................... Creative Affairs Associate
```

## SEAGAL-NASSO PRODUCTIONS
```
PHONE ........................................... 213-850-2940
FAX ............................................. 213-850-2935
```
Warner Hollywood Studios
1041 N. Formosa Ave.
West Hollywood, CA 90046

| | |
|---|---|
| TYPE | Motion Pictures |
| DEAL | Warner Bros. Pictures |
| CREDITS | On Deadly Ground - Under Siege I&II - Above The Law - The Glimmer Man - Fire Down Below |

```
Steven Seagal .............. Co-CEO/Director/Writer/Producer/Actor
Julius Nasso ................................. Co-CEO/Producer
Phillip Goldfine ....................................... President
Patricia Barron ............................... Executive Assistant
Andrew Gladston ............................... Creative Executive
Vera Sevic ..................... Personal Asst. to Mr. Seagal
```

## SEFTON PRODUCTIONS INTERNATIONAL
```
PHONE ........................................... 213-917-7874
FAX ............................................. 213-466-9593
```
1680 N. Vine Street, Ste. 727
Hollywood, CA 90028

| | |
|---|---|
| TYPE | Documentaries + Feature Direct to Video + Motion Pictures |
| CREDITS | James Dean, The Night Before - Imelda - James Dean: Race With Destiny - Wil. Shakespeare Docu. |

```
Dan Sefton ....................... President/Executive Producer
Priscilla Padilla ............... Production/Development Associate
Regan Dills .................... Dir., Financing & Joint-Venture
Sue Groves ............................... Dir., Development
Wil. Hall .............................. Actor/Executive Associate
```

# COMPANIES AND STAFF

**SEGAN COMPANY, THE LLOYD**
PHONE . . . . . . . . . . . . . . . . . . . . . . . . . 213-850-3130
FAX . . . . . . . . . . . . . . . . . . . . . . . . . . . 213-850-3133
Warner Hollywood Studios
1041 N. Formosa, Pickford Bldg. #208
W. Hollywood, CA 90046
TYPE          Motion Pictures
DEAL          New Line Cinema
CREDITS       The Bachelor - Blown Away - Judgment Night
Lloyd Segan . . . . . . . . . . . . . . . . . . . . . . . . . Producer
Stephen Hollocker . . . . . . . . . . . . . . . . . Vice President
Eaves Nye . . . . . . . . . . . . . . . . . . . . . . . Story Editor

**SEGGERMAN PRODUCTIONS, HENRY**
PHONE . . . . . . . . . . . . . . . . . . . . . . . . . 310-446-9750
FAX . . . . . . . . . . . . . . . . . . . . . . . . . . . 310-446-9850
EMAIL . . . . . . . . . . . . . . . . . . . . henrys@lytewave.net
2049 Linnington Ave.
Los Angeles, CA 90025-5901
TYPE          Motion Pictures
CREDITS       Leprechaun 3 - Evolver - The Paper Boy - Synapse -
              Progeny
Henry Seggerman . . . . . . . . . . . . . . . . . . . . Producer
Beverly Gray . . . . . . . . . . . . . . . . . . . . VP, Production

**SEGUE PRODS., INC.**
PHONE . . . . . . . . . . . . . . . . . . . . . . . . . 310-312-1828
FAX . . . . . . . . . . . . . . . . . . . . . . . . . . . 310-312-1868
11150 Santa Monica Blvd., Ste. 1200
Los Angeles, CA 90025
TYPE          Motion Pictures
CREDITS       Restoration - Ransom
Kip Hagopian . . . . . . . . . . . . . . . . Chairman/President
Pat Papero . . . . . . . . . . . . . . . . . . Executive Assistant

**SEGUIN PRODS., NICOLE**
PHONE . . . . . . . . . . . . . . . . . . . . . . . . . 310-657-5900
FAX . . . . . . . . . . . . . . . . . . . . . . . . . . . 310-657-2721
414 Westbourne
Los Angeles, CA 90048
TYPE          Motion Pictures + Television + Interactive Multimedia +
              Animation
CREDITS       Turn of the Screw - The West Side Waltz - Zandalee -
              Jersey Girl
Nicole Seguin . . . . . . . . . . . . . . . . . . . . . . . Producer

**SELDES FILMS**
PHONE . . . . . . . . . . . . . . . . . . . . . . . . . 310-449-3045
FAX . . . . . . . . . . . . . . . . . . . . . . . . . . . 310-586-8216
MGM/UA
2450 Broadway
Santa Monica, CA 90404
TYPE          Motion Pictures + Television
DEAL          MGM/UA
Elisabeth Seldes . . . . . . . . . . . . . . . . . . . . . Producer
David Kalisher . . . . . . . . . . . . . . . . . Dir., Development

***SELLERS PRODUCTIONS, DYLAN**
PHONE . . . . . . . . . . . . . . . . . . . . . . . . . 310-264-4130
3000 W. Olympic Blvd.
Santa Monica, CA 90404
TYPE          Motion Pictures + Television
CREDITS       Out to Sea - Passenger 57 - The Paper
Dylan Sellers . . . . . . . . . . . . . . . . . . . . . . . Producer
Bonny Giardina . . . . . . . . . . . . . . . . . Dir., Development

**SENNET PRODS., MARK**
PHONE . . . . . . . . . . . . . . . . . . . . . . . . . 310-887-5642
FAX . . . . . . . . . . . . . . . . . . . . . . . . . . . 310-887-5626
Citadel Entertainment
301 N. Canon Dr., Ste. 321
Beverly Hills, CA 90210
TYPE          Motion Pictures + Television
DEAL          Citadel Entertainment., LLC
CREDITS       Switched at Birth - Dying To Be Perfect - Legacy of Sin -
              Miracle on I-880
Mark Sennet . . . . . . . . . . . . . . . . . . . Executive Producer
John Marzullo . . . . . . . . . . . . . . . . Dir., Creative Affairs

**SEVEN ARTS PICTURES**
PHONE . . . . . . . . . . . . . . . . . . . . . . . . . 213-464-0225
FAX . . . . . . . . . . . . . . . . . . . . . . . . . . . 213-464-8305
7080 Hollywood Blvd., Ste. 511
Hollywood, CA 90028
TYPE          Motion Pictures
DEAL          Paramount Pictures- Motion Picture Group
CREDITS       Johnny Mnemonic - Never Talk To Strangers - Shattered
              Image
COMMENTS      Formerly CineVisions
Peter M. Hoffman . . . . . . . . . . . . . . . . . . . . Chairman
Colleen Camp . . . . . . . . . . . . . . . . . . Producer/Partner
Neil Canton . . . . . . . . . . . . . . . . . . . . Producer/Partner
Susan Hoffman . . . . . . . . . . . . . . . . . Producer/Partner
B.J. Miller . . . . . . . . . . . . . . . . . . . . Sr. Vice President
Eric Sandys . . . . . . . . . . . . . . . . . . Sr. VP, Production
Stephanie Poole . . . . . . . . . . . . . . . . . Dir., Development
Victor Teran . . . . . . . . . . . . . . . . . . . . . Development
Peter Bisanz . . . . . . . . . . . . . . . . . . . Executive Assistant
Victoria Clay . . . . . . . . . . . . . . . . . . . Executive Assistant
Brette Krinick . . . . . . . . . . . . . . . . . . Executive Assistant
Barbara Seretan . . . . . . . . . . . . . . . . . Executive Assistant

**SEVEN SUMMITS PICTURES & MGMT.**
PHONE . . . . . . . . . . . . . . . . . . . . . . . . . 213-655-0101
FAX . . . . . . . . . . . . . . . . . . . . . . . . . . . 213-655-2204
EMAIL . . . . . . . . . . . . . . . . . . . carthaycir@aol.com
8447 Wilshire Blvd., Ste. 200
Beverly Hills, CA 90211
TYPE          Motion Pictures + Television
CREDITS       Grandview USA - Zandalee - Linguini Incident - Pros &
              Cons of Breathing
William Blaylock . . . . . . . . . . . . . . . . . . . . . Partner
Sarah Jackson . . . . . . . . . . . . . . . . . . . . . . Partner
Paul Canterna . . . . . . . . . . . . . . . . . . . . . . Creative
Ben Levine . . . . . . . . . . . . . . . . . . . . . . . Creative
Louis Massicotte . . . . . . . . . . . . . . . . . . . Associate
Mariana Galvez . . . . . . . . . . . . . . . . . . . . Assistant

**SHADOWCATCHER ENTERTAINMENT**
PHONE . . . . . . . . . . . . . . . . . . . . . . . . . 206-328-6266
FAX . . . . . . . . . . . . . . . . . . . . . . . . . . . 206-328-6682
EMAIL . . . . . . . . . . . . . . . . email@shadowcathcherent.com
WEBSITE . . . . . . . . . . . . . . . http://www.shadowcatcherent.com
400 East Pine St., Ste. 315
Seattle, WA 98122
TYPE          Motion Pictures + Television
CREDITS       Smoke Signals - The Book of Stars
COMMENTS      LA Office (310) 358-3201
Larry Estes . . . . . . . . . . . . . . . . . . . . . . . Producer
Scott Rosenfelt . . . . . . . . . . . . . . . . . . . . . Producer
David Skinner . . . . . . . . . . . . . . . . . . . . . . Producer
Roger Baerwolf . . . . . . . . . . . . . Producer/VP, Development
Greg Mollner . . . . . . . . . . . . . . . Chief Operating Officer
Michael Lewis . . . . . . . . . . . . . . . . . . . . Story Editor
Pauline Tamblyn . . . . . . . . . . . . . . . . . . . . . Finance
Serena McDonald . . . . . . . . . . . . . . . . Executive Assistant
Peter Jensen . . . . . . . . . . . . . . . . . . Asst. to Producers

**SHADOWLANDS PRODUCTIONS**
PHONE . . . . . . . . . . . . . . . . . . . . . . . . . 818-501-6167
14225 Riverside Dr., Ste. #3
Sherman Oaks, CA 91423-2369
TYPE          Motion Pictures + Television
CREDITS       The Summer of Ben Tyler (Hallmark Hall of Fame)
Jeffrey R. Coates . . . . . . . . . . . . . . . . . . . . . Producer

**SHADOWPLAY FILMS**
PHONE . . . . . . . . . . . . . . . . . . . . . . . . . 310-478-1700
FAX . . . . . . . . . . . . . . . . . . . . . . . . . . . 310-478-2202
Hearst Ent.
1640 S. Sepulveda Blvd., 4th Floor
Los Angeles, CA 90025-7510
TYPE          Television
DEAL          Hearst Entertainment
CREDITS       Shadows of Desire - Jewels - Storm & Sorrow - Thrill -
              Hidden In Silence - Death on Everest
Hans Proppe . . . . . . . . . . . . . . . . . . . . . . . Producer

# COMPANIES AND STAFF

**SHAPIRO ENT. INC., RICHARD & ESTHER**
PHONE . . . . . . . . . . . . . . . . . . . . . . . . . . . . . 310-271-2202
FAX . . . . . . . . . . . . . . . . . . . . . . . . . . . . . . . 310-271-8990
335 N. Maple Dr., Ste. 245
Beverly Hills, CA 90210-3867

TYPE          Motion Pictures + Television
Richard Shapiro . . . . . . . . . . . . . . . . . . . . . . . . . Chairman
M. Jack Mayesh . . . . . . . . . . . . . . . . . . Chief Operating Officer
Esther Shapiro . . . . . . . . . . . . . . . . . . . . . . . President/CEO
Florie Shapiro . . . . . . . . . . . . . . . . . . . . . Dir., Development

**SHAPIRO PRODS., ARNOLD**
PHONE . . . . . . . . . . . . . . . . . . . . . . . . . . . . . 310-451-6270
FAX . . . . . . . . . . . . . . . . . . . . . . . . . . . . . . . 310-451-4634
520 Broadway, Ste. 220
Santa Monica, CA 90401

TYPE          Television
DEAL          CBS Entertainment
CREDITS       Rescue 911 - Scared Straight! - Scared Silent! - Break The
              Silence - The Story of Santa Claus
Arnold Shapiro . . . . . . . . . . . . . . . . . . . . . Executive Producer
Janine Iamunno . . . . . . . . . . . . . . . . . . . . Executive Assistant

**SHAPIRO PRODUCTIONS, ALLEN**
PHONE . . . . . . . . . . . . . . . . . . . . . . . . . . . . . 310-244-5845
FAX . . . . . . . . . . . . . . . . . . . . . . . . . . . . . . . 310-244-1447
10202 W. Washington Blvd., Lean Bld. 212
Culver City, CA 90232

TYPE          Motion Pictures + Interactive Multimedia
CREDITS       Universal Soldier - The Quick & The Dead - Air America
Allen Shapiro . . . . . . . . . . . . . . . . . . . . . . . President/CEO
Anne Attalla . . . . . . . . . . . . . . . . . . . . . . Creative Executive

**SHAPIRO PRODUCTIONS, ROBERT**
PHONE . . . . . . . . . . . . . . . . . . . . . . . . . . . . . 818-560-2712
FAX . . . . . . . . . . . . . . . . . . . . . . . . . . . . . . . 818-559-5561
Walt Disney Studios - Animation Building
500 S. Buena Vista St., 4th Fl.
Burbank, CA 91521-1897

TYPE          Motion Pictures
CREDITS       Pee-Wee's Big Adv. - Empire Of The Sun - Black Beauty -
              My Favorite Martian
Robert Shapiro . . . . . . . . . . . . . . . . . . . . . . . . President
Sarah Knight . . . . . . . . . . . . . . . . . . . . . . . . . . No Title

**SHATTER GLASS PRODS.**
PHONE . . . . . . . . . . . . . . . . . . . . . . . . . . . . . 213-662-4201
FAX . . . . . . . . . . . . . . . . . . . . . . . . . . . . . . . 213-661-6943
EMAIL . . . . . . . . . . . . . . . . . . . . . . spencertee@aol.com
2013 N. Vermont Ave.
Los Angeles, CA 90027

TYPE          Motion Pictures + Television
CREDITS       Screenwriters:On Film - Pump It Up/Fox - Life Styles Rich
              & Famous
COMMENTS      Encore Also: Music Videos.
Spencer Thornton . . . . . . . . . . . . . . Writer/Producer/Director
Valli Kleven . . . . . . . . . . . . . . . . . . . . . . . . . . . Writer
Sam Hill . . . . . . . . . . . . . . . . . . . . . . . . Production Manager

**SHELDON/POST COMPANY, THE**
PHONE . . . . . . . . . . . . . . . . . . . . . . . . . . . . . 818-760-8265
1437 Rising Glen Rd.
Los Angeles, CA 90069

TYPE          Motion Pictures + Television + Syndication
DEAL          Producers Ent. Group, Ltd., The/Clark Prods., Inc., Dick
CREDITS       Secrets of a Small Town - Mysteries of the Pyramids -
              Grizzly Adams And The Legend of Dark Mountain
COMMENTS      TV includes: Movies, Series, Sitcom, & Reality Programs .
              Sheldon/Post Tri-Media Intl. Prod. Unit In Canada.
David Sheldon . . . . . . . . . . . . . . . . Producer/Director/Writer
Ira Post . . . . . . . . . . . . . . . . . . . . . . . . . Executive Producer

**SHELTER ENTERTAINMENT**
PHONE . . . . . . . . . . . . . . . . . . . . . . . . . . . . . 310-724-8900
FAX . . . . . . . . . . . . . . . . . . . . . . . . . . . . . . . 310-724-8998
9255 Sunset Blvd., Ste. 1010
Los Angeles, CA 90069

TYPE          Motion Pictures + Television
Alan Iezman . . . . . . . . . . . . . . . . . . . . . . President/Producer
Ray McKigney . . . . . . . . . . . . . . . . . . . . . Manager/Producer
Caran Sealey . . . . . . . . . . . . . . . . . . . . . . Producer/Manager
Julie Guzman . . . . . . . . . . . . . . . . . . . . . Executive Assistant

**SHINBONE PRODUCTIONS**
PHONE . . . . . . . . . . . . . . . . . . . . . . . . . . . . . 310-319-6568
FAX . . . . . . . . . . . . . . . . . . . . . . . . . . . . . . . 310-319-6567
1316 3rd Street Promenade, Ste. 105
Santa Monica, CA 90401

TYPE          Motion Pictures
CREDITS       Fallen Angels - Hand That Rocks The Cradle - Eye For An
              Eye - The Relic
Rick Jaffa . . . . . . . . . . . . . . . . . . . . . . . . Writer/Producer
Amanda Silver . . . . . . . . . . . . . . . . . . . . . . Writer/Producer
Gibran Perrone . . . . . . . . . . . . . . . . . . . . Executive Assistant

**SHO FILMS**
PHONE . . . . . . . . . . . . . . . . . . . . . . . . . . . . . 213-665-9088
4470 Sunset Blvd., Ste. 192
Los Angeles, CA 90027

TYPE          Motion Pictures
CREDITS       Android - Critters I, II, III & IV - Slam Dance
Rupert Harvey . . . . . . . . . . . . . . . . . . . . . . . Co-President
Barry Opper . . . . . . . . . . . . . . . . . . . . . . . . . Co-President

**SHOELACE PRODUCTIONS, INC.**
PHONE . . . . . . . . . . . . . . . . . . . . . . . . . . . . . 212-243-2900
FAX . . . . . . . . . . . . . . . . . . . . . . . . . . . . . . . 212-243-2973
16 W. 19th St., 12th Fl.
New York, NY 10011

TYPE          Motion Pictures + Television
DEAL          Walt Disney Pictures/Touchstone Pictures
COMMENTS      Also: Cable.
Julia Roberts . . . . . . . . . . . . . . . . . . . . . . . Actor/Producer
Pliny Porter . . . . . . . . . . . . . . Pres., Production & Development
Suzanne Weinert . . . . . . . . . . . . . . . . . . . . VP, Development

**SHOGUN FILMS, LTD.**
PHONE . . . . . . . . . . . . . . . . . . . . . . . . . . . . . 818-904-9010
FAX . . . . . . . . . . . . . . . . . . . . . . . . . . . . . . . 818-787-2171
13601 Ventura Blvd., Ste. 263
Sherman Oaks, CA 91423

TYPE          Motion Pictures + Television + Documentaries +
              Interactive Multimedia
CREDITS       Gardish Destiny - Kalapari - Mortal Kombat (India)
COMMENTS      Producer in India - L.A. office for co-production.
R. Kalyanaraman . . . . . . . . . . . . . . . . . . . . . . . Chairman
Alain Berger . . . . . . . . . . . . . . . . . . . . Exec. Vice President

**SHOOTING GALLERY INC., THE**
PHONE . . . . . . . . . . . . . . . . . . . 212-243-3042/310-273-4141
FAX . . . . . . . . . . . . . . . . . . . . 212-647-1392/310-273-9879
WEBSITE . . . . . . . . . . . . . . . http://www.shootinggallery.com
145 Ave. of Americas, 7th Floor
New York, NY 10013

TYPE          Motion Pictures
CREDITS       Slingblade - Illtown - Drunks - New Jersey Drive - Layin
              Low - Niagara, Niagara - Henry Fool
COMMENTS      Also: 9350 Wilshire Blvd., #300 Beverly Hills, CA 90212
Larry Meistrich . . . . . . . . . . . . . . . . . . . . . Chairman/CEO
Steve Carlis . . . . . . . . . . . . . . . . . . . . . . President/CFO
Jonathan Marshall . . . . . . . . . . . . . . . . . . . General Counsel
Brandon Rosser . . . . . . . . . . . . . . . . . . . . Sr. Vice President
Joseph DiMartino . . . . . . . . . . . . . . . . . . . Sr. Vice President
David Tuttle . . . . . . . . . . Sr. VP, Gun for Hire Production Center
Bob Gosse . . . . . . . . . . . . . . . . . . . . Dir., Creative Affairs
Steve Bickel . . . . . . . . . . . . . . . . Pres., TSG International (LA)
Eamonn Bowles . . . . . . . . . . . . . . . . . . . Pres., TSG Pictures
Phil Carson . . . . . . . . . . . . . . . . . . . . Pres., TSG Records (LA)
David L. Bushell . . . . . . . . . . . . Exec. VP, TSG Productions/Producer
Bob Salerno . . . . . . . . . Exec. VP, Gun for Hire Production Center
Mary Sunshine . . . . . . . . . . . . . . . . . . VP, East Coast Post
Jim Powers . . . . . . . . . . . . . . . . . . . . . . Dir., Development
Lynda Murray . . . . . . . . . . . . . . . . . . Sr. VP, Production (LA)
Christopher Covert . . . . . . . . . . . . . . . . . . Music Supervisor
Jamey Pryde . . . . . . . . . . . . . . . . . . . Dir., Post Production
Rick Marchitto . . . . . . . . . . . . . . . . . . Film Delivery/Trailers
Beth P. Cohen . . . . . . . . . Exec. Dir., Gun for Hire Production Center

# COMPANIES AND STAFF

## SHORELINE ENTERTAINMENT

| | |
|---|---|
| PHONE | 310-551-2060 |
| FAX | 310-201-0729 |
| EMAIL | shoreline@shorelineentertainment.com |
| WEBSITE | http://www.shorelineentertainment.com |

1901 Ave. of the Stars, Ste. 1800
Los Angeles, CA 90067

TYPE      Motion Pictures + Television + Interactive Multimedia
CREDITS    The Continued Adventures Of Reptile Man - The Godson - Matter of Trust - Detour

Morris Ruskin . . . . . . . . . . . . . . . . . . . . . . . . . . . . . . . . . . . No Title
Lynn Mooney . . . . . . . . . . . . . . . . . . . . . . . . . . . . . . . . . . . No Title
George Marinos . . . . . . . . . . . . . . . . . . . . . . . . . . . . . . . . . No Title
Mary E. Skinner . . . . . . . . . . . . . . . . . . . . . . . . . . . . . . . . No Title
Juan Castro . . . . . . . . . . . . . . . . . . . . . . . . . . Dir., Development
Alexander Dix . . . . . . . . . . . . . . . . . . . . . . . . . . Dir., Acquisitions

## SHOWTIME NETWORKS INC.

| | |
|---|---|
| PHONE | 310-234-5200/212-708-1600 |
| WEBSITE | http://www.showtimeonline.com |

10880 Wilshire Blvd., Ste. 1500 & 1600
Los Angeles, CA 90024

TYPE      Television
CREDITS    Stargate SG-1 - The Outer Limits - More Tales of the City - Thanks of a Grateful Nation - Linc's - Lolita
COMMENTS   ALSO: 1633 Broadway, New York, NY 10019

Matthew C. Blank . . . . . . . . . . . . . . . . . . . . President/CEO (NY)
Jerry Offsay . . . . . . . . . . . . . . . . . . . . . . Pres., Programming (LA)
Larry Aidem . . . . . . . . . . . . . . Exec. VP, Business Development (NY)
Melinda Benedek . . . . . . . . . . . . . Exec. VP, Business Affairs (LA)
Jerry Cooper . . . . . . . . . . . . . . . . . Exec. VP, Finance/Operations (NY)
Matthew Duda . . . . . . . . . Exec. VP, Program Acquisitions & Planning (LA)
Ann Foley . . . . . . . . . . . . . . Exec. VP, East Coast Programming (NY)
Matthew Riklin . . . . . . Exec. VP, Program Enterprises & Distribution (LA)
Mark Zakarin . . . . . . . . . . . . . Exec. VP, Original Programming (LA)
Joan Boorstein . . . . . . . . . . . . . . . Sr. VP, Creative Affairs (LA)
Peter Keramidas . . . . . . . . . . . . . . . . . . Sr. VP, Programming (LA)
Frank Pintauro . . . . . . . . . . . . . . . Sr. VP, Family Programming (NY)
Judith Pless . . . . . . . . . . . . . . . Sr. VP, Business Development (NY)
Mike Rauch . . . . . . . . . . . . . Sr. VP, Motion Picture Production (LA)
Monica Foster . . . . . VP, Motion Picts./Series Development East Coast (NY)
Lori Kahn . . . . . . . . . . . . VP, Family & Children's Programming (NY)
Cynthia Bell . . . . . . . . . . . . . . . . . VP, Comedy Programming (LA)
Sharon Byrens . . . . . . . . . . . . . VP, Motion Picture Development (LA)
Katy Coyle . . . . . . . . . . . . . . . VP, Development West Coast (LA)
Anne Kurrasch . . . . . . . . . . . . . . . . . . VP, Business Affairs (LA)
Pancho Mansfield . . . . . . . . . . . . . . . . . . . . VP, Development (LA)
Deborah Scott-Spera . . . . . . . . . . . VP, Motion Pict. Development (LA)
John Vasey . . . . . . . . . . . . . . . . VP, Original Programming(LA)
Tom Christie . . . . . . . . . . . . . . . . . . Sundance Channel (NY)
Ann Gilmore . . . . . . . . . . Dir., Series & Original Programming (LA)
Pearlena Igbokwe . . . . . . . . . . . Dir., Original Programming (LA)
Vicki Letizia . . . . . . . . . Dir., Creative Affairs Motion Pictures (LA)
Kate Meyer . . . . . . . . . . . . Dir., Talent Relations & Awards (NY)
Jamie Padnos . . . . . . . . . . . . Dir., Programming & Planning (LA)
Dominique Williams . . . . . . . . . . . . . . . . Dir., Development (LA)
Michael Friedman . . . . . . . . . Mgr., Motion Picture Production (LA)
Vince Porter . . . . . . . . . . . Supervisor, Motion Picture Production (LA)

## SHUKOVSKY ENGLISH ENT.

| | |
|---|---|
| PHONE | 818-760-6100 |
| FAX | 818-760-5527 |
| WEBSITE | http://www.seetv.com |

CBS Studio Center
4024 Radford Ave.
Studio City, CA 91604

TYPE      Television
DEAL      CBS Entertainment
CREDITS    Murphy Brown - Love & War - Double Rush - The Louie Show - Ink

Diane English . . . . . . . . . . . . . . . . . . Writer/Exec. Producer
Joel Shukovsky . . . . . . . . . . . . . . . . . . . . Executive Producer
John Drinkwater . . . . . . . . . . . . . . . Exec. VP/General Counsel
Joe Fortunato . . . . . . . . . . . . . . . . . . . . . . . . Creative Affairs
James Koonce . . . . . . . . . Exec. Asst. to Diane English & Joel Shukovsky

## SIGNATURE

| | |
|---|---|
| PHONE | 310-244-8382 |
| FAX | 310-244-1433 |

10202 W. Washington Blvd., Astaire #1210
Culver City, CA 90232

TYPE      Motion Pictures
DEAL      Columbia Pictures
CREDITS    Maximum Risk - Time Cop - Double Team

Moshe Diamant . . . . . . . . . . . . . . . . . . CEO/Exec. Producer
Rudy Cohen . . . . . . . . . . . . . . . . . . . . . . . . . . . . Producer
Kevin Jones . . . . . . . . . . . . . . . . . . . . . . . . . . . . Producer
Limor Diamant . . . . . . . . . . . . . . . . . . . . . . . . . . Producer
Peter Nelson . . . . . . . . . . . . . . . . . . . . . . VP, Development
John Stevenson . . . . . . . . . . . . . . . . . . . . Dir., Development
Victoria Lucas . . . . . . . . . . . . . . . . . . . . . Dir., Development
James Portolese . . . . . . . . . . . . . . . . Development Associate

## SIGNATURE FILMS

| | |
|---|---|
| PHONE | 818-752-2991 |
| FAX | 818-752-1689 |
| EMAIL | robert.baker@mci2000.com/signaturefilms@hotmail.com |
| WEBSITE | http://www.signaturefilms.com |

10960 Ventura Blvd.
Studio City, CA 91604

TYPE      Motion Pictures + Television
CREDITS    Double Jeopardy - Payback - A Stolen Life

Robert Baker . . . . . . . . . . . . . . . . . . . . Producer/Owner
Ann Takach . . . . . . . . . . . . . . . . . . . . . Dir., Development

## SILVER HEART PRODUCTIONS

| | |
|---|---|
| PHONE | 818-754-4598 |

P.O. Box 1703
Burbank, CA 91507-1703

TYPE      Motion Pictures + Feature Direct to Video + Television + Syndication + Documentaries
CREDITS    Kaitsenko - Flamingo Dreams - Unsolved Mysteries

Michael David Jones . . . . . . . . . . . . . . . . . . . . . . . Producer
Donna Persico . . . . . . . . . . . . . . . . . . . . Dir., Development

## SILVER LION FILMS

| | |
|---|---|
| PHONE | 310-393-9177 |
| FAX | 310-458-9372 |
| EMAIL | slionfilms@aol.com |

715 Broadway, Ste. 310
Santa Monica, CA 90401

TYPE      Motion Pictures
CREDITS    Flashfire - The Air Up There - Pure Luck - Steel Dawn - Flipper - Gunmen - McHale's Navy - One Man's Hero

Lance Hool . . . . . . . . . . . . . . . . . . . . . . . . . . . . Producer
Conrad Hool . . . . . . . . . . . . . . . . . . . . . . . . . . . Producer

## SILVER PICTURES

| | |
|---|---|
| PHONE | 818-954-4490 |
| FAX | 818-954-3237 |

Warner Bros.
4000 Warner Blvd., Bldg. 90
Burbank, CA 91522-0001

TYPE      Motion Pictures + Television
DEAL      Warner Bros. Pictures
CREDITS    Die Hard 1-2 - Lethal Weapon 1-4 - Tales From the Crypt - Predator 1-2 - Executive Decision - Conspiracy Theory

Joel Silver . . . . . . . . . . . . . . . . . . . . . . . . . . . . Chairman
Dan Cracchiolo . . . . . . . . . . . . . . . . . . . Sr. VP, Production
Jennifer Gwartz . . . . . . . . . . . . . . . . . . . Sr. VP, Production
Steve Richards . . . . . . . . . . . . . . . . . . . . . Vice President
Pam Martin . . . . . . . . . . . . . . . . . . . . . . . VP, Operations
Percy Zuletta . . . . . . . . . . . . . . . . . . . . . Dir., Development
Rachel Bendavid . . . . . . . . . . . . . . . . . . . Creative Executive
Garrick Dion . . . . . . . . . . . . . . . . . . . . . . . . Story Editor

## SILVERCREEK ENTERTAINMENT

| | |
|---|---|
| PHONE | 818-879-1531 |
| FAX | 818-879-1007 |

5512 Evita Court
Agoura Hills, CA 91301

TYPE      Motion Pictures + Television
CREDITS    Caught in the Act - Sweet Justice - Hill Street Blues - Every Mother's Nightmare - Cracker - L.A. Docs
COMMENTS   Larry Garrison is also Pres. of Garrison Prods. Inc. Produces segments for primetime news magazine shows.

Larry Garrison . . . . . . . . . . . . . . . . . . . . Executive Producer
Scott Brazil . . . . . . . . . . . . . . . . . . . . . . Executive Producer

# COMPANIES AND STAFF

## SILVERFILM PRODS. INC.
```
PHONE ......................................... 212-355-0282
FAX ........................................... 212-421-8254
EMAIL ......................................... raysil@aol.com
```
510 Park Ave.
New York, NY 10022

TYPE         Motion Pictures
CREDITS     Crossing Delancey - Between The Lines - Fish in The Bathtub - Chilly Scenes of Winter

Raphael D. Silver ........................................ President
Joan Micklin Silver ...................... VP, Creative Affairs

## SILVERLINE PICTURES
```
PHONE ......................................... 818-752-3730
FAX ........................................... 818-752-3758
EMAIL ............................... SILVERLINE@earthlink.net
```
11846 Ventura Blvd., Ste 100
Studio City, CA 91604

TYPE         Motion Pictures + Television
CREDITS     Where Truth Lies - Dusting Cliff Seven

Leman Cetiner ................................... CEO/Producer
Axel Munch ............................... President/Producer
Dami Moir .............................. Dir., Acquisitions
Bryan Jenkins .......................... Head, Operations
Christopher Titpon ................... Executive Assistant
Gunter Heinlein ..................... Head, German Office

## SILVERMAN CO., THE FRED
```
PHONE ......................................... 310-826-6050
FAX ........................................... 310-207-5357
```
12400 Wilshire Blvd., Ste. 920
Los Angeles, CA 90025

TYPE         Television
CREDITS     Matlock - In the Heat of the Night - Perry Mason - Diagnosis Murder

Fred Silverman ........................................... President
Jaclyn Stern ................................... Dir., Talent
Casey O'Brien ............................. Dir., Development
Adriana Cevallos ..................... Development Assistant
Amber Waznis ........................ Development Assistant

## SILVERMAN PROD, LLOYD/PASSIONATE PICTS.
```
PHONE ......................................... 213-463-4600
FAX ........................................... 213-461-0600
```
Crossroads of the World
6671 Sunset Blvd., Bldg. 1584
Hollywood, CA 90028

TYPE         Motion Pictures + Television
CREDITS     Snow Falling On Cedars - Shattered Image - Pret A-Porter

Lloyd A. Silverman ......................... Partner/Producer
Ian Jessel ............................ Partner/Exec. Producer
Tom Gamble ............................................ Producer
Julian Bernard ........................................ Associate
Phillipe Frappier ..................................... Assistant

## *SIMIAN FILMS
```
PHONE ......................................... 310-285-2300
FAX ........................................... 310-285-2345
```
Castle Rock
335 N. Maple Drive, Ste. 350
Beverly Hills, CA 90210

TYPE         Motion Pictures
DEAL         Castle Rock Entertainment
CREDITS     Extreme Measures - Mickey Blue Eyes

Hugh Grant ................................... Actor/Producer
Elizabeth Hurley ...................................... Producer
Lisa Reeve ........................... Sr. VP, Production
Yael Oestreich ..................... Development Assistant

## SIMON PRODUCTIONS, RANDY
```
PHONE ......................................... 310-274-7440
FAX ........................................... 310-274-9809
```
1113 N. Hillcrest Rd.
Beverly Hills, CA 90210

TYPE         Motion Pictures
DEAL         Artisan Entertainment
CREDITS     Lover's Knot - Pi

Randy Simon ............................................ Producer

## SIMONDS CO., THE ROBERT
```
PHONE ......................................... 818-777-5445
FAX ........................................... 818-866-1404
```
100 Universal City Plaza
Bldg. 507A, Penthouse 1
Universal City, CA 91608-1085

TYPE         Motion Pictures
DEAL         Universal Pictures
CREDITS     Happy Gilmore - Problem Child I & II - Billy Madison - The Wedding Singer - Dirty Work - Half Baked

Robert Simonds ........................................ Producer
Rita Smith ........................... Associate Producer
Julia Dray ............................. VP, Creative Affairs
Amy Brown ........................................ Story Editor
Jessica Chavez ....................... Asst. to Ms. Smith
Tina Barr ......................... Asst. to Mr. Simonds
Kim Coleman ..................................... Receptionist

## SIMONS PRODS., DAVID A.
```
PHONE ......................................... 818-884-7823
FAX ........................................... 818-884-8553
EMAIL ......................................... dav4all@aol.com
```
5301 Parion Court
Woodland Hills, CA 91367

TYPE         Motion Pictures + Television + Syndication + Feature Direct to Video + Documentaries
CREDITS     American Detective - Equal Justice - Silence of the Heart - The Girl Who Spelled Freedom
COMMENTS    Rep. by Writers & Artists, Evan Corday.

David A. Simons .................... Writer/Executive Producer

## SIMSIE FILMS
```
PHONE ......................................... 310-271-0777
FAX ........................................... 310-271-5051
EMAIL ................................. simsie@earthlink.net
```
9803 Gloucester Drive
Beverly Hills, CA 90210

TYPE         Motion Pictures + Television + Feature Direct to Video
CREDITS     Patti Rocks - Reflections In The Dark

Gwen Field ............................................. Producer
Linda Jenkins ......................... VP, Creative Affairs
Andrew Pearson ....................... Dir., Development

## SINGER ENTERTAINMENT, JOSEPH M.
```
PHONE ......................................... 818-777-9675
FAX ........................................... 818-866-5092
```
100 Universal City Plaza, Bldg. 507 #2-A
Universal City, CA 91608

TYPE         Motion Pictures
DEAL         Universal Pictures
CREDITS     Doctor Dolittle - Mercury Rising - Dante's Peak - Daylight - Courage Under Fire - Dudley Do-Right

Joseph M. Singer ...................................... Producer
Susan Solomon .............. Sr. VP, Production (818-777-6455)
Jeff Levy .............. VP, Creative Affairs (NY) (212-605-2800)
Greg Frankovich ............ Dir., Development (818-777-8395)
Neil Weinberger ......... Dir., Creative Affairs (818-777-7748)
David Donegan ...................................... Story Editor
Tim Donovan ....................................... Story Editor
Karuna Venter ..................................... Story Editor

## SINGER PRODUCTIONS, CARLA
```
PHONE ......................................... 310-859-1107
FAX ........................................... 310-859-1665
```
8899 Beverly Blvd., Ste. 803
Los Angeles, CA 90048

TYPE         Motion Pictures + Television
CREDITS     Taken Away - Angel Flight Down - Cold Heart of a Killer

Carla Singer ............................... Executive Producer
Julie Wenberg ..................................... Story Editor
Brooke Driskill ............................. Creative Executive

## SINGER-WHITE ENTERTAINMENT
```
PHONE ......................................... 818-506-2400
FAX ........................................... 818-506-2409
EMAIL ............................... developmnet@pacificnet.net
```
12001 Ventura Place, Ste. 502
Studio City, CA 91604

TYPE         Television + Motion Pictures
CREDITS     She Cried No - Tempting Fate - Devil's Advocate - Love's Deadly Triangle

Sheri Singer ............................... Executive Producer
Steve White ............................... Executive Producer
Georgene Smith ....................... Mgr., Development
Melanie Chapman ................................. Story Editor

## SINGLE CELL PICTURES
PHONE . . . . . . . . . . . . . . . . . . . . . . . . . . . . . . . . . 310-385-6697
FAX . . . . . . . . . . . . . . . . . . . . . . . . . . . . . . . . . . . 310-248-6226
9229 Sunset Blvd., #615
West Hollywood, CA 90069

TYPE       Motion Pictures
DEAL       October Films
Michael Stipe . . . . . . . . . . . . . . . . . . . . . . . . . . . . . . . . Producer
Sandy Stern . . . . . . . . . . . . . . . . . . . . . . . . . . . . . . . . . Producer
Farley Ziegler . . . . . . . . . . . . . . . . . . . . . . . . . Creative Executive

## SINGLE SPARK PICTURES
PHONE . . . . . . . . . . . . . . . . . . . . . . . . . . . . . . . . . 310-315-4779
FAX . . . . . . . . . . . . . . . . . . . . . . . . . . . . . . . . . . . 310-315-4773
EMAIL . . . . . . . . . . . . . . . . . . . . . . . . . . . . singlspark@aol.com
3000 W. Olympic Blvd.
Santa Monica, CA 90404

TYPE       Motion Pictures + Television + Documentaries
CREDITS       Raw Footage - Survivors - Building Bombs - Blood Ties - The Life & Work of Sally Mann - The Fire This Time
Mark Mori . . . . . . . . . . . . . . . . . . . . . . . President/Producer/Director
Janet Monaghan . . . . . . . . . . . . . . . . . . . . . . . . . Dir., Development
Jim Hense . . . . . . . . . . . . . . . . . . . . . . . . . . . . Researcher/Writer
Yosi Rodriquez-Pozeilov . . . . . . . . . . . . . . . . . . . Research Associate
Joshua Kors . . . . . . . . . . . . . . . . . . . . . . . . . . . Asst. to Mark Mori

## SISTERLEE PRODUCTIONS INC.
PHONE . . . . . . . . . . . . . . . . . . . . . . . . . . . . . . . . . 818-954-7579
FAX . . . . . . . . . . . . . . . . . . . . . . . . . . . . . . . . . . . 818-954-2741
300 Television Plaza, Bldg. 136, Rm. 147
Burbank, CA 91505

TYPE       Television
DEAL       Warner Bros. Television Productions
CREDITS       A Different World - Living Single - Lush Life - For Your Love
Yvette Lee Bowser . . . . . . . . . . . . . . . . . . . . . . Executive Producer
Sean Dwyer . . . . . . . . . . . . . . . . . . . . . . . . . Development Associate

## SITTENFIELD PRODUCTIONS, JOAN
PHONE . . . . . . . . . . . . . . . . . . . . . . . . . . . . . . . . . 310-859-1107
FAX . . . . . . . . . . . . . . . . . . . . . . . . . . . . . . . . . . . 310-859-1665
869 Wooster St., Ste. 305
Los Angeles, CA 90035

TYPE       Motion Pictures + Television
DEAL       Singer Productions, Carla
CREDITS       On The Edge of Innocence - Gold Rush
COMMENTS       Also: 8899 Beverly Blvd., Ste. 803, LA, CA 90048
Joan Sittenfield . . . . . . . . . . . . . . . . . . . . Principal/Executive Producer

## SITTING DUCKS PRODS.
PHONE . . . . . . . . . . . . . . . . . . . . . . . . . . . . . . . . . 213-660-0861
FAX . . . . . . . . . . . . . . . . . . . . . . . . . . . . . . . . . . . 213-660-6021
1532 Micheltorena St.
Los Angeles, CA 90026

TYPE       Motion Pictures + Animation + Television + Interactive Multimedia + Feature Direct to Video
CREDITS       The Mouse and Monster (UPN) - Putnam Publishing - Sitting Ducks
Michael Bedard . . . . . . . . . . . . . . . . . . . . . . . . Executive Producer
Elizabeth Daro . . . . . . . . . . . . . . . . . . . . . . . . . Executive Producer
Ray Shenusay . . . . . . . . . . . . . . . . . . . . . . . Development Executive

## SKYFISH PRODUCTIONS
PHONE . . . . . . . . . . . . . . . . . . . . . . . . . . . . . . . . . 818-347-3773
11288 Ventura Blvd., Ste. 414B
Studio City, CA 91604-3791

TYPE       Motion Pictures
Kim Basinger . . . . . . . . . . . . . . . . . . . . . . . . . . . Actress/Producer
Robert Leffelman . . . . . . . . . . . . . . . . . . . . . . Asst. to Ms. Basinger

## SKYLARK FILMS LTD.
PHONE . . . . . . . . . . . . . . . . . . . . . . . . . . . . . . . . . 310-396-5753
FAX . . . . . . . . . . . . . . . . . . . . . . . . . . . . . . . . . . . 310-396-5753
EMAIL . . . . . . . . . . . . . . . . . . . . . . . . . . . . . . skyfilm@aol.com
1123 Pacific St., Ste. G
Santa Monica, CA 90405-1525

TYPE       Motion Pictures + Syndication + Television
DEAL       Adelson Productions, Orly
CREDITS       Terminal Justice - The Styx - Justice for None - Coal of the Heart
Bradford Pollack . . . . . . . . . . . . . . . . . . . . . . . . . . . . . Producer
Gregg Cooke . . . . . . . . . . . . . . . . . . . . . . . Co-Executive Producer
C.S. Drotman . . . . . . . . . . . . . . . . . . . . . . Development Executive
Jennifer Lively . . . . . . . . . . . . . . . . Development Associate/Story Analyst
Dawson Moore . . . . . . . . . . . . . . . Development Associate/Story Analyst

## SKYLINE PARTNERS
PHONE . . . . . . . . . . . . . . . . . . . . . . . . . . . . . . . . . 310-470-3363
FAX . . . . . . . . . . . . . . . . . . . . . . . . . . . . . . . . . . . 310-470-0060
10550 Wilshire Blvd., Ste. 304
Los Angeles, CA 90024

TYPE       Motion Pictures
CREDITS       Buddy Holly Story - The Lost Brigade - Cold Night Into Dawn - Cypress Edge
COMMENTS       Also: Financial Consulting.
Fred Kuehnert . . . . . . . . . . . . . . . . . . . Managing Partner/Producer
Tim Versacci . . . . . . . . . . . . . . . . . . . . . . . . . . . . . . . Producer
Doug Nelson . . . . . . . . . . . . . . . . . . . . . . . . . Producer/Director
John Speer . . . . . . . . . . . . . . . . . . . . . . . . . . . . . . Consultant
S.J. Chouinard . . . . . . . . . . . . . . . . . . . . . . . . Executive Assistant

## *SLADEK ENTERTAINMENT
PHONE . . . . . . . . . . . . . . . . . . . . . . . . . . . . . . . . . 213-934-9268
FAX . . . . . . . . . . . . . . . . . . . . . . . . . . . . . . . . . . . 213-934-7362
EMAIL . . . . . . . . . . . . . . . . . . . . . . . . . . . . dansladek@aol.com
8306 Wilshire Blvd., #510
Beverly Hills, CA 90211

TYPE       Motion Pictures + Television
CREDITS       Talos the Mummy - Sub Down - Silent Trigger - Hidden Assassin
Daniel Sladek . . . . . . . . . . . . . . . . . . . . . . . . . . . . . . . Producer

## SLAWSON PRODS., RUTH
PHONE . . . . . . . . . . . . . . . . . . . . . . . . . . . . . . . . . 914-876-4946
FAX . . . . . . . . . . . . . . . . . . . . . . . . . . . . . . . . . . . 914-876-4947
EMAIL . . . . . . . . . . . . . . . . . . . . . . . . . . . . . . . ruths@epix.net
64 Cedar Heights Road
Rhinebeck, NY 12572

TYPE       Television
CREDITS       Annie - Terror In The Family - Mom Swap - Ellen Foster
Ruth Slawson . . . . . . . . . . . . . . . . . . . . . . . . Executive Producer
Jennifer Schwartz . . . . . . . . . . . . . . . . . . . . Development Executive

## SLOANE/BORDEN PICTURES
PHONE . . . . . . . . . . . . . . . . . . . . . . . . . . . . . . . . . 213-665-7700
EMAIL . . . . . . . . . . . . . . . . . . . . . . . . . . . . . ikeborden@aol.com
4220 W. Newdale Drive
Los Angeles, CA 90027

TYPE       Motion Pictures
CREDITS       No Way Back
Morgan Sloane . . . . . . . . . . . . . . . . . . . . . . . . . . . . . . . . Partner
Michael Sweney Borden . . . . . . . . . . . . . . . . . . . . . . . . . . . Partner

## SMITH PRODUCTIONS INC., THOMAS G.
PHONE . . . . . . . . . . . . . . . . . . . . . . . . . . . . . . . . . 818-247-6082
1520 Hillcrest Ave.
Glendale, CA 91202

TYPE       Motion Pictures + Television + Documentaries
CREDITS       Honey, I Shrunk The Kids - Muppets 3D - The Arrival - Honey, I Shrunk the Audience 3D - M & M Adventure 3D
COMMENTS       Also: Theme Park Productions.
Thomas Smith . . . . . . . . . . . . . . . . . . . . . . . . . Producer/Director
Karen Winchester . . . . . . . . . . . . . . . . . . . . . . . . . . . Development

# COMPANIES AND STAFF

**SMITH-HEMION PRODS.**
PHONE . . . . . . . . . . . . . . . . . . . . . . . . . . . . . . . 213-871-1200
FAX . . . . . . . . . . . . . . . . . . . . . . . . . . . . . . . . . 213-464-8075
1438 N. Gower St., Box 15
Los Angeles, CA 90028-8306

TYPE          Television
CREDITS       Tony Awards - Clinton's Inaugural Gala - 50 Years of TV -
              Disney's Young Musicians - Snowden on Ice
COMMENTS      Also: Live & Special Events.
Gary Smith . . . . . . . . . . . . . . . . . . . . . . . . . . . Executive Producer
Dwight Hemion . . . . . . . . . . . . . . . . . . . Executive Producer/Director
Tony Michelman . . . . . . . . . . . . . . . . . . . . . . Dir., Filmed Division
Dann Netter . . . . . . . . . . . . . . . . . . . . . . . . . . Dir., Development

***SNAPDRAGON FILMS INC.**
PHONE . . . . . . . . . . . . . . . . . . . . . . . . . . . . . . 310-822-2505
FAX . . . . . . . . . . . . . . . . . . . . . . . . . . . . . . . . 310-822-7054
13428 Maxella Ave., Ste. 293
Marina del Rey, CA 90292

TYPE          Motion Pictures
CREDITS       Marvin's Room - Cemetary Club - Parents
Bonnie Palef . . . . . . . . . . . . . . . . . . . . Director/Producer/Writer

**SNEAK PREVIEW ENTERTAINMENT, INC.**
PHONE . . . . . . . . . . . . . . . . . . . . . . . . . . . . . . 213-962-0295
FAX . . . . . . . . . . . . . . . . . . . . . . . . . . . . . . . . 213-962-0372
EMAIL . . . . . . . . . . . . . . . . . . . . . . . sneak@primenet.com
Vine Tower Building, Seventh Floor
6305 Yucca Street
Los Angeles, CA 90028

TYPE          Motion Pictures
CREDITS       Bird of Prey - Tollbooth - Scorchers - Relax...It's Just Sex
COMMENTS      Also: Talent Management
Steven J. Wolfe . . . . . . . . . . . . . . . . . . . . Chairman/CEO/Producer
Lynette Prucha . . . . . . . . . . . . . . . . . . . . . . President/Writer
David Cohn . . . . . . . . . . . . . . . . . . . . . . . . . Talent Manager
Brian Benneker . . . . . . . . . . . . . . . . . . . . . Executive Assistant

**SNOW LEOPARD PRODUCTIONS**
PHONE . . . . . . . . . . . . . . . . . . . . . . . . . . . . . . 310-827-1220
FAX . . . . . . . . . . . . . . . . . . . . . . . . . . . . . . . . 310-821-5251
4727 La Villa Marina, Ste. C
Marina del Rey, CA 90292

TYPE          Motion Pictures + Television
C'esca Lawrence . . . . . . . . . . . . . . . . . . . . . . Producer/Co-Owner
Dan Tursi . . . . . . . . . . . . . . . . . . . . . . . . . Producer/Co-Owner
Ariel Levy . . . . . . . . . . . . . . . . . . . . . . . . . . . . . Producer
Tim Merritt . . . . . . . . . . . . . . . . . . . . . . . . . Dir., Development

**SOFRONSKI PRODS., BERNARD**
PHONE . . . . . . . . . . . . . . . . . . . . . . . . . . . . . . 310-244-5412
FAX . . . . . . . . . . . . . . . . . . . . . . . . . . . . . . . . 310-244-2472
TriStar TV
10202 W. Washington Blvd., Tristar 204
Culver City, CA 90232

TYPE          Television
DEAL          TriStar Television
CREDITS       Into Thin Air - Almost Golden: Jessica Savitch Story -
              Harvest of Fire - Mandela and deKlerk
Bernard Sofronski . . . . . . . . . . . . . . . . . . . . Executive Producer
Denny Flinn . . . . . . . . . . . . . . . . . . . . . . . . . . . . . Assistant

**SOLO ONE PRODUCTIONS**
PHONE . . . . . . . . . . . . . . . . . . . . . . . . . . . . . . 213-658-8748
FAX . . . . . . . . . . . . . . . . . . . . . . . . . . . . . . . . 213-658-8749
EMAIL . . . . . . . . . . . . . . . . . . . . . . . . . . . . jij@aol.com
8205 Santa Monica Blvd., Ste. 1279
Los Angeles, CA 90046-5912

TYPE          Motion Pictures + Television
CREDITS       In Her Defense - 90 Days at Hollyridge
Marlee Matlin . . . . . . . . . . . . . . . . . . . . . . Actress/Producer
Jack Jason . . . . . . . . . . . . . . . . . . . . . . . . . . . . . Producer

**SOLOMON/HACKETT PRODUCTIONS**
PHONE . . . . . . . . . . . . . . . . . . . . . . . . . . . . . . 310-551-2212
FAX . . . . . . . . . . . . . . . . . . . . . . . . . . . . . . . . 310-556-3760
Davis Entertainment
2121 Avenue of the Stars
Los Angeles, CA 90067

TYPE          Motion Pictures
DEAL          Davis Entertainment Co.
Michael Hackett . . . . . . . . . . . . . . . . . . . . . . . . . . Principal
David F. Solomon . . . . . . . . . . . . . . . . . . . . . . . . . Principal

**SOLT PRODUCTIONS, ANDREW**
PHONE . . . . . . . . . . . . . . . . . . . . . . . . . . . . . . 310-276-9522
FAX . . . . . . . . . . . . . . . . . . . . . . . . . . . . . . . . 310-276-0242
9121 Sunset Blvd.
Los Angeles, CA 90069

TYPE          Television
CREDITS       The History of Rock-n-Roll - The Best of Ed Sullivan -
              Comedy Club Superstars - First 50 Years of CBS
Andrew Solt . . . . . . . . . . . . . . . . . . . . . Producer/Writer/Director
Greg Vines . . . . . . . . . . . . . . . . . . . . . . . Sr. VP, Production
Cindy Frei . . . . . . . . . . . . . . . . . . . . . . . . VP, Development
Laura Law . . . . . . . . . . . . . . . . . . . . . . VP, International Sales

**SOMERS TEITELBAUM DAVID**
PHONE . . . . . . . . . . . . . . . . . . . . . . . . . . . . . . 310-203-8000
FAX . . . . . . . . . . . . . . . . . . . . . . . . . . . . . . . . 310-203-8099
EMAIL . . . . . . . . . . . . . . . . . . . . . . . postmaster@stdmgt.com
1925 Century Park East, Ste. 2320
Los Angeles, CA 90067

TYPE          Motion Pictures + Television + Syndication + Interactive
              Multimedia
CREDITS       Samantha - The Lovemaster - Bonds of Love - Life & Stuff
Alan Somers . . . . . . . . . . . . . . . . . . . . . . . . . . . . . Partner
Mark Teitelbaum . . . . . . . . . . . . . . . . . . . . . . . . . . . Partner
Alan David . . . . . . . . . . . . . . . . . . . . . . . . . . . . . . Partner
Chris E. Henze . . . . . . . . . . . . . . . . . . . . . . . Vice President
Tammi Chase . . . . . . . . . . . . . . . . . . . . . . . . . . . . Executive
Brad Fuller . . . . . . . . . . . . . . . . . . . . . . . . . . . . . Executive

**SONNENFELD/JOSEPHSON**
PHONE . . . . . . . . . . . . . . . . . . . . . . . . . . . . . . 818-560-0606
FAX . . . . . . . . . . . . . . . . . . . . . . . . . . . . . . . . 818-556-6662
500 S. Buena Vista St. Anim. 1A
Burbank, CA 91521-1854

TYPE          Motion Pictures
DEAL          Walt Disney Company, The
COMMENTS      Also: 500 Park Avenue, Ninth Floor, New York, NY
              10022 212-735-5361 Fax: 212-735-5340
Barry Sonnenfeld . . . . . . . . . . . . . . . . . . . . . . . . . . No Title
Barry Josephson . . . . . . . . . . . . . . . . . . . . . . . . . . No Title
Caroline Andoscia . . . . . . . . . . . . . . . . . . . . . . . . . No Title
Lisa Ellzey . . . . . . . . . . . . . . . . . . . . . . . . . . . . . No Title
Jason Anthony . . . . . . . . . . . . . . . . . . . . . . . . . No Title (NY)
Valerie Cornelison . . . . . . . . . . . . . . . . . . . . . . . . . No Title
Bill Eville . . . . . . . . . . . . . . . . . . . . . . . . . . . No Title (NY)
Bill Melton . . . . . . . . . . . . . . . . . . . . . . . . . . . . . No Title
Bryan Brucks . . . . . . . . . . . . . . . . . . . . . Asst. to Mr. Josephson
Shirley Lima . . . . . . . . . . . . . . . . . . . . . . Asst. to Ms. Andoscia
Mary Squillante . . . . . . . . . . . . . . . . . . . Asst. to Mr. Sonnenfeld

**SONY PICTURES ENTERTAINMENT**
PHONE . . . . . . . . . . . . . . . . . . . . . . . . . . . . . . 310-244-4000
FAX . . . . . . . . . . . . . . . . . . . . . . . . . . . . . . . . 310-244-2626
WEBSITE . . . . . . . . . . . . . . . . . . . . http://www.spe.sony.com/
10202 W. Washington Blvd.
Culver City, CA 90232-3195

TYPE          Motion Pictures + Television
COMMENTS      See also Columbia Picts. & Columbia TriStar Motion Picts.
              Group.
John Calley . . . . . . . . . . . . . . . . . . . . . . . . . President/CEO
Robert J. Wynne . . . . . . . . . . . . . . . . . . . . . Co-President/COO
Yuki Nozoe . . . . . . . . . . . . . . . . . . . . . . . Exec. Vice President
Ted Howells Jr. . . . . . . . . . . . . . . . . . . . . Exec. Vice Pres./CFO
Beth Berke . . . . . . . . . . . . . . . . . . . . Exec. VP, Human Resources
Jon Feltheimer . . . . . . . . . . . . . . . . . . . . . Exec. Vice President
Ronald Jacobi . . . . . . . . . . . . Exec. VP/General Counsel & Corp. Secretary
Yair Landau . . . . . . . . . . . Exec. VP, Corp. Development & Strategic Planning

# COMPANIES AND STAFF

**SONY PICTURES IMAGEWORKS**
PHONE . . . . . . . . . . . . . . . . . . . . . . . . . . . . 310-840-8000
FAX . . . . . . . . . . . . . . . . . . . . . . . . . . . . . . 310-840-8100
EMAIL . . . . . . don@spimageworks.com/production@spimageworks.com
WEBSITE . . . . . . . . . . . . . . . . . . . . . . . . http://www.spiw.com
9050 W. Washington Blvd.
Culver City, CA 90232
TYPE        Motion Pictures + Television + Documentaries +
            Animation + Interactive Multimedia + Feature Direct to
            Video
CREDITS     Godzilla - Starship Troopers - Contact - Anaconda
COMMENTS    Full service visual effects and digital animation. Also:
            Commercials.
Kenneth Williams . . . . . . . . . . . . . . President, Digital Studios Division
Ken Ralston . . . . . . . . . . . . . . . . . . . . . . . . . . . . President
Tim Sarnoff . . . . . . . . . . . . . . . . . Exec. VP/General Manager
Frank Foster . . . . . . . . . . . . . Sr. VP, Previsualization & Multimedia
Lincoln Hu . . . . . . . . . . . . . . . . . Sr. VP/Chief Technology Officer
Mary O'Hare . . . . . . . . . . . . . . Sr. VP, Business Affairs & Legal Affairs
Bill Schultz . . . . . . . . . . . . Sr. VP, Creative Technology & Digital Production
Debbie Denise . . . . . . . . . . . . . . . . . . . . . . . . Vice President
Ralph Horian . . . . . . . . . . . . . . . . . . . . . . . . . VP, Production
Stan Szymanski . . . . . . . . . . . . . . . . . . . . VP, Digital Production
Barry Weiss . . . . . . . . . . . . . . VP, Animation Production Administration
Jenny Fulle . . . . . . . . . . . . . . . . . . . . . . . . Executive Producer
Tracy Hauser . . . . . . . . . . . Exec. Producer, Pavlov,Commercial Division

**SOTO COMPANY, THE**
PHONE . . . . . . . . . . . . . . . . . . . . . . . . . . . . 213-468-2580
FAX . . . . . . . . . . . . . . . . . . . . . . . . . . . . . . 213-468-2588
6464 Sunset Blvd., Ste. 530
Hollywood, CA 90028
TYPE        Motion Pictures
CREDITS     Vietnam War Story/HBO - The Equalizer - The House of
            Ramon Iglesia
Luis Soto . . . . . . . . . . . . . . . . . . . . . . . Director/Producer
Laura Mola . . . . . . . . . . . . . . . . . . . . . . Producer/Writer

**SOUTH FORK PICTURES**
PHONE . . . . . . . . . . . . . . . . . . . . . . . . . . . . 310-395-7779
FAX . . . . . . . . . . . . . . . . . . . . . . . . . . . . . . 310-395-2575
1101 Montana Ave., Ste. B
Santa Monica, CA 90403
TYPE        Motion Pictures
CREDITS     She's The One - Slums of Beverly Hills - Long Time
            Nothing New
Robert Redford . . . . . . . . . . . . . . . . . . . . . . . . . . . Owner
Michael Nozik . . . . . . . . . . . . . . . . . . . . . . . . . . President
Lisa Bellomo . . . . . . . . . . . . Sr. VP, Development & Production
Linda Davis . . . . . . . . . . . . . . . . . . . . . . . . . Story Editor

**SOUTH SIDE FILMS**
PHONE . . . . . . . . . . . . . . . . . . . . . . . . . . . . 310-471-2758
EMAIL . . . . . . . . . . . . . . . . . . . . . . . karnage@primenet.com
1855 Westridge Rd.
Los Angeles, CA 90049
TYPE        Motion Pictures + Television
CREDITS     Blind Fury - One Woman's Courage - Vanishing Point -
            The Fixer
Charles Robert Carner . . . . . . . . . . . . . . . . Writer/Director
Jennifer Howe . . . . . . . . . . . . . . . . . . . . . . . . Assistant

**SOUTH, FRANK**
PHONE . . . . . . . . . . . . . . . . . . . . . . . . . . . . 213-634-1121
FAX . . . . . . . . . . . . . . . . . . . . . . . . . . . . . . 213-634-1131
5700 Wilshire Blvd., Ste. 478
Los Angeles, CA 90036
TYPE        Television
CREDITS     Cagney & Lacey - Equal Justice - Melrose Place - Models
            Inc.
COMMENTS    See Also: Melrose Prod.
Frank South . . . . . . . . . . . . . . . . . Writer/Producer/Director
Kristy Dobkin . . . . . . . . . . . . . . . . . . . Asst. to Mr. South

**SOUTHERN SKIES INC.**
PHONE . . . . . . . . . . . . . . . . . . . . . . . . . . . . 310-855-9833
FAX . . . . . . . . . . . . . . . . . . . . . . . . . . . . . . 310-855-0220
EMAIL . . . . . . . . . . . . . . . . . . . . . . . . edman99@aol.com
1104 S. Holt Ave., Ste. 302
Los Angeles, CA 90035
TYPE        Motion Pictures
CREDITS     Major League II - City Slickers - For the Boys
Ed Markley . . . . . . . . . . . . . . . . . . . . . . . . . . Producer

***SPANKY PICTURES, INC.**
PHONE . . . . . . . . . . . . . . . . . . . . . . . . . . . . 212-634-4440
FAX . . . . . . . . . . . . . . . . . . . . . . . . . . . . . . 212-634-4442
EMAIL . . . . . . . . . . . . . . . . . . . . . spankypics@earthlink.net
708 Broadway, 9th Floor
New York, NY 10003
TYPE        Motion Pictures + Television + Syndication
DEAL        New Line Cinema
CREDITS     Rounders - Life - Untitled Ted Demme Project - The Ref -
            Beautiful Girls
COMMENTS    Also: Music Videos.
Ted Demme . . . . . . . . . . . . . . . . . . . . . . . . . Co-Chairman
Joel Stillerman . . . . . . . . . . . . . . . . . . . . . . . Co-Chairman
Tracy Falco . . . . . . . . . . . . . . . . . . . . . Dir., Development

**SPECTACOR FILMS**
PHONE . . . . . . . . . . . . . . . . . . . . . . . . . . . . 310-271-9990
FAX . . . . . . . . . . . . . . . . . . . . . . . . . . . . . . 310-247-0412
9000 Sunset Blvd., Ste. 1550
West Hollywood, CA 90069
TYPE        Motion Pictures
CREDITS     Johnny 2.0 - The Invader - The Shadow Men - Thick &
            Thin
Ed Snider . . . . . . . . . . . . . . . . . . . . . . . . . . . . Partner
David Newlon . . . . . . . . . . . . . . . . . . . . . . President/CEO
Dino Gioia . . . . . . . . . . . . . . . . . . . . . . . . . . Controller
Jonathan Mundale . . . . . . . . . . . . . . . . . Dir., Development

**SPELLING FILMS INC.**
PHONE . . . . . . . . . . . . . . . . . . . . . . . . . . . . 213-965-5995
FAX . . . . . . . . . . . . . . . . . . . . . . . . . . . . . . 213-965-5993
5700 Wilshire Blvd., Ste. 375
Los Angeles, CA 90036-3659
TYPE        Motion Pictures
CREDITS     In & Out - Bound - Breakdown - The Mod Squad
Mitch Horwits . . . . . . . . . . . . . . . . . . . . . . . . . President
David J. Bloomfield . . . . . . . . . . Sr. VP, Business & Legal Affairs
Rene Garcia . . . . . . . . . . . . . . . . . . . . Sr. VP, Production
Denis Pregnolato . . . . . . . . . . Sr. VP, Production & Acquisitions
Andrew Golov . . . . . . . . . . . . . . . . . VP, Physical Production
Brenda Johns . . . . . . . . . . . . . . . . VP, Contract/Mktg. Admin.
Lynda Hongola . . . . . . . . . . . . . . Mgr., Business & Legal Affairs
Timothy Hill . . . . . . . . . . . . . . . . . . . . . . . . . Controller

**SPELLING TELEVISION, INC.**
PHONE . . . . . . . . . . . . . . . . . . . . . . . . . . . . 213-965-5700
FAX . . . . . . . . . . . . . . . . . . . . . . . . . . . . . . 213-965-5895
5700 Wilshire Blvd.
Los Angeles, CA 90036-3696
TYPE        Television
CREDITS     Melrose Place - Beverly Hills 90210 - 7th Heaven
Aaron Spelling . . . . . . . . . . . . . . . . Chairman of the Board/CEO
E. Duke Vincent . . . . . . . . . . . . . . . . . . . . . Vice Chairman
Jonathan C. Levin . . . . . . . . . . . . . . . . . . . . . President
James Conway . . . . . . . . . . . . . . . . . Exec. Vice President
Renate Kamer . . . . . . . . . . . . . . . . . . Sr. Vice President
Ken Miller . . . . . . . . . . . . . . . . . . Sr. VP, Post Production
Gail Patterson . . . . . . . . . . . . . . . . . . Sr. VP, Production
Ronald Sunderland . . . . . . . . . . Sr. VP, Business & Legal Affairs
Ron Taylor . . . . . . . . . . . . . . . . . . . Sr. VP, Development
Lorraine Jumelet . . . . . . . . . . . . . . . . . . . VP/Controller
Jennifer Nicholson . . . . . . . . . . . . . . . . VP, Series Development
Lougenia Patrick . . . . . . . . . . . . . . . VP, Series Business Affairs
Kristina Smith . . . . . . . . . . . . VP, Current Daytime Programming
Steve Tann . . . . . . . . . . . . . . . . VP, Current Programming
Robert Zinger . . . . . . . . . . . . . . . . . . . . VP, Legal Affairs

**SPI ENTERTAINMENT**
PHONE . . . . . . . . . . . . . . . . . . . . . . . . . . . . 310-827-1029
505 S. Beverly Dr., Penthouse
Beverly Hills, CA 90212
TYPE        Motion Pictures
CREDITS     Alien Predators - Deadtime Stories
Michael Sourapas . . . . . . . . . . . . . . . . . . . Producer/Writer
Jeffrey Delman . . . . . . . . . . . . . . . . . Producer/Director/Writer
Thomas McCurrie . . . . . . . . . . . . . . . . . . VP, Development
Elizabeth Fuller . . . . . . . . . . . . . . . . . . . . . Story Editor

**SPIKINGS ENTERTAINMENT**
PHONE . . . . . . . . . . . . . . . . . . . . . . . . . . . . 310-456-8039
FAX . . . . . . . . . . . . . . . . . . . . . . . . . . . . . . 310-456-1598
56 Malibu Colony Drive
Malibu, CA 90265
TYPE        Motion Pictures
CREDITS     Beyond Rangoon
Barry Spikings . . . . . . . . . . . . . . . . . . . . . . . . . Partner

# COMPANIES AND STAFF

## SPIN CYCLE ENTERTAINMENT
```
PHONE . . . . . . . . . . . . . . . . . . . . . . . . . . . . . . . . 818-777-8606
FAX . . . . . . . . . . . . . . . . . . . . . . . . . . . . . . . . . . 800-329-3925
EMAIL . . . . . . . . . . . . . . . . . . . . . . . . . . . steve@spincycle.net
WEBSITE . . . . . . . . . . . . . . . . . . . . . . http://www.spincycle.net
```
100 Universal City Plaza, MT-27
Universal City, CA 91608

TYPE — Animation + Television + Interactive Multimedia + Documentaries
DEAL — Universal Studios
CREDITS — Walt Disney World's 25th Anniversary
COMMENTS — Also: Web Site Design.

```
Stephen Jackson . . . . . . . . . . . . . . . . . . . . . . . . President/CEO
Kevin L.J. Davis . . . . . . . . . . . . . . . . . . Sr. VP/Creative Director
Gina Offerman . . . . . . . . . . . . . . . . . . . . Sr. VP/TV Development
Melissa Shenkin . . . . . . . . Sr. VP/Exec. in Charge of Production
John Tomich . . . . . . . . . . . . . . . . . . . . . . . . . . VP/Enhanced TV
Jake Carvey . . . . . . . . . . . . . . . . . . . . . VP, Animation & FX
Jonathan Grotenstein . . . . . . . . . . . . VP, New Media Development
James Saunders . . . . . . . . . . . . . . . . . . . . . . VP, Technology
Brenna Shenkin . . . . . . . . . . . . . . . . . . . . . . . . . . . Finance
Stephen Hyland . . . . . . . . . . . . . . . . . . . . . . . Graphic Design
Roland Plukas . . . . . . . . . . . . . . . . . . . . . . . . . Art Director
Nick Scaturro . . . . . . . . . . . . . . . . . . . . . . . Graphic Design
Jim Beard . . . . . . . . . . . . . . . . . . . . . . . . . . . . Production
Megan Odell . . . . . . . . . . . . . . . . . . Production Coordinator
Eric Baldwin . . . . . . . . . . . . . . . . . . . . . . . . . . Animation
Marco Mira . . . . . . . . . . . . . . . . . . . . . . . . . . . Animation
Diego Gorlato . . . . . . . . . . . . . . . . . . . . . . . . . Programmer
Brian May . . . . . . . . . . . . . . . . . . . . . . . . . . . Programmer
```

## SPRING CREEK PRODUCTIONS
```
PHONE . . . . . . . . . . . . . . . . . . . . . . . . . . . . . . . . 818-954-1210
FAX . . . . . . . . . . . . . . . . . . . . . . . . . . . . . . . . . . 818-954-2737
```
Warner Bros. Pictures
4000 Warner Blvd., Producers 7 #8
Burbank, CA 91522-0001

TYPE — Motion Pictures + Television
DEAL — Warner Bros. Pictures
CREDITS — Analyze This - Something To Talk About - Truman - First Time Felon - The Cherokee Kid

```
Paula Weinstein . . . . . . . . . . . . . . . . . . . . . . . President
Len Amato . . . . . . . . . . . . . . . . . . . . . Exec. Vice President
Robin Forman . . . . . . . . . . . . . . . . . . . . Exec. Vice President
Dana Goldberg . . . . . . . . . . . . . . . . . . . . VP, Development
Vanessa Colfman . . . . . . . . . . . . . . . . . . Dir., Development
Derek Dauchy . . . . . . . . . . . . . . . . . . . . . . . Story Editor
```

## SPRINGTIME!
```
PHONE . . . . . . . . . . . . . . . . . . . . . . . . . . . . . . . . 213-654-7755
FAX . . . . . . . . . . . . . . . . . . . . . . . . . . . . . . . . . . 213-654-8934
EMAIL . . . . . . . . . . . . . . . . . . . . . . . . martin@martinlewis.com
WEBSITE . . . . . . . . . . . . . . . . . . . . http://www.martinlewis.com
```
P.O. Box 461378
Los Angeles, CA 90046

TYPE — Motion Pictures + Television + Documentaries
CREDITS — The Secret Policeman's Other Ball - Wham! in China - Re-Meet The Beatles!

```
Martin Lewis . . . . . . . . . . . . . . Host/Writer/Producer/Director
Paul Klein . . . . . . . . . . . . . . . . . . . . . Exec. VP, Development
```

## SPUMCO
```
PHONE . . . . . . . . . . . . . . . . . . . . . . . . . . . . . . . . 818-550-5960
FAX . . . . . . . . . . . . . . . . . . . . . . . . . . . . . . . . . . 818-550-0320
EMAIL . . . . . . . . . . . . . . . . . . . . . . . . . . . bigshot@spumco.com
WEBSITE . . . . . . . . . . . . . . . . . . . . . . http://www.spumco.com
```
415 E. Harvard St., #204
Glendale, CA 91205

TYPE — Motion Pictures + Television + Animation
CREDITS — Ren & Stimpy Show - Bjork: I Miss You
COMMENTS — Also: Cartoons on the Internet.

```
John Kricfalusi . . . . . . . . . . . . . . . . Producer/Director/President
Steve Worth . . . . . . . . . . . . . . . . . . . . . . . . . . Producer
Kevin Kolde . . . . . . . . . . . . . . . . . . . . . . VP/General Manager
```

## SPYGAZE PICTURES
```
PHONE . . . . . . . . . . . . . . . . . . . . . . . . . . . . . . . . 310-395-8626
FAX . . . . . . . . . . . . . . . . . . . . . . . . . . . . . . . . . . 310-395-1401
EMAIL . . . . . . . . . . . . . . . . . . . . . . . . . . . spygaze@aol.com
```
710 Wilshire Blvd., Ste., 400
Santa Monica, CA 90401

TYPE — Motion Pictures + Television
CREDITS — High Stakes - Ultimate Betrayal - Trail of Tears

```
Donald Wrye . . . . . . . . . . . . . . . . . . . . . . . . . . President
```

## ST. CLARE ENTERTAINMENT
```
PHONE . . . . . . . . . . . . . . . . . . . . . . . . . . . . . . . . 310-229-2441
FAX . . . . . . . . . . . . . . . . . . . . . . . . . . . . . . . . . . 310-229-2443
```
1875 Century Park East, Ste. 1100
Los Angeles, CA 90067

TYPE — Television
DEAL — Walt Disney TV/Touchstone TV
CREDITS — Weird Science - Dream On - Sliders - Honey I Shrunk The Kids (series)

```
John Landis . . . . . . . . . . . . . . . . . . . . . . . . . . . Chairman
Leslie Belzberg . . . . . . . . . . . . . . . . . . . . . . COO/President
Bert Swartz . . . . . . . . . . . . . . . . . . . . President/Development
```

## STAMPEDE ENTERTAINMENT
```
PHONE . . . . . . . . . . . . . . . . . . . . . . . . . . . . . . . . 310-552-9977
FAX . . . . . . . . . . . . . . . . . . . . . . . . . . . . . . . . . . 310-552-9324
```
10345 W. Olympic Blvd., 3rd Floor
Los Angeles, CA 90064

TYPE — Motion Pictures
CREDITS — City Slickers - Heart & Souls - Tremors I & II

```
Nancy Roberts . . . . . . . . . . . . . . . . . . . . Partner/President
Ron Underwood . . . . . . . . . . . . . . . . . . . . . . . . . Partner
S.S. Wilson . . . . . . . . . . . . . . . . . . . . . . . . . . . . Partner
Brent Maddock . . . . . . . . . . . . . . . . . . . . . . . . . Partner
Lou Malacarne . . . . . . . . . . . . . . . . . . Exec. Vice President
Garett Berman . . . . . . . . . . . Exec. Asst./Development Associate
Greg Stevens . . . . . . . . . . . . Exec. Asst./Development Associate
```

## STAR LAND ENTERTAINMENT INC.
```
PHONE . . . . . . . . . . . . . . . . . . . . . . . . . . . . . . . . 213-651-1625
FAX . . . . . . . . . . . . . . . . . . . . . . . . . . . . . . . . . . 213-651-1627
EMAIL . . . . . . . . . . . . . . . . . . . . . . starland@starlandent.com
WEBSITE . . . . . . . . . . . . . . . . . . . . http://www.starlandent.com
```
8306 Wilshire Blvd., Ste. 7032
Beverly Hills, CA 90211

TYPE — Motion Pictures + Television + Syndication + Documentaries
CREDITS — All's Fair In Love & War - July 4th Triangle - The Stand Off - Love & War II
COMMENTS — Feature Films For Worldwide Theatrical Release.

```
Sartaj Khan . . . . . . . . . . . . . . . Producer/Director/Writer/Actor
Steven Halpern . . . . . . . . . . . . . . . . . . . . Writer/Producer
Sharon Choi . . . . . . . . . . . . . . . . . . . . . VP, Acquisitions
Gary Sohl . . . . . . . . . . . . . . . . . . . . . . . Dir., Operations
Tara Wetmur . . . . . . . . . . . . . . Dir., Development/Producer
```

## STARGATE ENTERTAINMENT INC.
```
PHONE . . . . . . . . . . . . . . . . . . . . . . . . . . . . . . . . 360-607-3044
FAX . . . . . . . . . . . . . . . . . . . . . . . . . . . . . . . . . . 360-608-4808
EMAIL . . . . . . . . . . . . . . . . . . . . . . strgate@stargate-ent.com
WEBSITE . . . . . . . . . . . . . . . . . . . . http://www.stargate-ent.com
```
11505 NE Fourth Plain Blvd., Ste. F1-403
Vancouver, WA 98662

TYPE — Motion Pictures
CREDITS — Flight of the Navigator - Lifeform

```
Mark H. Baker . . . . . . . . . . . . . . . . Writer/Director/Producer
Elizabeth Purcell . . . . . . . . . . . . . . . . . . . Asst. to Mr. Baker
```

## STARGAZER ENTERTAINMENT, INC.
```
PHONE . . . . . . . . . . . . . . . . . . . . . . . . . . . . . . . . 310-479-1200
FAX . . . . . . . . . . . . . . . . . . . . . . . . . . . . . . . . . . 310-473-9166
EMAIL . . . . . . . . . . . . . . . . . . . . . . . . . . . WMRMJ@aol.com
```
11828 La Grange Ave.
Los Angeles, CA 90025

TYPE — Motion Pictures + Television
CREDITS — Perfect Witness - Age Old Friends - AMC's Hywd. Report - Money Plays - Charlie Rose Specials (USA)

```
Wayne Rogers . . . . . . . . . . . . . . . . . . . . Executive Producer
Amy Rogers . . . . . . . . . . . . . . . . . . . . . Executive Producer
William Tannen . . . . . . . . . . . . . . . . . . . Executive Producer
```

## STARLIGHT PICTURES
```
PHONE .......................................... 702-870-7516
EMAIL ................................. ideamaster@aol.com
WEBSITE ..................... http://members.aol.com/ideamaster
```
1725 S. Rainbow Blvd., Ste. #2-186
Las Vegas, NV 89102

TYPE Motion Pictures
CREDITS Cardboard Angel - Shadow Dance - Benediction - Brainstorm Ballad

```
Gabriel Campisi ..................... Exec. Producer/Writer/Director
Anje Campisi ......................... Exec. Producer/Writer
Julio Espinoza ....................... Executive Producer
Steven Silvas ........................ Producer
Brian McNeal ........................ Development Executive
Earl T. Fox .......................... Financial Representative
```

## STARTOONS
```
PHONE .......................................... 708-335-3535
FAX ............................................ 708-335-3999
EMAIL ................................. Star2ns@aol.com
```
18147 Harwood Avenue
Homewood, IL 60430

TYPE Motion Pictures + Television + Animation + Interactive Multimedia
CREDITS Animaniacs - Fat Cats - Histeria

```
Jonathan D. McClenahan ............... Managing Director/CEO
Christine T. McClenahan .............. Executive Producer
Terry H. Hamilton .................... General Manager
```

## *STARTZ PRODUCTIONS, INC., JANE
```
PHONE .......................................... 212-545-8910
FAX ............................................ 212-545-8909
EMAIL ................................. gillmacken@aol.com
```
244 Fifth Avenue, Floor 11
New York, NY 10001

TYPE Motion Pictures + Feature Direct to Video + Animation + Television
CREDITS The Mighty - Indian and the Cupboard - The Magic Schoolbus - The Baby-Sitters' Club

```
Jane Startz .......................... President/Producer
Gillian MacKenzie .................... Dir., Development
```

## *STATE STREET PICTURES
```
PHONE .......................................... 310-369-5099
FAX ............................................ 310-369-8613
```
20th Century Fox
10201 West Pico Blvd., Trailer 769
Los Angeles, CA 90035

TYPE Motion Pictures + Television
DEAL Twentieth Century Fox-Fox 2000 (LA)
CREDITS Soul Food

```
Robert Teitel ........................ Producer
George Tillman Jr. ................... Director
Kathryn Tyus-Adair ................... VP, Production
Poppy Hanks .......................... Mgr., Production Administration
Gardenia Spiegel ..................... Asst. to Mr. Tillman
```

## STEELWORK FILMS
```
PHONE .......................................... 213-650-7220
FAX ............................................ 213-650-0093
```
8370 Yucca Trail
Los Angeles, CA 90046

TYPE Motion Pictures
CREDITS Little Odessa - The Arrival - The Substitute- Posse

```
Jim Steele ........................... President
```

## STEPPINSTONE ENTERTAINMENT
```
PHONE .......................................... 626-351-4334
FAX ............................................ 626-351-4335
EMAIL ................................. sse@steppinstone.com
WEBSITE ................................ http://www.steppinstone.com/
```
P.O. Box 8417
Universal City, CA 91618-8417

TYPE Motion Pictures + Television
CREDITS Ultraman - Puppet Master II - Predators From Beyond Neptune

```
King Wilder .......................... Partner/Director/Writer
Julie Avola .......................... Partner/Producer/Writer
```

## STERN PRODUCTION COMPANY, THE HOWARD
```
PHONE .......................................... 212-867-1200
FAX ............................................ 212-867-2434
```
10 E. 44th St.
New York, NY 10017

TYPE Motion Pictures + Television + Animation
CREDITS The Howard Stern E! Show

```
Howard Stern ......................... President
F.M. DeMarco ......................... Development
```

## STEVENS & ASSOCIATES
```
PHONE .......................................... 310-275-7541
FAX ............................................ 310-275-5929
```
9454 Wilshire Blvd., Ste. 600
Beverly Hills, CA 90212

TYPE Motion Pictures + Television
CREDITS Gunshy - This is L.S.A. - Money Shot

```
Neal Stevens ......................... President
Lorne Gorber ......................... Reader
Michael Haus ......................... Reader
Michelle Marburger ................... Reader
Giuseppina Di Raimondo ............... Development Assistant
```

## STEVENS COMPANY, THE
```
PHONE .......................... 213-634-2400/202-416-7960
FAX ............................ 213-937-6532/202-296-8344
```
Jess Morgan & Co.
5750 Wilshire Blvd., #590
Los Angeles, CA 90036

TYPE Motion Pictures + Television + Documentaries
CREDITS Thin Red Line - Kennedy Center Honors - AFI Salutes - Christmas in Washington
COMMENTS Also: JFK Center, Washington DC 20566

```
George Stevens Jr. ................... Partner/Writer/Producer/Director
Michael Stevens ...................... Partner/Writer/Producer/Director
Dottie McCarthy ...................... Exec. Asst. to George Stevens, Jr.
```

## STEWART TELEVISION, INC.
```
PHONE .......................................... 818-313-9394
FAX ............................................ 818-313-9514
EMAIL ................................. stewtv@aol.com
```
5525 Oakdale Ave., Ste. 275
Woodland Hills, CA 91364

TYPE Television
CREDITS Sports on Tap - Remember This

```
Sande Stewart ........................ Executive Producer
Bruce Burmester ...................... Director
```

## STF PRODUCTIONS, INC.
```
PHONE .......................................... 202-895-3100
FAX ............................................ 202-895-3096
EMAIL ................................. feedback@ari.net
WEBSITE ............................... http://www.amw.com
```
5151 Wisconsin Ave. N.W.
Washington, DC 20016

TYPE Television
CREDITS America's Most Wanted

```
Lance Heflin ......................... Executive Producer
Neal Freundlich ...................... Supervising Producer
Phil Lerman .......................... Co-Executive Producer
Gregg Klein .......................... Creative Producer
David Braxton ........................ Writer
```

## STICKS AND STONES
```
PHONE .......................................... 310-581-1992
FAX ............................................ 310-581-4994
```
2403 Main Street
Santa Monica, CA 90405

TYPE Motion Pictures

```
Blair Hayes .......................... No Title
Jonathan Weinstein ................... No Title
Preston Lee .......................... No Title
Amber Ventris ........................ No Title
Stacey Sutherland .................... No Title
```

# COMPANIES AND STAFF

## STIEFEL ENTERTAINMENT
PHONE . . . . . . . . . . . . . . . . . . . . . . . . . . . . . . 310-275-3377
FAX . . . . . . . . . . . . . . . . . . . . . . . . . . . . . . . . 310-275-8774
9255 Sunset Blvd., Ste. 610
Los Angeles, CA 90069

TYPE       Motion Pictures
DEAL       Warner Bros. Pictures
CREDITS       About Last Night - Stop Making Sense - Midnight in the Garden of Good and Evil

Arnold Stiefel . . . . . . . . . . . . . . . . . . . . . . . Chairman/Producer
Anita Zuckerman . . . . . . . . . . . . . . . . . . . . . Pres., Production
Erin Corzine . . . . . . . . . . . . . . . . . . . . . . . . Dir., Development
Alex Orellana . . . . . . . . . . . . . . . . . . . . . . Executive Assistant

## STILES-BISHOP PRODUCTIONS INC.
PHONE . . . . . . . . . . . . . . . . . . . . . . . . . . . 818-980-4483
12652 Killion
N. Hollywood, CA 91607

TYPE       Motion Pictures
CREDITS       Night Canvas - School for Speed (Pilot) - Men, Women & Money

Kathryn Bishop . . . . . . . . . . . . . . . . . . . . . . . . . President

## STONE CANYON INVESTMENTS, INC.
PHONE . . . . . . . . . . . . . . . . . . . . . . . . . . . 310-788-9555
FAX . . . . . . . . . . . . . . . . . . . . . . . . . . . . . 310-788-9559
EMAIL . . . . . . . . . . . . . . . . . jbrainard@stonecanyoninc.com
WEBSITE . . . . . . . . . . . . . . . . . . . http://stonecanyoninc.com
1800 Ave. of the Stars, Ste. 430
Los Angeles, CA 90067

TYPE       Motion Pictures + Animation
COMMENTS       Consultant to Medusa Film.

Ibrahim A. Moussa . . . . . . . . . . . . . . . . . . . . . . Chairman
Jana Brainard . . . . . . . . . . . . . . . . . . . . . . . VP, Acquisitions
Alessandra Sandron . . . . . . . . . Business Affairs Administration
Diana D'Alo . . . . . . . . . . . . . . . . . . . . . . . . . . . Assistant

## STONE STANLEY PRODUCTIONS
PHONE . . . . . . . . . . . . . . . . . . . . . . . . . . . 213-960-2599
FAX . . . . . . . . . . . . . . . . . . . . . . . . . . . . . 213-960-2437
Hollywood Center Studios
1040 N. Las Palmas, Bldg. 1
Hollywood, CA 90038

TYPE       Television
CREDITS       Legends of the Hidden Temple - Shop 'Til You Drop - Loveline - Big Deal

Scott A. Stone . . . . . . . . . . . . . . . . . . . . . Executive Producer
David G. Stanley . . . . . . . . . . . . . . . . . . . . Executive Producer
Heidi Cayn Freedman . . . . . . . . . VP/Exec. in Charge of Production
Melissa Butts . . . . . . . . . . . . . . . . . . . Executive Administrator

## STONE VS. STONE
PHONE . . . . . . . . . . . . . . . . . . . . . . . . . . . 212-941-1200
189 Franklin St., 3rd Floor
New York, NY 10013

TYPE       Motion Pictures + Television
CREDITS       Citizen X - The Negotiator

Robert Stone . . . . . . . . . . . . . . . . . . . . . . . . . . Producer
Webster Stone . . . . . . . . . . . . . . . . . . . . . . . . . Producer

## STONEFACE ENTERTAINMENT
PHONE . . . . . . . . . . . . . . . . . . . . . . . . . . . 310-203-1320
11041 Santa Monica Blvd., Ste. 302
Los Angeles, CA 90025

TYPE       Motion Pictures + Television
CREDITS       Between The Sheets
COMMENTS       Family Business.

Michael DeLuise . . . . . . . . . . . . Director/Actor/Exec. Producer
Michael Bendetti . . . . . . . . . . . . . . . . . . . Executive Producer
Peter DeLuise . . . . . . . . . . . . . . . . . . Writer/Producer/Actor

## STONEHENGE FILMS
PHONE . . . . . . . . . . . . . . . . . . . . . . . . . . . 213-634-8634
5757 Wilshire Blvd. Penthouse One
Los Angeles, CA 90036

TYPE       Motion Pictures + Television
CREDITS       Space - Fresh Horses - Key West - White Mile - Pronto
Dick Berg . . . . . . . . . . . . . . . . . . . . . . . . . . . . Chairman
Allan Marcil . . . . . . . . . . . . . . . . . . . . . . . . . . President
Ellie Ashburn . . . . . . . . . . . . . . . . . . . . . VP, Creative Affairs

## STONELOCK PICTURES
PHONE . . . . . . . . . . . . . . . . . . . . . . . . . . . 818-716-6356
FAX . . . . . . . . . . . . . . . . . . . . . . . . . . . . . 818-716-6866
5050 Serrania Avenue
Woodland Hills, CA 91364

TYPE       Motion Pictures + Television
CREDITS       In Dark Places
COMMENTS       A fully integrated finance/production company.
Beni Tadd Atoori . . . . . . . . . . . . . . . . . . . . . . . . . Partner
James Burke . . . . . . . . . . . . . . . . . . . . . . . . . . . Partner
H.J. Crane . . . . . . . . . . . . . . . . . . . . . . . . . . . . Partner

## STONEROAD PRODS. INC.
PHONE . . . . . . . . . . . . . . . . . . . . . . . . . . . 818-980-4820
EMAIL . . . . . . . . . . . . . . . . . . . bigevent1@photmail.com
11288 Ventura Blvd., Ste. 909
Studio City, CA 91604

TYPE       Motion Pictures + Television + Feature Direct to Video
CREDITS       Wrestling with God - Tomcat Angels
Jeanne M. Lange . . . . . . . . . . . . . . . . . Partner/Producer
Mike Cargile . . . . . . . . . . . . . . . . . Partner/Producer (818-781-5171)

## STORM ENTERTAINMENT
PHONE . . . . . . . . . . . . . . . . . . . . . . . . . . . 310-656-2500
FAX . . . . . . . . . . . . . . . . . . . . . . . . . . . . . 310-656-2510
EMAIL . . . . . . . . . . . . . . . . . . . . . . storment95@aol.com
225 Santa Monica Blvd., Ste. 601
Santa Monica, CA 90401

TYPE       Motion Pictures
CREDITS       Nevada - Hurlyburly - Lovelife - Big City Blues
H. Michael Heuser . . . . . . . . . . . . . . . . . . . President/CEO
Pamela S. Delaney Esq. . . . . . . . . . . . . . . Dir., Legal Affairs

## STORYBOOK ENTERTAINMENT
PHONE . . . . . . . . . . . . . . . . . . . . . . . . . . . 310-260-9990
FAX . . . . . . . . . . . . . . . . . . . . . . . . . . . . . 310-260-9990
220 San Vicente Blvd., Ste. 310
Santa Monica, CA 90402

TYPE       Motion Pictures + Television
CREDITS       Rebel Highway
Willie H. Kutner . . . . . . . . . . . . . . . . . . . . . . . President

## STORYBROOKE FILMS
PHONE . . . . . . . . . . . . . . . . . . . . . . . . . . . 310-553-9642
FAX . . . . . . . . . . . . . . . . . . . . . . . . . . . . . 310-553-4642
EMAIL . . . . . . . . . . . . . . . . . . . . . jbrooke@earthlink.net
10380 Tennessee Ave., Studio B
Los Angeles, CA 90064

TYPE       Motion Pictures + Television
CREDITS       Wind In The Wire - Plato's Run - The Dinosaur Hunter
James Brooke . . . . . . . . . . . . . . . . . . . . . . . . . Producer
Melanie Chartoff . . . . . . . . . . . . . . . . . . . . Writer/Producer

## STORYLINE ENTERTAINMENT
PHONE . . . . . . . . . . . . . . . . . . . . . . . . . . . 310-244-3222
FAX . . . . . . . . . . . . . . . . . . . . . . . . . . . . . 310-244-0322
TriStar Building
10202 W. Washington Blvd., #206
Culver City, CA 90232

TYPE       Motion Pictures + Television
DEAL       Columbia TriStar Television/Walt Disney TV/Touchstone TV
CREDITS       Rodgers & Hammerstein's Cinderella - Gypsy - Footloose - Serving In Silence

Craig Zadan . . . . . . . . . . . . . . . . . . . . . . . . . . Producer
Neil Meron . . . . . . . . . . . . . . . . . . . . . . . . . . Producer
Dave Mace . . . . . . . . . . . . . . . . . . . . . . . Dir., Development
Travis Knox . . . . . . . . . . . . . . . . . . . . . Creative Executive
Matt Murray . . . . . . . . . . . . . . . . . Asst. to Mr. Zadan/Mr. Meron

## STORYOPOLIS PRODUCTIONS
PHONE . . . . . . . . . . . . . . . . . . . . . . . . . . . 310-358-2525
FAX . . . . . . . . . . . . . . . . . . . . . . . . . . . . . 310-358-9551
EMAIL . . . . . . . . . . . . . . . . . . . storyopolis@storyopolis.com
116 N. Robertson Blvd., Plaza A
Los Angeles, CA 90048

TYPE       Motion Pictures + Television + Animation + Feature Direct to Video
DEAL       Warner Bros. Pictures
Fonda Snyder . . . . . . . . . . . . . . . . . . . . . . . . . President
Janet Salas . . . . . . . . . . . . . . . . . . . . . . Creative Executive

## STORYTELLER FILMS, LTD.
PHONE . . . . . . . . . . . . . . . . . . . . . . . . . . . . . . . . 310-277-7372
270 N. Canon Dr., Ste. 1398
Beverly Hills, CA 90210

TYPE | Motion Pictures + Television + Animation
CREDITS | Tracks of a Killer - Tall, Dark & Deadly - Jack Frost - Murder In Mind

Jeremy Paige . . . . . . . . . . . . . . . . . . . . . . . . . . . . . . . . Producer
Vicki Slotnick . . . . . . . . . . . . . . . . . . . . . . . . . . . . . . . Producer
Michael Cooney . . . . . . . . . . . . . . . . . . . . . . . . Writer/Director
Danielle Kutner . . . . . . . . . . . . . . . . . Asst. to Michael Cooney

## STRADER ENTERTAINMENT
PHONE . . . . . . . . . . . . . . . . . . . . . . . . . . . . . . . . 310-226-6166
EMAIL . . . . . . . . . . . . . . . . . . . . . . . . . . . . straderent@aol.com
171 Pier Avenue, Ste. 328
Santa Monica, CA 90405

TYPE | Motion Pictures + Television + Animation

Jim Strader . . . . . . . . . . . . . . . . . . . . . . . Producer (213-960-7983)
Scott Strader . . . . . . . . . . . . . . . . . . . . . Vice President (NYC)

## STRATFORD PRODS, INC., BERT
PHONE . . . . . . . . . . . . . . . . . . . . . . . . . . . . . . . . 212-757-2211
FAX . . . . . . . . . . . . . . . . . . . . . . . . . . . . . . . . . . 212-757-2213
221 W. 57th St., 10th Fl.
New York, NY 10019

TYPE | Motion Pictures + Television + Syndication + Animation + Feature Direct to Video
CREDITS | Noel (NBC) - Peppermint Rose - 12 Days of Christmas (NCB) - White Fang - Bingo & Molly

Bert Stratford . . . . . . . . . . . . . . . . . . . . . . . Co-Owner/Producer
Aura Sujaritchan . . . . . . . . . . . . . . . . . . . . Dir., Development

## STRATUM ENTERTAINMENT
PHONE . . . . . . . . . . . . . . . . . . . . . . . . . . . . . . . . 310-472-4217
FAX . . . . . . . . . . . . . . . . . . . . . . . . . . . . . . . . . . 310-472-9752
EMAIL . . . . . . . . . . . . . . . . . . . . . . . . . stratument@aol.com
747 Teakwood Rd.
Los Angeles, CA 90049

TYPE | Motion Pictures + Television
CREDITS | Infidelity
COMMENTS | Movies of the Week.

Gary Stretch . . . . . . . . . . . . . . . . . . . Chairman/Actor/Producer
Dianne Mandell . . . . . . . . . . . . . . . . . . . . President/Producer

## STUART PRODUCTIONS, INC., MEL
PHONE . . . . . . . . . . . . . . . . . . . . . . . . . . . . . . . . 310-785-9080
FAX . . . . . . . . . . . . . . . . . . . . . . . . . . . . . . . . . . 310-785-9179
EMAIL . . . . . . . . . . . . . . . . . . . . . . . . . . melfilm@aol.com
1551 S. Robertson Blvd.
Los Angeles, CA 90035

TYPE | Television + Documentaries
CREDITS | Willy Wonka & The Chocolate Factory - Making of the President

Mel Stuart . . . . . . . . . . . . . . . . . . . . . . . . . . . . . . . President

## STUDIO PRODUCTIONS
PHONE . . . . . . . . . . . . . . . . . . . . . . . . . . . . . . . . 213-856-8048
FAX . . . . . . . . . . . . . . . . . . . . . . . . . . . . . . . . . . 213-461-4202
EMAIL . . . . . . . . . . . . . . . . . . . . . . . . outayrmind@aol.com
650 N. Bronson Ave., Ste. 223
Hollywood, CA 90004-1404

TYPE | Animation + Motion Pictures + Television + Syndication
CREDITS | The Game Channel - Disney Club
COMMENTS | Also: Promos, 3D Animation, Cel Animation, Character Design through Flip Your Lid, Inc.

Steve Soffer . . . . . . . . . . . . . . . . . . . . . . . Executive Producer
Jay Jacoby . . . . . . . . . . . . . . . . . . . . . . . . . . Creative Director
Kit Hudson . . . . . . . . . . . . . . . . . . . . . . . . . . . . . . . Director
Gay Murdock . . . . . . . . . . . . . . . . . . . . . . . . . . . . Controller
Byron Chaney . . . . . . . . . . . . . . . . . . . . . . . . . . Art Director

## *STUDIOS USA
PHONE . . . . . . . . . . . . . . . . . . . . . . . . . . . . . . . . 818-777-1000
WEBSITE . . . . . . . . . . . . . . . . . . . . . . . http://unistudios.com
100 Universal City Plaza
Universal City, CA 91608-1085

TYPE | Television

Steve Rosenberg . . . . . . . . . . . . . . . Pres., Studios USA Television
Bob Fleming . . . . . . . . . . . . . . . . . . . . . . . . . . Group President
Vance Van Petten . . . . . . . . . . . Exec. VP, Business & Legal Affairs
Lonnie Burstein . . . . . . . . . . . . . . Sr. VP, First-Run Development

## *STUDIOS USA PICTURES
PHONE . . . . . . . . . . . . . . . . . . . . . . . . . . . . . . . . 818-777-1000
WEBSITE . . . . . . . . . . . . . . . . . . . . . . . http://unistudios.com
100 Universal City Plaza
Universal City, CA 91608-1085

TYPE | Television

Barbara Fisher . . . . . . . . . . . . . . . . . . . . . . . . . . . President
Bob Kelley . . . . . . . . . . . Exec. VP, Business Affairs & Administration
Randy Levinson . . . . . . . . . . . . . . . . . . Sr. VP, Creative Affairs
Angela Mancuso . . . . . . . . . . . . . . . . . . . . . Sr. VP, Production
Libby Beers . . . . . . . . . . . . . . . . . . . . . . . VP, Creative Affairs
Paulo de Oliveira . . . . . . . . . . . . . . . . . . . VP, Creative Affairs
Madeleine McBride . . . . . . . . VP, Production & Finance Administration
Joan Whitehead Evans . . . . . . . . . . . VP, Business & Legal Affairs

## *STUDIOS USA TELEVISION
PHONE . . . . . . . . . . . . . . . . . . . . . . . . . . . . . . . . 818-777-1000
WEBSITE . . . . . . . . . . . . . . . . . . . . . . . http://unistudios.com
100 Universal City Plaza
Universal City, CA 91608-1085

TYPE | Television

Ken Solomon . . . . . . . . . . . . . . . . . . . . . . . . . . . . President
Charles Engel . . . . . . . . . . . . . . . . . Exec. VP, Programming
Matthew N. Herman . . . . . . . . . . . . . . . Exec. VP, Production
Cheryl Bloch . . . . . . . . . . . . . . . . . Sr. VP, Drama Programming
Bill Hamm . . . . . . . . . . . . . . . . . . Sr. VP, Drama Programming
David Kissinger . . . . . . . . . . . . . . Sr. VP, Comedy Programming
Nancy Perkins . . . . . . . . . . . . . . . . . . . . . . . Sr. VP, Casting
Derek Platt . . . . . . . . . Sr. VP, Music, Creative & Business Affairs
Dave Beanes . . . . . . . . . . . . . . . . . . . . . . . . . VP, Production
Bruce Sandzimier . . . . . . . . . . . . . . . . . . VP, Post Production
Pat Wells . . . . . . . . . . . . . . . . . . . . . . VP, Drama Programming
Bari Halle . . . . . . . . . . . . . . . . . . . . . . . Production Executive
Rob Harland . . . . . . . . . . . . . . . . . . . . . Production Executive
Bob Minkoff . . . . . . . . . . . . . . . . . . . . . Production Executive
Megan Branman . . . . . . . . . . . . . . . . . . . . . . Dir., Casting
Kathy Busby . . . . . . . . . . . . . . . . . Dir., Comedy Programming
Tim De Luca . . . . . . . . . . . . . . . . . . . . . Dir., Post Production
Dava Waite . . . . . . . . . . . . . . . . . . . . . . . . . . Dir., Casting
Don Welty . . . . . . . . . . . . . . . Dir., Music Business Affairs
Debra Brause . . . . . . . . . . . . . Mgr., Comedy Programming
Shira Wertheimer . . . . . . . . . . . . . . . . Programming Executive

## STUN
PHONE . . . . . . . . . . . . . . . . . . . . . . . . . . . . . . . . 310-271-5858
FAX . . . . . . . . . . . . . . . . . . . . . . . . . . . . . . . . . . 310-271-9911
EMAIL . . . . . . . . . . . . . . . . . . . . . . . wyldoats@earthlink.net
9150 Wilshire Blvd., Ste. 201
Beverly Hills, CA 90212

TYPE | Motion Pictures + Television + Interactive Multimedia
CREDITS | The Gun Seller - The Diamond As Big As The Ritz - Found in the Street
COMMENTS | Also: 130 W. 57th St., Ste. 5C, NY, NY 10019; 10a Hall St., Bondi NSW 2026 Australia,001612.9365.5300

Susan Adler . . . . . . . . . . . . . . . . . . . . . . . . . . . . . . . Producer
Liza Oestreich . . . . . . . . . . . . . . . . . . . . . . . . VP, Development
Anna von Savoye . . . . . . . . . . . . VP, Finance & Business Admin.
Elliot Blair Esq . . . . . . . . . . . . . . . Business Affairs/Legal Counsel
Merelyn Hardaker . . . . . . . . . . . . Dir., Development (Australia)
Vaughn Sandman . . . . . . . . . . . . . . . . . . . . . . . Story Editor

## STUPIN PRODUCTIONS, PAUL
PHONE . . . . . . . . . . . . . . . . . . . . . . . . . . . . . . . . 310-979-8741
FAX . . . . . . . . . . . . . . . . . . . . . . . . . . . . . . . . . . 310-207-7998
12233 W. Olympic, Ste. 210
Los Angeles, CA 90064

TYPE | Motion Pictures + Television + Interactive Multimedia
DEAL | Columbia TriStar Television
CREDITS | Dawson's Creek - My Wildest Dreams - Fortune Hunter

Paul Stupin . . . . . . . . . . . . . . . . . . . . . . . Executive Producer
Ilka Rivard . . . . . . . . . . . . . . . . . . . . . . . . . Dir., Development

## SUGERMAN, ANDREW
PHONE . . . . . . . . . . . . . . . . . . . . . . . . . . . . . . . . 213-891-2670
Allied Cinema Corp.
3576 Dixie Canyon Ave.
Sherman Oaks, CA 91423

TYPE | Motion Pictures + Television
CREDITS | Savate - Payoff - Working Trash - Basic Training - Deadly Rivals - Love Kills

Andrew Sugerman . . . . . . . . . . . . . . . . . . . . . . . . . . . . Producer

# COMPANIES AND STAFF

**SULLIVAN COMPANY, THE**
PHONE . . . . . . . . . . . . . . . . . . . . . . . . . . . . . . . . . . . . . . 310-319-2026
FAX . . . . . . . . . . . . . . . . . . . . . . . . . . . . . . . . . . . . . . . . . . 310-393-2389
227 Broadway, Ste. 302
Santa Monica, CA 90401

TYPE         Motion Pictures + Television
DEAL         Atlantis Films
CREDITS     Dr. Quinn, Medicine Woman - California - The Trials of
Rosie O'Neill - The Tracey Thurman Story - USMA West
Point

Beth Sullivan . . . . . . . . . . . . . . . . . . . . . . . . . . . . . . . . . Executive Producer
Ron Green . . . . . . . . . . . . . . . . . . . . . . . . . . . . . . . . . . . . . . . . Development
Shelly Sterrett . . . . . . . . . . . . . . . . . . . . . . . . . . . . . . . . Executive Assistant

**SULLIVAN ENTERTAINMENT**
PHONE . . . . . . . . . . . . . . . . . . . . . . . . . . . . . . . . . . . . . . 310-247-0166
FAX . . . . . . . . . . . . . . . . . . . . . . . . . . . . . . . . . . . . . . . . . . 310-247-1945
9465 Wilshire Blvd., Ste. 605
Beverly Hills, CA 90212

TYPE         Motion Pictures + Television
CREDITS     Road to Avonlea - Under The Piano - Anne of Green
Gables

Kevin Sullivan . . . . . . . . . . . . . . . . . . . . . President/Exec. Producer (Toronto)
Trudy Grant . . . . . . . . . . . . . . . . . . . . . . . . . . Executive Producer (Toronto)
George Auge . . . . . . . . . . . . . . . . . . . . . . . Dir., Feature Development (LA)

**SUMMERS ENTERTAINMENT**
PHONE . . . . . . . . . . . . . . . . . . . . . . . . . . . . . . . . . . . . . . 213-665-5400
FAX . . . . . . . . . . . . . . . . . . . . . . . . . . . . . . . . . . . . . . . . . . 213-663-6679
5230 Linwood Drive
Los Angeles, CA 90027

TYPE         Motion Pictures + Television + Syndication
CREDITS     Stakeout 1&2 - Sandlot - Mystery Date - Vital Signs -
Dogfight
Cathleen Summers . . . . . . . . . . . . . . . . . . . . . . . . . . . . . . . . . . . Producer
Robert Fajardo . . . . . . . . . . . . . . . . . . . . . . . . . . . . . . . Creative Executive

**SUMMIT ENTERTAINMENT**
PHONE . . . . . . . . . . . . . . . . . . . . . . . . . . . . . . . . . . . . . . 310-315-6000
FAX . . . . . . . . . . . . . . . . . . . . . . . . . . . . . . . . . . . . . . . . . . 310-828-4132
2308 Broadway
Santa Monica, CA 90404

TYPE         Motion Pictures
Patrick Wachsberger . . . . . . . . . . . . . . . . . . . . . . . . . . . . . President/CEO
Bob Hayward . . . . . . . . . . . . . . . . . . . . . . . . . . . . . Chief Operating Officer
David Garrett . . . . . . . . . . . . . . . . . . . . Sr. Vice President (U.K. Office)
Heidi Lester . . . . . . . . . . . . . . . . . . . . . . . . . . . . . . Production Executive
Andrew Martin . . . . . . . . . . . . . . . . . . . . . . . . . . . . VP, Creative Affairs

**SUNBOW ENTERTAINMENT**
PHONE . . . . . . . . . . . . . . . . . . . . . . 212-886-4900/818-241-3100
FAX . . . . . . . . . . . . . . . . . . . . . . . . . 212-366-4242/818-241-7168
EMAIL . . . . . . . . . . . . . . . . . . . . . . . . . . . . postmaster@sunbow.com
100 Fifth Avenue
New York, NY 10011-4340

TYPE         Television + Animation
CREDITS     The Tick - The Mask - Salty's Lighthouse
COMMENTS   Deal with Sony Wonder Intl. Distr. Also: 1725 Victory
Blvd., Glendale, CA 91201

C.J. Kettler . . . . . . . . . . . . . . . . . . . . . . . . . . . . . . . . . . . . . . . President
Andrew Karpen . . . . . . . . . . . . . . . . . . . . . . . . . Chief Financial Officer
Andrea Miller . . . . . . . . . . . . . . . . . . . . . . . . . . . . . Sr. VP/Co-Production
Carole Weitzman . . . . . . . . . . . . . . . . . . . . . . . . . . . Sr. VP, Production
Geraldine Clarke . . . . . . . . . . . . . . . . . . . . VP, West Coast Production
Ken Olshansky . . . . . . . . . . . . . . . . . . . . . . . . . . . . VP, Development

**SUNDANCE INSTITUTE**
PHONE . . . . . . . . . . . . . . . . . . . . . . . . . . . . . . . . . . . . . . 310-394-4662
FAX . . . . . . . . . . . . . . . . . . . . . . . . . . . . . . . . . . . . . . . . . . 310-394-8353
EMAIL . . . . . . . . . . . . . . . . . . . . . . . . . . . . sundance@deltanet.com
WEBSITE . . . . . . . . . . . . . . . . . . . . . . . . . . http://www.sundance.org
225 Santa Monica Blvd., 8th Floor
Santa Monica, CA 90401

TYPE         Motion Pictures
CREDITS     Walking & Talking - Manny & Lo - Reservoir Dogs -
Smoke Signals

Nicole Gvillemet . . . . . . . . . . . . . . . . . . . . . . . . . . . . . . . Vice President
Kenneth Brecher . . . . . . . . . . . . . . . . . . . . . . . . . . . . Executive Director
Patricia Boero . . . . . . . . . . . . . . . . . . . . . Dir., International Projects
Geoffrey Gilmore . . . . . . . . . . Dir., Film Fest. Programming & Special Projects
Philip Himberg . . . . . . . . . . . . . . . . . . . . . . . . . Dir., Theatre Program
Michelle Satter . . . . . . . . . . . . . . . . . . . . Dir., Feature Film Program
Lynn Auerbach . . . . . . . . . . . . . . . . . Assoc. Dir., Feature Film Program
John Cooper . . . . . . . . . . . . . . . . . Assoc. Dir., Film Fest. Programming
Rebecca Yeldham . . . . . . . . . . . . . . . . . . . . Programmer, Film Festival
Heather Rae . . . . . . . . . . . . . . . . Native American Program Coordinator
Beth Nathanson . . . . . . . . . . . . . . . . . . Consultant, Special Projects
Shaz Bennett . . . . . . . . . . . . . . . . Program Assistant/Office Coordinator
Trevor Groth . . . . . . . . . . . . . . . . . . . . Asst. Programmer, Film Festival
Whitney Cook . . . . . . . . . . . . . . . . Asst. to Dir., Feature Film Program
Nanelle Culpepper . . . . . . . . . . . . . . . . . . . Asst. to Exec. Director
Mary Kerr . . . . . . . . . . . . . . . . . . . . . . . . Asst. to Dir., Film Festival
Judith Wexler . . . . . . . . . . . . . . . . . . . . . . . Asst. to Exec. Director

**SUNTAUR ENTERTAINMENT**
PHONE . . . . . . . . . . . . . . . . . . . . . . . . . . . . . . . . . . . . . . 213-656-3800
FAX . . . . . . . . . . . . . . . . . . . . . . . . . . . . . . . . . . . . . . . . . . 213-656-6311
EMAIL . . . . . . . . . . . . . . . . . . . . . . . . . . . . . . suntaurent@aol.com
1581 N. Crescent Hts. Blvd.
Los Angeles, CA 90046

TYPE         Motion Pictures + Television + Animation
CREDITS     Under One Roof
Paul Aaron . . . . . . . . . . . . . . . . . . . . . . . . . . Writer/Producer/Director
Michael Henry Brown . . . . . . . . . . . . . . . . . . . . . . . . . Writer/Producer
Rick Andreoli . . . . . . . . . . . . . . . . . . . . . . . . . . . Dir., Development
Jamie Kirakosian . . . . . . . . . . . . . . . . Dir., Finance & Business Affairs

**SUPPA PRODS., INC., RONALD**
PHONE . . . . . . . . . . . . . . . . . . . . . . . . . . . . . . . . . . . . . . 818-784-6369
FAX . . . . . . . . . . . . . . . . . . . . . . . . . . . . . . . . . . . . . . . . . . 818-784-6369
3737 Ventura Canyon Ave.
Sherman Oaks, CA 91423

TYPE         Motion Pictures
CREDITS     Paradise Alley - Defense Play - Riding the Edge - Maui
Heat
Ronald Suppa . . . . . . . . . . . . . . . . . . . . . . . . . . . . . Writer/Producer
Jolene Rae . . . . . . . . . . . . . . . . . . . . . . . . . . . . . . . VP, Development
Eric Harrington . . . . . . . . . . . . . . . . . . . . . . Dir., Creative Affairs

**SWEET LORRAINE PRODS. INC.**
PHONE . . . . . . . . . . . . . . . . . . . . . . . . . . . . . . . . . . . . . . 213-782-8582
FAX . . . . . . . . . . . . . . . . . . . . . . . . . . . . . . . . . . . . . . . . . . 213-782-8679
6399 Wilshire Blvd, Suite 803
Los Angeles, CA 90048

TYPE         Motion Pictures + Television
CREDITS     Where I Live - Homeboys in OuterSpace
Ehrich Van Lowe . . . . . . . . . . . . . . . . Exec. Producer/Writer/President
Robin Claire . . . . . . . . . . . . . . . . . . . . . . . . . . . . VP, Creative Affairs
Gary Feemster . . . . . . . . . . . . . . . . . . . . . . . . . . . Executive Assistant

**SWEETPEA ENTERTAINMENT**
PHONE . . . . . . . . . . . . . . . . . . . . . . . . . . . . . . . . . . . . . . 310-275-9859
FAX . . . . . . . . . . . . . . . . . . . . . . . . . . . . . . . . . . . . . . . . . . 310-275-9322
147 S. Almont Drive, Bugalow
Los Angeles, CA 90048

TYPE         Motion Pictures + Television + Syndication + Feature
Direct to Video + Animation
CREDITS     Gen 13 - Dungeons & Dragons
Courtney Solomon . . . . . . . . . . . . . . . . . . . . Chairman/President/Partner
Nelson Leong . . . . . . . . . . . . . . . . . . . . . . . . . . . . . . . . . . . . . Partner
Allan Zeman . . . . . . . . . . . . . . . . . . . . . . . . . . . . . . . . . . . . . . Partner
John Benitz . . . . . . . . . . . . . . . . . . . . . . . . . . . . . . . . . Co-Chairman
Ann Flagella . . . . . . . . . . . . . . . . . . . . . . . . . . . . . Creative Executive
James Dailey . . . . . . . . . . . . . . . . . . . . . . . . . . . . Asst. to President

# COMPANIES AND STAFF

**SYMPHONY ENTERTAINMENT, LLC**
PHONE . . . . . . . . . . . . . . . . . . . . . . . . . . . 310-656-9040
FAX . . . . . . . . . . . . . . . . . . . . . . . . . . . . . 310-656-9046
EMAIL . . . . . . . . . . . . . . . . . . . . . . . billg.414@aol.com
506 Santa Monica Blvd., #314
Santa Monica, CA 90401
TYPE         Motion Pictures + Television
CREDITS      Da - Nightbreaker - Judgment in Berlin - She Stood Alone:
             The Tailhook Scandal - Target Earth
COMMENTS     (Also: 920 S. Poplar St., Winston-Salem, N.C. 27101 tel:
             910-723-4383 fax: 910-723-4384

Sam Grogg . . . . . . . . . . . . . . . . . . . . . . . . . Partner/Chairman
William Greenblatt . . . . . . . . . . . . . . . . . . . Partner/President
Adoley Odunton . . . . . . . . . . . . . . . . . . . . . . . . . Producer
Blyth Daylong . . . . . . . . . . . . Dir., Production (North Carolina)

**SYNCHRONICITY PRODUCTIONS**
PHONE . . . . . . . . . . . . . . . 310-246-1477/212-704-0515
FAX . . . . . . . . . . . . . . . . . 310-246-9085/212-704-0945
EMAIL . . . . . . . . . . . . . . . . synchprodinc@earthlink.net
101 S. Robertson Blvd., Ste. 208
Los Angeles, CA 90048
TYPE         Motion Pictures + Television + Interactive Multimedia
CREDITS      Element of Truth - In Pursuit of Honor
COMMENTS     Also: 500 Fifth Ave., Ste. 1825, NY, NY 10110 Also:
             Commericals

Larry Peerce . . . . . . . . . . . . . . . . . . . . . . . . . . . No Title
Adam Peck . . . . . . . . . . . . . . . . . . . . . . . . . . . . No Title

**T-SQUARED PRODUCTIONS**
PHONE . . . . . . . . . . . . . . . . . . . . . . . . . . . 310-915-0055
FAX . . . . . . . . . . . . . . . . . . . . . . . . . . . . . 310-915-9109
3496 Wade St.
Los Angeles, CA 90066-1534
TYPE         Motion Pictures + Television + Interactive Multimedia
CREDITS      Kissing Miranda - Fried Green Tomatoes - Pyrates -
             Sweethearts

Tom Taylor . . . . . . . . . . . . . . . . . . . . . . Producer/Attorney

**T.H.A. - THOMAS HORTON ASSOCIATES INC.**
PHONE . . . . . . . . . . . . . . . . . . . . . . . . 805-963-3577
FAX . . . . . . . . . . . . . . . . . . . . . . . . . . 805-963-3157
EMAIL . . . . . . . . . . . . . . . . . . . . . . . . tha@sharktv.com
WEBSITE . . . . . . . . . . . . . . . . . . . http://www.sharktv.com
2020 Alameda Padre Serra, Ste. 201
Santa Barbara, CA 93103-1756
TYPE         Television + Documentaries
CREDITS      The Shark Files - Outer Bounds - Nature's Secret Worlds
COMMENTS     Post production in PAL or NTSC.

Thomas F. Horton . . . . . . . . . . . . . . . . . . . . . President
Jean Horton Garner . . . . . . . . . . . . . . . . . . Sr. Vice President
Jeff Kurr . . . . . . . . . . . . . . . . . . . . . . . . VP, Production
Kevin L. Rose . . . . . . . . . . . . . . . . . VP, Business & Legal Affairs

**TAE PRODUCTIONS**
PHONE . . . . . . . . . . . . . . . . . . . . . . . . 760-321-0024
FAX . . . . . . . . . . . . . . . . . . . . . . . . . . 760-325-3264
4741 E. Palm Canyon Dr., Ste. 171
Palm Springs, CA 92264
TYPE         Documentaries + Feature Direct to Video + Motion
             Pictures + Television + Interactive Multimedia +
             Syndication
CREDITS      Heaven & Earth - First Works - Terrorism: A World in
             Shadows - Victory in the Desert/General Colin Powell -
             Princess Grace, The Last Interview

Robert D. Kline . . . . . . . . . . . . . . . . . . . . . President/CEO
Bree Montana . . . . . . . . . . . . . . . . . . . . . . . Development
Anthony Pena . . . . . . . . . . . . . . . . . . . . . . . . . Production
Loretta Clements . . . . . . . . . . . . . . . . . . . Executive Assistant
Isa Zepeda . . . . . . . . . . . . . . . . . . . . . . . . . . . Assistant

**TAFFNER ENTERTAINMENT LTD.**
PHONE . . . . . . . . . . . . . . . . . . . . . . . . 213-937-1144
FAX . . . . . . . . . . . . . . . . . . . . . . . . . . 213-937-5095
1888 Century Park East., 19th Fl.
Los Angeles, CA 90067
TYPE         Television + Syndication + Motion Pictures +
             Documentaries
CREDITS      Three's Company - Too Close for Comfort - Rumpole at
             the Bailey

Don Taffner Jr. . . . . . . . . . . . . . . . Exec. VP/CEO (NY & LA)
Jeff Cotugno . . . . . . . . . . . . . . . . Chief Financial Officer (NY)
Emmet G. Lavery Jr. . . . . . . . . . . . . . VP, Business Affairs (LA)

**TAHSE PRODS., MARTIN**
PHONE . . . . . . . . . . . . . . . . . . . . . . . . 310-451-5164
FAX . . . . . . . . . . . . . . . . . . . . . . . . . . 310-394-2151
1364 Palisades Beach Rd.
Santa Monica, CA 90401
TYPE         Motion Pictures + Feature Direct to Video
CREDITS      The Lookalike - Matters of the Heart - Words by Heart -
             Kukla, Fran and Ollie

Martin Tahse . . . . . . . . . . . . . . . . . . . . . . . . . President
Michael Vodde . . . . . . . . . . . . . . . . . . . . . . VP, Development

**TAKES ON PRODUCTION**
PHONE . . . . . . . . . . . . . . . . . . . . . . . . 310-264-2474
EMAIL . . . . . . . . . . . . . . . . . . . . . . . amck@takeson.com
WEBSITE . . . . . . . . . . . . . . . . . . . http://www.takeson.com
1547 18th St.
Santa Monica, CA 90404
TYPE         Television
CREDITS      Tracey Takes On

Allan McKewon . . . . . . . . . . . . . . . . . . . . . Chairman/CEO
Stephanie Cone . . . . . . . . . . . . . . . . . . . . . . Co-Producer
Scott Hopkins . . . . . . . . . . . . . . . . . . . Financial Controller

**TAKOMA ENTERTAINMENT GROUP**
PHONE . . . . . . . . . . . . . . . . . . . . . . . . 818-505-9067
FAX . . . . . . . . . . . . . . . . . . . . . . . . . . 818-980-4776
11514 Sunshine Terrace
Studio City, CA 91604
TYPE         Television + Motion Pictures
CREDITS      Magnus Robot Fighter - Turok - The Winterhill Gang
COMMENTS     Motion Soundtracks, Music Supervision, Manufacturing,
             Marketing, Distributing of Movie Soundtracks.

Barry Levine . . . . . . . . . . . . . . . . . . . . . . . . President
Craig Besnoy . . . . . . . . . . . . . VP, Business Affairs/Development
Wendi Friedman . . . . . . . . . . . . . . . . . . . . . VP, Production
Leo Partible . . . . . . . . . . . . . . . . . . . . . . VP, Development
Serge Leenders . . . . . . . . . . . . . . . . . . . . . . . Producer
Brent Woods . . . . . . . . . . . . . . . . . . . . . Executive Assistant

**TALKING RINGS ENTERTAINMENT**
PHONE . . . . . . . . . . . . . . . . . . . . . . . . 702-227-3433
FAX . . . . . . . . . . . . . . . . . . . . . . . . . . 702-364-1101
EMAIL . . . . . . . . . . . . . . . . . . . . . . talkring@wizard.com
WEBSITE . . . . . . . . . . . . . . . . . http://www.scifistation.com
P.O. Box 80141
Las Vegas, NV 89180
TYPE         Motion Pictures + Television + Animation
CREDITS      The Time Machine - Darkside - 7 Faces of Dr. Lao -
             Puppetoon Movie
COMMENTS     Puppetoon Animation Studios.

Arnold Leibovit . . . . . . . . . . . . . . . . . . . Producer/Director
Barbara Schimpf . . . . . . . . . . . . . . . . . . . . . VP, Production

**TALKING WALL PICTURES, INC.**
PHONE . . . . . . . . . . . . . . . . . . . . . . . . 212-397-8686
FAX . . . . . . . . . . . . . . . . . . . . . . . . . . 212-397-0282
850 Seventh Ave., Ste. 805
New York, NY 10019
TYPE         Motion Pictures + Television
CREDITS      Signs of Life - Rising Son

John David Coles . . . . . . . . . . . . . . . . . . Director/President
Laura Zaccaro . . . . . . . . . . . . . . . . . . . . . VP, Development
Kevin Dreyfuss . . . . . . . . . . . . . . . . . Development Associate

**TAPESTRY FILMS INC.**
PHONE . . . . . . . . . . . . . . . . . . . . . . . . 310-275-1191
FAX . . . . . . . . . . . . . . . . . . . . . . . . . . 310-275-1266
EMAIL . . . . . . . . . . . . . . . . . . . . . . tapestryla@aol.com
9328 Civic Center Dr.
Beverly Hills, CA 90210
TYPE         Motion Pictures + Feature Direct to Video
CREDITS      Point Break - A Kid In King Arthur's Court - The Last
             Time I Committed Suicide

Peter Abrams . . . . . . . . . . . . . . . . . . . . Producer/Partner
Robert L. Levy . . . . . . . . . . . . . . . . . . . Producer/Partner
Louise Rosner . . . . . . . . . . . . . . . . . . . . . . . Producer
Natan Zahavi . . . . . . . . . . . . . . . . . . . . . . . . Producer
Jennifer Gibgot . . . . . . . . . . . . . . . . . Executive Vice President
Sherwood Jones . . . . . . . . . . . . . . . . Post Production Supervisor
Andrew Panay . . . . . . . . . . . . . . . . . . . . . Dir., Development
Alicia Hopkins . . . . . . . . . . . . . . . . . . . . . Business Affairs
Sophie Garrett . . . . . . . . . . . . . . . . . . Development Assistant
Helen Turnbull . . . . . . . . . . . . . . . . . . . Executive Assistant

# COMPANIES AND STAFF

**TARDY-GREEN PRODUCTIONS, LTD.**
PHONE . . . . . . . . . . . . . . . . . . . . . . . . . . . . . 213-850-2633
FAX . . . . . . . . . . . . . . . . . . . . . . . . . . . . . . . 213-850-2637
Warner-Hollywood Studios
1041 N. Formosa Ave., Formosa Bldg.
West Hollywood, CA 90046-6798
TYPE            Motion Pictures
Emese Tardy-Green . . . . . . . . . . . . . . . . . . . . . . . . . Producer
Jeanne Johnson . . . . . . . . . . . . . . . . . . . Dir., Development

**TARNOFF/LAZAR & CO.**
PHONE . . . . . . . . . . . . . . . . . . . . . . . . . 213-650-6887
FAX . . . . . . . . . . . . . . . . . . . . . . . . . . . 213-654-2388
EMAIL . . . . . . . . . . . . . . . . . . . . . . . jbtarnoff@aol.com
WEBSITE . . . . . . . . . . . . . . . . . . . http://www.newspeak.com
8640 Wonderland Ave.
Los Angeles, CA 90046
TYPE            Motion Pictures + Interactive Multimedia
CREDITS         Out of Bounds - Blood Oath - The Nature of the Beast -
                Trafficking
John Tarnoff . . . . . . . . . . . . . . . . . . . . . . . . . . . Producer
Ava Lazar . . . . . . . . . . . . . . . . . . . . . . . . . . . . Producer

**TASKA PRODUCTIONS**
PHONE . . . . . . . . . . . . . . . . . 212-980-7590/310-276-4330
532 LaGuardia Place, Ste. 243
New York, NY 10012
TYPE            Motion Pictures
CREDITS         Back in the USSR - Candles in the Dark
Ilmar Taska . . . . . . . . . . . . . . . . . . . . . President/Producer
Eva Banhidi . . . . . . . . . . . . . . . . . . . . . . . . . . . Producer

**TAURUS ENTERTAINMENT CO.**
PHONE . . . . . . . . . . . . . . . . . . . . . . . . . 213-993-7355
FAX . . . . . . . . . . . . . . . . . . . . . . . . . . . 213-993-7316
WEBSITE . . . . . . . . . . . . . . . http://www.taurus-entertainment.com
Sunset Gower Studios
1420 N. Beachwood Dr., Bldg. 50, Box 2
Hollywood, CA 90028
TYPE            Motion Pictures + Television + Syndication
CREDITS         Mastermind - Morella - Creepshow (TV Series) - Hot
                Springs Hotel
Stanley E. Dudelson . . . . . . . . . . . . . . . . . . . . . Chairman
James G. Dudelson . . . . . . . . . . . . . . . . . . . President/CEO
Robert F. Dudelson . . . . . . . . . . . . . . . . . . . President/COO
Ana Clavell . . . . . . . . . . . Exec. in Charge of Production & Post Production
Alex Fayvil . . . . . . . . . . . Dir., Development & Acquisitions
Lanny Horn . . . . . . . . . . . . . . . . . . . . . . . . Administration

**TAVEL ENTERTAINMENT**
PHONE . . . . . . . . . . . . . . . . . . . . . . . . . 310-278-6700
FAX . . . . . . . . . . . . . . . . . . . . . . . . . . . 310-278-6770
9171 Wilshire Blvd., Ste. 406
Beverly Hills, CA 90210
TYPE            Motion Pictures + Television
CREDITS         Ride The Wind - Family Album
Connie Tavel . . . . . . . . . . . . . . . . . . . . Owner/Producer
Roger Horn . . . . . . . . . . . . . . . . . . . . . . . . . . . No Title
Tim Johnson . . . . . . . . . . . . . . . . . . . . . . . . . . No Title
Vanessa Livingston . . . . . . . . . . . . . . . . . . . . . . No Title
Gina Matthews . . . . . . . . . . . . . . . . . . . . . . . . . No Title
Vera Mihailovich . . . . . . . . . . . . . . . . . . . . . . . No Title
Chris Ridenhour . . . . . . . . . . . . . . . . . . . . . . . No Title
Ann Marie Kanakis . . . . . . . . . . . Asst. to Mr. Johnson/Ms. Livingston
Robert Kyncl . . . . . . . . . . . . . Asst. to Mr. Horn/Ms. Mihailovich
Felicia Molinari . . . . . . . . . . . . . . . . . . Asst. to Ms. Tavel
Diane Paylor . . . . . . . . . . . . . . . . . . Asst. to Ms. Matthews

**TAYLOR PRODS., GRAZKA**
PHONE . . . . . . . . . . . . . . . . . . . . . . . . . 310-201-0806
FAX . . . . . . . . . . . . . . . . . . . . . . . . . . . 310-201-0711
EMAIL . . . . . . . . . . . . . . . . . . . . . grazka@earthlink.net
9899 Santa Monica Blvd., #206
Beverly Hills, CA 90212
TYPE            Motion Pictures + Television + Documentaries
CREDITS         The Operation - Voice In Exile - Rage - Tricks - The
                Mahalia Jackson Story - Prophecies
COMMENTS        Also: Cable.
Grazka Taylor . . . . . . . . . . . . . . . . . . . . . . . . . . Producer

***TBS SUPERSTATION**
PHONE . . . . . . . . . . . . . . . . . . . . . . . . . 404-885-4396
FAX . . . . . . . . . . . . . . . . . . . . . . . . . . . 404-885-4326
WEBSITE . . . . . . . . . . . . . . . http://www.tbssuperstation.com
1050 Techwood Drive, NW
Atlanta, GA 30318
TYPE            Television
Bill Burke . . . . . . . . . . . . . . . . . . . . . . . . . . President
Bill Cox . . . . . . . . . . . . . . . . . . . . Sr. VP, Programming
Jim Head . . . . . . . . . . . . . . . . . VP, Original Programming
Sophia Karteris . . . . . . . . . . . . . . . Sr. Program Executive
Barbara Lancaster . . . . . . . . . . . . . . . . . Asst. to Jim Head

**TEAM ENTERTAINMENT GROUP**
PHONE . . . . . . . . . . . . . . . . . . . . . . . . . 310-442-3500
FAX . . . . . . . . . . . . . . . . . . . . . . . . . . . 310-442-3501
12300 Wilshire Blvd., Ste. 400
Los Angeles, CA 90025
TYPE            Television + Motion Pictures + Feature Direct to Video +
                Documentaries
CREDITS         Total Recall(TV) - Sneak Previews - Amazing Tails
Drew S. Levin . . . . . . . . . . . . . . . . . . . . President/CEO
Paul Yamamoto . . . . . . . . . . . . . . . . . . Exec. Vice President
Eric S. Elias . . . . . . . . . . . . . . . Sr. VP, Business Affairs
Michael Latiner . . . . . . . . . . . . . . . . . . . . VP, Finance
Declan O'Brien . . . . . . . . . . . . . . . . . . VP, Development
Rob Morhaim . . . . . . . . . . . Dir., Development & Production

***TEAM TODD**
PHONE . . . . . . . . . . . . . . . . . . . . . . . . . 310-248-6001
FAX . . . . . . . . . . . . . . . . . . . . . . . . . . . 310-385-8072
9021 Melrose Ave., Ste. 301
Los Angeles, CA 90069
TYPE            Motion Pictures + Television
DEAL            New Line Cinema
CREDITS         Austin Powers - Now and Then
Jennifer Todd . . . . . . . . . . . . . . . . . . . . . . . . . Producer
Suzanne Todd . . . . . . . . . . . . . . . . . . . . . . . . . Producer
J.J. Klein . . . . . . . . . . . . . . . . . . . . . . . Vice President

**TELESCENE FILM GROUP., INC.**
PHONE . . . . . . . . . . . . . . . . . . . . . . . . . 310-821-5353
FAX . . . . . . . . . . . . . . . . . . . . . . . . . . . 310-577-6727
EMAIL . . . . . . . . . . . . . . . . . . . . . info@telescene.ca
WEBSITE . . . . . . . . . . . . . . . . . . http://www.telescene.ca
13323 Washington Blvd., Ste. 205
Los Angeles, CA 90066
TYPE            Motion Pictures + Television
CREDITS         The Hunger - Hiroshima - Student Bodies - AAN - Going
                to Kansas City
COMMENTS        Montreal: 514-737-5512 New York: 212-698-2025/Fax:
                212-698-2029
Robin Spry . . . . . . . . . . . . . . . . . . . President (Montreal)
Bruce Moccia . . . . . . . . . . . . . . . . Exec. Vice President (LA)
Paul Painter . . . . . . . . . . . Exec. Vice President/COO (Montreal)
Michael Yudin . . . . . . . . . . . . . Exec. Vice President (NY)
Chris Dalton . . . . . . . . . . . . . . . Head, Production (Montreal)
Anita Simand . . . . . . . . . . . . . Head, Creative Affairs (Montreal)
Diane Arcand . . . . . . . . . . . Assoc. Head, Production (Montreal)
Melanie Banders . . . . . . . . . . . . Development Coordinator (LA)

**TELEVEST**
PHONE . . . . . . . . . . . . . . . . . . . . . . . . . 212-468-3683
FAX . . . . . . . . . . . . . . . . . . . . . . . . . . . 212-468-4050
EMAIL . . . . . . . . . . . . . . . . . . . . . letor@televest.com
1675 Broadway, 14th Floor
New York, NY 10019
TYPE            Television
CREDITS         The Inheritance - Friends At Last - Is There Life Out There
                - The Staircase
Jeffrey S. Grant . . . . . . . . . . . Exec. VP/Dir., Broadcast Programming
Roseanne Leto . . . . . . . . . . . . . . . . . . . . VP, Programming
Nancy Florent . . . . . . . . . . . . . Programming Development Coordinator

# COMPANIES AND STAFF

**TELLING PICTURES INC.**
PHONE . . . . . . . . . . . . . . . . . . . . . . . . . . . . . . . 415-864-6714
FAX . . . . . . . . . . . . . . . . . . . . . . . . . . . . . . . . . 415-864-4364
EMAIL . . . . . . . . . . . . . . . . . . . . . . . . . tellingpix@aol.com
WEBSITE . . . . . . . . . . . . . . . . . . . . http://www.tellingpix.com
121 9th St.
San Francisco, CA 94103
TYPE          Motion Pictures + Television + Documentaries
CREDITS       Times of Harvey Milk - Common Thread: Stories From the
              Quilt - Where Are We - The Celluloid Closet
COMMENTS      Academy Award-winning documentaries.
Rob Epstein . . . . . . . . . . . . . . . . . . . . . . . Producer/Director
Jeffrey Friedman . . . . . . . . . . . . . . . . . . . Producer/Director

***TELVAN PRODUCTIONS**
PHONE . . . . . . . . . . . . . . . . . . . . . . . . . . . . . . . 818-777-3737
FAX . . . . . . . . . . . . . . . . . . . . . . . . . . . . . . . . . 818-866-5204
100 Universal City Plaza, 415-B
Universal City, CA 91608
TYPE          Motion Pictures + Television
DEAL          Universal Studios
CREDITS       Jingle All the Way - The Flintstones - Beethoven
Brian Levant . . . . . . . . . . . . . . . . . . Writer/Producer/Director
Allison Millican . . . . . . . . . . . . . . . . . . . . . . . . . Development
Eric Osmond . . . . . . . . . . . . . . . . . . . . . . . . . . . . . No Title

**TEMPLETON PRODUCTIONS**
PHONE . . . . . . . . . . . . . . . . . . . . . . . . . . . . . . . 310-248-6016
FAX . . . . . . . . . . . . . . . . . . . . . . . . . . . . . . . . . 310-858-1109
New Line Cinema
9021 Melrose, Ste. 300
Los Angeles, CA 90069
TYPE          Motion Pictures
DEAL          New Line Cinema
Anne Templeton . . . . . . . . . . . . . . . . . . . . . . . . . . Producer
Glenn Cockburn . . . . . . . . . . . . . . . . . . . . Creative Executive

**TEN THIRTEEN PRODUCTIONS**
PHONE . . . . . . . . . . . . . . . . . . . . . . . . . . . . . . . 310-369-1130
P.O. Box 900
Beverly Hills, CA 90213
TYPE          Television
DEAL          Twentieth Century Fox Television
CREDITS       X Files   Millennium
Chris Carter . . . . . . . . . . . . . . . . . . . . . . Executive Producer
Ken Horton . . . . . . . . . . . . . . . . . . . . . . . . . . . . . President

**TENTH PLANET PRODS.**
PHONE . . . . . . . . . . . . . . . . . . . . . . . . . . . . . . . 310-659-8001
FAX . . . . . . . . . . . . . . . . . . . . . . . . . . . . . . . . . 310-659-8029
WEBSITE . . . . . . . . . . http://www.tenthplanetproductions.com
833 N. La Cienega Blvd., Ste. 200
Los Angeles, CA 90069
TYPE          Motion Pictures + Television
CREDITS       Jenny McCarthy Show - MTV Movie Awards - VH1
              Fashion Awards
COMMENTS      Also: Music Videos & Commercials.
Joel Gallen . . . . . . . . . . . . . . . . . . . . . . . . . . . . President
Jay Karas . . . . . . . . . . . . . . . . . . . . Coordinating Producer

**TEOCALLI ENTERTAINMENT, INC.**
PHONE . . . . . . . . . . . . . . . . . . . . . . . . . . . . . . . 970-349-0500
FAX . . . . . . . . . . . . . . . . . . . . . . . . . . . . . . . . . 970-349-2813
P.O. Box 2767- 350 Country Club Dr. #108
Crested Butte, CO 81224-2767
TYPE          Motion Pictures + Television + Documentaries
CREDITS       The Legend of Billy the Kid - Billy Galvin - The Radicals
Bill Murto . . . . . . . . . . . . . . . . . . . . Chief Executive Officer
Robert A. Nowotny . . . . . . . . . . . . . . . . . . . . . . . President
Ed Callaway . . . . . . . . . . . . . . . . . . . . Development Executive

**TEPS PRODUCTIONS**
PHONE . . . . . . . . . . . . . . . . . . . . . . . . . . . . . . . 310-442-4781
FAX . . . . . . . . . . . . . . . . . . . . . . . . . . . . . . . . . 310-442-9507
11990 San Vicente Blvd., Ste. 200
Los Angeles, CA 90049
TYPE          Motion Pictures
CREDITS       Gilbert Grape - Mistress - When Sat. Night Comes - Dusk
              Til Dawn
Meir Teper . . . . . . . . . . . . . . . . . . . . . . . . . . . . . Producer

***TERRA BELLA ENTERTAINMENT**
PHONE . . . . . . . . . . . . . . . . . . . . . . . . . . . . . . . 213-655-2311
FAX . . . . . . . . . . . . . . . . . . . . . . . . . . . . . . . . . 213-655-0499
EMAIL . . . . . . . . . . . . . . . . . . . . . . . . artscircle@aol.com
Adam Leipzig
8170 Beverly Blvd., Ste. 108
Los Angeles, CA 90048
TYPE          Motion Pictures + Television
DEAL          PolyGram Filmed Ent./Interscope Communications Inc.
Adam Leipzig . . . . . . . . . . . . . . . . . . . . . . . . . . . . Producer

**TETRAFILMS INC.**
PHONE . . . . . . . . . . . . . . . . . . . . . . . . . . . . . . . 310-280-8000
10202 W. Washington Blvd.
Culver City, CA 90232
TYPE          Motion Pictures + Television
CREDITS       The Long Road - Bomber X - Daffodil
Bertrand Freeman . . . . . . . . . . . . . . . . . . . . . . . . Producer
Cassandra Freeman-Dayl . . . . . . . . . . . . Dir., Development

**THEATREX COMPANY, THE**
PHONE . . . . . . . . . . . . . . . . . . . . . . . . . . . . . . . 310-888-8023
9028 Sunset Blvd. PH 1
Los Angeles, CA 90069
TYPE          Motion Pictures + Television
CREDITS       Loss of Faith - Snide & Prejudice
Kai Hand . . . . . . . . . . . . . . . . . . . . . . . Manager/Producer
Tanya Monge . . . . . . . . . . . . . . . . . Assistant to Mr. Kai Hand

**THOMPSON ORGANIZATION, LARRY**
PHONE . . . . . . . . . . . . . . . . . . . . . . . . . . . . . . . 310-288-0700
FAX . . . . . . . . . . . . . . . . . . . . . . . . . . . . . . . . . 310-288-0711
335 N. Maple Dr., Ste. 361
Beverly Hills, CA 90210
TYPE          Motion Pictures + Television
CREDITS       Lucy & Desi:  Before the Laughter - Woman He Loved -
              Crimes of Passion
Larry Thompson . . . . . . . . . . . . . . . . . . . . . Chairman/CEO
Kelly LeBlanc . . . . . . . . . . . . . . Development, Motion Picts. & TV

**THOMPSON STREET PICTURES**
PHONE . . . . . . . . . . . . . . . . . . . . . . . . . . . . . . . 213-651-5813
FAX . . . . . . . . . . . . . . . . . . . . . . . . . . . . . . . . . 213-651-2613
Fox/Fox 2000
754 North Kilkea Dr., Ste. 101
Los Angeles, CA 90046
TYPE          Motion Pictures
CREDITS       Cool Runnings - Mr. Destiny - Angus Bethune - Young
              Harry Houdini
Susan B. Landau . . . . . . . . . . . . . . . . . . . . . . . . . Producer
Jeff Steele . . . . . . . . . . . . . . . . . . . . . . Asst. to Ms. Landau

**THOR PICTURES**
PHONE . . . . . . . . . . . . . . . . . . . . . . . . . . . . . . . 212-405-3080
FAX . . . . . . . . . . . . . . . . . . . . . . . . . . . . . . . . . 212-405-3223
300 E. 64th, Ste. 18B
New York, NY 10021
TYPE          Motion Pictures
CREDITS       Pentathlon
Dolph Lundgren . . . . . . . . . . . . . . . . . . . . . Actor/Producer
Katie Ladyko . . . . . . . . . . . . . . . . . . Asst. to Dolph Lundgren

**THREE GUYS FROM VERONA INC.**
PHONE . . . . . . . . . . . . . . . . . . . . . . . . . . . . . . . 818-509-2288
FAX . . . . . . . . . . . . . . . . . . . . . . . . . . . . . . . . . 818-509-2289
EMAIL . . . . . . . . . . . . . . . . . . . . . threeguys@earthlink.net
12423 Ventura Ct.
Studio City, CA 91604
TYPE          Motion Pictures + Television
CREDITS       The West Side Waltz - 1,000 Men And A Baby - Paul
              Anka Show
Stephen L. Bedell . . . . . . . . . . . . . . . . . . . . . . . . Producer
Clancy Grass . . . . . . . . . . . . . . . . . . . . . . . . . . . Producer
Burton Taylor . . . . . . . . . . . . . . . . . . . . . . . . . . . Producer
Kaz Akers . . . . . . . . . . . . . . . . . . . . . . . . . . . . . Associate

# COMPANIES AND STAFF

**THRESHOLD ENTERTAINMENT**
PHONE . . . . . . . . . . . . . . . . . . . . . . . . . . . . . . . 310-452-8899
FAX . . . . . . . . . . . . . . . . . . . . . . . . . . . . . . . . . 310-452-0736
WEBSITE. . . . . . . . . . . . . . . . . . . http://www.mortalkombat.com
1649 11th St.
Santa Monica, CA 90404
TYPE          Motion Pictures + Television + Animation + Interactive
              Multimedia
CREDITS       Mortal Kombat - Mortal Kombat Annihilation - Beowulf
COMMENTS      Also: Online Development.
Larry Kasanoff . . . . . . . . . . . . . . . . . . . . . . . . . . . . . . Producer
Alison Savitch . . . . . . . . . . . . . . . . . . . . . . . . . . . . . . Producer
Kim Lavery . . . . . . . . . . . . . . . . . . . . . . . Technology/Production
Susan Levin . . . . . . . . . . . . . . . . . . . . . . Development/Production
Joshua Wexler . . . . . . . . . . . . . . . . . . . . . Technology/Production
Elizabeth Pritscher . . . . . . . . . . . . . . . . . . Asst. to Mr. Kasanoff

**THUNDERBIRD PICTURES**
PHONE . . . . . . . . . . . . . . . . . . . . . . . . . . . . . . . 310-398-8486
FAX . . . . . . . . . . . . . . . . . . . . . . . . . . . . . . . . . 310-397-9545
3535 Inglewood Ave.
Los Angeles, CA 90066
TYPE          Motion Pictures + Television + Documentaries
CREDITS       Back In Business - Klash - Champions - Body and Soul
Peter McAlevey . . . . . . . . . . . . . . . . . . . . . President/Producer
Jason Rita . . . . . . . . . . . . . . . . . . . VP, Development & Production

**TIDEWATER ENTERTAINMENT, INC.**
PHONE . . . . . . . . . . . . . . . . . . . . . . . . . . . . . . . 310-201-9560
FAX . . . . . . . . . . . . . . . . . . . . . . . . . . . . . . . . . 310-201-9558
HBO
2049 Century Park East, Ste. 4313
Los Angeles, CA 90067
TYPE          Motion Pictures
CREDITS       The Fan - Crimson Tide - True Romance
Bill Unger . . . . . . . . . . . . . . . . . . . . . . . . . . . . . . . President
Shelagh O'Brien . . . . . . . . . . . . . . . . . . . . Executive Assistant

**TIG PRODUCTIONS, INC.**
PHONE . . . . . . . . . . . . . . . . . . . . . . . . . . . . . . . 818-954-4500
FAX . . . . . . . . . . . . . . . . . . . . . . . . . . . . . . . . . 818-954-4882
4000 Warner Blvd.
Burbank, CA 91522
TYPE          Motion Pictures
DEAL          Warner Bros. Pictures
Gregory Avellone . . . . . . . . . . . . . . . . . . . Development Executive

**TIGER PRODS.**
PHONE . . . . . . . . . . . . . . . . . . . . . . . . . . . . . . . 310-450-3197
FAX . . . . . . . . . . . . . . . . . . . . . . . . . . . . . . . . . 310-450-9979
EMAIL . . . . . . . . . . . . . . . . . . . . . . . . . . Tyger324@aol.com
324 Sunset Ave.
Venice, CA 90291
TYPE          Motion Pictures + Television
CREDITS       Journey of the Heart - The Yarn Princess - Ultimate
              Betrayal
Jim Noll . . . . . . . . . . . . . . . . . . . . . . . . . . . . . . . . . Producer
Gary Parker . . . . . . . . . . . . . . . . . . . . . . . Head, Development
Don White . . . . . . . . . . . . . . . . . . . . . . . . . . . . . . No Title

**TIME LIFE KIDS**
PHONE . . . . . . . . . . . . . . . . . . . . . . . . . . . . . . . 703-838-7000
FAX . . . . . . . . . . . . . . . . . . . . . . . . . . . . . . . . . 703-838-7192
2000 Duke Street
Alexandria, VA 22314
TYPE          Animation + Television
Mary Davis Holt . . . . . . . . . . . . . . . . . . . . . . . . . . President
Bridget Boel . . . . . . . . . . . . . . . . . . . . . . . . . Vice President
Madeline Boyer . . . . . . . . . . . . . . . . . . . VP, Brand Development

**TIME-LIFE VIDEO & TELEVISION**
PHONE . . . . . . . . . . . . . . . . . . . . . . . . . . . . . . . 703-838-7000
FAX . . . . . . . . . . . . . . . . . . . . . . . . . . . . . . . . . 703-838-7192
2000 Duke Street
Alexandria, VA 22314
TYPE          Television + Documentaries
Steve Janas . . . . . . . . . . . . . . . . . . . . . . . . . . . . . President
Lisa Kauffman . . . . . . . . . . . . . . VP, Acquisitions & Programming
Mark Stevens . . . . . . . . . . . . . . . . . . . . VP, Business Affairs

**TISCH CO., THE STEVE**
PHONE . . . . . . . . . . . . . . . . . . . . . . . . . . . . . . . 310-838-2500
FAX . . . . . . . . . . . . . . . . . . . . . . . . . . . . . . . . . 310-204-2713
3815 Hughes Ave.
Culver City, CA 90232-2715
TYPE          Motion Pictures + Television
CREDITS       Forrest Gump - The Postman - American History X -
              Corrina Corrina
Steve Tisch . . . . . . . . . . . . . . . . . . . . . . . . . . . . . Chairman
Danna Blesser . . . . . . . . . . . . . . . . . . . . . . . VP, Production
Kim Skeeters . . . . . . . . . . . . . . . . Controller/Business Affairs
Judd Payne . . . . . . . . . . . . . . . . . . . . . . . Dir., Development
David Blackman . . . . . . . . . . . . . . . . . . . Asst. to Steve Tisch
Rachel Evans . . . . . . . . . . . . . . . . . . . Asst. To Danna Blesser
Erin Ferdinand . . . . . . . . . . . . . . . . . . . . Asst. to Judd Payne
Cyrus Shepard . . . . . . . . . . . . . . . . . . . . Production Assistant

**TLC ENTERTAINMENT**
PHONE . . . . . . . . . . . . . . . . . . . . . . . . . . . . . . . 818-655-6155
FAX . . . . . . . . . . . . . . . . . . . . . . . . . . . . . . . . . 818-655-6254
EMAIL . . . . . . . . . . . . . . . . . . . . . . . . . . . . tlce@aol.com
CBS Studio Center
4024 Radford Ave.
Studio City, CA 91604-2101
TYPE          Television + Feature Direct to Video + Animation
CREDITS       The ALL NEW Captain Kangaroo - Secrets Adventures -
              McGee and Me!
George Taweel . . . . . . . . . . . . . . . . . . . . . Producer/Director
Rob Loos . . . . . . . . . . . . . . . . . . . . . . . . . Producer/Writer
Jonathan Chambers . . . . . . . . . . . . . . . . Production Executive
Brenda Salmon . . . . . . . . . . Exec. Asst. to Mr. Taweel & Mr. Loos

**TLN PRODUCTIONS**
PHONE . . . . . . . . . . . . . . . . . . 310-281-8000/615-320-7954
FAX . . . . . . . . . . . . . . . . . . . . . . . . . . . . 615-321-0345
EMAIL . . . . . . . . . . . . . . . . . . . . movieneff@earthlink.net
Martin, Inc.
144 McCarty Dr., Ste. 304
Beverly Hills, CA 90212
TYPE          Motion Pictures + Television + Documentaries
CREDITS       Running Mates - America's Music: The Roots of Country -
              Beatrice Wood: Mama of Dada - Piece of the Fed
COMMENTS      Also: 812 19th Ave. S., Nashville, TN 37203
Tom Neff . . . . . . . . . . . . . . . . . . . . . . . . . . . . . . President

**TOLLIN/ROBBINS PRODUCTIONS**
PHONE . . . . . . . . . . . . . . . . . . . . . . . . . . . . . . . 818-766-5004
FAX . . . . . . . . . . . . . . . . . . . . . . . . . . . . . . . . . 818-766-8488
EMAIL . . . . . . . . . . . . . . . . . . . . . . masonfett@earthlink.net
4133 Lankershim Blvd.
N. Hollywood, CA 91602
TYPE          Motion Pictures + Television + Documentaries
CREDITS       Goodburger - All That - Arli$$ - Cousin Skeeter - Kenan &
              Kel
Mike Tollin . . . . . . . . . . . . . . . . . . . . . . . Executive Producer
Brian Robbins . . . . . . . . . . . . . . . . . . . . . Executive Producer
Jonny Fink . . . . . . . . . . . . . . . . . . . . . . . . . . . . . . . Producer
Tracy Sullivan . . . . . . . . . . . . . . . . . . . . . . . . . . . . Producer
Steve McFeely . . . . . . . . . . . . . . . . . . . . . Dir., Development
Mason Gordon . . . . . . . . . . . . . . . . . . . . . . Office Manager
Jeremie Day . . . . . . . . . . . . . . . . . . . . . . Executive Assistant
Sharla Sumpter . . . . . . . . . . . . . . . . . . . . Executive Assistant

**TOO NUTS PRODUCTIONS, LTD.**
PHONE . . . . . . . . . . . . . . . . . . . . . . . . . . . . . . . 310-967-4532
EMAIL . . . . . . . . . . . . . . . . . . . . . . . . . TOADPIZZA@aol.com
WEBSITE . . . . . . . . . . . . . . . . . . . . . http://www.toadpizza.com
1511 Sawtelle Blvd., Ste. 288
Los Angeles, CA 90025
TYPE          Television + Animation + Interactive Multimedia
CREDITS       Toad Pizza - The Salivating Salamander - The Suburban
              Cowboys - Anonymouse
COMMENTS      Creatively entertaining while covertly educating.(TM) Also:
              Theatre & Children's Audiobook Production.
R. Scott Penza . . . . . . Exec. Producer/President/Sr. VP, Creative
Hadley Harper . . . . . . . . . . . . . . . . VP, Creative - Illustration
Daniel Simpson . . . . . . . . . . . . . . . . . . . . VP/Music Director
Ruth Chambers . . . . . . . . . . . . Dir., Photography/Sr. Creative
John Biehl . . . . . . . . . . . . . . . . . . . . Post Production Supervisor
Richard Irving . . . . . . . . . . . . . . . . . . . . . . . Casting Director
Robinette L. Lloyd . . . . . . . . . . . . . . . . . . . . . Casting Director

**TOPA FILMS**
PHONE . . . . . . . . . . . . . . . . . . . . . . . . 805-667-3900 x6833
FAX . . . . . . . . . . . . . . . . . . . . . . . . . . . . . 805-653-7151
EMAIL . . . . . . . . . . . . . . . . . . . . . . . . topa1001@aol.com
Santa Ventura Studios
5301 No. Ventura Ave.
Ventura, CA 93001
TYPE          Motion Pictures
Tom Craig . . . . . . . . . . . . . . . . . . . . . . . . . . . . . . Producer
Anka Brazzell . . . . . . . . . . . . . . . . . . . . Asst. to Tom Craig

**TOTEM PRODS.**
PHONE . . . . . . . . . . . . . . . . . . . . . . . . . . 213-650-4994
FAX . . . . . . . . . . . . . . . . . . . . . . . . . . . . . 213-650-1961
EMAIL . . . . . . . . . . . . . . . . . . . . . . . . totempro@aol.com
8009 Santa Monica Blvd.
Los Angeles, CA 90046
TYPE          Motion Pictures
CREDITS       True Romance - Days of Thunder - Crimson Tide - Top
              Gun - Enemy of the State
Tony Scott . . . . . . . . . . . . . . . . . . . . . . . . . Co-Chairman
Jerry Heiss . . . . . . . . . . . . . . . . . . . Exec. Asst. to Mr. Scott
Peter Toumasis . . . . . . . . . . . . . . . . . . . Asst. to Mr. Scott

**TOWNSEND ENT. CORP., THE**
PHONE . . . . . . . . . . . . . . . . . . . . . . . . 213-850-2421
Warner Hollywood Studios
1041 N. Formosa
W. Hollywood, CA 90046
TYPE          Motion Pictures + Television
CREDITS       Hollywood Shuffle - 5 Heartbeats - Meteor Man - The
              Parenthood
Robert Townsend . . . . . . . . . . . . Actor/Producer/Director/Writer
Loretha Jones . . . . . . . . . . . . . . . . . . . . . . . . . . Producer

**TRANCAS INTL. FILMS**
PHONE . . . . . . . . . . . . . . . . . . . . . . . . 310-553-5599
FAX . . . . . . . . . . . . . . . . . . . . . . . . . . . 310-553-0536
1875 Century Park East, Ste. 1145
Los Angeles, CA 90067
TYPE          Motion Pictures
CREDITS       Halloween Movies - Lion of the Desert - The Message
Moustapha Akkad . . . . . . . . . . . . . . President/Producer/Director
Malek Akkad . . . . . . . . . . . . . . . . Creative Develop. Director

***TRAVELER'S REST FILMS**
PHONE . . . . . . . . . . . . . . . . . . . . . . . . 818-777-3025
FAX . . . . . . . . . . . . . . . . . . . . . . . . . . . 818-866-2618
Universal
100 Universal City Plaza
Universal City, CA 91608
TYPE          Motion Pictures + Television
DEAL          Studios USA Television
Tom Thayer . . . . . . . . . . . . . . . . . . . . . . . . . President
Linda Messier . . . . . . . . . . . . . . . . . . . Executive Assistant

**TRAVIS GROUP, THE**
PHONE . . . . . . . . . . . . . . . . . . . . . . . . 818-508-4600
FAX . . . . . . . . . . . . . . . . . . . . . . . . . . . 818-508-4700
EMAIL . . . . . . . . . . . . . . . . . . mwtravis@earthlink.net
11326 Ventura Blvd., Ste. C
Studio City, CA 91604-3137
TYPE          Motion Pictures + Television
CREDITS       Going Under - A Bronx Tale - Time Flies When You're
              Alive - Blind Tom
Mark W. Travis . . . . . . . . . . . . . . . . . . . Director/Producer
Fred Johntz . . . . . . . . . . . . . . . . . . . . . Director/Producer
Warren de Mena . . . . . . . . . . . . . . . . . . . . . Development

**TRI-CROWN PRODS.**
PHONE . . . . . . . . . . . . . . . . . . . . . . . . 818-955-7337
FAX . . . . . . . . . . . . . . . . . . . . . . . . . . . 818-955-7338
3900 W. Alameda Ave., Ste. 700
Burbank, CA 91505
TYPE          Television + Interactive Multimedia + Documentaries
DEAL          PolyGram Television
CREDITS       Horseworld - When Stunts Go Bad 1 & 2 - Daredevils
              LIVE - Unmasked
Carol Sherman . . . . . . . . . . . . . . . . . Chief Executive Officer
Jeff Androsky . . . . . . . . . . . . Pres., Production/Program Development
Marty Iker . . . . . . . . . . . . Pre./Creative Dir., Tri-Crown Creative Group
Gary Kurtz . . . . . . . . . . . . . . . . . . VP, Program Development
Dan Weyand . . . . . . . . . . . . . . . . . . . . . . . VP, Production
Mike Androsky . . . . . . . . . . . . . . . . . . . . . Dir., Production
Christine Blake . . . . . . . . . . Dir., Program Development/Production
Armando Villalpando . . . . . . . . . Dir., Hispanic Div. Program Development
Joe Lewis . . . . . . . . . . . . . . . . . . . Supervisor, Post Production

**TRIBE**
PHONE . . . . . . . . . . . . . . . . . . . . . . . . 973-635-2660
FAX . . . . . . . . . . . . . . . . . . . . . . . . . . . 973-635-2654
EMAIL . . . . . . . . . . . . . . . . . . . . . . . . VCOakley@aol.com
244 Main Street
Chatham, NJ 07928
TYPE          Motion Pictures + Television + Documentaries
CREDITS       A Modern Affair - You Never Know - No Balls
Vern Oakley . . . . . . . . . . . . . . Director/Producer/President
Carol Trinker . . . . . . . . . . . . . . . . . . . . General Manager

**TRIBECA PRODUCTIONS**
PHONE . . . . . . . . . . . . . . . . . . . . . . . . 212-941-4040
FAX . . . . . . . . . . . . . . . . . . . . . . . . . . . 212-941-4044
375 Greenwich St., 8th Floor
New York, NY 10013
TYPE          Motion Pictures + Television + Interactive Multimedia
CREDITS       Faithful - Marvin's Room - Thunderheart - A Bronx Tale -
              Wag The Dog
Robert De Niro . . . . . . . . . . . . . . . . . . . . . . . Chairman
Jane Rosenthal . . . . . . . . . . . . . . . . . . . . . . . President
Brad Epstein . . . . . . . . . . . . . . . . . . . . Pres., Production
Amy Sayres . . . . . . . . . . . . . . . . . . . . . . VP, Production
Hardy Justice . . . . . . . . . . . . . . . . . . . Dir., Development
Nancy Lefkowitz . . . . . . . . . . . . . . . . Dir., Special Projects
Eric Schwarz . . . . . . . . . . . . . . . . . . . . . . Story Editor
Susannah Kaufman . . . . . . . . . Exec. Asst. to Jane Rosenthal
Kirsten Schatz . . . . . . . . . . . . Exec. Asst. to Brad Epstein

**TRICOAST ENTERTAINMENT**
PHONE . . . . . . . . . . . . . . . . . . . . . . . . 310-552-0888
FAX . . . . . . . . . . . . . . . . . . . . . . . . . . . 310-552-1888
EMAIL . . . . . . . . . . . . . . . . . . . . . . tricoast@worldsite.net
400 S. Beverly Dr., Penthouse
Beverly Hills, CA 90212
TYPE          Motion Pictures + Television + Documentaries
CREDITS       Temptation - Never Talk To Stangers - The Set Up -
              Escape From Atlantis
Marcy Levitas Hamilton . . . . . . . . . . . . . . . . . . . President
Strath Hamilton . . . . . . . . . . . . . . . . . . . . . . . . Director
Martin Wiley . . . . . . . . . . . . . . . . . . . . . Head, Production
Kevin Lee . . . . . . . . . . . . . . . . . Post Production Supervisor
Adam Ladygo . . . . . . . . . . . . . . . . . . . Executive Assistant

**TRICOR ENTERTAINMENT**
PHONE . . . . . . . . . . . . . . . . . . . . . . . . 818-763-0699
FAX . . . . . . . . . . . . . . . . . . . . . . . . . . . 626-441-0033
EMAIL . . . . . . . . . . . . . . . . . . Magiclantern@worldnet.att.net
1613 Chelsea Rd., Ste 329
San Marino, CA 91108-1821
TYPE          Motion Pictures + Television + Animation + Interactive
              Multimedia
Craig Darian . . . . . . . . . . . . . . . . . . . . . . . . . . Partner
Howard Kazanjian . . . . . . . . . . . . . . . . . . . . . . . Partner

# COMPANIES AND STAFF

**TRIDENT RELEASING INC.**
PHONE . . . . . . . . . . . . . . . . . . . . . . . . . . . . 213-655-8818
FAX . . . . . . . . . . . . . . . . . . . . . . . . . . . . . . 213-655-0515
EMAIL . . . . . . . . . . . . . . . . . . . info@tridentreleasing.com
WEBSITE . . . . . . . . . . . . . . . . . . http://www.tri-net.com/tri-net/
8401 Melrose Place, 2nd Fl.
Los Angeles, CA 90069
TYPE            Motion Pictures + Television + Syndication + Feature
                Direct to Video
CREDITS         Hit Me  - Hotel Shanghai - Heist - Love Kills - Left
                Luggage - The Unknown Cyclist

Jean Ovrum . . . . . . . . . . . . . . . . . . . . . . . . . . Co-President
Victoria Plummer . . . . . . . . . . . . . . . . . . . . . . . Co-President
Barbara Mannion . . . . . . . . . . . . . . . . . . . . VP, Acquisitions

**TRILOGY ENTERTAINMENT GROUP**
PHONE . . . . . . . . . . . . . . . 310-449-3095/310-449-3618
FAX . . . . . . . . . . . . . . . . . . . . . . . . . . . . . . 310-449-3195
2401 Colorado Ave., Ste. 100
Santa Monica, CA 90404-3061
TYPE            Motion Pictures + Television
DEAL            MGM/UA/Spelling Films
CREDITS         Moll Flanders - Robin Hood: Prince of Thieves - Backdraft
                - Magnificent Seven - Outer Limits - Poltergeist-The
                Legacy

Pen Densham . . . . . . . . . . . . . . . . Partner/Exec. Producer (310-449-8864)
Richard Barton Lewis . . . . . . . . . . . Partner/Exec. Producer (310-449-8826)
John Watson . . . . . . . . . . . . . . . . Partner/Exec. Producer (310-449-8885)
Guy McElwaine . . . . . . . . . . . . . . . . . . Pres., Motion Picts.
Mark Stern . . . . . . . . . . . . . . . . Pres., Production (310-449-8902)
Cheryl La Sasso . . . . . . . . . . . . . . Sr. VP, Production (310-586-8007)
Rhonda Moore . . . . . . . . . . . . . . . VP, TV Production (310-586-8237)
Lynne Symons . . . . . . . . . . . . . . . VP, TV Production (310-586-8067)
Bob Weber . . . . . . . . . . . . . . . . . . . VP, Corporate Affairs
Michael Birnbach . . . . . . . . . . . . . . . . . Dir., Development
Bryan Grant . . . . . . . . . . . . . . . . . . . . Dir., Development
Debra Greenfield . . . . . . . . . . . Independent Producer (310-449-8852)
Nora O'Brien . . . . . . . . . . . . . . . . . . In-House Coordinator
Jennifer Hare . . . . . . . . . . . . . . Producer's Associate to Pen Densham
Amy Hayes . . . . . . . . . . . . . . . Producer's Associate to John Watson
Alex Amin . . . . . . . . . . . . . . . . . . . . . . Script Coordinator

**TRIMARK PICTURES**
PHONE . . . . . . . . . . . . . . . . . . . . . . . . . . . . 310-314-2000
FAX . . . . . . . . . . . . . . . . . . . . . . . . . . . . . . 310-399-8246
EMAIL . . . . . . . . . . . . . . . . . . . trimark@trimarkpictures.com
WEBSITE . . . . . . . . . . . . . . . . . . http://www.trimarkpictures.com
2644 30th St.
Santa Monica, CA 90405-3009
TYPE            Motion Pictures
CREDITS         Kama Sutra - Eve's Bayou - Chinese Box - Slam
COMMENTS        A division of Trimark Holdings.

Mark Amin . . . . . . . . . . . . . . . . . . . . . . . . . Chairman/CEO
James Keegan . . . . . . . . . . . . . . . . . . . . . . . . Sr. VP/CFO
Cami Winikoff . . . . . . . . . . . Exec. VP/Chief Administrative Officer
Sergio Aguero . . . . . . . . . . . . . Exec. Vice President, International
Jonathon Komack Martin . . . . . . . . . . . . . . Exec. VP, Production
Tim Swain . . . . . . . . . . . . . . . . . . . . . . Exec. Vice President
Ray Price . . . . . . . . . . . . . . . . Sr. VP, Specialized Theatrical
Andrew Reimer . . . . . . . . . . . . . . Sr. VP, Worldwide Television
Shebnem Askin . . . . . . . . . . . . . . . . VP, Intl. Co-Productions
Peter Block . . . . . . . . . . . . . . . . . VP, Acquisitions Business Affairs
Bruce D. Eisen . . . . . . . . . . VP, Production Business Affairs/Music
Peter A. Marshall . . . . . . . . . . . . . . VP, Television Production
Darin Spillman . . . . . . . . . . . . . . . . . . . . VP, Production
Julie Schroeder . . . . . . . . . . . . . . . . . . . Dir., Development
Wayne Levin . . . . . . . . . . . . . . . . . . . Dir., Business Affairs
Julianne Kelley . . . . . . . . . . . . . . . . Dir., Music Department
Donna Solomon . . . . . . . . . . . . . . . . . . Mgr., Production
Joel High . . . . . . . . . . . . . . . . . . . . Music Dept. Coordinator

***TRINITY PICTURES, INC.**
PHONE . . . . . . . . . . . . . . . . . . . . . . . . . . . . 310-820-6733
FAX . . . . . . . . . . . . . . . . . . . . . . . . . . . . . . 310-207-6816
11600 San Vicente Blvd.
Los Angeles, CA 90049
TYPE            Documentaries + Feature Direct to Video + Motion
                Pictures
CREDITS         A Cry in the Wild - The Westing Game - The Dirt Bike Kid
                - Legend of the Lost Tomb - Da

Julie Corman . . . . . . . . . . . . . . . . . . . . . . . Chairman/CEO
Sean Cooney . . . . . . . . . . . . . . . . . . . . . Dir., Development
Catherine Corman . . . . . . . . . . . . . . . . Development Associate
Claude Hurwicz . . . . . . . . . . . . . . . . . Development Associate

**TRIUMPH PICTURES INC.**
PHONE . . . . . . . . . . . . . . . . . . . . . . . . . . . . 818-708-1384
FAX . . . . . . . . . . . . . . . . . . . . . . . . . . . . . . 818-996-1492
EMAIL . . . . . . . . . . . . . . . . . triumph@triumphpictures.com
8581 Santa Monica Blvd., #418
W. Hollywood, CA 90069
TYPE            Motion Pictures + Television
CREDITS         Jury Duty - 3 Ninjas Kick Back - Stone Cold - Lone Wolf
                McQuade - Steal the Sky
COMMENTS        Also: Commercials Development of new films and
                co-productions.

Yoram Ben-Ami . . . . . . . . . . . . . . . . . . . . . . . . President
Udi Nedivi . . . . . . . . . . . . . . . . . . . . . . . . . . . Producer
Ben Nedivi . . . . . . . . . . . . . . . . . . . . . . VP, Development
Prosper Pariente . . . . . . . . . . . . . . . . . . Overseas Projects
Dory Ben-Ami . . . . . . . . . . . . UK Office (01144-958486095)

**TRIVISION PICTURES INC.**
PHONE . . . . . . . . . . . . . . 213-655-5055/310-470-0095
FAX . . . . . . . . . . . . . . . . . . . . . . . . . . . . . . 310-470-0225
10590 Wilshire Blvd., Ste. 803
Los Angeles, CA 90024
TYPE            Motion Pictures + Television
DEAL            First Look Picts./Overseas Filmgroup
CREDITS         The Last Cowboy - Deadly Dance - Bloodsport II -
                Stranger In The House - Strip Search - Universal Cop - Set
                Up - Justice - Perfect Target
COMMENTS        Post Production Image Organization & Nu-Image.

Alexander Tabrizi . . . . . . . . . . . . . . . . . . . . . . . Chairman
Ros Hammer . . . . . . . . . . . . . . . . . . . . . . . . . . President
Peter Laipis . . . . . . . . . . . . . . . . . . Exec. Vice President
Anthony Esposito . . . . . . . . . . . . . . . . . . . . . . . Producer
George Saunders . . . . . . . . . . . . . . . . . . Producer/Director
Peter Yuval . . . . . . . . . . . . . . . . . . . . . . . . . . Producer
Joe Zito . . . . . . . . . . . . . . . . . . . . . . Producer/Director
Jon Broderick . . . . . . . . . . . . . . . . . . In-House Producer
Rebecca Morrison . . . . . . . . . . . . . . . . Creative Consultant
David Poland . . . . . . . . . . . . . . . . . . Creative Consultant
Teressa Tunney . . . . . . . . . . . . . . . . . Creative Consultant

**TROMA INC.**
PHONE . . . . . . . . . . . . . . 212-757-4555/213-960-4012
FAX . . . . . . . . . . . . . . . . 212-399-9885/213-960-4013
WEBSITE . . . . . . . . . . . . . . . . . . http://www.troma.com/home
Raleigh Studios
650 N. Bronson, Ste. 103
Los Angeles, CA 90004
TYPE            Motion Pictures
CREDITS         Sucker - Sgt. Kabukiman NYPD - Tromeo & Juliet -
                Bugged - Killer Condom - Canibal the Musical - Toxic
                Avenger
COMMENTS        NY office - 733 Ninth Ave., NY, NY 10019

Lloyd Kaufman . . . . . . . . . . . . . . . . . . . . . . . . President
Michael Herz . . . . . . . . . . . . . . . . . . . . . . Vice President
Patrick Cassidy . . . . . . . . . . . . . . . . Dir., Production/Acquisitions
Tony Rosen . . . . . . . . . . . . . . . . . . Dir., Video Aquistions
David Shultz . . . . . . . . . . . . . . . . . . . Dir., Operations (LA)
Jennifer Kennedy . . . . . . . . . . . . . . . . . . Head, Marketing
Josh Piezas . . . . . . . . . . . . . . . . . . . . . Business Affairs

**TRUE BLUE PRODS.**
PHONE . . . . . . . . . . . . . . . . . . . . . . . . . . . . 818-954-1626
FAX . . . . . . . . . . . . . . . . . . . . . . . . . . . . . . 818-954-1846
4000 Warner Blvd., Bldg. 5, Rm. 28
Burbank, CA 91522
TYPE            Motion Pictures + Television

Kirstie Alley . . . . . . . . . . . . . . . . . . . . . . Actor/Producer
Lee Ann Vasquez . . . . . . . . . . . . . . . . . Asst. to Ms. Alley
Will M. Smith . . . . . . . . . . . . . . . . . . . Executive Assistant

**TRUE FICTION PICTURES**
PHONE . . . . . . . . . . . . . . . . . . . . . . . . . . . . 212-684-4284
FAX . . . . . . . . . . . . . . . . . . . . . . . . . . . . . . 212-686-6109
12 W. 27th St., 12th Fl.
New York, NY 10001
TYPE            Motion Pictures
CREDITS         Amateur - The Unbelieveable Truth - Trust - Flirt - Simple
                Men - Henry Fool - The Book of Life

Hal Hartley . . . . . . . . . . . . . . . . . . . . . . . . . . Principal
Jerome Brownstein . . . . . . . . . . . . . . . . . . . . . Principal
Thierry Cagianut . . . . . . . . . . . . . . . . . . . . . . Producer
Matthew Myers . . . . . . . . . . . . . . . . . . . . . . . Producer
Chelsea Fuhrer . . . . . . . . . . . . . . . . . . Associate Producer

## TRUE PICTURES
PHONE . . . . . . . . . . . . . . . . . . . . . . . . . . 212-371-0514
FAX . . . . . . . . . . . . . . . . . . . . . . . . . . . . 212-262-4940
250 W. 57th St. Ste. 2207
New York, NY 10107

| | |
|---|---|
| TYPE | Motion Pictures |
| DEAL | Twentieth Century Fox-Fox 2000 (LA) |
| CREDITS | Me and Veronica |
| COMMENTS | Also: Theatre |

Leslie Urdang . . . . . . . . . . . . . . . . . . . . . . . . . Producer

## *TSE PRODUCTIONS, SIMON
PHONE . . . . . . . . . . . . . . . . . . . . . . . . . . 310-385-9331
FAX . . . . . . . . . . . . . . . . . . . . . . . . . . . . 310-385-9347
EMAIL . . . . . . . . . . . . . . . . . . . . . stpwest@earthlink.net
9060 Santa Monica Blvd., Ste. 106
Los Angeles, CA 90069

| | |
|---|---|
| TYPE | Feature Direct to Video + Motion Pictures + Television |
| CREDITS | Body Count - Distant Justice - Sweet Evil |

Simon Tse . . . . . . . . . . . . . . . . . . . . . . . Producer/CEO
Anthony Fu . . . . . . . . . . . . . . . . . . . . . Dir., Development

## TSPRODUCTIONS
PHONE . . . . . . . . . . . . . . . . . . . . . . . . . . 818-954-4999
FAX . . . . . . . . . . . . . . . . . . . . . . . . . . . . 818-954-4995
4000 Warner Blvd.
Burbank, CA 91522

| | |
|---|---|
| TYPE | Television |
| DEAL | Warner Bros. Pictures |
| CREDITS | Sinatra - Young at Heart |

Tina Sinatra . . . . . . . . . . . . . . . . . . . . . . . . . Producer

## TUDOR ENTERTAINMENT, INC.
PHONE . . . . . . . . . . . . . . . . . . . . . . . . . . 310-247-1660
FAX . . . . . . . . . . . . . . . . . . . . . . . . . . . . 310-859-1215
EMAIL . . . . . . . . . . . . . . . . . . . . . info@tudorgroup.com
WEBSITE . . . . . . . . . . . . . . . http://http://www.tudorgroup.com
9437 Santa Monica Blvd., Ste. 202
Beverly Hills, CA 90210-4612

| | |
|---|---|
| TYPE | Motion Pictures + Television |
| DEAL | Showtime Networks Inc. |
| CREDITS | Heads - Sahara - Next Door - The Fixer |

Martin Tudor . . . . . . . . . . . . . . . . . . Chief Executive Officer
Dailey Kennedy . . . . . . . . . . . . . . . . Chief Operating Officer
Andrea Simon . . . . . . . . . . . . . . . . . . . . . . . . . Manager
Pascal Gragaro . . . . . . . . . . . . . . . . . . Executive Assistant
Erica Leipheimer . . . . . . . . . . . . . . . . . Executive Assistant

## TULCHIN ENTERTAINMENT
PHONE . . . . . . . . . . . . . . . . . . . . . . . . . . 310-914-7900
FAX . . . . . . . . . . . . . . . . 310-914-7927/310-914-7928
EMAIL . . . . . . . . . . . . . . . . . . . . . entesquire@aol.com
WEBSITE . . . . . . . . . . . . http://http://www.medialawyer.com
11377 W. Olympic Blvd., 2nd Floor
Los Angeles, CA 90064

| | |
|---|---|
| TYPE | Motion Pictures + Television + Interactive Multimedia |
| CREDITS | Guy - To Sleep With Anger - Mona Must Die - The Mouse - Chicks, Man - Barbara Kopple Cannes Documentary |
| COMMENTS | Formerly Tulchin/Ades Entertainment |

Harris Tulchin . . . . . . . . . . . . . . . . . . . . . . . . . Producer
Carla Tulchin . . . . . . . . . . . . . . . . . Exec. Vice President
Josh Ryan . . . . . . . . . . . . . . . . . . . . . . . . Dir., Sales
Chris Bohjalian . . . . . . . . . . . . . . . . Administrative Assistant

## TURMAN-MORRISSEY COMPANY, THE
PHONE . . . . . . . . . . . . . . . . . . . . . . . . . . 310-244-4943
FAX . . . . . . . . . . . . . . . . . . . . . . . . . . . . 310-244-2332
10202 W. Washington Blvd.
Hepburn Building West, 2nd Floor
Culver City, CA 90232-3195

| | |
|---|---|
| TYPE | Motion Pictures + Television |
| DEAL | Columbia Pictures |
| CREDITS | Booty Call - American History X |

John Morrissey . . . . . . . . . . . . . . . . Partner (310-244-5044)
Lawrence Turman . . . . . . . . . . . . . . . Partner (310-244-5055)
Fiona Mackenzie . . . . . . . . . . . Dir., Development (310-244-3174)
Matthew Waldman . . . . . . . . . . . . . Creative & Office Manager
Jane Fitzgerald . . . . . . . . . . . Creative Executive (310-244-4840)

## TURNER ENTERTAINMENT GROUP
PHONE . . . . . . . . . . . . . . . . . . . . . . . . . . 404-827-1500
WEBSITE . . . . . . . . . . . . . . . . . . . . http://www.turner.com
1050 Techwood Dr., NW
Atlanta, GA 30318-5604

| | |
|---|---|
| TYPE | Television + Syndication + Documentaries + Interactive Multimedia |

Terence McGuirk . . . Chairman/Pres./CEO, Turner Broadcasting System, Inc.
Bill Burke . . . . . . . . . . . . . . . . President, TBS Superstation
Betty Cohen . . . . . . . . . . . . . . . President, Cartoon Network
Bradley Siegel . . . . . . . . . . . . . . . President, TNT & TCM
Robert Levi . . . . . . . . . . . . Exec. VP, Turner Ent. Networks
Vicky Miller . . . . . . . . . . . . Exec. VP, Finance & Planning
Tom Karsch . . . . . . . . . . . . . . General Mgr./Sr. VP, TCM
Terri Tingle . . . . . . . . . . . . . Sr. VP, Standards & Practices
Andrew Velcoff . . . . . . . . . . Sr. VP, General Counser, CNN
Teri Fournier . . . . . . . . . . . . . VP, Legal Affairs, CNN (LA)
Ken Schwab . . . . . . . . . . VP, Progam Planning & Acquisions
Scott Karol . . . . . . . . . . . . . . . . . . Legal Counsel (LA)

## TURNER NETWORK TELEVISION (TNT)
PHONE . . . . . . . . . . . . . . . . . . . . . . . . . . 310-551-6300
FAX . . . . . . . . . . . . . . . . . . . . . . . . . . . . 310-551-6344
WEBSITE . . . . . . . . . . . . . . . . . . . . http://www.turner.com
1888 Century Park East, 14th Floor
Los Angeles, CA 90067

| | |
|---|---|
| TYPE | Television |

Brad Siegel . . . . . . . . . . . . . . . . . . President, TNT & TCM
Robert DeBitetto . . . . . . . Exec. VP, Business Affairs, Originals
Julie Weitz . . . . . . . . . . . Exec. VP, Original Programming
Susan O. Gross . . . . . . . . . . . . Sr. VP, Business Affairs
Nick Lombardo . . . . . . . . . . . . . . . . Sr. VP, Production
Andre Carey . . . . . . . . . . . . . VP, Original Programming
Sandra Dewey . . . . . . . . . . . . . . . VP, Business Affairs
Iris Grossman . . . . . . . . . . . . . . VP, Talent & Casting
Jonathan Harris . . . . . . . . . . . . . . VP, Business Affairs
Jeffrey Levine . . . . . . . . . . . . VP, Original Programming
Kim Long . . . . . . . . . . . . . . . . . . . . VP, Production
Betsy Newman . . . . . . . . . . . . VP, Program Development
Spike Seldin . . . . . . . . . . . . . VP, Program Development
Jim Wilberger . . . . . . . . . . . . . . . . . VP, Production
Cindy Campbell . . . . . . . . . . . . Controller (404-885-4936)
Catherine George . . . . . . . . . . . . . . . . Dir., Production
Candace Snyder . . . . . . . . . . . . . . Dir., Post-Production
Cathy Wischner-Sola . . . . . . . . . . . . . . Dir., Development
Kat Slonaker . . . . . . . . . . . . . . . . . . Mgr., Production
Pam Pietroforte . . . . . . . . . . Exec. Asst. to Julie Weitz
Anne Marie Yantos . . . . . . . Asst. Development (Ms. Newman)
Dori Fram . . . . . . . . . . . . . . . Asst. to Iris Grossman
Dez Hunter . . . . . . . . . Asst. to Kim Long & Jim Willberger
Sharon Nelson . . . . . . . . . . . . . Asst. to Nick Lombardo

## TURNER ORIGINAL PRODUCTIONS
PHONE . . . . . . . . . . . . . . . . . . . . . . . . . . 404-827-2047
FAX . . . . . . . . . . . . . . . . . . . . . . . . . . . . 404-885-4433
WEBSITE . . . . . . . . . . . . . . . . . . . . http://www.turner.com/
1050 Techwood Dr. NW
Atlanta, GA 30318

| | |
|---|---|
| TYPE | Television + Documentaries |
| CREDITS | A Century of Women - The Native Americans - Moon Shot |

Pat Mitchell . . . . . . . . . . . . Pres., Turner Original Prods.
Teya Ryan . . . . . . . . . . . . Sr. VP & Exec. Producer(CNN)
Vivian Schiller . . . . . . . . . . . . . . Sr. VP/General Manager
Jacoba Atlas . . . . . . . . . . . . VP/Supervising Producer(LA)
Louis Lettes . . . . . . . . . VP, Business Affairs (404-885-0916)
Tom McMahon . . . . . . . . . . . VP/Supervising Producer(LA)
John Savage . . . . . . . . . . VP/Supervising Producer (Atlanta)
Cathe Neukum . . . . . . . Prod., Current Programming Specials
Tracy McArdle . . . . . . . Talent & Development Executive (LA)
Adrienne Bramhall . . . . . . . . . . . . . . . . Series Manager
Jody Gottlieb . . . . . . . . . . . . . . . . Production Manager
Lee Rivera . . . . . . . . . . . . . . . . . Legal (404-827-4945)
John Cooke . . . . . . . . . . . . . . Post Production Coordinator
Heather Donaldson . . . . . . . . . . . . Development Coordinator
Jennifer Hyde . . . . . . . . . . . . . . Development Coordinator
Bill Myers . . . . . . . . . . . . . . . . Mgr., Creative Services
Dan McKenzie . . . . . . Exec. Asst. to Ms. Atlas & Mr. McMahon (LA)
Julie Bitton . . . . . . . . . . . . . . . . . Asst. to Ms. Schiller
Ann Howard . . . . . . . . . . . . . . . . Asst. to Pat Mitchell

# COMPANIES AND STAFF

**TURTELTAUB-ORENSTEIN PRODS.**
PHONE . . . . . . . . . . . . . . . . . . . . . . . . . . . . . . 310-550-4525
9255 Sunset Blvd., Ste. 404
Los Angeles, CA 90069

TYPE        Television
CREDITS      Cosby

Saul Turteltaub . . . . . . . . . . . . . . . . . . . . Writer/Exec. Producer
Bernie Orenstein . . . . . . . . . . . . . . . . . . Writer/Exec. Producer

**TURTLE PRODUCTIONS, JON**
PHONE . . . . . . . . . . . . . . . 310-234-5347/310-234-5338
FAX . . . . . . . . . . . . . . . . . . . . . . . . . . . . 310-234-5345
Showtime Networks, Inc.
10880 Wilshire Blvd., #1101
Los Angeles, CA 90024

TYPE        Motion Pictures + Television
DEAL        Showtime Networks Inc.
CREDITS      The Minion - Arrival II - Fluke

Jon Turtle . . . . . . . . . . . . . . . . . . . . . . . . . . . . . . President
David Decker . . . . . . . . . . . . . . . . . VP/Head, Creative Affairs

**TWENTIETH CENTURY FOX**
PHONE . . . . . . . . . . . . . . . . . . . . . . . . . . 310-369-1000
WEBSITE . . . . . . . . . . . . . . . . . . . . . http://www.fox.com
10201 W. Pico Blvd.
Los Angeles, CA 90035

TYPE        Motion Pictures
COMMENTS   Mailing Address: P.O. Box 900 Beverly Hills, CA 90213.

William Mechanic . . . . . . . . . . . . . . . . . . . . . . . Chairman/CEO
Thomas Sherak . . . . . . . . . . . . . Chairman, 20th Domestic Film Group
Tom Rothman . . . . . . . . . . . . . . . . . . Pres., Worldwide Production
Steven Bersch . . . . . . . . . . . . . . . . . Exec. VP, Business Affairs
Elizabeth Gabler . . . . . . . . . . . . . . . . . . . Exec. VP, Production
Joe Hartwick . . . . . . . . . . . . . . . . Exec. VP, Feature Production
Sanford Panitch . . . . . . . . . . . . . . . . . . . Exec. VP, Production
Hutch Parker . . . . . . . . . . . . . . . . . . . . . Exec. VP, Production
Simon Bax . . . . . . . . . . . . . . . . . . . . . . . . . . . . . Sr. VP/CFO
Peter Cyffka . . . . . . . . . . . . . . . . . . . . . . . . Sr. VP, Finance
Daniel Ferleger . . . . . . . . . . . . . . . . . Sr. VP, Business Affairs
Ted Gagliano . . . . . . . . . . . . . . . . . . . Sr. VP, Post Production
Mark Resnick . . . . . . . . . . . . . . . . . . Sr. VP, Business Affairs
Peter Rice . . . . . . . . . . . . . . . . . . . . . . Sr. VP, Production
Tony Safford . . . . . . . . . . . . . . . . . . . . . Sr. VP, Productions
Bedi Singh . . . . . . . . . . . . . . . . . . . . . . Sr. VP/Deputy CFO
Ted Dodd . . . . . . . . . . . . . . . . . . . . . . . VP, Creative Affairs
Michael Jenkinson . . . . . . . . . . . . . . . . . . . . . VP, Production
Stephen Plum . . . . . . . . . . . . . . . . . . . . VP, Business Affairs
Victoria Rossellini . . . . . . . . . . . . . . . . . VP, Business Affairs
Sandi Black . . . . . . . . . . . . . . . . . . . . . . . Creative Executive
Carlos Kotkin . . . . . . . . . . . . . . . . . . . . . . Creative Executive
Emma Watts . . . . . . . . . . . . . . . . . . . . . . . Creative Executive
Serena Westwell . . . . . . . . . . . . . Exec. Dir., Talent Realtions
Nate Hooper . . . . . . . . . . . . . . . . . . . . . . . Dir., Development
Vanessa Morrison . . . . . . . . . . . . . . . . . . . . Dir., Development
Isabel Rosenthal . . . . . . . . . . . . . . . . . . . . Mgr., Acquisitions
Judy Fairly . . . . . . . . . . . . . . . . . . . . . . . . . . Story Editor

**TWENTIETH CENTURY FOX TELEVISION**
PHONE . . . . . . . . . . . . . . . . . . . . . . . . . . 310-369-1000
WEBSITE . . . . . . . . . . . . . . . . . . . . . http://www.fox.com
10201 W. Pico Blvd.
Los Angeles, CA 90067

TYPE        Television
CREDITS      X-Files - Chicago Hope - Simpsons

Sandy Grushow . . . . . . . . . . . . . . . . . . . . . . . . . . . President
Gary S. Newman . . . . . . . . . . . . . . . . . . . Exec. Vice President
Charlie Goldstein . . . . . . . . . . . . . Exec. VP, Production & Finance
Howard Kurtzman . . . . . . . . . . . Exec. VP, Business & Legal Affairs
Robert Barron . . . . . . . . . . . . . . . . . . . . . . . . Sr. VP, Finance
Kelly Cline . . . . . . . . . . . . . . . . . . . . . Sr. VP, Legal Affairs
Joel Hornstock . . . . . . . . . . . . . . . . . . . Sr. VP, TV Production
Edward Nassour . . . . . . . . . . . . . . . . . . Sr. VP, Post Production
David M. Robinson . . . . . . . . . . . . . . . . Sr. VP, Business Affairs
Mindy Schultheis . . . . . . . . . . . . Sr. VP, Comedy Development
Randy Stone . . . . . . . . . . . . . . . . . . . Sr. VP, Talent/Casting
Dana Walden . . . . . . . . . . . . . . . . . . Sr. VP, Head of Drama
Neal Baseman . . . . . . . . . . . . . . . . . . . . VP, Business Affairs
Alex Collett . . . . . . . . . . . . . . . . . . . . . . . . . . . . VP, Drama
Ada Goldberg . . . . . . . . . . . . . . . . VP, Business & Legal Affairs
Michael Hanel . . . . . . . . . . . . . . . . . . . . . . . . . VP, Comedy
Janie Kleiman . . . . . . . . . . . . . . . . VP, Television Production
Michelle Lautanen . . . . . . . . . . . . . . . . . . VP, Business Affairs
Sandra Ortiz . . . . . . . . . . . . . . . . . . . . . . VP, Business Affairs
Jeffrey Glaser . . . . . . . . . . . . . . . . . . . . . Exec. Dir., Drama
Emile Levisetti . . . . . . . . . . . . . . . . . . . Exec. Dir., Comedy
Jo Gard . . . . . . . . . . . . . . . . . . . Dir., Production Accounting
Beth Hoffman . . . . . . . . . . . . . . . . . . . Dir., Business Affairs
Diane Pachecho . . . . . . . . . . . . . . . . . . . . . Dir., TV Production
Marci Proietto . . . . . . . . . . . . . . . . . . . . . Associate Director
Lianne Siegel . . . . . . . . . . . . . . . . . . . . . . . Mgr., Comedy

**TWENTIETH CENTURY FOX-FOX 2000 (LA)**
PHONE . . . . . . . . . . . . . . . . . . . . . . . . . . 310-369-2041
FAX . . . . . . . . . . . . . . . . . . . . . . . . . . . . 310-369-4258
WEBSITE . . . . . . . . . . . . . . . . . . . . . http://www.fox.com
10201 W. Pico Blvd., Bldg. 78
Los Angeles, CA 90035

TYPE        Motion Pictures

Laura Ziskin . . . . . . . . . . . . . . . President (310-369-3722)
Kevin McCormick . . . . . . . . . . . Exec. VP, Production (310-369-4538)
Alex Gartner . . . . . . . . . . . . . . . Exec. VP, Production (310-369-2810)
Carla Hacken . . . . . . . . . . . . . . . Sr. Vice President (310-369-4550)
Ashley Kramer . . . . . . . . . . . . . . Sr. Vice President (310-369-4365)
Chris Vogler . . . . . . . . . . . . . . . . Story Consultant (310-369-3139)
Jack Leslie . . . . . . . . . . . . . . . . Dir., Development (310-369-2238)
Lisa Harrison . . . . . . . . . Talent Development & Relations Executive
Suzie Moldavon . . . . . . . . . . . . Creative Executive (310-369-4634)
Tracy Silbert . . . . . . . . . . . . . . Creative Executive (310-369-5345)
Chris Rico . . . . . . . . . . . . . . . . . . . 1st Asst. to Laura Ziskin
Lea Oggs . . . . . . . . . . . . . . . . . . . 2nd Asst. to Laura Ziskin
Nancy Covello . . . . . . . . . . . . . . . . Asst. to Kevin McCormick
Laura Williams . . . . . . . . . . . . . . . . . . . . . Asst. to J. Leslie
Saskia Young . . . . . . . . . . . . . . . . . . . . . Asst. to A. Kramer

**TWENTIETH CENTURY FOX-SEARCHLIGHT PICTS.**
PHONE . . . . . . . . . . . . . . . . . . . . . 310-369-4402/212-556-8245
FAX . . . . . . . . . . . . . . . . . . . . . . . 310-369-2359/212-556-8248
WEBSITE . . . . . . . . . . . . . . . . . . . . . http://www.fox.com
10201 W. Pico Blvd., Bldg. 38
Los Angeles, CA 90035

TYPE        Motion Pictures
CREDITS      The Ice Storm - The Full Monty - Oscar and Lucinda -
                 She's The One - Brothers McMullen - Two Girls and a Guy
COMMENTS   Also: 1211 6th Ave., 16th Fl., New York, NY 10036

Lindsay Law . . . . . . . . . . . . . . . . . . . . . . . . . . . . . . President
Joseph De Marco . . . . . . . . . . . . . . . . . . . Exec. Vice President
Claudia Lewis . . . . . . . . . . . . . . . . . . . . . Sr. VP, Production
Joe Pichirallo . . . . . . . . . . . . . . . . . . . . . . . . VP, Production
Jamie Taylor . . . . . . . . . . . . . . . . . . . . . . . VP, Legal Affairs
Gia Paladino . . . . . . . . . . . . . . . . . . . . . Counsel/Legal Affairs
Jill Gwen . . . . . . . . . . . . . . . . . . Exec. Dir., Finance & Admin.
Isabel Rosenthal . . . . . . . . . . . . . . Dir., Acquisitions & Production
J. Michael Stremel . . . . . . . . . . . . . . . . . . . Dir., Production (NY)
Lisa Fragner . . . . . . . . . . . . . . . . . . . . . . . Creative Executive
Matt Gannon . . . . . . . . . . . . . . . . . . . . . . . Creative Executive
Joshua Deighton . . . . . . . . . . . . . . . . . . Development/Production
Amber Husbands . . . . . . . . . . . . . . . . . . Development/Production
David Niederman . . . . . . . . . . . . . . . . . . Development/Production

# COMPANIES AND STAFF

**TWENTIETH TELEVISION**
PHONE . . . . . . . . . . . . . . . . . . . . . . . . . . . . . . . . 310-369-1000
FAX . . . . . . . . . . . . . . . . . . . . . . . . . . . . . . . . . . 310-369-1718
WEBSITE . . . . . . . . . . . . . . . . . . . . . . . . . . http://www.fox.com
2121 Ave. of the Stars
Los Angeles, CA 90067

TYPE       Television + Syndication
CREDITS      Access Hollywood - Student Bodies - The Magic Hour -
              Forgive or Forget

Rick Jacobson . . . . . . . . . . . . . . . . . . . . . . . . . . . . President/COO
Greg Nathanson . . . . . . Pres., Development, Fox TV Stations & Twentieth TV
Kevin Burns . . . . . . . . . . . . . . . . . . . . . . . . . . . . Sr. VP, Fox Star
Cliff Lachman . . . . . . . . . . . . . . . . . Sr. VP, Programming & Production
John McDonald . . . . . . . . . . . . . . . . Sr. VP, Programming Enterprises
David Shall . . . . . . . . . . . . . . . . . . Sr. VP, Business & Legal Affairs
Cheri Vincent . . . . . . . . . . . . . . . Sr. VP, Finance & Administration
Joey Carson . . . . . . . . . . . . . . . . Executive in Charge of Production
Lee Gonsalves . . . . . . . . . . . . . . . . . . . . . . . . . VP, Development

**TWILIGHT TIME FILMS**
PHONE . . . . . . . . . . . . . . . . . . . . . . . . . 310-888-3200 x261
FAX . . . . . . . . . . . . . . . . . . . . . . . . . . . . . . 310-888-3210
3 Arts Entertainment
9460 Wilshire Blvd., 7th Fl.
Beverly Hills, CA 90212

TYPE       Motion Pictures + Television
CREDITS      thirtysomething - My So-Called Life - Til There Was You -
              Significant Others Pilot - Cupid

Scott Winant . . . . . . . . . . . . . . . . . . . . . . . Producer/Director
Kelly McCarthy . . . . . . . . . . . . . . . . . VP, Production/Producer
Jenifer Catalano . . . . . . . . . . . . . . . . . . . . VP, Development
Robyn Andrews . . . . . . . . . . . . . . . . . . . . Production Associate

**TWIN BROTHERS PRODUCTIONS, INC**
PHONE . . . . . . . . . . . . . . . . . . . . . . . . . . . 310-275-1300
FAX . . . . . . . . . . . . . . . . . . . . . . . . . . . . . 310-275-1700
EMAIL . . . . . . . . . . . . . . . . . . . . . twinbros@directnet.com
Raleigh Studios
650 N. Bronson Ave., Ste. 215
Hollywood, CA 90004

TYPE       Motion Pictures + Interactive Multimedia + Television
CREDITS      Shattered - Carlito's Way - Das Boot The Director's Cut
Ortwin Freyermuth . . . . . . . . . . . . . . . . . . . . . . President/CEO

**TWO OCEANS ENTERTAINMENT GROUP**
PHONE . . . . . . . . . . . . . . . . . . . . . . . . . . . 818-501-6550
FAX . . . . . . . . . . . . . . . . . . . . . . . . . . . . . 818-501-6558
EMAIL . . . . . . . . . . . . . . . . . . . . . . . . twoceans@aol.com
15060 Ventura Blvd., Ste. 400
Sherman Oaks, CA 91403

TYPE       Motion Pictures + Television + Animation
CREDITS      Happily Ever After:Fairy Tales - When Danger Follows
              You Home - Baby Monitor: Soud of Fear
COMMENTS   Live Action, Animation/MOW's.
Meryl Marshall . . . . . . . . . . . . . . . . President/Exec. Producer
Susan Whittaker . . . . . . . . . . . . . VP, Development/Exec. Producer
Donna Brown Guillaume . . . . . . . . . . . . . . Executive Producer
Mary Pickert . . . . . . . . . . . . . . . . . . . . Development Associate

**TWO PAULS ENTERTAINMENT**
PHONE . . . . . . . . . . . . . . . . . . . . . . . . . . . 310-275-5501
FAX . . . . . . . . . . . . . . . . . . . . . . . . . . . . . 310-887-0155
301 North Canon Drive., Ste. 321
Beverly Hills, CA 90210

TYPE       Motion Pictures + Television
CREDITS      Lovers Knot - 919 5th Avenue
Paul A. Kaufman . . . . . . . . . . . . . . . . . . . . . . . . . . Producer
Paul Rauch . . . . . . . . . . . . . . . . . . Producer (212-986-5330)

**TWO ROADS PRODS., INC.**
PHONE . . . . . . . . . . . . . . . . . . . . . . . . . . . 212-261-9185
FAX . . . . . . . . . . . . . . . . . . . . . . . . . . . . . 212-459-3456
Hallmark Entertainment
1325 Ave. of the Americas, 21st Floor
New York, NY 10019

TYPE       Motion Pictures + Television
David V. Picker . . . . . . . . . . . . . . . . . . . . . . . . . . . Producer
Vicki Stein . . . . . . . . . . . . . . . . . . . . . . . Asst. to Mr. Picker

***TWO STEPP PRODUCTIONS**
PHONE . . . . . . . . . . . . . . . . . . . . . . . . . . . 818-567-6337
FAX . . . . . . . . . . . . . . . . . . . . . . . . . . . . . 818-567-6333
EMAIL . . . . . . . . . . . . . . . . . . . . . asteppprod@aol.com
Alan Stepp
316 North Maple St., Ste. 125
Burbank, CA 91505

TYPE       Animation + Motion Pictures + Television
CREDITS      Dancer, Texas-Pop. 81 - Willing to Kill - The Texas
              Cheerleader Story
Alan Stepp . . . . . . . . . . . . . . . . . . . . . . . . . . . . . . Producer

***UBU PRODUCTIONS**
PHONE . . . . . . . . . . . . . . . . . . . . . . . . . . . 818-655-5850
FAX . . . . . . . . . . . . . . . . . . . . . . . . . . . . . 818-655-8617
4024 Radford Ave., Bungalow #1
Studio City, CA 91604

TYPE       Motion Pictures + Television
DEAL       DreamWorks SKG
CREDITS      Spin City - Family Ties - Brooklyn Bridge
Gary David Goldberg . . . . . . . . . . . . . . . . . . Executive Producer
Alex Maggioni . . . . . . . . . . . . . . . . . . . . . . . VP, Development
Heather Green . . . . . . . . . . . . . . . . . . . . . . . . . . . . Assistant
Larry Reitzer . . . . . . . . . . . . . . . . . . . . . . . . . . . . . Assistant

**UFLAND PRODUCTIONS**
PHONE . . . . . . . . . . . . . . . . . . . . . . . . . . . 310-656-3031
FAX . . . . . . . . . . . . . . . . . . . . . . . . . . . . . 310-656-3073
534 21st Street
Santa Monica, CA 90402

TYPE       Motion Pictures + Television
CREDITS      Last Temptation of Christ - One True Thing - Snow Falling
              on Cedars
Harry J. Ufland . . . . . . . . . . . . . . . . . . . . . . . . . . . Producer
Mary Jane Ufland . . . . . . . . . . . . . . . . . . . . . . . . . . Producer

**UNA CHICA ENTERTAINMENT**
PHONE . . . . . . . . . . . . . . . . . . . . . . . . . . . 760-327-3517
FAX . . . . . . . . . . . . . . . . . . . . . . . . . . . . . 760-327-3371
100 S. Sunrise Way #507
Palm Springs, CA 92262

TYPE       Motion Pictures + Television + Documentaries + Feature
              Direct to Video
CREDITS      This Is Cuba - Snake Skin Jacket - Star Maps
Florence Figueroa . . . . . . . . . . . . . . . . . . . . Producer/Writer
Johnathan Scholz . . . . . . . . . . . . . . . . . . . . . . . . . . Producer
Mathew Jakositz . . . . . . . . . . . . . . . . . . Development Executive

**UNAPIX/A-PIX ENTERTAINMENT**
PHONE . . . . . . . . . . . . . . . . . . . 212-252-7711/818-981-8536
FAX . . . . . . . . . . . . . . . . . . . . . 212-252-7626/818-981-8537
200 Madison Ave., 24th Floor
New York, NY 10016

TYPE       Motion Pictures + Feature Direct to Video
CREDITS      Good Luck - Once A Thief - Men - P.U.N.K.S. - Happy
              Man
COMMENTS   Also: 4515 Van Nuys Blvd., Ste. 301, Sherman Oaks, CA
                 91403
Robert Baruc . . . . . . . . . . . . . . . . . . . . . . . . . . . . President
David Fox . . . . . . . . . . . . . . . . . . . President/CEO, Unapix
Alicia Reilly . . . . . . . . . . . . . . . . VP, Acquisitions & Production
Deborah Thompson-Duda . . . . . . . . . . VP, Acquisitions & Production (LA)

**UNDERWORLD ENTERTAINMENT**
PHONE . . . . . . . . . . . . . . . . . . . . . . . . . . . 310-247-0690
FAX . . . . . . . . . . . . . . . . . . . . . . . . . . . . . 310-247-0694
9200 Sunset Blvd. #1024
W. Hollywood, CA 90069

TYPE       Motion Pictures
DEAL       Universal Pictures
CREDITS      Menace II Society - Dead Presidents
Albert Hughes . . . . . . . . . . . . . . . . . . . . . . . . . . . . . Owner
Allen Hughes . . . . . . . . . . . . . . . . . . . . . . . . . . . . . Owner
Kevin Messick . . . . . . . . . . . . . . . . . . . . . . . . . . . President
Ethan Gross . . . . . . . . . . . . . . . . . . . . . . Creative Executive
Bryan Holdman . . . . . . . . . . . . . . . . . . . . . . . . Story Editor
AnnMarie Deringer . . . . . . . . . . . . . . . Asst. to the Hughes Bros.
Pamela Teschke . . . . . . . . . . . . . . . . . Asst. to Mr. Messick

**UNGER PRODUCTIONS INC.**
PHONE . . . . . . . . . . . . . . . . . . . . . . . . . . . . . . . . . 310-471-9624
FAX . . . . . . . . . . . . . . . . . . . . . . . . . . . . . . . . . . . . 310-440-2219
131 N. Bundy Dr.
Los Angeles, CA 90049-4108
TYPE          Motion Pictures
CREDITS       Silent Rage - Force Ten from Navarone - Don't Look Now
Anthony B. Unger . . . . . . . . . . . . . . . . . . . . . . . . . . . . President
Will McElroy . . . . . . . . . . . . . . . Asst., Production & Development

**UNISTAR INTL. PICTURES**
PHONE . . . . . . . . . . . . . . . . . . . . . . . . . . . . . . . . . 213-650-5061
FAX . . . . . . . . . . . . . . . . . . . . . . . . . . . . . . . . . . . . 213-650-7848
EMAIL . . . . . . . . . . . . . . . . . . . . . . . . . . . unistarpix@aol.com
8240 Mannix Dr.
Los Angeles, CA 90046
TYPE          Motion Pictures + Television
CREDITS       Midnight - Firestorm - True Story - Whatever Happened
              To Bobby Earl? - True Detective
Gloria Morrison . . . . . . . . . . . . . . . . . . . President/Exec. Producer
Gavin Carey . . . . . . . . . . . . . . . . . . . . . . . . . . . . . VP/Producer
David Francois . . . . . . . . . . . . . . . . . . . . VP/Office Management
Shane A. Snoke . . . . . . . . . . . . VP, Development/Assoc. Producer
Jason Morrison . . . . . . . . . . . . . . . . . . . . . . . . . . . Story Editor
Brian Zabawski . . . . . . . . . . . . . . . . . . . . . . . . . . . Story Editor

**UNITED ARTISTS PICTURES**
PHONE . . . . . . . . . . . . . . . . . . . . . . . . . . . . . . . . 310-449-3000
WEBSITE . . . . . . . . . . . . . . . . . . . . http://www.mgmua.com/
2500 Broadway St., 5th Fl.
Santa Monica, CA 90404-3061
TYPE          Motion Pictures
CREDITS       Supernova - The Scalper - Ronin
Frank Mancuso . . . . . . . . . . . . . . . . . . CEO/Chairman of the Board
Lindsay Doran . . . . . . . . . . . . . . . . . . . . . . . . . . . . . President
Jeff Kleeman . . . . . . . . . . . . . . . . . . . . . . Exec. VP, Production
Rebecca Pollack-Parker . . . . . . . . . . . . . . . . Exec. VP, Production
James Middleton . . . . . . . . . . . . . . . VP, Production & Development

**UNITED FILM**
PHONE . . . . . . . . . . . . . . . . . . . . . . . . . . . . . . . . 310-441-0900
FAX . . . . . . . . . . . . . . . . . . . . . . . . . . . . . . . . . . . . 310-474-7465
1990 Westwood Blvd., PH
Los Angeles, CA 90025
TYPE          Motion Pictures + Feature Direct to Video + Interactive
              Multimedia
CREDITS       Blind Trust - Skeletons- The Elevator - Wrong Turn
Brian Shuster . . . . . . . . . . . . . . . . . . . . . . . . . . . . . President
David Silberg . . . . . . . . . . . . . . . . . . . . . . . . . . VP, Production

**UNITED PARAMOUNT NETWORK (UPN)**
PHONE . . . . . . . . . . . . . . . . . . . . . . . . . . . . . . . . 310-575-7000
WEBSITE . . . . . . . . . . . . . . . . . . . . . . . . http://www.upn.com
11800 Wilshire Blvd.
Los Angeles, CA 90025
TYPE          Television
Dean Valentine . . . . . . . . . . . . . . . . . . . . . . . . . President/CEO
Layne Britton . . . . . . . . . . . . . . . . Exec. VP, Business Operations
Tom Nunan . . . . . . . . . . . . . . . . . . . . Exec. VP, Entertainment
Barbara Mannina . . . . . . . . . . . Sr. VP, Finance & Administration
June Baldwin . . . . . . . . . . . . . . . . . VP, Business Affairs & Legal
Kelly Edwards . . . . . . . . . . . . . . . . . . . VP, Comedy Development
Barry Gordon . . . . . . . . . . . . . . . . . VP, Business & Legal Affairs
Maira Suro . . . . . . . . . . . . . . . . . . . . . . VP, Drama Development
Judith Weiner . . . . . . . . . . . . . . . . . . . . . . . . . . . VP, Casting
John Levoff . . . . . . . . . . . . Exec. Producer, Movies & Mini-Series
James Bethea . . . . . . . . . . . . . . . Exec. Dir., Current Programming
Todd Lituchy . . . . . . . . . . . . . . . . . . . . Exec. Dir., Scheduling
Danielle Greene . . . . . . . . . . . . . . . . Mgr., Current Programming
Paul Spadone . . . . . . . . . . . . . . . . . . Mgr., Current Programming
Brad Sterling . . . . . . . . . . . . . . . . . Mgr., Comedy Development
Staci Albala . . . . . . . . . . . . . . . . . . . Asst. to Kelly Edwards
Jay Luchs . . . . . . . . . . . . . . . . . . . . . . Asst. to James Bethea
Christina Mack . . . . . . . . . . . . . . . . . Asst. to Dean Valentine
Lonnie Moore . . . . . . . . . . . . . . . . . . . . Asst. to Tom Nunan
Richard Remppel . . . . . . . . . . . . . . . . Asst. to Dean Valentine
Edwin Zane . . . . . . . . . . . . . . . . . . . . . . . Asst. to Maira Suro

**UNIVERSAL PICTURES**
PHONE . . . . . . . . . . . . . . . . . . . . . . . . . . . . . . . . 818-777-1000
WEBSITE . . . . . . . . . . . . . . . . . . http://www.universalstudios.com
100 Universal City Plaza
Universal City, CA 91608-1085
TYPE          Motion Pictures
COMMENTS      See Also Universal Studios
Casey Silver . . . . . . . . . . . . . . . . . . . . . . . . . . . . . Chairman
Chris McGurk . . . . . . . . . . . . . . . . . . . Chief Operating Officer
Jon Gumpert . . . . . . . . . . . . . . . . . . . . Executive Vice President
Jeffrey A. Korcheck . . . . . . . . . . Exec. VP, Business & Legal Affairs
Jim Burk . . . . . . . . . . . . . . . . Sr. VP, International Operations
Bahman Naraghi . . . . . . . . . . . . . . Sr. VP, Planning & Operations
James M. Horowitz . . . . . . . . . . . . . . . . . . VP, Business Affairs
Anthony Zummo . . . . . . . . . . . VP, Legal Affairs, Universal Picts.
Stacey Snider . . . . . . . . . . . . . . . . . . . . . . . Head, Production
Kevin Misher . . . . . . . . . . . . . Exec. VP, Universal Picts. Production
Don Zepfel . . . . . . . . Exec.VP, Physical Prod., Universal Picts. Production
Allison Brecker . . . . . . . . . . . . . . Sr. VP, Universal Picts. Production
Leonard Kornberg . . . . . . . . . . . . Sr. VP, Universal Picts. Production
Scott Stuber . . . . . . . . . . . . . . . Sr. VP, Universal Picts. Production
Peter Arnoff . . . . . . . . . . . . VP, Universal Picts. Prod. (East Coast)
Andrew Given . . . . . . . . VP, Physical Prod., Universal Picts. Production
Eric Hughes . . . . . . . . . . . . . . . . VP, Universal Picts. Production
Kool Marder . . . . . . . . . . VP, Physical Prod., Universal Picts. Production
Romy Kaufman . . . . . . . Exec. Story Editor, Universal Picts. Production
Lisa Alden . . . . . . . . . . . Dir., Development, Universal Picts. Production
Angelique Gonsalves . . . . . . Dir., Development, Universal Picts. Production
Holly Jenkinson . . . . . . . . Dir., Development, Universal Picts. Production
Greig McRitchie . . . . . . Dir., Feature Post Prod, Universal Picts. Production
Kathryn Miller . . . . . . . . . Dir., Development, Universal Picts. Production
Erik Palma . . . . . . . . . . . Dir., Development,Universal Picts. Prod.(East Coast)

**UNIVERSAL STUDIOS**
PHONE . . . . . . . . . . . . . . . . . . . . . . . . . . . . . . . . 818-777-1000
WEBSITE . . . . . . . . . . . . . . . . . . http://www.universalstudios.com
100 Universal City Plaza
Universal City, CA 91608-1085
TYPE          Motion Pictures + Television
Frank J. Biondi Jr. . . . . . . . . . . . . . . . . . . . . . Chairman/CEO
Ron Meyer . . . . . . . . . . . . . . . . . . . . . . . . . . President/COO
Bruce L. Hack . . . . . . . . . . . . . . . . . . . . . . . Exec. VP/CFO
Ken Kahrs . . . . . . . . . . . . . . . . . Sr. VP, Human Resources
Alice H. Lusk . . . . . . . . . . . Sr. VP/Chief Technology Officer
Karen Randall . . . . . . . . . . . . . . . . Sr. VP/General Counsel
Hellene Runtagh . . . . . . . . . . . . . . . . . . Sr. Vice President

**UNIVERSAL TELEVISION & NETWORKS GROUP**
PHONE . . . . . . . . . . . . . . . . . . . . . . . . . . . . . . . . 818-777-1000
WEBSITE . . . . . . . . . . . . . . . . . . http://www.universalstudios.com
100 Universal City Plaza
Universal City, CA 91608-1085
TYPE          Television
Blair Westlake . . . . . . . . . . . . . . . . . . . . . . . . . . . Chairman
Frederick Huntsberry . . . . . . . . . . . . . . . . . . . Chief Financial Officer
Tony Garland . . . . . . . . . . . . . President, Universal Studios Networks
Ned Nalle . . . . . . . . . . . . . President, Worldwide Television Production
Armando Nunez Jr. . . . . . . . . . . . . President, International Television
Peter Hughes . . . . . . . . . . . . . Exec. VP, International Television
Dan Filie . . . . . . . . . Sr. VP/Exec. in Charge, Dramatic Prod., WW & TV
Steve Jarmus . . . . . . . . . . . . . . . . . . . Sr. VP, Pay Television
Peter Schoenfeld . . . . . . . Sr. VP, Television Business Development
Philip Schuman . . . . . . . . . . . . . Sr. VP, Business & Legal Affairs
Trace Harris . . . . . . . . . . . VP, Television Business Development
Holly Leff Pressman . . . . . . . . . . . VP, Worldwide Pay Per View

**UPA PRODUCTIONS OF AMERICA**
PHONE . . . . . . . . . . . . . . . . . . . . . . . . . . . . . . . . 310-659-6004
FAX . . . . . . . . . . . . . . . . . . . . . . . . . . . . . . . . . . . . 310-659-4599
8640 Wilshire Blvd.
Beverly Hills, CA 90211
TYPE          Motion Pictures
Henry G. Saperstein . . . . . . . . . . . . . . . . . . . . . . Chairman/CEO
Dorothy Schechter . . . . . . . . . . . . . . . . . . . . . . Vice President

## UPLINGER ENTERPRISES
PHONE . . . . . . . . . . . . . . . . . . . . . . . . . . . 310-829-7886
FAX . . . . . . . . . . . . . . . . . . . . . . . . . . . . . 310-829-3446
EMAIL . . . . . . . . . . . . . . . . . . . . . . uplingertv@aol.com
930 Third St. #303
Santa Monica, CA 90403

| | |
|---|---|
| TYPE | Television + Syndication |
| DEAL | Millennium Television Network |
| CREDITS | Live Aid - Sport Aid - Earth 90 - Viva Terra Viva - Our Common Future - Millennium Television Network |
| COMMENTS | Also: Publishes Broadcasters Uplinger. |

Hal Uplinger . . . . . . . . . . . . . . . . . . . . . . . . . . President
Michael McLees . . . . . . . . . . . . . . . . . . . . . . Sr. Producer
Mike Appleton . . . . . . . . . . . . . . . . . . . Executive Producer
Jennifer Langlois . . . . . . . . . . . . . . . Administrative Assistant

## UPSTART ENTERTAINMENT
PHONE . . . . . . . . . . . . . . . . . . . . . . . . . . . 310-475-6025
FAX . . . . . . . . . . . . . . . . . . . . . . . . . . . . . 310-475-9844
10433 Wilshire Blvd., PH F
Los Angeles, CA 90024

| | |
|---|---|
| TYPE | Motion Pictures + Television + Syndication |
| CREDITS | She's Out of Control - The Bulkin Trail |

Michael J. Nathanson . . . . . . . . . . . . . . . . Writer/Producer
Amy Graves . . . . . . . . . . . . . . . . . . . . . Dir., Development

## UPSTREAM PICTURES
PHONE . . . . . . . . . . . . . . . . . . . . . . . . . . . 212-219-0355
FAX . . . . . . . . . . . . . . . . . . . . . . . . . . . . . 212-219-3409
P.O. Box 321 Prince St. Station
New York, NY 10012

| | |
|---|---|
| TYPE | Motion Pictures |
| CREDITS | City Unplugged |

Ilkka Jarvilaturi . . . . . . . . . . . . . . . . . . . Director/Producer
Sophie Kermarec . . . . . . . . . . . . . . . . . . . . . VP, Literary

## USA NETWORKS
PHONE . . . . . . . . . . . . . . 212-408-9100/310-277-0199
FAX . . . . . . . . . . . . . . . . 212-408-8228/310-201-2365
WEBSITE . . . . . . . . . . . . . . . . . . . http://usanetwork.com
1230 Avenue of the Americas
New York, NY 10020

| | |
|---|---|
| TYPE | Motion Pictures + Television |
| CREDITS | USA Series Originals - USA High - Silk Stalkings - La Femme Nikita - Big Easy - Sliders - Mystery Science Theatre 3000 |
| COMMENTS | Includes USA Networks & The Sci-Fi Channel. |

Stephen Brenner . . . . . . . . . . . . . . . . . . Pres., Operations
Stephen Chao . . . . . . . . . . . . . . . . . . . Pres., Programming
Rod Perth . . . . . . . . Pres., USA Networks Ent.(LA)/EVP Progr. USA Networks
Douglas Hamilton . . . . . . . . . . . . . CFO/Sr. VP, Administration
Tim Brooks . . . . . . . . . . . . . . . . . . . . . . Sr. VP, Research
David Armstrong . . . . . . . . . . . . . . . . VP, Program Acquistions
Gordon Beck . . . . . . . . . . . . . . . . . VP, Production & Sports
Jane Blaney . . . . . . VP, Program Scheduling & Acquisitions Development
Bonnie Hammer . . . . . . . . VP, Original Prod. & Current Programming (NY)
Medora Heilbron . . . . . . . . . . . . . . VP, Series Development (LA)
Neil Hoffman . . . . . . . VP, Programming & Strategic Programming (NY)
Monia Joblin . . . . . . VP, Orig. Prog./VP, Orig. Series Dev. Sci-Fi Channel
Richard Lynn . . . . . . . . VP, Business Affairs/General Counsel (NY)
Barry Schulman . . . . . . . . . . . . . . . . . . . VP, Programming
Ian Valentine . . . . . . . . . . . . VP, Long Form Programming (LA)
Fern Field . . . . . . . . . . . . . . . . Dir., Original Programming
Kate McArdle . . . . . . . . . . . . Dir., Long Form Programming

## USONIA PICTURES, INC.
PHONE . . . . . . . . . . . . . . . . . . . . . . . . . . . 310-476-2770
FAX . . . . . . . . . . . . . . . . . . . . . . . . . . . . . 310-476-5164
EMAIL . . . . . . . . . . . . . usoniapictures@worldnet.att.net
1000 Bel Air Rd.
Los Angeles, CA 90077

| | |
|---|---|
| TYPE | Motion Pictures |
| CREDITS | Executive Power - Double Exposure |

Richard J. Naegele . . . . . . . . . . . . . . . . . . . . President
Wm Brent Bell . . . . . . . . . . . . . . . . . . . . Vice President

## *UTOPIA FILMS
PHONE . . . . . . . . . . . . . . . . . . . . . . . . . . . 213-876-7075
FAX . . . . . . . . . . . . . . . . . . . . . . . . . . . . . 213-876-9988
EMAIL . . . . . . . . . . . . . . . . . . . . utopian@pacbell.net
7887 Hillside Ave.
Los Angeles, CA 90046

| | |
|---|---|
| TYPE | Motion Pictures + Television + Interactive Multimedia |
| CREDITS | Clubland - On the Line - Dead Dog Blues - The Price of Love - Deceoptions |

Guy J. Louthan . . . . . . . . . . . . . . . . . . . . . . Producer
John M. Leveson . . . . . . . . . . . . . . . . . VP, Development
Laura M. Chiasson . . . . . . . . . . . . . Development Assistant

## UTOPIA PICTS./CARL BORACK PRODUCTIONS
PHONE . . . . . . . . . . . . . . . . . . . . . . . . . . . 213-650-8053
FAX . . . . . . . . . . . . . . . . . . . . . . . . . . . . . 213-650-4733
1015 Gayley Ave., Ste. 1020
Los Angeles, CA 90028

| | |
|---|---|
| TYPE | Motion Pictures |
| CREDITS | Shiloh - Red Ribbon Blues - Across the Tracks |

Dale Rosenbloom . . . . . . . . . . . . . . Director/Writer/Producer
Carl Borack . . . . . . . . . . . . . . . . . . . . . . . . Producer
Lisa Vasconcellos . . . . . . . . . . . . . . . . . . . . Assistant

## VAL D'ORO ENTERTAINMENT
PHONE . . . . . . . . . . . . . . . . . . . . . . . . . . . 310-656-8555
FAX . . . . . . . . . . . . . . . . . . . . . . . . . . . . . 310-656-8560
EMAIL . . . . . . . . . . . . . . . . . . . . . valdoro@aol.com
1437 7th St., Ste. 200
Santa Monica, CA 90401

| | |
|---|---|
| TYPE | Motion Pictures + Television |

Steven E. de Souza . . . . . . . . . . . . . . . . . . . . President
Jeri Barchilon de Souza . . . . . . . . . . . . . . . Vice President
Pamela G. Coritz . . . . . . . . . . . . . . . . . . Office Manager
Michael Peterson . . . . . . . . . . . . . . . . . . Script Assistant

## VALENTE PRODS., RENEE
PHONE . . . . . . . . . . . . . . . . . . . . . . . . . . . 213-969-1541
13601 Ventura Blvd., Ste. 195
Sherman Oaks, CA 91423

| | |
|---|---|
| TYPE | Motion Pictures + Television |
| CREDITS | The Margaret Mitchell Story - Man From Left Field - Man Upstairs |

Renee Valente . . . . . . . . . . . . . . . . . . . . . . . Producer

## VANDERKLOOT FILM & TELEVISION INC.
PHONE . . . . . . . . . . . . . . . . . . . . . . . . . . . 404-221-0236
FAX . . . . . . . . . . . . . . . . . . . . . . . . . . . . . 404-221-1057
EMAIL . . . . . . . . . . . . . . vanderkloot@compuserve.com
WEBSITE . . . . . . . . . . . . . . http://www.magicklantern.com
750 Ralph McGill Blvd. NE
Atlanta, GA 30312

| | |
|---|---|
| TYPE | Motion Pictures + Television + Documentaries + Animation |
| CREDITS | The Big Adventure Series - Cumberland: An Island in Time |
| COMMENTS | Also: www.LITTLEMAMMOTH.com |

William VanDerKloot . . . . . . . . . . President/Producer/Director
Charlie Willis . . . . . . . . . . . . . . VP, Magick Lantern/President
Paul A. Johns . . . . . . . . . . . . . . . . . . . . . . Controller
Diane Simone . . . . . . . . . . . . . . Develop./Special Projects
Blaine Cone . . . . . . . . . . . . . . . . . 3D Animation Supervisor
Melissa Devereaux . . . . . . . . . . . . . Animation/SPX Producer
Kerry Kenemer . . . . . . . . . . . . . . . . . . . Designer/Director
Barbara Wunschel . . . . . . . . . Operations Director, Magick Lantern

## VANGUARD FILMS
PHONE . . . . . . . . . . . . . . . . . . . . . . . . . . . 310-888-8020
FAX . . . . . . . . . . . . . . . . . . . . . . . . . . . . . 310-306-4910
EMAIL . . . . . . . . . . . . . . . . vangrdprod@earthlink.net
WEBSITE . . . . . . . . . . . . . . . . http://vanguardfilms.com
1230 La Collina Dr.
Beverly Hills, CA 90210

| | |
|---|---|
| TYPE | Motion Pictures + Television + Documentaries |
| DEAL | DreamWorks SKG |
| CREDITS | 7 Years in Tibet - On The Road - Marley - Sarafina - Shrek - Galaxy High |

John Williams . . . . . . . . . . . . . . . . . . . . . . . Producer
Brandi McDougall . . . . . . . . . . . . Vice President (310-888-1843)
Wes Moore . . . . . . . . . . . . . . Vice President (SF) (415-921-0721)
Eric Bennett . . . . . . . . . . . . . . Vice President (310-888-8841)
Gwen Lighter . . . . . . . . . . . . . . . . . . . . . Vice President

**VANGUARD PRODUCTIONS**
PHONE . . . . . . . . . . . . . . . . . . . . . . . . . . . . . . . . . 310-306-4910
EMAIL . . . . . . . . . . . . . . . . . . . . . . . . vangrdprod@earthlink.net
WEBSITE . . . . . . . . . . . . . . . . . . . http://www.emamulti.com/vanguard
12111 Beatrice St.
Culver City, CA 90230

TYPE        Motion Pictures
CREDITS     We The People - The Bad Pack - Cross Dreams - Wanted
Terence M. O'Keefe . . . . . . . . . . . . . . . . . . . . . Writer/Producer/Director
Bennett J. Fidlow . . . . . . . . . . . . . . . . . . . . . . . . . . VP, Creative Affairs
Bruce Miyaki . . . . . . . . . . . . . . . . . . . . . . . . . . . . . . VP, Development
S. Drew Stotesbery . . . . . . . . . . . . . . . . . . . . . . . . . . VP, Production
Patrick Earls . . . . . . . . . . . . . . . . . . . . . . . . . . . . . . . . Development

**VAULT, INC., THE**
PHONE . . . . . . . . . . . . . . . . . . . . . . . . . . . . . . . . . 818-556-5175
FAX . . . . . . . . . . . . . . . . . . . . . . . . . . . . . . . . . . . 818-556-5202
3723 W. Olive Ave.
Burbank, CA 91505

TYPE        Motion Pictures + Television
CREDITS     The Last Supper - Campfire Tales
Matt Cooper . . . . . . . . . . . . . . . . . . . . . . . . Producer/Director/Writer
Lori Miller . . . . . . . . . . . . . . . . . . . . . . . . . . . . . . . . . . . Producer
David Cooper . . . . . . . . . . . . . . . . . . . . . . . . . . . Executive Producer
Bryan C. Bishop . . . . . . . . . . . . Development Assistant/Creative Executive

**VECCHIO ENT., JOSEPH S.**
PHONE . . . . . . . . . . . . . . . . . . . . . . . . . . . . . . . . . 818-906-0999
FAX . . . . . . . . . . . . . . . . . . . . . . . . . . . . . . . . . . . 818-788-9900
3599 Beverly Glen Terrace
Sherman Oaks, CA 91423

TYPE        Motion Pictures + Television
CREDITS     Oscar - Sunchaser - Wild Card - Westies - Stranger In A
            Strange Land - The Wanderer
Joseph S. Vecchio . . . . . . . . . . . . . . . . . . . . . . . . . . . . Producer
Julie Adams . . . . . . . . . . . . . . . . . . . . . . . . Adminstrative Assistant

**VENTANA FILMS**
PHONE . . . . . . . . . . . . . . . . . . . . . . . . . . . . . . . . . 213-876-3331
EMAIL . . . . . . . . . . . . . . . . . . . . . . . . . . . . . . . lafilm@aol.com
7440 Palo Vista Dr., Ste. 100
Los Angeles, CA 90046-1311

TYPE        Motion Pictures
CREDITS     Better Watch Out - Cabeza de Vaca - Cronos
COMMENTS    Also: Commercials.
Arthur H. Gorson . . . . . . . . . . . . . . . . . . . . President/Head, Production
Julio Solorzano . . . . . . . . . . . . . . . . . . . . . . . . . . . . . . . . Chairman
Bernard Nussbaumer . . . . . . . . . . . . . . . . . . . . . . . Sr. Vice President
Francisco Varese . . . . . . . . . . . . . . . . . . . . . . . . . . . . Field Producer

**VENTUREWEST PICTURES**
PHONE . . . . . . . . . . . . . . . . . . . . . . . . . . . . . . . . . 310-545-1011
FAX . . . . . . . . . . . . . . . . . . . . . . . . . . . . . . . . . . . 310-372-9810
8626 Skyline Dr.
Los Angeles, CA 90046

TYPE        Motion Pictures + Television
CREDITS     The Willies - Dream Team - Jurisdiction - Soldier of
            Fortune
Steven Gary Banks . . . . . . . . . . . . . . . . . . . . . . . . Partner/Producer
Terry Spazek . . . . . . . . . . . . . . . . . . . . . . . . . . . . Partner/Producer
Markus J. Woolley . . . . . . . . . . . . . . . . . . . . . . . . Partner/Producer
Mary Ann Ellis . . . . . . . . . . . . . . . . . . . . . . . . Development Executive

**VERDON-CEDRIC PRODS.**
PHONE . . . . . . . . . . . . . . . . . . . . . . . . . . . . . . . . . 310-274-7253
9350 Wilshire Blvd., Ste. 303
Beverly Hills, CA 90212

TYPE        Motion Pictures
COMMENTS    No Unsolicited Scripts.
Sidney Poitier . . . . . . . . . . . . . . . . . . . . Producer/Director/Writer/Actor
Susan Garrison . . . . . . . . . . . . . . . . . . . . Exec. Asst./Dir., Development

**VH1 (MUSIC FIRST)**
PHONE . . . . . . . . . . . . . . . . . . . . . 212-846-7800/310-752-8000
WEBSITE . . . . . . . . . . . . . . . . . . . . . . . . . . . http://www.vh1.com
1515 Broadway
New York, NY 10036

TYPE        Television
COMMENTS    Also: 2600 Colorado Ave., Santa Monica, CA 90404.
            Atlanta: 404-814-7800 & Chicago: 312-755-0310
John Sykes . . . . . . . . . . . . . . . . . . . . . . . . . . . . . . . . President
Mike Benson . . . . . . . . . . . . . . . . Sr. VP, Promotion & Program Planning
Jeffrey Gaspin . . . . . . . . . . . . . . . . . Sr. VP, Programming & Production
Wayne Isaak . . . . . . . . . . . . . . . . Sr. VP, Music & Talent Relations
Rob Barnett . . . . . . . . . . . . . . . . . . . . . . . . . VP, Program Planning
Bill Brand . . . . . . . . . . . . . . . . . . . . . VP, Programming & Production
Eddie Dalva . . . . . . . . . . . . . . . . VP, Acquisitions & Co-Productions
Linda Danner . . . . . . . . . . . . . VP/Creative Director, On-Air Promotion
Colleen Fahey Rush . . . . . . . . . . . . . . . . VP, Research & Planning
Bill Flanagan . . . . . . . . . . . . . . . . . . . . . . VP/Editorial Director
Bruce Gillmer . . . . . . . . . . . . . . . . . VP, Music & Talent Relations
Jill Newfield . . . . . . . . . . . . VP, Business Affairs & General Counsel
Michael Tierney . . . . . . . . . . . . . . . . . . VP, Music Programming
Lauren Zalaznick . . . . . . . . . . . VP, Original Programming & Development

**VIA ROSA PRODUCTIONS**
PHONE . . . . . . . . . . . . . . . . . . . . . . . . . . . . . . . . . 310-656-6252
FAX . . . . . . . . . . . . . . . . . . . . . . . . . . . . . . . . . . . 310-656-6256
506 Santa Monica Blvd., Ste. 217
Santa Monica, CA 90401

TYPE        Motion Pictures
DEAL        Touchstone Pictures
CREDITS     One Fine Day - A Thousand Acres - Deep End of the
            Ocean
Michelle Pfeiffer . . . . . . . . . . . . . . . . . . . . . . . . . . . . . Producer
Kate Guinzburg . . . . . . . . . . . . . . . . . . . . . . . . . . . . . Producer
Mary Kohnert . . . . . . . . . . . . . . . . . . . . . . . . . . . Development

**VIACOM ENTERTAINMENT GROUP**
PHONE . . . . . . . . . . . . . . . . . . . . . . . . . . . . . . . . . 323-956-5000
5555 Melrose Ave.
Hollywwod, CA 90038

TYPE        Motion Pictures + Television
Jonathan L. Dolgen . . . . . . . . . . . . . . . . . . . . . . . . . . . Chairman
Thomas McGrath . . . . . . . . . . . . . . . . . . . . . Exec. Vice President
Richard Cooperstien . . . . . . . . . . . . . . . . . VP, Business Development

**VIACOM PRODUCTIONS**
PHONE . . . . . . . . . . . . . . . . . . . . . . . . . . . . . . . . . 310-234-5000
FAX . . . . . . . . . . . . . . . . . . . . . . . . . . . . . . . . . . . 310-234-5059
10880 Wilshire Blvd., Ste. 1101
Los Angeles, CA 90024

TYPE        Television
CREDITS     Diagnosis Murder - Sabrina The Teenage Witch
Perry Simon . . . . . . . . . . . . . . . . . . . President, Viacom Television
Steven Gordon . . . . . . . . . . . . . . . . . . . Sr. VP, Creative Affairs
Beth Klein . . . . . . . . . . . . . . . . . . . . . Sr. VP, Casting & Talent
Adene Lacy . . . . . . . . . . . . . . . . . Sr. VP, Finance & Operations
David Lavin . . . . . . . . . . . . . . . . . . . Sr. VP, Business Affairs
Paul Mason . . . . . . . . . . . . . . . . . . . . . . Sr. VP, Production
Lorna Shepard . . . . . . . . . . . . . . . . . . Sr. VP, Business Affairs
Michele Conklin . . . . . . . . . . . . . . . . . . . VP, Creative Affairs
James Goodman . . . . . . . . . . . . . . . . . . . VP, Business Affairs
Victor Salant . . . . . . . . . . . . . VP, Controller of Production
Chris Sanagustin . . . . . . . . . . . . . . . . . Dir., Creative Affairs
Jim Fuller . . . . . . . . . . . . . . . . . . . . . . . . . . . . Story Editor

**VICTOR & GRAIS PRODS.**
PHONE . . . . . . . . . . . . . . . . . . . . . . . . . . . . . . . . . 310-247-1116
FAX . . . . . . . . . . . . . . . . . . . . . . . . . . . . . . . . . . . 310-247-1197
132B S. Lasky Dr.
Beverly Hills, CA 90212

TYPE        Motion Pictures + Television
CREDITS     Poltergeist - Marked For Death - Stephen King's
            Sleepwalkers
COMMENTS    Also: Publishing, Management.
Mark Victor . . . . . . . . . . . . . . . . . . . . . Producer/Writer/Manager
Michael Grais . . . . . . . . . . . . . . . . . . . . Producer/Writer/Manager
Mark Skelly . . . . . . . . . . . . . . . . . . . . . . . . . . . . . . . Producer

# COMPANIES AND STAFF

**VICTOR MOTION PICTURES**
PHONE . . . . . . . . . . . . . . . . . . . . . . . . . . . . 310-478-1806
FAX . . . . . . . . . . . . . . . . . . . . . . . . . . . . . . 310-478-1806
1506 Corinth Ave., Ste. 202
Los Angeles, CA 90025
TYPE          Motion Pictures
CREDITS       Victor's Big Score - Camp Stalag
COMMENTS      Accepts no submissions!
Brian Anthony . . . . . . . . . . . . . . . . . . . . . . Producer/Director
William A. Walker Jr. . . . . . . . . . . . . . . . . . . . Writer/Producer

**VICTORY ENTERTAINMENT, INC.**
PHONE . . . . . . . . . . . . . . . . . . . . . . . . . . . . 818-980-3200
FAX . . . . . . . . . . . . . . . . . . . . . . . . . . . . . . 818-980-9250
10153 1/2 Riverside Dr., Ste. 422
Toluca Lake, CA 91602
TYPE          Television + Motion Pictures
CREDITS       Silent Bomb - Issy's Planet
COMMENTS      No Unsolicited Scripts.
Kim Fields Freeman . . . . . . . . . . . . . . . . . . . . President/CEO
Darrell D. Miller . . . . . . . . . . . . . . . . COO/General Counsel
Dan Holton . . . . . . . . . . . . . . . . . . . . Sr. VP, Television
Linda Morris-Smith . . . . . . . . . . . . . . Sr. VP, Feature Films
Lisa Gonzalez . . . . . . . . . . . . . . . . . . . . . Office Manager

**VIDE-U PRODUCTIONS**
PHONE . . . . . . . . . . . . . . . . . . . . . . . . . . . . 310-276-5509
FAX . . . . . . . . . . . . . . . . . . . . . . . . . . . . . . 310-276-1183
EMAIL . . . . . . . . . . . . . . . . . . . . . . . . . brad3845@aol.com
9976 W. Wanda Dr.
Beverly Hills, CA 90210
TYPE          Motion Pictures + Television
DEAL          Showtime Networks Inc.
CREDITS       Dakota - The Lennon Conspiracy - Has Beens
COMMENTS      Also: Cable, Music Videos & Robots for the Industry.
Bradley Freidman . . . . . . . . . . . . . . . . . . Executive Producer
Fred Wietzsche . . . . . . . . . . . . . . . . . . . . . . . . . Director
Sandy Corner . . . . . . . . . . . . . . . . . . . . . . . . Development

**VIDEO DIMENSIONS INC.**
PHONE . . . . . . . . . . . . . . . . . . . . . . . . . . . . 213-466-6411
FAX . . . . . . . . . . . . . . . . . . . . . . . . . . . . . . 213-466-1557
EMAIL . . . . . . . . . . . . . . . . . . dwight@blackshearcomm.com
P.O. Box 2310
Hollywood, CA 90078
TYPE          Television + Interactive Multimedia + Documentaries
CREDITS       Eye on L.A. - Two on the Town
Dwight Blackshear . . . . . . . . . . . . . . . . . . Executive Producer
Stu Hall . . . . . . . . . . . . . . . . . . . . . . . . . . . . Producer

**VIENNA PRODUCTIONS**
PHONE . . . . . . . . . . . . . . . . . . . . . . . . . . . . 818-766-3572
FAX . . . . . . . . . . . . . . . . . . . . . . . . . . . . . . 818-766-6640
EMAIL . . . . . . . . . . . . . . . . . . . . . . . . . viennal@soca.com
8033 Sunset Blvd., Ste. 450
Los Angeles, CA 90046
TYPE          Motion Pictures + Television + Documentaries +
              Interactive Multimedia
CREDITS       Recess - Blue Angels - Thunder Over The Pacific - One
              Vision
Rob Stone . . . . . . . . . . . . . . . . . . . . . . . . . . President
Alex Eastburg . . . . . . . . . . . . . . . . . . . Development Executive

**VIEW ASKEW PRODUCTIONS, INC.**
PHONE . . . . . . . . . . . . . . . . . . . . . . . . . . . . 732-842-6933
FAX . . . . . . . . . . . . . . . . . . . . . . . . . . . . . . 732-842-3772
EMAIL . . . . . . . . . . . . . . . . . . . . . . . tooaskew@aol.com
WEBSITE . . . . . . . . . . . . . . . . . . . . http://www.viewaskew.com
69 Broad St.
Red Bank, NJ 07701
TYPE          Motion Pictures
DEAL          Miramax Films
CREDITS       Chasing Amy - Mallrats - Clerks
Kevin Smith . . . . . . . . . . . . . . . . . . . . . . . . . President
Scott Mosier . . . . . . . . . . . . . . . . . . . . . . . Vice President
Kim Loughran . . . . . . . . . . . . . . . . . . . Development Executive

**VIEWPOINT PRODUCTIONS**
PHONE . . . . . . . . . . . . . . . . . . . . . . . . . . . . 818-509-8966
3724 Vantage Ave.
Studio City, CA 91604
TYPE          Motion Pictures + Television
CREDITS       Convict Cowboy - The Lazarus Man - Black Fox
Ellen Levine . . . . . . . . . . . . . . . . . . . . . . . . . Partner
Carol Stanley . . . . . . . . . . . . . . . . . . . . . . . . . Partner

**VILLAGE ROADSHOW PICTURES**
PHONE . . . . . . . . . . . . . . . . . . 818-954-1998/310-282-5300
FAX . . . . . . . . . . . . . . . . . . . . 818-954-2249/310-282-0078
EMAIL . . . . . . . . . . . . . . . . . . . . . . . planbermam@aol.com
4000 Warner Blvd., Bldg. 139, Room 25
Burbank, CA 91522
TYPE          Motion Pictures + Television
DEAL          Warner Bros. Pictures
CREDITS       Matrix - Deep Blue Sea
COMMENTS      Also: c/o Village Roadshow Pictures, 2121 Avenue of the
              Stars, Ste. #1590, Los Angeles, CA 90067.
Bruce Berman . . . . . . . . . . . . . . . . . . . . . . Chairman/CEO
Greg Coote . . . . . . . . . . . . . . . . . . . . . . . President/COO
Bernie Goldmann . . . . . . . . . . . . . . . . . . Pres., Production
Jeffrey Hayes . . . . . . . . . . . . . . . . . . Pres., VRP Television
Robert Meyers . . . . . . . . . . . . . . . . . Pres., VRP Worldwide
Matt Bierman . . . . . . . . . . . . . . . . . . . Sr. VP, Production
Marina Glass . . . . . . . . . . . . . . . . . . . . . VP, Production
Kevin McMahon . . . . . . . . . . . . . . . . . VP, Creative Affairs
Dennis Shue . . . . . . . . . . . . . . . . . . . VP, Creative Affairs
Suzy Figueroa . . . . . . . . . . . . . . . Exec. Asst. to B. Berman
Cathleen Hoadley . . . . . . . . . . . . Exec. Asst. to B. Goldmann
Jason Traub . . . . . . . . . . . . . . . . . . . . . . . . No Title

**VILLARD PRODS., DIMITRI**
PHONE . . . . . . . . . . . . . . . . . . . . . . . . . . . . 310-229-4545
FAX . . . . . . . . . . . . . . . . . . . . . . . . . . . . . . 310-854-6044
EMAIL . . . . . . . . . . . . . . . . . . . . . . . . dvillard@loop.com
8721 Santa Monica Blvd., Ste. 100
Los Angeles, CA 90069-4511
TYPE          Motion Pictures
CREDITS       Flight of the Navigator - Once Bitten - In Love & War
Dimitri Villard . . . . . . . . . . . . . . . . . . . . . . . President
Wendy Colbert . . . . . . . . . . . . . . . . . . . . . . . . Assistant

**VISION FILMS**
PHONE . . . . . . . . . . . . . . . . . . . . . . . . . . . . 818-784-1702
FAX . . . . . . . . . . . . . . . . . . . . . . . . . . . . . . 818-788-3715
EMAIL . . . . . . . . . . . . . . . . . . . . visionfilms@earthlink.net
4626 Lemona Ave.
Sherman Oaks, CA 91403
TYPE          Television + Feature Direct to Video + Documentaries
CREDITS       Fatal Passion - Magic of SPFX - Alexandria - Movie Magic -
              Ushuaia - Flights Of Discovery
Stephen Rocha . . . . . . . . . . . . . . . . . . . . . . . President
Lise Romanoff . . . . . . . . . . . . . . . . . . . . . . Vice President

**VISION MEDIA/LXD INC.**
PHONE . . . . . . . . . . . . . . . . . . . . . . . . . . . . 310-589-0022
FAX . . . . . . . . . . . . . . . . . . . . . . . . . . . . . . 310-589-9301
EMAIL . . . . . . . . . . . . . . . . . . . . . . . . vmlxd@aol.com
29169 Heathercliff Rd., Ste. 220
Malibu, CA 90265
TYPE          Motion Pictures + Television
CREDITS       Lifestyles of Xtreme & Demented- Unspoken Truth - The
              Vow - 1000 White Women - Our Mother's Murder
Austin Hearst . . . . . . . . . . . . . . . . . . . . . Owner/Producer
Paul Taublieb . . . . . . . . . . . . . . . . . . . . . Owner/Producer
Penny Davidson . . . . . . . . . . . . . . . . . . Creative Executive
Pam Miller . . . . . . . . . . . . . . . . . . . . Motorsports Producer

**VISIONARY ENTERTAINMENT**
PHONE . . . . . . . . . . . . . . . . . . . . . . . . . . . . 213-848-9538
FAX . . . . . . . . . . . . . . . . . . . . . . . . . . . . . . 213-848-8614
1309 N. Harper Ave.
Los Angeles, CA 90046
TYPE          Motion Pictures + Television
CREDITS       Wigstock: The Movie
Tom Parziale . . . . . . . . . . . . . . . . . . . . . Partner/Producer
David Sweeney . . . . . . . . . . . . . . . . . . . . Partner/Producer
Audrey Hauson . . . . . . . . . . . . . . . . . Asst. to Tom Parziale

# COMPANIES AND STAFF

**VISTA STREET ENTERTAINMENT**
PHONE . . . . . . . . . . . . . . . . . . . . . . . . . . . . . . 310-556-3074
FAX . . . . . . . . . . . . . . . . . . . . . . . . . . . . . . . . . 310-556-8815
9831 W. Pico Blvd., Ste. 4
Los Angeles, CA 90035

| | |
|---|---|
| TYPE | Feature Direct to Video + Television + Interactive Multimedia + Motion Pictures + Syndication + Animation |
| CREDITS | Witchcraft 1-10 - Dead By Dawn - Strangers - Sisters - Sweet Evil |

Jerry Feifer . . . . . . . . . . . . . . . . . . . . . . . . . . . . . . . . . . President
Michael Feifer . . . . . . . . . . . . . . . . . . . . . . . . . VP, Production
Robyn Mellin . . . . . . . . . . . . . . . . . . . . . . . . . . . . . Producer

**VIVIANO ENTERTAINMENT**
PHONE . . . . . . . . . . . . . . . . . . . . . . . . . . . . . . 310-247-1221
FAX . . . . . . . . . . . . . . . . . . . . . . . . . . . . . . . . . 310-247-8734
EMAIL . . . . . . . . . . . . . . . . . . . . . . . . . . . bviviano@aol.com
9107 Wilshire Blvd., Ste. 500
Beverly Hills, CA 90210

| | |
|---|---|
| TYPE | Motion Pictures + Television + Animation + Feature Direct to Video + Documentaries |
| CREDITS | Bulletproof - Caught in the Act - Black Box - Three to Tango - Alibi |

Bettina Sofia Viviano . . . . . . . . . . . . . Producer/President/Literary Manager
Gregory Awada . . . . . . . . . . . . . . . . . . . . Dir., Development

***VOIGHT ENTERTAINMENT, JON**
PHONE . . . . . . . . . . . . . . . . . . . . . . . . . . . . . . 310-843-0223
FAX . . . . . . . . . . . . . . . . . . . . . . . . . . . . . . . . . 310-553-9895
EMAIL . . . . . . . . . . . . . . . . . . . . . . . . . . . . patfilm@aol.com
1901 Ave. of the Stars, Ste. 605
Los Angeles, CA 90067

| | |
|---|---|
| TYPE | Motion Pictures + Television + Documentaries |
| CREDITS | Tin Soldier - The Fixer - New York Wars |

Jon Voight . . . . . . . . . . . . . . . . . . . . . . . . . . . . . . . President
Patrick Ewald . . . . . . . . . . . . . . . . . . VP, Production & Development
Michael Pellettieri . . . . . . . . . . . . . . . . . . Development Associate
Justin Valentine . . . . . . . . . . . . . . . . . . . . Creative Consultant

**VON ZERNECK-SERTNER FILMS**
PHONE . . . . . . . . . . . . . . . . . . . . . . . . . . . . . . 818-766-2610
FAX . . . . . . . . . . . . . . . . . . . . . . . . . . . . . . . . . 818-766-7423
EMAIL . . . . . . . . . . . . . . . . . . . . . . . . . . . vzsfilms@aol.com
12001 Ventura Place, Ste. 400
Studio City, CA 91604

| | |
|---|---|
| TYPE | Television + Motion Pictures |
| CREDITS | Crazy Horse - Murder Live! - Robin Cook's Invasion |

Robert Sertner . . . . . . . . . . . . . . . . . . . . . . . . . . . . . . Partner
Frank von Zerneck . . . . . . . . . . . . . . . . . . . . . . . . . . . Partner
Randy Sutter . . . . . . . . . . . . . . . . . . . . . . Sr. VP, Production
Erik Storey . . . . . . . . . . . . . . . . . . . . . . . . VP, Development
Ted Babcock . . . . . . . . . . . . . . . . . . . . VP, Post Production
Peter Sadowski . . . . . . . . . . . . . . . . . . . . . . . VP, Production
Jean Abounader . . . . . . . . . . . . . . . . . . . . . . . . . . Producer
Rick Arredondo . . . . . . . . . . . . . . . . . . . . . . . . . . Producer
Richard Fischoff . . . . . . . . . . . . . . . . . . . . . . . . . . Producer
Rochelle Shaposhnick . . . . . . . . . . . . . . . . Dir., Development
Danielle von Zerneck Fearnley . . . . . . . . . . . . Dir., Development
Skates Naiman . . . . . . . . . . . . . . . . . . . . . . Dir., Production
Nancy S. Mouton . . . . . . . . . . . . . . . . . . . . Executive Assistant

**W.B. TELEVISION NETWORK**
PHONE . . . . . . . . . . . . . . . . . . . . . . . . . . . . . . 818-977-5000
FAX . . . . . . . . . . . . . . . . . . . . . . . . . . . . . . . . . 818-977-6336
c/o Warner Bros.
4000 Warner Blvd., Bldg. 34-R
Burbank, CA 91522-0001

| | |
|---|---|
| TYPE | Television |

Jamie Kellner . . . . . . . . . . . . . . . . . . . . . . . Head, Network
Garth Ancier . . . . . . . . . . . . . . . . . . . . . . Pres., Entertainment
Susanne Daniels . . . . . . . . . . . . . . . . . Exec. VP, Programming
Jordan Levin . . . . . . . . . . . . . . . . . . . . . . Sr. VP, Development
John Litvack . . . . . . . . . . . . . . . . . Sr. VP, Current Programming
John Maatta . . . . . . . . . . . . . . . . . . . . . . . . . Sr. VP, Legal
Mitchell Nedick . . . . . . . . . . . . . . . Sr. VP, Finance/Administration
Michael Ross . . . . . . . . . . . . . . . . . . . . Sr. VP, Business Affairs

**WACHS CO., THE ROBERT D.**
PHONE . . . . . . . . . . . . . . . . . . . . . . . . . . . . . . 310-276-1123
FAX . . . . . . . . . . . . . . . . . . . . . . . . . . . . . . . . . 310-276-5572
345 N. Maple Dr., Ste. 179
Beverly Hills, CA 90210

| | |
|---|---|
| TYPE | Motion Pictures + Television |
| CREDITS | Another 48 Hours - Beverly Hills Cop II - Raw - Coming to America |

Robert Wachs . . . . . . . . . . . . . . . . . . . . . . . . . . . . No Title
Sandra Reid . . . . . . . . . . . . . . . . . . . . . . . Executive Assistant

**WAGNER PRODS., INC., RAYMOND**
PHONE . . . . . . . . . . . . . . . . . . . . . . . . . . . . . . 310-278-1970
FAX . . . . . . . . . . . . . . . . . . . . . . . . . . . . . . . . . 310-274-2662
10377 Rochester Ave.
Los Angeles, CA 90024

| | |
|---|---|
| TYPE | Motion Pictures + Television + Animation |
| CREDITS | Turner & Hooch - Run - Fifty/Fifty |

Raymond Wagner . . . . . . . . . . . . . . . . . . President/Producer
Christine McBride . . . . . . . . . . . . . . . . . . Dir., Development

**WAISBREN ENTERPRISES, BRAD**
PHONE . . . . . . . . . . . . . . . . . . . . . . . . . . . . . . 818-506-3000
EMAIL . . . . . . . . . . . . . . . . . . . . . . . . waisbren@earthlink.net
P.O. Box 8741
Universal City, CA 91618

| | |
|---|---|
| TYPE | Motion Pictures + Television + Animation |
| CREDITS | NTV Thursday Special - Amazing Animals - World Star Quiz - Just for the Record |

Brad Waisbren . . . . . . . . . . . . . . . . . . . . . . . . . . . Producer
Marci Higer . . . . . . . . . . . . . . . . . . . . . . . . . . Development
David Bjerum . . . . . . . . . . . . . . . . . . . . . . . Business Affairs

**WALD ENTERTAINMENT INC., JEFF**
PHONE . . . . . . . . . . . . . . . . . . . . . . . . . . . . . . 310-289-0155
FAX . . . . . . . . . . . . . . . . . . . . . . . . . . . . . . . . . 310-289-1967
8900 Wilshire, Ste. 101
Beverly Hills, CA 90211

| | |
|---|---|
| TYPE | Motion Pictures + Television |
| CREDITS | 2 Days in the Valley - Switched at Birth - Behind Bars |

Jeff Wald . . . . . . . . . . . . . . . . . . . . . . . President/Chairman
Steven Thomas . . . . . . . . . . . . . . . . . . . . . . Vice President
Dana Gonshor . . . . . . . . . . . . . . . . . . . . . Executive Assistant

**WALLACH ENTERTAINMENT**
PHONE . . . . . . . . . . . . . . . . . . . . . . . . . . . . . . 310-278-4574
FAX . . . . . . . . . . . . . . . . . . . . . . . . . . . . . . . . . 310-273-0548
1400 Braeridge Drive
Beverly Hills, CA 90210

| | |
|---|---|
| TYPE | Television |
| CREDITS | Natl.Spelling Bee - Superdogs - Super Jocks - Gramblings White Tiger - If I Were President |

George Wallach . . . . . . . . . . . . . . . . . President/Personal Manager

**WALT DISNEY COMPANY, THE**
PHONE . . . . . . . . . . . . . . . . . . . . . . . . . . . . . . 818-560-1000
WEBSITE . . . . . . . . . . . . . . . . . . . . . . . . http://www.disney.com
500 S. Buena Vista St.
Burbank, CA 91521-0001

| | |
|---|---|
| TYPE | Motion Pictures |

Michael D. Eisner . . . . . . . . . . . . . . . . Chairman of the Board/CEO
Roy E. Disney . . . . . . . . . . . . . . . . . Vice Chairman of the Board
Louis M. Meisinger . . . . . . . . . . . . . . Exec. VP/General Counsel
Thomas O. Staggs . . . . . . . . . . . . . . . . . . . . Exec. VP/CFO
Sanford Litvack . . . . . . . . . . . Sr. Exec. VP/Chief of Corporate Operations
John F. Cooke . . . . . . . . . . . . . . . . . Exec. VP, Corporate Affairs
Peter E. Murphy . . . . . . . . . . . . Exec. VP/Chief Strategic Officer
John J. Garand . . . . . . . . . . . . . . . . Sr. VP, Planning & Control
Marsha L. Reed . . . . . . . . . . . . . . . . . . . . Corporate Secretary

# COMPANIES AND STAFF

## WALT DISNEY PICTURES/TOUCHSTONE PICTURES
PHONE . . . . . . . . . . . . . . . . . . . . . . . . . . . . . . . . . . . . . . 818-560-1000
WEBSITE . . . . . . . . . . . . . . . . . . . . . . . . . . . . http://www.disney.com
500 S. Buena Vista St.
Burbank, CA 91521-0001

TYPE         Motion Pictures

Joe Roth . . . . . . . . . . . . . . . . . . . . . . . . Chairman, Walt Disney Studios
Richard W. Cook . . . . . . . . . . Chairman, Walt Disney Motion Pictures Group
Donald DeLine . . . . . . . . . . . . . . . . . . . . . President, Touchstone Pictures
David E. Vogel . . . . . . . . . . . . . . . . . . . . President, Walt Disney Pictures
Peter Schneider . . . . . . . . . . Pres., Feature Animation & WD Theatrical Prods.
Kathy Nelson . . . . . . . . . . . . . . . . . . . . . . . . . . . . . President, Music
Bernardine Brandis . . . . . . Exec. VP, The Walt Disney Motion Pictures Group
Nina Jacobson . . . . . . . . . . . . . . . . . . Exec. VP, Prod, Walt Disney Picts.
Thomas Schumacher . . . . . . Exec. VP, Feature Animation & Theatrical Prods.
Mike Stenson . . . . . . . . . . . . . . . Exec. VP, Production, Touchstone Picts.
Steve Bardwil . . . . . . . . . . . . . . . . . . . . . . . . . Sr. VP, Legal Affairs
Kevin W. Breen . . . . . . . . . . . . . . . . . . . Sr. VP, Theatrical Animation
Tim Engel . . . . . . . . . . . . . . . Sr. VP, Production, Walt Disney Feature Animation
Todd Garner . . . . . . . . . . . . . . . . . . Sr. VP, Production, Touchstone Pics.
Bruce Hendricks . . . . . . . . . . . . . . . . . Sr. VP, Motion Picture Production
Scott Holtzman . . . . . . . . . . . . . . . . Sr. VP, Music Business/Legal Affairs
David McCann . . . . . . Sr. VP, Motion Picture & Television Post Prod.
Rob Moore . . . . . . . . . . . . . . . . . . . . . . Sr. VP, Planning & Analysis
Phillip Muhl . . . . . . . . . . . . . . . . . . . Sr. VP, Business & Legal Affairs
Michael Roberts . . . . . . . . . . . . . . . . Sr. VP, Production, Walt Disney Picts.
Jordi Ros . . . . . . . . . . . . . . . . . . . . . Sr. VP, Production, Touchstone Picts.
Marcia S. Ross . . . . . . Sr. VP, Casting, WD, Touchstone & Hollywood Picts.
Doug Carter . . . . . . . . . . . . . . . . . . . . . . . . . . . . VP, Business Affairs
William Clark . . . . . . . . . . . . . . . . . . VP, Participation & Residuals
Merritt D. Farren . . . . . VP, Business & Legal Affairs, Theme Park Productions
Chris Floyd . . . . . . . . . . . . . . . . . . . . . . . . . . . VP, Business Affairs
Steven W. Gerse . . . . . . . . . . . . . . . . . . . . . . . VP, Business Affairs
Stephanie J. Harris . . . . . . . . . . . . . VP, Credit & Title Administration
Andy Hill . . . . . . . . . . . . . . . . . . . . . . . . . . . . VP, Music Production
Gregg Hoffman . . . . . . . . . . . . . . . . . VP, Production, Walt Disney Picts.
Robert W. Johnson . . . . . . . . . . . . . . . . . . . . . . . VP, Labor Relations
Bob Lambert . . . . . . . . . . . . . . . . VP, New Technology & Development
Stuart Oken . . . . . . . . . VP, Creative Affairs, WD Theatrical Productions
Faith Raiguel . . . . . . . VP, Admin. & Operations, Walt Disney Feature Anim.
Marjorie Randolph . . . VP, Human Resources, Walt Disney Feature Animation
Howard Safenowitz . . . . . . . . . . . . . . . . . . . . . . . . VP, Business Affairs
Clark Spencer . . . . . . . . VP, Finance & Planning Analysis, WD Feature Anim.
Paul Steinke . . . . . . . . . . . . . . . . . . . . . . . VP, Production Finance
Mark Vahradian . . . . . . . . . . . . . . . . . . . . . VP, Touchstone Picts.
Paul Yanover . . . . . . . VP, Technology, Walt Disney Feature Animation
Ann Bowman . . . . . . . . . . . . . . . . . . . . . . . . . . . . . . . . . . Attorney
Joanne Cassidy . . . . . . . . . . . . . . . . . . . . . . . . . . . . . . . . . Attorney
Carolyn Clark . . . . . . . . . . . . . . . . . . . . . . . . . . . . . . . . . . Attorney
Sherri Feldman . . . . . . . . . . . . . . . . . . . . . . . . . . . . . . . . . Attorney
Beth Machlovitch . . . . . . . . . . . . . . . . . . . . . . . . . . . . . . . Attorney
Carol McDermott . . . . . . . . . . . . . . . . . . . . . . . . . . . . . . . Attorney
Liz McNicoll . . . . . . . . . . . . . . . . . . . . . . . . . . . Attorney, Music
James Meenaghau . . . . . . . . . . . . . . . . . . . . . . . . . . . . . . . Attorney
Gretchen O'Neal . . . . . . . . . . . . . . . . . . . . . . . . . Attorney, Music
Lee Parnell . . . . . . . . . . . . . . . . . . . . . . . . . . . . . . . . . . . . Attorney
Tiffany Prusia . . . . . . . . . . . . . . . . . . . . . . . . . . . . . . . . . . Attorney
Joe Quigley . . . . . . . . . . . . . . . . . . . . . . . . . . . . . . . . . . . Attorney
Kal Walthers . . . . . . . . . . . . . . . . . . . . . . . . . . . . . . . . . . Attorney
Paige Wright . . . . . . . . . . . . . . . . . . . . . . . . . . . . . . . . . . Attorney
Christy Callahan . . . . . . . . . . . . . . . . . . . . Dir., Touchstone Picts.
Jeff Daitch . . . . . . . . . . . . . . . . . . . . . . . . . Dir., Business Affairs
Sylvia J. Krask . . . . . . . . . . . . . . . . . . Dir., Music Business Affairs
Jessica Swirnoff . . . . . . . . . . . . . . . . . . Dir., Prod., Walt Disney Picts.
Kristin Burr . . . . . . . . . . . . . . . . . Creative Executive, Walt Disney Picts.
Jeffrey Clifford . . . . . . . . . . . . . . . Creative Executive, Walt Disney Picts.
Paige Goldberg . . . . . . . . . . . . . . . Creative Executive, Walt Disney Picts.
Jason Reed . . . . . . . . . . . . . . . . . Creative Executive, Touchstone Picts.
Doug Short . . . . . . . . . . . . . . . . . Creative Executive, Touchstone Picts.
Brigham Taylor . . . . . . . . . . . . . . . Creative Executive, Walt Disney Picts.

## WALT DISNEY TELEVISION ANIMATION
PHONE . . . . . . . . . . . . . . . . . . . . . . . . . . . . . . . . . . . . . . 818-560-5000
WEBSITE . . . . . . . . . . . . . . . . . . . . . . . . . . . . http://www.disney.com
500 S. Buena Vista Street
Burbank, CA 91521

TYPE         Television + Animation

Charles Hirschhorn . . . . . . . . . . . . . President, WDTV & WDTV Animation
Barry Blumberg . . . . . . . . . . . . . . . . . . . . . . . . Exec. Vice President
Sharon Morrill . . . . . . . . . . . . . . . . . . . . . . . . Exec. Vice President
Lenora Hume . . . . . . . . . . . . . . . . . . . . . Sr. VP, Intl. Production
Tom Ruzicka . . . . . . . . . . . . . . . . . . Sr. VP, Domestic Production
Mark Kenchelian . . . . . . . . . . . . . . . . . . . . . VP, Business Affairs
Bambi J. Moe . . . . . . . . . . . . . . . . . . . . . . . . . . . . . VP, Music
Joanna Spak . . . . . . . . . . . . . . . . . . . . . . . . . . . . . . VP, Finance

## WALT DISNEY TV/TOUCHSTONE TV
PHONE . . . . . . . . . . . . . . . . . . . . . . . . . . . . . . . . . . . . . . 818-560-5000
WEBSITE . . . . . . . . . . . . . . . . . . . . . . . . . . . . http://www.disney.com
500 S. Buena Vista St.
Burbank, CA 91521-0001

TYPE         Television

Charles Hirschhorn . . . . . . . . . President, WDTV & WDTV Animation
David Neuman . . . . . . . . . . . . . . . . . . . President, Walt Disney TV
Mitch Ackerman . . . . . . . . . . . . . . . . . . . . Sr. VP, TV Production
Peter Aronson . . . . . . . . . . . . . . . . . . . . . . Sr. VP, Network TV
Eugene Blythe . . . . . . . . . . . . . . . . . . . . . Sr. VP, TV Casting
Alan Duke . . . . . . . . . Sr. VP, Network TV Business & Legal Affairs
Robert W. Johnson . . . . . . . . . . . . . . . . . Sr. VP, Labor Relations
Janet Blake . . . . . . . . . VP, Writer Development & Special Projects
Frances Calfo . . . . . . . . . . . . . . . . . . . . . . . . . . . VP, Research
Howard Devine . . . . . . . . . . . . . . VP, Network TV Business Affairs
Ricka Fisher . . . . . . . . . . . . . . VP, Movies & Miniseries, Network TV
Grady Jones . . . . . . . . . . . . . . . . . . . . VP, Post Production, TV
Ted Kaye . . . . . . . . . . . . . . . . . . . . . . . VP, Videotape Production
Cheryl Melton . . . . . . . . . . . . . . . . . . . . . . . . . . VP, TV Music
Michael Moloney . . . . . . . . . . . . . . VP, Network TV Legal Affairs
Walter O'Neal . . . . . . . . . . . . . . . . . . VP, TV Production Finance
John Perry . . . . . . . . . . . . . . . . . . . . . . . . VP, Film Production
Joanna Spak . . . . . . . . . . . . . . . . . . . . VP, Network TV Finance
Paul Villadolid . . . . . . . . . . . . . . . . . . VP, Network TV Specials
Joella West . . . . . . . . . . . . . . . . . . VP, Network TV Business Affairs

## WALZ PRODUCTIONS, KEN
PHONE . . . . . . . . . . . . . . . . . . . . . . . . . . . . . . . . . . . 310-449-4001
FAX . . . . . . . . . . . . . . . . . . . . . . . . . . . . . . . . . . . . . 310-449-4006
EMAIL . . . . . . . . . . . . . . . . . . . . . . walzprods@earthlink.net
3000 W. Olympic Blvd.
Bldg. 5, Ste. 2102
Santa Monica, CA 90404

TYPE       Motion Pictures + Television
CREDITS     Adventures of Pete & Pete - Medusa, Dare to be Truthful - Tyler Madison's Coming to Town
COMMENTS   ALSO: 185 E. 85th St. #31-E, New York, NY 10028

Ken Walz . . . . . . . . . . . . . . . . . . . . . . . . . . . . . . . . . . . President
Catrina Gregory . . . . . . . . . . . . . . Dir., Development (310-449-4013)

## WANDERING MONKEY ENTERTAINMENT
PHONE . . . . . . . . . . . . . . . . . . . . . . . . . . . . . . . . . . 213-960-4096
FAX . . . . . . . . . . . . . . . . . . . . . . . . . . . . . . . . . . . . 213-960-4935
Raleigh Studios
5358 Melrose Ave., Ste. 300W
Hollywood, CA 90038

TYPE       Motion Pictures + Television
DEAL       Henson Company, Jim
CREDITS     Beyond Family - Read For The Stars

Dan Clark . . . . . . . . . . . . . . . . . . . . . . . . . . . . . Writer/Director
Don Asher . . . . . . . . . . . . . . . . . . . . . . . . . . . . . . . . . Producer
Dave Pressler . . . . . . . . . . . . . . . . Co-Producer/Character Designer

## WARD FILMS, INC., VINCENT
PHONE . . . . . . . . . . . . . . . . . . . . . . . . . . . . . . . . . . 213-850-5703
FAX . . . . . . . . . . . . . . . . . . . . . . . . . . . . . . . . . . . . 213-850-5743
1134 N. Gardner St.
Los Angeles, CA 90046

TYPE       Motion Pictures
DEAL       Interscope Communications Inc.
CREDITS     Map of the Human Heart

Vincent Ward . . . . . . . . . . . . . . . . . . . . . . . . . Producer/Director
Sarah Whistler . . . . . . . . . . . . . . . . . . . . . . . . Dir., Development
Ingrid Calame . . . . . . . . . . . . . . . . . . . . . . . Asst. to Mr. Ward

## WARDENCLYFFE ENTERTAINMENT
PHONE . . . . . . . . . . . . . . . . . . . . . . . . . . . . . . . . . . 310-273-9664
FAX . . . . . . . . . . . . . . . . . . . . . . . . . . . . . . . . . . . . 310-273-9658
EMAIL . . . . . . . . . . . . . . . . . . . . . . . . . . . . . clyffe@loop.com
9301 Wilshire Blvd., Ste. 501
Beverly Hills, CA 90210

TYPE       Motion Pictures
CREDITS     With or Without You - Iron Will - Survivors

Robert A. Schwartz . . . . . . . . . . . . . . . . . . . . . . . . . Producer
Maggie Soboil . . . . . . . . . . . . . . . . . . . . . . . . Dir., Development

# COMPANIES AND STAFF

## WARNER BROS. FEATURE ANIMATION

PHONE . . . . . . . . . . . . . . . . . . . . . . . . . . . . . . 818-977-7707
FAX . . . . . . . . . . . . . . . . . . . . . . . . . . . . . . . 818-977-7550
WEBSITE. . . . . . . . . . . . . . . . http://www.warnerbros.com
500 N. Brand Blvd., Ste. 1800
Glendale, CA 91203-1923

TYPE        Motion Pictures + Animation
CREDITS      Space Jam - Quest For Camelot - Iron Giant

Max Howard . . . . . . . . . . . . . . . . . . . . . . . . . . . . President
Dennis Edwards . . . . . . . . . . . . . . . . . . . . . . . . VP, Production
Amanda Seward . . . . . . . . . . . . . VP, Business Affairs & Operations
Daniel Crane . . . . . . . . . . . . . . . . . . . . . . . . . Dir., Finance
Laura Harkcom . . . . . . . . . . . . . . . . . . . . . Dir., Creative Affairs
Tamara Woolfork . . . . . . . . . . . . . . Dir., Business & Legal Affairs
Scott Grieder . . . . . . . . . . . . . . . . . . . . . Development Coordinator

## WARNER BROS. INTERNATIONAL TV PRODUCTION

PHONE . . . . . . . . . . . . . . . . . . . . . . . . . 818-977-5100
4000 W Alameda, 6th Floor
Burbank, CA 91505

TYPE        Television + Syndication + Feature Direct to Video +
               Animation

Catherine Malatesta . . . . . . . . . . . . . . . Sr. VP, Intl. Production
Adam Rosen . . . . . . . . . . . . . . . . . . . . Dir., Business Affairs
Dan Monta . . . . . . . . . . . . . . . . . . . . . . . . . Dir., Operations
Carola Ash . . . . . . . . . . . . . . . . . . . Mgr., Intl. Production, (UK)
Sarah Nettinga . . . . . . . . . . . . . . . . . . . . . . Mgr., Production
Christine Stegmeir . . . . . Mgr., Production Estimating & Auditing
Nestor Balaban . . . . . . . . . . . . . . . . . . . . Sr. Financial Analyst
Andrew Elkins . . . . . . . . . . . . Exec. Asst. to Catherine Malatesta
Kristen Stratton . . . . . . . . . . . . . . . . . . Production Administrator
Alice Pope . . . . . . . . . . . . . . . . . . . . . . . Asst. to Mr. Rosen

## WARNER BROS. PICTURES

PHONE . . . . . . . . . . . . . . . . . . . . . . . . . 818-954-6000
WEBSITE. . . . . . . . . . . . . . . . http://www.warnerbros.com
4000 Warner Blvd.
Burbank, CA 91522-0001

TYPE        Motion Pictures

Robert A. Daly . . . . . . . . . . . . . . . . . . . . Chairman/Co-CEO
Terry Semel . . . . . . . . . . . . . . . . . . . . . . . Chairman/Co-CEO
Barry A. Meyer . . . . . . . . . . . . Exec. VP/COO, Warner Bros., Inc.
Lorenzo Di Bonaventura . . . . . Pres., Worldwide Theatrical Production
Gary LeMel . . . . . . . . . . . . . . . . . . . . . . . President, Music
Doug Frank . . . . . . . . . . . . . Exec. VP, Business Affairs, Music
Robert Guralnick . . . . . . . . . . . Exec. VP, Theatrical Production
Tom Lassally . . . . . . . . . . . . . . Exec. VP, Theatrical Production
Steve Papzian . . . . . . . . . . . Exec. VP, Worldwide Feature Production
Diana Rathbun . . . . . . . . . . . . . . . . Sr. VP, Theatrical Production
Jeff Robinov . . . . . . . . . . . . . . . . Sr. VP, Theatrical Production
Courtenay Valenti . . . . . . . . . . . . . . Sr. VP, Theatrical Production
Clifford Werber . . . . . Sr. VP, Worldwide Co-Prods. & Acquisitions
William L. Young . . . . . . . . . Sr. VP, Worldwide Feature Production
Keith Zajic . . . . . . . . . . . . . . . Sr. VP, Business Affairs, Music
Michael Andreen . . . . . . . . . . . . . . . VP, Theatrical Production
Christopher deFaria . . . . . . . . . . . . . . . . VP, Feature Production
Bill Draper . . . . . . . . . . . . . . . . . . . . . VP, Feature Production
Basil Iwanyk . . . . . . . . . . . . . . . . . . . VP, Theatrical Production
Lynn Morgan . . . . . . . . . . . . . . . . . . . . VP, Feature Production
Mark Scoon . . . . . . . . . . . . . . . . . . . . . VP, Feature Production
Lionel Wigram . . . . . . . . . . . . . . . . . . VP, Theatrical Production
Ellen Schwartz . . . . . . . . . . . . . . . . Dir., Development, Music
Teresa Wayne . . . . . . . . . . . . . . . . Dir., Fesature Story Dept.
J. David Brewington Jr. . . . . . . . . . . . . . . Creative Executive
Polly Cohen . . . . . . . . . . . . . . . . . . . . . . Creative Executive
Steve Crystal . . . . . . . . . . . . . . . . . . . . . Creative Executive
Jessica Sandler . . . . . . . . . . . . . . . . . . . Creative Executive
Greg Silverman . . . . . . . . . . . . . . . . . . . Creative Executive

## WARNER BROS. TELEVISION PRODUCTIONS

PHONE . . . . . . . . . . . . . . . . . . . . . . . . . 818-954-6000
FAX . . . . . . . . . . . . . . . . . . . . . . . . . . . 818-954-7367
WEBSITE. . . . . . . . . . . . . . . . http://www.warnerbros.com
4000 Warner Blvd.
Burbank, CA 91522-0001

TYPE        Television

Tony Jonas . . . . . . . . . . . . . . . . . . . . . . . . . President
Gary Levine . . . . . . . . . . . . . . . . Exec. VP, Creative Affairs
Craig Hunegs . . . . . . . . . . . Exec. VP, Business & Financial Affairs
Andrew Ackerman . . . . . . . . . . . . . . . . . . Sr. VP, Production
Maria Grasso . . . . . . . . . . . . . . . Sr. VP, Comedy Development
Gregg Maday . . . . . . . . . . . . . . . . Sr. VP, Movies & Miniseries
Barbara Miller . . . . . . . . . . . . . . . . Sr. VP, Talent & Casting
Marjorie Nieset Neufeld . . . . . . . . . . . . . Sr. VP, General Counsel
Steve Pearlman . . . . . . . . Sr. VP, Drama Dev. & Current Programs
David Sacks . . . . . . . . . . . Sr. VP, Network Current Programming
Judy Zaylor . . . . . . . . . . . . Sr. VP, Drama & Comedy Productions
Lewis Abel . . . . . . . . . . . . . . . . . . . . . . . VP, Production
Henry Johnson . . . . . . . . . . . . . . . VP, Film & Tape Production
Trent Jones . . . . . . . . . . . . . . . . . VP, Current Programming
Lisa Lewis . . . . . . . . . . . . . . . . . . . . . VP, Post Production
Patrick Newcomb . . . . . . . . . . . . . . . . . . . . VP, Production
Ellen Rauch . . . . . . . . . . . . . . . . . . . . . . . VP, Production
Jim Botko . . . . . . . . . . . . . . . . . . Dir., Movies & Miniseries
Keith Cox . . . . . . . . . . . . . . . . . . Dir., Comedy Development
Len Goldstein . . . . . . . . . . . . . . . . Dir., Drama Development
Julia Gunn . . . . . . . . . . . . . . . . . . . . Dir., Current Programs
Melinda Hage . . . . . . . . . . . . . . . . . . Dir., Current Programs
Jane Segal . . . . . . . . . . . . . . . . Dir., Current Programming
Eric Timm . . . . . . . . . . . . . . . . . . . Dir., Current Programs
Pam Williams . . . . . . . . . . . . . . . Dir., Drama Development
Kary McHoul . . . . . . . . . . . . . . . Mgr., Comedy Development
Cheryl Morgan . . . . . . . . . . . . . . . . . Mgr., Creative Affairs

## WARNER BROS. TV ANIMATION

PHONE . . . . . . . . . . . . . . . . . . . . . . . . . 818-977-8700
FAX . . . . . . . . . . . . . . . . . . . . . . . . . . . 818-905-1692
WEBSITE. . . . . . . . . . . . . . . . http://www.warnberbros.com
15303 Ventura Blvd., Ste. 1200
Sherman Oaks, CA 91403

TYPE        Animation
CREDITS      Animaniacs - Tiny Toon Adventures - Batman - Superman
                 - Pinky & The Brain - Freakazoid

Jean MacCurdy . . . . . . . . . . . . . . . . . . . . . . . . President
Tom Ruegger . . . . . . . . . . . . . . . . . . . . . Executive Producer
Andrew Lewis . . . . . . . . . . . . . . . . Exec. VP/General Manager
Kathleen Helppie . . . . . . . . Sr. VP, Warner Bros. Classic Animation
Ken Duer . . . . . . . . . . . . . . . . . VP, Worldwide Production
Joey Franks . . . . . . . . . . . . . . . . . . . . VP, Creative Affairs

## WARNER SISTERS PRODS.

PHONE . . . . . . . . . . . . . . . 818-240-6674/813-441-4975
FAX . . . . . . . . . . . . . . . . . . 818-543-1515/813-441-4976
EMAIL . . . . . . . . . . . . . . . . . . . info@warnersisters.com
WEBSITE. . . . . . . . . . . . . . . . http://www.warnersisters.com
2469 N. Brand Blvd., Ste. 429
Glendale, CA 91203

TYPE        Motion Pictures + Television + Animation +
               Documentaries + Feature Direct to Video
COMMENTS   Also: 512 Cleveland St., Ste. 214, Clearwater, FL 33755

Cass Warner . . . . . . . . . . . . . . . . . . . . . . . CEO/President
Eric Sherman . . . . . . . . . . . . . . Exec. in Charge of Production
Karen Holly . . . . . . . . . . . . . . . . . . . . . . . Legal Affairs

## WARP FILMS

PHONE . . . . . . . . . . . . . . . . . . . . . . . . . 310-244-5355
FAX . . . . . . . . . . . . . . . . . . . . . . . . . . . 310-244-1898
Sony Pictures Entertainment
10202 W. Washington Blvd., Capra 103
Culver City, CA 90232

TYPE        Motion Pictures + Television
DEAL        Columbia Pictures
CREDITS      Crimson Tide - Bad Boys - Dangerous Minds

Lucas Foster . . . . . . . . . . . . . . . . . Producer (310-244-5393)
Brian Morewitz . . . . . . . . . . . . . . . . . . . . . VP, Production
Rebecca Jones . . . . . . . . . . . . . . . . . . . . . . . Story Editor
Steven Hein . . . . . . . . . . . . . . . . . . . . . Creative Executive
Shannon Ericson . . . . . . . . . . . . . . . . . . Asst. to Mr. Foster

**WATER STREET PICTURES**
PHONE . . . . . . . . . . . . . . . . . . . . . . . 310-581-0070/414-223-1060
FAX . . . . . . . . . . . . . . . . . . . . . . . . . . . . . . . . . . 414-226-4960
EMAIL . . . . . . . . . . . . . . . . . . . . . . . . . . tdgwsp@execpc.com
777 N. jefferson St.
Milwaukee, WS 53202
TYPE          Motion Pictures + Television
Chip Duncan . . . . . . . . . . . . . . . . . . . . . . . . . . . . . . . . . Producer
Lisa Gildehause . . . . . . . . . . . . . . . . . . . . . . . . . . . Development

**WATERMARK FILMS, INC.**
PHONE . . . . . . . . . . . . . . . . . . . . . . . . . . . . . . . 212-496-8480
FAX . . . . . . . . . . . . . . . . . . . . . . . . . . . . . . . . . . 212-787-4935
134 W. 80th St., Ste. 4R
New York, NY 10024
TYPE          Motion Pictures + Television
CREDITS       Goodbye, Lover - Blood Oranges - Dead Run
Chris Daniel . . . . . . . . . . . . . . . . . . . . . . . . . Principal/Producer
Mark Jupiter . . . . . . . . . . . . . . . . . . . . . . . . . Principal/Producer
Nicole Sors . . . . . . . . . . . . . . . . . . . . . . . . . Dir., Development
Brian Moriarty . . . . . . . . . . . . . . . . . . . . . . . . . . . Story Editor

**WEED ROAD PICTURES**
PHONE . . . . . . . . . . . . . . . . . . . . . . . . . . . . . . . 818-954-3771
FAX . . . . . . . . . . . . . . . . . . . . . . . . . . . . . . . . . . 818-954-3061
EMAIL . . . . . . . . . . . . . . . . . . . . . . weedroad@earthlink.net
4000 Warner Blvd., Bldg. 81, Ste. #115
Burbank, CA 91522
TYPE          Motion Pictures
DEAL          Warner Bros. Pictures
CREDITS       Deep Blue Sea
Akiva Goldsman . . . . . . . . . . . . . . . . . . . . . . . . . . . . Producer
Will Staeger . . . . . . . . . . . . . . . . . . . . . . . . Sr. Vice President
Varina Bleil . . . . . . . . . . . . . . . . . . . . . . . . Creative Executive
Stephanie Gisondi . . . . . . . . . . . . . . Story Editor/Executive Assistant

**WEINBERGER CO., ED.**
PHONE . . . . . . . . . . . . . . . . . . . . . . . . . . . . . . . 213-960-4506
Raleigh Studios
5300 Melrose Ave.
Los Angeles, CA 90038-3197
TYPE          Television
CREDITS       Amen - Dear John - Taxi - Mary Tyler Moore Show -
              Sparks - Good News
COMMENTS  MAIL: 650 N. Bronson, #333, L.A., CA 90004
Ed. Weinberger . . . . . . . . . . . . . . . . . . Writer/Director/Producer
Lynda Hudson . . . . . . . . . . . . . . . . . . Executive Asst./Producer

**WEINGROD/HARRIS PRODS.**
PHONE . . . . . . . . . . . . . . . . . . . . . . . . . . . . . . . 310-396-5937
FAX . . . . . . . . . . . . . . . . . . . . . . . . . . . . . . . . . . 310-450-4988
73 Market St.
Venice, CA 90291
TYPE          Motion Pictures
CREDITS       Space Jam - Twins - Kindergarten Cop - Falling Down -
              Trading Places
Timothy Harris . . . . . . . . . . . . . . . . . . . . . . . . Writer/Producer
Herschel Weingrod . . . . . . . . . . . . . . . . . . . . . Writer/Producer

**WEINSTOCK PRODUCTIONS**
PHONE . . . . . . . . . . . . . . . . . . . . . . . . . . . . . . . 310-888-3533
FAX . . . . . . . . . . . . . . . . . . . . . . . . . . . . . . . . . . 310-888-3516
Castle Rock Entertainment
335 N. Maple Dr., Ste. 135
Beverly Hills, CA 90210
TYPE          Motion Pictures
DEAL          Castle Rock Entertainment
CREDITS       Last Light
Charles Weinstock . . . . . . . . . . . . . . . . . . . . . . . . . . . Producer
Peggy Pierce . . . . . . . . . . . . . . . . . . . . . . . . . . Vice President

**WEINTRAUB PRODS., JERRY**
PHONE . . . . . . . . . . . . . . . . . . . . . . . . . . . . . . . 818-954-2500
FAX . . . . . . . . . . . . . . . . . . . . . . . . . . . . . . . . . . 818-954-1399
Warner Bros.
4000 Warner Blvd., Bung. 1
Burbank, CA 91522-0001
TYPE          Motion Pictures
DEAL          Warner Bros. Pictures
CREDITS       Vegas Vacation - The Specialist - Diner - Nashville - Karate
              Kid I, II, III & IV - Avengers
Jerry Weintraub . . . . . . . . . . . . . . . . . . . Producer (818-954-2335)
Chris Buchanan . . . . . . . . . . . . . . . . Sr. VP, Production (818-954-2374)
John Tomko . . . . . . . . . . . . . . . . . . Sr. VP, Production (818-954-4881)
Susan Ekins . . . . . . . . . . . . . . . VP, Physical Production (818-954-4272)
Glenn Abernathy . . . . . . . . . . . . . . . Creative Executive (818-954-6928)
Charlie Gogolak . . . . . . . . . . . . . . . Creative Executive (818-954-3824)
Lisa Rodriguez . . . . . . . . . . . . . . . . . Office Manager (818-954-1963)
Kimberly Pinkstaff . . . . . . . . . Exec. Asst. to Jerry Weintraub (818-954-2738)
Matt Broughton . . . . . . . . . . . . . . . . . . No Title (818-954-2374)
Jenny Lynn . . . . . . . . . . . . . . . . . . . . . No Title (818-954-6687)

**WEINTRAUB/KUHN PRODS.**
PHONE . . . . . . . . . . . . . . . . . . . . . . . . . . . . . . . 310-788-9380
FAX . . . . . . . . . . . . . . . . . . . . . . . . . . . . . . . . . . 310-788-0476
1900 Ave. of the Stars, Ste. 1440
Los Angeles, CA 90067
TYPE          Motion Pictures + Television + Documentaries + Feature
              Direct to Video
CREDITS       High Road to China - The New Adventures of Robin Hood
Fred Weintraub . . . . . . . . . . . . . . . . . . . . . . . . . . . . Producer
Tom Kuhn . . . . . . . . . . . . . . . . . . . . . . . . . . . . . . . . Producer
David Taber . . . . . . . . . . . . . . . . . . . . . . . Executive Assistant

**WEINY BRO PRODUCTIONS**
PHONE . . . . . . . . . . . . . . . . . . . . . . . . . . . . . . . 310-917-4441
FAX . . . . . . . . . . . . . . . . . . . . . . . . . . . . . . . . . . 310-917-4445
2121 Montana Ave., Ste. 4
Santa Monica, CA 90403
TYPE          Motion Pictures + Television
CREDITS       Glory Daze
COMMENTS  Also: Commercials.
Aaron M. Weinberg . . . . . . . . . . . . . . . . . . . . . . . . . . . Producer
Brian Sanders . . . . . . . . . . . . . . . . . . . . . . . . . . . Co-Producer

**WEISBERG PRODS., RONI**
PHONE . . . . . . . . . . . . . . . . . . . . . . . . . . . . . . . 310-235-5100
FAX . . . . . . . . . . . . . . . . . . . . . . . . . . . . . . . . . . 310-235-5767
Saban Entertainment
10960 Wilshire Blvd.
Los Angeles, CA 90024
TYPE          Motion Pictures + Television + Feature Direct to Video
DEAL          Saban Entertainment
CREDITS       Face Down - Following Her Heart - Promised A Miracle -
              Contagious
Roni Weisberg . . . . . . . . . . . . . . . . . Executive Producer (310-235-5478)
Holly Harter . . . . . . . . . . . . . . . . . . VP, Development (310-235-5471)
Robert Lane . . . . . . . . . . . . . . . . . . . . Development (310-235-5469)

**WEISMAN PRODUCTIONS, HOWARD J.**
PHONE . . . . . . . . . . . . . . . . . . . . . . . . . . . . . . . 310-452-8110
FAX . . . . . . . . . . . . . . . . . . . . . . . . . . . . . . . . . . 310-399-9278
EMAIL . . . . . . . . . . . . . . . . . . . . . . . . . . . HOWEIS@aol.com
213 Rose Avenue, 2nd Floor
Venice, CA 90291-2567
TYPE          Motion Pictures + Television
CREDITS       Lovestruck - The Kazooist - Follow You, Follow Me
Howard J. Weisman . . . . . . . . . . . . . . . . . . . . . . . . . . . Producer

**WEISWORLD PREMIERES**
PHONE . . . . . . . . . . . . . . . . . . . . . . . . . . . . . . . 310-285-1345
FAX . . . . . . . . . . . . . . . . . . . . . . . . . . . . . . . . . . 310-858-7956
9860 Wilshire Blvd.
Beverly Hills, CA 90210
TYPE          Motion Pictures + Television
DEAL          Merv Griffin Productions
CREDITS       The Ref - Rocket Gibraltar - Radiant City - Suddenly - The
              Christmas List
Jeff Weiss . . . . . . . . . . . . . . . . . . . . . . . . . . . . . . . . Producer
Robyn Latter . . . . . . . . . . . . . . . . . . . . . . . . . VP, Development

# COMPANIES AND STAFF

**WELLER/GROSSMAN PRODUCTIONS**
PHONE . . . . . . . . . . . . . . . . . . . . . . . . . . . . . . . . 818-755-4800
FAX . . . . . . . . . . . . . . . . . . . . . . . . . . . . . . . . . . . 818-755-4820
14144 Ventura Blvd., #200
Sherman Oaks, CA 91423

TYPE      Television + Documentaries + Syndication
DEAL      Home & Garden Television/A & E Television Networks/
          Discovery Networks/History Channel, The

Gary H. Grossman . . . . . . . . . . . . . . . . . . . . . . . Executive Producer
Robb Weller . . . . . . . . . . . . . . . . . . . . . . . . . . . Executive Producer
Joel Rizor . . . . . . . . . . . . . . . . . . . . . Exec. In Charge of Production
Debbie Supnik . . . . . . . . . . . . . . . . . . . . . . . . . . . . Development

**WELLS PRODUCTIONS, JOHN**
PHONE . . . . . . . . . . . . . . . . . . . . . . . . . . . . . . . . 818-954-1687
FAX . . . . . . . . . . . . . . . . . . . . . . . . . . . . . . . . . . . 818-954-3657
Warner Bros. Pictures
4000 Warner Blvd., Bldg. 138, Rm. 1206
Burbank, CA 91522-0001

TYPE      Motion Pictures + Television
DEAL      NBC Studios/Warner Bros. Pictures
CREDITS   ER

John Wells . . . . . . . . . . . . . . . . . . . . . . . . . . . . Producer/Writer
Kristin Harms . . . . . . . . . . . . . . . . . . . . . . . . . Pres., Production
Andrew Stearn . . . . . . . . . . . . . . . . . . VP, Television Development
Ted Broden . . . . . . . . . . . . . . . . . . . . . . . Dir., Feature Development
Susan Stofsky . . . . . . . . . . . . . . . . . . . . . Dir., Special Projects
Reeva Mandelbaum . . . . . . . . . . . . . . . . . . . . . . . Dir., Research
Julie Hullverson . . . . . . . . . . . . . . . . . . . . . Asst. to John Wells
Kristy Tautfest . . . . . . . . . . . . . . . . . . . . . Asst. to Kristin Harris
Ran Barker . . . . . . . . . . . . . . . . . . . . . . Asst. to Susan Stofsky

**WESSLER ENTERTAINMENT**
PHONE . . . . . . . . . . . . . . . . . . . . . . . . . . . . . . . . 310-248-6035
FAX . . . . . . . . . . . . . . . . . . . . . . . . . . . . . . . . . . . 310-858-0464
New Line Cinema
9056 Santa Monica, #300
Los Angeles, CA 90069

TYPE      Motion Pictures + Television
DEAL      New Line Cinema
CREDITS   Dumb And Dumber - Bushwacked - There's Something
          About Mary

Charles B. Wessler . . . . . . . . . . . . . . . . . . . . . . . . . President
Lali Kagan . . . . . . . . . . . . . . . . . . . . . . . . . Dir., Development
John Trozak . . . . . . . . . . . . . . . . . . . . . . . . . . . . . Assistant

**WESTBERG ENTERTAINMENT**
PHONE . . . . . . . . . . . . . . . . . . . . . . . . . . . . . . . . 213-874-5544
FAX . . . . . . . . . . . . . . . . . . . . . . . . . . . . . . . . . . . 213-874-7757
EMAIL . . . . . . . . . . . . . . . . . . . . . . . . . dwestman@aol.com
1604 N. Vista St.
Hollywood, CA 90046-2818

TYPE      Motion Pictures + Television
CREDITS   The Challenge - Night Passage - Self Portrait
David Westberg . . . . . . . . . . . . . . . . . . . . . . . President/COO

**WESTPORT FILM PARTNERS**
PHONE . . . . . . . . . . . . . . . . . . . . . . . . . . . . . . . . 310-840-5140
FAX . . . . . . . . . . . . . . . . . . . . . . . . . . . . . . . . . . . 310-373-8519
2125 Palos Verdes Dr. West
Palos Verdes Estates, CA 90274

TYPE      Motion Pictures
CREDITS   Second of Four - First Comes Love

Stephen C. Aristei . . . . . . . . . . . . . . . . . . . . . . General Partner
Joseph Janson . . . . . . . . . . . . . . . . . . . . . . . . . . . . . Partner
Karen Seiderman . . . . . . . . . . . . . . . . . . . . . . . . . . . Partner
Edward Seiderman . . . . . . . . . . . . . . . . . . . . . . . . . . Partner

***WESTWIND PRODUCTIONS, INC.**
PHONE . . . . . . . . . . . . . . . . . . . . . . . . . . . . . . . . 310-470-6949
FAX . . . . . . . . . . . . . . . . . . . . . . . . . . . . . . . . . . . 310-470-1832
1746 1/2 Westwood Blvd.
Los Angeles, CA 90024

TYPE      Motion Pictures + Television + Feature Direct to Video
CREDITS   Asylum (HBO) - One Man's Justice (HBO) - The Hit List
          (HBO)

William Webb . . . . . . . . . . . . . . . . . . . . . . . Producer/Director
Anna Worthins . . . . . . . . . . . . . . . . . . . . . . . . . . Development

***WHIDBEY ISLAND FILMS, INC.**
PHONE . . . . . . . . . . . . . . . . . . . . . . . . . . . . . . . . 818-988-1789
FAX . . . . . . . . . . . . . . . . . . . . . . . . . . . . . . . . . . . 818-787-1789
14658 Oxnard Street
Van Nuys, CA 91411

TYPE      Documentaries
CREDITS   Reverse Angle Documentary Series (Fear in America, -
          Education Wars) - National Desk Documentary Series -
          (The Politics of Medicine, Children of Divorce, - Redifining
          Racism: Fresh Voices from Black America)

Lionel Chetwynd . . . . . . . . . . . . . . . . . . . . . . . . . . . . Partner
Norman S. Powell . . . . . . . . . . . . . . . . . . . . . . . . . . . Partner
Conrad Denke . . . . . . . . . . . . . . . . . . . . . . . . . . . . . Partner

**WHITE PRODS., JEFFREY**
PHONE . . . . . . . . . . . . . . . . . . . . . . . . . . . . . . . . 213-956-5692
Paramount Pictures
5555 Melrose Ave., Von Sternberg 204
Hollywood, CA 90038

TYPE      Motion Pictures + Television
CREDITS   Beverly Hills 90210 - Sub Down - Nobody's Children -
          The Christmas Star - Flipper - Talos the Mummy

Jeffrey White . . . . . . . . . . . . . . . . . . . . . . . . . . . . . Producer
Sterling Belefant . . . . . . . . . . . . . . . . . . . . . . VP., Development
Cinjun Cajun Sinclair . . . . . . . . . . . . . . . . . . . . . . Story Analyst

**WHITE WOLF PRODS.**
PHONE . . . . . . . . . . . . . . . . . . . . . . . . . . . . . . . . 310-392-8220
FAX . . . . . . . . . . . . . . . . . . . . . . . . . . . . . . . . . . . 310-392-7794
2425 Main Street
Santa Monica, CA 90405

TYPE      Motion Pictures
CREDITS   Cannery Row - Major League I & II - King Ralph - The
          Program - Down Periscope

David S. Ward . . . . . . . . . . . . . . . . . . . . . . . . . . . . President

**WHITEWATER FILMS**
PHONE . . . . . . . . . . . . . . . . . . . . . . . . . . . . . . . . 310-575-5800
FAX . . . . . . . . . . . . . . . . . . . . . . . . . . . . . . . . . . . 310-575-5802
2232 Cotner Ave.
Los Angeles, CA 90064

TYPE      Motion Pictures + Television
CREDITS   Bad Boys - Distant Thunder - American Dreamer - Life
          Goes On

Rick Rosenthal . . . . . . . . . . . . . . . . . . . . . . . . . . . President
Jennifer Miller . . . . . . . . . . . . . . . . . . . . . . . . Dir., Development

**WHYADUCK PRODS., INC.**
PHONE . . . . . . . . . . . . . . . . . . . . . . . . . . . . . . . . 818-754-0535
12358 Ventura Blvd., #301
Studio City, CA 91604

TYPE      Motion Pictures + Television + Documentaries
CREDITS   Mother Night - WC Fields Straight Up (Emmy) - Mort Sahl
Robert B. Weide . . . . . . . . . . . . . . . . . . . . . President/Producer

**WICK, C.Z.**
PHONE . . . . . . . . . . . . . . . . . . . . . . . . . . . . . . . . 310-201-0812
FAX . . . . . . . . . . . . . . . . . . . . . . . . . . . . . . . . . . . 310-553-5019
2073 Kerwood Ave.
Los Angeles, CA 90025

TYPE      Motion Pictures + Television + Interactive Multimedia
DEAL      Columbia Pictures

C.Z. Wick . . . . . . . . . . . . . . . . . . . . . . . . . . . . . . . Producer
Ace Barrington . . . . . . . . . . . . . . . . . . . . . . . Asst. to Producer

**WIGUTOW PRODS., DAN**
PHONE . . . . . . . . . . . . . . . . . . . . . . . . . . . . . . . . 212-477-1328
FAX . . . . . . . . . . . . . . . . . . . . . . . . . . . . . . . . . . . 212-254-6902
534 La Guardia Place
New York, NY 10012

TYPE      Motion Pictures + Television
CREDITS   Brave New World - Peter Benchley's The Beast - Heaven
          Help Us

Dan Wigutow . . . . . . . . . . . . . . . . . . . . . . . . . Exec. Producer
Jennie Gusewelle . . . . . . . . . . . . . . . . . . . . . . Dir., Development
Nina Guckenberger . . . . . . . . . . . . . . . . . . . . . . . . Story Editor

## WILD FILMS INC.
PHONE . . . . . . . . . . . . . . . . . . . . . . . . . . . . . . . . . . 818-760-1020
FAX . . . . . . . . . . . . . . . . . . . . . . . . . . . . . . . . . . . . 818-760-1098
3624 Goodland Ave.
Studio City, CA 91604
TYPE        Motion Pictures + Television
CREDITS     Fox Cubhouse - Fast Forward - Best Revenge - Fox Kids
            PSA's
Nicky Noxon . . . . . . . . . . . . . . . . . . . . . . . . . . President/Producer
James Becket . . . . . . . . . . . . . . . . . . . . . . . . . . . Producer/Director
Steven Reich . . . . . . . . . . . . . . . . . . . . . . . . . . . Writer/Producer
Simon Barron . . . . . . . . . . . . . . . . . . . . . . . . . . . . . . . Producer
Betty Birney . . . . . . . . . . . . . . . . . . . . . . . . . . . . . . . . . Writer
Mary Lou Steinkraus . . . . . . . . . . . . . . . . . . . . . Associate Producer

## WILD THINGS PRODS.
PHONE . . . . . . . . . . . . . . . . . . . . . . . . . . . . . . . . . . 310-899-0787
FAX . . . . . . . . . . . . . . . . . . . . . . . . . . . . . . . . . . . . 310-394-4466
3955 Dixie Canyon Ave.
Sherman Oaks, CA 91423
TYPE        Motion Pictures + Television
DEAL        Nickelodeon/Nick at Nite/Nelvana Communications/
            Universal Pictures
CREDITS     Where the Wild Things Are - George and Martha - Really
            Rosie
Maurice Sendak . . . . . . . . . . . . . . . . . . . . . . . . . . . . . . Partner
John B. Carls . . . . . . . . . . . . . . . . . . . . . . . . . . . . . . . Partner

## WILDRICE PRODUCTIONS
PHONE . . . . . . . . . . . . . . . . . . . . . . . . . . . . . . . . . . 818-623-2898
FAX . . . . . . . . . . . . . . . . . . . . . . . . . . . . . . . . . . . . 818-623-2890
EMAIL . . . . . . . . . . . . . . . . . . . . . . . . . . . . . . wldrice@aol.com
4400 Coldwater Canyon, Suite 321
Studio City, CA 91604
TYPE        Motion Pictures + Television
CREDITS     About Sarah - Breaking Through - Sleeping With The
            Devil
Joel S. Rice . . . . . . . . . . . . . . . . . . . . . . . . . . . Executive Producer
Ronni Z. Rice . . . . . . . . . . . . . . . . . . . . . . . . . Exec. Vice President
Alison Clark . . . . . . . . . . . . . . . . . . . . . . . . . . . . Dir., Development
Erika Baldonado . . . . . . . . . . . . . . . . . . . . . . . . . . . . . Assistant

## WILDSMITH ENTERTAINMENT
PHONE . . . . . . . . . . . . . . . . . . . . . . . . . . . . . . . . . . 612-490-7836
FAX . . . . . . . . . . . . . . . . . . . . . . . . . . . . . . . . . . . . 612-490-7914
EMAIL . . . . . . . . . . . . . . . . . . . . . . . . . . clkingrey@stthomas.edu
3515 Owasso St., Ste. 312
Shoreview, MN 55126
TYPE        Motion Pictures + Television + Syndication
CREDITS     Toadies - Screams At Maybe Mansion - Haunted Cattle
            Drive
COMMENTS    Movies For The Ear - Audio Movies.
Connie Kingrey . . . . . . . . . . . . . . . . . . . . . . . . . . Writer/Producer
Jay Alton . . . . . . . . . . . . . . . . . . . . . . . . . . . . . Dir., Development

## WILDWOOD ENTERPRISES INC.
PHONE . . . . . . . . . . . . . . . . . . . . . . . . . . . . . . . . . . 310-395-5155
FAX . . . . . . . . . . . . . . . . . . . . . . . . . . . . . . . . . . . . 310-395-3975
1101 Montana Ave., Ste. E
Santa Monica, CA 90403
TYPE        Motion Pictures
DEAL        Walt Disney Company, The
CREDITS     Quiz Show - A River Runs Through It - Ordinary People -
            The Horse Whisperer
Robert Redford . . . . . . . . . . . . . . . . . . . . . . . . . . . . . . . . Owner
Michael Nozik . . . . . . . . . . . . . . . . . . . . . . . . . . . . . . . President
Wendy Taeuber . . . . . . . . . . . . . . . . . . . . . . . . . . . VP, Development
Damon Pennington . . . . . . . . . . . . . . . . . . . . . . . . Dir., Development

## WILSHIRE COURT PRODS.
PHONE . . . . . . . . . . . . . . . . . . . . . . . . . . . . . . . . . . 310-557-2444
FAX . . . . . . . . . . . . . . . . . . . . . . . . . . . . . . . . . . . . 310-557-0017
1840 Century Park East, Ste. 400
Los Angeles, CA 90067
TYPE        Television
CREDITS     Double Jeopardy - The Road to Galveston - My Antonia -
            Bad to the Bone
John J. McMahon . . . . . . . . . . . . . . . . . . . . . . . . . . . . . President
Jack Angeles . . . . . . . . . . . . . . . . . . . . . VP, Legal & Business Affairs
Stacy Mandelberg . . . . . . . . . . . . . . . . . . . . . . . . . VP, Development
Ed Milkovich . . . . . . . . . . . . . . . . . . . . . . . . . . . . . VP, Production
Ken Weikel . . . . . . . . . . . . . . . . . . . . . VP, Finance & Administration
Jodi Ticknor . . . . . . . . . . . . . . . . . . . . . . . . . . . . Dir., Development
Missy Pontious . . . . . . . . . . . . . . . . . . . . . . . . . . . Mgr., Development

## WINCHESTER PRODS., INC., MARGOT
PHONE . . . . . . . . . . . . . . . . . . . . . . . . . . . . . . . . . . 818-789-8150
FAX . . . . . . . . . . . . . . . . . . . . . . . . . . . . . . . . . . . . 818-789-6617
EMAIL . . . . . . . . . . . . . . . . . . . . . . . . . . . . . . sasmw@aol.com
5121 Longridge Avenue
Sherman Oaks, CA 91423
TYPE        Motion Pictures + Television + Documentaries
CREDITS     A Husband, A Wife and A Lover (CBS) - Brotherhood of
            Justice (ABC) - Coroner's Report
Margot Winchester . . . . . . . . . . . . . . . . . . . . . . . President/Producer

## WIND DANCER FILMS
PHONE . . . . . . . . . . . . . . . . . . . . . . . 818-560-1151/212-830-5820
FAX . . . . . . . . . . . . . . . . . . . . . . . . . 818-560-1107/212-830-5838
500 S. Buena Vista St., Bldg. 23
Burbank, CA 91521-2215
TYPE        Motion Pictures
COMMENTS    Also: 152 W. 57th St., 56th Fl., NY NY 10019
Susan Cartsonis . . . . . . . . . . . . . . . . . . . . . . . . . . . . . . President
Melissa Goddard . . . . . . . . . . . . . . Sr. Vice President (818-560-5675)
Marlene Adelstein . . . . . . . . . . . . . Vice President (NY) (212-830-5839)
Theresa Welty . . . . . . . . . . . . . . . . Vice President (818-560-5891)
Chris Durian . . . . . . . . . . . . . . . . . . . . . Story Editor (818-560-5898)

## WIND DANCER PROD. GROUP
PHONE . . . . . . . . . . . . . . . . . . . . . . . 818-560-5715/212-830-5820
FAX . . . . . . . . . . . . . . . . . . . . . . . . . 818-563-9674/212-830-5838
500 S. Buena Vista, Prod. Bldg., 3rd Fl.
Burbank, CA 91521-2215
TYPE        Motion Pictures + Television
CREDITS     Home Improvement - Thunder Alley - Soul Man
COMMENTS    Also: 152 W. 57th St., 56th Fl., NY NY 10019
Matt Williams . . . . . . . . . . . . . . . . . . . . . . . . . . Executive Producer
David McFadzean . . . . . . . . . . . . . . . . . . . . . . . . Executive Producer
Carmen Finestra . . . . . . . . . . . . . . . . . . . . . . . . . Executive Producer
Rick Leed . . . . . . . . . . . . . . . . President, Wind Dancer Production Group
Gayle Maffeo . . . . . . . . . . . . . . . . Sr. VP, Television, Wind Dancer TV
Dete Meserve . . . . . . . . . . . . . . . . Sr. VP, Wind Dancer Production Group
Pamela McCarthy . . . . . . . . . . Dir., Creative Affairs (Wind Dancer Theatre NY)
Vernon Sanders . . . . . . . . . . . . . Dir., TV Development, Wind Dancer TV
Kimberly Tushinsky . . . . . . . . . . . . . . Dir., Production, Wind Dancer TV
Joel Ruark . . . . . . . . . . . Managing Director (Wind Dancer Theatre NY)

## WINKLER FILMS
PHONE . . . . . . . . . . . . . . . . . . . . . . . . . . . . . . . . . . 310-858-5780
FAX . . . . . . . . . . . . . . . . . . . . . . . . . . . . . . . . . . . . 310-858-5799
211 S. Beverly Dr., Ste. 200
Beverly Hills, CA 90212
TYPE        Motion Pictures
CREDITS     Rocky - Goodfellas - Raging Bull - The Net - The Right
            Stuff
Irwin Winkler . . . . . . . . . . . . . . . . . . . . . . . Chief Executive Officer
Rob Cowan . . . . . . . . . . . . . . . . . . . . . . . . . . . . . . . President
SoYun Roe . . . . . . . . . . . . . . . . . . . . . . . . . . . . . VP, Production
Mary Lund . . . . . . . . . . . . . . . . . . . . . . . . . Asst. to Irwin Winkler

## WINSOME PICTURES, INC.
PHONE . . . . . . . . . . . . . . . . . . . . . . . . . . . . . . . . . . 213-934-9943
FAX . . . . . . . . . . . . . . . . . . . . . . . . . . . . . . . . . . . . 213-934-0304
EMAIL . . . . . . . . . . . . . . . . . . . . . . . . . . . winsomepix@aol.com
843 S. Sierra Bonita Ave.
Los Angeles, CA 90036-4703
TYPE        Motion Pictures + Television
CREDITS     Arctic Blue - Titanic - Rush Hour
Ross LaManna . . . . . . . . . . . . . . . . . . . . . . . . . . Writer/Producer
Lynn L LaManna . . . . . . . . . . . . . . . . Exec. VP, Business Affairs
Kathleen Rose . . . . . . . . . . . . . . . . . . . . . . . . . . . . VP, Development

## WINSTON PRODUCTIONS, STAN
PHONE . . . . . . . . . . . . . . . . . . . . . . . . . . . . . . . . . . 818-902-5639
FAX . . . . . . . . . . . . . . . . . . . . . . . . . . . . . . . . . . . . 818-902-3856
EMAIL . . . . . . . . . . . . . . . . . . . . . . . . . . . . SWinprod@aol.com
6930 Val Jean Ave., Ste. 201
Van Nuys, CA 91406
TYPE        Motion Pictures + Television
DEAL        DreamWorks SKG
CREDITS     Pumpkinhead - Ghosts - Jurassic Park - Cryptids - Hell
            Bent
Stan Winston . . . . . . . . . . . . . . . . . . . . . . . . . . Producer/Director
Brian Gilbert . . . . . . . . . . . . . . . . . . . . . . . . . . . . Vice President
David Greathouse . . . . . . . . . . . . . . . . . . . . . . . Creative Executive
Donna Jones . . . . . . . . . . . . . . . . . . . . . . . Development Assistant

# COMPANIES AND STAFF

**WITT, DAN**
PHONE . . . . . . . . . . . . . . . . . . . . . . . . . . . . . . . . 818-762-6600
FAX . . . . . . . . . . . . . . . . . . . . . . . . . . . . . . . . . . . 818-766-3657
Longbow Prods.
4181 Sunswept Dr., Ste. 100
Studio City, CA 91604
TYPE             Motion Pictures + Television
DEAL             Longbow Productions
CREDITS          A Killing in a Small Town - Nightmare Street - An
                 Unfinished Affair - Summer of Ben Tyler
Dan Witt . . . . . . . . . . . . . . . . . . . . . . . . . . . . . . Producer/Writer

**WITT-THOMAS FILMS**
PHONE . . . . . . . . . . . . . . . . . . . . . . . . . . . . . . . . 818-954-2545
FAX . . . . . . . . . . . . . . . . . . . . . . . . . . . . . . . . . . . 818-954-2660
4000 Warner Blvd., Producers 3, Room 20
Burbank, CA 91522
TYPE             Motion Pictures
DEAL             Warner Bros. Pictures
CREDITS          Dead Poets Society - Final Analysis - Mixed Nuts
Paul Junger Witt . . . . . . . . . . . . . . . . . . . . . . . . . . . Producer
Tony Thomas . . . . . . . . . . . . . . . . . . . . . . . . . . . . . Producer
Edward L. McDonnell . . . . . . . . . . . . . . . . . . . . . . President
Kim Roth . . . . . . . . . . . . . . . . . . . . . . . . . . . . Vice President
Sebastian Dungan . . . . . . . . . . . . . . . . . . . . Dir., Development
Kristel Laiblin . . . . . . . . . . . . . . . . . . . . . . . . Asst. to Ms. Roth
Justin Rosenblatt . . . . . . . . . . . . . . . . . Asst. to Mr. McDonnell
Bonnie Sporn . . . . . . . . . . . . . . . . . . Asst. to Sebastian Dungan

**WITT-THOMAS-HARRIS PRODUCTIONS**
PHONE . . . . . . . . . . . . . . . . . . . . . . . . . . . . . . . . 213-464-1333
FAX . . . . . . . . . . . . . . . . . . . . . . . . . . . . . . . . . . . 213-957-9886
Sunset/Gower Studios
1438 N. Gower St., Bldg. #35, 4th Fl.
Hollywood, CA 90028
TYPE             Television
DEAL             Warner Bros. Pictures
CREDITS          John Larroquette Show - The Golden Girls - Pearl - Soap -
                 Benson - Empty Nest
Paul Junger Witt . . . . . . . . . . . . . . . . . . . . . . . . . . . . Partner
Susan Harris . . . . . . . . . . . . . . . . . . . . . . . . . . . . . . . Partner
Tony Thomas . . . . . . . . . . . . . . . . . . . . . . . . . . . . . . Partner
Nina Wass . . . . . . . . . . . . . . . . . . . . . . . President, Television
Susan Palladino . . . . . . . . . . . . . . . . . . . . Exec. Vice President

**WOLF FILMS INC.**
PHONE . . . . . . . . . . . . . . . . . . . . . . . . . . . . . . . . 818-777-1236
WEBSITE . . . . . . . . . . . . . . . . . . . . . http://www.wolffilms.com
Universal TV
100 Universal City Plaza, Bldg. 69
Universal City, CA 91608-1085
TYPE             Motion Pictures + Television + Syndication
DEAL             Studios USA Television
CREDITS          Law & Order- New York Undercover- Players
Peter Jankowksi . . . . . . . . . . . . . . . . . . . . . . . . . . . President
Dick Wolf . . . . . . . . . . . . . . . . . . . . . . . . . . Executive Producer
Ed Sherin . . . . . . . . . . . . . . . . . Exec. Producer, Law & Order (NY)
Rene Balcer . . . . . . . . . . . . . . . Exec. Producer, Law & Order (LA)
Tony Ganz . . . . . . . . . . . . . . . . . . . . . . . . . . . . . . . Features
Sean Smith . . . . . . . . . . . . . . . . . Wolf Films Production Contact

**WOLF FILMS, FRED**
PHONE . . . . . . . . . . . . . . . . . . . . . . . . . . . . . . . . 818-846-0611
FAX . . . . . . . . . . . . . . . . . . . . . . . . . . . . . . . . . . . 818-846-0979
EMAIL . . . . . . . . . . . . . . . administration@fredwolffilms.com
WEBSITE . . . . . . . . . . . . . . . . . http://www.fredwolffilms.com
4222 W. Burbank Blvd.
Burbank, CA 91505
TYPE             Animation
CREDITS          Teenage Mutant Ninja Turtles - Zorro - The Fantasic
                 Voyages of Sinbad
COMMENTS         Also: c/o Bell House Montague Street, Dublin 2, Ireland
                 353-1-47-8-31991.
Fred Wolf . . . . . . . . . . . . . . . . . . . . . . . . . . . . . . . President
Bill Wolf . . . . . . . . . . . . . . . . . . . . . . . . . . . . . . . . Producer
Elizabeth Gibbar . . . . . . . . . . . . . . . . . . . . . . . . . . Controller
Cheryl Wadsworth . . . . . . . . . . . . . . . . . Dir., Administration
Liz Thompson . . . . . . . . . . . . . . . . . . . . Production Supervisor
Eamonn Lawless . . . . . . . . . . . . . . General Manager (Dublin)

**WOLFMILL ENTERTAINMENT**
PHONE . . . . . . . . . . . . . . . . . . . . . . . . . . . . . . . . 310-559-1622
FAX . . . . . . . . . . . . . . . . . . . . . . . . . . . . . . . . . . . 310-559-1623
EMAIL . . . . . . . . . . . . . . . . . . . . . . . cfmiller@primenet.com
9027 Larke Ellen Circle
Los Angeles, CA 90035-4222
TYPE             Animation + Television + Syndication
DEAL             ABC Entertainment/BKN Kids Network
CREDITS          Pocket Dragon Adventures - T.H.U.N.D.E.R. Agents -
                 Elfquest
Craig Miller . . . . . . . . . . . . . . . . . . . . . . . . . . . . . . . Partner
Marv Wolfman . . . . . . . . . . . . . . . . . . . . . . . . . . . . . Partner
Richard Rosen . . . . . . . . . . . . . . . . . . . . . . Business Affairs

**WOLPER ORG., THE**
PHONE . . . . . . . . . . . . . . . . . . . . . . . . . . . . . . . . 818-954-1421
FAX . . . . . . . . . . . . . . . . . . . . . . . . . . . . . . . . . . . 818-954-1593
EMAIL . . . . . . . . . . . . . . . . . . . . . . . . . . wolpster@aol.com
Warner Bros.
4000 Warner Blvd., Bldg. 14 Room X
Burbank, CA 91522-0001
TYPE             Motion Pictures + Television + Syndication +
                 Documentaries
DEAL             Warner Bros. Television Productions
CREDITS          Murder in the 1st - Surviving Picasso - Roots - Thornbirds -
                 LA Confidential
COMMENTS         Janet Burrows/Dev. Office fax: 818-954-2319; 4000
                 Warner Blvd., Bldg. 14, Rm. V.
David L. Wolper . . . . . . . . . . . . . . . . . . . . . . . . . . Chairman
Mark M. Wolper . . . . . . . . . . . . . . President/Exec. Producer
Janet Burrows . . . . . . . . . . . . VP, Development (818-954-3577)
Kevin Nicklaus . . . . . . . . . . . . . . . . . . . . . . . . . Story Editor
Jonathan Stein . . . . . . . . . . . . . . . . . Asst. to Mark Wolper

**WORKING TITLE FILMS**
PHONE . . . . . . . . . . . . . . . . . 310-777-3100/171-307-3000
FAX . . . . . . . . . . . . . . . . . . . . . 310-777-4698/171-307-3001
9333 Wilshire Blvd.
Beverly Hills, CA 90210
TYPE             Motion Pictures
CREDITS          Bean - Dead Man Walking - Fargo - 4 Weddings & A
                 Funeral - The Big Lebowski
COMMENTS         ALSO: Oxford House, 76 Oxford St., London WIN 9FD
Tim Bevan . . . . . . . . . . . . . . . . . . . . . . . . . . . . Co-Chairman
Eric Fellner . . . . . . . . . . . . . . . . . . . . . . . . . . . Co-Chairman
Liza Chasin . . . . . . . . . . . . . . . . . . . . Pres., Production  (US)
Debra Hayward . . . . . . . . . . . . . . . Head, Development (UK)
Kathy Greenberg . . . . . . . . . . VP, Development & Production (US)
Emily Cook . . . . . . . . . . . . . . . . . . . . . . . . . . . . Story Editor

**WORLD FILM SERVICES, INC.**
PHONE . . . . . . . . . . . . . . . . . . . . . . . . . . . . . . . . 212-632-3456
FAX . . . . . . . . . . . . . . . . . . . . . . . . . . . . . . . . . . . 212-632-3457
630 Fifth Ave., Ste. 1505
New York, NY 10111
TYPE             Motion Pictures
CREDITS          A Passage To India - The Dresser - Beautiful Thing
John Heyman . . . . . . . . . . . . . . . . . . Chief Executive Officer
Pamela Osowski . . . . . . . . . . . . . . . . . . . . . . Vice President
Roy Krost . . . . . . . . . . . . . . . . . . . . . . . . . . . . . . . . Canada
David Laserson . . . . . . . . . . . . . . . . . . . Dir., Development

**WORLD OF WONDER**
PHONE . . . . . . . . . . . . . . . . . . . . . . . . . . . . . . . . 213-463-7133
FAX . . . . . . . . . . . . . . . . . . . . . . . . . . . . . . . . . . . 213-463-7134
EMAIL . . . . . . . . . . . . . . . . . . . . . . . . . . wow@wavenet.com
6671 Sunset Blvd., #1590
Hollywood, CA 90028
TYPE             Motion Pictures + Television + Documentaries
CREDITS          Party Monster - Real Ellen Story - RuPaul Show - Vinyl
                 Justice - Supermodel - Turn On TV - Drop Dead Gorgeous
COMMENTS         Also:  Music Videos.
Fenton Bailey . . . . . . . . . . . . . . . . . . . . . . . Producer/Director
Randy Barbato . . . . . . . . . . . . . . . . . . . . . . Producer/Director

# COMPANIES AND STAFF

**WORLDWIDE PANTS INCORPORATED**
PHONE . . . . . . . . . . . . . . . . 212-975-5300/213-852-7970
FAX . . . . . . . . . . . . . . . . . . . 212-975-4780/213-852-7979
1697 Broadway
New York, NY 10019
TYPE        Television + Motion Pictures
CREDITS     Late Show with David Letterman - Everybody Loves
           Raymond - The Late, Late Show with Tom Snyder - The
           High Life
COMMENTS   Also: 7800 Beverly Blvd., Ste. 244 Los Angeles, CA
           90036
Rob Burnett . . . . . . . . . . . . . . . . . . . . . . . President/CEO
James Peterson . . . . . . . . . . . . . . . . . . . . Exec. VP/COO
David Letterman . . . . . . . . . . . . . . . . . . . . . Comptroller
Kate Adler . . . . . . . . . . . . . . . . . . . VP, Creative Affairs (LA)

**WORTH PRODS., MARVIN**
PHONE . . . . . . . . . . . . . . . . . . . . . . . . . . 310-273-0181
FAX . . . . . . . . . . . . . . . . . . . . . . . . . . . . 310-274-7378
9784 Drake Lane
Beverly Hills, CA 90210
TYPE        Motion Pictures + Television + Syndication + Interactive
           Multimedia
CREDITS     Gia - Diabolique - Malcolm X - The Rose - Lenny - Where's
           Poppa
Marvin Worth . . . . . . . . . . . . . . . . . . . . . . . . . Producer
Todd Schlank . . . . . . . . . . . . . . . . . . . . Asst. to Mr. Worth

**WRIGHT PRODUCTIONS, NORTON**
PHONE . . . . . . . . . . . . . . . . . . . . . . . . . . 818-990-3058
FAX . . . . . . . . . . . . . . . . . . . . . . . . . . . . 818-379-8511
13331 Moorpark St., Ste. 308
Sherman Oaks, CA 91423
TYPE        Motion Pictures + Television
CREDITS     Murderous Intent - Angel Flight Down - Rescue Flight 232
           - Sadie & Son
Norton Wright . . . . . . . . . . . . . . . . . Exec. Producer/Writer

***WRITE PLACE WRITE TIME**
PHONE . . . . . . . . . . . . . . . . . . . . . . . . . . 818-763-6618
FAX . . . . . . . . . . . . . . . . . . . . . . . . . . . . 818-763-2139
EMAIL . . . . . . . . . . . . . . . . . . . . . . . . . wpwt@aol.com
10500 Riverside Dr.
Toluca Lake, CA 91602
TYPE        Motion Pictures + Television + Documentaries
CREDITS     Mike Hammer: Private Eye
Robert B. Evans . . . . . . . . . . . . . . . . . . . . . . . Principal
Larry B. Williams . . . . . . . . . . . . . . . . . . . . . . Principal
Michele Wolford . . . . . . . . . . . . . . . . . . . . . . . Principal

**WYCHWOOD PRODUCTIONS**
PHONE . . . . . . . . . . . . . . . . . . . . . . . . . . 213-462-6400
FAX . . . . . . . . . . . . . . . . . . . . . . . . . . . . 213-465-6709
Propaganda Films
940 N. Mansfield Ave.
Hollywood, CA 90038
TYPE        Motion Pictures
DEAL        Propaganda Films
CREDITS     Con Air - General's Daughter
Simon West . . . . . . . . . . . . . . . . . . . . . Director/Producer
Jib Polhemus . . . . . . . . . . . . . . . . . . . . VP, Development
Amy Clark . . . . . . . . . . . . . . . . . . . . . Asst. to Simon West

**YAGYA PRODUCTIONS**
PHONE . . . . . . . . . . . . . . . . . . . . . . . . . . 310-230-4040
FAX . . . . . . . . . . . . . . . . . . . . . . . . . . . . 310-454-3703
EMAIL . . . . . . . . . . . . . . . . . . . . . billduke@billduke.com
WEBSITE . . . . . . . . . . . . . . . . . . . . http://billduke.com
P.O. Box 609
Pacific Palisades, CA 90272
TYPE        Motion Pictures + Television + Interactive Multimedia +
           Syndication
Bill Duke . . . . . . . . . . . . . . . . . . . . . . . . . President/CEO
Lynora Miller . . . . . . . . . . . . . . . . . . . Production Manager
Melissa Clark . . . . . . . . . . . . . . . . . . . . . . Chief Counsel
Timothy Hunter . . . . . . . . . . . . . . . . . . . . Office Assistant

**YELLEN COMPANY,, LINDA**
PHONE . . . . . . . . . . . . . . . . . . . . . . . . . . 310-474-2331
FAX . . . . . . . . . . . . . . . . . . . . . . . . . . . . 310-474-1291
10850 Wilshire Blvd., #817
Los Angeles, CA 90024
TYPE        Motion Pictures + Television
CREDITS     Northern Lights - Parallel Lives - Everybody Wins
COMMENTS   Agent - Frank Wuliger @ The Gersh Agency
           310-274-6611
Linda Yellen . . . . . . . . . . . . . . . . . . . . . . Director/Writer
Martin Yellen . . . . . . . . . . . . . . . . Exec. Vice President (NY)
Susanne Columbia . . . . . . . . . . . . Production & Development
Alicia Buchanan . . . . . . . . . . . . . . . Asst. to Linda Yellen

**YERKOVICH PRODS.**
PHONE . . . . . . . . . . . . . . . . . . . . . . . . . . 310-396-1200
EMAIL . . . . . . . . . . . . . . . . . . . . . . yerkovich@aol.com
46 Market St.
Venice, CA 90291
TYPE        Motion Pictures + Television
DEAL        Paramount Television Group
CREDITS     Miami Vice - Hill Street Blues - Private Eye - Hollywood
           Confidential - The Islands
Anthony Yerkovich . . . . . . . . . . . . . . . . . . . . . . President
Teresa Lin . . . . . . . . . . . . . . . . . . . . . . Head, Development

***YORK COMPANY, THE**
PHONE . . . . . . . . . . . . . . . . . . . . . . . . . . 818-846-9559
FAX . . . . . . . . . . . . . . . . . . . . . . . . . . . . 818-846-3993
EMAIL . . . . . . . . . . . . . . . . . . . . . . . Dyorkco@aol.com
Burbank Production Plaza
801 S. Main St., Ste. D
Burbank, CA 91506
TYPE        Motion Pictures + Television
CREDITS     La Cucaracha - Dragon: The Bruce Lee Story - Midnight
           Run
Dan York . . . . . . . . . . . . . . . . . . President/Producer/Writer

**YORKIN PRODUCTIONS, BUD**
PHONE . . . . . . . . . . . . . . . . . . . . . . . . . . 310-274-8111
FAX . . . . . . . . . . . . . . . . . . . . . . . . . . . . 310-274-8112
345 N. Maple Dr., Ste. 206
Beverly Hills, CA 90210
TYPE        Motion Pictures + Television + Syndication
DEAL        Paramount Pictures- Motion Picture Group
CREDITS     Intersection - Twice in a Lifetime - Blade Runner - All in
           the Family
Bud Yorkin . . . . . . . . . . . . . . . . . . . . . . . . . . President
Damon Carr . . . . . . . . . . . . . . . . . . . . . . . . . . Assistant

**YORKTOWN PRODS. INC.**
PHONE . . . . . . . . . . . . . . . . . . . . . . . . . . 310-264-4155
FAX . . . . . . . . . . . . . . . . . . . . . . . . . . . . 310-264-4167
3000 W. Olympic Blvd.
Santa Monica, CA 90404
TYPE        Motion Pictures + Television
CREDITS     Moonstruck - Bogus - For Richer or Poorer
Norman Jewison . . . . . . . . . . . . . . . . . . Director/Producer
Gayle Fraser-Baigelman . . . . . . . . . . . . . . . . . . . Producer
Dianne Hatlestad . . . . . . . . . . . . . . . . . Creative Assistant
Liz Broden . . . . . . . . . . . . . . . . . . Asst. to Norman Jewison

**YOU GO BOY PRODUCTIONS**
PHONE . . . . . . . . . . . . . . . . . . . . . . . . . . 310-244-6332
FAX . . . . . . . . . . . . . . . . . . . . . . . . . . . . 310-244-6399
10202 W. Washington, Hepburn East 1st Fl
Culver City, CA 90232
TYPE        Motion Pictures
DEAL        Columbia Pictures
Martin Lawrence . . . . . . . . . . . . . . . . . . . . . . . Chairman
Robert B. Lawrence . . . . . . . . . . . . . . . . Executive Director
Nilah Davis . . . . . . . . . . . . . . . . . . . . Production Executive
Jonah Hodge . . . . . . . . . . . . . . . . . . . . . . . . Story Editor
Regina Haynes . . . . . . . . . . . . . . . . . Development Assistant

# COMPANIES AND STAFF

**YOUNG ARTISTS PRODUCTIONS**
PHONE . . . . . . . . . . . . . . . . . . . . . . . . . . . . 213-464-8132
FAX . . . . . . . . . . . . . . . . . . . . . . . . . . . . . . 213-464-0827
6253 Hollywood Blvd., Ste. 822
Los Angeles, CA 90028-5320

TYPE — Animation + Documentaries + Motion Pictures + Television

Bryan Peele . . . . . . . . . . . . . . . . . . . . . . . . . . CEO/President
Marcus Durian . . . . . . . . . . . . . . . . . . . . . Jr. Creative Executive
Susanne Filkins . . . . . . . . . . . . . . . . . . . . Jr. Creative Executive

**ZAENTZ CO., THE SAUL**
PHONE . . . . . . . . . . . . . . . . . . . . . . . . . . . . 510-549-1528
FAX . . . . . . . . . . . . . . . . . . . . . . . . . . . . . . 510-486-2108
2600 10th St.
Berkeley, CA 94710

TYPE — Motion Pictures
CREDITS — One Flew Over the Cuckoo's Nest - Amadeus - The English Patient

Saul Zaentz . . . . . . . . . . . . . . . . . . . . . . . . . . . . . Producer

**ZANE BUZBY & CONAN BERKELEY PRODUCTIONS**
PHONE . . . . . . . . . . . . . . . . . . . . . . . . . . . . 213-876-5566
FAX . . . . . . . . . . . . . . . . . . . . . . . . . . . . . . 213-876-6668
EMAIL . . . . . . . . . . . . . . . . . . . . . . . zmail@earthlink.net
3446 Troy Drive
Los Angeles, CA 90068

TYPE — Television + Motion Pictures + Syndication
DEAL — Columbia TriStar Television

Zane Buzby . . . . . . . . . . . . . . . . . . . Director/Exec. Producer
Conan Berkeley . . . . . . . . . . . . . . . . . . . . Executive Producer
Teri Coleman . . . . . . . . . . . . . . . . . . . . . . . . Development

**ZANUCK CO., THE**
PHONE . . . . . . . . . . . . . . . . . . . . . . . . . . . 310-274-0261
FAX . . . . . . . . . . . . . . . . . . . 310-273-9217/212-688-1755
9465 Wilshire Blvd., Ste. 308
Beverly Hills, CA 90212

TYPE — Motion Pictures
CREDITS — Jaws - The Sting - The Verdict - Cocoon - Driving Miss Daisy - Rush - Deep Impact

Richard D. Zanuck . . . . . . . . . . . . . . . . . . . . . . . . Producer
Lili Fini Zanuck . . . . . . . . . . . . . . . . . . . . . Producer/Director
Phyllis Skolnik . . . . . . . . . . . . . . VP, Creative Affairs (East Coast)
Dean Zanuck . . . . . . . . . . . . . . . VP, Creative Affairs (West Coast)

**ZARING/CIOFFI ENTERTAINMENT, INC.**
PHONE . . . . . . . . . . . . . . . . . . . . . . . . . . . 310-826-8884
FAX . . . . . . . . . . . . . . . . . . . . . . . . . . . . . 310-826-8003
EMAIL . . . . . . . . . . . . . . . . . . . . . . . . . JRZ8884@aol.com
WEBSITE . . . . . . . . . . . . . . . . . . . http://www.stardays.com
1731 Barry Ave., Ste. 112
Los Angeles, CA 90025

TYPE — Motion Pictures + Television
CREDITS — Picture Perfect - Nervous Ticks - Enemy Camp
COMMENTS — Producing Partnership with Richard Karn Also: Sports Programs & Deal with ESPN.

Bianca Cioffi-Zaring . . . . . . . . . . . . . . . . . . Partner/Producer
John Zaring . . . . . . . . . . . . . . . . . . . . . . . Partner/Producer
Francesca Rollins . . . . . . . . . . . . . . . . . . . Dir., Development

**ZERO PICTURES**
PHONE . . . . . . . . . . . . . . . . . . . . . . . . . . . 310-285-7763
FAX . . . . . . . . . . . . . . . . . . . . . . . . . . . . . 310-450-0232
EMAIL . . . . . . . . . . . . . . . . . . . . . info@zeropictures.com
WEBSITE . . . . . . . . . . . . . . . . . . . http://zeropictures.com
171 Pier Ave., #317
Santa Monica, CA 90405

TYPE — Motion Pictures + Documentaries + Television + Animation
CREDITS — Hero, Lover Fool - The Wooden Gun - Mick and The Claw - The Invisibles - Dogstar - Lucinda's Spell

Cain Angelie . . . . . . . . . . . . . . . . . . . . . . . . . Filmmaker
Shana Betz . . . . . . . . . . . . . . . . . . . . . . . . . . Filmmaker
J.C. Brandy . . . . . . . . . . . . . . . . . . . . . . . . . . Filmmaker
Wic Coliman . . . . . . . . . . . . . . . . . . . . . . . . . Filmmaker
Jon Jacobs . . . . . . . . . . . . . . . . . . . . . . . . . . Filmmaker
Michael Kastenbaum . . . . . . . . . . . . . . . . . . . . . Filmmaker
Sophie Pegrom . . . . . . . . . . . . . . . . . . . . . . . . Filmmaker
Jaime Rotman . . . . . . . . . . . . . . . . . . . . . . . . . Filmmaker
Truman Weatherley . . . . . . . . . . . . . . . . . . . . . . Filmmaker
Thomas Zachmeier . . . . . . . . . . . . . . . . . . . . . . Filmmaker

**ZETA ENTERTAINMENT LTD.**
PHONE . . . . . . . . . . . . . . . . . . . . . . . . . . . 213-653-4077
FAX . . . . . . . . . . . . . . . . . . . . . . . . . . . . . 213-653-0737
EMAIL . . . . . . . . . . . . . . . . . . . . zetafilms@earthlink.net
8455 Beverly Blvd., Ste. 308
Los Angeles, CA 90048

TYPE — Motion Pictures
CREDITS — Physical Graffiti - Montana - Shiloh - The Big Squeeze - Guncrazy - Fist of the North Star

Zane W. Levitt . . . . . . . . . . . . . . . . . . . . . . CEO/Producer
Mark Yellen . . . . . . . . . . . . . . . . . . . . . President/Producer
Rowena Murphy . . . . . . . . . . . . . . . . Chief Financial Officer
Allyson Smith . . . . . . . . . . . . . . . . . . . . Head, Development

**ZIDE ENTERTAINMENT**
PHONE . . . . . . . . . . . . . . . . . . . . . . . . . . . 310-887-2999
FAX . . . . . . . . . . . . . . . . . . . . . . . . . . . . . 310-887-2995
EMAIL . . . . . . . . . . . . . . . . . . . . zidefilms@directnet.com
9100 Wilshire Blvd., Ste. 615 East
Beverly Hills, CA 90212

TYPE — Motion Pictures + Television
CREDITS — The Big Hit - Providence - East Grand Rapids High

Warren Zide . . . . . . . . . . . . . . . . . . . . . . . . . . Producer
Craig Perry . . . . . . . . . . . . . . . . . . Producer (310-887-2998)
JC Spink . . . . . . . . . . . . . . . Dir., Development (310-887-2990)

**ZIMMERMAN/BERG**
PHONE . . . . . . . . . . . . . . . . . . . . . . . . . . . 310-827-4480
FAX . . . . . . . . . . . . . . . . . . . . . . . . . . . . . 310-369-0618
20th Century Fox
10201 W. Pico Blvd., Bldg. 203, Rm. 10
Los Angeles, CA 90035

TYPE — Motion Pictures + Television
DEAL — Twentieth Century Fox Television
CREDITS — Roseanne - A Very Brady Sequel - Golden Girls - The Brady Bunch Movie - The Jetsons
COMMENTS — Moving at Press Time.

James Berg . . . . . . . . . . . . . . . . . . . . . . Writer/Producer
Stan Zimmerman . . . . . . . . . . . . . . . . . . . . Writer/Producer

**ZM PRODUCTIONS**
PHONE . . . . . . . . . . . . . . . . . . . . . . . . . . . 213-436-2300
FAX . . . . . . . . . . . . . . . . . . . . . . . . . . . . . 213-436-2399
3151 Cahuenga Blvd., West, Ste. 300
Los Angeles, CA 90068

TYPE — Motion Pictures + Television + Documentaries
CREDITS — Hearts of Darkness - Encino Man - The Cape - Frank Capra's American Dream

George Zaloom . . . . . . . . . . . . . . . . . . . . Executive Producer
Jean-Michel Michenaud . . . . . . . . . . . . . . . . Executive Producer
Charles Duncombe . . . . . . . . . . . . . . . . . . Producer/Writer
Chris Cowan . . . . . . . . . . . . . . . . . . . . . Executive Producer
Jeff Cvengros . . . . . . . . . . . . . . . . . . . . Head, Development
Michael Shevloff . . . . . . . . . . . . . . . . . . . Head, Production
Charles Steenreld . . . . . . . . . . . . . . . . Head, Business Affairs

**ZOLLO PRODUCTIONS**
PHONE . . . . . . . . . . . . . . . . . . . . . . . . . . . 212-957-1300
FAX . . . . . . . . . . . . . . . . . . . . . . . . . . . . . 212-957-1315
EMAIL . . . . . . . . . . . . . . . . . . . . . . . . . . zpi@aol.com
WEBSITE . . . . . . . . . . http://www.members.aol.com/zpi/index.html
257 W. 52nd St., 2nd Fl.
New York, NY 10019

TYPE — Motion Pictures + Television + Documentaries
CREDITS — Mississippi Burning - Ghosts of Mississippi - The Paper - Quiz Show - In The Gloaming
COMMENTS — Also: Theatre.

Frederick Zollo . . . . . . . . . . . . . . . . . . . . . . . . . Producer
Nicholas Paleologos . . . . . . . . . . . . . . . . . . . . . . Producer
Bostic Beard . . . . . . . . . . . . . . . . . . Executive, Creative Affairs

**ZUCKER BROTHERS PRODUCTIONS**
PHONE . . . . . . . . . . . . . . . . . . . . . . . . . . . 310-656-9200
FAX . . . . . . . . . . . . . . . . . . . . . . . . . . . . . 310-656-9220
1351 4th St., 3rd Floor
Santa Monica, CA 90401

TYPE — Motion Pictures
DEAL — Universal Pictures
CREDITS — Naked Gun 1, 2 & 3 - Airplane! - Ruthless People - Ghost - My Best Friend's Wedding

David Zucker . . . . . . . . . . . . . . . . . . . . . Producer/Director
Jerry Zucker . . . . . . . . . . . . . . . . . . . . . Producer/Director
Gil Netter . . . . . . . . . . . . . . . . . . . . . . President/Producer
Janet Zucker . . . . . . . . . . . . . . . . . . . . . . . . . . Producer

**ZWEIBEL, ALAN**
PHONE . . . . . . . . . . . . . . . . . . . . . . . . . . . . . . . . . 310-285-2374
FAX . . . . . . . . . . . . . . . . . . . . . . . . . . . . . . . . . . . 310-285-2386
Silly Robin Productions
335 N. Maple Dr., Ste. 135
Beverly Hills, CA 90210-3867
TYPE        Motion Pictures + Television
DEAL        Castle Rock Entertainment
CREDITS    It's Garry Shandling's Show - North - Dragnet - Bunny
           Bunny - The Story of Us
COMMENTS  Also:  Stageplays, Novels, and Magazine Pieces.
Alan Zweibel . . . . . . . . . . . . . . . . . . . . . . . . . . . . . Writer/Producer
Alice Kim . . . . . . . . . . . . . . . . . . . . . . . . . . . . . . . . . Assistant

# SECTION B.

# Companies with Studio Deals

# HAVE YOU BEEN ASKED TO COPY THIS BOOK?

## COPYRIGHT INFRINGEMENT IS A FEDERAL CRIME.

We offer rewards on information of illegal photocopying or distribution of any of our books. Please call our office.

*Your identity will be protected.*

**310-315-4815**

# STUDIO DEALS

## A & E Television Networks

| | |
|---|---|
| 44 Blue Productions, Inc. | 818-760-4442 |
| Jones Entertainment Group | 303-784-8250 |
| Weller/Grossman Productions | 818-755-4800 |

## ABC Entertainment

| | |
|---|---|
| Bedford Falls Co., The | 310-394-5022 |
| Bochco Prods., Steven | 310-369-2400 |
| Brillstein-Grey Ent. | 310-275-6135 |
| Clark Prods., Inc., Dick | 818-841-3003 |
| Edwards Yellen Entertainment | 213-466-3013 |
| Harpo Films Inc. | 310-278-5559 |
| Landsburg Co., The | 310-478-7878 |
| New Screen Concepts, Inc. | 203-961-0670 |
| Newman Prods., Launa | 310-442-5667 |
| O'Hara-Horowitz Productions | 818-986-7150 |
| Olmos Productions Inc. | 310-557-7010 |
| Panamort Television | 310-557-6920 |
| WolfMill Entertainment | 310-559-1622 |

## ABC Pictures

| | |
|---|---|
| Cairo/Simpson Productions, Inc. | 310-557-6939 |
| Demberg Productions, Lisa | 310-557-6908 |
| Raskoff Productions, Ken | 310-557-7700 |

## Adelson Productions, Orly

| | |
|---|---|
| Skylark Films Ltd. | 310-396-5753 |

## Alliance Entertainment

| | |
|---|---|
| Blue Relief, Inc. | 818-560-2255 |

## Alliance Television Productions

| | |
|---|---|
| Chanticleer Films | 213-462-4705 |
| LeFrak Prods. | 212-541-9444 |

## Anchor Bay Entertainment

| | |
|---|---|
| Magnum Motion Pictures, Inc. | 213-656-3922 |

## Artisan Entertainment

| | |
|---|---|
| Simon Productions, Randy | 310-274-7440 |

## Atlantis Films

| | |
|---|---|
| Old Beantown Films | 310-576-7719 |
| Rogers Entertainment | 310-820-0073 |
| Sullivan Company, The | 310-319-2026 |

## Batson Enterprises

| | |
|---|---|
| Roxaboxen | 310-559-9192 |

## Big Ticket Television

| | |
|---|---|
| Douthit Productions Ltd. | 310-917-1194 |

## BKN Kids Network

| | |
|---|---|
| WolfMill Entertainment | 310-559-1622 |

## Bonneville Worldwide Entertainment

| | |
|---|---|
| Gaslight Pictures | 818-379-8518 |

## Brillstein-Grey Ent.

| | |
|---|---|
| Daniel Productions, Jay | 818-760-5959 |

## Buena Vista Productions

| | |
|---|---|
| Burton Prods., Al | 213-954-7865 |

## Caravan Pictures

| | |
|---|---|
| Murphy Prods., Eddie | 212-399-9900 |

## Carsey-Werner Co., The

| | |
|---|---|
| Carlson, Matthew | 818-760-5054 |

## Castle Rock Entertainment

| | |
|---|---|
| Abilene Pictures | 310-888-3550 |
| Big Town Productions | 310-888-3506 |
| Bill Oakley & Josh Weinstein | 310-888-3529 |
| Blum Productions, Howard | 310-285-2300 |
| El Dorado Pictures | 310-244-8464 |
| Face Productions | 310-285-2300 |
| KiMina Entertainment | 310-550-0824 |
| Legacy Entertainment Inc. | 310-285-2300 |
| New Crime Productions | 310-396-2199 |
| Prufrock Pictures | 310-285-2360 |
| Simian Films | 310-285-2300 |
| Weinstock Productions | 310-888-3533 |
| Zweibel, Alan | 310-285-2374 |

## CBS Corporation

| | |
|---|---|
| Landsburg Co., The | 310-478-7878 |

## CBS Entertainment

| | |
|---|---|
| Bochco Prods., Steven | 310-369-2400 |
| Catfish Productions | 310-456-5365 |
| Clark Prods., Inc., Dick | 818-841-3003 |
| Greene Prods., Vanessa | 213-852-4425 |
| Lee Productions, Michele | 213-852-4094 |
| Mozark Productions | 818-655-5779 |
| Shapiro Prods., Arnold | 310-451-6270 |
| Shukovsky English Ent. | 818-760-6100 |

## Citadel Entertainment., LLC

| | |
|---|---|
| Grand Productions, Inc. | 310-887-5645 |
| Kaufman Co., The | 310-887-0150 |
| Roaring Fork Productions | 310-887-5643 |
| Sennet Prods., Mark | 310-887-5642 |

## Clark Prods., Inc., Dick

| | |
|---|---|
| Sheldon/Post Company, The | 818-760-8265 |

## Columbia Pictures

| | |
|---|---|
| 40 Acres & A Mule Filmworks Inc. | 718-624-3703 |
| Allied Stars | 310-244-5188 |
| Barwood Films | 212-765-7191 |
| First Kiss Productions | 310-244-5171 |
| First Street Films, Inc. | 310-244-7891 |
| Fountainbridge Films | 213-782-1177 |
| Fried Films | 310-244-8727 |
| Gittes, Inc. | 310-244-4333 |
| Hunt-Tavel Productions | 310-244-3144 |
| Imageries Entertainment | 310-244-6119 |
| JD Productions | 310-244-7590 |
| Lynn Productions, Tami | 818-888-8264 |
| Manifest Film Company | 310-244-4900 |

Out of the Blue . . . Entertainment . . . . . . . . . . 310-244-7800
Peters Entertainment . . . . . . . . . . . . . . . . . . . . . 818-954-2441
Rastar Productions . . . . . . . . . . . . . . . . . . . . . . . 310-244-7871
Signature . . . . . . . . . . . . . . . . . . . . . . . . . . . . . . 310-244-8382
Turman-Morrissey Company, The . . . . . . . . . . 310-244-4943
Warp Films . . . . . . . . . . . . . . . . . . . . . . . . . . . . . 310-244-5355
Wick, C.Z. . . . . . . . . . . . . . . . . . . . . . . . . . . . . . . 310-201-0812
You Go Boy Productions . . . . . . . . . . . . . . . . . . 310-244-6332

## Columbia TriStar Motion Picture Group

Original Film . . . . . . . . . . . . . . . . . . . . . . . . . . . 310-445-9000

## Columbia TriStar Television

Anderson Prods., Craig . . . . . . . . . . . . . . . . . . 310-841-2555
Blum Productions, Howard . . . . . . . . . . . . . . . 310-285-2300
Chris/Rose Prods. . . . . . . . . . . . . . . . . . . . . . . . 310-840-8384
Christmas Tree Entertainment, Inc. . . . . . . . . 310-840-8370
Crystal Beach Entertainment . . . . . . . . . . . . . . 310-840-8358
Dark Horse Ent. . . . . . . . . . . . . . . . . . . . . . . . . 818-777-5830
El Dorado Pictures . . . . . . . . . . . . . . . . . . . . . . 310-244-8464
Elephant Walk Entertainment . . . . . . . . . . . . . 310-887-3977
Hargrove Prods., Dean . . . . . . . . . . . . . . . . . . . 310-838-6841
Myerson Entertainment . . . . . . . . . . . . . . . . . . 310-550-7383
P.A.T. Productions . . . . . . . . . . . . . . . . . . . . . . 310-244-8881
Rice & Beans Prods. . . . . . . . . . . . . . . . . . . . . . 626-792-9171
Storyline Entertainment . . . . . . . . . . . . . . . . . . 310-244-3222
Stupin Productions, Paul . . . . . . . . . . . . . . . . . 310-979-8741
Zane Buzby & Conan Berkeley Productions . . . 213-876-5566

## Davis Entertainment Co.

Davis Classics . . . . . . . . . . . . . . . . . . . . . . . . . . 310-551-2266
Dogsmile Pictures . . . . . . . . . . . . . . . . . . . . . . . 310-551-2258
Equus Entertainment . . . . . . . . . . . . . . . . . . . . 310-551-2262
Jericho Entertainment . . . . . . . . . . . . . . . . . . . 310-282-6924
Solomon/Hackett Productions . . . . . . . . . . . . . 310-551-2212

## Digital Technoligies Media

Burrud Productions . . . . . . . . . . . . . . . . . . . . . 714-846-7174

## Dimension Films

Craven Films, Wes . . . . . . . . . . . . . . . . . . . . . . 818-752-0197
Grand Designs Entertainment . . . . . . . . . . . . . 310-656-7575

## Discovery Networks

44 Blue Productions, Inc. . . . . . . . . . . . . . . . . . 818-760-4442
Weller/Grossman Productions . . . . . . . . . . . . . 818-755-4800

## DreamWorks SKG

Apostle Pictures . . . . . . . . . . . . . . . . . . . . . . . . 212-541-4323
Bandeira Entertainment . . . . . . . . . . . . . . . . . . 213-866-3535
ImageMovers . . . . . . . . . . . . . . . . . . . . . . . . . . . 818-733-8313
Johnson Productions, Mark . . . . . . . . . . . . . . . 818-733-9872
Moll/Beallor Productions . . . . . . . . . . . . . . . . . 818-777-9000
Mozark Productions . . . . . . . . . . . . . . . . . . . . . 818-655-5779
Pacific Data Images . . . . . . . . . . . . . . . . . . . . . 650-846-8100
Remote Control Productions . . . . . . . . . . . . . . 310-656-9356
Roth/Arnold Prods. . . . . . . . . . . . . . . . . . . . . . . 310-315-4830
Sanford/Pillsbury Prods. . . . . . . . . . . . . . . . . . . 310-393-5225
UBU Productions . . . . . . . . . . . . . . . . . . . . . . . . 818-655-5850
Vanguard Films . . . . . . . . . . . . . . . . . . . . . . . . . 310-888-8020
Winston Productions, Stan . . . . . . . . . . . . . . . . 818-902-5639

## Film Roman, Inc.

Mischel Co., The . . . . . . . . . . . . . . . . . . . . . . . . 310-526-0321

## Finnegan-Pinchuk Company

Frankovich Prods., Inc., Peter . . . . . . . . . . . . . 310-447-3670

## First Look Picts./Overseas Filmgroup

Trivision Pictures Inc. . . . . . . . . . . . . . . . . . . . . 213-655-5055

## Fox 2000

Donley Productions, Maureen . . . . . . . . . . . . . 310-369-5418
Motor City Films . . . . . . . . . . . . . . . . . . . . . . . . 310-369-0360

## Fox Animation Studios

Common Ground Entertainment . . . . . . . . . . . 310-274-5186

## Fox Broadcasting Co.

Obst Prods., Lynda . . . . . . . . . . . . . . . . . . . . . . 310-369-2993
Rice & Beans Prods. . . . . . . . . . . . . . . . . . . . . . 626-792-9171

## Fox Entertainment Company

Schlatter Prods., George . . . . . . . . . . . . . . . . . . 213-655-1400

## Fox Family Channel

Fraser Prods., Woody . . . . . . . . . . . . . . . . . . . . 818-505-6050

## Fox Television Studios

Greenblatt Janollari Studio, The . . . . . . . . . . . 310-369-2026
LookAlike Productions . . . . . . . . . . . . . . . . . . . 310-444-8650
Mindless Entertainment . . . . . . . . . . . . . . . . . . 310-444-8549

## Fries Productions, Inc., Chuck

Avanti Enterprises . . . . . . . . . . . . . . . . . . . . . . . 213-466-2266

## Gaumont

Nomad Productions . . . . . . . . . . . . . . . . . . . . . 310-282-0660

## Genx Entertainment

Bregman Entertainment Co., The . . . . . . . . . . . 213-833-6207

## Goldwyn Films Inc.

Killer Films, Inc. . . . . . . . . . . . . . . . . . . . . . . . . 212-473-3950

## Granada Entertainment USA

Mr. Mudd . . . . . . . . . . . . . . . . . . . . . . . . . . . . . . 213-932-5656

## Greenblatt-Junollari/The Sullivan Co.

Rogers Entertainment . . . . . . . . . . . . . . . . . . . . 310-820-0073

## Griffin Group, The

Kosberg Prods., Robert . . . . . . . . . . . . . . . . . . . 310-285-1345

## Grosso-Jacobson Productions, Inc.

Glory Monty Prods. . . . . . . . . . . . . . . . . . . . . . . 310-274-4924

## Hallmark Entertainment

Blue Rider Pictures . . . . . . . . . . . . . . . . . . . . . . 310-314-8246

# STUDIO DEALS

## Hammer Film Productions Limited

Magnum Motion Pictures, Inc. . . . . . . . . . . . . . 213-656-3922

## HBO

Fried Films . . . . . . . . . . . . . . . . . . . . . . . . 310-244-8727

## HBO Original Programming

Albrecht/Read Management . . . . . . . . . . . . . . 213-461-3200
PB Management . . . . . . . . . . . . . . . . . . . . . 213-653-7284

## Hearst Entertainment

Auerbach Company . . . . . . . . . . . . . . . . . . . 310-478-1700
Brayton/Carlucci Productions . . . . . . . . . . . . . 310-478-1700
C.M. Two Productions . . . . . . . . . . . . . . . . . . 310-575-1291
Diana Kerew Productions . . . . . . . . . . . . . . . . 310-575-1272
Gleneagle Productions . . . . . . . . . . . . . . . . . 310-478-1700
JCS Entertainment Inc. . . . . . . . . . . . . . . . . . 310-575-1262
Rothstein Prods., Freyda . . . . . . . . . . . . . . . . 310-575-1264
Shadowplay Films . . . . . . . . . . . . . . . . . . . . 310-478-1700

## Henson Company, Jim

Angel/Brown Prods. . . . . . . . . . . . . . . . . . . . 213-960-8014
Wandering Monkey Entertainment . . . . . . . . . . 213-960-4096

## History Channel, The

Weller/Grossman Productions . . . . . . . . . . . . . 818-755-4800

## Hollywood Pictures

Parachute Entertainment, LLC. . . . . . . . . . . . . 212-691-1697

## Home & Garden Television

Weller/Grossman Productions . . . . . . . . . . . . . 818-755-4800

## Icon Productions Inc.

Paraview Inc. . . . . . . . . . . . . . . . . . . . . . . . 212-489-5343

## Interscope Communications Inc.

BallPark Productions . . . . . . . . . . . . . . . . . . 310-827-1328
Terra Bella Entertainment . . . . . . . . . . . . . . . 213-655-2311
Ward Films, Inc., Vincent . . . . . . . . . . . . . . . 213-850-5703

## Jaffe/Braunstein Films Ltd.

Chotzen/Jenner Productions . . . . . . . . . . . . . . 213-465-9877
March Hare Entertainment . . . . . . . . . . . . . . . 213-464-4100

## Kennedy/Marshall Company

Chesterfield Film Co., The . . . . . . . . . . . . . . . 310-260-6112

## King World Productions

Coffey/Ballantine . . . . . . . . . . . . . . . . . . . . 310-442-6315
Full Moon & High Tide Prods. Inc. . . . . . . . . . . 213-852-2626

## Longbow Productions

Kaylor Company, The (aka Edge Enter.) . . . . . 818-762-6600
Witt, Dan . . . . . . . . . . . . . . . . . . . . . . . . . 818-762-6600

## Mandalay Entertainment

Polone Company, The . . . . . . . . . . . . . . . . . . 310-309-5707

## Mandalay Pictures

Blum Productions, Howard . . . . . . . . . . . . . . . 310-285-2300

## MDP/Behaviour Worldwide

Mount/Kramer Company, The . . . . . . . . . . . . . 310-226-8374

## Merv Griffin Productions

Weisworld Premieres . . . . . . . . . . . . . . . . . . 310-285-1345

## MGM/UA

Danjaq Inc. . . . . . . . . . . . . . . . . . . . . . . . . 310-449-3185
David Ladd Films . . . . . . . . . . . . . . . . . . . . . 310-449-3410
FGM Entertainment . . . . . . . . . . . . . . . . . . . 310-358-1370
Seldes Films . . . . . . . . . . . . . . . . . . . . . . . . 310-449-3045
Trilogy Entertainment Group . . . . . . . . . . . . . 310-449-3095

## Millennium Television Network

Uplinger Enterprises . . . . . . . . . . . . . . . . . . . 310-829-7886

## Miramax Films

A Band Apart . . . . . . . . . . . . . . . . . . . . . . . 213-951-4600
aMuse Productions . . . . . . . . . . . . . . . . . . . . 310-209-6155
Craven Films, Wes . . . . . . . . . . . . . . . . . . . . 818-752-0197
FilmColony, Ltd. . . . . . . . . . . . . . . . . . . . . . 213-951-4650
Grand Designs Entertainment . . . . . . . . . . . . . 310-656-7575
Handprint Entertainment . . . . . . . . . . . . . . . . 213-655-2400
Konrad Pictures . . . . . . . . . . . . . . . . . . . . . 818-560-2700
Outerbanks Entertainment . . . . . . . . . . . . . . . 310-979-8747
View Askew Productions, Inc. . . . . . . . . . . . . . 732-842-6933

## Morgan Creek Prods.

Rankin/Bass Productions . . . . . . . . . . . . . . . . 212-582-4017

## Motion Pict. Corp. of America

Immortal Films . . . . . . . . . . . . . . . . . . . . . . 310-582-8300

## MTV Networks

Cheyenne 7 Prods. . . . . . . . . . . . . . . . . . . . . 818-954-7310

## Nash Entertainment

Rive Gauche International TV . . . . . . . . . . . . . 818-784-9912

## NBC Entertainment

Landsburg Co., The . . . . . . . . . . . . . . . . . . . 310-478-7878
O'Hara-Horowitz Productions . . . . . . . . . . . . . 818-986-7150

## NBC Studios

Barron/Pennette Prods. . . . . . . . . . . . . . . . . . 818-655-5960
Broadway Video (NY) . . . . . . . . . . . . . . . . . . 212-265-7621
Clark Prods., Inc., Dick . . . . . . . . . . . . . . . . . 818-841-3003
First Folio Films . . . . . . . . . . . . . . . . . . . . . 818-840-7741
Raskin Productions, Bonnie . . . . . . . . . . . . . . 818-840-7571
Wells Productions, John . . . . . . . . . . . . . . . . 818-954-1687

# STUDIO DEALS

## NBC Television Network

First Folio Films . . . . . . . . . . . . . . . . . . 818-840-7741

## Nelvana Communications

Wild Things Prods. . . . . . . . . . . . . . . . . . 310-899-0787

## New Line Cinema

Abilene Pictures. . . . . . . . . . . . . . . . . . . 310-888-3550
Apatow Productions . . . . . . . . . . . . . . . . 310-656-9122
Cunningham Prods. Inc. . . . . . . . . . . . . . 818-995-1585
Industry Entertainment . . . . . . . . . . . . . 213-954-9000
Langley Prods. . . . . . . . . . . . . . . . . . . . . 310-449-5300
Mojo Films . . . . . . . . . . . . . . . . . . . . . . . 310-248-6070
Rat Entertainment . . . . . . . . . . . . . . . . . 310-248-6040
Segan Company, The Lloyd . . . . . . . . . . 213-850-3130
Spanky Pictures, Inc. . . . . . . . . . . . . . . . 212-634-4440
Team Todd . . . . . . . . . . . . . . . . . . . . . . . 310-248-6001
Templeton Productions . . . . . . . . . . . . . 310-248-6016
Wessler Entertainment . . . . . . . . . . . . . . 310-248-6035

## New Line Television

Kahn Power Pictures(Formerly Odessa Pic). . . . 310-967-6566

## New Regency Television

Canterbury Films . . . . . . . . . . . . . . . . . . 310-550-0100

## NewStar Television

NewStar Media . . . . . . . . . . . . . . . . . . . . 310-786-1600

## Nickelodeon/Nick at Nite

Wild Things Prods. . . . . . . . . . . . . . . . . . 310-899-0787

## Oceans 2 Ent.

Roxaboxen . . . . . . . . . . . . . . . . . . . . . . . 310-559-9192

## October Films

Baer Entertainment Group . . . . . . . . . . . 310-777-3680
Butchers Run Films . . . . . . . . . . . . . . . . 818-777-7333
First Cold Press Productions . . . . . . . . . . 212-444-3215
Goatsingers, The . . . . . . . . . . . . . . . . . . 212-966-3045
Single Cell Pictures . . . . . . . . . . . . . . . . 310-385-6697

## Pacifica Entertainment

La Luna Films . . . . . . . . . . . . . . . . . . . . 310-285-9696

## Paramount Network Television

Bakula Productions, Inc. . . . . . . . . . . . . . 213-960-4005
Braga Productions . . . . . . . . . . . . . . . . . 213-956-5799

## Paramount Pictures- Motion Picture Group

Alphaville . . . . . . . . . . . . . . . . . . . . . . . . 213-956-4803
Badham Co., The . . . . . . . . . . . . . . . . . . 818-990-9495
Belisarius Prods. . . . . . . . . . . . . . . . . . . 213-956-8660
Berman Productions, Rick . . . . . . . . . . . 213-956-5037
Braga Productions. . . . . . . . . . . . . . . . . . 213-956-5799
Broadway Pictures (LA) . . . . . . . . . . . . . 213-956-5729
Broadway Video (NY) . . . . . . . . . . . . . . . 212-265-7621
C/W Productions . . . . . . . . . . . . . . . . . . 213-956-8150
Carr Enterprises, Allan . . . . . . . . . . . . . . 310-278-2490
Cort/Madden Company, The . . . . . . . . . . 213-956-5884

Eagle Nation Films . . . . . . . . . . . . . . . . . 213-956-5989
Evans Co., The Robert . . . . . . . . . . . . . . 213-956-8800
Flying Freehold Productions . . . . . . . . . . 213-956-8838
Goepp Circle Productions . . . . . . . . . . . . 213-956-4620
Icon Productions Inc. . . . . . . . . . . . . . . . 818-954-2960
Ladd Company, The . . . . . . . . . . . . . . . . 213-956-8203
Lakeshore Entertainment Corp. . . . . . . . . 213-956-4222
Leo Productions, Malcolm . . . . . . . . . . . 213-464-4448
London Company, Barry . . . . . . . . . . . . . 213-956-5066
Lyles Prods., A.C. . . . . . . . . . . . . . . . . . . 213-956-5819
Mandy Films, Inc. . . . . . . . . . . . . . . . . . 310-246-0500
Meyer/Jaffe Prods. . . . . . . . . . . . . . . . . . 213-956-5841
MTV Films . . . . . . . . . . . . . . . . . . . . . . . 323-956-8023
Mutual Film Co. . . . . . . . . . . . . . . . . . . . 213-871-5690
Neufeld Productions, Mace . . . . . . . . . . . 213-956-4816
Nickelodeon Movies . . . . . . . . . . . . . . . . 212-258-4985
OffRoad Entertainment . . . . . . . . . . . . . . 213-956-4425
Pacific Western Prods. . . . . . . . . . . . . . . 213-956-8601
Phase I Productions . . . . . . . . . . . . . . . . 310-393-6217
Rudin Prods., Scott . . . . . . . . . . . . . . . . . 213-956-4600
Say Unkel Entertainment . . . . . . . . . . . . 818-506-6015
Seven Arts Pictures . . . . . . . . . . . . . . . . 213-464-0225
Yorkin Productions, Bud . . . . . . . . . . . . . 310-274-8111

## Paramount Television Group

Act III Productions . . . . . . . . . . . . . . . . . 213-956-8587
Berman Productions, Rick . . . . . . . . . . . 213-956-5037
Bristol Cities . . . . . . . . . . . . . . . . . . . . . . 323-956-3513
Bungalow 78 Prods. . . . . . . . . . . . . . . . . 213-956-4440
Charles-Burrows-Charles . . . . . . . . . . . . 213-956-5961
Daly-Harris Productions . . . . . . . . . . . . . 213-956-8930
Eagle Nation Films . . . . . . . . . . . . . . . . . 213-956-5989
Ellison, Bob . . . . . . . . . . . . . . . . . . . . . . 213-956-4859
Fanaro-Nathan Prods. . . . . . . . . . . . . . . 213-956-8870
Floyd Johnson Productions, Charles . . . . 213-956-3606
Gibbons Enterprises, Leeza . . . . . . . . . . 213-956-4972
Grammnet Productions . . . . . . . . . . . . . . 213-956-5547
Grub Street Prods. . . . . . . . . . . . . . . . . . 213-956-4657
Pet Fly Prods. . . . . . . . . . . . . . . . . . . . . . 818-843-3594
Petrie Jr. & Co., Daniel . . . . . . . . . . . . . . 818-623-1600
Yerkovich Prods. . . . . . . . . . . . . . . . . . . . 310-396-1200

## Pearson All American

Ozma Productions . . . . . . . . . . . . . . . . . 310-656-1100

## Pearson Television Productions

Avenue Pictures . . . . . . . . . . . . . . . . . . . 310-996-6800

## Phoenix Pictures

Kingsgate Films, Inc. . . . . . . . . . . . . . . . 310-244-7004
Plurabelle Films . . . . . . . . . . . . . . . . . . . 310-244-6782
Rehme Productions . . . . . . . . . . . . . . . . . 310-477-5811

## PolyGram Filmed Ent.

Act III Productions . . . . . . . . . . . . . . . . . 213-956-8587
Egg Pictures . . . . . . . . . . . . . . . . . . . . . . 213-845-0300
Empire Pictures Inc. . . . . . . . . . . . . . . . . 213-463-1618
Havoc Inc. . . . . . . . . . . . . . . . . . . . . . . . 212-924-1629
Interscope Communications Inc. . . . . . . . 310-208-8525
Terra Bella Entertainment . . . . . . . . . . . . 213-655-2311

## Polygram Filmed Entertainment

Scott Free Productions . . . . . . . . . . . . . . 310-888-4100

## PolyGram Television

Prufrock Pictures . . . . . . . . . . . . . . . . . . 310-285-2360
Tri-Crown Prods. . . . . . . . . . . . . . . . . . . 818-955-7337

# STUDIO DEALS

## Proctor & Gamble Prods. Inc.

Logo Entertainment . . . . . . . . . . . . . . . . . . . . . . 310-276-6700

## Producers Ent. Group, Ltd., The

Sheldon/Post Company, The . . . . . . . . . . . . . 818-760-8265

## Propaganda Films

Blue Relief, Inc. . . . . . . . . . . . . . . . . . . . . . . . 818-560-2255
Boku Films . . . . . . . . . . . . . . . . . . . . . . . . . . . 213-993-2033
Wychwood Productions . . . . . . . . . . . . . . 213-462-6400

## Ruddy Morgan Organization, Inc., The

Brown Group, The . . . . . . . . . . . . . . . . . . . . . 310-581-4354
Canterbury Films . . . . . . . . . . . . . . . . . . . . . 310-550-0100

## Rysher Entertainment

Grant, Gil . . . . . . . . . . . . . . . . . . . . . . . . . . . . 310-309-5544
Johnson Prods., Don . . . . . . . . . . . . . . . . . . . 818-238-2200
Levinson/Fontana Company, LLC, The . . . . . . 212-206-3585
Papazian-Hirsch Entertainment . . . . . . . . . . . . 818-887-2400

## Saban Entertainment

Boz Productions . . . . . . . . . . . . . . . . . . . . 310-235-5401
Proud Mary Entertainment . . . . . . . . . . . . . . . . 213-658-0458
Weisberg Prods., Roni . . . . . . . . . . . . . . . . . 310-235-5100

## Showtime Networks Inc.

Imagination Productions Inc. . . . . . . . . . . . . . 310-315-4760
Paulson Prods., Daniel L. . . . . . . . . . . . . . . 310-234-5270
Samuelson Productions . . . . . . . . . . . . . . . . 310-208-1000
Tudor Entertainment, Inc. . . . . . . . . . . . . . . . 310-247-1660
Turtle Productions, Jon . . . . . . . . . . . . . . . . 310-234-5347
Vide-U Productions . . . . . . . . . . . . . . . . . . . 310-276-5509

## Sidney Kimmel Entertainment

Longfellow Pictures . . . . . . . . . . . . . . . . . . . 212-431-5550

## Singer Productions, Carla

Sittenfield Productions, Joan . . . . . . . . . . . . . 310-859-1107

## Sneak Preview Entertainment, Inc.

RoadKill Films . . . . . . . . . . . . . . . . . . . . . . . 213-962-0295

## Sony Pictures Entertainment

Gracie Films . . . . . . . . . . . . . . . . . . . . . . . . 310-244-4222
Henson Pictures, Jim . . . . . . . . . . . . . . . . . . 213-960-4096
Jaffilms . . . . . . . . . . . . . . . . . . . . . . . . . . . . 310-244-4700
Katie Face Prods. . . . . . . . . . . . . . . . . . . . . 310-244-6788
Mark Prods., Laurence . . . . . . . . . . . . . . . . . 818-560-6280
Mirage Enterprises . . . . . . . . . . . . . . . . . . . 310-244-2044
Radiant Productions . . . . . . . . . . . . . . . . . . 310-656-1400
Red Mullet, Inc. . . . . . . . . . . . . . . . . . . . . . . 310-244-3364
Red Wagon Prods. . . . . . . . . . . . . . . . . . . . . 310-244-4466

## Sony Television

Industry Entertainment . . . . . . . . . . . . . . . . . 213-954-9000
Platinum Studios, LLC . . . . . . . . . . . . . . . . . 310-276-3900

## Spelling Films

Trilogy Entertainment Group . . . . . . . . . . . . . 310-449-3095

## Storm Entertainment

Populuxe Pictures . . . . . . . . . . . . . . . . . . . . . 213-272-5537

## Studios USA Television

Renaissance Pictures . . . . . . . . . . . . . . . . . . 818-777-0088
Traveler's Rest Films . . . . . . . . . . . . . . . . . . 818-777-3025
Wolf Films Inc. . . . . . . . . . . . . . . . . . . . . . . . 818-777-1236

## Telescene Film Group/AAN

La-Mont Communications Inc. . . . . . . . . . . . . 310-577-6725

## Touchstone Pictures

Brownhouse Productions . . . . . . . . . . . . . . . . 213-650-2670
Colleton Company, The . . . . . . . . . . . . . . . . . 818-560-7190
Estevez Productions . . . . . . . . . . . . . . . . . . . 310-264-4199
Pilot Boy Productions . . . . . . . . . . . . . . . . . . 818-560-2853
Via Rosa Productions . . . . . . . . . . . . . . . . . . 310-656-6252

## TriStar Television

Sofronski Prods., Bernard . . . . . . . . . . . . . . . 310-244-5412

## Turner Network Television

Bleecker Street Films . . . . . . . . . . . . . . . . . . 213-993-7386
Gimbel Productions, Inc., Roger . . . . . . . . . . . 310-459-3838

## Twentieth Century Fox

Barnette Productions, Alan . . . . . . . . . . . . . . . 310-369-1000
Blue Horizon . . . . . . . . . . . . . . . . . . . . . . . . 310-656-6177
Blue Tulip Productions . . . . . . . . . . . . . . . . . 310-752-7900
Chako Film International . . . . . . . . . . . . . . . . 310-275-1543
Elephant Walk Entertainment . . . . . . . . . . . . . 310-887-3977
Equus Entertainment . . . . . . . . . . . . . . . . . . 310-551-2262
Goat Cay Productions, Inc. . . . . . . . . . . . . . . 212-247-6493
InFront Productions . . . . . . . . . . . . . . . . . . . 310-369-5890
Johnson Entertainment, Magic . . . . . . . . . . . . 310-369-1000
Langley Prods. . . . . . . . . . . . . . . . . . . . . . . . 310-449-5300
More/Medavoy Management . . . . . . . . . . . . . 213-969-0700
Mundy Lane Entertainment . . . . . . . . . . . . . . 310-369-5940
New Regency Prods. . . . . . . . . . . . . . . . . . . . 818-954-3044
OMNIBUS . . . . . . . . . . . . . . . . . . . . . . . . . . 310-369-7226
Schindler Prods., Deborah . . . . . . . . . . . . . . . 212-265-7760

## Twentieth Century Fox Film Corp.

Mutant Enemy, Inc. . . . . . . . . . . . . . . . . . . . . 310-579-5180

## Twentieth Century Fox Television

Ten Thirteen Productions . . . . . . . . . . . . . . . . 310-369-1130
Zimmerman/Berg . . . . . . . . . . . . . . . . . . . . . 310-827-4480

## Twentieth Century Fox-Fox 2000 (LA)

Bedford Falls Co., The . . . . . . . . . . . . . . . . . . 310-394-5022
Common Ground Entertainment . . . . . . . . . . . 310-274-5186
Diamond Heart Productions . . . . . . . . . . . . . . 310-369-3753
Dogstar Films . . . . . . . . . . . . . . . . . . . . . . . . 310-552-1518
Edmonds Entertainment . . . . . . . . . . . . . . . . 213-860-1550
Flat Penny Films . . . . . . . . . . . . . . . . . . . . . . 213-933-0991
Flower Films, Inc. . . . . . . . . . . . . . . . . . . . . . 310-285-0200
Friendly Productions . . . . . . . . . . . . . . . . . . . 310-369-3973
Isaac Productions, Sandy . . . . . . . . . . . . . . . 310-369-3528

# STUDIO DEALS

| | |
|---|---|
| Jacobs/Mutrux Prods. | 310-369-3181 |
| Knickerbocker Films | 310-369-3946 |
| Krane Group, The Jonathan | 310-278-0142 |
| Monarch Pictures | 310-369-1668 |
| Red Hour Films | 310-289-2565 |
| State Street Pictures | 310-369-5099 |
| True Pictures | 212-371-0514 |

## Twentieth Century Fox-Searchlight Picts.

| | |
|---|---|
| Good Machine | 212-343-9230 |
| Indican Productions | 212-274-1880 |

## Unapix Entertainemnt

| | |
|---|---|
| Fox Productions, Ted | 310-659-5016 |

## Universal Pictures

| | |
|---|---|
| All Girl Prods. | 818-777-7776 |
| Brillstein-Grey Ent. | 310-275-6135 |
| Butchers Run Films | 818-777-7333 |
| Clean Break Productions | 818-777-5977 |
| Daybreak Prods. | 818-777-0278 |
| Flat Penny Films | 213-933-0991 |
| Fortune Media Group, Inc. | 818-777-3063 |
| Haft Entertainment | 212-586-3881 |
| HyperFilms | 818-777-5617 |
| Jersey Films | 310-203-1000 |
| Katz Productions, Perry | 818-981-0232 |
| KiMina Entertainment | 310-550-0824 |
| Lobell-Bergman Prods. | 818-777-9944 |
| Moving Pictures | 310-576-0577 |
| Myron Productions, Ben | 310-360-1144 |
| Overbrook Entertainment | 818-777-2224 |
| Parkway Productions | 818-777-7107 |
| Raylin Entertainment | 818-777-6434 |
| Simonds Co., The Robert | 818-777-5445 |
| Singer Entertainment, Joseph M. | 818-777-9675 |
| Underworld Entertainment | 310-247-0690 |
| Wild Things Prods. | 310-899-0787 |
| Zucker Brothers Productions | 310-656-9200 |

## Universal Studios

| | |
|---|---|
| Dark Horse Ent. | 818-777-5830 |
| Edelson Productions | 818-733-0616 |
| Spin Cycle Entertainment | 818-777-8606 |
| Telvan Productions | 818-777-3737 |

## Universal Television

| | |
|---|---|
| Rose Productions, Lee | 310-659-2050 |

## Universal Television & Networks Group

| | |
|---|---|
| Angel Ark Productions | 818-777-2529 |
| Corymore Prods. | 818-777-1181 |
| Harris & Company | 818-777-3717 |
| Movicorp Holdings, Inc. | 310-553-4300 |

## Vega 7 Entertainment

| | |
|---|---|
| Populuxe Pictures | 213-272-5537 |

## Viacom

| | |
|---|---|
| Parachute Entertainment, LLC. | 212-691-1697 |

## Viacom Productions

| | |
|---|---|
| Bernbaum, Paul | 310-234-5085 |

| | |
|---|---|
| Clifford Prods., Patricia | 310-234-5074 |

## Von Zerneck-Sertner Films

| | |
|---|---|
| Germain Productions, Stephanie | 818-766-2610 |

## Walt Disney Company, The

| | |
|---|---|
| Bay Films | 310-829-7799 |
| Cappa Productions | 212-906-8800 |
| Caravan Pictures | 310-264-4400 |
| Estevez Productions | 310-264-4199 |
| Fogwood Films | 818-560-2880 |
| Forward Pass, Inc. | 310-571-3443 |
| Goldenring Productions | 818-560-7605 |
| Harpo Films Inc. | 310-278-5559 |
| Horseshoe Bay Productions | 310-587-0787 |
| Jacobs Prods., Michael | 818-560-6290 |
| Jacobson Company, The | 818-560-1600 |
| Junction Entertainment | 818-560-2800 |
| Kennedy/Marshall Company | 310-656-8400 |
| Lowry Productions, Hunt | 818-560-6790 |
| Mandeville Films | 818-560-1000 |
| Master Thespian Productions | 818-560-7711 |
| Mestres Productions, Ricardo | 818-560-Ext. |
| Montan Productions, Chris | 818-560-7485 |
| Paradox Prod., Inc. | 818-623-2855 |
| Rogow Productions, Stan | 818-560-5807 |
| Schiff Productions, Paul | 818-560-4423 |
| Sonnenfeld/Josephson | 818-560-0606 |
| Wildwood Enterprises Inc. | 310-395-5155 |

## Walt Disney Motion Pictures Group

| | |
|---|---|
| Blue Wolf Prods. Inc. | 310-451-8890 |
| Pixar Animation Studios | 510-236-4000 |

## Walt Disney Pictures/Touchstone Pictures

| | |
|---|---|
| Avnet-Kerner Co. | 310-838-2500 |
| Bruckheimer Films, Jerry | 310-664-6260 |
| DIC Entertainment | 818-955-5400 |
| Draizin Co., The | 818-972-4756 |
| Everyman Pictures | 310-244-8932 |
| Mendel Productions, Barry | 818-560-6747 |
| Meyers/Shyer Co., The | 818-560-4810 |
| Morra, Brezner, Steinberg & Tenenbaum | 310-385-1820 |
| Red Hen Productions | 818-560-1716 |
| Sandollar Prods. | 818-560-5820 |
| Saturn Films | 310-887-0900 |
| Shoelace Productions, Inc. | 212-243-2900 |

## Walt Disney Television

| | |
|---|---|
| Savage Studios Ltd. | 818-560-2316 |

## Walt Disney TV/Touchstone TV

| | |
|---|---|
| Burton Prods., Al | 213-954-7865 |
| Draizin Co., The | 818-972-4756 |
| FairDinkum Prods. | 310-586-8471 |
| Karz Entertainment | 818-560-4260 |
| Katz Entertainment Group, Barry | 212-977-1000 |
| Renfield Prods. | 818-733-0707 |
| St. Clare Entertainment | 310-229-2441 |
| Storyline Entertainment | 310-244-3222 |

## Warner Bros.

| | |
|---|---|
| HSI Entertainment | 310-452-9999 |
| Material | 818-954-1551 |
| Nava Films | 213-850-3155 |

# STUDIO DEALS

## Warner Bros. Feature Animation

Kirschner Prods., David . . . . . . . . . . . . . . . . . . . . 818-553-5511

## Warner Bros. Pictures

Atlas Entertainment . . . . . . . . . . . . . . . . . . . . . . . 310-724-7350
Aviator Films LLC . . . . . . . . . . . . . . . . . . . . . . . . . 818-558-5880
Baltimore/Spring Creek Pictures, LLC . . . . . . . 818-954-1210
Besame Mucho Pictures . . . . . . . . . . . . . . . . . . . 818-954-4555
Calm Down Productions, Inc. . . . . . . . . . . . . . . . 818-954-7614
Canton Company, The . . . . . . . . . . . . . . . . . . . . 818-954-2130
Copper Sky Productions . . . . . . . . . . . . . . . . . . . 310-827-9766
Di Novi Pictures . . . . . . . . . . . . . . . . . . . . . . . . . . 310-581-1355
Donner/Shuler-Donner Prods. . . . . . . . . . . . . . . See Section A
Fortis Films . . . . . . . . . . . . . . . . . . . . . . . . . . . . . . 310-659-4533
George Street Pictures . . . . . . . . . . . . . . . . . . . . 818-954-4361
Green Grass Blue Sky Company, Inc. . . . . . . . . 818-763-4182
Green Moon Productions . . . . . . . . . . . . . . . . . . 310-450-6111
Icon Productions Inc. . . . . . . . . . . . . . . . . . . . . . . 818-954-2960
Lynn Productions, Tami . . . . . . . . . . . . . . . . . . . 818-888-8264
Mad Chance . . . . . . . . . . . . . . . . . . . . . . . . . . . . . 818-954-3803
Madguy Films . . . . . . . . . . . . . . . . . . . . . . . . . . . 310-777-6515
Malpaso Prods. . . . . . . . . . . . . . . . . . . . . . . . . . . 818-954-3367
Maysville Pictures . . . . . . . . . . . . . . . . . . . . . . . . 818-954-4840
Miller/Boyett/Warren Productions . . . . . . . . . . . 818-954-7700
Nasser Entertainment Group . . . . . . . . . . . . . . . 818-505-8030
Ockrent Productions, Ltd. . . . . . . . . . . . . . . . . . . 212-636-5820
Outlaw Productions . . . . . . . . . . . . . . . . . . . . . . . 310-777-2000
Peters Entertainment . . . . . . . . . . . . . . . . . . . . . 818-954-2441
Riche/Ludwig Productions . . . . . . . . . . . . . . . . . 213-850-2777
Schumacher Prods., Joel . . . . . . . . . . . . . . . . . . 818-954-2508
Seagal-Nasso Productions . . . . . . . . . . . . . . . . . 213-850-2940
Silver Pictures . . . . . . . . . . . . . . . . . . . . . . . . . . . 818-954-4490
Spring Creek Productions . . . . . . . . . . . . . . . . . . 818-954-1210
Stiefel Entertainment . . . . . . . . . . . . . . . . . . . . . 310-275-3377
Storyopolis Productions . . . . . . . . . . . . . . . . . . . 310-358-2525
Tig Productions, Inc. . . . . . . . . . . . . . . . . . . . . . . 818-954-4500
TSProductions . . . . . . . . . . . . . . . . . . . . . . . . . . . 818-954-4999
Village Roadshow Pictures . . . . . . . . . . . . . . . . . 818-954-1998
Weed Road Pictures . . . . . . . . . . . . . . . . . . . . . . 818-954-3771
Weintraub Prods., Jerry . . . . . . . . . . . . . . . . . . . 818-954-2500
Wells Productions, John . . . . . . . . . . . . . . . . . . . 818-954-1687
Witt-Thomas Films . . . . . . . . . . . . . . . . . . . . . . . 818-954-2545
Witt-Thomas-Harris Productions . . . . . . . . . . . . 213-464-1333

## Warner Bros. Television Productions

Aviator Films LLC . . . . . . . . . . . . . . . . . . . . . . . . . 818-558-5880
Bent Outta Shape Productions . . . . . . . . . . . . . . 818-954-1978
Bickley Prods. . . . . . . . . . . . . . . . . . . . . . . . . . . . 818-954-2782
Bright-Kauffman-Crane Prods. . . . . . . . . . . . . . . 818-977-7777
Cheyenne 7 Prods. . . . . . . . . . . . . . . . . . . . . . . . 818-954-7310
Cowlip Productions . . . . . . . . . . . . . . . . . . . . . . . 818-954-3403
Kedzie Productions . . . . . . . . . . . . . . . . . . . . . . . 818-954-5454
Lussier, Paul . . . . . . . . . . . . . . . . . . . . . . . . . . . . 818-954-4483
Mirkin Vision . . . . . . . . . . . . . . . . . . . . . . . . . . . . 310-369-1963
Pico Creek Prods. . . . . . . . . . . . . . . . . . . . . . . . . 310-394-7522
Robinson Entertainment, Dolores . . . . . . . . . . . 310-441-7300
SisterLee Productions Inc. . . . . . . . . . . . . . . . . . 818-954-7579
Wolper Org., The . . . . . . . . . . . . . . . . . . . . . . . . . 818-954-1421

## Wilshire Court Productions

Ducks In A Row Entertainment Corporation . . 310-557-2444

## Working Title Films

Havoc Inc. . . . . . . . . . . . . . . . . . . . . . . . . . . . . . . 212-924-1629

# SECTION C.

# Companies Indexed by Type

# HAVE YOU BEEN ASKED TO COPY THIS BOOK?

## COPYRIGHT INFRINGEMENT IS A FEDERAL CRIME.

We offer rewards on information of illegal photocopying or distribution of any of our books.
Please call our office.

*Your identity will be protected.*

**310-315-4815**

## Animation

Addis Films, Michael
Albert Prods. Inc., Sydell
Allegro Films
Baer Animation Co. Inc.
Batfilm Prods., Inc.
Bennett Productions, Harve
Big Sky Entertainment
Blue Rider Pictures
Blue Tulip Productions
Braun Productions, David
Britt Allcroft Co., The
Buckeye Entertainment Group
Canal+ (U.S.)
Cannery, Inc., The
Cobblestone Films
Coffey/Ballantine
Cohen Productions Inc., Herman
Colossal Pictures
CPC Entertainment
Dark Horse Ent.
DIC Entertainment
Dockry Productions
Donner/Shuler-Donner Prods.
Double Eagle Ent.
Draizin Co., The
DreamWorks SKG
Enteraktion, Inc.
Film Roman, Inc.
Filmatic Adventures Inc.
Filmlight
Films By Jove
Fox Animation Studios
Freyer Productions, Ellen
Gaumont
Gerren Productions
Gracie Films
Grand Designs Entertainment
Green Communications
Green Moon Productions
Gullane Pictures
Hallmark Entertainment (NY)
Harvey Entertainment Company
HBO Animation
Hearst Ent. Licensing & Family Prog.
Henson Company, Jim
Holmes Run Entertainment
Hyperion Entertainment
Ideal Entertainment, Inc.
Ideal Movie Shoppe, LLC, The
Imagination Factory Inc.
Ink Tank, The
Iwerks Entertainment
Jumbo Pictures, Inc.
Keeshen Productions, Jim
Klasky Csupo Inc.
Knight Company, The
Kushner-Locke Co.
L.A. Animation
La Luna Films
Looking Glass Productions
Lower East Side Films
Lunaria Films
Marvel Studios
Matinee Entertainment
Melendez Productions, Bill
Meridian Entertainment, LLC
Midnight Sun Pictures
Mirisch Corporation
Mischel Co., The
Moffitt Associates, William
Montan Productions, Chris
Mutant Enemy, Inc.
National Lampoon
Nelvana Entertainment
Northern Lights Ent.
Ockrent Productions, Ltd.
Overbrook Entertainment
Pacific Data Images

Perennial Pictures Film Corp.
Philipico Pictures Co.
Platinum Studios, LLC
Playtime Productions
Popular Arts Ent., Inc.
Porchlight Entertainment
Post Office, The
Proud Mary Entertainment
R. Edwards Prods./R. Edwards Films
R.A.M.M. Entertainment, Inc
Rankin/Bass Productions
Raylin Entertainment
Red Wagon Prods.
Reinert Pictures, Rick
Remote Control Productions
Roaring Mouse Entertainment, Inc.
Ruby-Spears Prods.
Rust Productions, Patricia
Saban Entertainment
Sauce Entertainment
Savage Studios Ltd.
Scheimer Prods., Lou
Scholastic Entertainment
Schwartzberg & Company
Seguin Prods., Nicole
Sitting Ducks Prods.
Sony Pictures Imageworks
Spin Cycle Entertainment
Spumco
Startoons
Startz Productions, Inc., Jane
Stern Production Company, The Howard
Stone Canyon Investments, Inc.
Storyopolis Productions
StoryTeller Films, Ltd.
Strader Entertainment
Stratford Prods, Inc., Bert
Studio Productions
Sunbow Entertainment
Suntaur Entertainment
Sweetpea Entertainment
Talking Rings Entertainment
Threshold Entertainment
Time Life Kids
TLC Entertainment
Too Nuts Productions, Ltd.
Tricor Entertainment
Two Oceans Entertainment Group
Two Stepp Productions
VanDerKloot Film & Television Inc.
Vista Street Entertainment
Viviano Entertainment
Wagner Prods., Inc., Raymond
Waisbren Enterprises, Brad
Walt Disney Television Animation
Warner Bros. Feature Animation
Warner Bros. International TV Production
Warner Bros. TV Animation
Warner Sisters Prods.
Wolf Films, Fred
WolfMill Entertainment
Young Artists Productions
Zero Pictures

## Documentaries

44 Blue Productions, Inc.
A & E Television Networks
About Face Prods.
Albert Prods. Inc., Sydell
Allegro Films
America National Network, Inc.
American Movie Classics/Romance Classic
Arbus Prods., Inc., Loreen
Aspect Ratio Films
Associated Producers Group, Inc.
Atelier Pictures
Axelson-Weintraub Productions
B.S. Company, Inc., The

Beach House
Bell and Associates, Dave
Big Shoes Productions
Big Sky Entertainment
Blue Rider Pictures
Bright Street Pictures
Buckeye Entertainment Group
Bunim-Murray Productions, Inc.
Burlage/Edell Productions, Inc.
Burrud Productions
Byck, Dann
Cannery, Inc., The
Cinewest Productions
Cinnamon Prods. Inc.
City Entertainment
Colmano Productions, Marino
Communications Corp. of America
Cook Films
Cossette Productions
Crystal Pyramid Productions
Dockry Productions
Doumanian Prods., Jean
Earthbourne Films, Inc.
Earthworks Films, Inc.
Eleventh Day Entertainment
EMK Productions
Enzo Films
EO Productions International, Inc.
Evolve Entertainment
Farrell/Minoff Prods.
Feury Entertainment, Joseph
Film Garden Entertainment
Film Kitchen
Filmopolis Pictures
FilmRoos
Filmsmith
Fine Line Features
First Look Picts./Overseas Filmgroup
Fogwood Films
Foxstar Productions
Full Circle Ent. AKA Suzanne Bauman Prod
Galan Entertainment
Gerren Productions
Giddings Images Inc., Al
Gotham Entertainment
GRB Entertainment
Green Moon Productions
Greenhouse Film Group Ltd., The
Greif Company
Greystone Communications Group, Inc.
Greystone Films
Grinning Dog Pictures
Haft Entertainment
Hale Productions, Corky
Hallet Street Prods.
Hamilton Entertainment, Inc., Dean
Hampton Films, Inc.
Handprint Entertainment
Hansen, Edward D.
Haugland Productions, David
Havoc Inc.
Hellinger Films
History Channel, The
Hobel Productions
Hollywood Literary Retreat/Zoom Ent.
Illusion Entertainment Group
Imax Corporation
International Filmmakers Management, Inc
Intrepidus
Iwerks Entertainment
Jones Entertainment Group
Jurist Productions
Killer Films, Inc.
Krainin Productions Inc.
Lake Como Pictures
Landsburg Co., The
Langley Prods.
Leo Productions, Malcolm
Levinson/Fontana Company, LLC, The
Lilac Productions

Linden Prods.
Little Bear Films, Inc.
Logo Entertainment
LookAlike Productions
Lux Pictures
Lyles Prods., A.C.
Lynn Productions, Tami
Malpaso Prods.
Mandalay Television
Mars Prods. Corp.
Mesmerize Studios
Mischel Co., The
MKD Prods.
Moffitt Associates, William
Moll/Beallor Productions
Morrow-Heus Productions
MPH Entertainment, Inc.
National Geographic Television
Netter Digital Entertainment
Never A Dull Moment Prods.
New Screen Concepts, Inc.
Newman Prods., Launa
NewStar Media
Olmos Productions Inc.
Open Road Prods., Ltd.
Overbrook Entertainment
Palomar Pictures
Paraview Pictures
PDQ Directions, Inc.
Pirromount Pictures
Planet Girl Pictures
Plurabelle Films
Post Office, The
Premier Attractions
R.A.M.M. Entertainment, Inc
Really Big Shoe Prods.
Rive Gauche International TV
River Mill Productions
Roaring Mouse Entertainment, Inc.
Rosa Entertainment
Rose Prods. Inc., Alex
Rosenman Productions, Howard
Sachnoff-Lipman Entertainment
Sauce Entertainment
Savoir Faire Productions
Schwartz Productions, Steven
Schwartzberg & Company
Scripps Howard Prods.
Sefton Productions International
Shogun Films, Ltd.
Silver Heart Productions
Simons Prods., David A.
Single Spark Pictures
Smith Productions Inc., Thomas G.
Sony Pictures Imageworks
Spin Cycle Entertainment
SPRINGTIME!
Star Land Entertainment Inc.
Stevens Company, The
Stuart Productions, Inc., Mel
T.H.A. - Thomas Horton Associates Inc.
TAE Productions
Taffner Entertainment Ltd.
Taylor Prods., Grazka
Team Entertainment Group
Telling Pictures Inc.
Teocalli Entertainment, Inc.
Thunderbird Pictures
Time-Life Video & Television
TLN Productions
Tollin/Robbins Productions
Tri-Crown Prods.
Tribe
TriCoast Entertainment
Trinity Pictures, Inc.
Turner Entertainment Group
Turner Original Productions
Una Chica Entertainment
VanDerKloot Film & Television Inc.
Vanguard Films

Video Dimensions Inc.
Vienna Productions
Vision Films
Viviano Entertainment
Voight Entertainment, Jon
Warner Sisters Prods.
Weintraub/Kuhn Prods.
Weller/Grossman Productions
Whidbey Island Films, Inc.
Whyaduck Prods., Inc.
Winchester Prods., Inc., Margot
Wolper Org., The
World of Wonder
Write Place Write Time
Young Artists Productions
Zero Pictures
ZM Productions
Zollo Productions

## Feature Direct to Video

360 entertainment
A & E Television Networks
Active Entertainment
AEI-Atchity Edit./Ent. Intl. Inc.
Alpine Pictures
American New Wave Films
American World Pictures
Atelier Pictures
Atmosphere Entertainment Inc.
Baer Animation Co. Inc.
Barnette Productions, Alan
Bernstein Productions, Jay
Big Sky Entertainment
Blue Rider Pictures
Bonneville Worldwide Entertainment
Bottom Line Studio, Inc.
Brookwell McNamara Entertainment
Bubble Factory, The
Capital Arts Entertainment
Chiaramonte Films, Inc.
Children's Television Workshop
Chotzen/Jenner Productions
Cobblestone Films
Colmano Productions, Marino
Dancing Asparagus Prods.
DIC Entertainment
Dockry Productions
Double Eagle Ent.
Emby Eye
EO Productions International, Inc.
Farrell/Minoff Prods.
Feigelson Prods., Inc., J.D.
Film Roman, Inc.
Filmopolis Pictures
Filmwerks
First Look Picts./Overseas Filmgroup
Fox Animation Studios
Fox Productions, Ted
Foxboro Company, Inc., The
Freyer Productions, Ellen
Fries Film Group, Inc.
Goldbar Entertainment
Greystone Films
Hallet Street Prods.
Hallmark Entertainment (NY)
Hansen, Edward D.
Harvey Entertainment Company
Henson Company, Jim
Hollywood Network, Inc.
Hyperion Entertainment
Imagination Factory Inc.
Imperial Entertainment
Initial Entertainment Group
Jericho Entertainment
Ksproductions
Kushner-Locke Co.
L.A. Animation

Leo Films
Lighthouse Productions
Logo Entertainment
Londine Productions
Luger Productions, Inc., Lois
Magic Hour Pictures
Magnum Motion Pictures, Inc.
Manhattan Project Ltd., The
Mars Prods. Corp.
Meltzer Productions, Michael
Movicorp Holdings, Inc.
National Lampoon
Never A Dull Moment Prods.
Newman/Tooley Films
NewStar Media
Nichol Moon Films
Northstar Entertainment
Oliver Productions, Lin
Omega Entertainment
Open Road Prods., Ltd.
Overbrook Entertainment
Ovitz Productions, Mark H.
PDQ Directions, Inc.
Peacock Films/1st Miracle Pictures
Perennial Pictures Film Corp.
Philipico Pictures Co.
Pirromount Pictures
Playboy Entertainment Group Inc.
Popular Arts Ent., Inc.
Populuxe Pictures
Porchlight Entertainment
Post Office, The
Premier Attractions
Promark Entertainment Group
R.A.M.M. Entertainment, Inc
Red Hen Productions
Redler Entertainment, Dan
Regent Entertainment, Inc.
Renaissance Pictures
Rice & Beans Prods.
Roaring Mouse Entertainment, Inc.
Rocket Pictures
Rosen/Bender Prods.
Rough Diamond Productions
Rust Productions, Patricia
Rysher Entertainment
Scarlet Fire Films
Scheimer Prods., Lou
Sefton Productions International
Silver Heart Productions
Simons Prods., David A.
Simsie Films
Sitting Ducks Prods.
Sony Pictures Imageworks
Startz Productions, Inc., Jane
StoneRoad Prods. Inc.
Storyopolis Productions
Stratford Prods., Inc., Bert
Sweetpea Entertainment
TAE Productions
Tahse Prods., Martin
Tapestry Films Inc.
Team Entertainment Group
TLC Entertainment
Trident Releasing Inc.
Trinity Pictures, Inc.
Tse Productions, Simon
Una Chica Entertainment
Unapix/A-PIX Entertainment
United Film
Vision Films
Vista Street Entertainment
Viviano Entertainment
Warner Bros. International TV Production
Warner Sisters Prods.
Weintraub/Kuhn Prods.
Weisberg Prods., Roni
Westwind Productions, Inc.

# COMPANIES INDEXED BY TYPE

## Interactive Multimedia

Active Entertainment
Addis Films, Michael
Adelson Entertainment
Atelier Pictures
Atmosphere Entertainment Inc.
Baer Animation Co. Inc.
Bates Entertainment
Batfilm Prods., Inc.
Berk Schwartz Bonann Productions
Bonneville Worldwide Entertainment
Braun Productions, David
Brillstein-Grey Ent.
Britt Allcroft Co., The
Broadway Video (NY)
Brown Group, The
Buckeye Entertainment Group
Burrud Productions
Cairo/Simpson Productions, Inc.
Carascope Productions Inc.
Cherry Alley Productions
Chestnut Hill Prods.
Cobalt Moon
Coffey/Ballantine
Colossal Pictures
Communications Corp. of America
Craven Films, Wes
Creative Road Corp.
Crosby/Levy Co., The
Dark Horse Ent.
Dore Productions, Bonny
Double Eagle Ent.
Dream City Films
DreamWorks SKG
Empire Pictures Inc.
Enteraktion, Inc.
Film Roman, Inc.
Filmlight
Galan Entertainment
Gerren Productions
Giddings Images Inc., Al
H. Beale Company
Hamilton Entertainment, Inc., Dean
Heller Prods., Paul
Henson Company, Jim
Hobel Productions
Hollywood Network, Inc.
Holmes Run Entertainment
Hyperion Entertainment
IF/X Productions
Imagination Factory Inc.
Imaginazium
Immortal Films
Imperial Entertainment
IndieGal Productions, LLC
Initial Entertainment Group
Intrepidus
IXL
Jones Entertainment Group
Katz/Rush Entertainment
Knight Company, The
Kushner-Locke Co.
La Luna Films
Langley Prods.
Last Stand Pictures, Inc.
Lighthouse Productions
Listen To Your Mother Prods., Inc.
Loring Productions, Lynn
Maia Productions
Malpaso Prods.
Maple Palm Productions
Matinee Entertainment
Meltzer Productions, Michael
Midnight Sun Pictures
Milestone Pictures Inc.
Ministry of Film Inc., The
Moffitt Associates, William
Mountain Drive
Muse Productions, Inc.

MWG Prods.
National Geographic Television
National Lampoon
Neila Inc.
Neo Motion Pictures, Inc.
Newman Prods., Launa
NewStar Media
Nichol Moon Films
No Prisoners
OMS - One Mind Sound Productions
Paige Assoc., Inc., George
Palomar Pictures
Persistent Pictures, Inc.
Planet Girl Pictures
Platinum Studios, LLC
Popular Arts Ent., Inc.
Porchlight Entertainment
Premier Attractions
Red Hen Productions
Revelations Entertainment
Roaring Mouse Entertainment, Inc.
Rocket Pictures
Rogers Entertainment
Rosa Entertainment
Sauce Entertainment
Scholastic Entertainment
Schwartzberg & Company
Seguin Prods., Nicole
Shapiro Productions, Allen
Shogun Films, Ltd.
Shoreline Entertainment
Sitting Ducks Prods.
Somers Teitelbaum David
Sony Pictures Imageworks
Spin Cycle Entertainment
Startoons
Stun
Stupin Productions, Paul
Synchronicity Productions
T-Squared Productions
TAE Productions
Tarnoff/Lazar & Co.
Threshold Entertainment
Too Nuts Productions, Ltd.
Tri-Crown Prods.
Tribeca Productions
Tricor Entertainment
Tulchin Entertainment
Turner Entertainment Group
Twin Brothers Productions, Inc
United Film
Utopia Films
Video Dimensions Inc.
Vienna Productions
Vista Street Entertainment
Wick, C.Z.
Worth Prods., Marvin
Yagya Productions

## Motion Pictures

1492 Pictures
3 Arts Entertainment
360 entertainment
40 Acres & A Mule Filmworks Inc.
44 Blue Productions, Inc.
54th Street Productions
A Band Apart
Abatemarco Productions, Frank
Abilene Pictures
About Face Prods.
Acappella Pictures
Act III Productions
Action America Entertainment
Active Entertainment
Addis Films, Michael
Adelson Entertainment
Adelson Productions, Orly
AEI-Atchity Edit./Ent. Intl. Inc.

Affrime Productions, Mindy
Agamemnon Films Inc.
Alan Smithee Films
Albert Prods. Inc., Sydell
Albrecht & Assocs. Inc.
Alexander/Enright & Assocs.
Alive Films
All Girl Prods.
Allegro Films
Alliance Pictures
Alliance Television Productions
Alliance/LeMonde Entertainment
Allied Stars
Allyn Films
Alphaville
Alpine Pictures
AM Productions & Management
Amen Ra Films
America National Network, Inc.
American Filmworks
American New Wave Films
American World Pictures
American Zoetrope
Amphion/Nitestar Productions
aMuse Productions
Anderson Prods., Craig
Andre Prods., Inc., Blue
Angel Ark Productions
Angel/Brown Prods.
Apatow Productions
Apostle Pictures
Apple & Honey Productions, Ltd.
Appledown Films, Inc.
Arama Entertainment
Arkoff Intl. Pictures
Arnold Productions, Inc., Judy
Arrow Entertainment
Artisan Entertainment
Ascato Entertainment
AsIs Productions
Aspect Ratio Films
Asseyev Prods. Inc., Tamara
Associated Producers Group, Inc.
Asylum Films
Atelier Pictures
Atkinson Way Films
Atlas Entertainment
Atman Entertainment
Atmosphere Entertainment Inc.
Auerbach Company
Aurora Productions
Avanti Enterprises
Avenue Pictures
Aviator Films LLC
Avnet-Kerner Co.
Axelrod/Widdoes Productions
Axelson-Weintraub Productions
B.S. Company, Inc., The
Badham Co., The
Baer Animation Co. Inc.
Baer Entertainment Group
Bakula Productions, Inc.
Baldwin/Cohen Productions
BallPark Productions
Ballyhoo, Inc.
Baltimore Pictures, Inc.
Baltimore/Spring Creek Pictures, LLC
Bandeira Entertainment
Banner Entertainment
Barnette Productions, Alan
Barnstorm Films
Bartlett Prods., Juanita
Barwood Films
Bates Entertainment
Batfilm Prods., Inc.
Batjac Productions, Inc.
Bauer Company, The
Baum Productions, Carol
Baumgarten/Prophet Entertainment
Bay Films

# COMPANIES INDEXED BY TYPE

Beach House
Beacon Pictures
Bean And Cod Prods.
Bedford Falls Co., The
Belisarius Prods.
Bell and Associates, Dave
Belladonna Productions
Benedetti Productions, Inc., Robert
Benjamin Prods. Inc.
Bennett Productions, Harve
Berk Schwartz Bonann Productions
Berman Productions, Rick
Berner Films, Fred
Bernsen Prods. Inc., Harry
Bernstein Productions, Jay
Besame Mucho Pictures
Bettina Prods. Ltd.
Big Bang Films
Big Shoes Productions
Big Sky Entertainment
Big Town Productions
Bigel/Mailer Films
Black & White Productions
Black Sheep Entertainment
Black, Lawrence & Silverhardt Ent.
Black/Marlens Company, The
Blake Prods., Timothy
Bleecker Street Films
Blue Bay Productions
Blue Horizon
Blue Relief, Inc.
Blue Rider Pictures
Blue Tulip Productions
Blue Turtle, Inc.
Blue Wolf Prods. Inc.
Blueline Productions
Blum Productions, Howard
Blumberg Productions
BLURCO
Boardwalk Ent./Alan Wagner Prods., Inc.
Bobker Films, Daniel
Bodega Bay Prods., Inc.
Boku Films
Bona Fide Productions
Bonneville Worldwide Entertainment
Borchers, Donald P.
Bottom Line Studio, Inc.
Boyle-Taylor Prods.
Boyman Productions, Inc.
Boz Productions
Braga Productions
Brainstorm Media
Brandman Prods.
Braubach Productions
Braun Entertainment Group, Inc.
Braun Productions, David
Breen Prods., Paulette
Bregman Entertainment Co., The
Bregman Productions
Briggle Prods., Stockton
Bright Street Pictures
Brillstein-Grey Ent.
Bristol Cities
British Lion
Britt Allcroft Co., The
Broadway Pictures (LA)
Broadway Video (NY)
Brooksfilms, Ltd.
Brookwell McNamara Entertainment
Brown Group, The
Brownhouse Productions
Bruckheimer Films, Jerry
Bryan Films, James
BThree Films
Bubble Factory, The
Buckeye Entertainment Group
Bungalow 78 Prods.
Burlage/Edell Productions, Inc.
Burrud Productions
Burton Prods., Tim

Butchers Run Films
Byck, Dann
Byline Films
Byrum Power & Light
C/W Productions
Cafe Productions
Cairo/Simpson Productions, Inc.
Calm Down Productions, Inc.
Camera Marc
Canal+ (U.S.)
Cannell Motion Pictures
Cannery, Inc., The
Cannon & Associates, Reuben
Canterbury Films
Canton Company, The
Canton Productions, Maj
Capella Films Inc.
Capital Arts Entertainment
Capo Productions
Cappa Productions
Carascope Productions Inc.
Caravan Pictures
Carliner Prods., Mark
Carlson, Matthew
Carlson-Lehman Prods.
Carlyle Prods. & Mgmt.
Carr Enterprises, Allan
Carreras Productions
Carrie Productions
Carsey-Werner Co., The
Carter Company, The Thomas
Caruso-Mendelsohn Prods.
Castle Rock Entertainment
Catapult Films
Cates/Doty Productions
Catfish Productions
Cecchi Gori Pictures
Centropolis Streamline
Chako Film International
Chancellor Entertainment
Channel Productions
Channing Films LLC
Chanticleer Films
Chartoff Productions
Chase Prods., Stanley
Cherry Alley Productions
Chesler/Perlmutter Production
Chesterfield Film Co., The
Chestnut Hill Prods.
Cheyenne 7 Prods.
Chiaramonte Films, Inc.
Chicagofilms
Chotzen/Jenner Productions
Chris/Rose Prods.
Christmas Tree Entertainment, Inc.
Cine Grande Entertainment
Cine Paris
CineCity Pictures
Cinema Seven Prods.
CinePoint Productions, Inc.
Cinequanon Pictures Intl. Inc.
Cinergi Pictures Entertainment Inc.
Cinestage Productions
Cinetel Films
Cineville Inc.
Cinewest Productions
Cinnamon Prods. Inc.
Citadel Entertainment., LLC
City Entertainment
City Light Films
CLC Productions, Inc.
Clean Break Productions
Clifford Prods., Patricia
Cobalt Films International
Cobblestone Films
Codikow Films
Coffey/Ballantine
Cohen & Ryan Films, Inc.
Cohen Productions Inc., Herman
Cohen Productions, Martin B.

Colleton Company, The
Colmano Productions, Marino
Colomby/Keaton
Colossal Pictures
Columbia Pictures
Common Creed Entertainment Corp.
Common Ground Entertainment
Communications Corp. of America
Comsky Group Productions
Concorde/New Horizons Corp.
Concourse Prods.
Connection III Entertainment Corp.
Constantin Film Development Inc.
Cook Films
Copp And Goodman
Copper Sky Productions
Cort/Madden Company, The
Cosgrove-Meurer Prods.
Cossette Productions
Coyote Pass Productions
CPC Entertainment
Craven Films, Wes
Creative Group Prods., Inc.
Creative Road Corp.
Crosby/Levy Co., The
Crown International Pictures
Crystal Beach Entertainment
cTonic Fliks
Cuddihy, Christopher A.
Culver Films, Carmen
Cunningham Prods. Inc.
Curtis Prods., Dan
Dakota North Ent./Dakota Films
Daly-Harris Productions
Dancing Asparagus Prods.
Danger Filmworks
Danielson - Rosenthal Productions
Danika Productions, Inc.
Danjaq Inc.
Dark Horse Ent.
Dark Matter Productions
David Ladd Films
Davis Classics
Davis Entertainment Co.
Daybreak Prods.
De Laurentiis Company, Dino
De Passe Entertainment
Dee Gee Entertainment
Def Pictures
Deja View Productions, Inc.
Delaware Pictures
Demberg Productions, Lisa
Demo Productions, Inc.
DePew Productions
Desert Heart Prods.
Di Novi Pictures
Diamond Heart Productions
Diamondback Entertainment
DIC Entertainment
Dimension Films
Dinamo Entertainment
Distant Horizon
Dockry Productions
Dogsmile Pictures
Dogstar Films
Don Baer Prods. Inc.
Donley Productions, Maureen
Donner/Shuler-Donner Prods.
Dore Productions, Bonny
Double A Films
Double Eagle Ent.
Double Whammy Productions
Doumanian Prods., Jean
Douthit Productions Ltd.
Dragon Pictures
Draizin Co., The
Dream City Films
DreamWorks SKG
Dreyfuss/James Prods.
Driskill Entertainment

# COMPANIES INDEXED BY TYPE

Rankin/Bass Productions
Ransohoff Productions, Inc., Martin
Rastar Productions
Rat Entertainment
Raylin Entertainment
Razors Edge Productions, Inc.
Really Big Shoe Prods.
Rearguard Productions, Inc.
Recorded Picture Company
Red Diamond Company, The
Red Hen Productions
Red Hour Films
Red Mullet, Inc.
Red Strokes Entertainment
Red Wagon Prods.
Redeemable Features
Redler Entertainment, Dan
Reel Life Women
Regan Company, The
Regent Entertainment, Inc.
Rehme Productions
Reid Productions, Inc., Tim
Reinert Pictures, Rick
Remote Control Productions
Renaissance Pictures
Renfield Prods.
Revelations Entertainment
Revolution Entertainment
Rialto Films
Rice & Beans Prods.
Rich Productions, Lee
Riche/Ludwig Productions
Richulco, Inc.
Ridini Entertainment Corporation
Ridio Prods., Inc., Anthony
River Mill Productions
River One Films
RKO Pictures, Inc.
RoadKill Films
Roaring Fork Productions
Roaring Mouse Entertainment, Inc.
Robbins Entertainment
Robinson Entertainment, Dolores
Robinson Productions, Amy
Robson Entertainment
Rocket Pictures
Rocking Horse Prods.
Rodan Prods., Inc.
Rogers Entertainment
Rogow Productions, Stan
Rosa Entertainment
Roscoe Enterprises, Inc.
Rose Prods. Inc., Alex
Rose Productions, Lee
Rosemont Prods. International Ltd.
Rosen/Bender Prods.
Rosenberg, Helena Hacker
Rosenman Productions, Howard
Ross Production, Gary
Ross Productions, Hal
Ross, Herbert
Rossu Entertainment
Roth/Arnold Prods.
Rothstein Prods., Freyda
Rotman Productions, David
Rough Diamond Productions
Roxaboxen
RSO Films
Rubin * Burke Productions
Ruby-Spears Prods.
Ruddy Morgan Organization, Inc., The
Rudin Prods., Scott
Rumbleseat Prods.
Rupert Productions, Inc.
Russell Productions, Neil
Rust Productions, Patricia
S.E.R. Filmworks
Saban Entertainment
Sachs Productions, Gabe
Sacks Productions Inc., Alan

Saga Pictures Corporation
Saltire Entertainment
Samoset Inc./Sacret Inc.
Samuels Ent. Inc., Ron
Samuelson Productions
Sandollar Prods.
Sanford/Pillsbury Prods.
Santa Monica Pictures
Santiago Films
Saphier Productions
Sarabande Prods.
Saratoga Entertainment
Sarkissian Productions, Arthur
Saturn Films
Sauce Entertainment
Savage Studios Ltd.
Savoir Faire Productions
Say Unkel Entertainment
Scarlet Fire Films
Schachter Entertainment, Inc.
Scheimer Prods., Lou
Scherick Assocs., Edgar J.
Schiff Productions, Paul
Schindler Prods., Deborah
Scholastic Entertainment
Schumacher Prods., Joel
Schwartz Productions, Bernard
Schwartz Productions, Steven
Schwartzberg & Company
Scott Free Productions
Scripps Howard Prods.
Seagal-Nasso Productions
Sefton Productions International
Segan Company, The Lloyd
Seggerman Productions, Henry
Segue Prods., Inc.
Seguin Prods., Nicole
Seldes Films
Sellers Productions, Dylan
Sennet Prods., Mark
Seven Arts Pictures
Seven Summits Pictures & Mgmt.
Shadowcatcher Entertainment
Shadowlands Productions
Shapiro Ent. Inc., Richard & Esther
Shapiro Productions, Allen
Shapiro Productions, Robert
Shatter Glass Prods.
Sheldon/Post Company, The
Shelter Entertainment
Shinbone Productions
Sho Films
Shoelace Productions, Inc.
Shogun Films, Ltd.
Shooting Gallery Inc., The
Shoreline Entertainment
Signature
Signature Films
Silver Heart Productions
Silver Lion Films
Silver Pictures
Silvercreek Entertainment
Silverfilm Prods. Inc.
Silverline Pictures
Silverman Prod, Lloyd/Passionate Picts.
Simian Films
Simon Productions, Randy
Simonds Co., The Robert
Simons Prods., David A.
Simsie Films
Singer Entertainment, Joseph M.
Singer Productions, Carla
Singer-White Entertainment
Single Cell Pictures
Single Spark Pictures
Sittenfield Productions, Joan
Sitting Ducks Prods.
Skyfish Productions
Skylark Films Ltd.
Skyline Partners

Sladek Entertainment
Sloane/Borden Pictures
Smith Productions Inc., Thomas G.
Snapdragon Films Inc.
Sneak Preview Entertainment, Inc.
Snow Leopard Productions
Solo One Productions
Solomon/Hackett Productions
Somers Teitelbaum David
Sonnenfeld/Josephson
Sony Pictures Entertainment
Sony Pictures Imageworks
Soto Company, The
South Fork Pictures
South Side Films
Southern Skies Inc.
Spanky Pictures, Inc.
Spectacor Films
Spelling Films Inc.
SPI Entertainment
Spikings Entertainment
Spring Creek Productions
SPRINGTIME!
Spumco
Spygaze Pictures
Stampede Entertainment
Star Land Entertainment Inc.
StarGate Entertainment Inc.
Stargazer Entertainment, Inc.
Starlight Pictures
Startoons
Startz Productions, Inc., Jane
State Street Pictures
Steelwork Films
SteppinStone Entertainment
Stern Production Company, The Howard
Stevens & Associates
Stevens Company, The
Sticks And Stones
Stiefel Entertainment
Stiles-Bishop Productions Inc.
Stone Canyon Investments, Inc.
Stone vs. Stone
Stoneface Entertainment
Stonehenge Films
Stonelock Pictures
StoneRoad Prods. Inc.
Storm Entertainment
Storybook Entertainment
Storybrooke Films
Storyline Entertainment
Storyopolis Productions
StoryTeller Films, Ltd.
Strader Entertainment
Stratford Prods, Inc., Bert
Stratum Entertainment
Studio Productions
Stun
Stupin Productions, Paul
Sugerman, Andrew
Sullivan Company, The
Sullivan Entertainment
Summers Entertainment
Summit Entertainment
Sundance Institute
Suntaur Entertainment
Suppa Prods., Inc., Ronald
Sweet Lorraine Prods. Inc.
Sweetpea Entertainment
Symphony Entertainment, LLC
Synchronicity Productions
T-Squared Productions
TAE Productions
Taffner Entertainment Ltd.
Tahse Prods., Martin
Takoma Entertainment Group
Talking Rings Entertainment
Talking Wall Pictures, Inc.
Tapestry Films Inc.
Tardy-Green Productions, Ltd.

## Syndication

Harbor Lights Productions
Harding, Dave
Hobel Productions
Ideal Movie Shoppe, LLC, The
JCS Entertainment Inc.
Just Betzer Films Inc.
Katz/Rush Entertainment
Keeyumah Films
Keller Entertainment Group
King World Productions
Kushner-Locke Co.
Ladd Productions, Inc., Diane
Langley Prods.
Lavin Entertainment Group
Leach Ent. Enterprises, Inc.
Leo Productions, Malcolm
Levinson/Fontana Company, LLC, The
Lilac Productions
Logo Entertainment
Loring Productions, Lynn
Magic Hour Pictures
Manhattan Project Ltd., The
Maple Palm Productions
March Hare Entertainment
MDP Worldwide
Meridian Entertainment, LLC
Mesmerize Studios
Michael/Finney Prods., Inc.
Mindless Entertainment
National Lampoon
NewStar Television
North Hall Productions
P.A.T. Productions
Peacock Films/1st Miracle Pictures
Philipico Pictures Co.
PolyGram Filmed Ent.
Popular Arts Ent., Inc.
Producers Ent. Group, Ltd., The
R.A.M.M. Entertainment, Inc
Radio...With Pictures
Raylin Entertainment
Rearguard Productions, Inc.
Renaissance Pictures
Rive Gauche International TV
Ruby-Spears Prods.
Rupert Productions, Inc.
Rysher Entertainment
Scholastic Entertainment
Scripps Howard Prods.
Sheldon/Post Company, The
Silver Heart Productions
Simons Prods., David A.
Skylark Films Ltd.
Somers Teitelbaum David
Spanky Pictures, Inc.
Star Land Entertainment Inc.
Stratford Prods, Inc., Bert
Studio Productions
Summers Entertainment
Sweetpea Entertainment
TAE Productions
Taffner Entertainment Ltd.
Taurus Entertainment Co.
Trident Releasing Inc.
Turner Entertainment Group
Twentieth Television
Uplinger Enterprises
Upstart Entertainment
Vista Street Entertainment
Warner Bros. International TV Production
Weller/Grossman Productions
Wildsmith Entertainment
Wolf Films Inc.
WolfMill Entertainment
Wolper Org., The
Worth Prods., Marvin
Yagya Productions
Yorkin Productions, Bud
Zane Buzby & Conan Berkeley Productions

## Television

1492 Pictures
3 Arts Entertainment
360 entertainment
44 Blue Productions, Inc.
A & E Television Networks
Abatemarco Productions, Frank
ABC Daytime
ABC Entertainment
ABC Pictures
Abilene Pictures
About Face Prods.
Act III Productions
Action America Entertainment
Adam Productions
Addis Films, Michael
Adelson Entertainment
Adelson Productions, Orly
AEI-Atchity Edit./Ent. Intl. Inc.
Agamemnon Films Inc.
Alan Smithee Films
Albert Prods. Inc., Sydell
Albrecht & Assocs. Inc.
Albrecht/Read Management
Alexander/Enright & Assocs.
All American Communications, Inc.
All American Television, Inc.
Allegro Films
Alliance Television Productions
Alliance/LeMonde Entertainment
Allied Stars
Allyn Films
Alpine Pictures
AM Productions & Management
America National Network, Inc.
American Filmworks
American Movie Classics/Romance Classic
American New Wave Films
American Zoetrope
Amphion/Nitestar Productions
aMuse Productions
Anderson Prods., Craig
Andre Prods., Inc., Blue
Angel Ark Productions
Angel/Brown Prods.
Apostle Pictures
Apple & Honey Productions, Ltd.
Arbus Prods., Inc., Loreen
Arkoff Intl. Pictures
Arnold Productions, Inc., Judy
Artisan Entertainment
Ascato Entertainment
AsIs Productions
Aspect Ratio Films
Asseyev Prods. Inc., Tamara
Associated Producers Group, Inc.
Asylum Films
Atelier Pictures
Atkinson Way Films
Atlantis Films
Atlas Entertainment
Atmosphere Entertainment Inc.
Auerbach Company
Aurora Productions
Avanti Enterprises
Avenue Pictures
Aviator Films LLC
Avnet-Kerner Co.
Axelrod/Widdoes Productions
Axelson-Weintraub Productions
B.S. Company, Inc., The
Baer Animation Co. Inc.
Baerwald Prods., Susan
Bakula Productions, Inc.
Baldwin/Cohen Productions
BallPark Productions
Ballyhoo, Inc.
Baltimore Pictures, Inc.
Banner Assocs., Bob

Barnette Productions, Alan
Barron/Pennette Prods.
Bartlett Prods., Juanita
Barwood Films
Bates Entertainment
Batfilm Prods., Inc.
Bauer Company, The
Baumgarten/Prophet Entertainment
Bay Films
Beach House
Beacon Pictures
Bean And Cod Prods.
Bedford Falls Co., The
Belisarius Prods.
Bell and Associates, Dave
Bell-Phillip TV Prods., Inc.
Benedetti Productions, Inc., Robert
Benjamin Prods. Inc.
Bennett Productions, Harve
Bent Outta Shape Productions
Berk Schwartz Bonann Productions
Berman Productions, Rick
Bernbaum, Paul
Berner Films, Fred
Bernsen Prods. Inc., Harry
Bernstein Productions, Jay
Bettina Prods. Ltd.
Bickley Prods.
Big Daddy Productions
Big Shoes Productions
Big Sky Entertainment
Big Ticket Television
Bill Oakley & Josh Weinstein
Black & White Productions
Black Entertainment TV
Black, Lawrence & Silverhardt Ent.
Black/Marlens Company, The
Blake Prods., Timothy
Blanki & Bodi Prods., Inc.
Bleecker Street Films
Blue Relief, Inc.
Blue Rider Pictures
Blue Tulip Productions
Blue Turtle, Inc.
Blueline Productions
Blum Productions, Howard
Boardwalk Ent./Alan Wagner Prods., Inc.
Bochco Prods., Steven
Bodega Bay Prods., Inc.
Boku Films
Bonneville Worldwide Entertainment
Booker Productions, Bob
Bottom Line Studio, Inc.
Boyle-Taylor Prods.
Boyman Productions, Inc.
Boz Productions
Bradford Enterprises & Gemmy Prods.
Braga Productions
Brainstorm Media
Brandman Prods.
Braubach Productions
Braun Entertainment Group, Inc.
Braun Productions, David
Brayton/Carlucci Productions
Breen Prods., Paulette
Bregman Entertainment Co., The
Briggle Prods., Stockton
Bright Street Pictures
Bright-Kauffman-Crane Prods.
Brillstein-Grey Ent.
Bristol Cities
British Lion
Britt Allcroft Co., The
Broadway Video (NY)
Broido @ Alexander/Enright & Assoc.
Brookwell McNamara Entertainment
Brown Group, The
Brownhouse Productions
Bruckheimer Films, Jerry
Buckeye Entertainment Group

# COMPANIES INDEXED BY TYPE

Buena Vista Productions
Bungalow 78 Prods.
Bunim-Murray Productions, Inc.
Burlage/Edell Productions, Inc.
Burrud Productions
Burton Prods., Al
Butchers Run Films
Byck, Dann
Byrum Power & Light
C.M. Two Productions
Cafe Productions
Cairo/Simpson Productions, Inc.
Calm Down Productions, Inc.
Canal+ (U.S.)
Cannon & Associates, Reuben
Canterbury Films
Canton Company, The
Canton Productions, Maj
Capital Arts Entertainment
Carascope Productions Inc.
Carliner Prods., Mark
Carlson, Matthew
Carlson-Lehman Prods.
Carlyle Prods. & Mgmt.
Carrie Productions
Carsey-Werner Co., The
Carter Company, The Thomas
Cartoon Network
Caruso-Mendelsohn Prods.
Castle Rock Entertainment
Catapult Films
Cates/Doty Productions
Catfish Productions
CBS Entertainment
CBS Productions
Cecchi Gori Pictures
Chancellor Entertainment
Charles-Burrows-Charles
Chase Prods., Stanley
Cherry Alley Productions
Chesler/Perlmutter Production
Chesterfield Film Co., The
Chestnut Hill Prods.
Cheyenne 7 Prods.
Chicagofilms
Children's Television Workshop
Chotzen/Jenner Productions
Chris/Rose Prods.
Christmas Tree Entertainment, Inc.
Cine Paris
Cinewest Productions
Cinnamon Prods. Inc.
Citadel Entertainment., LLC
City Entertainment
Clark Prods., Inc., Dick
CLC Productions, Inc.
Clean Break Productions
Clifford Prods., Patricia
Cobalt Films International
Cobalt Moon
Cobblestone Films
Codikow Films
Coffey/Ballantine
Cohen & Ryan Films, Inc.
Cohen Productions Inc., Herman
Colmano Productions, Marino
Colossal Pictures
Columbia TriStar Television
Comedy Central
Common Creed Entertainment Corp.
Common Ground Entertainment
Communications Corp. of America
Comsky Group Productions
Concourse Prods.
Connection III Entertainment Corp.
Cook Films
Copp And Goodman
Copper Sky Productions
Cort/Madden Company, The
Corymore Prods.

Cosgrove-Meurer Prods.
Cossette Productions
Cowlip Productions
Coyote Pass Productions
CPC Entertainment
Craven Films, Wes
Creative Group Prods., Inc.
Creative Road Corp.
Crew Prods., Dick
Crosby/Levy Co., The
Crystal Beach Entertainment
Crystal Pyramid Productions
cTonic Fliks
Cuddihy, Christopher A.
Culver Films, Carmen
Cunningham Prods. Inc.
Curtis Prods., Dan
Dakota North Ent./Dakota Films
Daly-Harris Productions
Daniel Productions, Jay
Danielson - Rosenthal Productions
Dark Horse Ent.
Dark Matter Productions
Daydream Productions Inc.
De Laurentiis Company, Dino
De Passe Entertainment
Deja View Productions, Inc.
Delaware Pictures
Demberg Productions, Lisa
Demo Productions, Inc.
Desert Heart Prods.
Di Bona Prods., Vin
Diana Kerew Productions
DIC Entertainment
Dinamo Entertainment
Discovery Networks
Disney Channel
Disney Telefilms
Distant Horizon
Dockry Productions
Dogsmile Pictures
Dogstar Films
Don Baer Prods. Inc.
Donner/Shuler-Donner Prods.
Dore Productions, Bonny
Double Eagle Ent.
Double Whammy Productions
Doumanian Prods., Jean
Douthit Productions Ltd.
Draizin Co., The
Dream City Films
DreamWorks SKG
Driskill Entertainment
Dryer Prods., Fred
Ducks In A Row Entertainment Corporation
E! Entertainment Television
Eagle Nation Films
Earthbourne Films, Inc.
Earthworks Films, Inc.
Edelson Productions
Edmonds Entertainment
Edwards Yellen Entertainment
Effe Films, Inc.
Elephant Walk Entertainment
Eleventh Day Entertainment
Elkins Entertainment
Ellison, Bob
Emby Eye
EMK Productions
Empire Pictures Inc.
Enchanter Entertainment
Enlightened Witness, Inc./Levine Mgmt.
Enteraktion, Inc.
Entertainment Alliance, Inc., The
Entertainment Group, The
EntPro, Inc.
Enzo Films
EO Productions International, Inc.
Epiphany Productions, Inc.
Epstein Productions, Stefanie

Equinox Entertainment Ltd.
Erratic Entertainment, Inc.
Esparza-Katz Prods.
Evans Co., The Robert
Evolve Entertainment
Excelsior Pictures Corp.
Expect Miracles, Inc.
Eyemark Entertainment
FairDinkum Prods.
Fanaro-Nathan Prods.
Farrell/Minoff Prods.
Fat Chance Films
Fatima Production
Feigelson Prods., Inc., J.D.
Fenady Associates, Inc.
Feury Entertainment, Joseph
Film Garden Entertainment
Film Roman, Inc.
Filmatic Adventures Inc.
Filmlight
Filmopolis Pictures
FilmRoos
Films By Jove
FilmSaavy
Filmsmith
Filmwerks
Finnegan-Pinchuk Company
Firebrand Productions
First Entertainment LLC
First Folio Films
First Street Films, Inc.
Fischer Co., Preston Stephen
FitzGerald Prods. & Mgt.
Flashpoint Entertainment
Flat Penny Films
Floyd Johnson Productions, Charles
Fogwood Films
Force Ten Productions
Forrester Films
Foster Productions, David
Fountainbridge Films
Fourth Avenue Films
Fox Broadcasting Co.
Fox Family Channel
Fox Kids Network
Fox Productions, Ted
Fox Television Studios
Foxboro Company, Inc., The
Foxstar Productions
Frankovich Prods., Inc., Peter
Fraser Prods., Woody
Freedman Prods., Jack
Freyer Productions, Ellen
Fried Films
Fries Film Group, Inc.
Fries Productions, Inc., Chuck
Front Street Productions
Frost Prods., Mark
FTM Productions
Full Circle Ent. AKA Suzanne Bauman Prod
Full Moon & High Tide Prods. Inc.
Furst Films
FX Networks, LLC
Galan Entertainment
Galanty & Company
Gallant Entertainment, Inc.
Gallo Entertainment, Inc.
Gaslight Pictures
Gaumont
Gekko Film Corp
Gelfand Productions, Janna E.
Gendece Film Co.
Georgian Bay Prods.
Germain Productions, Stephanie
Gerren Productions
Gibbons Enterprises, Leeza
Giddings Images Inc., Al
Gilbert Associates, Ron
Gillen & Price
Gimbel Productions, Inc., Roger

# COMPANIES INDEXED BY TYPE

MacDonald Prods
Macht Ent. Group, Inc.
Magar Films, Inc., Guy
Magic Hour Pictures
Magnum Motion Pictures, Inc.
Maia Productions
MakeMagic Productions
Malpaso Prods.
Mandalay Television
Mandy Films, Inc.
Manhattan Pictures Ltd.
Manhattan Project Ltd., The
Manheim Company, The
Manifest Film Company
Manos Prods., Inc., James
Maple Palm Productions
March Hare Entertainment
Marino Film Group, Inc.
Marks Productions, Joan
Marmont Prods. Inc.
Mars Prods. Corp.
Marsh Entertainment
Marvel Studios
Marvin Productions, Niki
Marx Prods., Inc., Timothy
Mary Ann-LaGlo Productions
Mase/Kaplan Productions, Inc.
Matinee Entertainment
Matovich Productions
Matthau Company, Inc., The
Maynard Prods., Richard
Mayo/Gregg Entertainment
Maysville Pictures
McKissick/Gregory Prods.
MDP Worldwide
Media Four
Mega Films, Inc.
Melendez Productions, Bill
Melrose Prods.
Meltzer Productions, Michael
Mendillo/Form Productions
Meridian Entertainment, LLC
Meridian Films
Merlin Entertainment
Merv Griffin Productions
Mesmerize Studios
Messina Captor Films
Metafilmics Inc.
Metro-Goldwyn-Mayer/Worldwide TV
Meyer Prods., Patricia K.
Michael/Finney Prods., Inc.
Midnight Sun Pictures
Milestone Pictures Inc.
Miller Entertainment Group, Inc.
Miller/Boyett/Warren Productions
Mills Prods., Donna
Mindless Entertainment
Ministry of Film Inc., The
Mirisch Corporation
Mirkin Vision
Mischel Co., The
Mischer Productions, Don
Miss Universe L.P., LLLP
MKD Prods.
Moffitt Associates, William
Moffitt-Lee Prods.
Moll/Beallor Productions
Mont Blanc Prods.
Montage Entertainment
Montan Productions, Chris
Moonstone Entertainment
More/Medavoy Management
Moress-Nanas-Hart Entertainment
Morra, Brezner, Steinberg & Tenenbaum
Morrow-Heus Productions
Morton Prods., Jeff
Mount Olympus Entertainment
Mountain Drive
Movicorp Holdings, Inc.
Movie Development Corp.

Moving Pictures
Mozark Productions
MPH Entertainment, Inc.
MTV Networks
Mulberry Square Productions, Inc.
Mutant Enemy, Inc.
Mutual Film Co.
MWG Prods.
Myerson Entertainment
Myron Productions, Ben
Nash Entertainment
Nasser Entertainment Group
National Geographic Feature Films
National Geographic Television
National Lampoon
NBC Entertainment
NBC Studios
Nederlander Television & Film
Nelvana Entertainment
Neo Motion Pictures, Inc.
Nepotism Productions
Netter Digital Entertainment
Network Graphics Ltd.
Neu-man-films, Inc.
Neufeld Productions, Mace
Never A Dull Moment Prods.
New Amsterdam Entertainment, Inc.
New England Prods., Inc.
New Regency Prods.
New Screen Concepts, Inc.
Newland-Raynor Prods., Inc.
Newman Prods., Launa
Newman Productions, Carroll
NewStar Media
NewStar Television
Nexus Entertainment, Inc.
Nickelodeon/Nick at Nite
Night Flight Inc.
No Prisoners
Nolan/LaMonte-ITG
Norann Entertainment
North Hall Productions
Northstar Entertainment
O'Hara-Horowitz Productions
Obst Prods., Lynda
OffRoad Entertainment
Old Beantown Films
Oliver Productions, Lin
Olmos Productions Inc.
OMNIBUS
OMS - One Mind Sound Productions
Once Upon A Time Films, Ltd.
One Eight Five Film Productions, Inc.
One Voice Entertainment, Inc.
Open Door Entertainment
Open Road Prods., Ltd.
Orbit Entertainment Group
Out of the Blue . . . Entertainment
Outerbanks Entertainment
Ovitz Productions, Mark H.
Ozma Productions
P.A.T. Productions
P.O.V. Co.
Pachyderm Entertainment
Pacific Motion Pictures
Pacific Western Prods.
Paige Assoc., Inc., George
Palomar Pictures
Pamplin-Fisher Company
Panamort Television
Papazian-Hirsch Entertainment
Parachute Entertainment, LLC.
Paradox Prod., Inc.
Parami Productions
Paramount Domestic TV
Paramount International Television
Paramount Network Television
Paramount Television Group
Paraview Inc.
Parkway Productions

Patchett Kaufman Entertainment
Paulist Prods.
Paulson Prods., Daniel L.
PB Management
PBS
PDQ Directions, Inc.
Peacock Films/1st Miracle Pictures
Peak Productions
Pearson All American
Pearson Television Productions
Perennial Pictures Film Corp.
Perlman Productions
Permut Presentations
Persistent Pictures, Inc.
Persky Prods., Lester
Pet Fly Prods.
Petrie Jr. & Co., Daniel
Petrie Prods., Inc., Dorothea G.
Pfilmco, Inc.
Philipico Pictures Co.
Phoenix Pictures
Pico Creek Prods.
Picture Factory, The
Picturemaker Prods.
Pierce Co., The Frederick S.
Pilot Boy Productions
Planet Girl Pictures
Plaster City Productions
Platform Entertainment
Platinum Studios, LLC
Playtime Productions
Plurabelle Films
Poco Productions
Pola Co Productions
Polakoff Prods., Carol
Polone Company, The
Polson Company, The
PolyGram Filmed Ent.
PolyGram Television
Pompian Productions, Paul
Popular Arts Ent., Inc.
Porchlight Entertainment
Port Street Films
Post Office, The
Power Company, The Derek
Pratt Ent., Inc., Charles
Prelude Pictures
Principal Prods., Victoria
Producers Ent. Group, Ltd., The
Producers Group Studios
Production Partners, Inc.
Production Services
Promark Entertainment Group
Propaganda Films
Proud Mary Entertainment
Prufrock Pictures
Quince Prods., Inc.
Quinn Productions
R. Edwards Prods./R. Edwards Films
R.A.M.M. Entertainment, Inc
Radiant Productions
Radio...With Pictures
RadlerFilm
Radmin Company, The
Raffaella Productions, Inc.
Rambaldi Enterprises, David
Randan Prods., Inc.
Randwell Productions
Rankin/Bass Productions
Raskin Productions, Bonnie
Raskoff Productions, Ken
Raylin Entertainment
Razors Edge Productions, Inc.
Really Big Shoe Prods.
Rearguard Productions, Inc.
Red Diamond Company, The
Red Hour Films
Red Wagon Prods.
Redler Entertainment, Dan
Reel Life Women

# COMPANIES INDEXED BY TYPE

Rees Assocs., Marian
Regan Company, The
Regent Entertainment, Inc.
Rehme Productions
Reid Productions, Inc., Tim
Reinert Pictures, Rick
Remote Control Productions
Renaissance Pictures
Renfield Prods.
Revolution Entertainment
Rialto Films
Rice & Beans Prods.
Rich Productions, Lee
Richulco, Inc.
Ridini Entertainment Corporation
Ridio Prods., Inc., Anthony
Rive Gauche International TV
River Mill Productions
RKO Pictures, Inc.
Roaring Fork Productions
Roaring Mouse Entertainment, Inc.
Robinson Entertainment, Dolores
Rocking Horse Prods.
Rodan Prods., Inc.
Rogers Entertainment
Rogow Productions, Stan
Rosa Entertainment
Rose Prods. Inc., Alex
Rose Productions, Lee
Rosemont Prods. International Ltd.
Rosenberg, Helena Hacker
Rosenbloom Prods., Richard
Rosenman Productions, Howard
Ross Productions, Hal
Rossu Entertainment
Rothstein Prods., Freyda
Rotman Productions, David
Roundelay Prods.
Roxaboxen
Rubin * Burke Productions
Ruby-Spears Prods.
Ruddy Morgan Organization, Inc., The
Rupert Productions, Inc.
Russell Productions, Neil
Rust Productions, Patricia
Rysher Entertainment
S.E.R. Filmworks
Saban Entertainment
Sachnoff-Lipman Entertainment
Sachs Productions, Gabe
Sacks Productions Inc., Alan
Samoset Inc./Sacret Inc.
Samuels Ent. Inc., Ron
Samuelson Productions
Sandollar Prods.
Sanford/Pillsbury Prods.
Saphier Productions
Sarabande Prods.
Saratoga Entertainment
Sarkissian Productions, Arthur
Savage Studios Ltd.
Savoir Faire Productions
Say Unkel Entertainment
Schachter Entertainment, Inc.
Scheimer Prods., Lou
Scherick Assocs., Edgar J.
Schlatter Prods., George
Scholastic Entertainment
Schwartz Productions, Bernard
Schwartz Productions, Steven
Schwartzberg & Company
Scott Free Productions
Scripps Howard Prods.
Seguin Prods., Nicole
Seldes Films
Sellers Productions, Dylan
Sennet Prods., Mark
Seven Summits Pictures & Mgmt.
Shadowcatcher Entertainment
Shadowlands Productions

Shadowplay Films
Shapiro Ent. Inc., Richard & Esther
Shapiro Prods., Arnold
Shatter Glass Prods.
Sheldon/Post Company, The
Shelter Entertainment
Shoelace Productions, Inc.
Shogun Films, Ltd.
Shoreline Entertainment
Showtime Networks Inc.
Shukovsky English Ent.
Signature Films
Silver Heart Productions
Silver Pictures
Silvercreek Entertainment
Silverline Pictures
Silverman Co., The Fred
Silverman Prod, Lloyd/Passionate Picts.
Simons Prods., David A.
Simsie Films
Singer Productions, Carla
Singer-White Entertainment
Single Spark Pictures
SisterLee Productions Inc.
Sittenfield Productions, Joan
Sitting Ducks Prods.
Skylark Films Ltd.
Sladek Entertainment
Slawson Prods., Ruth
Smith Productions Inc., Thomas G.
Smith-Hemion Prods.
Snow Leopard Productions
Sofronski Prods., Bernard
Solo One Productions
Solt Productions, Andrew
Somers Teitelbaum David
Sony Pictures Entertainment
Sony Pictures Imageworks
South Side Films
South, Frank
Spanky Pictures, Inc.
Spelling Television, Inc.
Spin Cycle Entertainment
Spring Creek Productions
SPRINGTIME!
Spumco
Spygaze Pictures
St. Clare Entertainment
Star Land Entertainment Inc.
Stargazer Entertainment, Inc.
Startoons
Startz Productions, Inc., Jane
State Street Pictures
SteppinStone Entertainment
Stern Production Company, The Howard
Stevens & Associates
Stevens Company, The
Stewart Television, Inc.
STF Productions, Inc.
Stone Stanley Productions
Stone vs. Stone
Stoneface Entertainment
Stonehenge Films
Stonelock Pictures
StoneRoad Prods. Inc.
Storybook Entertainment
Storybrooke Films
Storyline Entertainment
Storyopolis Productions
StoryTeller Films, Ltd.
Strader Entertainment
Stratford Prods., Inc., Bert
Stratum Entertainment
Stuart Productions, Inc., Mel
Studio Productions
Studios USA
Studios USA Pictures
Studios USA Television
Stun
Stupin Productions, Paul

Sugerman, Andrew
Sullivan Company, The
Sullivan Entertainment
Summers Entertainment
Sunbow Entertainment
Suntaur Entertainment
Sweet Lorraine Prods. Inc.
Sweetpea Entertainment
Symphony Entertainment, LLC
Synchronicity Productions
T-Squared Productions
T.H.A. - Thomas Horton Associates Inc.
TAE Productions
Taffner Entertainment Ltd.
Takes On Production
Takoma Entertainment Group
Talking Rings Entertainment
Talking Wall Pictures, Inc.
Taurus Entertainment Co.
Tavel Entertainment
Taylor Prods., Grazka
TBS Superstation
Team Entertainment Group
Team Todd
Telescene Film Group., Inc.
TeleVest
Telling Pictures Inc.
Telvan Productions
Ten Thirteen Productions
Tenth Planet Prods.
Teocalli Entertainment, Inc.
Terra Bella Entertainment
Tetrafilms Inc.
Theatrex Company, The
Thompson Organization, Larry
Three Guys From Verona Inc.
Threshold Entertainment
Thunderbird Pictures
Tiger Prods.
Time Life Kids
Time-Life Video & Television
Tisch Co., The Steve
TLC Entertainment
TLN Productions
Tollin/Robbins Productions
Too Nuts Productions, Ltd.
Townsend Ent. Corp., The
Traveler's Rest Films
Travis Group, The
Tri-Crown Prods.
Tribe
Tribeca Productions
TriCoast Entertainment
Tricor Entertainment
Trident Releasing Inc.
Trilogy Entertainment Group
Triumph Pictures Inc.
Trivision Pictures Inc.
True Blue Prods.
Tse Productions, Simon
TSProductions
Tudor Entertainment, Inc.
Tulchin Entertainment
Turman-Morrissey Company, The
Turner Entertainment Group
Turner Network Television (TNT)
Turner Original Productions
Turteltaub-Orenstein Prods.
Turtle Productions, Jon
Twentieth Century Fox Television
Twentieth Television
Twilight Time Films
Twin Brothers Productions, Inc
Two Oceans Entertainment Group
Two Pauls Entertainment
Two Roads Prods., Inc.
Two Stepp Productions
UBU Productions
Ufland Productions
Una Chica Entertainment

# COMPANIES INDEXED BY TYPE

# SECTION D.

# Cross-Referenced Names

# HAVE YOU BEEN ASKED TO COPY THIS BOOK?

## COPYRIGHT INFRINGEMENT IS A FEDERAL CRIME.

We offer rewards on information of illegal photocopying or distribution of any of our books.
Please call our office.

*Your identity will be protected.*

## 310-315-4815

# CROSS-REFERENCED NAMES

Aaron, Paul . . . . . . . . . . . . . . . . . . . Suntaur Entertainment
Abatemarco, Frank . . . . . . . . . Abatemarco Productions, Frank
Abbott, Jonathan C. . . . . . . . . . . . . . . . . . . . . . . . . . . . PBS
Abbott, Michael . . . . . . . . . . . . . . . . . . . . . . . . . No Prisoners
Abdul-Jabbar, Kareem . . . . . . . . . . . . . . . . Kareem Productions
Abdy, Pamela . . . . . . . . . . . . . . . . . . . . . . . . . . . Jersey Films
Abel, Dawn . . . . . . . . . . . . . . . . . . . . Paramount Domestic TV
Abel, Lewis . . . . . . . . . Warner Bros. Television Productions
Abernathy, Glenn . . . . . . . . . . . . . . Weintraub Prods., Jerry
Abernethy, Jane M. . . . . . . . Lancit Media Entertainment, Ltd.
Abiragi, Christophe . . . . . . . . . . . . . . . Angel Ark Productions
Abounader, Jean . . . . . . . . . . . . Von Zerneck-Sertner Films
Abraham, Harriet . . . . . . . . . . . . . . . . . . . . . . ABC Daytime
Abraham, Marc . . . . . . . . . . . . . . . . . . . . . . Beacon Pictures
Abraham, Nancy . . . . . . . . . . . HBO Original Programming
Abramowitz, Lisa . . . . . . . . . . . . . . . . . Act III Productions
Abrams, Gerald W. . . . . . . . . . . . . . . . Evolve Entertainment
Abrams, Peter . . . . . . . . . . . . . . . . . . . Tapestry Films Inc.
Abrams, Stacy . . . . . . . . . . . . . . . . . . . Radmin Company, The
Abramson, Curt . . . . . . . . . . . . . . . . . CLC Productions, Inc.
Abramson, Richard G. . . . . . . . . . . . . Firestorm Pictures, Ltd.
Abramson, Stephen . . . . . . . . . . . . . . . . . New Line Cinema
Abril, Jason . . . . . . . . . . . . . . . . . . . . . . . Avnet-Kerner Co.
Aceste, Joan . . . . . . . . . . . . . . . . . . . . . . . . Comedy Central
Ackerman, Andrew . . . . . . Warner Bros. Television Productions
Ackerman, Mitch . . . . . . . . Walt Disney TV/Touchstone TV
Acosta, Mario E. . . . . . . . . . . . . Baer Entertainment Group
Acuna, Marvin V. . . . . . . . . . . . . . . . . Perlman Productions
Adams, Chase . . . . . . . . . . . . . . . . . . . . Phase I Productions
Adams, Christopher . . . . . . . . . . Horseshoe Bay Productions
Adams, Erik . . . . . . . . . . . . Abatemarco Productions, Frank
Adams, Julie . . . . . . . . . . . . . . . Vecchio Ent., Joseph S.
Adamson, Laird . . . . . . . . . . . . . . . . . . . Killer Films, Inc.
Adar, Ophir . . . . . . . . . . . Miller/Boyett/Warren Productions
Addis, Keith . . . . . . . . . . . . . . . . . . . Industry Entertainment
Addis, Michael . . . . . . . . . . . . . . . . . Addis Films, Michael
Addison, Anita . . . . . . . . . . . . . . . . . . . CBS Entertainment
Adelman, Barry . . . . . . . . . . . . . . Clark Prods., Inc., Dick
Adelson, Andrew . . . . . . . . . . . . . . . . Adelson Entertainment
Adelson, Gary . . . . . . . . . . . . . . . . . . . . aMuse Productions
Adelson, Orly . . . . . . . . . . . . . . . Adelson Productions, Orly
Adelstein, Marlene . . . . . . . . . . . . . . . . . Wind Dancer Films
Ades, Claudia Crown . . . . . . . . . . . . . . . . . Keeyumah Films
Ades, Richard . . . . . . . . . . . . . . . . . . . . . Keeyumah Films
Adilman, Glenn . . . . . . . . . . . . . . . . . . . . CBS Productions
Adio-Byrd, Kamafi . . . . . . . . . . . . . . . . . . . H2 Productions
Adler, Ben . . . . . . . . . . . . . . . . . . . . . . . Cobblestone Films
Adler, Jacqui . . . . . . . . . . . . . . . . . . . . . Cobblestone Films
Adler, Kate . . . . . . . . . . . . . Worldwide Pants Incorporated
Adler, Leslie . . . . . . . . . . . . . . . . . . . . . Prufrock Pictures
Adler, Susan . . . . . . . . . . . . . . . . . . . . . . . . . . . . . . . . Stun
Affrime, Mindy . . . . . . . . . . . . . . Affrime Productions, Mindy
Agin, Jonas . . . . . . . . . . . . . . . . . . . . . Lynch Entertainment
Agrama, Frank . . . . . . . . . . . . . . . . . . . . . . . Harmony Gold
Aguado, Kenneth . . . . . . . . Kings Road Entertainment Inc.
Aguero, Sergio . . . . . . . . . . . . . . . . . . . . Trimark Pictures
Aguilar, Michael . . . . . . . . . . Donner/Shuler-Donner Prods.
Ahdoot, Robert R. . . . . . . . . . . . . . . . . . . Cannery, Inc., The
Ahn, Paul . . . . . . . . . . . . . . . . . . . . . . . Burrud Productions
Ahrenberg, Staffan . . . . . . . . . . . . Saga Pictures Corporation
Ahrendt, Chad . . . . . . . . . . . . . . . . . Mark Prods., Laurence
Aidem, Larry . . . . . . . . . . . . . . . . . . Showtime Networks Inc.
Akers, Kaz . . . . . . . . . . . . . . Three Guys From Verona Inc.
Akers, Michael . . . . . . . . . . . . . . . . . . Grand Productions, Inc.
Akkad, Malek . . . . . . . . . . . . . . . . . . . . Trancas Intl. Films
Akkad, Moustapha . . . . . . . . . . . . . . . . Trancas Intl. Films
Alamdari, Homa . . . . . . . . . . . . . . . . . . . David Ladd Films
Alanne, Mikko . . . . . . . . . . . . . . Illusion Entertainment Group
Albala, Staci . . . . . . . . . . United Paramount Network (UPN)
Albanese, Tina . . . . . . . . . . . . . . . . . . . . Belisarius Prods.
Albelda, Randy . . . . . . . . . . . . . . . . . . . . . . Lupovitz Prods.
Albert, Kathryn . . . . . . . . . . . . Media Financial Corporation
Albert, Russ . . . . . . . . . . . . . . . . . . . . . . Mega Films, Inc.
Albert, Sydell . . . . . . . . . . . . . . . Albert Prods. Inc., Sydell
Albert, Trevor . . . . . . . . . . . . . . . . . . . . . . Ocean Pictures
Albrecht, Annie . . . . . . . . . . . . Albrecht/Read Management
Albrecht, Chris . . . . . . . . . . . . HBO Independent Productions
Albrecht, Chris . . . . . . . . . . . . HBO Original Programming
Albrecht, J.A. . . . . . . . . . . . . . . . Albrecht & Assocs. Inc.
Albrecht, Kurt . . . . . . . . . . . . . . . . . Hyperion Entertainment

Alden, Lisa . . . . . . . . . . . . . . . . . . . . . . Universal Pictures
Alexander, Beth . . . . . . . . . . . First Cold Press Productions
Alexander, Erin . . . . . . . . . . . . . . . . . . . . Red Hour Films
Alexander, Jason . . . . . . . . . . . . . . . . Angel Ark Productions
Alexander, Les . . . . . . . . . . . . . Alexander/Enright & Assocs.
Alexander, Marc . . . . . . . . . . . . . . Lynn Productions, Tami
Alexander, Marsha L. . . . . . . . . . . . . . Bubble Factory, The
Alexander, Tracey . . . . . . . . . . . . . . . Adelson Entertainment
Alexandria, Petra . . . . . . . . . . . . . . Mark Prods., Laurence
Alfano, JoAnn . . . . . . . . . . . . . . . . . . . . . . . . NBC Studios
Alfieri, Michael . . . . . . . . . . . . . . . . Permut Presentations
Alfieri, Richard . . . . . . . . . . . . . . . . . . . . . . . EntPro, Inc.
Allain, Stephanie . . . . . . . . . . . . . . . . Henson Pictures, Jim
Allard, Tony . . . . . . . . . . . . . . . . . . Pacific Motion Pictures
Allcroft, Britt . . . . . . . . . . . . . . . . . Britt Allcroft Co., The
Allcroft, Britt . . . . . . . . . . . . . . . . . . . . Gullane Pictures
Allen, Craig . . . . . . . . . . . . . . . . . . Henson Company, Jim
Allen, Luis . . . . . . . . . . . . . . . . . . . . . . Columbia Pictures
Allen, Sally . . . . . . . . . . . . . . . . . . . . BallPark Productions
Alley, Kirstie . . . . . . . . . . . . . . . . . . . . . True Blue Prods.
Allgood, Jeanne . . . . . . . . . . . . . . . . . . . Outlaw Productions
Allison, Carl . . . . . . . . . . . . . . . Miss Universe L.P., LLLP
Allison, Carol Diesel . . . . . . . . . . Image Organization, Inc.
Allyn, Sandra Smith . . . . . . . . . . . . . . . . . . . . Allyn Films
Allyn, William . . . . . . . . . . . . . . . . . . . . . . . . Allyn Films
Almadrones, Mark . . . . . . . . . . . . . . . Kardana Films, Inc.
Almeida, Michael . . . . . . . . . . . Hollywood Network, Inc.
Almond, Honi . . . . . . . . . . . . . . . . . . Di Bona Prods., Vin
Almond, Peter . . . . . . . . . . . . . . . . . . . . . Beacon Pictures
Aloe, Mary L. . . . . . . . . . . . . . . . Proud Mary Entertainment
Alonzo, Iris Dawn . . . . . . . . . . . Gross Points Entertainment
Alsop, Scott . . . . . . . . . . . . . . Ladd Productions, Inc., Diane
Alston, Howard . . . . . . . . . . . . . . . . . . . . . Marstar Prods.
Alterman, Kent . . . . . . . . . . . . . . . . . . . . Comedy Central
Altfeld, Sheldon I. . . . . . . . . . America National Network, Inc.
Alton, Jay . . . . . . . . . . . . . . . . . . Wildsmith Entertainment
Altounian, Brian . . . . . . . . . . . . . . . . Lynch Entertainment
Alvarez, Matt . . . . . . . . . . . . . . . . . . . . . Fine Line Features
Alvarez, Rick . . . . . . . . . . . . . . . . . . . . . . . Cinetel Films
Alward, Jennifer . . . . . . . . . . . . . . . . . Evolve Entertainment
Amato, Len . . . . . . . . . . Baltimore/Spring Creek Pictures, LLC
Amato, Len . . . . . . . . . . . . . . . . . Spring Creek Productions
Amato, Michael . . . . . . . . . . . . . Mount Royal Entertainment
Amatullo, Tony . . . . . . . . . . . . . . . . . Artisan Entertainment
Amelingmeier, Brent . . . . . . . . . Newmarket Capital Group
Amin, Alex . . . . . . . . . . . . . . . Trilogy Entertainment Group
Amin, Mark . . . . . . . . . . . . . . . . . . . . . . Trimark Pictures
Amritraj, Ashok . . . . . . . . . . . . . . . . Franchise Pictures Inc.
Amundson, Sarah . . . . . . . . . . . . . . Revolution Entertainment
Amurri, Franco . . . . . . . . . . . . . . . . . . . . . Effe Films, Inc.
Ancier, Garth . . . . . . . . . . . . . . W.B. Television Network
Anderman, Louis . . . . . . . . . . . . . . . . . . . . Miramax Films
Anderson, Craig . . . . . . . . . . . . . . . Anderson Prods., Craig
Anderson, James . . . . . . . . Lakeshore Entertainment Corp.
Anderson, Jenna . . . . . . . . Black, Lawrence & Silverhardt Ent.
Anderson, Melissa . . . . . . . . . . . Holcomb-Speed Productions
Anderson, Scott . . . . . . . . . . . Once Upon A Time Films, Ltd.
Anderson, Steve . . . . . . . . . . . . . . . . Enchantment Films, Inc.
Andoscia, Caroline . . . . . . . . . . . . . . . . Sonnenfeld/Josephson
Andraos, Nick . . . . . . . . . . . . . Equinox Entertainment Ltd.
Andraus, Julian . . . . . . . . . . . . . . . . . . . . . . . Jersey Films
Andre, Blue . . . . . . . . . . . . . . . . . . Andre Prods., Inc., Blue
Andreen, Michael . . . . . . . . . . . . . . . Warner Bros. Pictures
Andreen, Tracy . . . . . . . . . . . . . . . . . . . Mandalay Pictures
Andreoli, Rick . . . . . . . . . . . . . . . . . . Suntaur Entertainment
Andrews, Carol . . . . . . . . . . . . . . . . . . Hallet Street Prods.
Andrews, Robyn . . . . . . . . . . . . . . . . . . Twilight Time Films
Androsky, Jeff . . . . . . . . . . . . . . . . . . . . . . Tri-Crown Prods.
Androsky, Mike . . . . . . . . . . . . . . . . . . . . Tri-Crown Prods.
Andryc, Joel . . . . . . . . . . . . . . . . . . . . Fox Family Channel
Andryc, Joel . . . . . . . . . . . . . . . . . . . . Saban Entertainment
Angel, Dan . . . . . . . . . . . . . . . . . . . . . . Angel/Brown Prods.
Angeles, Jack . . . . . . . . . . . . . . . . . . . Wilshire Court Prods.
Angelie, Cain . . . . . . . . . . . . . . . . . . . . . . . . Zero Pictures
Angell, David . . . . . . . . . . . . . . . . . . . . Grub Street Prods.
Angsten, David . . . . . . . . . . AEI-Atchity Edit./Ent. Intl. Inc.
Ankeles, Alexander . . . . . . . . . . . . . . . . . . . . . Mad Chance
Ann-Margret . . . . . . . . . . . . . AM Productions & Management
Ansell, Julie . . . . . . . . . . . . . . . . . . . . . . . . . Gracie Films
Antal, Levy . . . . . . . . . . . . . . . . . . . . . . . Alliance Pictures

# CROSS-REFERENCED NAMES

<table>
<tr><td>Antholis, Kary</td><td>HBO Original Programming</td></tr>
<tr><td>Anthony, Brian</td><td>Victor Motion Pictures</td></tr>
<tr><td>Anthony, Cheryl</td><td>Bauer Company, The</td></tr>
<tr><td>Anthony, Jason</td><td>Sonnenfeld/Josephson</td></tr>
<tr><td>Antonelli, Frank</td><td>ITB CineGroup/Television</td></tr>
<tr><td>Antonini, Caryn</td><td>Platinum Studios, LLC</td></tr>
<tr><td>Apatow, Judd</td><td>Apatow Productions</td></tr>
<tr><td>Apatow, Mia</td><td>Apatow Productions</td></tr>
<tr><td>Apcar, Ara</td><td>Firestorm Pictures, Ltd.</td></tr>
<tr><td>Apodaca-Harms, Sonia</td><td>Braun Entertainment Group, Inc.</td></tr>
<tr><td>Appleton, Mike</td><td>Uplinger Enterprises</td></tr>
<tr><td>Aquila, Deborah</td><td>Paramount Pictures- Production Division</td></tr>
<tr><td>Arama, Elaine Ford</td><td>Arama Entertainment</td></tr>
<tr><td>Arama, Shimon</td><td>Arama Entertainment</td></tr>
<tr><td>Arbeeny, Karen Lee</td><td>Hinterland Entertainment</td></tr>
<tr><td>Arboleda, Ilan</td><td>Rose Prods. Inc., Alex</td></tr>
<tr><td>Arbus, Loreen</td><td>Arbus Prods., Inc., Loreen</td></tr>
<tr><td>Arcand, Diane</td><td>Telescene Film Group., Inc.</td></tr>
<tr><td>Archer, Michelle</td><td>Out of the Blue . . . Entertainment</td></tr>
<tr><td>Arechiga, Brenda</td><td>Lipper Productions, Ken</td></tr>
<tr><td>Arent, Laurie</td><td>Adelson Entertainment</td></tr>
<tr><td>Aries, Lolee</td><td>Film Roman, Inc.</td></tr>
<tr><td>Aristei, Stephen C.</td><td>Westport Film Partners</td></tr>
<tr><td>Ariyasu, Vicki</td><td>Klasky Csupo Inc.</td></tr>
<tr><td>Arkoff, Samuel Z.</td><td>Arkoff Intl. Pictures</td></tr>
<tr><td>Armstrong, Adrienne</td><td>Copper Sky Productions</td></tr>
<tr><td>Armstrong, David</td><td>USA Networks</td></tr>
<tr><td>Armstrong, Laura</td><td>New Line Cinema</td></tr>
<tr><td>Armstrong, Robin B.</td><td>Open Road Prods., Ltd.</td></tr>
<tr><td>Arnell, Joshua</td><td>Danger Filmworks</td></tr>
<tr><td>Arnoff, Peter</td><td>Universal Pictures</td></tr>
<tr><td>Arnold, Heather</td><td>Ballyhoo, Inc.</td></tr>
<tr><td>Arnold, Judy</td><td>Arnold Productions, Inc., Judy</td></tr>
<tr><td>Arnold, Kathryn</td><td>Cineville Inc.</td></tr>
<tr><td>Arnold, Sandy</td><td>Melendez Productions, Bill</td></tr>
<tr><td>Arnold, Susan</td><td>Roth/Arnold Prods.</td></tr>
<tr><td>Arnold, Tom</td><td>Clean Break Productions</td></tr>
<tr><td>Aronson, Letty</td><td>Doumanian Prods., Jean</td></tr>
<tr><td>Aronson, Peter</td><td>Walt Disney TV/Touchstone TV</td></tr>
<tr><td>Arpaci, Lale</td><td>Phil Alden Robinson</td></tr>
<tr><td>Arredondo, Rick</td><td>Von Zerneck-Sertner Films</td></tr>
<tr><td>Arroyo, Dawn</td><td>Goldcrest Films International, Inc.</td></tr>
<tr><td>Arsenault, Greg</td><td>Film Roman, Inc.</td></tr>
<tr><td>Artenstein, Isaac</td><td>Cinewest Productions</td></tr>
<tr><td>Arthur, Kristen</td><td>ABC Pictures</td></tr>
<tr><td>Arthur, Wendy</td><td>Luger Productions, Inc., Lois</td></tr>
<tr><td>Asbell, Steve</td><td>Mutual Film Co.</td></tr>
<tr><td>Aschenbrenner, Liz</td><td>Columbia Pictures</td></tr>
<tr><td>Ash, Carola</td><td>Warner Bros. International TV Production</td></tr>
<tr><td>Ashburn, Ellie</td><td>Stonehenge Films</td></tr>
<tr><td>Ashenafi, Aida</td><td>Sauce Entertainment</td></tr>
<tr><td>Asher, Don</td><td>Wandering Monkey Entertainment</td></tr>
<tr><td>Ashley, Heather</td><td>ITB CineGroup/Television</td></tr>
<tr><td>Ashton, Julie</td><td>Saban Entertainment</td></tr>
<tr><td>Asimow, Andrea</td><td>Parkway Productions</td></tr>
<tr><td>Askin, Shebnem</td><td>Trimark Pictures</td></tr>
<tr><td>Asner, Edward</td><td>Quince Prods., Inc.</td></tr>
<tr><td>Asseyev, Tamara</td><td>Asseyev Prods. Inc., Tamara</td></tr>
<tr><td>Atchity, Ken</td><td>AEI-Atchity Edit./Ent. Intl. Inc.</td></tr>
<tr><td>Atchity, Vincent</td><td>AEI-Atchity Edit./Ent. Intl. Inc.</td></tr>
<tr><td>Athas, Nick</td><td>Olmos Productions Inc.</td></tr>
<tr><td>Atherton, Heidi</td><td>Clark Prods., Inc., Dick</td></tr>
<tr><td>Atlas, Jacoba</td><td>Turner Original Productions</td></tr>
<tr><td>Atoori, Beni Tadd</td><td>Stonelock Pictures</td></tr>
<tr><td>Attalla, Anne</td><td>Shapiro Productions, Allen</td></tr>
<tr><td>Attanasio, Stacey</td><td>Meyers/Shyer Co., The</td></tr>
<tr><td>Attieh, Fida</td><td>Earthbourne Films, Inc.</td></tr>
<tr><td>Atwater, Martha</td><td>Scholastic Entertainment</td></tr>
<tr><td>Auerbach, Gary</td><td>Mindless Entertainment</td></tr>
<tr><td>Auerbach, Jeffrey</td><td>Auerbach Company</td></tr>
<tr><td>Auerbach, Lynn</td><td>Sundance Institute</td></tr>
<tr><td>Auerbach, Randy</td><td>Blue Tulip Productions</td></tr>
<tr><td>Auge, George</td><td>Sullivan Entertainment</td></tr>
<tr><td>Aulepp, Glenn</td><td>Post Office, The</td></tr>
<tr><td>Aurino, Karin</td><td>Alexander/Enright & Assocs.</td></tr>
<tr><td>Austen, Jane</td><td>Rossu Entertainment</td></tr>
<tr><td>Austin, Jeanne</td><td>1492 Pictures</td></tr>
<tr><td>Auty, Chris</td><td>Recorded Picture Company</td></tr>
<tr><td>Avallon, Susan</td><td>Columbia Pictures</td></tr>
<tr><td>Avellone, Gregory</td><td>Tig Productions, Inc.</td></tr>
<tr><td>Avnet, Jon</td><td>Avnet-Kerner Co.</td></tr>
<tr><td>Avola, Julie</td><td>SteppinStone Entertainment</td></tr>
<tr><td>Awada, Gregory</td><td>Viviano Entertainment</td></tr>
<tr><td>Axelman, Arthur</td><td>Rialto Films</td></tr>
<tr><td>Axelman, Matt</td><td>Rialto Films</td></tr>
<tr><td>Axelrod, Jonathan</td><td>Axelrod/Widdoes Productions</td></tr>
<tr><td>Axelson, John</td><td>Axelson-Weintraub Productions</td></tr>
<tr><td>Azusa, Dominique</td><td>Chotzen/Jenner Productions</td></tr>
<tr><td>Babcock, Ted</td><td>Von Zerneck-Sertner Films</td></tr>
<tr><td>Bachrach, Melissa</td><td>Montan Productions, Chris</td></tr>
<tr><td>Bacino, Mark</td><td>Green/Epstein Prods.</td></tr>
<tr><td>Badell-Slaughter, Cindy</td><td>CBS Entertainment</td></tr>
<tr><td>Baden, David</td><td>Craven Films, Wes</td></tr>
<tr><td>Bader, Jeff</td><td>ABC Entertainment</td></tr>
<tr><td>Bader, Jonathan</td><td>Interscope Communications Inc.</td></tr>
<tr><td>Badham, John</td><td>Badham Co., The</td></tr>
<tr><td>Badish, Ken</td><td>Active Entertainment</td></tr>
<tr><td>Baer, Amy</td><td>Columbia Pictures</td></tr>
<tr><td>Baer, Don</td><td>Don Baer Prods. Inc.</td></tr>
<tr><td>Baer, Jane</td><td>Baer Animation Co. Inc.</td></tr>
<tr><td>Baer, Matthew</td><td>Brillstein-Grey Ent.</td></tr>
<tr><td>Baer, Thomas</td><td>Baer Entertainment Group</td></tr>
<tr><td>Baer, Willi E.</td><td>Eternity Pictures, Inc</td></tr>
<tr><td>Baerwald, Susan</td><td>Baerwald Prods., Susan</td></tr>
<tr><td>Baerwolf, Roger</td><td>Shadowcatcher Entertainment</td></tr>
<tr><td>Bafia, Larry</td><td>Pacific Data Images</td></tr>
<tr><td>Baiers, Erik</td><td>Horseshoe Bay Productions</td></tr>
<tr><td>Bailey, Fenton</td><td>World of Wonder</td></tr>
<tr><td>Bailey, Sean</td><td>HorsePower Entertainment</td></tr>
<tr><td>Bain, Barnet</td><td>Metafilmics Inc.</td></tr>
<tr><td>Baizer, Josh</td><td>Mutual Film Co.</td></tr>
<tr><td>Bajaria, Bela</td><td>CBS Entertainment</td></tr>
<tr><td>Bakal, Matthew</td><td>Canton Company, The</td></tr>
<tr><td>Bakalar, Steven</td><td>H2 Productions</td></tr>
<tr><td>Bakalian, Peter</td><td>Rankin/Bass Productions</td></tr>
<tr><td>Baker, Allan</td><td>Oliver Productions, Lin</td></tr>
<tr><td>Baker, Claire</td><td>Schumacher Prods., Joel</td></tr>
<tr><td>Baker, Debbie</td><td>Miller/Boyett/Warren Productions</td></tr>
<tr><td>Baker, Dee</td><td>Miss Universe L.P., LLLP</td></tr>
<tr><td>Baker, George Woods</td><td>Intrepidus</td></tr>
<tr><td>Baker, Mark H.</td><td>StarGate Entertainment Inc.</td></tr>
<tr><td>Baker, Martin G.</td><td>Henson Company, Jim</td></tr>
<tr><td>Baker, Robert</td><td>Signature Films</td></tr>
<tr><td>Baker, Sondra</td><td>Chesterfield Film Co., The</td></tr>
<tr><td>Baker, Susan M.</td><td>Moll/Beallor Productions</td></tr>
<tr><td>Bakshi, Mark</td><td>Paramount Pictures- Production Division</td></tr>
<tr><td>Bakula, Scott</td><td>Bakula Productions, Inc.</td></tr>
<tr><td>Balaban, Bob</td><td>Chicagofilms</td></tr>
<tr><td>Balaban, Nestor</td><td>Warner Bros. International TV Production</td></tr>
<tr><td>Balcer, Rene</td><td>Wolf Films Inc.</td></tr>
<tr><td>Baldecchi, John</td><td>Mark Prods., Laurence</td></tr>
<tr><td>Baldonado, Erika</td><td>WildRice Productions</td></tr>
<tr><td>Baldwin, Alec</td><td>El Dorado Pictures</td></tr>
<tr><td>Baldwin, Eric</td><td>Spin Cycle Entertainment</td></tr>
<tr><td>Baldwin, Howard</td><td>Baldwin/Cohen Productions</td></tr>
<tr><td>Baldwin, June</td><td>United Paramount Network (UPN)</td></tr>
<tr><td>Baldwin, Karen</td><td>Baldwin/Cohen Productions</td></tr>
<tr><td>Bales, David</td><td>Goldstein Co., The</td></tr>
<tr><td>Balfe, Kelly</td><td>Caravan Pictures</td></tr>
<tr><td>Ball, Chris</td><td>Newmarket Capital Group</td></tr>
<tr><td>Ballantine, Jim</td><td>Coffey/Ballantine</td></tr>
<tr><td>Ballester, Roland</td><td>Galan Entertainment</td></tr>
<tr><td>Ballew, Denise</td><td>BThree Films</td></tr>
<tr><td>Balnicke, Janelle</td><td>National Geographic Television</td></tr>
<tr><td>Bamattre, Kristine</td><td>O'Hara-Horowitz Productions</td></tr>
<tr><td>Bamber, Audrey</td><td>Dreyfuss/James Prods.</td></tr>
<tr><td>Banderas, Antonio</td><td>Green Moon Productions</td></tr>
<tr><td>Banders, Melanie</td><td>Telescene Film Group., Inc.</td></tr>
<tr><td>Bandy, Eveleen</td><td>Icon Productions Inc.</td></tr>
<tr><td>Bangert, Charles</td><td>New Screen Concepts, Inc.</td></tr>
<tr><td>Banhidi, Eva</td><td>Taska Productions</td></tr>
<tr><td>Banks, Charlie</td><td>Bruckheimer Films, Jerry</td></tr>
<tr><td>Banks, Steven Gary</td><td>VentureWest Pictures</td></tr>
<tr><td>Banner, Bob</td><td>Banner Assocs., Bob</td></tr>
<tr><td>Banner, Chuck</td><td>Banner Assocs., Bob</td></tr>
<tr><td>Bannerman, Kevin</td><td>Fox Animation Studios</td></tr>
<tr><td>Baran, Jack</td><td>Merko Motion Pictures</td></tr>
<tr><td>Barbato, Randy</td><td>World of Wonder</td></tr>
<tr><td>Barbolak, Mark</td><td>Maple Palm Productions</td></tr>
<tr><td>Barder, Alex</td><td>Lobell-Bergman Prods.</td></tr>
</table>

# CROSS-REFERENCED NAMES

# CROSS-REFERENCED NAMES

Boero, Patricia . . . . . . . . . . . . . . . . . . . . . . Sundance Institute
Bogner, Nicholas . . . . . . . . . . . . . . . . . . . . . C/W Productions
Bohjalian, Chris . . . . . . . . . . . . . . . . . . . . . Tulchin Entertainment
Bonann, Gregory J. . . . . . . . . . . . . Berk Schwartz Bonann Productions
Bond, Cindy . . . . . . . . . . . . . . . . . . . . . . . . . . . Norann Entertainment
Bond, Derek . . . . . . . . . . . . . . . . . . . . . . . . . . Galan Entertainment
Bond, Tim . . . . . . . . . . . . . . . . . . . . . . . .Rough Diamond Productions
Bond, Vinette . . . . . . . . . . . . . . . . . . . . . . .De Passe Entertainment
Bonet, Rob . . . . . . . . . . . . . . . . . . . . . . . .Carr Enterprises, Allan
Bonfiglio, Lois . . . . . . . . . . . . . . . . . . . . . . Bleecker Street Films
Boorstein, Joan . . . . . . . . . . . . . . . . . . . Showtime Networks Inc.
Booth, Ron . . . . . . . . . . . . . . . . . . . . . . . . . Mont Blanc Prods.
Booton, Dana . . . . . . . . . . . . . . . . . . . . . . . . . Saban Entertainment
Borack, Carl . . . . . . . . . . . . . . . . Utopia Picts./Carl Borack Productions
Borchers, Donald P. . . . . . . . . . . . . . . . . . . . . .Borchers, Donald P.
Borden, Bill . . . . . . . . . . . . . . . . . . . . . . . First Street Films, Inc.
Border, W.K. . . . . . . . . . . . . . . . . . . . . . . Neo Motion Pictures, Inc.
Borja, Karen . . . . . . . . . . . . . . . . . . . . . . . First Street Films, Inc.
Borke, Susan . . . . . . . . . . . . . . . . . National Geographic Television
Borman, Moritz . . . . . . . . . . . . . . . . . . . . . . .Pacifica Entertainment
Boros, Stuart . . . . . . . . . . . . . .De Laurentiis Company, Dino
Borsiczky, Jessika . . . . . . . . . . . . . . . . . HBO NYC Productions
Borsten, Joan . . . . . . . . . . . . . . . . . . . . . . . . . . Films By Jove
Borza II, Donald . . . . . . . . . . . . Hamilton Entertainment, Inc., Dean
Bostick, Michael . . . . . . . . . . . . . . . . . . . . . Imagine Entertainment
Boswell, Donna . . . . . . . . . . . . . . . . . . . . . . Marvel Studios
Botko, Jim . . . . . . . . . . . . . Warner Bros. Television Productions
Botta, Pasquale . . . . . . . . . . . . . . . . . . . . Cinema Seven Prods.
Bottinelli, Connie . . . . . . . . . . . . . . . . . Grinning Dog Pictures
Botvinick, Mark . . . . . . . . . . . . . . . . . . . . . . . . . Blue Horizon
Botwick, Terry . . . . . . . . . . . . . . . . . . . . . . . . CBS Entertainment
Boule, Cliff . . . . . . . . . . . . . . . . . . . . . . . Pacific Data Images
Bowen, Sarah . . . . . . . . . . . . . . . . . . . . . . . Imagine Entertainment
Bowland, Debra . . . . . . . . . . . . . . . . . . . . . Marsh Entertainment
Bowles, Eamonn . . . . . . . . . . . . . . . . Shooting Gallery Inc., The
Bowles, Jill . . . . . . . . . . . . . . . . . . . . . . Bungalow 78 Prods.
Bowman, Ann . . . . . . Walt Disney Pictures/Touchstone Pictures
Bowman, Karri . . . . . . . . . . . . . .AM Productions & Management
Bowser, Yvette Lee . . . . . . . . . . . . . . . SisterLee Productions Inc.
Boyer, Madeline . . . . . . . . . . . . . . . . . . . . . . . . Time Life Kids
Boyer, Vikki . . . . . . . . . . . . . . .Hamilton Entertainment, Inc., Dean
Boyett, Robert L. . . . . . . . . . . . . . . Miller/Boyett/Warren Productions
Boyle, Barbara . . . . . . . . . . . . . . . . . . . . . . Boyle-Taylor Prods.
Boyle, David . . . . . . . . . . . . . . . . . . . . . . .Propaganda Films
Boyman, Marc . . . . . . . . . . . . . . . . . . Boyman Productions, Inc.
Brabetz, Melissa . . . . . . . . . . . . . . . . . . . . . . . . . . Filmsmith
Brada, Donald . . . . . . . . . . . . . . . .Metro-Goldwyn-Mayer Pictures
Bradford, Barbara Taylor . . . . . Bradford Enterprises & Gemmy Prods.
Bradford, Robert . . . . . . . . . . . . Bradford Enterprises & Gemmy Prods.
Bradley, Jeanie . . . . . . . . . . . . . . . Columbia TriStar Television
Brady, John . . . . . . . . . . . . . . . . . . . . . . .NewStar Media
Braga, Brannon . . . . . . . . . . . . . . . . . . . . Braga Productions
Brainard, Jana . . . . . . . . . . . . Stone Canyon Investments, Inc.
Braine, Tim . . . . . . . . . . . . . . . . . . . . . Popular Arts Ent., Inc.
Bramhall, Adrienne . . . . . . . . . . . . Turner Original Productions
Brams, Richard . . . . . . . . . . . . . . . . . . Scripps Howard Prods.
Brand, Bill . . . . . . . . . . . . . . . . . . . . . . . . VH1 (Music First)
Brand, Gary . . . . . . . . . . . . . . . . . . . . . . . . Fox Kids Network
Brandes, David . . . . . . . . . . . Apple & Honey Productions, Ltd.
Brandis, Bernardine . . . . . . . . Walt Disney Pictures/Touchstone Pictures
Brandman, Michael . . . . . . . . . . . . . . . . . . . . Brandman Prods.
Brandstein, Jonathan . . . . . . Morra, Brezner, Steinberg & Tenenbaum
Brandstrom, Charlotte . . . . . . . . . . . . . . . . . Enzo Films
Brandy, J.C. . . . . . . . . . . . . . . . . . . . . . . . . . Zero Pictures
Branman, Megan . . . . . . . . . . . . . . . . . Studios USA Television
Brantley, Chip . . . . . . . . . . . . . . . . . . . . . . . . . Dogstar Films
Branton, Michael . . . . . . . . . . . . . . . . . . . . . GRB Entertainment
Brassel, Bob . . . . . . . . . . . . . . . . . . . . . . . . DreamWorks SKG
Brassel, Richard . . . . . . . . . . . . . . . . . . . . Fountainbridge Films
Braubach, Mary Ann . . . . . . . . . . . . . . . . . Braubach Productions
Braun, Betsy . . . . . . . . . . . . . . . . . . . . . . . . PolyGram Television
Braun, David . . . . . . . . . . . . . . . . . . . . Braun Productions, David
Braun, Zev . . . . . . . . . . . . . . . . Braun Entertainment Group, Inc.
Braunstein, Howard . . . . . . . . . . . Jaffe/Braunstein Films Ltd.
Brause, Debra . . . . . . . . . . . . . . . . . . . . . Studios USA Television
Braxton, David . . . . . . . . . . . . . . . . . . . . STF Productions, Inc.
Brayton, Marian . . . . . . . . . . . . . . . Brayton/Carlucci Productions
Brazil, Scott . . . . . . . . . . . . . . . . . . . . Silvercreek Entertainment
Brazzell, Anka . . . . . . . . . . . . . . . . . . . . . . . . . . Topa Films
Brecher, Kaz . . . . . . . . . . . . . . . . . . . . . . . . . Mutual Film Co.

Brecher, Kenneth . . . . . . . . . . . . . . . . . . . Sundance Institute
Brecker, Allison . . . . . . . . . . . . . . . . . . . . . . .Universal Pictures
Breech, Bob . . . . . . . . . . . . . . . . . Kelley Productions, David E.
Breeker, Marnie . . . . . . . . . . . . . . . . . . . . . Mostow/Lieberman
Breen, Kevin W. . . . . . . . . . Walt Disney Pictures/Touchstone Pictures
Breen, Paulette . . . . . . . . . . . . . . . . . . . Breen Prods., Paulette
Bregman, Anthony . . . . . . . . . . . . . . . . . . . . . . Good Machine
Bregman, Buddy . . . . . . . . . . .Bregman Entertainment Co., The
Bregman, Martin . . . . . . . . . . . . . . . . . . . . Bregman Productions
Bregman, Michael . . . . . . . . . . . . . . . . . . Bregman Productions
Brehme, Paul . . . . . . . . . . . . . . . . . . . . . Mostow/Lieberman
Breidt, June . . . . . . . . . . . . . . . . . . . . . . . Live Action Pictures
Breil, Ilan . . . . . . . . . . . . . . Lasher, McManus & Robinson
Brener, Richard . . . . . . . . . . . . . . . . . . . . . New Line Cinema
Brennan, Shannon . . . . . . . . . . . .Cohen Productions, Martin B.
Brennan, Tom . . . . . . . . . . . . . . . . . . . . Atlas Entertainment
Brennan, Wendy . . . . . . . . . . . . . . . . . .Bubble Factory, The
Brenner, Robbie . . . . . . . . . . . . . . . . . . . . . . Miramax Films
Brenner, Stephen . . . . . . . . . . . . . . . . . . . . . USA Networks
Brent, Kimberly . . . . . . . . . . . . . . . . . . . Paradox Prod., Inc.
Brest, Martin . . . . . . . . . . . . . . . . . . . . . . City Light Films
Brewington Jr., J. David . . . . . . . . . . . Warner Bros. Pictures
Breziner, Salome . . . . . . . . . . . . . . . . . . . . .RoadKill Films
Brezner, Larry . . . . . . . . Morra, Brezner, Steinberg & Tenenbaum
Brezzo, Beppe . . . . . . . . . . . . . . . . . . Phase I Productions
Brice, Veronica . . . . . . . . . . . . . . . . . . . Rich Productions, Lee
Bridges, Jeff . . . . . . . . . . . . . . . . . . . . . . . . . .AsIs Productions
Briggle, Stockton . . . . . . . . . . . . . . . Briggle Prods., Stockton
Bright, Kevin S. . . . . . . . . . . . . . Bright-Kauffman-Crane Prods.
Bright, Skot . . . . . . . . . . . . . . . . . . . . . . Palomar Pictures
Brillstein, Bernie . . . . . . . . . . . . . . . . . . Brillstein-Grey Ent.
Briskey-Cohen, Amberwren . . . . . . . . . . Horseshoe Bay Productions
Briskman, Louis . . . . . . . . . . . . . . . . . . . . . . . CBS Corporation
Britt, David . . . . . . . . . . . . Children's Television Workshop
Britton, Layne . . . . . . . . . . . . . United Paramount Network (UPN)
Britton, Matt . . . . . . . . . . . . . . . . . Henson Company, Jim
Britton, Michael . . . . . . . . . . . Colmano Productions, Marino
Brizic Ilic, Sanja . . . . . . . . . . . . . . . . . . . Galanty & Company
Broadbent, Graham . . . . . . . . . . . . . . . . . . Dragon Pictures
Broadstreet, Jeff . . . . . . . . . . . . . . . . . . . Populuxe Pictures
Broccoli, Barbara . . . . . . . . . . . . . . . . . . . . . . . . Danjaq Inc.
Broccoli, Dana . . . . . . . . . . . . . . . . . . . . . . . . . Danjaq Inc.
Brockmann, Hans . . . . . . . . . . . . . Roscoe Enterprises, Inc.
Brockway, Joanna . . . . . . . . . . . . . . . . . . . NBC Entertainment
Broden, Liz . . . . . . . . . . . . . . . . . . . . . . Yorktown Prods. Inc.
Broden, Ted . . . . . . . . . . . . . . . . . . . Wells Productions, John
Broderick, Jon . . . . . . . . . . . . . . . . . . Trivision Pictures Inc.
Broderick, Suzanne . . . . . . . . . . . Elephant Walk Entertainment
Brodlie, Matt . . . . . . . . . . . . . . . . . . . . . . Miramax Films
Brodsky, Suzanne . . . . . . . . . . . Goldwyn Company, The Samuel
Broido, Joe . . . . . . . . . .Broido @ Alexander/Enright & Assoc.
Brokaw, Cary . . . . . . . . . . . . . . . . . . . . . Avenue Pictures
Bromiley, Bill . . . . . . . . . . . . . . . . Maple Palm Productions
Bromstad, Angela . . . . . . . . . . . . . . . . . . . . . . . NBC Studios
Brook, Harold . . . . . . . . . . . . . . . . . . . . . NBC Entertainment
Brook, Harold . . . . . . . . . . . . . . . . . . . . . . . . . NBC Studios
Brooke, James . . . . . . . . . . . . . . . . . . . . . Storybrooke Films
Brooks, Addie . . . . . . . . . . . . . . . . . . . . . Playtime Productions
Brooks, Brooke . . . . . . . . . . . . . . . Davis Entertainment Co.
Brooks, Garth . . . . . . . . . . . . . . . Red Strokes Entertainment
Brooks, James L. . . . . . . . . . . . . . . . . . . . . . Gracie Films
Brooks, Mel . . . . . . . . . . . . . . . . . . . . . . Brooksfilms, Ltd.
Brooks, Stanley M. . . . . . . . . . . .Once Upon A Time Films, Ltd.
Brooks, Tim . . . . . . . . . . . . . . . . . . . . . . . . USA Networks
Brooksbank, Steven . . . . . . . . . . . . . . . Platform Entertainment
Brookwell, David . . . . . . . . . Brookwell McNamara Entertainment
Brookwell, Rick . . . . . . . . . Greystone Communications Group, Inc.
Broom, Kerry . . . . . . . . . . . . . . . Harvey Entertainment Company
Broucek, Paul . . . . . . . . . . . . . . . . . . . . . . New Line Cinema
Broughton, Matt . . . . . . . . . . . . . . . . Weintraub Prods., Jerry
Brown Guillaume, Donna . . . . . . . . . . . . Longridge Enterprises
Brown, Amy . . . . . . . . . . . . . . . . . Simonds Co., The Robert
Brown, Billy . . . . . . . . . . . . . . . . . . . . . Angel/Brown Prods.
Brown, Cyndy . . . . . . . . . . . . . . . . . . . . . . CBS Entertainment
Brown, Danny . . . . . . . . . . . . . . . . . . Manifest Film Company
Brown, David . . . . . . . . . . . . . . . Manhattan Project Ltd., The
Brown, Dennis . . . . . . . . . . . . . . . . . . . . . . . . ABC Pictures
Brown, Jon . . . . . . . . . . . . . . . . . . . . . . .Brown Group, The
Brown, Jonah . . . . . . . . . . . . . . . . . Colleton Company, The
Brown, Judith . . . . . . . . . . . . . . . . . . . HBO NYC Productions

Brown, LaShan R. . . . . . . . . . . . . . . . . . . . . . Edmonds Entertainment
Brown, Michael Henry . . . . . . . . . . . . . . . . . Suntaur Entertainment
Brown, Paul D. . . . . . . . . . . . . . . . . . . . . . . . . . . . . Phoenician Films
Brown, S. Nicole . . . . . . . . . . . . . . . . . Hallmark Entertainment (LA)
Brown, Shelley . . . . . . . . . . . Metro-Goldwyn-Mayer/Worldwide TV
Brown, Stephen J. . . . . . . . . . . . . . . . . . . . Kopelson Entertainment
Brownet, Peter . . . . . . . . . . . . . . . . . . . . . . . . . Dockry Productions
Brownstein, Jerome . . . . . . . . . . . . . . . . . . . True Fiction Pictures
Bruce, Lisa . . . . . . . . . . . . . . . . . . . . . . . . . . . . . . . . Orenda Films
Bruckheimer, Bonnie . . . . . . . . . . . . . . . . . . . . . . . All Girl Prods.
Bruckheimer, Jerry . . . . . . . . . . . . . . . . Bruckheimer Films, Jerry
Brucks, Bryan . . . . . . . . . . . . . . . . . . . . . . Sonnenfeld/Josephson
Bruenell, Deborah . . . . . . . . . . . . . . . . . . . . . . Columbia Pictures
Brummond, Sheri . . . . . . . . . . Rosemont Prods. International Ltd.
Brunsmann, Keith . . . . . . . . . . . . . . . . . . . . . . . . . Nine By Nine
Brusasco, Joyce Marie . . . . . . . . . . . . . . . . . Newman/Tooley Films
Brustein, Richard C. . . . . . . . . . . . . . . . . . Di Bona Prods., Vin
Brustin, Michele . . . . . . . . . . . . . . . . . . . . Scripps Howard Prods.
Brustrom, Jeff . . . . . . . . . . . . . . . . . . . . . . . Fox Broadcasting Co.
Bryan, James . . . . . . . . . . . . . . . . . . . . . . . . . . Bryan Films, James
Buchanan, Alicia . . . . . . . . . . . . . . . . . . Yellen Company,, Linda
Buchanan, Chris . . . . . . . . . . . . . . . . . . . Weintraub Prods., Jerry
Buchanan, Eric . . . . . . . . . . . . . . . . . . . . . . De Passe Entertainment
Buchthal, Stanley F. . . . . . . . . . . Buckeye Entertainment Group
Buck, Nancy Jo . . . . . . . . . . . . . . . . . . . . Davis Entertainment Co.
Buckley, Christine . . . . . . . . . . . Lakeshore Entertainment Corp.
Budd, Robin . . . . . . . . . . . . . . . . . . . . . . . Bedford Falls Co., The
Buechler, John . . . . . . . . . . . . . . . . . . . . . Imageries Entertainment
Buelow, David . . . . . . . . . . . . . . . . . . . . . Johnson Prods., Don
Bukinik, Suzanne . . . . . . . . . . . . . . . . . . . . . . . ABC Entertainment
Bull, Tom . . . . . . . . . . . . . . . . . . . . . . . Production Partners, Inc.
Bullard, Conrad . . . . . . . . . . . . . . . . . . . . . . Gerren Productions
Bullard, Jim . . . . . . . . . . . . . . . . . . . . . . . George Litto Pictures
Bullas, Andrew . . . . . . . . . . . . . . . . . . . . . . Rossu Entertainment
Bullock, Bruce . . . . . . . . . . . . . . . . . . . . . . . . Dogsmile Pictures
Bullock, Gesine . . . . . . . . . . . . . . . . . . . . . . . . . . . . Fortis Films
Bullock, John . . . . . . . . . . . . . . . . . . . . . . . . . . . . . Fortis Films
Bullock, Sandra . . . . . . . . . . . . . . . . . . . . . . . . . . . . Fortis Films
Bulman, Regge . . . . . . . One Eight Five Film Productions, Inc.
Bunche Pierce, Nina . . . . . . . . . . . . . . . . . . . . . Belisarius Prods.
Bunim, Mary-Ellis . . . . . . . . . . . Bunim-Murray Productions, Inc.
Bunting, Clark . . . . . . . . . . . . . . . . . . . . . . . . . Discovery Networks
Buntzman, Mark . . . . . . . . . . . . . . . . . Movie Development Corp.
Buonincontri, Cara . . . . . . . . . . . . . . . Carascope Productions Inc.
Buono, Lisa . . . . . . . . . . . . . . . . . . . . . . . . . . . . . . . Egg Pictures
Burch, Curtis . . . . . . . . . . . . . . . . . . . . . . . . . . . . Latitude Films
Burditt, Ellen . . . . . . . . . . . . . . . . . . . . . . . . Mandalay Television
Bures, Stephen . . . . . . . . . . . . . . . . . . . . . . . . . . . . Saturn Films
Burford, Anne . . . . . . . . . Floyd Johnson Productions, Charles
Burk, Jim . . . . . . . . . . . . . . . . . . . . . . . . . . . . Universal Pictures
Burke, Bill . . . . . . . . . . . . . . . . . . . . . . . . . . . . TBS Superstation
Burke, Bill . . . . . . . . . . . . . . . . . . Turner Entertainment Group
Burke, James . . . . . . . . . . . . . . . . . . . . . . . . . Stonelock Pictures
Burke, Karey . . . . . . . . . . . . . . . . . . . . . . . . . NBC Entertainment
Burke, Patricia . . . . . . . . . Paramount Pictures- Production Division
Burke, Shawn . . . . . . . . . . . . . . . . . Rubin * Burke Productions
Burkin, Brian . . . . . . . . . . . . . . . . . . . . . . . . . . . Miramax Films
Burlage, Roger . . . . . . . . . . . . . Burlage/Edell Productions, Inc.
Burleigh, Stephen . . . . . . . . . . . . . . . . . . Daly-Harris Productions
Burmester, Bruce . . . . . . . . . . . . . . . . . . Stewart Television, Inc.
Burnett, Rob . . . . . . . . . . . . . . . . . Worldwide Pants Incorporated
Burnham-Kurta, Jacqueline . . . . . . . . . . . Creative Group Prods., Inc.
Burns, Kevin . . . . . . . . . . . . . . . . . . . . . . . Twentieth Television
Burns, Kevin J. . . . . . . . . . . . . . . . . . . . . . . . Foxstar Productions
Burns, Matthew M. . . . . . . . . . . . . . . . . . . Benjamin Prods. Inc.
Burns, Michael . . . . . . . . . . . . . . . . . . . . . . . . . HSX Films, Inc.
Burns, Peter . . . . . . . . . . . . . . . . Hart Sharp Entertainment, Inc.
Burr, Kristin . . . . . . . . Walt Disney Pictures/Touchstone Pictures
Burrows, James . . . . . . . . . . . . . . . . . . Charles-Burrows-Charles
Burrows, Janet . . . . . . . . . . . . . . . . . . . . . . . . Wolper Org., The
Burrows, John . . . . . . . . . . . . . . . . . Pompian Productions, Paul
Burrud, John . . . . . . . . . . . . . . . . . . . . . . . . . Burrud Productions
Burstein, Lonnie . . . . . . . . . . . . . . . . . . . . . . . . . . Studios USA
Burton, Al . . . . . . . . . . . . . . . . . . . . . . . . . . . Burton Prods., Al
Burton, Amanda . . . . . . . . . . . . . . . . . . . Earthbourne Films, Inc.
Burton, LeVar . . . . . . . . . . . . . . . . . . . . . . Eagle Nation Films
Burton, Tim . . . . . . . . . . . . . . . . . . . . . . . . . . Burton Prods., Tim
Busby, Kathy . . . . . . . . . . . . . . . . . . . . . . Studios USA Television
Bush, Nan . . . . . . . . . . . . . . . . . . . . . . . . . . Little Bear Films, Inc.
Bushell, David L. . . . . . . . . . . . . . . . . Shooting Gallery Inc., The

Butan, Marc . . . . . . . . . . . . . . . . . . . . . . . . . . . . HSX Films, Inc.
Butler, Alex . . . . . . . . . . . . . . . . . . . . . . Agamemnon Films Inc.
Butler, Karen . . . . . . . . . . . . . . . . . . . . . Porchlight Entertainment
Butler, Lola . . . . . . . . . . . . . . . . . . . . . . . . . . MacDonald Prods
Butler, Mark . . . . . . . . . . . . . . . . . . . . . Platform Entertainment
Butts, Melissa . . . . . . . . . . . . . . . . . . . . Stone Stanley Productions
Buzby, Zane . . . . . . . . Zane Buzby & Conan Berkeley Productions
Byck, Dann . . . . . . . . . . . . . . . . . . . . . . . . . . . . . . Byck, Dann
Byer, Heather . . . . . . . . . . . . . . . . . . . . . . Kopelson Entertainment
Byers, Mark . . . . . . . . . . . . . . . . . . . . ITB CineGroup/Television
Bynum, Jeff . . . . . . . . . . . . . . . . . . . . . . . . . . . Mutant Enemy, Inc.
Byrens, Sharon . . . . . . . . . . . . . . . . . . . Showtime Networks Inc.
Byrne, Gabriel . . . . . . . . . . . . . . . . . . . . . . . . . Plurabelle Films
Byrum, John . . . . . . . . . . . . . . . . . . . . . . Byrum Power & Light
Caan, Martin . . . . . . . . . . International Filmmakers Management, Inc
Caaro, Nigel . . . . . . . . . . . . . . . . Pearson Television Productions
Caceres, Juan . . . . . . . . . . . . . . . . . . . . . . Lower East Side Films
Caddow, Wally . . . . . . . . . . . . . . . . . . . . . . . . Dryer Prods., Fred
Cadiz, Sandra . . . . . . . . . . . . . . . . . . . . . . . . . . Greystone Films
Cadorette, Lee . . . . . . . . . . . . . . . . . . . . . . Fraser Prods., Woody
Cage, Nicolas . . . . . . . . . . . . . . . . . . . . . . . . . . . . . Saturn Films
Cagianut, Thierry . . . . . . . . . . . . . . . . . . . . . True Fiction Pictures
Cahan, Eric . . . . . . . . . . . . . . . . . . . . . . . . . . . . . Immortal Films
Cahn, Alice . . . . . . . . . . . . . . . . . . . . . . . . . . . . . . . . . . . . PBS
Cairo, Judy . . . . . . . . . . . . . . . . . Cairo/Simpson Productions, Inc.
Calabrese, Peter . . . . . . . . . . . . . Out of the Blue . . . Entertainment
Calabro, Beth . . . . . . . . . . . . . . . . . . . . . . . . . . Dimension Films
Calame, Ingrid . . . . . . . . . . . . . . . . . . . Ward Films, Inc., Vincent
Caldwell, Sara Coover . . . . . . . . . . . Amphion/Nitestar Productions
Calfo, Frances . . . . . . . . . . . . . . . . Walt Disney TV/Touchstone TV
Callahan, Christy . . . . . . . . . Walt Disney Pictures/Touchstone Pictures
Callaway, Ed . . . . . . . . . . . . . . . . . . Teocalli Entertainment, Inc.
Callaway, Megan . . . . . . . . . . . . . . . . . . . . Fox Broadcasting Co.
Callender, Colin . . . . . . . . . . . . . . . . . . . . HBO NYC Productions
Calley, John . . . . . . . . . . . . . . . . . . Sony Pictures Entertainment
Callison, Beverly . . . . . . . . . . . . . . . . . . Katz/Rush Entertainment
Calof, Grant . . . . . . . . . . . . . . . . . . . . . . Lobell-Bergman Prods.
Cameron, James . . . . . . . . . . . . . . . . . . . Lightstorm Entertainment
Camon, Alessandro . . . . . . . . . . . Pressman Film Corp., Edward R.
Camp, Colleen . . . . . . . . . . . . . . . . . . . . . . Seven Arts Pictures
Camp, Joseph . . . . . . . . . . . Mulberry Square Productions, Inc.
Campagna, Jeffrey H. . . . . . . . . Buckeye Entertainment Group
Campbell, Carey . . . . . . . . . . . . . . . . Arbus Prods., Inc., Loreen
Campbell, Cindy . . . . . . . . . . . Turner Network Television (TNT)
Campbell, David . . . . . . . . . . . . . . . . . . . . . Jumbo Pictures, Inc.
Campbell, Diane . . . . . . . . . . . . . . . . . . . Belladonna Productions
Campbell, Gretchen . . . . . . . . . . . . . . . . . . . Cappa Productions
Campbell, James . . . . . . . . . . . . . . . Castle Rock Entertainment
Campbell, Lana . . . . . . . . . . . . . . . . . Elephant Walk Entertainment
Campbell, Robert . . . . . . . . . . . . . . . . . . Banner Entertainment
Campbell, Tania . . . . . . . . . . . . . . . . . . . . . . . River One Films
Campfield, E.J. . . . . . . . . . . . . . . . . . . . . . High Road Productions
Campillo, Margo . . . . . . . . . . . . . . . . . Initial Entertainment Group
Campion, Berit . . . . . . . . . . . . . . . . . . . . Benjamin Prods. Inc.
Campisi, Anje . . . . . . . . . . . . . . . . . . . . . . . . . Starlight Pictures
Campisi, Gabriel . . . . . . . . . . . . . . . . . . . . . . . Starlight Pictures
Campus, Micheal . . . . . . . . . . . . . . . . . . . . Esparza-Katz Prods.
Candido, Johanna . . . . . . . . . . . . . . . . . . . . Saban Entertainment
Canellos, Jana . . . . . . . . . . . . . . . . . . . . . . . . . Colossal Pictures
Cannell, Stephen J. . . . . . . . . . . . . . Cannell Motion Pictures
Cannon, Reuben . . . . . . . . . . . . . Cannon & Associates, Reuben
Canter, Ross . . . . . . . . . . Morra, Brezner, Steinberg & Tenenbaum
Canterna, Paul . . . . . . . . . . . . . . Seven Summits Pictures & Mgmt.
Cantillon, Elizabeth . . . . . . . . . . . Johnson Productions, Mark
Canton, Maj . . . . . . . . . . . . . . . . . . . Canton Productions, Maj
Canton, Mark . . . . . . . . . . . . . . . . . . . . Canton Company, The
Canton, Neil . . . . . . . . . . . . . . . . . . . . . . Seven Arts Pictures
Caplan, Barbara . . . . . . . . . . . . . . . . . . . . . . . . PB Management
Capogrosso, Deborah . . . . . . . . . . . . . . . . . . . . Capo Productions
Capone, Sal . . . . . . . . . . . . . . . . . . . . . . . . . . . Avenue Pictures
Capretta, Juliette . . . . . . . . . . . . . . . . . . . . Aspect Ratio Films
Captan, Marion . . . . . . . . . . . . . . . . . . . . Green Communications
Captan, Talaat . . . . . . . . . . . . . . . . . . . . Green Communications
Captor, Roxanne Messina . . . . . . . . . . . . . Messina Captor Films
Carazza, Michael . . . . . . . . . . . . . . . . . . . Creative Road Corp.
Cardinale, Dagney . . . . . . . . . . . . . Rubin * Burke Productions
Cardinalli, Sean . . . . . . . . . . . . . . . . . . . Artisan Entertainment
Caren, Elisabeth . . . . . . . . . . . . . . . . . . . . Friendly Productions
Carey, Andre . . . . . . . . . . . . . . Turner Network Television (TNT)
Carey, Andrew . . . . . . . . . . . . . . . . . . . . . . Original Voices, Inc.

Carey, Anne . . . . . . . . . . . . . . . . . . . . . . . . . . . . . Good Machine
Carey, Chase . . . . . . . . . . . . . . . . . . . . Fox Broadcasting Co.
Carey, Gavin . . . . . . . . . . . . . . . . . . . . Unistar Intl. Pictures
Carey, Kathi . . . . . . . . . . . . . . . . . . . . . . . . . . . . . . Cine Paris
Carey, Tony . . . . . . . . . . . . . . . . . . . . . . Brillstein-Grey Ent.
Cargile, Mike . . . . . . . . . . . . . . . . . . . . StoneRoad Prods. Inc.
Carideo, Julie . . . . . . . . . . . . . . . . . . . . Jacobs/Mutrux Prods.
Carliner, Mark . . . . . . . . . . . . . . . . . . . Carliner Prods., Mark
Carliner, Rob . . . . . . . . . . . . . . . . . . . . . . Butchers Run Films
Carlis, Jeff . . . . . . . . . . . . . . . . . . . . . . . . . Fox Productions, Ted
Carlis, Steve . . . . . . . . . . . . . . . . . Shooting Gallery Inc., The
Carls, John B. . . . . . . . . . . . . . . . . . . . . . . . Wild Things Prods.
Carlson, Judith . . . . . . . . . . . . . . . . . . . Carlson-Lehman Prods.
Carlson, Martin . . . . . . . . . . . . . . . . . Fox Television Studios
Carlson, Matthew . . . . . . . . . . . . . . . . . . Carlson, Matthew
Carlson, Sandra . . . . . . . . . Green Grass Blue Sky Company, Inc.
Carlucci, Anne . . . . . . . . . . . . . . Brayton/Carlucci Productions
Carlyle, Phyllis . . . . . . . . . . . . . . . . Carlyle Prods. & Mgmt.
Carmel, David . . . . . . . . . . . . . . . . . . . . Industry Entertainment
Carner, Charles Robert . . . . . . . . . . . . . . . . . . South Side Films
Carnessale, Julianna . . . . . . . . . . . . . . . . . CBS Entertainment
Carney, Elizabeth . . . . . . . . . . . . . Crystal Beach Entertainment
Carolei, Linda . . . . . . . . . . . . . . . . . Diana Kerew Productions
Carollo, Gina . . . . . . . . . . . . . . . . . . . . . . . . . Cineville Inc.
Caron, Glenn Gordon . . . . . . . . . . . . . . . Picturemaker Prods.
Carosella, Cookie . . . . . . . . . . . . . . . . . . Mandeville Films
Carouso, Tom . . . . . . . . . . . . . . . . . . . Kardana Films, Inc.
Carpenter, Ben . . . . . . . . . . . . . Equinox Entertainment Ltd.
Carr, Allan . . . . . . . . . . . . . . . . . . Carr Enterprises, Allan
Carr, Damon . . . . . . . . . . . . . . . . . . Yorkin Productions, Bud
Carraro, Bill . . . . . . . . . . . . . . . . Diamondback Entertainment
Carreiro, Andi . . . . . . . . . . . . . . . . . . Gallo Entertainment, Inc.
Carrelli, Bari . . . . . . . . . . . . . . . . . . . . . . NBC Entertainment
Carreras, Raquel . . . . . . . . . . . . . . . . . Carreras Productions
Carreras, Raquel . . . . . . . . . . . . Mount/Kramer Company, The
Carrere, Tia . . . . . . . . . . . . . . . . . . . . . . . Phoenician Films
Carrigan, Taska . . . . . . . . . Children's Television Workshop
Carrillo, Sandi . . . . . . . . . . . . . . Scherick Assocs., Edgar J.
Carroll, Elizabeth . . . . . . . . . . . Metro-Goldwyn-Mayer Pictures
Carroll, Maggie . . . . . . . . . . . . . . . . . . . . . Red Hour Films
Carroll, Roland . . . . . . . . . . . . . . . . . . . . . . Alpine Pictures
Carroll, Ryan J. . . . . . . . . . . . . . . . . . . . . . Alpine Pictures
Carroll, Willard . . . . . . . . . . . . . . . Hyperion Entertainment
Carsey, Marcy . . . . . . . . . . . . . . . . Carsey-Werner Co., The
Carson, Joey . . . . . . . . . . . . . . . . . . . . Twentieth Television
Carson, Phil . . . . . . . . . . . . . . . . Shooting Gallery Inc., The
Carswell, Barbara . . . . . . . . . . . Jaffe/Braunstein Films Ltd.
Carter, Alan . . . . . . . . . . . . . . . . Macht Ent. Group, Inc.
Carter, Chris . . . . . . . . . . . . . . . . Ten Thirteen Productions
Carter, Doug . . . . . . . . Walt Disney Pictures/Touchstone Pictures
Carter, Marcia . . . . . . . . . . . . . . . . . . Rysher Entertainment
Carter, Thomas . . . . . . . . . . . Carter Company, The Thomas
Cartsonis, Susan . . . . . . . . . . . . . . . . . . . Wind Dancer Films
Cartwright, Evan . . . . . . . . . . . . Equinox Entertainment Ltd.
Caruso, Rocco . . . . . . . . . . . . . . Caruso-Mendelsohn Prods.
Caruso, Ruth . . . . . . . . . . . . . Pearson Television Productions
Carvey, Jake . . . . . . . . . . . . . . . . . Spin Cycle Entertainment
Casady, Guymon . . . . . . . . . . . . . . . . . . Propaganda Films
Casagrande, Jill . . . . . . . . . . . . . . . . . . . . Disney Channel
Casagrande, Nicole . . . . . . . . . Mestres Productions, Ricardo
Cascio, Michael . . . . . . . . . . . . . A & E Television Networks
Casemiro, Eryk . . . . . . . . . . . . . . . . . . Klasky Csupo Inc.
Casey, Patricia . . . . . . . . . . . . . . . . Kettledrum Films, Inc
Casey, Peter . . . . . . . . . . . . . . . . . . . Grub Street Prods.
Casey, Virginia . . . . . . . . . . . . . . . Film Garden Entertainment
Casper, Jeremy . . . . . . . . . Miller/Boyett/Warren Productions
Cassidy, Joanne . . . . . . Walt Disney Pictures/Touchstone Pictures
Cassidy, Patrick . . . . . . . . . . . . . . . . . . . . . . . Troma Inc.
Castle, Michael . . . . . . . . . . . . . . . . . . Production Services
Castleberry, Dustin . . . . . . . . . . . . . . . . . Concourse Prods.
Castro, Juan . . . . . . . . . . . . . . . . . . Shoreline Entertainment
Castronovo, T.J. . . . . . . . . . . . . . . . . Creative Road Corp.
Catalano, Anthony . . . . . . . . Green Grass Blue Sky Company, Inc.
Catalano, Frank . . . . . . . . . . Green Grass Blue Sky Company, Inc.
Catalano, Jenifer . . . . . . . . . . . . . . . . Twilight Time Films
Cates, Gilbert . . . . . . . . . . . . . . . . . . Cates/Doty Productions
Catmull, Dr. Edwin E. . . . . . . . . . . . Pixar Animation Studios
Cavallo, Lucy . . . . . . . . . . . . . . . . . . . CBS Entertainment
Cayago, Edgar . . . . . . . . . . . . . Cort/Madden Company, The
Cayn Freedman, Heidi . . . . . . . . . . . Stone Stanley Productions

Cayouette, Laura . . . . . . . . . . . . . . . Scarlet Fire Films
Cazen, Sue . . . . . . . . . . . . . . . . . . . Dockry Productions
Cazes, Lila . . . . . . . . . . . . . . . . . . . Lumiere Films Inc.
Cedrone, Cheryl . . . . . . . . Grossbart, Barnett Productions
Celentano, Jeff . . . . . . . . . . . . . . . . . Periscope Pictures
Cerezo, Cielo . . . . . . . . . . . . . . . . . . . . . Good Machine
Cerutti, Rosemarie . . . . . . . Bradford Enterprises & Gemmy Prods.
Cervantes, David . . . . . . . . . Donner/Shuler-Donner Prods.
Ceslik, Carolyn . . . . . . . . . . . . . . . . . CBS Entertainment
Cetiner, Leman . . . . . . . . . . . . . . . . . Silverline Pictures
Cevallos, Adriana . . . . . . . . . . . Silverman Co., The Fred
Chacamaty, Carol . . . . . . . . . . . . . . . Avnet-Kerner Co.
Chaffin, Stokely . . . . . . . . . . . . . . . . . . . . Original Film
Chalfin, Allan . . . . . . . . . . . . . . . Scripps Howard Prods.
Chamberlain, Robert . . . . . . . . . . . . . . . . Canal+ (U.S.)
Chambers, Ernest . . . . . . . . . . . . Merv Griffin Productions
Chambers, Jonathan . . . . . . . . . . . . . . . TLC Entertainment
Chambers, Ruth . . . . . . . . . . Too Nuts Productions, Ltd.
Chan, David . . . . . . . . . Children's Television Workshop
Chandler, Harry . . . . . . . . . . . . . . . . Dream City Films
Chandler-Ward, Jenna . . . . . . . . . Diamondback Entertainment
Chane, Peggy Howard . . . . . . . . . . . . . . CPC Entertainment
Chaney, Byron . . . . . . . . . . . . . . . . . . Studio Productions
Chang, Anita . . . . . . . . . . . . . . . . . . . Rat Entertainment
Chang, Arthur . . . . . . . . . . . . Kingman Films International
Chanley, Sandy . . . . . . . . . . . . Production Partners, Inc.
Channing-Williams, Simon . . . . . . . . Channing Films LLC
Channon, Brooke . . . . . . . . . . . . . . . CLC Productions, Inc.
Chao, Stephen . . . . . . . . . . . . . . . . . . . USA Networks
Chapin, Doug . . . . . . . . . . . . . . . . . . . . Krost/Chapin
Chapman, Carlynn . . . . . . . . . . . . . . . . . Marvel Studios
Chapman, Matthew . . . . . . . . . . . . . . . . . Asylum Films
Chapman, Melanie . . . . . . . . . Singer-White Entertainment
Chappelle, David . . . . . . . . . . . . . . . Pilot Boy Productions
Charette, Abbie A. . . . . . . . . . . . . . Saban Entertainment
Charles, Glen . . . . . . . . . . . . . Charles-Burrows-Charles
Charles, Les . . . . . . . . . . . . . . . . Charles-Burrows-Charles
Chartoff, Melanie . . . . . . . . . . . . . . . Storybrooke Films
Chartoff, Robert . . . . . . . . . . . . . . . . Chartoff Productions
Chase, Dauri . . . . . . . . . . Finnegan-Pinchuk Company
Chase, Debra Martin . . . . . . . . . . . Brownhouse Productions
Chase, Derek . . . . . . . . . . . . . . . . . Dryer Prods., Fred
Chase, Stanley . . . . . . . . . . . . . . . Chase Prods., Stanley
Chase, Tammi . . . . . . . . . . Somers Teitelbaum David
Chasey, Skip . . . . . . . . . . . . . . . . . Imagine Television
Chasin, Liza . . . . . . . . . . . . . . . . . . Working Title Films
Chaskin, Janis . . . . . . . . . . . . . . . . . . New Line Cinema
Chasle, Dama . . . . . . . . . . . . . . . . Arama Entertainment
Chasman, Julia . . . . . . . . . . . . . . . Industry Entertainment
Chatelain, Didier . . . . . . . . Cohen Productions Inc., Herman
Chavez, Jessica . . . . . . . . . . . Simonds Co., The Robert
Cheatle, Lori . . . . . . . . . . . . . . . . . . . Double A Films
Chekich, Elaine . . . . . . . . . . . . . . . Hinterland Entertainment
Cheng, John . . . . . . . . . . . . . . . . . . . Rat Entertainment
Cherkas, Vicki . . . . . . . . . . . . . . . . . . . Miramax Films
Chernin, Peter . . . . . . . . . . . . . . . Fox Broadcasting Co.
Chervisnky, Ann . . . . . . . . . . . . . . . . Fine Line Features
Chesler, Lewis . . . . . . . . . . . Chesler/Perlmutter Production
Chesman, Melissa . . . . . . . . . . . . . . Redeemable Features
Chetwynd, Lionel . . . . . . . . . . . Whidbey Island Films, Inc.
Cheung, Vince . . . . . . . . . . . . . . . . Rice & Beans Prods.
Chiara, Charles . . . . . . . . . . . . . . . . Dinamo Entertainment
Chiaramonte, Andrew . . . . . . . . . . . . Chiaramonte Films, Inc.
Chiaramonte, Deborah . . . . First Look Picts./Overseas Filmgroup
Chiasson, Laura M. . . . . . . . . . . . . . . . . . . Utopia Films
Chin, Curtis . . . . . . . . . . . . . . . . . Raskoff Productions, Ken
Chin, Elaine . . . . . . . . . . . . . . . . . . . . Dragon Pictures
Chin, Roberta . . . . . . . . . . . . . . . Golden Harvest Films
Chinich, Michael . . . . . . . . . . . . . . . . Northern Lights Ent.
Chmiel, Bob . . . . . . . . . . . . . . Paulson Prods., Daniel L.
Choi, Alan . . . . . . . . . . . . . . . . Lauren Productions, Andrew
Choi, Sharon . . . . . . . . . . . . Star Land Entertainment Inc.
Chong, Remy . . . . . . . . . . . . . . . . . . City Light Films
Chory, Elizabeth . . . . . . . . . . . . . . . . . Mega Films, Inc.
Chory, James A. . . . . . . . . . . . . . . . . . . Mega Films, Inc.
Chotzen, Yvonne . . . . . . . . . . . Chotzen/Jenner Productions
Chouinard, S.J. . . . . . . . . . . . . . . . . . . Skyline Partners
Choy, Vicky . . . . . . . . . . . . Citadel Entertainment., LLC
Christensen, Stens . . . . . . . . . . . Chako Film International
Christenson, Tim . . . . . . . . . . . . . Creative Group Prods., Inc.

# CROSS-REFERENCED NAMES

| | |
|---|---|
| Christian, Aurelio | Robson Entertainment |
| Christiansen, Robert W. | Chris/Rose Prods. |
| Christianson, Kim | Saban Entertainment |
| Christianson, Peggy J. | Disney Channel |
| Christianson, Vicki | Icon Productions Inc. |
| Christie, Tom | Showtime Networks Inc. |
| Christopher, Tony | Landmark Entertainment Group |
| Chu, Jeremy | Dockry Productions |
| Chuang, Richard | Pacific Data Images |
| Chubb, Caldecot | Alphaville |
| Chung, Heijin | Mestres Productions, Ricardo |
| Chuo, Monica | Goldwyn Company, The Samuel |
| Chvatal, Cynthia | High Horse Films |
| Chydzik, Natalia | Ladd Company, The |
| Cianfarini, Leda | Green Moon Productions |
| Ciccolini, Michael | ITB CineGroup/Television |
| Cicero, Sharon | Longbow Productions |
| Cieply, Michael | Byline Films |
| Cieply, Michael | Rastar Productions |
| Cincotta, Deborah | Mark Prods., Laurence |
| Cioffi-Zaring, Bianca | Zaring/Cioffi Entertainment, Inc. |
| Cipriano, Anthony | Lynch Entertainment |
| Cisneroz, Lisa | Jersey Films |
| Citrano, Laura | Blue Relief, Inc. |
| Claire, Robin | Sweet Lorraine Prods. Inc. |
| Claman, Danielle | Fox Broadcasting Co. |
| Clancy, Tad | Dockry Productions |
| Clar, Richard | Island-In-The-Sky Pictures |
| Clark, Alison | WildRice Productions |
| Clark, Amy | Wychwood Productions |
| Clark, Carolyn | Walt Disney Pictures/Touchstone Pictures |
| Clark, Dan | Wandering Monkey Entertainment |
| Clark, Dick | Clark Prods., Inc., Dick |
| Clark, Greg | Radmin Company, The |
| Clark, Melissa | Yagya Productions |
| Clark, Shannon | Mr. Mudd |
| Clark, Susan | Georgian Bay Prods. |
| Clark, William | Walt Disney Pictures/Touchstone Pictures |
| Clarke, Emma | Fine Line Features |
| Clarke, Geraldine | Sunbow Entertainment |
| Clary, Susan | Neu-man-films, Inc. |
| Clavell, Ana | Taurus Entertainment Co. |
| Clawson, Tim | Propaganda Films |
| Clay, Victoria | Seven Arts Pictures |
| Cleary, Beth | Saban Entertainment |
| Clements, Loretta | TAE Productions |
| Clements, Michael | Fox Broadcasting Co. |
| Clemmer, Ronnie D. | Longbow Productions |
| Clifford, Jeffrey | Walt Disney Pictures/Touchstone Pictures |
| Clifford, Patricia | Clifford Prods., Patricia |
| Cline, Kelly | Twentieth Century Fox Television |
| Clooney, George | Maysville Pictures |
| Close, Alex | Fried Films |
| Clyne, Timothy | Hallmark Entertainment (NY) |
| Coates, Carole | Kenwood Prods., Inc. |
| Coates, Jeffrey R. | Shadowlands Productions |
| Cobb, Melissa | Fox Animation Studios |
| Cochrane, Craig | Act III Productions |
| Cockburn, Glenn | Templeton Productions |
| Codikow, Stacy | Codikow Films |
| Coffey, Vanessa | Coffey/Ballantine |
| Cogan, Ron | Acappella Pictures |
| Cohen Esq., H. Jason | Cohen & Ryan Films, Inc. |
| Cohen, Adrianna A.J. | Milestone Pictures Inc. |
| Cohen, Amy | Maysville Pictures |
| Cohen, Andrew | Once Upon A Time Films, Ltd. |
| Cohen, Andy | Grade A Entertainment |
| Cohen, Beth P. | Shooting Gallery Inc., The |
| Cohen, Betty | Cartoon Network |
| Cohen, Betty | Turner Entertainment Group |
| Cohen, Bobby | Miramax Films |
| Cohen, Bruce | Jinks/Cohen Company, The |
| Cohen, Charles | Metro-Goldwyn-Mayer Pictures |
| Cohen, Dara | Red Hour Films |
| Cohen, David | Gallant Entertainment, Inc. |
| Cohen, Fred | King World Productions |
| Cohen, Garrett | Bell and Associates, Dave |
| Cohen, Hank | Metro-Goldwyn-Mayer/Worldwide TV |
| Cohen, Herman | Cohen Productions Inc., Herman |
| Cohen, Jay | Punch Productions |
| Cohen, Larry | Larco Productions, Inc. |
| Cohen, Martin B. | Cohen Productions, Martin B. |
| Cohen, Polly | Warner Bros. Pictures |
| Cohen, Richard | Baldwin/Cohen Productions |
| Cohen, Rob | Poco Productions |
| Cohen, Rudy | Signature |
| Cohen, Sadaf | Saban Entertainment |
| Cohen, Sheree | Himber Entertainment |
| Cohen, Stacy | Lowry Productions, Hunt |
| Cohen, Tom | Lightstorm Entertainment |
| Cohn, David | Sneak Preview Entertainment, Inc. |
| Cohn, Elie | Langley Prods. |
| Coifman, Vanessa | Baltimore/Spring Creek Pictures, LLC |
| Colamaria, Tom | Bunim-Murray Productions, Inc. |
| Colbert, Wendy | Villard Prods., Dimitri |
| Cole, Michael | Miramax Films |
| Coleman, Jeffrey | Metro-Goldwyn-Mayer Pictures |
| Coleman, Kim | Simonds Co., The Robert |
| Coleman, Laura | Goldwyn Company, The Samuel |
| Coleman, Teri | Zane Buzby & Conan Berkeley Productions |
| Coler, Douglas | Montivagus Prods. |
| Coles, John David | Talking Wall Pictures, Inc. |
| Coletta, Joanna | Melendez Productions, Bill |
| Colfman, Vanessa | Spring Creek Productions |
| Colgan, Brian | ABC Pictures |
| Colichman, Paul | Regent Entertainment, Inc. |
| Coliman, Wic | Zero Pictures |
| Collazo, Yesenia | Esparza-Katz Prods. |
| Collet, Christopher | Blue Tulip Productions |
| Colleton, Sara | Colleton Company, The |
| Collett, Alex | Twentieth Century Fox Television |
| Collett, Ellen | HBO Pictures |
| Collins, Clancy | Paramount Domestic TV |
| Collins, Dan | Chesler/Perlmutter Production |
| Collins, Dave | NewStar Television |
| Collins, Doug | Bristol Cities |
| Collins, George | Krost/Chapin |
| Colmano, Marino | Colmano Productions, Marino |
| Colomby, Harry | Colomby/Keaton |
| Colpaert, Carl-Jan | Cineville Inc. |
| Colt, Beth | Atkinson Way Films |
| Columbia, Susanne | Yellen Company,, Linda |
| Columbus, Chris | 1492 Pictures |
| Colvin, Deidra L. | Mundy Lane Entertainment |
| Colvin, Timothy | Agamemnon Films Inc. |
| Commins, Kevin | Chesler/Perlmutter Production |
| Compton, Michael | Clark Prods., Inc., Dick |
| Comsky, Cynthia | Comsky Group Productions |
| Comsky, David | Comsky Group Productions |
| Condon, Sarah | HBO Original Programming |
| Condren, Liz | Blue Wolf Prods. Inc. |
| Cone, Blaine | VanDerKloot Film & Television Inc. |
| Cone, Stephanie | Takes On Production |
| Conklin, Michele | Viacom Productions |
| Conley, Jana | Craven Films, Wes |
| Conlin, Sheila | Macht Ent. Group, Inc. |
| Connaughton, Tara | Longfellow Pictures |
| Connelly-Skorka, Paula | American Movie Classics/Romance Classic |
| Conner, Jeff | Pressman Film Corp., Edward R. |
| Conner, Lindsay | 54th Street Productions |
| Connery, Sean | Fountainbridge Films |
| Connor, Rich | Matthau Company, Inc., The |
| Conroy, Daneen | Moving Pictures |
| Conroy, Jen | Neo Motion Pictures, Inc. |
| Consales, Lisa M. | Gullane Pictures |
| Considine, Dennis | Logo Entertainment |
| Constantinidis, Maggie | Jaffilms |
| Constantino, Victor H. | Lowry Productions, Hunt |
| Conte, Courtney | Carsey-Werner Co., The |
| Conti, Chris | NBC Entertainment |
| Conway, Dyan | Rees Assocs., Marian |
| Conway, James | Spelling Television, Inc. |
| Coogan, Peter | Henson Company, Jim |
| Cook, Bob | CBS Enterprises |
| Cook, Carrie | Original Film |
| Cook, Chris | Cook Films |
| Cook, Emily | Working Title Films |
| Cook, Richard W. | Walt Disney Pictures/Touchstone Pictures |
| Cook, Robert | Eyemark Entertainment |
| Cook, Whitney | Sundance Institute |

# CROSS-REFERENCED NAMES

Cook, Winship . . . . . . . . . . . . . . . . . . . Feldman Co., Edward S.
Cook-Reiner, Tatum . . . . . . . . . . . . . . . . . Catfish Productions
Cooke, Gregg . . . . . . . . . . . . . . . . . . . . . . Skylark Films Ltd.
Cooke, John . . . . . . . . . . . . . . . . . Turner Original Productions
Cooke, John F. . . . . . . . . . . . . . . . . . Walt Disney Company, The
Cooke, Stuart . . . . . . . . . . . . . . . . . . Recorded Picture Company
Cookson, Shari . . . . . . . . . . . . . . . . . Bell and Associates, Dave
Coolidge, Martha . . . . . . . . . . . . . . . . . . . . . Ozma Productions
Cooney, Michael . . . . . . . . . . . . . . . . . StoryTeller Films, Ltd.
Cooney, Sean . . . . . . . . . . . . . . . . . . . Trinity Pictures, Inc.
Cooper, David . . . . . . . . . . . . . . . . . . . . . . . Vault, Inc., The
Cooper, Dona . . . . . . . . . . . . . . . . . . . . . . . . . ABC Daytime
Cooper, Jenna . . . . . . . . . . . . . . . . . . . . . Propaganda Films
Cooper, Jerry . . . . . . . . . . . . . . . . . Showtime Networks Inc.
Cooper, John . . . . . . . . . . . . . . . . . . . . Sundance Institute
Cooper, Kevin . . . . . . . . . . . . . . . . . . . American Zoetrope
Cooper, Kevin K. . . . . . . . . . . . . . . . . . . . . . . . . Bay Films
Cooper, Kyle . . . . . . . . . . . . . . . . . . . . . . Imaginary Forces
Cooper, Matt . . . . . . . . . . . . . . . . . . . . . . . Vault, Inc., The
Cooper, Susan . . . . . . . . . . . . . . . . . . . Saban Entertainment
Cooperstien, Richard . . . . . . . Viacom Entertainment Group
Coote, Greg . . . . . . . . . . . . . . . . Village Roadshow Pictures
Copeland, Ellie . . . . . . . . . . . . . . . . . . . Jumbo Pictures, Inc.
Copeland, John . . . . . . . . . . . . . Netter Digital Entertainment
Copeland, Karen Lee . . . . . . . . . . . Crystal Pyramid Productions
Copley, Andi . . . . . . . . . . . . . . . . . . . . . . Film Roman, Inc.
Copp, Rick . . . . . . . . . . . . . . . . . . . . . . . Copp And Goodman
Coppini, Robert . . . . . . . . Rosemont Prods. International Ltd.
Coppola, Adrienne . . . . . . . . . . . . . . Plaster City Productions
Coppola, Christopher . . . . . . . . . . . . . Plaster City Productions
Coppola, Susan . . . . . . . . . . . Lock 'N Load (Ubiquitous) Pics.
Corbin, Michael . . . . . . . . . Black, Lawrence & Silverhardt Ent.
Corda, Nikki . . . . . . . . . . . . . . . . . . . . . Empire Pictures Inc.
Corfino, Jon . . . . . . . . . . . . . . . . . . . . . Iwerks Entertainment
Coritz, Pamela G. . . . . . . . . . . . . . . Val D'Oro Entertainment
Corley, Al . . . . . . . . . . . . . . . . . . . . . . . Neverland Films, Inc.
Corman, Catherine . . . . . . . . . . . . . . . Trinity Pictures, Inc.
Corman, Cis . . . . . . . . . . . . . . . . . . . . . . . . . Barwood Films
Corman, Julie . . . . . . . . . . . . . Concorde/New Horizons Corp.
Corman, Julie . . . . . . . . . . . . . . . . . . . Trinity Pictures, Inc.
Corman, Roger . . . . . . . . . . . . . Concorde/New Horizons Corp.
Cornelison, Valerie . . . . . . . . . . . . . . Sonnenfeld/Josephson
Corner, Sandy . . . . . . . . . . . . . . . . . . . . Vide-U Productions
Corral, Pete . . . . . . . . . Columbia TriStar Motion Picture Group
Corrigan, Michael G. . . . . . . . . Metro-Goldwyn-Mayer Pictures
Corrigan, Sean . . . . . . . . . . . . . . . . . . . Parkway Productions
Cort, Robert . . . . . . . . . . . . . . . . . . Cort/Madden Company, The
Cortes, Ron . . . . . . . . . . . . . . . . . . . Bakula Productions, Inc.
Corzine, Erin . . . . . . . . . . . . . . . . . . . . Stiefel Entertainment
Corzo, Robert . . . . . . . . . . . . . . . . . . . . . Largo Entertainment
Cosenzo, Cindy . . . . . . . . . . . . . . . . . . . . Pacific Data Images
Cosgrove, Ben . . . . . . . . . . . . . . . . . . . . . Columbia Pictures
Cosgrove, John . . . . . . . . . . . . . . . . Cosgrove-Meurer Prods.
Cossette, John . . . . . . . . . . . . . . . . . Cossette Productions
Cossette, Mary . . . . . . . . . . . . . . . . . Cossette Productions
Cossette, Pierre . . . . . . . . . . . . . . . . Cossette Productions
Costanzo, Julie . . . . . . . . . . . . . . . . . . . American Zoetrope
Costigan, Michael . . . . . . . . . . . . . . . . . . Columbia Pictures
Coston, Suzanne . . . . . . . . . . . . . . De Passe Entertainment
Cotgrove, Leoni . . . . . . . . . . . . . Recorded Picture Company
Cotter, Colin . . . . . . . . . . . . . . . . . Initial Entertainment Group
Cotton, Nancy . . . . . . . . . . . . . . . . . . . . ABC Entertainment
Cotugno, Jeff . . . . . . . . . . . . . . . Taffner Entertainment Ltd.
Coughlin, Janine . . . . . . . . . . . . . . . . . . . . . . Atlantis Films
Coulter, Warren . . . . . . . . . . . . . . . . . Big Ticket Television
Courtney, Kerri . . . . . . . . . . . . . . . . . . . . . . Goatsingers, The
Courts, Roger . . . . . . . . . . . . . . . . Gregory Productions, Inc.
Coutanche, Michael . . . . . . . . . . . . . . . . . Alliance Pictures
Covello, Nancy . . . . . . . . . Twentieth Century Fox-Fox 2000 (LA)
Covert, Christopher . . . . . . . . . . . . . Shooting Gallery Inc., The
Cowan, Chris . . . . . . . . . . . . . . . . . . . . . . . ZM Productions
Cowan, Cindy . . . . . . . . . . . . . . . Initial Entertainment Group
Cowan, Jon . . . . . . . . . . . . . . . Granada Entertainment USA
Cowan, Rob . . . . . . . . . . . . . . . . . . . . . . . . . Winkler Films
Cowen, Jenny . . . . . . . . . . . . . . . . . . . Rees Assocs., Marian
Cowen, Ron . . . . . . . . . . . . . . . . . . . . . Cowlip Productions
Cowger, Eric . . . . . . . . . . . . . . . . . . . . NewStar Television
Cowles, Chris . . . . . . . . . . . . . . . . . . . . Apatow Productions
Cowling, Tim . . . . . . . . . . . . . . . . . . . . . Discovery Networks
Cox, Bill . . . . . . . . . . . . . . . . . . . . . . . . . TBS Superstation

Cox, Brian . . . . . . . . . . . . . . . . . . . . . . . . Distant Horizon
Cox, Cecil C. . . . . . . . . . . . . . . . Mundy Lane Entertainment
Cox, Joel . . . . . . . . . . . . . . . . . . . . . . . . . Malpaso Prods.
Cox, Keith . . . . . . . . . . Warner Bros. Television Productions
Cox, Michelle . . . . . . . . . . . . . . Master Thespian Productions
Cox, Penney Finkelman . . . . . . . . . . . . . . DreamWorks SKG
Coyle, Katy . . . . . . . . . . . . . . . . . . Showtime Networks Inc.
Cracchiolo, Dan . . . . . . . . . . . . . . . . . . . . Silver Pictures
Cracchiolo, Marianne . . . . . . . . . . . . . . Brillstein-Grey Ent.
Craig, Jennifer . . . . . . . . . . . . . . . First Cold Press Productions
Craig, Sharon . . . . . . . . . . . . . . . . . . . Fox Productions, Ted
Craig, Tom . . . . . . . . . . . . . . . . . . . . . . . . . . . Topa Films
Cramer, Peter . . . . . . . . . . . . . . . . . . . . . Daybreak Prods.
Crane, Daniel . . . . . . . . . . Warner Bros. Feature Animation
Crane, David . . . . . . . . . . . . . Bright-Kauffman-Crane Prods.
Crane, H.J. . . . . . . . . . . . . . . . . . . . . . . Stonelock Pictures
Crane, Jeff . . . . . . . . . . . . . . . . . . . . Leucadia Film Corp.
Crane, Peter . . . . . . . . . Producers Ent. Group, Ltd., The
Cranston, Bruce . . . . . . . . . . . . . . . . . . . DreamWorks SKG
Craven, Wes . . . . . . . . . . . . . . . . . . . . Craven Films, Wes
Creel, Leanna . . . . . . . . . . . . . . . . . . . . . HSX Films, Inc.
Crew, Dick . . . . . . . . . . . . . . . . . . . . . . Crew Prods., Dick
Crews, Kristel . . . . . . . . . . . . . . . . . . HBO NYC Productions
Crier, Cammie . . . . . . . . . . . . . . . . . . . . . Badham Co., The
Crofford, Keith . . . . . . . . . . . . . . . . . . . . Cartoon Network
Cronin, Mark . . . . . . . . . . . . . . . . . . Mindless Entertainment
Crooch, Joshua . . . . . . . . . . . . . . . . Open Road Prods., Ltd.
Crosby, Cathy Lee . . . . . . . . . . . . . . . . CLC Productions, Inc.
Crosby, John . . . . . . . . . . . . . . . . . . Crosby/Levy Co., The
Cross, Mindy . . . . . . . . . . . . . . . . . . . . Bubble Factory, The
Cross, Pippa . . . . . . . . . . . . . . . . . . . . . . . . Granada Film
Crowley, Jill . . . . . . . Green Management & Productions, Joan
Crowley, Patrick . . . . . . . . . . . . . . . . . New Regency Prods.
Cruce, Jeff . . . . . . . . . . . . . . . . . . . . . Renaissance Pictures
Cruise, Greg . . . . . . . . . . . . . . . . . Manhattan Pictures Ltd.
Crystal, Billy . . . . . . . . . . . . . . . . . . . . . . Face Productions
Crystal, Steve . . . . . . . . . . . . . . . . . Warner Bros. Pictures
Csupo, Gabor . . . . . . . . . . . . . . . . . . . . . Klasky Csupo Inc.
Cuaron, Alfonso . . . . . . . . . . . . . . . . Besame Mucho Pictures
Cubillas, Fernando . . . . . . . . . . . . . . Olmos Productions Inc.
Cucci, John . . . . . . . . . . . . . . . . . . . . . . . . Comedy Central
Cuddihy, Christopher . . . . . . . . . . Cuddihy, Christopher A.
Culpepper, Maryanne . . . . . . . National Geographic Television
Culpepper, Nanelle . . . . . . . . . . . . . . . . . Sundance Institute
Culver, Carmen . . . . . . . . . . . . . . . . . Culver Films, Carmen
Culver, Cordelia . . . . . . . . . . . . . . . . . Culver Films, Carmen
Cummins, Linda . . . . . . . . . . . . . . . . . Cinnamon Prods. Inc.
Cunningham, Bill . . . . . . . . . . . . . . . . . Omega Entertainment
Cunningham, Donna . . . . . . . . . . . . . . . . Fox Kids Network
Cunningham, Jennifer . . . . . . . . . . . . . Panamort Television
Cunningham, Noel . . . . . . . . . . . . . Cunningham Prods. Inc.
Cunningham, Sean S. . . . . . . . . . . . Cunningham Prods. Inc.
Cuperman, Rachel . . . . . . . . . . . . . . . Samuelson Productions
Curcio, Mark A. . . . . . . . . . . . . . . . . . Artisan Entertainment
Curnow, Dan . . . . . . . . . . . . . . . . . . . Gotham Entertainment
Curran, Robert . . . . . . . . Metro-Goldwyn-Mayer/Worldwide TV
Curtan, Deborah . . . . . . . . . . . . . . . . . Big Ticket Television
Curtis Hall, Vondie . . . . . . . . . . . . . . . . . . Motor City Films
Curtis, Dan . . . . . . . . . . . . . . . . . . . . . Curtis Prods., Dan
Curtis, Ellen . . . . . . . . . . . . . . . . . . . . . . . . . . FilmRoos
Curtis, Grant . . . . . . . . . . . . . . . . . . . Renaissance Pictures
Curtiss, Ron . . . . . . . . . . . . . . . . . . . . Pirromount Pictures
Cusack, John . . . . . . . . . . . . . . . . . . New Crime Productions
Cutler, Michael . . . . . . . . . . . . . . . . . Saban Entertainment
Cutler-Rubenstein, Devorah . . . . . . . . . . . . . H2 Productions
Cvengros, Jeff . . . . . . . . . . . . . . . . . . . . . ZM Productions
Cybulski, Kim . . . . . . . . . . . . . . Finnegan-Pinchuk Company
Cycmanick, Jonathan . . . . . . . . . . . Pratt Ent., Inc., Charles
Cyffka, Peter . . . . . . . . . . . . . . . . . . Twentieth Century Fox
Czernin, Pete . . . . . . . . . . . . . . . . . . . . . . Di Novi Pictures
D'Alo, Diana . . . . . . . . . . . . Stone Canyon Investments, Inc.
D'Amato, Robert . . . . . . . . . . . . . . . . Lynn Productions, Tami
D'Ambrosia, Joe . . . . . . . . . . . . . . . . . Nickelodeon Movies
D'Angelo, Carr . . . . . . . . . . . . . . . . . . Broadway Pictures (LA)
Dahan, Michael . . . . . . . . . . . . . . . . . . . . . Mutual Film Co.
Dailey, James . . . . . . . . . . . . . . . . . . Sweetpea Entertainment
Dainoff, Andrew . . . . . . . . . Black, Lawrence & Silverhardt Ent.
Daitch, Jeff . . . . . . . . . . . Walt Disney Pictures/Touchstone Pictures
Dalke, Traci . . . . . . . . . . Ruddy Morgan Organization, Inc., The
Dalton, Chris . . . . . . . . . . . . . . . . Telescene Film Group., Inc.

# CROSS-REFERENCED NAMES

Dalton, Robb . . . . . . . . . . . . . . . . . . Eyemark Entertainment
Dalva, Eddie . . . . . . . . . . . . . . . . . . . . . . VH1 (Music First)
Daly, Robert A. . . . . . . . . . . . . . . . . . . Warner Bros. Pictures
Daly, Tim . . . . . . . . . . . . . . . . . . . . Daly-Harris Productions
Damboulev, Yanko . . . . . . . . . . . . . . Saga Pictures Corporation
Damien, Tom . . . . . . . . . . . . . . . . . Erratic Entertainment, Inc.
Damon, Mark . . . . . . . . . . . . . . . . . . . . . . . MDP Worldwide
Danaher-Dorr, Karen . . . . . . . . . . . . . . . PolyGram Television
Dang, Minh . . . . . . . . . . . . . . . . . . . Jason Company, Melinda
Daniel, Antonio . . . . . . . . . . . . . . . . . . . . Mutual Film Co.
Daniel, Chris . . . . . . . . . . . . . . . . . . Watermark Films, Inc.
Daniel, Jay . . . . . . . . . . . . . . . . . . . Daniel Productions, Jay
Daniel, Sean . . . . . . . . . . . . . . . . . . . . . . . . . Alphaville
Daniel, Tiffany . . . . . . . . . . . . . . . Johnson Productions, Mark
Daniels, Bonnie . . . . . . . . . . . . . . . . . New Regency Prods.
Daniels, Susanne . . . . . . . . . . . . . . W.B. Television Network
Danielson, Lynn . . . . . . . . . . Danielson - Rosenthal Productions
Danielson, Wade W. . . . . . . . . . . . . . . . . . . . Nine By Nine
Danner, Linda . . . . . . . . . . . . . . . . . . . . . VH1 (Music First)
Dansby, Andrew . . . . . . . . . . . . . . Robinson Productions, Amy
Danska, Jennifer . . . . . . . . . . . . . . Davis Entertainment Co.
Dante, Joe . . . . . . . . . . . . . . . . . . . . . . . . Renfield Prods.
Danza, Tony . . . . . . . . . . . . . . . . . . . . . Katie Face Prods.
Dardano, Kristin . . . . . . . . . . . . . . . . . . . Mutual Film Co.
Dare, Karen . . . . . . . . . . . . . . . Lexington Road Productions
Darian, Craig . . . . . . . . . . . . . . . . . . Tricor Entertainment
Darley, Chris . . . . . . . . . . . . . . . . . Howard Prods. Inc., Al
Darnell, Mike . . . . . . . . . . . . . . . . . . Fox Broadcasting Co.
Daro, Elizabeth . . . . . . . . . . . . . . . . . . Sitting Ducks Prods.
Dauchy, Derek . . . . . . . . . . . . . . . Spring Creek Productions
Daugherty, George . . . . . . . . . . . . . . . . . . IF/X Productions
Dauphinee, Jim . . . . . . . . . . . . . . . . . Eyemark Entertainment
Davatzes, Nickolas . . . . . . . . . . . . . A & E Television Networks
Davey, Bruce . . . . . . . . . . . . . . . . . . . Icon Productions Inc.
David, Alan . . . . . . . . . . . . . . . . . Somers Teitelbaum David
David, Denise . . . . . . . . . . . . . . . . . MakeMagic Productions
David, Lorena . . . . . . . . . . . . . . . . . . Kingsize Entertainment
Davids, Daniel E. . . . . . . . . . . . . . . A & E Television Networks
Davids, Daniel E. . . . . . . . . . . . . . . . . . History Channel, The
Davids, Danny . . . . . . . . . . . . . Mestres Productions, Ricardo
Davidson, Boaz . . . . . . . . . . . . . . . . . . . . . . . . Nu Image
Davidson, Chris . . . . . . . . . . . . . . . . . . . CBS Entertainment
Davidson, Paul . . . . . . . . . . . . . . . . . Henson Pictures, Jim
Davidson, Penny . . . . . . . . . . . . . . . Vision Media/LXD Inc.
Davidson, Rachel . . . . . . . . . . . . . . . . . . Act III Productions
Davies, Michael . . . . . . . . . . . . . . . . . . . ABC Entertainment
Davis Holt, Mary . . . . . . . . . . . . . . . . . . . Time Life Kids
Davis, Bridget D. . . . . . . . . . . . . . . Edmonds Entertainment
Davis, Dorothy . . . . . . . . . . . . . . . . . . . . Avnet-Kerner Co.
Davis, Eugene . . . . . . . . . . . . . . . . . Rocking Horse Prods.
Davis, Gregg . . . . . . . . . . . . . . . . . . . . Parkwood Pictures
Davis, John A. . . . . . . . . . . . . . . . . Davis Entertainment Co.
Davis, Kevin L.J. . . . . . . . . . . . . . . Spin Cycle Entertainment
Davis, Linda . . . . . . . . . . . . . . . . . . . South Fork Pictures
Davis, Maril . . . . . . . . . . . . . . . . . Berman Productions, Rick
Davis, Nilah . . . . . . . . . . . . . . . . . . You Go Boy Productions
Davis, Warren . . . . . . . . . . . . . Motion Pict. Corp. of America
Davison, Doug . . . . . . . . . . . . . . . . . . . . . . Mad Chance
Day, Janette . . . . . . . . . . . . . . . . . . . . . . Granada Film
Day, Jeremie . . . . . . . . . . . . . . . . Tollin/Robbins Productions
Day, Kathy . . . . . . . . . . . . . . . . . . Neufeld Productions, Mace
Daylong, Blyth . . . . . . . . . . . . . Symphony Entertainment, LLC
Dayton, Arlene L. . . . . . . . . . . . . . . . . . . . Maraday Prods.
de Abreu, Carlos . . . . . . . . . . . . . . . Hollywood Network, Inc.
de Abreu, Janice . . . . . . . . . . . . . . . Hollywood Network, Inc.
De Bont, Jan . . . . . . . . . . . . . . . . . . . Blue Tulip Productions
De Castro, Cesar . . . . . . . . . . . . . . . . . . . Ruby-Spears Prods.
De Fina, Barbara . . . . . . . . . . . . . . . . . . . . Cappa Productions
De Koven, Lindy . . . . . . . . . . . . . . . . . . NBC Entertainment
De Koven, Lindy . . . . . . . . . . . . . . . . . . . . . . NBC Studios
De La Paz, Theresa . . . . . . . . . . . . . . . . . Rastar Productions
De Laurentiis, Dino . . . . . . . . . . . . De Laurentiis Company, Dino
De Laurentiis, Martha . . . . . . . . . . . De Laurentiis Company, Dino
De Laurentiis, Raffaella . . . . . . . . . Raffaella Productions, Inc.
De Luca, Michael . . . . . . . . . . . . . . . . . . . New Line Cinema
De Luca, Tim . . . . . . . . . . . . . . . . . . Studios USA Television
De Marco, Joseph . . . . . . . Twentieth Century Fox-Searchlight Picts.
De Marco, Kathy . . . . . . . . . . . . . . . Lower East Side Films
de Mena, Warren . . . . . . . . . . . . . . . . . Travis Group, The
De Meo, Paul . . . . . . . . . . . . . . . . . . . . . . Pet Fly Prods.

De Niro, Robert . . . . . . . . . . . . . . . . . . . Tribeca Productions
de Oliveira, Paulo . . . . . . . . . . . . . . . Studios USA Pictures
de Passe, Suzanne . . . . . . . . . . . . . . . De Passe Entertainment
de Puthod, Marie . . . . . . . . . . . Bregman Entertainment Co., The
De Souza, Bonnie . . . . . . . . . . . . . . . B.S. Company, Inc., The
de Souza, Jeri Barchilon . . . . . . . . . . . . Val D'Oro Entertainment
de Souza, Steven E. . . . . . . . . . . . . . Val D'Oro Entertainment
de Vallance, Denis . . . . . . . . . . . . . . . . . . L.A. Animation
Dean Anderson, Richard . . . . . . . . . . . . . . Gekko Film Corp
Dean, Lillian . . . . . . . . . . . . . . . . . . . . . . . . Fortis Films
Dean, Tomlinson . . . . . . . . . . . . . . . Persky Prods., Lester
Dean, Valerie . . . . . . . . . . . . . . . . . Jacobs/Mutrux Prods.
Dearth, Doug . . . . . . . . . . . . . . . . . . New Crime Productions
Deaton, Jennifer . . . . . . . . . . . . . . . . . Big Town Productions
Debeenie, Christina . . . . . . . . . . Nasser Entertainment Group
DeBitetto, Robert . . . . . . . . . . . Turner Network Television (TNT)
deBlois, Dick . . . . . . . . . . . . . . . Feigelson Prods., Inc., J.D.
DeBow, Jeni-Lynn . . . . . . . . . . . . . . . . . . Monarch Pictures
DeBrino, Robert J. . . . . . . . . . . . . . . . . . Canterbury Films
Decker, David . . . . . . . . . . . . . . . . Turtle Productions, Jon
DeCuir, Gabrielle . . . . . . . . . . . . . . . . . . NewStar Media
Dees, Christy . . . . . . . . . . . . . . . . . . . . FX Networks, LLC
deFaria, Christopher . . . . . . . . . . . . . . Warner Bros. Pictures
DeFina, Maggie . . . . . . . . . . . . . . . . Scripps Howard Prods.
Dehghani, Sam . . . . . . . . . . . . . . . . . . . . . Davis Classics
Deighton, Joshua . . . . . Twentieth Century Fox-Searchlight Picts.
Deitch, Donna . . . . . . . . . . . . . . . . . . Desert Heart Prods.
Deitchman, Beth . . . . . . . . . . . . . . . . . . . City Light Films
DeJan, Michael Leslie . . . . . . . . Johnson Entertainment, Magic
Dekker, Moira . . . . . . . . . . . . . . . . . Bochco Prods., Steven
Del Hierro, Joe . . . . . . . . . . . . . . . . . . . . Disney Telefilms
Del Prete, Deborah . . . . . . . . . . . . . . Dee Gee Entertainment
Delaney Esq., Pamela S. . . . . . . . . . . . . Storm Entertainment
Delaney, Lynn . . . . . . . . . . . . . . . Jaffe/Braunstein Films Ltd.
Delazerda, Elicia . . . . . . . . . Goldwyn Company, The Samuel
Delgado, Jose . . . . . . . . . . . . . . . . . . . . . . . Krost/Chapin
DeLine, Donald . . . . . . Walt Disney Pictures/Touchstone Pictures
della Valle, Martin . . . . . . . . . . . . . . . . . Atman Entertainment
Delman, Jeffrey . . . . . . . . . . . . . . . . . . . . SPI Entertainment
Delo, Mark . . . . . . . . . . . . . . . . . . . . . Mars Prods. Corp.
Delovich, Shirley . . . . . . . . . . . . De Laurentiis Company, Dino
DeLuise, Michael . . . . . . . . . . . . . . . Stoneface Entertainment
DeLuise, Peter . . . . . . . . . . . . . . . . . Stoneface Entertainment
DeMarco, F.M. . . . . . . . . . Stern Production Company, The Howard
Demberg, Lisa . . . . . . . . . . . . . . . Demberg Productions, Lisa
Demers, Bernard . . . . . . . . . . . . . . . . . . . Meridian Films
Demirer, Meltem . . . . . . . . . . . . . . . . . Artisan Entertainment
Demme, Ted . . . . . . . . . . . . . . . . . . . . Spanky Pictures, Inc.
Denise, Debbie . . . . . . . . . . . . . . . Sony Pictures Imageworks
Denke, Conrad . . . . . . . . . . . . . . . Whidbey Island Films, Inc.
Denkert, Darcie . . . . . . . . . . . . Metro-Goldwyn-Mayer Pictures
Densham, Pen . . . . . . . . . . . . . . . Trilogy Entertainment Group
DePew, Gary . . . . . . . . . . . . . . . . . . . . . DePew Productions
DequetteVille, Daryl . . . . . . . . . . . . . . Green Communications
Deringer, AnnMarie . . . . . . . . . . . . . Underworld Entertainment
DeRoy, Anna . . . . . . . . . . . . . . . . . . . Canton Company, The
Derrah, Jay . . . . . . . . . . . . . . . . . . Kennedy/Marshall Company
Derrick, Clyde . . . . . . . . . . . . . . . . Kennedy/Marshall Company
DeSantis, Anthony . . . . . . . . . . . . . . . . Cinestage Productions
DeSanto, F.J. . . . . . . . . . . . . . . . . . . . . Batfilm Prods., Inc.
DeSipio, Sally . . . . . . . . . . . . . . . . . . . Imagine Television
Desmond, Loretta . . . . . . . . . . . . . . . . . . . . . NBC Studios
Despres, Naomi . . . . . . . . . . . . . . . . Manifest Film Company
Deutch, Howard . . . . . . . . . . . . . . . . . . . . . H.R.D. Prods.
Deutchman, Ira . . . . . . . . . . . . . . . . . . Redeemable Features
Devendorf, Mark . . . . . . . . . . . . . . . . Chako Film International
Devereaux, Melissa . . . . . . . . VanDerKloot Film & Television Inc.
Devereux, Elizabeth . . . . . . . . . . . . . . . . . . . . 1492 Pictures
DeVille, Lorraine . . . . . . . . . . . . . Gimbel Productions, Inc., Roger
DeVincentis, D.V. . . . . . . . . . . . . . . . . New Crime Productions
Devine, Howard . . . . . . . . . . . . . Walt Disney TV/Touchstone TV
Devine, Zanne . . . . . . . . . . . . . . . . PolyGram Filmed Ent.
DeVito, Danny . . . . . . . . . . . . . . . . . . . . . . Jersey Films
Devoy, Peter . . . . . . . . . . . . . . . . Imagination Factory Inc.
Dew, Victoria . . . . . . . . . . . . . . . . . Besame Mucho Pictures
Dewart, Caleb . . . . . . . . . . . . . . . . . . BallPark Productions
Dewey, Sandra . . . . . . . . . . . . Turner Network Television (TNT)
Deyhle, Rolf . . . . . . . . . . . . . . . . . . . . . Capella Films Inc.
Di Bona, Vin . . . . . . . . . . . . . . . . . . . Di Bona Prods., Vin
Di Bonaventura, Lorenzo . . . . . . . . . . . . . Warner Bros. Pictures

# CROSS-REFERENCED NAMES

di Loreto, Dante . . . . . . . . . . . . . . . . . . . . . . . . . Aviator Films LLC
Di Novi, Denise . . . . . . . . . . . . . . . . . . . . . . . . . Di Novi Pictures
Di Raimondo, Giuseppina . . . . . . . . . . . . . . Stevens & Associates
Diamant, Limor . . . . . . . . . . . . . . . . . . . . . . . . . . . . . . . Signature
Diamant, Moshe . . . . . . . . . . . . . . . . . . . . . . . . . . . . . . Signature
Diaz, Joseph T. . . . . . . . . . . . . . Children's Television Workshop
Diaz-Santana, Miriam . . . . . . . . . . Germain Productions, Stephanie
DiBona, Cara . . . . . . . . . . . . . . . . . . . . . . . . Di Bona Prods., Vin
Dickens, Kimberly . . . . . . . . . . . . . . . . . . . Ascato Entertainment
Dickerman, Samuel . . . . . . . . . . . . . . . . . . . Radiant Productions
Dickson, Anthony . . . . . . . . . . . . . . . . . . . . Radiant Productions
Dickstein, Stephen . . . . . . . . . . . . . . . . . . . . . Propaganda Films
Diefenbach, Michael . . . . . . . . . . . . . . . . . . . . . . . . . . . . . . PBS
Dillman, Jack . . . . . . . . . . . . . . . . . . . . . . . . . Dockry Productions
Dills, Regan . . . . . . . . . . . . . . . Sefton Productions International
DiMartino, Joseph . . . . . . . . . . . . . . . Shooting Gallery Inc., The
Dimbort, Danny . . . . . . . . . . . . . . . . . . . . . . . . . . . . Nu Image
DiMento, Katie . . . . . . . . . . . . . . . . . . . . . . . . . Caravan Pictures
Dimitrijevich, Robert . . . . . . . . . . . . . . . . . . . . . Atelier Pictures
DiNallo, Barbara . . . . . . . . . . . . . . . . . . . . . . . . Canal+ (U.S.)
Dinerstein, David . . . . . . . . . . . . Paramount Specialty Division
DiNoto, Karen . . . . . . . . . . . . . . . . . . . . . . . Fox Kids Network
Dinsmore, Jamie . . . . . . . . . . . . . . . . . . . . . Rehme Productions
Dion, Garrick . . . . . . . . . . . . . . . . . . . . . . . . . . Silver Pictures
DiPasquale, Joseph A. . . . . . . . . . . . . . . . Bright Street Pictures
DiRaffaele, Michelle . . . . . . . . . . . . . . . . . . . Mandalay Pictures
DiSarro, David . . . . . . . . . . . . . . . . . . . . . . . Crew Prods., Dick
Disney, Roy E. . . . . . . . . . . . . . . . Walt Disney Company, The
Dix, Alexander . . . . . . . . . . . . . . . . . . . Shoreline Entertainment
Dixon, Tyrone D. . . . . . . . . . . . . . . . . . . . . . . . . . Def Pictures
Dixson, Alyss . . . . . . . . . . . . . . . . . . . . . . . . Rat Entertainment
Dobkin, Kristy . . . . . . . . . . . . . . . . . . . . . . . . . . South, Frank
Dockry, Nancy . . . . . . . . . . . . . . . . . . . . . . . Dockry Productions
Dodd, Ted . . . . . . . . . . . . . . . . . . . . . . Twentieth Century Fox
Dodson, James . . . . . . . . . . . . . . . . . . . . . . . Onelight Pictures
Dodson, Jolene . . . . . . . . . . . . . . . . . . Cosgrove-Meurer Prods.
Doel, Frances . . . . . . . . . . . . . . . Concorde/New Horizons Corp.
Doelger, Frank . . . . . . . . . . . . . . . . . . . . . HBO NYC Productions
Dogans, Ed . . . . . . . . . . . . . . . . . . Pompian Productions, Paul
Dohrmann, Sarah . . . . . . . . . . . . . . . . . . . . . Sarabande Prods.
Dolan, Beth . . . . . . . . . . . . . . . . . . . . . Coyote Pass Productions
Dolgen, Jonathan L. . . . . . . . . . . . Viacom Entertainment Group
Dolins, Cheryl . . . . . . . . . . . . . . . . . . . . . Grammnet Productions
Dollard, Jacqueline . . . . . . . . . . . . . . . . . . New Regency Prods.
Dombrow, John . . . . . . . . . . National Geographic Feature Films
Domingues, Tom . . . . . . . . . . . . . . . . . . Rees Assocs., Marian
Donahue, Kevin . . . . . . . . . . . . . Donner/Shuler-Donner Prods.
Donahue, Patrick . . . . . . . . . . . . . . . . . Bottom Line Studio, Inc.
Donahue, Sean . . . . . . . . . . . . . . . . . . . Bottom Line Studio, Inc.
Donald, Jefferson . . . . . . . . . . Peacock Films/1st Miracle Pictures
Donaldson, Cheryl . . . . . . . . . . . . . . Johnson Productions, Mark
Donaldson, Heather . . . . . . . . . . . . . Turner Original Productions
Donegan, David . . . . . . . . . . Singer Entertainment, Joseph M.
Doniger, Walter . . . . . . . . . . . . . . . . . . . . . . Bettina Prods. Ltd.
Donley, Maureen . . . . . . . . . . . . Donley Productions, Maureen
Donner, Richard . . . . . . . . . . . . . Donner/Shuler-Donner Prods.
Donohoe, Amanda . . . . . . . . Enlightened Witness, Inc./Levine Mgmt.
Donovan, Lisa . . . . . . . . . . . . . . . . . . . . . . Gross-Weston Prods.
Donovan, Tim . . . . . . . . . . . . Singer Entertainment, Joseph M.
Dooley, Maura . . . . . . . . . . . . . . . . . . . Henson Pictures, Jim
Doran, Lindsay . . . . . . . . . . . . . . . . . United Artists Pictures
Dore, Bonny . . . . . . . . . . . . . . . . . . . Dore Productions, Bonny
Dorfman, Marc . . . . . . . . . . . . . . . . . . . . . . Nichol Moon Films
Dornhecker, Shann . . . . . . . . . . . . . . . . . Arkoff Intl. Pictures
Dorr, Christopher . . . . . . . . . . . . . . . . . . Scott Free Productions
Doss, Arden . . . . . . . . . . . . . . . . . . . . . . . . Rastar Productions
Dossa, Andrea . . . . . . . . . . . . . . . . . . . . . . Cossette Productions
Doty, Dennis . . . . . . . . . . . . . . . . . . . . . Cates/Doty Productions
Dougherty, Jack . . . . . . . . . . . . . . . . . . . . . . . . . . . . . . . . PBS
Douglas, Cord . . . . . . . . . . . . . . . . . . Keller Entertainment Group
Douglas, David March . . . . . . . . . . Grand Designs Entertainment
Douglas, Jason . . . . . . . . . . . . . . . . . . Cobalt Films International
Douglas, Tim . . . . . . . . . . . . . . . . . Grand Designs Entertainment
Douglass, Jere . . . . . . . . . . . . . . . . . . . . Henson Pictures, Jim
Doumanian, Jean . . . . . . . . . . . . . . . . Doumanian Prods., Jean
Douthit, Randy . . . . . . . . . . . . . . . . . . . Douthit Productions Ltd.
Dowaliby, James M. . . . . . . . . Paramount International Television
Dowd, Jeff . . . . . . . . . . . . . . . . . . . . . . . . . . Palisades Pictures
Dowell, Raye . . . . . . . . . . . . . . . . . . . . . . . . . Motor City Films
Downey III, John . . . . . . . . . . . . . . . . Proud Mary Entertainment

Downey, M. Peter . . . . . . . . . . . . . . . . . . . . . . . . . . . . . . . . PBS
Doyle, Ned . . . . . . . . . . . . . . . . . . . . . Lightview Entertainment
Drachkovitch, Lasta . . . . . . . . . . . . . . . 44 Blue Productions, Inc.
Drachkovitch, Rasha . . . . . . . . . . . . . . . 44 Blue Productions, Inc.
Drachkovitch, Stephanie . . . . . . . . . . . . Buena Vista Productions
Draizin, Doug . . . . . . . . . . . . . . . . . . . . . . . . . Draizin Co., The
Draper, Bill . . . . . . . . . . . . . . . . . . . . . . Warner Bros. Pictures
Dray, Julia . . . . . . . . . . . . . . . . . . . . . Simonds Co., The Robert
Drechsler, Carol . . . . . . . . . . . . . . . . . . . . Force Ten Productions
Drenning, Tracie . . . . . . . . . . . . . . Netter Digital Entertainment
Drewe, Avery . . . . . . . . . . . . . . . . . . . . . . . . Belisarius Prods.
Dreyfuss, Kevin . . . . . . . . . . . . . . . . Talking Wall Pictures, Inc.
Dreyfuss, Richard . . . . . . . . . . . . . . . . . Dreyfuss/James Prods.
Drinkwater, John . . . . . . . . . . . . . . . . Shukovsky English Ent.
Driskill, Brooke . . . . . . . . . . . . . . . . . Singer Productions, Carla
Drotman, C.S. . . . . . . . . . . . . . . . . . . . . . . . Skylark Films Ltd.
Dryer, Fred . . . . . . . . . . . . . . . . . . . . . . . Dryer Prods., Fred
Dubelko, Bob . . . . . . . . . . . . . . . . . . Carsey-Werner Co., The
DuBose, Glenn . . . . . . . . . . . . . . . . . . . . . . . . . . . . . . . . . PBS
Dubovsky, Dana . . . . . . . . . . . . . . . American World Pictures
DuBow, Myron . . . . . . . . . . Playboy Entertainment Group Inc.
Dubrow, Chris . . . . . . . . . . . . . . . Millennium Mediaworks, Inc.
Dubrow, Chris . . . . . . . . . . . . . . . . . . . Pacifica Entertainment
Duda, Matthew . . . . . . . . . . . . . . . . . Showtime Networks Inc.
Dudar, Nanette . . . . . . . . . . . . . . . . . . . . . . . . . . . . . . . . PBS
Dudelson, James G. . . . . . . . . . . . . . Taurus Entertainment Co.
Dudelson, Robert F. . . . . . . . . . . . . . Taurus Entertainment Co.
Dudelson, Stanley E. . . . . . . . . . . . . . Taurus Entertainment Co.
Dudevoir, Leon . . . . . . . . . . . . . . . . . . . . . New Line Cinema
Duer, Ken . . . . . . . . . . . . . . . . . . Warner Bros. TV Animation
Duffy, Cella . . . . . . . . . . . . . . . . . . . . . . . Klasky Csupo Inc.
Dugas, Adam . . . . . . . . . . . . . . . . . . . . Boyle-Taylor Prods.
Duggan, Ervin S. . . . . . . . . . . . . . . . . . . . . . . . . . . . . . . . PBS
Duke, Alan . . . . . . . . . . . . . . Walt Disney TV/Touchstone TV
Duke, Bill . . . . . . . . . . . . . . . . . . . . . . . . . . Yagya Productions
Dunas, Ronald . . . . . . . . . . . . . . . . . Dunas Prods., Ronald S.
Dunbar, Maura . . . . . . . . . . . . . . . . . . . . . . ABC Entertainment
Duncan, Chip . . . . . . . . . . . . . . . . . . . . . . Water Street Pictures
Duncombe, Charles . . . . . . . . . . . . . . . . . . . . . . ZM Productions
Dungan, Sebastian . . . . . . . . . . . . . . . . . . . Witt-Thomas Films
Dungey, Channing . . . . . . . . . . . . . . . . . . . . . . . . . . . Material
Dunlap, Mary-Ann . . . . . . . . . . . . . . . . . . Lyles Prods., A.C.
Dunlop, Eddie . . . . . . . . . . . . Cannon & Associates, Reuben
Dunn, Jeff . . . . . . . . . . . . . . . . . . . . Nickelodeon/Nick at Nite
Dunn-Leonard, Barbara . . . . . . . R. Edwards Prods./R. Edwards Films
Duplat, Francois . . . . . . . . . . . . . . . . . Roscoe Enterprises, Inc.
Duplechien, Kimberlee . . . . . . . . . . . . . . . . . Quinn Productions
Dupont, Michelle . . . . . . . . . . . . . . . . Gross Points Entertainment
Dupont, Renee . . . . . . . . . . . . . . . . . Gross Points Entertainment
DuPre-Pesmen, Paula . . . . . . . . . . . . . . . . . . . . . 1492 Pictures
Durian, Chris . . . . . . . . . . . . . . . . . . . . . . . Wind Dancer Films
Durian, Marcus . . . . . . . . . . . . . . . . . Young Artists Productions
Durig, Greg . . . . . . . . . . . . . . . . . . . . . . Discovery Networks
Durk, Julie . . . . . . . . . . . . . . . . Donner/Shuler-Donner Prods.
Durrell, Angela . . . . . . . . . . . . . . . . . . . . . . Delaware Pictures
Durso, Kathleen . . . . . . . . . . . . . . Nasser Entertainment Group
Dusick Esq, Ken . . . . . . . . . . . . . . . . . Lee Productions, Michele
Duteil, Arnaud . . . . . . . . . . . . . . . . . . . . . . . . . Canal+ (U.S.)
Duvall, Robert . . . . . . . . . . . . . . . . . . . . . . Butchers Run Films
Dwek, Rob . . . . . . . . . . . . . . . . . . . . . . Fox Broadcasting Co.
Dwyer, Cathy . . . . . . . . . . Greenwood Avenue Entertainment
Dwyer, Sean . . . . . . . . . . . . . . . . . SisterLee Productions Inc.
Dwyer, Shawn . . . . . . . . . . . . . . . . . . . . NewStar Television
Dziak, Mark . . . . . . . . . . . . . . . . . . . . Plaster City Productions
Earls, Patrick . . . . . . . . . . . . . . . . . . . . . Vanguard Productions
East, Ted . . . . . . . . . . . . . . . . . . . . . . . . . . . Alliance Pictures
Eastburg, Alex . . . . . . . . . . . . . . . . . . . . . . Vienna Productions
Easton, Elliott . . . . . . . . Full Circle Ent. AKA Suzanne Bauman Prod
Eastwood, Clint . . . . . . . . . . . . . . . . . . . . . . . . Malpaso Prods.
Eastwood, Joseph . . . . . . . . . . . . . . . . . . . . . . . . . EntPro, Inc.
Ebbs, Donna Lee . . . . . . . . . . . . . . . . . King World Productions
Eberhard, Jude Pauline . . . . . . . . . . . . . . . Cinewest Productions
Echegoyen, Helena . . . . . . . . . . . . . . . . . . . . Motor City Films
Eckerle, Jeff . . . . . . . . . . . . . . . . . . . . . . Fox Broadcasting Co.
Economos, Greg . . . . . . . . . . . . . . . . . . . . . . Fox Kids Network
Ed Gernon . . . . . . . . . . . . . . . . . . . . . . . . . . . . Atlantis Films
Edelist, Evan . . . . . . . . . . . . . . . . . . . . . . . New Line Cinema
Edelman, Abra . . . . . . . . . . . . . . . . . Edelman Productions, Abra
Edelman, Matthew . . . . . . . . . . . . . . . . . . . . . Marvel Studios
Edelstein, Neal . . . . . . . . . . . . . . . . . . . . . Picture Factory, The

# CROSS-REFERENCED NAMES

# CROSS-REFERENCED NAMES

Fedro, Scott . . . . . . . . . . . . Morra, Brezner, Steinberg & Tenenbaum
Feemster, Gary . . . . . . . . . . . . . . Sweet Lorraine Prods. Inc.
Feghali, Chantal . . . . . . . . . . . . . . . . . . . . Mandalay Pictures
Feifer, Jerry . . . . . . . . . . . . . . . . . . Vista Street Entertainment
Feifer, Michael . . . . . . . . . . . . . . . . Vista Street Entertainment
Feige, Kevin . . . . . . . . . . . . . . . . . Donner/Shuler-Donner Prods.
Feigelson, J.D. . . . . . . . . . . . . . . . Feigelson Prods., Inc., J.D.
Feigen, Brenda . . . . . . . . . . . . . . . . . . . . . Reel Life Women
Feinberg, Petra . . . . . . . . . . . . . . . . . . Carlson-Lehman Prods.
Feingold, Rodd . . . . . . . . . . . . . . . . . . . Saban Entertainment
Feld, Kenneth . . . . . . . . . . . . . . . . . Pachyderm Entertainment
Feldman, Ed . . . . . . . . . . . . . . . . . . Feldman Co., Edward S.
Feldman, Elizabeth . . . . . . . . . . . Lasher, McManus & Robinson
Feldman, Jay . . . . . . . . . . . . . . . . . . . . . Discovery Networks
Feldman, Mark . . . . . . . . . . . . . . . E! Entertainment Television
Feldman, Michael . . . . . . . . . . . . . . . . . . . . Avenue Pictures
Feldman, Sherri . . . . . . . . . Walt Disney Pictures/Touchstone Pictures
Feldsott Reynolds, Kelley . . . . . . . . . . . . Channing Films LLC
Fellner, Eric . . . . . . . . . . . . . . . . . . . . . Working Title Films
Feltheimer, Jon . . . . . . . . . . . . . Columbia TriStar Television
Feltheimer, Jon . . . . . . . . . . . Sony Pictures Entertainment
Felton, Giles . . . . . . . . . . . . . . . . . Gold'n Hen Productions
Felton, Katie . . . . . . . . . . . . . . . . . . . . . . . . Jersey Films
Fenady, Andrew . . . . . . . . . . . . . . . Fenady Associates, Inc.
Fenady, John Duke . . . . . . . . . . . . . Fenady Associates, Inc.
Fenton, Suzanne . . . . . . . . . . . . . . . . KiMina Entertainment
Ferdinand, Erin . . . . . . . . . . . . . . . Tisch Co., The Steve
Ferguson, Brooks . . . . . . . . . . . . . . . . . . . . Blue Horizon
Ferguson, Ken . . . . . . . . . . National Geographic Television
Ferleger, Daniel . . . . . . . . . . . . . . Twentieth Century Fox
Ferneau, Laurie . . . . . . . . . . . . . . . . . . . Logo Entertainment
Fero, Lynn . . . . . . . . . . . . . . . . . . . Paramount Domestic TV
Ferraro, John . . . . . . . . . Paramount Pictures- Motion Picture Group
Ferrell, Lisa . . . . . . . . . . . . . . . . . . JCS Entertainment Inc.
Ferrero, Linda . . . . . . . . . . . . . . . . . . . . . . Hill/Fields Ent.
Ferriter, Christine . . . . . . . . . . . . . . . . . Klasky Csupo Inc.
Festa, Lou . . . . . . . . . . . . . . . . . . . . Pearson All American
Feury, Joseph . . . . . . . . . . . . . Feury Entertainment, Joseph
Fickman, Andy . . . . . . . . . . . . . . . . Middle Fork Productions
Fidlow, Bennett J. . . . . . . . . . . . . . . . Vanguard Productions
Field, Doug . . . . . . . . . . . . . . . . . . . . . . . NewStar Media
Field, Fern . . . . . . . . . . . . . . . . . . . . . . . . USA Networks
Field, Gwen . . . . . . . . . . . . . . . . . . . . . . . . Simsie Films
Field, Kevin . . . . . . . . . . . . . . . . . . . . . Maysville Pictures
Field, Sally . . . . . . . . . . . . . . . . . . . . . . . Fogwood Films
Field, Ted W. . . . . . . . . . . . . . Interscope Communications Inc.
Fielding, Lisa . . . . . . . . . . . . . . . . . . . Obst Prods., Lynda
Fields, Adam . . . . . . . . . . . . . . . . Fields Productions, Adam
Fields, Freddie . . . . . . . . . . . . . . Fields & Hellman Co., The
Fields, Freddie . . . . . . . . . . . . . . . . . . . . Fields Co., The
Fields, Joel . . . . . . . . . . . . . . . . . . . . . . Hill/Fields Ent.
Fields, Robert . . . . . . . . . . . . . . . . . . . . . . . Jake Films
Fierberg, Andrew . . . . . . . . . . . . . . . . . . . Double A Films
Figgis, Mike . . . . . . . . . . . . . . . . . . . . . . Red Mullet, Inc.
Figueroa, Florence . . . . . . . . . . . . . . Una Chica Entertainment
Figueroa, Suzy . . . . . . . . . . . . . . . Village Roadshow Pictures
Fili-Krushel, Patricia . . . . . . . . . . . . . . . . . . . ABC Daytime
Filie, Dan . . . . . . . . . . . Universal Television & Networks Group
Filkins, Susanne . . . . . . . . . . . . Young Artists Productions
Filus, Drew . . . . . . . . . . . . . . . . . . . . . . . . Jersey Shore
Fincioen, Joke . . . . . . . . . . . . . . . . Pacific Western Prods.
Fine, Delia . . . . . . . . . . . . . . . A & E Television Networks
Finerman, Wendy . . . . . . . . . . . . . Finerman Prods., Wendy
Finestra, Carmen . . . . . . . . . . . . . Wind Dancer Prod. Group
Fink, Jonny . . . . . . . . . . . . . . . . . Tollin/Robbins Productions
Finkelstein, Rick . . . . . . . . . . . . . . . . PolyGram Filmed Ent.
Finnegan, Patricia . . . . . . . . . . . . Finnegan-Pinchuk Company
Finnegan, William . . . . . . . . . . . . Finnegan-Pinchuk Company
Finnell, Michael . . . . . . . . . . . . . . . . . . . . Renfield Prods.
Finneran, Patricia . . . . . . . . . . . . . . . . . . . Peak Productions
Finnerty, James . . . . . . . . . . . . . . . . . . . . Fatima Production
Finney, Richard . . . . . . . . . . . . . . Michael/Finney Prods., Inc.
Firestone, Karen . . . . . . . . . . 40 Acres & A Mule Filmworks Inc.
Firste, John . . . . . . . . . . . . . . . . . . . . Dockry Productions
Fischer, A.B. . . . . . . . . . . . . . . . . . . . . . . Beacon Pictures
Fischer, Preston . . . . . . . . . Fischer Co., Preston Stephen
Fischer, Russel . . . . . . . . . Constantin Film Development Inc.
Fischler, Simon . . . . . . . . . . . . . . . Baldwin/Cohen Productions
Fischoff, Richard . . . . . . . . . . . . . Von Zerneck-Sertner Films
Fisher, Barbara . . . . . . . . . . . . . . . . . . Studios USA Pictures

Fisher, Ellen . . . . . . . . . . . . . . . . . Pamplin-Fisher Company
Fisher, John . . . . . . . . . . . . . . . HBO Original Programming
Fisher, Laurie . . . . . . . . . . . . . . . . Kuzui Enterprises, Inc.
Fisher, Lucy . . . . . . . . . . . . . . . . . . . . Columbia Pictures
Fisher, Lucy . . . . . . . . . Columbia TriStar Motion Picture Group
Fisher, Ricka . . . . . . . . . . . . . Walt Disney TV/Touchstone TV
Fisher, Robert W. . . . . . . . . . . . . . . Pamplin-Fisher Company
Fishman, Wendy . . . . . . . . . . . . . . . . . . CBS Entertainment
Fitzgerald, Adele . . . . . . . . . . . . . . . . . Parkway Productions
Fitzgerald, Jane . . . . . . . . . . . Turman-Morrissey Company, The
Fitzgerald, Jiles . . . . . . . . . . . . . Chesler/Perlmutter Production
Fitzgerald, Jim . . . . . . . . . . . . . . O'Hara-Horowitz Productions
FitzGerald, Lisa . . . . . . . . . . . . . FitzGerald Prods. & Mgt.
Fitzgerald, Susie . . . . . . . . . . . . . . . . Brillstein-Grey Ent.
FitzGibbon, Tom . . . . . . . . . . . . . . . . . . . . Atelier Pictures
Fitzsimmons, April . . . . . . . . . . . . . . . . . . Ozma Productions
Flagella, Ann . . . . . . . . . . . . . . . . Sweetpea Entertainment
Flaisher, Lynn . . . . . . . . Paramount Pictures- Production Division
Flanagan, Bill . . . . . . . . . . . . . . . . . . . . . VH1 (Music First)
Flanagan, Dayna . . . . . . . . . . . . . . . . . Bochco Prods., Steven
Flanigan, Steven R. . . . . . . . . . . . . . . Producers Group Studios
Fleary, Kim . . . . . . . . . . . . . . . . . . . . . H. Beale Company
Fleder, Gary . . . . . . . . . . . . . . . . . . . . . . . . Mojo Films
Fleisher, Mark . . . . . . . . . . . Metro-Goldwyn-Mayer Pictures
Fleming, Bob . . . . . . . . . . . . . . . . . . . . . . . Studios USA
Fleming, David . . . . . . . . Baumgarten/Prophet Entertainment
Fleming, Erik . . . . . . . . . . . . . . . . . Newman Prods., Launa
Fletcher, Angus . . . . . . . . . . . . . . . . Henson Company, Jim
Fletcher, April . . . . . . . . . . . . . . . Albrecht/Read Management
Flinn, Denny . . . . . . . . . . . . . . . . . Sofronski Prods., Bernard
Flint, Mike . . . . . . . . . . Producer & Management Ent. Group
Floeter, Rebecca . . . . . . . . . . . . . . . . . . Meyer/Jaffe Prods.
Florent, Nancy . . . . . . . . . . . . . . . . . . . . . . . . TeleVest
Floridis, Tad . . . . . . . . . . . . . . . . Schindler Prods., Deborah
Florio, Maria . . . . . . . . . . . . . . . . . . . Earthworks Films, Inc.
Flower, Buck . . . . . . . . . . . . . . . . . . . Hansen, Edward D.
Flower, Elizabeth . . . . . . . . . . . . . . . . . . . . . . Enteraktion
Floyd, Chris . . . . . . . Walt Disney Pictures/Touchstone Pictures
Flynn, Beau . . . . . . . . . . . . . . . . . . Bandeira Entertainment
Flynn, Mary Jo . . . . . . . . . . . . . . . . . Lighthouse Productions
Foley, Ann . . . . . . . . . . . . . . . . . . . Showtime Networks Inc.
Follmer, Brad . . . . . . . . . . . . . . . . . . Kopelson Entertainment
Fondrevay, Ashley . . . . . . . . . . . . . . . Scott Free Productions
Fong, Ramsey . . . . . . . . . . . . . . . . . . . Killer Films, Inc.
Fontana, Tom . . . . . . . . . . . . . . . . . . . . Fatima Production
Fontana, Tom . . . . . . . . Levinson/Fontana Company, LLC, The
Forby, Leilani . . . . . . . . . . . . . . . . . Artisan Entertainment
Forby, Marc . . . . . . . . . . . . . Alliance/LeMonde Entertainment
Ford, John . . . . . . . . . . . . . . . . . . . . . . Discovery Networks
Ford, Rebecca . . . . . . . . . . . . Metro-Goldwyn-Mayer Pictures
Forester, Ann . . . . . . . . . . . . . . . . . . Madsen Productions, Bill
Forester, Kevin D. . . . . . . . . . . . . . . . Bubble Factory, The
Form, Andrew . . . . . . . . . . . . . . . . Mendillo/Form Productions
Forma, Dominique . . . . . . . . . . . . . . . . . . . . Camera Marc
Forman, Michael . . . . . . . . . . . . . . . . . . . . . . NBC Studios
Forman, Robin . . . . . . . . . Baltimore/Spring Creek Pictures, LLC
Forman, Robin . . . . . . . . . . . . . . . Spring Creek Productions
Forrest, Marisa . . . . . . . . . . . . . . . . . . Kingsgate Films, Inc.
Forrest, Tom . . . . . . . . . . . . . . . . . . . . . Outlaw Productions
Forsdick, Larry . . . . . . . . . . . . . . . Paramount Domestic TV
Forsyth-Peters, Christine . . . . . . . . . Evans Co., The Robert
Forte, Deborah . . . . . . . . . . . . . . . . Scholastic Entertainment
Forte, Kate . . . . . . . . . . . . . . . . . . . . . . Harpo Films Inc.
Fortuna, Tom . . . . . . . . . . . . . . . . . . Front Street Productions
Fortunato, Beldeen . . . . . . . . . . . . . . . Jumbo Pictures, Inc.
Fortunato, Joe . . . . . . . . . . . . . . . Shukovsky English Ent.
Foster, Alan . . . . . . . . . . . . . . . . . . . . . . . . . . . . PBS
Foster, David . . . . . . . . . . . . . . . . Foster Productions, David
Foster, Frank . . . . . . . . . . . . . . . Sony Pictures Imageworks
Foster, Gary S. . . . . . . . . . . . . . . Horseshoe Bay Productions
Foster, Gregory A. . . . . . . . . . . Metro-Goldwyn-Mayer Pictures
Foster, Jodie . . . . . . . . . . . . . . . . . . . . . . . . Egg Pictures
Foster, Jonathan . . . . . . . . . . . . . . . . . . Longbow Productions
Foster, Lucas . . . . . . . . . . . . . . . . . . . . . . . . Warp Films
Foster, Monica . . . . . . . . . . . . . . . . Showtime Networks Inc.
Foster, Steven Kent . . . . . . . . . . . . . . Scott Free Productions
Foster, Tim . . . . . . . . . . . . . . . Motion Pict. Corp. of America
Foster, Wendell . . . . . . . . . . . . . . . . . . . ABC Entertainment
Fournier, Teri . . . . . . . . . . . . . . . . Turner Entertainment Group
Fowkes, Richard . . . . . . . . Paramount Pictures- Production Division

# CROSS-REFERENCED NAMES

Gardner, Darci . . . . . . . . . . . . . . . . . . . . . . . . . . . Northern Lights Ent.
Gardner, Dede . . . . . . . . . Paramount Pictures- Production Division
Gargaro, Alicia . . . . . . . . . . . . . . . . . . . . . . . . . . . . . . Metafilmics Inc.
Garinger, Judith . . . . . . . . . . . . . . . . . . . . . . . . . . . Phoenix Pictures
Garland, Tony . . . . . . . . . . . Universal Television & Networks Group
Garner, Jean Horton . . . . . . . T.H.A. - Thomas Horton Associates Inc.
Garner, Todd . . . . . . . Walt Disney Pictures/Touchstone Pictures
Garofalo, Chip . . . . . . . . . . . . . . . . . . . . . . Bodega Bay Prods., Inc.
Garofano, Michele . . . . . . . . . . . . . . Carascope Productions Inc.
Garon, Susan . . . . . . . . . . . . . . . . . . Calm Down Productions, Inc.
Garrett, David . . . . . . . . . . . . . . . . . . . . . . . . Summit Entertainment
Garrett, Rebecca . . . . . . . . . . . . . . . . . Jacobson Company, The
Garrett, Sophie . . . . . . . . . . . . . . . . . . . . . . Tapestry Films Inc.
Garrison, Janet . . . . . . . . . . . . . . . . . . . . . . . Rastar Productions
Garrison, Larry . . . . . . . . . . . . . . . . Silvercreek Entertainment
Garrison, Susan . . . . . . . . . . . . . . . . . . . . Verdon-Cedric Prods.
Gartner, Alex . . . . . . . . . Twentieth Century Fox-Fox 2000 (LA)
Garzilli, Richard . . . . . . . . . . . . . . . . . . . . . . . . . . Canal+ (U.S.)
Gaspin, Jeffrey . . . . . . . . . . . . . . . . . . . . . . . . VH1 (Music First)
Gasti, Ani . . . . . . . . . . . . . . . . . . . . . . . . . HBO NYC Productions
Gatins, George . . . . . . . . . . . . . . . . . . Baum Productions, Carol
Gatmaitan, Clem . . . . . . . . . . . . . . . . . Imperial Entertainment
Gatsby, Jill . . . . . . . . . . . . . . . . . . . . . . . . . . Expect Miracles, Inc.
Gauger, Christy . . . . . . . . . EO Productions International, Inc.
Gaulding, Shannon . . . . . . . . . . . . . . . . . . . . David Ladd Films
Gault, Willie . . . . . . . . . . . . . . . . . La-Mont Communications Inc.
Gayne, Matthew . . . . . . . . . . . . . . . . . . . . . . . . Big Bang Films
Geary, Robert . . . . . . . . . . . . . . . . . . . . . . . . Columbia Pictures
Geddie, Bill . . . . . . . . . . . . . . . . . . . . . . . . . . . . . . ABC Daytime
Geffen, David . . . . . . . . . . . . . . . . . . . . . . . . . DreamWorks SKG
Gelardo, Monica . . . . . . . . . . . . . . . . . . . . . Paradox Prod., Inc.
Gelber, Stephen . . . . . . . . . . . . . . . . . . . PolyGram Television
Geletko, Judy . . . . . . . . . . . . . . . . . . . . . . . . . Avenue Pictures
Gelfand, Janna E. . . . . . . . . . . . . . . Gelfand Productions, Janna E.
Gelineau, Melissa . . . . . . . . . . . . . . Daniel Productions, Jay
Geller, Nancy . . . . . . . . . . . . . . . HBO Original Programming
Gellis, Andrew . . . . . . . . . . . . . . . . . . . . . . . . . Imax Corporation
Gemmill, R. Scott . . . . . . . . . . . . . . . . . . . . Belisarius Prods.
Gendece, Brian . . . . . . . . . . . . . . . . . . . . Gendece Film Co.
Genier, Joe . . . . . . . . . . . . . . . . . Capital Arts Entertainment
Geniesse, Jan . . . . . . . . . . . . . . . . . . Imagine Entertainment
Geoffray, Jeff . . . . . . . . . . . . . . . . . . . . . . Blue Rider Pictures
George, Amber . . . . . . . . . . . . Razors Edge Productions, Inc.
George, Audrey . . . . . . . . . . . . . . . . . . . . . Auerbach Company
George, Bob . . . . . . . . . . . . . . . . . . . . Fraser Prods., Woody
George, Catherine . . . . . . . Turner Network Television (TNT)
George, Jacqueline . . . . . . . Razors Edge Productions, Inc.
Georgiou, Katerina . . . . . . . . . . . . . . . . . . . . . LeFrak Prods.
Geraldino, Ana Maria . . . . . . . . . . . . . . . . . . Act III Productions
Gerber, Brian . . . . . . . . . . . . . . . . . . . . . . . . . . . . . Alphaville
Gerber, David . . . . . . . . . . . . . . . . . Pearson All American
Gerlich, Garret G. . . . . . . . . . Metro-Goldwyn-Mayer Pictures
Germain, Stephanie . . . . . . . . Germain Productions, Stephanie
Gero, Jennifer . . . . . . . . . . . . . . . . . . . . . . . . . JLT Productions
Gerren, Jamal . . . . . . . . . . . . . . . . . . . . . . . Gerren Productions
Gerren, Michele . . . . . . . . . . . . . . . . . . . . . Gerren Productions
Gerren, Rudy . . . . . . . . . . . . . . . . . . . . . . . Gerren Productions
Gerse, Steven W. . . . . . . Walt Disney Pictures/Touchstone Pictures
Gerstel, Louis . . . . . . . . . . . . . . . . . . . . . Pirromount Pictures
Gertner, Jordan . . . . . . . . . . . . . . . . . . Muse Productions, Inc.
Gertz, Paul . . . . . . . . . . . . . . . . . . . Kirschner Prods., David
Ghammaski, Barbara . . . . . . . . Hit & Run Productions, Inc.
Ghassemi, Solmaz . . . . . . . . . . . . . . . . . . Burton Prods., Al
Gherardi, Laura . . . . . . . . . . . . . . . . . . . . Punch Productions
Giambarberee, Lisa . . . . . . . . . . . . . . . . Bubble Factory, The
Giannetti, Andrea . . . . . . . . . . . . . . . . . . . Columbia Pictures
Giardina, Bonny . . . . . . . . . . . . . Sellers Productions, Dylan
Gibbar, Elizabeth . . . . . . . . . . . . . . . . . . Wolf Films, Fred
Gibbons, Leeza . . . . . . . . . . . . . Gibbons Enterprises, Leeza
Gibbs, Tessa . . . . . . . . . . . . . . . . . . . . . . . . . . Granada Film
Gibgot, Adam J. . . . . . . . . . . . . . . . . . . . Equus Entertainment
Gibgot, Jennifer . . . . . . . . . . . . . . . . . Tapestry Films Inc.
Gibson, Jon . . . . . . . . . . . . . . . . . . . . . . . . Columbia Pictures
Giddings, Al . . . . . . . . . . . . . . . . . . Giddings Images Inc., Al
Giffen, Christina . . . . . . . . . . . . . . . . . . . . . Plurabelle Films
Gilardi Jr., Jack . . . . . . . . . . . . . . Baldwin/Cohen Productions
Gilbert, Brian . . . . . . . . . . . . . . . . Winston Productions, Stan
Gilbert, Bruce . . . . . . . . . . . . . . . . . . . American Filmworks
Gilbert, Jennifer . . . . . . . . . . . . . . . . . Midnight Sun Pictures
Gilbert, Julia . . . . . . . . . . . . . . . . . . . . . . Fox Family Channel

Gilbert, Ron . . . . . . . . . . . . . . . . . . . Gilbert Associates, Ron
Gilby, David . . . . . . . . . . . . . . . . . . . . . . . . . . . . Boku Films
Gildehause, Lisa . . . . . . . . . . . . . . . . . Water Street Pictures
Gilder, Steven . . . . . . . . . . . . . . . . . . . . . . Dark Horse Ent.
Gilgan, Regina . . . . . . . . . . . . . . . . . . . . . . . . . . Jersey Shore
Gill, Mark . . . . . . . . . . . . . . . . . . . . . . . . . . . . Miramax Films
Gillen, Anne Marie . . . . . . . . . . . . Revelations Entertainment
Gillen, Maria . . . . . . . . . . . . . . . . . . Scholastic Entertainment
Gillibrand, Dane . . . . . . . . . . . . . . . . . . . Dogsmile Pictures
Gillmer, Bruce . . . . . . . . . . . . . . . . . . . . . VH1 (Music First)
Gilmore, Ann . . . . . . . . . . . . . . . . . . Showtime Networks Inc.
Gilmore, Ford Lytle . . . . . . . . . . . . . . Goodman-Rosen Prods.
Gilmore, Geoffrey . . . . . . . . . . . . . . . . . Sundance Institute
Gilpin, Peri . . . . . . . . . . . . . . . . . . . . . . . . . . . . . Bristol Cities
Gilstrap, Suzy . . . . . . . . . . . . . . . . . . Imagine Entertainment
Gimbel, Roger . . . . . . . . . Gimbel Productions, Inc., Roger
Gingold, Chuck . . . . . . . . . . . . . . . . . . . . Discovery Networks
Gingold, Erika . . . . . . . . . . . . . . . . . . . . . Renaissance Pictures
Ginnane, Antony I. . . . . . . . . . . . . . . IFM Film Associates, Inc.
Ginsberg, Scot . . . . . . . . . . . . . . . . . . . . Permut Presentations
Ginsburg, Carolyn . . . . . . . . . . . . . . . . . . . ABC Entertainment
Ginsburg, Dana . . . . . . . . . . . . . . . . . . . Icon Productions Inc.
Ginsburg, David R. . . . . . . . . . . . . . . . . . . . . Alliance Pictures
Ginsburg, Marla . . . . . . . . . . . . . . . . . . . . . . . . . . . . Gaumont
Ginty, Robert . . . . . . . . . . . . . . . . . . . . . . . . . . . Ginty Films
Gioia, Dino . . . . . . . . . . . . . . . . . . . . . . . . . Spectacor Films
Gipson, Darrien Michele . . . . . . . . . . . . . . . . . Def Pictures
Gisondi, Stephanie . . . . . . . . . . . . . . . . Weed Road Pictures
Gitelson, Rick . . . . . . . . . . . . . . . . . . . . . . . . . . . Plotpoint Inc.
Githens, William E. . . . . . . . . . . . . . . . . . . . River One Films
Gitlin, Mimi Polk . . . . . . . . . . . . . . . . . . . . . Gitlin Productions
Gittelsohn, Amy S. . . . . . . . . . Columbia TriStar Television
Gittelsohn, Gary . . . . . . . . . . . . . . . . . . . . . . Marvel Studios
Gitter, Cynthia L. . . . . . . . . . . . . Hit & Run Productions, Inc.
Gittes, Harry . . . . . . . . . . . . . . . . . . . . . . . . . . . . . Gittes, Inc.
Given, Andrew . . . . . . . . . . . . . . . . . . . . . . Universal Pictures
Gladstein, Richard N. . . . . . . . . . . . . . . . . . FilmColony, Ltd.
Gladston, Andrew . . . . . . . . . . . . . . Seagal-Nasso Productions
Glaser, Jan . . . . . . . . . . . . . . Concorde/New Horizons Corp.
Glaser, Jeffrey . . . . . . . . . . Twentieth Century Fox Television
Glasgow, Ryan . . . . . . . . . . Associated Producers Group, Inc.
Glass, Marina . . . . . . . . . . . . . . . Village Roadshow Pictures
Glasser, Karen J. . . . . . . . . . . . . . . Icon Productions Inc.
Glasser, Shelly . . . . . . . . . . . . . . . Initial Entertainment Group
Glatter, Emily . . . . . . . . . . . . . . . . . . . . . . . New Line Cinema
Glatzer, Peter . . . . . . . . . . . . . . . . . . . . . Glatzer Productions
Glatzer, Susan . . . . . . . . . . . . . . . . . . . . . . . . . October Films
Glaze, Gail . . . . . . . . . . . . . . Chesler/Perlmutter Production
Glazer, Alan . . . . . . . . . . . . . . . . . . . . . . . Atlas Entertainment
Glazer, Jared . . . . . . . . . . . . . . . . . . . . . . . Mischel Co., The
Glazer, Ronald . . . . . . . . . Rive Gauche International TV
Gleason, Larry . . . . . . . . . . . . . . . . . . . . . Goldwyn Films Inc.
Gleason, Tom . . . . . . . . . . . . . . . . . Porchlight Entertainment
Glianna, Jennifer . . . . . . . . . . . . . . . . . . . . Brainstorm Media
Glickman, Jonathan . . . . . . . . . . . . . . . . . . Caravan Pictures
Glickman, Stuart . . . . . . . . . . . . . . . . Carsey-Werner Co., The
Glosser, Richard . . . . . . . . . . . Columbia TriStar Television
Glotzer, Liz . . . . . . . . . . . . . . . . Castle Rock Entertainment
Glover, Danny . . . . . . . . . . . . . . . . . . . . . . Carrie Productions
Glover, Jackie . . . . . . . . . . . . . . . HBO Original Programming
Glover, Nicholas . . . . . . . . . . . . . . . . . . . . . . Marvel Studios
Glucksman, Julie . . . . . . . . . . . . . . . . Imagine Entertainment
Glynn, Gavin . . . . . . . . . . . . . . . . . . . . . . Fox Broadcasting Co.
Goci, Jamison . . . . . . . . . . . . . . . . . Neo Motion Pictures, Inc.
Goddard, Gary . . . . . . . . . . . Landmark Entertainment Group
Goddard, Melissa . . . . . . . . . . . . . . . . . . Wind Dancer Films
Godfrey, Pamela . . . . . . . . . . . . . . . . . George Litto Pictures
Godfrey, Wyck . . . . . . . . . . . . . . . . . . Davis Entertainment Co.
Goebel, Larry . . . . . . . . . . . . . . . . . Image Organization, Inc.
Goemans, Edward . . . . . . . . . . . . . . . . . Rudin Prods., Scott
Goepel, Stephen . . . . . . . . . . . . . . . . . . . . . Loganworks Ltd.
Gogolak, Charlie . . . . . . . . . . . . . . . . Weintraub Prods., Jerry
Golchan, Frederic . . . . . . . . . . . . . . Golchan Prods., Frederic
Gold, Jeremy . . . . . . . . . . . . . . . . . . . . . Panamort Television
Gold, Nicole . . . . . . . . . . . . . . . . . Axelrod/Widdoes Productions
Gold, Ted . . . . . . . . . . . . . . . . Alliance Television Productions
Goldberg, Ada . . . . . . . . . . . Twentieth Century Fox Television
Goldberg, Amy . . . . . . . . . . . . . . . . . . Saban Entertainment
Goldberg, Dan . . . . . . . . . . . . . . . . . . . . Nash Entertainment
Goldberg, Dan M. . . . . . . . . . . . . . . . . . Northern Lights Ent.

# CROSS-REFERENCED NAMES

Goldberg, Dana . . . . . . . . . . . Baltimore/Spring Creek Pictures, LLC
Goldberg, Dana . . . . . . . . . . . . . . . . Spring Creek Productions
Goldberg, Gary David . . . . . . . . . . . . . . . . . . . UBU Productions
Goldberg, Leonard . . . . . . . . . . . . . . . . . . . . Mandy Films, Inc.
Goldberg, Mandy . . . . . . . . . . . . . . . Equinox Entertainment Ltd.
Goldberg, Paige . . . . . Walt Disney Pictures/Touchstone Pictures
Goldberg, Ralph . . . . . . . . . . . . . . . . . King World Productions
Goldberg, Rich . . . . . . . . . . . . . . . . . . . . . Magic Hour Pictures
Golde, Kenny . . . . . . . . . . . . . . . . . . . . . . . . . Greif Company
Golden, Julie . . . . . . . . . . . . . Lakeshore Entertainment Corp.
Golden, Ken . . . . . . . . . . . . . . . . . . . . Cinnamon Prods. Inc.
Golden, Kit . . . . . . . . . . . . . . . Manhattan Project Ltd., The
Golden, Nathan . . . . . . . . . . . . . . . Schlatter Prods., George
Golden, Peter . . . . . . . . . . . . . . . . . . . . . CBS Entertainment
Golden, Peter . . . . . . . . . . . . Golden & Associates Inc., Peter
Golden, Roger N. . . . . . . . . . . . . Bernsen Prods. Inc., Harry
Golden, Stan . . . . . . . . . . . . . . . . . . . . Saban Entertainment
Goldenberg, Jeff . . . . . . . . . . . . . . . . . . . . Brown Group, The
Goldenring, Jane . . . . . . . . . . . . . . . Goldenring Productions
Goldenson, Max . . . . . . . . . . . . . . . . . . . . . . . . MWG Prods.
Goldfine, Phillip . . . . . . . . . . . . . . . Seagal-Nasso Productions
Goldhammer, John . . . . . . . . . . . . . . . . . Di Bona Prods., Vin
Goldklang-Furie, Lori . . . . . . . . . . . . . . . . Columbia Pictures
Goldman, Alain . . . . . . . . . . . . . . . . . . . . Nomad Productions
Goldman, Gregg . . . . . . . . . Goldwyn Company, The Samuel
Goldman, Paul . . . . . . . . . . . . . . . . . . . Hearst Entertainment
Goldman, Scott . . . . . . . . . . . . . . . Adelson Productions, Orly
Goldman, Steven . . . . . . . . . . Paramount Television Group
Goldman, Wendy A. . . . . . . . . . . . . . . . Knight Company, The
Goldmann, Bernie . . . . . . . . . . . . Village Roadshow Pictures
Goldsman, Akiva . . . . . . . . . . . . . . . . . Weed Road Pictures
Goldsmith, David . . . . . . . . . . . . Goldsmith Company, The
Goldsmith, Melissa . . . . . . . . . . . . . . . . Katie Face Prods.
Goldsmith, Russell . . . . . Goldsmith Entertainment Company
Goldstein, Charlie . . . . . . . . . Twentieth Century Fox Television
Goldstein, Gary W. . . . . . . . . . . . . . . . . . Goldstein Co., The
Goldstein, Harel . . . . . . . . . . . . . . . . Goldbar Entertainment
Goldstein, Jamie . . . . . . . . . . . . . . . . Gold'n Hen Productions
Goldstein, Jerry . . . . . . . . Producer & Management Ent. Group
Goldstein, Joel . . . . . . . . . . . . . . . Gold'n Hen Productions
Goldstein, Judy . . . . . . . . . . . . . . . . . Appledown Films, Inc.
Goldstein, Julie . . . . . . . . . . . . . . . . . . . . . Miramax Films
Goldstein, Karen . . . . . . . . . . . . . . . . . . Big Town Productions
Goldstein, Len . . . . . . Warner Bros. Television Productions
Goldstein, Michael . . . . . . . . . . . . . . . . Evolve Entertainment
Goldstein, Wendi . . . . . . . . . . . . . . . . . CBS Entertainment
Goldstone, John . . . . . . . . . . . . . . . . . Canton Company, The
Goldwyn Jr., Samuel . . . . . . . . . Goldwyn Company, The Samuel
Goldwyn, Danny . . . . . . . . . . . . . . . . . . Playtime Productions
Goldwyn, John . . . . . . . . Paramount Pictures- Motion Picture Group
Golenberg, Jeff . . . . . . . . . . . . . . . . . . . 3 Arts Entertainment
Golightly, Norm . . . . . . . . . . . . . . . . . . . . . . Saturn Films
Golin, Steve . . . . . . . . . . . . . . . . . . . . . . Propaganda Films
Golod, Jerry . . . . . . . . . . . . . . . . . . Jaygee Productions Inc.
Golov, Andrew . . . . . . . . . . . . . . . . . . . Spelling Films Inc.
Gomez, Greg . . . . . . . . . . . . . . . . . . . Esparza-Katz Prods.
Gomez, Suzette . . . . . . . . . . . . . . . . . . . Bryan Films, James
Gonda, Kelly . . . . . . . . . . . . . . . Lexington Road Productions
Gonda, Lou . . . . . . . . . . . . . . . Lexington Road Productions
Gong, Sandy . . . . . . . . . . . . . . . . . . Fox Broadcasting Co.
Gonsalves, Angelique . . . . . . . . . . . . . . . Universal Pictures
Gonsalves, Lee . . . . . . . . . . . . . . . . . . Twentieth Television
Gonshor, Dana . . . . . . . . . Wald Entertainment Inc., Jeff
Gonzalez, Lisa . . . . . . . . . . . . . . . . Victory Entertainment, Inc.
Good, Christine . . . . . . . . . . . . . Bell and Associates, Dave
Goode, Kelly . . . . . . . . . . . . . . . . . . Lifetime Television (LA)
Gooding, Lisa . . . . . . . . . . . . . . . . Maple Palm Productions
Goodloe, Mills . . . . . . . . . . . . Donner/Shuler-Donner Prods.
Goodman, Adam . . . . . . . . . . . . . . . . . . . DreamWorks SKG
Goodman, Andrew . . . . . . . . . . Chesler/Perlmutter Production
Goodman, David . . . . . . . . . . . . . Castle Rock Entertainment
Goodman, David A. . . . . . . . . . . . . . . . . Copp And Goodman
Goodman, Gary . . . . . . . . . . . . . . . . . . Goodman-Rosen Prods.
Goodman, Gary S. . . . . . . . . . . . Interscope Communications Inc.
Goodman, Harlan . . . . . . Paramount Pictures- Production Division
Goodman, Ilyssa . . . . . . . . Bonneville Worldwide Entertainment
Goodman, James . . . . . . . . . . . . . . . . . Viacom Productions
Goodman, Jonas . . . . . . . . . . . . . . . . Front Street Productions
Goodman, Leah . . . . . . . . . . . . . . . . . Polson Company, The
Goodman-Robbins, Cathy . . . . . . . . . . Ministry of Film Inc., The

Goodson, Katie . . . . . . . . . . . . . . . . . . . . . . Dragon Pictures
Goodson, Liat . . . . . . . . . . . . . Sachs Productions, Gabe
Goodwin, Amanda . . . . . . . . . Atmosphere Entertainment Inc.
Gorak, Michael . . . . . . . . . . . . . . . . . . . . . Prufrock Pictures
Gorber, Lorne . . . . . . . . . . . . . . . . . . Stevens & Associates
Gordon, Abraham . . . . . . . . . . . . Capital Arts Entertainment
Gordon, Barry . . . . . . . . United Paramount Network (UPN)
Gordon, Bradley . . . . . . . . . . . Greenwald Prods., Robert
Gordon, Charles . . . . . . . . . . . . . . . . . . Daybreak Prods.
Gordon, Dan . . . . . . . . . . . . . . . . . . . Gordon Prods., Dan
Gordon, Jonathan . . . . . . . . . . . . . . . . . . . Miramax Films
Gordon, Mark . . . . . . . . . . . . . . . . . . . . Mutual Film Co.
Gordon, Mason . . . . . . . . . . . Tollin/Robbins Productions
Gordon, Richard . . . . . . . . . . . . . . . . . . Gendece Film Co.
Gordon, Shep . . . . . . . . . . . . . . . . . . . . . . . . Alive Films
Gordon, Steven . . . . . . . . . . . . . . . . . . Viacom Productions
Gordon, Stuart . . . . . . . . . . . . . . . . . . Red Hen Productions
Gorenc, Nick . . . . . . . . . . . . . . . . . . . . . . . . Cinetel Films
Gorfain, Louis . . . . . . . . . . . . New Screen Concepts, Inc.
Gorius, Leola . . . . . . . . . . . . . . . . . . . . CBS Productions
Gorlato, Diego . . . . . . . . . . . . . Spin Cycle Entertainment
Gorman, Sean . . . . . . . . . Harvey Entertainment Company
Gormley, Peggy . . . . . . . . . . . . . . . . . . . Goatsingers, The
Gorn, Ada . . . . . . . . . . . . . . . . . . . . . . . . Peak Productions
Gorson, Arthur H. . . . . . . . . . . . . . . . . . . . . Ventana Films
Gosling, Simon . . . . . . . . . . . . Recorded Picture Company
Gosse, Bob . . . . . . . . . . . . . . . . Shooting Gallery Inc., The
Gossett Jr., Louis . . . . . . . . . . . . . . . . . . Logo Entertainment
Gossett, Tracy . . . . . . . . . . . . . . . . . Messina Captor Films
Gottesman, Gerald . . . . . . . . . . . . . . . . . . Blue Rider Pictures
Gottlieb, David N. . . . . . . . . . . . . . Never A Dull Moment Prods.
Gottlieb, Jerry . . . . . . . . . . Quincy Jones*David Salzman Entertainment
Gottlieb, Jody . . . . . . . . . . . . . Turner Original Productions
Gottlieb, Lisa Hallas . . . . . . . . Never A Dull Moment Prods.
Gottlieb, Meyer . . . . . . . . . . Goldwyn Company, The Samuel
Gottsegen, Lee . . . . . . . . . . . . . . . . . . Punch Productions
Gough, Rick . . . . . . . . . . . . . . . Arbus Prods., Inc., Loreen
Gould, Lucinda . . . . . . . . . . . . . . . . . . . . . . . . . Jaffilms
Govreau, Linda . . . . . . . . . . . . . . Henson Company, Jim
Grabelsky, Alan . . . . . . . . . . . . . . . . HBO NYC Productions
Graboff, Marc J. . . . . . . . . . . . . . . . . . . CBS Entertainment
Grace, Michael L. . . . . . . . . . . . . . . . . MakeMagic Productions
Gracia, Margaret . . . . . . . . . . . . . . Haines Company, Randa
Graden, Brian . . . . . . . . . . . . . . . . . . . . . . MTV Networks
Graf, Beverly . . . . . . . . . . . . . . . . . . . . . . Abilene Pictures
Graf, Patricia . . . . . . . . . . . . . . . . . . . . . . Abilene Pictures
Gragaro, Pascal . . . . . . . . . . . . Tudor Entertainment, Inc.
Graham, Ellen . . . . . . . . . . . . . . . Diana Kerew Productions
Graham, Janet . . . . . . . . . . . . . . . . . . . . . . . HBO Pictures
Grais, Michael . . . . . . . . . . . . . . . . . . . Victor & Grais Prods.
Grammer, Kelsey . . . . . . . . . . . . . . . . Grammnet Productions
Granat, Cary . . . . . . . . . . . . . . . . . . . . . . Dimension Films
Granger, Donald . . . . . . Paramount Pictures- Production Division
Granirer, Marc . . . . . . . . . . . . . . . . . Johnson Prods., Don
Grant, Bryan . . . . . . . . . . . . Trilogy Entertainment Group
Grant, Bud . . . . . . . . . . . . . . . . . . Grant Productions, Bud
Grant, David . . . . . . . . . . . . . . . . . Fox Television Studios
Grant, Gil . . . . . . . . . . . . . . . . . . . . . . . . . . Grant, Gil
Grant, Glenda . . . . . . . . . . . . . . . . . . Hearst Entertainment
Grant, Hugh . . . . . . . . . . . . . . . . . . . . . . . . Simian Films
Grant, Jeffrey S. . . . . . . . . . . . . . . . . . . . . . . . TeleVest
Grant, Lee . . . . . . . . . . . . . . Feury Entertainment, Joseph
Grant, Trudy . . . . . . . . . . . . . . . . . Sullivan Entertainment
Grass, Clancy . . . . . . . . . . Three Guys From Verona Inc.
Grass, Steve . . . . . . . . . . . . . . . . . . . . Night Flight Inc.
Grasso, Maria . . . . . . . . Warner Bros. Television Productions
Graves, Amy . . . . . . . . . . . . . . . . . . Upstart Entertainment
Gray, Beverly . . . . . . . . . Seggerman Productions, Henry
Gray, Dawn . . . . . . . . . . . . . . . . . . . . . . . . . . Filmlight
Gray, Gretchen G. . . . . . . . . . . . . . . . . . . Atelier Pictures
Gray, Lauren . . . . . . . . . . . . . . . . . . . . . Comedy Central
Gray, Marianne . . . . . . . . . . . . . . . . Jacobs/Mutrux Prods.
Gray, Paul T. . . . . . . . . . . . . . . . . . . . . . . Atelier Pictures
Gray, Stephan . . . . . . . . . . . . . . . . . . . . . Gray Fox Films
Gray, Steven . . . . . . . . . . . . . . . . . . . . . . . . . . . . PBS
Gray, Thomas K. . . . . . . . . . . . . . . . . Golden Harvest Films
Grazer, Brian . . . . . . . . . . . . . . . . . . Imagine Entertainment
Grazer, Brian . . . . . . . . . . . . . . . . . . . . Imagine Television
Greathouse, David . . . . . . . . . . Winston Productions, Stan
Green, Alan R. . . . . . . . . . . . . Entertainment Alliance, Inc., The

# CROSS-REFERENCED NAMES

Green, Heather . . . . . . . . . . . . . . . . . . . . . . . . . . UBU Productions
Green, Jill . . . . . . . . . . . . . . . . . . . . . . Ockrent Productions, Ltd.
Green, Jim . . . . . . . . . . . . . . . . . . . . . . . . Green/Epstein Prods.
Green, Joan . . . . . . . . . . Green Management & Productions, Joan
Green, Matt . . . . . . . . . . . . . . . . . . . . . Pamplin-Fisher Company
Green, Michael C. . . . . . . . . Bonneville Worldwide Entertainment
Green, Misty . . . . . . . . . . . . . . . . . . . . . . . . . . . Beacon Pictures
Green, Paul H. . . . . . . . . . . . . . . . . . . . . . . . . .Propaganda Films
Green, Peter . . . . . . . . . . . . . . . . . . . . . . . . . . . Disney Telefilms
Green, Robert . . . . . . . . . . . . . . . . . . . . . Blue Tulip Productions
Green, Robin . . . . . . . . . . . . . . . . . Castle Rock Entertainment
Green, Ron . . . . . . . . . . . . . . . . . . . . . . Sullivan Company, The
Green, Stanley H. . . . . . . . . . . . . . . . . . . . . Burrud Productions
Greenberg, Harvey . . . . . . . . . . . . . . . . . . . . . . . Cineville Inc.
Greenberg, Kathy . . . . . . . . . . . . . . . . . . . . Working Title Films
Greenberg, Marc . . . . . . . . . . . . . . . . . . . Magic Hour Pictures
Greenblatt, Robert . . . . . . . . Greenblatt Janollari Studio, The
Greenblatt, William . . . . . . . . Symphony Entertainment, LLC
Greenburg, Michael . . . . . . . . . . . . . . . . . Gekko Film Corp
Greene, Danielle . . . . . . . . United Paramount Network (UPN)
Greene, Vanessa . . . . . . . . . . . . . . . Greene Prods., Vanessa
Greene, W. Michael . . . . . . . . . . . . . . . Hampton Films, Inc.
Greenfield, Barry . . . . . . . . . . . . . . . . . . Freedman Prods., Jack
Greenfield, Debra . . . . . . . . Trilogy Entertainment Group
Greenhut, Robert . . . . . . . . . . . . . . . Foundry Film Partners
Greenman, Cybelle . . . . . . . . . . . . . . . Artisan Entertainment
Greenspan, Alan. . . . . . . . . . . . . . . . . . . . . . . . Dogstar Films
Greenstein, Scott . . . . . . . . . . . . . . . . . . . . . . October Films
Greenwald, Nana . . . . . . . . . . . . . . . Kopelson Entertainment
Greenwald, Robert . . . . . . . . Greenwald Prods., Robert
Greenwald, Seena . . . . . . . . . . . . . . . Lynch Entertainment
Gregg, Judie . . . . . . . . . . . . . . . . . Mayo/Gregg Entertainment
Gregg, Rodman . . . . . . . . . . . . . . Mount/Kramer Company, The
Gregory, Catrina . . . . . . . . . . . . . . . . Walz Productions, Ken
Gregory, Cheryl . . . . . . . . . . . . . . McKissick/Gregory Prods.
Gregory, Glenn . . . . . . . . . . . . . . . . . . . . . .Propaganda Films
Gregory, Morgan . . . . . . . . . . . . . . . . . . . . . . . . Saturn Films
Gregory, Nancy . . . . . . . . . . . . . . . . Goldsmith Company, The
Gregory, Tamara . . . . . . . . Johnson Entertainment, Magic
Greif, Leslie . . . . . . . . . . . . . . . . . . . . . . . . . . . Greif Company
Grey, Brad . . . . . . . . . . . . . . . . . . . . . . . . Brillstein-Grey Ent.
Grey, Lawrence . . . . . . . . . . . . . Motion Pict. Corp. of America
Grieder, Scott . . . . . . . . Warner Bros. Feature Animation
Grieff, Barry . . . . . . . . . . . . . . . . . . . . . Broadway Video (NY)
Grierson, Tim . . . . . . . . . . . . . . . . . . . . . . Maysville Pictures
Griffin, Darrell . . . . . . . . . . . . . . . . . . KiMina Entertainment
Griffin, Greg . . . . . . . . . . . . . . . . . . Leider Co., The Jerry
Griffin, Peggy . . . . . . . . . . . . . . . . . . Cates/Doty Productions
Griffith, Beverly . . . . . . . . . . . . . . . . . . . . . . . . Jersey Films
Griffith, Melanie . . . . . . . . . . . . Green Moon Productions
Grillo, Michael . . . . . . . . . . . . . . . . . . . . . DreamWorks SKG
Grillo, Nick . . . . . . . . . . . . . . . . . . . . . . Rehme Productions
Grimaldi, Larry . . . . . . . . . . Brayton/Carlucci Productions
Grimaldi, Matthew . . . . . . . . . . . . . . . . Nichol Moon Films
Grimaldi, Maurizio . . . . . . . . . . . . . . . . . P.E.A. Films, Inc.
Grisanti, Melanie . . . . . . . . . . . . . . . .Jumbo Pictures, Inc.
Grivetti, Bruce . . . . . . . . . . . . . . . . . HBO NYC Productions
Grodnik, Daniel L. . . . . . . . . . . . . . . . . . Itasca Pictures, Inc.
Grogg, Sam . . . . . . . . . . . . Symphony Entertainment, LLC
Gronner, Carol . . . . . . . Ransohoff Productions, Inc., Martin
Gros, Robert . . . . . . . . . . . . . . . . . . . . . . CBS Productions
Gross, Anna . . . . . . . . . . . . . . . . . . . Cecchi Gori Pictures
Gross, Bill . . . . . . . . . . . . . . . . . . . . . .Jumbo Pictures, Inc.
Gross, Dan . . . . . . . . . . . . . . . . . . . . . . . Dimension Films
Gross, Ethan . . . . . . . . . . . . . . . Underworld Entertainment
Gross, Kenneth H. . . . . . . . . . . . . . . Gross Management, Ken
Gross, Kimberly . . . . . . . . . . . . . . . . . . Bubble Factory, The
Gross, Lloyd . . . . . . . . . . . . . . . . . . . . . . . . Enteraktion, Inc.
Gross, Marcy . . . . . . . . . . . . . . . . . . . . Gross-Weston Prods.
Gross, Matthew . . . . . . . . . . . . . . . . Kopelson Entertainment
Gross, Susan O. . . . . . . . . . . Turner Network Television (TNT)
Grossbard, Beth . . . . . . . . . . Grossbard Productions, Beth
Grossbart, Jack . . . . . . . . . . Grossbart, Barnett Productions
Grossman, Brad . . . . . . . . . . . . . . . . . Redeemable Features
Grossman, David . . . . . . . . Paramount Network Television
Grossman, Gary H. . . . . . . . . Weller/Grossman Productions
Grossman, Iris . . . . . . . . Turner Network Television (TNT)
Grossman, Sarahbeth . . . . . . . . . . . . . . . Ozma Productions
Grosso, Sonny . . . . . . . . Grosso-Jacobson Productions, Inc.
Grosso, Sonny . . . . . . . . .Producers Ent. Group, Ltd., The

Grotenstein, Jonathan . . . . . . . . . Spin Cycle Entertainment
Groth, Trevor . . . . . . . . . . . . . . . . . . . . Sundance Institute
Grove, Victoria . . . . . . . . . . . . . . . . . JCS Entertainment Inc.
Groves, Sue . . . . . . . . . . Sefton Productions International
Grunfeld, Jacqui . . . . . . . . . . . . . . . . . . . . . Fox Kids Network
Grushcow, Brian . . . . . . . . Motion Pict. Corp. of America
Grushow, Sandy . . . . . . . . Twentieth Century Fox Television
Gruskoff, Michael . . . . . . . . . . . . . . . . . Parallel Pictures
Guarino, Doug . . . . . . . . . . . . Braun Productions, David
Guber, Peter . . . . . . . . . . . . . . . . . . . . . Mandalay Pictures
Guber, Peter . . . . . . . . . . . . . . . . . . Mandalay Television
Guckenberger, Nina . . . . . . . . . . . Wigutow Prods., Dan
Guellati, Lamia . . . . . . . . . . . . . . . . . . Indican Productions
Guerra, Jim . . . . . . . . . . . . . . . . . . . . . . . . . . . . . . . . . . PBS
Guerrero, Dan . . . . . . . . . . . . .Guerrero & Company, Dan
Guggenheim, Barbara . . . . . . . . Double Whammy Productions
Gugliotta, Greg . . . . . . . . . . . . . . . . . . . Gaslight Pictures
Guido, Tony . . . . . . . . . . . . . . Hallmark Entertainment (NY)
Guidone, Kimberley . . . . . . . . . . . . . . . . . . . . . . . Jaffilms
Guidry, Cindy . . . . . . . . . . . . . . . . . . . . New Line Cinema
Guillaume, Donna Brown . . . Two Oceans Entertainment Group
Guillaume, Robert . . . . . . . . . . . . . . . Longridge Enterprises
Guillod, David . . . . . . . . . . . . . . . . Handprint Entertainment
Guinzburg, Kate . . . . . . . . . . . . . . . . Via Rosa Productions
Gummersall, Joshua . . . . . . . . . . . . . . Bedford Falls Co., The
Gumpert, Andrew . . . . . . . . Interscope Communications Inc.
Gumpert, Jon . . . . . . . . . . . . . . . . . . . . . . Universal Pictures
Gunloy, Tami . . . . . . . . . . . . . . Alexander/Enright & Assocs.
Gunn, Andrew . . . . . . . . . . . . Mestres Productions, Ricardo
Gunn, Julia . . . . . . . . . . . Warner Bros. Television Productions
Gunn, Patrick . . . . . . . . . . . . . . . . . . . . . . . . October Films
Gunning, Barbara . . . . . . . . . . . . . . . . . Gunning Co., The
Gunter, T.C. . . . . . . . . . . . . . . . . . . . . . . . . H2 Productions
Gunther, Dan . . . . . . . . . . . . . . . . Dark Matter Productions
Gunther, Lee . . . . . . . . . . . . Ideal Movie Shoppe, LLC, The
Guralnick, Robert . . . . . . . . . . . . . . Warner Bros. Pictures
Gurtiza, Jane. . . . . . . . . . . . . . . . . . . . Korova Entertainment
Gurvitz, Marc . . . . . . . . . . . . . . . . . . . . Brillstein-Grey Ent.
Gusewelle, Jennie . . . . . . . . . . . . . . . Wigutow Prods., Dan
Gusick, Ned . . . . . . . . . . . . . . . . . . . . Jacobs/Mutrux Prods.
Guthrie, Jeff . . . . . . . . . . . . . . . . . . . . . . . . . . . HBO Pictures
Guthrie, Robin . . . . . . . . . . . . . . . . Evans Co., The Robert
Gutierrez, Diego . . . . . . . . . . . . . . . . Mutant Enemy, Inc.
Gutman, Ilana . . . . . . . . . . . . . . . . Fields Productions, Adam
Guttierez, Ana . . . . . . . . Moress-Nanas-Hart Entertainment
Guttry, Thomas . . . . . . . . . . . . . . Popular Arts Ent., Inc.
Guy, Jasmine . . . . . . . . . . . . . . . . Black & White Productions
Guy, Patrick . . . . . . . . . . . . . . . . . . Lifetime Television (NY)
Guzman, Julie . . . . . . . . . . . . . . . . . . . Shelter Entertainment
Gvillemet, Nicole . . . . . . . . . . . . . . . . . . Sundance Institute
Gwartz, Jennifer . . . . . . . . . . . . . . . . . . . . . Silver Pictures
Gwen, Jill . . . . . . . . Twentieth Century Fox-Searchlight Picts.
Haag, Genevieve . . . . . . . . . . . . . . . . American Zoetrope
Haase, Kathleen . . . . . . . . Cinequanon Pictures Intl. Inc.
Habash, Michelle . . . . . . . . . . . Grossbard Productions, Beth
Haber, Dawn . . . . . . . . . . . . . . . . . Kuzui Enterprises, Inc.
Haber, Larry . . . . . . . . . . . . . . . . . Movicorp Holdings, Inc.
Hack, Bruce L. . . . . . . . . . . . . . . . . . . . . . Universal Studios
Hacken, Carla . . . . . . . . Twentieth Century Fox-Fox 2000 (LA)
Hackett, Elizabeth . . . . . . . . . . . . . . Licht/Mueller Film Corp.
Hackett, Michael . . . . . . . . . . Solomon/Hackett Productions
Hadar, Ronnie . . . . . . . . Hamilton Entertainment, Inc., Dean
Haffner, Craig . . . . . . . . Greystone Communications Group, Inc.
Haffner, Craig . . . . . . . . . . . . . . . . . . . . . . Greystone Films
Haft, Steven . . . . . . . . . . . . . . . . . . . . . . . Haft Entertainment
Hagan, Lisa . . . . . . . . . . . . . . . . . . . . . . . . . . . Paraview Inc.
Hagar, David W. . . . . . . . . Greenwood Avenue Entertainment
Hage, Melinda . . . . . . . . Warner Bros. Television Productions
Hageman, Kevin . . . . . . . . . . . . . . . . . . . . Dark Horse Ent.
Haggar, Paul . . . . . . . . Paramount Pictures- Production Division
Haggerty, Katharine . . . . . . . . . . . . . . . Driskill Entertainment
Hagopian, Chandra Joy . . . . . . . . . Finerman Prods., Wendy
Hagopian, Kip . . . . . . . . . . . . . . . . . . . . Segue Prods., Inc.
Hah, Justine . . . . . . . . . . . . . . . . . . . . . . . . . Amen Ra Films
Hahn, Helene . . . . . . . . . . . . . . . . . . . . . DreamWorks SKG
Hahn, Richard . . . . . . . . . . . . . . . East West Film Partners
Hahn, Shirley Honickman . . . . . . . . East West Film Partners
Haimes, Marc . . . . . . . . . . . . . . . . . . . . . DreamWorks SKG
Haimovitz, Jules . . . . . . . . . . . . . . King World Productions
Haines, Randa . . . . . . . . . . . . . . . Haines Company, Randa

# CROSS-REFERENCED NAMES

Hajdu, Steve . . . . . . . . . . . . . . . . . . Playboy Entertainment Group Inc.
Haldeman, E. Barry . . . . . . . Paramount Pictures- Production Division
Hale, Corky . . . . . . . . . . . . . . . . . . . . . . . . . Hale Productions, Corky
Hale, David R. . . . . . . . . . . . . . . . . . . . . . . . . 44 Blue Productions, Inc.
Halfon, Lianne . . . . . . . . . . . . . . . . . . . . . . . . . . . . . . . . . . Mr. Mudd
Halfon, Sheri . . . . . . . . . . . . . . . . . . . . . . . . . . . . . . . Avenue Pictures
Hall, Emilie . . . . . . . . . . . . . . . . . Sachnoff-Lipman Entertainment
Hall, Marilyn . . . . . . . . . . . . . . . . . . . . . . . . Hallet Street Prods.
Hall, Robyn . . . . . . . . . . . . . . . . . . . Action America Entertainment
Hall, Stu . . . . . . . . . . . . . . . . . . . . . . . . . . . . Video Dimensions Inc.
Hall, Wil. . . . . . . . . . . . . . . . . . . . . . Sefton Productions International
Halle, Bari . . . . . . . . . . . . . . . . . . . . . . . . . Studios USA Television
Halleen, Tom . . . . . . . . . . . . . . . . . . . . . . . . . . Fox Family Channel
Hallock, Jason . . . . . . . . . . . . . . . . . . . . . . . . . . . . Haft Entertainment
Halmi Jr., Robert . . . . . . . . . . . . . . . . . Hallmark Entertainment (NY)
Halmi Sr., Robert . . . . . . . . . . . . . . . . . Hallmark Entertainment (NY)
Halperin, Dan . . . . . . . . . . . . . . . . . . . . Epiphany Productions, Inc.
Halperin, Julia . . . . . . . . . . . . . . . . . . . . . . . . . RKO Pictures, Inc.
Halpern, Michael . . . . . . . . . . . . . . . . . . . . . . . . . . . . HBO Pictures
Halpern, Noreen . . . . . . . . . . . . . . . Alliance Television Productions
Halpern, Steven . . . . . . . . . . . . . . . . . . . Star Land Entertainment Inc.
Halsey Solomon, Christian . . . . . . . . . . Pressman Film Corp., Edward R.
Halsted, Dan . . . . . . . . . . . . . . . . . . . . . Illusion Entertainment Group
Hamada, Walter . . . . . . . . . . . . . . . . . . . . . . . . . . Columbia Pictures
Hamilton, Dean . . . . . . . . . . . . Hamilton Entertainment, Inc., Dean
Hamilton, Douglas . . . . . . . . . . . . . . . . . . . . . . . . . . . USA Networks
Hamilton, Jon . . . . . . . . . . . . . . . . . . . . . Erratic Entertainment, Inc.
Hamilton, Marcy Levitas . . . . . . . . . . . . . . . . . TriCoast Entertainment
Hamilton, Rod . . . . . . . . . . . . . . . . . . . . . . . . . . . . Cafe Productions
Hamilton, Strath . . . . . . . . . . . . . . . . . . . . . . TriCoast Entertainment
Hamilton, Terry H. . . . . . . . . . . . . . . . . . . . . . . . . . . . . . . Startoons
Hamm, Bill . . . . . . . . . . . . . . . . . . . . . . . . . Studios USA Television
Hamm, Michael . . . . . . . . . . . . . . . . . . . . . . . . . . Onelight Pictures
Hammer, Bonnie . . . . . . . . . . . . . . . . . . . . . . . . . . . . USA Networks
Hammer, Ros . . . . . . . . . . . . . . . . . . . . . . . . . Trivision Pictures Inc.
Hammond, Barbara . . . . . . . . . . . . . . . . . . Lower East Side Films
Hammond, Philip K. . . . . . . . . . . . . . . . . . . . . . . . . Alpine Pictures
Hamori, Andras . . . . . . . . . . . . . . . . . . . . . . . . . . Alliance Pictures
Hampton, Henry . . . . . . . . . . . . . . . . . . . . . . Hampton Films, Inc.
Hamsher, Jane . . . . . . . . . . . . . . . . . . . . . . . . . . . . . JD Productions
Hancock, Larry . . . . . . . . . . . . . . . . . . . . . . . . . . . . . NBC Studios
Hand, Kai . . . . . . . . . . . . . . . . . . Associated Producers Group, Inc.
Hand, Kai . . . . . . . . . . . . . . . . . . . . . . . . . Theatrex Company, The
Handel, Haya . . . . . . . . . . . . . . . . . . . . . . . . Fox Broadcasting Co.
Handley, Annette . . . . . . . . . . . . . . . . . . . . . Big Shoes Productions
Hanel, Michael . . . . . . . . . . . . . . Twentieth Century Fox Television
Hanks, Poppy . . . . . . . . . . . . . . . . . . . . . . . . . State Street Pictures
Hanley, Chris . . . . . . . . . . . . . . . . . . . . . . . . Muse Productions, Inc.
Hanley, Roberta . . . . . . . . . . . . . . . . . . . . . . Muse Productions, Inc.
Hannaway, Dorian . . . . . . . . . . . . . . . . . . . . . . . CBS Entertainment
Hannell, Geoff . . . . . . . . . . . . . . . . . . . . . . . . . . . . . NewStar Media
Hannon, Matt . . . . . . . . . . . . . . . . . . . . . . . . Banner Entertainment
Hanrahan, Martha . . . . . . . . . . . . . . . . . . . . . . . . . . . . NBC Studios
Hanratty, Dick . . . . . . . . . . . . . . . . . . . . . . . . . . . . . . . . . . . . . . PBS
Hansen, Ed . . . . . . . . . . . . . . . . . . . . . . . . . Hansen, Edward D.
Hansen, Laurie . . . . . . . . . . . . . . . . . . . . . . . . . . . Miracle Pictures
Hansen, Lisa . . . . . . . . . . . . . . . . . . . . . . . . . . . . . . Cinetel Films
Harari, Sasha . . . . . . . . . . . . . . . . . . . . . . . . . . . . Maia Productions
Harbonville, Christopher . . . . . . . . . . . . . . . Excelsior Pictures Corp.
Hardaker, Merelyn . . . . . . . . . . . . . . . . . . . . . . . . . . . . . . . . . . . Stun
Harding, Chris . . . . . . . . . . Bonneville Worldwide Entertainment
Harding, Dave . . . . . . . . . . . . . . . . . . . . . . . . . . . . Harding, Dave
Hare, Jennifer . . . . . . . . . . . . . . . . . . Trilogy Entertainment Group
Hargett, Hester . . . . . . . . . . . . . . . . . . . . Raffaella Productions, Inc.
Hargrove, Dean . . . . . . . . . . . . . . . . . . . . . Hargrove Prods., Dean
Harkcom, Laura . . . . . . . . . . . . . Warner Bros. Feature Animation
Harkin, Debra . . . . . . . . . . . . . . . . . . . . Fox Television Studios
Harkin, Shelley . . . . . . . . . . . . . . . . . . . . . . . . . . . Gullane Pictures
Harlan, Kristine . . . . . . . . . . . . . . . . . . . . . . . . . . MacDonald Prods
Harland, Rob . . . . . . . . . . . . . . . . . . . . . . . Studios USA Television
Harlin, Renny . . . . . . . . . . . . . . . . . . . . . . . . Midnight Sun Pictures
Harlow, Mike . . . . . . . . . . . . . . . . . . . . . . . . . . . . . . . Original Film
Harmon, Tom . . . . . . . . . . . . . . . . . . . . . . Macht Ent. Group, Inc.
Harms, Kristin . . . . . . . . . . . . . . . . . . . . . . . Wells Productions, John
Haro, Danny . . . . . . . . . . . . . . . . . . . . . . . Olmos Productions Inc.
Harper, Hadley . . . . . . . . . . . . . . . . . . . . Too Nuts Productions, Ltd.
Harper, Otis . . . . . . . . . . . . . . . . . . . . . . . . . . . Logo Entertainment
Harrah, Verna . . . . . . . . . . . . . . . . . . . . . . Middle Fork Productions
Harrington, Eric . . . . . . . . . . . . . . . . Suppa Prods., Inc., Ronald
Harris, Bill . . . . . . . . . . . . . . . . . . . . . . A & E Television Networks

Harris, Daniel . . . . . . . . . . . . . . . . . Mount Olympus Entertainment
Harris, Gail . . . . . . . . . . . . . . . . . . . . . . IndieGal Productions, LLC
Harris, Geoffrey . . . . . . . . . . . . . . . . . . . . . . . . . . NBC Entertainment
Harris, Greg . . . . . . . . . . . . . . . . . . . . . . . . . . . . CBS Entertainment
Harris, J. Todd . . . . . . . . . . . . . . . . . . . . . . . . Daly-Harris Productions
Harris, Jacqueline . . . . . . . . . . . . . . . . . . Looking Glass Productions
Harris, Jonathan . . . . . . . . . . . . . . . Turner Network Television (TNT)
Harris, Kirk . . . . . . . . . . . . . . . . . . . . . . . . . . . . . . . . . Film Kitchen
Harris, Lynn . . . . . . . . . . . . . . . . . . . . . . . . . . . . . . New Line Cinema
Harris, Mark R. . . . . . . . . . . . . . . . . . . . . Regent Entertainment, Inc.
Harris, Robert . . . . . . . . . . . . . . . . . . . . . . . . . . . Harris & Company
Harris, Russ . . . . . . . . . . . . . . . . . . . Perennial Pictures Film Corp.
Harris, Stephanie . . . . . . . . . . . . . . . . . . . . . . . . . Harpo Films Inc.
Harris, Stephanie J. . . . . . . . Walt Disney Pictures/Touchstone Pictures
Harris, Susan . . . . . . . . . . . . . . . . . Witt-Thomas-Harris Productions
Harris, Timothy . . . . . . . . . . . . . . . . . . . . . Weingrod/Harris Prods.
Harris, Todd . . . . . . . . . . . . . . . . . . . . . . . . . . . . . . Davis Classics
Harris, Trace . . . . . . . . . . . . . Universal Television & Networks Group
Harris, William . . . . . . . . . . . . . . . . . . . . . . Britt Allcroft Co., The
Harrison, Hal . . . . . . . . . . . . . . . . . Paramount Network Television
Harrison, Joan . . . . . . . . . . . . . . . . . . . . . . . . . . CBS Entertainment
Harrison, Lisa . . . . . . . . . . Twentieth Century Fox-Fox 2000 (LA)
Harron, Roberta . . . . . . . . . . . . . . . . . . Chesler/Perlmutter Production
Hart, Garry . . . . . . . . . . . . . . . . . . Paramount Network Television
Hart, Geno . . . . . . . . . . . . . . . . . . . . . . . . . . . . . . Hart Entertainment
Hart, James V. . . . . . . . . . . . . . . . Common Ground Entertainment
Hart, John . . . . . . . . . . . . . . . . . . . . . Hart Sharp Entertainment, Inc.
Hart, Monique . . . . . . . . . . . . . . . . . . . . . . . . . . CBS Entertainment
Hart, Scott . . . . . . . . . . . . . Moress-Nanas-Hart Entertainment
Hart, Una . . . . . . . . . . . . . . . . . . . . . . . Driskill Entertainment
Harter, Holly . . . . . . . . . . . . . . . . . . . . . . . Weisberg Prods., Roni
Hartford, Glen . . . . . . . . . . . . . R.A.M.M. Entertainment, Inc
Hartford, Scott . . . . . . . . . . . . . . . . . . . . . . . . . . Foxstar Productions
Hartley, Hal . . . . . . . . . . . . . . . . . . . . . . . . . . True Fiction Pictures
Hartley, Mariette . . . . . . . . . . . . . . . . . . . . . . . . . . Maraday Prods.
Hartley, Ted . . . . . . . . . . . . . . . . . . . . . . . . . . . RKO Pictures, Inc.
Hartounian, Michael . . . . . . . . . Metro-Goldwyn-Mayer/Worldwide TV
Hartwick, Joe . . . . . . . . . . . . . . . . . . . Twentieth Century Fox
Harvey, Rupert . . . . . . . . . . . . . . . . . . . . . . . . . . . . . . . . Sho Films
Haslett, Mark . . . . . . . . . . . . . . . . . . . . Cunningham Prods. Inc.
Hassitt, Nicholas . . . . . . . . . . . . . . . . . . . Hassitt Films, Nicholas
Hastings Edell, Elaine . . . . . . . . . . . . . Burlage/Edell Productions, Inc.
Haswell, Kim . . . . . . . . . . . . . . . . . . . Columbia TriStar Television
Hatlestad, Dianne . . . . . . . . . . . . . . . . . . . . . Yorktown Prods. Inc.
Haugland, David . . . . . . . . . . . . . . . . Haugland Productions, David
Haus, Michael . . . . . . . . . . . . . . . . . . . . . . . . . Stevens & Associates
Hauser, Tracy . . . . . . . . . . . . . . . . . . . . . Sony Pictures Imageworks
Hausmann, Greg . . . . . . . . . . . . . . . . . . . . . . . . Elkins Entertainment
Hauson, Audrey . . . . . . . . . . . . . . . . . . . . . Visionary Entertainment
Havens, Geno . . . . . . . . . . . . . . . . . . . . . . . . . . . . . Phoenician Films
Hawkins, Diana . . . . . . . . . Columbia TriStar Motion Picture Group
Hawkins, Linda . . . . . . . . . . . . . . . . . . . Newmarket Capital Group
Hawley, Kristin . . . . . . . . . . . . . . . . . . . . . Nelvana Entertainment
Hawley, Richard . . . . . . . . . . . . . . . . . . . . . . . . . . . Merchant-Ivory
Hawn, Goldie . . . . . . . . . . . . . . . . . . . . Cherry Alley Productions
Hay, Sandra . . . . . . . . . . . . . . . . . . . . . . . . . . . . . . Mountain Drive
Hay, Tina . . . . . . . . . . . . . . . . . . . . . . . . . . . Rudin Prods., Scott
Hayden, Laurette . . . . . . . . . . . . . . . . . . . . . Lifetime Television (LA)
Hayden-Jaffe, Karen . . . . . . . . . . . . . . . . . Looking Glass Productions
Hayes, Amy . . . . . . . . . . . . . . . . . . . . Trilogy Entertainment Group
Hayes, Blair . . . . . . . . . . . . . . . . . . . . . . . . . . . . Sticks And Stones
Hayes, Chip . . . . . . . . . . . . . . . . . . . . . . . . . . . . . . Melrose Prods.
Hayes, James Terry . . . . . . . . . . . . . . . . . . . Interland Entertainment
Hayes, Jeffrey . . . . . . . . . . . . . . . . . . . . Village Roadshow Pictures
Hayes, John . . . . . . . . . . . . . . . . . . . . . . . . . . . Apatow Productions
Hayes, Staci . . . . . . . . . . . . . . . . . . . . Samoset Inc./Sacret Inc.
Hayes, Steve . . . . . . . . . . . . . . . . . . . Keller Entertainment Group
Haynes, Regina . . . . . . . . . . . . . . . . . . . . You Go Boy Productions
Hayward, Bob . . . . . . . . . . . . . . . . . . . . . . . . . Summit Entertainment
Hayward, Debra . . . . . . . . . . . . . . . . . . . . . . Working Title Films
Hazan, Edward . . . . . . . . . . . . . . . . . . Ministry of Film Inc., The
Head, Jim . . . . . . . . . . . . . . . . . . . . . . . . . . . . . . TBS Superstation
Healy, Michael . . . . . . . . . . . . . . . . . . . . . . . . . . . Disney Channel
Heap, Jonathan . . . . . . . . . . . . . . . Rough Diamond Productions
Hearst, Austin . . . . . . . . . . . . . . . . . . . . . Vision Media/LXD Inc.
Heath, BJ . . . . . . . . . . . . . . . . . . . . . . . . . . . Carliner Prods., Mark
Hebble, Allison . . . . . . . . . . . . . . . . . . . . . . . . . . . . . . . Havoc Inc.
Heberer, Sandy . . . . . . . . . . . . . . . . . . . . . . . . . . . . . . . . . . . . . . PBS
Hecht, Albie . . . . . . . . . . . . . . . . . . . . . . . . . . . Nickelodeon Movies
Hecht, Albie . . . . . . . . . . . . . . . . . . . . . . Nickelodeon/Nick at Nite

# CROSS-REFERENCED NAMES

Holland, Savage Steve . . . . . . . . . . . . . . . . . . . . Savage Studios Ltd.
Hollander, Russell . . . . . . . . . . . . . . . . . . . . . Karz Entertainment
Hollar, John C. . . . . . . . . . . . . . . . . . . . . . . . . . . . . . . . . . . . PBS
Holliday, Susan J. . . . . . . . . . . . . . . . . . . . . . . . . CBS Corporation
Hollinger, Alicia . . . . . . . . . . . . . . . . . . R.A.M.M. Entertainment, Inc
Hollocker, Stephen . . . . . . . . . . . . . . . . Segan Company, The Lloyd
Holly, Karen . . . . . . . . . . . . . . . . . . . . . . . . Warner Sisters Prods.
Holman, David . . . . . . . . . . . . . . . . . Columbia TriStar Television
Holmberg, Erik . . . . . . . . . . . . . . . . . . . . . . . . New Line Cinema
Holmes, Herbert S.H. . . . . . . . . . . . . . . . Holmes Run Entertainment
Holmes, Preston . . . . . . . . . . . . . . . . . . . . . . . . . . . Def Pictures
Holmes, Tamara . . . . . . . . . . . . . . . . . . . . . . . Katie Face Prods.
Holst, Lynn . . . . . . . . . . . . . . . . . . . . . Hallmark Entertainment (NY)
Holstein, Laura . . . . . . . . . . . . . . . . . Donner/Shuler-Donner Prods.
Holt, Christopher . . . . . . . . . . . . . . . . Grand Designs Entertainment
Holt, David Barrington . . . . . . . . . . . . . . Henson Company, Jim
Holton, Dan . . . . . . . . . . . . . . . . . . . . . Victory Entertainment, Inc.
Holtzman, Scott . . . . . . . . Walt Disney Pictures/Touchstone Pictures
Hom, Rene . . . . . . . . . . . . . . . . . . . . . Newmarket Capital Group
Homer, Dru . . . . . . . . . . . . . . . . . . . . . . . . . . Gaslight Pictures
Hondrogen, Nicholas . . . . . . . . . . . . . . . . . . About Face Prods.
Hongola, Lynda . . . . . . . . . . . . . . . . . . . . . Spelling Films Inc.
Honore, Jimmy . . . . . . . . . . . . Columbia TriStar Motion Picture Group
Hool, Conrad . . . . . . . . . . . . . . . . . . . . . . . . . Silver Lion Films
Hool, Lance . . . . . . . . . . . . . . . . . . . . . . . . . . Silver Lion Films
Hooper, Marilyn . . . . . . . . . . . . . . . . . Power Company, The Derek
Hooper, Nate . . . . . . . . . . . . . . . . . . . . Twentieth Century Fox
Hope, Edward . . . . . . . . . . . . . . . . . . . . . . . Dockry Productions
Hope, Michael S. . . . . . . . . . . . . . . Harvey Entertainment Company
Hope, Ted . . . . . . . . . . . . . . . . . . . . . . . . . . . . . . Good Machine
Hopkins, Alicia . . . . . . . . . . . . . . . . . . . . . Tapestry Films Inc.
Hopkins, Anne . . . . . . . . . . . . . . . . . . . . . Rees Assocs., Marian
Hopkins, Scott . . . . . . . . . . . . . . . . . . . . . Takes On Production
Hopper, David . . . . . . . . . . . . . . . . . . . . . . . . . . . Mr. Mudd
Hopper, Laura . . . . . . . . . . . . . . . . . . . . . Brillstein-Grey Ent.
Horan, Arthur . . . . . . . . . . . . . . . . . . . . . . RKO Pictures, Inc.
Horberg, William . . . . . . . . . . . . . . . . . . . . Mirage Enterprises
Horenstein, Susanne . . . . . . . . . . . . . . . . . Fox Broadcasting Co.
Hori, Karen . . . . . . . . . . . . . . . . . . . . . . . . . . . Langley Prods.
Horian, Ralph . . . . . . . . . . . . . . . . . . . . Sony Pictures Imageworks
Horie, George . . . . . . . . . . . . . . . . . . . . Pacific Motion Pictures
Horn, Alan . . . . . . . . . . . . . . . . . . . . . Castle Rock Entertainment
Horn, Deloris . . . . . . . . . . . . . . . . . . . . Cherry Alley Productions
Horn, Lanny . . . . . . . . . . . . . . . . . . . . Taurus Entertainment Co.
Horn, Mitchell . . . . . . . . . . . . . . . . . . New Screen Concepts, Inc.
Horn, Roger . . . . . . . . . . . . . . . . . . . . . . . . . Tavel Entertainment
Horne, Andrew J. . . . . . . . . . . . . . . . . . . Edmonds Entertainment
Hornickel, Cindy . . . . . . . . . . . . . . . . . . . . . . New Line Cinema
Hornish, Rudy . . . . . . . . . . . . . . . . . . . . Grammnet Productions
Hornstein, Ellen . . . . . . . . . . . . . . . . . . Goepp Circle Productions
Hornstock, Joel . . . . . . . . . . . Twentieth Century Fox Television
Horovitz, Rachael . . . . . . . . . . . . . . . . . . . . Fine Line Features
Horowitz, James M. . . . . . . . . . . . . . . . . . . Universal Pictures
Horowitz, Lawrence . . . . . . . . . . . . . O'Hara-Horowitz Productions
Horowitz, Mark A. . . . . . . . . . . . . . . . . . . Alliance Pictures
Horowitz, Mark . . . . . . . . . . . . . . . . . . . . . . Belisarius Prods.
Horowitz, Mark B. . . . . . . . . . . . . . . . . . . Columbia Pictures
Horton, Drew . . . . . . . . . . . . . . . . . . . . . . Burrud Productions
Horton, Ken . . . . . . . . . . . . . . . . . . . . Ten Thirteen Productions
Horton, Peter . . . . . . . . . . . . . . . . . . . . . . . Pico Creek Prods.
Horton, Thomas F. . . . . . . . . T.H.A. - Thomas Horton Associates Inc.
Horvat, Aleks . . . . . . . . . . . . . . . . . . . . . . . . . . Santiago Films
Horwits, Mitch . . . . . . . . . . . . . . . . . . . . . . . Spelling Films Inc.
Horzepa, Steph . . . . . . . . . . . . . . . . . . . . . . Planet Girl Pictures
Hosbein, David . . . . . . . . . . . . . . . . . . . . Saratoga Entertainment
Houghton, Chip . . . . . . . . . . . . . . . . . . . . . . . . Imaginary Forces
Houser, Catherine . . . . . . . . . . . . . . . . . . . . . . . MTV Networks
Houston, Gregg . . . . . . . . . . . . . . . . . . . . . Nepotism Productions
Houston, Whitney . . . . . . . . . . . . . . . . . . . Brownhouse Productions
Hoven, Joan . . . . . . . . . . . . . . . . . . . . Carr Enterprises, Allan
Howard, Al . . . . . . . . . . . . . . . . . . . . . Howard Prods. Inc., Al
Howard, Ann . . . . . . . . . . . . . . . . . . . Turner Original Productions
Howard, Jeff . . . . . . . . . . . . . . . . . . . . Hill Productions, Debra
Howard, Lesley . . . . . . . . . . . . . . . . . . . . . . . . . . 1492 Pictures
Howard, Max . . . . . . . . . . . . . . . Warner Bros. Feature Animation
Howard, Meri . . . . . . . . . . . . . . . . . . . . . . . . CPC Entertainment
Howard, Molly Ann . . . . . . . . . . . . . . . . . Scott Free Productions
Howard, Ron . . . . . . . . . . . . . . . . . . . . . . Imagine Entertainment
Howard, Ron . . . . . . . . . . . . . . . . . . . . . . . Imagine Television
Howe, Jennifer . . . . . . . . . . . . . . . . . . . . . . . . South Side Films

Howells Jr., Ted . . . . . . . . . . . . . . . . Sony Pictures Entertainment
Howenstein, Bing . . . . . . . . . . . . . . . . . George Street Pictures
Howser, Dean . . . . . . . . . . . . . . . . . . . . Radio...With Pictures
Hoyer, Donn . . . . . . . . . . . . . . . . . . Schlatter Prods., George
Hoyle, Cathy . . . . . . . . . . . . . . . . . . . . . . . . . . Cobalt Moon
Hsiung, Cynthia . . . . . . . . . . . . . . . . . . . Renaissance Pictures
Hsiung, Susette . . . . . . . . . . . . . . . . . . . . . . Disney Channel
Hu, Lincoln . . . . . . . . . . . . . . . . . . Sony Pictures Imageworks
Hubbard, Beth Gotham . . . . . . . . . . . . . . . Gotham Entertainment
Hubbard, Michael . . . . . . . . . . . . . . . . . Gotham Entertainment
Hudgins, Jud . . . . . . . . . . . . . . . . . . . . . . . . . . Jersey Films
Hudson, Barbra . . . . . . . . . . . . . . . . . . . PDQ Directions, Inc.
Hudson, Kit . . . . . . . . . . . . . . . . . . . . . . . . Studio Productions
Hudson, Lynda . . . . . . . . . . . . . . . . . . . Weinberger Co., Ed.
Huffman, Aaron . . . . . . . . . . . . . . . . . . . . . Poco Productions
Hufnail, Mark . . . . . . . . . . . . . . . . . . . . MPH Entertainment, Inc.
Huggins, Erica . . . . . . . . . . . . . Interscope Communications Inc.
Hughes, Albert . . . . . . . . . . . . . . . . . . . Underworld Entertainment
Hughes, Allen . . . . . . . . . . . . . . . . . . . Underworld Entertainment
Hughes, Eric . . . . . . . . . . . . . . . . . . . . . . . . Universal Pictures
Hughes, Jennifer . . . . . . . . . . . . . . . . . . . . Blue Bay Productions
Hughes, Kimberly . . . . . . . . . . . . . . . . London Company, Barry
Hughes, Lindsey . . . . . . . . . . . . . . . . . . Polone Company, The
Hughes, Mary . . . . . . . . . Global Entertainment Network, Inc.
Hughes, Peter . . . . . . . . . Universal Television & Networks Group
Hull, Richard . . . . . . . . . . . . . . . . . . . . . . . Richulco, Inc.
Hull, Tony . . . . . . . . . . . . . . . . . . . . . . . . . DreamWorks SKG
Hullverson, Julie . . . . . . . . . . . . . . . . Wells Productions, John
Hume, Lenora . . . . . . . . . . . Walt Disney Television Animation
Humphrey, Christy . . . . . . . . . . . De Laurentiis Company, Dino
Humphreys, Martha D. . . . . . . . . . . . . . . Driskill Entertainment
Huncke, John . . . . . . . . . . . . . . . . . . . . . PolyGram Television
Hunegs, Craig . . . . . . . Warner Bros. Television Productions
Hung, Asa . . . . . . . . . . . . . . . . . . . . . . . . DreamWorks SKG
Hunka, Robert . . . . . . . . . . . . Columbia TriStar Television
Hunt, Gary . . . . . . . . . . . . . . . . . . . . . . . Hunt/Jaffe Prods.
Hunt, Helen . . . . . . . . . . . . . . . . . . . Hunt-Tavel Productions
Hunte, Karen Robinson . . . . . . . . . Out of the Blue . . . Entertainment
Hunter, Dez . . . . . . . . . . . . Turner Network Television (TNT)
Hunter, Leah . . . . . . . . . . . . . . . . . . Brownhouse Productions
Hunter, Les . . . . . . . . . . . . . . . . . . . . . . Pacific Data Images
Hunter, Pat . . . . . . . . . . . . . . . . . . . . . . . . . . . . . . . . . . PBS
Hunter, Robert C. . . . . . . . . . Ladd Productions, Inc., Diane
Hunter, Timothy . . . . . . . . . . . . . . . . . . . Yagya Productions
Hunter, Whitney . . . . . . . . . . . . . . . . . . . Periscope Pictures
Huntsberry, Frederick . . . . . . . Universal Television & Networks Group
Hurd, Gale Anne . . . . . . . . . . . . . . . . Pacific Western Prods.
Hurdelbrink, Amy . . . . . . . . . . . . . . . . . Dee Gee Entertainment
Hurley, Elizabeth . . . . . . . . . . . . . . . . . . . . . . . Simian Films
Hurwicz, Claude . . . . . . . . . . . . . . . . . . . Trinity Pictures, Inc.
Husbands, Amber . . . . . . . . . . . Twentieth Century Fox-Searchlight Picts.
Huston, Danny . . . . . . . . . . . . . . . Rough Diamond Productions
Hutchinson, Cathy . . . . . . . . . . . . . . . . . . . . Prufrock Pictures
Hutchinson, Troy . . . . . . . . . . . . . . . . . . . . Act III Productions
Hutensky, Steven . . . . . . . . . . . . . . . . . . . . . Miramax Films
Huth, Denise . . . . . . . . . . . . . . . . . . . . . Scott Free Productions
Huvane, Ruth-Ann . . . . . . . . . . . Columbia TriStar Television
Hyams, Peter . . . . . . . . . . . . . . . . . Hyams Prods., Inc., Peter
Hyde, Jennifer . . . . . . . . . . . . . . . . Turner Original Productions
Hyde, Wendi . . . . . . . . . . . . . . . . . . . . . . . FGM Entertainment
Hyder, Katherine . . . . . . . . Moress-Nanas-Hart Entertainment
Hyland, Stephen . . . . . . . . . . . . . . . . . Spin Cycle Entertainment
Hyman, Kevin . . . . . . . . . . . . . . . . . . . . . . Dimension Films
Hymes, Larry . . . . . . . . . . . . . . . . . . . . . . . Chanticleer Films
Iamunno, Janine . . . . . . . . . . . . . . . . . Shapiro Prods., Arnold
Iberri, Fred . . . . . . . . . . . . . . . . . . . . . . . . . . Fields Co., The
Iezman, Alan . . . . . . . . . . . . . . . . . . . . . . Shelter Entertainment
Igbokwe, Pearlena . . . . . . . . . . . . . . . . . Showtime Networks Inc.
Ige-Wong, Eileen . . . . . . . . . . . Paramount Network Television
Iglehart, Carrie . . . . . . . . . . . . . . Chesler/Perlmutter Production
Iker, Marty . . . . . . . . . . . . . . . . . . . . . . . . . Tri-Crown Prods.
Ildari, Hassan . . . . . . . . . . . . . . . . . . . . . . . . . Golden Quill
Ileen, Margo . . . . . . . . . . . . . . . . . . . . . . KiMina Entertainment
Imamoto, Jay . . . . . . . . Quincy Jones*David Salzman Entertainment
Immergut, Scott . . . . . . . . . . . . . . . . . . . . . . Sandollar Prods.
Imperiale, Jeannine . . . . . . . . . . . . . Keller Entertainment Group
Introcaso-Davis, Amy . . . . . . . . . . . . . . . Lifetime Television (NY)
Irmas, Matthew . . . . . . . . . . . . . . . . . . . . . . . . . . . Emby Eye
Irons, Camille . . . . . . . . . . . . . . . . . . . . . . . . . . Def Pictures
Irving, Richard . . . . . . . . . . . . . . . . . Too Nuts Productions, Ltd.

# CROSS-REFERENCED NAMES

Irwin, Carl .............................. Hansen, Edward D.
Isaac, Frank K. .......................... Largo Entertainment
Isaac, Sandy ................... Isaac Productions, Sandy
Isaacs, Stanley ............................. 360 entertainment
Isaacson, Mike ............... Hallmark Entertainment (NY)
Isaak, Wayne ........................... VH1 (Music First)
Isacksen, Peter ..................... Radio...With Pictures
Isenberg, Lynn ......... Hollywood Literary Retreat/Zoom Ent.
Ishakian, Nayiri ..................... Edelson Productions
Israel, Amy .............................. Miramax Films
Israel, Bob ......................... Aspect Ratio Films
Israel, Mark ................... Grand Productions, Inc.
Israel, Neal ......................... Aspect Ratio Films
Israelson, Susan ................... HBO NYC Productions
Israelson, Susan ......................... HBO Pictures
Isreal, Stephen ........... Associated Producers Group, Inc.
Ittner, Mark .......................... Fox Kids Network
Ittner, Mark ......................... Saban Entertainment
Iturralde, Jose-Maria ........... Fortune Media Group, Inc.
Iungerich, Lauren ......................... RKO Pictures, Inc.
Ivers, Jeff ............... Motion Pict. Corp. of America
Iverson, Jill ................... Montan Productions, Chris
Iverson, Scott ......... Bonneville Worldwide Entertainment
Ivory, James ........................... Merchant-Ivory
Iwamasa, Ken ............................. Krost/Chapin
Iwanyk, Basil ..................... Warner Bros. Pictures
Iwerks, Don ......................... Iwerks Entertainment
Izzicupo, Sunta ..................... CBS Entertainment
Jablin, David ............... Imagination Productions Inc.
Jacks, Jim ................................... Alphaville
Jackson, Becky ..................... Brillstein-Grey Ent.
Jackson, Dana ................... Hunt-Tavel Productions
Jackson, Kimiko ......................... Amen Ra Films
Jackson, Lisa ................... LookAlike Productions
Jackson, Sarah ........... Seven Summits Pictures & Mgmt.
Jackson, Stephen ............... Spin Cycle Entertainment
Jackson, Vikki ..................... Pilot Boy Productions
Jacobi, Ronald ............... Sony Pictures Entertainment
Jacobs Miller, Nancy ......... Film Garden Entertainment
Jacobs, David ......................... Roundelay Prods.
Jacobs, Holly ............................. ABC Daytime
Jacobs, Jane ................... Scripps Howard Prods.
Jacobs, Jay ................... Proud Mary Entertainment
Jacobs, Jeffrey ......................... Harpo Films Inc.
Jacobs, John ................... First Entertainment LLC
Jacobs, Jon ............................... Zero Pictures
Jacobs, Karen ......................... Mutual Film Co.
Jacobs, Katie ......................... Jacobs/Mutrux Prods.
Jacobs, Michael ................... Jacobs Prods., Michael
Jacobs, Michael D. ............... Porchlight Entertainment
Jacobs, Rick ................... Lifetime Television (LA)
Jacobson, Danny ......................... InFront Productions
Jacobson, Eric ................... Fox Television Studios
Jacobson, Jake ............... Paramount Network Television
Jacobson, Janet ............... Hallmark Entertainment (NY)
Jacobson, John ................... Hollywood Network, Inc.
Jacobson, Larry ......................... Fox Broadcasting Co.
Jacobson, Lawrence S. ........ Grosso-Jacobson Productions, Inc.
Jacobson, Lawrence S. ......... Producers Ent. Group, Ltd., The
Jacobson, Mark ............... London Company, Barry
Jacobson, Nina ........ Walt Disney Pictures/Touchstone Pictures
Jacobson, Rick ......................... Twentieth Television
Jacobson, Tom ................... Jacobson Company, The
Jacoby, Jay ......................... Studio Productions
Jaffa, Rick ......................... Shinbone Productions
Jaffe Kahn, Jan ............... Kahn Productions, Ronald J.
Jaffe, Barry ......................... Hunt/Jaffe Prods.
Jaffe, Bob ................................... Jaffilms
Jaffe, Michael ............... Jaffe/Braunstein Films Ltd.
Jaffe, Ryan ......................... Industry Entertainment
Jaffe, Stanley R. ............................. Jaffilms
Jaffe, Toby ......................... Ladd Company, The
Jaglom, Henry ........... Rainbow Film Co./Rainbow Releasing
Jago, Charmian ......................... Levinson, Mark
Jakoby, Don ......................... One Story Pictures
Jakositz, Mathew ................... Una Chica Entertainment
Jakubiak, Stephanie ........... Mestres Productions, Ricardo
Jam, Kia ................... Grand Designs Entertainment
James, Amanda ......................... Pacific Motion Pictures
James, Francesca ......................... ABC Daytime

James, Judith ................... Dreyfuss/James Prods.
James, Julie ......... Morra, Brezner, Steinberg & Tenenbaum
Jamieson, J.J. ......................... Avenue Pictures
Jamshidi, Goly ............... Concorde/New Horizons Corp.
Janas, Steve ................... Time-Life Video & Television
Janger, Lane ......................... Danger Filmworks
Janisch, John ................... Pearson All American
Jankowksi, Peter ......................... Wolf Films Inc.
Janollari, David ........... Greenblatt Janollari Studio, The
Janson, Joseph ................... Westport Film Partners
Janzen, Lisa ........................................ IXL
Japhet, Wendy ......................... Fogwood Films
Jaret, Seth ................... Revolution Entertainment
Jarmus, Steve ......... Universal Television & Networks Group
Jarvilaturi, Ilkka ......................... Upstream Pictures
Jason, Jack ......................... Solo One Productions
Jason, Melinda ................... Jason Company, Melinda
Javitz, Barbara ......................... Legend Entertainment
Jazan, Jorge ................... Double Whammy Productions
Jealous, Suzanne ......................... Arama Entertainment
Jeffers, Ian ................... Lauren Productions, Andrew
Jelline, Moe ................................... Original Film
Jenkel, Brad ................... Motion Pict. Corp. of America
Jenkins, Bryan ......................... Silverline Pictures
Jenkins, Linda ......................... Simsie Films
Jenkinson, Holly ......................... Universal Pictures
Jenkinson, Michael ............... Twentieth Century Fox
Jenner, William ................... Chotzen/Jenner Productions
Jennings, Heather ......................... Koch Co., The
Jensen, Erik ................... Cinequanon Pictures Intl. Inc.
Jensen, Peter ................... Shadowcatcher Entertainment
Jessel, Ian ........... Silverman Prod, Lloyd/Passionate Picts.
Jessen, Erik ................... Raffaella Productions, Inc.
Jewison, Norman ......................... Yorktown Prods. Inc.
Jimirro, James P. ......................... National Lampoon
Jinkins, Jim ......................... Jumbo Pictures, Inc.
Jinks, Dan ................... Jinks/Cohen Company, The
Jizba-Peterson, Susan ......................... Beacon Pictures
Joblin, Monia ......................... USA Networks
Jobs, Steven P. ................... Pixar Animation Studios
Joe, Jeanne Moy ......... First Look Picts./Overseas Filmgroup
Joffe, Roland ......................... Nomad Productions
Johanson, Cindy ........................................ PBS
Johns, Brenda ......................... Spelling Films Inc.
Johns, Geoff ................... Donner/Shuler-Donner Prods.
Johns, Paul A. ........... VanDerKloot Film & Television Inc.
Johnson, Ann ................... Jacobs Prods., Michael
Johnson, Bridget ................... New Regency Prods.
Johnson, Brooke Bailey ......... A & E Television Networks
Johnson, Brown ................... Nickelodeon/Nick at Nite
Johnson, Bruce D. ................... Porchlight Entertainment
Johnson, Chas. Floyd ........... Floyd Johnson Productions, Charles
Johnson, David ................... Metro-Goldwyn-Mayer Pictures
Johnson, Don ......................... Johnson Prods., Don
Johnson, Franklin ......................... Rysher Entertainment
Johnson, Greg ......................... Redeemable Features
Johnson, Henry ......... Warner Bros. Television Productions
Johnson, Jeanne ................... Tardy-Green Productions, Ltd.
Johnson, Joanna ......... Paramount Pictures- Motion Picture Group
Johnson, Keith ................... Grosso-Jacobson Productions, Inc.
Johnson, Lucy ......................... CBS Entertainment
Johnson, Magic ................... Johnson Entertainment, Magic
Johnson, Mark ................... Johnson Productions, Mark
Johnson, Mark S. ......................... Big Ticket Television
Johnson, Mark Steven ................... Horseshoe Bay Productions
Johnson, Nick ......................... Plaster City Productions
Johnson, Peter T. ......................... Fox Broadcasting Co.
Johnson, Robert ......................... Black Entertainment TV
Johnson, Robert ................................... Def Pictures
Johnson, Robert W. ........ Walt Disney Pictures/Touchstone Pictures
Johnson, Robert W. ........... Walt Disney TV/Touchstone TV
Johnson, Sheila ......................... Fox Television Studios
Johnson, Steven ......................... Korova Entertainment
Johnson, Susan ......................... Colomby/Keaton
Johnson, Tim ......................... Tavel Entertainment
Johnston, James ......................... Flying Freehold Productions
Johnston, Stephen R. ........... Goldcrest Films International, Inc.
Johntz, Fred ......................... Travis Group, The
Joli-Coeur, Allan ......................... Allegro Films
Jonas, Tony ............... Warner Bros. Television Productions

# CROSS-REFERENCED NAMES

Jones, Allen H. . . . . . . . . . . . . . . . . . . . . . . . . . . . . Production Services
Jones, Bruce . . . . . . . . . . . . . . . . . La-Mont Communications Inc.
Jones, Connie . . . . . . . . . . . . . . . . . . . . . . . Fox Broadcasting Co.
Jones, Damian . . . . . . . . . . . . . . . . . . . . . . . . . . . . Dragon Pictures
Jones, Dennis E. . . . . . . . . . . . . . . . Deja View Productions, Inc.
Jones, Donna . . . . . . . . . . . . . . . . . . . . . Winston Productions, Stan
Jones, Glenn R. . . . . . . . . . . . . . . . . . Jones Entertainment Group
Jones, Grady . . . . . . . . . . Walt Disney TV/Touchstone TV
Jones, Graham . . . . . . . . . . . . . . . . . . . . . . Blueline Productions
Jones, Jocelyn . . . . . . . . . . . . . . . . Recorded Picture Company
Jones, Kelley . . . . . . . . . . . . . . . . . . . . . . . . . . . . . . . . Allied Stars
Jones, Kevin . . . . . . . . . . . . . . . . . . . . . . . . . . . . . . . . . Signature
Jones, Loretha . . . . . . . . . . . . . . . . . Townsend Ent. Corp., The
Jones, Marilyn . . . . . . . . . . . . . . . . . . . . . Big Sky Entertainment
Jones, Michael David . . . . . . . . . . . . . Silver Heart Productions
Jones, Patrice . . . . . . . . . . . . . . . . . . . . . Douthit Productions Ltd.
Jones, Patricia . . . . . . . . . . . . . . . . . . . Schindler Prods., Deborah
Jones, Quincy . . . . . . . . . Quincy Jones*David Salzman Entertainment
Jones, Rebecca . . . . . . . . . . . . . . . . . . . . . . . . . . . . . . . Warp Films
Jones, Rich . . . . . . . . . . . . . . . . . . . . . . . . . . . . . . . . . Jersey Films
Jones, Sandra . . . . . . . . . . . . . . . Schwartz Productions, Bernard
Jones, Sherwood . . . . . . . . . . . . . . . . . . . . . Tapestry Films Inc.
Jones, Trent . . . . . . . . . Warner Bros. Television Productions
Jones, William . . . . . . . . . . Metro-Goldwyn-Mayer Pictures
Joniff, Sherry . . . . . . . . . . . . . . . . . . . . . . . Planet Girl Pictures
Jordan, David . . . . . . . . . . . . . . . . . . . . . . . . . . . Dimension Films
Jordan, Janice . . . . . . . . . . . . . . . . . . . . . . . . . . . Koch Co., The
Jordan, Michael H. . . . . . . . . . . . . . . . . . . . . . CBS Corporation
Jordan, Murray . . . . . . . . . . . . . . . . . . . . . . . . . . Langley Prods.
Jordan, Vanessa . . . . . . . . . . . . . . . . . Centropolis Streamline
Jorgensen, Rebekah . . . . . . . . . . . . . . Savoir Faire Productions
Josell, Jonathan . . . . . . . . . . . . . . . . . Maple Palm Productions
Joseph, Allison . . . . . . . . . . . . . . . . . . . . . . . . . . . . Def Pictures
Joseph, Rick . . . . . . . . . . . . . . . Sarkissian Productions, Arthur
Josephson, Barry . . . . . . . . . . . . . . . . . . Sonnenfeld/Josephson
Josey, Bill . . . . . . . . . . . . . . . . . . . . . . . . Saban Entertainment
Josten, Walter . . . . . . . . . . . . . . . . . . . . . . Blue Rider Pictures
Joundourian, Pari . . . . . . . . . . . . . . Double Whammy Productions
Juergens, Kate . . . . . . . . . . . . . . . . . . . . . . NBC Entertainment
Julian, Nanette . . . . . . . . . . . . . . . . . . Golchan Prods., Frederic
Jumelet, Lorraine . . . . . . . . . . . . . . . Spelling Television, Inc.
Jung, David . . . . . . . . . . . . . . . . . . . . . . . . . . Mandeville Films
Jupiter, Mark . . . . . . . . . . . . . . . . . . . . . Watermark Films, Inc.
Jurus, Marc . . . . . . . . . American Movie Classics/Romance Classic
Jurva, Suzanne . . . . . . . . . . . . . . . . . . . . . . . DreamWorks SKG
Justice, Hardy . . . . . . . . . . . . . . . . . . . . . . Tribeca Productions
Justice, Milton . . . . . . . . . . . . . . . . . . . . . . Indican Productions
Justice, Rebecca . . . . . . . . . . . . . . . . . . . . . . . Forrester Films
Juvonen, Nancy . . . . . . . . . . . . . . . . . . . . . Flower Films, Inc.
Kaczynski, Adolph . . . . . . . . . . . . . . . . . . . Dockry Productions
Kagan, Lali . . . . . . . . . . . . . . . . . . . . . . Wessler Entertainment
Kageff, Tom . . . . . . . . . . . . . . . . . . . . . . . Randwell Productions
Kahane, Nathan . . . . . . . . . . . . . . . . . . . Canton Company, The
Kahl, Kelly . . . . . . . . . . . . . . . . . . . . . . . . . CBS Entertainment
Kahl, Kristen . . . . . . . . . . . . . . . . . Maple Palm Productions
Kahn Power, Ilene . . . . . . Kahn Power Pictures(Formerly Odessa Pic)
Kahn, Harvey . . . . . . . . . . . . . . . . . . . Front Street Productions
Kahn, James . . . . . . . . . . . . . . . . . . . . . . . . . Melrose Prods.
Kahn, Janice . . . . . . . . . . . . . . . . . . . . . . Planet Girl Pictures
Kahn, Kyu . . . . . . . . . . . . . . . . . . . . . . . Broadway Pictures (LA)
Kahn, Linda . . . . . . . . . . . . . . . . . . . . Scholastic Entertainment
Kahn, Lori . . . . . . . . . . . . . . . . . . . . . . . Showtime Networks Inc.
Kahn, Ronald J. . . . . . . . . . . . . . . Kahn Productions, Ronald J.
Kahn, Sheldon . . . . . . . . . . . . . . . . . . . . Northern Lights Ent.
Kahrs, Ken . . . . . . . . . . . . . . . . . . . . . . . . . . . Universal Studios
Kaiser, Rachel . . . . . . . . . . . . . . . . . . . Jacobson Company, The
Kaiser, Tamara . . . . . . . . . . . . . . . . . . . . . . Fourth Avenue Films
Kalb, Steve . . . . . . . . . . . . . . . . . . . . . . . . Esparza-Katz Prods.
Kalins, Marjorie . . . . . . . . . . . . . Children's Television Workshop
Kalish, Barbara . . . . . . . . . . . . . . . . . . . Canton Company, The
Kalish, Leah . . . . . . . . . . . . . . . . . . . . . . . . . . . . . Imaginazium
Kalisher, David . . . . . . . . . . . . . . . . . . . . . . . . . . . Seldes Films
Kalmbach, Peter . . . . . . . . . . . . . . . . . . . . . . . . October Films
Kalos, Lauren . . . . . . . . . . . . . . . . . . . . . . . . . . . . . . . . . . PBS
Kalyanaraman, R. . . . . . . . . . . . . . . . . . . Shogun Films, Ltd.
Kamer, Renate . . . . . . . . . . . . . . . . Spelling Television, Inc.
Kamrowski, Andrew . . . . . . . . . . . . . . East West Film Partners
Kanakis, Ann Marie . . . . . . . . . . . . . . . . . . Tavel Entertainment
Kananack, Michael . . . . . . . . . . . . . . . . . Fries Film Group, Inc.
Kane, Peter . . . . . . . . . . . . . . . . . . . . Paramount Domestic TV

Kane, Tom . . . . . . . . . . . . . . . . . . . . . . . . . . . Phoenix Pictures
Kanemoto, Karen . . . . . . . . . . . . . . . . Paramount Domestic TV
Kang, Kiana . . . . . . . . . . . . . . . . . . . . . . . . Catfish Productions
Kanner, Cynthia . . . . . . . . . . . . . . . . . . . . . . . . . HBO Pictures
Kanyuck, Scott . . . . . . . . . . . . . . . . . . . . . . . New Line Cinema
Kaplan, Andrew J. . . . . . . . . . . . Columbia TriStar Television
Kaplan, Avram Butch . . . . . . . . . . Mase/Kaplan Productions, Inc.
Kaplan, Debby . . . . . . . . . . . . . . . . Bright-Kauffman-Crane Prods.
Kaplan, Howard . . . . . . . . . . . . . . . . . . . . Morgan Creek Prods.
Kaplan, Marty . . . . . . . . . . . . . . . . . . . . . . . . . Kaplan, Marty
Kaplan, Neil . . . . . . . . . . . . . . . . . . Black Sheep Entertainment
Kaplan, Rob . . . . . . . . . . . . . . . . . . . . . . . . . CBS Entertainment
Kaplin, Vivienne . . . . . . . . . . . . . . . . . . . Green/Epstein Prods.
Karabats, Peter . . . . . . . . . . . . . . . . . Clifford Prods., Patricia
Karabin-Hecomovich, Linda . . . . . . . . . . . Burrud Productions
Karas, Jay . . . . . . . . . . . . . . . . . . . . . . . . . . Tenth Planet Prods.
Karasic, Susan . . . . . . . . . . . . . . . . . . . . . . . . . . Nine By Nine
Karbelnikoff, Michael . . . . . . . . . . . . . . . . . . . . . . . HKM Films
Karchmer, Lara . . . . . . . . . . . . . . . . . . . . Mesmerize Studios
Karl, Elizabeth . . . . . . . . . . . . . . . . . . . . Force Ten Productions
Karlin, Allen . . . . . . . . . . . . . . . . . . . . . Savoir Faire Productions
Karlson, Nicolas . . . . . . . . . . . . . . . . . . . HBO NYC Productions
Karmazin, Mel . . . . . . . . . . . . . . . . . . . . . . . CBS Corporation
Karnowski, Tom . . . . . . . . . . . . . . . . . . . . . . . . . . . . Filmwerks
Karo, Rick . . . . . . . . . . . . Hearst Ent. Licensing & Family Prog.
Karol, Scott . . . . . . . . . . . . . . . . Turner Entertainment Group
Karpen, Andrew . . . . . . . . . . . . . . . . . . Sunbow Entertainment
Karpf, Merrill H. . . . . . . . . . . . . . . . . . King World Productions
Karras, Alex . . . . . . . . . . . . . . . . . . . . . . . . Georgian Bay Prods.
Karsch, Andrew . . . . . . . . . . . . . . . . . . . . Longfellow Pictures
Karsch, Tom . . . . . . . . . . . . . . . . Turner Entertainment Group
Karteris, Sophia . . . . . . . . . . . . . . . . . . . . . . TBS Superstation
Karz, Mike . . . . . . . . . . . . . . . . . . . . . . . . . Karz Entertainment
Karzan, Brooke . . . . . . . . . . . . . . . . . . Buena Vista Productions
Kasanoff, Larry . . . . . . . . . . . . . . . . . . . . Threshold Entertainment
Kashiba, Edwin . . . . . . . . . . . . . . . . . . . Scott Free Productions
Kassar, Mario . . . . . . . . . . . . . . . . . . . . . . . . . MK Productions
Kassirer, Allan M. . . . . . . . . . . . Kassirer Meyer Entertainment
Kastenbaum, Michael . . . . . . . . . . . . . . . . . . . . . . Zero Pictures
Kastner, Elliott . . . . . . . . . . . . . . . . . . . . . Cinema Seven Prods.
Kastner, Ron . . . . . . . . . . . . . . . . . . . Goldheart Pictures Corp.
Katcher, Michael A. . . . . . . . . . . . . . . . . . . CBS Entertainment
Kates, Michael . . . . . . . . . . Greenhouse Film Group Ltd., The
Katsky, Tracy . . . . . . . . . . . . . . . . . . . . . . . . . Sandollar Prods.
Katsotis, Rita . . . . . . . Quincy Jones*David Salzman Entertainment
Katz, Barry . . . . . . . . . . . . . . . Katz Entertainment Group, Barry
Katz, Campbell . . . . . . . . . . . . . . . . . . . . . . Katz Prods., Marty
Katz, Danica . . . . . . . . . . . . . . . . . . . . . . . . Film Roman, Inc.
Katz, David Bar . . . . . . . . . . . . . . . . . . . Lower East Side Films
Katz, Eileen . . . . . . . . . . . . . . . . . . . . . . . . . . Comedy Central
Katz, Gail . . . . . . . . . . . . . . . . . . . . . . . . . Radiant Productions
Katz, Marty . . . . . . . . . . . . . . . . . . . . . . . . . Katz Prods., Marty
Katz, Marvin S. . . . . . . . . . . . . . . . . . . . . . Hearst Entertainment
Katz, Perry . . . . . . . . . . . . . . . . . . . . Katz Productions, Perry
Katz, Raymond . . . . . . . . . . . . . . . . . . . Katz/Rush Entertainment
Katz, Robert . . . . . . . . . . . . . . . . . . . . . . Esparza-Katz Prods.
Katz, Stacy . . . . . . . . . . . . . . . . . . . . . . . . . . CineCity Pictures
Katzenberg, Jeffrey . . . . . . . . . . . . . . . . . . . DreamWorks SKG
Katzman, Jon . . . . . . . . . . . . . . . . . . . . . . New Regency Prods.
Kauffman, Lisa . . . . . . . . . . . . . . . . Time-Life Video & Television
Kauffman, Marta . . . . . . . . . . . . . . . Bright-Kauffman-Crane Prods.
Kaufman, Holden . . . . . . . . . . . Greenhouse Film Group Ltd., The
Kaufman, Karen . . . . . . . . . . . . . . . . . . . . . . Monarch Pictures
Kaufman, Kenneth . . . . . . . . . . . Patchett Kaufman Entertainment
Kaufman, Lloyd . . . . . . . . . . . . . . . . . . . . . . . . . . . Troma Inc.
Kaufman, Mark S. . . . . . . . . . . . . . . . . . . . . New Line Cinema
Kaufman, Muffett . . . . . . . . . . . . . . . . . . . . . . . . MKD Prods.
Kaufman, Paul A. . . . . . . . . . . . . . . . . . . . . Kaufman Co., The
Kaufman, Paul A. . . . . . . . . . . . . . . . Two Pauls Entertainment
Kaufman, Romy . . . . . . . . . . . . . . . . . . . . . Universal Pictures
Kaufman, Susannah . . . . . . . . . . . . . . . . . . Tribeca Productions
Kavandi, Ray . . . . . . . . . . . . . . . . . . . . . . . Filmopolis Pictures
Kaviar, Brent . . . . . . . . . . . . . . . . . . . . . . . . New Line Cinema
Kay, Julia . . . . . . . . . . . . . . . . . . . . . . . . . . . New Line Cinema
Kaye, Dale Eldridge . . . . . . . . . . . . . . Gold'n Hen Productions
Kaye, Ted . . . . . . . . . . . . . . Walt Disney TV/Touchstone TV
Kaylor, Kristi . . . . . . . . . . . Kaylor Company, The (aka Edge Enter.)
Kazanjian, Howard . . . . . . . . . . . . . . . . . . Tricor Entertainment
Keach, James . . . . . . . . . . . . . . . . . . . . . . Catfish Productions
Kearns, Lisa . . . . . . . . . . . . . . . . . . . . . . . . . . . . . Jersey Films

# CROSS-REFERENCED NAMES

Keating, Diane J. . . . . . . . . . . . . . . . . . . . . . New Line Cinema
Keaton, Diane . . . . . . . . . . . . . . . . . . . . . . . . . Blue Relief, Inc.
Keaton, Michael . . . . . . . . . . . . . . . . . . . . . . Colomby/Keaton
Keats, Laura . . . . . . . . . . . . . . . . . . . . IndieGal Productions, LLC
Keegan, James . . . . . . . . . . . . . . . . . . . . . . . . Trimark Pictures
Keel, John . . . . . . . . . . . . . . . . . . . . . . . . First Street Films, Inc.
Keeley, Richard . . . . . . . . . . . . . . . . . . . . . . . New Line Cinema
Keeley, Wayne . . . . . . . . . . . . . . . . . . . . . . Arrow Entertainment
Keenan, William . . . . . . . . . . . . . . . . . E! Entertainment Television
Keeshen, James F. . . . . . . . . . . . . . . . Keeshen Productions, Jim
Kehela, Karen . . . . . . . . . . . . . . . . . . . . . Imagine Entertainment
Keitel, Harvey . . . . . . . . . . . . . . . . . . . . . . . . Goatsingers, The
Keith, David . . . . . . . . . . . . . . . . . Diamondback Entertainment
Keith, Leah . . . . . . . . . . . . . . . . . . . . . . . . . . . Disney Telefilms
Keith, Paul . . . . . . . . . . . . . . . . . . . . . . . . Ladd Company, The
Keller, Eytan . . . . . . . . . . . . . . . . . . . . . . Fox Family Channel
Keller, Eytan . . . . . . . . . . . . . . . . . . . . . . . Fox Kids Network
Keller, Max . . . . . . . . . . . . . . . . . . Keller Entertainment Group
Keller, Micheline . . . . . . . . . . . . . . . Keller Entertainment Group
Kelley, Bob . . . . . . . . . . . . . . . . . . . . . . Studios USA Pictures
Kelley, David E. . . . . . . . . . . . . . Kelley Productions, David E.
Kelley, Julianne . . . . . . . . . . . . . . . . . . . . . . Trimark Pictures
Kellner, Jamie . . . . . . . . . . . . . . . . . W.B. Television Network
Kellogg-Joslyn, Mary . . . . . . . . . . . . . Buena Vista Productions
Kelly, Deveney . . . . . . . . . . . . . . . . Bell-Phillip TV Prods., Inc.
Kelly, Frank . . . . . . . . . . . . . . . . . . . . Paramount Domestic TV
Kelly, Michael . . . . . . . . . . . . . . . . . . . . . . . . . Marvel Studios
Kelly, Mick . . . . . . . . . . . . . . . . . . . . . Pacific Western Prods.
Kelly, Tim . . . . . . . . . . . . . . . National Geographic Television
Kemble, Tracey . . . . . . . . . . . . . . . . . . HBO NYC Productions
Kemp, Barry . . . . . . . . . . . . . . . . . . . . . . . Bungalow 78 Prods.
Kemp, Carroll . . . . . . . . . . . . . . . . . . . . . . . Acappella Pictures
Kemper, Barry . . . . . . . . . . . . . . . . . . . . . . . Imax Corporation
Kemper, Tom . . . . . . . . . . . . . . . . . . . . . . . . . Parallel Pictures
Kenchelian, Mark . . . . . . . . Walt Disney Television Animation
Kenemer, Kerry . . . . . . . . . VanDerKloot Film & Television Inc.
Kenneally, Rob . . . . . . . . . . . . . . . . . . . . Rysher Entertainment
Kennedy, Aryn . . . . . . . . . . . . . . . . Rust Productions, Patricia
Kennedy, Dailey . . . . . . . . . . . . . . . . Tudor Entertainment, Inc.
Kennedy, David . . . . . . . . . . . . . . . . . . . . Curtis Prods., Dan
Kennedy, Deborah . . . . . . . . . . . . . . . . . Radio...With Pictures
Kennedy, Jennifer . . . . . . . . . . . . . . . . . . . . . . . . . Troma Inc.
Kennedy, Kathleen . . . . . . . . . . . . Kennedy/Marshall Company
Kennedy, Kevin . . . . . . . . . . . . . . . . . . . . . . . . . Jersey Shore
Kennedy, Steve A. . . . . . . . . . . . . . Paulson Prods., Daniel L.
Kenny, Bryan A. . . . . . . . . . . . . . . . . . . Besame Mucho Pictures
Kenny, Saffron . . . . . . . . . . . . . . . . . . . . . . . Imaginary Forces
Kent, Chuck . . . . . . . . . . . . . . . . . . . . . . . . . Disney Channel
Kent, Linda L. . . . . . . . . . . . Grossbart, Barnett Productions
Keogh, Preston . . . . . . . . . . . . . . . . . First Entertainment LLC
Keohane, Jennifer . . . . . . . . . . . . . . . . . . . . Colomby/Keaton
Ker, Jonathon . . . . . . . . . . . . . . . . . . . . . . . Palomar Pictures
Keramidas, Peter . . . . . . . . . . . . . . . . Showtime Networks Inc.
Kerchner, Rob . . . . . . . . . . . . . . . . Capital Arts Entertainment
Kerew, Diana . . . . . . . . . . . . . . . . . . . Diana Kerew Productions
Keris, Roseann M. . . . . . . . . . . . Kelley Productions, David E.
Kerman, Thea . . . . . . . . . . . . . . . . Feigelson Prods., Inc., J.D.
Kermarec, Sophie . . . . . . . . . . . . . . . . . . . . Upstream Pictures
Kern, Elisabeth . . . . . . . . . . . . . . . . Neufeld Productions, Mace
Kern, Russell S. . . . . . . . . . . . . . . . . Producers Group Studios
Kerner, Bruce . . . . . . . . . . . . . . . . . . . . . Big Ticket Television
Kerner, Jordan . . . . . . . . . . . . . . . . . . . . . . . Avnet-Kerner Co.
Kerner, Nickole . . . . . . . . . . . . . . . . . . . Braubach Productions
Kerns, Valerie . . . . . . . . . . . . . . Common Ground Entertainment
Kerr, Mary . . . . . . . . . . . . . . . . . . . . . . . . . Sundance Institute
Kesler, Robert . . . . . . . . . . . . . . . . Action America Entertainment
Kessel, Robert . . . . . . . . . . . . . . . . . . . . . . . . Miramax Films
Kessell, Brad . . . . . . . . Paramount Pictures- Production Division
Kesselman, Josh . . . . . . . . . . . . . . . . . Jericho Entertainment
Kessler, Carolyn . . . . . . . . . . . . . . . . . . First Kiss Productions
Kessler, Gary . . . . . . . . . . . . . . . . . . . . . . . NBC Entertainment
Kettler, C.J. . . . . . . . . . . . . . . . . . . . . . . . Sunbow Entertainment
Keymah, T'Keyah Crystal . . . . . . . . . . . . . . . In Black World
Khan, Sartaj . . . . . . . . . . . . . . . . . . Star Land Entertainment Inc.
Khatami, Lontih . . . . . . . . . . . . . . . . . . Original Voices, Inc.
Kibbey, Chris . . . . . . . . . . . . . . . . . . . . . . . . . . No Prisoners
Kieser C.S.P., Father Ellwood E. . . . . . . . . . . . Paulist Prods.
Kim, Alice . . . . . . . . . . . . . . . . . . . . . . . . . Zweibel, Alan
Kim, Greg . . . . . . . . . . . . . . . Cinequanon Pictures Intl. Inc.
Kimball, Jack S. . . . . . . . . . . . . . . . . . . Green/Epstein Prods.

Kimoto, Shari . . . . . . . . . . . . . . . . . . . . . . . Avnet-Kerner Co.
Kindberg, Ann . . . . . . . . . . Patchett Kaufman Entertainment
King, Brett . . . . . . . . . . . . . . Paramount Network Television
King, Brian . . . . . . . . . . . . . . . . . . . . . . . Nomad Productions
King, Jacqueline . . . . . . . . . . . . . . . . . . Radiant Productions
King, John . . . . . . . . . . . . . . . . . Meridian Entertainment, LLC
King, Jonathan . . . . . . . . . . . . . . . . Mark Prods., Laurence
King, Michael . . . . . . . . . . . . . . . . . . . King World Productions
King, Roger . . . . . . . . . . . . . . . . . . . . King World Productions
King, Sara . . . . . . . . . . . . . . . . . . . . . . . . New Line Cinema
Kingrey, Connie . . . . . . . . . . . . . . . . Wildsmith Entertainment
Kirakosian, Jamie . . . . . . . . . . . . . . . . . Suntaur Entertainment
Kiratsoulis, Richard . . . . . . . . . . . . . . . . . . . MDP Worldwide
Kirk, Ryan . . . . . . . . . . . . . . Concorde/New Horizons Corp.
Kirkham, Julie . . . . . . . . . . . . . . . . . . . . . . . A Band Apart
Kirkpatrick, David . . . . . . . . . . . . . . . . Original Voices, Inc.
Kirkpatrick, Douglas . . . . . . . . . . . . . . . Original Voices, Inc.
Kirman, Roger . . . . . . . . . . . . . . . . . . . Big Ticket Television
Kirschenbaum, Jennifer . . . . . . . . . . . . . . . RKO Pictures, Inc.
Kirschner, David . . . . . . . . . . . . . . Kirschner Prods., David
Kirschner, Dick . . . . . . . . . . . . . . . . . . . . CBS Entertainment
Kirshbaum, Jeff . . . . . . . . . . . . . . . . . . . . . Cafe Productions
Kirven, Cindy . . . . . . . . . . . . . . . . Newmarket Capital Group
Kissinger, David . . . . . . . . . . . . . . . . Studios USA Television
Kistler, Martin . . . . . . . . . . . . . . . . . . . . . . . . Lux Pictures
Kitt, Sam . . . . . . . . . . . . . 40 Acres & A Mule Filmworks Inc.
Kiwitt, Peter . . . . . . . . . Metro-Goldwyn-Mayer/Worldwide TV
Klasky, Arlene . . . . . . . . . . . . . . . . . . . . . . Klasky Csupo Inc.
Kleeman, Jeff . . . . . . . . . . . . . . . . . . United Artists Pictures
Kleid, Debra J. . . . . . . . . . . . . . . . . . . . . . . . . Roxaboxen
Kleiman, Janie . . . . . . . . . . . Twentieth Century Fox Television
Klein, Allen . . . . . . . . . . . . . . . . Keller Entertainment Group
Klein, Amanda . . . . . . . . . . . . . . . . . . . . . . . October Films
Klein, Barbara . . . . . . . . . . . . . . . . . . . . . . . Forrester Films
Klein, Beth . . . . . . . . . . . . . . . . . . . . . . . Viacom Productions
Klein, Devin . . . . . . . . . . . . . . . . Carlyle Prods. & Mgmt.
Klein, Diane . . . . . . . . . . . . . . . . . . Fox Television Studios
Klein, Gregg . . . . . . . . . . . . . . . . . . . . STF Productions, Inc.
Klein, Howard . . . . . . . . . . . . . . . . . . . . 3 Arts Entertainment
Klein, J.J. . . . . . . . . . . . . . . . . . . . . . . . . . . . . Team Todd
Klein, Jennifer . . . . . . . . . . . . . . . . . . . . . . . . . . Bay Films
Klein, Paul . . . . . . . . . . . . . . . . . . . . . . . . . . SPRINGTIME!
Kleinbart, Philip . . . . . . . . . . . . . Greenwald Prods., Robert
Kleinman, Matt . . . . . . . . . . . . . . . . . . Big Sky Entertainment
Kleinman, Stuart . . . . . . . . . . . . . . . . . . . . . . . . Egg Pictures
Kleiser, Randal . . . . . . . . . . . . . . . . . Kleiser Prods., Randal
Kleven, Valli . . . . . . . . . . . . . . . . . . . . . Shatter Glass Prods.
Kline, Adam . . . . . . . . . . . . . . . . . . Kline Productions, Adam
Kline, Elizabeth . . . . . . . . . . . . . . . . Little Bear Films, Inc.
Kline, Robert D. . . . . . . . . . . . . . . . . . . . . TAE Productions
Klinenberg, Randy . . . . . . . . . . . . . . . . . . Movie Group, The
Klion, Jenny . . . . . . . . . . . . . . . . . . . Henson Pictures, Jim
Klubeck, Richard . . . . . . . . . . . . . . . . . Morgan Creek Prods.
Klyusner, Alex . . . . . . . . . . . . . . Cinequanon Pictures Intl. Inc.
Knapp, Ann . . . . . . . . . . . . . . . . . . . . . . Saban Entertainment
Knell, Catalaine . . . . . . . . . . . . . . . . . . . . . . . cTonic Fliks
Knell, Gary . . . . . . . . . . . . . . . Children's Television Workshop
Knight, Christopher W. . . . . . . . . . . . . . . . Knight Company, The
Knight, Sarah . . . . . . . . . . . . . . . Shapiro Productions, Robert
Knowles, Emmanuel . . . . . . . . . Mary Ann-LaGlo Productions
Knox, Travis . . . . . . . . . . . . . . . . . . . . Storyline Entertainment
Kobayashi, Mike . . . . . . . . . . . . . . . . . . . . HSI Entertainment
Koch Jr., Howard W. "Hawk" . . . . . . . . . . . . . . Koch Co., The
Koch, Mark W. . . . . . . . . . . . . . . . . . . . . . . Prelude Pictures
Kochoff, Anya . . . . . . . . . . . . . . . . Davis Entertainment Co.
Koegel, Michael . . . . . . . . . . . . . . . . . . . . FX Networks, LLC
Koenig, Teresa . . . . . . . . . National Geographic Television
Koenigsberg, Neil . . . . . . . . . . . . . . . . . . . . AsIs Productions
Koepple, Sarah . . . . . . . . . . . . . Alexander/Enright & Assocs.
Koffler, Pamela . . . . . . . . . . . . . . . . . . . . . . Killer Films, Inc.
Koga, David . . . . . . . . . . . . . . . . . . . . . . . . . Sandollar Prods.
Kogan, Taedra . . . . . . . . . . . . . . . . . . . Dinamo Entertainment
Koh, Aghi . . . . . . . . . Morra, Brezner, Steinberg & Tenenbaum
Koh, Wei . . . . . . . . . . . . . . . . . . . . . . . . . . . . First Light
Kohler, Warren . . . . . . . . . . . . . . . . Mendillo/Form Productions
Kohn, Jerry . . . . . . . . . . . . . . . Atmosphere Entertainment Inc.
Kohn, Michael . . . . . . . . . . . . . . Columbia TriStar Television
Kohnert, Mary . . . . . . . . . . . . . . . . . . . . Via Rosa Productions
Kolar, Evzen . . . . . . . . . . . . . . . . . . Kolar Productions, Inc.
Kolde, Kevin . . . . . . . . . . . . . . . . . . . . . . . . . . . . Spumco

# CROSS-REFERENCED NAMES

| | |
|---|---|
| Lane, Jennifer | Neo Motion Pictures, Inc. |
| Lane, Julie | George Street Pictures |
| Lane, Robert | Weisberg Prods., Roni |
| Lang, David | Broadway Video (NY) |
| Lang, Rocky | Harbor Lights Productions |
| Lange, Jeanne M. | StoneRoad Prods. Inc. |
| Langley, Donna | New Line Cinema |
| Langley, John | Langley Prods. |
| Langlois, Jennifer | Uplinger Enterprises |
| Lanier, Amy | Flat Penny Films |
| Lansbury, Angela | Corymore Prods. |
| Lansing, Sherry | Paramount Pictures- Motion Picture Group |
| Lantos, Robert | Alliance Pictures |
| Lanza Jr., John W. | Hyperion Entertainment |
| Lapara, Jerome | Island-In-The-Sky Pictures |
| LaPenna, Nick | Leach Ent. Enterprises, Inc. |
| Lapin, Chris | Konrad Pictures |
| LaPolla, Joe | History Channel, The |
| Lapuk, Steve | Brownhouse Productions |
| Lara, Joanne | Goldstreet Pictures Inc. |
| Largent, Lewis | MTV Networks |
| Larner, Drew | Morgan Creek Prods. |
| Larrivee, Lisa | Filmsmith |
| Larroquette, John | Port Street Films |
| Larson, Kristin | Parkway Productions |
| Larson, Steve | Hart Entertainment |
| Laserson, David | World Film Services, Inc. |
| Lasher, Estelle | Lasher, McManus & Robinson |
| Laskay, Jason | Laskay Drive |
| Lassally, Tom | Warner Bros. Pictures |
| Lasseter, John | Pixar Animation Studios |
| Lassiter, James | Overbrook Entertainment |
| Lathan, Stan | Def Pictures |
| Latiner, Michael | Team Entertainment Group |
| Latter, Robyn | Weisworld Premieres |
| Lauer, Joe | Pet Fly Prods. |
| Laughlin, Dana | Lifetime Television (LA) |
| Lauren, Andrew | Lauren Productions, Andrew |
| Lautanen, Michelle | Twentieth Century Fox Television |
| LaVaccare, MJ | Fox Broadcasting Co. |
| Laven, Arnold | Levy-Gardner-Laven Prods. |
| Laventhall, Donald | Red Wagon Prods. |
| Lavery Jr., Emmet G. | Taffner Entertainment Ltd. |
| Lavery, Kim | Threshold Entertainment |
| Lavin, David | Viacom Productions |
| Lavin, Linda | Lavin Entertainment Group |
| Law, Laura | Solt Productions, Andrew |
| Law, Lindsay | Twentieth Century Fox-Searchlight Picts. |
| Lawless, Eamonn | Wolf Films, Fred |
| Lawlor, Joe | Hearst Entertainment |
| Lawrence, Barbara | Black, Lawrence & Silverhardt Ent. |
| Lawrence, C'esca | Snow Leopard Productions |
| Lawrence, Martin | You Go Boy Productions |
| Lawrence, Michael | Krainin Productions Inc. |
| Lawrence, Robert | Maysville Pictures |
| Lawrence, Robert B. | You Go Boy Productions |
| Layne, Cooper | HorsePower Entertainment |
| Lazar, Andrew | Mad Chance |
| Lazar, Ava | Tarnoff/Lazar & Co. |
| Lazar, Robert | Norah Films |
| Lazzo, Mike | Cartoon Network |
| Leach, Robin | Leach Ent. Enterprises, Inc. |
| Leahy, Lori | Neo Motion Pictures, Inc. |
| Leahy, Mike | Neo Motion Pictures, Inc. |
| Leake, Craig | Scripps Howard Prods. |
| Lear, Norman | Act III Productions |
| Leary, Denis | Apostle Pictures |
| Leary, Kerry | Castle Rock Entertainment |
| Lebel, Lissa | Granada Film |
| LeBlanc, Kelly | Thompson Organization, Larry |
| Leblang, Steve | Fox Kids Network |
| Lechner, Jack | Miramax Films |
| LeDrew, Gaille | Chesler/Perlmutter Production |
| Ledworth, Simon | Hassitt Films, Nicholas |
| Lee, Andrew | Rastar Productions |
| Lee, Bryan | Columbia Pictures |
| Lee, Christopher | Columbia Pictures |
| Lee, Dabney | All Girl Prods. |
| Lee, Damon | Metro-Goldwyn-Mayer Pictures |
| Lee, David | Grub Street Prods. |
| Lee, Debra | Black Entertainment TV |
| Lee, Grant | Hit & Run Productions, Inc. |
| Lee, Kevin | TriCoast Entertainment |
| Lee, Michele | Lee Productions, Michele |
| Lee, Pat Tourk | Moffitt-Lee Prods. |
| Lee, Preston | Sticks And Stones |
| Lee, Rob | Elephant Walk Entertainment |
| Lee, Roy | Alphaville |
| Lee, Spike | 40 Acres & A Mule Filmworks Inc. |
| Lee, Stan | Marvel Studios |
| Lee, Susan D. | NBC Entertainment |
| Leed, Rick | Wind Dancer Prod. Group |
| Leeds, Linda | Merko Motion Pictures |
| Leeds, Liza | Scherick Assocs., Edgar J. |
| Leenders, Serge | Takoma Entertainment Group |
| Leeper, Susan | ABC Entertainment |
| Lees-Gonzalez, Laurel | RKO Pictures, Inc. |
| Leeves, Jane | Bristol Cities |
| LeFauve, Meg | Egg Pictures |
| Leff Pressman, Holly | Universal Television & Networks Group |
| Leffelman, Robert | Skyfish Productions |
| Lefkon, Roger | Merv Griffin Productions |
| Lefkowitz, Nancy | Tribeca Productions |
| Lefleur, Rachel | Dancing Asparagus Prods. |
| LeFrak, Francine | LeFrak Prods. |
| Lefranc, Jean-Martial | No Prisoners |
| Leguizamo, John | Lower East Side Films |
| Lehman, Naomi | Carlson-Lehman Prods. |
| Leibovit, Arnold | Talking Rings Entertainment |
| Leichter, Jon | PDQ Directions, Inc. |
| Leichter, Leo | PDQ Directions, Inc. |
| Leider, Jerry | Leider Co., The Jerry |
| Leifer, Stephanie | ABC Entertainment |
| Leighton, Michael W. | America National Network, Inc. |
| Leipheimer, Erica | Tudor Entertainment, Inc. |
| Leipzig, Adam | Terra Bella Entertainment |
| Leland Jr., Jed | Intl. Home Entertainment |
| Lemberger, Kenneth | Columbia Pictures |
| Lemberger, Kenneth | Columbia TriStar Motion Picture Group |
| Lemchen, Bob | Fox Television Studios |
| LeMel, Gary | Warner Bros. Pictures |
| Lemisch, Amy | Parkway Productions |
| Lemley, Jim | Icon Productions Inc. |
| Lenders, Nina | Flower Films, Inc. |
| Lenig, Christine | Cosgrove-Meurer Prods. |
| Lenser, Susan | Main Line Pictures |
| Lenzner, Emily | Blue Relief, Inc. |
| Leo, Malcolm | Leo Productions, Malcolm |
| Leonard, Brett | Filmlight |
| Leonard, Cassandra | HSX Films, Inc. |
| Leong, Nelson | Sweetpea Entertainment |
| Lerman, Phil | STF Productions, Inc. |
| Lerner, Avi | Nu Image |
| Lerner, Stuart | Mercury-Jet Pictures |
| Lescure, Pierre | Canal+ (U.S.) |
| Leshem, Matti | Cobalt Moon |
| Leshnick, Jennifer | Roth/Arnold Prods. |
| Leslie, Jack | Twentieth Century Fox-Fox 2000 (LA) |
| Lessans, Gregory | Rudin Prods., Scott |
| Lesser, Seymour | A & E Television Networks |
| Lesser, Seymour | History Channel, The |
| Lester, Heidi | Summit Entertainment |
| Lester, Mark L. | American World Pictures |
| Letizia, Vicki | Showtime Networks Inc. |
| Leto, Roseanne | TeleVest |
| Letterman, David | Worldwide Pants Incorporated |
| Lettes, Louis | Turner Original Productions |
| Letton, Valerie | aMuse Productions |
| Levant, Brian | Telvan Productions |
| Leveson, John M. | Utopia Films |
| Levi, Jo | Foundry Film Partners |
| Levi, Robert | Turner Entertainment Group |
| Levin, Daniel | Platform Entertainment |
| Levin, Drew S. | Team Entertainment Group |
| Levin, Gail | Disney Telefilms |
| Levin, Jonathan C. | Spelling Television, Inc. |
| Levin, Jordan | W.B. Television Network |
| Levin, Karen E. | Artisan Entertainment |
| Levin, Shira | Cappa Productions |
| Levin, Susan | Threshold Entertainment |

# CROSS-REFERENCED NAMES

Levin, Wayne .................... Trimark Pictures
Levine, Barry .......... Takoma Entertainment Group
Levine, Ben ......... Seven Summits Pictures & Mgmt.
Levine, Dan ..................... New Regency Prods.
Levine, David J. ..................... Konrad Pictures
LeVine, Deborah Joy ............... Kedzie Productions
Levine, Ellen .................. Viewpoint Productions
Levine, Gary ...... Warner Bros. Television Productions
Levine, Jeff ........................... Saturn Films
Levine, Jeffrey ........ Turner Network Television (TNT)
Levine, Lauren ...................... MTV Networks
Levine, Leslie M. ....... Hearst Ent. Licensing & Family Prog.
Levine, Mark .................. Manifest Film Company
Levine, Michael P. ..... Enlightened Witness, Inc./Levine Mgmt.
Levine, Thomas ..... Paramount Pictures- Production Division
Levinsky, Laura .......... Columbia TriStar Television
Levinsohn, Gary ..................... Mutual Film Co.
Levinson, Barry .......... Baltimore/Spring Creek Pictures, LLC
Levinson, Barry ...... Levinson/Fontana Company, LLC, The
Levinson, Josh ......................... Jersey Films
Levinson, Karen ................. HBO NYC Productions
Levinson, Mark ...................... Levinson, Mark
Levinson, Randy .................. Studios USA Pictures
Levinson, Robert .............. Intl. Home Entertainment
Levinson, Ron ...................... Levinson Prods., Ron
Levinson, Sandra S. ............ Intl. Home Entertainment
Levisetti, Emile ....... Twentieth Century Fox Television
Levitan, Josh .............. Ministry of Film Inc., The
Levitt, Zane W. .............. Zeta Entertainment Ltd.
Levoff, John ........ United Paramount Network (UPN)
Levy, Ariel ................. Snow Leopard Productions
Levy, Barbara ................. Levy/Weiss Productions
Levy, Barry ..................... Nelvana Entertainment
Levy, Debbie .................... Mostow/Lieberman
Levy, Frederick ................ Katz Prods., Marty
Levy, Jeff ......... Singer Entertainment, Joseph M.
Levy, John S. ..................... Columbia Pictures
Levy, Jules ................. Levy-Gardner-Laven Prods.
Levy, Jules A. ............... Revelations Entertainment
Levy, Lawrence ...................... Catapult Films
Levy, Lawrence B. ........... Pixar Animation Studios
Levy, Michael I. ................ Crosby/Levy Co., The
Levy, Robert ..................... NBC Entertainment
Levy, Robert L. ................... Tapestry Films Inc.
Levy, Shuki .................... Saban Entertainment
Lew, Jeff ...................... Mostow/Lieberman
Lew, Jeremy .............. Mount Royal Entertainment
Lew, Scott ....................... Beacon Pictures
Lewin, Deborah ................. Curtis Prods., Dan
Lewis, Alan ............. Hallmark Entertainment (NY)
Lewis, Andrew .......... Warner Bros. TV Animation
Lewis, Brad ...................... Pacific Data Images
Lewis, Claudia ...... Twentieth Century Fox-Searchlight Picts.
Lewis, Jim .................. Henson Company, Jim
Lewis, Joe ......................... Tri-Crown Prods.
Lewis, Kira .................. Fresh Produce Company
Lewis, Lenore R. ................ Gordon Prods., Dan
Lewis, Lisa ...... Warner Bros. Television Productions
Lewis, Marjorie ................... FGM Entertainment
Lewis, Martin ........................ SPRINGTIME!
Lewis, Michael ......... Shadowcatcher Entertainment
Lewis, Michael D. ................ New Line Cinema
Lewis, Patricia ..................... Brooksfilms, Ltd.
Lewis, Paul ...................... Fox Broadcasting Co.
Lewis, Richard ......... Interscope Communications Inc.
Lewis, Richard Barton ...... Trilogy Entertainment Group
Lewis, Simon R. ................ Lewis Prods., Simon
Lewis, Steven ................... Mandalay Television
Lexton, Lauren ............... Film Garden Entertainment
Ley, Brad ...................... Outlaw Productions
Lezama, Suzanna ....... Mase/Kaplan Productions, Inc.
Li, Rowena ................. Fortune Media Group, Inc.
Liber, Rodney ................. Blue Bay Productions
Lichstein, Laura .............. Lobell-Bergman Prods.
Licht, Andrew ................ Licht/Mueller Film Corp.
Lichtman, Jordan ................. Bubble Factory, The
Liddell, Mickey .................. Banner Entertainment
Lieber, Mark ...................... PolyGram Television
Lieberman, Hal .................... Mostow/Lieberman
Lieberman, Larry ..................... Comedy Central

Lieberman, Robert .......... Crystal Beach Entertainment
Lieblein, Dan ......................... October Films
Liebling, Deborah ................... Comedy Central
Liebman, Brett A. ................ Playtime Productions
Lifton, Stacy ....................... Fox Kids Network
Lighter, Gwen ........................ Vanguard Films
Lightstone, Ron ...................... NewStar Media
Lignier, Sharon .......... Castle Rock Entertainment
Lilliston, Bruce St. J. ............... Kushner-Locke Co.
Lima, Shirley .............. Sonnenfeld/Josephson
Limm, Cristi ...................... Mandeville Films
Lin, Teresa ....................... Yerkovich Prods.
Linardos, George .................... Red Hour Films
Linck, Daniel ...................... Loganworks Ltd.
Lincoln, Bill .................. Pearson All American
Lincoln, Catherine ................ Georgian Bay Prods.
Lindelof, Damon .................. Ladd Company, The
Lindeman, Doug ...................... Film Kitchen
Lindenbaum, Michael .......... Midnight Sun Pictures
Lindheim, Richard ........ Paramount Television Group
Lindstrom, Lisa .................... Avnet-Kerner Co.
Lingg, Kathy .......... Paramount Network Television
Lingner, Yun ........................... FilmRoos
Linke, Katharine .................. Di Bona Prods., Vin
Linson, Art ..................... Knickerbocker Films
Linson, John ................... Knickerbocker Films
Lipa, Joe ....................... Apostle Pictures
Lipari, Greg .......... Miracle Productions, Inc.
Lipman, Daniel .................... Cowlip Productions
Lipman, Joel ....... Sachnoff-Lipman Entertainment
Lipper, Ken .................. Lipper Productions, Ken
Lipstone, Howard .................. Landsburg Co., The
Lipton, James .................. Lipton Prods., James
Lipton, Leslie ....................... Krost/Chapin
Lipton, Leslie .................... Landsburg Co., The
Liroff, Marci .................. Liroff Productions, Marci
Lischak, William ...... First Look Picts./Overseas Filmgroup
Liska, Kathy .......... Donner/Shuler-Donner Prods.
Liss, Walter .................. Buena Vista Productions
List, Patrick .................. Hill Productions, Debra
Lister, Paul ...................... DreamWorks SKG
Little, Ellen ...... First Look Picts./Overseas Filmgroup
Little, Robert ...... First Look Picts./Overseas Filmgroup
Littlefield, Warren ................. NBC Entertainment
Littman, Jonathan .......... Bruckheimer Films, Jerry
Litto, Andria .................. George Litto Pictures
Litto, George .................. George Litto Pictures
Lituchy, Todd ........ United Paramount Network (UPN)
Litvack, John ............. W.B. Television Network
Litvack, Sanford .......... Walt Disney Company, The
Litvak, Alex ...................... Outlaw Productions
Litvinoff, Si .................. Litvinoff Productions, Si
Lively, Jennifer ..................... Skylark Films Ltd.
Livingston, Vanessa ............... Tavel Entertainment
Lloyd, Christopher ................. Grub Street Prods.
Lloyd, Lauren ..................... Columbia Pictures
Lloyd, Robinette L. ............ Too Nuts Productions, Ltd.
Lobell, Mike .................... Lobell-Bergman Prods.
LoCascio, Stephen .......... CinePoint Productions, Inc.
LoCascio, Steven .............. King World Productions
Locke, Peter ...................... Kushner-Locke Co.
Loesch, Margaret ............. Henson Company, Jim
Logan, Bob ...................... Loganworks Ltd.
Logan, Leroy .................... Phase I Productions
Logan, Lisa .............. Equinox Entertainment Ltd.
Logan-Torres, Shannon ..... Levinson/Fontana Company, LLC, The
Logigian, John .................. Doumanian Prods., Jean
Loh, Grace ................... New Crime Productions
Loman, Michael .......... Children's Television Workshop
Lombardo, Michael .......... HBO Original Programming
Lombardo, Nick .......... Turner Network Television (TNT)
Lombardo, Robin .......... Action America Entertainment
London, Barry ................. London Company, Barry
London, Robby ..................... DIC Entertainment
Long, Kim .......... Turner Network Television (TNT)
Longenecker, John .................. Live Action Pictures
Longi, Steven A. ................ Permut Presentations
Loos, Rob ....................... TLC Entertainment
Loparco, Elissa ................... New Regency Prods.
Lopker, Patrick T. ..................... Disney Channel

# CROSS-REFERENCED NAMES

Lorber, Marc . . . . . . . . . . . . . . . . . . . . . . . . . . . Phoenix Pictures
Lord, Tony . . . . . . . . . . . . . . . . . . . . . . . . . . Lord/Weaver Prods.
Lorenz, Carsten . . . . . . . . . . . . . . . . . . . . Miranda Entertainment
Loring, Lynn . . . . . . . . . . . . . . . . . . . . . Loring Productions, Lynn
Loubert, Patrick . . . . . . . . . . . . . . . . . . . . . Nelvana Entertainment
Loughran, Kim . . . . . . . . . . . . . . . . . . View Askew Productions, Inc.
Louis, Margret . . . . . . . . . . . . . . . . Hallmark Entertainment (NY)
Louthan, Guy J. . . . . . . . . . . . . . . . . . . . . . . . . . Utopia Films
Lovas, Jason . . . . . . . . . . . . . . . . . . . . . . . Filmopolis Pictures
Lovas, Zachary . . . . . . . . . . . . . . . . . . . . . . Filmopolis Pictures
Love, Sandi . . . . . . . . . . . . . . . . . . . . . . . Elkins Entertainment
Lovell, Dyson . . . . . . . . . . . . . . . . . . . . . . . . . Lovell, Dyson
Lovinger, Joanna . . . . . . . . . . . . . . . Epstein Productions, Stefanie
Lovitz, Jon . . . . . . . . . . . . . . . . . . . . Master Thespian Productions
Lowe, Gary A. . . . . . . . . . . . . . . . . America National Network, Inc.
Lowe, Kristin . . . . . . . . . . . . . . . . . . . . . . . . . . . Bay Films
Lowry, Hunt . . . . . . . . . . . . . . . . . . . . . . Lowry Productions, Hunt
Lowry, Richard . . . . . . . . . . . . . . . . . . . . . Legend Entertainment
Lubaroff, Rick . . . . . . . . . . . . . . . . . Illusion Entertainment Group
Luber, Matt . . . . . . . . . . . . . . . . . . . . Diamond Heart Productions
Lubin, Aaron . . . . . . . . . . . . . . . . . . . . . . Kopelson Entertainment
Lubin, Joel . . . . . . . . . . . . . . . . . . . . . . . Kingsgate Films, Inc.
Lucai, Victoria . . . . . . . . . . . . . . . . . . . . . . . . . A Band Apart
Lucas, Gus . . . . . . . . . . . . . . . . . . . . . . . . Fox Family Channel
Lucas, Jon . . . . . . . . . . . . . . . . . . . . . Petrie Jr. & Co., Daniel
Lucas, Victoria . . . . . . . . . . . . . . . . . . . . . . . . . . . Signature
Lucchesi, Gary . . . . . . . . . . . . . . . . . . . . Lucchesi Prods., Gary
Luchs, Jay . . . . . . . . . . . . . . . . United Paramount Network (UPN)
Lucken, Kimberlyn M. . . . . . . . . . . . . Krane Group, The Jonathan
Luddy, Tom . . . . . . . . . . . . . . . . . . . . . . . American Zoetrope
Ludlow, Graham . . . . . . . . . . . . . . . . Erratic Entertainment, Inc.
Ludovico, Teka . . . . . . . . . . . . . . . . . . . . . . . . . . Media Four
Ludwig, Susannah . . . . . . . . . . . . . . . . . . . . . . Giv'en Films
Ludwig, Tony . . . . . . . . . . . . . . . . . . . Riche/Ludwig Productions
Ludwin, Richard . . . . . . . . . . . . . . . . . . . . . NBC Entertainment
Luff, Brad . . . . . . . . . . . . . . . . . . . . . . . . . . . Original Film
Luger, Lois . . . . . . . . . . . . . . . . Luger Productions, Inc., Lois
Lumi Morgan, Marika . . . . . . . . . . . . . . . . . . . Patriot Pictures
Lund, Mary . . . . . . . . . . . . . . . . . . . . . . . . . . Winkler Films
Lundgren, Dolph . . . . . . . . . . . . . . . . . . . . . . . Thor Pictures
Lupariello, Joe . . . . . . . . . . . . . . Gibbons Enterprises, Leeza
Lupovitz, Dan . . . . . . . . . . . . . . . . . . . . . . . Lupovitz Prods.
Lurie, Jeffrey . . . . . . . . . . . . . . . . . . . . . Chestnut Hill Prods.
Lusitana, Donna E. . . . . . . Greystone Communications Group, Inc.
Lusk, Alice H. . . . . . . . . . . . . . . . . . . . . . . . Universal Studios
Lussier, Paul . . . . . . . . . . . . . . . . . . . . . . . . . Lussier, Paul
Lustgarten, Steve . . . . . . . . . . . . . . . . . . . . . . . . Leo Films
Lustig, William . . . . . . . . . . . . . . Magnum Motion Pictures, Inc.
Lux, Dan . . . . . . . . . . . . . . . . . . . . . . . Di Bona Prods., Vin
Lyles, A.C. . . . . . . . . . . . . . . . . . . . . . . . Lyles Prods., A.C.
Lynch Jr., Vernon . . . . . . . . . . . . . . . . . . Murphy Prods., Eddie
Lynch, David . . . . . . . . . . . . . . . . . . . . Picture Factory, The
Lynch, John . . . . . . . . . . . . . . . . . . . . . . Lynch Entertainment
Lynch, Tom . . . . . . . . . . . . . . . . . . . . . . . Lynch Entertainment
Lyne, Susan . . . . . . . . . . . . . . . . . . . . . . . ABC Entertainment
Lynn, Anthony J. . . . . . . . . . . Playboy Entertainment Group Inc.
Lynn, Brandy . . . . . . . . . . . . . . . . . . . . . . Lynch Entertainment
Lynn, Jenny . . . . . . . . . . . . . . . . . . Weintraub Prods., Jerry
Lynn, Julie . . . . . . . . . . . . . . . . . . . . . . Fresh Produce Company
Lynn, Richard . . . . . . . . . . . . . . . . . . . . . . . . . USA Networks
Lynn, Tami . . . . . . . . . . . . . . . . . . . Lynn Productions, Tami
Lynn-Nash, Helene . . . . . . . . . . . . . . . Anderson Prods., Craig
Lynne, Michael . . . . . . . . . . . . . . . . . . . . . New Line Cinema
Lyon, Gail . . . . . . . . . . . . . . . . . . . . . . . . . . . Jersey Films
Lyons, Ann . . . . . . . . . . . . . . . . . . IFM Film Associates, Inc.
Lyons, Jackie . . . . . . . . . . . . . . . . . . . . . . . ABC Entertainment
Lyons, Joseph T. . . . . . . . . . . . . . . . . Pamplin-Fisher Company
Lyons, Sidney H. . . . . . . . . . . . . . . . . . . . . CBS Entertainment
Lyttle, Larry . . . . . . . . . . . . . . . . . . . . . Big Ticket Television
Maatta, John . . . . . . . . . . . . . . . . . . W.B. Television Network
MacArthur, Doug . . . . . . . . . . . . . . . . Pachyderm Entertainment
MacCurdy, Jean . . . . . . . . . . . . . . . . Warner Bros. TV Animation
MacDonald, Laurie . . . . . . . . . . . . . . . . . . . DreamWorks SKG
MacDonald, Patty . . . . . . . . . . . . . . Cort/Madden Company, The
Macdonald, William J. . . . . . . . . . . . . . . . . MacDonald Prods
Mace, Dave . . . . . . . . . . . . . . . . . . . . . . Storyline Entertainment
Machlovitch, Beth . . . . . . . . Walt Disney Pictures/Touchstone Pictures
Macht, Jon . . . . . . . . . . . . . . . . . . . . . Macht Ent. Group, Inc.
Macias, Stephen F. . . . . . . . . . . . . . . . . Crosby/Levy Co., The
Macisco, Renee . . . . . . . . . . . . . . . . . . . . P.A.T. Productions

Mack, Christina . . . . . . . . . . . . . . . United Paramount Network (UPN)
Mack, Karen . . . . . . . . . . . Goldsmith Entertainment Company
Mack, Linda . . . . . . . . . . . . . . . . . . . . . . . . Beacon Pictures
Mackay, Anne-Marie . . . . . . . . . . . . . . . . . . . Palomar Pictures
MacKay, Catherine . . . . . . . . . . . . . . . . . . Pearson All American
Mackenzie, Fiona . . . . . . . . . . Turman-Morrissey Company, The
MacKenzie, Gillian . . . . . . . . . . . . Startz Productions, Inc., Jane
MacLeod-Hunter, Neill . . . . . . . . . . Scherick Assocs., Edgar J.
MacNair, Swanna . . . . . . . . . . . . . . . . . . . . Avnet-Kerner Co.
Maday, Charles . . . . . . . . . . . . . . . . . . . . History Channel, The
Maday, Gregg . . . . . . . . Warner Bros. Television Productions
Maddalena, Marianne . . . . . . . . . . . . . . . . Craven Films, Wes
Madden, David . . . . . . . . . . . . . . . Cort/Madden Company, The
Madden, Laura . . . . . . . . . . . . . . . . . . . . . . . Miramax Films
Madden, Molly . . . . . . . . . . . . . . . . . . . . 3 Arts Entertainment
Madden, Paul . . . . . . . . . . . . . . . . . Litvinoff Productions, Si
Maddock, Brent . . . . . . . . . . . . . . . . . Stampede Entertainment
Madigan, Alix . . . . . . . . . . . . . . . . . . . . . . . . . Fleece Films
Madonna . . . . . . . . . . . . . . . . . . . . . . . . . . . Madguy Films
Madsen, Bill . . . . . . . . . . . . . . . . . . Madsen Productions, Bill
Maes, Stacy . . . . . . . . . . . . . . . . . . . . Lightstorm Entertainment
Maffeo, Gayle . . . . . . . . . . . . . . . . . . Wind Dancer Prod. Group
Magagni-Seely, Alexis . . . . . . . . . . . . . . . . . . . . . HKM Films
Magar, Guy . . . . . . . . . . . . . . . . . . . . Magar Films, Inc., Guy
Magee, Heather . . . . . . . . . . . . . . . . . Mendel Productions, Barry
Maggioni, Alex . . . . . . . . . . . . . . . . . . . . . . UBU Productions
Magid, Karen . . . . . . . . . . Paramount Pictures- Production Division
Magleby, Monty . . . . . . . . . . . . . . . . . Leucadia Film Corp.
Magnatta, Costantino . . . . . . . . . Mount Olympus Entertainment
Magowan, James . . . . . . . . . . . . . . . . . . . . . . Lux Pictures
Magpiong, Bret . . . . . . . . . . . . . . . . . . . . Bubble Factory, The
Maguire, Ed . . . . . . . . . . . . . . . . . . . . . . . Mutual Film Co.
Mahmoud, Cindy . . . . . . . . . . . . . . . . Black Entertainment TV
Mailer, Michael . . . . . . . . . . . . . . . . . . . . Bigel/Mailer Films
Maio, Juliana . . . . . . . . . . . . . . . . . . . . . Lighthouse Productions
Maitland, Diana K. . . . . . . . . . . . . . . . . . . . . . Marstar Prods.
Maizes, Sarah . . . . . . . . . . . . . . . . . . . . Nelvana Entertainment
Majewski, George . . . . . . . . . . . . . . . . . . Rysher Entertainment
Makowski, Kevin . . . . . . . . . . . . . . . . . . . . Raylin Entertainment
Malacarne, Lou . . . . . . . . . . . . . . . . . Stampede Entertainment
Malaga, Laurie . . . . . . . . . . . . . . . . . . . . . . Propaganda Films
Malanga, Tom . . . . . . . . Metro-Goldwyn-Mayer/Worldwide TV
Malatesta, Catherine . . . . . . Warner Bros. International TV Production
Maliani, Michael . . . . . . . . . . . . . . . . . . . . . DIC Entertainment
Malin, Amir . . . . . . . . . . . . . . . . . . . . . . . Artisan Entertainment
Malina, Maggie . . . . . . . . . . . . . . . . . . . . Pacific Western Prods.
Malkovich, John . . . . . . . . . . . . . . . . . . . . . . . . . . Mr. Mudd
Mallmann, Stephan . . . . . . . . . . Recorded Picture Company
Malone, Nancy . . . . . . . . . . . . . . . . . . . . . . Lilac Productions
Mancini, Billy . . . . . . . . . . . . . . . . . . . . Firestorm Pictures, Ltd.
Mancini, Jennifer . . . . . . . . . . . . . . . Equinox Entertainment Ltd.
Mancuso Jr., Frank . . . . . . . . . . . . . . . . . . . FGM Entertainment
Mancuso, Angela . . . . . . . . . . . . . . . . . . Studios USA Pictures
Mancuso, Frank . . . . . . . . . . Metro-Goldwyn-Mayer Pictures
Mancuso, Frank . . . . . . . . . . . . . . . . . . United Artists Pictures
Mancuso, Renee . . . . . . . . . . . Lakeshore Entertainment Corp.
Mandabach, Caryn . . . . . . . . . . . . . . . Carsey-Werner Co., The
Mandel, David . . . . . . . . . . . Frankovich Prods., Inc., Peter
Mandelbaum, Reeva . . . . . . . . . . . . . . . Wells Productions, John
Mandelberg, Stacy . . . . . . . . . . . . . . . . . Wilshire Court Prods.
Mandell, Dianne . . . . . . . . . . . . . . . . . . Stratum Entertainment
Mandell, Molly . . . . . . . . . . . . . . . . Goepp Circle Productions
Manetti, Carolyn . . . . . . . . . . . . . . . . . . . . . New Line Cinema
Mangan IV, Thomas J. . . . . . . . . . . . . . . . . . River One Films
Manheim, Michael . . . . . . . . . . . . . . . Manheim Company, The
Manis, Brian D. . . . . . . . . . . . . . . . . . . . Peters Entertainment
Mann, Corrinne . . . . . . . . . . . . . . . . . . . . El Dorado Pictures
Mann, Cynthia . . . . . . . . . . . . . . . . Manos Prods., Inc., James
Mann, Dawne . . . . . . . . . . . . . . . Hallmark Entertainment (NY)
Mann, Michael . . . . . . . . . . . . . . . . . . . . . Forward Pass, Inc.
Mannina, Barbara . . . . . . . . . United Paramount Network (UPN)
Manning, Bob . . . . . . . . . . . . . . . . Equinox Entertainment Ltd.
Manning, Michelle . . . . . . . Paramount Pictures- Production Division
Mannion, Barbara . . . . . . . . . . . . . . . Trident Releasing Inc.
Manoogian, Peter . . . . . . . . . . . . . . . . Santa Monica Pictures
Manos Jr., James . . . . . . . . . . Manos Prods., Inc., James
Manriquez, Jenny . . . . . . . . . . . . . . . . First Street Films, Inc.
Mansfield, Pancho . . . . . . . . . . . . . . . Showtime Networks Inc.
Manship, David . . . . . . . . . . . . . . . . . . . . . . . . . Cine Paris
Manson, David . . . . . . . . . . . . . . . . . . . . . . Sarabande Prods.

McDermott, Eileen . . . . . . . . . . . . . . . . . . . Paulson Prods., Daniel L.
McDermott, Kathy . . . . . . . . . Columbia TriStar Motion Picture Group
McDermott, Mickey . . . . . . . . . . . . . . . . . . . . . Estevez Productions
McDermott, Sean . . . . . . . . . . . . . . . . . . . Myron Productions, Ben
McDonald, Carolyn . . . . . . . . . . . . . . . . . . . . . . Carrie Productions
McDonald, John . . . . . . . . . . . . . . . . . . . . . . Twentieth Television
McDonald, Mary-Liz . . . . . . . . . . . . . . Hallmark Entertainment (NY)
McDonald, Mike . . . . . . . . . . . . . . . . . . . . . Renaissance Pictures
McDonald, Serena . . . . . . . . . . . . . . . Shadowcatcher Entertainment
McDonell, Jenny . . . . . . . . . . . . . . . . . . . . . . . Gekko Film Corp
McDonnell, Courtney . . . . . . . . . . . . . . . . . . . . . . . A Band Apart
McDonnell, Edward L. . . . . . . . . . . . . . . . . . . Witt-Thomas Films
McDonnell, Robert . . . . . . . . . . . . . . . . . . . . . . . Meridian Films
McDougall, Brandi . . . . . . . . . . . . . . . . . . . . . . .Vanguard Films
McDougall, Ian . . . . . . . . . . . . . . Alliance Television Productions
McElroy, Will . . . . . . . . . . . . . . . . . . . . . . Unger Productions Inc.
McElwaine, Guy . . . . . . . . . . . . . . . . . Trilogy Entertainment Group
McEnroe, Katie . . . . . . . . . American Movie Classics/Romance Classic
McEveety, Steve . . . . . . . . . . . . . . . . . . . . . Icon Productions Inc.
McFadden, Jonathan . . . . . . . . . . . . . . Baldwin/Cohen Productions
McFadzean, David . . . . . . . . . . . . . . . . .Wind Dancer Prod. Group
McFeely, Steve . . . . . . . . . . . . . . . . . . Tollin/Robbins Productions
McFetridge, George . . . . . . . . . . . . . . . . . . . Brillstein-Grey Ent.
McGahey, Michael . . . . . . . . . . . . . . . . . . . . Friendly Productions
McGarry, Mark . . . . . . . . . . . . . . . . . . . . . . . Phoenician Films
McGauley, Victor . . . . . . . . . . . . . . . . . . . . . . . . Amen Ra Films
McGee, Lara . . . . . . . . . . . . . . . . . . . . . . . . . Gerren Productions
McGee, Trish . . . . . . . . . . . . . . . . . . . . . Scripps Howard Prods.
McGhee-Lazarou, Charisse . . . . . . . . . . . . . . . . NBC Entertainment
McGinley, John C. . . . . . . . . . . . . . . . . . . . . . . River One Films
McGinnis, J.R. . . . . . . . . . . . . . . . Paramount Network Television
McGinnis, Scott . . . . . . . . . . . . . . . . . . . . . . . 360 entertainment
McGivern, Fran . . . . . . . . . . . . . . . . . . . . . Pacifica Entertainment
McGloin, Ian . . . . . . . . . . . . . . . . . . . . . . . Rudin Prods., Scott
McGorrian, Carole . . . . . . . . . . . . . . Initial Entertainment Group
McGrail, Ann . . . . . . . . . . . . . . . . . . . . . . . . . . CBS Productions
McGrath, Judith . . . . . . . . . . . . . . . . . . . . . . . . MTV Networks
McGrath, Thomas . . . . . . . . . . . . . . . Viacom Entertainment Group
McGuire, Ginger . . . . . . . . . . . . . . . . . . Scholastic Entertainment
McGuire, John . . . . . . . . . . . . . . . . . . . . . . . . . . ABC Pictures
McGuirk, Terence . . . . . . . . . . . . . . Turner Entertainment Group
McGurk, Chris . . . . . . . . . . . . . . . . . . . . . . . Universal Pictures
McHale, Judith . . . . . . . . . . . . . . . . . . . . . . . Discovery Networks
McHenry, Doug . . . . . . . . . . . . . . . Elephant Walk Entertainment
McHoul, Kary . . . . . . . . . . . Warner Bros. Television Productions
McHugh, Amanda . . . . . . . . . . . . . . . . . . . . . . Blue Relief, Inc.
McHugh, Jon . . . . . . . . . . . . . . . . . . . . . . . . New Line Cinema
McIntyre, Pamela . . . . . . . . . . . . . . . . . . . . . . . . 1492 Pictures
McKairnes, Jim . . . . . . . . . . . . . . . . . . . . . . . CBS Entertainment
McKee, John . . . . . . . . . . . . . . . . . . . . . . . . . Caravan Pictures
McKenna, Charlotte . . . . . . . . . . . . . . . . . . . . Hellinger Films
McKenna, Nancy . . . . . . . American Movie Classics/Romance Classic
McKenzie, Dan . . . . . . . . . . . . . . . . Turner Original Productions
McKeown, Andrea . . . . . . . . . AEI-Atchity Edit./Ent. Intl. Inc.
McKewon, Allan . . . . . . . . . . . . . . . . . . . . . Takes On Production
McKigney, Ray . . . . . . . . . . . . . . . . . . . . . . Shelter Entertainment
McKimmie, Ilyse . . . . . . . . . . . . . . . . . . . . . Red Wagon Prods.
McKinnon, Laverne . . . . . . . . . . . . . . . . . . . . CBS Entertainment
McKinven, Mary Jane . . . . . . . . . . . . . . . . . . . . . . . . . . . . PBS
McKissick, Pam . . . . . . . . . . . . . . . McKissick/Gregory Prods.
McLain, Chuck . . . . . . . . . . . . . . . . . . . . C.M. Two Productions
McLaren, Jenny . . . . . . . . . . . . . . . . . . . . . . Mirage Enterprises
McLaughlin, Katie . . . . . . . . . . . . . . HBO Original Programming
McLaughlin, Lauren . . . . . . . . . . . . . . Lions Gate Films Production
McLees, Michael . . . . . . . . . . . . . . . . . . . . . Uplinger Enterprises
McLeroy, Val . . . . . . . . . . . . . . . . . . . . . . . Green/Epstein Prods.
McMahon, John J. . . . . . . . . . . . . . . . . . . . . Wilshire Court Prods.
McMahon, Kevin . . . . . . . . . . . . . . . Village Roadshow Pictures
McMahon, Tom . . . . . . . . . . . . . . . . Turner Original Productions
McManus, Marsha . . . . . . . . . Lasher, McManus & Robinson
McMenamin, Sophie . . . . . . . . . . . . . . . . . . FilmColony, Ltd.
McMinn, Robert . . . . . . . . . . . . . . . . . . . Lucchesi Prods., Gary
McNamara, Bernadette . . . . . . . . . . . . . . Bochco Prods., Steven
McNamara, John . . . . . . . . . . . . . . . . . . Mark Prods., Laurence
McNamara, Sean . . . . . . . . . Brookwell McNamara Entertainment
McNeal, Brian . . . . . . . . . . . . . . . . . . . . . . . . Starlight Pictures
McNeely, Milinda . . . . . . . . . . . . . . . Paramount Network Television
McNeil, Craig . . . . . . . . . . . . . . . .Granada Entertainment USA
McNeill, Angela W. . . . . . . . . . Mulberry Square Productions, Inc.
McNicoll, Liz . . . . . . . . . . . . . .Walt Disney Pictures/Touchstone Pictures

McNulty, Shannon . . . . . . . . . . . . . . . . . . Evans Co., The Robert
McNulty, Tom . . . . . . . . . . . . . . . . . Out of the Blue . . . Entertainment
McPherson, Stephen . . . . . . . . . . . . . . . . . . . . NBC Entertainment
McQuillan, Dara . . . . . . . . . . . . . . . . . . . . . . . . Merchant-Ivory
McRitchie, Greig . . . . . . . . . . . . . . . . . . . . . . . Universal Pictures
McWethy, Cindy . . . . . . . . . . . . . . . . . . . . . . . Beacon Pictures
Mead, Constance . . . . . . . . . . Asseyev Prods. Inc., Tamara
Mead, Shannon . . . . . . . . . . . . . . . . . . . . . . Burrud Productions
Meade, Kim . . . . . . . . . . . . . . . . . . . . . . . . . Periscope Pictures
Meador, Greg . . . . . . . . . . . . . . . . . . . . . . Iwerks Entertainment
Meadow, Cary . . . . . . . . . . . . . . . . . . . . . . . . Dimension Films
Meadow, Cary . . . . . . . . . . . . . . . . . . . . . . . . . Miramax Films
Meagher, Kevin . . . . . . . . . . . . . . . . . . Popular Arts Ent., Inc.
Meany, Maureen . . . . . . . . . . . . . . . . . . Cossette Productions
Mechanic, William . . . . . . . . . . . . . . . . . . Twentieth Century Fox
Medavoy, Brian . . . . . . . . . . . . . . . More/Medavoy Management
Medavoy, Mike . . . . . . . . . . . . . . . . . . . . . . .Phoenix Pictures
Medina, Benny . . . . . . . . . . . . . . . . . . . Handprint Entertainment
Medjuck, Joe . . . . . . . . . . . . . . . . . . . . . Northern Lights Ent.
Meeks, Shawnee . . . . . . . . . . . . . . . O'Hara-Horowitz Productions
Meenaghau, James . . . . . . . . . Walt Disney Pictures/Touchstone Pictures
Meerson, Steve . . . . . . . . . . . . . . . . . . . . . . .Meerson-Krikes
Mehlman, Gary . . . . . . . . . . . . . . . . . . Imageries Entertainment
Meier, Robin . . . . . . . . . . . . . . . . . . . . . . . . Rehme Productions
Meisinger, Louis M. . . . . . . . . . . . Walt Disney Company, The
Meistrich, Larry . . . . . . . . . . . . . . . Shooting Gallery Inc., The
Mejia, Vivien . . . . . . . . . . . . . . . . . . . Goldenring Productions
Mejia, Wayne . . . . . . . . . . . . . . . . Feigelson Prods., Inc., J.D.
Mekrut, John . . . . . . . . . . . . . . . . . . Say Unkel Entertainment
Meledandri, Chris . . . . . . . . . . . . . . . . .Fox Animation Studios
Melendez, Bill . . . . . . . . . . . . . . . . .Melendez Productions, Bill
Mellin, Robyn . . . . . . . . . . . . . . . . .Vista Street Entertainment
Mellner, Shirley . . . . . . . . . . . . . . . . . . . . . . . . .Hollane Corp.
Mellon, Mike . . . . . . . . . . . . . . . . . Paramount Domestic TV
Melniker, Benjamin . . . . . . . . . . . . . . . . Batfilm Prods., Inc.
Melton, Bill . . . . . . . . . . . . . . . . . . . . Sonnenfeld/Josephson
Melton, Cheryl . . . . . . . . . . . . . .Walt Disney TV/Touchstone TV
Meltzer, Benjamin . . . . . . . . . . . .Fries Productions, Inc., Chuck
Meltzer, Howard . . . . . . . . . . . . . . . . . Entertainment Group, The
Meltzer, Michael L. . . . . . . . . . . . .Meltzer Productions, Michael
Memel, Jana Sue . . . . . . . . . . . . . . . . . . . Chanticleer Films
Mendel, Barry . . . . . . . . . . . . . . . Mendel Productions, Barry
Mendelsohn, Carol . . . . . . . . . . . . . . . . . . . . Melrose Prods.
Mendelsohn, Eric . . . . . . . . . . . . . Caruso-Mendelsohn Prods.
Mendelsohn, Michael . . . . . . . . . . . . . . . . . . . Patriot Pictures
Mendez, Robert . . . . . . . . . . . . . . . Paramount Domestic TV
Mendillo, Stephen Tag . . . . . . . . . .Mendillo/Form Productions
Mentres, Agnes . . . . . . . . . . . . . . . . . . . . . . . Miramax Films
Menzies, Kathy . . . . . . . . . . . . . . . . . . . Firebrand Productions
Mercer, William . . . . . . . . . . . . . . .Mount Royal Entertainment
Merchant, Ismail . . . . . . . . . . . . . . . . . . . . . . . Merchant-Ivory
Mercurio, Jim . . . . . . . . . . . . . . . . . . . Montage Entertainment
Merians, Judith . . . . . . . . . . . . . . . . . . . . . Saban Entertainment
Merjos, Stavros . . . . . . . . . . . . . . . . . . . . . . . . HSI Entertainment
Mermet, Stephane . . . . . . . . . . . . . . . . . .Delaware Pictures
Meron, Neil . . . . . . . . . . . . . . . . . . . . . Storyline Entertainment
Merrick, R. . . . . . . . . . . . . . . . . . . . Leo Productions, Malcolm
Merrill, Dina . . . . . . . . . . . . . . . . . . . . . . RKO Pictures, Inc.
Merritt, Tim . . . . . . . . . . . . . . . . . . Snow Leopard Productions
Merschel, Sylvia . . . . . . . . . . . . . . . . . . . Production Services
Meserve, Dete . . . . . . . . . . . . . . . . Wind Dancer Prod. Group
Messer, Arnold . . . . . . . . . . . . . . . . . . . . . . .Phoenix Pictures
Messer, Fran . . . . . . . . . . . . . . . Moress-Nanas-Hart Entertainment
Messick, Jill . . . . . . . . . . . . . . . . . . . . . . . . . Miramax Films
Messick, Kevin . . . . . . . . . . . . . . . . . . Underworld Entertainment
Messier, Linda . . . . . . . . . . . . . . . . . . . . . Traveler's Rest Films
Messina, Michael . . . . . . . . . New Amsterdam Entertainment, Inc.
Messinger, Martin P. . . . . . . . . . . . . . . . . . . . . CBS Corporation
Mestres, Ricardo . . . . . . . . . . . . Mestres Productions, Ricardo
Methe, Jacques . . . . . . . . . . . . . . . . . . . . . . . . .Allegro Films
Metz, Marsha . . . . . . . . . . . . . Constantin Film Development Inc.
Meurer, Terry . . . . . . . . . . . . . . . . . . . . Cosgrove-Meurer Prods.
Meyer, Andy . . . . . . . . . . . . . . . . . . . . . . . Free Range Pictures
Meyer, Barry A. . . . . . . . . . . . . . . . . . . Warner Bros. Pictures
Meyer, Ellen . . . . . . . . . . . . . . . . Kassirer Meyer Entertainment
Meyer, Irwin . . . . . . . . . . . . . .Producers Ent. Group, Ltd., The
Meyer, Kate . . . . . . . . . . . . . . . . . . . . Showtime Networks Inc.
Meyer, Nicholas . . . . . . . . . . . . . . . . . . . . . Meyer/Jaffe Prods.
Meyer, Patricia K. . . . . . . . . . . . . . . Meyer Prods., Patricia K.
Meyer, Ron . . . . . . . . . . . . . . . . . . . . . . . . . Universal Studios

# CROSS-REFERENCED NAMES

Monty, Gloria . . . . . . . . . . . . . . . . . . . . . . . . . Glory Monty Prods.
Monville, Patricia . . . . . . . . . . . . . . . . . . . . . . . . . . Alpine Pictures
Moon, Cynthia . . . . . . . . . . . . . . . . . . . . . . . . . . Beacon Pictures
Moon, Lara . . . . . . . . . . . . . . . . . . . . . . . . . . . . . Codikow Films
Mooney, Lynn . . . . . . . . . . . . . . . . . . . Shoreline Entertainment
Mooney, Mary . . . . . . . . . . . . . . . . . . . Junction Entertainment
Moonves, Leslie . . . . . . . . . . . . . . . . . . . . . . . . CBS Corporation
Moonves, Leslie . . . . . . . . . . . . . . . . . . . . . . . CBS Entertainment
Mooradian, Greg . . . . . . . . . . . . . . . . . Finerman Prods., Wendy
Moore, Brad R. . . . . . . . . . . Hallmark Hall of Fame Productions, Inc.
Moore, Dawson . . . . . . . . . . . . . . . . . . . . . . Skylark Films Ltd.
Moore, Demi . . . . . . . . . . . . . . . . . . . . . . . . . . . Moving Pictures
Moore, Joanne . . . . . . . . . . . . . . . . . . . . . . . . Punch Productions
Moore, Lindy . . . . . . . . . . . . . . . . . . . . . Giddings Images Inc., Al
Moore, Lonnie . . . . . . . . . . . . . . United Paramount Network (UPN)
Moore, Rhonda . . . . . . . . . . . . . . . Trilogy Entertainment Group
Moore, Rob. . . . . . . . . Walt Disney Pictures/Touchstone Pictures
Moore, Wes . . . . . . . . . . . . . . . . . . . . . . . . . . . Vanguard Films
Moos, Betty . . . . . . . . . . . . . . . . . . . . . . . . . . . . Renfield Prods.
Moos-Hankin, Devorah . . . . . . . . . . . . . . . Bungalow 78 Prods.
Moose, Amanda . . . . . . . . . . . . . . . . . . . . . . . . . . . . . Alphaville
Morales, Charles . . . . . . . . . . . . . . . . . . C.M. Two Productions
Morales, Nan . . . . . . . . Paramount Pictures- Production Division
Moran, Leo . . . . . . . . . . . . . . . . . . Melendez Productions, Bill
Moran, Patrick . . . . . . . . . . . . . . . . . . . . . . New Line Cinema
Morayniss, John . . . . . . . . . . . Alliance Television Productions
More, Erwin . . . . . . . . . . . . . . . . More/Medavoy Management
Morea, Anne . . . . . . . . . . . . . . . . . . . Citadel Entertainment., LLC
Morelli, Rose Mary . . . . . . . . . . . . . . . . . . Hansen, Edward D.
Moreno, Margie . . . . . . . . . . . . . . . . . . . Mandalay Television
Moress, Stan . . . . . . . . . . . Moress-Nanas-Hart Entertainment
Moreton, Kevin . . . . . . . . . . . . . . . . Orbit Entertainment Group
Morewitz, Brian . . . . . . . . . . . . . . . . . . . . . . . . . . . . Warp Films
Morgan, Andre . . . . . . . . Ruddy Morgan Organization, Inc., The
Morgan, Cheryl . . . . . . . . . Warner Bros. Television Productions
Morgan, Hillary . . . . . . . . . . . . . . . . . . Blake Prods., Timothy
Morgan, John . . . . . . . . . . . . . . . . . . . . . . . . Renfield Prods.
Morgan, Lana . . . . . . . . . . . . . . . . Matthau Company, Inc., The
Morgan, Leslie . . . . . . . . . . . . . . . Diamond Heart Productions
Morgan, Lynn . . . . . . . . . . . . . . . . . . . . Warner Bros. Television
Morgan, Mark . . . . . . . . . . . . . . Motion Pict. Corp. of America
Morgan, Melissa . . . . . . . . . . . . . . . . . . . . Lumiere Films Inc.
Morgan, Scott Michael . . . . . . . . . . . . . . . . Kaufman Co., The
Morgan, William . . . . . . . . . . . . . . . . Last Stand Pictures, Inc.
Morhaim, Rob . . . . . . . . . . . . . . . . Team Entertainment Group
Mori, Mark . . . . . . . . . . . . . . . . . . . . . . Single Spark Pictures
Moriarty, Brian . . . . . . . . . . . . . . . . . . Watermark Films, Inc.
Moritz, Neal . . . . . . . . . . . . . . . . . . . . . . . . . . . Original Film
Morningstar, Shirley . . . . . . . . . . . . . . . . . . Harris & Company
Morra, Buddy . . . . . . Morra, Brezner, Steinberg & Tenenbaum
Morrill, Sharon . . . . . . . . . . Walt Disney Television Animation
Morris, Brent . . . . . . . . . . . . . . . . Rough Diamond Productions
Morris, Gloria L. . . . . . . . . . . . . . . . . . . . Landsburg Co., The
Morris, Myra . . . . . . . . Hallmark Hall of Fame Productions, Inc.
Morris-Smith, Linda . . . . . . . . . . . Victory Entertainment, Inc.
Morrison, Gloria . . . . . . . . . . . . . . . . . Unistar Intl. Pictures
Morrison, Jason . . . . . . . . . . . . . . . . . . Unistar Intl. Pictures
Morrison, Michael . . . . . . . . . . . . . . . . . . . NBC Entertainment
Morrison, Rebecca . . . . . . . . . . . . . . . . Trivision Pictures Inc.
Morrison, Vanessa . . . . . . . . . . . . . . Twentieth Century Fox
Morrissey, John . . . . . . . . . . Turman-Morrissey Company, The
Morrissey, John A. . . . . . . . Columbia TriStar Television
Morrow, Barry . . . . . . . . . . . . . . . . Morrow-Heus Productions
Morrow, Lynette . . . . . . . . . . . . . . . . . Mercury-Jet Pictures
Morton, Doug . . . . . . . . . . Motion Pict. Corp. of America
Morton, Jeff . . . . . . . . . . . . . . . . . . . . . Morton Prods., Jeff
Morton, Nicholas . . . . . . . . . . . . . . . . . . . . . Phoenix Pictures
Morton, Robert . . . . . . . . . . . . . . . . . . Panamort Television
Morton, Tracey . . . . . . . . . . . . . . Black Sheep Entertainment
Moses, Ben . . . . . . . . . . . . . . . . Bell and Associates, Dave
Moshay, Michele . . . . . . . . . . . . . . . . . . . PolyGram Television
Mosier, Scott . . . . . . . . . . . . . . . . View Askew Productions, Inc.
Moss, Bettina . . . . . . . . . . . . . . . . . . . . . . . . . . . HBO Pictures
Mossler, Helen . . . . . . . . . . . . . . . Paramount Network Television
Mostow, Fera . . . . . . . . . . Paramount Pictures- Production Division
Mostow, Jonathan . . . . . . . . . . . . . . . . . . Mostow/Lieberman
Mount, Thom . . . . . . . . . . . . . . . Mount/Kramer Company, The
Mountain, Erik . . . . . . . . . . . . . . . . . . . . . . MacDonald Prods
Moussa, Ibrahim A. . . . . . . . . Stone Canyon Investments, Inc.
Mouton, Nancy S. . . . . . . . . . . . . . Von Zerneck-Sertner Films

Moy, Karen . . . . . . . . . . Columbia TriStar Motion Picture Group
Moyer, Greg . . . . . . . . . . . . . . . . . . . . . Discovery Networks
Moyer, Jennifer . . . . . . . . . . . . . . . . . . . . . . . . . . . Alphaville
Moyer, Todd . . . . . . . . . . . . . . . . . . . . . . . . . . . No Prisoners
Mruvka, Alan . . . . . . . . . . . . . . . . Ministry of Film Inc., The
Mudd, Victoria . . . . . . . . . . . . . . . . . . Earthworks Films, Inc.
Mueller, Jeffrey . . . . . . . . . . . . . . . Licht/Mueller Film Corp.
Mueller, Laura . . . . . . . . . . . . . . . . . . Bandeira Entertainment
Muhl, Phillip . . . . . . . . Walt Disney Pictures/Touchstone Pictures
Muhlfriedel, Marina . . . . . . . . . . . . . . . Santa Monica Pictures
Mulay, James . . . . . . . . . . . . . . . . . . . . . . . . . . . 1492 Pictures
Munch, Axel . . . . . . . . . . . . . . . . . . . . . . Silverline Pictures
Mundale, Jonathan . . . . . . . . . . . . . . . . . . Spectacor Films
Mundy, Jason . . . . . . . . . . . . . . . Neo Motion Pictures, Inc.
Munoz, Jose . . . . . . . . . . . . . . . . Berman Productions, Rick
Munson, Linda . . . . . . . Evans Productions, Inc., Charles
Muraglia, Silvio . . . . . . . . . . Cine Grande Entertainment
Muraglia, Silvio . . . . . . . . . . . . . . Firestorm Pictures, Ltd.
Murakhver, Natalya . . . . . . . . . . . . . Kopelson Entertainment
Muraskin, Joan . . . . . . . . . . . . . . . Chancellor Entertainment
Murchison, John . . . . . . . . . . . . . . HBO Original Programming
Murdoch, Rupert . . . . . . . . . . . . . . . . Fox Broadcasting Co.
Murdock, Gay . . . . . . . . . . . . . . . . . . . . . . Studio Productions
Murillo, Lucia . . . . . . . . . . . . . . . . . . . . . Rudin Prods., Scott
Murphey, Michael . . . . . . . . . . . . . . . Bodega Bay Prods., Inc.
Murphy Jr., Ray . . . . . . . . . . . . . . . . . . Murphy Prods., Eddie
Murphy, Charles . . . . . . . . . . . . . . . . . Murphy Prods., Eddie
Murphy, Diane . . . . . . . . . Miller/Boyett/Warren Productions
Murphy, Don . . . . . . . . . . . . . . . . . . . . . . . . JD Productions
Murphy, Eddie . . . . . . . . . . . . . . . . . . Murphy Prods., Eddie
Murphy, Emily . . . . . . . . . . . . . . Entertainment Group, The
Murphy, Maggie . . . . . . . . . . . . . . . . . New Regency Prods.
Murphy, Pamela . . . . . . . . . . Hallmark Entertainment (LA)
Murphy, Peter E. . . . . . . . . . . . . Walt Disney Company, The
Murphy, Phillip . . . . . . . . . . . . . . . . . Paramount Domestic TV
Murphy, Richard G. . . . . . . . . . . . . Long Road Productions
Murphy, Rowena . . . . . . . . . . . . . . . . Zeta Entertainment Ltd.
Murray Quinn, Maureen . . . . . . . . . . Miss Universe L.P., LLLP
Murray, Charles . . . . . . . . . Johnson Entertainment, Magic
Murray, Dana . . . . . . . . . . . . . . . . . . Blue Bay Productions
Murray, Jeneane Fountaine . . . . . . . . Children's Television Workshop
Murray, Jonathan . . . . . . . . . Bunim-Murray Productions, Inc.
Murray, Karla . . . . . . . . . . . . . . . Remote Control Productions
Murray, Lynda . . . . . . . . . . . . . . . . Shooting Gallery Inc., The
Murray, Matt . . . . . . . . . . . . . . . . . . Storyline Entertainment
Murray, Patrick . . . . . . . . . . . . . . . . . . . . . Imax Corporation
Murray, Robert . . . . . . . . . . . . . . . . . . . . . . NewStar Media
Murthy, Karla . . . . . . . . . . . . . . . . . . . . . . . . . Paraview Inc.
Murto, Bill . . . . . . . . . . . . . . . Teocalli Entertainment, Inc.
Musso, Eugene . . . . . . . . . . . . . . . . Neverland Films, Inc.
Muterspaugh, Paul . . . . . . . Hallmark Hall of Fame Productions, Inc.
Mutrux, Gail . . . . . . . . . . . . . . . . . . Jacobs/Mutrux Prods.
Myers, Bill . . . . . . . . . . . . . . . . . Turner Original Productions
Myers, Cydrice . . . . . . . . . . . . . . . . . Angel Ark Productions
Myers, Kimberly . . . . . . . . . . . . . . . . Fox Television Studios
Myers, Matthew . . . . . . . . . . . . . . . . . . True Fiction Pictures
Myerson, Alan . . . . . . . . . . . . . . . . . . . . . DreamWorks SKG
Myerson, Edward . . . . . . . . . . . . . . . . Myerson Entertainment
Myerson, Rachel Tabori . . . . . . . . . . . Myerson Entertainment
Myman, Robert . . . . . . . . . . . . . . . . . . . . Adam Productions
Myron, Ben . . . . . . . . . . . . . . . . . . Myron Productions, Ben
Nabatoff, Alexandria . . . . . . . . . . . . . . . . . Motor City Films
Nadeau, Michael . . . . . . . . . . Motion Pict. Corp. of America
Nadel, Josh . . . . . . . . . . . . . . . . . . . . . . Scarlet Fire Films
Nadler, Marsha . . . . . . . . . . . . . . Neufeld Productions, Mace
Nadler, Maud . . . . . . . . First Look Picts./Overseas Filmgroup
Naegele, Richard J. . . . . . . . . . . . . . . . USONIA Pictures, Inc.
Naiman, Skates . . . . . . . . . . . . . . . Von Zerneck-Sertner Films
Naimy, Karen . . . . . . . . . . . . . . . . . . Merv Griffin Productions
Nakamori, Jennifer . . . . . . . . . . . . . R.A.M.M. Entertainment, Inc
Nalevansky, Steven . . . . . . . . . . . . . . . King World Productions
Nalle, Ned . . . . . . . . . Universal Television & Networks Group
Nanas, Herb . . . . . . . . . . . . Moress-Nanas-Hart Entertainment
Naraghi, Bahman . . . . . . . . . . . . . . . . . . . . Universal Pictures
Nash, Bruce . . . . . . . . . . . . . . . . . . . . . Nash Entertainment
Nash, Robyn . . . . . . . . . . . . . . . . . . . . . Nash Entertainment
Nasser, Jack . . . . . . . . . . . . . . . . Nasser Entertainment Group
Nasser, Joe . . . . . . . . . . . . . . . . Nasser Entertainment Group
Nassif, Lida . . . . . . . . . . . . . . . . . . . . . . . . . . . Egg Pictures
Nasso, Julius . . . . . . . . . . . . . . . . Seagal-Nasso Productions

# CROSS-REFERENCED NAMES

Nassour, Edward . . . . . . . . . . . . . . Twentieth Century Fox Television
Nastri, Vincent . . . . . . . . . . . . . Katz Entertainment Group, Barry
Nathan, Mort . . . . . . . . . . . . . . . . . . . . . . . Fanaro-Nathan Prods.
Nathanson, Beth . . . . . . . . . . . . . . . . . . . . . Sundance Institute
Nathanson, Greg . . . . . . . . . . . . . . . . . . . Twentieth Television
Nathanson, Michael . . . . . . . . . Metro-Goldwyn-Mayer Pictures
Nathanson, Michael J. . . . . . . . . . . . . . . . Upstart Entertainment
Nault, Bill . . . . . . . . . . . . . . . . . . . . . . . . . . . Fox Kids Network
Nava, Gregory . . . . . . . . . . . . . . . . . . . . . . . . . . . . Nava Films
Navis, Martin . . . . . . . . . . . . . . . . . . . . . . . . . . . All Girl Prods.
Nayar, Sunil . . . . . . . . . . . . . . . . . . . . . . . . . Fatima Production
Nayar, Sunil . . . . . . . . . . . . Levinson/Fontana Company, LLC, The
Neal, Carol . . . . . . . . . . . . . . . . . . Melendez Productions, Bill
Neber, Cynthia . . . . . . . . . . . . . . . Donner/Shuler-Donner Prods.
Necessary, Gary . . . . . . . . . . . . . . . Schlatter Prods., George
Nederlander, Gladys . . . . . . . . . . Nederlander Television & Film
Nedick, Mitchell . . . . . . . . . . . . . . . W.B. Television Network
Nedivi, Ben . . . . . . . . . . . . . . . . . . . . . Triumph Pictures Inc.
Nedivi, Udi . . . . . . . . . . . . . . . . . . . . . . Triumph Pictures Inc.
Needham, Edward M. . . . . . . . . . . . . . . . . Phase I Productions
Neeley, Lisa . . . . . . . . . . . . . . . . . . . . . . . . . . . HBO Pictures
Neely, Heather . . . . . . . . . . . . . . . . . . . . . . Mandy Films, Inc.
Neesan, Paul . . . . . . . . . . . . . . . . . . . . . . . . Mostow/Lieberman
Neff, Tom . . . . . . . . . . . . . . . . . . . . . . . . . . TLN Productions
Neilson, Jonas A. . . . . . . . . . . . . . . . . . Persky Prods., Lester
Neisser, Winifred White . . . . . . . . Columbia TriStar Television
Nelson, Anne R. . . . . . . . . . . . . . . . . . . . . . CBS Entertainment
Nelson, Doug . . . . . . . . . . . . . . . . . . . . . . . . Skyline Partners
Nelson, Eileen . . . . . . . . . . . . . . . . . Maynard Prods., Richard
Nelson, Jeffrey . . . . . . . . . . . . . Children's Television Workshop
Nelson, Kathy . . . . . . . . Walt Disney Pictures/Touchstone Pictures
Nelson, Lee . . . . . . . . . . . . . . . . . Orbit Entertainment Group
Nelson, Mark . . . . . . . . . . . . . . . . . . . . Scott Free Productions
Nelson, Patti Roberts . . . . . . . . . . . . Knickerbocker Films
Nelson, Peter . . . . . . . . . . . . . . . . . . . . . . . . . . . . Signature
Nelson, Ron . . . . . . . . . . . . . . . . . . . . . . . . DreamWorks SKG
Nelson, Sharon . . . . . . . . . . Turner Network Television (TNT)
Nelson, Terry . . . . . . . . . . . . . . . . . Having Had Prods., Inc.
Nemes, Scott . . . . . . . . . . . . . . . . . . . . . Parkway Productions
Nerenhausen, Malee . . . . . . . . . . . . . . . . . Phoenician Films
Nesvig, Jon . . . . . . . . . . . . . . . . . . . . . Fox Broadcasting Co.
Netscher, Laura . . . . . . . . . . . . . . . . . . Fountainbridge Films
Netter, Dann . . . . . . . . . . . . . . . . . . . . . Smith-Hemion Prods.
Netter, Douglas . . . . . . . . . . . . . . . Netter Digital Entertainment
Netter, Gil . . . . . . . . . . . . . . . . Zucker Brothers Productions
Netter, Jason . . . . . . . . . . . . . . . Netter Digital Entertainment
Nettinga, Sarah . . . . . . . Warner Bros. International TV Production
Neufeld, Mace . . . . . . . . . . . . . . . . . Neufeld Productions, Mace
Neufeld, Marjorie Nieset . . . . Warner Bros. Television Productions
Neukum, Cathe . . . . . . . . . . . . . . . Turner Original Productions
Neuman, David . . . . . . . . . . . Walt Disney TV/Touchstone TV
Neuman, Jeffrey R. . . . . . . . . . . . . . . . . Neu-man-films, Inc.
Neumeyer, Kari . . . . . . . . . . . . . . . Fortune Media Group, Inc.
Neuss, Wendy . . . . . . . . . . . . . . . Flying Freehold Productions
Neville, Lee . . . . . . . . . . . . . . . . . . . . . . Pirromount Pictures
Nevins, David . . . . . . . . . . . . . . . . . . . . . . . NBC Entertainment
Nevins, Sheila . . . . . . . . . . . . . . . . HBO Original Programming
Newburger, Patty . . . . . . . . . . . . . . . . . . . . . . Comedy Central
Newcomb, Patrick . . . . . . . Warner Bros. Television Productions
Newell, Mike . . . . . . . . . . . . . . . . . . . . . . . . . . Dogstar Films
Newfield, Jill . . . . . . . . . . . . . . . . . . . . . . VH1 (Music First)
Newland, John . . . . . . . . . . . . . . Newland-Raynor Prods., Inc.
Newlon, David . . . . . . . . . . . . . . . . . . . . . . . Spectacor Films
Newman, Adam . . . . . . . . . . . . . . . . . . . . . Cowlip Productions
Newman, Ari . . . . . . . . . . . . . . . . Media Financial Corporation
Newman, Barry . . . . . . . . . . . . . . . . . . . . Bean And Cod Prods.
Newman, Betsy . . . . . . . . . Turner Network Television (TNT)
Newman, Carroll . . . . . . . . . . . . Newman Productions, Carroll
Newman, Eric . . . . . . . . . . . . . . . . . Jacobson Company, The
Newman, Gary S. . . . . . . . . . Twentieth Century Fox Television
Newman, Jenifer . . . . . . . . . . . . . Newman Productions, Carroll
Newman, Peter . . . . . . . . . . . . . . . . . . Redeemable Features
Newman, Salli . . . . . . . . . . . . . . . . . . . . Firebrand Productions
Newman, Vincent . . . . . . . . . . . . . . . . . Newman/Tooley Films
Newman-Minson, Launa . . . . . . . . . . Newman Prods., Launa
Newmyer, Robert . . . . . . . . . . . . . . . . . . . Outlaw Productions
Nguyen, Robert . . . . . . . . . . . . . . . . . . . . . . . . All Girl Prods.
Nicholls, Craig . . . . . . . . . . . . . . . . . . . . Blue Rider Pictures
Nichols, Stephanie . . . . . . . . . . Ridio Prods., Inc., Anthony
Nicholson, Jennifer . . . . . . . . . . . . Spelling Television, Inc.

Nicita, Wallis . . . . . . . . . . . . . . . . . . . . . . . . . . La Luna Films
Nicklaus, Kevin . . . . . . . . . . . . . . . . . . . . . Wolper Org., The
Nickson, Robert . . . . . . . . . . . . . . . . . . . . . . . . Orenda Films
Nicolini, Christiane . . . . . . . . . Rive Gauche International TV
Nicolosi, Barbara R. . . . . . . . . . . . . . . . . . . . Paulist Prods.
Nides, Tina . . . . . . . . . . . . . . . . . . . . . Nides Productions, Tina
Niederhoffer, Galt . . . . . . . . . . . . . . . . . . . . . . . Giv'en Films
Niederman, David . . . . . . Twentieth Century Fox-Searchlight Picts.
Niemeyer, Scott . . . . . . . . . Motion Pict. Corp. of America
Nimoy, Leonard . . . . . . . . . . . . . . . . . . . . Rumbleseat Prods.
Niven, Fernanda . . . . . . . . . . . . . . . . Mark Prods., Laurence
Nix, Beverly . . . . . . . . . . . . . . . . Columbia TriStar Television
Nix, Carole . . . . . . . . . . . . . . . . . . . . . . New Regency Prods.
Noble, Paul . . . . . . . . . . . . . . . . . . . . . Lifetime Television (NY)
Nola, Rafaell . . . . . . . . . . . . . . . . . . Albert Prods. Inc., Sydell
Nolan, Jed . . . . . . . . . . . . . . . . . . . . . . . . . . . Alpine Pictures
Nolan, Laurie . . . . . . . . . . . . . . . . . . . . . . Nolan/LaMonte-ITG
Noll, Jim . . . . . . . . . . . . . . . . . . . . . . . . . . . . . Tiger Prods.
Nolte, Nick . . . . . . . . . . . . . . . . . . . . . Kingsgate Films, Inc.
Noonan, Dick . . . . . . . . . . . . . . . 44 Blue Productions, Inc.
Norman, Caresse . . . . . . . . . . . . . . . . . . . . . Madguy Films
Norman, Maria . . . . . . . . . . . . . . . . . . Kopelson Entertainment
Norman, Mark . . . . . . . . . . . . . . . . . . . . . . . Cartoon Network
Northrup, Curt . . . . . . . . . . . . . . . New Screen Concepts, Inc.
Norton, Robert . . . . . . . . . . . . . . . . . . Scott Free Productions
Norton, Terry . . . . . . . . . . . . . . . . . . . . . Northern Lights Ent.
Norville, Sonia . . . . . . . . . . . . . . . . . . . . . . Avnet-Kerner Co.
Nosek, Laslo . . . . . . . . . . . . . . . . . . . . . . . . Klasky Csupo Inc.
Novatt, Lynn . . . . . . . . . . . . . . . . . . . . . . . . Avenue Pictures
Noveck, Gregory . . . . . . . . . . . . . . . . Platinum Studios, LLC
Novelly, G. Michael . . . . . . . . . . . . . . . . PolyGram Television
Novick, Susan . . . . . . . . . . . . . . . . . . . . . . Outlaw Productions
Novo, Jose . . . . . . . . . . . . . . . . . . . . . . . . . . . Meridian Films
Nowotny, Robert A. . . . . . . . . . . . Teocalli Entertainment, Inc.
Noxon, Nicky . . . . . . . . . . . . . . . . . . . . . . . . . Wild Films Inc.
Noxon, Nicolas . . . . . . . . . . . National Geographic Television
Nozik, Michael . . . . . . . . . . . . . . . . . . . . South Fork Pictures
Nozik, Michael . . . . . . . . . . . . . . . Wildwood Enterprises Inc.
Nozoe, Yuki . . . . . . . . . . . . . . . . Sony Pictures Entertainment
Nugent, Nelle . . . . . . . . . . . . . . . Foxboro Company, Inc., The
Nugiel, Nellie . . . . . . . . . . . . . . . . . . . HBO NYC Productions
Numark, Clifford . . . . . . . . . . . . . . . . . KiMina Entertainment
Nunan, Tom . . . . . . . . . . . . United Paramount Network (UPN)
Nunez Jr., Armando . . . . . . . . Universal Television & Networks Group
Nunnari, Gianni . . . . . . . . . . . . . . . . . Cecchi Gori Pictures
Nuss, Bill . . . . . . . . . . . . . . . . . . . . . . . North Hall Productions
Nussbaum, Jodi . . . . . . . . . . . Children's Television Workshop
Nussbaumer, Bernard . . . . . . . . . . . . . . . . . . Ventana Films
Nuzzi, Dominick . . . . . . . . . . . . . . . . . . . . . . . . ABC Daytime
Nye, Barry . . . . . . . . . . . . . . . . National Geographic Television
Nye, Eaves . . . . . . . . . . . . . . . . . Segan Company, The Lloyd
O'Brien, Casey . . . . . . . . . . . . . . Silverman Co., The Fred
O'Brien, Declan . . . . . . . . . . . . . Team Entertainment Group
O'Brien, Jeanne . . . . . . . . . . . . . . . . . Radmin Company, The
O'Brien, Nora . . . . . . . . . . . . . . . . Trilogy Entertainment Group
O'Brien, Shelagh . . . . . . . . . . . Tidewater Entertainment, Inc.
O'Connell, Brian . . . . . . . . . . . . . . . . . . . . . . Ink Tank, The
O'Connor, Matthew . . . . . . . . . . . . Pacific Motion Pictures
O'Connor, Rachel . . . . . . . . . . . . . . . . . . Columbia Pictures
O'Corr, Steve . . . . . . . . . . . . . . . . Raffaella Productions, Inc.
O'Dea, Wendy . . . . . . . . . . . . . . . . . . . . . . NewStar Television
O'Donnell, Chris . . . . . . . . . . . . . . . . George Street Pictures
O'Donnell, Erin . . . . . . . . . . . . . . . . . . . . . . . . . Egg Pictures
O'Halloran, Michael . . . . . . . . . . . . . . . . . Braga Productions
O'Hara, Michael . . . . . . . . . . . . O'Hara-Horowitz Productions
O'Hare, Mary . . . . . . . . . . . . . . . . Sony Pictures Imageworks
O'Hehir, Claudia . . . . . . . . . . . . . . Kopelson Entertainment
O'Karma, Hank . . . . . . . . . . . . . . New Screen Concepts, Inc.
O'Keefe, Maureen . . . . . . . . . . . . . . . . . Crew Prods., Dick
O'Keefe, Sean . . . . . . . . . . . . . . . . . . . . . . . . . Original Film
O'Keefe, Terence M. . . . . . . . . . . . . . Vanguard Productions
O'Neal, Brian . . . . . . . . . . . . . . . . . . . . . . CBS Entertainment
O'Neal, Cleveland . . . . . . . . Connection III Entertainment Corp.
O'Neal, Gretchen . . . . . . Walt Disney Pictures/Touchstone Pictures
O'Neal, Walter . . . . . . . . . . . . . Walt Disney TV/Touchstone TV
O'Rourke, Erin . . . . . . . . . . . . Pressman Film Corp., Edward R.
Oakley, Bill . . . . . . . . . . . . . Bill Oakley & Josh Weinstein
Oakley, Vern . . . . . . . . . . . . . . . . . . . . . . . . . . . . . . . . Tribe
Oblinger, Leigh . . . . . . . . . . . . . . . . . Lucchesi Prods., Gary
Obst, Lynda . . . . . . . . . . . . . . . . . . . . . . . . Obst Prods., Lynda

# CROSS-REFERENCED NAMES

Ockrent, Mike . . . . . . . . . . . . . . . . . . . . Ockrent Productions, Ltd.
Odell, Megan . . . . . . . . . . . . . . . . . . . . . Spin Cycle Entertainment
Odunton, Adoley . . . . . . . . . . Symphony Entertainment, LLC
Oestreich, Liza . . . . . . . . . . . . . . . . . . . . . . . . . . . . . . . . . . . Stun
Oestreich, Yael . . . . . . . . . . . . . . . . . . . . . . . . . . . Simian Films
Offerman, Gina . . . . . . . . . . . . . . . . . . . Spin Cycle Entertainment
Offitzer, Mark . . . . . . . . . . . . . . . . . . . . . . . Broadway Video (NY)
Offsay, Jerry . . . . . . . . . . . . . . . . . . . . . Showtime Networks Inc.
Oggs, Lea . . . . . . . . . . . . Twentieth Century Fox-Fox 2000 (LA)
Oglesby, Marsha . . . . . . . . . . . . . . . . . . . . . . Avnet-Kerner Co.
Ohlmeyer, Don . . . . . . . . . . . . . . . . . . . . . NBC Entertainment
Ohlsen, Chris . . . . . . . . . . . . . . . . . . . . . River Mill Productions
Oken, Stuart . . . . . . Walt Disney Pictures/Touchstone Pictures
Okun, Sam . . . . . . . . . . . . . . . . . . . Erratic Entertainment, Inc.
Oleschak, Edward . . . . . . . . . . . . . Krane Group, The Jonathan
Olin, Lisa J. . . . . . . . . . . . . . . . . . . . . Goepp Circle Productions
Olivas, Xochitl L. . . . . . . . . . . . . . . . . . . Grammnet Productions
Oliver, Ann . . . . . . . . . . . . . . . . . . . . . . . . . . Movie Group, The
Oliver, Jack . . . . . . . . . . . . . . . . . . . . . . . . . . . . . Saturn Films
Oliver, Lin . . . . . . . . . . . . . . . . . . . . . Oliver Productions, Lin
Oliver-Frost, Lucas . . . . . Ruddy Morgan Organization, Inc., The
Olivo, Corrinne . . . . . . . . . . . . . . . . . Gilbert Associates, Ron
Olmos, Edward James . . . . . . . . . . . . . Olmos Productions Inc.
Olmstead, Patrick . . . . . . . . . . Mount/Kramer Company, The
Olshansky, Ken . . . . . . . . . . . . . . . . . . . . Sunbow Entertainment
Olshansky, Rick . . . . . . . . . . . . . . . . . . . . NBC Entertainment
Olson, Lee . . . . . . . . . . . . . . . . . . . . . . . Crew Prods., Dick
Omae, Roger . . . . . . . . . . . . . . . . . . . . . . . . DIC Entertainment
Oman, Chad . . . . . . . . . . . . . . . . . Bruckheimer Films, Jerry
Ondrus, Martin . . . . . . . . . . . . . . . Island-In-The-Sky Pictures
Oppenheimer, Brian . . . . Full Circle Ent. AKA Suzanne Bauman Prod
Opper, Barry . . . . . . . . . . . . . . . . . . . . . . . . . . . . Sho Films
Optican, Tony . . . . . . . . Metro-Goldwyn-Mayer/Worldwide TV
Ordesky, Mark . . . . . . . . . . . . . . . . . . . . . Fine Line Features
Orellana, Alex . . . . . . . . . . . . . . . . . . . . Stiefel Entertainment
Orenstein, Bernie . . . . . . . . . . . . . Turteltaub-Orenstein Prods.
Orenstein, Fern . . . . . . . . . . . . . . . . . . . . . CBS Entertainment
Orkin, Kenneth S. . . . . . . . . . . . . Chesterfield Film Co., The
Orlovsky, Alexander . . . . . . . . . . . . . . . . . . . . . Giv'en Films
Ormond, Julia . . . . . . . . . . . . . . . . . . . . . . Indican Productions
Oro, Edwin . . . . . . . . . . . . . . . . . . . . . . . . About Face Prods.
Orr, Joe . . . . . . . . . . . . . . . . . . . . . . . . . . . . . . . . Cobalt Moon
Ortiz, Sandra . . . . . . . . . . . . Twentieth Century Fox Television
Osborne, Gwen . . . . . . . . . . . . . . . . . . . . . Bubble Factory, The
Osborne, India . . . . . . . . . . . . . . . . . . . . . . . El Dorado Pictures
Osborne, Nick . . . . . . . . . . . . . . . . . . . . . . . Phoenix Pictures
Oseary, Guy . . . . . . . . . . . . . . . . . . . . . . . . . . Madguy Films
Oseransky, Bernard . . . . . . . . . . . . . . . Nepotism Productions
Osher, Robert . . . . . . . . . . . . . . . . . . . . . . . Miramax Films
Osmond, Eric . . . . . . . . . . . . . . . . . . . . . . Telvan Productions
Osowski, Pamela . . . . . . . . . . . . . . World Film Services, Inc.
Ostin, Michael . . . . . . . . . . . . . . . . . . . . . DreamWorks SKG
Ostin, Mo . . . . . . . . . . . . . . . . . . . . . . . . . DreamWorks SKG
Ostlund, Richard . . . . . . . . . . . . Lee Productions, Michele
Ostroff, Donna . . . . . . . . . . . . . . . . . . . . Mirage Enterprises
Ostrow, Randy . . . . . . . . . . . . . . . . . . . . . . . October Films
Ostrowski, Igor . . . . . . . . . . . . . . . . Open Door Entertainment
Oteyza, Manuel . . . . . . . . . . . . Common Ground Entertainment
Ottenhoff, Robert G. . . . . . . . . . . . . . . . . . . . . . . . . . . . PBS
Otto, John G. . . . . . . . . . . . . . . . . . . . . . . . . Mountain Drive
Otto, Linda . . . . . . . . . . . . . . . . . . . . . . . Landsburg Co., The
Otto, Narween . . . . . . . . . . . . . . . . . . . . . . . . . . . . BLURCO
Ouweleen, Michael . . . . . . . . . . . . . . . . . . . . Cartoon Network
Overby, Daria . . . . . . . . . . . . . . HBO Original Programming
Ovitz, Mark H. . . . . . . . . . . . . . . . Ovitz Productions, Mark H.
Ovrum, Jean . . . . . . . . . . . . . . . . . . . Trident Releasing Inc.
Owen, Tom . . . . . . . . . . . . . . . . . . . . . . . . . . Greif Company
Oxman, Steve . . . . . . . . . . . . . . . . . . . . Myerson Entertainment
Ozn, Robert . . . . . . . . . . . . . . . . One Voice Entertainment, Inc.
Paccone, Fred . . . . . . . . . . . . . . . . . . . . . Big Ticket Television
Pace, Bill . . . . . . . . . . . . . . . . . . . . . . . . . . Longbow Productions
Pace, Greg . . . . . . . . . . . . . . . . . . . . . . . . . El Dorado Pictures
Pachecho, Diane . . . . . . . . . . . Twentieth Century Fox Television
Padden, Preston . . . . . . . . . . . . . . . . . . . . . ABC Entertainment
Padilla, Priscilla . . . . . . . . . . Sefton Productions International
Padnick, Glenn . . . . . . . . . . . . . . . . . Castle Rock Entertainment
Padnos, Jamie . . . . . . . . . . . . . . . . . Showtime Networks Inc.
Page, David T. . . . . . . . . . . . . . . . . . . . . . Cannery, Inc., The
Page, Kathy . . . . . . . . . . . . . . . . . . . . Breen Prods., Paulette
Page, Langdon F. . . . . . . . . . . . . . . . . . . . . Cannery, Inc., The

Paige, George . . . . . . . . . . . . . . . . Paige Assoc., Inc., George
Paige, Jeremy . . . . . . . . . . . . . . . . . . StoryTeller Films, Ltd.
Paine, Curtis . . . . . . . . . . . . . . . . . . . . . . Crew Prods., Dick
Painter, Paul . . . . . . . . . . . . . . . . Telescene Film Group., Inc.
Pakula, Alan J. . . . . . . . . . . . . . . . . . . . . . Pakula Prods., Inc.
Paladino, Gia . . . . . . . . Twentieth Century Fox-Searchlight Picts.
Palef, Bonnie . . . . . . . . . . . . . . . . . . . . Snapdragon Films Inc.
Paleologos, Nicholas . . . . . . . . . . . . . . . . . Zollo Productions
Palermo, Gary . . . . . . . . . . . . . . . . . . . . . Palisades Pictures
Palladino, Susan . . . . . . . . . . Witt-Thomas-Harris Productions
Palma, Erik . . . . . . . . . . . . . . . . . . . . . . . Universal Pictures
Palmer, Amy . . . . . . . . . . . . . . . . . . . . . . . . . . Jersey Films
Palmer, Donalda . . . . . . . . . . Chesler/Perlmutter Production
Palmer, Glendon . . . . . . . . . . . . . . . Overbrook Entertainment
Palmer, Robert L. . . . . . . . . . . . . . . . . . Saban Entertainment
Palmer, Robin . . . . . . . . . . . . . . . . . . Lifetime Television (LA)
Palmer, Sara . . . . . . . . . . . . . . Equinox Entertainment Ltd.
Palmer, Wendy . . . . . . . . . . . . . . . . . . . . . Goldwyn Films Inc.
Palmieri, Hank . . . . . . . . . . National Geographic Feature Films
Pamplin, Rick . . . . . . . . . . . . . . . . . Pamplin-Fisher Company
Panajotovic, Ika . . . . . . . . . . . . . . . . . . Noble Productions Inc.
Panay, Andrew . . . . . . . . . . . . . . . . . . . . . Tapestry Films Inc.
Panitch, Sanford . . . . . . . . . . . . . . . . . Twentieth Century Fox
Panoff, Jaime . . . . . . . . . . . . . . . . . . . . Panamort Television
Papadeas, Paul . . . . . . . . . . . . . Rough Diamond Productions
Papazian, Robert . . . . . . . . . . Papazian-Hirsch Entertainment
Papero, Pat . . . . . . . . . . . . . . . . . . . . . . . Segue Prods., Inc.
Papinchak, Martina . . . . . . . . . . . . . . . . . Mandy Films, Inc.
Pappas, George . . . . . . . . . . . . . . . . . . Cinema Seven Prods.
Papriella, William . . . . . . . . . . . . . . . Baldwin/Cohen Productions
Papzian, Steve . . . . . . . . . . . . . . . . . Warner Bros. Pictures
Paquette, Eric . . . . . . . . . . . . . . . . . . . . . . Phoenix Pictures
Paradise, Lynette . . . . . . . . . . . . . . . . . . Carlson, Matthew
Pariente, Prosper . . . . . . . . . . . . . . . . . Triumph Pictures Inc.
Paris, Russ . . . . . . . . . . . . Columbia TriStar Motion Picture Group
Pariser, Michael . . . . . . . . . . . . . . . . Merko Motion Pictures
Parish, Heather . . . . . . . . 40 Acres & A Mule Filmworks Inc.
Park, Jane . . . . . . . . . . . . . . . . . . . . . . . Bandeira Entertainment
Parker, Craig . . . . . . . . . . . . . . . Ladd Productions, Inc., Diane
Parker, Gary . . . . . . . . . . . . . . . . . . . . . . . . . . . Tiger Prods.
Parker, Hope . . . . . . . . . . . . . . . . . Baer Animation Co. Inc.
Parker, Hutch . . . . . . . . . . . . . . . . . . Twentieth Century Fox
Parker, John . . . . . . . . . . . . . . . . Lemon Sky Productions, Inc.
Parkes, Walter . . . . . . . . . . . . . . . . . . . . . DreamWorks SKG
Parkinson, Jan . . . . . . . . Hallmark Hall of Fame Productions, Inc.
Parnell, Cheryl . . . . . . . . . . . . . Concorde/New Horizons Corp.
Parnell, Lee . . . . . . . . . Walt Disney Pictures/Touchstone Pictures
Parrent, Joanne . . . . . . . . . . . . . . . . . . . . . . Reel Life Women
Parry, Kathryn Sommer . . . . . . . . . . . . . . . . . . . Ksproductions
Parsons, Clive . . . . . . . . . . . . . . . . Film and General Prods.
Parsons, Danielle . . . . . . . . . . Motion Pict. Corp. of America
Partible, Leo . . . . . . . . . . . . . Takoma Entertainment Group
Parton, Dolly . . . . . . . . . . . . . . . . . . . . . . . Sandollar Prods.
Parziale, Tom . . . . . . . . . . . . . . . . . . . Visionary Entertainment
Pascal, Amy . . . . . . . . . . . . . . . . . . . . . . . Columbia Pictures
Paseornek, Michael . . . . . . . . . . Lions Gate Films Production
Pasquin, John . . . . . . . . . . . . . . . . . . . . Paradox Prod., Inc.
Pasternack, Dan . . . . . . . . . . Granada Entertainment USA
Patchett, Tom . . . . . . . . . . Patchett Kaufman Entertainment
Patel, Riaz . . . . . . . . . . . . . . . . . . . . . . . . . . . Chicagofilms
Patillo, Toni . . . . . . . . . . . . . . . . . . . . . De Passe Entertainment
Patmore, Suzanne . . . . . . . . . . . . . . . . . . . Mutual Film Co.
Patric, Jason . . . . . . . . . . . . . . . . . . . . . . . . . Fleece Films
Patricia, Tom . . . . . . . . . . . . . . . . . . Mandalay Television
Patrick, Lougenia . . . . . . . . . . . . . Spelling Television, Inc.
Patrick, Robert . . . . . . . . . . . . . . . . . . . . . . 360 entertainment
Patrick, Shari . . . . . . . . . . . . . . . . . . . . . . . Comedy Central
Patterson, Bill . . . . . . . . . . Roaring Mouse Entertainment, Inc.
Patterson, Gail . . . . . . . . . . . . . . . Spelling Television, Inc.
Paul, D.J. . . . . . . . . . . . . . . . . . . . . . . . . . Ocelot Films, Inc.
Paul, Greg . . . . . . . . . . . . . . . . . . Castle Rock Entertainment
Paul, Jonathan . . . . . . . . . . . . . . . . . Excelsior Pictures Corp.
Paul, Pam . . . . . . . . . Ruddy Morgan Organization, Inc., The
Paulson, Daniel L. . . . . . . . . . . . . . . Paulson Prods., Daniel L.
Paulson, Elizabeth . . . . . . . . . Ladd Productions, Inc., Diane
Pavich, Frank . . . . . . . . . . . . . . . . . . . . . Aviator Films LLC
Pavlick, Christopher . . . . . . . . . . . Moll/Beallor Productions
Paxton, Tajamika . . . . . . . . . . . . . . . . . . . . . . . . MTV Films
Paylor, Diane . . . . . . . . . . . . . . . . . . . . . Tavel Entertainment
Payne, Judd . . . . . . . . . . . . . . . . . . . . . . Tisch Co., The Steve

　　　　253　　　　©1998 Hollywood Creative Directory Vol. 34

# CROSS-REFERENCED NAMES

Peardon, Nancy . . . . . . . . . . . . . . . . . . . . . . Forward Pass, Inc.
Pearlman, Barbara . . . . . . . . . . . . . . . . . . . . . . . . MKD Prods.
Pearlman, Steve . . . . . . . Warner Bros. Television Productions
Pearlmutter, Donna . . . . . . . . . . . . . . . . . . . . . HBO Pictures
Pearson, Andrew . . . . . . . . . . . . . . . . . . . . . . . . Simsie Films
Peck, Adam . . . . . . . . . . . . . . . . . . . Synchronicity Productions
Peckham, Jennifer . . . . . . . . Cinequanon Pictures Intl. Inc.
Pederson, Alec . . . . . . . . . . . . . . . . . . . . . . Mostow/Lieberman
Pedowitz, Mark . . . . . . . . . . . . . . . . . . . . . . ABC Entertainment
Peele, Bryan . . . . . . . . . . . . . . . . . . . Young Artists Productions
Peerce, Larry . . . . . . . . . . . . . . . . . Synchronicity Productions
Peerce, Madeline . . . . . . . . . . . . . . . . . . . . CBS Entertainment
Pegrom, Sophie . . . . . . . . . . . . . . . . . . . . . . . . . Zero Pictures
Peirson, George . . . . . . . . . . . . . . . . . . . . . . . Alpine Pictures
Pele, Linda . . . . . . . . . . . . . . . . . . . . . . . . Dockry Productions
Pellegrini, Danny . . . . . . . . . . . . . . . . . . . . . Konrad Pictures
Pellettieri, Michael . . . . . . . . . . . Voight Entertainment, Jon
Pelman, Aaron . . . . . . . . . . . . . . . . . Manheim Company, The
Peltier, Melissa Jo . . . . . . . . . . . . . . MPH Entertainment, Inc.
Pena, Anthony . . . . . . . . . . . . . . . . . . . . . . . . TAE Productions
Pendorf, James . . . . . . . . . . . . . . . . . . . . . . . Distant Horizon
Penn-Kraus, Rick . . . . . . . . . . . . . . . . . . . . . . NewStar Media
Pennette, Marco . . . . . . . . . . . . . . . . Barron/Pennette Prods.
Pennington, Damon . . . . . . . . . . . Wildwood Enterprises Inc.
Pennington, Nicole . . . . . . . . . . . . . . . . . . . . . A Band Apart
Penza, R. Scott . . . . . . . . . . . . . . Too Nuts Productions, Ltd.
Pepe, Barbara . . . . . . . . . . . . . . . . E! Entertainment Television
Percelay, David . . . . . . . . . . . . . . . . Scripps Howard Prods.
Perebinossoff, Philippe . . . . . . . . . . . . . . ABC Entertainment
Perez, Carlos . . . . . . . . . . . . . . . Castle Rock Entertainment
Pergola, Chris . . . . . . . . . . . . . . . . . . . . . . . Comedy Central
Perini, Jennifer . . . . . . . . . . . . . . . . . . . . . . . . ImageMovers
Perkins, George W. . . . . . . . . . . . . New England Prods., Inc.
Perkins, Nancy . . . . . . . . . . . . . . . . Studios USA Television
Perkins, Rowland . . . . . . . . . . . . . . . . . . Double Eagle Ent.
Perlman, Laurie . . . . . . . . . . . . . . . . . . Perlman Productions
Perlmutter, David . . . . . . . . Chesler/Perlmutter Production
Perlstein, Patti . . . . . . . . . . . . . . . . . . Fries Film Group, Inc.
Permut, David . . . . . . . . . . . . . . . . . . . . Permut Presentations
Perrone, Gibran . . . . . . . . . . . . . . . . . . Shinbone Productions
Perry Davis, Penny . . . . . . . . . . . . . . Rocking Horse Prods.
Perry, Craig . . . . . . . . . . . . . . . . . . . . . . . Zide Entertainment
Perry, Jeanne . . . . . . . . . . . . . . . . . . . Britt Allcroft Co., The
Perry, Jeanne . . . . . . . . . . . . . . . . . . . . . . . Gullane Pictures
Perry, John . . . . . . . . . . . Walt Disney TV/Touchstone TV
Perry, Sean E. . . . . . . . . . . . . . . . . . King World Productions
Perryman, Jacquie . . . . . . . . . . . . . . PolyGram Filmed Ent.
Persico, Donna . . . . . . . . . . . . . . . . Silver Heart Productions
Persinger, Marshall . . . . . . . . . . . . . . Fresh Produce Company
Persky, Lester . . . . . . . . . . . . . . . . . . . . Persky Prods., Lester
Person, Yolanda . . . . . . . . . . . . . . . . Colleton Company, The
Perth, Rod . . . . . . . . . . . . . . . . . . . . . . . . . . . USA Networks
Peruggi, Rita . . . . . . . . . . . . . . . . . . Henson Company, Jim
Pesci, Priscilla . . . . . . . . . . . . . . . . . . . . . Gray Fox Films
Peternel, Timothy . . . . . . . . . . . . . . Muse Productions, Inc.
Peters, David . . . . . . . . . . . . . . . . . . Montage Entertainment
Peters, Jon . . . . . . . . . . . . . . . . . . . . . Peters Entertainment
Peters, Michael . . . . . . . . . . . . . . . . . . Heller Prods., Paul
Petersen, William . . . . . . . . . . . . . . . . . High Horse Films
Petersen, Wolfgang . . . . . . . . . . . . . . Radiant Productions
Peterson, Bonnie . . . . . . . . . . . Leo Productions, Malcolm
Peterson, Clark . . . . . . . . . . . . . . Image Organization, Inc.
Peterson, James . . . . . . . . . . Worldwide Pants Incorporated
Peterson, Joel . . . . . . . . . . . . . . . Bodega Bay Prods., Inc.
Peterson, Michael . . . . . . . . . . . . Val D'Oro Entertainment
Petrie Jr., Dan . . . . . . . . . . . . . . . Petrie Jr. & Co., Daniel
Petrie, Dorothea G. . . . . . . . Petrie Prods., Inc., Dorothea G.
Pettinato, J.P. . . . . . . . . . . . . . . . . . . . . . . . . Cinetel Films
Peyrot, Maureen . . . . . . . . . . . . . . . . Imagine Entertainment
Peyser, Michael . . . . . . . . . . . . . . . . Blue Tulip Productions
Pfeffer, Andrew . . . . . . . . . . . . . . . . . . . . . . . Pfilmco, Inc.
Pfeiffer, Michelle . . . . . . . . . . . . . . . . Via Rosa Productions
Philip, Michael . . . . . . . . . . . . . . . . . . . Nichol Moon Films
Philips, Todd . . . . . . . . . . . . . . . . Krainin Productions Inc.
Phillips, Don . . . . . . . . . . . . . . . . Neo Motion Pictures, Inc.
Phillips, Drew . . . . . . . . . . . Cinequanon Pictures Intl. Inc.
Phillips, Laura A.S. . . . . . . . . . . . . . . . . . Hellinger Films
Phillips, Lil . . . . . . . . . . . . . . . . . . . Davis Entertainment Co.
Phillips, Louis M. . . . . . . . . . . . . . . Henson Pictures, Jim
Phillips, Mark . . . . . . . . . . . . . . . . . . . . . Night Flight Inc.

Phillips, Michael . . . . . . . . . . . . . . . Lighthouse Productions
Phillips, Peter . . . . . . . . . . . . . . . . . . . . Pakula Prods., Inc.
Phillips, William . . . . . . . . . . . . . . . . Bochco Prods., Steven
Pichirallo, Joe . . . . . Twentieth Century Fox-Searchlight Picts.
Picker, David V. . . . . . . . . . . . . . . . . Two Roads Prods., Inc.
Pickert, Mary . . . . . . . . . . Two Oceans Entertainment Group
Piepeir, Paul . . . . . . . . . . . . . . . . . . . . . Iwerks Entertainment
Pierce, Frederick S. . . . . . . . . . . . . Pierce Co., The Frederick S.
Pierce, Keith . . . . . . . . . . . . . . . Pierce Co., The Frederick S.
Pierce, Nina Bunche . . . . . . . . Floyd Johnson Productions, Charles
Pierce, Peggy . . . . . . . . . . . . . . . . . . . Weinstock Productions
Pierce, Richard . . . . . . . . . . . . . . Pierce Co., The Frederick S.
Pietri, Didier . . . . . . . . . . . . . . . . . . . . . . . . . ABC Pictures
Pietroforte, Pam . . . . . . . . Turner Network Television (TNT)
Piezas, Josh . . . . . . . . . . . . . . . . . . . . . . . . . . . Troma Inc.
Pike, Kristine K. . . . . . . . . . . . . . . . . . . . . . . . . . Intrepidus
Pillsbury, C.J. . . . . . . . . . . . . . . . Equinox Entertainment Ltd.
Pillsbury, Gayle . . . . . . . . . . . . . . . . . . . Imagine Television
Pillsbury, Sarah . . . . . . . . . . . . . . . Sanford/Pillsbury Prods.
Pilon, Ryan . . . . . . . . . . . . . . . . . . . . . . Goldstein Co., The
Pinchuk, Jason . . . . . . . . . . . . . . . . Demberg Productions, Lisa
Pinchuk, Sheldon . . . . . . . . . . . . Finnegan-Pinchuk Company
Pine, Steve . . . . . . . . . . . . . . . . . Nasser Entertainment Group
Pink, Steve . . . . . . . . . . . . . . . . . . . New Crime Productions
Pinkney, Rose Catherine . . . . . . . Paramount Network Television
Pinkstaff, Kimberly . . . . . . . . . . . . Weintraub Prods., Jerry
Pinnolis, Toni . . . . . . . . . . . . . . . . . . . . . . . . . . British Lion
Pintauro, Frank . . . . . . . . . . . . . . . . Showtime Networks Inc.
Piper, Sonja . . . . . . . . . . . . . . . . . . . . . . . ABC Entertainment
Pirro, Mark . . . . . . . . . . . . . . . . . . . . . . Pirromount Pictures
Pisano, Michael . . . . . . . . . . . . . . . . . . . . . . Blue Turtle, Inc.
Pistor, Julia . . . . . . . . . . . . . . . . . . . . . Nickelodeon Movies
Pitts, Randolph . . . . . . . . . . . . . . . . . . . . . Lumiere Films Inc.
Plass, Nikol . . . . . . . . . . . . . . . . . . . . . . Outlaw Productions
Platnick, Adam . . . . . . . . . . . . . . . . . . . . Mandalay Pictures
Platt, Derek . . . . . . . . . . . . . . . . . . . Studios USA Television
Platt, John . . . . . . . . . . . . . . . . . . . . . . . Crew Prods., Dick
Platt, Polly . . . . . . . . . . . . . . . . . Carsey-Werner Co., The
Plavin, Sid . . . . . . . . . . . . . . . . . . . Copper Sky Productions
Plec, Julie . . . . . . . . . . . . . . . . . . . . Outerbanks Entertainment
Pless, Judith . . . . . . . . . . . . . . . . . . Showtime Networks Inc.
Plotkin, Andrew . . . . . . . . . . . . . . . . . . Rysher Entertainment
Plotner, Alan . . . . . . . . . . . . . . . . Rotman Productions, David
Plukas, Roland . . . . . . . . . . . . . . . . . Spin Cycle Entertainment
Plum, Stephen . . . . . . . . . . . . . . . . . Twentieth Century Fox
Plummer, Victoria . . . . . . . . . . . . . . Trident Releasing Inc.
Poe, Rudy . . . . . . . . . . . . . . . . . . Eleventh Day Entertainment
Pogue, Brian . . . . . . . . . . . . . . . . Dancing Asparagus Prods.
Pogue, John . . . . . . . . . . . . . . . . . . . . . . . . . . . . Poguefilm
Poitier, Sidney . . . . . . . . . . . . . . . . . . . Verdon-Cedric Prods.
Pokarney, Christy . . . . . . . . . . . . . . . . Omega Entertainment
Polak, Richard . . . . . . . . . . . . . . . . . . . Cinestage Productions
Polakoff, Carol . . . . . . . . . . . . . . . . . . Polakoff Prods., Carol
Poland, David . . . . . . . . . . . . . . . . . Trivision Pictures Inc.
Polhemus, Jib . . . . . . . . . . . . . . . . . . . Wychwood Productions
Polk, Patrik-Ian . . . . . . . . . . . . . . . . Edmonds Entertainment
Poll, Martin . . . . . . . . . . . . . . . . . . . . . . . . . Hollane Corp.
Pollack, Bradford . . . . . . . . . . . . . . . . . . . Skylark Films Ltd.
Pollack, Debra . . . . . . . . . . . . . . . Newmarket Capital Group
Pollack, Jeff . . . . . . . . . . . . . . . . . . . Handprint Entertainment
Pollack, Sydney . . . . . . . . . . . . . . . . . . . Mirage Enterprises
Pollack-Parker, Rebecca . . . . . . . . . . United Artists Pictures
Pollak, Kevin . . . . . . . . . . . . . . Calm Down Productions, Inc.
Pollison, David . . . . . . . . . . . . . . . . . . Renaissance Pictures
Pollock, Camille . . . . . . . . . . . . . . . . Persky Prods., Lester
Pollock, Dale . . . . . . . . . . . . . . . . . Open Door Entertainment
Pollock, Dale . . . . . . . . . . . . . . . . . . . . . . Peak Productions
Pollock, James B. . . . . . . . R. Edwards Prods./R. Edwards Films
Pollock, Lani . . . . . . . . . . . . . . . . . . Meyers/Shyer Co., The
Pollok, Stuart . . . . . . . . . . . . . . . . . . . Saltire Entertainment
Polone, Judith A. . . . . . . . . . . . . . . . . Polone Company, The
Polson, Beth . . . . . . . . . . . . . . . . . . . . Polson Company, The
Polstein, Claire Rudnick . . . . . . . . . . . . . New Line Cinema
Pomerance, Ruth . . . . . . . . . . . . . . . . Kopelson Entertainment
Pomerantz, Kathy S. . . . . . . . . . . . . . . . . Rosa Entertainment
Pompian, Paul . . . . . . . . . . . . . . . . Baldwin/Cohen Productions
Pompian, Paul . . . . . . . . . . . . . . . . Pompian Productions, Paul
Ponder, Zina . . . . . . . . . . . . . . . . . . Revelations Entertainment
Pongracic, Lisa . . . . . . . . . . . . . . . . . . . . . . DreamWorks SKG
Pontious, Missy . . . . . . . . . . . . . . . . . . Wilshire Court Prods.

# CROSS-REFERENCED NAMES

| | |
|---|---|
| Pool, Marci | Fox Television Studios |
| Poole, Rebecca | Nickelodeon Movies |
| Poole, Stephanie | Seven Arts Pictures |
| Pope, Alice | Warner Bros. International TV Production |
| Pope, Braxton | Mischel Co., The |
| Pope, David | Danjaq Inc. |
| Pope, Randy | Krofft Pictures Corp., Sid & Marty |
| Popofsky, Kaye | Interscope Communications Inc. |
| Porter, Christine | Ginty Films |
| Porter, Kurt | Burrud Productions |
| Porter, Pliny | Shoelace Productions, Inc. |
| Porter, Vince | Showtime Networks Inc. |
| Portier, Teena | Sacks Productions Inc., Alan |
| Portolese, James | Signature |
| Post, Ira | Sheldon/Post Company, The |
| Poster, Meryl | Miramax Films |
| Poticha, Eric | Bonneville Worldwide Entertainment |
| Potiker, Gwen | NBC Studios |
| Pottash, Bruce | Paramount Domestic TV |
| Potter, Barr | Largo Entertainment |
| Potter, Bridget | NBC Entertainment |
| Potter, Richard | Dimension Films |
| Potts, Suzanne | Columbia TriStar Motion Picture Group |
| Poul, Alan | Boku Films |
| Powell, Anne M. | LookAlike Productions |
| Powell, Brian | New Crime Productions |
| Powell, Corey | Hyperion Entertainment |
| Powell, Holly | Greenblatt Janollari Studio, The |
| Powell, Marykay | Rastar Productions |
| Powell, Norman S. | Whidbey Island Films, Inc. |
| Power, Derek | Kahn Power Pictures(Formerly Odessa Pic) |
| Power, Derek | Power Company, The Derek |
| Power, Ilene Kahn | Power Company, The Derek |
| Powers, Jim | Shooting Gallery Inc., The |
| Pozmantier, Laurie | Alliance Television Productions |
| Prager, Matt | HBO Pictures |
| Prakash, Manjari | Nederlander Television & Film |
| Prat, Olivier | Excelsior Pictures Corp. |
| Pratt Jr., Charles | Pratt Ent., Inc., Charles |
| Pratt, Chuck | Melrose Prods. |
| Pratt, Curt | Parkway Productions |
| Pregnolato, Denis | Spelling Films Inc. |
| Presser, Matt | Kassirer Meyer Entertainment |
| Pressler, Dave | Wandering Monkey Entertainment |
| Pressman, Andy | Arrow Entertainment |
| Pressman, Edward R. | Pressman Film Corp., Edward R. |
| Prezioso, Gayle | Legacy Entertainment Inc. |
| Price, Jody | Gillen & Price |
| Price, Ray | Trimark Pictures |
| Priemer, John | Crystal Beach Entertainment |
| Prigann, Aisha | Rose Productions, Lee |
| Prince, Adam | Butchers Run Films |
| Prince, Pam | Media Four |
| Prince, Tom | Bubble Factory, The |
| Principal, Victoria | Principal Prods., Victoria |
| Pritchard, David B. | Film Roman, Inc. |
| Pritscher, Elizabeth | Threshold Entertainment |
| Pritzker, Gigi | Dee Gee Entertainment |
| Proft, Pat | Proft, Pat |
| Proietto, Marci | Twentieth Century Fox Television |
| Prophet, Melissa | Baumgarten/Prophet Entertainment |
| Proppe, Hans | Shadowplay Films |
| Prucha, Lynette | Sneak Preview Entertainment, Inc. |
| Pruett, Cynthia | Constantin Film Development Inc. |
| Prunier, Christy | Phoenix Pictures |
| Prusia, Tiffany | Walt Disney Pictures/Touchstone Pictures |
| Pryde, Jamey | Shooting Gallery Inc., The |
| Pullman, Bill | Big Town Productions |
| Purcell, Elizabeth | StarGate Entertainment Inc. |
| Puritz, Elle | Lavin Entertainment Group |
| Purohit, Yogini | Galan Entertainment |
| Purves, Catherine | Cort/Madden Company, The |
| Pusavat, Keith | Producer & Management Ent. Group |
| Putnam, Kerith | HBO NYC Productions |
| Quattrone, Kathy | PBS |
| Quattrone, Mike | Discovery Networks |
| Quested, John | Goldcrest Films International, Inc. |
| Quigley, Joe | Walt Disney Pictures/Touchstone Pictures |
| Quinn, Frank | Comedy Central |
| Quinn, John | Quinn Productions |
| Quinn, Tom | Goldwyn Company, The Samuel |
| Quinn, Tracy | Producers Ent. Group, Ltd., The |
| Quiroz, Eva | Burton Prods., Tim |
| Rabin, Ian | Ridio Prods., Inc., Anthony |
| Rabiner, Steven | Castle Rock Entertainment |
| Rabins, Sandy | DreamWorks SKG |
| Radcliffe, Mark | 1492 Pictures |
| Rader, Rhoades | Ladd Company, The |
| Radford, Bonne | DreamWorks SKG |
| Radler, Kitty | RadlerFilm |
| Radler, Robert | RadlerFilm |
| Radmin, Linne | Radmin Company, The |
| Radziwill, Anthony | HBO Original Programming |
| Rae, Heather | Sundance Institute |
| Rae, Jolene | Suppa Prods., Inc., Ronald |
| Rae, Tammy | Gelfand Productions, Janna E. |
| Rafelson, Bob | Marmont Prods. Inc. |
| Rafofsky, Joshua | Lord/Weaver Prods. |
| Raiguel, Faith | Walt Disney Pictures/Touchstone Pictures |
| Raimi, Sam | Renaissance Pictures |
| Raimo, Michell | Miramax Films |
| Rain, Molly | Rudin Prods., Scott |
| Rainey, Jim | Pirromount Pictures |
| Rains, Mark | Macht Ent. Group, Inc. |
| Raitt, Jayson | Metro-Goldwyn-Mayer/Worldwide TV |
| Rajski, Peggy | Rajski Productions, Peggy |
| Raleigh, Judy | Matthau Company, Inc., The |
| Ralston, Ken | Sony Pictures Imageworks |
| Ramati, Lonnie | Phase I Productions |
| Rambaldi, David | Rambaldi Enterprises, David |
| Rambaldi, Neil | Rambaldi Enterprises, David |
| Ramirez, Lynnette | Fountainbridge Films |
| Ramis, Harold | Ocean Pictures |
| Ramos, Gus | American New Wave Films |
| Ramsey, Jade | Motion Pict. Corp. of America |
| Ramsey, Shari | Belisarius Prods. |
| Ranan, Judy | Citadel Entertainment, LLC |
| Rand, Alisandra M. | Firestorm Pictures, Ltd. |
| Randall, Gary | Grand Productions, Inc. |
| Randall, Karen | Universal Studios |
| Randell, Maggie | Grub Street Prods. |
| Randolph, Marjorie | Walt Disney Pictures/Touchstone Pictures |
| Raney, Paul | Scripps Howard Prods. |
| Rankel, Brian | Horseshoe Bay Productions |
| Rankin, Arthur | Rankin/Bass Productions |
| Ransohoff, Martin | Ransohoff Productions, Inc., Martin |
| Ransom, Dru A. | Phase I Productions |
| Raphael, David | Excelsior Pictures Corp. |
| Raphael, Sally Jessy | March Hare Entertainment |
| Rapke, Jack | ImageMovers |
| Rapp, Jerry | Looking Glass Productions |
| Rappa, Dominick | Mount/Kramer Company, The |
| Rappa, Ray | Creative Road Corp. |
| Rappaport, Daniel | 3 Arts Entertainment |
| Rardin, Amy | Obst Prods., Lynda |
| Rask, Julia | Morrow-Heus Productions |
| Raskin, Bonnie | Raskin Productions, Bonnie |
| Raskoff, Ken | Raskoff Productions, Ken |
| Rastatter, Maria | CBS Productions |
| Ratay, Mark | Gregory Productions, Inc. |
| Rathbun, Diana | Warner Bros. Pictures |
| Ratner, Brett | Rat Entertainment |
| Rauch, Ellen | Warner Bros. Television Productions |
| Rauch, Mike | Showtime Networks Inc. |
| Rauch, Paul | Two Pauls Entertainment |
| Raucher, Jennifer | Barwood Films |
| Raval, Manish | Immortal Films |
| Raven, Abbe | A & E Television Networks |
| Raven, Abbe | History Channel, The |
| Ravine, Vince | Green Communications |
| Rawley, Peter | Fortune Media Group, Inc. |
| Ray, Bingham | October Films |
| Raymond, Kevin | Kedzie Productions |
| Raynor, Lynn | P.O.V. Co. |
| Raynor, Milton T. | Newland-Raynor Prods., Inc. |
| Read, Bob | Albrecht/Read Management |
| Reagan, Darren | Marstar Prods. |
| Record, Laurie | Jersey Films |
| Record, Timothy | Finerman Prods., Wendy |
| Redford, Robert | South Fork Pictures |

# CROSS-REFERENCED NAMES

Redford, Robert . . . . . . . . . . . . . . . . . . . Wildwood Enterprises Inc.
Redler, Dan . . . . . . . . . . . . . . . . . . . . . Redler Entertainment, Dan
Redmon, Diana . . . . . . . . . . . . . . . . . . . . . Merv Griffin Productions
Reed, Graham . . . . . . . . . . . . . . . . . . . . . . . . . Mostow/Lieberman
Reed, Jason . . . . . . . . . . . . Walt Disney Pictures/Touchstone Pictures
Reed, Marsha L. . . . . . . . . . . . . . . . . . Walt Disney Company, The
Reed, Nikki . . . . . . . . . . . . . . . . . . . . . . . Junction Entertainment
Reeder, David . . . . . . . . . . . . . . . . . . . . . . . . . Poco Productions
Rees, Brennan . . . . . . . . . . . . . . . Illusion Entertainment Group
Rees, Marian . . . . . . . . . . . . . . . . . . . . . Rees Assocs., Marian
Reeve, Lisa . . . . . . . . . . . . . . . . . . . . . . . . . . . Simian Films
Regan, Judith . . . . . . . . . . . . . . . . . . . . . Regan Company, The
Rehme, Robert . . . . . . . . . . . . . . . . . . . . . Rehme Productions
Reich, Steven . . . . . . . . . . . . . . . . . . . . . . . . Wild Films Inc.
Reichel, Stephane . . . . . . . . . . . . . . . . . . . . . . Allegro Films
Reid Levin, Debby . . . . . . . . . . . . . . . . . . . GRB Entertainment
Reid, Dana . . . . . . . . . . . . . . . . . . . . . . . Artisan Entertainment
Reid, Eric . . . . . . . . . . . . . . . . . Lakeshore Entertainment Corp.
Reid, Lisa . . . . . . . . . . . . . . . . . . . . . . . . . . Sandollar Prods.
Reid, Melissa . . . . . . . . . . . . . . . . . . . . . . . Red Wagon Prods.
Reid, Sandra . . . . . . . . . . . . . . . . . . Wachs Co., The Robert D.
Reid, Tim . . . . . . . . . . . . . . . . . . . . . Reid Productions, Inc., Tim
Reid, Tori L. . . . . . . . . . . . . . . . . . . Reid Productions, Inc., Tim
Reidy, Maureen J. . . . . . . . . . . . . . . . Miss Universe L.P., LLLP
Reilly Jr., Edward . . . . . . . . . . . . Concorde/New Horizons Corp.
Reilly, Alicia . . . . . . . . . . . . . . . . . Unapix/A-PIX Entertainment
Reilly, Kevin . . . . . . . . . . . . . . . . . . . . . . Brillstein-Grey Ent.
Reimer, Andrew . . . . . . . . . . . . . . . . . . . . . Trimark Pictures
Reiner, Rob . . . . . . . . . . . . . . . . . . Castle Rock Entertainment
Reiner, Susan . . . . . . . . . . . . . . . . . . . . . . . Avnet-Kerner Co.
Reinert, Carole . . . . . . . . . . . . . . . . . . Reinert Pictures, Rick
Reinert, Rick . . . . . . . . . . . . . . . . . . . . Reinert Pictures, Rick
Reinking, Mark Hunter . . . . . . . . . . . . . . . . . . Moving Pictures
Reisman, Michael . . . . . . . . . . . . . . . . . . . . . . . . Alphaville
Reiss, Ariel . . . . . . . . . . . . . . . . . . . . . . . . . H2 Productions
Reitman, Ivan . . . . . . . . . . . . . . . . . . . . Northern Lights Ent.
Reitzer, Larry . . . . . . . . . . . . . . . . . . . . . . . . UBU Productions
Relyea, Robert . . . . . . . . . . . . . . Metro-Goldwyn-Mayer Pictures
Rembert, Grey . . . . . . . . . . . . . . . . . . . . . . . DreamWorks SKG
Remesar, Luis . . . . . . . . . . . . . . . . . . . Coyote Pass Productions
Remiro-Jordan, Maria . . . . . . . . . . . . . . . . . . . Langley Prods.
Remppel, Richard . . . . . . . . . United Paramount Network (UPN)
Rende, George . . . . . . . . . . . . . . . . . . . . . . Canterbury Films
Resh, Julie . . . . . . . . . . . . . . . . . . . . . . . Fox Family Channel
Resnick, Gina . . . . . . . . . . . . . . . . . . . GMR Productions, Inc.
Resnick, Mark . . . . . . . . . . . . . . . . Twentieth Century Fox
Resnick, Noel . . . . . . . . . . . Lancit Media Entertainment, Ltd.
Revitte, Joe . . . . . . . . . . . . . . . . . . . . . . Fine Line Features
Reynolds, Burt . . . . . . . . . . AM Productions & Management
Reynolds, Fred . . . . . . . . . . . . . . . . . . . . . . CBS Corporation
Reynolds, Jerry . . . . . . . . . . . Perennial Pictures Film Corp.
Rhodes, Annie . . . . . . . . . . . . . . . . . . . . . . . Mostow/Lieberman
Rhodes, Matthew . . . . . . . . . . . . . . . Persistent Pictures, Inc.
Rhodes, Scott . . . . . . . . . . . . . . . . . . . . . . ABC Entertainment
Ribeiro, Chantal . . . . . . . . . . . . . . . . . . Cinema Seven Prods.
Ricca, Greg . . . . . . . . . . . . . . . . . . . . . . . . . MTV Networks
Rice, Craig . . . . . . . . . . . . . . . . . . . . . River Mill Productions
Rice, Dorothy . . . . . . . . . . . . . . . . . . . Chase Prods., Stanley
Rice, Joel S. . . . . . . . . . . . . . . . . . . . . . WildRice Productions
Rice, Peter . . . . . . . . . . . . . . . . . . . . Twentieth Century Fox
Rice, Ronni Z. . . . . . . . . . . . . . . . . . . . . WildRice Productions
Rice, Wayne . . . . . . . . . . . . . . . . . Master Thespian Productions
Rich, David . . . . . . . . . . . . . . . . . . . . . Bean And Cod Prods.
Rich, Gerry . . . . . . . . . . . . . . . . . . . . . . . Goldwyn Films Inc.
Rich, Lee . . . . . . . . . . . . . . . . . . . . . . Rich Productions, Lee
Richards, Alicia . . . . . . . . . . . . . . . . . . . Kettledrum Films, Inc
Richards, Steve . . . . . . . . . . . . . . . . . . . . . . . Silver Pictures
Richardson, Lisa . . . . . . . . . . . . . . . . . . Pacific Motion Pictures
Richardson, Mike . . . . . . . . . . . . . . . . . . . . Dark Horse Ent.
Richbourg, Eli . . . . . . . . . . . . . . . . . Schumacher Prods., Joel
Riche, Alan . . . . . . . . . . . . . . . . . . . Riche/Ludwig Productions
Riche, Wendy . . . . . . . . . . . . . . . . . . . . . . . . . ABC Daytime
Richman, Carrie . . . . . . . . . . . . . . . . . . . . Columbia Pictures
Richmond, Aaron . . . . . . . . . . . . . . Capital Arts Entertainment
Richter, Andrew . . . . . . . . . Bonneville Worldwide Entertainment
Rico, Chris . . . . . . . . . . . . Twentieth Century Fox-Fox 2000 (LA)
Ridenhour, Chris . . . . . . . . . . . . . . . . . . . Tavel Entertainment
Ridini, Maryann . . . . . . . . . . Ridini Entertainment Corporation
Ridio, Anthony . . . . . . . . . . . . . . Ridio Prods., Inc., Anthony
Ridio, Kelly . . . . . . . . . . . . . . . . Ridio Prods., Inc., Anthony

Ridley, Jane . . . . . . . . . . . . . . . . . . . . . . . Aviator Films LLC
Rieber, John . . . . . . . . . . . . . . . . E! Entertainment Television
Rigg, Jean . . . . . . . . . . . . . . . . . . . . . Lifetime Television (NY)
Riklin, Matthew . . . . . . . . . . . . . . . . . . Showtime Networks Inc.
Riley, Sahara . . . . . . . . . . . . . . Playboy Entertainment Group Inc.
Rink, JoAnn . . . . . . . . . . . . . . . . . . . . . . . . Brandman Prods.
Rinzel, Alison . . . . . . . . . . . . . . . . . . . . . . . CBS Entertainment
Ripley, James . . . . . . . . . . . . . . . . . . . . . . . Enteraktion, Inc.
Ripp, Martha . . . . . . . . . . . . . . . . . . . . . Jumbo Pictures, Inc.
Ripps, Hillary Anne . . . . . . . . . . . . . . . . . . Chanticleer Films
Risher, Sara . . . . . . . . . . . . . . . . . . . . . . . . New Line Cinema
Rissner, Dan . . . . . . . . . . . . . . . . . Neufeld Productions, Mace
Risucci, Christopher . . . . . . . . . . . . . . Oliver Productions, Lin
Rita, Jason . . . . . . . . . . . . . . . . . . . . . . Thunderbird Pictures
Ritt, Martina . . . . . . . . . . . . . . . . . . . . . . . Enteraktion, Inc.
Ritter, John . . . . . . . . . . . . . . . . . . . . . . . . Adam Productions
Riva, J. David . . . . . . . . . . . Associated Producers Group, Inc.
Rivard, Ilka . . . . . . . . . . . . . . . . . . . . . Stupin Productions, Paul
Rivas, Ivan . . . . . . . . . . . . . . . . . . . . . . . Elkins Entertainment
Rivera, Lee . . . . . . . . . . . . . . . . . Turner Original Productions
Riviere, Sylvie De La . . . . . . . . . . . . . . . . . . CPC Entertainment
Rivkin, Charles H. . . . . . . . . . . . . . . . Henson Company, Jim
Rizor, Joel . . . . . . . . . . . . . . . . . Weller/Grossman Productions
Roach, James A. . . . . . . . . . . . . . . . . . Bochco Prods., Steven
Roach, Jay . . . . . . . . . . . . . . . . . . . . . . . Everyman Pictures
Roach, John . . . . . . . . . . . . . . . . . . . . . Force Ten Productions
Robbins, B.J. . . . . . . . . . . . . . . . . . . . . . . . . . . Jake Films
Robbins, Brian . . . . . . . . . . . . . . . . Tollin/Robbins Productions
Robbins, Lance H. . . . . . . . . . . . . . . . . Fox Family Channel
Robbins, Lance H. . . . . . . . . . . . . . . . . . Saban Entertainment
Robbins, Mary . . . . . . . . . . . . . . . . . Goat Cay Productions, Inc.
Robbins, Mitchell B. . . . . . . . . . . . . . . Robbins Entertainment
Robbins, Richard . . . . . . . . . Producer & Management Ent. Group
Robbins, Tim . . . . . . . . . . . . . . . . . . . . . . . . . . Havoc Inc.
Roberson, Bud . . . . . . . . . . . America National Network, Inc.
Roberson, Julia . . . . . . . . . . . . . . . . . . . . . Eagle Nation Films
Robert, Geri . . . . . . . . . . . . . . . . . . . . . . . . . . Fried Films
Roberts, Julia . . . . . . . . . . . . . . . . Shoelace Productions, Inc.
Roberts, Marilyn . . . . . . . . . . . . . . . . . . . . . . . . Poguefilm
Roberts, Mark . . . . . . . . . . . . . . . . . . . Kingsize Entertainment
Roberts, Michael . . . . . . . Walt Disney Pictures/Touchstone Pictures
Roberts, Nancy . . . . . . . . . . . . . . . . . . Stampede Entertainment
Roberts, Susan . . . . . . . . . . . . . . . . . . Kirschner Prods., David
Robertson, Shauna . . . . . . . . . . . . . . . . . . . Everyman Pictures
Robinov, Jeff . . . . . . . . . . . . . . . . . . . . . Warner Bros. Pictures
Robinson, Adam . . . . . . . . . . . . . . . . . . . . . FilmColony, Ltd.
Robinson, Amy . . . . . . . . . . . . . . Robinson Productions, Amy
Robinson, Bill . . . . . . . . . . . . . . . . . . . . . . . Blue Relief, Inc.
Robinson, Bob . . . . . . . . . Ransohoff Productions, Inc., Martin
Robinson, David M. . . . . . . . . Twentieth Century Fox Television
Robinson, Dolores . . . . . . . . . Robinson Entertainment, Dolores
Robinson, Elizabeth . . . . . . . . . Lasher, McManus & Robinson
Robinson, Gary . . . . . . . . . . . . . . . Granada Entertainment USA
Robinson, James G. . . . . . . . . . . . . . . . Morgan Creek Prods.
Robinson, Phil Alden . . . . . . . . . . . . . . . Phil Alden Robinson
Robinson, Randy . . . . . . . . . . . . . . . . . . . Randwell Productions
Robson, Sybil A. . . . . . . . . . . . . . . . . . . . Robson Entertainment
Rocco, Marc . . . . . . . . . . . . . . . . . . . . . . . . . Camera Marc
Rocha, Stephen . . . . . . . . . . . . . . . . . . . . . . . . Vision Films
Roche, Tim . . . . . . . . . . . . . . . . . . . . . . . . MK Productions
Roda, Jeffrey . . . . . . . . . . . . . Hart Sharp Entertainment, Inc.
Roddy, Jessica . . . . . . . . . . . . . . Castle Rock Entertainment
Rodgers, Christine . . . . . . . . . . . . . . . . . . One Story Pictures
Rodgers, David . . . . . . . . . . . . . . . . . . . . . One Story Pictures
Rodgers, Johnathan . . . . . . . . . . . . . . . . . Discovery Networks
Rodman, Simone D. . . . . . . . . . . . . . . . . . Rumbleseat Prods.
Rodrigue, Nena . . . . . . . . . . . . . . . . . . . . Imagine Television
Rodriguez, Kathy . . . . . . . . . Gelfand Productions, Janna E.
Rodriguez, Lisa . . . . . . . . . . . . . . . Weintraub Prods., Jerry
Rodriquez-Pozeilov, Yosi . . . . . . . . . . . . . . Single Spark Pictures
Rodwick, Leigh . . . . . . . . . . . . . . . . . . . . Acappella Pictures
Roe, Nick . . . . . . . . . . . . . . . . . . . . . . . . . C/W Productions
Roe, SoYun . . . . . . . . . . . . . . . . . . . . . . . . . . Winkler Films
Roedy, William . . . . . . . . . . . . . . . . . . . . . . . . MTV Networks
Roesler, Sharon . . . . . . . . . . . . . . . . . . . High Road Productions
Roessler, Craig . . . . . . . . Metro-Goldwyn-Mayer/Worldwide TV
Roewe, Jay . . . . . . . . . . . . . . . . . . . . . . . . . . HBO Pictures
Roffer, Steven . . . . . . . . . . . . . . . . . . . . . . . . . HyperFilms
Rogan, Tom . . . . . . . . . . . . . . . . . Film Garden Entertainment
Rogers, Amy . . . . . . . . . . . . . . . . . Stargazer Entertainment, Inc.

| | |
|---|---|
| Rogers, Peter | Lakeshore Entertainment Corp. |
| Rogers, Phil | Philipico Pictures Co. |
| Rogers, Scott | Kolar Productions, Inc. |
| Rogers, Stephanie | Philipico Pictures Co. |
| Rogers, Wayne | Stargazer Entertainment, Inc. |
| Rogow, Stan | Rogow Productions, Stan |
| Rohner, Franklin B. | Bochco Prods., Steven |
| Rohrer, Susan | S.E.R. Filmworks |
| Rollins, Francesca | Zaring/Cioffi Entertainment, Inc. |
| Rollman, Eric | Saban Entertainment |
| Romaine, Michelle | Haines Company, Randa |
| Roman, Phil | Film Roman, Inc. |
| Romanoff, Lise | Vision Films |
| Rona, Andrew | Dimension Films |
| Rooker, Melissa | Malpaso Prods. |
| Rooker, Tom | Malpaso Prods. |
| Roos, Bram | FilmRoos |
| Roos, Fred | F.R. Productions |
| Root, Antony | Granada Entertainment USA |
| Ros, Jordi | Walt Disney Pictures/Touchstone Pictures |
| Rosas, Dora | Dakota North Ent./Dakota Films |
| Rose, Alex | Rose Prods. Inc., Alex |
| Rose, Andrew | Little Bear Films, Inc. |
| Rose, David | Santa Monica Pictures |
| Rose, Jane | Rotman Productions, David |
| Rose, Kathleen | Winsome Pictures, Inc. |
| Rose, Kevin L. | T.H.A. - Thomas Horton Associates Inc. |
| Rose, Lee | Rose Productions, Lee |
| Rose, Merry | Beacon Pictures |
| Rose, Rachel | Centropolis Streamline |
| Rose, Sara | Goldwyn Films Inc. |
| Roseanne | Full Moon & High Tide Prods. Inc. |
| Rosemont, David A. | Rosemont Prods. International Ltd. |
| Rosemont, Norman | Rosemont Prods. International Ltd. |
| Rosen, Adam | Warner Bros. International TV Production |
| Rosen, Barry | Goodman-Rosen Prods. |
| Rosen, Carole | HBO Original Programming |
| Rosen, Douglas | Chesterfield Film Co., The |
| Rosen, Josie | Horseshoe Bay Productions |
| Rosen, Lon | Johnson Entertainment, Magic |
| Rosen, Manette Beth | Rosen/Bender Prods. |
| Rosen, Richard | WolfMill Entertainment |
| Rosen, Shanna | Demberg Productions, Lisa |
| Rosen, Steve | Kushner-Locke Co. |
| Rosen, Tony | Troma Inc. |
| Rosenbalm, R.C. | Populuxe Pictures |
| Rosenberg, Gary A. | Parallel Pictures |
| Rosenberg, Helena Hacker | Rosenberg, Helena Hacker |
| Rosenberg, Julia | Alliance Pictures |
| Rosenberg, Max J. | Rearguard Productions, Inc. |
| Rosenberg, Michael | Imagine Entertainment |
| Rosenberg, Paul | Saratoga Entertainment |
| Rosenberg, Rick | Chris/Rose Prods. |
| Rosenberg, Scott Mitchell | Platinum Studios, LLC |
| Rosenberg, Steve | Studios USA |
| Rosenberg, Thomas | Lakeshore Entertainment Corp. |
| Rosenblatt, Bart | Neverland Films, Inc. |
| Rosenblatt, Beth | Miramax Films |
| Rosenblatt, Justin | Witt-Thomas Films |
| Rosenbloom, Dale | Utopia Picts./Carl Borack Productions |
| Rosenbloom, Richard | Rosenbloom Prods., Richard |
| Rosenblum, Gail | Miss Universe L.P., LLLP |
| Rosenblum, John Frank | Lighthouse Productions |
| Rosenbush, Barry | First Street Films, Inc. |
| Rosencrans, Suzanne | New Line Cinema |
| Rosendahl, Carl | Pacific Data Images |
| Rosene, Lori | Meridian Films |
| Rosenfeld, Daniel | Madguy Films |
| Rosenfeld, Madelon | Jurist Productions |
| Rosenfeld, Michael | Brillstein-Grey Ent. |
| Rosenfeld, Michael | National Geographic Television |
| Rosenfeld, Mike | Kenwood Prods., Inc. |
| Rosenfelt, Adam | HSI Entertainment |
| Rosenfelt, Karen | Paramount Pictures- Production Division |
| Rosenfelt, Scott | Shadowcatcher Entertainment |
| Rosenman, Howard | Rosenman Productions, Howard |
| Rosenstein, Nina | HBO Original Programming |
| Rosenthal, Isabel | Twentieth Century Fox |
| Rosenthal, Isabel | Twentieth Century Fox-Searchlight Picts. |
| Rosenthal, Jane | Tribeca Productions |
| Rosenthal, Mark | MTV Networks |
| Rosenthal, Rick | Whitewater Films |
| Rosett, Daniel | Metro-Goldwyn-Mayer Pictures |
| Rosetti, Richard P. | Playboy Entertainment Group Inc. |
| Rosin, Katherine | Lions Gate Films Production |
| Rosner, Louise | Tapestry Films Inc. |
| Ross, Damon | Nickelodeon Movies |
| Ross, Gary | Ross Production, Gary |
| Ross, Hal | Ross Productions, Hal |
| Ross, Herbert | Ross, Herbert |
| Ross, Kenneth | Mount/Kramer Company, The |
| Ross, Laurie | Propaganda Films |
| Ross, Lisa M. | Neila Inc. |
| Ross, Marcia S. | Walt Disney Pictures/Touchstone Pictures |
| Ross, Marcy | Henson Company, Jim |
| Ross, Matt | CBS Entertainment |
| Ross, Michael | W.B. Television Network |
| Ross, Nancy M. | Neila Inc. |
| Ross, Rich | Disney Channel |
| Ross, Stanley Ralph | Neila Inc. |
| Ross, Zana | Eternity Pictures, Inc |
| Rossellini, Victoria | Twentieth Century Fox |
| Rosser, Brandon | Shooting Gallery Inc., The |
| Rossi, Carol | Keller Entertainment Group |
| Rossi, Dave | Berman Productions, Rick |
| Rossi, Jim | Howard Prods. Inc., Al |
| Rossow, Jim | Pacific Western Prods. |
| Rossu, Alex | Rossu Entertainment |
| Rosten, Peter | Kingman Films International |
| Rotenberg, Michael | 3 Arts Entertainment |
| Roth, Craig Davis | Daly-Harris Productions |
| Roth, Donna | Roth/Arnold Prods. |
| Roth, Joe | Walt Disney Pictures/Touchstone Pictures |
| Roth, Kim | Witt-Thomas Films |
| Roth, Myron | All American Communications, Inc. |
| Roth, Peter | Fox Broadcasting Co. |
| Rothbard, Robert | Miracle Productions, Inc. |
| Rothberg, Naomi | Lynch Entertainment |
| Rothkin, Barbara | Lifetime Television (NY) |
| Rothman, Tom | Twentieth Century Fox |
| Rothschild, Cheryl Birch | Paramount Network Television |
| Rothstein, Freyda | Rothstein Prods., Freyda |
| Rothstein, Richard | Carter Company, The Thomas |
| Rothstein, Richard | NBC Entertainment |
| Rotman, David | Rotman Productions, David |
| Rotman, Jaime | Zero Pictures |
| Roumel, Katie | Killer Films, Inc. |
| Roven, Charles | Atlas Entertainment |
| Rovner, Robert | Granada Entertainment USA |
| Rovner, Susan | ABC Entertainment |
| Rowe, Chris | Banner Assocs., Bob |
| Rowe, Michelle | Chanticleer Films |
| Rowe, Tom | Pacific Motion Pictures |
| Rowlee, Teresa | Renaissance Pictures |
| Roy, Melanie | HBO Original Programming |
| Roybal, Mark | Rudin Prods., Scott |
| Rozenfeld, Kim | ABC Entertainment |
| Ruark, Joel | Wind Dancer Prod. Group |
| Rubin, Alyse | Kennedy/Marshall Company |
| Rubin, Barbara M. | Rysher Entertainment |
| Rubin, David | Mirage Enterprises |
| Rubin, Jerry | Kushner-Locke Co. |
| Rubin, Kimberly | Greenwald Prods., Robert |
| Rubin, Marjorie | Rubin * Burke Productions |
| Rubinstein, Richard P. | New Amsterdam Entertainment, Inc. |
| Rubio, Jack | Film Kitchen |
| Ruby, Joseph | Ruby-Spears Prods. |
| Ruddy, Al | Ruddy Morgan Organization, Inc., The |
| Rudin, Scott | Rudin Prods., Scott |
| Rudnick, Arnold | Lucchesi Prods., Gary |
| Rudnicki, Stefan | NewStar Media |
| Rudolph, Alan | Raincity |
| Rudolph, Ellen | HBO Pictures |
| Rudolph, Matt | Lakeshore Entertainment Corp. |
| Ruegger, Tom | Warner Bros. TV Animation |
| Rugolo-Judd, Gina | More/Medavoy Management |
| Ruiz, Antonio | E! Entertainment Television |
| Ruiz, Manuel | Lux Pictures |
| Runstrom, Michael | Alan Smithee Films |
| Runtagh, Hellene | Universal Studios |

| | |
|---|---|
| Rush, Herman | Katz/Rush Entertainment |
| Rush, Jordan | KiMina Entertainment |
| Ruskin, Kevin | Davis Classics |
| Ruskin, Morris | Shoreline Entertainment |
| Ruskin, Susan | Middle Fork Productions |
| Russ, Mark | Obst Prods., Lynda |
| Russell, Ann | High Horse Films |
| Russell, Michael | CinePoint Productions, Inc. |
| Russell, Neil | Russell Productions, Neil |
| Russo, Sylvester | King World Productions |
| Russo, Tom | Paramount Network Television |
| Rust, Patricia | Rust Productions, Patricia |
| Rustam, Mr. Mardi | Mars Prods. Corp. |
| Rustam, Sarah | Mars Prods. Corp. |
| Rustemagic, Ervin | Platinum Studios, LLC |
| Ruta, Nick | Baldwin/Cohen Productions |
| Ruzicka, Tom | Walt Disney Television Animation |
| Ruzzin, Gregory | Nine By Nine |
| Ryan, Chris | CBS Entertainment |
| Ryan, Daniela | Samuelson Productions |
| Ryan, Hilary | George Litto Pictures |
| Ryan, Josh | Tulchin Entertainment |
| Ryan, Meg | Prufrock Pictures |
| Ryan, Mix | Iwerks Entertainment |
| Ryan, Teya | Turner Original Productions |
| Ryan-Shearman, Jennifer | Cohen & Ryan Films, Inc. |
| Rydell, Mark | Concourse Prods. |
| Ryder, Aaron | Newmarket Capital Group |
| Saade, John | Dakota North Ent./Dakota Films |
| Saatjian, Wendy | Paulson Prods., Daniel L. |
| Saavedra, Craig M. | FilmSaavy |
| Saban, Haim | Fox Family Channel |
| Saban, Haim | Fox Kids Network |
| Saban, Haim | Saban Entertainment |
| Sabath, Barry | Blue Wolf Prods. Inc. |
| Sabellico, Steve | Crew Prods., Dick |
| Sacchi, John | Lobell-Bergman Prods. |
| Sacharow, Michele | Reid Productions, Inc., Tim |
| Sachnoff, Marc | Sachnoff-Lipman Entertainment |
| Sachs, Claudia | Caravan Pictures |
| Sachs, Gabe | Sachs Productions, Gabe |
| Sachs, Karen | Brookwell McNamara Entertainment |
| Sachs, Patty | Proft, Pat |
| Sacks, Alan | Sacks Productions Inc., Alan |
| Sacks, David | Warner Bros. Television Productions |
| Sadeghi, Jennifer | Adelson Entertainment |
| Sadowski, Peter | Von Zerneck-Sertner Films |
| Sadowsky, Nina R. | Prufrock Pictures |
| Safavi, Mandy | Kingman Films International |
| Safenowitz, Howard | Walt Disney Pictures/Touchstone Pictures |
| Safford, Tony | Twentieth Century Fox |
| Safran, Don | Rastar Productions |
| Safran, Nancy | Red Wagon Prods. |
| Sagerian, Melissa | Propaganda Films |
| Sahlberg, Ryan | Equinox Entertainment Ltd. |
| Saigh, Rita | Nasser Entertainment Group |
| Saintex, Tony | Rossu Entertainment |
| Saiz, Rita | America National Network, Inc. |
| Sajak, Pat | P.A.T. Productions |
| Sakai, Richard | Gracie Films |
| Salant, Victor | Viacom Productions |
| Salas, Janet | Storyopolis Productions |
| Salas, Marian | Cine Grande Entertainment |
| Saler, John | Lake Como Pictures |
| Salerno, Bob | Shooting Gallery Inc., The |
| Sales, Daniel | Cinequanon Pictures Intl. Inc. |
| Salinas, Xavier | Esparza-Katz Prods. |
| Sallan, Bruce | Davis Entertainment Co. |
| Salloum, Glen | Blue Tulip Productions |
| Salmo, Frederick E. | Davis Classics |
| Salmon, Brenda | TLC Entertainment |
| Salmon, Charles | Intrepidus |
| Salob, Lorin B. | Pearson All American |
| Saltz, Harry | Moving Pictures |
| Saltzman, Stephen | Double Eagle Ent. |
| Salvino, Frank | Initial Entertainment Group |
| Salzberg, Diane | Picturemaker Prods. |
| Salzman, David | Quincy Jones*David Salzman Entertainment |
| Samaha, Elie | Phoenician Films |
| Sampson, Vivian | Blanki & Bodi Prods., Inc. |
| Samson, Josh | Furst Films |
| Samson, Joshua | Glatzer Productions |
| Samuels, Ron | Samuels Ent. Inc., Ron |
| Samuelson, Marc | Samuelson Productions |
| Samuelson, Peter | Samuelson Productions |
| Sanagustin, Chris | Viacom Productions |
| Sanchez, Martha | Curtis Prods., Dan |
| Sanchini, Rae | Lightstorm Entertainment |
| Sanderlin, Ann Marie | Mestres Productions, Ricardo |
| Sanders, Bill | Big Ticket Television |
| Sanders, Brian | Weiny Bro Productions |
| Sanders, Jay | Lightstorm Entertainment |
| Sanders, Ken | Image Organization, Inc. |
| Sanders, Lissa | Braun Productions, David |
| Sanders, Scott | Mandalay Television |
| Sanders, Vernon | Wind Dancer Prod. Group |
| Sanderson, Lisa | Red Strokes Entertainment |
| Sandin, Scott | Capital Arts Entertainment |
| Sandler, Jessica | Warner Bros. Pictures |
| Sandman, Vaughn | Stun |
| Sandron, Alessandra | Stone Canyon Investments, Inc. |
| Sandru, Corina A. | Chris/Rose Prods. |
| Sands, Lauren | Donley Productions, Maureen |
| Sands, Rick | Miramax Films |
| Sandys, Eric | Seven Arts Pictures |
| Sandzimier, Bruce | Studios USA Television |
| Sanford, Midge | Sanford/Pillsbury Prods. |
| Sanger, Alex | Caravan Pictures |
| Sanger, Jonathan | C/W Productions |
| Sanitsky, Bob | PolyGram Television |
| Sano, Dana | New Line Cinema |
| Santa Croce, Anthony | Ascato Entertainment |
| Santana, Victor | Once Upon A Time Films, Ltd. |
| Santor, Louis | New Regency Prods. |
| Santos, Christopher | Punch Productions |
| Saperstein, Frank | Matinee Entertainment |
| Saperstein, Henry G. | UPA Productions of America |
| Saperstein, Richard | New Line Cinema |
| Saphier, Patricia | CBS Entertainment |
| Saphier, Peter | Saphier Productions |
| Saralegui, Jorge | Material |
| Saranec, Christopher | NBC Studios |
| Sardini, Ann | Children's Television Workshop |
| Sarkissian, Arthur | Sarkissian Productions, Arthur |
| Sarnoff, Ann | Nickelodeon/Nick at Nite |
| Sarnoff, Bret | Carsey-Werner Co., The |
| Sarnoff, Tim | Sony Pictures Imageworks |
| Sass, Stephen J. | NBC Studios |
| Satter, Michelle | Sundance Institute |
| Sauer, Steve | Media Four |
| Saunders, George | Trivision Pictures Inc. |
| Saunders, James | Spin Cycle Entertainment |
| Saunders, Tatiana | Amen Ra Films |
| Savage, John | Turner Original Productions |
| Savage, Stephanie | Flower Films, Inc. |
| Savas, Michael | Davis Entertainment Co. |
| Savitch, Alison | Threshold Entertainment |
| Sayre, Cyndi | Pola Co Productions |
| Sayres, Amy | Tribeca Productions |
| Scalem, James | PBS |
| Scanlan, Dana | Kushner-Locke Co. |
| Scanlan, Kristy | Pacific Western Prods. |
| Scanlon, Caitlin | Beacon Pictures |
| Scannell, Herb | Nickelodeon/Nick at Nite |
| Scaton, Barry | Saban Entertainment |
| Scaturro, Nick | Spin Cycle Entertainment |
| Schachter, Ted | Schachter Entertainment, Inc. |
| Schaefer, Fred | Porchlight Entertainment |
| Schaeffer, James | Main Line Pictures |
| Schaeffer, Paul | Mandalay Pictures |
| Schaer, Josh | Lobell-Bergman Prods. |
| Schaer, Valerie | ABC Daytime |
| Schaffel, Robert | High Road Productions |
| Schamus, James | Good Machine |
| Schapiro, Angela P. | IndieGal Productions, LLC |
| Schapiro, Ken | Artisan Entertainment |
| Schatz, Kirsten | Tribeca Productions |
| Schechter, Dorothy | UPA Productions of America |
| Scheidlinger, Rob | OMNIBUS |
| Scheimer, Erika | Scheimer Prods., Lou |

# CROSS-REFERENCED NAMES

| | |
|---|---|
| Scheimer, Lou | Scheimer Prods., Lou |
| Scheinman, Andrew | Castle Rock Entertainment |
| Schenck, Jeff | Regent Entertainment, Inc. |
| Scherer, Ken | Frost Prods., Mark |
| Scherick, Edgar J. | Scherick Assocs., Edgar J. |
| Schiff, Paul | Schiff Productions, Paul |
| Schiff-Abrams, Zach | Pressman Film Corp., Edward R. |
| Schiffer, Holly | Common Creed Entertainment Corp. |
| Schiffer, Michael | BallPark Productions |
| Schiffman, Barbara | Dancing Asparagus Prods. |
| Schiller, Vivian | Turner Original Productions |
| Schimmel, Elizabeth | Lakeshore Entertainment Corp. |
| Schimpf, Barbara | Talking Rings Entertainment |
| Schindel, Barry | Kardana Films, Inc. |
| Schinderman, Jay | Punch Productions |
| Schindler, Deborah | Schindler Prods., Deborah |
| Schipper, Ted | Mount Royal Entertainment |
| Schiro, Victor | Dryer Prods., Fred |
| Schisgal, Murray | Punch Productions |
| Schlank, Todd | Worth Prods., Marvin |
| Schlatter, George | Schlatter Prods., George |
| Schlatter, Maria S. | Schlatter Prods., George |
| Schlesinger, Adam | Doumanian Prods., Jean |
| Schlichter, Brian K. | Lancaster Gate Ent. |
| Schliewen, Heather | Rogers Entertainment |
| Schmidt, Ann-Cathrin | Boardwalk Ent./Alan Wagner Prods., Inc. |
| Schmidt, John | October Films |
| Schmidt, Ron | Green Communications |
| Schmidt, William | Edelson Productions |
| Schmoeller, Gary | Filmwerks |
| Schneider, Don | Phase I Productions |
| Schneider, Peter | Walt Disney Pictures/Touchstone Pictures |
| Schneider, William G. | America National Network, Inc. |
| Schnitzer, Robert | Movicorp Holdings, Inc. |
| Schoenfeld, Peter | Universal Television & Networks Group |
| Schoenhals, Kai P. | Open Door Entertainment |
| Scholz, Johnathan | Una Chica Entertainment |
| Schreiber, Amanda | Haft Entertainment |
| Schreiner, Rheinhardt | American New Wave Films |
| Schrock, Laura | Big Ticket Television |
| Schroeder, Adam | Rudin Prods., Scott |
| Schroeder, Julie | Trimark Pictures |
| Schube, Peter | Henson Company, Jim |
| Schuhart-Zito, Susan | Bradford Enterprises & Gemmy Prods. |
| Schulman, Barry | USA Networks |
| Schulman, Catherine | Lobell-Bergman Prods. |
| Schulman, Mark | 3 Arts Entertainment |
| Schulman, Michael | Mendel Productions, Barry |
| Schultheis, Mindy | Twentieth Century Fox Television |
| Schultz, Amy | Raskin Productions, Bonnie |
| Schultz, Bill | Sony Pictures Imageworks |
| Schultz, Michelle | Columbia Pictures |
| Schultz, Murray | Blue Rider Pictures |
| Schultze, Alexandra | Roscoe Enterprises, Inc. |
| Schumacher, Joel | Schumacher Prods., Joel |
| Schumacher, Thomas | Walt Disney Pictures/Touchstone Pictures |
| Schuman, Philip | Universal Television & Networks Group |
| Schur, Jacki | Nasser Entertainment Group |
| Schwab, Ken | Turner Entertainment Group |
| Schwam, Carla | First Look Picts./Overseas Filmgroup |
| Schwartz, Al | Clark Prods., Inc., Dick |
| Schwartz, Bernard | Schwartz Productions, Bernard |
| Schwartz, Brian M. | Ocean Pictures |
| Schwartz, Doris | RKO Pictures, Inc. |
| Schwartz, Douglas | Berk Schwartz Bonann Productions |
| Schwartz, Ellen | Warner Bros. Pictures |
| Schwartz, Jennifer | Slawson Prods., Ruth |
| Schwartz, Jill | Pearson Television Productions |
| Schwartz, Marty E. | Anderson Prods., Craig |
| Schwartz, Robert | Gleneagle Productions |
| Schwartz, Robert A. | Wardenclyffe Entertainment |
| Schwartz, Robin | NBC Entertainment |
| Schwartz, Russell | HBO Independent Productions |
| Schwartz, Sander | Columbia TriStar Television |
| Schwartz, Steven | Schwartz Productions, Steven |
| Schwartz, Teri | Cherry Alley Productions |
| Schwartz, Todd | Lifetime Television (NY) |
| Schwartzberg, Louis | Schwartzberg & Company |
| Schwarz, Anne | Fox Broadcasting Co. |
| Schwarz, Eric | Tribeca Productions |
| Schwarz, Kristine J. | Phase I Productions |
| Schweickert, Joyce | Fresh Produce Company |
| Schwenker, Kenneth | Oak Island Films, Inc. |
| Schwerin, Peter | Dimension Films |
| Schwimer, Scott E. | Crown International Pictures |
| Scoon, Mark | Warner Bros. Pictures |
| Scoon, Valerie | Harpo Films Inc. |
| Scorsese, Martin | Cappa Productions |
| Scott, Art | L.A. Animation |
| Scott, Bambi Lynn | Laskay Drive |
| Scott, Cedric | Mary Ann-LaGlo Productions |
| Scott, Jason D. | Hunt-Tavel Productions |
| Scott, Nathan | MDP Worldwide |
| Scott, Pippa | Linden Prods. |
| Scott, Ridley | Scott Free Productions |
| Scott, Tony | Scott Free Productions |
| Scott, Tony | Totem Prods. |
| Scott-Spera, Deborah | Showtime Networks Inc. |
| Scotti, Anthony J. | Harvey Entertainment Company |
| Scruggs, H.E. | Leucadia Film Corp. |
| Scudder, Kat | Material |
| Scurlock, Aliana | Hollane Corp. |
| Seagal, Steven | Seagal-Nasso Productions |
| Sealey, Caran | Shelter Entertainment |
| Seeley, Carrie | Amen Ra Films |
| Seferian, Susan | Northern Lights Ent. |
| Sefton, Dan | Sefton Productions International |
| Segal, Amy | Equinox Entertainment Ltd. |
| Segal, Debbie | Katz Entertainment Group, Barry |
| Segal, Douglas | Atlas Entertainment |
| Segal, Jane | Warner Bros. Television Productions |
| Segan, Allison | Mutual Film Co. |
| Segan, Lloyd | Segan Company, The Lloyd |
| Segars, Charles | DreamWorks SKG |
| Seggerman, Henry | Seggerman Productions, Henry |
| Seguin, Nicole | Seguin Prods., Nicole |
| Seidelman, Arthur Allan | EntPro, Inc. |
| Seiderman, Edward | Westport Film Partners |
| Seiderman, Karen | Westport Film Partners |
| Seitz, Kathrin | Nickelodeon Movies |
| Selak, Chris | Mandalay Television |
| Seldes, Elisabeth | Seldes Films |
| Seldin, Spike | Turner Network Television (TNT) |
| Selig, Keri | Cort/Madden Company, The |
| Sellers, Arlene | Lantana Productions |
| Sellers, Dylan | Sellers Productions, Dylan |
| Sellitti, Tom | Apostle Pictures |
| Selzer, Elizabeth | Greenwald Prods., Robert |
| Semel, Mitchell R. | CBS Entertainment |
| Semel, Terry | Warner Bros. Pictures |
| Semon, Sam | CBS Entertainment |
| Sendak, Maurice | Wild Things Prods. |
| Senders, Roger | CBS Entertainment |
| Sengupta, Momita | MTV Films |
| Sennet, Mark | Sennet Prods., Mark |
| Seno, Kathryn | Ginty Films |
| Septien, Al | Aurora Productions |
| Seretan, Barbara | Seven Arts Pictures |
| Serna, Pepe | Delaware Pictures |
| Serpico, Jim | Apostle Pictures |
| Serritello, Toni | Movicorp Holdings, Inc. |
| Sertner, Robert | Von Zerneck-Sertner Films |
| Service, Deborah | Fox Broadcasting Co. |
| Serwatka, Dave | Comedy Central |
| Severini, Mark | Palisades Pictures |
| Severson, Chris | Barnette Productions, Alan |
| Sevic, Vera | Seagal-Nasso Productions |
| Sevilla, Enid N. | Paulist Prods. |
| Seward, Amanda | Warner Bros. Feature Animation |
| Seymour, Jane | Catfish Productions |
| Shackelford, Carrie | H.R.D. Prods. |
| Shaevitz, Geoff | Riche/Ludwig Productions |
| Shafer, Martin | Castle Rock Entertainment |
| Shafton, Randy | Baumgarten/Prophet Entertainment |
| Shah, Ash R. | Imperial Entertainment |
| Shah, Sundip R. | Imperial Entertainment |
| Shah, Sunil R. | Imperial Entertainment |
| Shall, David | Twentieth Television |
| Shamberg, Carla Santos | Jersey Films |
| Shamberg, Michael | Jersey Films |

# CROSS-REFERENCED NAMES

Shane Leighton, Michael . . . . . . . . . America National Network, Inc.
Shane, Reid . . . . . . . . . . . . . . . . . . . Paramount Network Television
Shane, Rick . . . . . . . . . . . . . . . . . . . Promark Entertainment Group
Shanti, Alys . . . . . . . . . . . . . . . . . . . . . . . . . . . . . Hill/Fields Ent.
Shapiro, Allen . . . . . . . . . . . . . . . . . . Shapiro Productions, Allen
Shapiro, Arnold . . . . . . . . . . . . . . . . . . . Shapiro Prods., Arnold
Shapiro, Cynthia B. . . . . . . . . . . . . . . Bell and Associates, Dave
Shapiro, Esther . . . . . . . . Shapiro Ent. Inc., Richard & Esther
Shapiro, Florie . . . . . . . . . Shapiro Ent. Inc., Richard & Esther
Shapiro, Greg . . . . . . . . . . . . . . . . . . . . Kingsgate Films, Inc.
Shapiro, Jon . . . . . . . . . . . . . . . . . . . . Ideal Entertainment, Inc.
Shapiro, Julie . . . . . . . . . . . . . . . . . . . . . . Rysher Entertainment
Shapiro, Lisa . . . . . . . . . . . . . . . Pressman Film Corp., Edward R.
Shapiro, Paul . . . . . . . . . . . . . . . . . . . . . . Big Ticket Television
Shapiro, Peter . . . . . . . . . . . . . . . . . . Ideal Entertainment, Inc.
Shapiro, Richard . . . . . . . . Shapiro Ent. Inc., Richard & Esther
Shapiro, Robert . . . . . . . . . . . . . . Shapiro Productions, Robert
Shapiro, Susan . . . . . . . . . . . . . . . . . . . . . . . . . . Cineville Inc.
Shaposhnick, Rochelle . . . . . . . . . . Von Zerneck-Sertner Films
Shardo, J C . . . . . . . . . . . . . . . . . . . . . JCS Entertainment Inc.
Shariat, Far . . . . . . . . . . . . . . . . . . . . . . . . . . . . . Mad Chance
Sharon, Roee . . . . . . . . . . . . . . . . . . . . . . . . . . . . Norah Films
Sharp, Jeff . . . . . . . . . . . . . . . . Hart Sharp Entertainment, Inc.
Sharp, Jim . . . . . . . . . . . . . . . . . . . . Fox Television Studios
Sharp, Jim . . . . . . . . . . . . . Greenblatt Janollari Studio, The
Sharp, Todd . . . . . . . International Filmmakers Management, Inc
Shaw, Anthony . . . . . . . . . . . . . . . . . . . . . . . Corymore Prods.
Shaw, David . . . . . . . . . . . . . . . . . . . . . . . . . Corymore Prods.
Shaw, James M. . . . . . . . . . . . . . . . . . . . . . . . MTV Networks
Shaw, Kathy . . . . . . . . . . . . . . . . . . . . Bottom Line Studio, Inc.
Shaw, Lizzy . . . . . . . . . . . . . . . . . . . . Pacific Motion Pictures
Shaw, Robert . . . . . . . . . . . . . . . O'Hara-Horowitz Productions
Shaw-Kolar, Deborah . . . . . . . . . . . . . Kolar Productions, Inc.
Shaye, Robert . . . . . . . . . . . . . . . . . . . . . . . New Line Cinema
Shayne, Bob . . . . . . . . . . . . . . . . . . B.S. Company, Inc., The
Shayne, Dylan . . . . . . . . . . . . . . . . . B.S. Company, Inc., The
Shea Jr., Henry M. . . . . . . . . . . . . . . . Persistent Pictures, Inc.
Shea, Fran . . . . . . . . . . . . . . . . . . . E! Entertainment Television
Shea, Melanie . . . . . . . . . . . . . . . . . . . . . Savage Studios Ltd.
Shearer, Peg . . . . . . . . . . . . . . . . . . . . . Scott Free Productions
Sheehan, Robert . . . . . . . . . . . . . Paramount Television Group
Sheeser, Trilby . . . . . . . . . . . . . . . . . . . . . . Mandeville Films
Sheets, Tom . . . . . . . . . . . . . . . . . . . . . . Fox Broadcasting Co.
Sheffer, Hogan . . . . . . . . . . . . . . . Johnson Productions, Mark
Sheinberg, Bill . . . . . . . . . . . . . . . . . . . . Bubble Factory, The
Sheinberg, Jon . . . . . . . . . . . . . . . . . . . . Bubble Factory, The
Sheinberg, Sid . . . . . . . . . . . . . . . . . . . . Bubble Factory, The
Sheldon, David . . . . . . . . . . . . . . Sheldon/Post Company, The
Sheldon, Laurie . . . . . . . . . . . . . . . . . . Northern Lights Ent.
Shellen, Chris . . . . . . . . . . . . . . . Cort/Madden Company, The
Shelton, Marla L. . . . . . . . . . . . . . . . . . . . . . Merchant-Ivory
Shenkin, Brenna . . . . . . . . . . . . . . . . Spin Cycle Entertainment
Shenkin, Melissa . . . . . . . . . . . . . . . . Spin Cycle Entertainment
Shenusay, Ray . . . . . . . . . . . . . . . . . . . . . Sitting Ducks Prods.
Shepard, Cyrus . . . . . . . . . . . . . . . . . . . Tisch Co., The Steve
Shepard, Lorna . . . . . . . . . . . . . . . . . . . . . Viacom Productions
Shepherd, Max . . . . . . . . . . . . . . Equinox Entertainment Ltd.
Shepley, Scott . . . . . . . . . . . . . . . . . . . . . Iwerks Entertainment
Sher, Stacey . . . . . . . . . . . . . . . . . . . . . . . . . . . Jersey Films
Sherak, Thomas . . . . . . . . . . . . . . . . . Twentieth Century Fox
Sherak, William . . . . . . . . . . . . . . . . . Davis Entertainment Co.
Sheridan, Bill . . . . . . . . . . . . . . . . . . . . . . . Mega Films, Inc.
Sheridan, Rene . . . . . . . . . . Red Diamond Company, The
Sherin, Ed . . . . . . . . . . . . . . . . . . . . . . . . . . . Wolf Films Inc.
Sherkow, Daniel A. . . . . . . . . . . . . . . . . . Randan Prods., Inc.
Sherman, Carol . . . . . . . . . . . . . . . . . . . . . . Tri-Crown Prods.
Sherman, Eric . . . . . . . . . . . . . . . . . . . Warner Sisters Prods.
Sherman, Melissa . . . . . . . . . . . . . . . . . . . . Sarabande Prods.
Sherman, Sidney . . . . . . . . . . . . . . . . . . . . Rosa Entertainment
Sherman, Tom . . . . . . . . . . . . . . . . . . . . . . ABC Entertainment
Sherren, Thomas . . . . . . . . . Dakota North Ent./Dakota Films
Shertzer, Loren . . . . . . . . . . . . . . . . . . . . . . . . . Blue Horizon
Sherwood, Jennifer . . . . . . . . . . . . . . . . . . . . Dimension Films
Shestack, Jon . . . . . . . . . . . . . . . . . . . . . . . . Beacon Pictures
Shevick, Jerry . . . . . . . . . . . . . . . . . . . Hearst Entertainment
Shevloff, Michael . . . . . . . . . . . . . . . . . . . . ZM Productions
Shields, Brent . . . . . . . . . . Hallmark Hall of Fame Productions, Inc.
Shiff, Tony . . . . . . . . . . . . . . . . . . . . . . . . . Palomar Pictures
Shils, Barry . . . . . . . . . . . . . . . . . . . . Goldstreet Pictures Inc.
Shine, Vidette . . . . . . . . . . . . . . . . . . . . . Arama Entertainment

Shintani, Roberta . . . . . . . . . . . . . . . De Laurentiis Company, Dino
Shipton, Christine . . . . . . . . . . . . . Alliance Television Productions
Shirazi, Donna . . . . . . . . . . . . . Connection III Entertainment Corp.
Shirazi, Mahsa . . . . . . . . . . . . . Connection III Entertainment Corp.
Shire, Seth I. . . . . . . . . . . . . . . . . . . . . . . . . . . . River One Films
Shirley, Marvin . . . . . . . . . . . . . . . . . . . . . . . . CBS Enterprises
Shirley, Marvin . . . . . . . . . . . . . . . . . . . . Eyemark Entertainment
Shoemaker, Jay . . . . . . . . . . . . . . . . . . . . . . American Zoetrope
Shoenfelt, John . . . . . . . . . . . . . . Lancaster Productions, David
Shofet, Ari . . . . . . . . . . . . . . . . . . . . . . . . . . Maia Productions
Shor, Hilary . . . . . . . . . . . . . . . . . . . Hit & Run Productions, Inc.
Short, Doug . . . . . . . Walt Disney Pictures/Touchstone Pictures
Short, Trevor . . . . . . . . . . . . . . . . . . . . . . . . . . . . . Nu Image
Shrater, Paul . . . . . . . . . . . . . . . . . . . Morrow-Heus Productions
Shue, Dennis . . . . . . . . . . . . . . . . . . Village Roadshow Pictures
Shukovsky, Joel . . . . . . . . . . . . . . . Shukovsky English Ent.
Shuler-Donner, Lauren . . . . . . . . Donner/Shuler-Donner Prods.
Shultz, David . . . . . . . . . . . . . . . . . . . . . . . . . . . . Troma Inc.
Shultz, Harriet . . . . . . . . . . . . . . . . . . . . . . . . . . MTV Networks
Shumaker, Dresden . . . . . . . . . . . . . . . . . Mostow/Lieberman
Shure, Alice . . . . . . . . . Evans Productions, Inc., Charles
Shuster, Brian . . . . . . . . . . . . . . . . . . . . . . . . . . . United Film
Shuster, Phil . . . . . . . . . . . . . . . . . . . . . Addis Films, Michael
Shwarzstein, Meyer . . . . . . . . . . . . . . . . . . Brainstorm Media
Shyer, Charles . . . . . . . . . . . . . . . . . Meyers/Shyer Co., The
Sidebottom, Dina . . . . . . . . . . . . . . Daniel Productions, Jay
Sidlow, Carol . . . . . . . . . . . . . . . . . . . . . . . . Face Productions
Siebert, Steven . . . . . . . . . . . . . . . . . Lighthouse Entertainment
Siebert, Steven . . . . . . . . . . . . . . . . . . . . . . Motor City Films
Siegel, Brad . . . . . . . . . . . . . . Turner Network Television (TNT)
Siegel, Bradley . . . . . . . . . . . . . . Turner Entertainment Group
Siegel, Debbie . . . . . . . . . . . . . . . . . . . . . . . . Hill/Fields Ent.
Siegel, Lianne . . . . . . . . . . Twentieth Century Fox Television
Siegel, Michael . . . . . . . . . . . . . . . . . . . . Brillstein-Grey Ent.
Siegler, Jess . . . . . . . . . . . . . . . . . . . . . . . . . . Ballyhoo, Inc.
Siegler, Scott . . . . . . . . . . . . . . Granada Entertainment USA
Siek, Rainer . . . . . . . . . . . . . . . . . . . . . . . . . CBS Enterprises
Siemann, Renee A. . . . . . . . . . . . . Rothstein Prods., Freyda
Sienega, Corey . . . . . . . . . . . . . . . . . . Kirschner Prods., David
Sierernich, Chris . . . . . . . . . . . . . Millennium Mediaworks, Inc.
Sievernich, Chris . . . . . . . . . . . . . . . . . Pacifica Entertainment
Sighvatsson, Sigurjon . . . . . . . . Lakeshore Entertainment Corp.
Silberg, David . . . . . . . . . . . . . . . . . . . . . . . . . . . United Film
Silberman, Mickey . . . . . . . . . . . . . . . . . . . . Belisarius Prods.
Silbert, Tracy . . . . . . . . . Twentieth Century Fox-Fox 2000 (LA)
Silbert, Wendy . . . . . . . . . . . . . . . . . . . . . . . . . . . . . Jaffilms
Silfen, Lori . . . . . . . . . . . . . . . . . . . . . . . . . New Line Cinema
Sillan, Diane . . . . . . . . . . . . . . . . . . Green Moon Productions
Silvas, Steven . . . . . . . . . . . . . . . . . . . . . . . Starlight Pictures
Silver, Alain . . . . . . . . . . . . . . . . . . . Plaster City Productions
Silver, Amanda . . . . . . . . . . . . . . . . . . . . Shinbone Productions
Silver, Caryn . . . . . . . . . . . . . . . . . . . . . . . . Greystone Films
Silver, Casey . . . . . . . . . . . . . . . . . . . . . . . Universal Pictures
Silver, Gary . . . . . . . . . . . . . . . . . . . . . . . . CBS Entertainment
Silver, Jeffrey . . . . . . . . . . . . . . . . . . . . . . . Outlaw Productions
Silver, Joan Micklin . . . . . . . . . . . . . . . . . Silverfilm Prods. Inc.
Silver, Joel . . . . . . . . . . . . . . . . . . . . . . . . . . . Silver Pictures
Silver, Joshua . . . . . . . . . . . . . . . . . . . . . . Jericho Entertainment
Silver, Raphael D. . . . . . . . . . . . . . . . . . Silverfilm Prods. Inc.
Silver, Rob . . . . . . . . . . . . . . . . . . . . . Manhattan Pictures Ltd.
Silverhardt, Jerald J. . . . . . . . . Black, Lawrence & Silverhardt Ent.
Silverman, Fred . . . . . . . . . . . . . . . Silverman Co., The Fred
Silverman, Geoff . . . . . . . . . . . . . . . . . Pearson All American
Silverman, Greg . . . . . . . . . . . . . . . . . . Warner Bros. Pictures
Silverman, Lloyd A. . . . . . Silverman Prod, Lloyd/Passionate Picts.
Silverman, Nancy D. . . . . . . . . . . . . . . . . . . Disney Telefilms
Silverman, Rich . . . . . . . . . . . . . . . . . . . . . 3 Arts Entertainment
Silverstone, Alicia . . . . . . . . . . . . . . . . . . . First Kiss Productions
Simand, Anita . . . . . . . . . . . . . . . Telescene Film Group., Inc.
Simchowitz, Stefan . . . . . . . . . . . . . . . Bandeira Entertainment
Simensky, Linda . . . . . . . . . . . . . . . . . . . . . Cartoon Network
Simmons, Russell . . . . . . . . . . . . . . . . . . . . . . . . Def Pictures
Simon, Andrea . . . . . . . . . . . . . . . . . Tudor Entertainment, Inc.
Simon, Annie . . . . . . . . . . . . . . . . . . . . . . Playtime Productions
Simon, Bill . . . . . . . . . . . . . . . . . . . . Clark Prods., Inc., Dick
Simon, Brenda . . . . . . . . . . . . . . . . . . Enchanter Entertainment
Simon, Bryan W. . . . . . . . . . . . . . . . . . . . . Montivagus Prods.
Simon, David L. . . . . . . . . . . . . . . . . . . . . . DreamWorks SKG
Simon, Erin . . . . . . . . . . . . . . . . . . . . . . Clean Break Productions
Simon, Jim . . . . . . . . . . . . . . . . . . . . . . . . . . . L.A. Animation

# CROSS-REFERENCED NAMES

Spielberg, Steven . . . . . . . . . . . . . . . . . . . . . . . DreamWorks SKG
Spies, James . . . . . . . . . . . . . . . . . . . . . . . . . . . . . Camera Marc
Spikings, Barry . . . . . . . . . . . . . . . . . . . . Spikings Entertainment
Spikings, Rebecca . . . . . . . . . . . . . . . . . . Midnight Sun Pictures
Spillman, Darin . . . . . . . . . . . . . . . . . . . . . . . . Trimark Pictures
Spillum, Jack . . . . . . . . . . . . . . . . . . . . . . . Jumbo Pictures, Inc.
Spink, JC . . . . . . . . . . . . . . . . . . . . . . . . . . . Zide Entertainment
Spinks, Lynwood . . . . . . . . . . . . . . . . . . . . . . . . . . . HyperFilms
Spiroff, Tom . . . . . . . . . . . . . . . . . . . . . . Bakula Productions, Inc.
Sporer, Andrea . . . . . . . . . . . . . . . . . . . . Scholastic Entertainment
Sporn, Bonnie . . . . . . . . . . . . . . . . . . . . . . . . Witt-Thomas Films
Sporn, David . . . . . . . . . . . . . . . . . . . . . . . . . New Line Cinema
Spoto, Lou . . . . . . . . . . . . . . . . . . . . . . . Scott Free Productions
Spragens, Lee . . . . . . . . . . . . . . . . . . . . . . . . . Act III Productions
Sprecher, Samantha . . . . . . . . . . . . . . . . . Schiff Productions, Paul
Springer, Linda . . . . . . . . Paramount Pictures- Production Division
Spry, Robin . . . . . . . . . . . . . . . . . . Telescene Film Group., Inc.
Spungin, Scott . . . . . . . . . Metro-Goldwyn-Mayer/Worldwide TV
Spurgeon, Van . . . . . . . . . . . . . . . . . . . . . . . Nomad Productions
Squillante, Mary . . . . . . . . . . . . . . . . . . . Sonnenfeld/Josephson
Squyres, Phil . . . . . . . . . . . . . . . . . Columbia TriStar Television
Stabler, Steve . . . . . . . . . . . . . . . . Motion Pict. Corp. of America
Stack, Thomas . . . . . . . . . . . . . . . . . . . . . . Columbia Pictures
Staeger, Will . . . . . . . . . . . . . . . . . . . . . Weed Road Pictures
Staggs, Thomas O. . . . . . . . . . . . . . . Walt Disney Company, The
Stanford Brown, Georg . . . . . . . . . . . . Nexus Entertainment, Inc.
Stanford Grossman, Halle . . . . . . . . . . Henson Company, Jim
Stangel, Suzzanne . . . . . . . . . . . . . . Schlatter Prods., George
Stanley, Carol . . . . . . . . . . . . . . . . . Jaygee Productions Inc.
Stanley, Carol . . . . . . . . . . . . . . . . . Viewpoint Productions
Stanley, Cathryn . . . . . . . . . . . . . . . . . . . . . . Moving Pictures
Stanley, Cheryl . . . . . . . . . . . . . . . . More/Medavoy Management
Stanley, David G. . . . . . . . . . . . . . . Stone Stanley Productions
Stanley, Tracee . . . . . . . . . . . . . . . . . . . . . Phoenician Films
Starger, Martin . . . . . . . . . . . . . . . . . . . . . . Marstar Prods.
Stark, Michael . . . . . . . . . . . . . . . Hickox Productions, Inc., Bryan
Stark, Ray . . . . . . . . . . . . . . . . . . . . . . . . . . Rastar Productions
Stark, Steve . . . . . . . . . . . . . . . . Paramount Network Television
Starkey, Steve . . . . . . . . . . . . . . . . . . . . . . . . . . ImageMovers
Starling, Brandon . . . . . . . . . Miller/Boyett/Warren Productions
Startz, Jane . . . . . . . . . . . . . . . . . Startz Productions, Inc., Jane
Stearn, Andrew . . . . . . . . . . . . . . . . Wells Productions, John
Stearns, Neil . . . . . . . . . . . . . . . . . . . Clark Prods., Inc., Dick
Steel, Eric . . . . . . . . . . . . . . . . . . . . . . . . . Rudin Prods., Scott
Steele, Jeff . . . . . . . . . . . . . . . . . . Thompson Street Pictures
Steele, Jim . . . . . . . . . . . . . . . . . . . . . . . . . . Steelwork Films
Steenreld, Charles . . . . . . . . . . . . . . . . . . . . . ZM Productions
Steffek, Kurt . . . . . . . . . . . . . . . . . . . . . . . . . MTV Networks
Stegmeir, Christine . . . . . . Warner Bros. International TV Production
Stein, David . . . . . . . . . . . . Lakeshore Entertainment Corp.
Stein, Gene . . . . . . . . . . . . . . . . . . . . . . . CBS Entertainment
Stein, Jennifer . . . . . . . . . . . . . . . . . . . . . . . . . Lotus Pictures
Stein, Joel . . . . . . . . . . . . . . . . . . . . . Howard Prods. Inc., Al
Stein, Jonathan . . . . . . . . . . . . . . . . . . . . . . Wolper Org., The
Stein, Susan . . . . . . . . . . . . . . . . . . . . . . . Radiant Productions
Stein, Vicki . . . . . . . . . . . . . . . . . . . . Two Roads Prods., Inc.
Steinberg, Andrew . . . . . . . . . . . . . . . . . . Kushner-Locke Co.
Steinberg, Christina . . . . . . . . . . . . . . . Junction Entertainment
Steinberg, David . . . . . . . . Morra, Brezner, Steinberg & Tenenbaum
Steinberg, Dawn . . . . . . . . . . . . . . . . . Big Ticket Television
Steinberg, Robert . . . . . . . . . . . . . . . . . . . Scarlet Fire Films
Steinhardt, Michael . . . . . . . . . . . Baer Entertainment Group
Steinke, Paul . . . . . . . . . . . Walt Disney Pictures/Touchstone Pictures
Steinkraus, Mary Lou . . . . . . . . . . . . . . . . . . Wild Films Inc.
Steinman, Alan . . . . . . . . . . . . . . Daydream Productions Inc.
Steinman, Sheryl . . . . . . . . . . . . . . Daydream Productions Inc.
Steir, Amie . . . . . . . . . . . . . . . . . . . . . . . . . . . . MTV Films
Stella, Raymond . . . . . . . . . . . . . . . . . Manhattan Pictures Ltd.
Steloff, Ellen . . . . . . . . . . . . . . . . . . . . . Lake Como Pictures
Stelzer, Peter . . . . . . . . . . . . . . . . . . . . . On Stilts Productions
Stenson, Mike . . . . . . . . . . Walt Disney Pictures/Touchstone Pictures
Stephan, Allan . . . . . . . . . . Full Moon & High Tide Prods. Inc.
Stephan, Andrew . . . . . . . . . . . . . . . . . . . . . . Ocean Pictures
Stephen, Elizabeth . . . . . . . . . . . . . . . . . . Avnet-Kerner Co.
Stephen, Tim . . . . . . . . . . . . . . . . . . . . . . Adam Productions
Stephenson, Gary . . . . . . . . . . . . . . . . . Lynch Entertainment
Stephenson, John . . . . . . . . . . . . . . Henson Company, Jim
Stepp, Alan . . . . . . . . . . . . . . . . . . . . Two Stepp Productions
Sterling, Brad . . . . . . . . . . . United Paramount Network (UPN)
Sterling, Victoria . . . . . . . . . . . . . . . . . . Fourth Avenue Films

Stern, Amanda . . . . . . . . . . . . . . . . . . . Midnight Sun Pictures
Stern, Cori . . . . . . . . . . . . . . . . . . . . . . Saban Entertainment
Stern, Howard . . . . . . . . . Stern Production Company, The Howard
Stern, Jaclyn . . . . . . . . . . . . . . . . . Silverman Co., The Fred
Stern, Jay . . . . . . . . . . . . . . . . . . . . . . . . . New Line Cinema
Stern, Mark . . . . . . . . . . . . . . . . Trilogy Entertainment Group
Stern, Nancy . . . . . . . . . . . . . . . . . . . . LookAlike Productions
Stern, Sandra . . . . . . . . . . . . . . . Columbia TriStar Television
Stern, Sandy . . . . . . . . . . . . . . . . . . . . . Single Cell Pictures
Sternberg, Marc . . . . . . . . . . . . . . . . . . . . . Daybreak Prods.
Sterrett, Shelly . . . . . . . . . . . . . . . . Sullivan Company, The
Stevens Jr., George . . . . . . . . . . . . . . Stevens Company, The
Stevens, Amber . . . . . . . . . . . . . . . . . . . . . . . . Mojo Films
Stevens, Amy . . . . . . . . . . . . . . . . . . . . . . . C/W Productions
Stevens, Andrew . . . . . . . . . . . . . . . Franchise Pictures Inc.
Stevens, Greg . . . . . . . . . . . . . . . . . . Stampede Entertainment
Stevens, Mark . . . . . . . . . . . . . . Time-Life Video & Television
Stevens, Michael . . . . . . . . . . . . . . . . Stevens Company, The
Stevens, Neal . . . . . . . . . . . . . . . . . . Stevens & Associates
Stevenson, Damian . . . . . . . . . . . . . . Kopelson Entertainment
Stevenson, John . . . . . . . . . . . . . . . . . . . . . . . . . Signature
Stewart, Allyn . . . . . . . . . . . . . . . . . . . . . . . . . . . . Jaffilms
Stewart, Annie . . . . . . . . . . . . . . . . . . . . . Red Mullet, Inc.
Stewart, Denise . . . . . . . . . . . . . . . . . Brillstein-Grey Ent.
Stewart, Jason . . . . . . . . . . . . . . . . . . Fox Broadcasting Co.
Stewart, Lyle . . . . . . . . . Paramount International Television
Stewart, Patrick . . . . . . . . . . . . . Flying Freehold Productions
Stewart, Sande . . . . . . . . . . . . . . . Stewart Television, Inc.
Stickle, Erin . . . . . . . . . . . . . . . . . Double Whammy Productions
Stiefel, Arnold . . . . . . . . . . . . . . . . . . . Stiefel Entertainment
Stier, Geoff . . . . . . . . . . . . . . . . . . . . . . . Mirage Enterprises
Stigwood, Robert . . . . . . . . . . . . . . . . . . . . . . . . RSO Films
Stiller, Ben . . . . . . . . . . . . . . . . . . . . . . . . . Red Hour Films
Stillerman, Joel . . . . . . . . . . . . . . . . . Spanky Pictures, Inc.
Stine, Jane . . . . . . . . . . . . Parachute Entertainment, LLC.
Stipe, Michael . . . . . . . . . . . . . . . . . . . Single Cell Pictures
Stockstill, Doris . . . . . . . . . . . . . . . . . Hargrove Prods., Dean
Stoddard, George . . . . . . . . . . . . . . Maynard Prods., Richard
Stoff, Erwin . . . . . . . . . . . . . . . . . . . . . . . 3 Arts Entertainment
Stofsky, Susan . . . . . . . . . . . . . . . . . Wells Productions, John
Stogel, Lauren . . . . . . . . . . . . . . . . Porchlight Entertainment
Stokdyk, Danielle S. . . . . . . . . . . Columbia TriStar Television
Stoll, Rand . . . . . . . . . . . . . . . . All American Television, Inc.
Stoller, Bryan Michael . . . . . . . . . . . Northstar Entertainment
Stone, Alexandra . . . . . . . . . . . . . . Recorded Picture Company
Stone, Dan . . . . . . . . . . . . . . . . . . Persistent Pictures, Inc.
Stone, Michelle . . . . . . . . . . . . . . . . . . . . . . Fogwood Films
Stone, Oliver . . . . . . . . . . . . . . Illusion Entertainment Group
Stone, Randy . . . . . . . . . Twentieth Century Fox Television
Stone, Rob . . . . . . . . . . . . . . . . . . . . . . . Vienna Productions
Stone, Robert . . . . . . . . . . . . . . . . . . . . . . . Stone vs. Stone
Stone, Scott A. . . . . . . . . . . . . . . . Stone Stanley Productions
Stone, Webster . . . . . . . . . . . . . . . . . . . . . . Stone vs. Stone
Storey, Erik . . . . . . . . . . . . . . . . . Von Zerneck-Sertner Films
Storey, Jennifer . . . . . . . . . . . . . . . . . . . Indican Productions
Storrier, John . . . . . . . . . . . . . . . All American Television, Inc.
Stotesbery, S. Drew . . . . . . . . . . . . . . Vanguard Productions
Stott, Jeffrey . . . . . . . . . . . . . . . . . Castle Rock Entertainment
Stott, Lisa . . . . . . . . . . . . . . . . . . . . Midnight Sun Pictures
Stovin, Jesse . . . . . . . . . . . . . . . . . . . . . . Gullane Pictures
Strader, Jim . . . . . . . . . . . . . . . . . . . . . . Strader Entertainment
Strader, Scott . . . . . . . . . . . . . . . . . . . . . Strader Entertainment
Stratford, Bert . . . . . . . . . . . . . . Stratford Prods, Inc., Bert
Stratton, Dene . . . . . . . . . . . . . . . . . . . . . . DIC Entertainment
Stratton, Kristen . . . . . . Warner Bros. International TV Production
Strauss, Carolyn . . . . . . . . . . . . . . HBO Independent Productions
Strauss, Carolyn . . . . . . . . . . . . . . . HBO Original Programming
Strauss, Fred . . . . . . . . . . . . . Communications Corp. of America
Strauss, Peter E. . . . . . . . . . . . . . . . . . . Movie Group, The
Strauss, Ricky . . . . . . . . . . . . . . . . . . . . . Columbia Pictures
Strauss, Scott . . . . . . . . . . . . . . . . . . . . . . Outlaw Productions
Streisand, Barbra . . . . . . . . . . . . . . . . . . . . . . Barwood Films
Streit, Eric . . . . . . . . . . . . . . . . Axelson-Weintraub Productions
Stremel, J. Michael . . . . Twentieth Century Fox-Searchlight Picts.
Stretch, Gary . . . . . . . . . . . . . . . . . . . Stratum Entertainment
Strichartz, Deborah . . . . . . . . . . . . . . . . . Gullane Pictures
Striegel, Stephanie . . . . . . . . . . . . . . . . . New Line Cinema
Stringer, Helen . . . . . . . . . . . . . . . . . Pearson All American
Stroh, Ernst Etchie . . . . . . . . . . . . . Moonstone Entertainment
Stroh, Kandice . . . . . . . . . . . . . . . . . . . Itasca Pictures, Inc.

Stroh, Yael . . . . . . . . . . . . . . . . . . Moonstone Entertainment
Stroman, Gwenn . . . . . . . . . . . . . . . . . . Flower Films, Inc.
Stromberg, Winston . . . . . . . . . Licht/Mueller Film Corp.
Stromer, Lisa . . . . . . . . . . . . . . . . . . . . . . Catapult Films
Stronach, John . . . . . . . . . . . . . . . . Agamemnon Films Inc.
Strong, Patrick . . . . . . . . . . . . . . . Blake Prods., Timothy
Strudwick, Tom . . . . . . . . . . . . . . . . . Goldwyn Films Inc.
Strype, Fred . . . . . . . . . . . . . . . . . . Raindance Pictures
Strzelecka, Joanna . . . . . . . . . . . Open Door Entertainment
Stuart, John W. . . . . . . . . . . . . . . Golden Harvest Films
Stuart, Katherine . . . . . . . . . . . . . . . Curtis Prods., Dan
Stuart, Mel . . . . . . . . . . . . Stuart Productions, Inc., Mel
Stuart, William . . . . . . . . . . . . . . . . Aurora Productions
Stuber, Scott . . . . . . . . . . . . . . . . . . Universal Pictures
Stupin, Paul . . . . . . . . . . . . . . Stupin Productions, Paul
Styles, Yvonne . . . . . . . . . . . . . . . . . . . . . . . . Gaumont
Suarez, Flody . . . . . . . . . . . . . . . . . . NBC Entertainment
Suckle, Richard . . . . . . . . . . . . . . . . Atlas Entertainment
Suddelson, Eric . . . . . . . . . . . . . . . . . Mutual Film Co.
Sudmeier, Michael . . . . . . . . . . . . . . . Rastar Productions
Sugar, Bonnie . . . . . . . . . . . . . . . Greenwich Entertainment
Sugerman, Andrew . . . . . . . . . . . . . . Sugerman, Andrew
Suhl, Sean . . . . . . . . . . Dakota North Ent./Dakota Films
Sujaritchan, Aura . . . . . . . . . . Stratford Prods, Inc., Bert
Sulaimani, Alex . . . . . . . . . Lakeshore Entertainment Corp.
Sullenger, Betsy . . . . . . . . . . . Middle Fork Productions
Sullivan, Beth . . . . . . . . . . . . . . . Sullivan Company, The
Sullivan, Heather . . . . . . Kahn Power Pictures(Formerly Odessa Pic)
Sullivan, Kevin . . . . . . . . . . . . . . . Sullivan Entertainment
Sullivan, Susan . . . . . . . . . Arnold Productions, Inc., Judy
Sullivan, Tara . . . . . . . . . . Blum Productions, Howard
Sullivan, Tim . . . . . . . . . . . . . . . King World Productions
Sullivan, Tracy . . . . . . . . . . . . . Tollin/Robbins Productions
Summers, Cathleen . . . . . . . . . . . Summers Entertainment
Sumpter, Sharla . . . . . . . . . . . . Tollin/Robbins Productions
Sunderland, Ronald . . . . . . . . . Spelling Television, Inc.
Sunshine, Mary . . . . . . . . . . . . . Shooting Gallery Inc., The
Sunshine, Randi . . . . . . . . . . . . . . . Randan Prods., Inc.
Supa, Tom . . . . . . . . . . . . . . . . Henson Pictures, Jim
Supnik, Debbie . . . . . . . . . . Weller/Grossman Productions
Suppa, Ronald . . . . . . . . . . . . . . Suppa Prods., Inc., Ronald
Suro, Maira . . . . . . . . . United Paramount Network (UPN)
Surowicz, Kim . . . . . . . . . . . . . . . . . . . . . HyperFilms
Suser, Andrew . . . . . . . . . . . . . . . Clark Prods., Inc., Dick
Susskind, Andrew . . . . . . . . . . . Legacy Entertainment Inc.
Sussman, Ben . . . . . . . . . . . . Foster Productions, David
Sussman, Peter . . . . . . . . . . . . . . . . . . . Atlantis Films
Sutherland, Rowan . . . . . . . . R.A.M.M. Entertainment, Inc
Sutherland, Stacey . . . . . . . . . . . . . . Sticks And Stones
Sutter, Randy . . . . . . . . . . . Von Zerneck-Sertner Films
Swafford, Jeff . . . . . . . . . . . . . . . . . . . . A Band Apart
Swain, Tim . . . . . . . . . . . . . . . . . . . Trimark Pictures
Swallow, Karen . . . . . . . . . . . . . . . . . . . . . 1492 Pictures
Swan, Robert . . . . . . . . . . . . . . . . . Kushner-Locke Co.
Swanson, Neely . . . . . . . . . Kelley Productions, David E.
Swartz, Bert . . . . . . . . . . . . . . . . St. Clare Entertainment
Sweeney, Anne . . . . . . . . . . . . . . . . . . Disney Channel
Sweeney, David . . . . . . . . . . . . . . Visionary Entertainment
Sweeney, Mary . . . . . . . . . . . . . . . . Picture Factory, The
Sweney Borden, Michael . . . . . . . . . Sloane/Borden Pictures
Swirnoff, Jessica . . . . . Walt Disney Pictures/Touchstone Pictures
Swope, Mel . . . . . . . . . . Metro-Goldwyn-Mayer/Worldwide TV
Sykes, John . . . . . . . . . . . . . . . . . . VH1 (Music First)
Sykes, Laurie . . . . . . . . . . . . HBO Original Programming
Sykes, Rosemary . . . . . . . . . . . Lifetime Television (NY)
Sylvester, Doug . . . . . . . . . . E! Entertainment Television
Symes, John . . . . . . . . Metro-Goldwyn-Mayer/Worldwide TV
Symons, Kel . . . . . . . . . . Neufeld Productions, Mace
Symons, Lynne . . . . . . . . . . Trilogy Entertainment Group
Syvan, Lemore . . . . . . . . . . . . Goldheart Pictures Corp.
Szimonisz, Greg . . . . . . . . . . . . Dreyfuss/James Prods.
Szymanski, Stan . . . . . . . . . Sony Pictures Imageworks
Taber, David . . . . . . . . . . . . . . . Weintraub/Kuhn Prods.
Tabrizi, Alexander . . . . . . . . . . . . . Trivision Pictures Inc.
Taeuber, Wendy . . . . . . . . . . . Wildwood Enterprises Inc.
Taffner Jr., Don . . . . . . . . . . . . Taffner Entertainment Ltd.
Taglianetti, Alan . . . . . . . . . Foxboro Company, Inc., The
Tahse, Martin . . . . . . . . . . . . . . . . Tahse Prods., Martin
Takach, Ann . . . . . . . . . . . . . . . . . . . . . Signature Films
Takahashi, Drew . . . . . . . . . . . . . . . . Colossal Pictures

Talbert-Weller, Kathy . . . . . . . . . . . . . NBC Entertainment
Talbott, Chris . . . . . . . . . . . . . . . . . . . . . . . Havoc Inc.
Taloni, Nadine . . . . . . . . . . . . . . Green Moon Productions
Tamasy, Paul . . . . . . . . . . . . . . Open Road Prods., Ltd.
Tamblyn, Pauline . . . . . . . . . Shadowcatcher Entertainment
Tanen, Ned . . . . . . . . . . . . . . . . . . . Channel Productions
Tang, Deborah . . . . . . . . . . . . . . Black Entertainment TV
Tann, Steve . . . . . . . . . . . . . . . . . Spelling Television, Inc.
Tannebaum, Ted . . . . . . Lakeshore Entertainment Corp.
Tannen, William . . . . . . . . . . Stargazer Entertainment, Inc.
Tannenbaum, Eric . . . . . . . . . Columbia TriStar Television
Tannenbaum, Jeremy . . . . . . . . . . . Enchanter Entertainment
Tannenbaum, Jill . . . . . . . . . . . . . . . Playtime Productions
Tannenbaum, Thomas D. . . . . Christmas Tree Entertainment, Inc.
Tanning, Hay . . . . . . . . . . . . . . . Network Graphics Ltd.
Tao, Stephen . . . . . . . . . . . . . . . . . . . ABC Entertainment
Tapanes, Patty . . . . . . . . Goldcrest Films International, Inc.
Tapert, Robert . . . . . . . . . . . . . . . . Renaissance Pictures
Taran, Maureen . . . . . . . Katz Entertainment Group, Barry
Tarantino, Quentin . . . . . . . . . . . . . . . . A Band Apart
Tardy-Green, Emese . . . . . . . Tardy-Green Productions, Ltd.
Targon, Jodi . . . . . . . . . . . . . . . . . Roth/Arnold Prods.
Tarnoff, John . . . . . . . . . . . . . . . . Tarnoff/Lazar & Co.
Tarnofsky, Dawn . . . . . . . . . . . Lifetime Television (NY)
Tarpy, Leah . . . . . . . . . . . . Johnson Productions, Mark
Tarquinio, Rosemary . . . . . . . . . . . . Kushner-Locke Co.
Tarses, Jamie . . . . . . . . . . . . . . . . . ABC Entertainment
Tartikoff, Lilly . . . . . . . . . . . . . . . H. Beale Company
Taska, Ilmar . . . . . . . . . . . . . . . . . Taska Productions
Tassler, Nina . . . . . . . . . . . . . . . . . CBS Productions
Tate, Shoshanna . . . . . . . . . . . . Manhattan Pictures Ltd.
Tate, Stephen A. . . . . . . . . . . . . Manhattan Pictures Ltd.
Taub, Lori-Etta . . . . . . . . . . . Finnegan-Pinchuk Company
Tauber, James . . . . . . . . . . . . . . . . . Propaganda Films
Taublieb, Paul . . . . . . . . . . . . . . . Vision Media/LXD Inc.
Taubman, Lawrence . . . . . . . . . . . . . CineCity Pictures
Tautfest, Kristy . . . . . . . . . . . Wells Productions, John
Tavares, Michael . . . . . . . . . . . . . . . . . . . . Danjaq Inc.
Tavel, Connie . . . . . . . . . . . . . . . Hunt-Tavel Productions
Tavel, Connie . . . . . . . . . . . . . . . . . Tavel Entertainment
Taweel, George . . . . . . . . . . . . . . . . . TLC Entertainment
Taylor, Alix . . . . . . . . . . . . . . . . . . Craven Films, Wes
Taylor, Brigham . . . . . Walt Disney Pictures/Touchstone Pictures
Taylor, Burton . . . . . . . . . . Three Guys From Verona Inc.
Taylor, Chris . . . . . . . . . . . . . . . . . Largo Entertainment
Taylor, Dan . . . . . . . . . . . Metro-Goldwyn-Mayer Pictures
Taylor, Deborah J. . . . . . . . . America National Network, Inc.
Taylor, Grazka . . . . . . . . . . . . . . . Taylor Prods., Grazka
Taylor, Jamie . . . . . Twentieth Century Fox-Searchlight Picts.
Taylor, Lance B. . . . . . . . . . . . . . . Fox Broadcasting Co.
Taylor, Lynne Harris . . . . . . . . . . Black Entertainment TV
Taylor, Michael . . . . . . . . . . . . . . . . Boyle-Taylor Prods.
Taylor, Minna . . . . . . . . . . . . . . . . . Fox Broadcasting Co.
Taylor, Quinn . . . . . . . . . . . . . . . . . ABC Entertainment
Taylor, Ron . . . . . . . . . . . . . . . . Spelling Television, Inc.
Taylor, Tom . . . . . . . . . . . . . . . . T-Squared Productions
Taylor, Toper . . . . . . . . . . . . . . . . Nelvana Entertainment
Taylor, Yvette . . . . . . . . . . . . . . . . . . . . All Girl Prods.
Taylor, Zanthe . . . . . . . . . . . . . . . . . . . . . . . . Material
Teachey, Julia . . . . . . . . . . . . . . . . . . Carreras Productions
Teaton, Kenneth . . . . . . . . . Foxboro Company, Inc., The
Teele, Cynthia . . . . . . . . . . . . . . . Paramount Domestic TV
Teeter, Richard A. . . . . . . . . . Proud Mary Entertainment
Teets, Edward . . . . . . . . . . . . . . . . . . . . Phoenix Pictures
Tehranian, Yalda . . . . . . . . Metro-Goldwyn-Mayer Pictures
Teicher, Allison . . . . . . . . . . . . . Lifetime Television (LA)
Teicher, Allison . . . . . . . . . . . . . Lifetime Television (NY)
Teicher, Debbie . . . . . . . . . . . . . . . . . . . . . NBC Studios
Teicher, Karen . . . . . . . . . . . . . . . . Mandalay Pictures
Teitel, Robert . . . . . . . . . . . . . . . . . State Street Pictures
Teitelbaum, Mark . . . . . . . . . . . Somers Teitelbaum David
Tellem, Nancy . . . . . . . . . . . . . . . . . CBS Entertainment
Tellem, Nancy . . . . . . . . . . . . . . . . . . . CBS Productions
Templeton, Anne . . . . . . . . . . . . . . Templeton Productions
Templeton, Gary . . . . . . . . . . . . . . . . P.A.T. Productions
Tenenbaum, Stephen . . . . . Morra, Brezner, Steinberg & Tenenbaum
Tennenbaum, Andrew R. . . . . . . . . . Flashpoint Entertainment
Tenser, Marilyn J. . . . . . . . . . Crown International Pictures
Tenser, Mark . . . . . . . . . . . . . Crown International Pictures
Tenzer, Michael . . . . . . . . . . . . . . . . NBC Entertainment

# CROSS-REFERENCED NAMES

| | |
|---|---|
| Teper, Meir | Teps Productions |
| Teran, Victor | Seven Arts Pictures |
| Terkuhle, Abby | MTV Networks |
| Teschke, Pamela | Underworld Entertainment |
| Tetrick, Michael | NewStar Television |
| Thale, Joy | Mary Ann-LaGlo Productions |
| Thayer, Tom | Traveler's Rest Films |
| Theodoropoulos, Nicholas | Bedford Falls Co., The |
| Theros, Tamiko D. | Blue Turtle, Inc. |
| Thomas, Bradley | Motion Pict. Corp. of America |
| Thomas, Brady | Castle Rock Entertainment |
| Thomas, Dave | Maple Palm Productions |
| Thomas, Grant | Dancing Asparagus Prods. |
| Thomas, Jeff | Rysher Entertainment |
| Thomas, Jeremy | Recorded Picture Company |
| Thomas, Leslie | Raylin Entertainment |
| Thomas, Philip E. | Cherry Alley Productions |
| Thomas, Rob | All Girl Prods. |
| Thomas, Scott | Marvel Studios |
| Thomas, Steven | Wald Entertainment Inc., Jeff |
| Thomas, Tony | Witt-Thomas Films |
| Thomas, Tony | Witt-Thomas-Harris Productions |
| Thomason, Harry | Mozark Productions |
| Thomopoulos, Anne | HBO Original Programming |
| Thompsen, Sonya | New Line Cinema |
| Thompson, Courtney | Clean Break Productions |
| Thompson, Ian | Samuelson Productions |
| Thompson, Larry | Thompson Organization, Larry |
| Thompson, Liz | Wolf Films, Fred |
| Thompson, Richard | Bennett Productions, Harve |
| Thompson-Duda, Deborah | Unapix/A-PIX Entertainment |
| Thoms, Donald | PBS |
| Thomson, Julie | Pacific Western Prods. |
| Thoren, Terry | Klasky Csupo Inc. |
| Thornton, Spencer | Shatter Glass Prods. |
| Thorsen, Jeff | Moffitt-Lee Prods. |
| Thos, Francois | Goldwyn Films Inc. |
| Thro, Holly | Sanford/Pillsbury Prods. |
| Thumm, Karen | Moving Pictures |
| Ticknor, Jodi | Wilshire Court Prods. |
| Tierney, Michael | VH1 (Music First) |
| Till, Stewart | PolyGram Filmed Ent. |
| Tillman Jr., George | State Street Pictures |
| Tilson, Gregg | Kaufman Co., The |
| Timberman, Sarah | Columbia TriStar Television |
| Timm, Eric | Warner Bros. Television Productions |
| Tingle, Terri | Turner Entertainment Group |
| Tisch, Steve | Tisch Co., The Steve |
| Titpon, Christopher | Silverline Pictures |
| To, Tony | Ascato Entertainment |
| Tobias, Glen | Enchanter Entertainment |
| Tochterman, David | Carsey-Werner Co., The |
| Todd, G. Evan | Keith Barish Prods. |
| Todd, Jennifer | Team Todd |
| Todd, Suzanne | Team Todd |
| Todhunter, Jennifer | Out of the Blue . . . Entertainment |
| Toffler, Van | MTV Films |
| Toffler, Van | MTV Networks |
| Toll, Jim | Keller Entertainment Group |
| Toll, Roger | Columbia Pictures |
| Tollefson, Joyce | Fountainbridge Films |
| Tollefson, Rhonda | Fountainbridge Films |
| Tollin, Mike | Tollin/Robbins Productions |
| Tollinger, Jane | Lifetime Television (NY) |
| Tolmach, Matthew | Columbia Pictures |
| Tom, Nancy J. | Principal Prods., Victoria |
| Tomich, John | Spin Cycle Entertainment |
| Tomko, John | Weintraub Prods., Jerry |
| Tompkins, Andy | Porchlight Entertainment |
| Tooley, Tucker | Newman/Tooley Films |
| Topham, Neil | NewStar Media |
| Topper, Norman | Rankin/Bass Productions |
| Topping, Marguerite | Lussier, Paul |
| Torigian, Rosemary | Ridio Prods., Inc., Anthony |
| Torii, Tom | Pressman Film Corp., Edward R. |
| Torme, Tracy | Cheyenne 7 Prods. |
| Torres, Peter | Palisades Pictures |
| Tortora, Tim | Harpo Films Inc. |
| Toumasis, Pete | Scott Free Productions |
| Toumasis, Peter | Totem Prods. |
| Towey, Desmond | Expect Miracles, Inc. |
| Townsend, Jim | Hamilton Entertainment, Inc., Dean |
| Townsend, Robert | Townsend Ent. Corp., The |
| Trabulus, Mark | Gimbel Productions, Inc., Roger |
| Tracy, Beth | Belisarius Prods. |
| Tracy, Brett | Loring Productions, Lynn |
| Tracy, Marta | E! Entertainment Television |
| Tran, Bic | Lakeshore Entertainment Corp. |
| Traub, Jason | Village Roadshow Pictures |
| Traub, Tom | Daly-Harris Productions |
| Traugott, Peter | Brillstein-Grey Ent. |
| Travis, Mark W. | Travis Group, The |
| Treinish, Dan | New Line Cinema |
| Tremayne, Serina | Moll/Beallor Productions |
| Trias, Jhoanna | Fox Productions, Ted |
| Tribuch, Michael | Schachter Entertainment, Inc. |
| Trinker, Carol | Tribe |
| Triplett, Bruce | IF/X Productions |
| Troy, Kim | Lightstorm Entertainment |
| Trozak, John | Wessler Entertainment |
| Truesdell, Keith | Production Partners, Inc. |
| Truett, Cecily | Lancit Media Entertainment, Ltd. |
| Trunkey, Christopher | Kings Road Entertainment Inc. |
| Tsao, Andrew | First Folio Films |
| Tse, Simon | Tse Productions, Simon |
| Tucci, Stanley | First Cold Press Productions |
| Tucker, Jodi | Dancing Asparagus Prods. |
| Tudor, Martin | Tudor Entertainment, Inc. |
| Tugend, Jennie Lew | JLT Productions |
| Tulchin, Carla | Tulchin Entertainment |
| Tulchin, Harris | Tulchin Entertainment |
| Tumminia, James | Paige Assoc., Inc., George |
| Tunney, Teressa | Trivision Pictures Inc. |
| Turk, Scott A. | River Mill Productions |
| Turman, Lawrence | Turman-Morrissey Company, The |
| Turnbull, Helen | Tapestry Films Inc. |
| Turner, Cheri | Image Organization, Inc. |
| Tursi, Dan | Snow Leopard Productions |
| Turteltaub, Jon | Junction Entertainment |
| Turteltaub, Saul | Turteltaub-Orenstein Prods. |
| Turtle, Jon | Turtle Productions, Jon |
| Tusan, Cary | Parkwood Pictures |
| Tushinsky, Kimberly | Wind Dancer Prod. Group |
| Tusk, Mark | New Line Cinema |
| Tuttle, David | Shooting Gallery Inc., The |
| Twardosz, Sebastian | C/W Productions |
| Twigg, Tara | Pacific Motion Pictures |
| Tyler, Marianne | Bennett Productions, Harve |
| Tyndall, Shanna | Gaslight Pictures |
| Tyrer, William | Newmarket Capital Group |
| Tyus-Adair, Kathryn | State Street Pictures |
| Ufland, Harry J. | Ufland Productions |
| Ufland, Mary Jane | Ufland Productions |
| Ujlaki, Steve | Chesler/Perlmutter Production |
| Ukai, Clara | DreamWorks SKG |
| Ulloa, Ronald | Hearst Entertainment |
| Ulman, Karyn | DIC Entertainment |
| Underwood, Ron | Stampede Entertainment |
| Ungar, Gary | Exile Entertainment |
| Unger, Anthony B. | Unger Productions Inc. |
| Unger, Bill | Tidewater Entertainment, Inc. |
| Uniacke, Caspar | Gitlin Productions |
| Unkel, Robert | Say Unkel Entertainment |
| Uplinger, Hal | Uplinger Enterprises |
| Urdang, Leslie | True Pictures |
| Ursini, Amedeo A. | Jazz Pictures, Inc. |
| Uslan, Michael | Batfilm Prods., Inc. |
| Ussenko, Kenneth | Savoir Faire Productions |
| Vacca, Claudine | Baumgarten/Prophet Entertainment |
| Vachon, Christine | Killer Films, Inc. |
| Vahabzadeh, Youssef | Blue Turtle, Inc. |
| Vahradian, Mark | Walt Disney Pictures/Touchstone Pictures |
| Vajna, Andrew | Cinergi Pictures Entertainment Inc. |
| Valdivia, Laura | Goat Cay Productions, Inc. |
| Valente, Renee | Valente Prods., Renee |
| Valenti, Courtenay | Warner Bros. Pictures |
| Valenti, Jon | Berk Schwartz Bonann Productions |
| Valentine, Dean | United Paramount Network (UPN) |
| Valentine, Ian | USA Networks |
| Valentine, Justin | Voight Entertainment, Jon |

# CROSS-REFERENCED NAMES

|  |  |
|---|---|
| Valentine, Tanya | Saban Entertainment |
| Valeo, Michael | Robinson Entertainment, Dolores |
| Valldejuli, Priscilla | Cherry Alley Productions |
| Vallely, Julie | Dogstar Films |
| Vallen, Maria | Krane Group, The Jonathan |
| Vallin, Katherine | Interland Entertainment |
| Valois, Rob | Henson Pictures, Jim |
| Van Damme, Jean-Claude | Long Road Productions |
| van de Bunt, Dirk W. | Carsey-Werner Co., The |
| Van Doren, Doug | Red Mullet, Inc. |
| Van Herle, Inge | RKO Pictures, Inc. |
| Van Kempen, Michelle | Film Garden Entertainment |
| Van Leeuwen, Chako | Chako Film International |
| Van Lowe, Ehrich | Sweet Lorraine Prods. Inc. |
| Van Nostrand, Amy | Daly-Harris Productions |
| Van Petten, Vance | Studios USA |
| van Roden, Peter | Henson Company, Jim |
| Vance, Ladd | Ministry of Film Inc., The |
| Vance, Marilyn | Ministry of Film Inc., The |
| VanDerKloot, William | VanDerKloot Film & Television Inc. |
| Vanderwier, Terry | Hickox Productions, Inc., Bryan |
| Vane, Norman Thaddeus | American New Wave Films |
| Vann, Bruce | Largo Entertainment |
| Varese, Francisco | Ventana Films |
| Vargas, Peggy | MK Productions |
| Vasconcellos, Lisa | Utopia Picts./Carl Borack Productions |
| Vasey, John | Showtime Networks Inc. |
| Vasilatos, Jerry | Amphion/Nitestar Productions |
| Vasilovich, Guy | Film Roman, Inc. |
| Vasquez, Lee Ann | True Blue Prods. |
| Vaughn, Robert | Chesler/Perlmutter Production |
| Vecchio, Joseph S. | Vecchio Ent., Joseph S. |
| Veilleux, Rene | Double A Films |
| Vein, Jon | Film Roman, Inc. |
| Vela, Luz Maria | Cannery, Inc., The |
| Velcoff, Andrew | Turner Entertainment Group |
| Venter, Karuna | Singer Entertainment, Joseph M. |
| Venter, Ronell | Oak Island Films, Inc. |
| Ventimiglia, Gary | Madguy Films |
| Ventris, Amber | Sticks And Stones |
| Ver Wiel, Chris | Nichol Moon Films |
| Verdin, Julia | Rough Diamond Productions |
| Vergara, Dolly M. | Imperial Entertainment |
| Vermilion, Kevin | Codikow Films |
| Verno, Helen | Columbia TriStar Television |
| Vernon, Lori Imbler | Chartoff Productions |
| Veronis, Nick | Avenue Pictures |
| Versacci, Tim | Skyline Partners |
| Victor, Daniel | Children's Television Workshop |
| Victor, Mark | Victor & Grais Prods. |
| Vidov, Oleg | Films By Jove |
| Vigman, Siow | Di Bona Prods., Vin |
| Vila, Scott | Paramount Network Television |
| Villadolid, Paul | Walt Disney TV/Touchstone TV |
| Villalobos, Ligiah | Esparza-Katz Prods. |
| Villalpando, Armando | Tri-Crown Prods. |
| Villandry, Victoria | Longbow Productions |
| Villard, Dimitri | Villard Prods., Dimitri |
| Villegas, Jenni | FGM Entertainment |
| Vincent, Cheri | Twentieth Television |
| Vincent, E. Duke | Spelling Television, Inc. |
| Vincent, T. | El Dorado Pictures |
| Vines, Amie | Cohen Productions, Martin B. |
| Vines, Greg | Solt Productions, Andrew |
| Vinnedge, Syd | All American Communications, Inc. |
| Vinson, Day | Cairo/Simpson Productions, Inc. |
| Vinson, Tripp | Bruckheimer Films, Jerry |
| Viscidi, Marcus | Lemon Sky Productions, Inc. |
| Visvydas, Julie | Boz Productions |
| Vitale, Ruth | Paramount Specialty Division |
| Viviano, Bettina Sofia | Viviano Entertainment |
| Vliet, Whitney | Hallmark Entertainment (NY) |
| Voci, Joe | Mandalay Television |
| Vodde, Michael | Tahse Prods., Martin |
| Vogel, David E. | Walt Disney Pictures/Touchstone Pictures |
| Vogel, Marvin | Manhattan Pictures Ltd. |
| Vogler, Chris | Twentieth Century Fox-Fox 2000 (LA) |
| Voight, Jon | Voight Entertainment, Jon |
| Voiku, Beth | Lumiere Films Inc. |
| Vokulich, Richard | Fox Broadcasting Co. |
| Volat, Lorne | Diamond Heart Productions |
| Voltmer, Ted | Norann Entertainment |
| Von Arx, Debbie | Beacon Pictures |
| von Gal, Peter | Hallmark Entertainment (NY) |
| von Savoye, Anna | Stun |
| Von Seyfried, Henry | American New Wave Films |
| von Zerneck, Frank | Von Zerneck-Sertner Films |
| Vresilovic, John | Aspect Ratio Films |
| Wacek, Ed | Raffaella Productions, Inc. |
| Wachs, Robert | Wachs Co., The Robert D. |
| Wachsberger, Patrick | Summit Entertainment |
| Wadsworth, Cheryl | Wolf Films, Fred |
| Wagner, Alan | Boardwalk Ent./Alan Wagner Prods., Inc. |
| Wagner, Elizabeth | Boardwalk Ent./Alan Wagner Prods., Inc. |
| Wagner, Marti | Boardwalk Ent./Alan Wagner Prods., Inc. |
| Wagner, Paula | C/W Productions |
| Wagner, Raymond | Wagner Prods., Inc., Raymond |
| Wagner, Samantha | Equinox Entertainment Ltd. |
| Wagner, Susan | Boardwalk Ent./Alan Wagner Prods., Inc. |
| Wahl, Michael | Ideal Movie Shoppe, LLC, The |
| Wain, Margot | CBS Entertainment |
| Wainrib, Andrew | Mont Blanc Prods. |
| Waisbren, Brad | Waisbren Enterprises, Brad |
| Waite, Dava | Studios USA Television |
| Wakeman, Jill | Manifest Film Company |
| Walby, Steve | Baer Animation Co. Inc. |
| Wald, Jeff | Wald Entertainment Inc., Jeff |
| Walden, Dana | Twentieth Century Fox Television |
| Waldman, Matthew | Turman-Morrissey Company, The |
| Waldron, Jamie | Pearson All American |
| Wali, Hynndie | Melrose Prods. |
| Walker Jr., William A. | Victor Motion Pictures |
| Walker, Dana | Scripps Howard Prods. |
| Walker, Darrell | Mandalay Pictures |
| Walker, Eldridge | Paramount Pictures- Production Division |
| Walker, Timothy P. | Hearst Ent. Licensing & Family Prog. |
| Walkes, Bess | Bungalow 78 Prods. |
| Walkup, Carrie | Lions Gate Films Production |
| Wall, Barbara | Fox Broadcasting Co. |
| Wall, Heidi | Dream City Films |
| Wall, Kevin | IXL |
| Wall, Matt | October Films |
| Wallace, Jeff | Bandeira Entertainment |
| Wallace, Rick | Parami Productions |
| Wallach, Barry | Eyemark Entertainment |
| Wallach, George | Wallach Entertainment |
| Wallach, Lou | Fox Television Studios |
| Walley, Jim | Comedy Central |
| Wally, David J. | City Light Films |
| Walsh, Adriana | Enteraktion, Inc. |
| Walsh, Tom | Enteraktion, Inc. |
| Walsh-Gruber, Loretta | Peters Entertainment |
| Walters, Barbara | ABC Daytime |
| Walters, Happy | Immortal Films |
| Walters, Kent | Camera Marc |
| Walthers, Kal | Walt Disney Pictures/Touchstone Pictures |
| Walz, Ken | Walz Productions, Ken |
| Wanderman, Wendy | 3 Arts Entertainment |
| Wang, Edward C. | Gittes, Inc. |
| Ward, David S. | White Wolf Prods. |
| Ward, Jason | Nasser Entertainment Group |
| Ward, Julie | Big Daddy Productions |
| Ward, Kelly Ann | Gray Fox Films |
| Ward, Noreen | Good Machine |
| Ward, Peter | Blue Tulip Productions |
| Ward, Vincent | Ward Films, Inc., Vincent |
| Ware, Clyde | Delaware Pictures |
| Wargowski, Jim | NewStar Television |
| Waricha, Joan | Parachute Entertainment, LLC. |
| Warner, Cass | Warner Sisters Prods. |
| Warner, Keith | Codikow Films |
| Warner, Steve | Lifetime Television (NY) |
| Waronker, Lenny | DreamWorks SKG |
| Warren, Michael | Miller/Boyett/Warren Productions |
| Warren, Ryan | C/W Productions |
| Wartlieb, Jack | NewStar Television |
| Washington, Denzel | Mundy Lane Entertainment |
| Washington, Hayma (Screech) | Buena Vista Productions |
| Washington, Tracey | Nexus Entertainment, Inc. |
| Wass, Nina | Witt-Thomas-Harris Productions |

# CROSS-REFERENCED NAMES

| | |
|---|---|
| Waters, Don | Enteraktion, Inc. |
| Waterson, Trevor | Razors Edge Productions, Inc. |
| Waterston, Sam | Atkinson Way Films |
| Watkins, Bonnie | Icon Productions Inc. |
| Watson, John | Trilogy Entertainment Group |
| Watson, Julie | Belisarius Prods. |
| Watson, Peter | Recorded Picture Company |
| Watson, Scott | Red Hen Productions |
| Watts, Emma | Twentieth Century Fox |
| Waud, George | Act III Productions |
| Wax, Gary | Initial Entertainment Group |
| Wax, Sandra | Disney Channel |
| Wayne, Martye | Krainin Productions Inc. |
| Wayne, Michael A. | Batjac Productions, Inc. |
| Wayne, Teresa | Warner Bros. Pictures |
| Waznis, Amber | Silverman Co., The Fred |
| Wear, Donald | Discovery Networks |
| Weatherley, Truman | Zero Pictures |
| Weathers, Rich | America National Network, Inc. |
| Weathersby, Cassius Vernon | Londine Productions |
| Weathersby, Nadine | Londine Productions |
| Weaver, Doug | Icon Productions Inc. |
| Weaver, Katina | Entertainment Alliance, Inc., The |
| Weaver, Matthew | Lord/Weaver Prods. |
| Weaver, Megan | Roth/Arnold Prods. |
| Weaver, Ron | Bell-Phillip TV Prods., Inc. |
| Weaver, Sigourney | Goat Cay Productions, Inc. |
| Webb, Janelle | Expect Miracles, Inc. |
| Webb, Lucy | Calm Down Productions, Inc. |
| Webb, William | Westwind Productions, Inc. |
| Weber, Bob | Trilogy Entertainment Group |
| Weber, Bruce | Little Bear Films, Inc. |
| Weber, Jeff | Common Creed Entertainment Corp. |
| Weber, Marco | Centropolis Streamline |
| Wechsler, Nick | Industry Entertainment |
| Wechsler, Ron | Roxaboxen |
| Wedaa, Jim | Jacobson Company, The |
| Weed, Gene | Clark Prods., Inc., Dick |
| Weeks, Denise | Braun Productions, David |
| Wegner, Laura | Saban Entertainment |
| Wei, Inness | RKO Pictures, Inc. |
| Weide, Robert B. | Whyaduck Prods., Inc. |
| Weidner, Warren | Grinning Dog Pictures |
| Weikel, Ken | Wilshire Court Prods. |
| Weinberg, Aaron M. | Weiny Bro Productions |
| Weinberg, Robert | Dancing Asparagus Prods. |
| Weinberger, Ed. | Weinberger Co., Ed. |
| Weinberger, Neil | Singer Entertainment, Joseph M. |
| Weiner, Andrew | Goldwyn Films Inc. |
| Weiner, Judith | United Paramount Network (UPN) |
| Weiner, William S. | New Regency Prods. |
| Weinert, Suzanne | Shoelace Productions, Inc. |
| Weingrod, Herschel | Weingrod/Harris Prods. |
| Weinstein, Bob | Dimension Films |
| Weinstein, Bob | Miramax Films |
| Weinstein, David | Rossu Entertainment |
| Weinstein, Harvey | Miramax Films |
| Weinstein, Jonathan | Sticks And Stones |
| Weinstein, Josh | Bill Oakley & Josh Weinstein |
| Weinstein, Nina | Scripps Howard Prods. |
| Weinstein, Paula | Baltimore/Spring Creek Pictures, LLC |
| Weinstein, Paula | Spring Creek Productions |
| Weinstock, Charles | Weinstock Productions |
| Weinstock, Ronnie | Film Garden Entertainment |
| Weintraub, Barbara | Axelson-Weintraub Productions |
| Weintraub, Fred | Weintraub/Kuhn Prods. |
| Weintraub, Jerry | Weintraub Prods., Jerry |
| Weintraub, Lloyd | Di Bona Prods., Vin |
| Weintraub, Lori | Krane Group, The Jonathan |
| Weir, Andrea | Entertainment Group, The |
| Weir, Innes | Neufeld Productions, Mace |
| Weisbarth, Michael | Alliance Television Productions |
| Weisberg, Roni | Weisberg Prods., Roni |
| Weiser, Donna | Fox Broadcasting Co. |
| Weisgal, Jonathan | Jersey Shore |
| Weisman, Howard J. | Weisman Productions, Howard J. |
| Weisman, Straw | Scarlet Fire Films |
| Weiss Lurie, Christina | Levy/Weiss Productions |
| Weiss, Barry | Sony Pictures Imageworks |
| Weiss, Bob | Broadway Pictures (LA) |
| Weiss, Jason | OMNIBUS |
| Weiss, Jeff | Weisworld Premieres |
| Weiss, Megan | Maysville Pictures |
| Weissberger, Kathi | Pearson All American |
| Weissman, Lauren C. | Danika Productions, Inc. |
| Weitz, Julie | Turner Network Television (TNT) |
| Weitzman, Carole | Sunbow Entertainment |
| Weitzman, Marc | Bandeira Entertainment |
| Weitzman, Marjorie | InFront Productions |
| Welch, Steve | Dakota North Ent./Dakota Films |
| Weller, Robb | Weller/Grossman Productions |
| Wellins, Alyson | Miramax Films |
| Wellner, Barbara | Goodman-Rosen Prods. |
| Wells, John | Wells Productions, John |
| Wells, Pat | Studios USA Television |
| Wells, Patrick C. | River Mill Productions |
| Welsh, Barbara Hunter | CBS Entertainment |
| Welsh, Richard E. | Hallmark Hall of Fame Productions, Inc. |
| Welteke, Daniela | Fox Television Studios |
| Welty, Don | Studios USA Television |
| Welty, Theresa | Wind Dancer Films |
| Wenberg, Julie | Singer Productions, Carla |
| Wenokur, Bob | Kushner-Locke Co. |
| Werber, Clifford | Warner Bros. Pictures |
| Werkman, S. Russell | Revelations Entertainment |
| Werner, Peter H. | Joyful Noise Unlimited, A |
| Werner, Sharon | HBO NYC Productions |
| Werner, Tom | Carsey-Werner Co., The |
| Wernick, Jeff | DIC Entertainment |
| Wernick, Sandy | Brillstein-Grey Ent. |
| Wernig, Marcus | Driskill Entertainment |
| Wertheimer, Shira | Studios USA Television |
| Wesche, Jason | First Light |
| Wesley, James | Lifetime Television (NY) |
| Wesley, Tim | Meridian Entertainment, LLC |
| Wessler, Charles B. | Wessler Entertainment |
| West, Donald | Associated Producers Group, Inc. |
| West, Joella | Walt Disney TV/Touchstone TV |
| West, Simon | Wychwood Productions |
| Westberg, David | Westberg Entertainment |
| Westergaard, Troy | Katie Face Prods. |
| Westin, David | ABC Entertainment |
| Westlake, Blair | Universal Television & Networks Group |
| Weston, Ann | Gross-Weston Prods. |
| Weston, Brad | Merlin Entertainment |
| Westphal, John | Big Ticket Television |
| Westwell, Serena | Twentieth Century Fox |
| Wetmur, Tara | Star Land Entertainment Inc. |
| Wexelblatt, Linda | Producers Ent. Group, Ltd., The |
| Wexler, Joshua | Threshold Entertainment |
| Wexler, Judith | Sundance Institute |
| Weyand, Dan | Tri-Crown Prods. |
| Whedon, Joss | Mutant Enemy, Inc. |
| Whelan, Stephen | City Light Films |
| Whifler, Graeme | Cafe Productions |
| Whistler, Sarah | Ward Films, Inc., Vincent |
| Whitacre, William L. | Pamplin-Fisher Company |
| Whitaker, Christine | National Geographic Feature Films |
| Whitaker, Jim | Imagine Entertainment |
| White, Andrew | Malpaso Prods. |
| White, Benji | Mojo Films |
| White, Brenda | Golden Quill |
| White, Brett | ABC Entertainment |
| White, Don | Tiger Prods. |
| White, Elizabeth | HBO Original Programming |
| White, Jeffrey | White Prods., Jeffrey |
| White, Karen | Red Wagon Prods. |
| White, Kolleen | Dunas Prods., Ronald S. |
| White, Marla | Longbow Productions |
| White, Sean | Brillstein-Grey Ent. |
| White, Steve | Singer-White Entertainment |
| White, Whitney | Ocean Pictures |
| Whitehead Evans, Joan | Studios USA Pictures |
| Whitehead, Glenn | HBO Pictures |
| Whitmore, Brandi | Krost/Chapin |
| Whitney, Rae | Banner Assocs., Bob |
| Whittaker, Susan | Two Oceans Entertainment Group |
| Whittington, Rebecca | Cosgrove-Meurer Prods. |
| Wick, C.Z. | Wick, C.Z. |
| Wick, Doug | Red Wagon Prods. |

# CROSS-REFERENCED NAMES

| | |
|---|---|
| Wicks, Sean | Mad Chance |
| Widdoes, James | Axelrod/Widdoes Productions |
| Wieringa, Jan | Harmony Pictures |
| Wietzsche, Fred | Vide-U Productions |
| Wigan, Gareth | Columbia Pictures |
| Wigan, Gareth | Columbia TriStar Motion Picture Group |
| Wigor, Bradley | Helios Prods. |
| Wigram, Lionel | Warner Bros. Pictures |
| Wigutow, Dan | Wigutow Prods., Dan |
| Wilberger, Jim | Turner Network Television (TNT) |
| Wilcox, Leslie | Iwerks Entertainment |
| Wilder, King | SteppinStone Entertainment |
| Wiley, Martin | TriCoast Entertainment |
| Wilhite, Thomas | Hyperion Entertainment |
| Wilk, Andrew Carl | National Geographic Television |
| Wilkens, Marlena | Caravan Pictures |
| Wilkerson, Michelle | Bernbaum, Paul |
| Wilkes, Deon | Donner/Shuler-Donner Prods. |
| Wilkins, Wendy | Dakota North Ent./Dakota Films |
| Williams, Abdul | Monarch Pictures |
| Williams, Dan | Apple & Honey Productions, Ltd. |
| Williams, Dominique | Showtime Networks Inc. |
| Williams, Ellyn | March Hare Entertainment |
| Williams, John | Vanguard Films |
| Williams, Kenneth | Sony Pictures Imageworks |
| Williams, Larry B. | Write Place Write Time |
| Williams, Laura | Twentieth Century Fox-Fox 2000 (LA) |
| Williams, Lindsay | Finerman Prods., Wendy |
| Williams, Marsha | Blue Wolf Prods. Inc. |
| Williams, Matt | Wind Dancer Prod. Group |
| Williams, Pam | Warner Bros. Television Productions |
| Williams, Richard | Persistent Pictures, Inc. |
| Williams, Robin | Blue Wolf Prods. Inc. |
| Williams, Shaun | Scott Free Productions |
| Williams, Stephanie | Gitlin Productions |
| Williams, Ty | Outerbanks Entertainment |
| Williams, Wayne S. | Cannell Motion Pictures |
| Williamson, Glenn | DreamWorks SKG |
| Williamson, Kevin | Outerbanks Entertainment |
| Williger, David S. | P.A.T. Productions |
| Willis, Charlie | VanDerKloot Film & Television Inc. |
| Wilson, Adam | Mutant Enemy, Inc. |
| Wilson, Brad | Greystone Films |
| Wilson, Caren | Bernsen Prods. Inc., Harry |
| Wilson, Ed | CBS Enterprises |
| Wilson, Ed | Eyemark Entertainment |
| Wilson, John | PBS |
| Wilson, Jonathan | Hyams Prods., Inc., Peter |
| Wilson, Kate | Egg Pictures |
| Wilson, Michael | Danjaq Inc. |
| Wilson, Molly | HBO Pictures |
| Wilson, Rob | Illusion Entertainment Group |
| Wilson, S.S. | Stampede Entertainment |
| Wilson, Stacy C. | Banner Entertainment |
| Winant, Scott | Twilight Time Films |
| Winch, Jack | Associated Producers Group, Inc. |
| Winchester, Karen | Smith Productions Inc., Thomas G. |
| Winchester, Margot | Winchester Prods., Inc., Margot |
| Winfrey, Oprah | Harpo Films Inc. |
| Winikoff, Cami | Trimark Pictures |
| Winitsky, Alex | Lantana Productions |
| Winkler, Henry | FairDinkum Prods. |
| Winkler, Henry | Schwartzberg & Company |
| Winkler, Irwin | Winkler Films |
| Winn, Courtney | Grade A Entertainment |
| Winship, Dorian | Lifetime Television (NY) |
| Winston, Stan | Winston Productions, Inc. |
| Winston, Susan | Blanki & Bodi Prods., Inc. |
| Winter, Aurora | Porchlight Entertainment |
| Winter, Ralph | Common Creed Entertainment Corp. |
| Winteringham, Tim | Hill/Fields Ent. |
| Wischner-Sola, Cathy | Turner Network Television (TNT) |
| Wise, Stephanie | Metro-Goldwyn-Mayer/Worldwide TV |
| Wiseman, John | Paramount Pictures- Production Division |
| Wishnick, Gil-Adrienne | Promark Entertainment Group |
| Wisne, Pamela | Kelley Productions, David E. |
| Wiss, Brad | Di Novi Pictures |
| Witlin, Alixandre | City Entertainment |
| Witt, Dan | Witt, Dan |
| Witt, Paul Junger | Witt-Thomas Films |
| Witt, Paul Junger | Witt-Thomas-Harris Productions |
| Witt, Renee | Fine Line Features |
| Witt, Renee | New Line Cinema |
| Witten, Brian | New Line Cinema |
| Wittenberg, Jess | Castle Rock Entertainment |
| Wixson, Keith | De Passe Entertainment |
| Wizan, Joe | Phase I Productions |
| Wizan, Steve | Phase I Productions |
| Wlasic, Tina | Metro-Goldwyn-Mayer/Worldwide TV |
| Woertz, Gregory | Pressman Film Corp., Edward R. |
| Wohl, Linda | Paramount Pictures- Production Division |
| Woinsky, Orin | Outlaw Productions |
| Wolf, Abby | Mostow/Lieberman |
| Wolf, Bill | Wolf Films, Fred |
| Wolf, Dick | Wolf Films Inc. |
| Wolf, Fred | Wolf Films, Fred |
| Wolf, Marc | Di Novi Pictures |
| Wolfe, Elizabeth | PBS |
| Wolfe, Steven J. | Sneak Preview Entertainment, Inc. |
| Wolfe, Tom | Immortal Films |
| Wolff, Jolene | Marmont Prods. Inc. |
| Wolfman, Marv | WolfMill Entertainment |
| Wolford, Michele | Write Place Write Time |
| Wolfson, Tina | Cannery, Inc., The |
| Wolinsky, Judith | Rainbow Film Co./Rainbow Releasing |
| Wollman, Don | Clark Prods., Inc., Dick |
| Wolman, Adam | ABC Entertainment |
| Wolper, David L. | Wolper Org., The |
| Wolper, Mark M. | Wolper Org., The |
| Wolpert, Megan | Konrad Pictures |
| Wolsh, Deborah | Rothstein Prods., Freyda |
| Wolters, John | ABC Entertainment |
| Wong, Chi-Li | AEI-Atchity Edit./Ent. Intl. Inc. |
| Wong, David | IF/X Productions |
| Wong, Max | Beacon Pictures |
| Wong, Ronald J. | Green Grass Blue Sky Company, Inc. |
| Wood, Andrea | Alliance Pictures |
| Wood, Doris | Manhattan Project Ltd., The |
| Wood, Lara | Kopelson Entertainment |
| Woods, Brent | Takoma Entertainment Group |
| Woods, Jake | Newman/Tooley Films |
| Woods, Mel | Fox Family Channel |
| Woods, Mel | Fox Kids Network |
| Woods, Mel | Saban Entertainment |
| Woods, Susan | Rehme Productions |
| Woodward, Ali | Prufrock Pictures |
| Woodward, Josh | Meridian Entertainment, LLC |
| Woodward, Karen | Baumgarten/Prophet Entertainment |
| Woolfork, Tamara | Warner Bros. Feature Animation |
| Woolley, Markus J. | VentureWest Pictures |
| Woosley, Tom | Hirsch Company, Inc., S. |
| Wooton, Patty | Pacific Data Images |
| Wordham, Heather | Harris & Company |
| Work, Channing | Mestres Productions, Ricardo |
| Worth, Lauren | Equinox Entertainment Ltd. |
| Worth, Marvin | Worth Prods., Marvin |
| Worth, Steve | Spumco |
| Worthington, Jennifer | Bruckheimer Films, Jerry |
| Worthins, Anna | Westwind Productions, Inc. |
| Wright, Ian | Macht Ent. Group, Inc. |
| Wright, Michael | CBS Entertainment |
| Wright, Michelle | Interscope Communications Inc. |
| Wright, Norton | Wright Productions, Norton |
| Wright, Paige | Walt Disney Pictures/Touchstone Pictures |
| Wright, Richard | Lakeshore Entertainment Corp. |
| Wroblewski, Gretchen Hayduk | Hart Sharp Entertainment, Inc. |
| Wrye, Donald | Spygaze Pictures |
| Wulbrun, Karyn | Krost/Chapin |
| Wulfe, Kym | Interscope Communications Inc. |
| Wunschel, Barbara | VanDerKloot Film & Television Inc. |
| Wyatt, Kevin | Nomad Productions |
| Wycoff, Susan | Columbia TriStar Television |
| Wylie, Melissa | MWG Prods. |
| Wyman, Mark | Columbia Pictures |
| Wynne, Robert J. | Sony Pictures Entertainment |
| Yacoub, Lila | FilmColony, Ltd. |
| Yamamoto, Paul | Team Entertainment Group |
| Yamashita, Jane | Mirkin Vision |
| Yang, Janet | Manifest Film Company |
| Yankelevits, Donny | HBO Original Programming |

# CROSS-REFERENCED NAMES

Yanover, Michael I. . . . . . . . . . . . . . . . . . . . . Matinee Entertainment
Yanover, Paul . . . . . . . . . Walt Disney Pictures/Touchstone Pictures
Yantek, Greg . . . . . . . . . . . . . . . . . . . . . . . . . . . ABC Entertainment
Yantos, Anne Marie . . . . . . . . . . . . Turner Network Television (TNT)
Yee, Joan . . . . . . . . . . . . . . . . . . . . . . . . . . . . . CBS Entertainment
Yeldell, Eric . . . . . . . . . . . . . . . . . . . . . . . . . Fox Broadcasting Co.
Yeldham, Rebecca . . . . . . . . . . . . . . . . . . . . Sundance Institute
Yellen, Linda . . . . . . . . . . . . . . . . . . . . . . . Yellen Company,, Linda
Yellen, Mark . . . . . . . . . . . . . . . . . . . . . Zeta Entertainment Ltd.
Yellen, Martin . . . . . . . . . . . . . . . . . . . . . . Yellen Company,, Linda
Yellen, Nicholas . . . . . . . . . . . . . Edwards Yellen Entertainment
Yellin, Douglas . . . . . . . . . . . . . . . . . . . . . . Iwerks Entertainment
Yerkovich, Anthony . . . . . . . . . . . . . . . . . . . . . . Yerkovich Prods.
Yerxa, Ron . . . . . . . . . . . . . . . . . . . . . . . . Bona Fide Productions
Yoelin, Naomi . . . . . . . . . . . . . . . . . Capital Arts Entertainment
Yoo, Susan . . . . . . . . . . . . . . . . . Baumgarten/Prophet Entertainment
York, Dan . . . . . . . . . . . . . . . . . . . . . . . . . . York Company, The
Yorkin, Bud . . . . . . . . . . . . . . . . . . . . . . Yorkin Productions, Bud
Yorn, Julie . . . . . . . . . . . . . . . . . . . . . . . . . Industry Entertainment
Yorn, Rick . . . . . . . . . . . . . . . . . . . . . . . . . Industry Entertainment
Yoshinaga, Yumi . . . . . . . . . . . Lakeshore Entertainment Corp.
Yost, Elizabeth . . . . . . . . . . . . . . . . . . . . . Gleneagle Productions
Young, Alison . . . . . . . . . . . . . . . . . . . . . . Byrum Power & Light
Young, Ann C. . . . . . . . . . . . . . . . . . . . . . . Berner Films, Fred
Young, John Sacret . . . . . . . . . . . . . . . . Samoset Inc./Sacret Inc.
Young, Saskia . . . . . . . . . . Twentieth Century Fox-Fox 2000 (LA)
Young, Suzanne . . . . . . . . . . . . . . . . . . . . . . . . . . HBO Pictures
Young, William L. . . . . . . . . . . . . . . . . . . . Warner Bros. Pictures
Yudin, Michael . . . . . . . . . . . . . . . . Telescene Film Group., Inc.
Yuval, Peter . . . . . . . . . . . . . . . . . . . . . . Trivision Pictures Inc.
Zabawski, Brian . . . . . . . . . . . . . . . . . . . . Unistar Intl. Pictures
Zabel, John . . . . . . . . . . . . . . . . . . . . . . . . . Mandalay Pictures
Zaccaro, Laura . . . . . . . . . . . . . . . . Talking Wall Pictures, Inc.
Zachary, Susan . . . . . . . . . . Rosemont Prods. International Ltd.
Zachmeier, Thomas . . . . . . . . . . . . . . . . . . . . . Zero Pictures
Zadan, Craig . . . . . . . . . . . . . . . . . . . . . Storyline Entertainment
Zaentz, Saul . . . . . . . . . . . . . . . . . . . . . Zaentz Co., The Saul
Zagala, Cecille . . . . . . . . . . . . . . . . . Baldwin/Cohen Productions
Zahavi, Natan . . . . . . . . . . . . . . . . . . . . . . Tapestry Films Inc.
Zajic, Keith . . . . . . . . . . . . . . . . . . . . . . . Warner Bros. Pictures
Zak, John . . . . . . . . . . . . . . . . . . . . . Bell-Phillip TV Prods., Inc.
Zakarin, Mark . . . . . . . . . . . . . . . . . . . . . Showtime Networks Inc.
Zakin, Isabelle . . . . . . . . . . . . . . . . . . . . . . . . IF/X Productions
Zaks, Laurie . . . . . . . . . . . . . . . . . . . . . . . . . CBS Entertainment
Zalaznick, Lauren . . . . . . . . . . . . . . . . . . . . . VH1 (Music First)
Zalenski, Emily . . . . . . . . . . Pressman Film Corp., Edward R.
Zaloom, George . . . . . . . . . . . . . . . . . . . . . . . ZM Productions
Zand, Stacy . . . . . . . . . . . . . . . . . . . . . . . . Peters Entertainment
Zane, Edwin . . . . . . . . . . . United Paramount Network (UPN)
Zanitsch, Noel . . . . . . . . . . . . . . . . . . . Image Organization, Inc.
Zanuck, Dean . . . . . . . . . . . . . . . . . . . . . . . . Zanuck Co., The
Zanuck, Lili Fini . . . . . . . . . . . . . . . . . . . . . . Zanuck Co., The
Zanuck, Richard D. . . . . . . . . . . . . . . . . . . . . Zanuck Co., The
Zappy, Leah . . . . . . . . . . . . . . . . . . . . . . . . . . Brooksfilms, Ltd.
Zarghami, Cyma . . . . . . . . . . . . . . . Nickelodeon/Nick at Nite
Zaring, John . . . . . . . . . . . . . . Zaring/Cioffi Entertainment, Inc.
Zarpas, Chris . . . . . . . . . . . . . . . . . . . . . . . Scott Free Productions
Zarrow, Aaron . . . . . . . . . . . . . . . . . . . Moll/Beallor Productions
Zauber, Kirsten . . . . . . . . . . . . . . . . . . . . . . . CPC Entertainment

Zaylor, Judy . . . . . . . . . . . . . . Warner Bros. Television Productions
Zebrowski-Heller, Kathy . . . . . . . . . . . . . . . . . Heller Prods., Paul
Zee, Teddy . . . . . . . . . . . . . . . . . . . . . . Davis Entertainment Co.
Zeegen, Heather . . . . . . . . . . . . . . . . . . . . . . . . . Original Film
Zella, Jeff . . . . . . . . . . . . . . . . . . . . . . . . . Brillstein-Grey Ent.
Zelman, David J. . . . . . . . . . . . . . . . Isaac Productions, Sandy
Zelon, David . . . . . . . . . . . . . . . . . . . . . . . . Mandalay Pictures
Zeman, Allan . . . . . . . . . . . . . . . . . . Sweetpea Entertainment
Zemeckis, Robert . . . . . . . . . . . . . . . . . . . . . . . ImageMovers
Zenga, Bo . . . . . . . . . . . . . . . . . . . . . . . . . . . Boz Productions
Zepeda, Isa . . . . . . . . . . . . . . . . . . . . . . . . . . . TAE Productions
Zepeda, Susana R. . . . . . . . . . . . . . . . . . . . . . Nava Films
Zepfel, Don . . . . . . . . . . . . . . . . . . . . . . . . . . Universal Pictures
Zerr, David . . . . . . . . . . . . . . . . . . . . . Mark Prods., Laurence
Zide, Warren . . . . . . . . . . . . . . . . . . . . . . . Zide Entertainment
Ziegler, Farley . . . . . . . . . . . . . . . . . . . . . . Single Cell Pictures
Ziering, Barbara . . . . . . . . . . . . . . . Keeshen Productions, Jim
Zigler, Trisha . . . . . . . . . . . . . . . . . . . . . . . Scarlet Fire Films
Zimbert, Jonathan A. . . . . . . . . . . . . . . . . . Morgan Creek Prods.
Zimmerly, Deborah . . . . . . . . . . . . IndieGal Productions, LLC
Zimmerman, Derk . . . . . . . . . . . . . . . . . . . . . CBS Corporation
Zimmerman, Ray . . . . . . . Columbia TriStar Motion Picture Group
Zimmerman, Stan . . . . . . . . . . . . . . . . . . . . . Zimmerman/Berg
Zinger, Robert . . . . . . . . . . . . . . . . . Spelling Television, Inc.
Zinkin, Ben . . . . . . . . . . . . . . . . . . . . . . . . . New Line Cinema
Zinman, Richard . . . . . . . . . . . . . . . . . . . . . . . Fried Films
Zinner, Peter . . . . . . . . . . . . . . . . Braun Productions, David
Zinnes, Andrew . . . . . . . . . . . . . . . . . . . . Act III Productions
Zipperman, Barbara . . . . . . . . . . . . . . Fox Animation Studios
Ziskin, Laura . . . . . . . . . Twentieth Century Fox-Fox 2000 (LA)
Ziskin, Ron . . . . . . . . . . . . . . . . . . . . . . . . . . . NewStar Media
Ziskin, Ron . . . . . . . . . . . . . . . . . . . . . . . NewStar Television
Zito, Joe . . . . . . . . . . . . . . . . . . . . . . . . Trivision Pictures Inc.
Zito, Stephen . . . . . . . . . . . . . . . . . . . . . . . . Belisarius Prods.
Zivot, Louis . . . . . . . . . . . . . . . . . . . . . . Mercury-Jet Pictures
Zlotnik, Carmi . . . . . . . . . . . . . . . . . . . . . . . HBO Animation
Zlotnik, Carmi . . . . . . . . . . . . . HBO Independent Productions
Zlotnik, Carmi . . . . . . . . . . . . . . HBO Original Programming
Zollo, Frederick . . . . . . . . . . . . . . . . . . . . . . . . Zollo Productions
Zonker, David K. . . . . . . . . . . . . . Jones Entertainment Group
Zotnowski, Kathy . . . . . . . . . OMS - One Mind Sound Productions
Zoumas, Michael . . . . . . . . . . . . . . . . . . . . . . . Avenue Pictures
Zubrick, Nadja . . . . . . . . . . . . . . . . . . . . . Missel Prods., Renee
Zucker, David . . . . . . . . . . . . . . . . Zucker Brothers Productions
Zucker, Janet . . . . . . . . . . . . . . . . Zucker Brothers Productions
Zucker, Jerry . . . . . . . . . . . . . . . . Zucker Brothers Productions
Zucker, Jody . . . . . . . . . . . . . Paramount Network Television
Zuckerman, Anita . . . . . . . . . . . . . . . . . Stiefel Entertainment
Zuckerman, Nora . . . . . . . . . . . . . . . . . . . . Roth/Arnold Prods.
Zuker, Lori . . . . . . . . . . . . . . . . . . . Overbrook Entertainment
Zuletta, Percy . . . . . . . . . . . . . . . . . . . . . . . . . Silver Pictures
Zulfer, Catherine . . . . . . . . . . . Playboy Entertainment Group Inc.
Zummo, Anthony . . . . . . . . . . . . . . . . . . . . . . . Universal Pictures
Zupan, Lisa . . . . . . . . . . . . . . . . . . . . . Finerman Prods., Wendy
Zurbrugg, Shauna . . . . . . . . . . . . . . . . . . . . . NewStar Media
Zusmann, Kaye . . . . . . . . . . . . . . . Gibbons Enterprises, Leeza
Zweibel, Alan . . . . . . . . . . . . . . . . . . . . . . . . . Zweibel, Alan
Zwick, Edward . . . . . . . . . . . . . . . . . . . . . . Bedford Falls Co., The

# SECTION E.

# TV Shows and Staff

# TV SHOWS AND STAFF

**3RD ROCK FROM THE SUN (NBC/30 mins.)**
PHONE . . . . . . . . . . . . . . . . . . . . . . . . . . . . . . . . . . 818-760-6057
4024 Radford Avenue
Studio City, CA 91604
PROD.CO:    Carsey-Werner Co., The

Marcy Carsey . . . . . . . . . . . . . . . . . . . . . . . . . . . . Executive Producer
Caryn Mandabach . . . . . . . . . . . . . . . . . . . . . . . . . Executive Producer
Bill Martin . . . . . . . . . . . . . . . . . . . . . . . . . . . . . Executive Producer
Mike Schiff . . . . . . . . . . . . . . . . . . . . . . . . . . . . . Executive Producer
Bonnie Turner . . . . . . . . . . . . . . . . . . . . . . . . . . . Executive Producer
Terry Turner . . . . . . . . . . . . . . . . . . . . . . . . . . . . Executive Producer
Tom Werner . . . . . . . . . . . . . . . . . . . . . . . . . . . . Executive Producer
David Sacks . . . . . . . . . . . . . . . . . . . . . . . . . . . . . Co-Exec. Producer
Bob Kushnell . . . . . . . . . . . . . . . . . . . . . . . . . . . Supervising Producer
Christine Zander . . . . . . . . . . . . . . . . . . . . . . . . . Supervising Producer
Patrick Kienlen . . . . . . . . . . . . . . . . . . . . . . . . . . . . . . . Producer
Marc Hirschfeld . . . . . . . . . . . . . . . . . . . . . . . . . . . . . . . . Casting

**ALL MY CHILDREN (ABC/60 mins.)**
PHONE . . . . . . . . . . . . . . . . . . . . . . . . . . . . . . . . . . 212-456-0800
320 West 66th Street
New York, NY 10023
PROD.CO:    ABC Daytime

Jean Dadario-Burke . . . . . . . . . . . . . . . . . . . . . . . Executive Producer
Heidi Adam . . . . . . . . . . . . . . . . . . . . . . . . . . . Supervising Producer
Ginger Smith . . . . . . . . . . . . . . . . . . . . . . . . . . Supervising Producer
Judy Wilson . . . . . . . . . . . . . . . . . . . . . . . . . . . . . . . . . . Casting

***ALL MY LIFE (NBC/30 mins.)**
PHONE . . . . . . . . . . . . . . . . . . . . . . . . . . . . . . . . . . 818-977-8215
FAX . . . . . . . . . . . . . . . . . . . . . . . . . . . . . . . . . . . 818-977-8211
4000 Warner Blvd., Bldg. 160, Ste. 200
Burbank, CA 91522
PROD.CO:    Bright/Kauffman/Crane Prods./Warner Bros. Television
            Productions

Kevin S. Bright . . . . . . . . . . . . . . . . . . . . . . . . . . Executive Producer
David Crane . . . . . . . . . . . . . . . . . . . . . . . . . . . . Executive Producer
Marta Kauffman . . . . . . . . . . . . . . . . . . . . . . . . . Executive Producer
Stephen Nathan . . . . . . . . . . . . . . . . . . . . . . . . . Executive Producer
Ira Ungerleider . . . . . . . . . . . . . . . . . . . . . . . . . Executive Producer
Tony Sepulveda . . . . . . . . . . . . . . . . . . . . . . . . . . . . . . . . Casting

**ALLY MCBEAL (Fox/60 mins.)**
PHONE . . . . . . . . . . . . . . . . . . . . . . . . . . . . . . . . . . 310-727-2100
FAX . . . . . . . . . . . . . . . . . . . . . . . . . . . . . . . . . . . 310-727-2468
Twentieth Century Fox
10201 W. Pico Blvd.
Los Angeles, CA 90035
PROD.CO:    David E. Kelley Prods.

David E. Kelley . . . . . . . . . . . . . . . . . . . . . . . . . . Executive Producer
Jeffrey Kramer . . . . . . . . . . . . . . . . . . . . . . . . . . Co-Exec. Producer
Jonathan Pontell . . . . . . . . . . . . . . . . . . . . . . . . . Co-Exec. Producer
Mike Listo . . . . . . . . . . . . . . . . . . . . . . . . . . . . . . . . . . Producer
Jeanie Bachrach . . . . . . . . . . . . . . . . . . . . . . . . . . . . . . . . Casting

**ANOTHER WORLD (NBC/60 mins.)**
PHONE . . . . . . . . . . . . . . . . . . . . . . . . . . . . . . . . . . 212-213-7149
1268 E. 14th St.
Brooklyn, NY 11230
PROD.CO:    Proctor & Gamble Prods. Inc.

Charlotte Savitz . . . . . . . . . . . . . . . . . . . . . . . . . Executive Producer
Scott Collishaw . . . . . . . . . . . . . . . . . . . . . . . . . . . . . . . . Producer
Leslie Kwartin . . . . . . . . . . . . . . . . . . . . . . . . . . . . . . . . Producer
Carole Shure . . . . . . . . . . . . . . . . . . . . . . . . . . . . . . . . . Producer
Jimmy Bohr . . . . . . . . . . . . . . . . . . . . . . . . . . . . . . . . . . Casting

***ANY DAY NOW (Lifetime/60 mins.)**
PHONE . . . . . . . . . . . . . . . . . . . . . . . . . . . . . . . . . . 310-556-7500
Lifetime Television
2049 Century Park East
Los Angeles, CA 90067
PROD.CO:    Spelling Entertainment Group, Inc.

Nancy Miller . . . . . . . . . . . . . . . . . . . . . . . . . . . Executive Producer
Gary Randall . . . . . . . . . . . . . . . . . . . . . . . . . . . Executive Producer
Ulrich/Dawson/Kritzer Casting . . . . . . . . . . . . . . . . . . . . . . . . Casting

***ARMY SHOW, THE (WB/60 mins.)**
PHONE . . . . . . . . . . . . . . . . . . . . . . . . . . . . . . . . . . 213-850-2762
1041 N. Formosa
Santa Monica Bldg., Ste. 111
Los Angeles, CA 90046
PROD.CO:    Castle Rock Entertainment

J.J. Wall . . . . . . . . . . . . . . . . . . . . . . . . . . . . . . Executive Producer

**AS THE WORLD TURNS (CBS/60 mins.)**
CBS Broadcast Center
524 W. 57th St.
New York, NY 10019
PROD.CO:    Proctor & Gamble Prods. Inc.

Felicia Minei Behr . . . . . . . . . . . . . . . . . . . . . . . Executive Producer
Terry Cacavio . . . . . . . . . . . . . . . . . . . . . . . . . . . . . . . . Producer
Vivian Gundaker . . . . . . . . . . . . . . . . . . . . . . . . . . . . . . . Producer
Mikie Heilbrun . . . . . . . . . . . . . . . . . . . . . . . . . . . . . . . . Casting

**BABYLON 5 (TNT/60 mins.)**
PHONE . . . . . . . . . . . . . . . . . . . . . . . . . . . . . . . . . . 818-504-3135
FAX . . . . . . . . . . . . . . . . . . . . . . . . . . . . . . . . . . . 818-504-3195
8615 Tamarack Ave.
Sun Valley, CA 91352
PROD.CO:    Babylonian Prods.

J. Michael Straczynski . . . . . . . . . . . . . Executive Producer/Creator/Writer
Douglas Netter . . . . . . . . . . . . . . . . . . . . . . . . . Executive Producer
John Copeland . . . . . . . . . . . . . . . . . . . . . . . . . . . . . . . . Producer
Fern Champion . . . . . . . . . . . . . . . . . . . . . . . . . . . . . . . . Casting
Mark Paladini . . . . . . . . . . . . . . . . . . . . . . . . . . . . . . . . . Casting

**BAYWATCH (UPN/Syndicated/60 mins.)**
PHONE . . . . . . . . . . . . . . . . . . . . . . . . . . . . . . . . . . 310-302-9164
FAX . . . . . . . . . . . . . . . . . . . . . . . . . . . . . . . . . . . 310-302-9190
5433 Beethoven St.
Los Angeles, CA 90066
PROD.CO:    Baywatch Production Co.

Gregory J. Bonann . . . . . . . . . . . . . . . . . . . . . . . Executive Producer
David Hasselhoff . . . . . . . . . . . . . . . . . . . . . . . . Executive Producer
Doug Schwartz . . . . . . . . . . . . . . . . . . . . . . . . . Executive Producer
Susan Glicksman . . . . . . . . . . . . . . . . . . . . . . . . . . . . . . . Casting

***BENBEN SHOW, THE (CBS/30 mins.)**
PHONE . . . . . . . . . . . . . . . . . . . . . . . . . . . . . . . . . . 818-954-7550
FAX . . . . . . . . . . . . . . . . . . . . . . . . . . . . . . . . . . . 818-954-7248
4000 Warner Blvd., Bldg. 136, Rm. 101
Burbank, CA 91522
PROD.CO:    Warner Bros. Television Productions/CBS Productions

Robert Borden . . . . . . . . . . . . . . . . . . . . . . . . . . Executive Producer
Brian Benben . . . . . . . . . . . . . . . . . . . . . . . . . . Co-Exec. Producer

**BEVERLY HILLS 90210 (Fox/60 mins.)**
PHONE . . . . . . . . . . . . . . . . . . . . . . . . . . . . . . . . . . 213-965-5700
Spelling Television
5700 Wilshire Blvd., #575
Los Angeles, CA 90036
PROD.CO:    Spelling Television Inc

John Eisendrath . . . . . . . . . . . . . . . . . . . . . . . . . Executive Producer
Jason Priestley . . . . . . . . . . . . . . . . . . . . . . . . . Executive Producer
Aaron Spelling . . . . . . . . . . . . . . . . . . . . . . . . . Executive Producer
E. Duke Vincent . . . . . . . . . . . . . . . . . . . . . . . . Executive Producer
Paul Waigner . . . . . . . . . . . . . . . . . . . . . . . . . . Executive Producer
Michael Cassutt . . . . . . . . . . . . . . . . . . . . . . . . . . . . . . . Producer
Laurie McCarthy . . . . . . . . . . . . . . . . . . . . . . . . . . . . . . . Producer
Betty Reardon . . . . . . . . . . . . . . . . . . . . . . . . . . . . . . . . Producer
Doug Steinberg . . . . . . . . . . . . . . . . . . . . . . . . . . . . . . . . Producer
Vicki Huff . . . . . . . . . . . . . . . . . . . . . . . . . . . . . . . . . . Casting

**BOLD AND THE BEAUTIFUL, THE (CBS/30 mins.)**
PHONE . . . . . . . . . . . . . . . . . . . . . . . . . . . . . . . . . . 213-852-4138
FAX . . . . . . . . . . . . . . . . . . . . . . . . . . . . . . . . . . . 213-655-8760
7800 Beverly Blvd.
Los Angeles, CA 90036
PROD.CO:    Bell-Phillip TV Prods., Inc.

Bradley Bell . . . . . . . . . . . . . . . . . . . . . . . . . . . Executive Producer
John C. Zak . . . . . . . . . . . . . . . . . . . . . . . . . . . Supervising Producer
Deveney Marking Kelly . . . . . . . . . . . . . . . . . . . . . . . . . . . Producer
Rhonda Friedman . . . . . . . . . . . . . . . . . . . . . . . Coordinating Producer
Christy Elaine Dooley . . . . . . . . . . . . . . . . . . . . . . . . . . . . Casting

**BOY MEETS WORLD (ABC/30 mins.)**
PHONE . . . . . . . . . . . . . . . . . . . . . . . . . . . . . . . . . . 818-760-5981
FAX . . . . . . . . . . . . . . . . . . . . . . . . . . . . . . . . . . . 818-508-3656
Touchstone Television
500 S. Buena Vista St.
Burbank, CA 91521
PROD.CO:    Touchstone Television/Michael Jacobs Prod.

Michael Jacobs . . . . . . . . . . . . . . . . . . . . . . . . . Executive Producer
Bob Tishner . . . . . . . . . . . . . . . . . . . . . . . . . . . Co-Exec. Producer
Karen MacKain . . . . . . . . . . . . . . . . . . . . . . . . . . . . . . . Producer
Sally Stiner . . . . . . . . . . . . . . . . . . . . . . . . . . . . . . . . . Casting

# TV SHOWS AND STAFF

***BRIMSTONE (Fox/60 mins.)**
PHONE . . . . . . . . . . . . . . . . . . . . . . . . . . . . . . . 818-954-6000
4000 Warner Blvd.
Burbank, CA 91522
PROD.CO:    Warner Bros. Television Productions/SisterLee
        Productions Inc.
Chad S. Hoffman . . . . . . . . . . . . . . . . . . . . . . . Executive Producer

***BROTHER'S KEEPER (ABC/30 mins.)**
PHONE . . . . . . . . . . . . . . . . . . . . . . . . . . . . . . . 818-777-1000
Universal Studios
100 Universal City Plaza, Bldg. 507
Universal City, CA 91608
PROD.CO:    Universal Television & Networks Group
John Axelrod . . . . . . . . . . . . . . . . . . . . . . . . . . Executive Producer
Donald Todd . . . . . . . . . . . . . . . . . . . . . . . . . . Executive Producer
James Widdoes . . . . . . . . . . . . . . . . . . . . . . . . Executive Producer

***BUDDY FARO (CBS/60 mins.)**
PHONE . . . . . . . . . . . . . . . . . . . . . . . . . . . . . . . 818-655-4890
FAX . . . . . . . . . . . . . . . . . . . . . . . . . . . . . . . . . 818-655-8630
4024 Radford Ave., Norvet Bldg. 3rd Fl.
Studio City, CA 91604
PROD.CO:    Spelling Television, Inc./Worldvision Enterp., Inc.
Mark Frost . . . . . . . . . . . . . . . . . . . . . . . . . . . . Executive Producer
Charles Haid . . . . . . . . . . . . . . . . . . . . . . . . . . Co-Exec. Producer
Victor Schu . . . . . . . . . . . . . . . . . . . . . . . . . . . Producer

**BUFFY THE VAMPIRE SLAYER (WB/60 mins.)**
PHONE . . . . . . . . . . . . . . . . . . . . . . . . . . . . . . . 310-315-4100
FAX . . . . . . . . . . . . . . . . . . . . . . . . . . . . . . . . . 310-579-5353
P.O. Box 900
Beverly Hills, CA 90213-0900
PROD.CO:    Twentieth Century Fox
Gail Berman . . . . . . . . . . . . . . . . . . . . . . . . . . Executive Producer
Sandy Gallin . . . . . . . . . . . . . . . . . . . . . . . . . . Executive Producer
Fran Rubel Kuzui . . . . . . . . . . . . . . . . . . . . . . Executive Producer
Kaz Kuzui . . . . . . . . . . . . . . . . . . . . . . . . . . . . Executive Producer
Joss Whedon . . . . . . . . . . . . . . . . . . . . . . . . . . Executive Producer
David Greenwalt . . . . . . . . . . . . . . . . . . . . . . . Co-Exec. Producer
Gareth Davies . . . . . . . . . . . . . . . . . . . . . . . . . Producer
David Solomon . . . . . . . . . . . . . . . . . . . . . . . . Co-Producer

**CAROLINE IN THE CITY (NBC/30 mins.)**
PHONE . . . . . . . . . . . . . . . . . . . . . . . . . . . . . . . 818-760-5960
FAX . . . . . . . . . . . . . . . . . . . . . . . . . . . . . . . . . 818-655-4120
4024 Radford
Fourth Floor, Norvet Bldg.
Studio City, CA 91604
PROD.CO:    Three Sisters Ent./Barron/Pennette Prods./CBS
        Entertainment
Marco Pennette . . . . . . . . . . . . . . . . . . . . . . . . Executive Producer
Michael Sardo . . . . . . . . . . . . . . . . . . . . . . . . . Executive Producer
Faye Oshima Belyeu . . . . . . . . . . . . . . . . . . . . Co-Exec. Producer

***CHARMED (WB/60 mins.)**
PHONE . . . . . . . . . . . . . . . . . . . . . . . . . . . . . . . 213-965-5700
Spelling Television
5700 Wilshire Blvd., Ste. 575
Los Angeles, CA 90036
Constance M. Burge . . . . . . . . . . . . . . . . . . . . Executive Producer
Aaron Spelling . . . . . . . . . . . . . . . . . . . . . . . . . Executive Producer
E. Duke Vincent . . . . . . . . . . . . . . . . . . . . . . . . Executive Producer

**CHICAGO HOPE (CBS/60 mins.)**
PHONE . . . . . . . . . . . . . . . . . . . . . . . . . . . . . . . 310-369-3708
10201 W. Pico Blvd.
Los Angeles, CA 90035
PROD.CO:    David E. Kelley Prods./Twentieth Century Fox Television
Bill D'Ella . . . . . . . . . . . . . . . . . . . . . . . . . . . . . Executive Producer
John Tinker . . . . . . . . . . . . . . . . . . . . . . . . . . . Executive Producer
Rob Corn . . . . . . . . . . . . . . . . . . . . . . . . . . . . . Co-Exec. Producer
James C. Hart . . . . . . . . . . . . . . . . . . . . . . . . . Co-Exec. Producer
John Heath . . . . . . . . . . . . . . . . . . . . . . . . . . . Co-Exec. Producer
Tim Kring . . . . . . . . . . . . . . . . . . . . . . . . . . . . . Supervising Producer
Dawn Prestwich . . . . . . . . . . . . . . . . . . . . . . . Supervising Producer
Nicole Yorkin . . . . . . . . . . . . . . . . . . . . . . . . . . Supervising Producer
Debi Manuriller . . . . . . . . . . . . . . . . . . . . . . . . Casting

**CLUELESS (UPN/30 mins.)**
PHONE . . . . . . . . . . . . . . . . . . . . . . . . . . . . . . . 213-956-1669
FAX . . . . . . . . . . . . . . . . . . . . . . . . . . . . . . . . . 213-862-1116
Paramount
5555 Melrose Ave.
Hollywood, CA 90038
PROD.CO:    A Cockamamie Prod./Paramount Network Television
Tim O'Donnell . . . . . . . . . . . . . . . . . . . . . . . . . Executive Producer
Brad Johnson . . . . . . . . . . . . . . . . . . . . . . . . . Co-Exec. Producer
Dan Dugan . . . . . . . . . . . . . . . . . . . . . . . . . . . Producer
Lisa Mionie . . . . . . . . . . . . . . . . . . . . . . . . . . . Casting
Eileen Stringer . . . . . . . . . . . . . . . . . . . . . . . . . Casting

***CONRAD BLOOM (NBC/30 mins.)**
PHONE . . . . . . . . . . . . . . . . . . . . . . . . . . . . . . . 818-840-7500
3000 W. Alameda Ave.
Burbank, CA 91523
PROD.CO:    Three Sisters Ent./Pennette Prods./NBC Studios
Marco Pennette . . . . . . . . . . . . . . . . . . . . . . . . Executive Producer

**COSBY (CBS/30 mins.)**
PHONE . . . . . . . . . . . . . . . . . . . . . . . . . . . . . . . 718-706-5701
FAX . . . . . . . . . . . . . . . . . . . . . . . . . . . . . . . . . 718-706-5322
Kaufman Astoria Studios
34-12 36th Street
Astoria, NY 11106
PROD.CO:    Carsey-Werner Co., The
Marcy Carsey . . . . . . . . . . . . . . . . . . . . . . . . . Executive Producer
William H. Cosby . . . . . . . . . . . . . . . . . . . . . . . Executive Producer
Caryn Mandabach . . . . . . . . . . . . . . . . . . . . . . Executive Producer
Tom Straw . . . . . . . . . . . . . . . . . . . . . . . . . . . . Executive Producer
Tom Werner . . . . . . . . . . . . . . . . . . . . . . . . . . . Executive Producer
Adam Belanoff . . . . . . . . . . . . . . . . . . . . . . . . . Supervising Producer
Joanne Curley . . . . . . . . . . . . . . . . . . . . . . . . . Producer
Vanessa Middleton . . . . . . . . . . . . . . . . . . . . . Producer
Brett Goldstein . . . . . . . . . . . . . . . . . . . . . . . . . Casting

***COSTELLO (Fox/30 mins.)**
PHONE . . . . . . . . . . . . . . . . . . . . . . . . . . . . . . . 818-560-5685
FAX . . . . . . . . . . . . . . . . . . . . . . . . . . . . . . . . . 818-560-1722
500 S. Buena Vista, Bldg. 22
Burbank, CA 91521
PROD.CO:    Touchstone Television/Winddancer
Carmen Finestra . . . . . . . . . . . . . . . . . . . . . . . Executive Producer
Cheryl Holliday . . . . . . . . . . . . . . . . . . . . . . . . . Executive Producer
David McFadzean . . . . . . . . . . . . . . . . . . . . . . Executive Producer
Matt Williams . . . . . . . . . . . . . . . . . . . . . . . . . . Executive Producer
Deborah Barylski . . . . . . . . . . . . . . . . . . . . . . . Casting

***CUPID (ABC/60 mins.)**
PHONE . . . . . . . . . . . . . . . . . . . . . . . . . . . . . . . 310-842-8662
9336 W. Washington Blvd.
Culver City, CA 90232
PROD.CO:    Mandalay Television/Columbia TriStar Television
Scott Sanders . . . . . . . . . . . . . . . . . . . . . . . . . Executive Producer
Joe Voci . . . . . . . . . . . . . . . . . . . . . . . . . . . . . . Executive Producer
Scott Winant . . . . . . . . . . . . . . . . . . . . . . . . . . Executive Producer

**DAWSON'S CREEK (WB/60 mins.)**
PHONE . . . . . . . . . . . . . . . . . . . . . . . . . . . . . . . 310-979-8735
FAX . . . . . . . . . . . . . . . . . . . . . . . . . . . . . . . . . 310-207-7998
12233 W. Olympic, Ste. 210
Los Angeles, CA 90064
PROD.CO:    Granville Prod.
Paul Stupin . . . . . . . . . . . . . . . . . . . . . . . . . . . Executive Producer
Kevin Williamson . . . . . . . . . . . . . . . . . . . . . . . Executive Producer
Jon Feldman . . . . . . . . . . . . . . . . . . . . . . . . . . Co-Exec. Producer
Greg Prange . . . . . . . . . . . . . . . . . . . . . . . . . . Supervising Producer
David Semel . . . . . . . . . . . . . . . . . . . . . . . . . . . Producer
Mike White . . . . . . . . . . . . . . . . . . . . . . . . . . . . Producer

**DAYS OF OUR LIVES (NBC/30 mins.)**
PHONE . . . . . . . . . . . . . . . . . . . . . . . . . . . . . . . 818-972-0917
FAX . . . . . . . . . . . . . . . . . . . . . . . . . . . . . . . . . 818-972-0972
3400 Riverside Dr., Ste. 780
Burbank, CA 91505
PROD.CO:    Columbia Pictures
Ken Corday . . . . . . . . . . . . . . . . . . . . . . . . . . . Executive Producer
Tom Langan . . . . . . . . . . . . . . . . . . . . . . . . . . . Co-Exec. Producer
Steve Wyman . . . . . . . . . . . . . . . . . . . . . . . . . . Supervising Producer
Jeanne Haney . . . . . . . . . . . . . . . . . . . . . . . . . Coordinating Producer
Janet Spellman-Rider . . . . . . . . . . . . . . . . . . . . Coordinating Producer
Fran Bascom . . . . . . . . . . . . . . . . . . . . . . . . . . Casting

**DHARMA & GREG (ABC/30 mins.)**
PHONE . . . . . . . . . . . . . . . . . . . . . . . . . . . . . . . . . . . . 310-369-7174
FAX . . . . . . . . . . . . . . . . . . . . . . . . . . . . . . . . . . . . . . . 310-369-8087
Twentieth Century Fox Television
10201 W. Pico Blvd.
Los Angeles, CA 90035
PROD.CO:      Twentieth Century Fox Television
Dottie Dartland . . . . . . . . . . . . . . . . . . . . . . . . . Executive Producer
Chuck Lorre . . . . . . . . . . . . . . . . . . . . . . . . . . . . Executive Producer
Bill Prady . . . . . . . . . . . . . . . . . . . . . . . . . . . . . . Co-Exec. Producer
Regina Stewart . . . . . . . . . . . . . . . . . . . . . . . . . Co-Exec. Producer
Randy Cordray . . . . . . . . . . . . . . . . . . . . . . . . . . . . . . . . Producer
Nikki Valko . . . . . . . . . . . . . . . . . . . . . . . . . . . . . . . . . . . . Casting

**DIAGNOSIS MURDER (CBS/60 mins.)**
PHONE . . . . . . . . . . . . . . . . . . . . . . . . . . . . . . . . . . . . 818-756-1272
FAX . . . . . . . . . . . . . . . . . . . . . . . . . . . . . . . . . . . . . . . 818-901-7477
700 Balboa Avenue
Van Nuys, CA 91406
PROD.CO:      Viacom Productions
Lee Goldberg . . . . . . . . . . . . . . . . . . . . . . . . . . . Executive Producer
Dean Hargrove . . . . . . . . . . . . . . . . . . . . . . . . . Executive Producer
William Rabkin . . . . . . . . . . . . . . . . . . . . . . . . . Executive Producer
Fred Silverman . . . . . . . . . . . . . . . . . . . . . . . . . Executive Producer
Dick Van Dyke . . . . . . . . . . . . . . . . . . . . . . . . . Executive Producer
David Bennett Carren . . . . . . . . . . . . . . . . . . . Supervising Producer
J. Larry Carroll . . . . . . . . . . . . . . . . . . . . . . . . . Supervising Producer
Jacquelyn Blain . . . . . . . . . . . . . . . . . . . . . . . . . . . . . . . Producer
Victoria Burrows . . . . . . . . . . . . . . . . . . . . . . . . . . . . . . . . Casting

***DILBERT (UPN/30 mins.)**
PHONE . . . . . . . . . . . . . . . . . . . . . . . . . . . . . . . . . . . . 310-841-0601
FAX . . . . . . . . . . . . . . . . . . . . . . . . . . . . . . . . . . . . . . . 310-841-2922
9696 Culver Blvd., Ste. 101
Culver City, CA 90232
PROD.CO:      Columbia TriStar Television
Larry Charles . . . . . . . . . . . . . . . . . . . . . . . . . . . Executive Producer
Scott Adams . . . . . . . . . . . . . . . . . . . . . . . Co-Exec. Producer/Creator
David Silverman . . . . . . . . . . . . . . . . . . . . . . . . . Co-Exec. Producer
Steven Sustarsic . . . . . . . . . . . . . . . . . . . . . . . . Co-Exec. Producer
Jeff Kahn . . . . . . . . . . . . . . . . . . . . . . . . . . . . . . Supervising Producer
Richard Raynis . . . . . . . . . . . . . . . . . . . . . . . . . Supervising Producer
Jeffrey Goldstein . . . . . . . . . . . . . . . . . . . . . . . . . . . . . . . Producer
Ned Goldreyer . . . . . . . . . . . . . . . . . . . . . . . . . Coordinating Producer

***DIRESTA (UPN/30 mins.)**
PHONE . . . . . . . . . . . . . . . . . . . . . . . . . . . . . . . . . . . . 213-956-5000
FAX . . . . . . . . . . . . . . . . . . . . . . . . . . . . . . . . . . . . . . . 213-862-1460
5555 Melrose Ave., Mae West, Ste. 10
Hollywood, CA 90038
PROD.CO:      Paramount Network Television
Matt Goldman . . . . . . . . . . . . . . . . . . . . . . . . . . Executive Producer
David Babcock . . . . . . . . . . . . . . . . . . . . . . . . . . Co-Exec. Producer
Mark H. Ovitz . . . . . . . . . . . . . . . . . . . . . . . . . . . . . . . . . Producer
Tammy Billik . . . . . . . . . . . . . . . . . . . . . . . . . . . . . . . . . . . Casting

**DR. KATZ PROFESSIONAL THERAPIST (Comedy Central/30 mins.)**
PHONE . . . . . . . . . . . . . . . . . . . . . . . . . . . . . . . . . . . . 212-512-8900
FAX . . . . . . . . . . . . . . . . . . . . . . . . . . . . . . . . . . . . . . . 212-512-8968
HBO Downtown Productions
1114 Avenue of the Stars
New York, NY 10036
PROD.CO:      Tom Snyder Productions/HBO Downtown Productions/
              Popular Arts Entertainment
Tim Braine . . . . . . . . . . . . . . . . . . . . . . . . . . . . . Executive Producer
Nancy Geller . . . . . . . . . . . . . . . . . . . . . . . . . . . Executive Producer
Tom Snyder . . . . . . . . . . . . . . . . . . . . . . . . . . . . Executive Producer
John Fisher . . . . . . . . . . . . . . . . . . . . . . . . . . . . Supervising Producer
Niki Hebert . . . . . . . . . . . . . . . . . . . . . . . . . . . . Coordinating Producer

**DREW CAREY SHOW, THE (ABC/30 mins.)**
PHONE . . . . . . . . . . . . . . . . . . . . . . . . . . . . . . . . . . . . 818-954-3878
FAX . . . . . . . . . . . . . . . . . . . . . . . . . . . . . . . . . . . . . . . 818-954-3979
4000 Warner Blvd.
Burbank, CA 91522
PROD.CO:      Mohawk Prods./Warner Bros. Television Productions
Drew Carey . . . . . . . . . . . . . . . . . . . . . . . . . . . . Executive Producer
Clay Graham . . . . . . . . . . . . . . . . . . . . . . . . . . . Executive Producer
Bruce Helford . . . . . . . . . . . . . . . . . . . . . . . . . . Executive Producer
Bruce Rasmussen . . . . . . . . . . . . . . . . . . . . . . . Executive Producer
Diane Burroughs . . . . . . . . . . . . . . . . . . . . . . . . Co-Exec. Producer
Joey Gutierez . . . . . . . . . . . . . . . . . . . . . . . . . . . Co-Exec. Producer
Deborah Oppenheimer . . . . . . . . . . . . . . . . . . . Co-Exec. Producer
Richard Baker . . . . . . . . . . . . . . . . . . . . . . . . . . . . . . . . . Producer
Rick Messina . . . . . . . . . . . . . . . . . . . . . . . . . . . . . . . . . . Producer
Joanne Koehler . . . . . . . . . . . . . . . . . . . . . . . . . . . . . . . . . Casting
Barbara Miller . . . . . . . . . . . . . . . . . . . . . . . . . . . . . . . . . . Casting

**DUE SOUTH (CTV/60 mins.)**
PHONE . . . . . . . . . . . . . . . . . . . . . . . . . . . . . . . . . . . . 416-967-1174
FAX . . . . . . . . . . . . . . . . . . . . . . . . . . . . . . . . . . . . . . . 416-967-1782
121 Bloor St. East, #1400
Toronto, Ontario M4W3M5
PROD.CO:      Alliance Communications Corp.
Paul Gross . . . . . . . . . . . . . . . . . . . . . . . . . . . . . Executive Producer
R.B. Carney . . . . . . . . . . . . . . . . . . . . . . . . . . . . Co-Exec. Producer
Frank Siracusa . . . . . . . . . . . . . . . . . . . . . . . . . . . . . . . . . Producer
Marissa Richmond . . . . . . . . . . . . . . . . . . . . . . . . . . . . . . . Casting

***EARLY EDITION (CBS/60 mins.)**
PHONE . . . . . . . . . . . . . . . . . . . . . . . . . . . . . . . . . . . . 310-342-7727
1000 Corporate Pointe, Ste. 202
Culver City, CA 90231
PROD.CO:      Columbia TriStar Television
Bob Brush . . . . . . . . . . . . . . . . . . . . . . . . . . . . . Executive Producer
Jeff Melvoin . . . . . . . . . . . . . . . . . . . . . . . . . . . . Executive Producer
Carol Kritzer . . . . . . . . . . . . . . . . . . . . . . . . . . . . . . . . . . . Casting

***ENCORE! ENCORE! (NBC/30 mins.)**
PHONE . . . . . . . . . . . . . . . . . . . . . . . . . . . . . . . . . . . . 213-956-5000
5555 Melrose Ave., Wilder Bldg., 2nd Fl.
Los Angeles, CA 90038
PROD.CO:      Paramount Network Television
David Angell . . . . . . . . . . . . . . . . . . . . . . . . . . . . Executive Producer
Peter Casey . . . . . . . . . . . . . . . . . . . . . . . . . . . . Executive Producer
Anne Flett-Giordano . . . . . . . . . . . . . . . . . . . . . Executive Producer
David Lee . . . . . . . . . . . . . . . . . . . . . . . . . . . . . . Executive Producer
Chuck Ranberg . . . . . . . . . . . . . . . . . . . . . . . . . Executive Producer
Valerie Curtin . . . . . . . . . . . . . . . . . . . . . . . . . . . . . . . . . . Producer
Mary Fukuto . . . . . . . . . . . . . . . . . . . . . . . . . . . . . . . . . . . Producer
Jon Sherman . . . . . . . . . . . . . . . . . . . . . . . . . . . . . . . . . . Producer
Jeff Greenberg . . . . . . . . . . . . . . . . . . . . . . . . . . . . . . . . . . Casting

**ER (NBC/60 mins.)**
PHONE . . . . . . . . . . . . . . . . . . . . . . . . . . . . . . . . . . . . 818-954-6000
4000 Warner Blvd.
Burbank, CA 91522
PROD.CO:      Constant C. Prods./Amblin Entertainment/Warner Bros.
              Television Productions
Michael Crichton . . . . . . . . . . . . . . . . . . . . . . . . Executive Producer
Carol Flint . . . . . . . . . . . . . . . . . . . . . . . . . . . . . Executive Producer
John Wells . . . . . . . . . . . . . . . . . . . . . . . . . . . . . Executive Producer
Lydia Woodward . . . . . . . . . . . . . . . . . . . . . . . . Executive Producer
Christopher Chulack . . . . . . . . . . . . . . . . . . . . . Co-Exec. Producer
Walon Green . . . . . . . . . . . . . . . . . . . . . . . . . . . Co-Exec. Producer
Neal Baer . . . . . . . . . . . . . . . . . . . . . . . . . . . . . . . . . . . . . Producer
Lance Gentile . . . . . . . . . . . . . . . . . . . . . . . . . . . . . . . . . . Producer
John Levey . . . . . . . . . . . . . . . . . . . . . . . . . . . . . . . . . . . . Casting
Barbara Miller . . . . . . . . . . . . . . . . . . . . . . . . . . . . . . . . . . Casting

# TV SHOWS AND STAFF

**EVERYBODY LOVES RAYMOND (CBS/30 mins.)**
PHONE . . . . . . . . . . . . . . . . . . . . . . . . . . . . . . . 818-954-7770
FAX . . . . . . . . . . . . . . . . . . . . . . . . . . . . . . . . . 818-954-7905
4000 Warner Blvd., Trailer 45
Burbank, CA 91522
PROD.CO:     Where's Lunch Prods.
Rory Rosegarten . . . . . . . . . . . . . . . . . . . . . . Executive Producer
Philip Rosenthal . . . . . . . . . . . . . . . . . . . . . . Executive Producer
Stu Smiley . . . . . . . . . . . . . . . . . . . . . . . . . . Executive Producer
Cindy Chupack . . . . . . . . . . . . . . . . . . . . . . . Co-Exec. Producer
Ellen Sandler . . . . . . . . . . . . . . . . . . . . . . . . Co-Exec. Producer
Kathy Ann Stumpe . . . . . . . . . . . . . . . . . . . . Co-Exec. Producer
S. Jeremy Stevens . . . . . . . . . . . . . . . . . . . Supervising Producer
Lisa Helfrich-Jackson . . . . . . . . . . . . . . . . . . . . . . . . Producer
Stewart Lyons . . . . . . . . . . . . . . . . . . . . . . . . . . . . . Producer
Ray Romano . . . . . . . . . . . . . . . . . . . . . . . . . . . . . . Producer
Lew Schneider . . . . . . . . . . . . . . . . . . . . . . . . . . . . . Producer
Lisa Miller . . . . . . . . . . . . . . . . . . . . . . . . . . . . . . . . . Casting

***FANTASY ISLAND (ABC/60 mins.)**
PHONE . . . . . . . . . . . . . . . . . . . . . . . . . . . . 310-244-4000
9336 W. Washington Blvd.
Culver City, CA 90232
PROD.CO:     Mandalay Television/Columbia TriStar Television
Barry Josephson . . . . . . . . . . . . . . . . . . . . . . Executive Producer
Barry Sonnenfeld . . . . . . . . . . . . . . . . . . . . . . Executive Producer

***FEELIN' ALL RIGHT (Fox/30 mins.)**
PHONE . . . . . . . . . . . . . . . . . . . . . . . . . . . . 818-655-5598
4024 Radford Ave., Bldg. 3
Studio City, CA 91604
PROD.CO:     Carsey-Werner Co., The
Mark Brazill . . . . . . . . . . . . . . . . . . . . . . . . . Executive Producer
Marcy Carsey . . . . . . . . . . . . . . . . . . . . . . . . Executive Producer
Caryn Mandabach . . . . . . . . . . . . . . . . . . . . . Executive Producer
Bonnie Turner . . . . . . . . . . . . . . . . . . . . . . . . Executive Producer
Terry Turner . . . . . . . . . . . . . . . . . . . . . . . . . Executive Producer
Tom Warner . . . . . . . . . . . . . . . . . . . . . . . . . Executive Producer
Joshua Sternin . . . . . . . . . . . . . . . . . . . . . . Co-Executive Producer
Jeff Ventimilia . . . . . . . . . . . . . . . . . . . . . . . Co-Executive Producer
Linda Wallen . . . . . . . . . . . . . . . . . . . . . . . . Co-Executive Producer
Liberman/Hirschfeld Casting . . . . . . . . . . . . . . . . . . . . . Casting

***FELICITY (WB/60 mins.)**
PHONE . . . . . . . . . . . . . . . . . . . . . . . . . . . . 310-277-1665
3322 La Cienega Place
Los Angeles, CA 90016
PROD.CO:     Imagine Television/Touchstone Television
JJ Abrams . . . . . . . . . . . . . . . . . . . . . . . . . . Executive Producer
Brian Grazer . . . . . . . . . . . . . . . . . . . . . . . . . Executive Producer
Ron Howard . . . . . . . . . . . . . . . . . . . . . . . . . Executive Producer
Tony Krantz . . . . . . . . . . . . . . . . . . . . . . . . . Executive Producer
Matt Reeves . . . . . . . . . . . . . . . . . . . . . . . . . Executive Producer

***FOR YOUR LOVE (WB/30 mins.)**
PHONE . . . . . . . . . . . . . . . . . . . . . . . . . . . . 818-954-3638
FAX . . . . . . . . . . . . . . . . . . . . . . . . . . . . . . 818-954-2680
300 Television Plaza, Bldg. 136. Rm. 143
Burbank, CA 91505
PROD.CO:     SisterLee Productions Inc./Warner Bros. Television
             Productions
Yvette Leebowser . . . . . . . . . . . . . . . . . . . . . . Executive Producer

**FRASIER (NBC/30 mins.)**
PHONE . . . . . . . . . . . . . . . . . . . . . . . . . . . . 213-956-3100
FAX . . . . . . . . . . . . . . . . . . . . . . . . . . . . . . 213-862-3200
5555 Melrose Ave.
Hollywood, CA 90038
PROD.CO:     Grub Street Prods.
David Angell . . . . . . . . . . . . . . . . . . . . . . . . . Executive Producer
Peter Casey . . . . . . . . . . . . . . . . . . . . . . . . . Executive Producer
David Lee . . . . . . . . . . . . . . . . . . . . . . . . . . . Executive Producer
Christopher Lloyd . . . . . . . . . . . . . . . . . . . . . . Executive Producer
Jay Kogen . . . . . . . . . . . . . . . . . . . . . . . . . Supervising Producer
Jeff Richman . . . . . . . . . . . . . . . . . . . . . . . . Supervising Producer
Robert Greenberg . . . . . . . . . . . . . . . . . . . . . . . . . . . Producer
Maggie Randell . . . . . . . . . . . . . . . . . . . . . . . . . . . . . Producer
Jeff Greenberg . . . . . . . . . . . . . . . . . . . . . . . . . . . . . . Casting

**FRIENDS (NBC/30 mins.)**
PHONE . . . . . . . . . . . . . . . . . . . . . . . . . . . . 818-977-7943
Warner Bros. Television
4000 Warner Blvd.
Burbank, CA 91522
PROD.CO:     Bright/Kauffman/Crane Prods./Warner Bros. Television
             Productions
Kevin S. Bright . . . . . . . . . . . . . . . . . . . . . . . Executive Producer
David Crane . . . . . . . . . . . . . . . . . . . . . . . . . Executive Producer
Marta Kauffman . . . . . . . . . . . . . . . . . . . . . . Executive Producer
Adam Chase . . . . . . . . . . . . . . . . . . . . . . . . . Executive Producer
Michael Curtis . . . . . . . . . . . . . . . . . . . . . . . . Executive Producer
Greg Malins . . . . . . . . . . . . . . . . . . . . . . . . . Executive Producer
Todd Stevens . . . . . . . . . . . . . . . . . . . . . . . . . . . . . . Producer
Wendy Knoller . . . . . . . . . . . . . . . . . . . . . . Coordinating Producer
Leslie Litt . . . . . . . . . . . . . . . . . . . . . . . . . . . . . . . . . Casting
Barbara Miller . . . . . . . . . . . . . . . . . . . . . . . . . . . . . . . Casting

**GENERAL HOSPITAL (ABC/60 mins.)**
PHONE . . . . . . . . . . . . . . . . . . . . . . . . . . . . 310-557-7777
FAX . . . . . . . . . . . . . . . . . . . . . . . . . . . . . . 310-557-3150
4151 Prospect Ave.
Los Angeles, CA 90027
PROD.CO:     ABC Daytime
Wendy Riche . . . . . . . . . . . . . . . . . . . . . . . . Executive Producer
Lisa Levinson . . . . . . . . . . . . . . . . . . . . . . . . . . . . . . . Producer
Carol Scott . . . . . . . . . . . . . . . . . . . . . . . . . . . . . . . . Producer
Marty Vajts . . . . . . . . . . . . . . . . . . . . . . . . Coordinating Producer
Mark Teschner . . . . . . . . . . . . . . . . . . . . . . . . . . . . . . Casting

**GUIDING LIGHT (CBS/60 mins.)**
PHONE . . . . . . . . . . . . . . . . . . . . . . . . . . . . 212-975-4321
CBS
51 W. 52nd St.
New York, NY 10019
PROD.CO:     Proctor & Gamble Prods. Inc.
Paul Rauch . . . . . . . . . . . . . . . . . . . . . . . . . Executive Producer
Roy Steinberg . . . . . . . . . . . . . . . . . . . . . . . . . . . . . . Producer
Alexandra Johnson . . . . . . . . . . . . . . . . . . Coordinating Producer
Glenn Daniels . . . . . . . . . . . . . . . . . . . . . . . . . . . . . . . Casting

***GUYS LIKE US (UPN/30 mins.)**
PHONE . . . . . . . . . . . . . . . . . . . . . . . . . . . . 310-202-3383
9336 W. Washington Blvd.
Los Angeles, CA 90232
PROD.CO:     Columbia TriStar Television
Barry O'Brien . . . . . . . . . . . . . . . . . . . . . . . . Executive Producer
Dan Schneider . . . . . . . . . . . . . . . . . . . . . . . Executive Producer

***HOLDING THE BABY (Fox/30 mins.)**
PHONE . . . . . . . . . . . . . . . . . . . . . . . . . . . . 310-369-1000
10201 W. Pico Blvd.
Los Angeles, CA 90035
PROD.CO:     Twentieth Century Fox Television
Howard J. Morris . . . . . . . . . . . . . . . . . . . . . . Executive Producer

**HOME IMPROVEMENT (ABC/30 mins.)**
PHONE . . . . . . . . . . . . . . . . . . . . . . . . . . . . 818-560-5715
500 S. Buena Vista St.
Burbank, CA 91521
PROD.CO:     Touchstone Television/Wind Dancer Prod. Group
Bruce Ferber . . . . . . . . . . . . . . . . . . . . . . . . Executive Producer
Carmen Finestra . . . . . . . . . . . . . . . . . . . . . . Executive Producer
David McFadzean . . . . . . . . . . . . . . . . . . . . . Executive Producer
Elliot Shoenman . . . . . . . . . . . . . . . . . . . . . . Executive Producer
Matt Williams . . . . . . . . . . . . . . . . . . . . . . . . Executive Producer
Laurie Gelman . . . . . . . . . . . . . . . . . . . . . . . . Co-Exec. Producer
Gayle S. Maffeo . . . . . . . . . . . . . . . . . . . . . . . . . . . . . Producer
Allan Padula . . . . . . . . . . . . . . . . . . . . . . . . . . . . . . . Producer
Deborah Barylski . . . . . . . . . . . . . . . . . . . . . . . . . . . . . Casting

**HONEY, I SHRUNK THE KIDS - THE TV SHOW (Syndicated/60 mins.)**
PHONE . . . . . . . . . . . . . . . . . . . . . . . . . . . . 213-993-9933
FAX . . . . . . . . . . . . . . . . . . . . . . . . . . . . . . 213-993-9939
6255 Sunset Blvd., Ste. 1112
Los Angeles, CA 90028
PROD.CO:     St. Clare Entertainment
Leslie Belzberg . . . . . . . . . . . . . . . . . . . . . . . Executive Producer
John Landis . . . . . . . . . . . . . . . . . . . . . . . . . Executive Producer
Ed Naha . . . . . . . . . . . . . . . . . . . . . . . . . . . . Co-Exec. Producer
Jonathan Hackett . . . . . . . . . . . . . . . . . . . . . . . . . . . . Producer
Brenda Lilly . . . . . . . . . . . . . . . . . . . . . . . . . . . . . . . . Producer
Bert Swartz . . . . . . . . . . . . . . . . . . . . . . . . . . . . . . . . Producer
Tammy Billik . . . . . . . . . . . . . . . . . . . . . . . . . . . . . . . . Casting

***HUGHLEYS, THE (ABC/30 mins.)**
PHONE . . . . . . . . . . . . . . . . . . . . . . . . . 818-655-5000
4024 Radford Ave.
Studio City, CA 91604
PROD.CO:    Greenblatt Janollari Studio, The
Dave Becky . . . . . . . . . . . . . . . . . . . . . . Executive Producer
Bob Greenblatt . . . . . . . . . . . . . . . . . . . . Executive Producer
David Janollari . . . . . . . . . . . . . . . . . . . . Executive Producer
Chris Rock . . . . . . . . . . . . . . . . . . . . . . . Executive Producer
Michael Rotenberg . . . . . . . . . . . . . . . . . Executive Producer
Matt Wickline . . . . . . . . . . . . . . . . . . . . . Executive Producer

***HYPERION (WB/60 mins.)**
PHONE . . . . . . . . . . . . . . . . . . . . . . . . . 818-954-6000
4000 Warner Blvd.
Burbank, CA 91522
PROD.CO:    Warner Bros. Television Productions
Joseph Dougherty . . . . . . . . . . . . . . . . . . Executive Producer

**JAG (CBS/60 mins.)**
PHONE . . . . . . . . . . . . . . . . . . . . . . . . . 805-294-5500
FAX . . . . . . . . . . . . . . . . . . . . . . . . . . . 805-294-8549
28343 Ave. Crocker, #1
Valencia, CA 91355
PROD.CO:    Belisarius Prods./Paramount Network Television
Donald P. Bellisario . . . . . . . . . . . . . . . . Executive Producer
Chas. Floyd Johnson . . . . . . . . . . . . . . . . Co-Exec. Producer
Stephen Zito . . . . . . . . . . . . . . . . . . . . . Co-Exec. Producer
Larry Moskowitz . . . . . . . . . . . . . . . . . . Supervising Producer
Mark Horowitz . . . . . . . . . . . . . . . . . . . . . . . . . . Producer
Julie Watson . . . . . . . . . . . . . . . . . . . . . . . . . . . Producer
Melissa Skoff . . . . . . . . . . . . . . . . . . . . . . . . . . . . Casting

**JAMIE FOXX SHOW (WB/30 mins.)**
PHONE . . . . . . . . . . . . . . . . . . . . . . . . . 818-954-5264
Warner Bros. Television
4000 Warner Blvd.
Burbank, CA 91522
PROD.CO:    Foxxhole Prods./Bent Outta Shape Productions/Warner
            Bros. Television Productions
Bentley Kyle Evans . . . . . . . . . . . . . . . . Executive Producer
Marcus King . . . . . . . . . . . . . . . . . . . . . Executive Producer
Sandy Frank . . . . . . . . . . . . . . . . . . . . . Co-Exec. Producer
Bennie Richburg . . . . . . . . . . . . . . . . . . Co-Exec. Producer
Drew Brown . . . . . . . . . . . . . . . . . . . . . . . . . . . . Producer
Jamie Foxx . . . . . . . . . . . . . . . . . . . . . . . . . . . . Producer
DeeDee Bradley . . . . . . . . . . . . . . . . . . . . . . . . . Casting
Barbara Miller . . . . . . . . . . . . . . . . . . . . . . . . . . . Casting

**JUST SHOOT ME (NBC/30 mins.)**
PHONE . . . . . . . . . . . . . . . . . . . . . . . . . 818-760-5760
9150 Wilshire Blvd., #350
Beverly Hills, CA 90210
Bernie Brillstein . . . . . . . . . . . . . . . . . . Executive Producer
Brad Grey . . . . . . . . . . . . . . . . . . . . . . . Executive Producer
Steven Levitan . . . . . . . . . . . . . . . . . . . Executive Producer
Jack Burditt . . . . . . . . . . . . . . . . . . . . . Co-Exec. Producer
Eileen Conn . . . . . . . . . . . . . . . . . . . . . Co-Exec. Producer
Andrew Gordon . . . . . . . . . . . . . . . . . . . Co-Exec. Producer
Marsh McCall . . . . . . . . . . . . . . . . . . . . Supervising Producer
Brian Medavoy . . . . . . . . . . . . . . . . . . . . . . . . . . Producer
Erwin More . . . . . . . . . . . . . . . . . . . . . . . . . . . . Producer
Gina Rugolo-Judd . . . . . . . . . . . . . . . . . . . . . . . . Producer
Kevin Slattery . . . . . . . . . . . . . . . . . . . . . . . . . . Producer
Bruce Rand Berman . . . . . . . . . . . . . . . Coordinating Producer
Deborah Barylski . . . . . . . . . . . . . . . . . . . . . . . . . Casting

***KING OF QUEENS (CBS/30 mins.)**
PHONE . . . . . . . . . . . . . . . . . . . . . . . . . 310-244-3343
10202 W. Washington Blvd.
David Lean Bldg., Ste. 410
Culver City, CA 90232
PROD.CO:    Columbia TriStar Television/CBS Productions
Michael Weithorn . . . . . . . . . . . . . . . . . Executive Producer
Stacie Lipps . . . . . . . . . . . . . . . . . . . . . Co-Exec. Producer
Tony Sheehan . . . . . . . . . . . . . . . . . . . . Co-Exec. Producer
David Litt . . . . . . . . . . . . . . . . . . . . . . . . . . . . . Producer
Annette Sahakian . . . . . . . . . . . . . . . . . . . . . . . . Producer
Lisa Miller . . . . . . . . . . . . . . . . . . . . . . . . . . . . . Casting

**KING OF THE HILL (Fox/30 mins.)**
PHONE . . . . . . . . . . . . . . . . . . . . . . . . . 310-229-2476
10201 W. Pico Blvd.
Los Angeles, CA 90035
PROD.CO:    Twentieth Century Fox Television
Greg Daniels . . . . . . . . . . . . . . . . . . . . . Executive Producer
Mike Judge . . . . . . . . . . . . . . . . . . . . . . Executive Producer
Howard Klein . . . . . . . . . . . . . . . . . . . . Executive Producer
Michael Rotenberg . . . . . . . . . . . . . . . . Executive Producer
Richard Appel . . . . . . . . . . . . . . . . . . . . Executive Producer
Jonathan Collier . . . . . . . . . . . . . . . . . . Co-Exec. Producer
Jonathan Aibel . . . . . . . . . . . . . . . . . . . Supervising Producer
Glenn Berger . . . . . . . . . . . . . . . . . . . . Supervising Producer
Joe Boucher . . . . . . . . . . . . . . . . . . . . . . . . . . . Producer
Johnny Hardwick . . . . . . . . . . . . . . . . . . . . . . . . Producer
Norm Hiscock . . . . . . . . . . . . . . . . . . . . . . . . . . Producer
Paul Lieberstein . . . . . . . . . . . . . . . . . . . . . . . . . Producer
Alan Cohen . . . . . . . . . . . . . . . . . . . . . . . . . . . Co-Producer
Alan Freedland . . . . . . . . . . . . . . . . . . . . . . . . Co-Producer
Mark McJimsey . . . . . . . . . . . . . . . . . . . . . . . . Co-Producer
Julie Mosberg . . . . . . . . . . . . . . . . . . . . . . . . . . . Casting

***L.A. DOCS (CBS/60 mins.)**
PHONE . . . . . . . . . . . . . . . . . . . . . . . . . 818-655-5000
4024 Radford Ave.
Studio City, CA 91604
PROD.CO:    Columbia TriStar Television/CBS Productions
John Lee Hancock . . . . . . . . . . . . . . . . . Executive Producer
Mark Johnson . . . . . . . . . . . . . . . . . . . . Executive Producer

**LAW & ORDER (NBC/60 mins.)**
PHONE . . . . . . . . . . . . . . . . . . . . . . . . . 818-777-1236
100 Universal City Plaza, Bldg. 69
Universal City, CA 91608
PROD.CO:    Wolf Films Inc./Universal Television & Networks Group
Rene Balcer . . . . . . . . . . . . . . . . . . . . . Executive Producer
Ed Sherin . . . . . . . . . . . . . . . . . . . . . . . Executive Producer
Dick Wolf . . . . . . . . . . . . . . . . . . . . . . . Executive Producer
Kathy McCormick . . . . . . . . . . . . . . . . . Co-Exec. Producer
Arthur Forney . . . . . . . . . . . . . . . . . . . . Supervising Producer
Billy Fox . . . . . . . . . . . . . . . . . . . . . . . . . . . . . Producer
Lewis H. Gould . . . . . . . . . . . . . . . . . . . . . . . . . . Producer
Jeffrey Hayes . . . . . . . . . . . . . . . . . . . . . . . . . . Producer
David Shore . . . . . . . . . . . . . . . . . . . . . . . . . . . Producer
Lynn Kressel . . . . . . . . . . . . . . . . . . . . . . . . . . . Casting
Suzanne Ryan . . . . . . . . . . . . . . . . . . . . . . . . . . Casting

***LEGACY (UPN/60 mins.)**
PHONE . . . . . . . . . . . . . . . . . . . . . . . . . 310-576-7719
FAX . . . . . . . . . . . . . . . . . . . . . . . . . . . 310-576-0799
227 Broadway, Ste. 300
Santa Monica, CA 90401
PROD.CO:    Atlantis Films
Chris Abbott . . . . . . . . . . . . . . . . . . . . . Executive Producer

***LINC'S (Showtime/30 mins.)**
PHONE . . . . . . . . . . . . . . . . . . . . . . . . . 804-862-2250
One New Millenium Studios
Petersbury, VA 23805
PROD.CO:    Showtime Networks Inc./Reid Productions, Inc., Tim
Susan Fales-Hill . . . . . . . . . . . . . . . . . . Executive Producer
Tim Reid . . . . . . . . . . . . . . . . . . . . . . . . Executive Producer
Pat Golden . . . . . . . . . . . . . . . . . . . . . . . . . . . . . Casting

***LIVING IN CAPTIVITY (Fox/30 mins.)**
PHONE . . . . . . . . . . . . . . . . . . . . . . . . . 310-369-1000
10201 W. Pico Blvd.
Los Angeles, CA 90035
PROD.CO:    Twentieth Century Fox
Diane English . . . . . . . . . . . . . . . . . . . . Executive Producer
Joel Shukovsky . . . . . . . . . . . . . . . . . . . Executive Producer

***LOT, THE (AMC/30 mins.)**
PHONE . . . . . . . . . . . . . . . . . . . . . . . . . 516-396-3000
150 Crossways Park West
Woodbury, NY 11797
PROD.CO:    American Movie Classics/Romance Classic
Paula Connelly-Skorka . . . . . . . . . . . . . . Executive Producer

# TV SHOWS AND STAFF

**MAD ABOUT YOU (NBC/30 mins.)**
PHONE . . . . . . . . . . . . . . . . . . . . . . . . . . . 310-202-1234
9336 W. Washington Blvd.
Culver City, CA 90232
PROD.CO:    Nuance Prods./TriStar Television/InFront Productions
Danny Jacobson . . . . . . . . . . . . . . . . . . . . . Executive Producer
Victor Levin . . . . . . . . . . . . . . . . . . . . . . . Executive Producer
Paul Reiser . . . . . . . . . . . . . . . . . . . . . . . . Executive Producer
Roger Director . . . . . . . . . . . . . . . . . . . . . . Co-Exec. Producer
Helen Hunt . . . . . . . . . . . . . . . . . . . . . . . . Co-Exec. Producer
Mary Connelly . . . . . . . . . . . . . . . . . . . . . Supervising Producer
Bob Heath . . . . . . . . . . . . . . . . . . . . . . . . Supervising Producer
Lissa Levin . . . . . . . . . . . . . . . . . . . . . . . Supervising Producer
Maria Semple . . . . . . . . . . . . . . . . . . . . . Supervising Producer
William Cosentino . . . . . . . . . . . . . . . . . . . . . . . . . Producer
Craig Knizek . . . . . . . . . . . . . . . . . . . . . . . . . . . . Producer
Michael Martineau . . . . . . . . . . . . . . . . . . . . . . . . . Producer
Bonnie Zane . . . . . . . . . . . . . . . . . . . . . . . . . . . . . Casting

**MAD TV (Fox/60 mins.)**
PHONE . . . . . . . . . . . . . . . . . . . . . . . . . . . 213-860-8999
FAX . . . . . . . . . . . . . . . . . . . . . . . . . . . . . 213-860-8997
5842 W. Sunset Blvd., Bldg. 11
Los Angeles, CA 90028
PROD.CO:    Quincy Jones*David Salzman Entertainment
Quincy Jones . . . . . . . . . . . . . . . . . . . . . . Executive Producer
David Salzman . . . . . . . . . . . . . . . . . . . . . Executive Producer
Steven Haft . . . . . . . . . . . . . . . . . . . . . . . . Co-Exec. Producer
John Irwin . . . . . . . . . . . . . . . . . . . . . . . . . . . . . Producer

***MAGGIE DAY (Lifetime/30 mins.)**
PHONE . . . . . . . . . . . . . . . . . . . . . . . . . . . 213-956-3838
FAX . . . . . . . . . . . . . . . . . . . . . . . . . . . . . 213-862-0800
5555 Melrose Ave., Trailer 33
Hollywood, CA
PROD.CO:    Paramount Network Television
Dan O'Shannon . . . . . . . . . . . . . . . . . . . . . Executive Producer
Daphne Pollan . . . . . . . . . . . . . . . . . . . . . . Co-Exec. Producer
David Menteer . . . . . . . . . . . . . . . . . . . . . . . . . . . Producer

***MAGGIE WINTERS (CBS/30 mins.)**
PHONE . . . . . . . . . . . . . . . . . . . . . . . . . . . 310-369-8184
FAX . . . . . . . . . . . . . . . . . . . . . . . . . . . . . 310-369-7378
10201 W. Pico, Bldg. 41, Ste. 300
Los Angeles, CA 90035
PROD.CO:    Greenblatt Janollari Studio, The
Bob Greenblatt . . . . . . . . . . . . . . . . . . . . . Executive Producer
David Janollari . . . . . . . . . . . . . . . Executive Producer (310-369-0367)
Kari Lizer . . . . . . . . . . . . . . . . . . . . . . . . . Executive Producer

**MAGNIFICENT SEVEN, THE (CBS/60 mins.)**
PHONE . . . . . . . . . . . . . . . . . . . . . . . . . . . 310-449-3095
FAX . . . . . . . . . . . . . . . . . . . . . . . . . . . . . 310-449-3195
2401 Colorado Ave., #100
Santa Monica, CA 90404
PROD.CO:    Mirisch Corporation/Trilogy Entertainment Group
Pen Densham . . . . . . . . . . . . . . . . . . . . . . Executive Producer
Richard Barton Lewis . . . . . . . . . . . . . . . . . Executive Producer
Walter Mirisch . . . . . . . . . . . . . . . . . . . . . Executive Producer
John Watson . . . . . . . . . . . . . . . . . . . . . . Executive Producer
Holly Powell . . . . . . . . . . . . . . . . . . . . Casting (310-369-7743)

**MALCOLM & EDDIE (UPN/30 mins.)**
PHONE . . . . . . . . . . . . . . . . . . . . . . . . . . . 213-993-7930
FAX . . . . . . . . . . . . . . . . . . . . . . . . . . . . . 213-993-7066
1438 N. Gower St., Bldg. 35, Rm. 264
Hollywood, CA 90028
PROD.CO:    TriStar Television/Jeff Franklin Prods.
Jeff Franklin . . . . . . . . . . . . . . . . . . . . . . . Executive Producer
Jerry Perzigian . . . . . . . . . . . . . . . . . . . . . Executive Producer
Cheryl Alu . . . . . . . . . . . . . . . . . . . . . . . . . Co-Exec. Producer
Roxie Wenk Evans . . . . . . . . . . . . . . . . . . . . . . . . . Producer
Pat Melton . . . . . . . . . . . . . . . . . . . . . . . . . . . . . Casting

***MARTIAL LAW (CBS/60 mins.)**
PHONE . . . . . . . . . . . . . . . . . . . . . . . . . . . 310-369-1000
10201 W. Pico Blvd.
Los Angeles, CA 90035
PROD.CO:    Twentieth Century Fox Television/CBS Productions
Carlton Cuse . . . . . . . . . . . . . . . . . . . . . . Executive Producer
Andre Morgan . . . . . . . . . . . . . . . . . . . . . Executive Producer
Stanley Tong . . . . . . . . . . . . . . . . . . . . . . Executive Producer

**MELROSE PLACE (Fox/60 mins.)**
PHONE . . . . . . . . . . . . . . . . . . . . . . . . . . . 805-295-3333
FAX . . . . . . . . . . . . . . . . . . . . . . . . . . . . . 805-295-3334
5700 Wilshire Blvd.
Los Angeles, CA 90036
PROD.CO:    Darren Star Prods./Spelling Television Inc
Frank South . . . . . . . . . . . . . . . . . . . . . . . Executive Producer
Aaron Spelling . . . . . . . . . . . . . . . . . . . . . Executive Producer
E. Duke Vincent . . . . . . . . . . . . . . . . . . . . Executive Producer
Carol Mendlesohn . . . . . . . . . . . . . . . . . . . Co-Exec. Producer
Chuck Pratt . . . . . . . . . . . . . . . . . . . . . . Co-Executive Producer
James Kahn . . . . . . . . . . . . . . . . . . . . . . Supervising Producer
Chip Hayes . . . . . . . . . . . . . . . . . . . . . . . . . . . . . Producer
Debra Rubinstein . . . . . . . . . . . . . . . . . . . . . . . . . . Casting

***MERCY POINT (UPN/60 mins.)**
PHONE . . . . . . . . . . . . . . . . . . . . . . . . . . . 310-244-7796
10202 W. Washington Blvd.
Culver City, CA 90232
PROD.CO:    Columbia TriStar Television/Mandalay Entertainment
Peter Guber . . . . . . . . . . . . . . . . . . . . . . . Executive Producer
Scott Saunders . . . . . . . . . . . . . . . . . . . . . Executive Producer
David Simkins . . . . . . . . . . . . . . . . . . . . . Executive Producer
Joe Voci . . . . . . . . . . . . . . . . . . . . . . . . . . Executive Producer

**MILLENNIUM (Fox/60 mins.)**
PHONE . . . . . . . . . . . . . . . . . . . . . . . . . . . 310-369-1000
FAX . . . . . . . . . . . . . . . . . . . . . . . . . . . . . 310-369-1308
P.O. Box 900
Beverly Hills, CA 90213
PROD.CO:    Twentieth Century Fox/TCFV Canadian Prods. Inc.
Chris Carter . . . . . . . . . . . . . . . . . . . . . . . Executive Producer
Ken Horton . . . . . . . . . . . . . . . . . . . . . . . . Co-Exec. Producer
John Kousakis . . . . . . . . . . . . . . . . . . . . . . Co-Exec. Producer
Thomas J. Wright . . . . . . . . . . . . . . . . . . . . . . . . . . Producer
Nan Dutton . . . . . . . . . . . . . . . . . . . . . . . . . . . . . . Casting
Coreen Mayrs . . . . . . . . . . . . . . . . . . . . . . . . . . . . Casting

**MOESHA (UPN/30 mins.)**
PHONE . . . . . . . . . . . . . . . . . . . . . . . . . . . 213-956-2500
FAX . . . . . . . . . . . . . . . . . . . . . . . . . . . . . 213-862-1910
5555 Melrose Ave., Modular Bldg.
Los Angeles, CA 90038
PROD.CO:    Big Ticket Television
Sara V. Finney . . . . . . . . . . . . . . . . . . . . . Executive Producer
Vida Sprears . . . . . . . . . . . . . . . . . . . . . . Executive Producer
Calvin Brown Jr. . . . . . . . . . . . . . . . . . . . . Co-Exec. Producer
Jim Tripp-Haith . . . . . . . . . . . . . . . . . . . . . . . . . . . Producer
Kim Hardin . . . . . . . . . . . . . . . . . . . . . . . . . . . . . . Casting

**NANNY, THE (CBS/30 mins.)**
PHONE . . . . . . . . . . . . . . . . . . . . . . . . . . . 310-202-1234
TriStar Television
9336 W. Washington Blvd.
Culver City, CA 90232
PROD.CO:    Sternin/Fraser Ink, Inc./TriStar Television/High School
              Sweethearts
Fran Dresher . . . . . . . . . . . . . . . . . . . . . . Executive Producer
Peter Marc Jacobson . . . . . . . . . . . . . . . . . Executive Producer
Diane Wilk . . . . . . . . . . . . . . . . . . . . . . . . Executive Producer
Frank Lombardi . . . . . . . . . . . . . . . . . . . . . Co-Exec. Producer
Caryn Luces . . . . . . . . . . . . . . . . . . . . . . . Co-Exec. Producer
Nastaran Dibai . . . . . . . . . . . . . . . . . . . . Supervising Producer
Jeffrey B. Hodes . . . . . . . . . . . . . . . . . . . Supervising Producer
Kathy Landsberg . . . . . . . . . . . . . . . . . . . . . . . . . . Producer
Dorothy Lyman . . . . . . . . . . . . . . . . . . . . . . . . . . . Producer
Ivan Menchell . . . . . . . . . . . . . . . . . . . . . . . . . . . Producer

**NASH BRIDGES (CBS/60 mins.)**
PHONE . . . . . . . . . . . . . . . . . . . . . . . . . . . 415-782-4100
FAX . . . . . . . . . . . . . . . . . . . . . . . . . . . . . 415-263-4343
Treasure Island
440 California Ave., Bldg. 2
San Fransisco, CA 94130
PROD.CO:    Carlton Cuse Prods./Don Johnson Co.
Carlton Cuse . . . . . . . . . . . . . . . . . . . . . . Executive Producer
Don Johnson . . . . . . . . . . . . . . . . . . . . . . Executive Producer
Jim Hirsch . . . . . . . . . . . . . . . . . . . . . . . . Co-Exec. Producer
Robert Papazian . . . . . . . . . . . . . . . . . . . . Co-Exec. Producer
John Wirth . . . . . . . . . . . . . . . . . . . . . . . . Co-Exec. Producer
Reed Steiner . . . . . . . . . . . . . . . . . . . . . . Supervising Producer
Andrew Dettmann . . . . . . . . . . . . . . . . . . . . . . . . . Producer
Jed Seidel . . . . . . . . . . . . . . . . . . . . . . . . . . . . . . Producer
Daniel Truly . . . . . . . . . . . . . . . . . . . . . . . . . . . . . Producer
Geoffrey Hemwall . . . . . . . . . . . . . . . . . . . . . . . . Co-Producer
John Aiello . . . . . . . . . . . . . . . . . . . . . . . . . . . . . . Casting

# TV SHOWS AND STAFF

***NET, THE (USA/60 mins.)**
PHONE . . . . . . . . . . . . . . . . . . . . . . . . . . 310-204-2025
3961 Landmark St., Ste. 300
Culver City, CA 90232
PROD.CO:    USA Networks
Rob Cowan . . . . . . . . . . . . . . . . . . . . . . . Executive Producer
Patrick Hasburgh . . . . . . . . . . . . . . . . . . Executive Producer
Irwin Winkler . . . . . . . . . . . . . . . . . . . . . Executive Producer
Karen Rea . . . . . . . . . . . . . . . . . . . . . . . . . . . . . . Casting

**NEWS RADIO (NBC/30 mins.)**
PHONE . . . . . . . . . . . . . . . . . . . . . . . . . . 213-993-7369
FAX . . . . . . . . . . . . . . . . . . . . . . . . . . . . 213-993-7993
1438 N. Gower, Box 32
Los Angeles, CA 90028
PROD.CO:    Brillstein-Grey Ent.
Bernie Brillstein . . . . . . . . . . . . . . . . . . . Executive Producer
Brad Grey . . . . . . . . . . . . . . . . . . . . . . . . Executive Producer
Paul Simms . . . . . . . . . . . . . . . . . . . . . . . Executive Producer
Joe Furey . . . . . . . . . . . . . . . . . . . . . . . . . Co-Exec. Producer
Josh Lieb . . . . . . . . . . . . . . . . . . . . . . . . . Co-Exec. Producer
Drake Satner . . . . . . . . . . . . . . . . . . . . . Supervising Producer
Bonnie Zane . . . . . . . . . . . . . . . . . . . . . . . . . . . . . Casting

***OH BABY (Lifetime/30 mins.)**
PHONE . . . . . . . . . . . . . . . . . . . . . . . . . . 310-202-1234
10202 W. Washington Blvd.
Myrna Loy Bldg., 2nd Floor
Culver City, CA 90232
PROD.CO:    Columbia TriStar Television
Susan Beavers . . . . . . . . . . . . . . . . . . . . Executive Producer
Bob Stevens . . . . . . . . . . . . . . . . . . . . . . Executive Producer
Barbara Stoll . . . . . . . . . . . . . . . . . . . . . . . . . . . . Producer

**ONE LIFE TO LIVE (ABC/60 mins.)**
PHONE . . . . . . . . . . . . . . . . . . . . . . . . . . 212-456-3582
FAX . . . . . . . . . . . . . . . . . . . . . . . . . . . . 212-456-2755
56 W. 66th Street
New York, NY 10023
PROD.CO:    Capital Cities/ABC Daytime
Jill Farren Phelps . . . . . . . . . . . . . . . . . . Executive Producer
Mary O'Leary . . . . . . . . . . . . . . . . . . . . . . . . . . . Producer
Jennifer Pepperman . . . . . . . . . . . . . . . Coordinating Producer
Julie Madison . . . . . . . . . . . . . . . . . . . . . . . . . . . . . Casting

**OUTER LIMITS, THE (Showtime/60 mins.)**
PHONE . . . . . . . . . . . . . . . . . . . . . . . . . . 604-299-7119
FAX . . . . . . . . . . . . . . . . . . . . . . . . . . . . 604-299-7157
2400 Boundary Road
Burnady, Vancouver V5M 323
PROD.CO:    Atlantis Films/Trilogy Entertainment Group
Pen Densham . . . . . . . . . . . . . . . . . . . . . Executive Producer
Richard Barton Lewis . . . . . . . . . . . . . . . Executive Producer
John Watson . . . . . . . . . . . . . . . . . . . . . . Executive Producer
Carlton Eastlake . . . . . . . . . . . . . . . . . . . Co-Exec. Producer
Brad Markowitz . . . . . . . . . . . . . . . . . . . Supervising Producer
Chris Ruppenthal . . . . . . . . . . . . . . . . . . Supervising Producer
Brent Karl Clackson . . . . . . . . . . . . . . . . . . . . . . . Producer
Bette Chadwick . . . . . . . . . . . . . . . . . . . . . . . . . . . Casting
Mary Jo Slater . . . . . . . . . . . . . . . . . . . . . . . . . . . . Casting
Paul Weber . . . . . . . . . . . . . . . . . . . . . . . . . . . . . . Casting

***PACIFIC BLUE (USA/60 mins.)**
PHONE . . . . . . . . . . . . . . . . . . . . . . . . . . 310-827-2453
FAX . . . . . . . . . . . . . . . . . . . . . . . . . . . . 310-827-1332
12636 Beatrice Street
Los Angeles, CA 90066
PROD.CO:    North Hall Productions, Inc.
Bill Miss . . . . . . . . . . . . . . . . . . . . . . . . . Executive Producer
Paul Brown . . . . . . . . . . . . . . . . . . . . . . . Supervising Producer
John Moranville . . . . . . . . . . . . . . . . . . . . . . . . . . . Producer

**PARENT 'HOOD, THE (WB/30 mins.)**
PHONE . . . . . . . . . . . . . . . . . . . . . . . . . . 213-850-2420
FAX . . . . . . . . . . . . . . . . . . . . . . . . . . . . 213-850-2404
Warner - Hollywood Studios
1041 N. Formosa, Bldg. 222
W. Hollywood, CA 90046
PROD.CO:    Warren & Rinsler Prods./Townsend Ent. Corp., The/
        Warner Bros. Television Productions
Dennis Rinsler . . . . . . . . . . . . . . . . . . . . Executive Producer
Mark Warren . . . . . . . . . . . . . . . . . . . . . Executive Producer
Robert Townsend . . . . . . . . . . . . . . . . . . Executive Producer
Loretha Jones . . . . . . . . . . . . . . . . . . . . . Executive Producer
Greg Fields . . . . . . . . . . . . . . . . . . . . . . . Co-Exec. Producer
Eunetta Boone . . . . . . . . . . . . . . . . . . . . Supervising Producer
Barry Douglas . . . . . . . . . . . . . . . . . . . . Supervising Producer
Al Sonja L. Rice . . . . . . . . . . . . . . . . . . . . . . . . . . Producer
Tim Steele . . . . . . . . . . . . . . . . . . . . . . . . . . . . . . Producer
Barbara Miller . . . . . . . . . . . . . . . . . . . . . . . . . . . . Casting
Kevin Scott . . . . . . . . . . . . . . . . . . . . . . . . . . . . . . Casting

**PARTY OF FIVE (Fox/60 mins.)**
PHONE . . . . . . . . . . . . . . . . . . . . . . . . . . 310-244-7261
FAX . . . . . . . . . . . . . . . . . . . . . . . . . . . . 310-244-2330
10202 W. Washington Blvd., Garland Bldg.
Culver City, CA 90232
PROD.CO:    Keyser/Lippman Prods./High Prod. Inc.
Christopher Keyser . . . . . . . . . . . . . . . . . Executive Producer
Amy Lippman . . . . . . . . . . . . . . . . . . . . . Executive Producer
John Romano . . . . . . . . . . . . . . . . . . . . . Executive Producer
Ken Topolsky . . . . . . . . . . . . . . . . . . . . . Executive Producer
Tammy Ader . . . . . . . . . . . . . . . . . . . . . . Co-Exec. Producer
P.K. Simonds . . . . . . . . . . . . . . . . . . . . . . Co-Exec. Producer
Dan Attias . . . . . . . . . . . . . . . . . . . . . . . . . . . . . . Producer
Paul Marks . . . . . . . . . . . . . . . . . . . . . . . . . . . . . . Producer
Steve Robman . . . . . . . . . . . . . . . . . . . . . . . . . . . . Producer
Meg Liberman . . . . . . . . . . . . . . . . . . . . . . . . . . . . Casting
Liberman/Hirschfeld Casting . . . . . . . . . . . . . . . . . . Casting
Patrick Rush . . . . . . . . . . . . . . . . . . . . . . . . . . . . . Casting

**PORT CHARLES (ABC/30 mins.)**
PHONE . . . . . . . . . . . . . . . . . . . . . . . . . . 310-557-7777
FAX . . . . . . . . . . . . . . . . . . . . . . . . . . . . 310-557-3150
4151 Prospect Ave.
Los Angeles, CA 90027
PROD.CO:    ABC Daytime
Wendy Riche . . . . . . . . . . . . . . . . . . . . . . Executive Producer
Hope Smith . . . . . . . . . . . . . . . . . . . . . . . . . . . . . . Producer
Mercer Burrows . . . . . . . . . . . . . . . . . . Coordinating Producer
Mark Teschner . . . . . . . . . . . . . . . . . . . . . . . . . . . . Casting

**PRACTICE, THE (ABC/60 mins.)**
PHONE . . . . . . . . . . . . . . . . . . . . . . . . . . 213-993-5321
FAX . . . . . . . . . . . . . . . . . . . . . . . . . . . . 213-993-5598
846 N. Cahuenga Blvd.
Los Angeles, CA 90038
PROD.CO:    David E. Kelley Prods.
David E. Kelley . . . . . . . . . . . . . . . . . . . . Executive Producer
Jeffrey Kramer . . . . . . . . . . . . . . . . . . . . . Co-Exec. Producer
Robert Breech . . . . . . . . . . . . . . . . . . . . Supervising Producer
Ed Redlich . . . . . . . . . . . . . . . . . . . . . . . . . . . . . . Producer
Gary Strangis . . . . . . . . . . . . . . . . . . . . . . . . . . . . Producer
Janet Gilmore . . . . . . . . . . . . . . . . . . . . . . . . . . . . Casting
Megan McConnell . . . . . . . . . . . . . . . . . . . . . . . . . . Casting

**PROFILER (NBC/60 mins.)**
PHONE . . . . . . . . . . . . . . . . . . . . . . . . . . 818-503-4200
FAX . . . . . . . . . . . . . . . . . . . . . . . . . . . . 818-503-6390
7333 Radford Ave.
N. Hollywood, CA 91605
PROD.CO:    Sander/Moses Prods./NBC Studios
Kim Moses . . . . . . . . . . . . . . . . . . . . . . . Executive Producer
Ian Sander . . . . . . . . . . . . . . . . . . . . . . . Executive Producer
Steve Feke . . . . . . . . . . . . . . . . . . . . . . . . Co-Exec. Producer
George Geiger . . . . . . . . . . . . . . . . . . . . . Co-Exec. Producer
Cynthia Saunders . . . . . . . . . . . . . . . . . . Supervising Producer
Charles Holland . . . . . . . . . . . . . . . . . . . . . . . . . . Producer
John Niss . . . . . . . . . . . . . . . . . . . . . . . . . . . . . . . Producer
Lorie Zerweek . . . . . . . . . . . . . . . . . . . . . . . . . . . Producer
Anthony Barnao . . . . . . . . . . . . . . . . . . . . . . . . . . . Casting

# TV SHOWS AND STAFF

**PROMISED LAND (CBS/60 mins.)**
PHONE . . . . . . . . . . . . . . . . . . . . . . . . . . . . 818-508-3420
FAX . . . . . . . . . . . . . . . . . . . . . . . . . . . . . . 818-508-2053
12711 Ventura Blvd., Ste. 210
Studio City, CA
PROD.CO:     Merlot Film Prod./Promised Land
Steve Smith . . . . . . . . . . . . . . . . . . . . . . . . Executive Producer
Martha Williamson . . . . . . . . . . . . . . . . . . Executive Producer
Jon Anderson . . . . . . . . . . . . . . . . . . . . . . . Co-Exec. Producer
Bill Schwartz . . . . . . . . . . . . . . . . . . . . . . . Supervising Producer
David Giella . . . . . . . . . . . . . . . . . . . . . . . . . . . . . . . . . Casting

***RUDE AWAKENING (Showtime/30 mins.)**
PHONE . . . . . . . . . . . . . . . . . . . . . . . . . . . . 213-860-3170
FAX . . . . . . . . . . . . . . . . . . . . . . . . . . . . . . 213-860-3171
Hollywood Centre Studios
1040 N. Las Palmas, Bldg. 9
Los Angeles, CA 90038
PROD.CO:     Mandalay Television/Showtime Networks Inc.
Pam Eels . . . . . . . . . . . . . . . . . . . . . . . . . . Executive Producer
Scott Sanders . . . . . . . . . . . . . . . . . . . . . . Executive Producer
Joe Voci . . . . . . . . . . . . . . . . . . . . . . . . . . . Executive Producer
Eric Dawson . . . . . . . . . . . . . . . . . . . . . . . . . . . . . . . . . . Casting

**SABRINA THE TEENAGE WITCH (ABC/30 mins.)**
PHONE . . . . . . . . . . . . . . . . . . . . . . . . . . . . 213-956-2600
FAX . . . . . . . . . . . . . . . . . . . . . . . . . . . . . . 213-862-1533
5555 Melrose Ave., Trailer 35
Hollywood, CA 90038
PROD.CO:     Viacom Productions
Paula Hart . . . . . . . . . . . . . . . . . . . . . . . . . Executive Producer
Holly Hester . . . . . . . . . . . . . . . . . . . . . . . . Executive Producer
Miriam Trogdon . . . . . . . . . . . . . . . . . . . . . Executive Producer
Carrie Honigblum . . . . . . . . . . . . . . . . . . . . Co-Exec. Producer
Renee Phillps . . . . . . . . . . . . . . . . . . . . . . . Co-Exec. Producer
Ken Koch . . . . . . . . . . . . . . . . . . . . . . . . . . . . . . . . . . Producer
Rick Millikan . . . . . . . . . . . . . . . . . . . . . . . . . . . . . . . . . Casting

***SAVED BY THE BELL: THE NEW CLASS (NBC/30 mins.)**
PHONE . . . . . . . . . . . . . . . . . . . . . . . . . . . . 818-840-2250
FAX . . . . . . . . . . . . . . . . . . . . . . . . . . . . . . 818-840-2254
3000 W. Alameda, Rm. 2138, Studio 9
Burbank, CA 91523
PROD.CO:     Peter Engel Prods.
Peter Engel . . . . . . . . . . . . . . . . . . . . . . . . . Executive Producer
Bennett Tramer . . . . . . . . . . . . . . . . . . . . . . Co-Exec. Producer
Tony Soltis . . . . . . . . . . . . . . . . . . . . . . . . . Supervising Producer
Diane Ranaldi . . . . . . . . . . . . . . . . . . . . . . . Coordinating Producer
Chris Conte . . . . . . . . . . . . . . . . . . . . . . . . . . . . . . . . . Producer
Robin Lippin . . . . . . . . . . . . . . . . . . . . . . . . . . . . . . . . . Casting

***SECRET DIARY OF DESMOND PFEIFFER, THE (UPN/30 mins.)**
PHONE . . . . . . . . . . . . . . . . . . . . . . . . . . . . 213-956-5000
FAX . . . . . . . . . . . . . . . . . . . . . . . . . . . . . . 213-862-0270
5555 Melrose Ave.
Lucy Bungalow, Rm. 107
Hollywood, CA 90038
PROD.CO:     Paramount Network Television
Barry Fanaro . . . . . . . . . . . . . . . . . . . . . . . . Executive Producer
Mort Nathan . . . . . . . . . . . . . . . . . . . . . . . . . Executive Producer
Marica Govens . . . . . . . . . . . . . . . . . . . . . . . . . . . . . . Producer
Greg Orson . . . . . . . . . . . . . . . . . . . . . . . . . . . . . . . . . . Casting

***SECRET LIVES OF MEN (ABC/30 mins.)**
PHONE . . . . . . . . . . . . . . . . . . . . . . . . . . . . 213-464-1333
1438 N. Gower St., Bldg. 35, 4th Fl.
Hollywood, CA 90028
PROD.CO:     Witt-Thomas-Harris Productions
Susan Harris . . . . . . . . . . . . . . . . . . . . . . . . Executive Producer
Tony Thomas . . . . . . . . . . . . . . . . . . . . . . . . Executive Producer
Nina Wass . . . . . . . . . . . . . . . . . . . . . . . . . . Executive Producer
Paul Junger Witt . . . . . . . . . . . . . . . . . . . . . Executive Producer

***SEVEN DAYS (UPN/60 mins.)**
PHONE . . . . . . . . . . . . . . . . . . . . . . . . . . . . 213-956-5000
5555 Melrose Ave.
Los Angeles, CA 90038
PROD.CO:     Paramount Network Television
Christopher Crowe . . . . . . . . . . . . . . . . . . . Executive Producer

***SEVENTH HEAVEN (WB/60 mins.)**
PHONE . . . . . . . . . . . . . . . . . . . . . . . . . . . . 213-965-5700
Spelling Television
5700 Wilshire Blvd., #575
Los Angeles, CA 90036
PROD.CO:     Northshore Productions/Spelling Television Inc
Brenda Hempton . . . . . . . . . . . . . . . . . . . . . Executive Producer
Aaron Spelling . . . . . . . . . . . . . . . . . . . . . . . Executive Producer
E. Duke Vincent . . . . . . . . . . . . . . . . . . . . . . Executive Producer
Cathy Lepard . . . . . . . . . . . . . . . . . . . . . . . . . . . . . . . Producer
Joe Wallenstein . . . . . . . . . . . . . . . . . . . . . . . . . . . . . Producer
Cheryl Stein . . . . . . . . . . . . . . . . . . . . . . . . . Coordinating Producer
Vickie Huff . . . . . . . . . . . . . . . . . . . . . . . . . . . . . . . . . . Casting

***SEX AND THE CITY (HBO/30 mins.)**
FAX . . . . . . . . . . . . . . . . . . . . . . . . . . . . . . 718-937-4675
42-22 22nd St.
Long Island City, NY 11101
PROD.CO:     HBO
Darren Star . . . . . . . . . . . . . . . . . . . . . . . . . Executive Producer
Barry Jossen . . . . . . . . . . . . . . . . . . . . . . . . Co-Exec. Producer
Michael Patrick King . . . . . . . . . . . . . . . . . . Co-Exec. Producer
Billy Hopkins . . . . . . . . . . . . . . . . . . . . . . . . . . . . . . . . . Casting

***SILK STALKINGS (USA/60 mins.)**
PHONE . . . . . . . . . . . . . . . . . . . . . . . . . . . . 818-508-3477
FAX . . . . . . . . . . . . . . . . . . . . . . . . . . . . . . 818-508-3356
12711 Ventura Blvd., Ste. 330
Studio City, CA 91604
PROD.CO:     Stu Segal Prods.
Kim LeMasters . . . . . . . . . . . . . . . . . . . . . . Executive Producer
Stu Segal . . . . . . . . . . . . . . . . . . . . . . . . . . . Executive Producer
Barbara Claman . . . . . . . . . . . . . . . . . . . . . . . . . . . . . . Casting

**SIMPSONS, THE (Fox/30 mins.)**
PHONE . . . . . . . . . . . . . . . . . . . . . . . . . . . . 310-369-1000
10201 W. Pico Blvd.
Los Angeles, CA 90035
PROD.CO:     Gracie Films/Twentieth Century Fox Television/Film
             Roman, Inc.
James L. Brooks . . . . . . . . . . . . . . . . . . . . . Executive Producer
Matt Groening . . . . . . . . . . . . . . . . . . . . . . . Executive Producer
Mike Scully . . . . . . . . . . . . . . . . . . . . . . . . . Executive Producer
Dan Greaney . . . . . . . . . . . . . . . . . . . . . . . . Supervising Producer
Ron Hauge . . . . . . . . . . . . . . . . . . . . . . . . . . Supervising Producer
Colin ABV Lewis . . . . . . . . . . . . . . . . . . . . . . . . . . . . . Producer
Mike Mendel . . . . . . . . . . . . . . . . . . . . . . . . . . . . . . . Producer
Bonnie Pietila . . . . . . . . . . . . . . . . . . . . . . . Producer/Casting
Richard Raynis . . . . . . . . . . . . . . . . . . . . . . . . . . . . . . Producer
Richard Sakai . . . . . . . . . . . . . . . . . . . . . . . . . . . . . . . Producer
Denise Sirkot . . . . . . . . . . . . . . . . . . . . . . . . . . . . . . . Producer

***SINS OF THE CITY (USA Networks/60 mins.)**
PHONE . . . . . . . . . . . . . . . . . . . . . . . . . . . . 305-899-8089
12100 No. East 16th Ave., Ste. 200
No. Miami, CA 33161
PROD.CO:     Alliance Communications Corp./Chesler/Perlmutter
             Production
Lewis Chesler . . . . . . . . . . . . . . . . . . . . . . . Executive Producer
Steve Feke . . . . . . . . . . . . . . . . . . . . . . . . . . Executive Producer
Oscar Costo . . . . . . . . . . . . . . . . . . . . . . . . . Co-Exec. Producer
Hank McCann . . . . . . . . . . . . . . . . . . . . . . . . . . . . . . . Casting
Lori Wyman . . . . . . . . . . . . . . . . . . . . . . . . . Casting (Miami)

**SISTER SISTER (WB/30 mins.)**
PHONE . . . . . . . . . . . . . . . . . . . . . . . . . . . . 213-956-4525
FAX . . . . . . . . . . . . . . . . . . . . . . . . . . . . . . 213-862-1092
Paramount
5555 Melrose Avenue
Hollywood, CA 90038
PROD.CO:     Paramount Television Group/De Passe Entertainment
Suzanne Coston . . . . . . . . . . . . . . . . . . . . . . Executive Producer
Suzanne de Passe . . . . . . . . . . . . . . . . . . . . Executive Producer
Rick Hawkins . . . . . . . . . . . . . . . . . . . . . . . . Executive Producer
Irene Dreayer . . . . . . . . . . . . . . . . . . . . . . . . Co-Exec. Producer
Felicia Henderson . . . . . . . . . . . . . . . . . . . . Co-Exec. & Supervising Producer
Regina Hicks . . . . . . . . . . . . . . . . . . . . . . . . . . . . . . . . Producer
Laura Lynn . . . . . . . . . . . . . . . . . . . . . . . . . . . . . . . . . . Producer
Rushion McDonald . . . . . . . . . . . . . . . . . . . . . . . . . . . Producer
Monica Swann . . . . . . . . . . . . . . . . . . . . . . . . . . . . . . . Casting

## SLIDERS (Sci-Fi/60 mins.)
PHONE . . . . . . . . . . . . . . . . . . . . . . . . . . . . 818-733-0459
FAX . . . . . . . . . . . . . . . . . . . . . . . . . . . . . . 818-866-2177
Universal Television
100 Universal City Plaza, 480/3
Universal City, CA 91608
PROD.CO:     Universal Television & Networks Group

David Peckinpah . . . . . . . . . . . . . . . . . . . . Executive Producer
Bill Dial . . . . . . . . . . . . . . . . . . . . . . . . . Co-Exec. Producer
Ed Ledding . . . . . . . . . . . . . . . . . . . . . . . . . . . . . Producer
Jerry O'Connell . . . . . . . . . . . . . . . . . . . . . . . . . . . Producer
Barbara Claman . . . . . . . . . . . . . . . . . . . . . . . . . . . Casting

## SMART GUY, THE (WB/30 mins.)
PHONE . . . . . . . . . . . . . . . . . . . . . . . . . . . . 818-560-6994
FAX . . . . . . . . . . . . . . . . . . . . . . . . . . . . . . 818-560-3073
500 S. Buena Vista Street
Burbank, CA 91521
PROD.CO:     Danny Kallis Prods./De Passe Entertainment/Walt Disney
             TV/Touchstone TV

Suzanne Coston . . . . . . . . . . . . . . . . . . . . Executive Producer
Suzanne de Passe . . . . . . . . . . . . . . . . . . . Executive Producer
Danny Kallis . . . . . . . . . . . . . . . . . . . . . . Executive Producer
Bob Young . . . . . . . . . . . . . . . . . . . . . . . Executive Producer
Irene Dreayer . . . . . . . . . . . . . . . . . . . . . Co-Exec. Producer
Tim Maile . . . . . . . . . . . . . . . . . . . . . . . Co-Exec. Producer
Doug Tuber . . . . . . . . . . . . . . . . . . . . . . Co-Exec. Producer
Patty Gary-Cox . . . . . . . . . . . . . . . . . . . . . . . . . . Producer
Ralph Greene . . . . . . . . . . . . . . . . . . . . . . . . . . . Producer
Adam Lapidus . . . . . . . . . . . . . . . . . . . . . . . . . . . Producer
Monica Swann . . . . . . . . . . . . . . . . . . . . . . . . . . . Casting

## *SOF: SPECIAL OPS FORCE (UPN/60 mins.)
PHONE . . . . . . . . . . . . . . . . . . . . . . . . . . . . 805-257-8300
FAX . . . . . . . . . . . . . . . . . . . . . . . . . . . . . . 805-257-8320
24937 Tibbitts Ave.
Valencia, CA 91355
PROD.CO:     Neil Russell Prods./Bruckheimer Prods./Rysher
             Entertainment

Jerry Bruckheimer . . . . . . . . . . . . . . . . . . . Executive Producer
Robert McCoullough . . . . . . . . . . . . . . . . . . Executive Producer
Neil Russell . . . . . . . . . . . . . . . . . . . . . . Executive Producer
Greg Strangis . . . . . . . . . . . . . . . . . . . . . Executive Producer
Sam Stangis . . . . . . . . . . . . . . . . . . . . . . . . . . . . Producer
Lou DiGiamo . . . . . . . . . . . . . . . . . . . . . . . . . . . . Casting
Andrea Kenyon . . . . . . . . . . . . . . . . . . . . . . . . . . . Casting
Dianne Young . . . . . . . . . . . . . . . . . . . . . . . . . . . Casting

## SPIN CITY (ABC/30 mins.)
PHONE . . . . . . . . . . . . . . . . . . . . . . . . . . . . 212-336-6420
FAX . . . . . . . . . . . . . . . . . . . . . . . . . . . . . . 212-336-6997
Chelsea Piers
West 23rd St., Hudson River Pier 62
New York, NY 10011
PROD.CO:     Mountie Productions/DreamWorks Television

Michael J. Fox . . . . . . . . . . . . . . . . . . . . . Executive Producer
Bill Lawrence . . . . . . . . . . . . . . . . . . . . . Co-Exec. Producer
Bonnie Finnegan . . . . . . . . . . . . . . . . . . . . . . . . . . Casting

## *SPORTS NIGHT (ABC/30 mins.)
PHONE . . . . . . . . . . . . . . . . . . . . . . . . . . . . 818-560-1000
Walt Disney Studios
500 S. Buena Vista, Stage 6, 5th Fl.
Burbank, CA 91521
PROD.CO:     Imagine Television

Rob Scheidlinger . . . . . . . . . . . . . . . . . . . . Executive Producer
Tommy Schlamme . . . . . . . . . . . . . . . . . . . . Executive Producer
Aaron Sorkin . . . . . . . . . . . . . . . . . . . . . . Executive Producer

## STAR TREK: DEEP SPACE NINE (UPN/60 mins.)
PHONE . . . . . . . . . . . . . . . . . . . . . . . . . . . . 213-956-5000
Paramount
5555 Melrose Ave.
Hollywood, CA 90038
PROD.CO:     Paramount Television Group

Ira Steven Behr . . . . . . . . . . . . . . . . . . . . . Executive Producer
Rick Berman . . . . . . . . . . . . . . . . . . . . . . Executive Producer
Ronald D. Moore . . . . . . . . . . . . . . . . . . . . Co-Exec. Producer
Hans Beimler . . . . . . . . . . . . . . . . . . . . . . Supervising Producer
Peter Lauriston . . . . . . . . . . . . . . . . . . . . . Supervising Producer
Junie Lowry-Johnson . . . . . . . . . . . . . . . . . . . . . . . . Casting
Ron Suma . . . . . . . . . . . . . . . . . . . . . . . . . . . . . . Casting

## STAR TREK: VOYAGER (UPN/60 mins.)
PHONE . . . . . . . . . . . . . . . . . . . . . . . . . . . . 213-956-5000
Paramount
5555 Melrose Ave.
Hollywood, CA 90038
PROD.CO:     Paramount Television Group

Rick Berman . . . . . . . . . . . . . . . . . . . . . . Executive Producer
Brannon Braga . . . . . . . . . . . . . . . . . . . . . Executive Producer
Peter Lauritson . . . . . . . . . . . . . . . . . . . . . Supervising Producer
Joe Menosky . . . . . . . . . . . . . . . . . . . . . . Supervising Producer
Merri Howard . . . . . . . . . . . . . . . . . . . . . Co-Supervising Producer
Junie Lowry-Johnson . . . . . . . . . . . . . . . . . . . . . . . . Casting
Ron Surma . . . . . . . . . . . . . . . . . . . . . . . . . . . . . . Casting

## *STARGATE SG-1 (Showtime/60 mins.)
PHONE . . . . . . . . . . . . . . . . . . . . . . . . . . . . 604-654-1600
FAX . . . . . . . . . . . . . . . . . . . . . . . . . . . . . . 604-654-2900
2400 Boundary Road
Burnaby, BC V5M323
Richard Dean Anderson . . . . . . . . . . . . . . . . . Executive Producer
Jonathan Glassner . . . . . . . . . . . . . . . . . . . Executive Producer
Michael Greenburg . . . . . . . . . . . . . . . . . . . Executive Producer
Brad Wright . . . . . . . . . . . . . . . . . . . . . . Executive Producer
N. John Smith . . . . . . . . . . . . . . . . . . . . . . . . . . . Producer
Carol Kelsay . . . . . . . . . . . . . . . . . . . . . . . . . . . . Casting

## STEVE HARVEY SHOW, THE (WB/30 mins.)
PHONE . . . . . . . . . . . . . . . . . . . . . . . . . . . 818-760-5588
FAX . . . . . . . . . . . . . . . . . . . . . . . . . . . . 818-655-8579
4024 Radford, Bldg. 8
Studio City, CA 91604
PROD.CO:     Stan Lathan TV/Winifred Hervey Prods. Inc./Columbia
             Pictures Television/Brillstein-Grey Ent.

Bernie Brillstein . . . . . . . . . . . . . . . . . . . . Executive Producer
Brad Grey . . . . . . . . . . . . . . . . . . . . . . . Executive Producer
Winifred Hervey . . . . . . . . . . . . . . . . . . . . Executive Producer
Stan Lathan . . . . . . . . . . . . . . . . . . . . . . Executive Producer
Walter Allen Bennett Jr. . . . . . . . . . . . . . . . . Co-Exec. Producer
Manny Basanesse . . . . . . . . . . . . . . . . . . . . . . . . . . Producer
B. Mark Seabrooks . . . . . . . . . . . . . . . . . . . . . . . . . Producer
Monica Swann . . . . . . . . . . . . . . . . . . . . . . . . . . . Casting

## SUDDENLY SUSAN (NBC/30 mins.)
PHONE . . . . . . . . . . . . . . . . . . . . . . . . . . . 818-954-3332
FAX . . . . . . . . . . . . . . . . . . . . . . . . . . . . 818-954-3371
Warner Bros. Television
4000 Warner Blvd.
Burbank, CA 91505
PROD.CO:     Warner Bros. Television Productions

Gary Dontzig . . . . . . . . . . . . . . . . . . . . . . Executive Producer
Steven Peterman . . . . . . . . . . . . . . . . . . . . Executive Producer
Jeanette Collins . . . . . . . . . . . . . . . . . . . . Co-Exec. Producer
Mimi Friedman . . . . . . . . . . . . . . . . . . . . . Co-Exec. Producer
Becky Hartman Edwards . . . . . . . . . . . . . . . . . Co-Exec. Producer
Chuck Tatham . . . . . . . . . . . . . . . . . . . . . . Co-Exec. Producer
Christopher Vane . . . . . . . . . . . . . . . . . . . . Co-Exec. Producer
Frank Pace . . . . . . . . . . . . . . . . . . . . . . . . . . . . . Producer
Barbara Miller . . . . . . . . . . . . . . . . . . . . . . . . . . . Casting
Tony Sepulveda . . . . . . . . . . . . . . . . . . . . . . . . . . . Casting

## SUNSET BEACH (NBC/30 mins.)
PHONE . . . . . . . . . . . . . . . . . . . . . . . . . . . 818-526-2700
FAX . . . . . . . . . . . . . . . . . . . . . . . . . . . . 818-526-7129
3000 West Alameca Ave.
Burbank, CA 91523
PROD.CO:     Spelling Television, Inc.

Aaron Spelling . . . . . . . . . . . . . . . . . . . . . Executive Producer
Gary Tomlin . . . . . . . . . . . . . . . . . . . . . . Executive Producer
E. Duke Vincent . . . . . . . . . . . . . . . . . . . . Executive Producer
Lisa Hesser . . . . . . . . . . . . . . . . . . . . . . Supervising Producer
Mary Kelly Weir . . . . . . . . . . . . . . . . . . . . . . . . . . Producer
Sue Silkiss . . . . . . . . . . . . . . . . . . . . . . Coordinating Producer
Harriet Greenspan . . . . . . . . . . . . . . . . . . . . . . . . . Casting

## *TO HAVE AND TO HOLD (CBS/60 mins.)
PHONE . . . . . . . . . . . . . . . . . . . . . . . . . . . 310-444-8468
1440 S. Sepulveda, Ste. 322
Los Angeles, CA 90025
PROD.CO:     Greenblatt Janollari Studio, The/CBS Productions

Bob Greenblatt . . . . . . . . . . . . . . . . . . . . . Executive Producer
David Janollari . . . . . . . . . . . . . . . . . . . . . Executive Producer
Scott Shepherd . . . . . . . . . . . . . . . . . . . . . Executive Producer
Joanne T. Waters . . . . . . . . . . . . . . . . . . . . Supervising Producer
Carol Kritzer . . . . . . . . . . . . . . . . . . . . . . . . . . . Casting
Robert A. Ulrich . . . . . . . . . . . . . . . . . . . . . . . . . . Casting

**TOUCHED BY AN ANGEL (CBS/60 mins.)**
PHONE . . . . . . . . . . . . . . . . . . . . . . . . . . . . . . 818-508-3420
FAX . . . . . . . . . . . . . . . . . . . . . . . . . . . . . . . . . 818-508-3464
12711 Ventura Blvd., Ste. 210
Studio City, CA 91604
PROD.CO:      Caroline Film Prods./CBS Productions
Martha Williamson . . . . . . . . . . . . . . . . . . . . . Executive Producer
Jon Anderson . . . . . . . . . . . . . . . . . . . . . . . . . Co-Exec. Producer
R.J. Colleary . . . . . . . . . . . . . . . . . . . . . . . . . . Co-Exec. Producer
Burt Pearl . . . . . . . . . . . . . . . . . . . . . . . . . . . . Co-Exec. Producer
Robert J. Visciglia Jr. . . . . . . . . . . . . . . . . . . . . . . . . . Producer
David Giella . . . . . . . . . . . . . . . . . . . . . . . . . . . . . . . . Casting

***TRINITY (NBC/60 mins.)**
PHONE . . . . . . . . . . . . . . . . . . . . . . . . . . . . . . 818-954-6000
4000 Warner Blvd.
Burbank, CA 91522
PROD.CO:      Warner Bros. Television Productions
Mathew McNair . . . . . . . . . . . . . . . . . . . . . . . Executive Producer
John Wells . . . . . . . . . . . . . . . . . . . . . . . . . . . Executive Producer

***TWO GUYS, A GIRL, AND A PIZZA PLACE (ABC/30 mins.)**
PHONE . . . . . . . . . . . . . . . . . . . . . . . . . . . . . . 310-369-3280
10201 W. Pico Blvd., Bldg. 3
Los Angeles, CA 90067
PROD.CO:      In Front/Twentieth Century Fox Television
Danny Jacobson . . . . . . . . . . . . . . . . . . . . . . . Executive Producer
Marjorie Weitzman . . . . . . . . . . . . . . . . . . . . . Executive Producer

**UNHAPPILY EVER AFTER (WB/30 mins.)**
PHONE . . . . . . . . . . . . . . . . . . . . . . . . . . . . . . 818-560-1000
Touchstone Television
500 S. Buena Vista St.
Burbank, CA 91521
PROD.CO:      Touchstone Television
Ron Leavitt . . . . . . . . . . . . . . . . . . . . . . . . . . . Executive Producer
Arthur Silver . . . . . . . . . . . . . . . . . . . . . . . . . . Executive Producer
Marcy Vosburgh . . . . . . . . . . . . . . . . . . . . . . . Executive Producer
Stewart Burns . . . . . . . . . . . . . . . . . . . . . . . . . . . . . . . Producer
Christina Lynch . . . . . . . . . . . . . . . . . . . . . . . . . . . . . . Producer
Hariette Regan . . . . . . . . . . . . . . . . . . . . . . . . . . . . . . . Producer
Tammy Billik . . . . . . . . . . . . . . . . . . . . . . . . . . . . . . . . . Casting

**USA HIGH (USA/ 30 mins.)**
PHONE . . . . . . . . . . . . . . . . . . . . . . . . . . . . . . 213-468-3751
FAX . . . . . . . . . . . . . . . . . . . . . . . . . . . . . . . . . 213-468-3799
1438 N. Gower, Courtyard Box 29
Hollywood, CA 90028
PROD.CO:      Peter Engel Prods./NBC Enterprises/Rysher
                Entertainment
Peter Engel . . . . . . . . . . . . . . . . . . . . . . . . . . . Executive Producer
Leslie Eberhard . . . . . . . . . . . . . . . . . . . . . . . Co-Exec. Producer
Sue Feyk . . . . . . . . . . . . . . . . . . . . . . . . . . . . . . . . . . . Producer
Patricia Noland . . . . . . . . . . . . . . . . . . . . . . . . . . . . . . . Casting

***VENGEANCE UNLIMITED AKA MR. CHAPEL (ABC/60 mins.)**
PHONE . . . . . . . . . . . . . . . . . . . . . . . . . . . . . . 818-954-2589
FAX . . . . . . . . . . . . . . . . . . . . . . . . . . . . . . . . . 818-777-0129
3701 W. Oak St., Bldg. 4R
Burbank, CA 91505
PROD.CO:      McNamara Paper Products/Warner Bros. Television
                Productions
John McNamara . . . . . . . . . . . . . . . . . . . . . . . Executive Producer

**VERONICA'S CLOSET (NBC/30 mins.)**
PHONE . . . . . . . . . . . . . . . . . . . . . . . . . . . . . . 818-977-7943
Warner Bros. Television
4000 Warner Blvd.
Burbank, CA 91522
PROD.CO:      Bright/Kauffman/Crane Prods./Warner Bros. Television
                Productions
Kevin S. Bright . . . . . . . . . . . . . . . . . . . . . . . . Executive Producer
David Crane . . . . . . . . . . . . . . . . . . . . . . . . . . Executive Producer
Marta Kauffman . . . . . . . . . . . . . . . . . . . . . . . Executive Producer
Rob Ulin . . . . . . . . . . . . . . . . . . . . . . . . . . . . . Executive Producer
Kirstie Alley . . . . . . . . . . . . . . . . . . . . . . . . . . . . . . . . . Producer
Mark S. Greenberg . . . . . . . . . . . . . . . . . . . . . . . . . . . . Producer
Wendy Knoller . . . . . . . . . . . . . . . . . . . . . . . Coordinating Producer
Leslie Litt . . . . . . . . . . . . . . . . . . . . . . . . . . . . . . . . . . . Casting
Barbara Miller . . . . . . . . . . . . . . . . . . . . . . . . . . . . . . . . Casting

**VIPER (Syndicated/60 mins.)**
PHONE . . . . . . . . . . . . . . . . . . . . . . . . . . . . . . 818-526-0930
FAX . . . . . . . . . . . . . . . . . . . . . . . . . . . . . . . . . 818-526-0906
3100 W. Burbank Blvd., Ste. 200
Burbank, CA 91505
PROD.CO:      Paramount Network Television
Danny Bilson . . . . . . . . . . . . . . . . . . . . . . . . . Executive Producer
Paul De Meo . . . . . . . . . . . . . . . . . . . . . . . . . . Executive Producer
Robert Benjamin . . . . . . . . . . . . . . . . . . . . . . . . . . . . . . Producer
Trish Robinson . . . . . . . . . . . . . . . . . . . . . . . . . . . . . . . . Casting
April Webster . . . . . . . . . . . . . . . . . . . . . . . . . . . . . . . . . Casting

**WALKER: TEXAS RANGER (CBS/60 mins.)**
PHONE . . . . . . . . . . . . . . . . . . . . . . . . . . . . . . 818-752-9292
FAX . . . . . . . . . . . . . . . . . . . . . . . . . . . . . . . . . 818-752-9131
11969 Ventura Blvd., 3rd Floor
Studio City, CA 91604
PROD.CO:      Amadea Film Prods./CBS Productions
Aaron Norris . . . . . . . . . . . . . . . . . . . . . . . . . . Executive Producer
Chuck Norris . . . . . . . . . . . . . . . . . . . . . . . . . . Executive Producer
Gordon Dawson . . . . . . . . . . . . . . . . . . . . . . . Co-Exec. Producer
Lisa Clarkson . . . . . . . . . . . . . . . . . . . . . . . Supervising Producer
Bruce Cervi . . . . . . . . . . . . . . . . . . . . . . . . . . . . . . . . . . Producer
John Lansing . . . . . . . . . . . . . . . . . . . . . . . . . . . . . . . . . Producer
Shari Rhodes . . . . . . . . . . . . . . . . . . . . . . . . . . . . . . . . . Casting

**WAYANS BROTHERS, THE (WB/30 mins.)**
PHONE . . . . . . . . . . . . . . . . . . . . . . . . . . . . . . 213-993-7925
FAX . . . . . . . . . . . . . . . . . . . . . . . . . . . . . . . . . 213-993-7946
Warner Bros. Television
1438 N. Gower, Bldg. 48, 3rd Fl., Box 47
Hollywood, CA 90028
PROD.CO:      Next To Last Prods./Baby Way Prods./Warner Bros.
                Television Productions
Phil Kellard . . . . . . . . . . . . . . . . . . . . . . . . . . . Executive Producer
Tom T. Moore . . . . . . . . . . . . . . . . . . . . . . . . . Executive Producer
Josh Goldstein . . . . . . . . . . . . . . . . . . . . . . . . Co-Exec. Producer
Robert Bruce . . . . . . . . . . . . . . . . . . . . . . . Supervising Producer
Phil Bearman . . . . . . . . . . . . . . . . . . . . . . . . . . . . . . . . . Producer
Ernest Johnson . . . . . . . . . . . . . . . . . . . . . . . . . . . . . . . Producer
Leah Daniels-Butler . . . . . . . . . . . . . . . . . . . . . . . . . . . . Casting
Barbara Miller . . . . . . . . . . . . . . . . . . . . . . . . . . . . . . . . Casting

***WILL & GRACE (NBC/30 mins.)**
PHONE . . . . . . . . . . . . . . . . . . . . . . . . . . . . . . 818-760-5000
4024 Radford Ave., Bungalow 8
Studio City, CA 91604
PROD.CO:      Three Sisters Ent./NBC Studios
David Kohan . . . . . . . . . . . . . . . . . . . . . . . . . . Executive Producer
Max Mutchnik . . . . . . . . . . . . . . . . . . . . . . . . . Executive Producer
Tim Kaiser . . . . . . . . . . . . . . . . . . . . . . . . . . . . . . . . . . Producer

***WIND ON THE WATER (NBC/60 mins.)**
PHONE . . . . . . . . . . . . . . . . . . . . . . . . . . . . . . 818-700-7300
FAX . . . . . . . . . . . . . . . . . . . . . . . . . . . . . . . . . 818-700-7338
8411 Canoga Ave.
Canoga Park, CA 91304
PROD.CO:      Wind On Water Productions/NBC Studios
Zalman King . . . . . . . . . . . . . . . . . . . . . . . . . . Executive Producer
Charles Rosin . . . . . . . . . . . . . . . . . . . . . . . . . Executive Producer
Stuart Sheslow . . . . . . . . . . . . . . . . . . . . . . . . Executive Producer

**WORKING (NBC/30 mins.)**
PHONE . . . . . . . . . . . . . . . . . . . . . . . . . . . . . . 818-760-5222
FAX . . . . . . . . . . . . . . . . . . . . . . . . . . . . . . . . . 818-508-2397
4024 Radford Ave.
Studio City, CA 91604
PROD.CO:      NBC Studios
Michael Davidoff . . . . . . . . . . . . . . . . . . . . . . . Executive Producer
Bill Rosenthal . . . . . . . . . . . . . . . . . . . . . . . . . Executive Producer
Matt Goldman . . . . . . . . . . . . . . . . . . . . . . . . . Co-Exec. Producer
Werner Waliar . . . . . . . . . . . . . . . . . . . . . . . . . . . . . . . . . Producer
Cami Patton . . . . . . . . . . . . . . . . . . . . . . . . . . . . . . . . . . Casting

# TV SHOWS AND STAFF

**X-FILES (Fox/60 mins.)**
PHONE . . . . . . . . . . . . . . . . . . . . . . . . . . . . . . . . . . 310-369-1000
FAX . . . . . . . . . . . . . . . . . . . . . . . . . . . . . . . . . . . . . 310-369-1978
P.O. Box 900
Beverly Hills, CA 90213
PROD.CO:    Twentieth Century Fox/Ten Thirteen Productions
Chris Carter . . . . . . . . . . . . . . . . . . . . . . . . . . . Executive Producer
Frank Spotnitz . . . . . . . . . . . . . . . . . . . . . . . . . . Co-Exec. Producer
Vince Gilligan . . . . . . . . . . . . . . . . . . . . . . . . . Supervising Producer
Rob Bowman . . . . . . . . . . . . . . . . . . . . . . . . . . . . . . . . Producer
J.P. Finn . . . . . . . . . . . . . . . . . . . . . . . . . . . . . . . . . . . Producer
Kim Manners . . . . . . . . . . . . . . . . . . . . . . . . . . . . . . . . Producer
Paul Rabwin . . . . . . . . . . . . . . . . . . . . . . . . . . . . . . . . Producer
Coreen Mayrs . . . . . . . . . . . . . . . . . . . . . . . . . . . . . . . . Casting

**YOUNG AND THE RESTLESS, THE (CBS/60 mins.)**
PHONE . . . . . . . . . . . . . . . . . . . . . . . . . . . . . . . . . . 213-852-2532
FAX . . . . . . . . . . . . . . . . . . . . . . . . . . . . . . . . . . . . . 213-653-0361
7800 Beverly Blvd.
Los Angeles, CA 90036
PROD.CO:    Columbia TriStar Television
William J. Bell . . . . . . . . . . . . . . . . . . . . . . . . . Sr. Executive Producer
Edward Scott . . . . . . . . . . . . . . . . . . . . . . . . . . . Executive Producer
David Shaughnessy . . . . . . . . . . . . . . . . . . . . . . . . . . . . . Producer
Nancy Wiard . . . . . . . . . . . . . . . . . . . . . . . . . Coordinating Producer
Meryl O'Loughlin . . . . . . . . . . . . . . . . . . . . . . . . . . . . . . Casting

— **Doug Belgrad, Sr. V.P. Production, Columbia Pictures**





| DESCRIPTION | ITEM CODE | PRICE | SHIP |
| --- | --- | --- | --- |
| HCD Book/Single Issue | HCD-BK-0 | **$49.50** | $4.00 |
| HCD Book/1-Yr. Subscription | HCD-BK-1 | **$120.00** | $12.00 |
| HCD Book/2-Yr. Subscription | HCD-BK-2 | **$210.00** | $24.00 |
| HCD Mailing Labels/Single Printing | HCD-LA-0 | **$350.00** | $8.00 |
| HCD Mailing Labels/1-Yr. Subscription | HCD-LA-1 | **$750.00** | $24.00 |
| HCD Mailing Labels On Disc/Single Issue | HCD-LD-0 | **$550.00** | $3.50 |
| HCD Mailing Labels On Disc/1-Yr. Subscription | HCD-LD-1 | **$850.00** | $10.50 |
| HCD Online/1-Yr. Subscription | HCD-OL-1 | **$99.00** | N/A |

— **Michael Halpern, V.P., HBO Pictures**



| DESCRIPTION | ITEM CODE | PRICE | SHIP |
| --- | --- | --- | --- |
| HAD Book/Single Issue | HAD-BK-0 | **$49.50** | $4.00 |
| HAD Book/1-Yr. Subscription | HAD-BK-1 | **$79.00** | $8.00 |
| HAD Book/2-Yr. Subscription | HAD-BK-2 | **$139.00** | $16.00 |
| HAD Mailing Labels/Single Printing | HAD-LA-0 | **$250.00** | $8.00 |
| HAD Mailing Labels/1-Yr. Subscription | HAD-LA-1 | **$425.00** | $16.00 |
| HAD Mailing Labels On Disc/Single Issue | HAD-LD-0 | **$350.00** | $3.50 |
| HAD Mailing Labels On Disc/1-Yr. Subscription | HAD-LD-1 | **$500.00** | $7.00 |
| HAD Online/1-Yr. Subscription | HAD-OL-1 | **$89.00** | N/A |

# http://www.hcdonline.com

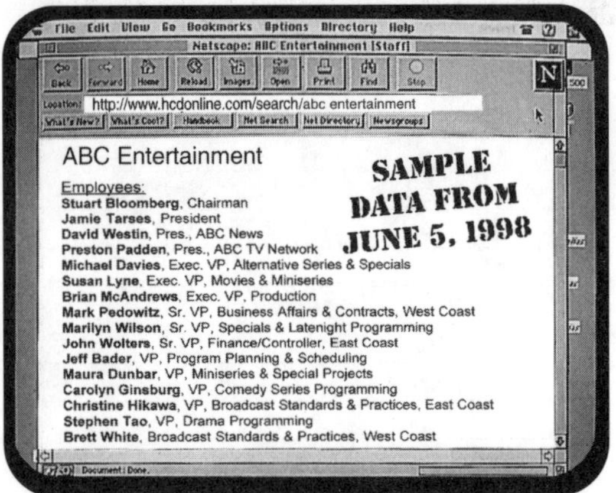


**"I get contacted by so many people in the industry . . . The HCD gives me info I never had before. I look up a name and BAM, there it is!"**

— **Harry Knowles. Founder**
**Ain't It Cool News**

## CALL US FOR A FREE TRIAL

## UPDATED EVERY FRIDAY

**BONUS: FREE** *HOLLYWOOD NEW MEDIA DIRECTORY ONLINE* **WITH PURCHASE OF** *HOLLYWOOD EXECUTIVE LIBRARY* **ONLINE!**
(until Sept. 1, 1998)

| DESCRIPTION | ITEM CODE | PRICE |
|---|---|---|
| HEL   Hollywood Executive Library/1-year | HEL-OL-1 | $199.00 |
| HCD  Hollywood Creative Directory/1-year | HCD-OL-1 | $99.00 |
| HAD  Hollywood Agents & Managers Directory/1-year | HAD-OL-1 | $89.00 |
| HDD  Hollywood Distributors Directory/1-year | HDD-OL-1 | $79.00 |
| HND Hollywood New Media Directory/1-year | HND-OL-1 | $69.00 |

## MAILING LISTS ON LABELS & ON DISC

## LABEL SPECIFICATIONS

Avery Laserjet labels, 3-up, 30 per page, 1 x 2-5/8" per label.
Can be sorted by Last Name, Company, Address, City, Zip.

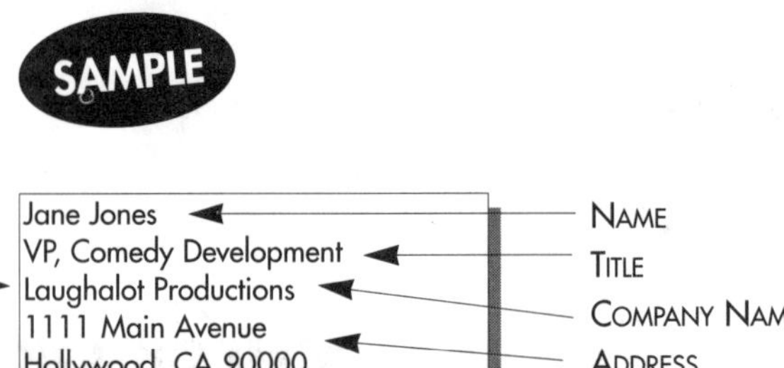


| DESCRIPTION | ITEM CODE | PRICE | SHIP |
|---|---|---|---|
| HCD  Mailing Labels/Single Printing | HCD-LA-0 | $350.00 | $8.00 |
| HCD  Mailing Labels/1-Yr. Subscription | HCD-LA-1 | $750.00 | $24.00 |
| HCD  Mailing Labels On Disc/Single Issue | HCD-LD-0 | $550.00 | $3.50 |
| HCD  Mailing Label Disc/1-Yr. Subscription | HCD-LD-1 | $850.00 | $10.50 |
| HAD  Mailing Labels/Single Printing | HAD-LA-0 | $250.00 | $8.00 |
| HAD  Mailing Labels/1-Yr. Subscription | HAD-LA-1 | $425.00 | $16.00 |
| HAD  Mailing Labels On Disc/Single Issue | HAD-LD-0 | $350.00 | $3.50 |
| HAD  Mailing Labels On Disc/1-Yr.Subscription | HAD-LD-1 | $500.00 | $7.00 |
| HDD  Mailing Label/Single Printing | HDD-LA-0 | $225.00 | $3.50 |
| HDD  Mailing Labels On Disc/Single Issue | HDD-LD-0 | $325.00 | $3.50 |
| HND  Mailing Labels/Single Printing | HND-LA-0 | $175.00 | $3.50 |
| HND  Mailing Labels On Disc/Single Issue | HND-LD-0 | $275.00 | $3.50 |

## DISC SPECIFICATIONS (LABELS ON DISC)

★ ASCII, Text File, delimited by quotation marks. Comes in a 3.5" High Density Disc (1.44MB). Works best with Microsoft Word.
ONLY WORKS ON IBM OR IBM COMPATIBLE SYSTEMS

★ Does not include mailmerge title software program. Only includes mailmerge data: name, company name and address.

# ORDER FORM
## ALL ORDERS MUST BE PRE-PAID

| TITLES | ITEM | PRICE | QTY. | TOTAL |
|---|---|---|---|---|
| | | | | |
| | | | | |
| | | | | |
| | | | | |
| | | | | |
| | | | | |
| | | | | |
| | | | | |
| | | | | |
| | | | | |

❏ VISA ❏ MC ❏ AMEX

| | |
|---|---|
| | SUBTOTAL |
| | CA RESIDENTS ADD 8.25% TAX |
| | SHIPPING ($4.00 PER BOOK UNLESS OTHERWISE SPECIFIED) |
| | TOTAL ENCLOSED |

CARDHOLDER NAME

CARD NUMBER

SIGNATURE                                        EXPIRATION

## ONLINE SUBSCRIBERS:
*EMAIL ADDRESS NECESSARY FOR ONLINE SUBSCRIBERS.*

Email Address

Add password

## SHIP TO:

NAME                                        COMPANY

TELEPHONE

STREET ADDRESS        (UPS does not deliver to post office boxes.)

CITY                                        STATE                ZIP

## CHECK OR MONEY ORDER TO:

**HOLLYWOOD CREATIVE DIRECTORY**
3000 W. Olympic Blvd • Suite 2525 • Santa Monica, CA 90404-5041

## CREDIT CARD ORDERS:

Phone: **310-315-4815** or **800-815-0503** (outside California) FAX: **310-315-4816**
EMAIL: hcd@HollyVision.com

## CANADA & FOREIGN:

Sent Airmail. Payable in U.S. Dollars or on funds drawn on a U.S. Bank.
Canada: Multiply U.S. shipping X 2. Foreign: Multiply U.S. shipping X 4.

## U.S. ORDERS:

Sent UPS Ground (Allow 3 days in CA and 5-10 days out-of-state).
Please enclose proper tax and shipping.

# WORKSHEET



| NAME | COMPANY | PHONE # | FAX # |
|------|---------|---------|-------|
|      |         |         |       |